To John, Sarah, and Adam

The study of human development across the lifespan is especially interesting because the reader is also the subject. While students are learning about development in their course, they are also dealing with developmental changes on a personal level. This textbook serves as a guide for students as they study the different phases of life. It offers multiple perspectives with which to view and understand the characteristic changes that make life so interesting. A number of practical applications and solutions to common problems in development have been included to encourage students to apply the material to their own lives.

Furthermore, I have made a deliberate effort to provide readers with an appreciation of the importance of the cultural context. Increased mobility and greater access to information about people living in various countries or cultures has expanded our understanding of the ways in which culture can affect the quality and significance of behavior across the lifespan. Development no longer can be viewed solely from the perspective of a single culture.

This book provides an overview of the basic principles and theories that describe the physical, cognitive, social, and personality changes that occur during various developmental periods of the lifespan. *Lifespan Human Development* can be used to support introductory developmental courses even if students are encountering the basic concepts of psychology for the first time. Each new term is introduced with a clear, concise definition and followed by concrete applications and examples. This book provides a foundation in psychological and developmental theory and research practices that beginning students need. It also offers practical applications, telling the reader about children, adolescents, and adults they could meet in everyday life. Because multicultural issues are systematically integrated into each chapter, this textbook would be an asset in courses that have multicultural awareness as one of their behavioral and course objectives.

CHANGES TO THIS EDITION

Beginning with the Prologue, which is new to this edition, human development is compared to a long journey. Just as people setting off on an adventure may want to prepare themselves by reading up on what they might see in their travels, this textbook provides readers with descriptive previews of human development across the lifespan. I have inserted "snapshots," in the form of vignettes and personal examples, to illustrate the changes and concerns of each developmental stage of life. Each Part Opener includes a graphic link that locates the reader on the journey of life. As is in the previous edition, the importance of culture is high-lighted with Focus on Culture inserts.

Each chapter has been updated and revised to reflect current issues and concerns. Each chapter contains new topics that replace outdated ones; new topics include media influences on children, the school experience, adolescent stressors, resolving marital conflicts, assisted suicides, and ethical dilemmas in caring for elderly people. This edition provides four new types of boxed inserts that offer students various perspectives on development. The *Health Perspective* provides insight into developmental changes that can affect health and well-being. The *Educational Perspective* focuses on issues related to the way people learn across the lifespan. The *Personal Perspective* includes practical applications and suggestions for dealing with selected problems. And, to help students appreciate the way in which scientists look at issues in human development, the *Research Perspective* offers examples of how questions about development are studied. All of these Perspective boxes are easy to read and relate to material discussed in the chapter. Topics addressed in the Perspective boxes include bias in psychological research, the impact of socioeconomic stress on health, comforting babies, cross-cultural influences on moral judgements, women's ways of knowing, family therapy, sexual harassment, and dealing with the return of adult children.

I have expanded the pedagogical features by introducing *Recaps,* which provide short summaries at strategic places within the chapter. *Key terms* are defined in the text in a running glossary and are listed at the end of each chapter with a page reference showing where the term is introduced and defined. Additionally in the index, the numbers of the pages where these key terms are defined appear in boldface. Also new to this edition are 75 tables that highlight and summarize concepts and stages for a quick review and study aid.

PEDAGOGICAL FEATURES

Readability   One of the strongest features of *Lifespan Human Development* is its readability. Students will find the writing in this book to be lively and descriptive, with numerous examples that highlight issues and illustrate concepts. Additionally, important technical terms are introduced in bold type and are defined immediately in the text and again in the running glossary.

Part Openers   Each part is introduced by a short explanation of the developmental issues that will be addressed in subsequent chapters. Connections are made between the material previously presented and that to be presented in subsequent chapters. A graphic element illustrates the portion of the lifespan featured in the part.

Chapter Outlines and Opening Vignettes   At the beginning of each chapter is an overview, in outline form, of the major topics and issues included in the chapter. The overview is followed by two short narratives describing real-life examples of issues and behaviors that occur during the stage of development featured in the chapter. The characters in these opening vignettes are used as examples to illustrate concepts within the chapter. One of the vignettes reflects the experience of growing up in a cultural context that is different from the dominant culture or in a different cultural setting altogether.

Perspective Boxes   Distributed throughout the text are boxes that offer some practical applications of human development from one of four perspectives: Health, Education, Personal, and Research. A list of topics included in the boxed features follows the Table of Contents.

Focus on Culture   Strategically placed within each chapter, these elements are designed to maintain awareness of and stimulate thought about the impact of culture on development. Instructors may want to use these as lecture openers, as catalysts for class discussion, or as essay questions on an exam.

Brief Review   Every chapter concludes with a brief review of the major topics covered in the chapter, organized into short, bulleted paragraphs.

Key Terms   At the end of each chapter is a list of key terms that can be used as a quick review or test of the concepts and issues presented within the chapter. Page numbers identify the places where the terms are first defined.

Review Questions   At the end of each chapter, readers are challenged to answer the review questions. Students who cannot answer the questions are invited to reread the chapter.

Observational Activity   At the end of each chapter is an out-of-class activity that helps create real-life experiences from which to apply the material presented in the chapter. Additional observational activities are included in the Instructor's Manual.

Running Glossary   The chapter-by-chapter glossary, a lifespan dictionary in miniature, defines important terms in the margin of the page on which the term is first introduced. Glossary items are also identified in the index by a boldfaced page number.

Supplements   An Instructor's Manual contains suggestions for lecture topics, media, classroom discussions, activities, and essay questions. The test bank includes multiple-choice items that have been carefully coordinated with the textbook and reflect its commitment to multicultural issues. The test questions are also available in computerized form. The accompanying Study Guide for students contains chapter outlines, learning objectives, multiple-choice and true or false practice tests, vocabulary exercises, flash cards for self testing, and valuable study tips.

ORGANIZATION OF THE BOOK

The sixth edition features eight major parts, introduced by a discussion of issues, theories, and methods in Chapter 1. With the exception of Part Eight, which covers death, dying, and bereavement, each part covers the physical, cognitive, personality, and social development of the individual in one of the broad stages of growth.

Chapter 1, "Lifespan Development: Issues, Theories, and Methods," deals with the concerns of lifespan developmental psychology, summarizes major theories of development, and provides an overview of how research on human development is conducted.

Part One, "The Beginning Years," follows the development of the individual from conception through the second year of life. Chapter 2 describes the mechanisms of genetics, the many dimensions of prenatal development, and the birth process. Chapter 3 describes the characteristics of the newborn and the infant's rapid physical and cognitive development during the first two years. The infant's social and personality development are described in Chapter 4, which also includes a discussion of early language behavior.

Part Two, "The Exploring Years," takes the child to age six. Physical, cognitive, and language development are detailed in Chapter 5, and personality and social development are presented in Chapter 6.

Part Three, "The Learning Years," follows the developing person through the grade-school years to pubescence. Chapter 7 describes physical growth, cognition, and learning, and Chapter 8 examines personality and social development.

Part Four, "The Transition Years," treats the physical changes that occur at puberty and their effects on the adolescent's personality and social life. Chapter 9 describes the adolescent's attainment of physical maturity, as well as changes in cognitive and moral-ethical development. In Chapter 10, the issues of identity and personality are explored.

Part Five, "The Decision Years," presents the major developmental tasks confronting people as they make the transition to early adulthood. Chapter 11 focuses on physical, cognitive, and personality changes experienced by young adults, and Chapter 12 examines parenting and family relations and occupational development.

Part Six, "The Reassessment Years," takes the individual through the middle years of adult life, from approximately 40 to 65. Physical, cognitive, and personality development are described in Chapter 13. Chapter 14 examines midlife marital and family relations as well as experiences and adjustments at work.

Part Seven, "The Golden Years," completes the lifespan with a discussion of issues and changes that occur in late adulthood. Chapter 15 explores various factors that influence physical and cognitive adaptation in the later years as well as issues of identity and personality adjustment among the elderly. Chapter 16 focuses on family life, social relations, and adjustment to retirement.

Part Eight, "The Final Years," consists of one chapter (17) in which the changes that occur as people die and experience bereavement are discussed. The impact of death on individuals of various ages across the lifespan is described.

ACKNOWLEDGMENTS

Writing a successful textbook requires an interst in the subject matter, a commitment of time and energy, and a lot of help from other people. As is true in many aspects of work, many people have contributed to the success of this book and should be recognized for their efforts. Several instructors of developmental psychology contributed in-depth evaluations of the manuscript. For their thoughtful reviews and many suggestions, I thank the following individuals: Carol Lynn Davis, University of Southern Maine; Cynthia de Saint Victor, University of Toledo; Annie M. Dunn, Montgomery College; Vivian N. Harper, San Joaquin Delta College; Bert Hayslip, Jr., University of North Texas; Jackie Hill, Chattanooga State Technical Community College; Julie Kontos, Bloomsburg University; Robert Lawyer, Delgado Community College; Lyla S. Maynard, Des Moines Area Community College; Nancy Billings Meyer, Northeast Iowa Community College; Jeffrey L. Nagelbush, Ferris State University; Sherrill Richarz, Washington State University; Rosemary R. Price, Rancho Santiago College; Gary L. Schilmoeller, University of Maine; Sheila B. Shields, Forsyth Technical Community College; Paul S. Silverman, University of Montana; Robert B. Stewart, Jr., Oakland University; Elizabeth Stine, University of New Hampshire; Leonard T. Volenski, Seton Hall University; Deborah R. Winters, New Mexico State University;

Elizabeth A. Yost, Belmont University; and Martha S. Zlokovich, Southeast Missouri State University.

I could not have written this textbook without the help and encouragement of my husband, John Bernard. While I worked away on my laptop computer, John kept the Gormly homefires burning. In the process, he has become a first rate cook and a great coach. His patience, kindness, and well-placed sense of humor kept me writing and earned him a spot in heaven. I probably would never have cultivated my interest in developmental psychology were it not for my children, Adam John and Sarah Anne; they have been a source of inspiration and pride. I am also grateful to my sisters and brothers and my mother, Helen McLaren, for their patience and suggestions.

The editorial staff of Harcourt Brace also deserves mention. For their dedication and support in bringing my manuscript to its final production, my thanks go to acquisitions editor Jo-Anne Weaver, project editor Charlie Dierker, production manager Serena Barnett Manning, art director Peggy Young, and photo editor Sandra Lord. Thanks are also owed to copy editor Jennifer Moorhouse, proofreader Susan Swain, and photo researcher Steve Lunetta.

One of the many rewards of working on a textbook is the opportunity to form new relationships with the people who keep me on target and stimulate my thinking. I have been fortunate to have worked with Carolyn Smith, who was my development editor on this edition. Her attention to detail in the manuscript has improved the textbook and helped me as a writer. I also have gained a friend in the process.

To the Student

This is a book about the lifespan, some of which you have already experienced, some of which is ahead of you. You may be interested in human development because you want to understand your own development (or perhaps that of your roomate or a friend, your children or another relative). You may also be eager to learn about the years ahead. Some of the material that you will read about in these 17 chapters will not stay in your immediate memory after this course is finished, although I hope you will remember most of the material until you have taken your final exam. However, in the future, when you find yourself in situations with infants, children, and other adults of varying ages, I hope you will remember something about what you have read. It is then that you will be glad that you have kept your textbook as a reference. If you have children to raise, you may find yourself devouring the material in Parts One through Four. If you are working with the elderly or living with your aging parents, then Parts Seven and Eight may become your favorite segment of the book.

I hope that you will find this text enjoyable and informative. I welcome any suggestions or comments you have about your text. Please send them to the Psychology Editor, Harcourt Brace College Publishers, 301 Commerce Street, Suite 3700, Fort Worth, Texas 76102.

Anne V. Gormly

Over the course of her professional life, Anne Gormly has been a student, teacher, therapist, researcher, and administrator. She is currently an administrator at Trenton State College in Trenton, New Jersey. She earned a B.A. in mathematics from Rhode Island College and a Ph.D. in psychology from the University of Illinois. For the past 20 years, Dr. Gormly has taught courses in child development, parenting, and human development. Her research interests have included fertility motivation, attitudes and social behavior, and parenting.

Dr. Gormly is the proud parent of two adult children, Adam and Sarah. Her husband, John, who is also a psychologist and college professor, has been her friend and partner for more than thirty years. She was raised in a large family and has an identical twin sister. She lives in Princeton, New Jersey, and loves to travel and learn about how people live their lives. When she can, Dr. Gormly travels to a small island in the Caribbean to think about the beauty of life.

BRIEF CONTENTS

TABLE OF CONTENTS

PART III: THE LEARNING YEARS 252

PART V: THE DECISION YEARS   416

PART VIII: THE END OF THE JOURNEY   650

CHAPTER 17   THE FINAL JOURNEY OF LIFE: DEATH, DYING, AND BEREAVEMENT   652

PERSPECTIVE BOXES

Have you ever been to Machu Picchu? I haven't, but I hope to visit there someday. I have read several travel articles about this city high in the mountains of Peru. From time to time I wonder about what it would be like to be there. Some people who have made the journey have shared their perspectives with me about this city. When I finally get there, I will know where to obtain maps and other travel information.

So how does traveling to Peru relate to reading a lifespan human development text? Good question. In many ways you are in the same situation. But instead of contemplating a journey to the Andes mountains, you may be thinking about your journey through life. Life can be perceived as a series of adventures and experiences on the way to a distant destination. In fact, many cultures portray life using the metaphor of a journey. All of you have begun your trip through life and have made it at least to late adolescence or early adulthood. Those of you in your middle or even late adulthood years are more experienced travelers in life and, as a result, will have gathered more information that can help you in the rest of your life journey.

If you accept my metaphor, then by analogy this text can serve as your guidebook. Every one of you will hopefully live a long life during which you will experience the many changes that define the different stages of life. I have written this textbook to give you an idea of what the journey ahead of you will be like.

No experienced traveler would set off on a journey without the benefit of a detailed map to show the way. Therefore, throughout this textbook I have included a variety of aids to help you see where you are going. At the beginning of each major segment of the lifespan, I will describe that particular segment of the journey ahead of you. Within each chapter you will find a chapter outline of the material you will cover in your readings.

I have a friend who talks about his quest as a spirited teenager to walk across the United States. Leaving from New York City on a sunny day in August, he got as far as the Brooklyn Bridge and then stopped. He says he got distracted on his journey. When you are absorbed by the scenery, it is sometimes easy to lose your perspective. To help you stay focused, I have included a Recap, or brief section review, at selected points in each chapter. You will also find several charts that summarize key points. At the end of each chapter, there is a Brief Review section, a series of Review Questions, and Key Terms, all designed to help you remember what you have read.

As you read each chapter you will learn about the landmarks for each segment of the life journey. The terrain of life is marked by changes in physical, social, cognitive, emotional, and personality characteristics. Not all segments of life share the same degree of change.

Nor will all people make the journey in the same way. Some people never fulfill their travel plans. They may get distracted along the way, or die prematurely. In Chapter 17, you will learn more about the end of the journey. Even when people travel the same distance and reach the same final destination, their experiences vary considerably. For example, two people taking the same trip to the Grand Canyon may have very different experiences depending on whether they fly or drive or if they travel through the northern or southern states to reach their destination.

Where it is appropriate, I will point out the factors or elements that can alter the quality of a person's experience. Some people set their course in life and reach it without much interference. Others may have many obstacles to overcome before they reach their destinations. Throughout life there are many turning points from which we must decide how to proceed. While some people may make certain choices and go on, others linger. But unlike an actual trip, life is a journey we must take—one way or another.

People usually see what they expect to see. To help you broaden your perspective on what you will learn, I have included a series of boxes that offer one of four perspectives on development. Information in the *Health Perspective* boxes examine development from the point of view of people interested in health and health-care careers. The *Education Perspective* boxes provide a look at development from the teaching perspective. The *Research Perspective* boxes highlight the issues and problems associated with studying developmental changes. Finally, the *Personal Perspective* boxes offer practical applications for people at a particular phase of life.

If you would like to really enjoy your armchair travels through the lifespan, then take advantage of the *Observational Activity* that I have included at the end of each chapter. These activities are designed to help you get a firsthand look at selected aspects of life. In some activities you will be asked to observe people, and in others you will be directed to talk with people about their experiences. Either way, completing the activities will help you personalize your experience of lifespan development.

I hope that you enjoy your life and that this guidebook will increase your excitement about the journey ahead. It may also help you reconsider the ground you have already covered and understand it a little better. As you enter different segments of the lifespan, I hope that you will reread those chapters that pertain to where you are in your travels.

Let your enrollment in this course be your passport, this book be your guide, and, to borrow from an old Irish saying, "may the road of life rise up to greet you." Enjoy your travels.

Lifespan
Human Development

CHAPTER 1

Lifespan Development: Issues, Theories, and Methods

It had been nearly 3 years since Ellie had seen her four children and grandchildren all together. The last time was at their father's funeral. Now the occasion was a happier one: the celebration of her youngest daughter's second marriage. As she waited for the ceremony to begin she couldn't help but remember the painful divorce and custody battles that Kathleen endured many years ago. At the time Ellie worried that perhaps she herself had neglected her responsibilities as a parent. Perhaps Kathleen's failed marriage was a result of some problem with her upbringing. But, now those concerns seem so far away. Her grandson Jack, now 14, appeared to be happy about the new marriage; the groom's 20-year-old son, Greg, gets along very well with Jack.

During the festivities, which were held in her eldest daughter's garden, Ellie realized how lucky she has been to have had such a long life and loving family. All of her adult children were alive and healthy, and most of them had children of their own. There were rumors that Paula's daughter Lori and her boyfriend Jeff were on the verge of announcing their engagement. Her son Stephen had just become a father last spring for the first time and seemed to be challenged by the role his wife expected him to take in caring for the new baby. Ellie remembered what a difficult child Stephen had been and quietly chuckled to herself. Life did have its own rewards!

Thousands of miles away on the island of Bali, Wayan, first-born male in his family, joined his extended family to offer prayers at the temple on Pagerwesi, the day set aside for the protection of the family, the village, and the world at large. His family was large by Balinese standards; his 3 sons and 4 daughters had all married and together had produced 31 grandchildren so far.

Each child born to his family was a cause for much celebration and dancing. In Bali, babies are considered most holy since they represent unblemished innocence. As children grow into adults they lose this holiness until they gradually reclaim it through their death and rebirth. Like other Balinese people, Wayan believed that he would be reborn into his family after the passage of five generations. Thus, he viewed his declining health and age with reverence and expectation.

Ellie and Wayan viewed their families from different cultural perspectives. Yet each realized that their descendants would not be following their footsteps exactly, but instead would continue to grow and change throughout their lives, just as Ellie and Wayan had done and would continue to do. It was this sense of change that added to the excitement and that was indeed cause for celebration.

THE LIFESPAN APPROACH

Each person's journey from birth to death is distinguished from all others by its unique life events and accomplishments. For some people, this journey is a long one punctuated by pleasant memories and perhaps some regrets. For others who face more difficult circumstances, the journey may be a shorter one. No matter how different our lives may be, we all share in the human experience of birth, growth, and change.

ASSUMPTIONS UNDERLYING MY VIEW OF THE LIFESPAN

Often, authors bring their biases and assumptions to their writing. Throughout my study of development and my life experiences I have developed a set of beliefs about life that will undoubtedly emerge in this book. So let me identify them for you.

First of all, I am an eternal optimist when it comes to human development. I believe each person has the ability to change, and I celebrate this fact whenever I can. Human beings are amazingly adaptable. Given the right circumstances and a little push, people will surprise themselves with their progress.

Secondly, even though some types of change are easier in some parts of the lifespan than others, change does occur across all age groups. Adaptability and change is not just a characteristic of the young. I am delighted every time I have an older adult in my classroom because it supports my belief that you are never to old to learn. I once had an 81-year-old student who taught us all about what it is like to be elderly.

I believe that people are active agents in their lives. Certainly, we are affected by events that occur outside of our control, but we also react and respond to our experiences. We often select and sometimes create the settings and circumstances in which meaningful life events occur. Just by choosing to spend time in a college environment and taking courses, you are setting a path for yourself in life that will create new and different opportunities in the future.

I like to use practical and concrete examples to illustrate aspects of the lifespan. If you can apply what you are reading to your own lives you will learn more easily and hopefully retain more of what you learn for a longer time.

LIFESPAN DEVELOPMENTAL PSYCHOLOGY

developmental psychology
The study of the physical, cognitive, personality, social, and emotional changes that occur over the lifespan.

The field of **developmental psychology** has emerged to help us understand and explain the predictable and common changes and differences in human behavior that characterize different facets of life. While many characteristics change with age, others remain remarkably stable. Developmental psychologists are interested in intra-individual differences—that is, the course of or lack of change in body, thought, emotions, and behavior a person experiences over the course of his or her life; they are also interested in the differences among people of different ages and life circumstances, or inter-individual differences. For example, researchers have studied changes that occur in sexual behavior from adolescence to late adulthood and found a gradual decline in sexual activity with age beginning in young adulthood. However, these inter-individual differences may not describe the intra-individual changes that occur for any specific individual. It may be the case that a person is sexually active throughout the majority of his or her lifespan.

Some of the changes that developmental psychologists study are obvious—for example, the 3 inches grown by the toddler in the 2nd year of life. Other changes, such as sociability or self-esteem, are not as visible because the tools we use to measure these changes are not as precise as the rulers we use to measure height. This focus on change is what makes developmental psychology unique. Whereas other areas of psychology may be concerned with the way memory operates or the nature of human social interaction, only developmental psychology concentrates on the changes in memory or social interaction over the course of the entire lifespan.

Take a moment to consider the task of a lifespan developmental psychologist in more detail. Suppose that you were asked to write a person's biography. You would probably want to describe and explain all the changes and events in that person's life. It would take a long time and a lot of research to cover all the major behaviors and events that characterize the subject of your biography. To simplify your task, you might decide to limit your biography to the behaviors and relevant events within a specified period of time or age—say early childhood. Another way to simplify the biography would be to examine a specific behavior and describe the way your subject has changed with respect to this behavior. For example, you might focus on changes in intellectual ability over the person's life. Either approach—the study of a specific age period or the in-depth study of a certain behavior over time—would produce useful information. However, to capture the essence of the person and to appreciate the way behavior develops over time, the lifespan developmentalist seeks to combine both approaches.

Developmental psychologists today recognize the importance of viewing development from the **lifespan perspective** (see Table 1–1). A lifespan view of development takes into consideration all the changes that occur over time as a result of many interacting factors. Many behaviors develop at different times and rates in a person's life and have an influence on changes that occur later in life. For example, Ellie felt somewhat guilty when Kathleen's first marriage did not work because she believed that she had not provided her daughter with the necessary earlier life experiences to help her in her later life. Psychologists recognize that a person's ability to experience intimacy with another person in young adulthood is influenced by the quality of that person's relationship with his or her parents as a young infant and child. The parent-child relationship, in turn, is influenced by the infant's physical health and maturity at birth. Childhood and adolescent successes

lifespan perspective
The view that development occurs throughout the course of life as a result of a changing interaction of physical, biological, social, historical, cultural, and psychological influences.

CHARACTERISTICS OF THE LIFESPAN PERSPECTIVE

Development represents the study of changes in behavior over the whole lifespan.

Development is affected by many interacting factors.

Change occurs throughout the different phases of the lifespan.

The impact of change is cumulative; earlier events affect later development.

Development occurs within contexts and cultures.

TABLE 1–1

or failures in making friends and establishing a good self-concept will also affect the person's willingness to share himself or herself with another person in adulthood. The degree to which the person's culture permits or encourages close contact and expression of emotions is another factor that may have an effect on the quality and form of intimacy expressed in young adulthood.

The lifespan approach to development has provided challenges to the way we perceive and study human development (Brim & Kagan, 1980; Featherman, 1983; Gergen, 1980; Labouvie, 1982). Researchers look at the way changes can and do occur at all ages, not just during the earlier years of life. Because development is seen as the cumulative effect of many different changes occurring at different times, lifespan research often involves the study of individuals over long periods of time. As a result of this long-range research, conclusions can be drawn about the different patterns and sequences in behavior. The lifespan approach also considers the influence that social setting and historical times have on development. For example, people who grew up in the United States during the 1940s and 1950s would be expected to have a different attitude toward sexuality than people who grew up in the 1960s, when sexual behavior was more openly discussed, or in the late 1980s, when the AIDS epidemic changed people's attitude toward sexual behavior.

The lifespan approach acknowledges that change occurs throughout life and asserts that behavior can be corrected or remedied in the adult years. This view contrasts with the belief that behavior is relatively fixed and unchangeable after childhood. Intervention programs have been aimed primarily at the young, but the lifespan perspective presents the prospect of intervention programs throughout adulthood as well. For example, people typically learn to read and write during childhood; however, many people reach adulthood without having learned these literacy skills. The belief that changes in learning occur throughout the lifespan encouraged intervention programs aimed at teaching adults how to read and write.

THE CONTEXT OF DEVELOPMENT

contextual view
The view that development and behavior must be understood in terms of the setting or context in which they occur.

One viewpoint that complements the lifespan perspective is the **contextual view,** which proposes that behavior must be understood in terms of the total setting or context against which it occurs (Sameroff, 1983). Development is seen as a dynamic, changing process in which the individual and the environment continuously interact. The individual is both affected by the environment and participates in changing the environment. Thus behavior cannot be interpreted out of its context—and the contexts are many. The lives of Ellie and Wayan today can be understood only in light of their health and physical status (biological context), their family network and roles as parents, children, and siblings (family context), their friendships (social context), the cultures in which they live (cultural context), the times during which they grew up and the present (historical context), their financial and work status (economic context), and their abilities to deal with new challenges (intellectual context). Change in one system affects the context of other systems, which in turn can have an impact on yet other systems. Should Ellie's health decline from disease or stroke, this could no doubt influence her contact with her family, perhaps change her financial status, and reduce her intellectual activities.

THE IMPACT OF CULTURE ON DEVELOPMENT

The 81-year-old student in my class entered adulthood at the start of the Great Depression. He could not get a job and at the same time was responsible for contributing to his family's economic survival. The younger students in the class heard a vivid example of the impact that growing up in a different historical time had on their classmate. Each generation has its own challenges and expectations. Imagine how your life would have been different if you had grown up before television was invented.

culture
The representation of shared values and beliefs, knowledge, and experience of a group of people that are passed on through language and customs to people living within the culture.

Another equally powerful influence on our development is the culture within which we live. **Cultures** represent the shared values and beliefs, knowledge, and experience of a group of people that are passed on through language and customs. Often we may not be aware of the extent to which our culture has shaped our experiences. Take a simple example. To the question, "On which day does a new week begin?" many people may answer, "Sunday." Your calendar begins a new week with Sunday—everyone you know would agree that Sunday is the first day of the week. But some readers may answer "Monday" and be equally correct. In many countries, calendars mark the beginning of a new week with Monday. Your experience of a new week depends upon your cultural expectation and experiences.

Where people are born and brought up can have a profound influence on the changes that occur in life. The physical geography and climate of a country can determine the economic and political stability that emerges. Countries that have many natural resources are likely to become prosperous and be able to provide their citizens with better medical, health, and educational resources, which can alter the courses of their lives. Children born in countries with high rates of starvation are likely to have shorter lifespans than those born into wealthier countries. Adults living in highly industrialized and technological societies may be forced to retire at earlier ages than those living in agricultural or non-technological societies.

Human development cannot be studied in a cultural vacuum because it is guided by cultural norms, values, and expectations. For example, in Western culture, particularly in the United States, competition and achievement are highly valued. Children are exposed to many situations in which they learn the value of competition and achievement. However, in some non-Western and Native American cultures, cooperation is valued over competition and achievement. To understand children's behavior in competitive or achievement-orientated situations, it is necessary to ask about their cultural context (Rogoff & Morelli, 1989).

Even within the same country, people may experience different subcultures based on their gender, race, ethnic origin, or religious affiliation. Within the United States, a long history of racial and ethnic prejudice and discrimination have created qualitatively different social and economic environments for some Americans, most notably African Americans, Hispanic Americans, and Asian Americans. If we are to have a good understanding of development, it is important to recognize the impact that cultures and subcultures can have on the human experience.

Throughout this text you will learn more about the influence that culture has on development across the lifespan. As you read, ask yourself: Would this be true in all cultures and countries? For men and women alike? You will also learn about the similarities in development among people of different backgrounds and gender.

How parents care for their children is influenced by the culture in which they live. Bathing in the local river is a common event for this Brazilian mother.

RECAP

The intra-individual and inter-individual changes in behavior that occur throughout life are the subject of study for developmental psychologists. Changes are both quantitative and qualitative and occur as a result of several interacting factors. The cultural context in which people live can have a profound effect on development. Change occurs throughout all facets of the lifespan and has a cumulative effect.

THE STUDY OF HUMAN DEVELOPMENT

Developmental psychologists are interested in two fundamental issues: (1) Is development a continuous series of changes or a series of discontinuous changes that occur throughout the lifespan? and (2) What determines development: biology or environment?

THE CONTINUITY OF DEVELOPMENT

When my children were young, I looked forward to their visits to the pediatrician, where they would be weighed and measured. When my son Adam was 3 years old his pediatrician predicted that he would be 6 feet tall when he stopped growing. He was able to make this prediction (which turned out to be correct!) by referring to normative growth charts. These charts represent the average height and weight for boys and for girls of differing ages from birth to adolescence. As children grow older, their height and weight increases until it levels off in middle childhood for girls and in late adolescence for boys. Looking at the growth charts it would seem as if the changes in physical development from birth until adolescence represent continuous growth. However, a closer look at physical development over this period will reveal that these changes are not entirely continuous, but rather come in spurts. From early infancy, children may grow in a discontinuous but overall predictable rate until they reach age 6, at which point growth slows until about age 10, when another growth spurt occurs.

Some psychologists believe that growth is gradual, stable, and continuous. They argue that the transformations that we see represent a long, gradual sequence of changes that begin in early childhood and culminate in adulthood in complex and mature behavior. Once a person reaches maturity, change does not occur. Personality, for example, is viewed by many psychologists as developing in the earlier parts of the lifespan and remaining stable throughout adulthood.

Other psychologists disagree; they believe that growth is discontinuous. Growth is described as occurring in stages that are qualitatively different from one another. Like physical development, there may be periods of little change followed by periods of rapid and dramatic change. Moreover, although individuals may vary in the rate at which they develop, the order of development from one stage to another is the same for all people.

Whether developmental change is continuous or discontinuous is a topic of controversy which will not be resolved with a simple answer. Earlier developmental researchers assumed that growth and change occurred as a result of biological maturation; their goal was to identify and describe the stages in which changes emerged with maturation. More recent researchers, however, while acknowledging the discontinuity of development, do not agree that these changes can be explained by stages.

DETERMINANTS OF DEVELOPMENT

The question of what determines development is one of the oldest controversies in the recorded history of the human race. Even the ancient Greeks speculated about this issue. In contemporary times the controversy has centered around two major factors: heredity and environment. **Heredity** refers to the genetic program that is passed along from parents to offspring at conception. **Environment** is a more broadly defined concept. Generally, it refers to the vast array of experiences to which the individual is exposed from the time of conception until death. These experiences may be biological in nature, such as exposure to disease, drugs, or inadequate nutrition. Or they may be primarily social, such as interactions with family members, peers, teachers, or exposure to the media and community culture.

Historically, the controversy over what determines development often has taken an extreme form, with one group of researchers arguing for heredity as the primary factor in development and an opposing group of researchers arguing just as forcefully for the unique role of the environment. In this extreme form, however, the **heredity-environment** (or nature-nurture) **issue** has proven not to be very fruitful for understanding development. Instead, investigators have argued that development can be better understood only in terms of the interaction between genetic and experiential forces (Anastasi, 1958; Angoff, 1988).

Today, most agree that neither heredity nor environment alone can adequately explain the complicated way in which each of us grows and develops. At the same time, however, it is not assumed that each of these factors plays an equal role in all aspects of development. Certain behaviors, such as walking, can best be explained by the process of maturation that is guided by our genetic blueprint. Other

heredity
The genetic program that is transmitted from parents to offspring at conception.

environment
An array of experiences to which individuals are exposed from conception to death.

heredity-environment issue
The controversy in psychology concerning the relative contribution of heredity or genetics (nature) versus experience or environment (nurture) in the development of the person.

Health Perspective

THE IMPACT OF SOCIOECONOMIC STATUS ON HEALTH

Some cultures have rigid social systems or castes into which people are born and in which they remain throughout their lives. While most Americans reject the idea of a caste system, they readily acknowledge the impact that different socioeconomic backgrounds can have on many aspects of development. For example, children who live in poverty are more likely than children from upper income levels to show intellectual deficits and behavioral problems (Duncan, Brooks-Gunn, & Kato Klebanov, 1994). Socioeconomic status (SES) is usually assessed by a combination of determinants, such as economic status (measured by income), social status (mea-

sured by degree of education), and work status (measured by occupation) (Dutton & Levine, 1989).

The impact of SES on health is of particular interest today because of the high costs of providing health care. For a long time, researchers have recognized the pronounced effect that poverty can have on people's chances for survival throughout the lifespan. People living below the poverty level suffer higher rates of mortality and disease than people with discretionary incomes. Poor people are more likely to be malnourished, to have little or no access to early prenatal care, and to receive limited medical treatment for chronic conditions. But the impact of SES on health is more complicated than it appears. SES and health appear to be related at all levels of socioeconomic status and not just for people who live below the poverty line (Adler et al., 1994). People who live at the highest SES level enjoy better health than people who come

from the SES level just below them—which raises the following question: What factors are at work within socioeconomic levels that influence health?

Adler and colleagues (1994) identified several possible attitudes and behaviors that have a direct effect on physical health and well being but that operate differently at various levels of SES. Among the health behaviors that Adler identified, smoking is the most deadly. Smoking behavior is inversely related to SES: the higher the SES level, the less people smoke, regardless of their level of education. Furthermore, the higher the SES, the lesser the likelihood for people to start smoking in the first place—and the greater the chances they would stop smoking if they had already started. A similar effect has been found for obesity and lack of physical activity: The higher the SES level, the greater amount of time people spend in physical activity.

In addition to actual health behaviors, Adler identified two

---

age-normative events
The influences of biological and maturational growth on development.

history-normative events
The influences on personal development of major historical events, such as wars, economic depressions, and epidemics.

nonnormative events
Events occuring at any time that have a serious impact on a person's life.

behaviors, however, such as wearing a sari or a business suit, or playing polo or stickball, are best explained by examining the influence of the individuals and society we encounter. Thus, the critical question concerning development is not which factor—heredity or environment—is responsible for our behavior, but how these two general factors interact to propel us along our unique developmental paths.

The relative importance of heredity and environment may change across the lifespan. According to Baltes, Reese, and Lipsitt (1980), there are three types of influences on lifespan development: (1) **age-normative influences,** such as biological and maturational growth; (2) **history-normative influences,** including major historical events such as wars, economic depressions, and epidemics; and (3) **nonnormative influences**—events that can occur at any time and which have a serious impact on people's lives. These include the death of a spouse or child, psychological characteristics that appear to relate SES to health: Depression and hostility. The prevalence of depression is much higher among people from lower SES levels. Similarly, hostility towards others was found to be inversely related to SES. Both depression and hostility have been linked to coronary disease and contribute to levels of psychological stress.

Psychological stress was the another category of behaviors that Adler et. al. (1994) identified as linked to SES and health. Stress refers to both the types of situations that require adaptation or adjustment, such as the loss of a spouse or birth of a child, and to the state that occurs when too many demands are made on a person at one time. People from lower SES are exposed to more stressful life events and have fewer resources available to them to help them cope with stressful situations.

Adler's review suggests that more remains to be done in the way of education and prevention. More research is needed to understand the role that specific variables play in promoting or discouraging healthy behaviors. In addition to behaviors, health is influenced by the quality of the physical environment in which people live. People from lower socioeconomic levels are more likely to live in settings with chipping lead based paint, polluted air and water, overcrowding, and high crime levels. These conditions have a demonstrated relationship to health. So while we may not have a caste system, it is clear that the socioeconomic status level people live in can have a profound effect on how healthy they are.

People who live in poverty are exposed to more stressful life events and have fewer resources to help them deal with adversity.

accidents or illness, divorce, career changes, or even lucky wins in a sweepstakes (see Figure 1–1). In adulthood the role of age-normative influences is sharply reduced, and the influence of nonnormative and history-normative influences is much stronger than in childhood.

THE ROLE OF THEORY

During the first half of this century most of the research in developmental psychology sought to discover and chart the course of development. Investigators often followed a specific line of inquiry—for example: When do most children produce their first word? At what age do most children learn to read? The aim of this research approach was to describe the milestones of development, not to explain

FIGURE 1–1

Developmental influences across the lifespan. The relative importance of various influences is believed to shift during the lifespan as shown in this hypothetical profile. Age-normative, history-normative, and nonnormative influences interact to produce age-related changes in development.

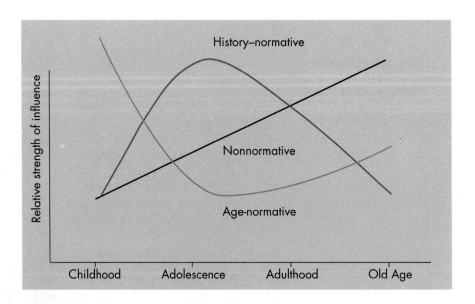

how the changes occurred. As the discipline of developmental psychology matured, researchers were no longer satisfied with simply describing the emergence and development of behaviors and skills. They wanted to understand the basis of development—to explain why specific behaviors emerged at particular times. This shift in focus from questions of "what" and "when" to "why" and "how" heralded the emergence of formal theory in the study of human development.

The Functions of Theory   Psychologists use theory to guide them in their study of development. A **theory** is a set of coherent, interrelated statements, laws, and principles that describe, define, and predict specific aspects of some phenomenon—in our case, human development. The four key functions that theory plays for researchers is presented in Table 1–2. In the study of human development, there are a variety of theories, some of which seek to identify universal principles governing all of development. Others focus on only one aspect—for example, personality or intellectual development. Some theories cover the whole lifespan, whereas others are concerned with a much smaller time frame. Thus, theories of development vary considerably in their scope. They also vary in their ability both to generate testable research ideas and to integrate data derived from research into a coherent and meaningful framework.

theory
A set of interconnected statements that integrate information within a field of inquiry and suggest new relationships among the phenomena under study.

FUNCTION OF THEORIES			
DESCRIPTIVE FUNCTION	**DELIMITING FUNCTION**	**GENERATIVE FUNCTION**	**INTEGRATIVE FUNCTION**
The description of the conditions under which the phenomena being studied occur.	The setting of limits or boundaries within which particular phenomena will be described and explained.	The suggestion of possible relationships among theoretical ideas.	The bringing together of existing data into an integrated, logically consistent body of knowledge.

TABLE 1–2

FOCUS ON CULTURE

Most of the theories within psychology have been developed by psychologists and researchers from Western cultures (United States, Canada, and Europe). Most of the theories do not explicitly address the issue of cultural variations. Past research to test these theories has been collected primarily from people living in industrialized countries. In what ways might the cultural perspective of the theorists and the people studied affect the theory that emerges to explain human behavior?

Assumptions of Developmental Theories   Developmental theories differ in the assumptions they make about the nature of the human organism. Some theories, for example, view human beings as basically passive, reactive, and ultimately responsive to the impact of environmental stimulation. Such theories place a great deal of emphasis on the influence of reward and punishment as factors shaping development. By contrast, other theories view the human organism as inherently active. Instead of being shaped by the environment, the individual ultimately is responsible for shaping or constructing the environment. As mentioned earlier, theories also differ in the degree to which they view development as a continuously unfolding process or a series of discontinuous and discrete series of changes.

RECAP

Developmental psychologists have focused on two issues: Is growth continuous or discontinuous? and What is the relative influence of heredity and environment on development? Theories fulfill four functions: They describe developmental phenomena; they provide a way of focusing attention on specific aspects of change; they generate new ideas; and they integrate existing ideas. Theories differ in the way they view humans (passive versus active) and developmental change (continuous versus discontinuous).

THEORETICAL PERSPECTIVES: A QUICK OVERVIEW

Within the field of developmental psychology, three major theoretical perspectives have impacted the way development is viewed: psychoanalytic theory, cognitive theory, and social learning theory. Within each of these broad perspectives are more specific theories focusing on different aspects of behavior and development. Later chapters will discuss some of these theories in greater detail and where appropriate offer a critique of specific aspects of these theories. For now, however, a brief introduction to these theoretical perspectives will help illustrate how they have influenced the ways in which psychologists have come to understand human development.

PSYCHOANALYTIC THEORIES

psychoanalytic theories
Theories based on the ideas of Freud that stress the importance of unconscious motivation and early experience in personality development.

Psychoanalytic theories of development are concerned primarily with personality and emotional development. They focus on the way in which people's emotional and biological needs adapt to the requirements of the society in which they live. Traditionally, psychoanalytic theories have placed a great deal of emphasis on the role of early experience in the development of adult personality. As a result, this perspective has stimulated much research on early-childhood socialization processes. Most of this research has derived from the theories of Sigmund Freud and Erik Erikson.

Freud: Psychosexual Development

Sigmund Freud (1856–1939) was a Viennese physician who specialized in what were called "nervous" or "mental" diseases. (Today Freud would probably be called a psychiatrist.) Freud believed that the adult personality is profoundly affected by unconscious drives and desires that are frustrated primarily during the early part of life. He believed that personality developed first at the level of the **id,** when the infant's interaction with the world focuses on satisfying basic survival needs for food, comfort, and stimulation. Later, the developing infant must learn to balance the need for immediate gratification with the desire for approval and acceptance from the people who provide for those needs, namely parents. The **ego** component of personality develops as children learn how to satisfy their pleasure-based needs from a rational, planning perspective. Finally, as a result of negotiating with parents and other caregivers, children also learn values, rules, and expectations regarding their behavior. The incorporation of these values and attitudes represents the **superego** component of the personality. The superego consists of what is commonly referred to as the conscience, or the moral values that when followed produce the ideal self.

Another feature of Freud's theory was the assumption that stimulation of different parts of the body is sexually arousing to children as they develop. Freud defined sexuality as any type of bodily stimulation that is pleasurable, and he proceeded to demonstrate how the sexuality of adolescence and adulthood concludes a long and orderly sequence of stages of **psychosexual development.**

In Freud's theory, the first stage of psychosexual development is the oral stage. At birth the oral region is very sensitive to any kind of stimulation. Newborn infants will instinctively suck on any object brought to the mouth, even when they are not hungry. According to Freud, the lips and mouth are the source of sexual pleasure. Freud believed that adults could become stuck, or fixated, in any one of the psychosexual stages. If the fixation was at the oral stage, people would develop an oral character; for example, they might be excessively and passively dependent on other people for attention.

At some point in the 2nd year, the anal area replaces the oral area as the primary source of gratification. This shift from the oral stage to the anal stage coincides with the neurological development of the anal sphincter muscles, a development that enables children to hold onto or let go of the contents of their bladder and bowels. Adults with an anal character personality may be obstinate and stingy (unwilling to give in), engage in hoarding behavior, or be compulsive.

The next stage of psychosexual development, occurring between the ages of 3 to 5 or 6 years, is called the phallic stage. Freud postulated that during this stage sexual gratification is achieved through genital stimulation, or masturbation. In other words, gratification is achieved without regard to the feelings of others—it is a self-centered approach to sexuality.

During the elementary-school years, the child enters the next period of psychosexual development, the latency stage. This is the time when much of the

---

id

According to Freud, an innate part of the personality system governing the expression of our most basic biological and emotional urges.

ego

In Freudian theory, the part of the personality system that is responsible for realistic adaptation to the world.

superego

In Freudian theory, the part of the personality system encompassing one's conscience and set of moral values.

psychosexual development

According to Freud's theory of personality, stages in which psychological energy is focused on one of five erogenous zones: oral, anal, phallic, latency, and genital. Failure to develop in one stage inhibits later development.

psychic energy formerly invested in sexual desires is displaced or channeled to other behaviors—for example, mastering culturally relevant skills, including those specifically related to school. From a psychosexual perspective, this is a quiet period. Very little of the child's energy is directed toward sexual gratification.

With the advent of adolescence, however, sexual desires burst forth once again, and the person enters into Freud's final psychosexual stage, the genital stage. In contrast to the phallic period, sexual gratification is now based on true intimacy—that is, people mutually sharing their sexual feelings with each other.

According to Freud, at every stage of psychosexual development the individual is confronted with the same basic conflict—how to give expression to one's sexual and aggressive instincts or needs in a way that is acceptable both to the self and to society.

Erikson: Psychosocial Development   Erik Erikson (1902–1994) was one of the first psychoanalysts to challenge the Freudian assumption that virtually all the interesting and important events in personality development had occurred by the time children started school. Erikson believed that the personality continued to develop throughout the entire lifespan.

psychosocial development
Theories of personality development that emphasize the importance of social and cultural experiences.

Unlike Freud, Erikson was primarily concerned with the way in which **psychosocial** rather than psychosexual forces influence the person's development. In his theory he describes a series of life crises or turning points that occur in response to demands that society places on the developing individual—that is, demands to conform to adult expectations about self-expression and self-reliance.

Erikson was born in Denmark, studied in Germany and Austria, and ultimately came to live in the United States. His personal experiences in several different cultures helped to shape his theory of personality. He stressed the importance and influence of cultural traditions and values on the way in which children are reared and on the quality of social interactions that affect personality development.

In contrast to Freud, Erikson's first interest was children, and his earliest scientific observations were drawn from their play behavior. In his own psychoanalytic theory Erikson showed that the sequence of bodily sensations Freud had identified were also reflected in a sequence of social experiences that had meaning for children within a given culture (Erikson, 1963). The stage of oral gratification, for example, is also the stage at which the infant establishes (or fails to establish) a sense of trust in the nurturing figure. The stage of anal control is also the time when the child gains control of other impulses that become the object of parental discipline. For Erikson, moving from the oral to the anal stage also equals means moving from a relationship with a nurturing parent, whom one learns to trust or mistrust, to a relationship with a disciplining (toilet-training) parent, from whom one derives feelings of autonomy or shame.

Erikson agreed with Freud's belief that early experience exerts a continuing influence on development. We do not simply graduate from the oral stage with its crisis of trust completely resolved. The crisis becomes less critical but is, nevertheless, re-experienced in all later stages of development.

Whereas Freud believed that the final psychosexual crisis occurred in adolescence, Erikson saw additional psychosocial crises developing in adulthood. Indeed, Erikson's theory is one of the few theories of development that extend throughout the lifespan. He has written extensively, not only on personality development in childhood and adolescence, but, as we shall see in later chapters in this book, on the normal changes that occur in the developing and aging adult (see Table 1-3).

COGNITIVE THEORIES

cognitive development
Changes in a variety of intellectual operations such as representational thought, logical reasoning, problem solving, planning, memory, and abstract thought.

Cognitive development refers to the orderly changes that occur in the way people understand and cope with their world. Cognition includes the process of thinking and the accumulation of knowledge; it also includes problem solving, memory skills, and creativity. Our understanding of cognitive development has changed dramatically in the past 50 years. At one time most people in Western societies

FREUD, ERIKSON, AND PIAGET: STAGES OF DEVELOPMENT						
	FREUD		**ERIKSON**		**PIAGET**	
AGE	**STAGE**	**FOCUS**	**STAGE**	**FOCUS**	**STAGE**	**FOCUS**
Birth to 1½ years	Oral	Oral pleasure	Trust	Social support	Sensorimotor	Understanding through sensory physical contact
1–3 years	Anal	Control of bodily functions	Autonomy versus doubt	Establishing independence	Sensorimotor/ preoperational	Development of language and other symbols to guide under standing
3–6 years	Phallic	Sex role identification; moral development	Initiative versus guilt	Development of self-care skills	Preoperational	Use of a prelogical system of reasoning
6–12 years	Latent	Repression of sexuality	Industry versus inferiority	Mastery of culturally relevant skills	Concrete operations	Systematic logical manipulation of symbols with a concrete reference
12–18 years	Genital	Heterosexual interest	Identity versus identity confusion	Definition of self	Formal operations	Abstract thought and hypothetical reasoning
Young adulthood	—	—	Intimacy versus isolation	Establishing meaningful relationships	—	—
Middle adulthood	—	—	Generativity versus stagnation	Caring for others	—	—
Late adulthood	—	—	Integrity versus despair	Life evaluation; seeking of self-fullfillment	—	—

TABLE 1–3

Dash indicates no specific focus for this period.
Source: From *Child Development,* by S. Ambron and N. Salkind, 1984, New York: Holt, Rinehart & Winston.

considered children to be miniature adults, at least as far as intelligence was concerned. Children were thought to differ from adults only in the quantity of knowledge they had managed to acquire. Cognitive research, however, began to demonstrate that children think and learn in ways that are quite different from adults.

Piaget: Cognitive Development

Jean Piaget (1896–1980), a Swiss psychologist, biologist, and philosopher, studied the way children think when presented with problems to solve. He found that what children know makes a different kind of sense than what adults know. For example, if one were to ask a group of adults what makes something alive, the answers probably would focus on the biological processes of plants and animals, such as cell multiplication; preschool age children, however, often attribute life to anything that moves. Somewhat older children, in contrast, tend to restrict the concept of life to objects that move of their own accord, such as the wind or a river, as opposed to objects that are capable of movement only if impelled by some force—for example, a bicycle or a car. Not until early adolescence, around 11 or 12 years, is the child's concept of life restricted to living plants and animals.

As children develop, they replace one set of assumptions with another, thereby reorganizing and reconstructing their base of knowledge. Piaget introduced two concepts to explain how people learn to adapt to their world. **Assimilation** is the process by which a person uses existing knowledge to comprehend new information. For example, young children usually learn about animals first through their experiences with pets; when they are confronted with non-pet animals such as goats or skunks, they use their existing knowledge about their pets to understand and direct their behaviors towards these new non-pet animals. Very quickly, in the case of the skunk, they learn that their knowledge of animals does not conform

assimilation

Within Piaget's theory, the process by which a person understands new information by applying their existing knowledge.

Many years ago, people thought that children were like miniature adults. They dressed them in adult-like clothes and assumed that they thought like adults. Today, we recognize the qualitative difference between childhood and adulthood.

Jean Piaget (1896–1980) formulated a stage theory of cognitive development describing the qualitative changes that occur in thought and reasoning from infancy to adulthood.

accommodation

Within Piaget's theory, the process of changing existing conceptions as a result of new experiences.

sensorimotor stage

Piaget's first stage of cognitive development; intelligence at this time is defined primarily in terms of the infant's motor and sensory actions.

preoperational thought

Within Piaget's theory, the second stage of cognitive development that begins at around 2 years of age and ends at around 6 or 7 years; characterized by the emergence of representational thinking but the absence of logical reasoning.

entirely with their immediate experience; their pet cat never smelled so bad! At this point of discovery, **accommodation,** or the modification of existing knowledge, occurs. Now the child has two understandings about animals; one for animals that are pets and one for non-pet animals. Through repeated interactions with their environment, people gradually build and change their concepts about their world. According to Piaget, the interplay of assimilation and accommodation forms the basis of cognitive processes.

Children undergo many changes in their understanding before they finally adopt adult assumptions about the world (Piaget, 1970a). Like Freud, Piaget formulated a sequence of stages of development to represent these changes. The stages refer to levels of mental reasoning, showing how the child constructs knowledge differently at each stage of development (see Table 1–3).

According to Piaget, in the first stage of cognitive development, thinking is limited to immediate sensory experience and motor behaviors; hence the name **sensorimotor stage.** Children learn about their bodies and the immediate environment through direct manipulation and experimentation. They do not think about things they cannot see or touch.

During Piaget's stage of **preoperational thought,** children become increasingly more capable of thinking using symbols such as words to represent the objects and events they experience. For example, 4-year-old Raoul, through symbolic play, uses a cigar box to represent a cart and uses a stick to represent the horse that pulls the cart. Although the ability to mentally represent experiences emerges

concrete operations
Piaget's third stage of cognitive development, characterized by the development of logical thought and the ability to manipulate symbols.

formal operations
Piaget's fourth and final stage of cognitive development that emerges during adolescence or later; characterized by abstract, logical, and hypothetical reasoning.

information-processing theory
A theory of thinking and cognitive development compared to the functions of a computer, concerning how people process information.

in the second stage of development, children's representations remain limited by adult standards. Children can represent only states of being; they cannot conceive of something changing from one state to another. It is during Piaget's third major period of cognitive development, the stage of **concrete operations,** that children become capable of thinking about how things change—and not only how they appear at different times.

The final stage of cognitive development in Piaget's theory is **formal operations,** what we usually call abstract thought. In the concrete operational stage, children master the ability to think about things. In the formal operational stage, however, adolescents master the ability to think about thoughts. They can reason about things they have not actually experienced, even about things that have no concrete existence—for example, hypothesizing about what life would be like in the year 2050.

Later chapters will address other psychologists' arguments for an additional stage of thought beyond Piaget's formal operations. This stage emerges in adulthood and is distinctively different from the way younger adults and children think.

Information-Processing Theories   Piaget's theory provides a way to understand how thinking develops and changes. Another way of understanding cognition is to study the ways in which people receive, represent, and process information (Kail & Bisanz, 1982). This approach to cognition is called the **information-processing theory.**

In this theory an analogy is often drawn between the way people think and the way computers work (not a far-fetched comparison, since people invented computers). Psychologists interested in this theory study the way people of different

Symbolic play is characteristic of preoperational thought. These boys are pretending to shave their make-believe beards.

ages accept new information, store the information in memory, and then retrieve or remember it.

Information processing is not specifically a developmental theory with defined stages or changes over time. The study of how people process information involves many interacting processes: attention, perception, memory, reasoning, and problem solving. Unlike Piaget, information-processing theorists believe that many of the basic processes for registering, storing, and processing information do not change with age (Siegler, 1983). What does change is the capacity, efficiency, and speed with which people process information (Kail & Bisanz, 1982). A young child may only be able to attend to a stimulus or task for a short period of time, but an older child or adult can sustain interest and attention for a greater duration. Likewise, an adult who has developed the ability to group common features together can remember and think about ideas more efficiently than a child, who considers ideas individually.

An example of the information-processing approach is the study of memory. One of the more important aspects of memory development is the acquisition of memory strategies. Even infants show a capacity for remembering things (such as a mother's face, the sound of a father's voice, and a favorite toy). This kind of memory is mostly involuntary—it "just happens." We see or hear something, and then recognize it later when it is presented again. Recognition memory appears not to change very much across the lifespan. However, some age differences do occur in recognition memory, depending on the type of information people are asked to recognize (Park, Puglisi, & Smith, 1986).

What does change with development is deliberate memory—that is, a planned attempt to remember something (Brown, 1975). For example, if children of varying ages are read a list of groceries to buy, they are likely to engage in different activities or strategies to help them remember what they are supposed to purchase. Preschool children are unlikely to realize that they need to do anything special to remember the list; as a result, they will forget many of the items. Somewhat older children may think to say the items aloud, often over and over again, as the list is read. This strategy, called verbal rehearsal, is quite effective in helping people remember things. The important point is that, with development, people become increasingly aware that they need to do something special in order to remember things. Ann Brown (1975, 1979) has pointed out that much of what we call memory development involves coming to know when, where, and how to process information in order to remember it.

Simply understanding the hardware of the computer, or the biological or neurological processes by which information is processed in humans, is not enough. The cultural context and demands must be examined as well. For example, ethnic minority families often must prepare their children to function in more than one culture—the majority ethnic culture and their own ethnic culture (Harrison, Serafica, & McAdoo, 1984; Harrison, Wilson, Pine, Chan, & Buriel, 1990). These children must must develop a greater cognitive flexibility to learn two different languages and sets of customs and be able to switch between one culture to another. To understand the cognitive development of children from ethnic minorities, it is critical to understand the cognitive demands of functioning in different cultures.

Social Learning Theories

social learning theory

Based on learning principles, a school of thought that recognizes that people learn by observing and imitating others.

reinforcement

The term that describes any stimulus that follows a behavior and results in the recurrence of that behavior.

Most of the theories we have discussed have focused on changes that occur over an extended period of time. The psychoanalytic theories of Freud and Erikson call attention to changes in personality and emotional behavior, while the Piagetian and information-processing theories are concerned with changes in thinking and problem solving. By contrast, instead of looking at changes in people's behavior as they age, **social learning theorists** pay attention to the way in which behavior is acquired. Development is viewed as the accumulated effects of learning. Behavior changes as people learn new responses as a result of experiences with different people in different settings—the mother's back or lap, the kitchen, the classroom, the playground, the workplace, the church, the social club, and so forth. The difference between what children and adults learn in these settings is a quantitative one; adults have learned many more behaviors or responses to a larger number of specific people and situations than have children.

From a social learning perspective, there are no developmental "stages" in learning; people at different ages do not have access to different kinds of learning mechanisms. The way people learn holds true for people of all ages, and even for animals. Development is seen as continuous rather than discontinuous across the lifespan.

Behavior is acquired primarily through the process of **reinforcement.** Behavior that is reinforced with pleasant consequences will more likely be repeated. Likewise, behavior that results in unpleasant or punishing consequences is likely to be discontinued. Reinforcement is the term used to describe any stimulus or reaction that follows a behavior and results in the recurrence of that behavior. To change behavior, you must alter the consequences to the learner of that behavior. In later chapters we will discuss in more detail the ways in which behavior can be changed by changing the consequences of the behavior. But for now, consider the case of the charming Lianna. At age 6, Lianna has learned that the way to get her grandfather to take her for a ride in his canoe is to smile sweetly at him and say, "I love your canoe!" Every time she had done this in the past her reward was—you guessed it!—a ride in the canoe with her grandfather. Her sweet behavior was increased because she liked what followed it, the ride. If, on the other hand, her grandfather ignored her response, she would probably persist until it was clear her strategy was not working and then try a different strategy.

While the nature of reinforcement varies from person to person and can include physical rewards such as food or money, social learning theorists Albert Bandura and Walter Mischel give greater recognition to the role of social reinforcements in stimulating behavior changes. Approval, acceptance, and criticism may be far more powerful reinforcers in your life than food or physical relief.

Social learning theorists also recognize the importance of thoughts and emotional reactions on behavior. For example, a person who experiences fear about going to a doctor may delay making an appointment or undergoing medical tests, possibly jeopardizing his or her own health.

Perhaps the greatest contribution of social learning theory is its recognition that responses can be acquired without exposure to direct reinforcement (Bandura, 1977). Much of what children learn occurs through their natural tendency to imitate or model the behavior of others. If they witness a model (such as a parent) being rewarded, their imitation of the model's behavior will increase.

Social learning theory suggests that much of what children learn occurs through their natural tendency to observe and imitate those people around them.

This is so, according to Bandura, because in imitating models, children temporarily identify with them and consequently "share" in either the pleasure of being reinforced or the discomfort of being punished—a phenomenon known as vicarious reinforcement. Social learning theorists believe that vicarious reinforcement is as strong an influence of behavior as direct reinforcement.

Much of the research in social learning theory has sought to specify the conditions that enhance learning through imitation and modeling. For example, researchers have shown that people are more likely to imitate a model whom they admire and perceive as being similar to themselves than someone who is not highly regarded and is considered to be different. Parents or caregivers are children's most effective models during the early periods of development. Later, as the person's world broadens, peers, co-workers, and other significant people outside the family become effective models. Later chapters will address social learning explanations of many behavioral patterns that are important in Western culture—among them aggression and gender-role behavior.

FOCUS ON CULTURE

Social learning theory has been used to explain the impact that living in a particular culture has on behavior. People learn by watching and imitating other people; the more often people interact with one another, the greater the likelihood that they will adopt similar behaviors, particularly if these behaviors are rewarded. Think of examples of vicarious reinforcement of particular behaviors within your own culture or subculture.

RECAP

Three theories that have influenced the study of human development include psychoanalytic, cognitive, and social learning (see Table 1–4). Freud and Erikson view development in terms of stages that emerge in reactions to either psychosexual or psychosocial forces. Erikson's view of psychosocial development encompasses the lifespan, while Freud's stages end in late adolescence. Cognitive theories describe development in terms of how people understand their world. Piaget depicted developmental changes in the way knowledge is acquired and understood by using four qualitatively different stages. Information theories focus on how people receive and retrieve information. Social learning theorists view development as the accumulation of learned behavior that is acquired as a result of social reinforcement and exposure to role models.

METHODS OF STUDYING DEVELOPMENT

It took Freud a lifetime to formulate his ideas and observations about behavior into a theory. It might take at least that long to assess the usefulness of his proposals. To evaluate a theory like Freud's, the researcher must design and conduct studies of various kinds. Most of the information in this book is based on findings from research studies designed to evaluate or test some aspect of a theory. But theories are usually stated in rather general terms. In order to conduct a research study, the investigator must first define the specific question or problem to be explored. The problem may be very broad—for example, the nature of cognitive development; or it may be quite specific, such as the relationship between parental

A COMPARISON OF THEORIES

THEORETICAL VIEW	ADVANTAGES	DISADVANTAGES
Psychoanalytic theories	Sees personality development as occuring in stages; emphasizes the importance of early childhood experiences; introduced the concept of unconscious motivation.	Based on clinical records which do not lend themselves to scientific testing; concepts are difficult to define and measure; provides a negative view of development because the theory was derived from pathological examples.
Cognitive theories	Focuses on the active nature of humans; provides new techniques for assessing cognitive changes; highlights the differences in thought processes between children and adults.	Piaget may have underestimated children's capabilities; no recognition of unconscious factors; deemphasizes environmental influences; stages may not be universal.
Social learning theories	Emphasizes environmental influences on behavior; concepts are easily tested; provides many practical applications.	Seems to depersonalize development; no attention is given to biological factors; ignores inner thought and unconscious factors.

TABLE 1–4

use of physical punishment and the emergence of self-control among preschoolers. Regardless of its scope, the statement of the problem defines the area under study.

Defining the problem, of course, is only the first step in research (see Table 1–5). Once the problem is defined, it must be reformulated into a statement about the relationship between variables—for example, the relationship between physical punishment (one variable) and self-control (a second variable). In turn, the variables must be operationalized—that is, clearly defined in ways that will allow the researcher to observe and measure the variables. When this has been accomplished, the researcher must consider the methods and strategies by which the phenomena in question will be studied.

Developmental researchers can choose from many data collection methods and research strategies. Consider, for example, the question of the relationship between violence on television and the expression of aggression among children. If you were a social scientist interested in this problem, you might want to gather information about this issue by observing children in their homes. Or you might want to create a more controlled situation in a laboratory in which children are exposed to television programs depicting varying degrees of aggression. Yet another strategy would be to compare children's aggression in doll or fantasy play and assess their exposure to specific television shows. You might want to investigate the effect of television violence over extended periods, repeatedly testing the same individuals at different ages; or you may decide to use samples of children of different ages and test each sample only once. Each strategy focuses on the same general problem—the relationship between television violence and childhood aggression—yet each uses a different approach.

DATA COLLECTION TECHNIQUES

The first step in answering research questions is to decide what type of information is needed and how this information will be collected. Before choosing a technique for collecting data, researchers must be clear about what they wish to accomplish. This, of course, requires familiarity with the strengths and weaknesses of the various data collection methods. In this section we will describe several methods in detail (they are summarized in Table 1–6).

STEPS IN CONDUCTING A RESEARCH STUDY
1. Define the problem or question to be studied.
2. Define the relationship between and among the variables of the problem.
3. Define the variables in a way that will permit measurement or observation (operationalize the variables).
4. Select a research strategy to collect the data.
5. Collect and analyze the data.
TABLE 1–5

METHODS OF DATA COLLECTION		
TYPE	**ADVANTAGES**	**DISADVANTAGES**
Interview	Flexible, rich source of subjective information	Possibility of distortion of information through memory lapse or bias; heavy reliance on verbal skills; dependent on subject's motivation to respond
Observation	Provides a detailed description of behavior; can provide practical applications	Does not answer the cause/effect question; no way to observe internal psychological events; cannot evaluate behaviors that occur infrequently or irregularly
Clinical method	Provides rich detail about individuals	Difficulty in generalizing to others; subject to the biases of the clinician
Standardized testing	Provides a basis for comparing people's scores; offers a means of assessment and tracking	Limited by culture-bound tests that rely heavily on verbal skills; can only measure narrow range of behaviors

TABLE 1–6

interview technique
A data-collection strategy involving a one-to-one dialogue between subject and investigator.

Interview Techniques   One way to collect information is by means of **interview techniques** in which the researcher usually asks the subject a variety of questions in a one-to-one dialogue. In most interviews, the format is flexible. The interviewer begins by asking relatively standard questions, but then pursues other ideas as they are introduced during the interview.

The interview technique can be a rich source of data for the researcher. By talking with people directly you may be able to learn more about a person's thought processes, fantasies, hopes, and concerns. Trained interviewers can conduct in-depth inquiries of subjective phenomena not ordinarily available for direct observation or manipulation.

Despite its obvious advantages, this approach also has some drawbacks. For one thing, the lack of standardization inherent in most interviews almost ensures that the questioning process will vary slightly from one individual to another. Information from a particularly talkative or unique subject could distort the conclusions a researcher may draw. Also, reliance on language as a medium of communication limits this technique to subjects who speak the same language and have sufficient language skills—possibly eliminating subjects from other language cultures, young children, and people with language problems. Finally, because valid interviews require good rapport between subject and investigator, this technique is highly susceptible to motivational factors. Results obtained from a child who feels dominated by the researcher, for example, or from an adult who is suspicious of the researcher's objectives, may be distorted and thus of questionable value.

observational technique
A data-collection strategy in which the ongoing behavior of individuals is recorded with as little interaction between observers and subjects as possible.

naturalistic observation
The organized study of people in their natural environment.

Observational Techniques   A second way of collecting data is through **observational techniques** that record the ongoing behavior of individuals with as little interaction between observer and subjects as possible. Observations may be made under naturalistic conditions or controlled conditions. **Naturalistic observation** means recording behavior in "real-world" conditions, with no attempt by the researcher to impose constraints on subjects' behavior. Unobtrusively observing the

Observing behavior in a controlled setting is one way to collect data. These researchers are monitoring the aggressive behavior of a child through a one-way mirror.

daily activities of nursing-home residents or street children in Rio de Janeiro would be examples of naturalistic observation. By contrast, controlled observation involves limiting the environmental scope under which observations are made or imposing conditions on subjects that are not ordinarily experienced in that particular setting. Observing how children play together in a university psychology lab, for example, would constitute one form of controlled observation.

In reality, the distinction between naturalistic and controlled observation is somewhat misleading. The difference between these two approaches is more a matter of degree than the traditional definitions suggest. These two categories of observation actually represent opposite poles on a single continuum—with the naturalistic end characterized by lower levels of investigator intervention and the controlled end by higher levels of investigator intervention (Willems & Alexander, 1982).

Observational procedures are particularly useful when the goal of research is to determine exactly what people are doing in a specific setting—for example, how children interact with one another in the playground or how parents discipline their children in the home. Moreover, to the extent that researchers refrain from imposing themselves on their subjects or the context in which the observation is taking place, this procedure is also very useful for determining how children and adults function in their everyday world—a goal that often has important practical implications.

The major limitation of the observational approach, however, is that it usually does not answer the question of cause and effect. Observational techniques provide us with information about what is happening, but not about how or why. This is because observational procedures do not allow for the kind of experimental control necessary for determining how research variables are related causally to one another.

Observational procedures have two other limitations. First, they tell us little about the internal, psychological experiences of subjects—their thoughts, beliefs, fantasies, and so forth. Observational procedures are also inefficient when studying behaviors that occur infrequently or irregularly in the subject's everyday life (such as altruism). In such a situation the observer would be forced to wait a long time before the behavior of interest was demonstrated. Despite these limitations, however, observational techniques have proven fundamental to the study of life-span human development.

clinical method

Combines naturalistic observation and interview techniques; researchers ask questions and collect information specific to the individual being studied.

Clinical Method   The **clinical method** involves collecting information from case studies of selected individuals. The clinical method combines naturalistic observation and interview techniques to allow researchers to ask questions and collect information specific to each individual they are studying. Piaget relied heavily on the use of case studies to learn about cognitive functioning. Piaget gave children problems to solve, observed their behaviors, and asked them open-ended questions about how they solved the problems. Each child would be presented with the same problem, but the questions Piaget asked would depend on the answers given; very often in the clinical method no two people are asked exactly the same questions. Unlike naturalistic observation, the subjects are usually not in their natural environment. Often they are observed in a laboratory or in a clinic or hospital setting. Case studies provide a more detailed view of individual behaviors and can be a rich source of new insights about behavior.

One drawback of using the clinical method to obtain information is that its results cannot easily be applied to other groups of people. Also, clinical method data is subject to the bias of the person conducting the case study. Often, information is selectively attended to or ignored depending on the interests of the clinician.

standardized test

A test whose material, administration, scoring, and evaluation have been so designed that it can be given reliably at different times and places by different examiners.

Standardized Tests   A different technique for gathering data is the use of standardized tests. The material, administration, scoring, and evaluation of a **standardized test** have been designed so that the same test can be given with confidence to different people at different times and places by different examiners (Cronbach, 1970). Standardized tests are developed by giving the test material to hundreds or thousands of individuals to establish performance levels associated with different ages—called age norms. When the test then is given to a subject in a research study, his or her performance is compared with the age norms derived from the original standardization sample. In this way, the researcher can tell whether the subject is performing above, below, or at about the same level as the majority of individuals of a given age.

Many standardized tests are used to collect developmental data. Some of the most common are intelligence tests (e.g., Stanford-Binet, Wechsler Intelligence Scale for Children, Wechsler Adult Intelligence Scale, etc.), achievement tests (e.g., California Achievement Tests, Iowa Test of Basic Ability, etc.), and personality tests (e.g., Minnesota Multiphasic Personality Inventory, or MMPI, etc.). Standardized tests are used widely in developmental research. They are also used, however, for many practical purposes—for example, grade-level tracking, clinical assessment, vocational interest evaluation, and so forth.

The choice of a particular test depends on many factors, the most obvious of which is the investigator's objective. You would not choose an intelligence test, for example, if you wanted to study personality. The theoretical orientation of the researcher also influences the choice of a test. For example, the Rorschach test, which is assumed to measure hidden and unconscious aspects of personality, is used almost exclusively by psychoanalytically oriented investigators.

One drawback to standardized tests is that they are not sensitive to cultural differences. Many of the standardized tests used today have established norms for people living in Western societies, and do not take into consideration the cultural or ethnic background of the test taker. As we shall see, the application of standardized tests in the United States has resulted in some rather heated controversies—including the use of intelligence tests and standardized achievement tests by school systems for assigning students to ability "tracks."

CORRELATION AND CAUSATION

Once data have been collected, researchers must analyze it to see to what extent the questions they have raised have been answered by the gathered information. Consider the following hypothetical finding: A researcher who has used interview and observational techniques to obtain her data reports that children who score high in imaginative ability are more likely to come from homes that contain many storybooks and other symbolic play material. Just what does this statement imply? Has the researcher shown that the development of imagination is somehow causally linked to playing with certain types of toys? The answer is no. All that has been established is that children's imagination and the presence of storybooks and symbolic play material tend to occur simultaneously in this study. In other words, a positive **correlation** (or association) exists between these two variables.

correlation
A measure of the degree to which two factors vary together.

It could well be the case that children who are creative and imaginative cause their parents to buy storybooks or to bring symbolic play materials into the home. Or it could be that children who are not particularly creative are less interested in storybooks, and hence their parents do not purchase them. With correlational data, one cannot and should not determine causation. In order to answer the question of what causes a behavior to occur, the researcher would have to use **experimental techniques.**

experimental technique
Data-collection strategies in which one set of variables (called independent variables) is manipulated in order to observe its influence on a second set of variables (dependent variables).

Experimental Techniques   In experimental research, the investigator manipulates one dimension of behavior—called the independent variable—and observes its influence on another dimension of behavior—the dependent variable. To the extent that the experimental manipulation leads to changes in subjects' behavior, the experimenter is justified in assuming a cause-effect relationship between the independent and dependent variables.

Take, for example, a study by Andrew Meltzoff (1988a). Meltzoff wanted to determine whether infants could understand what they viewed on television, and whether watching television would affect their behavior. Infants aged 14 months and 24 months were exposed to one of three conditions. In one condition infants saw the experimenter on a television set produce a novel toy, one the infants had never seen before. The experimenter pulled the toy apart and then reassembled it. In the second condition infants simply saw the experimenter on the television without the novel toy. In the third condition infants saw the experimenter on television handle the novel toy but not disassemble or assemble it. Then all the infants were presented with the actual novel toy and were observed to see whether or not they pulled it apart. (In a second, related study, infants who were exposed to the experimental conditions were observed 24 hours later to see whether they would remember and imitate an action they had seen on television the day before.) In both studies, all infants who had seen the experimenter pull apart the toy on television imitated the action. Those who did not see the toy disassembled did not pull it apart. In this experiment, the dependent variable was the behavior of pulling apart the toy because it depended on whether or not the infants had seen the experimenter do so on television.

The experimental approach is clearly the most appropriate method to use when the overriding concerns of the investigator are maintaining control over research variables and establishing cause-effect relationships. In addition, this procedure is quite useful for studying behavior that occurs infrequently or irregularly in everyday life. In such situations, researchers can devise experiments that are more likely to bring out the behavior so that it can be studied. Certain types of behavior, however, are not open to experimental manipulation. One would not, for example, purposely expose children to abuse simply to see what effect it had on their development.

Another limitation of experimental techniques is that they tell us what children can do under relatively restricted laboratory conditions but not what they actually do in their ordinary lives. This has prompted some critics to argue that researchers are painting an artificial picture of development through experimental procedures. As one prominent researcher (Bronfenbrenner, 1977) has said, experimental laboratory research is the "science of the strange behavior of children in strange situations with strange adults" (p. 513). The same also could be said for the experimental study of adult development.

FOCUS ON CULTURE

Most, but not all, of the developmental research that is reported in American and European professional journals has used subjects living in industrialized, English-speaking countries. Some of the data collection techniques available in developmental psychology are difficult to adapt for use in nonindustrialized societies; for example, asking children to put together puzzles when these toys are not part of their experience or giving them tests that have been translated from English to their native language may not make any sense. How does this limitation affect our understanding of human development?

ISSUES IN DATA COLLECTION

Once a researcher has specified what will be studied and the type of data to collect, the next step is to consider how and when data collection will occur. For example, suppose you wanted to study test-taking anxiety and have decided to use a self-report test to collect your information. Your next concern would be to decide whom you will include in your study. Will the subjects you use be representative of the general population? Will you use people of different ages and backgrounds? How will you recruit the subjects? Will you collect data from them once or over

Research Perspective

BIAS IN PSYCHOLOGICAL RESEARCH

One of the hallmarks of the scientific method is its quest for knowledge that is free from moral, political, or social values (Sherif, 1979). However, critics suggest that scientific research indeed reflects biases of both the experimenter and the current political and cultural climate (Riger, 1992). This can be seen in my own experience as a researcher.

About 20 years ago I focused my research activities on the frequency, situational determinants, and consequences of emotional responses. I used women as subjects because I had discovered in a previous study that men are reluctant to discuss their emotions in much detail, especially to a female experimenter. The women in my study kept daily records of their emotional experiences for 1 month, noting the emotions they experienced, the context in which they occurred, and their consequences. The study was a productive one. However, when I submitted it to a professional journal, I was surprised to learn that while the editors could not fault the study, they didn't consider the topic significant enough to warrant publication. After recovering from the shock, I decided to pursue research topics that were more mainstream and therefore more likely to be published.

My experience highlights the influence that bias can have on scientific research. In the 1970s the editorial boards of professional journals were composed primarily of male researchers who were predisposed to value the topics and types of research that they considered to fall within the domain of science. Women's emotional experiences did not qualify. Despite the advantages of interview techniques for generating detailed information, particularly about personal thoughts and feelings, they produce data that are harder to quantify and conditions that resist rigorous control. At the time most of the psychological scientists used the physical sciences as a standard for research; they were

an extended period? The question of sampling will have an important influence on the type of information you collect.

RESEARCH DESIGNS

Because development implies a change in behavior over time, the developmental researcher must address the problem of how to study behaviors that, by definition, are changing. To accomplish the difficult and complex task of describing and explaining behavioral change over the lifespan, the researcher must gather information about individuals at different levels of development. Three principal research designs are used for this task: cross-sectional, longitudinal, and sequential designs.

cross-sectional design
A type of research design in which groups of individuals are compared at different ages on some measure at the same point in time.

Cross-Sectional Design
In **cross-sectional design,** individuals of different ages are tested or observed at the same point in time. The findings—observed group differences in behavior at different ages—are then used to draw inferences and conclusions about the nature of development for people in general. For example, if a psychologist wants to compare the level of moral reasoning of 30- and 60-year-olds, she might interview subjects in those age categories within the relatively

interested in precise measurements of observable behavior. Since subjective experiences are frequently not observable and are difficult to measure, reviewers with this bias could not very easily evaluate the merit of studying women's emotions. There is a sequel to my story: Although I did not continue my research on emotional experiences, current journals have published several studies by other researchers on this topic.

Despite the frequent complaints that psychological studies have focused too much research attention on white men to the exclusion of other groups of subjects, the problem still exists. In a review of 14,542 articles reported in six psychology journals between 1970 and 1989, Sandra Graham (1992) found that only 526 of them addressed African American subjects. Her analysis also revealed decreasing coverage of African American research. A similar finding has been reported for research involving or relevant to women (Crawford & Marecek, 1989). In the field of medicine and public health, this bias is even more pronounced. The health issues that have been heavily researched have used men as their subjects. One consequence of this bias is that the conclusions and treatment programs derived from research conducted on men cannot be safely generalized to women. For example, the mortality rate for coronary disease in women has risen, while the rate for men has declined. This is due in part to more aggressive diagnostic and treatment approaches being offered to men but not to women.

It can be argued that it is impossible for researchers to prevent their values from intruding into their work; their interest in a particular research question and their motivation to pursue a certain kind of research program reflect what is important to them. However, it is possible to recognize the gaps in psychology's attempt to study human behavior. The issues and characteristics of groups of people who are underrepresented in research need to be addressed (Reid, 1993) and new research should be encouraged. Research concerning women, who represent half of the human population, needs to be expanded to accurately reflect their experiences.

short period of a week or two. If the 30-year-olds demonstrated higher levels of moral reasoning than the 60-year-olds, the researcher might conclude that young adults are morally more sensitive than older adults. She might go further and hypothesize that adults lose their ability to draw moral conclusions as they age.

Because a cross-sectional study usually can be carried out over a short period, it has the advantage of being quick and relatively inexpensive. Moreover, it gives the psychologist a good overview of the developmental phenomena under investigation. Yet this research design has some limitations. For one thing, because this approach measures a person's behavior at only one point in time, it tells little, if anything, about the historical antecedents of the behavior—that is, the earlier experiences that prompted the behavior. And it tells nothing about behavioral stability—whether behavior observed at one time will repeat itself during a future observation. These limitations are linked to the fact that the cross-sectional design tells more about differences among age groups than about development within individuals (Baltes, Reese, & Nesselroade, 1977).

Another problem with this approach is that people from different age groups differ not only in chronological age but also in the historical period in which they were born and brought up. In other words, age groups in cross-sectional research constitute different generations, or cohorts. A **cohort** is a group of individuals born

cohort
A group of individuals born during the same time period who presumably were exposed to similar experiences during the socialization process.

Cohorts from the 1960s may share similar characteristics because of social and political experiences they have in common.

during the same period who presumably share many general societal experiences that could influence aspects of their development.

For example, think about the impact of growing up in the United States during the era of computers, computer-aided instruction, and video devices and games. People today are exposed to a much broader range of information than ever before. We may expect today's young adults, compared with people born 50 or 60 years ago, to have a different attitude toward technology. It would be difficult, however, to know whether this difference is the result of developmental changes or simply of differences in training and exposure to computers and other technological advances.

Longitudinal Design   To overcome many of the problems inherent in cross-sectional designs, researchers sometimes adopt another strategy—**longitudinal design.** This method involves repeatedly testing the same group of individuals over a period of time. The time span involved and the elapsed time between testings vary, depending on the problem being investigated. For example, in one study (Ramsay, Campos, and Fenson, 1979) the development of bimanual handedness (preference for the right or left hand in manual tasks) was examined using infants who were assessed for hand preference at monthly intervals from 10 months of age

longitudinal design

A research design in which the same group of individuals is repeatedly tested over a period of time.

A longitudinal study of the influence of television on children's development would probably require testing groups of children from infancy through childhood and early adolescence.

until a clear preference for one hand or the other was found—usually around the age of 18 months. McCall, Eichorn, and Hogarty (1977), in their investigation of developmental transitions in early mental growth, needed a lengthier time frame. These researchers tested children monthly between the ages of 1 and 15 months; every 3 months thereafter until they were 2½ years old; and then every 6 months until the children were 5 years old.

Other research questions require even longer periods of study, particularly for those interested in development across the lifespan. In such cases, the time between testings usually is measured in years, and sometimes even in decades. In the earlier example of moral reasoning, we may decide to test adults every 10 years, from 30 to 60 years of age, to see what changes occur in the level of moral reasoning as the subjects age.

Longitudinal research has many advantages. Probably the most important one is that it provides a good picture of development within individuals and not simply an overview of differences among age groups. Furthermore, in following the development of a specific behavior over a given period, researchers are able to answer questions about the developmental stability of that behavior. In addition, they can often determine what earlier conditions or experiences influenced the development of the behavior in question (Schaie & Hertzog, 1982).

For all its benefits, however, the longitudinal approach has some serious drawbacks that limit its usefulness. Perhaps its greatest disadvantage is that it requires substantial investments of time and money. Consider, for example, the plight of the researcher who is committed to investigating the course of mental growth across the entire lifespan using a longitudinal design. The researcher faces an impossible task if he or she plans to collect the data personally. If the researcher begins testing infant subjects early in his or her research career, say at age 25, by the time the subjects are themselves 65 and entering old age, the researcher most likely will be dead. Indeed, even less extreme time commitments are often prohibitive from a practical standpoint. For this reason, short-term longitudinal studies—usually no more than 5 years in length—are most common.

Longitudinal research also presents methodological difficulties. Because such research continues for months or years, some subjects invariably will drop out or be lost over the course of the experiment. It is now well known that this loss of subjects does not occur in a random fashion. Participants who see a longitudinal project through to its conclusion are usually more cooperative, more motivated, more persistent, and more competent than those who drop out along the way. Thus at the end of a longitudinal study, the remaining subject sample may be biased, thereby making it difficult to draw valid conclusions about the more general population.

Another problem with this approach results from the repeated testing of subjects over long periods. When subjects receive the same or similar tests more than once, they often become "test wise"—particularly when the time between tests is relatively short. In such cases, subjects will perform better on later tests, not because of the effects of development but because of the effects of repeated practice.

A final, more subtle problem with the longitudinal strategy is that some changes in individuals are caused by the period of measurement rather than by the effects of development. Consider, for example, a hypothetical study that examines age-related changes in sexual attitudes among Americans during adulthood. Teenage subjects interviewed in the 1950s would probably have displayed relatively conservative attitudes regarding sexual behavior. Interviewed today, some 40 years later, these same subjects would undoubtedly be more permissive in their attitudes. This finding could be interpreted to mean that sexual attitudes become less conservative from adolescence to middle-adulthood. However, times have changed since the 1950s; American society as a whole has become more permissive regarding the expression of sexuality. The observed change in this hypothetical study could very well reflect a historical change rather than a normal developmental change occurring during adulthood. The point is that the longitudinal design in itself does not necessarily enable one to make sound generalizations about the effects of development.

Sequential Design   To meet the challenges of collecting data across the lifespan, researchers have developed a complex research design called **sequential design** that combines cross-sectional and longitudinal techniques (Schaie & Hertzog, 1982, 1983) (see Table 1–7). A sequential design starts out resembling a cross-sectional study in that groups of subjects of different ages are tested at the same time. The groups of subjects are retested at specific intervals, as is the case with a longitudinal design. With each new testing period, however, new subjects are added to make up for subjects who may have dropped out of the study.

By comparing the changes over time, age-related differences can be identified. Because different cohorts of subjects are used, history-related changes can be examined by comparing samples of subjects born in different years. Sequential designs are more efficient because researchers can collect information about a fairly long period of development in a relatively short time.

sequential design
A research design that combines cross-sectional and longitudinal techniques; groups of subjects of different ages are tested at the same time and retested at future times.

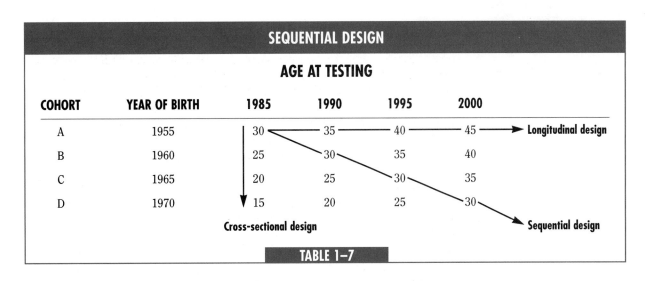

		SEQUENTIAL DESIGN				
		AGE AT TESTING				
COHORT	**YEAR OF BIRTH**	**1985**	**1990**	**1995**	**2000**	
A	1955	30	35	40	45	Longitudinal design
B	1960	25	30	35	40	
C	1965	20	25	30	35	
D	1970	15	20	25	30	Sequential design
		Cross-sectional design				

TABLE 1–7

ETHICAL CONSIDERATIONS IN RESEARCH

In planning a research project, one of the most important things the investigator must keep in mind is its potential effect on the subjects participating in the experiment. Does the research design in any way expose the individuals to possible physical or psychological harm? If some risk is involved, is it worthwhile in light of the proposed goals of the project?

Ethics in psychological research recently has become a controversial issue; in large part this is because researchers are more aware of the negative consequences that sometimes result from the procedures used in studying human beings. Consider, for example, the following hypothetical studies:

> A researcher is interested in studying the effects of punishment on children's problem-solving behavior. Punishment is operationalized as a 5-volt electric shock delivered to the child's palm whenever the child makes a mistake on a test item.
>
> In a second experiment, a researcher decides to explore developmental trends in children's cheating behavior. The young subjects are not told that the experimental setting has been designed to facilitate their cheating on a test, nor do they know that the researcher is watching them through a one-way mirror.
>
> A third study is designed to evaluate the effect of environmental control on the mortality rate of nursing-home residents. Two groups of elderly adults are recruited. One group—the experimental condition—is given responsibility and control over scheduling its daily activities; the other group—the control condition—is exposed to the usual nursing-home procedure, which entails little personal responsibility and environmental control.

Each of the above examples raises a question about research ethics. In the first example, the question is obvious: Is it necessary to use electric shock to study the effect of punishment on children's learning? Clearly the answer is no. Even if one argues that a 5-volt shock is mild and unlikely to cause any physical damage, one cannot ignore the potential for psychological trauma to the child in such a situation.

The problems in the second example are somewhat less obvious. Observing subjects without their knowledge and without their fully understanding the nature of the experiment not only undermines trust but may well place these individuals at risk for psychological harm (for instance, acute embarrassment and negative self-evaluation) should they later find out that others have observed them cheating.

Even the intervention study described in the third experiment raises an important question about ethical research practices. If the new intervention technique proves to be successful in reducing the mortality rate of nursing-home residents (or at least postpones death for a short time), is it ethical to withhold it from the control group? If it is not, how are we to gauge the effects of the new technique without employing a control group?

Evaluating the ethics of a particular research study can be a complicated task. While some studies (such as the first experiment described) clearly violate standard ethical guidelines for research with humans, others fall in an ethical "gray area." The final decision on whether to employ a research procedure is usually made by a research ethics peer review board. This board, which is found in virtually every research institution, reviews all research proposals involving human subjects for possible violations of standard ethical practices.

It is generally recognized that research involving children and other relatively powerless groups (e.g., the retarded, prisoners, inmates in mental institutions, nursing-home residents, etc.) poses even greater potential ethical problems for the investigator. For children, parental consent is always required before participation in research is allowed. Yet parental consent is no guarantee that the child will participate voluntarily. Sometimes subtle pressures (from parents, peers, teachers, or researchers) are enough to coerce the child into participating when he or she really does not want to. Such coercion, whether used with children or others, is in clear violation of research ethics (see Table 1–8).

AN OVERVIEW OF THE ROAD AHEAD

This chapter introduced some of the theories, issues, and questions that interest developmental psychologists, along with the methods they use to seek answers to these questions. Now it is time to examine the changes that occur over the lifespan, organized in this textbook according to the following periods:

Prenatal Experience	Conception to birth
Birth through Infancy	0–2 years
Early Childhood Years	2–6 years
Middle Childhood	6–12 years
Adolescence	12–18 years
Early Adulthood	18–40 years
Middle Adulthood	40–65 years
Late Adulthood	65 years and older
Death	At any time

ETHICAL STANDARDS FOR DEVELOPMENT PSYCHOLOGISTS

1. No matter how young the subject, the child has rights that supersede the rights of the investigator. In the conduct of their research, investigators measure each operation they propose against this principle and are prepared to justify their decision.

2. The investigator uses no research operations that may harm the child either physically or psychologically. Psychological harm, to be sure, is difficult to define; nevertheless, its definition remains a responsibility of the investigator.

3. The informed consent of parents or of those legally designated to act in loco parentis is obtained, preferably in writing. Informed consent requires that the parent be given accurate information on the profession and institutional affiliation of the investigator and on the purpose and operations of the research, albeit in layman's terms. The consent of parents is not solicited by any claim of benefit to the child. Not only is the right of parents to refuse consent respected, but parents must be given the opportunity to refuse.

4. The investigator does not coerce a child into participating in a study. The child has the right and should be given the opportunity to refuse to participate in a study.

5. When investigators are in doubt about possible harmful effects of their efforts, or when they decide that the nature of their research requires deception, they submit their plan to an ad hoc group of colleagues for review. It is the group's responsibility to suggest other feasible means of obtaining the information. Psychologists have a responsibility to maintain not only their own ethical standards but also those of their colleagues.

6. The child's identity is concealed in written and verbal reports of the results, as well as in informal discussions with students and colleagues.

7. Investigators do not assume the role of diagnostician or counselor in reporting their observations to parents or those in loco parentis. They also do not report test scores or information given by a child in confidence, although they recognize a duty to report general findings to parents and others.

8. Investigators respect the ethical standards of those who act in loco parentis (e.g., teachers or superintendents of institutions).

9. The same ethical standards apply to children who are control subjects and to their parents as to those who are experimental subjects. When the experimental treatment is believed to benefit the child, the investigator considers an alternative treatment for the control group instead of no treatment.

10. Payment in money, gifts, or services for the child's participation does not annul any of the above principles.

11. Teachers of developmental psychology present the ethical standards of conducting research on human beings to both their undergraduate and graduate students. Like the university committees on the use of human subjects, professors share responsibility for the study of children on their campuses.

TABLE 1–8

Source: From "Statement of the Division of Developmental Psychology of the American Psychological Association," 1968, *Society for Research in Child Development Newsletter,* pp. 1–3.

Within each of these periods you will learn about the changes in the areas of physical, cognitive, social, emotional, and personality development. In the chapters that address changes in adulthood, you will learn about the importance of family and occupational changes. Because death can occur at any age and has an impact on everyone involved, issues related to death, dying, and bereavement are addressed in a single chapter that considers all phases of the lifespan.

To get a feel for the journey ahead, you may want to skim through all the chapters now. Because this is an introductory lifespan development textbook, you will be getting just a taste of the many changes and experiences that define each phase of life. As you learn about each period of development, I urge you to consider what you have already learned about life through your own personal journey. I also hope that you will be encouraged to learn more.

BRIEF REVIEW

The scientific study of human development is a relatively new field that focuses on the physical, social, and cognitive changes that occur in behavior over the course of a person's life. Issues of particular concern to lifespan researchers are the cumulative effects of changes across the lifespan, the contexts, including culture, in which change occurs, and the degree of change that can occur at any age.

Development is influenced by the interaction of heredity and environment. Across the lifespan, age-normative, history-normative, and nonnormative events exert different influences on development.

Many theories of human development have been proposed during the twentieth century, and each has supporters. Scientific theories have a descriptive and explanatory role. They also serve to define the area of study, to provide a basis from which to test hypotheses, and to provide a framework for understanding the data gathered by researchers.

Sigmund Freud and Erik Erikson based their theories of development on psychosexual/psychosocial factors. Freud proposed that there were five stages in psychosexual development—oral, anal, phallic, latency, and genital—and that failure to develop in one stage inhibited later development. Erikson believed that social forces exert a strong influence on an individual's movement from one stage of life to the next. Building on Freud's stages, Erikson proposed eight psychosocial stages throughout the entire lifespan.

Jean Piaget developed a theory of cognitive, or intellectual, development that specified how an individual's thought processes differ at various ages. Piaget identified four stages from birth through adolescence: sensorimotor, preoperational thought, concrete operations, and formal operations. An alternative view of cognitive development is provided by information-processing theory. This perspective is concerned with how information flows through a cognitive system and with developmental changes in attention, memory, and problem-solving capacities.

Social learning theory attributes primary importance to environmental factors and asserts that development consists of what an individual learns throughout life. Social learning theorists focus on the influence of direct reinforcement, observation, and imitation on the acquisition of new behavior.

Researchers use a variety of techniques to collect data. The most commonly used techniques include interviews, naturalistic observation, clinical methods, and standardized tests. Correlations between behaviors do not mean that one variable caused another, only that two or more variables are related to one another in some way.

The basic research designs available to the developmental psychologist include the cross-sectional, longitudinal, and sequential designs. The cross-sectional design involves testing different age groups at a single point in time. Longitudinal designs test the same sample of people more than once over a longer period. Sequential design involves both cross-sectional and longitudinal techniques.

Researchers in human development must be especially aware of ethical considerations. In any study involving children or, indeed, any living subjects, adverse short- or long-term effects must be minimized and appropriate consent obtained.

KEY TERMS

accommodation (18)
age-normative events (10)
assimilation (17)
clinical method (27)
cognitive development (16)
cohort (31)
concrete operations (19)
contextual view (6)
correlation (28)

cross-sectional design (30)
culture (7)
developmental psychology (4)
ego (14)
environment (9)
experimental technique (28)
formal operations (19)
heredity (9)
heredity-environment issue (9)

history-normative events (10)
id (14)
information-processing theory (19)
interview technique (25)
lifespan perspective (5)
longitudinal design (32)
naturalistic observation (25)
nonnormative events (10)
observational technique (25)

preoperational thought (18)   reinforcement (21)   standardized test (27)
psychoanalytic theory (13)   sensorimotor stage (18)   superego (14)
psychosexual development (14)   sequential design (34)   theory (12)
psychosocial development (15)   social learning theory (21)

REVIEW QUESTIONS

If you can answer these questions, you have a good understanding of the material in this chapter. If a question seems difficult, go back to the text and review the topic.

1. How does the lifespan approach differ from other ways of studying human behavior?

2. Why is it important to include culture and gender in the study of development?

3. Describe the heredity-environment (nature-nurture) controversy.

4. What are the four functions of a theory in psychology? List and describe them.

5. What are the assumptions underlying theories of development?

6. Distinguish between the id, ego, and superego. Name the psychosexual stages of development proposed by Freud.

7. Describe three ways in which Erikson's theory of personality development differs from Freud's.

8. Name Piaget's stages of cognitive development. Describe the way thinking occurs within each stage.

9. How do information-processing theorists study human cognition?

10. Describe the social learning theory view of development.

11. Compare and contrast the advantages and disadvantages of using the cross-sectional and longitudinal research designs. Give an example of each design. Describe the sequential design.

12. What is meant by the statement, "Correlation is not causation"?

13. Why is it important to use cohorts in the study of development?

14. Describe the following methods of data collection: interview, observation, clinical method, standardized test.

15. Describe the ethical considerations that researchers must consider when conducting research using people.

OBSERVATIONAL ACTIVITY

CHANGES IN BEHAVIOR ACROSS THE LIFESPAN
The purpose of this activity is to familiarize yourself with the degree of change in a person's life by using an informal method of collecting data. Select a friend, relative, or even yourself as the subject of your study.

Your aim is to gather information and evidence about the changes in your subject's life. You can begin by collecting a series of photos of your subject, perhaps from family albums or yearbooks. Baby books are also a good source of information about the early years of a person's life. You may want to narrow your focus of study by limiting yourself to a few areas of change (e.g., physical size, interests or activities, school performance, friendships).

You can collect more information by interviewing your subject. You will need to consider what kind of questions you want answered before you actually conduct the interview.

After you have collected as much information as you can, write a description of the changes that have occurred in your subject's life and when they occurred.

The most interesting part of this activity is your own critique of your "study."

1. What problems did you encounter in collecting your "data?"

2. What possible biases are there in your description of your subject?

3. How would you do this "study" differently if you had the time and resources to do so?

4. What did you gain in doing this activity?

The Beginning Years

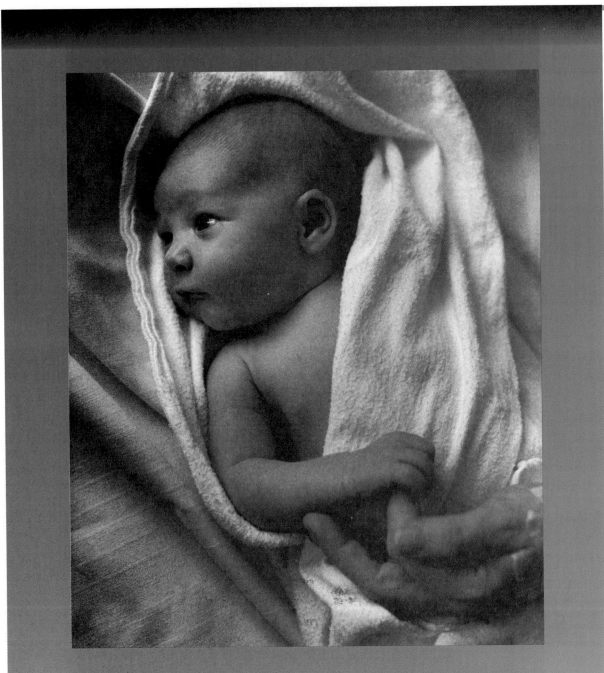

The journey of life begins at conception with the union of an egg and sperm, establishing the genetic blueprint that guides the emergence of a unique individual. The next three chapters begin the study of development by examining the changes that occur during the prenatal and early infancy portion of the lifespan. Just as the overall quality of any journey is affected by travel arrangements and circumstances surrounding the departure, the quality of a person's life is influenced by both genetic and environmental factors. In Chapter 2 you will learn how genetic heritage can affect physical development and behavior. This chapter describes the passage of the unborn child from conception to birth, and emphasizes the importance of a healthy prenatal environment and a safe birth to development in early infancy. Chapter 3 discusses the growing capabilities of infants to discover and quickly master first their own bodies and then their surroundings. Finally, Chapter 4 focuses on the social and emotional maturation of infants and the role that caregivers play in nurturing children.

Genetics, Pregnancy, and Birth

Thirty-five-year old Jane had all but given up on being a mother. She and Louis had been married for 4 years and had tried practically every technique and recommendation offered to them about the best ways to get pregnant. At first, Jane figured that their difficulty in conceiving was due to their busy work schedules. Later she began to think something might be wrong with her, but her doctor reassured her that both she and Louis were fine. And then, just when she had begun to investigate adoption, she learned that she was pregnant. Now she was 6½ months into the pregnancy and proudly displaying their baby's first picture: the sonogram, from which Jane and Louis learned they were expecting a boy. Because of her age, Jane underwent amniocentesis, a prenatal diagnostic procedure to rule out genetic disorders. Louis accompanied her on prenatal office visits and the two of them were registered for birth preparation classes at the hospital. Louis was quite involved with the upcoming birth; in fact, he proudly told his friends, "We're pregnant."

Two and a half months later, with Louis as her coach, Jane gave birth to Aaron. Jane and Louis finally realized the joy of bringing a new life into the world.

In contrast, pregnancy and birth for the !Kung San people is a an event dictated by custom and tradition. Husbands are relatively uninvolved during the pregnancy and birth is a solitary experience for mothers. Because this was her second pregnancy, Nomawele, whose name meant "mother of twins," recognized the signs of labor and impending birth. In this African community, it was the custom for a pregnant woman to select and prepare an isolated spot away from the village in which to give birth. Nomawele had already prepared herself a grassy spot in the veld for just this moment.

As her mother had done when she was born, Nomawele slowly retreated to her carefully chosen spot without telling anyone where she was going or asking for help. !Kung women were expected to approach childbirth without fear. As the pains of contraction quickened she silently lowered herself into a crouching position. It was hard physical work, but soon she felt the relief of watching her son slowly emerge from her body onto the soft grass beneath her.

Using the sharp end of a stick, Nomawele severed the cord that had connected the two of them over the months. She then wrapped her newborn son in her scarf. After a short rest she would return to her village and wait for her husband to receive and name their child.

Two babies, born in very different cultures and settings, begin their lives through the universal process of childbirth. The preface of their lives actually began with their genetic heritage and with their early days of life inside their mothers' bodies. What experiences and circumstances will influence their development? We will first consider genetic contributions.

THE GENETIC FOUNDATIONS OF LIFE

chromosomes
Rodlike structures containing long segments of genes.

genes
Segments of specifically arranged molecules of deoxyribonucleic acid (DNA) that govern cell activity.

deoxyribonucleic acid (DNA)
Found within genes, a protein molecule made up of sugar, phosphate, and bases.

MECHANICS OF HEREDITY

Lifespan development begins when the genetic material from both parents unites to form a new human cell. The essential ingredients for this transmission of genetic information is imbedded within each of our cells. The nucleus of each cell contains rodlike structures called **chromosomes;** there are 46 chromosomes arranged in pairs within body cells. A chromosome is made up of long segments called **genes,** which are responsible for the formation of body proteins that affect the activity of the cell. It is estimated that each chromosome contains from 20,000 to 100,000 genes. Genes, acting either separately or in combination with other genes, are responsible for directing the physical changes in the body that ultimately affect the psychological and physical development occurring throughout the lifespan.

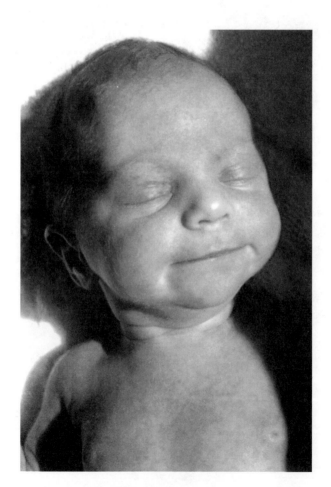

From the early moments of life, genes influence the physical changes in the body.

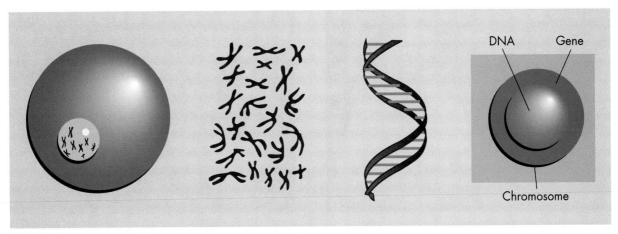

FIGURE 2-1

A human cell, far left. The dark mass within the cell is the nucleus containing the chromosomes. An enlargement of some chromosomes is depicted in the second drawing. Chromosomes contain deoxyribonucleic acid, or DNA, the basic chemical of heredity. A portion of the DNA molecule is shown in the third drawing from the left. At each level of the spiral (or rungs of the ladder) are particular chemical pairs. The arrangement of these pairs along the DNA molecule determines which kinds of protein will be formed in the cell. The relationship of DNA, gene, and chromosome is shown in the picture on the far right.

FIGURE 2-2

Conception occurs when the genetic materials from the egg and sperm unite.

germ or sex cell
The egg or sperm cell.

zygote
The fertilized egg.

Genes consist of specific arrangements of molecules of **deoxyribonucleic acid, or DNA.** The DNA molecule consists of a chain of sugar, phosphate, and four bases: adenine, thymine, cytosine, and guanine. These bases are arranged in spiral-staircase fashion—a structure often referred to as a double helix. Genetic instructions on each gene are determined by the arrangement of the molecules of these bases; any rearrangement of these bases changes the genetic instructions to the body. The arrangement of DNA molecules in gene groupings on different chromosomes within the cell creates a complex genetic code. Each arrangement directs the production of body proteins that influence growth throughout life (see Figure 2-1).

There are two kinds of cells within our bodies—those that direct the growth of the body and those that are responsible for reproduction. **Germ or sex cells,** also known as the egg or sperm cells, differ from body cells in that they contain only half the number of chromosomes—23 instead of 46. When the egg and sperm unite and fuse their genetic material at conception, the 23 chromosomes from each of the germ cells couple to produce 23 pairs of chromosomes in the resulting **zygote,** or fertilized egg. Thus, each parent contributes half the chromosomal material (see Figure 2-2).

A few hours after fertilization the newly formed cell duplicates its nucleus and divides into two identical cells. These two cells then become four, the four cells

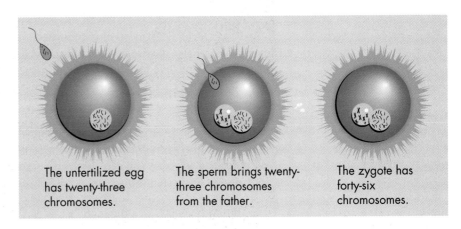

The unfertilized egg has twenty-three chromosomes.

The sperm brings twenty-three chromosomes from the father.

The zygote has forty-six chromosomes.

Monozygotic (identical) twins develop from a single fertilized egg and have the same genetic makeup. Dizygotic (fraternal) twins develop from two separate fertilized eggs and have different genetic blueprints. Can you tell from these photographs which twin pairs are monozygotic?

mitosis
Process of cell reproduction in which the nucleic material is duplicated and the cell divides into two separate, identical cells.

meiosis
The process of cell division by which germ cells are formed.

become eight, and so on. This process of cell reproduction is called **mitosis.** In mitosis the genetic material within the cell nucleus is duplicated, and the cell splits into two genetically identical cells. By this process cells grow and develop throughout life. As old cells deteriorate they are replaced by new ones, each one preserving the genetic blueprint contained in the original cell formed at conception (see Figure 2–1).

Germ cells, like all other cells, originate from the 46-chromosome cell that began life, but germ cells are produced by a different process of cell division called **meiosis.** Before meiosis begins, the germ cell has 46 chromosomes, as do other cells. In meiosis the chromosomes duplicate themselves as the cell divides, producing two new cells. After the first division the cells divide again, but they do not duplicate themselves as they did on the first cell division. When the second division is complete there are four cells, each with 23 chromosomes, or half the number found in the original cell.

Just before the chromosomes separate, there is a rearrangement and exchange of DNA molecules between the two pairs of chromosomes in a process known as crossing over—which creates a new sequence of genetic information. This new genetic pattern, while a mixture of the genetic contributions from each parent, does not match that of either parent because the DNA messages have been scrambled. This is why we can say that with the exception of identical twins, no two people, even from the same family, have the same genetic makeup.

SEX CHROMOSOMES

sex chromosome
The chromosome that determines the gender of the person.

Among the 23 pairs of chromosomes found in each cell is a special chromosome pair that is responsible for characteristics associated with an individual's sexual development. There are two kinds of **sex chromosomes.** The larger one is called the X chromosome, and the much smaller one is known as the Y chromosome. Females have two X chromosomes, and males have one X and one Y chromosome. Thus, all the cells in females include an XX pair and all the cells in males an XY pair. However, the germ or sex cell from the mother—the egg—contains only the X chromosome, whereas the germ cell from the father—the sperm—can contain either an X or a Y chromosome. The gender of the offspring—female (XX) or male (XY)—depends on whether the sperm that penetrates the cell contains an X or a Y chromosome. Thus, since the mother can contribute only one type of sex chromosome, the gender of the offspring is determined by the father.

TWINS

I happen to have a special interest in twins because I have an identical twin sister, Mary. If you were to meet us both, you would have difficulty distinguishing between us; we both excel in mathematics and have the ability to recall information by forming vivid mental pictures. We have naturally curly hair, the same bend in our noses, and similar cowlicks in our hair. Yet my sister and I don't for a minute understand why people have trouble telling us apart. It was not until we reached early adolescence that we fully understood the special significance we have for each other. Mary is my genetic clone or duplicate.

monozygotic twins
Identical twins formed from one egg that divides into two separate beings.

Identical or **monozygotic twins** are formed when the zygote divides during the process of mitosis to form two separate cells. These two cells, which contain identical genetic material because they originate from the same zygote, continue to grow and develop into two separate beings. Identical twins are always the same gender, since their heredity is the same. Monozygotic twins occur about once in every 250 conceptions. It is not known why some zygotes separate in the process of mitosis, but identical twinning is not influenced by the age or health of the mother, nor is it controlled by heredity.

dizygotic twins
Fraternal twins formed when two eggs are fertilized at the same time by two different sperm.

My father and my aunt were fraternal twins. **Fraternal** or **dizygotic twins** are formed when the mother's body releases two egg cells, each with its own chromosomal arrangement. These two eggs are then fertilized by two different sperm cells (see Figure 2–3). The result is two offspring born at the same time but with entirely different genetic codes. Like my father and aunt, fraternal twins may be of opposite sexes. The tendency to conceive dizygotic twins appears to be influenced by race, heredity, the mother's age, and the number of previous pregnancies she has had. In the United States, women are statistically more likely to give birth to fraternal twins if they are themselves dizygotic twins who are African American, are between the ages of 35 and 40, and have had at least four children. Women who take fertility drugs are also more likely to conceive fraternal twins.

FOCUS ON CULTURE

In many African cultures, the birth of twins is cause for much celebration. Twins are viewed as a gift, a symbol of fertility. Names are given to twins that identify them as special throughout their lifetime. Twins are the focus of many special rituals and customs within their community. For example, it is the custom among the Iteso people that twins are required to taste the first fruits of a harvest (Karp, 1987).

GENETIC TRANSMISSION

Dominant and Recessive Genes
The chromosome pairs contain the genetic code that results, over time, in recognizable differences in physical characteristics and behaviors. What is inherited is not a particular trait or characteristic such as intelligence or curly hair, but rather the biochemical instructions to cells to either produce or not produce specific proteins that would ultimately result in intelligent actions or curly hair.

genotype
The actual genetic arrangement contained in the cell; one's genetic makeup.

In describing the action of the genes it is helpful to define two terms. **Genotype** refers to the actual genetic arrangement contained in the cells of an

FIGURE 2–3

Except for monozygotic twins, it is impossible for any two people to have the exact same genetic makeup.

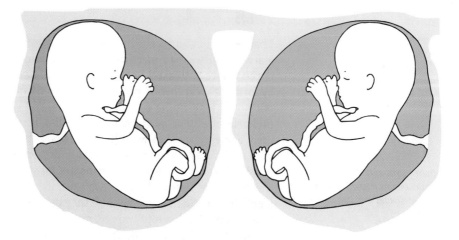

Fraternal twins can be as different as any two siblings born separately.

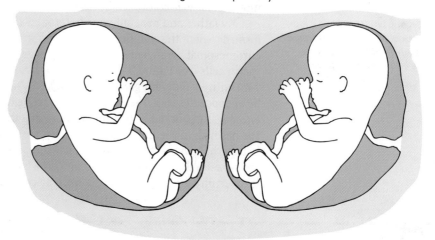

Monozygotic twins are generally identical.

phenotype
The expressed and observable characteristics of a person based on the genotype.

allele
A single gene in a pair of genes, or alleles.

individual. **Phenotype** refers to the observable characteristics of an individual that result from the genotype. Although much more is known today about how the specific actions of chromosomes and genes cause inherited physical characteristics, very often the specific genotype for many of the characteristics observed in people are not precisely known. Many of the characteristics associated with personality and intelligence, for example, represent a complex interaction of many behaviors that change with age, each of which may represent the action of many, many genes. For less complex traits, such as eye color or blood type, it is easier to describe the genetic code, or genotype.

The gene factors that contribute to the genotype are arranged in pairs within the chromosomes. Half of the gene pair is from the mother, and half is from the father. These gene pairs are called **alleles.** Some traits or characteristics, such as eye color, are known to result from a single gene pair. It is possible to receive a gene from the father for brown eyes and a gene from the mother for blue eyes.

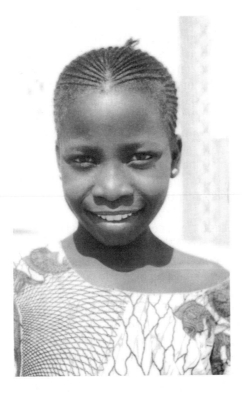

Genes determine skin, hair, and eye color, the shape of the nose, and the curliness and texture of this girl's hair.

dominant gene
The gene that is expressed when paired with the same or a different gene.

recessive gene
The gene that is expressed only when paired with a similar recessive gene or in the absence of a dominant gene.

These two genes, one directing blue eye color and the other brown eye color, would compose the genotype. The actual color of the eyes would represent the phenotype.

In this example, the eyes would be brown since the gene for brown eye color is known to be dominant over the blue-eyed gene. A **dominant gene** is one that is physically expressed whenever it is present in a gene pair; it is the gene that prevails in the phenotype. A **recessive gene** is one that is physically expressed only when it is paired with a similar recessive gene or in the absence of a dominant gene (see Table 2–1).

Many traits are known to function according to the principles of dominance and recessiveness. Certain physical defects are carried on the recessive gene and are expressed in the offspring only when both parents carry the recessive gene. PKU (phenylketonuria), hemophilia, sickle-cell anemia, and color blindness are a few disorders carried on recessive genes.

AN EXAMPLE OF DOMINANCE AND RECESSIVE TRAIT TRANSMISSION		
	BROWN-EYED GENE	**BLUE-EYED GENE**
Brown-eyed gene	Brown-eyed child	Brown-eyed child
Blue-eyed gene	Brown-eyed child	Blue-eyed child
TABLE 2–1		

Sex-Chromosome Abnormalities For most people, the sex-chromosome pattern is a normal *XX* or *XY*. However, in some people a defective arrangement of the sex chromosomes results in significant abnormalities. For example, Turner's syndrome is characterized by an XO genotype, indicating a missing sex chromosome. This defect occurs in about 1 in 2,000 females, who tend to show limited sexual development, short stature, webbed necks, and—although no overall mental retardation occurs—specific cognitive defects in spatial abilities.

Females with additional *X* chromosomes—*XXX, XXXX,* or *XXXXX*—have increasing physical and mental disabilities with each additional *X* chromosome. Klinefelter's syndrome, *XXY,* involves an additional *X* chromosome in the male genotype. Occurring in 2 in 1,000 births, this disorder results in tall men, stunted sexual development, and, in some cases, mild retardation and personality disturbances.

Perhaps the most controversial and best known sex-chromosome abnormality is the genotype *XYY,* sometimes called "supermale" disorder. This chromosomal pattern is found in males and was originally thought to lead to criminality because early studies found a higher incidence of the genotype in men convicted of violent and aggressive crimes. Since then this association has been questioned because there was control group sampling of nonincarcerated males. Traits that are known to be associated with *XYY* include tall stature, poor coordination, low intelligence, and facial acne. Witken believes that the elevated crime rate shown by *XYY* men is related not so much to increased levels of aggression as to low intelligence (Plomin & DeFries, 1980; Witken et al., 1976).

Fragile X Syndrome, or Fra-X, is usually found in about one in every 1,000 *XY* males, but the disorder can also occur in females with an *XX* genotype (about one in every 2,500). In these individuals the *X* chromosome appears to be thin and easily broken—hence the name "fragile." Fra-X, the most common human chromosomal abnormality associated with mental retardation (Hagerman & Silverman, 1991), is also the most variable in its phenotype. Females with the Fra-X genotype may show very little deficiency, although mental retardation is found in about one third of reported cases. Males with the Fra-X genotype may display varying degrees of mental retardation, language deficiencies, and poor motor coordination (Lachiewicz, Spiridigliozzi, Gullion, Ransford, & Roa, 1994); yet some males with Fra-X appear normal.

CULTURAL AND ETHNIC VARIATIONS IN GENETIC DISORDERS

Most people think that because a characteristic or trait is genetically determined, the impact of culture or environment is minimal. While genetic programming may assign the biological mechanisms that produce a particular trait, the phenotype is shaped by the cultural environment. The frequency of expression of some genetic disorders may be linked to some features associated with certain cultural groups. For example, social customs that restrict marriages among people from different religions or ethnic groups may limit the gene pool and increase the chances of a recessive disorder emerging, as in the following examples.

Tay-Sachs Disease Infants born with Tay-Sachs disease are more likely to be descendants of eastern European or Ashkenazi Jews; it is inherited by about 1 in every 3,000 Jewish children in the United States. People with this disorder lack an enzyme to break down fat, which allows harmful wastes to accumulate. Eventually, brain and nerve cells degenerate, resulting in mental and physical retardation and usually death by age 5. Tay-Sachs disease is neither preventable nor curable. It is detectable, however, through prenatal diagnosis. Why does it occur primarily in eastern European Jews? Jews who adhere to the restrictions against marrying non-Jewish people are more likely to restrict their gene pool, thus increasing the chances of marrying someone who also carries the recessive gene for Tay-Sachs.

Sickle-Cell Anemia   The blood cells of people afflicted with sickle-cell anemia, unlike the normal round cells, are elongated and curved. These sickle-shaped blood cells clog the blood vessels and prevent the delivery of oxygen. As a result, people with sickle-cell anemia experience severe pain in the abdomen, back, and limbs. They are susceptible to infection and, in some cases, die before reaching adulthood. Sickle-cell anemia is found in people of African descent, especially those from the coastal and central areas of Africa. It also affects some people of Arabian, Greek, Maltese, Sicilian, Turkish, and southern Asian descent. In the United States, 1 in every 625 African Americans and 1 in every 1,000 to 1,500 Hispanics inherits this disorder (March of Dimes, 1983).

To develop this disorder a child must receive a recessive sickle-cell gene from each parent. If the child inherited only one sickle-cell gene, then he or she would be a carrier of the disorder but would not have the disease. If you are a carrier of sickle-cell anemia, you run a 25% risk of risk of passing on the disorder to your offspring if your mate is also a carrier. However, sickle-cell carriers also can have advantages: they have a much higher than average resistance to malaria, a deadly disease commonly found in coastal areas, especially in Africa, where the risk of contracting malaria and dying from it is much greater than the 1 in 4 risk of producing an offspring with sickle-cell anemia.

Thalassemia (Cooley's Anemia)   About 1 in every 400 descendants of people from the eastern Mediterranean regions of Africa, Asia, and southern Europe—tropical or subtropical climates—are born with thalassemia, a common recessive blood disorder that results in severe anemia. Infants born with this disease appear listless, have poor appetites, and are susceptible to infections. If it is not treated, the disease results in an enlarged spleen and liver. Thalassemia is detectable before birth and is treated by frequent blood transfusions and careful monitoring.

Cystic Fibrosis   People who inherit two recessive genes for cystic fibrosis lack an enzyme that is necessary to control the amount of mucus the body produces. Mucus collects in the lungs and digestive tract and eventually leads to death, usually before the age of 30. In the United States, cystic fibrosis is most common among Caucasians of northern European descent.

Phenylketonuria (PKU)   PKU is caused by a recessive gene that interferes with the metabolism of the protein phenylalanine, so that the protein accumulates in the brain and causes brain damage. About 1 in every 15,000 newborns are afflicted with PKU; 1 in every 80 Caucasian births are carriers of the disorder. Although PKU is found in almost all ethnic groups, it is most common in babies of northern European descent and rare in babies from black, Jewish, or Asian families. PKU is detectable before birth and can be treated if detected early in life.

RECAP

The foundation of life rests within the cell nucleus, where the genetic material is arranged among 23 pairs of chromosomes that contain thousands of genes. The action of the genes is directed by the DNA molecules that make up the gene. The sex chromosome determines gender and carries certain characteristics. Except for identical twins, no two individuals have the exact same pattern of genes. While dominant genes are more likely to be expressed in the phenotype than recessive genes, many genetic disorders are the result of the expression of recessive genes. Occasionally, the sex chromosome is defective and abnormalities result. Different ethnic and cultural groups have a higher incidence of certain genetic disorders.

THE INFLUENCE OF GENETICS ON BEHAVIOR

Even though my twin sister Mary and I are genetically identical, we have not developed identically. I am slightly taller, heavier (I am sorry to have to admit it!), and generally healthier than my sister. I have often puzzled over our differences. Clearly, the influence of genetics is not as straightforward as it might appear. Today we know enough about the action of the genes and the DNA molecules to conclude that the environment is a contributing factor in the biochemical genetic coding that directs growth. Recent studies have even suggested that there is a genetic component to one's social environment (Plomin & Neiderhiser, 1992; Chipuer, Plomin, Pedersen, McClearn, & Nesselroade, 1993). The ways in which people interact with their environment are influenced by genetically based characteristics, such as personality, which in turn affect the types of experiences they have.

Many researchers in the field of behavior genetics (the study of the effects of heredity on behavior) believe that much of the individual variation that emerges throughout life can be explained by genetic differences. However, the fact that genes influence behavior does not mean that nothing can be done to change behavior. Although it is difficult and often undesirable to change the genetic code that may direct behavior, it is possible to alter the environment in which the genes operate. For example, diabetes is an inherited disease, some forms of which can be controlled by managing the dietary intake of sugar and fats. By changing the nutritional environment, the consequences of the genetic disorder can be modified.

UNRAVELING THE GENETIC THREAD

Chemists, biologists, psychologists, and counselors are teaming up to study the influences of genetic and environmental factors on behavior. The task is, of course, a very complex one because the answer depends on which behavior is studied. A second complication arises when researchers seek to answer the question of how genetic factors influence growth and change by conducting experiments. Following the lead of Gregor Mendel, the monk who discovered the laws of genetics by selectively cross-breeding different varieties of sweet pea plants, a researcher might crossbreed animals with known pedigrees and characteristics and then observe the phenotypes of the offspring. However, ethical and practical constraints

Research Perspective

THE HUMAN GENOME PROJECT

An enormous research project is under way in several locations in the United States that is likely to have a profound effect on our understanding of genetic influence. The Genome Project, a 15 year effort being funded by the U.S. Department of Defense and the National Institutes of Health, aims to decipher the human genetic blueprint. The researchers' first goal is to map the location of over 100,000 genes on the 23 chromosome pairs within the human cell nucleus. Then they will work on specifying the sequence of the components of DNA, the basic building block of genes. To understand the scope of this long range project, imagine unraveling all of the DNA strands within the cell nucleus; their entire length would measure approximately 6 feet. So far, researchers have been successful in mapping and sequencing less than half an inch of that DNA (Yarris, 1992): So far less than 2,000 genes have been mapped. Locating a gene on a chromosome involves not only identifying which chromosome carries that gene, but where on that chromosome the gene resides. All of this work is tedious and time consuming. We can expect to see faster progress in the future as a result of the use of high speed computers and new biochemical procedures to help isolate and reproduce millions of copies of DNA strands being used in the Genome research (Holzman, 1992).

Even though the project is nowhere near completion, the researchers have made some discoveries that shed light on certain kinds of genetic disorders. For example, in 1989 the gene responsible for cystic fibrosis was located. This enabled researchers to develop a test to identify the probability of the cystic fibrosis gene in an embryo. Other discoveries include the identification of the gene for Huntington's chorea, Duchenne's muscular dystrophy, and familial Alzheimer's disease (Martin, 1987). More than 4,000 diseases, including cancer and heart disease, are believed to result from a breakdown in the genetic process (Yarris, 1992). With a detailed genetic map as a guide, medical researchers will be greatly assisted in developing new ways to diagnose and prevent these diseases.

The next generation may owe its longevity to the outcome of the Human Genome Project, but it will also have to address a number of ethical issues. When it is possible to know each person's genetic map, what precautions will be needed to ensure that people carrying "bad" genes are not disenfranchised or treated with prejudice? Would genetic screening be a requirement for marriage? For employment? For health benefit eligibility? Anticipating these questions, the Human Genome Project has dedicated some of it research funds to examining the social, legal, and ethical implications of their research.

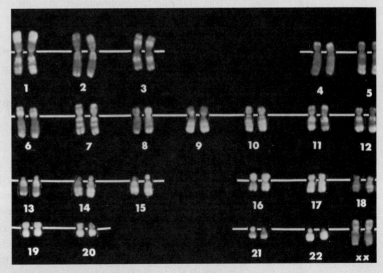

The aim of the Genome Project is to map the location of genes on the 23 chromosome pairs within the human cell nucleus.

prevent the use of selective breeding when studying humans. The specific environments in which animals are raised can be controlled more carefully and compared. For example, dogs that are known to be quite even-tempered can be exposed to a stressful physical environment, such as one with bright lights and noise, and compared with animals of the same breed raised in a nonstressful setting.

A second way to study the impact of genetics is to examine characteristics and traits that occur within a particular family. This requires the construction of a family tree—a description of all the individuals in several generations within a family. For example, Sir Francis Galton (1869) attempted to prove that giftedness or genius was inherited by referring to the number of gifted people who were related to other gifted individuals in the same family. Studying inherited characteristics using family trees requires extensive research and accurate records, which often are not available. Furthermore, in the family tree studies, the effect of the environment on a trait cannot always be separated from genetic influences because relatives often share similar environments as well as genes.

A third approach is to study monozygotic (identical) and dizygotic (fraternal) twins. Since identical twins have the same genetic makeup, any characteristics governed primarily by heredity would affect both identical twins. Thus, a high rate of concordance or similarity would be expected. Fraternal twins are no more alike than siblings, and thus a lower rate of similarity would be expected for a genetic trait.

By comparing the degree of similarity in certain characteristics between identical and fraternal twins, researchers can identify possible hereditary contributions. The impact of the environment can be assessed by comparing the similarities between twin pairs who are reared in the same environment by the same parents (that is, reared together) with twin pairs who are raised in different environments. The difficulties with this approach lie in finding sufficient numbers of twins separated at birth and in following up on the twins throughout their lives.

Yet another approach that is used to distinguish the contributions of genetics from those of the environment is to study adopted children who have no genetic connection to their adoptive parents. If adopted children are more like their biological parents than their adoptive parents, the contributions of heredity are underscored. If they resemble their adoptive parents more than their biological parents, the environmental contribution is seen as stronger.

PHYSICAL APPEARANCE AND DISORDERS

If you look at pictures of yourself and compare them to pictures of your parents at the same age, you will no doubt see some similarities. This is because heredity has a strong influence on physical appearance and body shape. The shape of your body, the color of your skin, eyes, and hair as well as blood type, bone structure, and metabolism are all guided by the genetic program contained in the DNA molecules. However, even with simple physical characteristics such as hair color, the environment can have an altering effect. The actual color of your hair, for example, can change as a result of malnutrition or exposure to excessive radiation (and of course to any chemical preparation you may apply to purposely change the color of your hair).

When our son Adam was born, he looked just like my husband did in his baby picture. However, as a child, Adam seemed to resemble my side of the family more.

Now that he is an adult, Adam clearly resembles my husband and I suspect he will look more like his father as he ages. Our genes direct the sequence and form of physical development over a lifetime. Height, facial features, body proportion, and even the age at which your hair begins to turn gray is controlled by your genes. My twin sister and I began to gray, need reading glasses, lose our waistlines, and develop wrinkles at about the same age. You may be able to look at members of your own family and see physical resemblances that appear across generations. The observation that many physical characteristics are inherited is not new. Today, however, researchers are more informed about the process of genetic influence.

Historically, researchers relied almost exclusively on phenotypes (observable characteristics) as indicators of genotype. They were unable to assess the ways in which chromosomal and genetic changes influenced development. Consequently erroneous conclusions about the genetic origins of behavior were sometimes drawn, as was originally the case with **Down syndrome.** People diagnosed with Down syndrome have 47 chromosomes instead of the normal 46. The phenotypic characteristics of this disorder include short stature, a flattened skull, oval-shaped, slanting eyes with an extra fold of skin over the eyelid, a large, protruding tongue, a short neck, and mental and motor retardation. It was the physical characteristics of slanting eyes and folded eyelids that led British physician Langdon Down in 1867 to erroneously conclude that the syndrome was limited to offspring from the Mongoloid racial group. In fact, at one time the disorder was referred to as Mongolism. Today it is recognized that the disorder is the result of the addition of an extra chromosome to the twenty-first chromosome pair (hence, the disorder is referred to as trisomy 21) and is unrelated to membership in any racial group.

Down syndrome occurs in approximately 1 of every 600 to 700 babies and is more frequently found in children born to older mothers (Cicchetti & Beeghly, 1990). Evidence also suggests that a defect in the father's sperm may result in the extra chromosome in the offspring (Magenis, Overton, Chamberlin, Brady, & Lovrein, 1977).

When studying the influence of genetics on physical appearance and disorders, researchers can agree on a description of the phenotype. In the case of blood type, for example, certain laboratory tests performed on a blood sample yield results that can be used to determine whether a particular blood sample is type A+ or O+. This degree of clarity in defining the phenotype is not always possible when studying the effects of heredity on more complex characteristics such as personality and intelligence. Let's examine the evidence for the influence of genetics on these two psychological domains.

PERSONALITY

Personality is a person's unique pattern of response and adjustment to his or her environment. One of the difficulties in examining the influence of genetics on more complex arrangements of behavior such as personality and intelligence is that the environment also has a significant influence on behavior. If we examine the relationship between parent and child on a specific trait such as aggressiveness, for example, we may find that an aggressive parent has an aggressive child. We cannot confidently attribute this similarity to heredity, however, since the same parent also teaches the child aggressive behavior through their example. To identify genetic influences on personality such as aggression, behavioral

Down syndrome

A chromosomal abnormality caused by an additional chromosome in the twenty-first pair. People diagnosed with Down syndrome have 47 chromosomes instead of the normal 46.

geneticists would use the comparison studies of monozygotic and dizygotic twins discussed earlier.

Heredity has been found to influence several behavioral traits and personality adaptations. Infant temperament, for example, which is related to the child's level of activity, sleep patterns, emotionality, irritability, and sociability, has been found to be strongly influenced by genetics (Buss & Plomin, 1984; Plomin, 1989; Robinson, Kagan, Reznick, & Corley, 1992; Wilson & Matheny, 1983). Some studies also suggest a genetic basis for the personality trait of extraversion-introversion. People who are friendly, uninhibited, and outgoing with others would be described as extraverted, while people who tend to be shy, withdrawn, and anxious with others would be described as introverted.

Since 1979, psychologists at the University of Minnesota have been studying identical twins who were separated at birth and reared in different environments. One of the researchers, Thomas Bouchard (1984, 1990), reports that early results from this longitudinal study indicate that these twins are similar in their medical histories, intelligence test scores, temperaments, and fears. In some cases, the scores of identical twins on many psychological and ability tests were closer than would be expected for the same person taking the same test twice. The twins were also found to be more alike in a wide range of interests, tastes, and experiences that are usually considered to be determined by environmental influences. For example, separated twins entered the same occupations, married women with the same names, and wore the same types of rings on their fingers. Because I am a twin, many people ask me if my sister and I share such similarities. Indeed we do. Even though my sister lives over 300 miles away, and we do not talk on a regular basis, we often select the same birthday cards for relatives, buy each other similar presents, and anticipate each other's phone calls.

In addition to personality characteristics, some types of mental illness are also considered to be influenced by genetic factors. Many researchers believe that the predisposition to *schizophrenia,* a form of mental illness, has a genetic basis. The incidence of this disorder in the general population is about 1%. If one parent has schizophrenia, the likelihood that the children will develop the illness is 8%; if both parents are diagnosed as schizophrenic, the incidence increases to 39% (Gottesman, 1991; Gottesman & Shields, 1982). Forty-seven percent of people with a schizophrenic identical twin have also been diagnosed as schizophrenic (Kinney & Matthysse, 1978).

Although researchers have provided much evidence to suggest that certain personality characteristics and patterns of adjustment are influenced by heredity, they disagree about the degree to which these characteristics are controlled by genetics. The same twin studies that support the contributions of genetics to development also provide support for the influence of environmental factors. Identical twins reared in different environments are not as similar as identical twins reared in the same environment (Plomin, 1989).

INTELLIGENCE

Is intelligence inherited? Is the ability to deal effectively with abstract problems passed along through genes? The question of the origins of intelligent behavior is one of the most widely studied and controversial issues in psychology. Francis Galton (1869) noted that prominent public figures seemed to run in families.

Bright and distinguished people seemed to produce bright and distinguished off-spring. Our intuitive understanding from such observations is that intelligence has a genetic basis. However, the amount and type of influence heredity has on intelligence is a more difficult question to answer.

Part of the difficulty in demonstrating a genetic basis for intelligence lies in the many different ideas about what intelligence actually means. Most studies of intelligence have used the standardized IQ (intelligence quotient) test as a measure of intelligence, and performance on these tests seems to be influenced by genetic factors. Twin studies have provided one basis for this conclusion. Plomin and DeFries (1980), for example, report that genetic differences explain only about 50% of the variance in IQ scores; the other 50% of the variance is caused by environmental factors.

Studies comparing the IQ scores of adopted children with those of their biological and adoptive parents provide further support for the influence of genetics on IQ. Overall, research has found a closer relationship in intelligence between adopted children and their biological parents than between these children and their adoptive parents (DeFries & Plomin, 1978). Later studies by the same researchers, however, have found that both heredity and the adoptive family environment contribute to the cognitive ability of adopted children. For example, the adoptive mother's responsiveness to her child was significantly correlated with measures of infant intelligence (DeFries, Plomin, Vandenberg, & Kuse, 1981).

RECAP

The influence of genetics on behavior is measured by using animal selective breeding, family history, twin, and adoption studies. Genetics has a strong influence on physical attributes and the occurrence of some diseases and disorders. Down syndrome is an example of a disorder caused by a chromosomal defect; other physical attributes are the result of a single gene. The influence of genetics is more prominent in intelligence and personality characteristics such as extraversion-introversion and shyness. Certain types of schizophrenia also have demonstrated a genetic link.

THE PROCESS OF CONCEPTION

Now that you have a better understanding of genetic contributions and mechanisms, it is time to examine how human reproductive systems serve as the vehicles for conception.

REPRODUCTIVE SYSTEMS

Female Reproductive System   It is believed that human females are born with several hundred thousand immature eggs, or ova, which are housed in one of two ovaries. When the female reaches sexual maturity, and a mature egg is released from one of the female's ovaries and conducted through one of the two fallopian tubes approximately every 28 days in a process called **ovulation** (see Figure 2–4). The fallopian tubes provide a passageway for the egg into the woman's uterus, which is lined with blood.

ovulation
The process in which a sexually mature female's ovaries release one egg approximately every 28 days into one of her two fallopian tubes.

FIGURE 2–4

Ovulation, fertilization, and implantation. The ovary releases an egg into the fallopian tube, where it is penetrated by a sperm. The zygote begins cell division as it moves down the fallopian tube toward the uterus. When the cluster of cells has formed a hollow ball, it is called a blastocyst. Six days after conception the blastocyst begins to implant itself in the wall of the uterus.

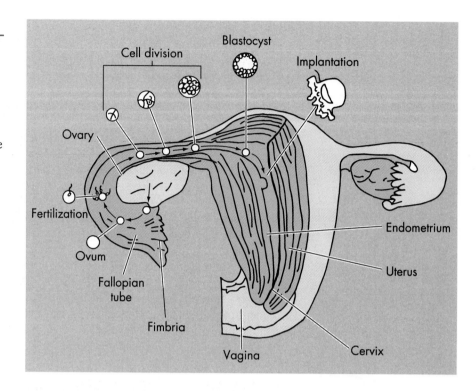

Each month, the lining of the uterus is filled with blood in preparation to receive a fertilized egg. If sexual intercourse should occur during the time the egg is en route to the uterus, fertilization and conception are possible. If the egg is not fertilized, it is released during the process of menstruation, when the lining of the uterus is shed.

Male Reproductive System   The reproductive organs for males include the testes, which produce germ cells known as sperm; the penis, which helps deliver the sperm into the woman's uterus; and the prostate gland, which produces a milky substance in which sperm are carried. During intercourse the male releases millions of sperm that swim upward through the vagina towards the cervix, and then into the uterus and the fallopian tubes in search of a ripened egg (see Figure 2–5).

CONCEPTION

fertilization
During conception, the process in which the egg and sperm cell fuse their nuclei to become the first cell of life.

If one of the sperm contacts and penetrates the wall of the egg cell, conception occurs. The two germ cells (the egg and sperm cells) fuse their nuclei to form the first cell of life, a process called **fertilization.** Fertilization of the egg by the sperm usually occurs in the fallopian tube, and the resulting new cell is called a zygote. While only one sperm penetrates the egg during conception, the process is not as simple as it seems. Many sperm never make it to the fallopian tube; once in the vicinity of the egg, several hundreds of sperm must surround the surface of the egg, acting as biochemical catalysts to break down the outer shell so that a sperm can penetrate the egg.

FIGURE 2–5

The male reproductive system.

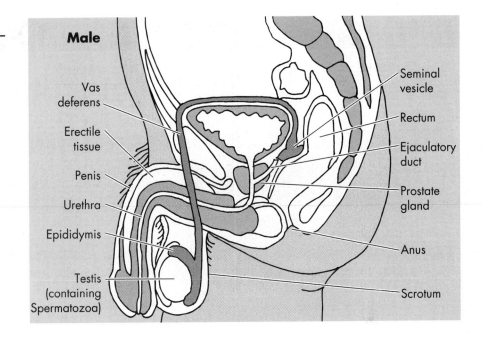

Male

Vas deferens
Erectile tissue
Penis
Urethra
Epididymis
Testis (containing Spermatozoa)

Seminal vesicle
Rectum
Ejaculatory duct
Prostate gland
Anus
Scrotum

INFERTILITY

infertility
Inability to conceive or difficulty in conceiving a child.

While most couples who want to have children are able to conceive through normal sexual intercourse, about one in six couples cannot. (Sokoloff, 1987). The reasons for **infertility**, the inability to conceive a child, are related to problems either in the man or in the woman, or sometimes in both. In some cases the reasons are simply not understood.

Infertility can have long-term effects on the lives of people who want to become parents but cannot. Couples may experience a loss of self-esteem, feel inadequate as men or women, or blame each other for the failure to conceive. In some cultures, such as that of China, some couples face the prospect of living out their lives without children or grandchildren, who will provide future links to their ancestry and will maintain the rituals of ancestor worship that are an important aspect of their culture. Such a situation can cause increasing distress as people grow older. Fortunately, as a result of recent advances in reproductive technology there are several alternative ways to help couples reproduce. A description of some of these techniques can be found in Table 2–2.

PRENATAL DEVELOPMENT

STAGES OF PRENATAL DEVELOPMENT

When Nomawele first suspected that she was pregnant, she announced the news to her husband, who immediately told his father that his family was about to expand. Everyone was very pleased. The onset of pregnancy is a physiological event, but it is also a psychological one. For the mother, there is the recognition that she has the responsibility of carrying a new life. Pregnancy also signals the creation of a new family. Fortunately, nature provides the prospective mother and father a period of time to prepare for their changing roles.

ALTERNATIVE MEANS OF CONCEPTION

PROCEDURE	WHAT HAPPENS
Artificial insemination	Sperm from either the male partner or a donor is inserted into the mother's uterus for conception.
In vitro fertilization	Egg of mother is surgically removed and fertilized by sperm from either the male partner or a donor in a petri dish; the fertilized egg is then implanted in the mother's uterus.
Egg transfer	An egg from a donor woman is fertilized through artificial insemination using the male partner's sperm and then inserted into the prepared uterus of the female.
	A second technique involves the artificial insemination of a donor by the male partner. After conception the fertilized egg is removed from the donor and transplanted to the female partner.
Surrogate womb	A woman agrees to be artificially inseminated by the would-be father, carrying the child the duration of the pregnancy. Upon birth, the child is adopted by the father and his partner.

TABLE 2–2

ovum stage
The first stage of prenatal development lasting 10 to 14 days after conception.

differentiation
Within 2 weeks after fertilization, the process in which growth of the cell becomes more specialized.

blastocyst
The hollow sphere of cells that forms within a week after fertilization of the egg by the sperm.

embryonic stage
The 6 weeks following the implantation of the ovum into the uterine wall.

placenta
A blood-filled structure that supplies the unborn child with nutrients.

The normal human pregnancy lasts 9 months, or 266 days. The zygote changes in shape and size at a rapid rate during the time from conception to birth. It is helpful to divide the pregnancy into three stages, during which the ovum is transformed into the embryo, and then into a fetus (see Table 2–3).

The **ovum stage,** also called the germinal stage, begins at conception in the mother's fallopian tube and ends with the implantation of the zygote in the uterine wall. This stage lasts approximately 2 weeks. During this time the developing ovum, or fertilized egg, is rapidly growing—through the process of mitosis— while it travels to the uterus.

Once the ovum is fertilized by the sperm, the mother's body begins preparing the lining of the uterine wall with a rich blood supply to provide for the developing new life over the 9-month gestation period. At this time the mother may not even be aware of her pregnancy since she has not yet missed a menstrual period. By about the 6th day the ovum has reached the uterus, and the process of implantation begins (see Figure 2–4).

At about the time that the ovum enters the uterus, the developing cells, now numbering approximately 32, start a process of **differentiation:** The cells, triggered by genetic instructions, assume different functions. A week after fertilization the cells form into a hollow ball called a **blastocyst.** Some of the inner cells of the blastocyst will form the body of the baby, while the outer cells will form the placenta, umbilical cord, and amniotic sac, the structures that house and protect the baby during prenatal development. At this time the cell mass is no larger than the size of the period at the end of this sentence. When the blastocyst imbeds itself into the blood-rich wall of the uterus, the ovum stage ends and the embryonic stage begins.

The **embryonic stage** (from the Greek word meaning "to swell") lasts approximately 6 weeks. During this time the life-support systems—the placenta, umbilical cord, and amniotic sac—are refined. The part of the embryo attached to the uterine wall becomes the **placenta.** This blood-filled, spongy mass is an amazing organ that supplies the embryo with all its nutrients and carries off all its waste

STAGES OF PRENATAL DEVELOPMENT		
STAGE	**LENGTH OF TIME**	**CHARACTERISTIC EVENTS**
Ovum	First 2 weeks	Rapid growth of the fertilized egg, which passes through the fallopian tube to the uterus. The blastocyst forms and embeds itself in the uterine lining.
Embryonic	2–8 weeks	The placenta, umbilical cord, and amniotic sac develop. Through the process of cell differentiation the basic physical structures are formed. Head, heart, limbs, and the digestive and nervous systems have begun to function in their primitive forms.
Fetal	8–40 weeks	Bone cells replace embryonic cartilage. Organs and structures grow and develop. **3rd month:** Teeth buds appear; limbs and fingers move; the genitals are formed. Average weight is 3 ounces and length is 3 inches. **4th month:** Mother feel fetal movement; the face appears human-like; average weight is 6 ounces and length is 5 inches. **5th month:** Fetus reacts to extrauterine noise, increases activity, and sleeps; fingers and toenails emerge; lanugo (fine hair) covers the skin; average weight is close to 1 pound and length is 12 inches. **6th month:** Grasping reflex and hiccuping are possible; eyes and eyelids are formed; occasional breathing occurs; average weight is close to 2 pounds and length is 14 inches. **7th month:** Fetus could survive if born; average weight is 3 pounds and length is 16 inches. **8th–9th months:** Rapid weight gain occurs; the fat layer in skin develops; average weight at birth is 7½ pounds and length is 20 inches.

TABLE 2–3

umbilical cord
The structure that links the embryo to the placenta.

amniotic sac
A membrane filled with a salty fluid that surrounds and protects the embryo.

ectoderm
The outer layer of the embryo from which the skin, sense organs, and nervous system develop.

mesoderm
The middle layer of the embryo from which the circulatory, excretory, skeletal, and muscular systems develop.

products. The embryo is linked to the placenta through the **umbilical cord,** a tough, hoselike structure made up of two arteries and one vein surrounded by a jellylike substance (see Figure 2–6).

The placenta, which grows in size during pregnancy, has two sets of blood vessels connected to it, one set going to the baby through the umbilical cord and the other set going to the mother's circulatory system. However, there is no direct link between these two blood systems. The semipermeable membrane in the vessels allows nutrients and other elements to pass through the blood vessel walls. Through this indirect passage the embryo receives oxygen, proteins, and other essential ingredients for growth. Carbon dioxide is removed from the embryo by the same means. However, the placenta cannot prevent certain viruses, bacteria, and harmful chemicals from affecting the developing embryo.

During the embryonic stage the amniotic sac develops and encloses the embryo. The **amniotic sac** is a membrane filled with amniotic fluid, a salty solution acts as a cushion for the embryo, protecting it from jolts, shocks, and the effects of gravity. The fluid is maintained at a constant temperature, warmed by the mother's body.

The embryo grows rapidly during this period, developing the basic structures of most of the parts of the body. As differentiation progresses, cells begin to assume distinct forms and functions. The head, heart, arms, legs, and nervous system are but a few of the systems that are developing.

By the end of the 1st month three distinct layers are formed in the embryo: the **ectoderm,** or outer layer, from which the skin, sensory organs, and nervous system develop; the **mesoderm,** or middle layer, from which the circulatory,

FIGURE 2–6

The embryo. As the embryo's blood circulates through the placenta it picks up oxygen and nutrients and discharges wastes into the mother's blood without actually mixing with it. The amniotic fluid protects the embryo from being bounced around in the uterus and also helps regulate its temperature.

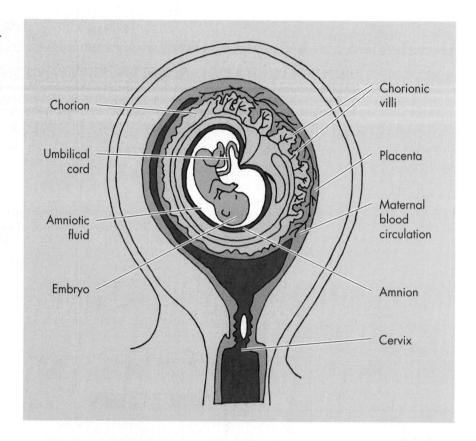

Chorion

Umbilical cord

Amniotic fluid

Embryo

Chorionic villi

Placenta

Maternal blood circulation

Amnion

Cervix

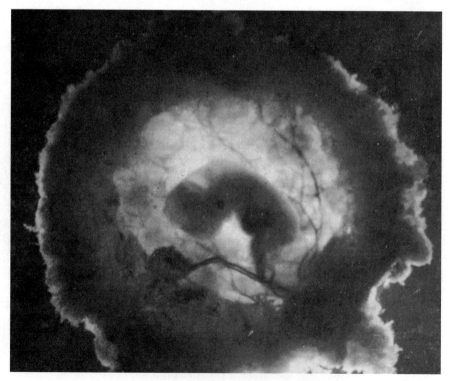

The human embryo at 7 weeks is surrounded by the amniotic sac.

endoderm

The inner layer of the embryo from which the digestive, respiratory, and glandular systems develop.

cephalocaudal

A pattern of growth that begins first in the region of the head and proceeds toward the extremities; literally, head to toe.

excretory, skeletal, and muscular systems evolve; and the **endoderm,** or inner layer, from which the digestive, respiratory, and glandular systems emerge. The heart has begun to beat; a simple brain is functioning; and the liver, digestive tract, and kidneys have emerged. At this point the embryo is only ¼ inch long. The mother may still be unaware of the new life within her body.

By the end of the 2nd month almost all the structures of the baby have been formed, and a few, such as the heart, are even functioning. The embryo is about 1¼ inches long. Most of this length is in the head, which can be clearly distinguished. The emergence of growth from the head down is characteristic of the **cephalocaudal** (head to toe) pattern that is seen throughout development. A primitive tail emerges during this stage, only to disappear as the spinal cord develops (see Figure 2–7).

Because of the rapid changes in the physiological structures and of the primitive nature of the developing organs, the embryo is extremely vulnerable. A slight environmental intrusion (such as a virus or drug) at this stage of growth can have a gross effect on later development. For this reason the embryonic stage is viewed as a critical period in development.

FIGURE 2–7

The embryonic and fetal stages. This is a life-size illustration of the growth of the human embryo and fetus from 14 days to 15 weeks.

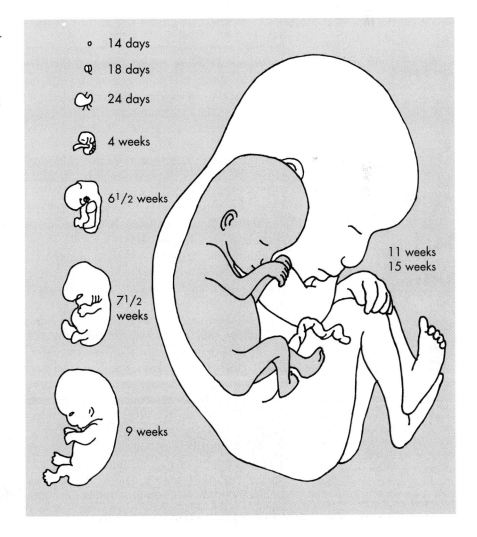

14 days
18 days
24 days
4 weeks
6¹/2 weeks
7¹/2 weeks
9 weeks
11 weeks
15 weeks

In this photo of a 4½-month-old human fetus, you can see the appearance of bones. It is during the fetal period that body structures develop in size.

critical period
A time of growth and development during which the organism is changing and is most vulnerable to outside influence.

During the 5th month of prenatal life, the face and hands assume human characteristics. The maturation of the nervous system and muscular system allows the fetus to perform simple reflex actions such as sucking its thumb.

A **critical period** is any time in which the organism's parts are emerging or changing and hence are most sensitive to outside environmental stimuli. Critical periods occur throughout the lifespan, not just in the prenatal period. For instance, when the sensory organs are forming the embryo is most vulnerable to the rubella, or German measles, virus. If the virus is transmitted to the embryo by way of the placenta at this stage of development, severe defects in the eyes or ears may result. If the same virus were transmitted at a later time in development, when the sensory organs were already formed, no defects develop in the baby's sensory systems.

Technically, the **fetal stage** begins with the appearance of the first real bone cells, which replace the embryonic cartilage. This stage begins at approximately the 8th week and lasts until birth, which occurs about 38 to 40 weeks after conception. During this time completion of bodily structures takes place. The primitive organs and systems of the body assume form and grow in size. By the 3rd month of pregnancy the fetus is 3 inches long and weighs about 3 ounces. It can make primitive breathing movements and when stimulated will even suck. Despite this activity, the mother does not yet feel the fetus inside her body.

Up to this point in development, it would be impossible to detect the gender of the baby by examining the genitals, for both male and female fetuses develop genitals from the same type of gonadal tissue. During the 3rd month, however, the genitals emerge as a result of a biochemical sequence initiated by the genetic messages on the sex chromosomes. If the fetus is female—that is, has an *XX* genotype—no hormones are released into the uterine environment and the primitive gonadal tissue develops into ovaries. If the fetus is male, with an *XY* genotype, the genes on the *Y* chromosome trigger the release of male hormones that cause the development of the testicles and penis from the primitive gonadal tissue.

By the 4th month, the fetus is 6 inches in length and weighs 6 ounces. Looking much like an astronaut in space, the fetus moves about, swimming and floating in the amniotic fluid attached to the placenta by the umbilical cord. It is during this month that many mothers begin to feel the fetus's movement within them. This sensation, called **quickening,** is hard to detect at first because it feels like a mere flicker, but later the suspicion of fetal movement is confirmed by strong, hard kicks by the fetus.

During the 5th and 6th months of pregnancy, fetal activity increases. The fetus sucks its thumb and responds to loud extrauterine noises with a startle reaction. It experiences both wakefulness and sleep, even choosing a favorite position in which to rest. Although the fetus receives oxygen from the placenta, it occasionally makes irregular breathing movements. Sometimes the fetus even develops hiccups, much to the amazement of the mother.

By the 7th month, the fetus has a chance of survival outside the womb if it is born prematurely. The fetus is said to be *viable* at this age, although it has been possible to sustain fetuses born as early as 23 weeks after conception. Even at 28 weeks, however, the risks associated with premature birth are high, and special environments are necessary to protect the prematurely born infant while it continues to grow outside the uterus (Kleiman, 1984).

From the 8th month until birth, the fetus gains weight rapidly. The skin, previously red and wrinkled, fills out with fat, and the fetus increases in size at the rate of ½ pound per week. The fetus is now so large that its once comfortable amniotic sac provides very cramped living quarters. By the end of this period the

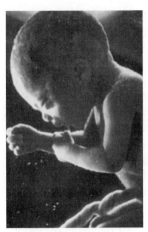

At seven months the fetus has a chance of surviving outside the uterus if born prematurely.

fetal stage
The last stage of prenatal development when all major bodily systems are completed.

quickening
The experience of feeling the fetus's movement in the uterus.

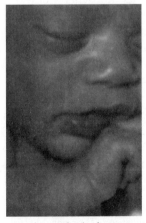

At eight months the fetus gains weight rapidly at a rate of half a pound a week.

fetus will weigh an average of 7 pounds and will be about 20 inches in length. The fetus is now ready for birth. Before discussing labor and delivery, however, let's take a look at some of the ways that the environment may influence the developing child during the mother's pregnancy.

EFFECTS OF THE PRENATAL ENVIRONMENT

When my husband John and I were expecting our daughter Sarah, I was teaching a course on child development and was well aware of the importance of providing our developing child with a safe prenatal environment. I was very careful about my body and the things I put into it; I even reduced my caffeine consumption. I consulted my doctor before taking any over-the-counter medicines, and I took special prenatal vitamins.

In my mother's time people rarely considered how their lifestyles might affect an unborn child. Then it was assumed that the fetus was cut off from the outside world and safe from harm within the mother's body. But in the early 1960s this belief was shattered by medical research that linked the birth of grossly deformed babies to the drug thalidomide, prescribed to their pregnant mothers to alleviate morning sickness. These babies were born either without limbs or with embryonic-like flippers. When thalidomide was taken during the critical period of limb formation (27 to 40 days after conception), the drug drastically altered the normal course of limb development (Taussig, 1962). When taken much later in pregnancy, little or no effects were found in the newborn.

The thalidomide crisis caused researchers and obstetricians to take a closer and more conservative look at the substances to which the unborn child might be exposed in the uterus. People could no longer assume that only substances beneficial to the offspring crossed the placenta. Researchers began to focus on what substances can cross the placental barrier, and how these substances impact development—questions that may take a lifetime of research to answer. This is especially true for substances that pass the placental barrier but do not display an effect until the offspring reaches maturity. Longitudinal studies specifically aimed at the effects of the prenatal environment are few and rather recent. Thus most of what is known about the effects of the prenatal environment on development is concerned with the more immediate effects on the infant or young child.

Maternal Conditions The most obvious source of outside influence is the mother herself. Her health, age, and nutrition all affect the condition of the baby. The optimal time to bear children is between 20 and 35 years of age (Rugh & Shettles, 1971). Women in this age category have fewer complications in pregnancy and easier labors and deliveries than either older or younger mothers.

In the United States, for teenage mothers under 18 years of age, the risk of infant death is twice as high compared with mothers in their twenties. Teenage mothers also are more likely to give birth to low-birthweight infants (Brown, 1983). In part, this results from a lack of early prenatal medical care and inadequate nutrition before and during pregnancy (Lewit, 1992). The majority of pregnant teenagers come from poor families and therefore are less likely than more affluent teenagers to terminate a pregnancy through abortion and or receive access to prenatal care. Very young teenagers who are still developing physically face even greater risks.

In recent years, the number of women giving birth after the age of 40 has risen sharply. Today, more American women are seeking careers and choosing to delay pregnancy; second marriages have also contributed to the increase in the number of older women becoming first-time mothers. In the past, women over 35 were warned that they risked a greater proportion of children with birth defects, stillborns, and low-birthweight or premature infants. However, recent studies suggest that these risks are not related to age itself but to conditions that coexist with increasing age, such as hypertension and diabetes (Kopp & Kaler, 1989). When pregnant women over 40 were compared with pregnant women in their twenties and thirties and the two groups were matched for maternal weight, smoking, and the number of pregnancies, there were no greater risks for older women (Spellacy, Miller, & Winegar, 1986). Provided that the woman is well nourished, is in good health, and seeks adequate prenatal care, a successful pregnancy and healthy baby are likely.

One risk associated with older pregnancy is that of giving birth to a child with Down syndrome. With each year after the age of 35, the risk of conceiving a Down syndrome child increases dramatically. For example, the incidence of children with Down syndrome for women aged 35 is 1 in 400; for women aged 40 it is 1 in 105; and for women aged 48 it is 1 in 12. One theory holds that since a woman is born with all the eggs that are necessary for bearing children, by the time she is 35, her eggs are also 35 years old: The older the egg, the greater the chance that it has been exposed to physical or chemical agents that may damage the chromosomal material in the egg.

In recent years, the majority of Down syndrome births have occurred among women younger than 35. This may be the result of routine amniocentesis screening for Down syndrome among women older than 35, but not younger women (Racine, Joyce, & Grossman, 1992). Although most cases of Down syndrome seem to be the result of a faulty egg, it is now estimated that about 5% of the cases can be attributed to a faulty chromosome contributed by the father (Abroms & Bennett, 1981; Antonarakis & Down Syndrome Collaborative Group, 1991; Holmes, 1978).

Maternal Nutrition   The developing fetus receives its nutrients from the mother's body and thus depends on her for an adequate prenatal diet. Research has linked the mother's diet with the health of the newborn (Cravioto, DeLicardie, & Birch, 1966; Drillien & Ellis, 1964; Lester, Garcia-Coll, Valcarcel, Hoffman, & Brazelton, 1986; Vore, 1973). It is now believed that inadequate nutrition poses the greatest potential threat to fetal development. Since much of the prenatal period is a critical time in the development of brain cells, insufficient nutrients can affect the entire nervous system. A poorly developed nervous system can have negative consequences throughout the lifespan.

The importance of prenatal nutrition has not always been recognized. It was once believed that since the developing baby's nutritional needs would be met first, the mother did not have to worry about her diet. However, this misconception was corrected after World War II studies revealed that babies born in European countries, where food shortages were most severe, had lower birthweights. Also, the incidence of stillbirths and premature births increased. These early studies triggered more extensive research on the effects of inadequate diet on the developing fetus.

Because more than 86% of all babies are born in third-world countries in which adequate nutrition is a serious daily problem, the culture in which a child is born can have a significant impact on its development (Lozoff, 1989). Severe maternal malnutrition can have a profound effect on the development of the baby's nervous system. Lower levels of intellectual functioning are frequently found in babies born to poorly nourished mothers (Winick, 1976). In particular, animal proteins usually found in meat and egg products appear to be essential to adequate brain development. Often these proteins are missing in the diets of mothers living in poverty, primarily because they are a relatively expensive food source.

Rigid or restrictive diets during pregnancy can also be hazardous to the fetus. The recommended weight gain during pregnancy has increased from 15 to 20 pounds to 25 to 30 pounds—although the optimal gain will vary considerably depending on the size and normal weight of the mother.

The mother's ability to nourish her unborn child begins to develop in her early teens and twenties. It takes time for the body to build up the necessary nutritional reserves for pregnancy. Thus, the mother's diet in earlier years can be as important to the fetus's development and survival as her diet during pregnancy (Wyden, 1971).

Mother's Emotional State   One myth about pregnancy is that whatever the mother is feeling will be experienced by the unborn child and will have a lasting effect. Research has discounted this belief. We know that there is no direct neural connection between the mother and fetus that would directly communicate the mother's emotional state to the fetus. However, a woman experiencing emotional stress does experience hormonal changes. Under states of high emotional arousal the adrenal glands secrete hormones into the blood, and these hormones can pass through the placenta. Thus, indirectly, the mother's emotional state does register in the intrauterine environment.

Fear of pregnancy and childbirth can be a potent source of maternal distress. Among the !Kung, young girls are taught not to fear childbirth as part of their preparation for womanhood and birth. Within industrialized countries many maternity nurses recognize that the more relaxed the mother is during labor and delivery, the easier and shorter the process of giving birth will be. Highly anxious mothers who are sensitive to pain and fearful about the delivery process have more difficult deliveries and also have more irritable babies. In an extensive study, Stott and Latchford (1976) found a greater increase in behavioral disorders and chronic illness in children of mothers who had experienced stress during pregnancy. Other studies have linked excessive maternal stress during the time when the fetus's upper jaw and mouth are forming to the development of a cleft palate, harelip, and other physical defects (Norbeck & Tilden, 1983; Strean & Peer, 1956).

It is difficult to attribute all these disorders solely to the effects of prenatal emotional stress in the mother since the same stress may be present postnatally to affect the baby's cultural, social, and emotional environment. The presence of an emotionally supportive person during labor and delivery has been shown to significantly reduce the length of labor and signs of fetal distress (Sosa, Kennel, Klaus, Robertson, & Urrutia, 1980). In the case of an already anxious mother, the presence of a reassuring spouse or family member will help reduce the negative effects of emotional stress on the newborn.

TERATOGENS

The effect of the drug thalidomide on the developing fetus was mentioned earlier as an example of how the unborn child is influenced by the environment. The scientific study of defects or deformities in newborns caused by the influence of the environment during pregnancy is known as *teratology,* and the specific environmental agents that cause the abnormalities are called **teratogens.** Teratogens may take the form of drugs, poisons, diseases, chemicals, or radiation. The effect of teratogens will depend upon the substance and the timing of prenatal exposure. Generally, the first 3 months of prenatal development (called the first trimester) are the most critical time for development and hence the period of greatest vulnerability for the developing child. Let's examine some of the known teratogens.

teratogens

Specific environmental agents that cause abnormalities in the developing fetus.

Drugs   Maternal use of drugs poses two potential dangers to the fetus. First, the drug dose is prescribed for an adult. Even when filtered through the mother's body, the dose nonetheless crosses the placenta to the fetus and may be too high for the unborn child. Second, the fetus's liver cannot break down the drug the same way the mother's liver does, so the chemical action of the drug on the fetus may be different.

Adults often take prescribed and over-the-counter drugs—including aspirin, antihistamines, antibiotics, barbiturates, and caffeine, to name only a few—assuming they are safe. Most drugs taken during pregnancy are not associated with fetal defects. However, when taken in large amounts or in conjunction with other drugs, they may cause teratogenic effects. For example, a woman who daily took 10 to 15 aspirins and smoked more than a pack of cigarettes gave birth to a grossly deformed infant that lived only about an hour (Benawra, Mangurten, & Duffell, 1980). Research has found that regular use of aspirin is associated with low birthweight, infant mortality, and poor mental and physical development (Barr, Streissguth, Darby, & Sampson, 1990).

Antibiotics, particularly streptomycin and tetracycline, have been associated with minor defects in infants' teeth and bones. The United States Food and Drug Administration warns against the use of popular tranquilizers during the first months of pregnancy, saying they may cause cleft palate and other defects. While drug manufacturers dispute some of these claims, physicians usually follow a conservative strategy, recommending little or no prescribed or over-the-counter medication during the early months of pregnancy.

Caffeine, a drug contained in coffee, tea, chocolate, and cola drinks, is another substance under scrutiny as a teratogen. Although animal studies on the effects of caffeine on prenatal development are still being done, results so far show an increase in birth defects in litters of animals given large doses of caffeine. So far the evidence for the effects on human infants is inconclusive. Acting as a stimulant to the central nervous system, caffeine can cause sleeplessness, irritability, anxiety, and disturbances in heart rhythm and rate. Preferring to err on the cautious side, the United States Department of Health and Human Services urges pregnant women to watch their consumption of foods and drugs containing caffeine.

Heroin and morphine are addictive drugs, and habitual maternal use of these drugs during pregnancy often produces newborns who exhibit symptoms of withdrawal from the drugs—hyperactivity, tremors, vomiting, fever, and a shrill cry—and are likely to have a low birthweight (Zelson, 1973). Similar symptoms have been found in babies whose mothers are taking methadone (Zelson, Lee, & Casalino, 1973).

In addition to these physiological symptoms, early mother-child interaction is greatly disrupted by the effects of these drugs. Irritable babies are harder to care for, and addicted mothers often have difficulty establishing a bond with them. Poor prenatal care and nutrition add to the difficulties of the newborn.

fetal alcohol syndrome (FAS)
A pattern of abnormal growth and development in children of chronic alcoholic mothers.

Alcohol   The long-suspected connection between heavy alcohol consumption during pregnancy and faulty development in the unborn child has been scientifically substantiated (Jones & Smith, 1973). Researchers have noted a pattern of abnormal growth and development in the children of chronic alcoholic mothers. This pattern, called **fetal alcohol syndrome (FAS),** has been the subject of much research (see Clarren & Smith, 1978). FAS includes four basic kinds of abnormalities: (1) growth deficiencies, both pre- and postnatally, (2) facial malformations, (3) central nervous system dysfunctions, and (4) certain malformations of the eyes, ears, mouth, and heart. It is believed that alcohol passes directly to the fetus and adversely affects the fast-growing tissues, either killing the fetal cells or slowing their growth. Not surprisingly, the brain, which grows throughout pregnancy, is the most affected organ. Some FAS infants are even born with the odor of alcohol on their breath.

As with drug use, the dangers of excessive alcohol use to the unborn child are increased by poor nutrition and prenatal care. One study (Sokol, Miller, & Reed, 1980) reported that the risks of a growth-retarded infant are doubled if the woman drinks or smokes and are quadrupled if she does both. Other research has suggested that fathers who consume large amounts of alcohol just prior to conception increase the risk of fetal alcohol syndrome in their children (Merewood, 1991). The growth retardation accompanying FAS lasts throughout life, with significantly above average deficiencies in height and weight (Luke, 1977).

Fetal alcohol syndrome is the most common cause of mental retardation, exceeding Down syndrome (Streissguth et al., 1991), affecting an estimated 1 in 700 children—and the effects appear to be long term. In one study FAS infants were found to be slower and less efficient in processing information (Jacobson, Jacobson, Sokol, Martier, & Ager, 1993). Alcohol consumption during pregnancy has also been found to have an affect on attention and reaction time in preschool-age children (Streissguth et al., 1984). Four-year-olds whose mothers were moderate drinkers (that is, who drank an average of two drinks per day before realizing they were pregnant and an average of five drinks per week during pregnancy) performed slower and with poorer attention on a task that required them to press a key whenever the figure of a cat appeared on a display board. In a different study involving a comparison of FAS and normal 11-year olds, FAS children were found to perform more poorly in school and to display more problematic behavior such as overactivity, low attention span, and academic difficulties (Olson, Sampson, Barr, Streissguth, & Bookstein, 1992). Numerous studies support the view that there is no safe level of alcohol consumption during pregnancy (Streissguth, Barr, Sampson, Darby, & Martin, 1989). Even moderate drinking can produce symptoms similar to FAS. The best recommendation is that pregnant women completely abstain from alcohol.

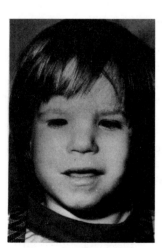

Children with fetal alcohol syndrome are distinguished by malformations of the face, ears, eyes, and mouth. They also exhibit mental deficiencies.

Health Perspective

COCAINE-ADDICTED BABIES

Cocaine is reported to be the number one illicit drug used by women of childbearing age in the United States (Schutter & Brinker, 1992). Cocaine (including crack) is a highly addictive substance that acts as a stimulant to the nervous system. The past 10 years have seen an alarming increase in cocaine addiction in the United States, along with a rise in prenatal exposure to cocaine. The incidence of cocaine use during pregnancy varies considerably, with significantly higher rates reported among poor mothers in urban inner city settings (Hawley & Disney, 1992). The average hospital costs for the delivery and care of cocaine-exposed infants is $13,222, compared to the $1,297 average for nonexposed infants (Calhoun & Watson, 1991). But as the number of cocaine-exposed infants increases, the long-term consequences are likely to impact the schools as well.

The effects of cocaine exposure on the newborn are both direct and indirect (Lester et al., 1991). When the drug passes through the placenta, the direct impact of cocaine on the developing nervous system of the fetus results in cardiac arrhythmias (erratic heart rates), high blood pressure, and seizures. In addition, newborns whose mothers used cocaine throughout their pregnancies are likely to be born addicted to cocaine and may experience withdrawal symptoms.

Even if babies are not born addicted to cocaine, they may experience indirect effects from their mothers' cocaine use. Cocaine constricts the placental blood vessels in pregnant women, impeding the flow of essential nutrients and oxygen to the fetus and interfering with normal fetal growth. As a result, many cocaine-exposed infants are born with a low birthweight and are smaller and shorter in size than nonexposed infants (Alessandri, Sullivan, Imaizumi, & Lewis, 1993; Lester et al., 1991). This is especially true if the mother continued to use cocaine during all three trimesters of pregnancy. The risks of stillbirth and infant mortality are also higher for cocaine babies.

Cocaine use may impede the normal development of the brain and nervous system during the prenatal stages. As a result, cocaine-exposed babies

---

Smoking and Nicotine   Aside from the obvious health hazard smoking presents to the mother, it poses additional hazards to the unborn child. Cigarette smoke contains carbon monoxide and nicotine. Nicotine first stimulates and then depresses the body's functioning. The effect on mother and fetus is an increase in blood pressure and a decrease in the amount of oxygen available in the placenta. Carbon monoxide also reduces the amount of placental oxygen. Because the fetus needs more oxygen as it grows, oxygen deprivation has its most severe effect during the latter months of pregnancy. The greater the exposure and duration of cigarette smoking, the more harmful it is to the unborn child.

The effects of maternal smoking include low-birthweight babies, higher rates of miscarriage and spontaneous abortion, and a greater risk of premature delivery. The more the mother smokes, the less the baby weighs at birth. Women who smoke heavily are twice as likely to deliver low-birthweight babies as nonsmoking mothers, regardless of the length of pregnancy (Aaronson & MacNee, 1989; Frazier, Davis, Goldstein, & Goldberg, 1961). Even if a pregnant woman does not smoke, but is exposed to cigarette smoke at home or work, the fetus can be affected. Inhaling other people's cigarette smoke is associated with have numerous neurological problems. Infants who are directly affected by cocaine are easily overstimulated, have a shrill cry, and are fretful, tense, and jittery (Chasnoff, Burns, Schnoll, & Burns, 1985; Lester et al., 1991). Those who are indirectly affected by the drug appear to be depressed, nonresponsive, or listless.

Cocaine exposure influences the infant's arousal system. Alessandri and his colleagues (1993) compared the learning performance of a matched sample of cocaine-exposed and nonexposed infants between the ages of 4 and 8 months. The infants who were exposed to cocaine had smaller birth weights and lengths. They were also less aroused and interested in a novel learning task. While nonexposed infants expressed joy at successfully making an event happen (using their arms to cause the playing of a Sesame Street song), cocaine-exposed infants showed very few positive emotions. When infants were not rewarded by hearing the song, the cocaine infants were unresponsive, in comparison to the nonexposed infants who expressed their anger and frustration.

Some cocaine-exposed babies may seem normal at birth but acquire behavioral problems later on in their development. Many appear unable to control the effects of distractions around them. They have difficulty relating well to others and are easily irritated. They have extreme difficulty remaining calm and alert at the same time. Since most learning occurs when children are alert and attentive, cocaine-exposed infants are likely to have difficulty in a learning environment.

Most of the research on cocaine-exposed infants has come from studies done with poor mothers in urban settings. The long-term effects of cocaine exposure are intermingled with the effects of growing up in an economically and socially deprived environment. Many of the mothers continue their drug habit after delivery, which may also contribute to the behavioral symptoms children display. Cocaine abuse is not restricted to poor people; varying estimates put the rate of use of cocaine among American middle- and upper-income women between 5 and 26%. However, poorer mothers are more likely to use clinics in large urban hospitals where much of the research has been conducted. More research on a broader sample of mothers is needed to determine the long-term consequences of cocaine exposure on development.

low birthweight, infant mortality, and later deficits in mental functioning (Makin, Fried, & Watkinson, 1991). If a women does smoke during pregnancy but stops during the 3rd trimester, she greatly reduces the effect of smoking on the fetus (Li, Windsor, Perkins, Goldenberg, & Lowe, 1993).

Diseases Some viruses and bacteria that cause diseases in the mature adult can cross the placenta and invade the developing fetus. Depending on the stage of pregnancy, maternal diseases can cause varying degrees of birth defects.

In 1964 and 1965 more than 20,000 babies were born in the United States with birth defects during an outbreak of rubella, or German measles. The pregnant mothers may have experienced mild, flulike symptoms and a rash from this highly contagious disease. The offspring exposed to rubella during the first 3 months of prenatal development were born with such defects as blindness, deafness, heart, nerve, and brain defects, and mental retardation. Fortunately, a vaccine against the rubella virus was developed in 1969. However, pregnant women cannot be vaccinated since the fetus will be directly affected. Only when the woman is sure she will not get pregnant for at least 3 months is the vaccination recommended during the childbearing years.

At one time, chicken pox, mumps, measles, and infectious hepatitis were linked with birth defects. However, a thorough study (Siegel, 1973) compared 409 pregnant women infected with one of these viral diseases with a matched sample of uninfected women and found no differences between their offspring in birth defects, although maternal infection was likely to increase the chances of an early delivery.

Sexually transmitted diseases also pose a threat to the developing child. Untreated maternal syphilis also may cross the placenta and cause deformities in the developing child. Gonorrhea and active genital herpes can be transmitted to the baby during delivery and result in blindness or severe brain damage. When sexually transmitted diseases are diagnosed during pregnancy, treatment of the mother can reduce the risks to the child. For example, if syphilis is treated with penicillin early in the pregnancy, the probability of risks to the newborn during the birth process are reduced (Grossman, 1986).

AIDS (acquired immune deficiency syndrome) and HIV have also been found to pass through the placenta and infect the fetus. Infants may also become HIV positive by being exposed to the mother's infected blood during delivery. In fact, 80% of all children with AIDS contracted the disease during either their mothers' pregnancy or delivery (Health Information Network, 1987).

However, not all HIV infected mothers transmit the virus to their babies. Of the approximately 7,000 babies born in the United States to HIV infected mothers each year, between 70 and 85% escape infection (Glausiusz, 1994). Why some infants contract the virus and others don't is not fully understood. Infection by the AIDS virus may depend on the strain of virus to which the fetus is exposed. Or the levels of HIV in some mothers' blood may be high at the time of pregnancy. It could also be that uninfected but HIV exposed infants have acquired antibodies from their mothers during pregnancy that help them fight off the virus. The answer to the question of why some babies are infected by their HIV mothers while others are not will help guide the prevention and treatment programs that must be developed to combat the spread of this dreaded disease (Glausiusz, 1994).

Hormones   In the United States between 1945 and 1970, a synthetic hormone called diethylstilbestrol, or DES, was used to maintain pregnancies in women who showed signs of miscarrying. The effects of DES on the offspring were not apparent at birth or even shortly thereafter. It was not until years later, when the female offspring of women who had taken DES during pregnancy had reached puberty, that the teratogenic effects of the hormone became apparent. Some developed rare forms of vaginal and cervical cancer. While this hormone is no longer used for pregnant women, we still do not know whether other hormones taken during pregnancy may have teratogenic effects.

The development of male and female characteristics during the 3rd month of pregnancy is dependent on a specific hormonal environment. A pregnant woman taking hormones for medical reasons may be disturbing the in utero hormonal balance. For example, Reinisch (1981) reports that women who received male hormones during the first 3 months of pregnancy had children who were rated as more aggressive when compared to children of women who did not take any hormones.

Radiation and Environmental Hazards   During early pregnancy, repeated exposure to X rays, especially in the abdominal or pelvic region, may endanger the fetus. The fact that radiation can destroy very sensitive growing cells was tragically demonstrated in the survivors of the atomic bombings of Hiroshima and Nagasaki, Japan, when great increases in miscarriages, stillborns, and gross deformities in live births were found. While X rays used in medical diagnosis contain a far lower dose of radiation, not enough is known about the effects of exposure. The effects of radiation are cumulative, so the recommendation for pregnant women is to avoid X rays when possible.

Another source of danger to the unborn child are environmental pollutants and toxic industrial wastes. High doses of these contaminants have been shown to cause defects in animals and in utero children exposed to them. For example, researchers have found that mothers who had eaten fish contaminated with the industrial chemical PCB (polychlorinated biphenyl) gave birth to children with lower birthweights and smaller heads, often after shorter pregnancies (Fein, Jacobson, Jacobson, Schwartz, & Dowler, 1984). Furthermore, PCB-exposed children who appeared normal at birth were tested at 7 months of age, and they showed less preference for novel stimuli compared with children who had not been exposed to the chemicals prenatally (Jacobson, Fein, Jacobson, Schwartz, & Dowler, 1985).

It is difficult for a person to know whether fish or other foods, air, water, or soil has been contaminated. While people in childbearing years cannot avoid all possible environmental toxins, they can become more aware of reports of toxic wastes and take precautions to avoid contact with them. Just as Jane and Louis had done during in preparation for Sarah's birth, couples can make simple changes in their daily habits to maximize the chances of a healthy birth.

Teratogens: A Note of Reassurance   After reading about the many possible side effects of chemicals, diseases, and other substances on the developing fetus, you may find yourself becoming alarmed, particularly if you are already pregnant. You can relax a bit by putting the information about teratogens in perspective. Although there are many possible causes for abnormality in children—including teratogens, genetic disorders, and the health of the mother—note that 95% of all live births in the United States are healthy and well-formed. Furthermore, not all birth defects are serious ones. Educating parents and caution during pregnancy will help to keep this live-birth success rate high.

FOCUS ON CULTURE

In impoverished countries, infant death rates are higher than in the more developed countries. However, even among wealthier industrialized nations, infant mortality rates vary considerably. The United States, for example, ranks 18th for infant mortality among 25 industrialized countries. Within the United States, African American infants have a much higher death rate than white infants, primarily because of poor access to adequate health care and nutrition.

Harmless ultrasound waves are sent through the uterus of the pregnant woman to determine the size, location, and number of fetuses that are developing.

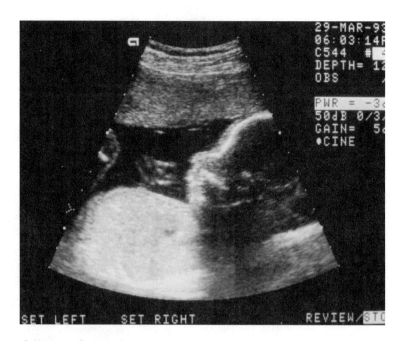

GENETIC COUNSELING

genetic counselors
Specialists who provide and interpret medical information about genetics to prospective parents.

Several years ago my twin sister's baby died within hours after birth due to a very rare recessive genetic disorder. Before she and her husband attempted another pregnancy, they sought the help of a **genetic counselor** to determine the risks of having another child with the same disorder. Fortunately, there are a growing number of genetic and prenatal tests available that can identify the presence of a genetic disorder and also assess the status of the fetus while still in the uterus.

PRENATAL DIAGNOSTIC TECHNIQUES

TECHNIQUE	DESCRIPTION
Amniocentesis	Performed after the 14th week of pregnancy; a sample of amniotic fluid is extracted; fetal cells are analyzed for metabolic and chromosomal defects.
Chorionic villus sampling (CVS)	A sample of villi from the chorion membrane surrounding the placenta is extracted during the 5th and 10th weeks of pregnancy; fetal cells are analyzed.
Ultrasound sonography	High frequency sound waves are bounced through the uterus to form a picture of the fetus; the pictures, called sonograms, are used to confirm multiple births and detect physical abnormalities.
Fetoscopy	A narrow tube is inserted through an incision in the uterus; a view of the fetus and placenta is possible.
Alpha-fetoprotein (AFP) screening	Blood samples extracted through fetoscopy between the 16th and 18th week of pregnancy are analyzed for levels of alpha-fetoprotein to determine defects in the spinal cord or brain.

TABLE 2–4

Genetic counselors work with prospective parents to recommend and then interpret the results of genetic tests. Information about the probability of their children inheriting certain genetic traits or disorders may help a couple decide when and whether they want to have children. Genetic counselors are also interested in identifying factors that adversely affect the quality of the prenatal environment and thus the unborn child. The aim of the genetic counselor is to provide as much information as possible to the parents in order to maximize the chances of giving birth to a healthy child.

Several methods exist to provide a couple with information about its genetic heritage. One involves taking a family history, noting any medical problems or diseases that have occurred in the parents' families. Another facet of genetic counseling includes the detection of genetic carriers of certain diseases through laboratory analysis of the parents' blood, urine, or perspiration. For couples who are already expecting, a **prenatal diagnosis** can inform them of chromosomal disorders, diseases, or other defects in the developing fetus. Using **amniocentesis** (see Figure 2–8), a procedure usually performed after the 14th week of pregnancy,

prenatal diagnosis
The use of medical techniques to provide information about the unborn child.

amniocentesis
A prenatal test of the amniotic fluid to determine the presence of defects in the unborn child.

FIGURE 2–8

Amniocentesis. Amniotic fluid is removed from the amniotic sac and analyzed to reveal a variety of chromosomal and metabolic disorders.

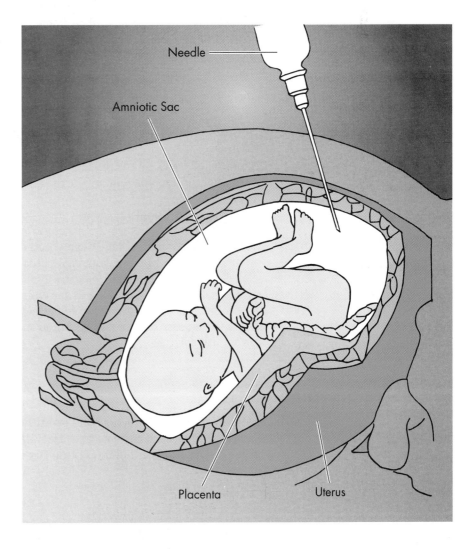

Needle

Amniotic Sac

Placenta   Uterus

FOCUS ON CULTURE

Genetic counseling is a luxury not found in less developed societies. Indeed, because many of the technical procedures used in prenatal diagnosis are expensive, people living in industrialized countries without medical insurance are denied access to these techniques. These parents often approach pregnancy and birth with a much more fatalistic attitude and are less able to medically and emotionally prepare for the care of children with genetic or metabolic disorders.

a small amount of amniotic fluid surrounding the fetus is withdrawn through a long, hollow syringe inserted into the uterus through the mother's abdomen. The fluid contains discarded skin cells from the developing fetus. After these cells have been allowed to grow, they are analyzed to learn about the chromosomal, genetic, and metabolic characteristics of the unborn child. The gender of the offspring and about 200 chromosomal and metabolic defects can be diagnosed. Other types of prenatal diagnostic tests are described in Table 2–4. These and other prenatal diagnostic tests are usually performed on women with comparatively high risks of genetic or chromosomal defects. This includes women over the age of 35 and women with a family history of genetic or metabolic disorders. However, 97% of these high-risk women find that their fetus is free of any suspected defect.

> ### RECAP
>
> The process of conception occurs when the egg and sperm unite, usually as a result of sexual intercourse. Alternate methods of contraception include artificial insemination, in vitro semination, egg transfer, and surrogate wombs. The prenatal period is divided into three stages during which the ovum is implanted in the uterus, the embryo differentiates the cell functions and lays down the structural foundation of life, and the fetus develops the organs and systems necessary for survival outside the uterus. The health, age, and emotional status of the mother can influence fetal development. Teratogens are harmful environmental agents that cross the placenta and cause defects and disorders in the fetus. Numerous genetic and prenatal diagnostic techniques exist to help prospective parents determine the risks of giving birth to an infant with a genetic disorder or birth defects.

BIRTH

Birth signals the end of the fetal period and the beginning of infancy. It is a moment of life and death: The fetus must be expelled in order to continue life. In some cultures, rituals and customs associated with death are also performed during birth in acknowledgment of this critical transition.

THE ONSET OF BIRTH

When I was pregnant with my first child and already well past my due date, I asked my obstetrician what initiated the process of labor. I did not get a clear answer to my question because my doctor didn't know; it is still unclear precisely what triggers the beginning of birth. One hypothesis is that the placenta ceases to provide nourishment, causing the fetus to release hormones that initiate the birth process.

Even though the precipitating factors may not be known, the actual onset of the birth process is relatively easy to detect. The uterus begins to contract regularly, and these contractions increase in strength. The mother may have a slight bloody "show" or may discharge some amniotic fluid. At this point **labor,** the process of expelling the baby, has begun.

labor
The process of expelling the baby from the uterus.

STAGES OF LABOR

Like the term of a pregnancy, labor also is divided into three stages (see Figure 2–9). During the first stage the **cervix,** the opening to the uterus, is dilated by the action of the increasingly stronger uterine contractions. This stage, which may take from 2 to 24 hours, is the longest and most difficult stage of labor. Mothers who have had previous deliveries tend to have shorter labors than first-time mothers.

cervix
The opening to the uterus.

At the beginning of the second stage of labor the cervix is completely open, and the baby is ready to be expelled through the vaginal birth canal into the world. An alert and unanesthetized mother can assist in this process by pushing down with her abdominal muscles. This stage lasts an average of 2 hours.

The baby's head appears first at the opening of the vagina; this is called **crowning.** For women who give birth in American hospitals, it is at this point that an **episiotomy,** a surgical incision in the skin around the vaginal opening, may be performed to ease the baby's passage. The baby's head is then delivered, usually face down, and the nasal passages are cleared of mucus to permit normal breathing. The shoulders and the rest of the body quickly follow the head. The umbilical cord, still attached to the placenta, must now be clamped and cut. As soon as the newborn's lungs receive air through the unclogged nasal passages, the umbilical cord's function of delivering oxygen from the placenta ends. A jellylike substance inside the cord closes off the oxygen supply line.

crowning
During the birth process, the moment at which the baby's head first appears at the opening of the vagina.

episiotomy
A surgical incision made in the skin around the vaginal opening to ease delivery of the baby.

Once the infant has emerged, its condition can be evaluated. To assess the newborn's physical condition, a scoring system developed in 1953 by Virginia Apgar is routinely used in most U.S. hospitals. The newborn is rated 60 seconds after birth, and then again 5 and 10 minutes after birth (see Table 2–5). The highest Apgar score is a 10; a score of 7 of more indicates that the newborn is in no immediate danger; any score below 7 indicates some problem, and a score of 4 or less 0 indicates a critical, life-threatening condition.

Within 20 minutes after the delivery of the baby the mother may experience another strong contraction. This begins the third stage of labor: the delivery of the placenta, umbilical cord, and membranes, after which birth process is complete.

CHILDBIRTH METHODS

Methods of childbirth vary considerably, depending on the cultural traditions and economic development of the country in which a mother gives birth. In some cultures birth is considered a natural event. It occurs at home, often with family members present to assist with the process. A common practice around the world

FIGURE 2–9

Birth of a baby. (a) During the first stage of labor, a series of stronger and stronger contractions dilates the cervix, the opening to the mother's womb. (b) During the second stage, the baby's head moves down the birth canal and emerges from the vagina. (c) During the brief third stage, the placenta and umbilical cord are expelled from the womb. Then the cord is severed.

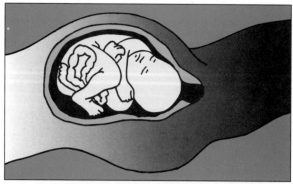

(a) First stage

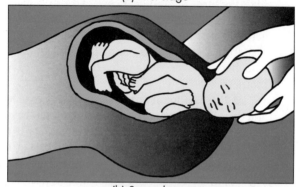

(b) Second stage

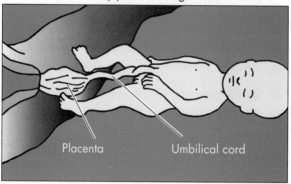

Placenta   Umbilical cord

(c) Third stage

is the assistance of midwives, who are trained to recognize danger signs during labor and to deliver babies (Seager & Olson, 1986).

How a woman gives birth is also shaped by culture. Some women traditionally squat or crouch during labor. Eskimo women used to sit on their knees while giving birth. Japanese women used to stand in a thatched hut to give birth; today, most Japanese women give birth in hospitals. As was the case for Nomawele, the birth experience may be a solitary one, away from the village but not apart from the community. In some cultures, women give birth among their sisters and mother. Some cultures, such as the Ngoni in East Africa, forbid the presence of men during childbirth; some Ngoni women even conceal their pregnancy from their husbands for as long as possible (Read, 1960, 1968).

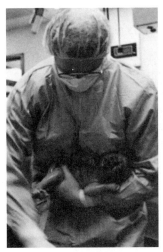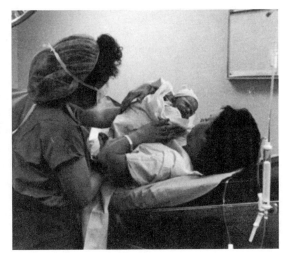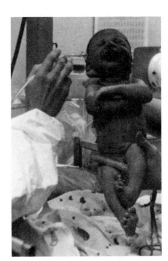

Seconds after birth (left), the newborn's cry announces its arrival. The new parents' initial contact (center) with their newborn is likely to be a very special and tender moment. Within minutes after delivery (right), the attending physician examines the newborn and assigns an Apgar rating.

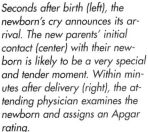

prepared childbirth
Method of childbirth in which both parents are prepared to deal with the various aspects of labor and delivery.

Lamaze method
A type of prepared childbirth involving lectures and specific exercises and routines.

Other cultures, including our own, encourage fathers to attend and sometimes participate in delivery.

In most developed countries today, the process of birth is viewed as a medical condition; most women give birth in a hospital or clinic. Often, the mother receives medication to ease her pain during labor: Some women take mild painkillers to help them relax between contractions; others receive anesthesia that blocks out all sensation from the waist down; and some may be completely anesthetized at the actual moment of birth.

A popular method of delivery used in hospitals is called **prepared childbirth** because the parents are prepared for the birth by going to classes for about 6 weeks before the expected delivery date. Parents-to-be learn about the stages of labor, hospital procedures, and specific exercises and routines to use during labor. The most popular method of prepared childbirth is the Lamaze method, named after physician Fernand Lamaze (1981). One advantage of the **Lamaze method** is that

APGAR SCALE			
	SCORE		
SIGN	**0**	**1**	**2**
Heart rate	No heartbeat	Under 100 beats per minutes	100 to 140 beats per minute
Respiratory effort	No breathing for 60 seconds	Irregular and shallow	Strong breathing and crying
Muscle tone	Flaccid and limp	Weak movement of limbs	Strong movement of limbs
Reflex response	No response to stimuli	Weak response	Strong reactions to stimuli
Color	Body and limbs are blue and pale	Body is pink, extremities are blue	Body and limbs are both pink

TABLE 2–5

women require lower dosages of medication during labor and delivery and hence are more active and alert during the birth process. Some women practicing the Lamaze method take no drugs at all.

In the United States, many couples have the option of giving birth in a family-oriented setting rather than in the sickroom atmosphere of a hospital. **Birthing rooms** are homelike settings that are medically equipped but casually decorated to create a more relaxed atmosphere. Unlike the traditional hospital setting, labor and delivery both take place in the birthing room; these are usually found in birthing centers, which are frequently near but separate from hospitals. The centers focus on the needs of prospective parents and provide complete prenatal and delivery services to families.

birthing rooms

Homelike settings in hospitals or birthing centers designed for both labor and delivery.

FOCUS ON CULTURE

Childbirth practices within a culture are influenced by contemporary attitudes and resources available. Having a baby at home was once standard practice in the United States and is still the norm in many other cultures. Improved medical technology has increased the chances for survival for some infants, but it has also removed the birth process from the family home, often to replace it with a sterile and strange hospital environment.

COMPLICATIONS

Although most deliveries normally occur headfirst, sometimes the baby appears at the vagina in a **breech,** or buttocks-first, position. This position presents difficulties for both mother and child because the vaginal opening may not be wide enough to accommodate the baby without damage to the spinal cord. Unlike the brain, which is well protected by the skull during birth, the spinal cord is more vulnerable to damage in the birth canal.

When it looks as if there may be danger to the baby, the physician may perform a **cesarean section.** In this procedure a surgical incision is made through the mother's abdominal wall into the uterus from which the newborn is extracted. The cesarean newborn looks better than a vaginally delivered baby, since it has not had to make the journey through the tight vaginal passage. However, the procedure poses additional stresses and risks to the mother and baby: For example, the mother may develop an infection at the location of the incision and may also require a prolonged convalescence from the surgery.

Another complication can result from the use of drugs during labor and delivery. Since the drugs administered to the mother also pass through the placenta, the newborn may also experience the effects of the drugs at birth. Further, a mother who is totally anesthetized during delivery cannot aid the delivery by pushing down with her abdominal muscles. The delivery therefore may take longer or require the use of forceps, a clamplike set of tongs used to extract the baby.

Anoxia, or lack of oxygen, is one final complication that may endanger the baby during the birth process. This happens when the newborn has difficulty making the transition to breathing on its own. Anoxia can cause severe brain damage, resulting in impaired motor and mental development. The longer the brain is deprived of oxygen, the more severe the damage. One reason the newborn

breech birth

A delivery in which the baby appears in a buttocks-first position.

cesarean section

A surgical procedure used when vaginal delivery poses a danger to the baby. An incision is made through the mother's abdominal wall into the uterus.

anoxia

Lack of oxygen to the baby at birth.

may not be breathing results from the early release of meconium, a sticky green substance secreted from the baby's bowels. Usually, meconium is secreted after delivery, but in one in ten newborns, meconium is released during labor. When these infants are born, their lungs cannot absorb oxygen because they have inhaled meconium (Halle, 1994).

The immediate effects of mild anoxia are greater irritability and tension in the baby's body. Decreased sensitivity to pain and visual stimulation have also been reported. Long-term effects include lowered mental functioning and learning disabilities (Epstein, Cullinan, Lessen, & Lloyd, 1980), and higher risks for chronic lung disorders such as asthma (Halle, 1994). Follow-up studies on anoxic children indicate a deficit in cognitive skills at age 3, with slighter results at age 7 (Corah, Anthony, Painter, Stern, & Thurston, 1965; Graham, Ernhart, Thurston, & Craft, 1962). Behavioral problems, however, were also found in the 7-year-old children who were anoxic at birth.

Low-Birthweight Infants

Low birthweight is the most common birth problem, affecting 1 in every 12 babies born each year in the United States. Seventy percent of infant deaths are attributable to a birthweight under 2,500 grams, or 5 pounds, 8 ounces. Very low-birthweight infants are those weighing less than 3 pounds, 5 ounces. Throughout the world, and especially in countries in which famine and poor nutrition are widespread, low-birthweight babies are more common. In India and Pakistan, for example, more than 30% of births are low-birthweight infants (Seager & Olson, 1986).

There are two categories of low birthweight. Most of the low-birthweight infants fall into the category of **short-gestation-period** (or preterm) **babies,** born before the full 38 weeks of a normal pregnancy. Babies born after only 23 weeks of gestation have been known to survive birth.

Small-for-date (or growth-retarded) **babies** are born after the full 9 months of gestation but are too small because of a slowdown or halt of prenatal growth. Maternal malnutrition, overuse of drugs, alcohol, smoking, and exposure to certain diseases as well as poor prenatal care have been suggested as causes of small-for-date babies. The risks to such infants are great since they are more susceptible to illness early in life and often experience difficulties in breathing. Some preterm babies do not have enough fat to keep them warm so they must be kept in heated incubators. The lower the birthweight, the greater the risks for the infant. Research suggests that low birthweight has long-term effects on motor, mental, social, and emotional development. A fuller discussion of low-birthweight infants will be presented in the next chapter.

short-gestation-period babies
Infants born before the full 38 weeks of development; also referred to as preterm babies.

small-for-date babies
Infants born after the full period of gestation but who weigh less than 2,500 grams or 5 lbs. 8 oz.; also referred to as growth-retarded babies.

BRIEF REVIEW

Growth and development are guided by genetic programming. Genes, made up of DNA molecules, are specifically arranged on the chromosomes, which are found in the nucleus of every living cell.

Cultural and ethnic groups face different risks of inheriting genetic diseases and disorders. Selective mating based on membership in racial, ethnic, or religious groups increases the risks of inheriting recessive genes that are responsible for these disorders.

Sex chromosomes determine gender and other sex-linked characteristics. Other physical features such as eye and skin color, height, body proportion, and certain diseases are inherited through the genes and chromosomes. Research evidence suggests a genetic influence on personality and intelligence. The environment and genetic code interact to produce most of the characteristics of human behavior.

Conception describes the process in which the egg and sperm unite to form the zygote. Alternative methods of conception involve use of donated egg, sperm, or womb. The new cell grows by a process known as mitosis. Genetic variation in the germ cell occurs through a process known as meiosis.

Prenatal development involves three stages of growth. In the ovum stage the growing zygote enters the uterus and embeds itself in the uterine wall. In the embryo stage the cells differentiate into different systems and organs. The fetal stage refers to the last stage of prenatal development, during which the fetus grows and develops until its birth.

The prenatal period is a critical period of development in which the unborn child is vulnerable to environmental influences. The physical condition of the mother is one source of environmental influences on the baby. Teratogens—specific environmental agents such as drugs, bacteria, viruses, chemicals, and radiation—also can affect prenatal development. Many agents are known to cross the placenta and adversely affect the unborn child.

Prenatal diagnosis using amniocentesis is one aspect of genetic counseling, which provides information to parents about certain characteristics, including possible genetic diseases or birth defects, of the fetus. Other tests include chorionic villus sampling, alpha-fetoprotein screening, fetoscopy, and ultrasound sonography.

The birth process, like prenatal development, involves three stages. The first stage, labor, results in the dilation of the cervix. The second stage refers to the actual delivery of the baby. During the third stage, the placenta and umbilical cord are delivered.

Possible complications of birth include breech birth, cesarean section, anoxia, and low birthweight. Drugs used in labor and delivery can reduce the alertness of the newborn and interfere with the mother's ability to participate in the delivery.

Prepared childbirth classes and new methods of delivery can help parents be more involved, relaxed, and informed during and after the birth of the baby. Birthing centers are homelike settings with access to medical care which focus on the needs of families during labor and delivery.

KEY TERMS

allele (48)
alpha-fetoprotein screening (74)
amniocentesis (75)
amniotic sac (61)
anoxia (80)
birthing rooms (80)
blastocyst (60)
breech birth (80)
cephalocaudal (63)
cervix (77)
cesarean birth (80)
chromosome (44)
critical period (64)
crowning (77)
differentiation (60)
dominant gene (49)
DNA (44)

Down syndrome (55)
dizygotic twins (47)
ectoderm (61)
embryonic stage (60)
endoderm (63)
episiotomy (77)
fertilization (58)
fetal alcohol syndrome (FAS) (69)
fetal stage (65)
gene (44)
genetic counseling (74)
genotype (47)
germ cell (45)
infertility (59)
labor (77)
Lamaze method (79)
meiosis (46)

mesoderm (61)
mitosis (46)
monozygotic twins (47)
ovulation (57)
ovum stage (60)
phenotype (48)
placenta (60)
prenatal diagnosis (75)
prepared childbirth (79)
quickening (65)
recessive gene (49)
sex chromosome (46)
short-gestation-period babies (81)
small-for-date babies (81)
teratogen (68)
umbilical cord (61)
zygote (45)

REVIEW QUESTIONS

If you can answer these questions, you have a good understanding of the material in this chapter. If a question seems difficult, go back to the text and review the topic.

1. Describe the relationship among genes, chromosomes, DNA, and the zygote.

2. What is mitosis? What is meiosis? Why can we say that, with the exception of identical twins, no two people are genetically alike?

3. Distinguish between monozygotic and dizygotic twins. Why are they of interest to people who study the influence of genetics on behavior?

4. Contrast the influence of dominant and recessive genes on behavior.

5. Describe three genetic disorders that occur more frequently in particular cultural, racial, or ethnic groups.

6. What does it mean when we say that a trait is sex linked? Give two examples of sex-linked traits.

7. Describe four ways to study the influence of genetics on behavior.

8. Describe the process of conception. What is in vitro fertilization? egg transfer? womb surrogacy?

9. Describe the three stages of prenatal development. Identify the major changes that occur in each stage.

10. How effective is the placenta in protecting the fetus during pregnancy?

11. What is meant by a critical period? Give an example of a critical period in prenatal development.

12. Describe the potential impact of the mother's age on pregnancy and birth.

13. Why is nutrition an important factor in prenatal development?

14. What are teratogens? Give examples of three types of teratogens.

15. What is genetic counseling? Name two techniques used in prenatal diagnosis.

16. Describe the three stages of labor.

17. Describe three methods of childbirth. What impact do they have on the fetus?

18. What is anoxia?

19. Name two categories of low-birthweight infants and describe the risks to the newborn for each category.

OBSERVATIONAL ACTIVITY

CHANGES IN OBSTETRICAL CARE: A GENERATION GAP

Over the past 20 years there has been considerable change in obstetric care. Attitudes toward pregnancy have changed as well as hospital procedures during labor and delivery. To become aware of these changes in prenatal care and methods of childbirth you will need to locate two or more mothers who are willing to be interviewed by you. Locate at least one mother who gave birth 20 or more years ago. Your own mother or an aunt may be a good choice. Also locate a mother who has given birth within the past 5 years. A relative or friend would be more likely to cooperate with your interview.

Explain to each mother that you would like to learn about the changes that have occurred over the years in attitude and treatment during pregnancy and delivery. If you can, tape the interview so that you can listen more attentively to what their responses are during the interview instead of taking notes. After eliciting their cooperation, ask them the following questions (you may want to ask other questions in addition to these):

1. When you were pregnant, what recommendations did your doctor give you about your pregnancy?

2. Did you change your eating habits during pregnancy? If so, why?

3. Were there some things you didn't do when you were pregnant? For example, did you stop smoking or strenuous physical activity?

4. What special plans did you and your husband make in preparation for the birth of the baby?

5. What was your husband doing during the labor? Was he with you? Did you want him there?

6. What do you remember about the way you were treated by the nurses and hospital staff during labor?

7. Did you receive medication while in labor?

8. Were you able to see the birth of the baby?

9. After the birth, how much contact did you have with your baby while you were in the hospital?

After collecting this information from the mothers, compare their responses. What changes can you identify? What new insight or information did you gain for yourself?

CHAPTER 3

Infancy: Physical, Perceptual, and Cognitive Development

Hannah's father never dreamed he would spend so much time watching a baby. But he was enchanted by Hannah, his first-born child. He loved her new-baby smell and her skin was the softest he had every felt. When he held her in his arms, she seemed so tiny and helpless. But he knew better. Hannah had a gaze that was mesmerizing. Even when she was as young as 2 weeks, she would look at him so intently that if she had asked for anything, he would have given it to her.

Now that Hannah was 6 months old, she had mastered the art of letting her wants be known. She would smile and coo when her father gave her the stuffed bear that squeaked, and she would cry when she wanted more attention or was frustrated. Her little hands were busy all the time, fingering toys, touching her body—especially her mouth—and reaching for the toy figures on the mobile over her crib. Hannah's curiosity was growing daily.

Li Wei's nursery looked very different from Hannah's. Li Wei and her family lived in China in a small village not far from the town where her mother and father worked. From her early days of life she slept with her parents so that her mother could respond immediately to her cry. When she was 3 months old Li Wei accompanied her mother to work and stayed in the infant nursery established for employees with young children. Twice a day until she was 15 months of age, her mother would stop her work to breast-feed Li Wei.

Li Wei was left in the good care of "aunties," women who were chosen on the basis of their patience and demonstrated ability to carefully meet the needs of young infants. Like Hannah, Li Wei showed a keen interest in her environment. She particularly liked the multicolored quilt her grandmother had made for her. In her quiet moments she often fingered the different colors and patterns of each square. The bright paper flowers that decorated the nursery were also a favorite.

Despite their emergence into different cultures, Hannah and Li Wei demonstrated remarkable similarity in their travels during their first 2 years of life. Over time they gradually acquired many new skills. They learned how to roll over, to sit and stand up, and later to climb out of their cribs. They learned how to tell their caregivers what did and did not want. They learned how to use the toys and other objects they found in their explorations of their playrooms and nurseries. In just 2 short years Li Wei and Hannah had emerged as capable, inquisitive, and active children.

THE NEONATE

Infancy is like a new adventure, full of excitement and surprises. Starting at birth and spanning a period of two years, infancy is filled with change; babies begin to establish themselves in a physical and social world. Without the benefit yet of language skills, infants nonetheless learn both to adapt to and manipulate objects and people. Infants become more aware of their surroundings and acquire new ways of participating in the many aspects of their expanding world.

Even among babies born to healthy, well-nourished mothers, the period of weeks following birth is a vulnerable one. During this time infants are referred to as **neonates.** Their entry into the world represents a major life transition. While in its mother's uterus, the fetus acquires nutrition and oxygen through the placenta. At birth the newborn's own respiratory and digestive systems assume the functions previously performed by the mother. The newborn, once warmed by the mother's body, now must rely on active movement and crying to maintain an adequate body temperature. Even the newborn's body movements, which were held in check by the mother's cramped uterus, must now be controlled by the baby's developing nervous system.

neonate
The infant during the first 4 weeks of life.

PHYSICAL APPEARANCE

When Adam, my first child, was born his skin was blotchy and wrinkled and his head was pointed. And I thought he looked beautiful! Contrary to their parents' opinions, newborn babies are often anything but beautiful. A peek through a newborn nursery window will reveal a variety of funny-looking infants.

The baby's skin, while soft, is also relatively free of fat, giving it a certain looseness. It seems to hang off the bones and is sometimes folded over. The baby's body may be covered with fine hair, called **lanugo.** Sometimes the baby's body is also covered in a cheese-like substance, called **vernix caseosa.** This substance, secreted by the hair follicles on the body, helps to protect the infant's thin skin while in the amniotic sac. Infants often appear blotchy red in color because the capillaries are visible through the thin, unfatted layer of skin.

lanugo
Fine hair covering a newborn's body.

vernix caseosa
A cheese-like substance covering the newborn's skin.

Similarly, the head and face of the newborn are not particularly attractive. The neonate's eyes are puffy because of fluid accumulated from its head-down position during the birth process. The bones of the skull may have come together, a process known as **molding,** during the neonate's tight squeeze through the mother's pelvis. The head may be misshapen, pointed, or lopsided, as the open spaces in the skull—the **fontanelles**—come together to protect the brain during the birth passage. Some infants have flattened noses or ears that are pressed close to the skull as evidence of the tight passage.

molding
The coming together of the bones of the newborn's skull during the birth process.

fontanelles
Open spaces in a neonate's skull.

The neonate's irises appear to be gray-blue in Caucasian infants and brown in non-Caucasian newborns. By about 12 months the genetically coded color of the iris emerges. The neonate may sometimes appear cross-eyed because the eye muscles are not yet strong enough to maintain coordination. The tear ducts are not fully functional, so that although the neonate cries, there are no tears. The eyes have a glassy look to them.

The head is proportionately the largest part of the baby's body, an example of the cephalocaudal, or head to toe, growth pattern upon which we will elaborate in a following section. It is so large the newborn seems to have trouble holding the head on its body; indeed, the neck muscles are not strong enough to support the head for any length of time. The tiny arms and legs and minuscule buttocks add to the top-heavy look of the neonate.

The average newborn born in the United States weighs 7½ pounds and is about 20 inches in length. Within the first 4 days of life, the neonate's birthweight decreases an average of 6 to 9%, mainly due to loss of body fluids. It takes about 10 days for infants to regain this weight. By that time the neonate's digestive system is functioning regularly, and the mother and infant are on regular feeding schedules.

When the neonate is born, the spinal cord may still be curled from the fetal position in the mother's womb. Within a few days after birth, the backbone stretches out, resulting in an increase in length.

PHYSIOLOGICAL FUNCTIONING

Respiration and Circulation   At birth, air fills the infant's lungs, and the artery through the umbilical cord that has carried oxygen from the placenta to the fetus closes off. The neonate's breathing during the first weeks of life is often irregular. The rapid, shallow, regular breaths often observed in newborns may stop suddenly, a condition called **apnea.** This brief halt in breathing results in a buildup of carbon dioxide in the blood, which then causes the brain to stimulate breathing. Sometimes the neonate breathes deep, irregular breaths. Coughs, sneezes, and wheezes are not uncommon and help to clear mucus from the nasal or throat passages.

A healthy heart rate for the newborn is between 120 and 150 beats per minute. Just as the lungs replaced the umbilical cord as the vehicle by which oxygen is brought into the neonate's body, a new circulatory system replaces the umbilical circulation system. Because of the oxygen now delivered through the lungs, the infant has more red blood cells than are needed. As the neonate's body destroys the surplus red blood cells, a by-product known as bilirubin accumulates in its body. The newborn's liver cannot break down the accumulated bilirubin fast enough, and the result is a condition called **physiological neonatal jaundice.** This causes the skin to appear yellow in about 55 to 70% of newborns who have this condition. Usually the jaundice disappears after a few days of exposure to fluorescent light, the rays of which help to break down the bilirubin.

Digestion   The neonate does not begin digesting food immediately. Many newborns have difficulty sucking in nourishment because of the mucus remaining in the throat after birth. Moreover, it generally takes 2 or 3 days for the mother's breasts to begin secreting milk. In the interim a thin, watery, yellowish substance called **colostrum** is secreted. Newborns are encouraged to ingest the colostrum because it is a high-protein food source and contains antibodies that help the newborn resist infections. Some of the weight loss neonates experience directly after birth is because of the difficulty they have sucking nourishment during their mother's transition from secreting colostrum to milk.

Temperature Regulation   The newborn's body temperature is not very stable during the first week of life. In addition, because the neonate's thin skin lacks a layer of insulating fat, heat is more readily lost. In fact, newborns lose heat 4 times

apnea
A condition in which regular breathing suddenly stops.

physiological neonatal jaundice
A condition frequently found in neonates in which the baby's skin appears yellow.

colostrum
A thin, watery, yellowish substance secreted from a new mother's breasts.

FOCUS ON CULTURE

In the Highland region of Ecuador it is the custom for new mothers to seclude themselves and their newborns from the sun and from other people for a period of 42 days (McKee, 1987). It is believed that exposure to the sun will produce a grippe-like illness in nursing mothers and have an even worse effect on the health of newborns. The sun is viewed as unhealthy for infants, especially since they are unable to regulate their body temperatures.

as fast as adults (Bruck, 1961). One way the infant regulates its body temperature is through activity and crying. For prematurely born infants, however, temperature regulation in a heated incubator is essential for survival since these infants have greater difficulty maintaining an even body temperature.

States of Consciousness Babies spend a lot of their time in the early weeks of life sleeping. But if you look carefully, as Hannah's father did, you will notice that infants seem to have different levels of sleeping and wakefulness. In 1959, Peter Wolff documented the fact that newborns experienced six separate states of consciousness. This was a landmark discovery in one sense because his findings contradicted the then-popular belief that the newborn was not attentive or alert to the objects or people in its environment. By maintaining an 18-hour vigil over newborn babies and by carefully recording their activities, Wolff was able to detect different states of alertness and activity (described in Table 3–1). Neonates also differ widely within the first 5 days of life in their attentiveness to stimuli. Birns (1973)

STATES OF CONSCIOUSNESS IN INFANTS

STATE	CHARACTERISTIC	DURATION/DAY
Regular sleep	Smooth and even breathing accompanied by very little motor activity. Eyes are closed and unmoving; face is still and relaxed.	8–9 hours
Irregular sleep	Even breathing accompanied by periodic body movement, facial grimacing, and smiles. Eyes are closed but show rapid eye movement.	8–9 hours
Drowsiness	Breathing that is even but faster than regular sleep. Eyelids are droopy, either open or shut with a glazed appearance. There is more motor activity than regular sleep, but less than irregular sleep. Breathing is even and faster than regular sleep.	Varying
Alert inactivity	Even breathing and open eyes. Face is relaxed and attentive; there is very little movement. Infant is able to learn and interact with others.	15 minutes at a time, up to 2–3 hours per day
Waking activity	Irregular breathing and sporadic bursts of motor activity. Eyes are open, and face may be relaxed or grimaced. There is very little crying.	2–3 hours
Crying state	Awake with eyes open. Crying is accompanied by motor activity and facial grimace.	1–2 hours

TABLE 3–1

Source: From "Observations on Newborn Infants," by P. H. Wolff, 1959, *Psychosomatic Medicine, 21,* pp. 110–118. Adapted with permission.

found that newborns were rather consistent in their reactions. Babies who responded vigorously to one stimulus reacted with an equal amount of intensity to all stimuli consistently over 5 days of testing.

SENSORY AND PERCEPTUAL SYSTEMS OF THE NEONATE

sensation
The ability to respond to and be aware of stimuli.

Discovering Infant Capabilities   **Sensation** refers to the ability to respond to and be aware of stimuli. If you wanted to discover how well adults or children could see, hear, or respond to different stimuli, you would probably present them with different sights, sounds, or objects and ask them to describe their experience. But newborns and infants cannot directly tell us what they see, hear, or feel because they have not yet acquired the language skills to do so. Therefore, other more indirect methods of studying infants' sensory and perceptual systems have been developed.

One way to indirectly measure the extent to which newborns are capable of responding to light, sound, or odors is to measure their physiological reactions when different stimuli are presented. Heart and breathing rates and muscular movements are some of the physiological measures typically used by researchers. First researchers must determine the newborn's unstimulated physiological rates, typically monitored while the infant is sleeping—which, as you recall, is most of the time. Then the awake newborn's physiological reactions are recorded by presenting a tone, sound, or other stimulus. If there is a noticeable change in the

About one third of an infant's day is spent in regular sleep.

physiological rate of responding, it is inferred that the newborn must have heard or seen the stimulus.

Fantz (1958, 1961, 1965) used a different method of studying infants' reactions to visual stimuli. He placed the infant in a specially designed booth that allowed him to watch the infant's eyes and measure how long the infant would look at different pictures. This method is called the *preferential looking technique.* It has been improved by using infrared lights that enable researchers to tell not only how long a picture is viewed but also what specific aspects or features of a picture newborns look at (Maurer & Salapatek, 1976). More recently, video cameras have also been used to measure and record infant eye movement and facial expression.

Yet another way to determine the extent to which newborns can see or hear is to observe whether they reach out for objects presented to them or turn their heads in response to sound. In some studies, newborns' sucking responses are used as a measure of their attentiveness to stimuli. Using a pacifier rigged to the focusing apparatus of a slide projector, researchers have found that newborns will suck harder and faster to bring specific pictures into focus.

To help them interpret the measures of attentiveness to various physical stimuli, researchers rely on **habituation,** the process by which people become familiar with a stimulus and also less sensitive to it. The principle can be demonstrated by a two-step testing procedure. In the first step a sound such as a buzzer is presented several times, and the baby's startle reaction, breathing, and heart rate are recorded. Over repeated presentations the baby's reactions change and diminish as if it were becoming bored by the noise. Heart rate and respiration may slow down and eventually, after several presentations, the startle reaction disappears. If, however, a new sound (for example, a ringing bell) is presented, the baby perks up and responds with a startle and a change in heart rate and respiration. By using ultrasound to measure fetal movements, researchers have demonstrated that habituation also occurs during the prenatal period (Madison, Madison, & Adubato, 1986).

Vision

Both my grandmother and my mother erroneously believed that children are blind at birth; this belief affected their interactions with newborns, whom they believed could not see them. Researchers have since developed new ways to measure visual behavior in the neonate and it is now widely accepted that newborns can indeed see. The question is how much and how well. Wolff's (1959) study of newborn states illustrated how young infants could focus on an object held before their faces. If that object is moved, the infant can also visually follow it by moving its eyes and head (Brazelton, 1973).

When bright light is presented, the iris constricts. In dim light, the iris widens to let in more light. This automatic reaction is called the **pupillary reflex.** The neonate has a primitive pupillary reflex responding to gross changes in light. While researchers have discovered that newborns can tell the difference between the brightness or darkness of light, they do not know whether newborns can see and distinguish between colors. Clearly, however, this capacity has developed by a few months of age (Bornstein, 1985; Dannemiller, 1989).

Binocular fixation, the ability to simultaneously use both eyes to focus on an object, is present in some newborns at birth. By 2 months of age the infant readily uses both eyes to look at an object. The range within which a newborn can see an object clearly is limited to about 7 to 15 inches at birth. This occurs because the newborn lacks **visual accommodation**—that is, the eye's ability to change the

---

habituation
The process by which a person becomes familiar with a stimulus and decreasingly reacts to it.

pupillary reflex
The automatic opening or closing of the iris in response to light.

binocular fixation
The ability to simultaneously use both eyes to focus on an object.

visual accommodation
The eye's ability to change the shape of the lens to obtain a clear focus.

Researchers have found that babies like to look at figures with strong contrasts and complex and symmetrical designs. Toy manufacturers have capitalized on these findings.

visual acuity
The ability to distinguish between different features of an object.

shape of the lens to bring objects at varying distances into clear focus. By about 4 months of age the infant becomes capable of visual accommodation (Haynes, White, & Held, 1965).

The ability to distinguish between different features of an object is called **visual acuity.** At birth newborns have poor visual acuity. The normal adult measure of acuity is 20/20; reports of newborn acuity have ranged from 20/150 to 20/800 (Banks & Salapatek, 1983).

Researchers are also asking the question: "What do newborns like to look at?" The most common answer to this question is "The human face." For example, newborns can tell the difference between facial expressions (Field, Woodson, Greenberg, & Cohen, 1982) and can even match other people's facial expressions by changing their own (Field et al., 1982; Meltzoff & Moore, 1977, 1983). For example, infants have been known to open their mouths and stick out their tongue in response to watching a person make the same gesture.

Researchers have also discovered that newborns choose to look at figures with strong contrasts, as well as symmetrical and complex designs (Fantz, 1961). Infants also prefer visual patterns that are irregular rather than regular, curved rather than straight, symmetrical rather than asymmetrical, and concentric rather than nonconcentric (Olson & Sherman, 1983). By measuring eye movements, Haith (1980) demonstrated that newborns prefer to scan the edges and contours of complex shapes. Even when they are in the dark, newborns scan their visual environment.

Hearing   Research on fetuses and prematurely born infants has provided evidence that the ability to hear develops several weeks before full-term birth (Aslin, Pisoni, & Jusczyk, 1983). The study of newborns' hearing, however, is limited by techniques available to researchers. Using habituation responses, researchers have learned that newborns can distinguish between loud and soft sounds and high and low pitches, and in fact are more sensitive to higher pitched sounds (Aslin et al., 1983). They can also locate a sound in space and turn their heads in the direction of the noise (Brody, Zelago, & Chaika, 1984). They even can discriminate between the sound of their mother's voice and unfamiliar voices within twelve hours of birth (DeCasper & Fifer, 1980).

Using changes in heart rate as a measure of attention, researchers have found that neonates respond more to complex patterns of vowel sounds than to continuous presentations of the same sound (Clarkson & Berg, 1983). This finding suggests that infants may be encouraged from the very beginning of life to attend to the complexity of human speech (Aslin et al., 1983). This probably comes as no surprise to parents of newborn infants: One way parents learn to calm a crying infant is by talking to it quietly but steadily.

Smell, Taste, and Touch   Newborns react to strong odors, such as those of ammonia and fresh onion. An infant is able to detect the smell of his or her mother's breast as early as 6 to 10 days after birth (MacFarlane, 1978).

Newborns can distinguish between different tastes such as sugar, lemon, salt, and quinine. They have a preference for sweet tastes and will suck longer and slower at fluids laced with sucrose (Lipsitt, 1975). Because the taste buds of newborns are more widely distributed on the tongue than are those of older infants, they are more sensitive to strong tastes.

Another well-developed newborn sensitivity is touch. Many of the early behaviors of neonates are triggered by a touch to the skin. For example, stroking the cheek of a newborn will result in the baby turning its head in the direction of the stroked cheek. Since the newborn's skin is soft and pleasant to touch, tactile stimulation is frequent during the early weeks and months of life. Some researchers maintain that touching the newborn immediately after birth triggers an affectionate caretaking response in adults (Klaus & Kennell, 1982).

At one time it was thought that newborns were not particularly sensitive to pain. In fact, infant boys are circumcised without the benefit of anesthesia, primarily because of the dangers of using pain-killing drugs on very young infants. However, it is now known that newborns do indeed suffer from physical distress. Male newborns emit a sharp, stressful cry during circumcision (Porter, Porges, & Marshall, 1988). In addition, their heart rate and blood pressure accelerates during the painful procedure, suggesting distress. Fortunately, pediatricians are responding to this changed view of neonatal pain sensitivity and are seeking ways to prevent unnecessary trauma in newborns.

BEHAVIORAL RESPONSES: THE REFLEXES

Even though newborns come into this world naked, they aren't without skills. Their cell nuclei, carrying their parents' genetic heritage, equips newborns with sensory systems that allow them to detect a variety of surrounding stimuli. And they possess a set of behavioral responses that enable them to primitively respond to certain stimuli in specific ways. **Reflexes** are automatic and unlearned responses to particular stimuli in the environment. The newborn's pupillary reaction to bright light is one example. Other reflexes that are present at birth and remain throughout development include the breathing, knee jerk, eye blink, gagging, and sneezing reflexes. Controlled by the central nervous system, reflexes are often used to assess its status and development. An absent knee jerk or pupillary reflex would suggest some damage to the nervous system.

reflexes
Automatic and unlearned responses to particular stimuli in the environment.

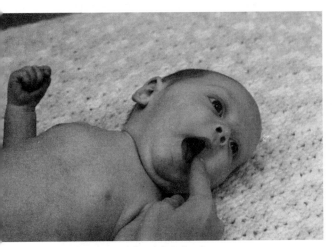

The rooting reflex (left) helps the newborn locate the mother's breast. The newborn will turn its head in the direction of whatever touches its cheek. The Moro reflex (right) is released by a loud noise or sudden loss of support.

neonatal reflexes
Automatic responses that are present in the early weeks and months of life.

In addition to the essential physiological reflexes, the infant possesses a variety of **neonatal reflexes,** automatic responses that are present only in the early weeks and months of life. These neonatal reflexes help the infant adapt to the physical environment and disappear quickly as the newborn's brain matures. Reflexes that change or disappear when the nervous system has matured are referred to as *marker reflexes.* Pediatricians look for changes in these marker reflexes in their examination of neonates and infants.

Some neonatal reflexes appear to have an adaptive function. They include the *sucking reflex,* which is elicited whenever an object touches the newborn's lips. Whether the object is the mother's nipple, a bottle nipple, or a finger, the infant will respond to this stimulus by sucking. The *rooting reflex,* in which a stroke to

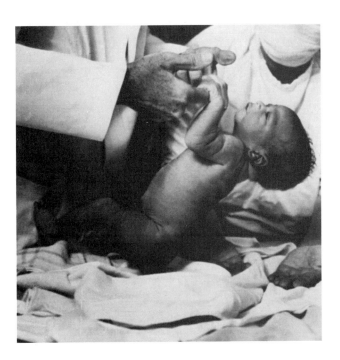

The palmar grasp is so strong that this newborn can be lifted to a standing position by the strength of its hold on the physician's fingers.

the baby's cheek causes the baby to turn its head in the direction of the stroke, often occurs in conjunction with the sucking reflex. Sucking and rooting assist survival by enabling the infant to locate and receive food. By about 3 months of age, these reflexes are replaced by more deliberate and voluntary actions. Other neonatal reflexes, which are described in Table 3–2, do not have such an obvious adaptive function.

THE PRETERM INFANT: A SPECIAL CASE

Although most infants are born after 38 to 40 weeks of prenatal development, some are born earlier—at one time referred to as premature babies. However, this term is misleading, since some babies born after a full 9 months of gestation still are quite small. Today the term low birthweight is used to describe infants who are born weighing less than 2,500 grams, or approximately 5 pounds (see Chapter 2). Infants born before 37 weeks of gestation are referred to as preterm.

In years past, the chances of survival for an infant born prematurely were low. However, newer methods of caring for the neonate have resulted in a much higher survival rate. In 1981, Henig reported an 80 to 85% survival rate of preterm infants with birthweights between 1,000 to 1,500 grams (2 to 3 pounds). In addition, 50 to 60% of preterm infants with very low birthweights of 750 to 1,000 grams (1 to 2 pounds) were also surviving, although 11% of this group experienced serious problems such as mental retardation, blindness, or cerebral palsy.

NEONATAL REFLEXES

REFLEX	STIMULATION	RESPONSE	AGE OF DISAPPEARANCE
Rooting	Stroke on the cheek	Turns head in direction of touch	3 months
Sucking	Object (nipple, finger) placed in the mouth	Rhythmic sucking of the object	3 months
Moro	Sudden loss of support or loud noise	Arms and legs extend outward, followed by a quick return to the body with back arched	3–5 months
Palmar grasp	Object placed in hand and pressed against the palm	Strong grasping	Weakens at 3 months; gone by 12 months
Babinski	Sole of foot is stroked from toe to the heel	Toes fan out and curl as foot turns inward	6 months
Babkin	Pressure on palms of both hands	Head turns to the side and mouth opens	3 months
Stepping	Upright infant is held under arms on a flat surface	Stepping movements, lifting one foot after the other	3 months
Swimming	Infant is placed facedown in water	Paddling and swimming movements	5 months

TABLE 3–2

Although preterm and low-birthweight babies are born occur in all socioeconomic levels, the rates are the highest among impoverished mothers, especially those who are members of an ethnic minority group (Kopp & Kaler, 1989; Neel & Alvarez, 1991). The effects of premature birth are compounded by the difficulties poor mothers have in helping their children attain normal levels of health and development. They live in less protective environments and have limited access to the medical and social support services and intervention programs aimed at reducing negative long-term consequences of prematurity (Bradley et al., 1994; Liaw & Brooks-Gunn, 1993).

Preterm infants are more vulnerable to complications and delays in development. Furthermore, boys are more likely than girls to experience delays in both mental and motor development as a result of premature birth (Braine, Heimer, Wortis & Freedman, 1966). The younger and smaller infants are at birth, the more problems they encounter later in development (Wilcox & Skjoerven, 1992). This is because many of the infant's physical systems are not yet developed or functioning, and the infant may have additional medical problems resulting from poor neonatal care.

Although individual differences vary greatly among both full-term and preterm infants in their capacity to respond to their environment, preterm infants as a group demonstrate striking contrasts. For example, preterm infants spend less time in the state of alertness. They sleep more than full-term infants, and, when they are alert, it is difficult for them to maintain this state (Goldberg, Brachfield, & DiVitto, 1980). They are also less responsive to sights and sounds around them (Friedman, Jacobs, & Werthmann, 1981; Hernandez, 1981). Motor development in preterm babies is somewhat delayed, especially during the second half of the first year, when noticeable changes in an infant's motor development occur (Hunt &

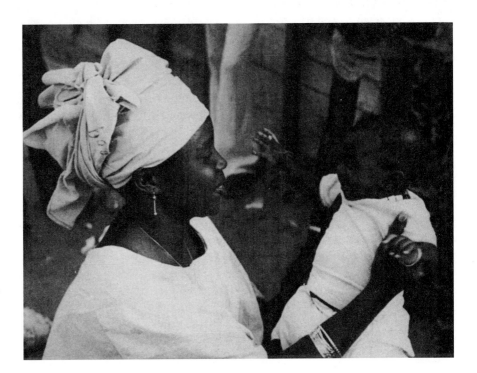

Physical stimulation contributes to infants' physical development. This loving exchange between mother and child is likely to encourage a healthy emotional relationship.

PARENTS OF PREMATURE INFANTS

A friend of mine recently gave birth to her first child, Eric. Her son was born 6 weeks early and weighed just under 4 pounds. Eric's parents were very grateful for the efforts of the obstetric and pediatric staff who helped their preterm baby survive the precarious birth. Fortunately, they live near a large hospital that was able to meet the baby's medical needs. Eric was placed in a neonatal intensive care unit (NICU), a conglomerate of blinking, beeping monitors, catheters, electrodes, and lights, all connected to the tiny baby. Eric's parents recognized the necessity of the NICU but were also frightened by it. When they dreamed of having their first child, they never thought about the possibility that it would take place in such an intimidating setting.

In addition, it was very awkward for Eric's parents to hold and cuddle him in the NICU. However, the helpful nursing staff showed them how to safely handle Eric, and they were able to overcome their apprehensions about hurting him. When he was removed from the NICU, his parents were able to rock him in the rocking chair provided in the neonatal nursery.

Holding, cuddling, rocking, and generally stimulating preterm infants is important for their growth. Today, many neonatal care physicians and nurses recognize the benefits to both the parents and the infant in establishing early contact. They encourage new parents to spend time with their preterm or low-birthweight baby, and to hold, talk to, and care for the infant in every possible way. Hospitals have tried to simulate a normal home environment by involving family members in the regular care of the infant and by placing colorful mobiles over the NICU.

Fortunately for Eric and his parents, they were able to talk about their concerns about taking care of a preterm baby. Not all parents are as fortunate. Especially after the return home from the hospital, when there are no trained staff to guide new parents, the task of caring for a preterm infant may seem overwhelming. The parents may have mixed feelings about their newborn. They may feel guilty because the infant did not reach full term or normal weight.

Rhodes, 1977). Many of these differences between full-term and preterm infants diminish or disappear with age. Some researchers have argued that preterm infants should not be compared to full-term infants in terms of developmental status.

When age is measured from conception rather than from birth, the early developmental differences in motor behavior between preterm and full-term infants are diminished. In a national study involving the records of 555 preterm infants, the development of very premature children equaled that of normal children when a correction was made to account for their early arrival. By age 2, the development of preterm infants was equivalent to or better than that of normal children even without such a correction (Den-Ouden, Rijken, Brand, Verloove-Vanhorick, & Ruys, 1991).

The effects of early environment on preterm infant development is studied by many researchers (Barrera, Rosenbaum, & Cunningham, 1986; Beckwith & Parmalee, 1986). It is clear that the special environment of the preterm and low-birthweight infant results in different social interactions between the infant and its caregiver. Interestingly, studies have found that preterm infants stimulated either by rocking or visual/auditory stimulation show greater gains in weight

They may be disappointed that their scrawny infant does not look like normal babies. And yet, they also feel nurturant towards their baby.

All of these feelings are understandable. But parents' perceptions of their infants affects the way they respond. In one study of premature stereotyping, researchers Stern and Hildebrandt (1986) labeled a group of full-term infants as either "premature" or "full term" and observed the caregivers' reactions to these babies. The "premature" infants were touched less, described as smaller, finer-featured, and not as cute, and were less liked by their caregivers than infants labeled as "full term." As a result of what the researchers believe to be a self-fulfilling prophecy, the "premature"-labeled infants proved to be less active with their caregivers.

The care of a tiny infant does present additional problems. However, when caregivers recognize the importance of caring contact in the early days of a newborn's life, many of the difficulties can be reduced. Par-

ents of premature infants need to be reminded that although their infants are behind in development, with adequate nutrition and stimulation most infants eventually catch up to their peers by the age of 5 or 6.

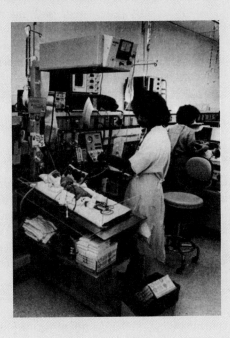

The special hospital treatment of the preterm and low-birthweight infant results in higher rates of survival. One problem with this environment is that it makes it difficult for parents to have direct contact with their newborn.

and overall development than preterm infants not receiving such treatment (Field & Schanberg, 1990; Goldberg, 1979). The long-term consequences of premature birth can be offset by careful monitoring and the use of intervention programs that support and educate the parents about the best way to care for and stimulate their frail infants (Olds & Kitzman, 1993). In the next chapter you will learn more about the impact of preterm birth on the infant's emotional and social development.

FOCUS ON CULTURE

A lifespan developmentalist is interested in how different factors affect development. Cultural attitudes, resources, and values exert a significant influence on the care infants receive. For example, would you expect an infant born in China, Saudi Arabia, or Chile to develop differently than an infant born in the United States? What information would you need to know about a culture to be able to answer this question?

RECAP

The neonate is in a state of vulnerability and adjustment during the first month of life. Its physical appearance may include the presence of lanugo, vernix caseosa, molding of the head, and crossed eyes. Its breathing may be irregular. But despite their fragile appearance, newborns are born with sensory and perceptual systems that allow them to respond to some of the physical stimuli around them. Using a variety of experimental techniques, researchers are beginning to assess newborn capabilities in vision, hearing, taste, smell, and touch. Neonatal reflexes are automatic responses that help the developing nervous system adapt to its physical environment. Preterm infants, however, require special care to help them adjust in the early weeks of life. Later developmental deficiencies are often observed in infants born prematurely.

THE INFANT

PHYSICAL GROWTH

General Principles   For both of my children, Adam and Sarah, I regularly documented their early development by recording various physical and psychological milestones in their baby books. It seemed that in the early months, there was something new to add every week. Later, their rate of growth slowed. But looking back at their baby pictures I am reminded of the dramatic sequence of changes in size, shape, and physical capabilities that occurred in the first few months of their lives.

The changes in infancy occur with such regularity that a careful observer can accurately guess an infant's age by noting its degree of physical and motor development (Alley, 1983a). As infants grow physically, they also gain increasing control over their bodies. The order of both physical and motor development follows two basic patterns: cephalocaudal, the progression of growth from head to foot, and proximodistal, the progression of growth from the center of the body to the periphery (Gesell, 1954).

In the **cephalocaudal pattern,** development occurs earlier and more rapidly in the head and upper parts of the body than in lower parts of the body. As I mentioned earlier, the proportionately large head of the newborn is an example of cephalocaudal development. **Proximodistal growth,** on the other hand, occurs earlier and more rapidly in the center of the body than in the extremities. For example, infants will gain control over their arms before they can use their fingers reliably. Before Adam could grab the figures on his crib mobile, he could hit them with his forearm and hand.

These general patterns of growth continue throughout development but are more apparent during infancy because physical change is more frequent. Individual infants, of course, may differ greatly from one another in rate of growth and onset of motor skills during the early years. These general patterns are derived from observing growth in many infants from different environments over time.

Differentiation, which describes the change in growth and development from simple, general reactions to those that are more complex and specific, can be seen

cephalocaudal
Pertaining to the pattern of growth that proceeds in a head-to-toe direction.

proximodistal
Pertaining to the pattern of growth that proceeds from the center to the outer or peripheral parts of the body.

differentiation
(1) Changes in growth and development from simple, general forms to more complex, specific ones. (2) Within 2 weeks after fertilization, the process in which growth of the cell becomes more specialized.

in the infant's changing reactions to a visual stimulus. Initially, Li Wei's interest in her colorful baby quilt was evident because she would move her arms and legs excitedly whenever she saw it; when she was older, she began to finger specific blocks in the quilt. Differentiation refers to children's increasing voluntary control over their bodies, which is regulated by the brain. With the maturity of the brain comes greater control over voluntary movement and hence a more specific response to stimuli.

Changes in Size and Proportion

By the 4th or 5th month of life, the infant has doubled its birthweight; by the age of 1 year, its weight has tripled. Because height is slower to change, it is not until age 4 that the length of the body has doubled. This is why children appear round and plump during infancy. Boys are generally taller and heavier than girls during infancy because they have more muscle and bone.

Even though bone cells first appear during the fetal stage of development, it takes a while before true bones emerge. At birth the infant's skeletal system is mostly soft cartilage, so the bones are more flexible. This skeletal flexibility makes the birth passage easier for mother and child. During infancy, different bones harden, or ossify, at different rates. The age at which the cartilage turns into bone is used to determine the maturity of the child. By comparing the rate of ossification between boys and girls, we see that even though boys are heavier and taller than girls in infancy, girls actually mature faster. In fact, at birth girls are 4 weeks ahead of boys in skeletal development (Tanner, 1970).

Brain Development

During infancy, the brain is growing rapidly. At birth, the brain is about 25% of its adult weight; by 3 months of age it is 40%; by 6 months it is 50%; and by 2 years of age it is 75% of its adult size. The neurons increase in size and density and develop a protective sheath of fatty cells called **myelin.** The myelin covering stabilizes the neurons and permits a faster transmission of neural messages, making it easier for infants to control their behavior. At birth the neurons within the cortex are not myelinized, and hence the neural messages between the cortex and other parts of the nervous system are not reliably transmitted.

The cerebral cortex, the portion of the brain responsible for voluntary control and thought, develops during infancy. By the 1st month of life, the section of the cortex controlling motor development begins to function; by 3 months of age, the sensory areas of the cortex are more fully developed. This neurological development allows infants to coordinate responses controlled by their motor cortex with their visual responses. Thus, the infant can now look at and touch an object at the same time, although precise eye-hand coordination will develop somewhat later (see Figure 3–1). The onset and refinement of sensory and motor events in infancy are correlated with growth and changes in the nervous system. Researchers are even suggesting that spurts in brain growth are correlated with spurts in cognitive development (Fischer, 1987; Kagan, 1982).

Sudden Infant Death Syndrome (SIDS)

Sudden Infant Death Syndrome **(SIDS)** is the name given to the sudden and unexpected death of seemingly healthy babies between the ages of 3 weeks and 1 year. The major cause of infant deaths, SIDS—or crib death, as it was formerly called—is responsible for more than one third of the deaths in this age group in the United States (Wilson &

myelin
The protective sheath covering the neurons.

Sudden Infant Death Syndrome (SIDS)
A sudden and unexpected death of a seemingly healthy infant between the ages of 3 weeks and 1 year.

FIGURE 3–1

The development of dendrites in the human occipital cortex: (A) the newborn; (B) the 3-month-old; (C) the 2-year-old.

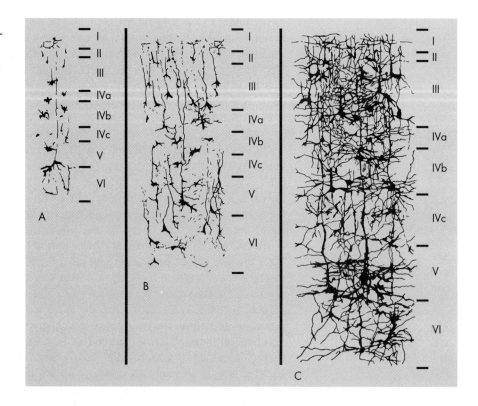

Neidrich, 1991). The tragedy of SIDS is that the syndrome is neither predictable nor preventable.

In the typical SIDS case, the baby, usually between 2 and 4 months of age, when put to bed appears healthy or may have signs of a slight cold. Some time later, the baby is found dead, usually with no signs of a struggle or discomfort. An autopsy may reveal at most a minor upper respiratory inflammation but nothing serious enough to cause death.

Who are the SIDS victims? Many are boys, especially those who are born prematurely. The rate of incidence of SIDS is also higher among the poor than the well-to-do, and it is higher among minority non-whites (predominantly African Americans) than among whites (Valdes-Dapena, 1980). Many of the SIDS victims die during the winter months, which suggests that cold, wet weather may be a factor. SIDS infants also are often placed on their stomachs when put to bed and wrapped very warmly with bed covers (Cotton, 1990). Infants of young mothers are most susceptible to SIDS. Further, the incidence of SIDS is higher among infants whose mothers smoke tobacco or use cocaine. Researchers now believe that SIDS probably has more than one cause, even though the actual process of death may be similar. It is now believed that SIDS victims are not as normal or healthy a group as was previously thought. Many have subtle physiological defects that are detectable only after death. A sizable number of the infants are found to have abnormalities in the central nervous system that had caused difficulty from birth. Other studies point to the possibility of lesions in the respiratory area of the brain stem as a factor in SIDS.

The hypothesis that apnea (cessation of breathing) causes SIDS has received much attention in the news, and many people have erroneously concluded that apnea is the cause of most SIDS cases. Many, but not all, SIDS babies have episodes of apnea while they are asleep. When apnea episodes are prolonged (10 to 20 seconds in duration) this condition may lead to anoxia, cardiac arrest, and death. However, only about 5% of SIDS victims seem to have had a history of severe apneic episodes (Valdes-Dapena, 1980).

Nutrition and Feeding Practices   Just as adequate nutrition is critical for neurological growth during the prenatal period, it is equally important during infancy. Inadequate nutrition can have a cumulative effect on development of the nervous system and hence affect the individual throughout life. Infants born to poorly nourished mothers and/or into households with inadequate diets are likely to carry these deficiencies into adulthood. For young mothers, the impact of poor diet can be passed on to offspring, who stand a greater chance of being born prematurely because of the mother's inability to nourish the placenta.

Inadequate nutrition can lead to significant declines in motor and cognitive skills that persist well into adolescence (Pollitt, Gorman, Engle, Martorell, & Rivera, 1993). Pollitt and his colleagues conducted an 8-year longitudinal study and a cross-sectional follow-up study using two groups of Guatemalan children. One group received protein-rich supplementary feedings during childhood while the other group did not. During adolescence and young adulthood, the children who had received the protein supplement outperformed those in the control group on all measures of reading, vocabulary, and numerical skill.

But the impact of malnutrition on development is a complex one, since the social and economic factors that contribute to an inadequate diet can also cause a decline in cognitive skills (Duncan, Brooks-Gunn, & Klevanov, 1994; Ricciuti, 1993). Poverty often leads to disruptions in the family, lack of access to good schools, and unsafe neighborhoods, all of which detract from normal intellectual development. Furthermore, malnourished children tend to be less active than well-nourished children, thus eliciting less positive responses from their caregivers. Not surprisingly, the motor development of malnourished children is delayed as a result.

FOCUS ON CULTURE

Customs and beliefs about breast-feeding vary in different cultures. The image of the nursing mother and child is respected in many societies, in which breast milk is believed to be a special food. Ecuadorians believe that women who have sexual intercourse while they are lactating will produce less milk. They also protect their infants from being harmed by milk that might have been "burned" by the sun by expressing some milk from their breasts before feeding (McKee, 1987).

Breast or Bottle?   As the infant's body grows, so does its need for nutrients, particularly protein. Milk is the primary source of protein for the infant during the 1st year of life. In the United States, most infants are either breast-fed by their mother or receive a cow's milk formula from a bottle. In most other countries, breast-feeding is the norm.

From a purely physiological viewpoint, breast milk is the ideal food for the baby. One reason is that it is more readily digested by the infant than cow's milk. In addition, the child is less likely to be allergic to the milk produced by its mother. Breast milk also contains the mother's antibodies and immunities, which help protect the infant from diseases. Research has discovered that breast milk contains a factor that seems to promote growth by increasing the absorption of folic acid by the infant's body (Colman, Helliarachy, & Herbert, 1981).

Breast-feeding has advantages for the mother. First, the infant's sucking stimulates her uterus, which promotes a quicker return to its normal prepregnancy size. Breast-feeding is readily available to the infant; in less developed areas this is important because access to clean water or facilities to sterilize bottles may not be available. As its nutritional needs increase, the infant sucks harder and longer, and the mother's body compensates by producing greater quantities of milk, free of charge. During nursing many women report great satisfaction from the intimate skin-to-skin, eye-to-eye contact. A similar degree of contact can, of course, be achieved in bottle-feeding. In a study by Richards and Bernal (1971), however, it was found that breast-fed babies were held, touched, and talked to more during feeding than bottle-fed infants—but this result may reflect personality differences between mothers who decide to breast-feed and those who choose bottle-feeding.

Not all women experience pleasure in breast-feeding. Some are unable to nurse because it is too painful or fatiguing, or because they are in poor health and cannot keep up with the additional nutritional demands of breast-feeding. Depending on cultural attitudes about breast-feeding, some women may feel embarrassed about exposing their breasts or may not want to be tied down by their baby's feeding schedule. Career commitments and an inflexible work setting may conflict with the need to be physically available to the child. Unlike Li Wei's mother, described in the opening story of this chapter, many women are not able to breast-feed at their place of employment. Some mothers may want to share the care and feeding of the infant with the father and prefer to bottle-feed. Obviously, there are many factors that influence the choice of bottle or breast as a source of nutrition. New parents, therefore, must balance the benefits and restrictions in light of their own situation. The long-term psychological benefits of breast- versus bottle-feeding are not known.

Culture also influences how long an infant is breast-fed. In some cultures, such as the African !Kung, infants are breast-fed until age 3. In the United States, infants are usually breast-fed for a much shorter length of time. Whether the infant is breast- or bottle-fed, by about 6 to 8 months most American mothers usually begin to wean the child to drinking from a cup. By 8 months the first tooth has appeared, and infants begin to bite on their mother's nipple. The mother and infant may both be ready for a change in the feeding pattern. By this age, infants show increasingly greater interest and curiosity in their physical world and in new foods. The recommended approach to weaning is a gradual one in which the child is offered a cup instead of the breast or bottle. Toward the end of the first year most infants are eager to feed themselves.

Self-Feeding and Diet.   The average 1-year-old has six to eight teeth and sufficient hand-eye coordination to self-feed. When my daughter Sarah was about 16 months old, she loved to feed herself raw peppers, frozen blueberries, and Cheerios. Between her regular meals and snacks, she seemed to be eating little bits

FOCUS ON CULTURE

In many predominantly agricultural countries it is a common practice for mothers to carry their infants with them as they go about their daily activities. Babies are tied to the mother's side, back, or front; they are in close contact with their mothers and only inches away from their main source of nourishment, her breasts. In most Western countries infants do not have such ready access. Many infants are fed on a schedule set by the mother rather than by their own needs.

of food most of the day. Because growth is rapid during infancy, the amount of food infants eat is more than their actual bodily size would suggest.

The long-term impact of an inadequate diet and starvation on physical and mental functioning is a common concern. An equally serious problem occurs when a child is encouraged to overeat by being offered foods containing large amounts of sugar and fats. During the 1st year of life the number of fat cells in a baby's body is determined by how much it eats. After the 1st year this number remains the same no matter how much a person eats. Later, as a person consumes an excess of calories, the fat cells expand, resulting in overweight. Thus, the number of fat cells developed during the first year of life theoretically can influence later tendencies toward obesity (Harding, 1971). Chubby babies are more likely than average weight babies to become overweight adults. Not all fat babies grow up to be obese adults, but most pediatricians recommend diets that are not loaded with sugar during infancy.

MOTOR DEVELOPMENT

Friends and relatives who have watched an infant grow from birth are likely to use the ages that the baby rolls over, sits up, or takes its first step as an index of the

Infant motor development proceeds more rapidly in the upper portion of the body. This baby has greater control over his head than he does over his legs and lower body.

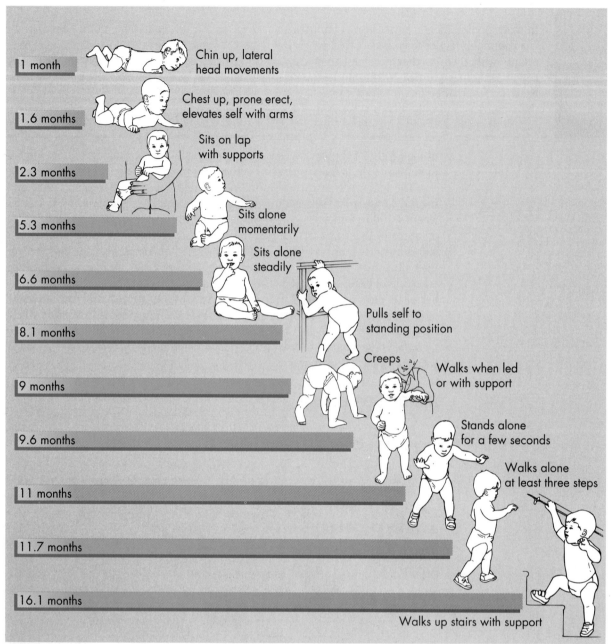

FIGURE 3–2

The development of locomotion in infants.

child's overall development. Changes in a child's ability to use his or her body are numerous and obvious, but they are not good predictors of changes in other types of development. For example, children who sit up and walk at early ages do not necessarily develop language or other cognitive skills at an earlier rate. For healthy infants, motor skills seem to occur in a regular progression in development.

The two major motor skills that develop in infancy are prehension, the ability to grasp and hold an object, and locomotion, the ability to move from one place to

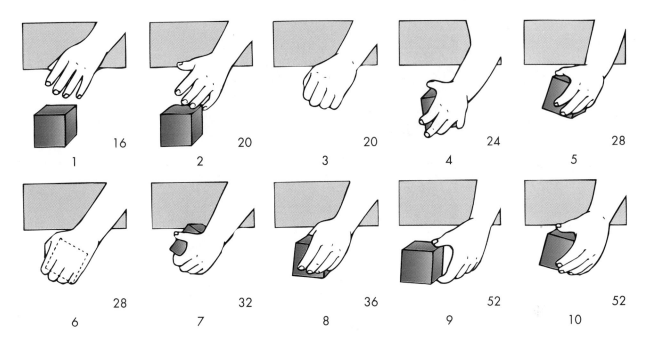

16	20	20	24	28
1	2	3	4	5
28	32	36	52	52
6	7	8	9	10

FIGURE 3–3

Ten types of grasping behavior: (1) no contact; (2) contact only; (3) primitive squeeze; (4) squeeze grasp; (5) hand grasp; (6) palm grasp; (7) superior palm grasp; (8) inferior forefinger grasp; (9) forefinger grasp; (10) superior forefinger grasp. The number in the lower right indicates the child's age in weeks at which these stages normally appear.

another. These skills emerge in an orderly sequence that follows cephalocaudal and proximodistal growth patterns. In the case of reaching and grasping, the infant progresses from the gross hand control of the palmar grasp to a more refined grasp of smaller objects, using its thumb and forefingers in a pincer grasp. In moving from one place to another, the infant first sits up, then stands; standing is followed by creeping, assisted walking, and finally unassisted walking. These sequences of locomotor and prehensive development are illustrated in Figures 3–2 and 3–3.

The order of motor events is believed to result from maturational factors. The growth of the nervous system, in particular the network of neurons, permits greater control over the large and small muscles controlling body movement. The center in the brain that integrates neural messages from the parts of the body also develops so that the infant can coordinate its control over specific body parts.

The role of experience in the onset of motor skills has been the subject of many studies. Dennis (1940), for example, researched Native American Hopi babies, who are bound to a cradle board during the first 9 months of life. Because of this restriction, the babies cannot practice motor skills such as rolling over or moving their hands or feet. However, this restricted early motor experience did not affect their motor development. Dennis found no differences in age of walking or other motor skills when he compared the cradled infants with nonrestricted infants.

Gesell and Thompson (1929) used identical twin girls in their study of motor development. One twin was given specific training and practice in stair climbing for 6 weeks, beginning when she was 46 weeks old. The other twin received no practice. At 53 weeks both twins could climb the stairs but the practiced twin could climb them faster. After only 2 weeks' practice, the untrained twin was climbing at the same rate as the twin who had practiced climbing. Practice and training, therefore, seemed not to affect overall motor development.

Later studies by White (1971) have emphasized the role of the environment in the development of reaching. For an infant to be able to reach for and grasp an

Although this Navajo infant's motor activity is restricted by being tied to a cradle board, her motor development most likely will not be affected.

object, it must first develop eye-hand coordination. For such coordination to occur, however, the infant must first look at its hand, then at the object, and then, after repeated object and hand viewing, coordinate its actions to reach for and locate the object. Only then can the infant successfully grasp the object. When the physical-visual environment was made more stimulating by introducing colorful objects, White found that infants reached for these objects at an earlier age than infants in a less-enriched visual environment. It can be concluded that the sequence of motor development is broadly guided by maturational factors and refined by the specific experiences of the infant in its physical environment.

The Impact of Culture on Physical Development   There are marked similarities in the timing and sequence of infant sensory and motor development across cultures. Perhaps this is why in the past researchers paid little attention to the influence that differing cultures have on early physical development. Today, however, psychologists recognize the importance and necessity of examining culture as a factor in infant development (Garcia-Coll, 1990; Rogoff & Morelli, 1989).

People from different cultures vary in their attitudes, expectations, and behaviors regarding childrearing. In addition, different cultures provide different kinds of resources to assist parents in the care of their young. The feeding of infants provides some good examples. Among middle-class parents in the United States slimness is valued; consequently, they are concerned with diet and weight.

Another example can be seen in breast- versus bottle-feeding. The choice to breast-feed may be dictated as much by cultural prohibitions against women exposing their breasts in public as by the health benefits to the infant. How long and openly an infant is nursed depends on the norm within the culture.

It has been noted in several studies (Kilbride, 1980; Super, 1981) that African infants routinely surpass American infants in the rate at which they learn how to sit and to walk, but not to crawl or climb stairs. In order to make sense of these differences in motor development, you need to know something about the culture in which the infants grow. African mothers encourage their infants to sit on the ground by propping them up with rolled blankets; they deliberately give their babies practice supporting themselves by putting them in a specially prepared hole in the ground. Crawling is not encouraged by African mothers because parents want their children to stay nearby them as they work in the village, and stairs are not commonly found in African homes.

The sleep habits of infants among rural Kenyan families were also compared to sleeping patterns of children in industrialized cultures (Super & Harkness, 1972). Most parents in the United States pride themselves on being able to get their young infants to sleep through the night. Feedings are delayed until late evening, and prolonged late afternoon naps are disrupted to encourage the infant to sleep later into the morning. However, in rural Kenya infants spend most of their time with their mothers, day and night. They are carried on the mothers' backs and are allowed to sleep and nurse whenever they want. As a result, young Kenyan infants adjust their wake-sleep cycle to their natural level of hunger. They typically do not sleep through the night as American babies do, nor is this a characteristic that Kenyan mothers value. Instead Kenyan babies sleep for short periods, usually about 3 hours, during the 1st month.

The gender of a child is biologically determined by its chromosomes, but the significance of its gender is emphasized by the values and traditions within its culture. In many cultures female infants are viewed as more fragile, and consequently are not bounced around or handled as much as male infants. This bias is significant because physical stimulation, as mentioned previously, is an important ingredient in early growth and development.

A final way that culture affects development in infancy is through the resources a country offers its people. Children born into economically impoverished communities are clearly at risk for malnutrition or starvation, both of which have dire consequences for growth. Infant mortality rates vary across and within national boundaries. In the United States, for example, African-American infant mortality rates are higher than the overall rate for the country (Garcia-Coll, 1990).

FOCUS ON CULTURE

Rattles are found around the world and are many infants' first toys. They take advantage of infants' tendency to grasp objects and their interest in locating sounds. Cultures vary in the way they construct rattles. American rattles are most likely to be made of plastic, while other rattles reflect the natural resources of the culture. Gourds, shells, rattan, hemp, and cane are popular raw materials for rattles. In some cultures, rattles are also used to frighten off evil spirits and promote health.

PERCEPTUAL DEVELOPMENT

When my son Adam was 2 months old I loved to watch him in his crib as he seemingly gazed at the animal mobile suspended above him. I knew he could see the figures, but I wondered what he was "thinking" about as he watched the shapes move. He obviously recognized the figures; he would smile and kick his feet and wave his arms while looking at the yellow spotted dog and the blue striped cat suspended above him. What interested me then, as it still does today, is how infants interpret all of the information they gather from their senses. This question has also stimulated a great deal of infant research.

Perception involves the organization and interpretation of sensory information. Perceptual capabilities develop rapidly during the early months of life. Infants as young as 1 to 2 months selectively attend to shapes, contours, patterns, and colors. At 3 months, infants prefer to look at familiar sights; by 4 months they can discriminate between different speech sounds (Eimas & Miller, 1992). By 6 months, infants scan, touch, and manipulate objects, actively acquiring information about their properties. For example, in one study researchers found that 6-month-old infants could distinguish an unfamiliar object from a familiar one by touching it and detecting whether it was hot or cold (Bushnell, Shaw, & Strauss, 1985).

Face Perception   Perhaps the earliest thing a newborn sees is a face. Doctors, nurses, eager parents, and, later, other family members are likely to present themselves face-to-face to the infant early in life. Research (Meltzoff & Moore, 1977, 1983) has demonstrated that newborns ranging in age from a few hours to 3 weeks are able to imitate simple facial responses modeled by adults. In fact, newborns only hours old can recognize their mother's face, regardless of whether it is presented to them live or on video (Bushnell, Sai, & Mullin, 1989; Field, Cohen, Garcia, & Greenberg, 1984; Walton, Bower, & Bower, 1992). In addition to their face recognition ability, newborns have exhibited a preference for looking at faces that are familiar to them. A study by Walton and Bower (1993) demonstrated that newborns preferred to look at a composite of faces they had seen rather than one of faces they had never seen. In one study (Carpenter, 1975) infants as young as 2 weeks looked longest at their mother when she was talking to them, and preferred to look at their mother's face rather than at either strangers' faces or the mother's face while listening to strangers' voices. Reissland (1988) studied newborns in a rural Nepalese hospital within their 1st hour of life and found that neonates would imitate the facial expressions of adult models. These ages for facial perception are younger than earlier studies on infant perception would suggest (Caron, Caron, Caldwell, & Weiss, 1973; Maurer & Salapatek, 1976).

By the age of 3 months the infant is reliably able to distinguish the familiar mother's face from other facial patterns. By 4 months of age infants perceive differences in facial expression, particularly when the face they are looking at is smiling (Kuchuk, Vibbert, & Bornstein, 1986). By 7 months of age infants can tell the difference between a happy face and a fearful one (Ludemann & Nelson, 1988; Nelson & Dolgin, 1985).

Depth Perception   The answer to the question, "When can the infant perceive that an object has depth or solidity?" depends on which infant response is used to

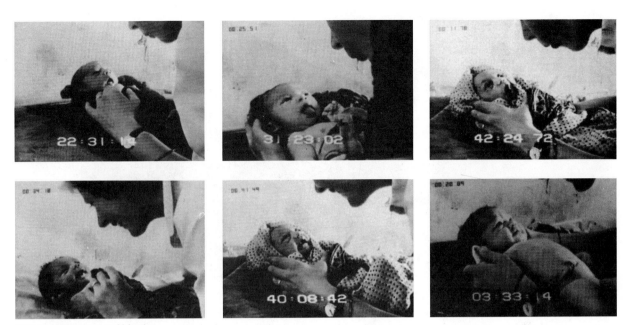

Within the first hours of life, these Nepalese babies demonstrated that they were capable of imitating facial expressions.

assess depth perception. In a classic study by Gibson and Walk (1960), infants 6 to 14 months of age were placed on an apparatus called the *visual cliff*. The apparatus was a raised table with a shallow side and a side that appeared to drop off. In fact, the "deep" side was covered with glass. The infant's mother was stationed at the "deep" end of the apparatus and tried to coax the infant to reach her. Even though infants felt the solid glass under them they would not cross over the "cliff," indicating that the infants perceived depth.

By using a decrease in the infant's heart rate as an index of attention, Campos, Bertenthal, and Caplovitz (1982) discovered that infants begin to focus their attention on the deep side of the apparatus by about 3 months of age but do not appear to fear falling. It is not until 8 months of age, having had experiences with locomotion and falls and spills, that the infant shows fear when on the deep side.

However, this conclusion has been challenged by research by Rader and associates (Rader, Bausano, & Richards, 1980). Twenty-two infants between 4 and 8½ months of age who were trained to use a walker and who could crawl to their mothers on request were tested on the visual cliff apparatus. When infants were tested in their walkers, they were as likely to move into the deep end as they were to move into the shallow end of the visual cliff. However, infants who had been crawling at an early age (before 6½ months) were more likely to crawl to the deep end, while those who learned to crawl at or older than 6½ months were remain in the shallow area. Infants who learn to crawl before 6½ months do so by using tactile cues (how the floor feels) rather than visual cues (how the floor looks). Infants who learn to crawl at an older age rely more on visual cues. Thus, Rader argues, depth perception is less influenced by motor experience than Campos and colleagues suggest.

Finally, it may be that the infant's mother may be communicating her emotions to the infant. Using a modified version of the visual cliff apparatus, Sorce and his associates found that if a mother's emotional response was joy or interest,

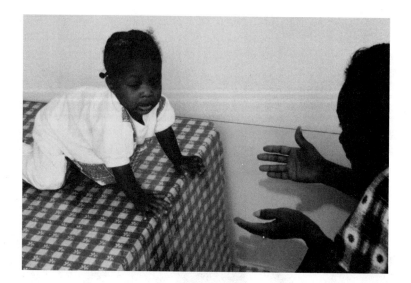

Gibson and Walk used the visual cliff apparatus to assess the depth perception of infants. Even though crawling infants can feel solid glass beneath them, they do not cross over the "cliff" to meet their mother.

infants were more likely to cross over the visual cliff. If the mother expressed fear or anger, the 12-month-old infants did not cross (Sorce, Emde, Campos, & Klinnert, 1985).

RECAP

During infancy growth is rapid and proceeds from head to toe and from the center of the body outward. Through differentiation, growth evolves from the general to the specific. The nervous systems changes rapidly, underscoring the need for an adequate supply of protein. Sudden Infant Death Syndrome affects seemingly healthy infants during the early months of life. The advantages of breast milk over cow's milk make it an ideal food during infancy; however, not all mothers are willing or able to breast-feed their infants. Infants acquire the ability to grasp and hold objects and to move from one place to another. The order and timing of motor skills is primarily controlled by maturation. Infants are capable of organizing their perceptions and are particularly good at recognizing faces. Depth perception emerges between 3 and 8 months of age.

COGNITIVE DEVELOPMENT

So far we have learned that infants are quite skilled at collecting information about their world. Through their sensory systems, infants taste, smell, see, touch, and hear their world. Growing motor skills give the baby greater access to people and objects. But how does the infant make sense out of this information and its world? Such questions focus on the infant's cognitive skills. **Cognition** is the process by which a person acquires and organizes information and knowledge about the world. It is the process by which we learn. The perceptual skills of the infant are just one example of an infant's attempt to organize the information about the physical world.

cognition
The process by which a person acquires and organizes information and knowledge.

Infant Memory   Researchers now recognize that young infants are very active processors of information (Olson & Sherman, 1983). They attend, select, perceive, and remember hundreds of pieces of information from their everyday world. Researchers became interested in the memory capabilities of infants as a result of habituation studies. Recall that infants (and adults) will grow bored and appear disinterested with an object that is presented to them frequently. If that same object is presented again at a later time, infants will often become excited again—as if they recognize the object. Parents who recognize this fact will be able to extend the lifetime of new toys by periodically boxing up some toys and reintroducing them at a later time. In order to have recognized an object, the infant must have encoded or stored in memory its important features. Using the habituation technique to assess memory, Swain, Zelazo, and Clifton (1993) found that newborns who heard a certain speech sound 1 day after birth remembered that sound 24 hours later.

Being able to recognize a familiar object is just one indication of memory. Recalling previously learned responses is another. In a cleverly designed experiment, researchers taught 3-month-old infants to turn a mobile overhanging their cribs by kicking their feet (Rovee-Collier, 1984). Several weeks later, after not having had any practice with their kick-start mobiles, the infants quickly remembered how to get them spinning. Infants who had not had the training sessions could not make the mobile turn. Even infants as young as 8 weeks are capable of retaining the mobile training over a 2-week period (VanderLinde, Morrongiello, & Rovee-Collier, 1985). Older infants remember events longer than younger ones (Bhatt, Rovee-Collier, & Weiner, 1994; Rovee-Collier, 1993).

Piaget's Theory   Perhaps one of the most innovative views about how infants and young children make sense of their world is that of Jean Piaget. Central to Piaget's theory of cognitive development is the idea that knowledge is constructed as people interact with their environment. The basic structures necessary for acquiring information about the world—for example, the sensory and motor systems—are present at birth in a primitive fashion. As infants use these structures, they develop, making it possible for them to gain more knowledge about the world. Thus Piaget's theory stresses the contribution of both biological and environmental factors as infants' actions set the stage for further knowledge and learning. Piaget postulated two processes to explain how knowledge is acquired through interaction with the environment: assimilation and accommodation.

Assimilation is the process by which the person uses existing knowledge, or schemes, to absorb new information about the environment. Piaget used the term **scheme** to describe an action sequence. For example, a baby presented with a rattle may look at it and then grasp it; this action sequence could be labeled the "look and grasp" scheme. When presented with an object other than a rattle—say a rubber ring—the infant, using the existing "look and grasp" scheme, would assimilate the new object.

As soon as the "look and grasp" scheme is applied to the rubber ring, however, the infant may notice some differences. For example, the ring doesn't make a noise like the rattle, and it has a different shape as well. Through the experience of interacting with the rubber ring, the infant will modify his or her existing "look and grasp" scheme to include a "look, grasp, and listen" scheme. Changing existing schemes as a result of new experiences is called **accommodation.**

assimilation
The process by which a person, using existing knowledge, comprehends new information about the environment.

scheme
Term used by Piaget to describe an action sequence.

accommodation
The changing of existing schemes as a result of new experiences.

Education Perspective

WHAT DO INFANT IQ TESTS TELL US?

Is my baby developing normally? What predictions can be made about my baby's future development? These are two questions often asked by parents. For years psychologists have been interested in creating a test that would assess the intelligence of infants while also predicting their future intellectual skills. The first such infant test was developed by Arnold Gesell (1925), who wanted to provide pediatricians with a way to determine whether an infant was developing normally. In the Gesell test, assessments are made in four areas: language, motor, adaptive, and personal/social skills. By comparing an infant's performance on a variety of nonverbal tasks to national norms, the examiner can determine the infant's *developmental quotient,* or DQ. With a DQ as a guide, pediatricians can identify and offer early intervention programs to infants with developmental abnormalities.

Another commonly used test is the Bayley Scales of Infant Development (Bayley, 1969, 1993). The test is divided into three subtests that measure motor development, mental development, and behavior in infants from 1 to 42 months old. Motor development involves the assessment of fine (ability to manipulate small objects, hand-eye coordination) and large (sitting, crawling, etc.) motor development. The infant behavior rating is based on the examiner's observations of the infant during the testing (interest in the task, restlessness, quickness of response, etc.). The mental subtest includes measures of the following abilities, among others:

Attention to visual and auditory stimuli

Babbling and vocalizations during the testing

Memory for hidden objects (object permanence)

Knowledge of named objects

Persistence in completing a task

Following directions

Imitating actions

Bayley scales are useful because they provide a fairly accurate assessment of the developmental status of infants. However, neither the Bayley nor the Gesell tests are good predictors of subsequent intellectual performance, for several reasons. First, the infant tests are primarily nonverbal and rely heavily on sensory-motor responses. In contrast, the older child and adult versions of IQ tests emphasize verbal skills. Thus, the two tests measure different behaviors, and this fact alone would explain the failure of infant tests to predict later IQ test scores (Bornstein & Sigman, 1986). A second problem is that scores on infant scales are not as reliable as later assessments. Scores can vary widely, depending on the infant's state of alertness and mood and the quality of the testing environment. Generally, the younger the infant, the less reliable the assessment.

More recently, researchers have measured infant information processing skills (by assessing habituation and recognition memory) to predict later intelligence. The advantage of using information processing skills as a measure of intelligence is that these skills are less subject to influence by the infant's socioeconomic environment or by the quality of the infant's parenting. Results from several studies suggest that habituation and recognition memory are indeed fairly accurate predictors of later IQ scores (Benson, Cherny, Haith, & Fulker, 1993; McCall & Carriger, 1993). Although the predictions are not perfect, infant measures of information processing provide a promising avenue for understanding the continuity of mental development from early infancy to adulthood.

By watching and following the moving objects of the mobile, this baby is acquiring new schemes and gaining knowledge about the world around him.

According to Piaget, assimilation and accommodation occur simultaneously. When reaching for the rubber ring, the infant is using the existing scheme; at the moment of contact with the ring it is changing that scheme in light of the information gathered by his or her senses. Throughout life, humans are constantly striving to establish a balance between perceptions and understanding of their actual experiences. Piaget called this process **equilibration.** Sometimes this balance is achieved through assimilation, sometimes through accommodation. Both accommodation and assimilation help infants develop increasingly complex schemes that enable them to adapt to their world.

equilibration

Piaget's term for the process by which one strives to establish a balance between perceptions and understanding of the world and actual experiences.

As their physical structures develop, children progress through different stages in which they use increasingly symbolic or conceptual schemes to guide their actions. The first stage, the sensorimotor stage, begins at birth and continues to 2 years of age. The infant interacts with its world primarily using sensory and motor schemes. Since Piaget viewed cognitive growth as a process, he placed a great deal of emphasis on the sensorimotor stage as the foundation for later symbolic thought.

The changes that occur in the various substages of the sensorimotor stage reflect qualitative differences in children's understanding of their world at different ages. Age alone, however, does not determine which substage characterizes the child. One 12-month-old infant may be functioning at the fourth substage (coordination of secondary schemes, 8–12 months) while another may be at the next substage (tertiary circular reactions, 12–18 months). However, Piaget believed that the sequence of the stages and substages is the same for all people even though the speed at which each stage is completed may vary. Table 3–3 lists the approximate ages for and describes each of the six distinct substages within the sensorimotor period.

By the end of the sensorimotor period at age 2, the infant has accomplished several major cognitive tasks: The infant has become familiar with his or her own body; has learned that events are preceded by some cause; has acquired **object permanence,** the knowledge that objects still exist even when they are not in sight; and is capable of using symbols in language and thought. Let's examine in detail the progressive changes in the infant's structures, or schemes, during this period of cognitive growth.

object permanence

The knowledge that objects still exist even when they are not in sight.

Substage 1: Reflex (0–1 month).   The reflex stage was originally called "exercising the ready-made sensorimotor schemes" because the infant reacts to environmental stimuli using simple reflexes, or schemes that are present at birth and even prenatally. The neonatal reflexes of sucking, grasping, and rooting are but a few of the ready-made ways of responding available to the newborn. By using or assimilating ready-made schemes, the infant also changes or accommodates them with actual experiences. For example, at birth the infant will suck on any object placed in its mouth. By the end of this substage, however, the infant may refuse to suck on anything but the nipple it has used most. For this reason, mothers who plan to supplement breast-feeding with a bottle are advised to introduce the bottle nipple to the infant in the early days of life to ensure that the baby will accept the bottle in the 3rd or 4th week.

PIAGET'S STAGES OF COGNITIVE GROWTH: THE SENSORIMOTOR PERIOD

SUBSTAGE	APPROXIMATE AGE	CHARACTERISTICS
1. Reflex	0–1 month	Ready-made schemes are used; reflexes are initiated both internally and environmentally.
2. Primary circular reactions	1–4 months	Goal-directed behavior is present, but internal goals are prevalent; infant repeats learned schemes.
3. Secondary circular reactions	4–8 months	Goals are more directly related to the environment; infant uses trial-and-error more often, still depends on chance to learn responses, and develops a primitive concept of objects.
4. Coordination of secondary schemes	8–12 months	Orientation to environment increases; infant distinguishes between goals and methods for achieving them; shows originality in combining two or more learned schemes.
5. Tertiary circular reactions	12–18 months	Curiosity begins, and novel stimuli are important; infant experiments with environment, systematic with trial and error.
6. Invention of new means through mental combination	18–24 months	Problem solving begins; infant begins to develop insights; can think without action.

TABLE 3–3

Substage 2: Primary Circular Reactions (1–4 months).

The term *circular* refers to the infant's tendency to repeat activities or schemes that create a desirable action. In effect, the infant's reactions are maintained by its action. These circular reactions are first noticed with the infant's own body rather than with objects in the environment; hence they are called *primary*. Li Wei watching her hand as she moves it back and forth while lying in her crib is one example of a primary circular reaction. Her random movements of her hand and arm result in her hand coming into view. This action of moving the hand over the body into the visual range is repeated often in an infant's day.

The child in this substage will not look for an object that has been taken from sight, but will stare at the place where the object was last seen. While this action reflects a primitive visual attempt to locate an object, it does not reflect object permanence.

Substage 3: Secondary Circular Reactions (4–8 months).

The circular actions in this substage seem to be focused more on objects and events outside, or *secondary* to, the infant's own body. For example, after months of watching, foot kicking, and organizing his motor schemes, my son Adam accidentally discovered that the animal shapes on the mobile would move when he moved his arms and legs, causing the crib to shake. This event caused him pleasure, so Adam would repeat the action of moving his arms and legs and watching the mobile figures shake. His own activity was a means to an end. Piaget used the term *motor meaning* to describe the infant's first understanding of objects through the specific motor actions it uses in the presence of those objects.

Modifications in the object permanence scheme are also made in this substage. When an object is only partially hidden, the infant will search for it. When the object is completely hidden, however, the infant will not search for it, even if he or she has seen the toy being hidden.

Substage 4: Coordination of Secondary Schemes (8–12 months).

Infants at the fourth substage are much more intentional in their actions. No longer are they content to repeat schemes; they now use their accumulated knowledge and schemes to produce an effect. For example, at 7 months Piaget's son Laurent

During the secondary circular reaction substage (4 to 8 months), infants may recognize a favorite toy as long as it is in full view. However, when it is hidden from sight, infants may act as if the toy never existed.

had perfected his "hitting at things" scheme to the point where he would hit objects to remove them as obstacles. In trying to reach a matchbox that was obstructed by a pillow (placed in front of the matchbox by Piaget), Laurent hit the pillow until it was out of his way (Piaget, 1952). Several schemes were thus coordinated to accomplish this goal: The looking, hitting, reaching, and grasping schemes culminated in Laurent getting the matchbox. Thus, in this substage, no longer is some effect achieved by chance and then simply repeated. For the first time the young child is capable of using well-practiced schemes to achieve aims that have been conceived ahead of time. Should these behaviors fail to achieve the desired goal, however, the child still is unable to alter his or her routine to increase the chances of success.

Object permanence emerges in this substage in a specific form called *contextually bound object permanence*. If the infant sees an object being hidden, it will search where the object was last seen. If the object is moved from one hiding place to another, the infant will continue to look in the original hiding place even though the object was seen being placed elsewhere.

AB error

The infant's inability to locate an object that has been visibly put in a different hiding place.

Psychologists refer to the infant's inability to locate the displaced object as the $\overline{AB}$ (A not B) **error,** which Piaget used to prove the development of object permanence. He believed that 8- to 12-month-old infants must rely on their sensorimotor actions to define an object since they have not yet developed the capacity to represent objects symbolically. However, other researchers explain the $\overline{AB}$ error in terms of infants' limited memory skills. Infants look for the toy under the first pillow (A) and not the second pillow (B) because they do not remember the second hiding place (Bjork & Cummings, 1984; Cummings & Bjork, 1983). As infants develop, their capability for holding items in short-term memory increases so that 14- to 16-month-old infants can remember hiding places longer than do younger infants (Schacter & Moscovitch, 1984).

One study compared the performance of adult amnesic patients who were asked to locate an object that had been moved to a new hiding place with the performance of 8- to 10-month-old infants who were given a similar task (Schacter, Moscovitch, Tulving, McLachlan, & Freedman, 1986). The adults demonstrated significant memory deficits yet were able to represent objects symbolically and recognize their permanence. The infants had not yet acquired object permanence and had limited memory capabilities. However, the amnesic adults generally did not perform the object search tasks any better than the 8- to 10-month-old infants. Thus the researchers concluded that the $\overline{AB}$ error in infants may not reflect an immature object concept but rather a memory deficit.

During the fourth substage, the infant also advances in its understanding of meaning. Instead of acknowledging an object or event by simple motor activity (as was the case in the earlier substage), the infant now activates more specific schemes in response to a signal event. For example, the sound of the refrigerator door opening may signal mealtime to the infant so that it activates the schemes associated with eating—such as crawling to the mother or reaching for the food—even though food has not yet been presented. This type of understanding of objects and events by the infant is called *signal meaning*.

Substage 5: Tertiary Circular Reactions (12–18 months).

Infants in the tertiary circular reaction substage are very exciting to watch because they are curious and actively engaged in trying out new ways to accomplish their goals. The physical structures have matured to the point that the infant is capable of moving about on foot as well as climbing. New schemes are created to achieve desired aims through active exploration and experimentation. During this fifth substage, my daughter Sarah loved to drop things while seated in her high chair; she would pick up a spoon, drop it on the floor, and wait for a response. She would bang various toys, foods, and utensils on her metal eating tray while listening to the sound. Then she would systematically drop each object while waiting to hear the sound it made as it hit the floor. She soon discovered that different shapes made different sounds. Sarah even roped me into her playful experimentation— she would watch my face and even wait for my reaction as she hurled objects from her high chair.

By this substage object permanence has improved to the point that the baby will look for an object in the last place it was found and search for it in other hiding places that have been observed. If the infant cannot see the object being moved from one hiding place to the next, however, then the infant cannot find it. For example, if the mother pretends to have a ball in her right hand but switches it to the left hand behind her back, the infant will look in the right hand for the ball. Not finding it, the infant will be at a loss. The infant's inability to form a mental representation of the ball being transferred from one hand to the other prevents the successful solving of this problem.

Substage 6: Invention of New Means through Mental Combinations (18–24 Months).

The sixth substage represents the transition to symbolic thought. The ability to represent internally certain events that are not actually perceived by the child's sense organs is called *symbolic thought*. The infant now applies symbolic meaning to the objects and events in his or her world. In other words, the infant can now think about properties of events or objects not just by engaging in sensory or motor actions but by forming a mental picture or image to help achieve a desired outcome. For example, at this stage Laurent was able to figure out how to reach a piece of bread that was out of his reach by mentally combining the action of reaching with the action of using a stick as an extension of his arm. Then he picked up the stick and used it to draw the bread toward him.

Although younger infants have demonstrated that they can imitate the actions of others, Piaget believed that it is not until this last stage of sensorimotor development that infants exhibit *deferred imitation*—the ability to imitate an action in the absence of the model demonstrating that action. In order for infants to copy a model's actions, they must have some representational image of the model's actions to guide their response. Older siblings provide a rich source of novel behaviors for the active 2-year-old to copy. Infants in day care may acquire new behaviors by watching and imitating their peers. Hanna and Meltzoff (1993) trained a 14-month-old "expert" to demonstrate specific actions with five different objects. Then they exposed a group of 14- to 18-month-old infants to the "peer expert." Five minutes later the subjects were presented with the objects and observed. The majority of infants imitated the behavior of the expert peer. In a similar study, infants who had observed an expert peer in a day-care setting imitated the behavior in their homes after a 2-day delay. Television can also serve as a source of imitative behavior, as demonstrated by Meltzoff's (1988a) study of 14- and 24-month old infants who imitated novel behaviors they had seen on TV the day before (see Chapter 1).

Object permanence is complete at this substage, as evidenced by the infant's continued search for objects that have been secretly hidden. Language skills emerge during this time as the infant associates both the verbal responses of others and its own verbalizations with the objects and people in its world. By the age of 2 the child has replaced many of its infant sensory motor reactions with symbolic verbal actions.

Evaluating Piaget's Theory

When Piaget began his study of young children, much of what we recognize today regarding infant memory and perceptual abilities was as yet unknown. Piaget was truly a pioneer in the field of cognitive development. However, not all researchers have supported his views. For example, Piaget maintained that the ability to imitate develops with age; yet, as mentioned earlier, researchers (Meltzoff & Moore, 1977, 1983; Reissland, 1988) have found that infants 2 weeks old and younger could imitate facial expressions and that newborns are able to remember faces and sounds (Eimas & Miller, 1992; Swain et al., 1993). Further research (Abravanel & Gingold, 1985; Meltzoff, 1985, 1988a, 1988b, has found that under certain conditions 9-, 12-, and 14-month-old infants will imitate actions after a delay. For example, in one study (Meltzoff, 1988b) infants observed an adult engage in novel behaviors (rattle an orange plastic egg, push a button that produced a beeping noise, and fold down a wooden hinge). The infants not only imitated the novel actions immediately after watching the adult, but they also were able to reproduce these actions after a 24-hour delay.

Piaget's estimate of the age at which object permanence emerges has also been challenged by a number of researchers (Wellman, Cross, & Bartsch, 1987). Infants as young as 3½ months are able to represent and reason about objects they cannot see. In one study (Baillargeon & DeVos, 1991) infants watched a toy car roll along a track that was partly hidden by a screen. A large toy mouse was placed behind the screen seemingly on the track in the path of the rolling car. Infants looking at the mouse on the track expressed surprise when the car emerged from behind the screen because they had represented the mouse as being on the track and thus an obstacle to the car. Nevertheless, although Piaget may have underestimated infants' abilities to make sense out of their world, he has presented developmental psychology with a rich theory to stimulate further research.

Learning in Infancy

There is much evidence that newborns and infants demonstrate their ability to learn early in life. They make changes in their behavior to adapt to their immediate surroundings, and when these changes "work," they repeat them as they adjust to new situations. This is **learning**—a relatively permanent change in behavior as a result of reinforced practice. Several types of learning occur in infancy.

learning
A relatively permanent change in behavior as a result of reinforced practice.

Classical Conditioning.

When my son Adam was 2 years old he had an unfortunate learning experience. It happened when the water to our house had been shut off for a short time for repairs. Later, after the water had been restored, Adam went into the bathroom and flushed the toilet; a very loud and frightening noise occurred as a result of the air in the pipes. He was terrified and ran out of the bathroom. Subsequently, he was afraid to flush the toilet. His experience illustrates the principles of classical conditioning, which occurs when a new stimulus—such as the act of flushing the toilet—coincides with an unconditioned or unlearned stimulus (UCS) and automatically evokes an unconditioned or unlearned response (UCR)—such as when the loud noise produced a fear reaction. After several pairings the new stimulus, called the conditioned stimulus (CS)—the flushing of the toilet in my son's case-produces a conditioned response (CR)—Adam's fear—very similar to the unconditioned response (UCR).

Watson and Raynor (1920) demonstrated that fears could be classically conditioned when they exposed an infant to a white rat while at the same time sounding a loud noise (see Figure 3–4). In another classic study, Jones (1924) illustrated how children's fears could be eliminated by using a classical conditioning model. A young boy who had a fear of furry animals was given milk and crackers; each day while the boy ate the crackers, a rabbit was brought closer and closer to him until he no longer displayed any fear. Eventually, the boy was able to pet the rabbit

FIGURE 3–4

The classical conditioning of a fear response to a rat. Watson and Raynor conditioned a baby to fear the rat by pairing the presence of the rat with a sudden loud noise that produced a startle and fear response.

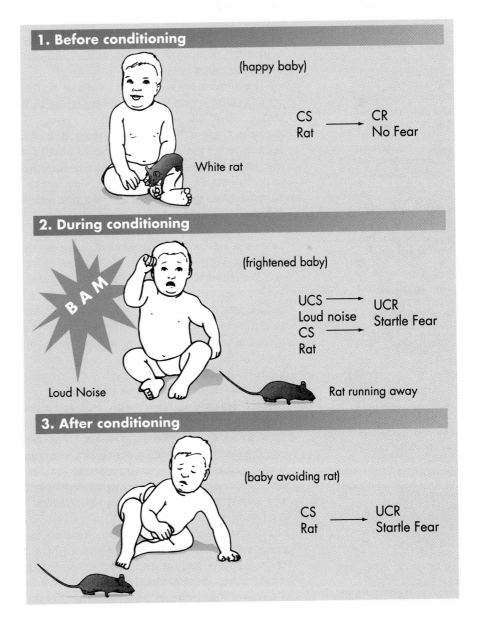

1. Before conditioning

(happy baby)

White rat

CS Rat → CR No Fear

2. During conditioning

BAM

(frightened baby)

Loud Noise

Rat running away

UCS Loud noise → UCR Startle Fear
CS Rat →

3. After conditioning

(baby avoiding rat)

CS Rat → UCR Startle Fear

while eating the crackers. In a different study, Lipsitt and Kaye (1964) conditioned infants to suck whenever they heard a pure tone. For the most part, classically conditioned responses have been demonstrated using reflexive responses—such as eye blinking, startling, and sucking—that are automatically evoked by specific stimuli.

It has been difficult to clearly establish how readily neonates learn behaviors through classical conditioning (Sameroff & Cavanagh, 1979), because the experiments performed to date have used very small samples of infants. A second difficulty is that the experiments must be conducted on alert, awake infants during the early months of life—the very period when infants usually spend much of their time asleep or feeling drowsy.

Operant Conditioning.

operant conditioning
A form of learning in which the learner acquires a behavior as a result of its consequences.

reinforcement
The term that describes any stimulus following a behavior that results in its repetition.

positive reinforcement
A stimulus that follows a behavior and increases the frequency of that behavior.

negative reinforcement
A process whereby the removal of an aversive stimulus results in an increase in a certain behavior.

punishment
A process whereby the application of an aversive stimulus after a behavior decreases its frequency.

Operant conditioning is a learning process in which the learner repeats behaviors that have resulted in a positive outcome (reinforcement) and eliminates behaviors that have resulted in a negative outcome (punishment). The famous psychologist B. F. Skinner was a pioneer in the study of this form of learning.

Reinforcement is the term used to describe a stimulus that follows a behavior and results in that behavior being repeated. **Positive reinforcement** refers to a stimulus that follows a behavior and increases the frequency of that behavior. For example, giving a dose of sugared water to an infant when it turns its head to the left will result in the infant turning its head to the left more frequently; the sugared water is the positive reinforcement. **Negative reinforcement** occurs whenever the frequency or likelihood of a behavior increases as a result of the removal of a stimulus. For example, when a person who has a headache takes some aspirin (the behavior) and the headache goes away, that person is more likely to repeat the behavior of taking aspirin the next time a similar situation occurs. In this case the aspirin is a negative reinforcement since it removed the unpleasantness of the headache.

Punishment is the process whereby an aversive stimulus is applied after a particular response, causing the response to decrease in frequency. For example, if a child is sent to her room every time she spits, one would expect to see a reduction in spitting—assuming that being sent away is unpleasant to the child. Punishment and negative reinforcement both involve unpleasant consequences, but they differ in their timing with respect to the behavior. In punishment, the behavior is followed by an unpleasant event; in negative reinforcement, the unpleasant event comes before the behavior. Skinner and other psychologists recognize that although punishment is one way to change unwanted behavior, it is not the most effective one to use with children. It is better to teach children desired behaviors through reinforcement than to eliminate behaviors through punishment.

Operant conditioning describes the consequence-based learning involved in the Rovee-Collier (1984) study mentioned earlier, in which 8-week- and 3-month-old infants were trained to turn a mobile. The infant's behavior of kicking resulted in a positive reinforcement—the mobile turning—that increased the infant's kicking behavior.

The success of operant conditioning in changing infants' behavior also depends on the nature and complexity of the behavior to be changed and the ability of the infant to perform the behavior. Kicking is a simple response for even very young infants. If infants had been required to grasp the mobile to make it turn, the 8-week-old infants would most likely not have been able to make the mobile work.

Even young infants are capable of acquiring new behaviors by watching others. This infant may be beginning a career in computing at a young age.

observational learning

A form of learning in which behavior change occurs as a result of watching others engage in specific behaviors.

Observational Learning.   **Observational learning** refers to a change in behavior as a result of watching others engage in specific behaviors. Kaye and Marcus (1978) point out that as infants become older they become more skillful at imitating models because they have greater voluntary control over their bodies. The behaviors infants imitate parallel their developing motor skills. Older infants are capable of symbolically representing and thinking about what they have seen and hence are better able to recall and match the model at a later date. Recall the research studies by Meltzoff (1988a, 1988b) and Reissland (1988) that demonstrated infants' ability to imitate real and videotaped models. Because infants require a great deal of physical care, they have many opportunities to attend to and observe people from whom they can learn new behaviors through observational learning. Learning by imitation is a powerful way for infants to expand their behavioral repertoire. In later chapters you will find more information about how children and adults acquire social behaviors by observing others.

BRIEF REVIEW

The neonate's physical appearance may seem unattractive as a result of the birth experience. The skin may be wrinkled and the head misshapen.

In addition, the newborn's physiological systems must adjust to extrauterine life. Respiration and circulation of oxygen from the lungs to the heart and brain begin when the umbilical cord is cut. It may take several days for the digestive system to function smoothly.

Newborns experience six separate states of consciousness. The infant is most attentive to its environment during the alert inactivity state.

Methods for studying infant capabilities include measuring physiological responses, changes due to habituation, preferential looking, and other behaviors that signal infants' interest in objects.

Although there are limits to the newborn's visual skills, the infant can see at birth and prefers to look at complex, symmetrical, high-contrast designs.

The newborn's behavioral responses include neonatal reflexes, which are responses triggered by specific stimuli in the environment. These neonatal reflexes disappear with the maturation of the nervous system.

BRIEF REVIEW

Premature babies are not fully developed and require special environments for survival. Often, they lag behind full-term infants in their motor development and may experience long-term deficits in mental development.

Physical growth in infancy follows a cephalocaudal (head to toe) and proximodistal (center to extremities) pattern. The infant develops more specific, controlled behaviors as the nervous system matures. Sudden Infant Death Syndrome (SIDS) is a disorder that seems to be related to central nervous system development.

An adequate diet with sufficient protein is important in infancy to ensure physical and neurological growth. Breastfeeding has many physiological advantages over bottle-feeding, but many mothers prefer to bottle-feed. Overfeeding in infancy can lead to obesity in later life.

Motor development is guided by maturation and follows a predictable sequence. Prehension and locomotion are two major motor skills acquired during infancy. The environment can influence an infant's interest in exercising motor skills.

Perception involves the interpretation of sensory information. Infants recognize faces at a young age and are able to imitate facial gestures. Infants also perceive depth at an early age.

Infants are capable of visually recognizing objects because they encode features of the objects into memory. Memory is evident in infants and newborns. The older the infant, the longer information is remembered.

According to Piaget, during the sensorimotor period the infant acquires object permanence, learns to control its body and to understand cause and effect, and begins to think in images. Schemes are assimilated and accommodated by the infant to adapt to the environment.

Infants demonstrate their ability to learn new behavior through classical and operant conditioning and through observational learning. Reinforcement is any stimulus that increases the frequency of a behavior. Punishment reduces the frequency of a behavior. Much of the behavior children acquire occurs through observational learning.

KEY TERMS

AB error (116)
accommodation (111)
apnea (87)
assimilation (111)
binocular fixation (90)
cephalocaudal (98)
cognition (110)
colostrum (87)
differentiation (98)
equilibration (113)
fontanelles (86)
habituation (90)

lanugo (86)
learning (118)
molding (86)
myelin (99)
negative reinforcement (120)
neonatal reflexes (93)
neonate(s) (86)
object permanence (114)
observational learning (121)
operant conditioning (120)
physiological neonatal jaundice (87)
positive reinforcement (120)

proximodistal (98)
punishment (120)
pupillary reflex (90)
reflexes (92)
reinforcement (120)
sensation (89)
scheme (111)
Sudden Infant Death Syndrome
    (SIDS) (99)
vernix caseosa (86)
visual accommodation (90)
visual acuity (91)

REVIEW QUESTIONS

If you can answer these questions, you have a good understanding of the material in this chapter. If a question seems difficult, go back to the text and review the topic.

1. Describe the physical condition of the neonate.

2. What is apnea?

3. Describe the six states of consciousness in the infant.

4. In what ways can researchers discover the sensory and perceptual capabilities of infants? What is habituation?

5. Describe the visual capabilities of the newborn. What is binocular fixation? What is visual accommodation?

6. Describe at least five neonatal reflexes. Why is it important to monitor the development of neonatal reflexes?

7. What are the two types of premature infants? Describe the differences in responding between full-term and preterm infants.

8. What is Sudden Infant Death Syndrome (SIDS)? What are the characteristics of infants at risk for SIDS?

9. List the advantages of breast-feeding.

10. What are the two major motor skills infants acquire in the first two years of life? What role does experience play in the development of motor skills?

11. Describe the infant's ability to perceive faces and depth.

12. What is cognition? How do researchers measure infant memory?

13. Define and give an example of assimilation, accommodation, and scheme. What is equilibration?

14. Name and describe the six substages of the sensorimotor period.

15. What is object permanence? At what age does it develop?

16. Describe the three ways that infants learn new behaviors. Give an example of each way of learning.

OBSERVATIONAL ACTIVITY

THE CHILD'S UNDERSTANDING OF OBJECT PERMANENCE

Piaget has detailed the acquisition of object permanence in his theory of cognitive development. With each substage the child demonstrates a more thorough understanding of the idea that objects exist even when they are not visible. In this activity you will be asked to observe a young infant between the ages of 6 months and 2 years. You may be able to find a baby in this range among the children of your friends and relatives, or you might try a local infant day-care center or nursery. (Your school may offer a day-care service for students and staff.) Be sure to obtain permission from the center's director before you begin your observation. Try also to learn the chronological age of the infant you are observing.

Once you have selected an infant, observe that infant while he or she is playing with toys in the playpen or on the floor. Using the following questions as a guide, notice the infant's reactions to the objects.

1. Does the infant notice the toys? How does he/she react?

2. Does the infant pick up any of the toys?

3. Does the infant repeat any actions with his/her body and the toy?

Now, cover the toys with a cloth or blanket and observe the baby's reaction. Does the infant know that the toys are still there? Does the infant search for the toys? Describe the infant's attempts to locate the toys.

On the basis of your observations identify which substage in the sensorimotor period best describes your infant's behavior. Summarize your findings and describe what you have learned in doing this activity. Share this with your classmates. How might an awareness of infants' development of object permanence help an early-child-care teacher?

About 2 years before Alec was born, his mother gave birth to a baby girl with a serious heart defect. The baby lived only 2 days, but she had a significant impact on Alec's life. Alec's parents were both distraught and confused about the death of the baby. A year later, after Alec was conceived and throughout the pregnancy, his mother prayed for a healthy baby. Fortunately, Alec was healthy, though small. During his 1st year of life, his mother insisted on being the only one to care for Alec, afraid that he might catch something from a sitter. Alec's father was "allowed" to fill in for his mother from time to time. At 6 months, Alec was quite familiar with his mother's care. Whenever his father held him, Alec would cry and reach out for his mother. His mother interpreted Alec's strong preference for her as a sign of his love and attachment to her and was not concerned by his behavior.

By his 1st birthday, relatives described Alec as fussy and irritable and avoided bothering him as much as they could. He would not let others pick him up, and when his mother did leave him with a sitter he would scream helplessly and unconsolingly for a very long time. Eventually, he would exhaust himself and wait for his mother.

Kia was also timid with people, but her circumstances provided her with ways to overcome her temperament. She was born in Embu, Kenya, into a family that already had four other children. At 3 months of age, it was apparent to her parents and siblings that Kia was slow to warm to people and new situations. She spent her days in the close company of her mother and older sisters. They took turns carrying her about the village and nearby fields. Whenever she encountered a new situation or met a stranger, it took a while for her to adjust. Her family helped Kia become comfortable with others by giving her many opportunities to interact with people who let her express herself at her own pace.

Perhaps it was because of Kia's shyness with others that her mother and sisters spent much of their time together talking and singing to Kia. Her mother could easily elicit a smile from Kia just by speaking softly. By 12 months of age, Kia was quite a talker herself. She could say her sisters' names and the names of the foods she liked. She even knew the names of the crops her family grew.

Over the months since birth, both Kia and Alec interacted with people and objects in unique ways. They established themselves within their families and learned to express themselves in their emotional exchanges with others. Their styles of interacting gradually became part of their emerging personalities.

One of the challenges in describing development from a lifespan perspective is to capture and convey the essence of multidirectional and multidetermined changes. One way would be to require you to observe an infant daily for the course of the infant's life. Then you would see how changes in one system, such as perception, are related to and affect the changes in other behaviors, such as cognitive or social skills. But you would be very old by the time the course requirement was completed.

Chapter 3 addressed the infant's capacity to take in, interpret, and respond physically and psychologically to events and stimuli. But that was really only half the story. Like Alec and Kia, infants display their own unique reactions to people and objects—they interact with people in different ways and with different consequences. Thus, to get a true picture of the emerging infant we must consider the social and emotional changes—responses that both influence and are influenced by the physical, perceptual, and cognitive changes discussed in Chapter 3. Furthermore, infants' social, emotional, and personality development is affected by the cultural and social context in which they are developing.

EARLY SOCIAL INTERACTIONS: BIDIRECTIONAL INFLUENCE

unidirectional view
The view of development that considers the child to be a passive recipient of the parents' actions.

bidirectional view
The view of development maintaining that the parents and the child actively influence each other.

In my early years as a college professor, whenever I discussed childrearing practices I would focus on what parents could do to help teach their children appropriate behaviors. It was not until I became a mother myself that I realized how much students were missing. As a result of raising my two very different children, I discovered that children have a profound influence on the kind of care they receive. Like Kia and Alec, different children generate different reactions.

Until the late 1950s, most of the studies of infant behavior in the United States focused primarily on the effects of different child-rearing practices. Most of the changes in infant behavior were considered to result from either maturation or the way the parents treated the child. This view of development, in which the child was considered a passive recipient of the parents' actions, was based on a **unidirectional view**. In the 1950s, however, Piaget's theory and research began to impact the way developmental psychologists viewed the infant. As noted in the last chapter, Piaget believed that infants are active and involved participants in their own development. Later research focused on the infant's abilities to respond selectively to experiences. As you learned in Chapter 3, infants are quite capable of responding to their physical and social world using their sensorimotor skills.

With this new view of the infant as an active agent in the parent-child interaction came a need for a different model of development. Richard Bell (1968; Bell & Harper, 1980) views the unidirectional model as too simplistic and emphasizes the ways in which the child's actions affect the parent's caregiving behavior. Thus in the **bidirectional view** of development the parent and child both actively influence each other; the infant's behavior determines the parent's response. For example, because of Kia's shyness her mother would talk to her in a quiet voice; Alec's whimper would discourage his family from picking him up. Rather than simply focusing on one side of the interaction, developmental psychologists study both participants, and the sequential nature of their interactions.

FOCUS ON CULTURE

Throughout the world, young children have a recognizable influence on their caregivers. For example, Japanese mothers believe that infants are initially independent and autonomous, responding only to their own internal body rhythms. To encourage their dependence, mothers devote a great deal of energy responding to their infants (Fogel, Toda, & Kawai, 1988).

THE INFANT'S CONTRIBUTION

Physical Characteristics   From the moment of birth, newborns and their parents are primed to form a powerful, affectionate bond. Many of the infant's actions are instrumental to the formation of this bond. Numerous researchers (Condon & Sander, 1974; Meltzoff & Moore, 1983; Reissland, 1988) have shown that newborns in the 1st hours of life engage in behaviors that complement the parent's actions. In one study (Condon & Sander, 1974), the infants were shown to move in rhythm to their mother's voice, creating a synchronized "dance" with her. An infant will also engage in eye-to-eye contact with the caregiver whose face is within 8 to 9 inches away (the distance at which newborns can best focus on an object). The feeding position provides many opportunities for parents and infants to gaze into each other's eyes. In addition, the infant sucking at the mother's breast triggers the release of the hormones oxytocin and prolactin, which some researchers believe act as a chemical releaser of affectionate maternal behavior. The cry and voice of the infant also stimulate the nursing mother's blood flow to her breasts. Further, mothers have been known to be able to distinguish their own babies from among several by their unique smell (MacFarlane, 1975). Parents also quickly learn to distinguish the cry of their own babies from other infants.

The quality of care infants receive from parents or caregivers from the moment of birth contributes to the development of a powerful affectional bond.

Brazelton (1981) suggests that the very shape of the infant evokes a more nurturant response in adults. The large head and small, soft body of the newborn produce protective and cuddling behaviors in humans. One study examined how the shape of the infant's body influenced adults' willingness to care for children (Alley, 1983b). The study found that caretaking responses decreased as the proportion of head to body decreased; that is, as the shape of the child lost its "babyish" look, adults were less likely to engage in caregiving behavior.

The physical attractiveness of an infant may affect the care it receives. In one study (Ritter, Casey, & Langlois, 1991) adults were asked to rate the attractiveness, age, and developmental capabilities of 6-month-old infants. Adults rated the less attractive infants as older than the attractive infants; they also overestimated the accomplishments of the less attractive infants (e.g., sit up, stand, talk, drink from a cup).

Several studies have found that mothers of preterm infants spend more time stimulating their infants than do mothers of full-term infants (Brachfeld, Goldberg, & Sloman, 1980; DiVitto & Goldberg, 1979; Stern & Hildebrandt, 1986). Other research (Greene, Fox, & Lewis, 1983) has indicated that mothers of full-term ill newborns spent less time in social interactions and more time in caregiving behavior than did mothers of healthy infants. The sick infants were also less responsive and attentive than their healthy counterparts. Furthermore, the mothers' behavior seemed to be influenced by the behavior of their babies, even after the illness had subsided. At 3 months of age the infants were no longer ill or unresponsive, and yet the mothers continued to compensate or be affected by the neonatal behavior of their infants. Recall that Alec, whom you met in the opening vignette, was born small and considered vulnerable by his mother; as a result, his mother responded to him in an overly protective manner long after his birth.

The long-term consequence of these early parent-child interactions could be a restrictive or overprotective style of parenting. The conclusion from studies of

Parents of high-risk preterm infants need special encouragement and instructions on how to handle and stimulate their infants in the early days of life.

high-risk infants and their interactions with their parents is that special attention and encouragement may be needed for the parents of ill newborns in order to promote a healthy parent-infant bond, as well as to encourage the infant's development (Barrera, Rosenbaum, & Cunningham, 1986; Goldberg, Perrotta, Minde, & Corter, 1986).

Infants are born with differing temperaments and sensitivities to their physical and social environment. By observing parents interacting with their babies, pediatric specialists can identify difficult or disruptive parent-child patterns and help parents develop new ways of responding to their infants. For example, an irritable baby may be hypersensitive to noise or touch. The parent who is unaware of the infant's temperament may actually irritate the infant by frequently picking it up or by placing it in a noisy setting. In one study (Lasky, Tyson, Rosenfeld, & Gant, 1984) infants who required neonatal intensive care were observed interacting with their mothers at 1 year of age; a similar observation was made of infants with normal neonatal experiences. Mothers of the normal infants were more likely to play with, talk to, comfort, smile, and directly face their babies than were mothers of the high-risk infants. The normal infants were also more likely to smile back at their mothers.

FOCUS ON CULTURE

The positions and amount of time infants are carried is influenced by child-rearing practices within a culture. Parents living in Western societies transport their infants in carriages, baby carriers, strollers, and backpacks. In contrast, infants living in nontechnological cultures spend the majority of their days strapped to their parent (or a sibling). Thus, infant and caregiver have many opportunities to become acquainted with each other's smell, voice, appearance, and touch.

Temperament   By his first birthday, others were calling Alec difficult; Kia was characterized as timid from her earliest months of life. For centuries parents have described their newborns in terms of their temperament, and the study of infant temperament is one of the most exciting areas of research in human development.

temperament
A person's inborn, characteristic way of responding to stimuli.

Temperament refers to a person's inborn, characteristic way of responding to stimuli. Temperament is believed to be the first manifestation of what will later be called "personality"—what results from the interaction of genetic or biological heritage with individual experience. Because newborns have not been exposed to the many social experiences that influence personality, whatever individual differences exist must be the result of inborn genetic factors and/or neonatal experiences.

Interest in infant temperament was triggered both by Bell's (1968) research on the infant's contribution to the parent-child relationship and the results of the New York Longitudinal Study (NYLS) reported by Thomas and Chess (1977). This 20-year study tracked the temperament and behavior of 136 people from early infancy into adolescence. Parents were asked to describe precisely how their infants reacted during specific routines of daily living such as feeding, bathing, sleeping, and responding to people. The infants were also observed at home. The researchers found that newborns differed on nine qualities of behaving and reacting, and that these differences sometimes continued into childhood (see Table 4–1).

Thomas and Chess (1977) found that certain of these qualities tended to occur together and could be grouped into three patterns of infant temperament: *easy, difficult,* and *slow-to-warm.* The easy baby has regular patterns of eating and sleeping, comfortably approaches new people and objects, adapts readily to changes in the environment, reacts with moderate to low intensity, and typically is in a good mood. The difficult baby (like Alec) has irregular patterns of eating and sleeping, withdraws from new people and objects, adapts slowly to changes, has intense reactions, and is often irritable. The slow-to-warm baby (like Kia) has a low activity level, tends to withdraw when presented with an unfamiliar object, reacts with a low level of intensity, and slowly adapts to changes. Easy babies represented 40 percent of the total NYLS sample; 10 percent were difficult children, and slow-to-warm babies made up 15 percent of the sample. The remaining 35 percent did not fit easily into one of the established patterns and showed a mixture of behavioral patterns.

Most of the data from the Thomas and Chess study come from parents' reports about their infants' behavior. Data from the Louisville Twin Study, a longitudinal study of young twins, suggests that infant temperament can be readily detected by observers as well as by parents (Matheny, Riese, & Wilson, 1985; Wilson & Matheny, 1983). By observing and videotaping infants in the laboratory during a standardized set of interactions with strangers, Wilson and Matheny found that infants differed in their emotional reactions, attention, and receptivity to strangers and that these differences paralleled differences reported by the parents in describing their infants' reactions at home.

CHARACTERISTICS OF INFANT TEMPERAMENT

1. Level of activity

2. Rhythmicity or regularity of biological functions such as sleep, activity, eating, and elimination

3. Approach or withdrawal, based on the child's initial reaction to new stimulation

4. Adaptability or the child's flexibility of behavior following the initial reaction to a new situation

5. Intensity of reaction

6. Threshold of responsiveness, or the level of stimulation necessary to evoke a response

7. Quality of mood, or the amount of pleasant behavior compared to unpleasant behavior

8. Distractibility, or the degree to which extraneous stimulation disrupts ongoing behavior

9. Attention span and persistence, or the length of time the infant maintains activity and tolerates difficulty

TABLE 4–1

In a different study Matheny and associates (1985) found that measurements of a newborn's temperament could be used to predict whether that infant would have a strong emotional reaction to stimuli presented at the age of 9 months. They discovered that irritable, difficult-to-soothe newborns were more likely to be fussy and distressed in the laboratory test than more easygoing newborns.

Another study found a relationship between newborns' physical activity and later measures of activity at 4 to 8 years of age (Korner et al., 1985). The most animated neonates became the more active children and were perceived by their parents as more likely to approach new experiences.

Kagan (1989; Kagan & Snidman, 1991) reported on the persistence of the temperamental characteristic of inhibition. Infants who were described as socially inhibited or shy based on observations during their infancy continued to be described as timid up to the age of 8. Likewise, uninhibited or socially outgoing infants also showed these characteristics in childhood.

Thomas and Chess (1977) also found that parents were quite influenced by whether a child was easy, difficult, or slow to warm in infancy. An easy child more often than not made parents feel competent in their roles, whereas a difficult, irritable child caused some parents to doubt their abilities to care for their infant. The degree of "fit" between parents' expectations regarding their infant's behavior and the actual behavior of the infant also plays an important role in the family's adjustment. Difficult behavior on the baby's part is less of a problem for parents when, for whatever reason, they expected such behavior to emerge. It is the disconfirmation of expectations—such as when a baby who manifests difficult behavior is born to parents who expect an "easy" baby—that produces problems in the ongoing social interaction between parent and child.

In a recent longitudinal study conducted in the Netherlands (van den Boom & Hoeksma, 1994), researchers observed mother-infant interactions from birth to 6 months of age. When the infants were 15 days old, ratings were used to classify them as either irritable or nonirritable. Observers then made monthly home visits

Difficult or irritable babies withdraw from people and are slow to adapt to new situations. Often the parents of difficult babies doubt their abilities to care for their children.

Personal Perspective

COMFORTING BABY DURING MEDICAL PROCEDURES

One of the most disturbing sounds to parents (worse even than the early morning alarm clock) is their baby's crying. This cry is both a signal and a powerful reinforcer. Usually, the caregiver perceives the baby's cry as a sign of discomfort and proceeds to alleviate the situation. If the baby is hungry, the parent offers a bottle; if the baby is tired or wearing soiled diapers, a different remedy is in order. But what can a parent do when the discomfort the baby feels is due to necessary medical procedures? Inoculations, blood samples, and throat cultures may seem fairly harmless to adults, but they are extremely distressing to the young infant. Infants with serious illnesses may be subjected to even more painful procedures.

When these procedures cannot be avoided, there are some things that parents and medical professionals can do to comfort infants and reduce their pain. Psychologist Rosemary Campos (1993) culled the research on infant reactions to painful stimulation and derived five practical suggestions for reducing the aversive effects of medical procedures:

1. Create an environment that promotes relaxation and reduces stress. Infants who are hungry and tired are likely to experience more pain during medical procedures than infants who are fed and content. Therefore, to reduce painful experiences, make sure the procedure is done when the infant is in a comfortable position, is well fed and relaxed, and is not already crying. The setting should be quiet and not chaotic (a condition many emergency treatment rooms cannot meet).

2. Distract the infant's attention from the painful procedure. (Most parents are already familiar with this strategy.) Diverting the infant's attention to toys, colorful displays, or sounds reduces pain. To increase alertness to distracting objects, it is best to position the infant upright on one's shoulder.

3. Giving infants a dose of sucrose helps to reduce pain. The use of "sugar water" has been popular with mothers and grandmothers in a variety of cultures as a means of soothing cranky babies. Now research has established that sucrose has a calming effect that lasts beyond its actual ingestion. Thus, to reduce the painful effect of procedures, give the infant sucrose beforehand.

4. Reduce irregular or intermittent stimulation. Rhythmical or continuous touch is more effective in reducing arousal than irregular handling or stimulation. Sometimes, the occasional touch, even a tender stroke, can produce a startle response in infants that can intensify their pain. The combination of touching and talking to infants can be aversive.

5. Provide infants with a way to control or cope with their pain. Giving an infant a pacifier to suck on during a painful procedure is comforting and lets the infant do something about the pain. Another way to enhance infants' sense of control is to hold them in skin-to-skin contact. This allows the caregiver to detect and respond to subtle changes in respiration or positioning.

Campos cautions that not all of these techniques will work for all infants. There is considerable variability in infants' responses to stress and pain. For some infants, providing a pacifier may help, while other infants require a combination of soothing techniques to reach a similar level of comfort.

during which they recorded the behavior of both mother and baby. Irritable infants displayed less positive social behavior and more passivity compared to nonirritable ones. However, by the time the infants were 6 months old, most of these differences had disappeared. Despite the changing reactions of the infants over the 6-month period, the mothers displayed a consistent pattern of interaction. Mothers of irritable infants were generally less involved with the infants and primarily provoked by negative emotions. In contrast, mothers of nonirritable infants looked at their infants more often and reacted to positive emotions with more stimulation and responsiveness than mothers of irritable babies. Clearly, the early temperamental behaviors of these infants had influenced their mothers' child-rearing attitudes.

Infant Emotions   A growing number of studies reveal that infants have a much more complex emotional life than was previously thought (Tronick, 1989). By carefully observing infants' reactions to people and situations in early life, researchers are discovering that infants go through stages in their emotional development in much the same way as in physical and cognitive growth (Greenspan, 1984). In fact, most researchers see emotional and cognitive development as very closely linked (Sroufe, 1979). Experiencing the world, the infant not only understands it, but reacts to it emotionally with joy, anger, and even anxiety.

Stages of Emotional Development.   For a theory of emotional development to be meaningful from a lifespan perspective, it must relate the emergence of affect (emotion) with concurrent changes in social and cognitive development. Sroufe (1979) has combined the results of several empirical studies of infant social, emotional, and cognitive development to describe stages of emotional development (see Table 4–2).

Beginning with a lack of emotional response in Stage 1, infants progress with an increasingly more complex display of emotional reactions. As infants interact more with the people around them, they form emotional attachments and learn to expect their caregivers to be responsive to their needs. By the time children reach age 3, they have acquired a sense of themselves as a result of their social interactions with family members. Emotions are experienced as they engage in role-play and fantasy. The child experiences pride and guilt as a by-product of a natural inclination to practice newly developing skills and to evaluate the performance of these skills using other people's standards (Stipek, 1983).

Assessing Infant Emotions.   As with most age-related sequences it is important to keep in mind that infants' emotional reactions may vary. Furthermore, the assessment of infant emotional reactions is complicated by the fact that infants cannot tell us what they are feeling—their reactions must be inferred from their behavior. Several researchers have used facial expression to measure emotional experience. Izard (1979, 1991), for example, has studied videotapes of infants reacting to a wide variety of situations—such as when being given an ice cube or having a favorite toy taken from them. Based on these observations, he and his colleagues have developed a coding system to identify different emotions by rating different facial responses. For example, anger is indicated when the eyebrows are lowered sharply and drawn together, the eyes are narrowed or squinted, and the mouth is open in an angular, squarish shape.

STAGES OF EMOTIONAL DEVELOPMENT		
STAGE	**AGE**	**CHARACTERISTIC**
1	1 month	No true emotions shown, reacts to external stimuli
2	1–3 months	Reacts with a social smile, displays interest in outside world
3	3 months	Displays such positive and negative emotions as rage, frustration, joy, and delight; engages in reciprocal social exchanges
4	7–9 months	Engages in social play and elicits social responses from others
5	9–12 months	Displays strong attachment to caregiver and ambivalence and wariness toward strangers
6	12–18 months	Actively explores and engages the environment; displays strong emotions of joy and anger
7	18–36 months	Experiences anxiety when separated from caregiver; frustration and anger are common; self-awareness emerges
8	3 years	Forms view of self; experiences pride and guilt

TABLE 4–2

Using a similar coding system for facial expressions, Stenberg, Campos, and Emde (1983) demonstrated that specific facial expressions of anger could be reliably detected in 7-month-old infants. In this study infants were given a teething biscuit. Once the infant began to suck on the biscuit, the biscuit was removed and held just beyond the child's reach. This sequence was repeated several times. Since only the infant's face was videotaped, raters had no contextual cues as to what specific emotion the infant might have been experiencing. Using only the eyes, mouth, and eyebrows for facial cues, raters were able to reliably assess the angry emotional reactions.

Infants not only imitate facial expressions of emotion, they also learn where and when to express their feelings. The learning process occurs daily through countless face-to-face interactions with their parents (Malatesta, Culver, Tesman, & Shepard, 1989; Malatesta, Grigoryev, Lamb, Albin, & Culver, 1986; Termine &

FOCUS ON CULTURE

Western psychologists have primarily studied the emotions that are expressed within their shared culture—namely, anger, fear, sadness, contempt, joy, excitement, guilt, and shame. Other cultures selectively reinforce and value different emotional states. For example, the Utku Eskimo value *naklik,* a feeling associated with the desire to nurture and protect another; the Japanese value *amae,* a feeling of mutual interdependence with another person; and the Ifalukians of Micronesia consider *song,* justified rage, as a primary human emotion (Kagan, 1984).

Izard, 1988). A smiling infant is likely to elicit more smiles from others. Furthermore, once it is clear that the infant likes the interaction, as evidenced by the smile, people continue in their playful exchanges until the infant grows tired or bored. Emotions serve as a powerful reinforcer of behavior. In Alec's case, described at the beginning of the chapter, whenever he grimaced or cried, he was reinforced because people backed away or stopped "bothering" him. Alec's relatives also were discouraged in their attempts to stimulate him.

PARENTS' CONTRIBUTION

Much has been written about the early influence of parents on the developing child's personality. Freud first called attention to the importance of the first 5 years of a child's life in his theory of psychosexual stages of personality development: oral, anal, phallic, latency, and genital. Personality first develops during the *oral stage,* when young infants receive food and satisfy their sensual needs by sucking, gumming, and biting. Freud believed that infants who are allowed to fulfill their psychosexual needs will develop an optimistic view of the self and the world. Those infants whose oral needs are frustrated are likely to become fixated on these needs later in life.

Freud's theory was later elaborated upon and reinterpreted by Erikson (1963, 1968), who suggested that the foundation of personality is laid in infancy as the child interacts with parents. The early social interactions between parent and child form the basis for the first psychosocial "crisis" in development, which Erikson labeled *basic trust versus mistrust.* The term **crisis** refers to a turning point, a time of increased vulnerability, as well as a time for potential growth.

During the stage of basic trust versus mistrust, infants learn whether they can rely on other people to meet their needs. If the baby's physical needs are met in a consistent and affectionate manner by the caregiver or mother, then the baby comes to interpret the world as a safe place. Infants trust their caregivers, and this positive orientation applies to themselves as well as to others.

crisis

In Erikson's theory of psychosocial development, a turning point in life in which a person may be more vulnerable to damage or growth.

A sense of trust emerges when parents predictably and warmly meet the infant's needs.

If, however, infants are less fortunate and experience neglectful, inconsistent, or abusive treatment at the hands of parents or other caregivers, then they are likely to acquire a mistrustful outlook toward others. If cries are ignored, or needs for touching and cuddling are not recognized, then infants may interpret their world as a neglectful and unfriendly place. Mistrustful infants will also lack confidence and consider themselves unworthy of attention. In Erikson's theory, a healthy resolution of the trust-versus-mistrust conflict is represented by infants learning to trust themselves and others. A certain amount of mistrust, however, is seen as healthy since the child has discovered that not everyone or everything responds in a predictable manner. Overall, however, the child's basic trust encourages continued interaction with people and surroundings.

Parents play a particularly important role in the child's acquisition of basic trust or mistrust. Since parents structure the physical and social environment for young children, the characteristic manner in which parents interact with infants can strongly affect infants' early experiences. What characteristics are associated with being a "good" parent? How does an effective caregiver behave toward his or her child? These questions are useful but difficult to answer specifically because we know that parental behavior is influenced by the child's characteristics as well as by the parents' own personality and individual history.

FOCUS ON CULTURE

Most parents learn how to take care of children by watching their own parents take care of them, and perhaps by practicing these skills by caring for younger siblings. The specific child-rearing strategies that are learned are part of the cultural heritage that is passed on from one generation to another. Behaviors that may be considered "good" parenting behaviors in one culture may not be considered appropriate in others. The length of time an infant is nursed is one example of a child-rearing practice that varies from culture to culture.

Data from studies on parent-child interactions are also difficult to interpret because of the way in which the data are collected. If you ask parents in an interview or questionnaire to describe their behavior with their children, their answers may reflect how they *think* they should respond rather than how they actually *do* respond. The very act of observing parent-child interaction in the home or in a laboratory may alter it. The best approach for such study is to combine observational with interview or questionnaire data (Wachs & Gruen, 1982).

By observing parents and children interacting in the home and in the laboratory and by assessing the child's social and cognitive development, some broad conclusions about parental influence in the child's development have been drawn. Parents who stimulate their infants—those who talk to, cuddle, and express warm positive emotions with their babies—generally have more responsive and socially competent children (Belsky, Lerner, & Spanier, 1984; Clarke-Stewart, 1973; Crockenberg, 1983). Furthermore, the more sensitive attention and stimulation the infant receives, the earlier and more accelerated will be his or her performance on tests of cognitive development (Yarrow, Rubenstein, & Pedersen, 1975). Similar findings have been reported on the parent-child interactions among the Embu in Kenya (Sigman, Neumann, Jansen, & Bwibo, 1989). Infants who were talked to frequently and who had a great deal of social interaction with adults were more advanced mentally and showed more positive emotions than infants who were less involved with people.

Additional information about the effects of parental interactions on the child comes from studies of parents known to have personality disturbances or difficulties. In particular, mothers who are depressed are likely to interact with their infants in an inconsistent and unresponsive manner. Research by Zahn-Waxler, Cummings, McKnew, and Radke-Yarrow (1984) has found that children with a bipolar (manic-depressive) parent display problems in social interactions as early as 18 months of age. However, children of parents with bipolar disorder may themselves have an inherited tendency toward emotional difficulties that may contribute to the problems in social interactions.

In several different studies, Cohn and Tronick (1983, 1988) demonstrated that infants as young as 3 months of age respond to the affective quality of the parent's interaction. In one study (1983) infants were exposed to two experimental conditions: (1) normal mother, in which the mother responded to the infant in her usual way, and (2) depressed mother, in which the mother made no emotional facial expressions while interacting with her child. Compared to the normal mother condition, infants in the depressed mother condition spent more time in a state of distress and less time demonstrating positive emotions. In a different study, comparisons were made in the quality of the emotional interaction between depressed and nondepressed mothers and their 2-month-old infants (Cohn, Campbell, Matias, & Hopkins, 1990). The mothers were videotaped in a laboratory where they were asked to play with their babies. Researchers found that depressed mothers were more negative with their babies, displaying emotions of anger, irritation, and sadness. The babies of the depressed mothers were fussier and cried more than the babies of the nondepressed mothers. In a similar laboratory study conducted by Pickens and Field (1993), 3-month old infants of depressed mothers displayed more sadness and anger than infants of nondepressed mothers.

Whether the caregiver is satisfied or feels competent to perform the parenting role can also influence the quality of the parent-child interaction (Teti & Gelfand, 1991). For example, Lerner and Galambos (1985) found that mothers who were very satisfied with their roles displayed more warmth and acceptance of their

Infants can be distressed by the emotional states of their parents. Angry, hostile parents present a powerful model to their children.

children than did mothers who were dissatisfied with their parenting. We know that infants are affected by the emotional behavior of their parents both directly and indirectly. Directly, parents model specific emotional reactions and selectively reinforce their infant's emotional responses. Indirectly, young children are affected by angry exchanges that they witness even though the emotion is not directed at them (Cummings, Iannotti, & Zahn-Waxler, 1985). Thus parents who argue and fight with each other may also contribute to the distress of their young children.

EFFECTS OF SOCIAL SUPPORT

Additional social support and information about infants and their care seem to help parents establish a more positive style of interacting with their children. In Chapter 6, you will learn more about parents who physically abuse or neglect their children; often abusive parents have both unrealistic expectations of children and inappropriate ideas about proper care. In the United States a large number of child-abuse victims are preterm births, a fact suggesting that disturbance in the parent-child interaction may have had an early origin. In a study comparing the effects of stress and social support on mothers of preterm and full-term infants, it was found that mothers who were experiencing greater stress were less positive in their attitudes and behavior, while mothers with greater support from the father, family members, and community were significantly more positive in their attitude toward their infants (Crnic, Greenberg, Ragozin, Robinson, & Basham, 1983). Numerous other studies have documented the positive effect that social support and intervention programs can have in changing the quality of child care (Spiker, Ferguson, & Brooks-Gunn, 1993).

Parents who receive social support are likely to be more sensitive to their infant's needs and thus provide a more secure and stable emotional atmosphere for their children (Crittenden, 1985; Crockenberg & McCluskey, 1986). The most helpful types of social support come from close friends and relatives who offer empathy and understanding to the parents. However, neighbors and community workers are also important because they can provide parents with assistance and needed information on how best to care for their children. Through early intervention, potentially negative parent-child interactions can be altered to promote a more satisfactory relationship for both.

RECAP

The quality of the social interaction between infant and caregiver is influenced by their own individual characteristics. Inborn temperament can also affect the way in which people respond to the infant. Three types of infant temperament have been identified: easy, difficult, and slow-to-warm. Emotional response changes throughout infancy. Both Freud and Erikson emphasized the importance of parental behavior in the development of the child's personality. Personality characteristics of the parents can also affect children's responses. Social support is an important ingredient for sensitive parental behaviors.

THE FIRST SOCIAL RELATIONSHIP: PARENT-CHILD ATTACHMENT

attachment
An affectionate emotional bond between parent (or caregiver) and child.

As a new parent, one of the things that first struck me was how dependent my baby was on me and my husband for basic care. Without someone to care for them, infants would not survive. Social contact early in the child's life is also important for healthy personality development. Infants come to define themselves through their interactions with their parents. Physical touching and handling teach infants limits, such as where their own body ends and another person's begins. Learning to distinguish oneself as physically separate from another is an important step in establishing a self-concept. As a result of frequent social and emotional exchanges with parents, the infant acquires a particular style or orientation that some researchers believe extends into later childhood (Sroufe, 1978). Let's pause on our journey to look more closely at this important first social relationship.

THE STUDY OF ATTACHMENT

Imagine entering Kia's village and seeing a group of young infants between the ages of 8 months and 1 year gathered together in a room. Then suppose the parents of these infants entered the room. Without even waiting to see which parent paired up with which infant, you could probably accurately match the parents and infants simply by noticing their reactions—the affectionate emotional bond between parent and child called **attachment**. Virtually all infants form an attachment to their caregiver, although the quality of the attachment may vary widely.

Attachment refers to an affectional tie that the infant forms with another specific person, bonding them together in space, enduring over time, and fostering survival (Bowlby, 1969). Physically immature and unable to care for itself, the human infant without an adult to feed and protect it would surely die. The attachment is mutual between both baby and parents. This means that the parents are very much interested in being with or near their infant, a state that ensures care and protection during the most vulnerable period of development. For example, Alec's mother spent a good deal of her time focused on her baby; this provided her with a sense of purpose and relieved her concerns about his welfare. Early and frequent contact and familiarity with the caregiver create an affectionate relationship.

At one time it was assumed that feeding, not the contact itself, provided the essential basis for the development of attachment. This belief was confronted in several classic experiments with infant monkeys conducted by Harlow and colleagues (1962; Harlow & Harlow, 1966). The experimenters constructed two surrogate "monkey" mothers. One of the substitute mothers was made out of wire mesh and the other was covered with a terry cloth fabric. In the center of each figure was a slot to attach a feeding bottle. Separated from their biological mothers at birth, the baby monkeys were reared by both types of surrogate mothers. Some were fed only by the wire mesh mother, and others were fed by the terry cloth mother. Harlow found that all the monkeys developed a clinging attachment to the terry cloth mother even when they were not fed by her. The baby monkeys preferred to spend their time between feedings close to or clinging to this soft, cloth mother; furthermore, the monkeys seemed to derive a sense of safety and security in the presence of the terry cloth mother. The wire mesh mother was ignored by the baby monkeys except at feeding time.

These studies demonstrated the importance of physical contact for the attachment bond. But Harlow's study of infant monkeys also produced another striking finding: He found that as these baby monkeys—who were essentially raised from birth in the laboratory—matured, they displayed very inappropriate sexual and maternal behavior. They did not engage in typical mating behavior, and the female monkeys proved to be neglectful and abusive mothers. They would not feed or cuddle their young, and some even attacked their babies. Harlow attributed this highly disruptive behavior to the lack of social contact with other monkeys during development. It seems that the laboratory-raised monkeys did not have the opportunity to establish healthy social behaviors.

Attachment Behaviors   Seeking the contact and closeness of the parent or caregiver is one behavior that indicates attachment. Other attachment behaviors include showing distress when separated from the attachment figure and expressing relief or joy upon reunion. Even if there is no physical contact, the infant displays a clear preference for the caregiver by seeking eye contact or by being especially attentive to the sound of his or her voice. In the example of a room full of babies one would most likely use these behaviors to identify the infant's parents.

Parents display a similar, though more subtle, set of attachment behaviors. In the case of the children and parents gathered in a room in Kia's village, the parents likely would seek and establish eye contact followed by physical contact. If the infant was not immediately located, the parent would have a worried or concerned look and would then smile when the baby was found. The bond is, therefore, a reciprocal process, for both are interested in maintaining closeness to each other.

Another characteristic of attachment behavior is the use of attachment figures as a secure base from which to explore the physical and social environment. The toddler in a new situation may remain close to his or her parent until feeling secure enough to venture out and explore. Visual contact with the parent may be sufficient to ensure comfort. Becoming afraid or upset during exploration, the toddler will return to the caregiver's side for comfort. Infants vary in the extent to which they use their parents for security and source of comfort.

DEVELOPMENT OF ATTACHMENT

Attachment is an organized system of parental and child behaviors that have an emotional quality. When psychologists speak about attachment they refer not to a specific set of behaviors but to the way a parent and child respond to each other. These behaviors change as the child's cognitive, social, and emotional skills develop. Because it is a process, attachment is not immediately present at birth but rather develops gradually from the first moment of contact.

John Bowlby (1969) detailed four phases occurring in the first few years of life during which the infant gradually directs more attention and effort toward being physically close to his or her caregiver (see Table 4–3). In the first *preattachment* phase (0–3 months), the infant appears to be interested in anyone. The primary caregiver is not distinguished from others. It is not until about 2 to 3 months of age that the infant consistently discriminates the caregiver from other people.

During the *attachment-in-the-making phase* (3–6 months of age), a unique relationship is forming between the baby and his or her primary caregiver. The infant smiles and vocalizes more frequently and intensely to the caregiver. Although the infant may be relatively receptive to strangers, the baby clearly is able to distinguish between the caregiver and other people.

BOWLBY'S PHASES OF INFANT ATTACHMENT		
PHASE	**AGE**	**CHARACTERISTICS**
Preattachment	0–3 months	Interested in everyone; eventually distinguishes the caregiver from others
Attachment in the making	3–6 months	Increase in smiling and vocalizations to the primary caregiver; clearly discriminates the mother from others
Clear-cut attachment	6–12 months	Displays separation distress and stranger anxiety; is clearly attached to the caregiver
Goal-corrected partnership	12–24 months	Attempts to anticipate and manipulate the caregiver's behavior; displays a more complex interplay of cognitive, social, and emotional behaviors

TABLE 4–3

The *clear-cut attachment phase* emerges between 6 and 12 months of age, when the infant is able to move around by crawling, creeping, and walking. These locomotor skills allow the infant to actively seek out and become physically close to his or her parent. During this time infants also generally acquire object permanence and thus recognize that a person continues to exist even when out of sight. The infant has also learned how to hold his or her parents' attention through vocalization and crying.

At this point the infant has an expanding repertoire of behaviors designed to keep the parents close at hand. When the mother and father leave the room or go out for an evening, the infant is likely to show signs of distress or to protest by crying. This reaction is called **separation distress** and usually peaks in intensity around 12 months.

A similar apprehension is present when a stranger approaches or interacts with the infant. **Stranger anxiety** refers to the infant's general wariness of unfamiliar people, which usually peaks in intensity around 8 to 10 months of age. Stranger anxiety can occur in response to people who are not necessarily strangers but who merely appear to the infant to be different from the attachment figure. If Mother is a light-skinned, blonde woman who speaks softly to the baby, then a dark-haired, dark-skinned uncle who smells of aftershave and speaks in a deep voice may well trigger a wariness reaction from the baby. The discrepancy between the infant's schemes of Mother and Uncle is too great. The different reaction to the stranger tells us that the infant has made a conceptual distinction between the caregiver and other people.

When my daughter Sarah was about this age, she showed no stranger anxiety whatsoever when my twin sister came for a visit. This was despite the fact that during her 1st year Sarah had very little contact with my sister. Since my sister and I look identical and have similar voices and ways of expressing ourselves, Sarah saw few differences that might trigger stranger anxiety.

The last phase in the development of attachment according to Bowlby is the *goal-corrected partnership phase* (12–24 months), which represents a more

separation distress
The infant's protest or crying when separated from the caregiver.

stranger anxiety
An infant's general wariness of unfamiliar people.

Loving, stimulating, and playful interactions between infant and caregiver are important in the formation of attachment. This father's game of peek-a-boo with his baby is one example.

complex interplay of cognitive, social, and emotional behavior. The attachment between the infant and caregiver becomes much more complicated. The infant may initiate attempts to influence the attachment figure in fairly sophisticated ways—such as by trying to anticipate the parents' actions and subsequently influence their behavior. An example is the infant who protests by crying and holding onto the father or mother when the babysitter arrives. The infant has figured out that the babysitter's arrival means that father and mother will leave; the infant also has learned that by crying and holding onto the father or mother, they may change their plans and stay home.

THE FATHER AND OTHER ATTACHMENT FIGURES

Until recently many researchers assumed the father's involvement with the care of the infant to be minimal. However, there have been significant changes in the degree to which men are caring for their young infants (Cordes, 1983). More men are participating in the birth of their babies, and this early contact with their infants seems to be important for later involvement.

Are there differences in the way infants respond to each parent? Observations in the laboratory and at home indicate that infants react positively to both mothers and fathers, but the quality of the father's involvement seems to be an important determinant of the infant's reaction to him (Cox, Owen, Henderson, & Margand, 1992; Parke, 1979). With the exception of breast feeding, fathers are capable of performing most child-care routines and responding to infant cues that signal the need for care (Parke, 1979).

There are certain differences, however, between the ways mothers and fathers interact with their babies. Parke and Sawin (1980) observed American mothers and fathers with their infants in the hospital, and found that fathers were just as likely as mothers to hold, rock, cuddle, smile at, talk to their babies, and look directly into their babies' faces. When the infants were older, however, the same parents were observed at home, and the parents' style of interacting with the infants was noticeably different. Mothers were more involved in routine child care, while fathers more often were engaged in playful stimulation of the infant (Parke & Tinsley, 1987). Fathers tended to take more interest in their infant sons than in their daughters. This may have been because the father's style tended to be more physical, involving playful wrestling. Mothers were more likely to use a toy in playing with their infants. In a study examining how new mothers and fathers use toys with their 8-month-old infants, Power and Parke (1983) found that fathers were more physical in their use of toys, while mothers paid more attention to the infant's indications of interest in a particular toy.

These differences in style may be related to the father's less frequent contact with the infant, which, in turn, could affect his ability to interpret the baby's nonverbal messages. In examining families where the role of caregiver was assumed by the father rather than the mother, researchers have found that fathers who are the primary caregivers act more like traditional mothers—they are responsive to their infants' subtle cues, and imitate their infants' facial expressions and vocalizations (Field, 1978). In a similar study of Swedish fathers, Lamb and his associates found that fathers who were primary caregivers interacted more with their daughters, whereas fathers who were secondary caregivers interacted more with their sons (Lamb, Frodi, Hwang, Frodi, & Steinberg, 1982). When fathers assume the role of primary caregiver, they still play with their infants in a more arousing manner than mothers do (Lamb & Oppenheim, 1989). Interestingly, when mothers become employed they become more playful with their infants (Cox et al., 1992).

As was true for Kia, many young children receive care not only from their parents but from older siblings as well. In some other cultures and in some subcultures within our own society, infants and toddlers are cared for predominantly by siblings or older children. Does the infant form a similar attachment to the caregiver who is also a child?

A study by Stewart (1983) suggests that infants do in fact become attached to their older siblings, and display prominent attachment behaviors toward the

Infants can form attachments to siblings as well as to their parents and caregivers.

siblings when the parents are not present. Stewart observed 54 mothers of infants aged 10 to 20 months and the infants' older siblings, who ranged in age from 30 to 58 months. He used a modified version of Ainsworth's Strange Situation (described in the next section) in which the older sibling was also introduced when the infant was separated from the mother. More than half of the 4-year-old children were both active and effective in caring for their younger siblings who were distressed by the mother's absence. The older sibling comforted the infant and reassured the baby of the mother's eventual return. The infant was calmed by the sibling's efforts and returned to play activities. When a stranger entered, the infant used the sibling as a secure base for exploration. However, even though the infants responded to the siblings in a manner similar to the way they responded to the mothers, Stewart claims that the sibling attachment does not replace the attachment to the parent.

PATTERNS OF ATTACHMENT

In order to gain a better understanding of the attachment process, Ainsworth and her colleagues (Ainsworth, Bell, & Stayton, 1971) developed a method of studying attachment behaviors by observing the child with his or her parent, usually the mother, in specific situations. The *Strange Situation* method has been used by Ainsworth and her associates to study hundreds of children at varying ages. In this procedure, the mother and baby are brought into an observation room that is well supplied with toys. The mother puts the baby down and sits on a chair. After 3 minutes, a female stranger enters and begins a conversation with the mother. The stranger then tries to play with the baby, and the mother quietly leaves the room but leaves her handbag on the chair to signal that she will return. The mother is gone for 3 minutes, and during this time the stranger reacts to the infant either by giving comfort if it protests the parent's absence or by engaging it in play with the toys. Then the mother returns and the stranger leaves. After 3 minutes the mother leaves again; this time the infant is left alone in the observation room. In the last 6 minutes of this standardized observation the stranger returns and again attempts to interact with the infant, after which the parent returns and the stranger departs. Throughout the 20-minute testing period, the infant's behaviors are observed and recorded by trained researchers. On the basis of the quality and pattern of infant behavior, Ainsworth and her associates (1978) identified three categories of attachment behavior: **secure attachment (Type B)** and two varieties of **insecure attachment: avoidant (Type A)** and **resistant (Type C)**. More recently, a third type of insecure pattern, the **disorganized-disoriented attachment (Type D)**, has been described by Main and Solomon (1990). The characteristic behaviors of each of these types of attachment is described in Table 4–4.

The hallmark of securely attached infants is their ability to use their attachment figures to regain their source of security when stressed; this allows them to move forth into the world once again through exploration and play. Most of the children observed by Ainsworth and her colleagues displayed the securely attached pattern. Approximately 7–15% of infants in a normal North American sample displayed an insecure-resistant attachment (Ainsworth, Blehar, Waters, & Wall, 1978). Main and Solomon (1990) found that about 5% of infants display an insecure-disorganized-disoriented pattern of attachment.

secure attachment (Type B)
A pattern of attachment in which infants use their parents as a base of security in a strange situation and to regain their source of security when stressed.

insecure-avoidant attachment (Type A)
An attachment pattern in which infants have trouble using their parents as a base for exploration and avoid contact with them when reunited.

insecure-resistant attachment (Type C)
An attachment pattern in which infants seem to be upset when their parents leave but resistant and anxious in their presence when reunited. These infants have difficulty using their parents as a base for exploration.

insecure-disorganized-disoriented attachment (Type D)
A pattern of attachment in which infants seem confused when reunited with their caregivers and display inconsistent behaviors.

PATTERNS OF ATTACHMENT

NAME	TYPE	CHARACTERISTIC BEHAVIOR
Secure attachment	B	Stays close to parent in new situations; is distressed by separation and receptive upon reunion; prefers the parent to strangers
Insecure-avoidant attachment	A	Ignores the parent as a base of support; is not distressed by separation and avoids contact on reunion; does not distinguish between strangers and parent for contact
Insecure-resistant attachment	C	Appears anxious and distressed in the presence of parent; does not use parent as a base of support; is upset when separated but not comforted by reunion; resists contact with strangers
Insecure-disorganized-disoriented attachment	D	Seems afraid, dazed, and confused; displays inconsistent behavior after reunion with parent; seeks contact with and then avoids the parent

TABLE 4–4

INDIVIDUAL DIFFERENCES IN ATTACHMENT PATTERNS

Is infant attachment a universal characteristic? Does it occur in all cultures? The answer seems to be yes. Strange Situation research has been done in numerous cultures; by 12 months of age, infants universally display strong emotional attachments to their caregivers (Bretherton, 1985). However, the quality and type of attachment seems to be influenced by the specific child-rearing patterns predominant in the culture. For example, in Japan mothers are rarely separated from their infants; they spend much of their time talking to and touching their infants. Consequently, Japanese babies are more distressed by the presence of a stranger and separation from their mothers (Miyake, Chen, & Campos, 1985). German infants show a higher incidence of avoidant attachment when compared to American infants (Grossman, Grossman, Spangler, Suess, & Unzner, 1985). German parents deliberately discourage their infants from clinging and becoming emotionally dependent because they value independence and obedience.

Another question asked about attachment behavior is why some infants are securely attached to one or more caregivers and other infants are insecurely attached. Some researchers believe that the differences in attachment patterns among infants can be explained in terms of the differences in infant temperament (Calkins & Fox, 1992; Kagan, 1982, 1984)—for example, infants with a difficult temperament would be less likely to establish a secure attachment. Even in secure attachments infants with difficult temperaments are likely to react differently than easy-temperament infants to their caregivers (Belsky & Rovine, 1987). Other researchers (Sroufe, 1985) argue that temperament is not a factor at all in attachment patterns.

Perhaps attachment differences can be explained by examining differences in the parents' behavior. In one study (Weber, Levitt, & Clark, 1986) researchers

Japanese mothers are rarely separated from their infants. They spend much of their time talking to and touching their infants. Consequently, Japanese babies tend to be more distressed by strangers or a separation from their mothers.

found that mothers' temperament was linked to the attachment patterns of their infants. For example, infants whose mothers rated themselves as less adaptable cried more often during the separation and reunion phases of the Strange Situation procedure. Other studies have found that mothers of avoidant infants did enjoy physical contact with their babies (Egeland & Farber, 1984) and that mothers of insecurely attached infants expressed more negative and less positive emotions (Radke-Yarrow, Cummings, Kuczynski, & Chapman, 1985).

Ainsworth and her colleagues (1978) report that the type of attachment an infant forms is influenced by the quality of the caregiver-child interaction. Caregivers who responded sensitively to their infants during the 1st year of life were likely to have securely attached infants. When the caregivers were insensitive, insecure relationships more often resulted. Thus, caregivers who are insensitive, unavailable, and inconsistent in their responses to their infants are more likely to promote an insecure-resistant attachment (Cassidy & Berlin, 1994).

Isabella (1993) conducted naturalistic observations of mothers interacting with their infants at 1, 4, and 9 months of age. He found that mothers of securely attached infants were more sensitive and responsive to their infants on all observations, and less rejecting at the 1- and 9-month visit. Mothers of the insecure-avoidant infants were more rejecting and became more rejecting over time. Mothers of the insecure-resistant infants were the least sensitive to their infants and most rejecting at 1 month of age. These studies and others suggest that the nature of the attachment relationship is jointly influenced by both the infant and the caregiver.

What are the long-term consequences of the different patterns in attachment? From the descriptions you have read of securely and insecurely attached infants you might predict that securely attached infants would be more trusting of others and hence have more success in later relationships. This prediction has received much support from research findings (Bretherton, 1985). Furthermore, securely attached infants engage in more autonomous exploration and problem solving, which may contribute to their persistence and increased attention span when considering tasks. Securely attached children get along better with peers and preschool teachers, while insecurely attached children have been found to avoid contact with their preschool peers. Generally, the securely attached infant seems more likely to emerge in early childhood as more self-reliant with a more positive self-image. Insecure-resistant infants become accustomed to an unavailable caregiver; the long-term consequences of this attitude is often "clingy" children who as adults are preoccupied with their romantic relationships (Cassidy & Berlin, 1994).

Margaret Ricks (1985) has suggested an even longer term consequence of attachment patterns. She maintains that adults model their attachment relationship with their children after the type of attachment they experienced with their parents. For example, mothers of securely attached infants had more positive recollections of their childhood relationships with their mothers, fathers, and peers than did mothers of infants who were judged to be insecurely attached. Thus the prospect exists that during the 1st few years of life the infant is acquiring attitudes, emotions, and behaviors that may extend their influence well into adulthood and indeed succeeding generations.

ISSUES IN FOSTER CARE

During World War II people were quite concerned about the health and welfare of children living in the bomb-targeted major cities of Great Britain. As a measure of precaution, a nationwide program was instituted in which children were relocated to villages and towns in the countryside. This meant that children were often separated from their parents and placed in the care of unfamiliar adults. Because of the extreme circumstances involved, the separation of infants from their caregivers was considered to be the lesser of two evils. After the danger of attack was over, the children were reunited with their parents. Thus, the separation was, for most children, only temporary and fortunately had no long-term adverse effects.

In the United States, a similar forced separation occurs when children are placed in foster care. Although our culture places a high value on preserving the integrity of a family, in some circumstances it may be necessary to remove a child from his or her parents. When a parent is severely depressed or physically incapable of providing appropriate care for a child, or when a parent is abusive or neglectful, the child may be temporarily removed from the family for his or her own protection.

Rather than place a child in an institutional setting, which may be too impersonal and understaffed to meet the child's developmental needs, the social welfare agency involved may seek a foster home for the child. Foster parents are screened by social welfare agencies and receive payment for their care of a child. The placement in a foster home is intended to be a temporary situation, but unfortunately many children often remain in foster care for several years rather than only weeks or months. Often several different foster parents may care for a single child.

One of the major concerns regarding foster care is its disruption on the infant's social and emotional development. It takes time and a continuous caring

Education Perspective

TEACHING PARENTS TO FORM HEALTHY ATTACHMENTS WITH THEIR INFANTS

The long-term consequences of insecure-attachment relationships are not yet fully known, but the general understanding is that it is much better for infants to form a secure relationship with their parents or caregivers than an insecure one. Most people become parents with little preparation or direct education about how best to foster a healthy secure relationship with their infants. In an attempt to circumvent the development of insecure attachments, a variety of intervention programs have emerged to teach new parents how to promote secure attachments.

Lieberman, Weston, and Pawl (1991) of the University of California conducted a study of 100 Spanish-speaking immigrant mothers from Mexico and Central America. The mothers and their 12-month-old infants participated in an intervention study for 1 year. All of the infants were assessed to have established an anxious (resistant) attachment to their mothers. At the beginning of the study the mothers and infants were videotaped and interviewed by the researchers. Then throughout the year, each mother-infant pair was visited on a weekly basis by a trained bicultural, bilingual "intervenor."

During the visits, the intervenor would teach the mothers how to respond affectionately and responsively to their infants. Concrete examples and suggestions based on each child's needs were demonstrated during the visits. The intervenor would provide the mothers with information about what they could realistically expect their children to be able to do for their ages; they helped the mothers set reasonable expectations and encouraged them to let their infants explore and enjoy their contact with the mothers. Mothers were encouraged to talk about their concerns about how to deal with their infants and were given help in resolving some of their parenting conflicts.

At the end of the intervention program, mothers and infants were assessed again. In particular, the researchers measured the mothers' ability to empathize and respond to their infants' needs. They also assessed changes in the infants' emotional responses to their mothers. Lieberman and her associates found that the infants in the intervention program were less resistant, avoidant, and angry with their mothers. Furthermore, the mothers responded with greater empathy and more positively to their infants at the end of the program.

Although the mothers changed the way they interacted with their infants, they did not change their child-rearing attitudes. The researchers believed this was because the mothers' attitudes were heavily influenced by their cultural beliefs about how to care for children. For example, most of the mothers believed that it was very important for their children to be obedient, that they firmly suppress any aggression in their children, and that parents are the final authority in the home. These beliefs are consistent with strongly held values in Latino cultures.

relationship for an infant to establish an emotional attachment with his or her caregiver. In the case of foster care the infant may be abruptly removed from the parents' care and thrust into the arms of a total stranger—at an age when the infant cannot comprehend the reasons for the loss of his or her original caregivers. This event alone could be distressing to both parents and child.

Because a foster care placement is temporary, the foster parent may be urged not to establish a close emotional bond with the child. It is argued that it is too difficult for infants to separate from a caregiver with whom an attachment has been established. Most foster parents do not receive specialized training or supervision; thus, it may be too much to expect that they could be aware of and respond to the need to be affectionate, stimulating, and consistent in the care of an infant who will be with them only temporarily.

RECAP

Attachment represents an affectionate reciprocal relationship between the caregiver and the infant. Behaviors that signal an attachment relationship include use of the caregiver as a base of support and exploration, stranger anxiety, separation distress, and an affectionate reunion after separation. Attachment develops during the first 2 years of life and is most evident between 6 and 12 months of age. Infants form attachments to both parents and often to siblings. Four different patterns of attachment have been described: secure, insecure resistant, insecure avoidant, and insecure disorganized-disoriented. Both infant and parental characteristics contribute to the development of attachment, which appears to have long-term consequences. Children placed in foster care are vulnerable because the temporary nature of these programs discourages the forming of attachments.

DEVELOPMENT OF SELF

Does a young infant have a view of itself? When and how does this view develop? These questions, while intriguing, have not generated as much research as they have speculation and theory. The sense of self involves a recognition of one's separateness from others as well as a conceptual image of one's characteristic behaviors. The development of a self-concept follows a sequence that begins with the recognition of one's physical self, followed by the ability to describe oneself and seek recognition from others, and ending with an ability to evaluate and react to one's self (Stipek, Gralinski, & Kopp, 1990; Stipek, Recchia, & McClintic, 1992). Many psychologists view the development of self as a process occurring throughout development and one that closely parallels cognitive, social, and emotional development (Lewis & Brooks-Gunn, 1979; Maccoby, 1980).

The development of self-awareness is tied to the child's early attachment with his or her parents. With the security so provided, the 1-year-old explores more and more aspects of his or her physical and social world. For example, Kia's attachment to her mother allows her to try out new toys and meet new people in different settings; in the process she learns something new about how she can and does function in the world with each new adventure.

Beginning about the age of 18 months, children enter what Freud called the *anal stage* of personality development. It is during this stage that children develop their egos as they learn to balance their needs against the demands of their new environment. During this stage the focus for sensual stimulation and gratification shifts from the mouth to the anal region. This shift corresponds with infants' interest in releasing and controlling their bowels. Toilet training is typically the

The attention that this young boy receives from those around him can contribute to his sense of self.

event highlighting children's active attempt to gratify their need for anal stimulation. During the anal stage children learn how to delay gratification of their sensual anal needs until there is a suitable opportunity (that is, until they are on the toilet). If parents or caregivers are too harsh or rigid in their toilet training attempts, Freud believed that children will become "stuck" at the anal stage of personality development and display traits such as stubbornness, extreme orderliness, or defiant messiness in later adult life.

 Erikson (1968) considered the period from 1½ to 3 years of age to be critical for the child's development of a sense of self. He referred to this stage as the crisis of *autonomy versus shame and doubt.* The psychosocial crisis of this period centers on the child's attempts at self-control. A successful resolution of this crisis leads the toddler to develop a sense of his or her own autonomy, including a realistic view of what he or she is capable of performing. In establishing basic competency, the infant begins to see himself or herself as distinct from the caregiver. At the same time, the toddler is learning to comply with social constraints or rules established by parents and other adults. The child's sense of autonomy is very much influenced by parental demands, which, if they conform to the child's capabilities to comply, cause the child to acquire a sense of self-worth. If, however, the parents have placed unrealistic or overly rigid demands on the young child, he or she may fail to comply and consequently may acquire a sense of shame and doubt about his or her own competence to deal effectively with people and objects. For example, parents who expect their toddlers to be able to toilet train themselves or to have consideration for their parents' feelings may be setting the stage for their toddlers to fail to live up to their expectations and hence feel a sense of shame.

According to Erikson, a successful resolution of this crisis requires a balance between what the child can and should do (autonomy), and what the child cannot and should not do (shame and doubt). Based on Erikson's theory, I might be concerned that the overprotective environment that Alec's mother has created may contribute to his growing sense of distrust in his own abilities to cope with new people in his environment. The less experience he has in dealing with new people, the more doubtful Alec will be about new social situations.

Setting reasonable limits for children during this period allows them to gain positive experience with people and objects that add to their sense of self. With a healthy sense of autonomy, infants are able to regulate their own actions with increasingly greater ease. Often the talking 2-year-old will assert a newfound sense of self by saying "No!" and resisting the caregiver's attempts to regulate his or her activities. By saying "No!" the child is expressing a desire to separate from the caregiver. Parents who allow their toddlers a certain amount of self-expression and choice encourage their children's development of a sense of autonomy (Crockenberg & Litman, 1990).

As pointed out earlier, researchers can only indirectly measure self-awareness in infants who have not yet acquired language skills. One technique, initially used with animals (e.g., Gallup, 1977), measures the infant's recognition of his or her image in a mirror. The mother surreptitiously puts an orange dot on the child's nose; during a pretest, the observer rates how often the infant touches his or her nose. Then the infant is placed before a mirror, and observers again record the frequency of nose touching. In studies using this technique (Bertenthal

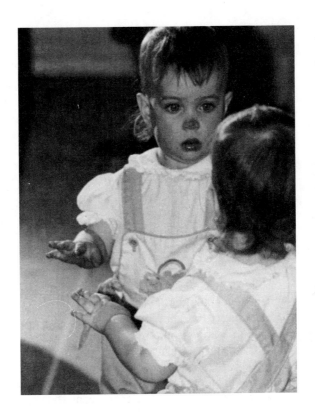

One way to measure self-awareness in infants is to observe their reactions to a dot placed on their nose. If this infant touches her nose and not the mirror-image of her nose, this may indicate that she recognizes herself in the mirror.

& Fischer, 1978; Lewis & Brooks-Gunn, 1979) it was found that by 18 months of age infants touched their noses significantly more frequently in front of the mirror. In contrast, younger infants did not try to locate the distinctive orange dot on their own body, although they often pointed to the dot in the mirror as if it existed on another person. For infants to realize that the dot was on their own nose, they must have possessed a primitive scheme of what they looked like, knowledge that allowed them to recognize the discrepancy between the mirror image and their self-concept.

Another way of measuring self-awareness is to assess the child's use of self-referent words, such as "I," my," or "mine." By observing young infants between the ages of 13 to 24 months, Kagan (1981) discovered a significant increase in 19- to 24-month-olds in the use of both these self-referent words and words that occur while the child performs a particular action. For example, as a little girl was climbing a chair, she might describe her actions by saying "up." In a different study (Levine, 1983), 2-year-old boys who had a more advanced sense of self, as measured by pronoun use and by mirror recognition, claimed toys as their own and were able to interact more positively with other 2-year-olds than were boys who had a less mature view of themselves. Levine concluded that the possessiveness of a 2-year-old actually may reflect the child's attempt to interact socially with another child, and thus, greater self-awareness.

The sense of self begins in infancy but develops in complexity with cognitive and social maturity. Other aspects of the child's self-concept will be explored in Chapter 6.

> **RECAP**
>
> The infant's concept of self emerges during the first 2 years of life with a physical self-recognition; this is followed later by a view of the self from the perspective of others. During the anal stage, according to Freud, the infant develops an ego primarily through the experiences of toilet training, which require a balance between satisfying immediate physical needs and meeting the demands of parents and society for cleanliness and order. Erikson focused on the importance of parental encouragement in the establishment of a sense of autonomy versus a sense of shame or doubt. Research on self-awareness has focused on infants' self-recognition abilities and their later use of self-referent words.

PARENT-CHILD COMMUNICA- TION: EARLY LANGUAGE SKILLS

The word infancy stems from the Latin word *infans,* meaning "without language." Infancy generally ends at age 2; this also is the age by which most infants begin to communicate in their native language. They may not yet be able to converse fluently, but they do use words to convey their meaning.

The language spoken within a country or community is an important and distinctive part of any culture. Learning to communicate in a language takes exposure and practice. New speakers must master several components: the sounds that are used, the meaning of the words, and the rules for making words and combining words into sentences (Rice, 1989). For a young infant, learning a language can take many years. However, even before toddlers have acquired all the formal aspects of their native language, they are capable of communicating with their parents. For example, from birth Alec was quite capable of conveying his needs and preferences through expressions of pleasure and displeasure, his hand and body movements, and stiffness. These early patterns of communication through sound and gestures are believed to be important precursors to language acquisition. Bruner (1978) sees language mastery as involving the parent as much as the child. At the least, in order to develop speech, the child must hear the native language spoken in social interactions with the parents (Slobin, 1982).

EARLY LANGUAGE BEHAVIOR

Children throughout the world speak in many different languages. Although the words they learn differ, the onset and pace with which they learn their native languages is similar across different cultures (Bowerman, 1981). During the first 6 months of life, the young infant gradually practices and expands a growing repertoire of sounds and gestures. By engaging in a synchronous exchange of body movement and sounds with his or her parents, the infant communicates awareness and interest.

At birth, the most prominent infant vocalizations are in the form of crying. Smiling and cooing are also common ways in which infants communicate pleasure. By 2 months of age the infant makes cooing sounds that contain many of the basic sounds of all languages, not just those of the native culture.

babbling

A repetitive combination of sounds common to infants 4 to 5 months of age.

expressive jargon

The speech pattern in which infants between 6 months and 1 year engage; it resembles the intonation and sounds of adult speech, yet is meaningless in content.

Early Speech By 4 to 5 months of age, the infant produces more sounds and strings them together to produce **babbling**, a repetitive combination of sounds such as "la-la-la" or "ba-ba-ba." The babbling sounds have no special meaning, but the infant appears to enjoy such vocalizations and playfully repeats them. Gesturing by pointing to a desired person or object then becomes part of the infant's pre-speech behavior. At first the infant engages in language play only when alone, but as the infant grows older he or she involves parents and familiar adults in a playful exchange of sounds (Kuczaj, 1982). However, infants will babble without encouragement or response from their caregivers. Children of deaf parents engage in the same babbling behavior as children of hearing parents (Lenneberg, 1967). Furthermore, an infant's activity during the babbling stage has no clear connection to later language development. Early babblers do not become early or more fluent speakers.

By about 6 months, infants gradually produce only the sounds contained in the languages they hear (Lenneberg, 1967). For the child with English-speaking parents, numerous conversations and social interactions encourage the child to acquire and produce the sounds specific to English and to drop those sounds required for other languages. If there are no verbal interactions by this age (for example, if the child is deaf), the child gradually loses the capability to communicate verbally.

Between 6 months and 1 year, infants engage in a speech pattern that sounds like adult conversation; this is termed **expressive jargon** because it resembles the intonation and sounds of adult speech yet is meaningless in content. The infant engaging in expressive jargon is learning to control speech and to use sound patterns to engage parents in social interaction. Often children will vocalize while smiling or laughing with their parents.

By 1 year of age, the infant's first words emerge. Infants first talk about what they know. They label their toys, food, parents and siblings, and the objects they use on a daily basis (such as shoe, cup, spoon, and cap). They also use words such as "all gone," "more," "bye-bye," and "no." These first words are typically concrete nouns spoken in the actual presence of the objects they represent and hence are more readily understood by others.

By 15 to 18 months of age, the infant's use of one-word utterances carries additional meaning. Linguists have debated whether the use of one word to convey meaning implies the acquisition of true language. Alec said "More!" to mean "I want more milk"; this was conveyed by the emphasis and intonation of the word and its context. His mother understood him perfectly and responded by giving him more milk.

By the age of 2 years, children generally are creating two-word combinations such as "Dada bye-bye" and "cookie gone." The child at this stage is combining words into a primitive sentence, which reflects the beginning of true language behavior. The meaning of the sentence is less restricted to the mother's interpretation; other adults are now able to understand the infant's use of words.

As adults use language in their interactions with the infant, they facilitate the infant's learning and later production of the language by the model they present to the infant (Snow, 1981). The more experience the infant has with the language, the greater the child's fluency.

This grandmother enjoys the playful exchange of words and sounds with her grandchild. Some researchers believe that these early verbal interactions encourage language development in children.

PARENT-CHILD SPEECH

Baby Talk   When talking to an infant, people tend to use a different way of speaking than when talking with adults or older children. You might say something like "Whadda whadda snookums, whosa happy baby?" Try it! Raise and lower the pitch of your voice in a singsong fashion while gazing into the infant's eyes and smiling. This is referred to as **baby talk** or infant-directed speech (Fernald, 1989). Researchers believe that infant-directed speech is an important tool in teaching language to infants. It also may be useful in gaining infants' attention and modulating their emotional arousal (Fernald, 1989). Infants as young as 2 days old prefer the sound of baby talk to adult-directed speech (Cooper & Aslin, 1990). Furthermore, baby talk appears in different language cultures: It has been observed in infant-parent interactions in French, Italian, German, Japanese, and British homes (Fernald et al., 1989).

baby talk
Adult speech directed at infants that includes raising and lowering of the pitch of one's voice.

Motherese   Most of the studies of early parent-infant language behavior have focused on the quality of the mother's speech to her baby. Through myriad verbal and nonverbal interactions, mothers help infants fine-tune their language skills. The term **motherese** refers to the short, grammatically simple baby talk that mothers and other caregivers use when talking with their infants. The parent repeats and expands those utterances made by the baby. For example, when Alec says "bah-bah," his mother replies, "Where is your bottle?" Often the caregiver uses more commands and questions and fewer pronouns, verbs, and modifiers when talking to the infant. As the child's capacity for language advances, the parent increases the complexity of verbal exchanges (Furrow, Nelson, & Benedict, 1979; Slobin, 1975).

motherese
The short, grammatically simple, baby talk that mothers and other caregivers use when talking with their infants.

Some studies of motherese have focused on the function of verbal exchanges in promoting social interactions between the parent and child. When parents talk to their infants, they are not trying to teach them how to speak the language so much as using language to make contact and playfully communicate with them (Molfese, Molfese, & Carrell, 1982). Furthermore, the infant's verbal responses seem to elicit the parent's verbal interactions. The parent and child appear to take turns "talking" to each other. What the parent talks about is influenced by the child's linguistic and cognitive level and, most important, by the child's interests. Parents of a toddler, for example, learn to make the "rrrr" sound of trucks if their child shows particular interest in them.

Mothers vary in the amount of talking they do with their infants. In the United States, some middle-class mothers expand or rephrase what their infants say into complete sentences in an attempt to help them acquire language. However, it is not clear that these efforts are at all necessary. Samoan parents, for example, do not involve themselves in teaching language to their infants; they believe that infants will communicate when they are ready. Despite these differences in approach to language, Samoan and American children acquire language at the same age (Ochs, 1982).

Cultural values and settings may also affect the quality of mother-infant verbal interactions in other ways. In a laboratory study in which Japanese and American mothers were videotaped interacting with their 3-month-old infants, researchers (Fogel, Toda, & Kawai, 1988) found that Japanese mothers were more likely to reduce their own vocalizations and lean their bodies closer and touch their infants when their babies smiled, looked, or spoke. In contrast, American mothers spent most of their time verbally interacting, with their faces up close to their babies. The researchers explained the differences between the Japanese and American styles of interaction in terms of their cultures. Japanese mothers were more likely to communicate their feelings through nonverbal means (looming and touching), which is consistent with the tradition in Japanese culture to indirectly express emotions. Americans are more likely to directly communicate emotion, and hence the mothers were more likely to verbally communicate their feelings.

It is not certain whether more frequent exposure to child-directed language leads to greater speaking ease or early fluency (Gleitman, Newport, & Gleitman, 1984). It is known, however, that early language exchanges have an effect on the child's social skills and help to establish an affectionate bond between parent and child.

BRIEF REVIEW

The infant's earliest social interactions are with parents, who not only care for the child but are affected by the child's behavior. In the bidirectional view of development infants are seen as active agents in their socialization.

The child's physical appearance, health, and maturity may influence a parent's initial reaction and bonding with the infant. The child's temperament may be described as easy, difficult, or slow-to-warm. Different temperaments elicit differing reactions from the caregiver.

The young infant is capable of expressing a progressively greater variety of emotions during the first 2 years of life. The infant's emotional development is closely related to cognitive development. One way to assess infant emotions is to rate the changes in facial expressions in response to different emotional experiences.

The early social interactions between parent and child form the basis for Erikson's first psychosocial crisis of basic trust versus mistrust. A consistent and affectionate caregiver helps the child develop self-confidence and trust in others. Abusive, inconsistent, or neglectful parents may foster a sense of mistrust in the infant.

Since the parent's behavior is influenced by the temperament of the child, it is difficult to specify precisely what parental characteristics are necessary to promote healthy personalities in children. However, research on parent-child interactions suggests that parents who stimulate, touch, and hold their infants and express warm, positive emotions are likely to have more responsive and socially competent children. Social support to parents in stressful situations also may encourage a positive parent-child relationship.

The attachment between parent and child begins at birth but is clearly established by the age of 6 to 12 months. Attachment is indicated by the child's seeking contact with the caregiver, the amount of comfort and affection displayed in parent-child interactions, the degree of distress shown when they are separated or when a stranger is present, and the extent to which a child can use the parent to recover from stress and begin to explore the environment once again.

Children may have more than one attachment figure, including the father and siblings. Fathers and mothers tend to interact with their infants in different ways.

Four patterns of attachment have been observed: securely attached, insecure-resistant, insecure-avoidant, and insecure-disorganized-disoriented attachment. Most children are securely attached and use the attachment figure as a base of security from which to explore the world.

Individual differences in patterns of attachment occur as a result of cultural, developmental, and temperamental differences among infants. Differences in maternal behavior also result in different attachment patterns. The long-term consequences of attachment have been found in cognitive, social, and emotional development.

The toddler begins to separate from the parent and to develop a sense of autonomy. If the demands on the child for self-control are too rigid, he or she may develop a feeling of shame and self-doubt.

By 18 months of age, infants are able to recognize their images in a mirror. The sense of self is established later in infancy and continues to develop throughout childhood.

Early language behavior begins in infancy as the child communicates by crying, cooing, and gesturing. Baby talk or infant-directed speech is useful in helping infants learn a language. Motherese is the term that describes a particular way that parents have of talking to their babies to maintain social contact with them.

KEY TERMS

attachment (139)
babbling (153)
baby talk (154)
bidirectional view (126)
crisis (135)
expressive jargon (153)

insecure-avoidant attachment (144)
insecure-disorganized-disoriented attachment (144)
insecure-resistant attachment (144)

motherese (154)
secure attachment (144)
separation distress (141)
stranger anxiety (141)
temperament (129)
unidirectional view (126)

REVIEW QUESTIONS

If you can answer these questions, you have a good understanding of the material in this chapter. If a question seems difficult, go back to the text and review the topic.

1. Explain the difference between the unidirectional and bidirectional views of development.

2. What characteristics of infants may affect the quality of care they receive?

3. Describe the three types of infant temperament identified by Thomas and Chess. What behaviors are used to measure infant temperament?

4. List and explain the eight stages of infant emotional development.

5. Discuss Erikson's crisis of trust versus mistrust.

6. What parental characteristics promote healthy development in young children?

7. What is attachment? What behaviors are used to signify that a child has formed an attachment? Describe Bowlby's four phases in the development of attachment.

8. Define and give an example of stranger anxiety and separation distress. At what ages are they likely to occur?

9. Describe Ainsworth's Strange Situation procedure.

10. Describe four types of attachment patterns.

11. What is autonomy? According to Erikson, how does an infant develop autonomy?

12. What is the sequence for developing a self-concept? How are researchers able to study self-awareness in infants?

13. Describe the ways in which infants communicate during the first 18 months of life. What is expressive jargon? What is the significance of baby talk?

14. What is motherese? What impact does culture have on the way infants and their parents communicate?

OBSERVATIONAL ACTIVITY

ATTACHMENT BEHAVIORS

The purpose of this observation is for you to gain a better understanding of the behaviors that signal the infant's development of an attachment to his or her caregiver. You will need to observe a mother or father with an infant between 1 and 2 years of age for about 30 minutes in a setting such as an infant day-care center, a church nursery, a pediatrician's waiting room, or a play area in a shopping mall. Ideally, you want to find a place where the toddler is allowed some freedom to move about while in the presence of the parent. Be sure to get permission from the people in charge before you do your observation.

While observing the mother or father and child, take notice of the following behaviors:

1. Physical contact. How often does the child touch or hold the parent? Who initiates the contact? Under what circumstances do the parent and child make contact with each other?

2. Exploration behavior. Does the child move away from the parent and examine toys, people, or objects in the room? Does the parent encourage the child's exploration?

3. Use of parent as a secure base. Does the infant use the parent for comfort or security? Does the child make eye contact or verbal contact while playing with toys? What is the parent's reaction?

4. Stranger reactions. How does the infant respond to unfamiliar people who make contact with it? What emotional reaction can you see in the infant's face? Does the infant return to the parent?

5. Separation anxiety. If the parent leaves the immediate area, observe the infant's reaction. Does the infant protest or cry? What is the infant's reaction when the parent returns?

Stay long enough to collect the information you need to describe the attachment behavior. Summarize your observations and share the summary with your class. What insights did you gain in doing this activity?

The Exploring Years

Life's journey from 2 to 6 years assumes a delightful quality. Babies become children and begin to express their thoughts about the world; it is a time of curiosity and exploration. The physical immaturity that typified infancy gives way to a growing range of physical and motor skills. During this time, young children rapidly acquire and demonstrate new social skills and learn to communicate their needs. They expand their travels from the home to the playground and classroom, and thus broaden their views of themselves and their immediate environment. An individual's experiences during early childhood lay the foundation for his or her personality and later learning. In the next two chapters you will sample some of the characteristic changes in physical, cognitive, social, and personality development. As you travel through this exciting period of the lifespan, keep in mind the following two questions: What changes typically occur? How do these changes relate to overall development throughout the lifespan?

CHAPTER 5

Early Childhood: Physical, Cognitive, and Language Development

By the time Rachel was 2 she was starting to look more like a child and less like a baby. She had a lot of energy, which she directed at exploring her playroom.

About the same time, Rachel's mother decided to return to work part-time. Since Rachel was now toilet trained and liked to play with other children, her parents decided to enroll her in a preschool program. They had visited a number community programs and interviewed their staffs; their major concern was that Rachel would receive the care and attention she needed to make the transition from home to a safe environment in a stimulating school. After much consideration, they selected Mrs. Riddering's Nursery School.

Rachel's teacher was a kind and very wise grandmother who guided children toward mastery and discovery in a well-conceived, structured setting. She had taught hundreds of preschool-aged children and knew how to capitalize on children's natural curiosity and energy. But she had her rules, too. One basic rule for the children in the play yard: Before a child could use the swing set, she had to be able to seat herself unassisted. By her 3rd birthday, Rachel prided herself on the fact that, after much practice and determination, she could seat herself on the swing. By the time she was 4, she could climb to the top of the jungle gym and proclaim, "I made it to the top of the mountain!" Rachel had found a new world to discover.

In New Delhi, 4-year-old Anand quietly listened to his grandmother as she read stories to him in Hindi. In India fifteen languages are spoken. Anand's family spoke three of them; Hindi was their first language. Anand's father wanted him to learn as many languages as he could. He believed that in order to be successful in a multilingual culture such as India, it was important for people to know more than just one language. Ever since he was an infant, his father spoke to him in English while his mother spoke to him in Hindi.

Anand was the only son in his family. He and his older sister spent most of their free time in their parents' shop. Together, they would help out by stacking bags of beans and rice on the shelves. Anand liked to pretend that they were bags of coins. He counted the bags as he put them "in the bank" (on the shelf). Even as Anand and his sister played, they were learning about numbers and quantities.

Rachel and Anand live in different cultures, yet they share many characteristics. They both like to play and in doing so learn new skills that will assist them later. Both children were maturing physically at the same time that their cognitive abilities were expanding to include a rich fantasy life. The settings in which they expressed their exploratory skills are influenced by their cultural contexts, but the pattern of growth is universal.

PHYSICAL DEVELOPMENT

SIZE AND PROPORTION

My children never wore out their clothes during infancy; they just outgrew them. But as their rate of growth slowed during early childhood, they were also more mobile and active. My son Adam frequently wore out the tips of his shoes because he loved to drag his feet while riding on his Big Wheel.

Assuming an adequate diet and health, average 2-year-olds will have quadrupled their birthweight and increased their height by two thirds. Compared to the rapid growth in height and weight during the first 2 years of life, growth appears to level off during the next 4 years. From ages 2 to 3 the average child grows by 4 pounds and 3 inches a year. Between 4 to 6 years of age the rate of growth has slowed down to 2½ inches in height a year, while body weight grows by 5 to 7 pounds a year. By age 6 the average child weighs 48 pounds and is 46 inches tall (Watson & Lowrey, 1967).

By age 2½ for boys and 1¾ for girls, children have achieved one half of their predicted adult height; but for the most part, boys and girls are similar in their physical development during the preschool years (see Table 5–1).

Of course, there is considerable variation across cultures in children's physical growth. After reviewing more than 200 studies of preschool-aged children

PHYSICAL GROWTH, AGES 3 TO 6 (50TH PERCENTILE)

Age	HEIGHT (INCHES)		WEIGHT (POUNDS)	
	Boys	Girls	Boys	Girls
3	38	37.75	32	31.75
3.5	39	39	34	34
4	40.75	40	36	36
4.5	42	42	38	38
5	43	43	41	41
5.5	45	44	45	44
6	46	46	48	47

TABLE 5–1

Source: From *Growth and development of children* (5th ed.), by E. H. Lowrey, 1967, Chicago: Year Book Medical Publishers, Inc. Reprinted with permission.

around the world, Meredith (1978) concluded that much of this variation relates either to ethnic origin or nutrition. In the United States, African American children are taller than Caucasian children, who are, in turn, taller than Asian American children. Urban, middle-class, and first-born children are taller than rural, lower-class, and later-born children. Furthermore, Meredith found that children whose mothers smoked during pregnancy are on the average ½ inch shorter at age 6 than are children whose mothers did not smoke. A poorly nourished child can be expected to be smaller and to develop at a slower rate. It is also possible that a child experiencing extreme emotional stress will grow more slowly than average.

FOCUS ON CULTURE

Physical development can be slowed by poor diet, malnutrition, starvation, or disease, all of which can occur in any culture. Climate and geography can also be limiting factors. People who grow up in high altitudes where the oxygen level is lower tend to be smaller than others; less exposure to vitamin D, found in sunlight, can also limit physical growth. People living in some countries, such as Iceland and Scandinavia, have very little exposure to sunlight during the winter months.

MOTOR COORDINATION

Gross Motor Coordination

Although the changes in the child's motor development may not appear to be as dramatic as the changes in size and proportion in the first 2 years of life, the early childhood period from 2 to 6 years is highlighted by increasingly more coordinated neuromuscular ability. Children's large muscles and leg and arm joints are also growing during this period, thus increasing their susceptibility to injury.

Recall that during the sensorimotor period, infants use their bodies and practice body motions so that by age 2 they have increasing skill and mastery of their body. The term *toddler* has been applied to infants between the ages of 1 to 2 years as they first begin to walk, because their gait is initially unsteady and they appear to "toddle." With practice, however, they walk more steadily and are able to start and stop movements with ease. The 2-year-old is likely to be clumsy, and spills and falls are common occurrences. However, by 5 years old the child walks, runs, climbs, and jumps with grace. Skipping, walking on a balance beam, and hopping on one foot are other milestones achieved by the end of this period. With practice in play, the preschool-aged child masters the skill of throwing and catching a ball with increasing poise and accuracy. Even though young children learn to control the movement of their large arm and shoulder muscles, they may not be able to throw a ball with as much strength or accuracy as older children. Overall, the degree of mastery that young children display over their bodies is quite impressive (see Table 5–2 and Figure 5–1).

Fine Motor Coordination

Fine motor skills involve the use and control of smaller muscles in the fingers and are harder for young children to master than gross motor skills involving larger muscles. Imagine the difficulty you might have if you were asked to tie a shoe or write your name while wearing thick gloves. You

MOTOR AND MANIPULATIVE SKILLS IN EARLY CHILDHOOD

GENERAL ABILITY	SPECIFIC ABILITY	AGE OF ONSET
Running		
Running involves a brief period of no contact with the supporting surface.	First run	2–3 years
	Efficient and refined run	4–5 years
	Speed of run increases	5 years
Jumping		
Jumping takes three forms:	Jumps down from low object with both feet	2 years
1. Jumping for distance	Jumps off floor with both feet	28 months
2. Jumping for height	Jumps for distance (about 3 feet)	5 years
3. Jumping from a height	Jumps for height (about 1 foot)	5 years
It involves a 1- or 2-foot takeoff with a landing on the same foot.		
Hopping		
Hopping involves a 1-foot takeoff with a landing on the same foot.	Hops up to three times on preferred foot	3 years
	Hops from four to six times on same foot	4 years
	Hops from eight to ten times on the same foot	5 years
	Hops distance of 50 feet in about 11 seconds	5 years
	Hops skillfully with rhythmical alteration	6 years
Galloping		
The gallop combines a walk and a leap with the same foot leading throughout.	Basic but inefficient gallop	4 years
	Gallops skillfully	6 years
Skipping		
Skipping combines a step and a hop in rhythmic alteration.	One-footed skip	4 years
	Skillful skipping about 20% of the time	5 years
	Skillful skipping for most of the time	6 years

GENERAL ABILITY	SPECIFIC ABILITY	AGE OF ONSET
Catching		
Catching involves receiving force from an object with the hands, moving from large to progressively smaller balls.	Chases ball; does not respond to aerial ball	2–3 years
	Responds to aerial ball with delayed arm movements	2–3 years
	Needs to be told how to position arms	3–4 years
	Fear reaction (turns head away)	3–4 years
	Basket catch using the body	3 years
	Catches using the hands only with a small ball	5 years
Kicking		
Kicking involves imparting force to an object with the foot.	Kicks with leg straight and little body movement (kicks at the ball)	2–3 years
	Flexes lower leg on backward lift	3–4 years
	Greater backward and forward swing with definite arm opposition	4–5 years
	Mature pattern (kicks through the ball)	5–6 years
Striking		
Striking involves imparting force to objects in an overarm, sidearm, or underhand pattern.	Faces object and swings in a vertical plane	2–3 years
	Swings in a horizontal plane and stands to the side of the object	4–5 years
	Rotates the trunk and hips and shifts body weight forward; mature horizontal patterns	6–7 years
Throwing		
Throwing involves imparting force to an object in the general direction of intent.	Body faces target, feet remain stationary, ball thrown with forearm extension only	2–3 years
	Same as above but with body rotation added	$3\frac{1}{2}$–5 years
	Steps forward with leg on same side as the throwing arm	5–6 years
	Mature throwing pattern	$6\frac{1}{2}$ years
	Boys exhibit more mature pattern than girls	6 years and older

TABLE 5–2

Source: From *Motor development experiences for young children* (pp. 65–66), by D. L. Gallahue, 1976, New York: John Wiley & Sons. Adapted with permission.

FIGURE 5–1

Running styles of 18- and 36-month-old youngsters. Changes in body proportion as well as changes in coordination help account for the difference in styles.

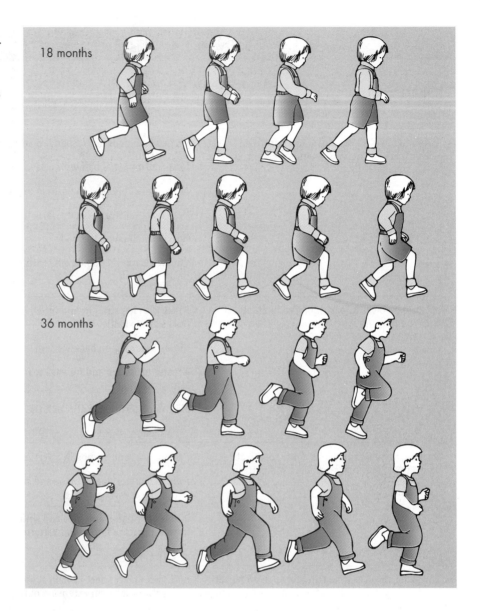

18 months

36 months

probably would not be able to hold the pen or grasp the shoelace as easily and would not be as coordinated in your actions.

The 2-year-old has fat fingers, and the neurons in the fingers are not yet fully covered by myelin, the protective and insulating neuron sheath. By 4 years of age this myelinization is complete, and the result can be seen in the ease with which a 4-year-old can use a crayon or pencil to copy a figure or write on the walls. By age 4 children can use child-size scissors, put together puzzle pieces, and make paintings with a brush. By age 5 they can manage buttons and zippers, use chopsticks or a fork, spoon, and knife while eating; some may even be able to tie shoelaces.

Like Rachel and Anand, much of young children's skill in fine motor activities is a result of everyday practice in play. While maturation of the nervous system is necessary for the development of fine motor coordination, experience in

The differences in size and shape among young children illustrate the variation in growth rates during the 2- to 6-year-old period.

handedness
A person's basic preference for the use of one hand over the other.

The use of scissors requires fine motor control and coordination, which improves with growth and practice.

manipulating objects helps children develop fine motor skills. For example, picking up and sorting the beans in his father's shop gives Anand more experience with handling small objects. The more opportunities children have to use tools and utensils, crayons, brushes, and scissors, the greater will be their ease and proficiency with these tools.

Handedness, the basic preference for the use of one hand over the other for manipulating objects, develops during early childhood. While most young children display a consistent preference for one hand by the age of 5 (Goodall, 1980), some children begin to rely on the use of one hand as young as 6 months (Shucard & Shucard, 1990). In one study, girls who showed a consistent hand preference also tested higher on measures of intellectual development; this finding did not hold true for boys. About one in every 10 children is left-handed (Coren & Halpern, 1991; Hardyck & Petrenovick, 1977). Handedness appears to be influenced by genetics or the prenatal environment rather than training. Thus, attempts to alter the child's natural preference may be frustrating and futile. The obvious difficulties for the left-handed child in writing and manipulating right-handed objects may be offset by the greater ambidexterity often found in left-handed children (K. Fischer, 1987).

FOCUS ON CULTURE

In the United States and other industrialized countries, toys for preschool-aged children are a big business. Parents are told that toys will help their children develop perceptual-motor and cognitive skills. However, children do not need specially made toys to acquire these skills. Children living in nonindustrialized cultures play with objects such as gourds, stones, reeds, and maize, all of which are a part of their physical environment. Using these "toys," children learn to use and manipulate objects while learning about their physical environment and their relationship to it.

The early childhood years are highlighted by increasingly more coordinated movement, most often seen during play.

RECAP

Between 2 and 6 years of age, a child's growth rate slows relative to its rate during infancy. Physical development is influenced by nutrition and genetics. Gross motor skills rapidly increase and are enhanced by practice. Fine motor skills take longer to develop because they are dependent on the myelinization of neurons. Handedness is demonstrated by age 5.

COGNITIVE DEVELOPMENT

PIAGET'S PREOPERATIONAL CHILD

By the time my daughter Sarah was 2 years old, she was very clever in manipulating her parents. She had learned to get her way by playfully smiling as she snuggled into her father's lap with a book in her hand. Even before the second birthday children show signs of increased ability to adapt to the many different features of their world. As we saw in Chapter 3, Piaget's first stage of cognitive growth, the sensorimotor stage, describes how children understand their world through sensory and motor actions, or schemes. Their knowledge is limited to a here-and-now understanding of the objects and people with whom they interact. Piaget believed that it was not until the end of the sensorimotor stage that children begin to break out of their restricted view of the world by mentally representing these people and objects. *Deferred imitation*—that is, imitation of actions in the absence of a model—signals the beginning of **symbolic representation** (or function). In order for children to imitate a model's actions without a concrete

symbolic representation
The ability to create and use symbols or images to represent something that is not present.

example directly in front of them, they must be able to represent the model's action in some form of mental picture or image. For example, in order for a child to imitate the karate movements the day after watching a karate movie, the child must construct a mental picture of the stylized action.

When children are capable of mentally representing events, objects, or people, they can think about these things without having to act on them using their senses or body. Symbolic representation is one distinguishing characteristic of the **preoperational stage** of cognitive development, the second major stage in Piaget's theory of cognitive development. This stage describes thought that occurs before children are capable of operations—the logical mental manipulation and transformation of information. The preoperational child can mentally represent information gathered through the senses but does not yet integrate this information with other knowledge in a logical manner. (See Table 5–3 for a summary of the characteristics of the preoperational thinker.) True symbolic thought involves both representation and operations (Piaget, 1952a).

Symbolic Representation
As toddlers, both of my children recognized the meaning of the golden arches: They represented the fast-food restaurant that they loved to visit. The ability to represent an event mentally, referred to as symbolic representation, enables children to increase their sphere of activity to include past and future events as well as present ones. The degree of correspondence between the children's mental representation and the real object or event can vary from a concrete mental picture of an object to a highly abstract representation in the form of a word.

Children readily acquire and use more and more complex **symbols** throughout the preoperational period. Children's use of words to represent thoughts about the past and future also increases with age. In fact, it was Piaget's view that the ability to represent events mentally precedes the development of language. Before children can learn to use words, Piaget believed, they must acquire their own symbols to represent familiar objects in their environment.

Symbolic Play and Imitation
When Sarah rode her Big Wheel, she was pretending to drive a real vehicle. When she poured tea from her toy teapot, nothing came out, but she was very careful not to spill it. Many examples of the use of symbols to represent reality can be seen in children's play. Preschool-aged children gradually spend more of their time in **symbolic play,** by pretending and engaging in make-believe. When Anand and his sister play together, they often pretend that to run a shop, using props like a table to represent the shop's counter and different colored blocks for the sale items. In this game of make-believe the two children are also imitating the actions of their parents. Again, mental representation allows children to imitate actions they observed some time in the past. For example, when Rachel puts her hand on her hip and points her finger at her sister while saying "Now go to sleep, baby!" she is imitating actions she has seen her parents perform many times.

Children as young as 2 have been shown to incorporate and understand the meaning of pretense in their play. In a series of experiments, Harris and Kavanaugh (1993) examined the ability of 2-year-olds to follow the activities of an adult who poured make-believe tea from a pot over a toy animal. After watching the pretend episode, the children were asked about what they had seen. Most of

preoperational stage
Piaget's second stage of cognitive development that begins around 2 years of age and ends around 6 or 7 years; characterized by the emergence of symbolic representational thinking but the absence of logical reasoning.

symbol
A gesture, drawing, or word that represents something else; according to Piaget, a type of mental representation that is unique to the child's experience.

symbolic play
Child's play involving the use of symbols to represent reality, such as make-believe or pretend games.

the children realized that the toy animal had gotten "wet" because the "tea" that was poured over it. They were quite capable of following the pretense and recognizing the consequences of the pretend actions. And the children used the words poured and wet even though no liquid was involved at all.

In symbolic play the child can often work out conflicts encountered in the real world. By pretending to be "mother" in a game of house, Rachel is able to express some of her displeasure at the way people, namely her sister who plays the "baby," respond to her. She can structure her time as the "mother" in whatever way she chooses, which may not be so easy for her to do in reality. The use of pretense and fantasy in play increases with age so that 4-year-old children not only incorporate fantasy into much of their play but they join in pretend play with other children (Howes, 1985). Social pretend play requires greater cognitive skill because the child must simultaneously coordinate his or her actions with those of another child and maintain the pretense. Thus Rachel must be aware of her sister's pretend role of "baby" and adjust her pretend role of "mother" to her sister's actions.

What Is Real?   When Rachel referred to the jungle gym as a mountain it was clear to her that it was not really a mountain. But do young children typically make the distinction between reality and their mental representations? This question has puzzled both parents and researchers for many decades.

Consider this example. Four-year-old Ben ran to his father and said, "There's a baby dinosaur sleeping in my toy box!" His father thought he was telling a tall tale, but Ben persisted: "I really did see a baby dinosaur!" The next day when his father was cleaning Ben's toy box he discovered a very large, dead beetle! Ben actually saw a dead bug but he mentally represented it as a sleeping dinosaur.

Piaget (1929) claimed that children do not distinguish between real and mental entities. Children will attribute feelings and intentions to objects that are not

In pretend play, children share their fantasies and coordinate their actions with one another based on pretense. This young boy has just arrived on his "horse" to visit with his friend, who also recognizes the "horse" pretense.

animism
The tendency of young children to attribute animate characteristics to inanimate objects.

realism
The tendency to attribute real physical properties to merely concepts.

alive, a characteristic Piaget referred to as **animism.** For example, 3-year-olds might say that the ocean is asleep or that a flower is bad when it wilts. **Realism** refers to children's tendency to attribute real physical properties to mental events. A 3-year-old believes that a dream is as tangible and real as a picture in a book.

LIMITATIONS OF THE PREOPERATIONAL THINKER

In many ways young children seem to be progressing in their ability to think about things. However, preoperational children may present somewhat of a puzzle to those who listen to their ideas. The way in which they combine ideas and draw conclusions is difficult for adults to understand because their thinking is not logical. Anyone familiar with Winnie-the-Pooh, a character from the children's book by A. A. Milne (1926), will recognize how Pooh's thinking is that of a preoperational child.

FOCUS ON CULTURE

Belief in Santa Claus, fairies and elves, and magic is common among young children. Children's reliance on magical beliefs to explain events in their real world decreases with age and with their growing ability to test the physical explanations for events (Phelps & Woolley, 1994). Folktales are a means of communicating the values and beliefs of a culture. Very often, folktales involve animals who represent gods or other spirits. For example, many Asian parents tell their children *jatakas,* tales that describe Buddha's previous births in the form of animals such as an ox-calf, a rabbit, a quail, a parrot, and a deer. These stories have appeal to children and adults alike, particularly for Buddhists who believe in their rebirth as animals or other living things.

Animism refers to the child's attribution of feeling and other human characteristics to animals and other inanimate objects. Do you think this boy believes elephants can talk?

Education Perspective

CHILDREN'S DRAWINGS: WHAT DO THEY MEAN?

At age 4, my daughter Sarah loved to draw. Her favorite pastime was to use her crayons and magic markers. One morning I noticed a face on the wall directly next to her bed. It was a happy face partially hidden by Sarah's bed pillow. When I asked about her "mural," Sarah replied simply and sweetly, "Oh, that is my friend Molly."

Sarah had drawn a circle with a curved line, two smaller circles and several other lines. To her these shapes and lines represented a face. The picture of the face is a symbol she used to represent her mental image of her friend Molly.

Young children love to draw—even on the walls. Most teachers recognize that drawing is an activity that children spontaneously initiate. People have long been fascinated by the way children busy themselves with a crayon. Does the drawing mean anything to the child? Why does the child draw? Psychologists have used children's artwork to gain insight into their mental world. Clinical psychologists and therapists use children's drawings, especially pictures they draw of themselves, to indicate children's emotional reactions and views of themselves.

Cognitive and developmental psychologists consider children's drawing to represent their mastery and use of graphic symbols to communicate their view of the world (Gardner, 1980). For example, young children typically draw objects and people in proportion to their importance to them. The more important the object or person is to the child, the larger it is drawn. This characteristic is understood to be an example of their egocentric perspective (defined in the following section). Robert Coles (1967) in his study of the effects of prejudice on children describes how a young black girl who was exposed to frightening discrimination and mob violence never used the color black or brown to draw people; white people were drawn larger and more realistically than black people.

When children first begin to draw, their drawings look like scribbles, in the same way that their early attempts at language sound like babbling or gibberish. But with practice and greater fine motor control they perfect their use of lines and shapes and use them to represent things (Matthews, 1990). If you ask a 4-year-old, the child will usually tell you what the picture shows. By age 5 or 6 a child will be able to draw a body showing head, arms, legs, hands, feet, face, hair, and clothes. Their drawings become more complex and detailed, paralleling their increasingly more complex cognitive skills

(Pemberton, 1990).

Young children tend to draw what they know rather than what they actually see. Up to about the age of 7 or 8 years children rely on mental images to guide their drawings. In one study (Freeman & Janikoun, 1972), children ranging in age from 5 to 9 years were shown a cup with a flower painted on it. The cup was positioned so that the children could not see the handle of the cup. When asked to draw what they see, children under 7 drew the cup with a handle and without a flower. Eight- and 9-year olds, however, drew what they had actually seen—the cup with a flower, without a handle.

At age 7 or 8 children can draw in perspective, with nearer objects being larger and objects in the background smaller. An important acquisition for children is the ability to see the same scene from several points of view. At 9 or 10, children can draw an object not only as they see it, but as it would be seen by someone on the opposite side of the object and by someone to their right or left.

Children's drawings provide teachers and parents with a way to understand the child's view of the world. By encouraging children to put their ideas onto paper, they may be able to discover characteristics of children that might otherwise be hidden. If in fact a picture is worth a thousand words, then preschool children's drawings have quite a bit to tell us.

One day when he was out walking, he came to an open place in the middle of the forest, and in the middle of this place was a large oak-tree, and, from the top of the tree, there came a loud buzzing-noise. Winnie-the-Pooh sat down at the foot of the tree, put his head between his paws and began to think.

First of all he said to himself: "That buzzing-noise means something. You don't get a buzzing-noise like that, just buzzing and buzzing, without its meaning something. If there's a buzzing-noise, somebody's making a buzzing-noise, and the only reason for making a buzzing-noise that I know of is because you're a bee."

Then he thought another long time, and said: "And the only reason for being a bee that I know of is making honey." And then he got up, and said: "And the only reason for making honey is so as I can eat it." So he began to climb the tree. (pp. 5–6)

Pooh's thinking resembles that of a rational thinker even though the scope of his thinking is limited to what he wants to accomplish.

Egocentrism   One of the limitations of the preoperational child's thought processes is called **egocentrism,** the inability to distinguish easily between one's own perspective and other perspectives. Pooh cannot conceive of any reason for bees to make honey other than for him to eat it. The young child often acts as if other people see the child's world the same way he or she does. Four-year-old Anand would delight his grandmother by covering his eyes and saying, "You can't see me!" If he cannot see his grandmother, he assumes that she cannot see him. Another common example of egocentrism occurs when children report that the sun or moon follows them when they walk.

Young children also engage in **egocentric speech;** they talk to themselves either in the company of other children or alone. Piaget observed that the proportion of egocentric utterances in children's speech decreases with increased social interactions. By the age of 7, the child is aware of the listener and adjusts speech so that the listener will be able to understand. Piaget interprets this change from egocentric to a social speech as evidence of the child's growing intellectual ability to mentally consider more than one viewpoint at a time.

Concreteness   A second limitation of preoperational children's thinking is their reliance on physical objects or events. Most of children's mental representations—that is, their symbols—refer to concrete objects and events that they can mentally manipulate. For example, children may use a stick as a symbol of a real gun, a machete, or sword. An older child or adult may use a word to symbolize the process of aggression or a more abstract event without a physical referent.

Centration   Children in the preoperational period also have a tendency to focus their attention on one detail or aspect of an event, a process called **centration.** Because they center their attention on a particular perceptual aspect, young children are often unable to accurately process information about an event.

Piaget illustrated the centration characteristic in his famous conservation of continuous quantity experiment, in which a child is presented with two identical glass containers that have been filled to exactly the same level with colored liquid. One of the containers is identified as the child's, the other as the experimenter's. After the child acknowledges that the two glasses contain the same amount of liquid, the experimenter pours the contents of his or her container into a tall, thin

egocentrism
The inability to easily distinguish one's own perspective from that of others.

egocentric speech
Speech that is uttered when the child is alone or is not trying to communicate.

concreteness
The overreliance on physical objects or events to guide thought.

centration
Piaget's term for the process of focusing attention on a single detail or aspect of an object or event.

container. When asked, "Who has more to drink, or do we have the same amount?" the preoperational child will usually respond that the tall, thin container holds more liquid because the child is centering his or her attention on the height of the liquid in the container. Another child may be centered on the width of the container and respond that the shorter, fatter container has more liquid.

In both cases, children base their judgment on one dimension and not both height and width. If such children could *decenter*—that is, shift attention from one aspect of this problem (height of the liquid) to another (width of the container)—they would be able to think the problem through and conclude that the containers contain the same amount of liquid. This knowledge—that so long as nothing has been added or subtracted the amount of liquid in the containers remains the same—is referred to as *conservation of quantity.*

The principle of conservation can be observed in real-world as well as experimental settings. Suppose you are giving a birthday party for your 3-year-old and you do not have enough of the same-sized clear plastic glasses for all the children. You supplement your supply with glasses of several different sizes. To make sure that each child believes that the amount of juice in each glass is the same, pour juice to the same level in each glass. However, if there is a 7- or 8-year-old at the party, you can be certain that he or she will grab the shortest and widest glass!

Conservation—again, comprehending that physical properties remain the same so long as nothing has been added or taken away—occurs with other areas in addition to quantity of liquid. For example, *conservation of number* occurs when children recognize that the number of objects remains the same even if the objects are rearranged. The area, weight, and volume of physical objects are other characteristics for which conservation applies. (Conservation will be discussed in more detail in Chapter 7.)

Irreversibility   Another limitation of young children's thought processes is called **irreversibility,** their inability to mentally reverse their thinking and return

conservation
The recognition that characteristics of objects remain the same so long as nothing is added or subtracted.

irreversibility
The child's inability to reverse his or her thinking.

In Piaget's conservation of continuous quantity task, the preoperational child confuses the height of the liquid with its amount, and thus does not see the equality of the two amounts.

to the point of origin. Older children and adults are able to solve the water-level problem described above because they can think back through the steps to when both containers contained the same amount of liquid. They know that as long as no liquid was added or subtracted, the containers must hold equal amounts. In the water-level task, preoperational children do not demonstrate conservation of quantity with liquid, partly because they center their attention on one perceptual attribute and partly because they do not reverse their thinking.

transductive reasoning
Unlike inductive or deductive reasoning, the reasoning of children from the particular to the particular.

Transductive Reasoning   A final limitation of preoperational thinking can be seen in the way children reason. Instead of reasoning from the particular to the general (inductive reasoning) or from the general to the particular (deductive reasoning), as adults do, the preschooler engages in what Piaget called **transductive reasoning**—that is, reasoning from the particular to the particular. For example, Rachel has a dog named JoJo who is exceptionally friendly with children. However, Brutus, the dog down the street, is not so friendly. Using transductive reasoning, however, Rachel may think otherwise:

> JoJo is a dog (particular). JoJo is friendly (particular). Brutus is a dog (particular). Therefore, Brutus is friendly.

Preoperational children may be just as convinced of the soundness of their logic as adults using deductive or inductive reasoning, even though such conclusions are obviously inaccurate. The quote from Winnie-the-Pooh, "the only reason for making honey is so as I can eat it" is another example of a conclusion reached by transductive reasoning. Because two events occur together, the young child thinks they are connected. That some events occur by chance is incomprehensible to the preoperational child. If one asks, "Why does the moon shine?" The response may be "To light my bedroom at night when I am in it." This type of thinking is both amusing and confusing to people far removed from the preoperational child's level of transductive reasoning.

While there are numerous examples of transductive reasoning in young children, research has demonstrated that when the problem is purely fictional and is not based on any practical knowledge, 4-year-olds can reason deductively (Hawkins, Pea, Glick, & Scribner, 1984). For example, 4-year-old children could solve this problem:

> Merds laugh when they are happy.
> All animals that laugh don't like mushrooms.
> Do merds like mushrooms? (No)

They could not, however, solve the following problem because the conclusion contradicts their daily experience with glasses:

> Glasses bounce when they fall.
> Everything that bounces is made of rubber.
> Are glasses made of rubber? (Yes)

CONCEPTUAL UNDERSTANDING

By the age of 4, children seem to be able to think about things beyond their own experience. The way they understand their world, however, is different from the

CHARACTERISTICS OF THE PREOPERATIONAL THINKER

CONCEPT	CHARACTERISTIC
Animism	Tendency to attribute animate characteristics to inanimate objects
Realism	Tendency to attribute real physical properties to mental events
Egocentrism	Inability to see things from another person's perspective
Concreteness	Overreliance on physical objects or events
Centration	Focus of attention is directed to a single aspect or detail
Irreversibility	Inability to mentally reverse the order of thoughts
Transductive reasoning	Reasoning from the particular to the particular
Symbolic representation	The ability to create and use symbols or images to represent objects, people, or events

TABLE 5–3

conceptualization of older children and adults. Gradually, over the period of time from 2 to 6 years old, children develop a fuller understanding of the more abstract concepts such as time, number, and groupings.

Time Although young children may use words reflecting an understanding of time (such as minute, hour, day, or week), they often confuse the concepts of time and space. Piaget (1927/1971) illustrated this confusion by using the following task, in which two tracks are presented to the child. On Track I a car is moved from point *a* to point *d* while simultaneously a second car is moved on Track II from point *a* to point *b* (see Figure 5–2A). Both cars travel for the same duration of time (½ second), yet preoperational children are distracted by their perception of space and describe the car on Track I as "taking longer." Even when the car on Track II is moved twice (see Figure 5–2B), children still maintain that the car on Track I took longer than the car on Track II. Their perception that the first car is ahead of the second car influences their judgment of duration.

It is not until age 10 that the child understands that movements that begin and end at the same moment take the same amount of time, and that objects can move over unequal distances in the same amount of time by varying the speed at which they travel.

Usually children comprehend time by referring to the movement of a clock's hands. In fact, many preschool and kindergarten teachers instruct children to tell time by calling their attention to the movement of the big and little hands of the clock. For example, my son Adam's 5-year-old friend Ray once asked me to tell him when it was 5 o'clock since he had to go home at that time. Noticing that he was wearing a new and rather spectacular digital watch that displayed the hour clearly, I asked Ray why he did not just look at his own watch for the time. He replied quite

FIGURE 5–2

Understanding time. In diagram A, an object is moved from point *a* to point *d* in ½ second while a second object is moved from point *a* to point *b* in the same amount of time. Preoperational children describe the object that moved from *a* to *d* as taking longer. In diagram B, an object moved from *a* to *d* in ½ second is still judged to take longer when compared to an object moved from *a* to *b* to *c* in 1 second.

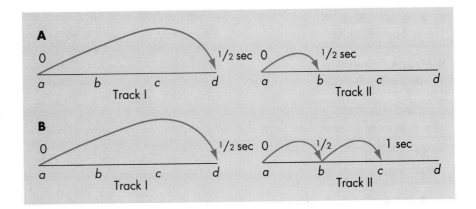

simply, "My watch doesn't have 5 o'clock on it." In fact, it was only 4:07 P.M., and he did not see any 5 on the watch! An older child or an adult would not be so dependent on the spatial arrangement of the numbers on the clock to determine time.

FOCUS ON CULTURE

A child who grew up in the United States may have heard the phrase "time is money" more than once. Time is an important factor in industrialized countries that measure success in terms of production per unit of time. However, time is not valued in the same way in cultures whose productivity is governed more by their climate and geography than by schedules or timetables. In the Caribbean, for example, time is viewed merely as a general guide; when someone says they will come to visit, it is often without a specific time reference. Young children's understanding of time then must be considered in context of time within their culture.

Number   By the age of 2, a child can count two objects; by age 4, four objects. By age 6, the child's capacity for assigning a number to a series of objects has greatly increased. Counting involves assigning objects a number and placing these objects in order. Children learn to count skillfully through practice. However, the development of skilled counting depends on the child not only acquiring but also coordinating separate skills such as knowing how to tag items, how to group items, and when to stop counting (Wilkinson, 1984). These component skills are first acquired separately and later coordinated to achieve accurate counting. In a series of studies in which preschool children were given counting tasks, it was found that when a task required very few component skills, children performed well. When many skills were involved their performance was lower and more variable (Wilkinson, 1984).

Piaget (1952a) explained the child's understanding of number concepts as a special type of conservation. Conservation, described earlier in the water-level task, now occurs in a different form—when the child recognizes that numbers of objects remain the same as long as nothing is added or subtracted. Piaget constructed a series of tests of the child's ability to conserve number, involving two parallel rows of objects, such as pennies (see Figure 5–3). At first, the two rows are the same length and have the same number of coins. After the child has

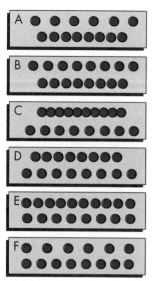

FIGURE 5–3

Children under the age of 5 generally judge the longer lines in rows A through D to have more objects, and rows E and F to have an equal number. By 5 or 6, children are able to use both the length and density of the line to judge its number.

classification

The process of sorting objects into categories.

examined the rows, the examiner shortens or lengthens one of them without removing any of the coins and asks the child, first, which row has more coins in it and, second, *why* one row has more coins than another row.

Young children appear to acquire conservation of number in stages (Brainerd, 1978). In Stage I, children's numerical judgments are dominated by the relative length of the two rows. For rows A through D in Figure 5–3, children under 5 years of age incorrectly report that the longer line has more coins, and that lines E and F contain the same number. By about age 5 or 6, children enter Stage II, in which they now consider the density of the coins as well as the length of the rows in making a number judgment. The child in Stage II recognizes that denser means more and so judges denser lines in E and F to be more numerous. However, the Stage II child does not coordinate density and length and thus judges lines A through D on length alone. It is not until age 6 or 7 that true number conservation is attained and children use both density and length to accurately judge and explain which lines have more coins.

If an older child or adult were given a similar task of judging rows A through F, they would most likely count and/or match the coins one-to-one in each row to determine which has more. Young children do not spontaneously use matching and counting to judge number. Rather, they rely more on gross perceptual features such as the length of the row. However, the child can accurately determine the number of coins if encouraged to use matching or counting (Fuson, Secada, & Hall, 1983).

Classification   Imagine that you entered your bedroom and found that all of the contents of your drawers had been emptied onto the floor. Immediately (after you recovered from the shock) you would probably begin to restore order by grouping different items together—the socks in one pile, shirts in another, underwear in a third pile, and so forth. Once you had separated the clothes, you might sort them even further by color—light colors in one pile, dark colors in another. The useful process of sorting objects into categories or classes is called **classification** (Inhelder & Piaget, 1970).

True classes have four properties:

1. Classes are mutually exclusive: No article of clothing can belong to both the sock pile and the shirt pile.

2. The class is defined by its *intension*—that is, by the characteristics held in common by the members of the class (for example, "sockness").

3. A class is also determined by *extension:* All of the members of the group fit the definition of the class. In our example, all of the items are made of cloth and worn on the feet.

4. Intension must define extension, meaning that the defining characteristics of a class determines what objects may be included within it. For example, if only dark socks are included in one pile, then white socks would not be considered part of that class.

When young children are given a similar task of sorting a collection of objects into piles that are alike or "go together," they typically do not form true classes.

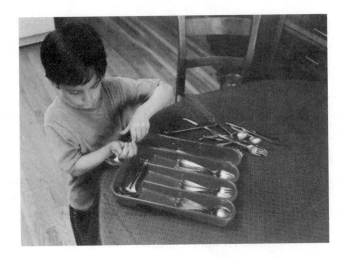

Children can sort items by shape and size when they recognize that objects belong to distinct and separate categories that are defined by specific qualities. For example, a fork has qualities that distinguish it from a knife or spoon.

For example, in sorting colorful shapes, the child will begin by sorting on the basis of color (all red shapes in one pile, all yellow shapes in another), and then switch to a different criterion, such as shape (all triangles in one pile, all squares in another) to finish. At other times the child may group some of the red shapes but exclude the red triangles. One reason children have difficulty sorting items into groups is that they limit their attention to one dimension of the task (Howe & Rabinowitz, 1991). Thus, the task of sorting items on the basis of shape *and* color becomes too difficult for them. When more meaningful objects are used in a classification task, young children will often group objects together on a thematic basis, associating them by events. For example, a man and a car may be grouped together because the man drives the car.

Children older than 7 are more likely to form classes on the basis of truly defined, or *taxonomic,* categories. For example, a car and truck would be grouped together as both being vehicles (Markman & Hutchinson, 1984). Gradually during early childhood children become able to successfully group and even subdivide groups. However, it is not until the end of this period that children are able to form true classes.

CRITICISM OF PIAGET'S VIEWS

Piaget's views about the cognitive skills of young children have been the subject of much research and disagreement. Generally, researchers have challenged the accuracy of Piaget's estimates of the age at which children achieve conceptual understanding (Flavell, Miller, & Miller, 1993).

Egocentrism   According to Piaget, young children are unable to take another person's viewpoint and hence are very limited in their ability to display empathy toward another person's experiences. However, research on empathy and altruism (Zahn-Waxler, Cummings, McKnew, & Radke-Yarrow, 1984) suggests that children as young as 2 are able to express sympathy toward a hurt or upset child. Furthermore, Lempers, Flavell, and Flavell (1977) reported that young children know that other people have their own perceptions. When presenting a picture to another person, children as young as 2½ would turn the picture so that it faced the viewer rather than themselves. Other researchers (Gelman & Shatz, 1978) have found that 4-year-olds adjust their language depending on whether they are talking to 2-year-olds, peers, or adults.

Piaget used a "three mountains test" to illustrate the young child's egocentrism. The child is seated in front of a three dimensional display of three differently colored mountains, each topped with a different object (a house, a cross, and a person). A toy doll is placed across from the child. Because they are unable to assume another perspective, Piaget argued that children functioning at the preoperational level could not accurately describe what the doll "sees" while looking at the display. But other researchers (Newcombe & Huttenlocher, 1992) have found that the age at which children can regard the viewpoint of another varies depending on the complexity of the task used to assess this ability. If young children are asked to make judgments about what a person sees while looking at a simple rather than a complex array of objects, they are more likely to be able to accurately reflect the other person's perspective; when they are allowed to manipulate or rename the objects in the display, they are more successful in demonstrating perspective-taking ability (Yaniv & Shantz, 1998, 1991).

Realism   Some researchers have also challenged Piaget's views on childhood realism. Wellman and Estes (1986) tested the abilities of 3- to 5-year-olds to distinguish a real object (like a cookie) from a mental representation of the object (like thinking about a cookie). They found that children as young as 3 years old could distinguish between real and mental entities. In a different study in which 3- and 4-year-olds were questioned about the differences between a rock, a person, and a doll, it was found that the children understood that people are alive but rocks are not (Gelman, Spelke, & Meck, 1983).

Children are also able to distinguish between appearances and reality. Flavell, Green, & Flavell (1986) found that 3-year-old children understood the difference between the apparent identity of an object (e.g., a rock) and its real identity (e.g., a sponge shaped like a rock).

Understanding of Number   Research has also questioned Piaget's view that young children are limited to gross perceptual information in determining number. Hudson (1983) presented kindergarten-aged children with drawings of two sets of related objects such as squirrels and nuts, birds and worms, and kids and bikes. In all of the drawings there were fewer nuts, worms, and bikes than squirrels, birds, or kids. The children were tested using the following two types of questions: "Here are some squirrels and here are some nuts. How many more squirrels than nuts are there?" and "Here are some birds and here are some worms. Suppose the birds all race over, and each one tries to get a worm. Will every bird get a worm? How many birds won't get a worm?" The children were much more successful in establishing correspondence between numbers when they were asked the "won't get" questions. The standard question of "how many more than" was misunderstood by the kindergarten-aged children.

RECAP

During the preoperational stage children acquire the ability to mentally represent objects and events with symbols. The use of symbolic function is prevalent in children's pretend play. Researchers have not supported Piaget's claim that young children do not distinguish between real and mental events. Preoperational thinkers are unable to reverse their thoughts, are egocentric in their perspective, rely heavily on concrete examples, and are unable to shift their focus of attention to more than one aspect or object. Their thinking is dominated by transductive reasoning, or reasoning from the particular to the particular. Children's understanding of concepts of time, number, and classification improves throughout the early childhood period. Numerous researchers have criticized Piaget for underestimating the capabilities of the young child.

INFORMATION PROCESSING

If you were to spend a morning in the company of a bunch of preschool-aged children, you would probably be struck by how much they seemed to comprehend about their world. Because of their teeming curiosity and penchant for asking "Why?" your impression of young children would most likely focus on their abilities to speculate about their world rather than the limitations in their thinking.

However, Piaget's theory of cognitive development underscores the limitations in the way young children make sense of their world. While Piaget has contributed significantly to our understanding of the stages in cognitive functioning, modern developmental psychologists are taking a different and more positive look at cognitive processes in children. Instead of seeking to identify the child's limitations, some researchers are asking, "What capacities do young children have to process information?" In seeking answers, psychologists have studied how children attend to and remember information.

Children's attention is influenced by their interest in the material. As a result, most children's books are colorfully designed.

Attention   As any parent or preschool teacher will tell you, as children grow their abilities to pay attention increases. Whereas 3-year-olds are easily distracted, 6-year-olds can focus their attention on a game or book for 20 to 30 minutes. In addition, the way children look at things becomes more efficient. Older children learn to focus on relevant or important features of a task and to ignore the irrelevant ones (Lane & Pearson, 1982). As a result, older children generally need less time to select important information. Furthermore, older children are better at selecting information because they seem to have developed strategies to guide their selections.

In a study by Elaine Vurpillot (1968), children were given pictures of house windows to compare. As Figure 5–4 shows, some pairs of windows in each house are the same, and some pairs of windows are different. The children were asked whether the pairs of houses were the same or different. Vurpillot evaluated the way in which the children arrived at their answers: By measuring the reflections in their eyes, she could tell what they were looking at, how long, and in what

FIGURE 5–4

A pair of different houses (top row) and a pair of identical houses (bottom row) used in Vurpillot's study of children's attention.

sequence. She found that children under the age of 6 were not very efficient or accurate in their scanning of the windows. They did not examine all features of the windows, whereas older children were more complete and systematic in their visual scanning.

Memory   Infants and young children are active processors of information. Their skill and efficiency in selecting what information to attend to increases with age. So too does their ability to remember the information they have acquired. Memory is an important cognitive skill that actually involves two different processes.

working memory
Temporary storage of information that is available for several seconds to several minutes (also called short-term memory).

secondary memory
A more permanent storage of information, which includes items that have been transferred from the working memory (also known as long-term memory).

Working memory, also known as short-term memory, refers to the temporary storage of information that is available for only several seconds to several minutes. For example, telephone numbers are usually remembered only for the short time it takes to dial the number. **Secondary** (or long-term) **memory** accommodates a more permanent storage of information, and includes items that have been transferred from working memory. For example, the theme of a movie or book or the main characters in a play would be items that might be transferred to long-term memory.

There are several ways to assess memory capacity in children. Recognition memory is measured by presenting various stimuli and asking the child to pick out the ones he or she has seen before. The second way to assess memory is to ask the child to recall specific information, such as the name of Rachel's nursery school teacher. A recall memory task is much more difficult than a recognition task. For an item to be recalled, it must be first stored in secondary memory and then later retrieved. This is a more complex process than recognition, which simply requires matching what was seen or known before with what is presented.

Infants and young children are fairly good at recognizing familiar stimuli, especially visual stimuli (Fagan, 1982). On recognition tasks, 2-year-olds average 81% correct and 4-year-olds 92% correct. However, on a recall task, 2-year-olds remembered only an average 23% of the items and 4-year-olds an average 35% of items (Myers & Perlmutter, 1978). Recall is harder than recognition at all ages. Part of the difficulty for young children is due to the fact that they do not classify items for memory storage, thus making it more difficult to remember them. Older children and adults realize that in order to remember a lot of information, they have to group items and then develop a way to rehearse and memorize the groups. In short, younger children have more trouble because they are not as efficient in processing material for memory.

Most of the earlier research on recall memory involved verbal responses in which children were asked to recall objects or words. A 1948 study of Soviet children found that children younger than 4 do not have deliberate strategies for remembering things (Istomina, 1975). Furthermore, the Soviet children had better recall of items in a play situation than for tasks in which they were told to remember something.

The same study was later repeated using American children (Weissberg & Paris, 1986). In one condition children were asked to play a game in which they were to run an errand to a pretend grocery store and buy five items. In a second condition children were asked to remember five words in a lesson-like setting. The American children, aged 3 to 7 years, all recalled more words when they were presented as a lesson than when the task was embedded in a shopping game. Of course, with age, children improved in their recall. The reasons that children of all ages did better on recall in the lesson setting was that they rehearsed and repeated the five items more deliberately than did children in the game setting. Thus, Istomina's findings were not supported by later study.

The American study is especially interesting to a lifespan researcher because it compares the performance of Soviet children in 1948 (before children's television programs and extensive preschool education programs) with that of American preschoolers in the 1980s. Are the improvements in memory due to culture? To differences in history? Or to differences in context? Weissberg and Paris reasoned that children in the game setting were distracted from the memory task by the objects and people involved in the game and hence did not recall as much as the children who were deliberately trying to remember the five items.

When my son Adam was just a toddler, I was surprised to discover that he could describe our family dog who died when Adam was barely a year old. Recent studies on the memory capacities of very young children suggest that infants as young as several months can recall specific and repeat actions such as playing with a toy in a novel way (Bauer & Mandler, 1992). Other researchers such as Katherine Nelson (1990, 1993) are studying the ways in which young children recall special events in their lives. Three-year-olds remember special events such as the day the hurricane struck, their first pony ride, or a special birthday party; the more unusual the event, the greater detail is recalled.

RECAP

Children's ability to process information increases with maturity and experience. Older children are better at selecting important features of a task and sustaining their attention over time than younger children. Similarly, children improve their efficiency in recognizing and recalling information stored in both short- and long-term memory.

LANGUAGE DEVELOPMENT

Have you ever tried to learn a second language? If so, you can appreciate the ease with which young children seem to acquire their first language. Fluency in another language requires learning an entirely new vocabulary, the rules for putting the words together in a sentence, pronunciation, and comprehension of the spoken version of the language. Some adults find this task to be the most difficult they have tried; many never even attempt it. Yet for young children acquiring a language seems to come naturally.

Any experienced traveler will tell you that being able to speak the language of a country makes the journey much easier and more interesting. Likewise, children's mastery of their native language opens many conceptual doors. It allows them to consider objects, people, and events beyond their immediate experience; language skills let them communicate their needs and manipulate people to help them achieve their goals. Language also provides children with a wealth of stories and songs that delight and inform them for a lifetime. It is through language that cultures and traditions are maintained.

STRUCTURE OF LANGUAGE

phoneme
The basic unit of sound in a given language.

Language has five components, which are listed in Table 5–4. The first element involves the production of the basic units of sound, or **phonemes.** Human beings are capable of producing sounds with their mouth and vocal cords and of discriminating among sounds through hearing. Each language is produced by a combination of a specific set of phonemes. In the English language there are 45 phonemes; other languages use different numbers of phonemes to produce the sounds specific to the language.

THE STRUCTURE OF LANGUAGE	
COMPONENT	**CHARACTERISTIC**
Phoneme	The basic unit of sound
Morpheme	The basic unit of meaningful sound
Syntax	The rules for combining morphemes and words to form clauses and sentences
Semantics	The understanding of the meaning of words and sentences
Pragmatics	The rules for expressing language in a social context

TABLE 5–4

morpheme
The smallest unit of meaningful sound in a given language.

Within each language community phonemes are combined and arbitrarily assigned meaning by its users—the second component of language. The smallest unit of meaningful sound is called a **morpheme.** Thus the sound "Ma" when repeated becomes "MaMa," which means Mother in English and several other languages. A word is one example of a morpheme. Endings and prefixes such as *s, ed, ing, pre,* and *un* are also examples of morphemes, since they add meaning to the root word. Many words are composed of more than one morpheme. The word breakfast, for example, is composed of two morphemes, break and fast, each of which carries a separate meaning. The meanings of the utterances of a language have to be learned within the language culture.

syntax
The rules of a language by which words and morphemes are combined to form larger clauses and sentences.

Another language component is **syntax,** or the rules by which words and morphemes are combined to form larger clauses and sentences. Syntax is sometimes referred to as the grammar of the language. Each language has its own set of rules that a person must learn in order to understand and be able to produce the language.

semantics
The study of the meanings of words and sentences within a language.

The fourth component of language, **semantics,** refers to the rules governing the meanings of words and sentences. When people are stuck for the "right" word to convey a particular meaning, they are struggling to find the semantically correct term. For example, consider the two sentences: "The writer dragged the pen across the paper" and "The writer slid the pen across the paper." Both of these sentences are syntactically similar and correct, yet they convey very different meanings. Likewise, the sentence "The elephant spoke softly and carried a big stick" would be interpreted either as a joke or as a misprint because the meaning is not clear. As far as we know, elephants do not speak.

pragmatics
The rules for using the language in a social context.

The last component of language is **pragmatics,** the rules for using the language in a social context. This includes learning how to interpret the intended meaning of a grammatical statement through the intonation and gestures of the speaker. For example, in grammatical terms, "Have you washed your hands?" is a question that requires either a "yes" or a "no" response. The intended meaning, however, is really a demand: "Wash your hands."

LANGUAGE ACQUISITION

How do children learn language? The process is a gradual one beginning in the early months of life and developing through the many verbal and nonverbal

		AVERAGE NUMBER OF WORDS UNDERSTOOD	AVERAGE NUMBER OF SPOKEN WORDS	AVERAGE LENGTH OF SPOKEN SENTENCES
AGE	MILESTONE			
Birth	Startles to sharp noises	0	0	0
3–6 months	Interest in sounds, plays with saliva, responds to voices; first words are understood; first instructions understood	3	0–5	1
6–9 months	Babbles with a string of consonants	12	10–15	1
9–12 months	Imitates sounds and comprehends words	50	20–25	2
1 year	Says first words clearly	100	20–25	2
15 months	Speaks two-word sentences	>300	200–275	3
18 months	Says first sentence	>750	400–450	3
21 months	Proficient at naming things	>800	>500	3
2 years	Two-word phrases are common	>1,000	800–900	3
3 years	Grammar similar to informal adult speech	>1,000	>900	>3

MILESTONES IN LANGUAGE DEVELOPMENT DURING THE FIRST 3 YEARS

TABLE 5–5

Source: Adapted with permission from *Educating the Infant and Toddler* by B. White, 1988, Lexington, MA: Lexington Books.

exchanges infants have with their caregivers. Early cooing and babbling is replaced by one-word utterances at 1 year of age. In just a short period of time between ages 2 and 6, remarkable events occur: Children not only increase their vocabulary to an average of between 8,000 and 14,000 words (Carey, 1977), but they also master the basic grammatical rules or syntax of their native language. Children in different language communities around the world appear to progress through similar identifiable stages in their acquisition of language skills. Table 5–5 lists the major language-development milestones in the first 3 years of life.

Semantic Development   One day the toddler is delighting relatives with one word recitations—usually "Mama," "Dada," or "bye-bye"—but before long the size of the child's vocabulary has grown to hundreds of words. The rate at which children understand word and sentence meaning varies during the early childhood period. Early in their semantic development children slowly add new words to their vocabularies, but by the age of 3 they rapidly acquire new words (see Table 5–5). **Active vocabulary** refers to the words the child can actually say and use, while **passive** (or receptive) **vocabulary** refers to the words that are understood, as indicated by the child's actions in response to the words. Passive vocabularies are usually larger than active vocabularies, even for adults, since recognition occurs earlier than production.

active vocabulary
Words that a child actually says and uses.

passive vocabulary
Words that are understood, as indicated by the child's actions in response to the words.

Between the ages of 2 and 6, children's vocabularies increase dramatically. This enables them to communicate more effectively with others.

The first words children learn are largely used to represent people, objects (nouns), actions (verbs such as "jump," "eat," and "go") and states (modifiers such as "fat," "dirty," and "there"). Usually concrete, the words refer to immediate actions or objects in the child's experience. Later, prepositions (such as "in" and "on") emerge to indicate locations. Personal and possessive pronouns (such as "I," "me," or "mine") also appear at age 2.

Gradually, with practice and exposure to new words, children increase the types of words they use. Sometimes the words are used to label different classes of objects children have mentally created. For example, when Anand was 2 he referred to all gray-haired men as "Grampa." This use of one word to symbolize a larger class of objects than normally intended by adults is called **overextension.** This may result from the child limiting the number of properties used to define the class (e.g., gray hair and male for Grampa) as opposed to the larger number used by adults. Other researchers believe that many overextensions may represent the child's early use of metaphors; that is, using figurative language to draw an analogy to another object or person (Gardner, 1974; Mendelson, Robinson, Gardner, & Winner, 1984). Thus, Anand may be using the term "Grampa" metaphorically and not actually believe that gray-haired men are the same as his grandfather.

Young children also use words in overrestrictive fashion when they refer to a smaller set of properties than adults would use for the same word. This phenomenon is called **underextension.** For example, Rachel uses the word *blanket* to refer to the small, yellow blanket she regularly takes to bed with her. However, she does not use the word **blanket** to refer to any other blanket.

By about 2 years of age children communicate by combining two words. Linguists and psychologists debate whether the production of two-word strings represents the child's first sentence. By combining two words children are able to express a much wider variety of thoughts (see Table 5–6). For example, "Dada

overextension

The use of one word to symbolize a larger class of objects than what adults normally intend with a word.

underextension

Children's use of words in an overrestrictive fashion when they refer to a smaller set of properties than adults would for the same word.

MEANINGS CONVEYED IN TWO-WORD UTTERANCES

MEANING	EXAMPLE
Identification	"See doggie"
Location	"House there"
Repetition	"More milk"
Nonexistence	"Allgone cookie"
Negation	"Not doggie"
Possession	"Mommy hat"
Attribution	"Big ball"
Agent action	"Baby run"
Agent object	"Daddy book"
Agent location	"Sit chair"
Action object	"Put cup"
Question	"Where doll?"

TABLE 5–6

Source: From "Children and language: They learn the same way all around the world," by D. Slobin, July 18, 1972, *Psychology Today.* Reprinted with permission.

telegraphic speech
Abbreviated speech containing only the most informative words (similar to the sentence structure used in sending a telegram).

byebye" may represent a shortened version of "Daddy has gone away." Two-word utterances such as this are referred to as **telegraphic speech** since they resemble the abbreviated form used when sending a telegram.

Even though two-word utterances express greater meaning, they do not conform to the grammatical rules that apply to sentences. Thus, it is difficult to determine whether children have acquired the rules of syntax. They seem to appreciate the importance of word order (as in "Dada byebye" to mean "Daddy has gone" and "Byebye Dada" to mean "Goodbye, Daddy"), but do not use it consistently. Furthermore, depending on the context, the same two-word utterance can have entirely different meanings. For example, "mommy's sock" was used by a child to refer to the mother's sock and in another context to refer to the mother putting the sock on the child (Bloom, 1970).

Word Meanings
Four-year-old Anand learned about ten new words a day in Hindi, and almost as many new English words. Most children between the ages of 2 and 6 acquire an average of eight new words a day. This is a remarkable feat considering the complexity of the learning task. Learning a word requires that children associate the sound of a particular word or label with a concept. For example, a child who has a pet dog will use the word "dog" to refer to the pet; "dog" may also be used to refer to other pets that are dogs. This connection is quite specific to the animal as a whole and not to events, objects, or activities associated

with dogs. For example, children do not use the word "dog" to refer to a dog's tail (part of the body), or to the dog's leash (object used with dogs) even though they may have heard the term "dog" used in connection with tail and leash.

A question asked by many researchers (Merriman & Bowman, 1989; Waxman & Kosowski, 1990) is, "How do children learn specific word meanings so quickly and easily?" One answer is that children have certain cognitive biases that lead them to prefer some word meanings over others. As discussed in Chapter 4, the first types of words children produce are nouns—thus expressing a noun-category bias. When a new and unfamiliar word is presented as a noun in a sentence, children are prone to understand this word in terms of category relations (Waxman & Kosowski, 1990). For example, if you say to a 2- or 3-year-old, "This is a koobo," they are likely to understand a "koobo" as an object because it is used as a noun in the sentence.

Children also tend to construct mutually exclusive or nonoverlapping referents or attributes for different words. For example, the word "cow" is separate or mutually exclusive from the word "horse" or "farm." Through a process of elimination, children learn the meanings of new words by matching them to objects or referents they do not already know. Thus, if children were shown a picture of a donkey (an unfamiliar word) and a cow (a word they know) and were asked to point to the donkey, they would most likely point correctly to the donkey (and demonstrate a knowledge of the word "donkey"). By process of elimination, the word "donkey" would be assigned to the object they cannot name (Taylor & Gelman, 1988).

FOCUS ON CULTURE

Words allow us to communicate our experiences to others. They also reflect shared cultural experiences. For example, in the Eskimo language at least four words are used to describe snow—a central part of Eskimo life—compared to the single English word. Linguist Benjamin Whorf (1956) argued that the concepts and words used within a language culture influence the speaker's ability to perceive the environment. Thus, Eskimos perceive four different types of snow because they have the appropriate words within their language. Other linguists disagree with Whorf's theory about the causal relationship between language and perception.

Syntactical Development   As children move beyond two-word utterances to produce longer strings of words, they display a growing mastery of the grammatical rules within a language. Most children (and adults) acquire rules of syntax without actually being able to articulate these rules. For example, a 4-year-old can invert the auxiliary verb in the sentence "Daddy is sleeping" to produce the question "Is Daddy sleeping?" without being able to state the grammatical rule.

After a period in which they learn the rules that govern sentence production, children tend to overuse these rules and frequently produce new, linguistically incorrect combinations of words. This process is called **overregulation,** because the child is attempting to make language more regular than it actually is. For example, Rachel has learned to add an *s* to the end of a word to indicate more than one. She engages in overregulation when she pluralizes *mouse* and *foot* to produce *mouses* and *foots*. Such "errors" indicate that the child is learning the grammatical rules; their exceptions (such as *mice* or *feet*) take longer to learn.

overregulation
The child's tendency to overuse the rules of a language to produce new and nongrammatical combinations of words.

Even though children may have demonstrated correct usage of a rule (such as the rule for creating plural words) in the past, they seem to regress to nongrammatical usage when they learn the rule for producing words. Thus, before Rachel learned the rule about adding an *s*, she used the words *mice* and *feet*. Parents and preschool teachers may be concerned about their children's seeming regression in language development. However, this is only a short-term loss in grammatical fluency that seems to be part of the process by which children acquire more sophisticated language skills. Moreover, overregularization is not very common. After analyzing 11,521 irregular past tense utterances by 83 children, Marcus and his colleagues (1992) concluded that overregularization errors occurred in about 2.5% of the utterances. By about age 7, most children have learned the rules—including their exceptions—of their language and no longer tend to overregularize.

Children approximately 3½ are able to reorder the words of a sentence to express a new idea. Children produce longer sentences, and they can construct a negative sentence or ask a question by rearranging the order of the words in a sentence (e.g., "Daddy is not eating" or "Why is the baby eating?"). In the earlier stages of sentence construction, the child conveyed a question or negation by intonation or by adding a word to the front or end of the sentence, as in "Baby eat?" or "No daddy eat."

transformational rules
Rules that allow the child to translate the basic meaning of a sentence to make it grammatically correct.

In order to construct negations and questions, the child must learn **transformational rules,** which are used to translate the basic meaning of a sentence to make it grammatically correct. For example, the rule for negation involves moving a negative word such as *no* or *not* to a position in front of the verb. Yes/no questions are created by either moving the first auxiliary verb of a sentence to the initial position or, if there is no auxiliary verb, adding one. For example, "Baby is sleeping" becomes "Is baby sleeping?"; or "Anne runs" becomes "Does Anne run?" *Wh* questions are formed by adding a *wh* word such as *why, what, where,* or *when* to a yes/no question—for example, "Why does Anne run?" and "Where is baby sleeping?" Children learn the transformational rule for yes/no questions before they learn the rule for *wh* questions.

By age 5, children also learn how to use the active and passive voices. They have learned the basic subject-verb-object (SVO) order of an active sentence but have difficulty interpreting a passive-voice sentence. For example, consider the following two sentences.

1. The dog chased the cat. (active voice)

2. The cat was chased by the dog. (passive voice)

When asked to select a picture depicting sentence 2 (Bellugi, 1970), 3-year-olds selected the picture of a cat chasing the dog. The passive voice violates the normal S-V-O order in a sentence, and hence the children are confused. By 5 years of age, children are able to interpret passive-voice sentences.

Children learn increasingly complex and sophisticated sentence structures as they get older. Their utterances become longer, and they begin to combine sentences together and embed parts of sentences in others. For example, a child may say, "My teddy that Nana gave me is brown and fat," thus constructing a sentence containing two ideas: (1) My Nana gave me a teddy, and (2) My teddy is brown and fat. By about age 6, children are able to construct simple compound sentences using the conjunction *and:* "Mary hit the ball and Johnny ran."

THEORIES OF LANGUAGE ACQUISITION

At least four different theories have been offered by psychologists and psycholinguists to answer the question as to how language develops (see Table 5–7). One theory, the **behavioral approach,** emphasizes reinforcement and imitation as the basic processes for acquiring language skills (Whitehurst & Valdez-Menchaca, 1988). Skinner (1957) believed that language is a form of behavior that is acquired in the same way as all other behaviors: through its consequences (reward and punishment). If a little girl accidentally says something approximating the word "cookie" and receives a cookie, or says "Dada" and receives a hug from her father, she is more likely to continue her language efforts. By imitating her parents' speech she receives further encouragement.

The behavioral approach has its limitations. Although the quality of the child's language environment is an important factor in language development, it does not explain how children can and do say things they have never heard before. The 2½-year-old is likely to make up sentences such as "Daddy hurted self" and "Kitty goed home," which are clearly not the result of pure imitation but instead reflect overregularization. Furthermore, most parents reward children for the truthfulness of their statements rather than their grammatical correctness (R. Brown, 1970). In response to "Kitty goed home," the parent is likely to respond with agreement if, in fact, the cat went home.

Another theory, the **nativist** (or rationalist) **approach,** views language development as a natural, biological consequence of physical maturation. One advocate of this view is Chomsky (1968), who maintains that humans are born with an innate tendency to acquire language, just as they possess an innate capacity to learn to walk. Chomsky believes that all languages share certain basic structural characteristics. Even though languages differ on the surface (e.g., different words, word orders) they have a common universal grammar that consists of rules and principles for generating sentences and meaning.

Likewise, people have inherited the biological structures (namely the central nervous system) to process these common linguistic features. Chomsky called the

behavioral approach
A theory that emphasizes reinforcement and imitation as the basic process for acquiring language skills.

nativist approach
A theory that views language development as a natural, biological consequence of physical maturation.

THEORY	PERSPECTIVE
Behavioral	Language is acquired through reinforcement and imitation.
Nativist	Language is a maturational event guided by the LAD and the maturing brain.
Interactionist	Language is both a biological and cognitive event that is influenced by experience.
Cognitive	Language is a direct result of cognitive maturity.

THEORIES OF LANGUAGE DEVELOPMENT

TABLE 5–7

mental blueprint for acquiring language the *language acquisition device,* or LAD. The LAD contains a universal grammar composed of rules that apply to all languages. It processes linguistic information and helps the child gain an understanding of the vocabulary and rules of spoken language. Chomsky argues that without this inborn capability children would be unable to process the sentences they hear. The LAD permits the acquisition of grammatical rules that allow the child to translate and later produce sentences. As the brain matures, children acquire greater skill in understanding and producing language.

This view of the innate capacity for language has been supported by Lenneberg (1967), who suggests that language development parallels neurological changes that occur as a result of maturation. He points to the fact that children of all cultures learn language at about the same age and make the same kinds of errors in their language production. Lenneberg points to the changes in the organization of the brain around 3 years of age that aid children in their ability to understand as well as produce language. The rapidness with which children master their language between 2 and 3 years of age is hard to explain without reference to changes in children's overall neurological capacity to process information.

While Chomsky's theory has influenced how language development is viewed, his ideas have not been universally accepted. LAD is based on the assumption of a universal grammar learned by all children; yet despite efforts by linguists, this universal grammar has not been proven. Language development appears to take longer than it should if it were primarily under biological or maturational control. For example, the use of the passive voice does not typically occur until well into middle childhood.

interactionist approach
A theory that focuses on the ways in which children learn language rules based on experience.

Indeed, the nativist approach seems to ignore children's experiences and cognitive capabilities. Theorists using the **interactionist approach** (Berko, 1958; Brown, 1973; Ervin, 1964) have accepted the nativist view of language development but have focused on the ways in which children learn the rules of the language. These theorists reject the empirical view that the child acquires language simply by imitation and practice. They argue that the child who correctly imitates an adult by saying "The kitty went home" does not necessarily display a comprehension of grammatical rules. However, when saying "Kitty goed home," the child has demonstrated mastery of a specific grammatical rule: Add *ed* to form the past tense of a verb. Interactionists focus their study of language development on the way children acquire concepts and meanings attached to words. Although innate biological mechanisms such as a LAD may guide language development, interactionists place equal importance on the role of experience.

cognitive approach
A view of language acquisition that language is a direct result of cognitive development.

A third view of language acquisition is called the **cognitive approach** because it holds that language is a direct result of cognitive development. Piaget (1926) considered the child's ability to represent actions mentally as the necessary foundation for language. Once having formed a mental scheme, the child can apply a linguistic label to it. In fact, symbolic representation emerges at the end of the sensorimotor period at 1½ to 2 years, the age at which children begin to master language.

Vygotsky (1962) presented a different view. He believed that thought and language originate from two separate roots, a preintellectual stage and a prelinguistic stage. At about age 2 these two lines of development meet and language and thought merge. At this point what children think influences what they want to say. Further, language helps them arrange their thoughts and communicate them.

Vygotsky believed that thinking is an activity that depends on both inner speech (talking to oneself) and overt speech (talking with other people). This union of language and thought helps explain children's rapid use of new words at a time when their curiosity about people and things is so intense. It seems that overnight a child has learned to talk and has so much to say. While Piaget believed that language is a manifestation of cognitive development, Vygotsky believed that language and cognition develop quite separately.

BILINGUALISM: ARE TWO LANGUAGES BETTER THAN ONE?

Today many children grow up in families and communities in which two or more languages are spoken. Some children, even in the United States where English is the primary language, are exposed to several languages and can selectively speak in any of them. For example, Anand responds in English to his father and speaks Hindi to his mother.

Prior to 1962 many American parents, teachers, and researchers thought that exposing children to two languages would confuse them and delay their language acquisition. But Peal and Lambert (1962) shifted the view of bilingualism from a negative to a positive one. Their research contradicted previous studies claiming that bilingual children did not perform as well on intelligence tests as children who spoke one language. In fact, Peal and Lambert found that bilingual children had *higher* cognitive abilities than monolingual children. Their sample included "balanced" bilingual children—that is, children who knew two languages equally well. Earlier studies compared monolingual children with bilingual children who knew very little English but had greater familiarity with a second language. Also, it is important to remember that differences in cognitive abilities between monolinguals and bilinguals may reflect differences in social variables (such as socioeconomic and educational levels of parents) as well as differences in language learning.

What are the cognitive advantages to young children in learning two languages? Research has shown that bilingual children who acquired their second language at an early age were more flexible in their use of labels for words (Oren, 1981). Bilingual children are also better at noticing grammatical and semantic errors (Galambos & Goldin-Meadow, 1990; Ricciardelli, 1992). Compared to monolinguals, bilingual children are more creative storytellers but have smaller vocabularies in both languages (Doyle, Champagne, & Segalowitz, 1978).

Vygotsky (1962) believed that people will fully understand their own language only when they can contrast it to another language. Bilingual children learn that there is not a fixed relationship between words and the world around them—words and sentences change depending on the language system being spoken. Some researchers (Diaz, 1985; Hakuta, 1987) believe that bilingualism helps children learn about languages. They become more flexible in thinking because they learn to see the world from two different perspectives and from two different cultures. They learn that language is arbitrary, that the name of an object can be changed so long as other people agree to rename the object. For some children learning two languages may also add to their sense of self-esteem and help them learn about their cultural heritage. Thus it appears that learning two languages simultaneously can prove to be an asset rather than a liability for children.

Research Perspective

IS THERE AN OPTIMAL TIME TO LEARN A LANGUAGE?

Most children rapidly acquire the basics of their native language between the ages of 2 and 4 years. Some linguists argue that this is evidence for a critical period for language acquisition, a time during which children are most likely to acquire the words and rules of the language they hear spoken. Children, therefore, who have had little or no exposure to a language during this period would not be expected to master language very easily, if at all. Other theorists argue that a language can be learned at any time in development, not just in the early years. The issue of the existence of a critical period for language development is difficult to resolve through sys-

tematic research, since it would be ethically impossible to experimentally restrict a child from an opportunity to learn language. However, clinical case studies often present data that shed light on the issue. The case of Genie provides an example.

Genie was born in 1957 in Los Angeles. When she was 13½ years old, she was found and identified as a totally unsocialized "wild child" (Curtiss, 1977). For most of her life she had been tied naked to a potty chair, hidden away from all people. Her father hated the child from birth and was himself seriously disturbed. He thought Genie was mentally retarded because she was slow in walking, so at age 20 months he locked her in a small room, strapped her to the potty chair, and ordered that no family member talk to her. He would bark at her like a dog and beat her if she made any noises or sounds. Her blind mother was terrified by her husband and made no attempt to help Genie until after the father died, which

was shortly after the mother applied for public assistance and Genie came to the attention of social welfare workers.

Genie was immediately hospitalized. Even though she was well into puberty, she was so malnourished that she weighed only 59 pounds. She did not talk and the only sounds she did make were animal-like. She could not stand or walk alone and was not toilet trained. Doctors at the hospital were not very optimistic about her ability to develop normally after such a long and hideously deprived experience.

After a stay in the hospital, Genie went to live in a foster home. Over a period of 6 years following her rescue she made remarkable progress in her ability to use language to communicate. Within a short time after hearing language spoken, she began to imitate words and gradually she acquired a small vocabulary in much the same way that a 1-year-old normally begins to use words. Within a year after she began special

RECAP

Units of sound, or phonemes, acquire meaning when used to communicate in a given language. These meaningful units, or morphemes, are combined into phrases and sentences according to a set of agreed upon grammatical rules—the syntax of a language. The meanings of words and their expressions vary from one culture to another and must be learned. Children gradually acquire and use words during the early childhood period through exposure and practice. Despite a bias for learning treatment, she started to use simple two-word sentences, at first using only nouns such as "little dog" and then later including verbs, such as "eat cookie." Gradually she learned to produce longer sentences.

One interesting aspect of Genie's language production is that she acquired language in much the same sequence that young children do when learning language. For example, she made the same errors of overregulation, acquired nouns before verbs, and used "no" at the beginning of a sentence to form a negative.

However, Genie never did advance beyond the level of a 5-year-old in her language acquisition. At age 25 she was speaking in telegraphic sentences. She was not able to use negative auxiliary verbs correctly (*isn't, haven't, hasn't*), and she had great difficulty forming past-tense sentences. Furthermore, she could not use personal pronouns, did not comprehend the difference between active and passive voice, and did not spontaneously ask questions.

Genie's case study offers support for environmental and biological views of language acquisition. She contradicted the belief that language cannot develop after puberty, casting some doubts on the idea of a critical period for language acquisition. However, her mastery of the language was clearly deficient, suggesting that her early abuse and linguistic, physical, and emotional deprivation severely harmed her development. The fact that the early steps in Genie's language development were so much like young children's suggests that they may be biologically determined. Genie's story also suggests that in order for language to develop fully, children must be exposed to language and encouraged to use it at an earlier age than puberty.

A different approach to studying the existence of a critical period for the acquisition of language is to compare the ease with which deaf people learn sign language. Sign language has similar components to spoken language; meaning is communicated by a series of gestures and facial expressions that are combined according to a set of "grammatical" rules. But, unlike people who speak a language, deaf people vary in terms of their first exposure to sign language. Some deaf children learn sign language early in life, while others are not exposed to it until they are well into school or even adolescence. If there is critical period in which language can best be learned, you would expect to find performance differences among deaf signers based on the age at which they first learned the language. And in fact, a number of such studies have shown that children who learn sign language at an early age are better "signers" than those who learn it at a later age— even better than their deaf parents who taught them to sign (Johnson & Newport, 1989; Newport, 1991).

certain types of words, children make errors of extension in the learning process. The acquisition of grammatical rules and mastery of complex sentences increases with age. A variety of theories attempt to explain the sequence and timing of language acquisition. Children who learn more than one language do not differ in their language skills from monolingual speakers; in fact, bilingualism may prove to be more of an asset to them.

PRESCHOOL AND DAY-CARE PROGRAMS

When my son Adam was about 2½ years old, I began my career as a college professor. I was also faced with the challenge of finding adequate day care at a time when very little was available. Fortunately, I found a combined day care and nursery school program with flexible hours and a competent and caring staff to meet my son's needs.

In 1990, 53% of U.S. mothers with children under the age of 1 and 60% of mothers with children under the age of 3 were employed outside the home (Children's Defense Fund, 1992). An estimated 5.1 million children under the age of 6 were enrolled in day-care centers (Hoffreth, Brayfield, Diech, & Holcomb, 1990). Divorce, separation, and economic changes in the family have resulted in more parents leaving the day-to-day care of their children to other people. Enrollment in day care has also increased for children whose mothers who are not employed; in 1990, 33% of families with a mother who was not employed outside of the home used some sort of day-care program for their preschool-aged children (Hofferth et al., 1990) (see Table 5–8).

TYPES OF PROGRAMS

Preschool programs in the United States can be divided into two broad categories: nursery school and day care. Choosing a program is important to both parents and children and depends upon the individual needs of the family and the availability of community programs.

PRIMARY FORM OF CHILD CARE FOR ALL CHILDREN UNDER AGE 5

TYPE OF CHILD CARE	TOTAL PERCENTAGE	EMPLOYED MOTHER (PERCENTAGE)	NONEMPLOYED MOTHER (PERCENTAGE)
Center	20.5	26.5	14.7
Parent	46.3	29.9	65.2
Relative (child's home)	5.9	6.3	5.2
Relative (other home)	8.7	11.3	5.5
In-home provider	3.0	3.7	2.2
Family day care	10.7	18.6	2.6
Other*	4.9	3.6	4.6
Total	100	100	100

TABLE 5–8

*Includes children enrolled in activities or lessons, and those cared for by their mothers while working.
Source: *National Child Care Survey, 1990*, p. 59, by S.L. Hofferth, A. Brayfield, S. Deich, and P. Holcomb, 1991. Washington, DC: Urban Institute Press. Copyright 1991 by the Urban Institute and the National Association for the Education of Young Children.

With increased numbers of U.S. mothers in the workforce, more young children attend some type of nursery school or day-care program.

Nursery Schools   Most nursery schools generally offer a program of educational enrichment for children who have reached age 3 and have been toilet-trained. Children typically attend nursery school 3 to 5 half-days a week. While the aims of nursery schools vary depending on the philosophy of the school, most nursery schools include preparation for kindergarten and elementary school as part of their curricula. They emphasize teaching appropriate social skills and enriching the child's intellectual experiences.

Most nursery school teachers are college-educated and trained in child development. Some nursery school programs, called cooperative nursery schools, are operated by parents who take turns working in the school either as assistants to the teachers or by building or repairing school equipment or facilities. However, a half-day, part-time, or cooperative nursery school schedule may be practically impossible to manage for working parents. As an alternative, many parents turn to day care for their preschool-age children.

Day Care   Day-care programs are designed to provide care for children for the entire day, on a year-round basis. Three types of day care are typical. In *home day care,* children receive care in their own home by someone other than a relative. Typically, the setting is not child oriented. There are no special activity areas, few planned activities, and little—if any—structured programming. The daily activities are varied and informal. Usually there is an older adult sitter who takes care of one or two children, so the adult-to-child ratio is quite high. As a result, the child in this type of day care has very little interaction with other children. Most children whose parents both work outside the home are cared for in their own home, either by another parent or by a relative (Hofferth et al., 1990).

Family day care involves small groups of up to six children in the private home of another person. About 18% of all employed women in the United States use family day care for their children. People who run family day-care centers usually are younger than home care sitters and lack professional child care experience (Clarke-Stewart & Gruber, 1984). Children in family day-care centers (typically homes that have been rearranged with more playrooms, etc.) have contact with other children, who usually come from similar ethnic and socioeconomic backgrounds.

The third type of program is the *day-care center,* a licensed facility providing care to 13 or more children on an all-day basis, 5 or more days a week, year-round. In all types of day care, children's ages range from newborn to 13 years, although most of the children are of preschool age. Day-care centers are used by about 26% of working mothers with preschool children in the United States (Hoffreth et al., 1990). The day-care center is child oriented both in its activities and its physical facilities. In many ways day-care centers are similar to nursery schools. The teachers are usually trained in child care, there are several children, and more than one adult is involved in the care of the children. The major difference presented by day-care is the time that children spend in the center: an average of 8 hours every day, compared to fewer than 3 hours a day in the nursery school.

When most of today's college students were babies, they were cared for in their homes by their mothers. Today, the situation has changed dramatically. Preschool programs and day care are no longer seen as unusual or a last resort for working parents. Instead, these programs are viewed by many as a necessity for the economic survival of the family, especially when single parents are involved. Some nonemployed parents want to enroll their children in preschool programs because of the cognitive and social benefits associated with high quality programs (Silverstein, 1991). Because of this demand for preschool programs, parents and educators are concerned about their long-term effects on children's development (Belsky & Rovine, 1988; Belsky, Lerner, & Spanier, 1984; Blum, 1983; Etaugh, 1980; Fraiberg, 1977; Kagan, Kearsley, & Zelazo, 1978; Ruopp, Travers, Glantz, & Coelen, 1979; Scarr, 1984; Silverstein, 1991; Zigler & Gorden, 1982).

Evaluating Preschool Programs

American researchers began to focus their attention on preschool and day-care programs in the mid-1970s, when their enrollment increased dramatically. Initially, the research focused on one issue: Is day care bad for children? (Belsky, 1984). To answer this question, researchers studied the effects of day-care and preschool programs on children's intellectual, social, and emotional development. The popular belief at the time was that the home was the best place to raise young children and the mother was the best person to do it. However, most of the studies found little evidence of negative effects on children enrolled in programs outside the home.

Building on the conclusion that day care is not bad for children, current research on day care is directed toward determining under what conditions children fare best in day care (Silverstein, 1991). However, studying day care's effects on development and identifying the necessary conditions for quality care present some difficulties. For one thing, most of the studies conducted on preschool programs have used children enrolled in day care rather than nursery school. Day-care centers tend to have a more regular enrollment, and—since many of them are sponsored by universities—they present easier access to researchers. The conclusions drawn from studying children of college-educated parents, however, may not apply to all children.

Another problem with studying the effects of preschool programs is deciding what behaviors to examine and the duration of the research. Most of the studies look at the immediate or short-term impact of preschool and not its long-term effects. Yet the impact of preschool programs may not be felt immediately, such as the example of the Head Start program.

Begun in the sixties to enrich the disadvantaged child's knowledge of basic skills before enrollment in public school, Head Start programs provided preschool-aged children with experiences of which they were deprived in their home environments: listening to stories; using scissors; playing with blocks, puzzles, and shapes; writing with pencils; playing pretend games; learning songs; and so on. Most of the evaluative studies that compared Head Start children with neighborhood children who were not enrolled in the program found some immediate gains in IQ and other school-related skills. However, these initial gains did not persist when the children entered school. In a large-scale follow-up study, the long-term effects of 14 different programs similar to Head Start were examined. Even though the programs varied in the way they were implemented (e.g., degree of parental involvement, amount of contact with the child), they all had positive long-term effects, some lasting as long as high school (Lazar & Darlington, 1982). Apparently, the impact of Head Start incubated over the intervening years.

The cultural context in which children enter preschool is another important variable to keep in mind when evaluating these programs. In contrast to the United States, many Western European countries have provided quality preschool programs to parents at a nominal cost for many years. In Sweden, for example, about 70% of children under age 4 are enrolled in day-care centers and one third of infants enter day care during their 1st year of life (Andersson, 1992). Furthermore, Swedish children receive high quality care. A longitudinal study of Swedish children found that children who had entered day care during their first year of life received higher teacher ratings on cognitive, social, and emotional competencies when they were 8 and 13 years of age when compared to children who had entered day care at a later age (Andersson, 1992). However, the children who did not participate in day care during their 1st year were able to benefit from the early stimulation characteristic of Swedish infant care programs even though they differed from the group of infants who participated in day care at an earlier age.

EFFECTS ON DEVELOPMENT

As previously mentioned, prior to 1980, most of the research on the developmental effects of preschool programs studied high-quality university-sponsored demonstration programs (Etaugh, 1980). More recently, researchers have extended their study of preschool effects to infants in a variety of nonmaternal care programs. The major concerns have been how day care affects (1) the emotional bond to the mother, (2) the child's cognitive skills, and (3) the development of social skills.

Emotional Bonds   Several studies have examined the attachment behavior of children reared at home with those of children reared in day-care centers. Most of these studies have found that day care does not disrupt the child's emotional bond to the mother (Belsky & Steinberg, 1978). Kagan and associates (1978) created a high-quality day care center to service 33 infants, who were enrolled in the program between the ages of 3 and 5 months. These infants were studied over a period of 2½ years. On the basis of data collected on these infants, the authors concluded:

> Day care and home reared infants did not differ in their emotional responses to their mothers. Although some children may display some distress at being separated from their mothers at nursery school or at the day care center, this reaction appears to be transient and not different from the distress reaction of home reared children.

When the supplementary child-care arrangements are stable and of a reasonable quality, infants and young children's emotional ties to their mothers are not disturbed or diminished (Belsky, 1984).

However, in a longitudinal study of 1-year-old infants and their attachment behavior toward their mothers and fathers, Belsky and Rovine (1988) found that extensive nonmaternal and nonpaternal care in the 1st year resulted in insecure attachment patterns for a small group of children. The researchers used Ainsworth's Strange Situation to measure infants' reactions to their fathers and mothers upon reunion. They found that infants who received 20 or more hours of care per week displayed more avoidance of their mothers on reunion. Sons whose mothers were employed on a full-time basis were more likely to be insecurely attached to both parents. However, the impact of day care on infants' attachments to their parents is complicated by a number of factors, not the least of which is the parents' satisfaction with and the actual quality of the child-care arrangements. When parents are confident that their children are receiving good care, the quality of their relationships with their infant is likely not to be diminished by the separation. Children left in the hands of insensitive, unstable, or harsh caregivers are more likely to develop negative emotional reactions (Vaughn, Gove, & Egeland, 1980).

Cognitive Skills   Two secondary aims of some day-care programs are to enrich or enhance the child's awareness of the world and to stimulate the development of the child's cognitive skills. Most of the studies on day care indicate that for middle-class children quality nonmaternal care does not appear to have either an adverse or beneficial effect on the child's intellectual or cognitive functioning (Belsky & Steinberg, 1978; Etaugh, 1980).

In a study using a sample of day-care centers more representative than the overused superior university-based programs, McCartney (1984) found that verbal interactions with day-care workers enhanced children's language skills. Other studies (Caughy, DiPietro, & Strobino, 1994; Ramey & Mills, 1977; Ramey & Smith, 1977) have found that high-quality, education oriented day-care programs offered to children from low-income families prevent the decline in intellectual performance frequently found in home-reared children living in poverty. One study (Caughy et al., 1994) compared the cognitive performance of children from impoverished and stimulating home environments who had been enrolled in day care during the first 3 years of life. The researchers found that children from impoverished families did better on reading recognition and mathematics performance at age 5 and 6 than did children from more stimulating home environments. The impact of day care on cognitive development for children who come from a stimulating home setting was relatively minimal. However, the contrast was greater for children whose home settings were less stimulating relative to their day-care experience. During the first 3 years of life, day care provided impoverished children with a richer foundation for later cognitive development.

Social Skills   Most of the programs for preschool-aged children have the development of social skills as one of their major aims. The results of many studies show that day-care children interact more with their peers than do home-raised children. However, these interactions include both positive and negative aspects (Belsky, 1984; Belsky & Steinberg, 1979; Howes & Olenick, 1986). This is especially true for children who begin day care before the age of 2. While the day-care children were more likely to share their toys, they also engaged in more fights than home-reared children. In fact, children who enter day care before the age of 2 are reported to be more aggressive and less cooperative with adults than later-entering children (Haskins, 1985; Largman, 1976). However, these behaviors may result from several factors, such as the length of stay in the center, the quality of the home environment, and the cultural context.

In a longitudinal study conducted by Howes (1990), children who entered low-quality child care as infants had the most difficulty getting along with their peers as preschoolers. Teachers rated these children as more easily distracted, less considerate of others, and unable to apply themselves to their schoolwork.

CONDITIONS FOR QUALITY DAY CARE

Research on day care indicates that it is not bad for children. But not all day-care programs are the same. There are considerable differences in quality among the many preschool programs available to families, especially those with low incomes (Phillips, Voran, Kisker, Howes, & Whitebook, 1994). High-quality day-care programs are characterized by the following:

1. Low child-to-adult ratio: 4 to 6 infants and toddlers per adult and 8 to 10 3- to 5-year-olds per adult (Ruopp & Travers, 1982)

2. Day-care workers who are trained in childhood education (Ruopp & Travers, 1982)

3. Responsive, affectionate, and stimulating day-care workers (Howes & Rubenstein, 1985).

In one study (Howes & Olenick, 1986), children who attended high-quality day-care centers were found to be more compliant than those in inferior programs. Researchers also found that parents who placed their children in low-quality day-care centers were less involved and interested in their children's compliance when compared to the parents of children enrolled in high-quality day-care centers. This finding suggests that the quality of care a child receives at home may indirectly affect the quality of his or her day care. After reviewing the research on the developmental effects of day care and its quality, Belsky (1984) concluded that it is not where the child is reared that is so important but how the child is treated: Day-to-day experiences most significantly influence development.

BRIEF REVIEW

The rate of growth levels off during early childhood years as the child's body approximates the shape and proportion of an adult. The length of the child's body increases, mostly in the legs.

Gross motor skills also become more coordinated, allowing the child to run, hop, skip, and jump. Fine motor skills, which involve the use of the fingers and small muscles, take longer to develop. By 4 years of age most children are able to handle tools and toys requiring fine motor precision.

In contrast to Piaget's preoperational period, children in the sensorimotor stage are able to represent objects, events, and people symbolically. At this point, young children are able to mentally represent their experience by means of language, gestures, deferred imitation, drawing, and symbolic play.

Young children also become able to tell the difference between physical and mental realities. They can distinguish between what an object actually is and how it appears.

Preoperational thought is characterized by several limitations. Preoperational children are egocentric (unable to perceive another's point of view), center their attention on one perceptual attribute at a time, and are unable to use abstract symbols. Also, children engage in transductive reasoning, and cannot mentally reverse their thinking.

Preoperational children equate time with space and distance. Although most children can count by age 5, they have difficulty mastering conservation of number because they understand number in terms of gross perceptual cues such as density or length. Although young children can group objects together, they do not form true classes based upon logical properties.

Young children attend to information in a haphazard manner and are distracted by irrelevant stimuli. They are not as selective about what they notice. Their memory is limited by their inabilities to group items together and to use rehearsal to process the information.

Language development involves the acquisition of sounds (or phonemes); learning the meanings of words (or morphemes) and the rules of syntax (combining words into sentences); and using language in a social context. Children begin to acquire language skills at age 2, and by 6 have mastered the essentials of their native language. Psychologists and linguists have developed several different theoretical approaches to understanding language acquisition.

Acquiring two languages simultaneously during early childhood has demonstrated cognitive benefits. Bilingual children are more flexible in labeling words and develop a greater appreciation for language learning.

Preschool and day care are increasingly common experiences for young children. Overall, research on day care indicates no adverse effects on development, although more recent studies suggest that day care may affect infants' attachment to parents. High-quality day-care programs are staffed by trained caregivers who interact positively and frequently with the children.

KEY TERMS

active vocabulary (186)
animism (171)
behavioral approach (191)
centration (173)
classification (178)
cognitive approach (192)
concreteness (173)
conservation (174)
egocentric speech (173)
egocentrism (173)
handedness (167)

interactionist approach (192)
irreversibility (174)
morphemes (185)
nativist approach (191)
overextension (187)
overregulation (189)
passive vocabulary (186)
phonemes (184)
pragmatics (185)
preoperational stage (169)
realism (171)

semantics (185)
secondary memory (183)
symbol (169)
symbolic play (169)
symbolic representation (168)
syntax (185)
telegraphic speech (188)
transductive reasoning (175)
transformational rules (190)
underextension (187)
working memory (183)

REVIEW QUESTIONS

If you can answer these questions, you have a good understanding of the material in this chapter. If a question seems difficult, go back to the text and review the topic.

1. Compare the average size of 3-year-olds to that of 6-year-olds. What accounts for the differences?

2. What activities and behaviors are under gross motor control? What activities are under fine motor control?

3. What is symbolic representation? Give an example.

4. Give an example of animism in children. Give an example of realism.

5. List the limitations of preoperational thought. Give examples of egocentrism and centration.

6. What is meant by conservation in Piaget's theory? Describe one way to measure conservation in young children.

7. How do preschoolers understand the concepts of time and number?

8. How are classes defined? At what age are children likely to form true classes?

9. Describe the five components of language.

10. What is overextension? Underextension? Give an example of telegraphic speech.

11. What explanations have been offered to explain how children between the ages of 2 and 6 acquire new words so quickly?

12. Define transformational rules and overregulation.

13. Compare and contrast four theories of language acquisition.

14. What evidence is there for a critical period in the development of language?

15. What are the benefits of bilingualism?

16. Describe the types of preschool programs available and explain how they differ.

17. Describe the effects of attending preschool programs on children's cognitive, social, and emotional development.

OBSERVATIONAL ACTIVITY

PIAGETIAN TASKS

In this chapter you learned of several limitations in the child's understanding. This activity focuses on classification and number. You will need to locate a 4-year-old who is willing to "play some games" with you. Be sure to get permission from the child's parent before you ask the child to play your games.

1. **Classification task.** Using construction paper, cut out an assortment of shapes (circles, squares, and triangles) of different sizes (small, medium, and large) and of different colors (red, yellow, and blue). Mix up the shapes in front of the child and ask the child to make piles of the pieces that go together. (You may want to illustrate the task for the child.) As the child arranges the different groups, note the dimension the child uses to sort the pieces. After finishing, ask the child to name the

piles. Then ask the child if there is any other way the shapes can be rearranged, and if so, to go ahead and make new piles. Continue with the task as long as the child has different ways of classifying the objects.

2. **Number.** Reread the section on conservation of number and refer to Figure 5–2 for the arrangement of the coins. Ask the child to tell you whether the rows have the same number of coins, and if not, which row has more. Note the answer for each arrangement depicted in Figure 5–2. Ask the child to tell you why he or she thinks the row selected has more coins.

Compile the answers to the two tasks and describe the child's level of understanding. Share your observations with your classmates. Were you surprised by the performance of the child? What did you learn from doing this activity?

CHAPTER 6

Early Childhood: Personality and Social Development

Andre's parents were naturalized American citizens who had immigrated from Venezuela and were fortunate to live in a safe section of the city. Andre was the youngest of three children. By the time he was 3 years old, his parents decided it was time to enroll him in a day-care program. They were eager for him to spend time with other children, particularly with other boys since his sisters seemed to dominate him at home.

He was fully toilet-trained, could communicate sufficiently in English and Spanish, and was fairly well coordinated. However, the day-care program at the local Catholic church proved to be a rude awakening for Andre. To his dismay, the other children in the classroom did not immediately acknowledge his presence, as had always been his experience at home. He approached a table where several children were putting together puzzles. Cautiously picking up one of the pieces that a boy named Jonathan was using, he suddenly found Jonathan grabbing it out of his hand! Andre began to cry, as much in surprise as in indignation over the lost puzzle piece. The teacher, noticing the crisis, interceded by introducing Andre to the other children, who by now were regarding intently the crying newcomer. "Let's all welcome Andre, boys and girls!" coached the teacher.

By 7:00 A.M. 4-year-old Midori was in her assigned chair in the Buddhist preschool not far from her family's apartment in Kyoto. Midori's parents wanted her to learn how to work and play cooperatively with her peers; they also wanted to encourage her independence. On this day, Midori was bothered by a little boy named Kikou who had placed a pillow in his trousers, pretending to have a big butt. When he started to throw flash cards, Midori tried to get the Fukei-sensei to reprimand Kikou, but the teacher instead nicely urged her to work out the problem with Kikou, which eventually she did.

Andrew and Midori represent two children in two different cultures developing social skills that will help them get along with others and develop new ways of viewing themselves as people. Through their interactions with family members and with significant people outside the home, young children learn the expected attitudes, behaviors, and emotional responses that are valued by their culture and community. In learning to get along with others, children add new dimensions to their emerging personalities. Some newly acquired personal and social skills have enduring qualities that will influence later childhood and adulthood adjustments. Other characteristics are unique to the early childhood period and have little obvious or direct influence on development across the lifespan. Preschool play activities, for example, provide rich opportunities for children to practice cognitive and social behaviors, but they do not directly correspond to adult development.

THE DEVELOPMENT OF SELF

Who are you? When did you first have a sense of yourself as a person? While you may be able to answer the first question, you probably cannot answer the second. This is because we acquire our first sense of who we are during the early childhood period beginning at age 2. As you remember from our discussions in Chapter 4, early childhood memories are not easily recalled. Thus, even though children as young as 18 months show signs of having a conception of themselves, they cannot articulate that experience until later on in childhood.

By the end of early childhood, children have acquired the ability to stand apart and view themselves from another person's perspective. They are able to describe themselves as different from other children by listing their unique characteristics, especially the fact that their names are different. Young children first define themselves in terms of their physical characteristics and activities, such as "I have curly hair," "I sleep in a bunk bed," "I go to nursery school," and "I ride a tricycle" (Keller, Ford, & Meachem, 1978). Later, after 5 years of age, children employ more psychological descriptions of themselves—for example, "I am smart" or "I am happy."

How do children like Andre and Midori come to form a view of themselves? What factors influence a child's self-concept? Are there similarities in the way children describe themselves? And how does this early childhood self-concept affect later development? Let's explore some answers to these questions.

SELF-CONCEPT DEFINED

personality

The characteristic behavior of an individual; the pattern of beliefs, actions, and feelings that distinguishes one person from another.

self-concept

A person's sense of his or her identity, including physical and psychological traits; the way a person views oneself.

self-esteem

The value people place on their self-concept.

Personality generally refers to the characteristic way that a person behaves—the pattern of beliefs, actions, and feelings that distinguishes one person from another. Part of one's personality includes the way a person views oneself, or the **self-concept.** The process of discovering one's personal picture of self is a gradual one. A child does not wake up suddenly and discover who he or she really is. In fact, although a person's self-concept begins in early childhood, the process of self-discovery is one which continues throughout the lifespan. Older children and adults learn to judge themselves depending on the value they place on their self-concepts; in other words they develop **self-esteem.**

The development of the self-concept is closely related to the child's growing cognitive, emotional, and social skills (Lewis & Brooks-Gunn, 1979; Maccoby, 1980, 1984). With age, children develop a more complex understanding of themselves; they distinguish between themselves as objects of knowledge and as recipients of experiences (Bullock & Lutkenhaus, 1990). For example, children can talk about being a member of a soccer team and also share how they feel when they score a winning goal. According to Bruner (1984), children's views of themselves develop through the many verbal and nonverbal interactions with caregivers, especially the mother. Other theorists such as Freud (1924), Erikson (1963), and Vygotsky (1978), however, view personality and the child's concept of self as a product of a broader socialization process. Through the various and daily interactions with parents, peers, older siblings, and other adults, children learn to respond to people in ways that are appropriate to the family in particular and the culture in general.

Freud believed that the basic foundation of adult personality was formed by the time the child reached the age of 6. He placed particular emphasis on the experiences associated with toilet training and sexual socialization during the early childhood period. As you learned in Chapter 4, it is during the anal stage that children learn to delay the gratification of their immediate needs until there is an appropriate time and place. During the phallic stage, which begins at age 3, the focus of energy shifts from the anal region to the genitals. Freud believed that children find pleasure in stimulating their genitals and experience a sexual desire for the parent of the opposite sex. This romantic and sexual attraction toward the opposite-sex parent triggers a rivalrous relationship with the same-sex parent, a situation Freud referred to as the Oedipal conflict.

In the case of the little boy, the attraction to his mother is a direct result of her caregiving. It is less clear why the little girl should prefer the father over the mother as her object of attention. Freud believed that children in the phallic stage become aware of genital differences; they realize that some people have penises and others do not. He developed the concept of *penis envy* to explain why a little girl would shift her focus of attention to her father (who has a penis) and away from her mother (who has no penis). According to Freud, the little girl blames her mother for not providing her with a penis.

As a result of this rivalrous relationship with their same-sex parent, children experience both guilt and fear. In an attempt to deal with these emotions, young children assume the characteristics of the feared same-sexed parent; this helps to reduce the anxiety associated with having a powerful competitor in the parent. In the process children acquire their parent's values and expectations of what is right and wrong and develop the beginnings of a conscience. According to Freud, this is when the last component of the personality, the *superego,* develops. It is also through this process of identification with the same-sex parent that children acquire a more detailed understanding about what it means to be a girl or a boy. (Gender identity will be discussed in more detail shortly since it is such an important part of self-definition.)

IDENTIFICATION

By the time Andre was 4 years old, his relatives had noticed the way he imitated his father. He echoed his father's opinions about the Boston Red Sox and scolded his sister using tones and gestures similar to those used by his dad. Andre followed his father everywhere he could, and openly imitated him at the dinner table. It was very obvious that Andre wanted to be like his father.

identification
The process by which a child assumes the beliefs, behaviors, desires, or values of another person as his or her own.

One reason for this observed similarity between children and their parents is **identification,** the process by which a person takes on the beliefs, desires, and values of another person. Freud was one of the earlier theorists to emphasize the important role that identification plays in the child's developing personality. One way children cope with their fears of losing their parents' love or being punished for errors or social transgressions is based on their belief that they will not be admonished or rejected if they act like or assume characteristics of their parents. By defensively aligning themselves with a parent, usually of the same gender, children acquire such characteristics as gender- and culture-appropriate behaviors, self-control, prosocial forms of aggression, guilt feelings, and adult standards for assessing the goodness or badness of an act (Mischel, 1970; Sears, Rau, & Alpert, 1965).

Later social learning theorists expanded on Freud's concept of identification by focusing on the process by which children assume characteristics of their

FOCUS ON CULTURE

Among the Bamana people living in Mali it is customary to name children after a respected person within their community, usually an elder. The qualities of the namesake become a part of the child's identity. For example, children also take the status of their namesake within the family. Thus, if a boy were named after his grandfather, then he would be addressed as "father" by his father. Furthermore, a close kinship develops between children and their namesakes (Arnoldi, 1987).

parents. According to the theorists, identification is learned; it is the consequence of children observing and imitating the actions of other people, namely their parents and older siblings. Children are selectively rewarded for imitating culturally approved behaviors and punished or ignored for inappropriate conduct. While children frequently identify with the parent of the same gender, sometimes they model their behavior after the parent of the opposite gender, a finding which cannot be explained from the psychoanalytic perspective. The process of identification includes two subprocesses: (1) imitation of parental actions, and (2) incorporation of these behaviors into the child's view of the self. Children are not just copying adult actions, but rather using the adult characteristics to describe themselves. Although there is not clear agreement about what motivates children to identify with their parents (Mischel, 1970), there has been much research on which parental characteristics foster the identification process.

Children are more likely to identify with the parent who is similar to them in physical or psychological characteristics. Parents who are nurturing and warm, while at the same time seen as powerful by the child, are more likely to function as models. Children are likely to identify with parents or adults who can do things they admire. For example, Andre wanted to be able to lift heavy weights like his father while Midori wanted to be able to read like her mother.

The 2- to 3-year-old is very exciting to watch because the child coordinates growing perceptual, motor, cognitive, and language skills to make things happen. Nothing seems to deter the active, inquisitive child who, by age 4, has mastered the mighty question "Why?": "Why do the stars twinkle?" "Why do we have to go to bed?" Like Andre, young children insert themselves in the middle of social exchanges. A common example of this boundless yet intrusive enthusiasm is when children interrupt their parent in the middle of a telephone conversation. Egocentric children cannot yet conceptualize that their parent might not want to talk to them while they are also on the phone.

Erik Erikson (1963) theorized that children develop their personality by resolving various developmental crises at different stages in life. These crises focus on the conflicts between the child and the social environment, which places demands and restrictions upon the child's behavior. As you learned in Chapter 4, Erikson suggests that children first learn to either trust or mistrust themselves and others; then they proceed to resolve issues related to their own sense of autonomy versus shame and doubt.

Once children have resolved the second crisis and are convinced of their ability to be separate, they become more assertive in their activities. Children initiate play with other children; they pursue their own interests in the family by asking to help. Midori's attempt to change Kikou's behavior is one example of initiative.

This 3-year-old wants his mother's attention, especially when she is on the telephone. The egocentric child cannot imagine that his or her mother would prefer talking to another person.

Sometimes children's initiative and persistence can get them into trouble.

In this stage of Erikson's theory, which lasts from 3 to 6 years of age, children are eager and ready to learn how to cooperate in working with others to make things happen. They welcome the guidance and assistance offered by grown-ups, which also helps children demonstrate their own abilities. Because of their exuberance, this is the perfect time for parents to begin to teach children more about social rules and expected behaviors. For example, when Midori's teacher urged her to work things out with Kikou, she was also helping the child develop a sense of herself as a member of group, an important value in the Japanese culture (Tobin, Wu, & Davidson, 1989). In other words, the teacher was helping Midori to develop appropriate social behavior.

At the same time, children's enthusiasm and initiative may result in actions that earn them reprimands instead of praise. Consequently, they may experience a

FOCUS ON CULTURE

In rural villages, such as in the Philippines, Mexico, and Japan, parents entrust the care of their young children to older children between 6 and 8 years of age (Whiting & Edwards, 1988). While these child caregivers generally are nurturant and responsible minders of their younger siblings, they may become frustrated and aggressive with the children, especially when the length of time spent caring for children is too long or if they are unable to control their charges. How might child caregivers affect the development of a sense of initiative in young children under their care?

sense of guilt—partly a result of the child's limited cognitive skills. For example, not long after Andre's mother had expressed delight at the painting he made in day-care, he duplicated the design on his bedroom wall. His mother, however, was not at all amused. "Don't you know you are not supposed to draw on the walls?" she demanded. Quite clearly, Andre did not understand this rule. Having been praised for his previous design, he naively copied it on his bedroom wall in the hope of additional praise. His mother's response, however, would more likely result in feelings of guilt than a positive sense of initiative and accomplishment.

In Erikson's view, a small amount of guilt over transgressions is normal and helps the child gain self-control over future actions. However, if parents consistently overreact to the child's activities, the child may be overburdened with guilt and lose the sense of initiative. By clearly setting some limits and rules for self-expression, parents and teachers can help the child achieve a healthy resolution of the crisis of initiative versus guilt.

RECAP

Children's developing self-concept is affected by their growing cognitive skills and by the socializing attempts made by parents and teachers during the early childhood. Freud explained the process of identification as a means of resolving the Oedipal conflict and acquiring a superego. Through identification and observation of role models, children assume characteristics that are valued in the family and culture. Erikson emphasized the importance of a balance between initiative and guilt.

GENDER DEVELOPMENT

sex
The male or female gender of a person determined by physical and chromosomal characteristics.

gender identity
The recognition and acceptance of one's own gender.

gender typing
The process by which children acquire the culturally expected behaviors for their gender.

Sex refers to whether a person is male or female based on physical and chromosomal characteristics. The term *gender* refers to a broader view of male and female differences that include socialized traits and expectations. Although the difference between the sexes is a very obvious characteristic, it usually is not until age 2 or 3 that young children become aware of and use sex as a dimension by which to classify people (Serbin & Sprafkin, 1986), although children as young as 1½ show a preference for gender-based toys (Fagot, 1986). Once children become aware of their sex, they quickly learn to label themselves as boy or girl. Gender awareness and **gender identity,** the recognition and acceptance of one's own gender, are considered to be important cognitive events. Knowing about gender helps children learn which behaviors are considered to be appropriate and expected of males and females. These gender expectations vary according to the culture and time period in which children are reared (Jacklin, 1989).

Gender typing refers to the process by which children acquire the culturally expected attitudes and behaviors for their gender. Through daily interactions and exposure to these customs, traditions, and activities, children learn how males and females in their culture should behave. Identification with the parent of the same gender helps children learn how to perform a male or female role in their culture. For example, when a little girl aligns herself with her mother and pretends to be her doll's mother, or when a young boy imitates his father's interest in hunting,

Young children often will assume prominent characteristics of their parents. This boy has copied his father's dress behavior.

they are practicing the gender-typed skills of their culture. These characteristics in turn become part of a child's self-concept.

Gender Identity

gender constancy
The recognition that one's gender does not change.

Gender identity develops in stages. First, the child recognizes his or her own sex but may not yet understand that it is an unchanging characteristic. **Gender constancy** is achieved only when the child realizes that boys always grow up to be men and girls always grow up to be women. When my son Adam was 3 years old, he knew he was a boy; he was fascinated with his penis and touched it regularly. One day he asked me, "When you grow up, Mommy, will you be a man?" Obviously, Adam had not yet achieved gender constancy. The concept that one's sex does not change is difficult for the young child to master—one reason for which may be that the child is familiar with many physical characteristics that *do* change with age.

Researchers measure gender constancy by asking children to match gender properties (such as *plays with trucks* or *plays with dolls*) with a gender category of male or female. When you ask a 4-year-old the question, "If a boy wears a dress will he be a boy?" the answer is likely to be "No." But if you ask children "What do boys wear?" they are able to answer appropriately. They recognize that boys play with trucks and do not wear dresses, and girls play with dolls and do wear dresses (Gelman, Collman, & Maccoby, 1986). Thus the age at which gender constancy is determined may vary depending on how the question is asked.

Children develop an awareness that their own gender does not change before they realize that the same gender constancy applies to other children (Gouze & Nadelman, 1980; Marcus & Overton, 1978). According to Kohlberg (1966), gender constancy is a by-product of the child's cognitive development. By age 6, most children have accepted the notion that one's sex does not change. Gender constancy may not be necessary, however, for a child to acquire a sense of gender identity (Martin & Halverson, 1981; Martin & Little, 1990). Since young children are typically oriented to the present, when you ask them, "What sex are you?" they are able to respond quite readily, "I am a boy" or "I am a girl."

GENDER ROLES

Even though by 3 years of age the child has acquired gender identity, it is not until age 4 or 5 that the child can reliably identify the gender of other people. Usually this distinction is made on the basis of gender stereotypes that predominate in the culture. Specific clothing, hairstyle, colors, and behaviors are associated with the female gender in particular. For example, if you ask a 4- or 5-year-old to explain how she knows that a particular child is a girl, she might reply, "Because she has long hair, is dressed in pink, and is playing with dolls." This response reflects the fact that children not only have learned that there are two genders, but also that boys and girls differ in the way they act and how they are dressed (Picariello, Greenberg, & Pillemer, 1990). These attributed differences form the basis of **gender roles,** the pattern of behaviors considered to be appropriate for males and females within a particular culture. Every culture defines the gender roles of men and women somewhat differently and attempts to socialize its young to fit these roles at an early age.

When people use stereotypes to make judgments, they infer a variety of related attributes from a single characteristic. For example, if you saw a person wearing a skirt, you might expect her to display other feminine traits. Martin and her colleagues (Martin & Little, 1990; Martin, Wood, & Little, 1990) conducted a series of studies to assess children's ability to identify and relate different characteristics associated with **gender stereotypes.** They were interested in whether the presence of one masculine or feminine characteristic would suggest the presence of other gender stereotypes. Children of different ages were told that a child (whose sex was not identified) possessed either a characteristic that was

gender role
The pattern of behaviors considered to be appropriate for the male and female within a particular culture.

gender stereotype
The broad, exaggerated characteristics associated with each gender.

Children acquire culturally expected gender behaviors through their interactions with others of the same sex.

stereotypically masculine ("liked to play with trucks"), or feminine ("liked to play with dolls"). They were then asked to predict whether the child in the story would possess other masculine or feminine traits. Martin found that while children made stereotypical judgments, they did not make them consistently. Children were more likely to make stereotypical judgments based on characteristics associated with their own sex but not on characteristics associated with the opposite sex. According to Martin,, from ages 4 to 6 children seem to be able to make more indirect and complex associations for their own sex, but not until age 8 do they learn the complex associations relevant to the opposite sex (Martin, Wood, & Little, 1990). Furthermore, she found that older children were more extreme in their stereotypic judgments than younger children.

FOCUS ON CULTURE

Some cultures rigidly distinguish between gender roles by defining appropriate dress and behavior for men and women. For example, in Saudi Arabia and other Muslim countries, women are not allowed to drive cars, to be seen in public without a veil, or to have any direct contact with men other than their husbands. Men, on the other hand, are allowed more freedom in public places. Young children growing up in these cultures can easily learn their gender roles because the adults clearly demonstrate the differences in expected gender behaviors.

Whatever the culture, children's knowledge of gender stereotypes increases with age, although children as young as 2 appear to adopt gender stereotypes (Smith & Daglish, 1977; Weinraub et al., 1984). Young children not only learn what behaviors are appropriate for girls and boys, they are also not very accepting of other children who do not conform to these expected behaviors (Stoddart & Turiel, 1985). When you ask 5- to 7-year-olds if it is all right for a boy to wear a barrette while playing football or for a girl to wear a boy's suit, they will most likely answer, "No."

Gender-role expectations change according to the circumstances within a particular culture. For example, at one time the gender-role stereotype for girls in the United States included the expectation that little girls did not play baseball. Today, that expectation has changed; Little Leagues now include girls as well as boys. In fact, a much wider range of behaviors is accepted as appropriate to either sex in the United States. Even though gender roles still exist in all modern cultures, they are becoming more flexible to allow for greater individual differences (Tavris & Wade, 1984). Table 6–1 summarizes the different aspects of gender development in all children.

FOCUS ON CULTURE

Twenty years ago most American psychologists believed that acquiring appropriate gender-role behaviors was an important developmental goal. Today, many people are questioning the merits of channeling children into gender stereotypes. Given that today's young parents were raised at a time when traditional gender-role behaviors were highly valued and encouraged, how might their experiences affect the way they raise their children?

ASPECTS OF GENDER DEVELOPMENT

ASPECT	DESCRIPTION	DEVELOPMENT
Gender awareness	Recognition that people can be classified as either male or female	Occurs at about age 2 or 3
Gender identity	Recognition and acceptance of one's own gender	Related to cognitive awareness of the category of gender and the acquisition of what it means to be male or female in the culture; begins at age 2 and is firmly established by age 3
Gender typing	The process by which children learn expected gender behaviors	Process begins very early in life and involves socialization of the culturally accepted behaviors. Family, peers, and media contribute to the socialization
Gender constancy	Recognition that one's gender does not change	Constancy is obtained first with one's own gender and later for other people's gender. It is a by-product of cognitive development and is firmly established by age 6
Gender roles	The pattern of behaviors considered appropriate for males and females	Follows gender constancy; aspects are apparent as young as age 3 and become more prominent by age 6
Gender stereotypes	Broad, exaggerated, categorical characteristics associated with gender	Demonstrated in children as young as 2 or 3, but appears with greater complexity and strength in older children

TABLE 6–1

SEX-RELATED DIFFERENCES

Gender roles ascribe specific behaviors to each sex. But are these differences in behavior based on biological factors, or are they the result of socialization? It is difficult to separate the influence of genetic biological factors from the influence of early learning. By examining reported differences in behavior between males and females in widely different cultures and environments, researchers have been able to draw some conclusions about universal differences in the behavior of the two sexes.

On the basis of their comprehensive review of thousands of published studies, psychologists Maccoby and Jacklin (1974; Jacklin, 1989; Maccoby, 1990) concluded that there are very few behavioral differences that can be attributed to gender alone. The differences that do appear include characteristics that occur in almost every culture, such as aggression and certain cognitive skills. Some sex related differences in personality and social behavior have been reported by some researchers. However, many of these differences occur as a by-product of the settings and social context in which behaviors are observed. For example, preschool-aged girls playing with other girls are unlikely to display passive behavior;

however, when they are playing with preschool-aged boys, girls are more likely to be passive in play (Wasserman & Stern, 1978).

Aggression   The most consistent finding of research on sex differences indicates that males are more physically aggressive than females from an early age (Block, 1983; Maccoby & Jacklin, 1974, 1980). This conclusion is supported by naturalistic and laboratory studies of children and adults as well as by numerous animal studies. Males engage in more rough-and-tumble play, are more likely to imitate aggression when it is modeled, and exhibit more antisocial behavior than females. Although the accumulated evidence suggests that boys are more aggressive, it has been suggested that boys express their aggression overtly, whereas girls are more concerned about their aggressive tendencies and thus more likely to censor their expression of aggression (Brodzinsky, Messer, & Tew, 1979). However, McCabe and Lipscomb (1988) studied the informal speech of nursery school children and found no sex differences in the use of verbal aggression. In a similar study of children in grades 1, 3, 5, and 7, McCabe and Lipscomb found that only 5th-grade boys produced more verbally aggressive comments than girls.

Cognitive and Intellectual Skills.   Maccoby and Jacklin (1974) found support for female superiority in verbal skills. Girls learn to speak and read earlier and have fewer difficulties in reading when compared to boys. Later in childhood, girls also score better on tests of spelling, grammar, and verbal comprehension. However, a recent analysis by Feingold (1988) of sex differences in aptitude test scores

The most consistent research finding on sex differences indicates that males are more aggressive than females even from an early age.

reported between 1960 and 1983 suggests a decline in cognitive differences. No differences were reported between boys' and girls' performances on verbal reasoning, arithmetic, or ability to interpret figural configurations.

While adolescent boys and men excel on tests that require them to visualize objects in different spatial orientations, girls and women do not (Feingold, 1988). In a study in which the spatial abilities of 1,800 school children were assessed, boys outperformed girls by the age of 10 and continued to do better on tests of spatial ability to age 18 (Johnson & Meade, 1987). Some studies have found, however, that this visual-spatial superiority depends on the particular test used and does not emerge until at least the 10th grade (Tavris & Wade, 1984).

Men and adolescent boys tend to show greater mathematical ability than women and adolescent girls, although there seems to be no such sex difference in the childhood years (Maccoby & Jacklin, 1974). This difference in mathematical ability is not as widely supported as the other three differences noted above (Tobias, 1982), however, and has even been the subject of much controversy. While Feingold (1988) reported an overall decline in sex differences in recent years, the one exception found was in mathematics. High school males scored higher than females in upper level mathematics skills. In part this decline has been attributed to parental gender-stereotyped expectations that females were not as adept as males in mathematical skills (Eccles, Adler, & Kaczala, 1982).

In examining these studies it is important to remember that the evidence supporting sex differences in certain traits and skills does not answer the question of whether these traits are innate or learned. The fact that boys as a group are more aggressive than girls may be the result of differing parental expectations. A girl who is aggressive may be reprimanded or punished, while a boy may be expected and encouraged to act aggressively. In one study in which 13- to 14-month-old children were observed with adults in a play group, adults were more likely to respond to girls when they used gestures or gentle touches or talked softly, whereas the boys received adult attention when they used physical means or when they cried, whined, or screamed (Fagot, Hagen, Leinbach, & Kronsberg, 1985). Eleven months later when the researchers observed the children again, they found that boys were more assertive and girls talked more to their preschool teachers.

Other Sex Differences   Aside from aggression and the three cognitive skills discussed above, what other psychological differences between males and females can be supported by research results? Maccoby and Jacklin (1974) found little consistent evidence to support some of the traditional gender-role stereotypes. For example, there was no evidence to support the view that girls are more sociable than boys or that girls are more suggestible. In a review of studies examining sex differences, Deaux (1984) concludes that sex differences are less pervasive than previously thought. There are greater differences among girls and boys as individuals than there are group gender differences. Eagly (1983) expresses concern that many laboratory studies reporting sex differences may be biased in the direction of one sex or the other. Subjects tested in a laboratory do not necessarily provide information on what members of the two sexes actually do in natural settings.

GENDER-ROLE SOCIALIZATION

After my daughter Sarah was born, I realized that for her I would serve as an example of what a female should be like. As a concerned parent, I wanted her to view herself and her body in a positive and healthy perspective; I also wanted her to be able to relate to others without being limited by gender stereotypes. When she was 4 years old, I enrolled her in a preschool program that provided a learning environment designed to promote gender equality rather than stereotypes. The teachers (male and female) did not allow any books or toys in the classroom that presented or reinforced gender stereotypes; daily activities were designed to enhance positive characteristics for boys and girls equally.

Teacher and parental models are a potent source of information about the behavior expected of males and females. Young children are surrounded by numerous examples of gender appropriate behavior. From the very beginning of life, parents perceive and treat their newborn boys and girls differently (Stern & Karraker, 1989; Vogel, Lake, Evans, & Karraker, 1991). For example, parents interviewed within a day of their child's birth rated girls as smaller and softer than boys (Rubin, Provenzano, & Luria, 1974). Fathers described their sons as stronger and harder and their daughters as more delicate, even though there were no objective differences between the male and female newborns.

At birth, cultures place different values on the gender of a child. In some countries, such as Japan, Pakistan, China, and India, the birth of a male child is cause for much celebration while the birth of a female is ignored. If parents have a preference for the sex of their child before birth, this can affect their interest in and involvement with their offspring. In a longitudinal study conducted among Swedish parents, researchers Stattin and Klackenberg-Larsson (1991) found that parents spent less time playing with their children when the sex of the child did not match their prebirth preference for a particular sex. The quality of the parent-child relationship was more negative among the parents whose gender expectations for their children were not met. Furthermore, the long-term negative consequences of this relationship were more pronounced for female than for male children. Fathers in particular were bothered by the birth of a daughter when they expected a son, and this attitude seemed to influence the parent-child relationship.

During early childhood, children may be differentially rewarded for gender-appropriate behavior. Boys are discouraged from playing with dolls and encouraged to explore and manipulate objects. Girls are encouraged to stay close to home and mother and to be nurturant, while they are discouraged from being aggressive or physical (Block, 1983). Despite the numerous studies highlighting the specific ways in which parents selectively encourage different behavior from girls and boys, research by Maccoby and Jacklin (1987) suggests that in recent years parents have reduced their stereotyping of their children. They appear to treat little girls and boys in much the same ways. By studying 275 children from birth to the 1st grade, for example, the researchers found that parents seemed to be equally warm, nurturing, and accepting or restrictive of boys and girls. The only exception was that fathers tended to offer their children more gender-stereotyped toys and were more likely to engage in rough play with their sons than with their daughters.

Young children spend a good deal of their time playing in self-selected gender-segregated groups (Maccoby & Jacklin, 1987). Girls prefer to play with other girls and engage in different types of behaviors than boys playing with other boys. Substantially different subcultures develop within the all-girl and all-boy play groups. For example, boys are more likely to play in larger groups while girls play in small groups of two or three playmates. Boys engage in rougher and more active, aggressive, and competitive forms of play away from adult supervision, while girls

Despite the fact that parents selectively encourage different behaviors in their sons and daughters, parents' gender stereotyping of their children has decreased.

are more likely to play more cooperatively and to focus their play on developing relationships (DiPietro, 1981; Eaton & Enns, 1986; Maccoby & Jacklin, 1987). By age 3, children show a definite preference for toys that are considered by others to be gender appropriate. Naturalistic studies in which toddlers were observed in their homes suggest that children as young as 2 have a preference for gender-stereotyped toys (Eisenberg, Wolchik, Hernandez, & Pasternack, 1985; O'Brien & Huston, 1985).

Parents also contribute to the gender-socialization of their children by providing them with some gender-typed toys. Eisenberg and her colleagues video-taped mothers and fathers in their homes as they interacted with their 1- to 2-year-old children. They rated children's toys as either masculine (trucks, toy hammers and other tools, balls), feminine (dolls, cleaning and kitchen tools, stuffed animals) or neutral (clay, puzzles, books). Parents of boys chose neutral or masculine toys for their children to use during their interaction, while parents of girls picked more neutral toys. By selecting "girl" or "boy" toys, parents channel their children toward one gender orientation and away from another. Often, how-ever, the decision about what toy to buy for a child is influenced not only by the gender appropriateness of the toy, but by the child's interest and enthusiasm for the toy. Thus, in the case of toy selection and availability, children may influence their own socialization.

The influence of gender-role training on the child's self-concept is substantial, particularly during early childhood when early views of self are being formed. Block (1983) suggests that gender-differentiated socialization also has a profound impact on the child's cognitive development. She argues that males are systemat-ically exposed to more opportunities for independent problem solving—which

Parents serve as powerful gender-role models for their children.

leads to different competencies for males than for females. These skill differentials result in different self- and worldviews that have lifetime impacts. (We will concentrate on the long-term influence of sex differences on self-concept later in this book.)

Gender-role behavior is not fixed, but rather changes throughout the lifespan. Thus, while 3-year-old Andre may believe it is not appropriate for a boy to like to take care of babies, it is quite likely that he will become more nurturant and display these more "feminine" role behaviors when he reaches adulthood (Nash & Feldman, 1981). Furthermore, children are exposed to their parents as gender-role

AGENTS OF GENDER-ROLE SOCIALIZATION	
AGENT	**IMPACT**
Parents	Selectively reward gender-role behaviors; provide gender-specific toys and encourage gender-typed activities; serve as role models for gender role
Teachers	Selectively reward gender-role behaviors; encourage gender-typed behaviors in group settings through gender segregation; serve as gender-role models; teach children about gender equality
Peers	Reinforce gender stereotypes in play activities; preference for same-sex play partners limits knowledge about opposite sex playmates; provide a forum for practicing gender role
Media	Promote gender stereotypes through television and movies; promote beliefs about gender and offer gender-role models; advertise gender-typed toys

TABLE 6–2

models at different times in their parents' gender-role development. Most children acquire their gender roles by observing parents who are themselves young adults. Developmentally, this is the time of the lifespan when adults are most rigid in their interpretation of expected gender-role behaviors—in most cultures when women are involved predominantly in childbearing and domestic activities while men provide economic support to the family. In many industrialized countries, however, this may also be the time when women may return to the workforce. Children who first learn about gender roles when their mothers go back to work and their fathers become more involved in child care may develop a different view of gender-role behaviors than children whose mothers remain at home while their fathers are relatively uninvolved in their care.

RECAP

Gender development begins with awareness of the two sexes and recognition of one's gender identity. Once gender constancy is achieved, children learn gender roles and stereotypes through a process known as gender typing. Very few sex-related differences have been documented; those which have include differences in aggression and selected cognitive and intellectual skills. Children learn what behaviors are appropriate for males and females by selective exposure and reinforcement of gender-specific behaviors in the family, in the classroom, and on the playground.

THE CHILD IN THE FAMILY

Many years ago—before I had children and only dreamed about what it would be like to be a parent—I envisioned my role as someone who took care of the needs of a young child. I never realized how much of my time would be spent in teaching my children how to get along with others—a powerful and time-consuming role. Many people approach parenthood as I did, without a clear idea about the extent of its responsibilities. However, with parenthood comes on-the-job-training. Usually, during the child's 2nd year of life, the parent's role shifts in emphasis from that of primary caregiver to major socializing agent. At this point, parents become more deliberate in the task of teaching young children how to control their anger, how to dress themselves, and what rules must be followed to get along with other family members. Later, as children approach school age, parents teach them how to be polite, follow instructions, and get along with other children.

THE CONTEXTS OF PARENTHOOD

The task of socializing children requires a number of years and extends well beyond early childhood. The quality and effectiveness of the parenting that children receive is influenced by the several interacting contexts within which it occurs. Raising children is a family affair; the family context shapes the way parents discipline and express affection to their children. As the chapter on early adulthood discusses, even the decision to have a child is often influenced by family pressures or by the parental role models in the family.

Most parents rely on their own childhood socialization by their parents to guide them in what to teach their children. Families offer support by baby-sitting, offering advice on how to care for a sick child, or tips on discipline. The quality of the parents' marriage is another factor that influences the parenting process. One study found evidence that fathers experiencing marital discord were more negative and less accepting of their daughters (Kerig, Cowan, & Cowan, 1993).

The degree to which parents are effective in raising their children is influenced by children's own reactions and by the broader social context in which the family is embedded (Belsky, 1984; Weinraub & Wolf, 1983). For example, irritable children often resist their parents' efforts to restrict their behavior, making the parents' job even more difficult. The social context of parenting also includes the attitudes and services that may or may not be available to assist new, single, or working parents. The availability of parent leave policies in the workplace, affordable preschool programs, and health-care services offers parents valuable support, especially for those with low incomes. Poverty places additional demands on parents who must ensure the safety and survival of their children in a hostile inner-city environment (Musick, 1994). Social support is particularly important to parents who are themselves children or adolescents.

Cultural values and expectations about how children should behave influence the training parents give to their children. Child-rearing practices vary considerably from culture to culture, parent to parent, and even over time for the same parents. Cultural values influence how parents should respond to their children; geographic and economic conditions determine the context in which parents rear their children. For example, parents living in agricultural communities may leave the care of their young children to older siblings or elders while tending to crops or herding animals. Climate and geographic terrain may dictate the amount of time parents spend dressing and protecting their children from the elements (Whiting & Edwards, 1988). In countries where infant mortality is high, such as India and sub-Saharan Africa, the focus of parental activities may be on keeping their children alive by providing them with adequate diets and a hygienic environment.

Cultures also vary considerably in the types of social behaviors they encourage in children. Self-reliance, for example, is a highly valued characteristic in the American culture that parents are expected to teach their children. In contrast, Khalapur mothers in north India continue to hand-feed their 4- and 5-year-old children (Whiting & Edwards, 1988). In Japan, parents send their young children (like Midori) to a nursery school because they believe it is a necessary part of their training in the Japanese culture to learn how to be a member of a group rather than totally self-reliant (Tobin, Wu, & Davidson, 1989). These three different approaches to self-reliance are all acceptable within their respective cultures.

THE PARENTING RESPONSIBILITIES

In most (but not all) cultures, the responsibility for raising children is assigned to their parents. This responsibility is a broad one (see Table 6–3). In the United States, parents are expected to provide for the physical and psychological care and safety of their children. Obviously, parents must ensure that children are fed and are free from physical harm, but they are also expected to meet the children's security needs. One way in which parents provide a secure setting is through a

PARENTAL RESPONSIBILITIES

ISSUE	PARENTAL ACTIVITY
Physical care	Provide warmth, food, and look after health needs
Safety and security	Provide a predictable, orderly, and structured setting; protect from physical harm and fears
Advocacy	Represent the needs of the child in the community; seek out opportunities and relevant services; provide affection and warmth
Self-regulation	Teach child how to dress, bathe, and feed self; establish daily routines and structure time; control emotions
Social skills	Teach social rules of etiquette and communication; encourage compliance and a respect for the importance of rules
Cultural values	Convey culturally held attitudes, values, customs, and traditions

TABLE 6-3

predictable and orderly home environment. Parents are expected to establish daily routines and schedules for eating, sleeping, and bathing that allow children to anticipate their care and consequently feel secure (Musick, 1994). Parents serve as the primary advocates for their children, seeking out opportunities that will enhance their safety and well-being and encourage their development. It is also assumed that parents will love their children, although a small number of parents do physically abuse and neglect their children.

Parents are expected to discipline their children and teach them how to regulate their emotions and care for themselves according to social norms of behavior that change according to the age of the child. They are expected to serve as their children's first teacher. For example, parents teach their children to value other people's possessions, to refrain from being nasty (biting, screeching, kicking, and so on), and to avoid interrupting adults. As children mature, parents increase the complexity of their requests and expectations for compliance (Gralinski & Kopp, 1993). Later on in middle childhood, schoolteachers are expected to supplement parents' socializing efforts in addition to teaching children cognitive skills.

Parents must accomplish several tasks if they are to be successful in socializing their children. Children must be encouraged and taught skills and attitudes that will enable them to live healthy and productive lives as adults. Parents are also responsible for transmitting cultural values and traditions, including etiquette and appropriate social behavior. In the day-to-day tasks of teaching and providing for their children's care, parents may often lose sight of the ultimate goal of socialization and become distracted by a more immediate goal of teaching their children to be compliant and pleasant in their interactions. In fact, child-rearing practices often focus on ways to teach children to be obedient and responsive to their adult teachers. As Bell (1968; Bell & Harper, 1980) has pointed out, parents are influenced by their children just as children are influenced by their parents.

New parents are likely to be anxious and somewhat rigid in their style of child rearing. With experience, however, they are likely to become more relaxed and less demanding. Also, since parents adjust their behaviors to the characteristics of the child, the socialization practices to which the easy child is exposed are likely to be quite different from the parental practices used with a more difficult child. Nevertheless, a few generalizations can be made regarding overall parenting styles among American parents.

PARENTING STYLES

discipline

The strategies used by parents to induce children to comply with their rules.

Most people describe their child-rearing practices in terms of discipline. **Discipline** in this sense refers to parents' strategies for getting children to obey their rules and respect their authority. It includes the selective use of rewards and punishments for obedience or disobedience of rules set by the parents. However, parents teach children how to get along with others by their own actions as well as by instruction. Often when parents describe how they interact with their children they describe their intentions and their disciplinary efforts—but they neglect their own impact as models of appropriate behavior. For this reason, in the study of parental behaviors it is important to observe the parent-child interaction as well as to collect parents' self-reports of child-rearing practices.

The way in which parents care for their children is influenced by their culture.

Early research on parental styles identified two basic dimensions on which parents differ: loving warmth versus hostility, and permissiveness versus authoritarian control (Schaefer & Bayley, 1963). The warm, loving parent is accepting, supportive, rewarding, praising and comforting, and expresses interest in the child. The hostile parent is described as critical, derogatory, insensitive, and generally unappreciative of the child's company. The permissive parent does not clearly state or enforce rules and frequently gives in to the child's demands, while the authoritarian parent imposes strict, arbitrary demands and applies a high degree of control in disciplining the child.

Later correlational research by Baumrind (1967, 1971, 1980) examined the way in which parental styles affect the developing social competencies of young children. By observing the behavior of children enrolled in nursery schools, she was able to classify them in terms of their independence and social competence. Socially competent children were rated as friendly, cooperative, and able to assert themselves in an individual and creative fashion without being irresponsible (Baumrind, 1977). Baumrind then assessed the styles of the parents of these preschool children by evaluating them according to the following seven characteristics:

Provide clear rules

Firmly enforce rules

Expect children to help out with chores

See themselves as the infallible authority

Encourage independence and self-assertion

Use explanations and reason

Encourage social conformity

By studying data collected from 300 families, Baumrind (1978) found three common styles of parenting, which she labeled as authoritarian, permissive, and authoritative:

authoritarian parent
A parent that values obedience as a virtue and favors punitive, forceful measures to curb self-will.

1. The **authoritarian parent** values obedience as a virtue and favors punitive, forceful measures to curb self-will at points in which the child's actions or beliefs conflict with what the parent considers to be right. The authoritarian parent views the child as a subordinate and restricts his or her autonomy, discouraging verbal give and take. Authoritarian parents may be very concerned and protective, or they may be neglecting.

permissive parent
A parent who behaves in an affirmative, acceptant, and benign manner toward the child's impulses and actions.

2. The permissive prototype of adult control requires the parent to behave in an affirmative, acceptant, and benign manner toward the child's impulses and actions. **Permissive parents** see themselves as resources for the child but not as active agents responsible for shaping and altering the child's ongoing and future behavior. The immediate aim of the ideologically aware permissive parent is to free the child from restraint as much as is consistent with survival. Some permissive parents are very protective and loving, while others are self-involved and offer freedom as a way of evading responsibility for the child's development.

authoritative parenting

A style of parenting that attempts to direct the child's activities in a rational, issue-oriented manner.

3. The **authoritative parent** attempts to direct the child's activities in a rational, issue-oriented manner. He or she encourages dialogue, shares with the child the reasoning behind the parental policy, and solicits the child's objections when the child refuses to conform. Both autonomous self-will and disciplined conformity are valued by the authoritative parent. Therefore, this parent exerts firm control when the young child disobeys, but does not hem the child in with restrictions. The authoritative parent enforces the adult perspective, but recognizes the child's individual interests and special ways. Such a parent affirms the child's present qualities, but also sets standards for future conduct, using reason as well as power and shaping by regimen and reinforcement to achieve parental objectives.

In general, Baumrind found that children of authoritative parents seem to be the most self-reliant, self-controlled, explorative, and content. Children of authoritarian parents, however, showed little independence, and were more discontented, withdrawn, and distrustful. Children of permissive parents seemed to be the least self-reliant, self-controlled, or explorative of the entire group of children studied.

While Baumrind's general conclusions hold true for both boys and girls, some gender differences in the effects of parenting styles were observed. Authoritarian parenting seemed to be more damaging to boys than to girls. For example, sons of authoritarian parents were less likely to be independent and self-reliant and more likely to be angry and defiant. Also, authoritative parenting was more strongly associated with self-reliance and achievement in girls than boys.

uninvolved parent

An uncommitted parent who appears quite indifferent to a child's need for discipline or affection.

Other researchers have identified a fourth parenting style, the **uninvolved parent** (Maccoby & Martin, 1983). This parent is not very committed to being a parent and appears quite indifferent to the child's need for discipline or affection. The uninvolved parent is more focused on his or her own comfort than on the care of the child. The main effect on children of this indifferent style is a lowered self-esteem often accompanied by aggressive and disagreeable behavior.

It is important to keep in mind that parents vary considerably in the way they respond to and direct their children. In a two-parent family the child is likely to be influenced by parents who use different socialization practices. Even in the same family parents differ in the way they respond to different children. In one study (Dunn, Plomin, & Daniels, 1986) in which mothers were observed with their two children when the children were each 2 years old, little similarity was found in the mothers' disciplinary actions with the children. Even when dealing with the same child, it is unreasonable to expect that parents will use the same style all the time. Children differ in the type of parental reaction they elicit. For example, a temperamentally difficult child is likely to encourage a parental response that is more controlling and restrictive when compared to a child with an easygoing temperament. Furthermore, as children mature, the type of care and supervision they require from parents also changes.

Again, the cultural context in which parenting occurs can greatly influence how adults care for their children. Lin and Fu (1990) examined the difference and similarities in child-rearing practices among Chinese, immigrant Chinese, and Caucasian American parents and found that the Chinese and immigrant Chinese parents tended to rate higher on parental control, encouragement of

Chinese parents encourage independence in their child-rearing practice.

independence, and emphasis on achievement when compared with the Caucasian American parents.

CHILDREARING PRACTICES: ENCOURAGING COMPLIANCE

When my children were in preschool, my husband and I thought twice about bringing them to my Aunt Mary's home because we knew we would be spending much of our time worrying about their behavior. My aunt had lots of accessible knickknacks and did not like "unruly" children. Since Adam and Sarah were naturally curious and enjoyed a fair amount of freedom in our home, we knew that Aunt Mary's home was not a comfortable place for them. At about the time that toddlers learn to resist and say "No," parents begin to develop their disciplinary

FOCUS ON CULTURE

It is important to keep in mind that in many cultures, and within ethnic subcultures in the United States, children are raised within extended family networks. Living within the family household may be grandparents, aunts and uncles, and/or cousins, all of whom may play a significant part in socialization. In this context, the view of parents as solely responsible for socializing their children may not be appropriate.

strategies. Parents seek to control their children's behavior in a number of ways. One way is to punish unwanted behaviors and reward desirable ones. A second strategy is to teach children how to control their own behavior by providing them with a set of rules and guidelines. For example, my husband and I had a variety of rules for Adam and Sarah: No body parts outside of the car window; do not talk with your mouth full; and don't run in the house.

Exercising self-restraint requires the ability to refrain from acting on impulse or out of self-interest. For example, Midori may want to grab a desired toy from the hands of a classmate, but she has learned to control herself. Children who demonstrate self-control are able to delay gratification of their needs. As children develop their ability to think conceptually, they also increase their ability to delay gratification. They can wait in the line for a turn on the swing, or they can wait until the teacher has stopped talking to ask their question.

The method of parental control used during early childhood has an impact on the child's developing personality. Common sense suggests that parents use a variety of techniques to encourage compliance from their children. What particular disciplinary strategies are most effective with children? How effective is punishment in shaping children's behavior?

The most effective form of discipline for children occurs when parents are warm, nurturant, and consistent in their use of rationally based demands (Lamb, 1982c). When parents' responses to behavior are predictable, it is easier for children to learn what is expected of them. By giving children a rational explanation about the consequences to other people of their actions, parents are more likely to instill appropriate social skills. For example, when Andre grabs a toy from another child, his mother is likely to frown and tell him, "It is not nice to take things without asking. If you grab things, other children won't want to play with you." In order for a reasoning strategy to be effective, the explanations given must match the intellectual level of the child. Also, a short explanation will be more effective than a longer one when disciplining young children.

punishment
A process whereby the application of an aversive stimulus following a particular response decreases the frequency of that response.

Punishment   Parents frequently use some sort of **punishment** to control and socialize their young children. While punishment is effective for eliminating some behaviors and establishing new ones, it can also have undesirable effects. Parents use a variety of punishments, including actually hitting or hurting the child, verbal criticism or rebuke, withdrawal of love or attention, and withholding privileges.

Children who are harshly punished at home are more likely to be aggressive with other children and teachers. Furthermore, children—especially boys—who are harshly punished or receive unresponsive parenting are more likely to become antisocial delinquents in adolescence (Loeber & Dishion, 1983; Loeber & Stouthamer-Loeber, 1986; Shaw & Bell, 1993). Although the parent's use of physical punishment temporarily inhibits the child's undesired behavior, it also provides the child with a very potent model of aggression (Bandura, 1977). Children controlled by physical force learn not only that aggression is an effective way for parents to obtain what they want, but, at the same time, how to use it themselves in other situations.

A second problem with harsh or physical punishment, or with its too frequent use, is that children learn to avoid the punitive parent, thus reducing that parent's opportunity to correct inappropriate behavior. Punishment is also likely

Personal Perspective

TEACHING PEOPLE HOW TO BE PARENTS

Raising children is perhaps the single most important job a person will have in a lifetime—yet it is one that most people are poorly prepared to handle. Few are knowledgeable in child development or how to effectively influence behavior. In fact, by virtue of taking this course in human development, you are already more well-informed about these issues than most parents.

Some attempts have been made to offer parent education programs, which vary according to the population of parents they address: adolescent mothers, poorly educated parents, or new parents in general. Since the responsibilities of parents change as children age, some parent education programs specialize in different facets of parenting. For parents of infants and young children, many parent programs try to teach them how to observe, stimulate, comfort, and oversee the emotional and cognitive development of their young children. An example of one such program is the Missouri New Parents as Teachers Project (NPAT). By working directly with new parents in their very early days as caregivers, specially trained teachers were able to change the home environment of young children for the better (White, 1988). Begun in 1982, a model parent education program was established in each of four types of Missouri school districts: urban, suburban, small town, and rural. One full-time and two part-time parent educators were trained to serve between 60 to 100 families in each district. The parent educators met with each family twice a month, once in the home and once with a small group at a school, until the babies were 5 months old. After that, the parent educators visited each home once a month, while the parents met in groups every 6 weeks (Meyerhoff & White, 1986). Mothers were primarily involved in the parent education, but fathers, grandparents, and baby-sitters were all encouraged to participate.

Parents were given basic information on effective parenting practices, stages in infant and child development, and stimulating learning activities for young children. A resource center containing books, magazines, toys, and videotapes was made available to parents. The social and intellectual progress of children in the project was carefully monitored—along with the parents' knowledge and awareness of child development.

The project was extraordinarily successful. Compared to a control group of children, project children were more advanced in social, intellectual, and linguistic skills. Furthermore, the parents in the NPAT project were more knowledgeable about the capabilities of young children than the control group of parents who were not enrolled in the parent education project.

to suppress rather than change behavior. A young girl who is punished for biting her nails may temporarily stop the nail-biting behavior but is unlikely to give it up completely. In addition, punishment sometimes results in the opposite response from the one that parents desire. For example, punishing a child for whining, crying, or clinging—all forms of dependent behavior—may actually result in increased dependence (Yarrow, Campbell, & Burton, 1968).

Punishment can be used effectively. First, the sooner the punishment follows an undesired action, the more effective it will be. When a child is punished immediately after breaking a rule he or she is more likely to associate the punishment with the act. Second, if also provided with a reason when punished, children

Other parent education programs specialize in teaching parents how to gain behavioral control of their children or use discipline more effectively. These programs are based on learning principles and aim to equip parents with skills to cope with children's noncompliance (Wierson & Forehand, 1994). Most parents ineffectively confront noncompliance by demanding that the child obey, but then do not act on their threats or they call attention to unwanted behaviors and thus reinforce them. Parents need to learn how to use positive strategies to encourage desirable behaviors while applying disciplinary techniques to eliminate unwanted behaviors.

The first step for parents is to get their children's attention so that they can teach them to behave. Many children disobey or engage in deviant behavior as a way of getting their parents' attention. Parents need to learn how to pay attention to their children when they are behaving, thereby eliminating children's attention-getting negative behavior. In other words, parents should be trained to catch their children being good rather than bad.

A second strategy for parents is to use verbal praise and approval to reinforce good behavior. For example, "I really liked how you put your toys away" or "You are being very nice to your sister; I like that." Because parental attention is so reinforcing, they need to learn when not to give it; parents need to ignore minor unwanted behavior. So long as children's behavior does not present a danger to themselves or others, simply walking away can have the effect of extinguishing the behavior. However, parents must be consistent and persistent in ignoring the undesirable behavior; if they finally give in and scold the child, they will end up rewarding the very behavior they were attempting to eliminate.

One highly effective behavioral technique that parents can use to discourage unwanted behavior is called **time out.** This disciplinary strategy involves removing the noncompliant child from the reinforcing setting. This may mean sending a child to his or her bedroom or putting the child on a chair in the corner for a period of time. Time out is a form of punishment that does not involve aversive or aggressive behavior; it is also an effective way to prevent parents from yelling at (and consequently reinforcing) unwanted behavior.

Finally, parents need to give their children clear commands that can be followed; if parents are vague or confusing about what they want their child to do, then parents may incorrectly interpret the child's lack of response as defiance rather than as a sign that the command was not understood.

Since there is no way to train parents to deal with every specific problem that may occur, the best strategy is to equip parents with general skills that they can apply across a range of situations and ages. Once parents learn that they can deal with their children in a positive way, the task of raising children becomes more enjoyable all around.

time out
A strategy for changing behavior by removing a person from the setting in which the behavior occurred.

are more likely to change their behavior. Third, inconsistent punishment is less effective than consistent punishment. Finally, the more affectionate and nurturant parents are, the more effective they will be in using punishment to change the child's behavior.

Alternatives to Punishment   Parents have other ways of dealing with disruptive and inappropriate behavior. Sometimes when Andre is misbehaving, his mother may gently but firmly remove him from the situation and put him in a quiet place such as his room. By removing the child from the setting, the disruptive behavior is not reinforced by this attention. It is important that the time-out area be an

Children who are physically or harshly punished by their parents are more likely to be aggressive with others outside of the home.

unrewarding but not aversive place. Sending the disruptive child out to play may actually reinforce his actions if the child would rather be playing. Thus, rather than get into the unpleasant business of having to physically remove my son from the room when he was acting up, my husband and I taught him to remove himself by telling him, "Go to your room and stay there until you can act like a decent human being." Adam knew that "decent human being" meant that he would not be yelling or physically aggressive. If he came out of his room and continued his "indecent" behavior, we would send him back again with the same message. Eventually, Adam learned to control himself and would often go to his room for time out without a prompt from his parents.

Sometimes parents are effective in controlling disruptive behavior in their children by anticipating the child's actions and preventing their occurrence by managing the situation (Patterson, 1980). In an observational study of mothers and their 2½-year-olds in a supermarket, Holden (1983) found that mothers used two types of control. In **reactive control,** parents respond to their children's disruptive behavior; for example, when the toddler grabs a box of cookies off the shelf, a reactive parent might return the product and restrain the child in the shopping cart. In **proactive control,** parents avoid potential conflict by distracting their children before the disruptive behavior begins; for example, a parent may provide the toddler with a favorite toy while cruising the cookie aisle. Preventing or eliminating undesirable behaviors in young children is only part of the parent's function. Parents also teach the child what *is* appropriate behavior—and the best way to do this is to catch them being good. Rewarding a child for appropriate behavior encourages positive behaviors that contribute to the child's socialization. An additional bonus for parents who use positive reinforcement is that they are learning what the child does right instead of focusing their attention on what the child does

reactive control

A parent's negative response to children's disruptive behavior.

proactive control

A parent's avoidance of a potential conflict by distracting children before disruptive behavior begins.

wrong, as in the case with punishment. Also, children are more likely to imitate parents who provide them with positive rewards.

Children are also more likely to cooperate with a parent who has been cooperative with them in the past. Parpal and Maccoby (1985) observed how 3½-year-old children complied with their mothers' requests to put away toys after they had experienced one of three kinds of interactions in their laboratory. Some of the children and mothers had played freely for 15 minutes as they would at home; some of the children had played with their mothers while they acted responsively, letting the child initiate all the play with toys and cooperating with the child's intentions; and some of the children had played alone without any interaction with their mothers, who were kept busy filling out a questionnaire. Children were more likely to comply after the noninteractive session and after the responsive play. In both of the sessions the mothers did not attempt to control their children. Children received neither reinforcement for compliance nor punishment for noncompliance. Thus, the children who complied were allowed to take a dominant role in the play setting. Children whose parents are less controlling and more cooperative in their interactions are more likely to be compliant.

RECAP

The quality of care parents provide their children is influenced by the family, cultural, economic, and social contexts in which parenting occurs. Parents are expected to provide for the physical and psychological needs of their children and to teach them how to get along with other people in the community. Four different parenting styles have been identified: authoritarian, permissive, authoritative, and uninvolved. Disciplinary tactics that involve the use of reason, clearly stated rules, and positive reinforcement are more effective in encouraging compliance. Punishment, while effective, encourages aggression and resentment. Alternatives to punishment include the use of time out, preventing unwanted behavior, and teaching appropriate behavior.

THE CHANGING FAMILY

At one time the traditional nuclear family consisted of parents and children living together; the father typically worked while the mother remained at home to care for the children and the household. Today, however, this description of families is no longer representative. Families throughout the world are smaller and include fewer extended relatives such as grandparents, aunts, uncles, or cousins (Seager & Olson, 1986). Mothers as well as fathers are often employed outside of the home, and fathers are now assuming more child-care responsibilities than a generation or two ago. Furthermore, with more marriages ending in divorce, a greater number of children live in single-parent households.

Maternal Employment   Today more children than ever before have mothers in the workforce. For example, in 1950 only 12% of married women with children younger than 6 years worked outside of the home. Today, more than half of preschool-aged children have mothers who work outside of the home. Many of these mothers are employed part-time rather than full-time. However, for single mothers (divorced or never married) with children younger than 6, the percentage who are employed full time is much higher (Clarke-Stewart, 1982).

While many mothers work because they have to—that is, for economic reasons—many women are choosing to combine both motherhood and a career. The mother's decision to work is influenced by a number of factors, including the quality and availability of child care, the support and cooperation of the spouse, the type of employment available, the degree of self-fulfillment in the job, and the age of the child. Additionally, since most out-of-home child care is costly, many mothers find that any profit from a second income is often used to pay for child care.

Effects.   Child care is the first priority for parents when the mother returns to work. In the United States, most of the young children whose mothers are employed are cared for at home by a parent, relative, or neighbor (Hoffreth, Brayfield, Deich, & Holcomb, 1990). Over 60% of American children are cared for in some form of day care outside the home. In Chapter 5 we examined the impact of day care on young children; the overall research results suggest that quality day care does not cause any adverse effects and may even enhance the development of young children from low-income families.

The concern that employed mothers may have less contact with and hence reduced impact on their preschool children seems not to be supported by the research data (Crockenberg & Litman, 1991; Hayes & Kammerman, 1983; Richards & Duckett, 1994; Zaslow, Pederson, Suwalsky, & Rabinovich, 1989). The quality of care that children receive may depend on their parents' type of job and satisfaction with their work (Greenberger, O'Neil, & Nagel, 1994). More challenging, stimulating, or complex jobs were associated with better parenting; parents provided flexible discipline and were warm and responsive to their children. Mothers who had challenging jobs involving a lot of interactions with people provided better quality explanations to their children than other mothers. In a different study (Crockenberg & Litman, 1991) researchers found that mothers who worked longer hours used more guidance and were more responsive to their children. In general, if mothers are satisfied with their work roles, there appear to be no adverse effects of employment on the way they care for their children (Benn, 1986; Lerner & Galambos, 1985).

Instead, children of working mothers may benefit from the mother's dual career. Aside from enhancing the family's economic status, the employed mother provides a less stereotyped female model for her children. Children, especially daughters, whose mothers are employed are likely to have a broader and less stereotyped view of the female gender role. Teenage daughters whose mothers are employed are more likely than daughters of nonemployed mothers to name their mother as the person they would most like to be like (Huston-Stein & Higgins-Trenk, 1978). School-aged daughters of working mothers display greater academic achievement and score higher in self-esteem than do daughters whose mothers are not employed. Results from a study that analyzed the daily activities of 295 10- to 13-year-old children found that youths whose mothers were employed spent more time doing their homework with their mothers and more time alone with their fathers than youths whose mothers were not employed (Richards & Duckett,

1994). Compared to children of mothers who were not employed, children of employed mothers spent no less time with their family, parents, friends, or by themselves.

Furthermore, in families in which the mother works outside the home, the father often has more responsibility for child care or domestic activities. This increased involvement of men in traditionally feminine activities also presents a less traditional gender-role model to the children. Research by Gold and her colleagues (Gold & Andres, 1978c; Gold, Andres, & Glorieux, 1979) compared 4-year-old, middle-class children whose mothers has been employed since their children's birth with a comparable group of children whose mothers who were not employed. The children of employed mothers showed better social adjustment and had more egalitarian views of the male and female gender roles. For school-aged children the impact of maternal employment is evidenced by greater flexibility in gender-role definition when the mother is satisfied with her role as an employee (Gold & Andres, 1978b).

Maternal employment outside of the home has an impact on how the family functions. School-aged children of working mothers are also more likely to share in household chores, have more training in independence, and learn to be more responsible (Hoffman, 1974). The families of working mothers are also more structured and are characterized by more clear-cut rules. There is a division of the work among all family members—although not an equal distribution, since mothers who work outside the home still do more housework than other family members.

Divorce   According to one U.S. Census report, each year more than a million children experience the divorce of their parents. In the majority of the cases, custody of these children is awarded to the mothers, although there is an increase in

Mothers who work outside of the home may depend on day-care centers to provide for their children. Other mothers rely on family members to take care of their children in the home.

the number of fathers granted custody. As a result, many children spend a portion of their growing years in a single-parent household. The psychological effects on children of having one parent instead of two are diverse and very much dependent on the reason for a parent's absence. However, most of the single-parent households are a result of divorce.

Divorce is an unpleasant and stressful period for all involved because the basic structure and function of the family are temporarily shaken and disorganized. Most researchers examining the impact of divorce view it as a process extending over several years rather than a single event marked by the divorce decree (Hetherington, 1979; Hetherington, Cox, & Cox, 1982; Hetherington, Stanley-Hagan, & Anderson, 1989; Wallerstein, 1991; Wallerstein & Kelley, 1980).

The initial stage of the divorce process begins with the parents' decision to divorce and their subsequent separation. This period is usually the most stressful time for parents and children and lasts for about 1 year. In families experiencing multiple stresses, the initial period may, in fact, last longer.

The transition period is the second stage in the divorce process and lasts approximately 2 to 3 years; it is marked by a variety of social, economic, and structural changes in the family. For example, during this time divorced people reestablish a dating relationship, and many remarry. There usually is a substantial decline in the family's standard of living, which may require the custodial parent to seek new employment or to move to a less expensive residence.

Despite these tangible transitions, most children appear to function at a normal developmental level. Wallerstein and her colleagues (Wallerstein, 1987; Wallerstein & Kelly, 1980) have conducted several longitudinal studies of children experiencing divorce. They reported that for many children, return to normalcy occurred even when the parent-child relationships were not especially improved. However, about 25% of the children did experience anger and depression that affected their school performance and overall social adjustment. Ten years after the divorce, when the children studied were in their late teens, Wallerstein (1987) found that some children still reported feelings of sadness, guilt, or helplessness. Boys more than girls seemed to have difficulty in establishing relationships with their peers. Ten years after the divorce, some children still missed their fathers and harbored fears of being abandoned.

Wallerstein and Kelly also described a third stage in the divorce process that generally occurred about 5 years after the marital breakup. During this period, many parents stabilize their families or start new ones by remarrying. For some children these new family structures represent a return to a normal family, but for others the new situations are not better than the pre-divorce family situation.

Overall, children's reaction to the disruptive set of transitions that occur when parents divorce depends on the children's age at the time of the divorce, their gender, and the quality of the parent-child relationship before and throughout the divorce process. During this time children react to the tension and conflict in the family in a number of ways. The most commonly reported reactions of children during this time are anger, fear, depression, and guilt (Hetherington, 1979). Children experience several changes in their lives: the loss of a parent, family upheaval and fighting, change and uncertainty in the parent-child relationships, change of residence, and the perceived threat of abandonment. Children experience concerns and stresses at a time when parents are least available to provide support or encouragement because of their own personal distress (Nelson,

1993). The biggest concern of children during this period is what will happen to them as a result of the divorce. Even if the family has experienced a number of problems, most children prefer the familiar home and family members to a divorce (Hetherington et al., 1989; Wallerstein & Kelly, 1980). "Who will take care of me?" "Where will I sleep?" "Will I see my father?" are typical concerns expressed by both young children and adolescents. Children are also likely to react to divorce with anger. Young children are likely to display this anger through aggression in school, while older adolescents are likely to blame the parents rather than themselves for the family breakup. Adolescent boys who do not establish a good relationship with their fathers after the divorce are likely to take out their disappointment and frustration on their custodial mothers (Wallerstein, 1987).

Because of their cognitive immaturity, young children may have difficulty comprehending the reason for the parents' breakup and are more likely to blame themselves for the divorce. The egocentric, preoperational child may think, "Daddy and Mommy are angry at each other because I have been naughty." Young children also fantasize that their parents will be reconciled (Wallerstein & Kelly, 1980).

However, for some children their inability to conceptualize their parents' divorce may be a blessing in disguise. Ten years after divorce, these children have fewer memories of their fears surrounding the divorce. In comparison, children whose parents divorced during their adolescent period of development had more

Children are more likely to adjust to their parents' divorce if there is less hostility between the parents.

detailed memories of the conflict and anguish surrounding the breakup of the marriage (Wallerstein, Corbin, & Lewis; 1988). Older children are better able to understand the divorce and have greater access to peers and other adults for support during the family crisis. Despite these resources, however, adolescents also experience pain and anger during the initial stages. Later they are able to accurately assign responsibility for the breakup to one or both parents and to cope with the immediate effects on their own lives (such as having to assume greater responsibility in household activities or receiving less spending money). Some, in fact, are able to gain greater maturity and independence during their parents' divorce (Wallerstein & Kelly, 1980).

Boys generally have more difficulty adjusting to their parents' divorce than girls, and the negative effects seem to last longer. Hetherington (1979), found that boys whose parents had divorced were often aggressive, lacking in self-control, dependent, and anxious. These characteristics were reported by teachers in school as well as by the parents (Zill & Peterson, 1982). Two years after the divorce, however, these disruptive behaviors had declined. Since most of the children of divorce live with their mothers, it is not surprising to note that custodial mothers have more difficulty dealing with their sons than with their daughters (Colletta, 1978; Hetherington et al., 1982). In addition, boys receive less positive support and nurturance and are viewed more negatively by mother, teachers, and peers following a divorce (Hetherington et al., 1982; Santrock & Tracy, 1978). Immediately following a divorce fathers usually have more contact with their children than they did before the divorce. However, this contact rapidly diminishes so that by the 2nd year after a divorce children rarely see their father (Furstenberg, Nord, Peterson, & Zill, 1983).

The quality of the parent-child relationship before and after a divorce is a critical factor in children's adjustment. Hess and Camara (1979) report that adjustment is easier when there is less hostility between the parents and when the child is able to maintain a good relationship with both parents. Because of the increased stress associated with a divorce, parents are often not as effective in their parenting roles in comparison to parents from intact families. They are often less affectionate, less consistent in discipline, poorer at communication, and less inclined to make maturity demands of their children (Hetherington et al., 1982). Custodial mothers are likely to be more indulgent but less available to their children.

Research by Ahrons and Wallisch (1986) on the relationship between divorced spouses suggests that not all partners remain hostile and antagonistic. In fact half of the couples studied were either cooperative or friendly with each other. The consequences of divorce for children are considerably reduced when the parents maintain a good relationship regardless of whether both parents share in the custody of their children or not (Kline, Tschann, Johnston, & Wallerstein; 1989).

Single-Parent Families   Most single-parent families in the United States are headed by women as a result of bearing children out of wedlock or becoming divorced, separated, or widowed. (In most situations, the single-parent family is a result of divorce.) More than one out of two African American children lives in a single-mother household. In 1988, 51% of African American children, 27% of Hispanic children, and 16% of white children were living solely with their mothers (SRCD Newsletter, 1991).

The most significant characteristic of single-parent families is the condition of economic stress, for which there are several reasons. Child support payments often are not adequate to meet children's needs and in many families payments are never made. Single mothers often work full-time at low-paying jobs such as clerks or cashiers, and often work longer hours than comparable married working mothers. Compared to married mothers, single mothers were also found to receive substantially less help in the form of offers to baby-sit or to run household errands from friends or neighbors (Weinraub & Wolf, 1983). Single fathers typically receive help with child care or household chores from concerned friends or relatives, whereas the single mother generally assumes these duties unassisted.

There are some positive aspects to single parent families. With no second adult to share the responsibilities, single-parent families have children who are likely to become more independent, more responsible, and more active in family decision making than children in two-parent homes (Weiss, 1979). Despite the increased pressures and reduced social supports, many single mothers are able to function relatively effectively in their parental roles. This is especially the case when the parents have resolved their differences enough to support the custodial parent (both financially and psychologically) in the care of the children. In families where the children are encouraged to spend time with the noncustodial parent and where children have warm relationships with other adults, the anticipated negative effects of living in a single-parent family do not occur.

Stepparent Families   Closely tied to the increase in the number of divorces and single parent families in the United States is the growing number of stepparent

When adults with children remarry, the result is a larger, more varied family. Young children born into a reconstituted family thus acquire much older stepsiblings.

reconstituted family
A family created when adults with children remarry.

families. It is estimated that at least one out of every three children growing up today will have a stepparent before they reach the age of 18. The remarriage of adults with children creates a **reconstituted family,** which can include a stepfather or stepmother, stepsiblings, and even stepgrandparents. Very little research has been done on reconstituted families. However, there are some common characteristics and difficulties which distinguish them from other families (Hetherington et al., 1989; Vishner & Vishner, 1978).

Members of a reconstituted family must make more adjustments to new family members. Some or even all members of the reconstituted family have had to deal with the disruption of a close relationship, which may strain parent-child relations. Stepparents enter their new parenting role without the benefit of having already established a close relationship with their stepchild. Furthermore, children often resist or resent their parent's new spouse. Stepmothers have to overcome the biases against them set up by fairy tales such as *Cinderella* and *Hansel and Gretel* and sometimes by the children's biological parent, who may be resentful of the stepparent (Nelson & Nelson, 1982). Children in reconstituted families often belong to two households, their mother's and their father's, each of which may include stepparents and stepsiblings. The difficulties in coordinating the activities of one household are amplified when there are two sets of families with differing rules and activities (Hetherington, Cox, & Cox, 1982).

The adjustments children make may differ depending on their gender. In one study, boys and girls in intact families were compared with children whose mothers were divorced and single, or divorced and remarried (Santrock, Warshak, Lindberg, & Meadows, 1982). Boys in stepfather families displayed more competent social behavior than boys in intact families, whereas girls in stepfather families were more anxious than girls in intact families. Boys in reconstituted families showed more warmth to their stepfathers than did girls.

The overall impact of growing up in a stepfamily depends on the relationships that develop between stepparents and stepchildren. Most of the research studies have focused on stepfather families where the biological mother has custody of the children. Until recently, very little research has been done on stepmother families, probably because it had been more common in the past for mothers to be awarded custody of children in a divorce. In one study it was found that girls who have frequent visits with their biological nonresident mothers are more likely to have a less positive relationship with their stepmothers (Clingempeel & Segal, 1986). However, the longer stepdaughters lived with their father and stepmother, the more positive were the stepdaughter-stepmother relationships. Overall, children in stepfamilies as compared with children in nuclear families demonstrate little difference in adjustment or cognitive functioning.

CHILD ABUSE

child abuse
Physical or emotional injury, sexual abuse, and negligent treatment or maltreatment of children under the age of 18 by adults entrusted with their care.

Incidence   While many parents provide a warm and safe environment for their children, there are an alarming number of cases reported of children being physically, sexually, or psychologically abused or neglected by their parents or stepparents. **Child abuse** includes physical or emotional injury, sexual abuse, and negligent treatment or maltreatment of children under the age of 18 by adults entrusted with their care. Since many incidents of child abuse go unreported, accurate statistics are difficult to compile. In 1994, 2.9 million cases of child abuse and neglect were reported in the United States; of these reports, physical abuse accounted for 30% and child neglect for 47% (McCurdy & Daro, 1994). In 1990, the U.S. Advisory Board on Child Abuse declared that child abuse was at a level of national emergency.

Causes   Abusive treatment of children by people entrusted with their care is a growing social problem. Instead of viewing child abuse as an isolated action on the part of a disturbed parent, many professionals are exploring the multiple factors that determine maltreatment. Belsky (1980), for example, believes that child abuse results from a combination of several factors, including stresses experienced by the parents, certain behaviors of the abused child, dysfunctional patterns of family interaction, stress-inducing social forces such as unemployment and isolation, and cultural values that promote abuse.

Many abusive parents were themselves mistreated in childhood, which suggests that these parents may have learned a dysfunctional way of caring for children (Spinetta & Rigler, 1972). Some parents still believe that "to spare the rod is to spoil the child" and that the best way to train a child to obey is through the harsh physical discipline they have seen their own parents use. Abusive parents have little patience with their children. They often have unrealistic expectations and are upset when the child does not live up to them. For example, an abusive parent may interpret a 2-year-old's fantasy as a deliberate lie or become angry when the 2-year-old wets his or her pants or spills milk. Often, abusive parents are upset when the child does not supply them with love or emotional support, something a child usually seeks from the parents. Abusive parents are more likely than nonabusive parents to believe that they can do nothing to change the way they treat their children; they also tend to believe that their children have more control than they do over the quality of care they provide (Bugental, Blue, & Cruzcosa, 1989).

Social-cultural stresses such as poverty, unemployment, and lack of contact with church, neighborhood, or community groups also are associated with child abuse (Hashima & Amato, 1994). Some studies (Burgess, 1979; Gil, 1970; Pelton, 1978) report more child abuse in lower socioeconomic families. Being poor means that parents may have greater difficulty providing for the needs of their children; Zigler (1980) points out that low-income families are not inherently abusive, but rather experience more stressful living conditions.

Another factor contributing to child abuse is the social norm that condones the use of physical punishment to discipline children, particularly within the context of the family. Not too many years ago, corporal punishment was an integral part of many school systems. Over half the incidences of child abuse appear to have begun as a disciplinary action that got out of control. For this reason many professionals target the broader social network as the true culprits in child abuse.

Effects on Children   There is no question that child abuse is bad for children. In some cases abusive treatment is fatal. Surprisingly, until recently there has been very little research on the developmental effects of abuse. Most of the earlier studies described the characteristics of abused children without drawing comparisons to nonabused children (Belsky, Lerner, & Spanier, 1984). Maltreated and abused children are often described as aggressive, irritable, clingy, and difficult to manage. While you may be quick to infer that these characteristics are the result of being abused, you must also consider that they may be its cause. Overburdened and stressed parents are more likely to abuse their children, particularly the most troublesome child. Low-birthweight infants and hyperactive or mentally retarded children have a higher risk of abuse. One reason may be that these children are less alert, less responsive, more difficult to care for, and less attractive, thus making greater demands on the parents (Belsky, 1980; Belsky, et al., 1984).

Results from studies using control groups of nonabused children suggest that abused children are generally more emotionally distressed, more socially inhibited and withdrawn, more difficult to manage, and more likely to display aggression in many different settings (Belsky et al., 1984; Main & George, 1985; Oldershaw, Walters, & Hall, 1986). In one study (Klimes-Dougan & Kistner, 1990), abused preschool-aged children displayed more aggression and withdrawal from peers than nonabused children. The abused children were also more likely to antagonize other children. Because abused children are frequently raised in a climate of family violence, they may become sensitized to adult anger. In another study (Hennessy, Rabideau, Cicchetti, & Cummings, 1994), abused and nonabused children were exposed to videotaped segments of adults in both angry and friendly interactions. Compared to the nonabused children, abused children were found to be more fearful of angry adult interactions and were particularly sensitive to whether the anger between the adults had been resolved.

Emotional and physical maltreatment can also affect on school performance. One study (Eckenrode, Laird, & Doris, 1993) compared the academic performances of abused and nonabused children. Children who were abused had lower scores on standardized tests and poorer grades, and were more likely to repeat a grade than nonabused children. Additionally, maltreated children were more likely to be referred for disciplinary action and suspensions. Neglected children showed the poorest outcome on academic performance, while physically abused children showed the most disciplinary problems.

Sexually Abused Children

In 1973 the U.S. Congress passed the Child Abuse Prevention and Treatment Act, making sexual activities with a child a crime. Sexual abuse involves two elements: sexual activities involving a child and an abusive condition (Finkelhor, 1994). (See Table 6–4.) In 1978, the child abuse act was amended to include sexual abuse as child abuse (Congressional Record, 1978). Approximately 11% of the 2.9 million cases of reported child abuse in the United States in 1993 involved sexual abuse (McCurdy & Daro, 1994). Finkelhor (1994) of the Family Violence Research Program at the University of New Hampshire points out that most sexual abuse estimates rely on reports to child welfare agencies and thus underestimate the problem. Using adult memories of childhood experiences, Finkelhor reports that 20% of women and between 5 to 10% of men experienced some form of sexual abuse as children. Most cases involve the sexual molestation of a child by an adult who is known to the child; three quarters of child molesters are friends, neighbors, or relatives.

While more than 90% of child molesters are men, women have been known to sexually abuse young boys and to participate in organized sexual abuse of children. However, boys are more likely to be molested by male strangers or casual acquaintances (Tierney & Corwin, 1983). In the case of incest, the sexually active abuser is often a parent or a parental figure, and the victim is usually a female child. In two thirds of the incest cases, the offender is not the biological parent but the stepfather.

DEFINITIONS OF CHILD SEXUAL ABUSE

Sexual Activity Involving a Child (Activities Intended to Sexually Stimulate)

Contact sexual abuse	Touching the sexual portions of the child's body, or the child touching the sexual portions of a partner's body; involves either penetration or nonpenetration (fondling, kissing, or touching sexual portions)
Noncontact sexual abuse	Exhibitionism, voyeurism, and using the child in pornography; could include verbal sexual harassment or propositioning

Abusive Conditions (Unequal Power Relationship without Consent)

The child's partner has a considerable age or maturational advantage over the child

The child's partner is in a position of authority or in a caretaking relationship with the child

The activities are carried out against the child using force or trickery

TABLE 6–4

Source: From "Current Information on the Scope and Nurture of Child Sexual Abuse," by D. Finkelhor, 1994 (Summer/Fall), *The Future of Children, 4,* pp. 31–53. Adapted with permission.

Perhaps the most devastating aspect of sexual abuse is that children are often tricked into participating in the activity and believe the act to be their fault. When the offender is a parent, relative, or friend, the child not only experiences the trauma and stress of the sexual molestation, but also is forced to keep a secret for fear of getting the grown-up in trouble. The young victims experience a severe conflict when they are subjected to habitual sexual activity with an adult upon whom they depend. Secrecy may also be obtained when the molester threatens harm to the child for revealing the abuse. In some cases, children who have been sexually abused are also physically abused and even killed by the offenders. Many parents, perhaps because sexual abuse is too horrifying to accept, dismiss the child's attempts to tell them about the incident as lies.

The terror, shame, guilt, inhibited rage, and anxiety that are typical reactions of victims of sexual abuse often stay with these victims throughout their childhood and into their adult years. The effects of incestuous activities, for example, are often reflected in poor sexual adjustment in later life. Often the victims have difficulty trusting others and establishing intimate relationships.

FOCUS ON CULTURE

The United States has a particularly high rate of reported physical violence in the family, and specifically child abuse, compared to other countries. What aspects of the American culture might contribute to the high rate of reported abuse? To what extent has exposure to violence on TV or in the media affected the incidence or reporting of child abuse?

Health Perspective

SYMPTOMS OF CHILD ABUSE

Health care professionals are often the first to suspect and detect signs of child abuse and neglect. Because children usually do not talk about their maltreatment and parents frequently deny the existence of abuse, the responsibility for identifying child abuse in its early stage frequently falls on the nurses and physicians who see the abused child in a hospital emergency room or physician's treatment room. State laws require that physicians report their suspicions of child abuse and take steps to ensure that identified children are protected from further harm. The earlier the diagnosis of abuse is made, the better the outcome for the child.

The nature of the physical ailment or injury often can be a sign of abuse. Unexplained eye damage is a common finding in battered children. Multiple bruises, burns, lacerations, and abrasions in various stages of healing are other signs of frequent, recurring abuse. If a child displays a painful inability to move certain parts of the body, this might suggest dislocations or fractures. Head injuries may

be diagnosed through neurological tests. Many children who die as a result of battering have human bite marks on their bodies. Nonaccidental poisoning is another common co-occurrence in child abuse cases. Neglected children frequently appear malnourished, underweight, and unclean.

Another source of suspicion of child abuse is the parent's behavior. Often the parent's account of a child's injury does not explain the symptoms. For example, a parent of a 2-month-old infant with multiple bruises and fractures might explain the injuries as a result of the infant rolling out of a crib. Sometimes an abused child may be brought in for medical treatment of a cold or flu when the child has severe bruises that the parent seems to ignore. Some abusing parents will delay seeking medical help for their injured child; when they do seek help they are reluctant to provide information about the child to medical

personnel. The abused child is often described by the parents as "bad" or "different" and may indeed appear different either physically or emotionally. Abusive parents often have unrealistic expectations of their children and overreact emotionally to them when they disobey or act immaturely.

When child abuse is suspected, physicians are urged to hospitalize the child to assess the degree of injury and provide protection from additional abuse. X rays may reveal previous incidents of abuse and provide documentation of injuries. Many hospitals have established child abuse committees to assess suspected cases of child abuse and neglect. The committees—usually composed of a pediatrician, nurse, social worker, psychiatrist, and hospital administrator—attempt to determine whether the child has been abused and also provide suggestions for managing the child's care.

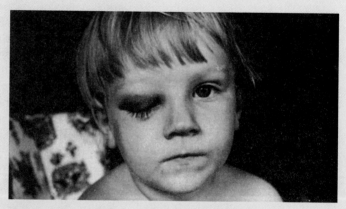

Unexplained injuries are sometimes a sign of child abuse.

RECAP

Children are raised in a variety of family situations. The impact of maternal employment on children's development depends on the quality of child-care arrangements, the mother's type of job, the degree of social support, and the socioeconomic status of the family. Children whose parents divorce must cope with the loss of family harmony and parental support over a period of time before, during, and after the breakup of the marriage. If normalcy is restored to the parent-child relationship, children are less adversely affected. Single parent and stepparent families place additional demands on the parent-child relationship. Child abuse, including sexual abuse, has both immediate and long-term harmful effects.

THE CHILD'S SOCIAL WORLD

Life's journey assumes a more social quality during the preschool years. Children begin to spend more time with other children and in the process discover that they can influence others. Children develop an ever-growing battery of social skills that influence their contact with other people. They learn how to bully another child, how to raise their voice to get attention, and how to persuade a babysitter to let them stay up later. As was the case for Midori and Andre, attendance at a preschool program gives them an opportunity to develop ways of getting along or disagreeing with children their own age. One social behavior that becomes particularly noticeable during the preschool years is aggression.

AGGRESSION

aggression
Behaviors intended to hurt another person.

instrumental aggression
Behaviors designed to accomplish an end.

hostile aggression
Behaviors designed to harm or hurt another person, usually as a reaction of anger or frustration.

Usually, the term **aggression** refers to behaviors intended to hurt another person. Preschool children often engage in aggressive behavior as a means of achieving some end; this type of aggression is referred to as **instrumental aggression.** For example, when Jonathan wanted the puzzle piece Andre had, he shoved him and grabbed the piece from him. **Hostile aggression** occurs when the child deliberately intends to harm or hurt another person, as when a child hits someone out of anger. Many acts of hostile aggression are the result of frustration.

Most children younger than 2 have outbursts of anger and may engage in instrumental aggression. Often the child is only interested in getting a toy rather than trying to hurt or dominate. In fact, most of the young child's aggression occurs during social play amid struggles over toys or control of space. Many observant parents and preschool teachers, for example, have learned that putting more than three children together in a small room is likely to result in a fight or squabble. Interestingly, the children who are the most sociable and competent are also the ones more frequently involved in fights (Maccoby, 1980).

After the age of 6 or 7, children change the form of their aggressive behaviors from physical to verbal attacks on others. They also learn other more socially acceptable ways of resolving disputes. Hence, the frequency of overtly aggressive behaviors declines as the child ages. Parents who respond to their children's aggression by physically punishing them actually encourage aggression by their example.

A different way of understanding aggression is to study the differences in the way children assimilate and process social information. Dodge (1986) believes that some children display aggressive behavior because they have not developed the social skills to direct their attention to relevant social cues and interpret them correctly. For example, one study (Dodge & Tomlin, 1987) reported that socially rejected aggressive children are less attentive to social cues than their less aggressive peers. Aggressive children are also more likely to misinterpret the intentions of their peers and act more aggressively and inappropriately toward them (Dodge & Price, 1994). For example, a child may believe that other children are saying unfavorable things about him when they are really not and then respond aggressively. Aggressive children also expect to gain more interpersonal and instrumental rewards as a result of their aggression than their less aggressive and more socially competent peers.

The cultural setting in which children are raised also influences the type and frequency of aggression they display. Fry (1988) observed 3- to 8-year-olds from two Zapotec-speaking communities in Mexico. One community was selected because it was a peaceful, nonviolent community; by comparison, the second community had a higher level of violence, such as spouse and child abuse and fighting. In play and other interactions, the children who grew up in the peaceful community engaged in far less aggression than did those who grew up in the more violent community.

Television is one potent source of modeled aggression from which children learn to value and accept violence.

The Impact of Media Violence   Another potent source of modeled aggression for young children living in industrialized countries—especially the United States—are the aggressive actions presented by the media. One of the most pervasive media sources is television. When children watch cartoons or other television programs, they are exposed to numerous examples of violence and aggression. The fact that many of these programs are fiction and pure fantasy does not dilute their potency as models of behavior for children. In fact, young children often do not make the distinction between fantasy and reality during the preschool period. After viewing such aggressive behaviors as hitting and fighting on television, for example, young children imitate these actions during their free play with peers (Freidrich & Stein, 1974). Children who are already more aggressive compared to their peers become even more aggressive when they watch violence on TV (Stein & Friedrich, 1975). TV programming thus provides examples and reinforcement for aggression in children. Chapter 8 discusses the impact of TV on children's development in more detail.

A second potential source of modeled aggression are computer video games. Many of the games directly reward the aggressive behavior by the computer character who assaults and kills opponents in fantasy battles using a variety of weapons. Computer video games are interactive; they require the user to make some sort of response (moving the joy stick or pushing buttons). While not all video games reinforce aggressive behavior, many do by awarding higher scores to the players who kill or immobilize more opponents.

PROSOCIAL BEHAVIOR

prosocial behavior
Positive actions that are directed toward other people.

As children mature, they acquire alternative ways to accomplish their goals—ways that are more socially acceptable than aggressive behavior. In addition to learning new social skills, young children also become aware of the hurtfulness of their aggressive actions. As they develop more positive feelings toward others and become aware of people's feelings, they begin to inhibit their aggression. The development of **prosocial behavior,** positive actions that are directed toward other people, occurs as a result of socialization and the child's growing self-awareness.

empathy
The ability to perceive and share the emotional responses of another person.

Empathy   When Japanese parents were asked what they felt were the most important things for their children to learn in preschool, sympathy, empathy, and a concern for others topped their lists (Tobin, Wu, & Davidson, 1989). The first step in the development of prosocial behavior begins when the child is able to empathize with another person. According to Feshbach (1974), **empathy** includes "the shared emotional responses which the child experiences on perceiving another's emotional reaction." Further, she suggests that empathy involves three components: (1) The child must be aware of the emotional reaction in another; (2) the child must be able to assume the perspective and role of another person; and (3) the child must be able to experience some emotional reaction as a consequence of seeing another person's reaction. Young children have a rudimentary awareness of different social roles as early as 2 to 3 years of age (Hoffman, 1981; Watson & Amgott-Kwan, 1983).

Several studies have demonstrated that children as young as 2 are able to recognize emotional states in other children and respond to them in a caring way

The ability to empathize involves awareness of another's emotional distress. Researchers have found that children as young as 2 respond to distress in other children.

(Denham, 1986; Iannotti, 1985; Zahn-Waxler, Iannotti, & Chapman, 1982). Zahn-Waxler and her colleagues (Zahn-Waxler, Cummings, McKnew, & Radke-Yarrow, 1984) found that children whose mothers were themselves more empathic and disciplined their children when they caused distress in others were more likely to engage in prosocial activities such as comforting, protecting, or defending others.

Other researchers (Dunn, 1983; Garner, Jones, & Palmer, 1994) have examined the role that early sibling interactions play in the development of empathy and later prosocial behaviors. Most children have brothers and sisters with whom they share similar interests and activities. Because of this common interest and familiarity, it is easier for siblings to understand each other's experiences and to practice and refine their empathic skills. Dunn reports that children who are encouraged at a young age to cooperate and be kind toward their siblings are more likely to be advanced in their development of prosocial behaviors. (Sibling relationships will be discussed in more detail in Chapter 8.)

Altruism   When people recognize the emotional reactions of other people and respond to them with acts of kindness without any expected reward or benefit to themselves, they are engaging in **altruistic behavior.** Helping, comforting, protecting, defending, or sharing are all considered to be altruistic actions. With encouragement from parents and the opportunity to practice these behaviors, young children have been known to display altruism toward other children at an early age. Despite the restrictions placed on children's understanding of other people's situations by their cognitive immaturity and egocentrism, they can acquire the prosocial behaviors that foster altruism.

Parents who actively talk to their children about how other people feel and at the same time discipline them for causing distress to others have children

altruistic behavior

Recognizing the emotional reactions of other people and responding to them with acts of kindness without any expected reward or personal benefit.

who display higher rates of altruism at an early age. When a child's attention is called to his or her actions and the effect they have on another, the child is more likely to be able to share the aggrieved person's distress at the time. When Andre shoved Jonathan in nursery school, the teacher disapproved of his actions and called his attention to how he had distressed Jonathan. Then she asked Andre to help Jonathan pass out the cupcakes for the class party. By doing so, the teacher was teaching Andre that hurtful actions are not acceptable and that only helpful behavior is rewarded. The effectiveness of adult models in teaching altruistic behavior to children also depends on the nature of the children's relationship to the model. If the model has an affectionate and nurturant relationship with the child, then the child is more likely to imitate the model's altruistic behaviors.

SOCIAL PLAY

play
Behavior performed for its own sake, dominated and controlled by the player.

When we see young children together, we often notice that they seem to be having fun; they spend a good deal of their time playing with each other and by themselves. **Play** can be defined as pleasurable behavior performed for its own sake, dominated and controlled by the player (Weisler & McCall, 1976). Play is likely to occur only in a familiar atmosphere in which children feel safe and are neither tired nor hungry.

The Function of Play
Play is not only fun, it can be beneficial. Piaget believed that play lets children practice their understanding of their world; in the sensorimotor period children play by manipulating objects and learning about the limits of their bodies within their physical world. Later on during the early childhood period children practice their symbolic understanding by engaging in pretend play and make believe. Vygotsky (1978) viewed play as a means by which children learn new ways of extending their own thinking within their immediate world. Freud believed that play was important because it allows children (and adults) to relieve their emotions and tensions.

Play allows children the opportunity to experiment with social encounters, discover new elements of their environment, and become familiar with the tools (like pencils, hammers, and cooking utensils) that they will later learn to use in productive activities. Through play, children can test social rules with minimal consequences. When Kikou pretended to have a big butt by placing a pillow in his trousers, he learned that other people, like Midori, may take offense, but the consequences of this offense were minimal compared to what they may be if he did the same thing as an older child in school or as an adult on the job. Play lets children explore the ways in which people get along with one another. Children approach and learn to play with their peers; as children mature emotionally and develop new cognitive skills, the ways in which they play with each other also change. For example, as children develop the ability to think symbolically they incorporate make-believe in their play. The importance of play in children's development is recognized in many cultures. Some cultures, such as Japanese culture (Tobin et al., 1989), value children's play as a means for children to enjoy each other and to learn social skills. Other cultures, such as American culture, view play as a way for children to practice and enhance their growing cognitive skills.

solitary play

Independent play, without reference to what any other children are doing.

onlooker play

A type of social play in which children watch others play without involving themselves in the activity.

parallel play

When children play within sight and earshot of another but play independently.

associative play

Play involving two or more children using the same equipment and participating in the same games but each in their own way.

cooperative play

Play in which children are able to accept and respond to ideas and actions that are not originally their own and are capable of sharing toys, organizing games, and making friends.

functional play

A type of cognitive play in which children engage in simple, repetitive muscle movements with or without the use of objects.

Social Aspects of Play   One of the earliest studies of children's play was conducted by Parten (1932). Based on her observations of children she reported the following sequence in the development of social play: **solitary play, onlooker play, parallel play, associative play,** and **cooperative play** (described in Table 6–5). Cooperative play reflects children's growing capacity to accept and respond to ideas and actions that are not originally their own. Over time, young children become more social in their play. Children between the ages of 2 and 3 spend most of their time in solitary or parallel play, while 5-year-olds spend more of their time in associative and cooperative play (Barnes, 1971). However, the progression from solitary to cooperative play is not necessarily uninterrupted (Rubin, Watson, & Jambor, 1982). Older children may spend time in solitary or parallel play if they attend preschool programs that encourage them to draw, play with puzzles, or build things on their own. Furthermore, the type of activities children engage in across all of Parten's play categories become more sophisticated as children mature cognitively.

Types of Play Activities   The kinds of activities children engage in when they play varies depending on children's cognitive maturity and gender, and the settings in which they play. Four types of cognitive play can be identified (Smilansky, 1968). In **functional play** children amuse themselves by simple repetitive muscle movements with or without objects, such as rolling a ball back and forth, running, or hopping about. Functional play is more commonly seen in young children under 2 years of age.

CHARACTERISTICS OF PLAY

Social Aspects of Play

Solitary play	Plays alone without reference to what other children are doing
Onlooker play	Watches other children play without being directly involved
Parallel play	Plays independently but within sight and earshot of another child
Associative play	Plays with two or more children using the same equipment and games, but in an individual way
Cooperative play	Play involves sharing of playthings and ideas about how to play

Types of Cognitive Play Activities

Functional play	Involves simple repetitive muscle movements with or without objects
Constructive play	Involves creation or construction
Make-believe play	Everyday or imaginary roles are acted out
Games with rules	Rules, goals, and structures are applied to activities

TABLE 6–5

constructive play

A type of cognitive play involving creating or constructing something.

make-believe play

A type of cognitive play in which everyday or imaginary roles are acted out; also referred to as pretend play.

games with rules

A type of cognitive play in which rules, goals, and structures are applied to activities.

sociodramatic play

A type of play that combines make-believe play and games with rules.

Constructive play emerges between 3 and 6 years of age and involves creating or constructing something like a picture puzzle, a drawing, or a roadway in the sandbox. During the preoperational period, children are capable of using symbols in their play. This is also the time when children are likely to engage in **make-believe play** in which they act out everyday and imaginary roles. Through pretend play, children practice what it would be like to be the leader of the village, to be the parent, or to be a dragon slayer or Teenage Mutant Ninja Turtle.

The last category of cognitive play, **games with rules,** is most commonly observed among 6- to 12-year-old children. In this type of play, rules, goals, and structure are created and applied to activities. This category includes a host of games as such as tag, hopscotch, baseball, cricket, board games, marbles, cat's cradle—games which we learn in childhood and remember all our lives. **Sociodramatic play** involves a blend of make-believe and games with rules, such as when children play "school": one child is the teacher, several children are the students, and perhaps another child is the teacher's aide. All must follow the rules of school and stay in their roles while they play.

By the age of 3 or 4, children spend much of their time in play groups segregated by gender, and the type of play they engage in differs within these gender-segregated groups (Maccoby & Jacklin, 1987). Some of the time adults structure gender groups for play, but more often it is the children themselves who create them. As was mentioned earlier in this chapter, boys and girls differ in their play activities within the groups. Boys engage in more rough-and-tumble and competitive play, while girls prefer cooperative, turn-taking activities.

The physical setting in which children live can have a profound effect on play activities. For example, children who live in crowded, urban areas with safe access to playgrounds or parks have greater opportunity to play with other children, while children who live in remote areas or isolated suburban homes may spend more of their play time by themselves. Children who live near or on water are likely to play water games like Marco Polo or water tag; children living in impoverished countries are likely to turn natural resources such as pebbles, nuts, and dried grasses into play materials. Access to jungle gyms and swings or sports fields will likewise affect the type of play activity of children. Whatever the setting, children throughout the world enjoy play and develop as a result of it.

BRIEF REVIEW

A child's self-concept gradually develops from the ages of 2 to 6 through numerous social interactions. Part of the child's self-concept includes gender identity and the development of gender-appropriate behaviors.

According to Freud's phallic stage of personality development, children acquire a superego and identify with the same-sexed parent. Erikson believes that young children experience a developmental crisis of initiative versus guilt: Overcritical reactions to a young child's initiative can result in their feeling a sense of guilt.

Through the process of identification, children assume characteristics of their parents, including gender-appropriate behaviors. Gender-role behaviors are learned by observation of models and through reinforcement. Although there are few strong differences between the sexes on most psychological characteristics, males have been consistently found to be more aggressive than females.

Children are socialized to culture specific gender-roles through their interactions with people in the family, community, and school.

Parents socialize children within the family by disciplining inappropriate behaviors and reinforcing what is socially acceptable. Four styles of parenting have been observed: authoritarian, authoritative, permissive, and uninvolved. The most effective style of parenting is one that combines firm control with warmth.

Discipline includes the use of punishment when children do not obey. Punishment is most effective, however, when rationally and consistently applied. Alternatives to punishment include managing the situation and catching the child being good.

In families in which mothers are employed outside the home, the children benefit from a more flexible female role model. Divorce produces stresses for both children and parents that lasts for about 1 to 2 years. Single-parent families have multiple stresses that affect the parent-child relationship, including financial difficulties. Stepfamilies have the added difficulties of adjusting to new family members along with different rules and parenting styles.

Child abuse is a serious problem demonstrated by a parent's inappropriate use of physical punishment, often resulting from stresses that overburden the caregiver's ability to cope with children. Abused children usually show more aggressive and avoidant behaviors. Treatment of child abuse involves providing abusive families with community support and re-education.

Sexually abused children are molested or coerced into performing sexual acts. Often sexual abuse can be prevented by teaching children to say "no" to anyone who would touch them in sexual ways.

Children display physical aggression in their play activity. By 6 years of age the frequency of aggression decreases as the child acquires self-control and alternative ways to cope with frustration.

Prosocial behavior develops in early childhood when the child becomes aware of other people's feelings. Empathy precedes the development of altruistic behavior. Parents can encourage sharing, helping, and other prosocial behaviors by providing positive examples and expressing disapproval of actions that cause distress in others.

Play is pleasurable activity performed for its own sake, dominated and controlled by the player. Play serves several functions, including teaching children about their physical and social environments, relieving tension, and learning how to get along with other people.

Social play develops according to the following progression: solitary play, onlooker play, parallel play, associative play, and cooperative play. Types of play activities include functional play, constructive play, make-believe play, and play with rules. The physical setting influences the types of play activity that emerge.

KEY TERMS

aggression (243)
altruistic behavior (246)
associative play (248)
authoritarian parenting (224)
authoritative parenting (225)
child abuse (238)
constructive play (249)
cooperative play (248)
discipline (223)
empathy (245)
functional play (248)
games with rules (249)
gender constancy (211)

gender identity (210)
gender role (212)
gender stereotype (212)
gender typing (210)
hostile aggression (243)
identification (207)
instrumental aggression (243)
make-believe play (249)
onlooker play (248)
parallel play (248)
permissive parenting (224)
personality (206)
play (247)

proactive control (230)
prosocial behavior (245)
punishment (227)
reactive control (230)
reconstituted family (238)
self-concept (206)
self-esteem (206)
sex (210)
sociodramatic play (249)
solitary play (248)
time out (229)
uninvolved parenting (225)

REVIEW QUESTIONS

If you can answer these questions, you have a good understanding of the material in this chapter. If a question seems difficult, go back to the text and review the topic.

1. Discuss the development of self from the perspectives of Erikson and Freud.

2. Define identification. How does identification occur in young children?

3. Distinguish between gender identity, gender constancy, gender typing, and gender roles. Give an example of each of these concepts.

4. What factors influence the gender roles children adopt? What is the impact of culture on gender socialization?

5. Discuss the differences in behavior demonstrated by males and females.

6. Describe the contexts that affect the quality of parenting. What responsibilities of parenthood are typically expected with the American culture?

7. Describe Baumrind's three styles of parenting. Which style is most effective and why? Are there other parenting styles that have been identified? If so, describe them.

8. What is discipline? How do parents effectively control their children's behavior?

9. Discuss the pros and cons of using physical punishment to control or change children's behavior. What are the alternatives to punishment?

10. What effect does maternal employment have on children's development? What are some of the benefits to children whose mothers are employed outside of the home?

11. Describe the three stages in the divorce process. What problems are children likely to encounter during each stage?

12. How do children of different ages react differently to the divorce of their parents?

13. What is the impact on children of living in a single-parent household?

14. Describe the adjustments that must be made by children living in a reconstituted family. What adjustments must be made by the parents?

15. What is child abuse? What are some of the causes of child abuse? What characteristics define children who are more likely to be abused?

16. What is sexual abuse and how can it be prevented?

17. Give examples of instrumental and hostile aggression. Identify at least three sources through which young children learn to be aggressive.

18. Describe the components of empathy. What is the influence of cognitive development on empathic behavior?

19. Identify and explain (using examples) each of the categories of social play. Describe four types of cognitive play and give an example of each.

OBSERVATIONAL ACTIVITY

GENDER TYPING IN YOUNG CHILDREN'S PLAY

When young children play together they often act out the gender roles to which they are exposed in the family and on television. In many ways, children practice gender-appropriate behaviors in play. The purpose of this observation is for you to observe young children at play and to identify examples of gender-role behavior in their activities.

For this observation, choose a playground or an indoor play area where children are allowed to play on their own. You will want to observe a group of girls and boys, at least two of each sex. Local nursery schools, day-care centers, or church nursery groups are good places to locate a group of 2- to 6-year-olds. Be sure to obtain permission to observe the children from the teacher or director. Your school may even have a drop-in day-care center that you could use for this activity.

When you have found a group of preschoolers, spend at least 30 minutes observing them. Notice the games they play. Children at this age often use a lot of imagination and fantasy in their play. Use the following questions to guide your observations:

1. Are the girls and boys playing similar games? In what behaviors do they engage? How are they different?

2. Notice the type and frequency of aggressive actions, both verbal and physical. How do the boys and girls differ in the amount or type of aggression displayed?

3. Do the children play pretend games? Do they imitate adult roles such as mother, father, firefighter, or nurse?

4. How do the boys treat the girls? How do the girls treat the boys? Are there differences? Similarities?

5. Do the children seem to have an understanding of their own gender? How do you know? What do they do or say that would suggest that they know how girls or boys should act?

Stay long enough to collect the information you need to draw some comparisons between the girls' and boys' behavior in play. What differences did you notice? Are these differences consistent with your view of gender-appropriate behaviors? In what ways are the two sexes alike? Summarize your observations and draw some conclusions about the way young children acquire gender-appropriate behavior. Be sure to include the personal insights you have gained in your own understanding of gender roles.

The Learning Years

The road through life takes a major turn at the age of 6, when most children begin their formal education. The first day of school is very important for most children: It marks their entry into the world of learning and opens the way for an expanded array of new experiences. Middle childhood begins with entrance into school and ends at about age 12. During this 6-year period, children refine their language and motor skills and discover new arenas in which to test out the social skills they acquired during early childhood. Throughout these school years, children have many opportunities to strengthen and expand their abilities to think and solve problems. From a lifespan perspective, middle childhood is when children meet and make new friends, learn about their community and culture, and, most importantly, form a more detailed impression of themselves. The influence of parents continues to be important but is balanced by children's experiences outside the home.

In middle childhood, competencies are developed that pave the way for maturity and independence in adolescence and young adulthood. The methods children use to confront and solve problems during middle childhood often predicts their ability to cope with adult challenges in the future. As you read about the social and personal landscape of childhood, recall your experiences and draw parallels to your own journey.

CHAPTER 7

Middle Childhood: Physical Growth, Cognition, and Learning

It was a big day in 7-year-old Ian's life when he came home from his Rhode Island school and proudly announced, "I can read!" He was not the fastest reader, but with practice, Ian found he could read the words on the video games and comic books like his older brother Billy. He also was learning how to add and subtract. He could now go into the local candy store and buy baseball cards and bubble gum on his own. In addition, his second-grade teacher, Mrs. McNulty, was helping him learn how to write his name and how to draw dinosaurs. He looked up to her and the other teachers because they seemed to know how to do so many things.

Ian's parents noticed that his thinking was becoming more like their own—he had become "reasonable." Instead of insisting that things be done his way, as he had when he was 4 and 5 years old, he was now open to suggestion and could see things from other people's points of view. His mother learned that Ian could follow her instructions. At times, he even generated his own rules—on his bedroom door he had posted the sign "No girls or babies allowed in."

In a small village not far from the coconut plantation on the island of Nevis, 7-year-old Sienna sorted coconut shells into different categories according to color and texture. Her family made jewelry from the shells to sell in local gift shops on the small Caribbean island. When Sienna was not in school, her friends could find her at her family's workshop organizing the shells.

Sienna was proud of the work she did; she was fast and accurate in her sorting, and looked forward to the time when she would be able to paint designs on the shell pieces. She liked to draw pictures of the island flowers and bring them to school to show her teachers. Everyone who knew Sienna recognized her artistic talents and encouraged her by praising her work. She liked that very much. Her teacher provided her with paints and brushes and let her have a place to leave her work to dry. Many days Sienna would stay after school to work on her coconut creations.

PHYSICAL GROWTH

From ages 6 to 12, the developmental period known as middle childhood, Ian and Sienna can be expected to steadily expand their cognitive skills. As they grow in size, strength, and coordination, they will acquire greater skill and poise in moving about in their physical and social environments. Middle childhood is punctuated with numerous examples of children's mastery of ideas, skills, and tools—part of the enlarged competencies that will eventually transform them into adults within their communities.

SIZE AND PROPORTION

During middle childhood, physical growth becomes more uniform. Instead of large spurts in height or weight, size increases gradually from age 6 to about 10 or 12 (Meredith, 1987), although smaller growth spurts occur frequently during this period (Lampl, Veldhuis, & Johnson, 1992). Height increases from an average of 47 inches at age 6 to about 59 inches at age 12. Weight gain also occurs at a relatively constant rate of about 5 to 6 pounds per year during middle childhood. The average American 6-year-old weighs approximately 45 pounds, while the average 12-year-old weighs 86 pounds. This weight gain is a result of growth in muscles and bone tissues, accompanied by a gradual decrease in fatty tissue as children grow taller and leaner. Body proportions change gradually over this 6-year span as the child develops a more adult-like body.

Between the ages of 6 and 8, the myelinization of neurons is approaching completion, and by 8 years of age the brain is nearly its mature size. In addition, brain waves reflecting electrical activity increase in frequency, producing a more mature level of brain activity (Epstein, 1980).

Notable gender differences in growth occur during the school years. By age 12, girls are 2 years ahead of boys in height and weight, even though boys are heavier at birth than girls. Between the ages of 9 and 10, girls experience a prepubescent growth spurt. They grow taller and retain more fatty tissue than boys. As a result, girls develop softer, rounder contours, while boys' bodies are becoming more muscular and angular. Boys also have greater forearm strength than girls, even though the average girl is taller and heavier.

One sure way to estimate children's age is to check their teeth. The loss of baby teeth and the eruption of permanent teeth are signs of middle childhood. Beginning at age 5 or 6, children start to lose their teeth; girls typically lose their teeth earlier than boys. By age 12, the larger, permanent teeth are developed, giving the child's face a more grown-up look.

School-age children vary greatly in size. For example, if a 7-year-old of average height were to stop growing for 2 years, the child would still be within the normal range for height at age 9 (Tanner, 1978). In the United States, heredity rather than diet seems to account for most of the differences in size among children. However, in other areas of the world, environment may be a contributing factor. Meredith (1982) found a consistent difference in size between school-age children from urban and rural settings. Urban children were, on the average, taller and heavier than rural children. He attributed this difference to a greater access to health, nutritional, and medical resources in the urban settings.

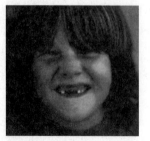

An obvious physical change that occurs in the school years is the loss of baby teeth. Soon this 5-year-old will be sprouting permanent teeth.

FOCUS ON CULTURE

Children who grow up in Zaire or Bangladesh—where poverty and conditions of famine and disease are routine—can be expected to be significantly smaller and developmentally lag behind children of the same age from more prosperous countries such as the United States. Lack of adequate nutrition can delay or interfere with skeletal, muscular, and neurological growth.

MOTOR DEVELOPMENT

The day my daughter Sarah learned to ride her two-wheel bicycle was a significant milestone in her life. The ability to operate a bicycle signifies that children have gained sufficient coordination and muscle strength to balance and maneuver like an adult. Their legs are long enough to reach the pedals and their muscles are strong enough to control their bodies. Children acquire greater precision in gross motor skills; they can run, jump, hop, and skip with grace and agility. The child of 6 can also jump rope, row a boat, and operate a weaving loom. Fine motor precision takes a little longer, as evidenced by the child's improvement in handwriting from the first to the sixth grade. With greater hand and finger control, school-aged children can learn to play the piano and other musical instruments, sew, construct models from kits, or, like Sienna, paint detailed pictures. With practice, many children perform these skills nearly as well as adults.

During middle childhood, children often practice and refine their motor skills by playing on sports teams. By joining local football, baseball, or soccer leagues, children learn to follow rules and to cooperate with their fellow team members while becoming more skilled. Many children gain a sense of self-esteem through their athletic achievements. Accumulated ribbons and trophies provide tangible evidence of their growing competencies. Not all children, however, distinguish themselves through motor skills. Some find other arenas in which to display their abilities and competence. In many agricultural cultures, school-age children are expected to join their parents in field work or fishing, and as they work they too become more skilled at throwing fishnets or using a hoe. Whatever the cultural context, physical maturity, practice, and encouragement are all important in helping children become more proficient in using their motor skills.

PHYSICAL FITNESS

A national survey of over 8,800 children between the ages of 10 and 18 revealed that American children are fatter and less physically fit today than in the 1960s (U.S. Public Health Service, 1984). **Physical fitness** refers to the body's optimal level of functioning and is measured in terms of heart rate, muscular strength, and lung capacity. It is during the school years that many children acquire the physical skills (e.g., swimming, tennis, running) that they will continue to use throughout their adult lives. Physical fitness habits learned in childhood can help prevent adult disorders such as high blood pressure, obesity, and heart disease. Despite the fact that children in middle childhood are better coordinated and have the time to

physical fitness
The body's degree of optimal functioning measured by heart rate, muscular strength, and lung capacity.

There is considerable variation in height among school-age children.

develop fitness skills, many do not. Many American children spend a large amount of their in-school and after-school time being physically inactive (e.g., watching television or playing computer games). In addition, children who watch television are inundated by commercials for fattening snack foods (Carruth, Goldberg, & Skinner, 1991).

There is more than one major drawback to the lack of physical fitness in childhood. Many children are aware of how they look to others, especially to peers. A physically unfit and overweight child is not only unhealthy, but may also be unpopular. Generally, the larger, more muscular child is popular with peers, in part because he or she is more likely to be adept in sports and physical games.

OBESITY IN CHILDHOOD

obesity
Weight that is at least 20% heavier than the ideal weight based on a person's height, age, and gender.

There are many immediate and long-term hazards associated with obesity in childhood. **Obesity** is defined as weight that is 20% or heavier than the ideal weight based on a person's height, age, and gender. According to one report (Gortmaker, Dietz, Sobol, & Wehler; 1987; Kolata, 1986) there has been a 50% increase in the number of obese school-age children. Furthermore, 40% of children who are obese at age 7 become obese adults. However, childhood obesity is not always a predictor of weight problems in adulthood; many obese children are not obese as adults, and many obese adults were not overweight as children (Roche, 1981).

One popular theory about obesity is that it is a hereditary condition; fat adults are likely to have fat children who in turn will become fat adults. Results from a longitudinal study of adopted children and their biological and adoptive parents suggest that genetic factors play a very important role in obesity (Stunkard, et al., 1986). Adopted children were more similar in weight and body build to their biological parents than to the adoptive parents who raised and fed them. If one parent is obese, the risk of having an obese child is estimated at 40 to 50% (LeBel & Zuckerman, 1981). If both parents are obese, the risk increases to 80% (Mayer, 1975). However, these figures must be interpreted with caution because overweight parents are also likely to overfeed their children and to serve as models of overeating. In fact, a variety of factors in addition to heredity contribute to childhood obesity (see Table 7–1).

Diet and eating behaviors are other significant factors in obesity. People who consume more food than their bodies need accumulate excess fat. Obese people who have been overweight since childhood have up to twice as many fat cells in their bodies as nonobese people (Hirsch, 1975; Winick, 1975). Clearly, diets that are high in fat and carbohydrates (such as fast food and snacks) add to the problem of maintaining normal weight.

A low level of physical activity is a third contributor to obesity. Obese children do not move as often or as vigorously as nonobese children; hence they do not burn up excess calories and fat as quickly. Dietz has suggested that television viewing is the second strongest predictor (after infant obesity) of obesity (Kolata, 1986). When children spend long hours in front of the television they not only are inactive, they also eat more. Attractively presented commercials promote a host of snack foods, many of which are shown being eaten by thin people, thus encouraging viewers to eat without concern about weight gain.

FACTORS CONTRIBUTING TO CHILDHOOD OBESITY

Heredity	Overweight adults are likely to have overweight children; children resemble their parents in body type and weight.
Diet	Diets high in fat and carbohydrates result in weight increases; overfeeding in infancy may increase the number of fat cells in the body.
Physical activity	Lack of physical activity increases the storage of fat in body cells.
Television	Viewing television is a sedentary activity; unhealthy and frequent snacking is promoted through commercials.

TABLE 7–1

Obesity carries a negative stereotype in American culture. It has long been known that young children have negative attitudes toward obesity—even overweight children express such attitudes (Lerner & Korn, 1972; Reaves & Roberts, 1983). Researchers in one study (Young & Avdze, 1979) wondered if the behavior of an obese child would reduce the negative image caused by obesity. The results showed that the child of average weight is very much preferred to the obese child, but that the "obedient" obese child was preferred to the "disobedient" normal-weight child. Thus, a child's behavior can override the negative attitude toward obesity, but only if the behavior is "good."

Good behavior, unfortunately, will not completely solve the social stigma of a child's obesity. Another researcher (Sallade, 1973) found that, according to

A low level of activity is one factor in obesity. Watching television competes with other more physical activities and is one of the strongest predictors of obesity.

a self-concept scale, obese children in the third, fourth, and fifth grades had poorer self-images than average-weight children. If children express negative attitudes toward their obese peers (and they often do), the results may have profound consequences for the social adjustment of these children.

RECAP

During middle childhood children grow in size, strength, and both large and fine motor coordination. Physical fitness contributes to a child's self-concept and health; however, not all children are fit. A growing number of children are obese as a result of poor diet, lack of exercise, and genetic factors. Obesity in children can contribute to negative stereotypes and reduced self-esteem.

COGNITIVE GROWTH

Around the age of 6 or 7, children appear to make a remarkable shift in their ability to understand and think in a rational, logical manner. They become reasonable! Parents and teachers often recognize the transition from prelogical to logical thought when the child responds to rules and requests, or when the child supplies a reason for his or her behavior that is guided by logic. For example, 5-year-old Lisa might explain a sunset by referring to magic or some other fantasy such as "the sun goes to bed at night," whereas 7-year-old Ian is likely to recognize that the sun is inanimate and may even be able to explain why he does not see the sun at night.

PIAGET'S THEORY: CONCRETE OPERATIONAL THOUGHT

concrete operations
Piaget's third stage of cognitive development, characterized by the development of logical thought and the ability to manipulate symbols.

Some of the notable changes in children's thought processes were described by Piaget in his theory of cognitive development. He believed that, by age 7, children enter the third stage of cognitive development: **concrete operations.** This stage is characterized by the acquisition of several conceptual skills that permit logical manipulation of symbols (see Table 7–2). Many of the limitations of preoperational thinking (described in Chapter 5) disappear as children begin to think logically.

This stage is labeled *concrete* because children's thinking is still limited by their reliance on what they can observe—that is, tangible, concrete objects or events. For example, a 6- or 7-year-old may have difficulty understanding democracy, since a political system is an abstract concept referring to a variety of actions the child cannot actually see. However, if the teacher were to lead the class in an election based on democratic principles, the children might be able to understand the concept of democracy through their real-life elective experience. The challenge for many parents and educators is to make lessons concrete enough for students to understand. Piaget maintained that the ability to logically manipulate abstract and unobservable concepts does not emerge until about age 11 or 12, when the child enters the last stage of cognitive development, **formal operations.**

formal operations
Within Piaget's theory, being able to deal with problems on an abstract level, form hypotheses, and to reason from propositions that are contrary to fact.

Decentration and Reversibility   Even though children reason primarily according to what they directly perceive, they become more flexible in their use of that information. Unlike preoperational thinkers, children are now able to shift their

Learning throughout Life

One distinguishing human characteristic is the capacity for learning. It emerges in the early stages of life, when infants display an awareness of their immediate environment, and continues in later months and years when they actively explore and manipulate their world. The knowledge and experiences from childhood create a foundation for learning later in life. Some learning occurs as a result of direct instruction and applied lessons, while other skills are acquired by watching and imitating those around us. We learn how to communicate, how to use the tools of our culture, how to view ourselves, and how to pass on our knowledge to the next generation. Whether learning is deliberate or unintentional, it occurs at all stages of life and in a variety of contexts.

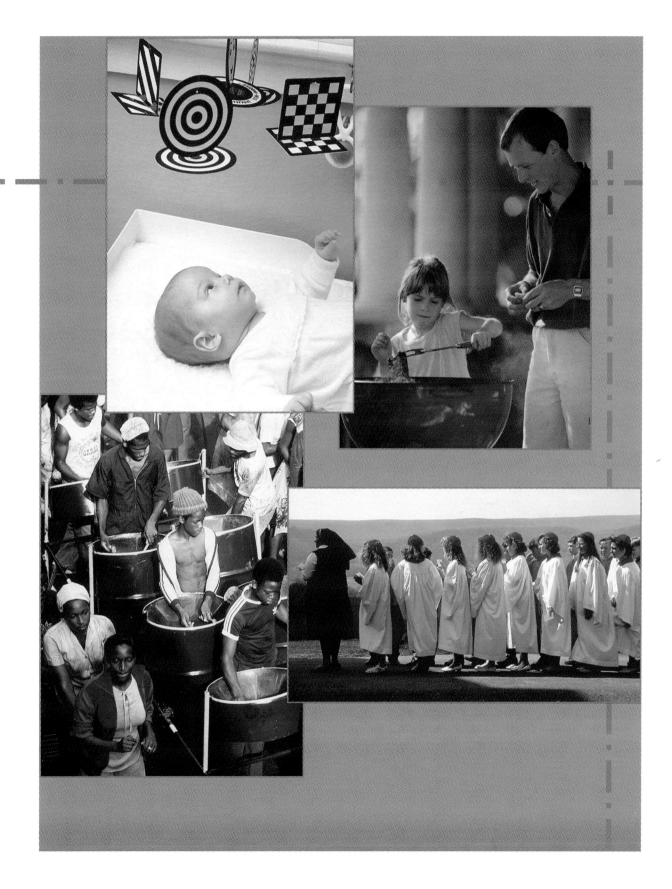

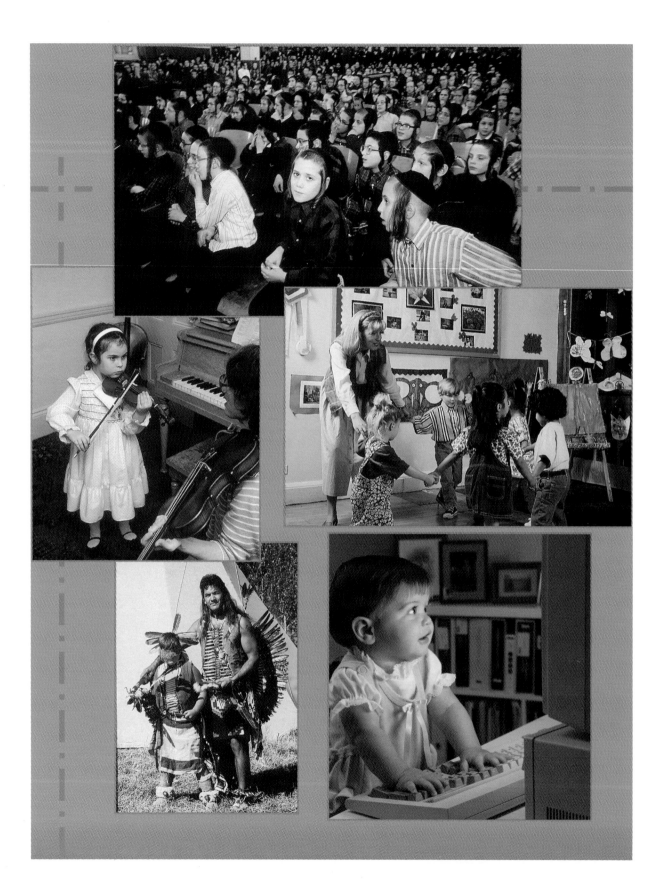

CHARACTERISTICS OF CONCRETE OPERATIONAL THINKERS	
CHARACTERISTIC	**DESCRIPTION**
Concreteness	To focus thinking on people, objects, or events with which one has had direct, hands-on experience.
Decentration	The ability to shift the focus of attention from one attribute to another.
Reversibility	The ability to mentally retrace one's thoughts or actions; to think backwards.
Conservation	The recognition that certain physical properties remain the same despite changes in their outward appearance; occurs for weight, number, volume, length, area, liquids, and mass.
Horizontal decalage	Conservation of different physical characteristics occurs at different times and ages.
Classification	The ability to define classes or categories and to list all members of the category; also the ability to arrange classes or categories in hierarchical order.

TABLE 7–2

decentration

According to Piaget, the child's ability to shift his or her attention from one perceptual attribute to another.

reversibility

According to Piaget, the child's ability to mentally retrace his or her actions or thoughts—to think backward.

attention from one perceptual attribute to another. This process, **decentration,** actually begins before the period of concrete operational thought but becomes more generalized and is applied to increasingly more complex problems during middle childhood.

A second accomplishment during the concrete operational period is **reversibility,** the ability to mentally retrace or reverse actions. For example, in the conservation problem described in Chapter 5, the child is presented with two identical containers filled with identical amounts of liquid. When the liquid in one container is poured into a taller, thinner container, concrete operational thinkers recognize that no change has been made in the amounts of liquid because they can mentally retrace the steps in the sequence of pouring the liquid from the original container to the taller one. In addition, because they are now able to decenter, children can shift their perceptual focus to include the height and width of the fluid in the containers. Hence, they are able to judge them as equivalent.

Conservation Skills   In recognizing that the amount of liquid has remained the same even though the container has changed, children demonstrate the achievement of conservation of liquid quantity. With the general understanding that some aspects of an object or substance do not change even though its shape may be transformed, children introduce some stability to their perceptions of the physical world. The acquisition of conservation skills allows children to make logical predictions about what will happen to physical objects with which they come in daily contact.

Piaget and Inhelder (1969) maintained that all children go through the same stages in mastering conservation of the different characteristics of objects. However, children do not achieve conservation of all characteristics at the same ages (see Table 7–3). The idea that children acquire conservation of different

THE DEVELOPMENT OF CONSERVATION

TYPE	THE CHILD IS SHOWN:	THE EXPERIMENTER:	THE CHILD RESPONDS:	AGE (IN YEARS) CONSERVATION IS USUALLY ACHIEVED
Liquid	two equal short, wide glasses of water and agrees that they hold the same amount	pours water from the short, wide glass into the tall, thin one and asks if one glass holds more water than the other.	*Preoperational child:* The tall glass has more. *Concrete operational child:* They hold the same amount.	6
Number	two rows of checkers and agrees that both rows have the same number.	spreads out the second row and asks if one row has more checkers than the other.	*Preoperational child:* The longer row has more checkers. *Concrete operational child:* The number of checkers in each row hasn't changed.	6
Length	two sticks and agrees that they are the same length.	moves the bottom stick and asks if they are still the same length.	*Preoperational child:* The bottom stick is longer. *Concrete operational child:* They're the same length.	6–7

TYPE	THE CHILD IS SHOWN:	THE EXPERIMENTER:	THE CHILD RESPONDS:	AGE (IN YEARS) CONSERVATION IS USUALLY ACHIEVED
Area	two boards with six wooden blocks and agrees that the blocks on both boards take up the same space.	scatters the blocks on one board and asks if one board has more unoccupied space.	*Preoperational child:* blocks on board B take up more space. *Concrete operational child:* They take up the same amount of space.	7–8
Matter	two equal balls of clay and agrees they are the same.	rolls one ball of clay into a sausage and asks if one has more clay.	*Preoperational child:* The long one has more clay. *Concrete operational child:* They both have the same amount.	7–8
Volume	two balls of clay put in two glasses equally full of water and says the level is the same in both.	flattens one ball of clay and asks if the water level will be the same in both glasses.	*Preoperational child:* The water in the glass with the flat piece won't be as high as the water in the other glass. *Concrete operational child:* Nothing has changed; the levels will be the same in each glass.	11–12

TABLE 7–3

horizontal decalage
Piaget's belief that children acquire conservation of different physical characteristics at different ages.

characteristics at different ages is referred to as **horizontal decalage.** Piaget believed that children in all cultures learn to conserve different quantitative characteristics in the same invariant order, although the *rate* at which they acquire the concepts may vary as a function of specific experiences (e.g., whether they have attended school or had experience with physical substances). Thus, conservation of number is achieved before quantity, and conservation of quantity occurs before weight conservation, which precedes volume conservation (Brainerd, 1978).

Cross-cultural Variations in Conservation Skills

Cross-cultural research using Piagetian tasks has not uniformly supported the view that all children acquire conservation skills in the same sequence or at a similar age (Dasen, 1977; Price-Williams, 1981). Most of the studies in support of Piaget's theory have focused on children living in industrialized and relatively literate cultures. When children living in non-Western unindustrialized cultures are tested on conservation tasks, they generally lag behind children from industrialized countries by about 1 year (Price-Williams, 1981). For example, Nigerian children were found to achieve conservation by age 8 (Price-Williams, 1981). In some studies the lag is a significant one; Greenfield (1966) tested Senegalese children on a series of conservation tests and found that most had not achieved conservation by the age of 11 or 12.

The meaning of this developmental lag has been the subject of much debate, most of which has focused on the testing procedures used to assess concrete operational skills. Recall that Piaget interviewed children during the assessments and, depending on their answers, asked other questions to determine whether the children understood the concept being tested. When non-native researchers test children on the Piagetian tasks, children do not do as well as children who are tested by someone from their own culture and in their own language (Nyiti, 1976, 1982). Also, children living in non-Western cultures may find the idea of testing in itself to be strange and unfamiliar; they may be uncertain about how they should respond, or the meaning of their performance to the "foreign" tester. When children are trained for conservation tasks, their performance improves (Dasen, Ngini, & Lavallee, 1979).

Classification Skills

As a parent, I particularly enjoyed it when my children were old enough to appreciate categories; this was because they now had the skills to organize and order their toys and belongings. I would invite them to play "Let's put all the toys that go together in their own special place," which was my way of getting them to pick up the playroom (and it worked!). During the concrete operational period, children demonstrate their understanding of true classes by coordinating the two crucial properties of class intension and class extension. Unlike the preoperational child, the concrete operational thinker is able to define a class **(class intension)** and list all of the members of that class **(class extension).** Throughout the school years, children become more skilled at making groupings and relating them to one another. One of the most frequent pastimes of children between the ages of 6 and 12 is collecting things and arranging them in relation to each other. Seven-year-old Sienna has been collecting seashells, rocks, and pieces of glass from along the Nevisian beaches for 2 years and has arranged them using several dimensions: color, size, shape, and texture. She carefully arranged each beach gem on her shelf, demonstrating a fairly sophisticated understanding of classification and arrangement of elements in a hierarchy.

class intension
The ability of a thinker to define a class.

class extension
The ability of a thinker to list all the members of a particular class.

In many cultures, school-age children like Sienna are expected to participate in the family's work. They may be weavers, tailors, pot-makers, animal herders, baby-sitters, or traders. Work activities provide children with daily practice in such skills as counting, classifying, manipulating physical matter, judging spatial distances, and role-playing, all of which can contribute to their overall cognitive development.

Cognitive Skills in Action: Children's Humor   The use of humor illustrates children's expanded cognitive skills in action. Young children are notorious for telling bad jokes—jokes that adults consider off-color or too obvious. A joke that is obvious to an adult may not be immediately obvious to an 8-year-old or even understandable to a 5-year-old. The ability to tell and understand a joke develops with the child's growing ability to think and manipulate ideas.

Children in the stage of concrete operations are able to appreciate a joke because they can consider several ideas at once. They appreciate puns because they recognize that words can have more than one meaning, and they can simultaneously consider these double meanings. Consider the following joke from a children's riddle book:

Q: How do you stop a bull from charging?
A: Take away his credit card.

To appreciate this joke, a child must first have accumulated enough experience in the culture to identify a charging bull and a credit card charge. A 4- or 5-year-old may not yet have learned the meaning of these words. Secondly, the child must recognize the incongruity in the idea that a bull can use a credit card. A child of 4 or 5 is unlikely to understand this joke, whereas the 8- or 9-year-old will. To an adult, this joke may be funny the first time it is told, after which it presents no challenge and loses its value.

As children develop their cognitive skills, they also appreciate the humor in jokes they tell one another.

Jokes are funny to the extent that they involve some incongruity, some unexpected situation or outcome. The pleasure of a joke comes from figuring it out (McGhee, 1979). It must be moderately complex or challenging to be considered funny, however. If the joke is too difficult or beyond the listener's level of cognitive understanding—or too obvious or easy—it is unlikely to be considered funny.

In one study, school-age children's senses of humor were measured and related to their overall competence in school (Masten, 1986). Children who were better at producing, understanding, and appreciating humor were viewed by their teachers as more attentive, cooperative, and generally more competent in the classroom. Their peers viewed these children as more popular, outgoing, and happy.

As school-age children become less egocentric and better able to perceive another person's perspective, they delight in telling jokes that fool the listener, particularly when the listener is an adult. Consider this "knock, knock" joke my daughter Sarah loved to tell her father:

Knock, knock!

Who's there?

Banana.

Banana who?

Knock, knock!

Who's there?

Banana.

Banana who?

. . . and so on several times until Sarah saw that her father was growing tired of the joke, at which point she would say:

Knock, knock!

Who's there?

Orange.

Orange who?

Orange you glad I didn't say "Banana"?

Sarah's ability to see her father's perspective and judge his annoyance with the repetition helped her to tell and appreciate this joke. Also, in telling the joke, Sarah took pleasure in putting something over her father—in assuming the authority role. She, rather than her father, was the one with the answers.

Children use jokes to entertain as well as tease others. The older the child, the more aware he or she is of the entertainment value of a joke (Fowles & Glanz, 1977). Children realize that not only is it fun to tell a joke, it is also fun to hear one. The 12-year-old recognizes that a joke would be spoiled for the listener if it is heard too often, and so only tells the joke sparingly and privately to maximize their enjoyment.

Perspective Taking and Social Cognition

I remember the day Adam, then 7 years old, asked me what I thought about the New York Mets. I was impressed he recognized that I might have thoughts about the Mets, and that our thoughts may be different. By about age 6 or 7, children begin to demonstrate a realization that others often perceive the world differently than they do. At this time children begin to differentiate between their thoughts and the way others think about an object, person, or event. As they start to move away from the typical egocentric thinking of the early childhood years, children recognize the possibility that their view of things may not necessarily reflect other people's views; in fact, they are now in a position to benefit from other people's perspectives on issues. Parents and teachers often notice that 7-year-olds are open to adult input, and often solicit adult opinions on problems they are facing.

The loss of egocentrism also means that children now can consider other people in their actions. For example, they are able to understand what it is like to be a parent and what behaviors are expected of a mother or father (Watson & Amgott-Kwan, 1983). They can assume another's position and imagine what it is like to be that person. When a teacher admonishes a 7-year-old child for his aggressive behavior by asking, "How do you think Benjamin feels when you shove him?" the child is likely to be able to answer the question and correct his or her behavior. As egocentrism diminishes, cooperation with others increases as the child becomes more aware of how his or her actions affect others.

Assuming another viewpoint is closely related to the comprehension and use of social-relational terms. For a girl to understand that she is her sister's sister, for example, or her mother's daughter, she must grasp the nature of reciprocal relationships. This, in turn, implies the mastery of reversibility in thinking, one aspect of concrete operational thought. Obviously, the development of this ability to decenter from oneself and to take the role of others has important consequences for

During the years from 6 to 12, children gradually become more aware of and learn to care about other people.

the child's ability to understand other's feelings and to function socially. Hence, cognitive growth facilitates the development of social behavior and morality.

social cognition

The child's knowledge and understanding of social relationships and reactions.

This knowledge about social relationships and reactions is one aspect of **social cognition.** It may be generally described as awareness and understanding of how other people think, feel, and see things; what they intend; and how to describe other people. It also includes the recognition of oneself as seen by others. Social cognitive skills are primitive in the preoperational child, but some 3- and 4-year olds can assume another person's visual perspective in a familiar environment (Shantz, 1983). From the ages of 6 to 12, children gradually obtain a fuller understanding of others and their relationship to them. For example, children as young as 5 or 6 infer how people are feeling based on their behavior, but it is not until about age 9 that children view the behavior of another as indicative of personality traits that are consistent across time and situations (Rholes & Ruble, 1984). As you will discover when you read Chapter 8, children's growing awareness of other people affects their relationships with and acceptance by peers and their view of themselves, which, in turn, affect their interactions as adults.

MORAL REASONING

Ten-year-old Judy was quite upset when her girlfriends at school began to make fun of the way Albert carried his books. Although she did think that Albert carried his books in an odd way, she didn't think it was right to tease him. However, she didn't want her friends to reject her or, worse, make fun of her. Judy truly was in a dilemma about what behavior was right and wrong in this situation. In this case Judy's behavior (not teasing Albert) was not in conflict with her belief that it was wrong to tease. Her reasoning about morality is consistent with her moral behavior.

moral reasoning

A person's ideas or judgments about whether some action is right or wrong, based on a set of rules.

moral behavior

How a person behaves or acts when confronted with a moral situation.

But for many children there is a big difference between **moral reasoning,** the person's judgments about the appropriateness of an action based on some set of rules, and **moral behavior,** the actions in which a person engages. Moral reasoning is a cognitive function. As children become more capable of thinking abstractly, coordinating more than one idea, and seeing other perspectives besides their own, they are also able to make more sophisticated moral judgments. However, even though children understand and accept moral standards defining right and wrong, they do not always act on these standards. For example, 10-year-old Sally knows that it is wrong for her to use her brother's stereo without first obtaining his permission. When her friends were visiting and wanted to hear a new record, however, Sally played it on her brother's stereo, even though she was fully aware that she was doing something wrong. This discrepancy between moral reasoning and moral behavior is normal and to be expected during middle childhood.

premoral judgment

The first stage in Piaget's development of moral reasoning during which 2- to 5-year-old children do not possess cognitive structures necessary for moral judgments and are unaware of the need for rules.

Stages of Moral Reasoning Piaget (1965) believed that the essence of morality is found in the child's respect for rules. Rules of appropriate conduct dictate whether an action is right or wrong. By studying the changes in the way children use rules in playing a game of marbles, he was able to distinguish three stages in the development of moral reasoning (Table 7–4). In the first stage, **premoral judgment,** characteristic of ages 2 to 5, children do not possess the cognitive structures necessary to make moral judgments. They are not aware of rules or the

PIAGET'S STAGES OF MORAL REASONING		
STAGE	**AGE**	**DESCRIPTION**
Premoral judgment	2–5	Not aware of rules or the need for them; no moral judgments are made.
Moral realism	5–10	Rules are regarded as sacred and unchangeable; rules are used as guidelines for behavior and are viewed as the absolute authority. Actions are judged by their consequences rather than by the actor's intentions.
Autonomous morality	10+	Awareness that rules are made to meet people's needs and can be changed; children make up their own rules. Actions are judged by the actor's intentions.

TABLE 7–4

need for them. When playing marbles, for example, the child at this stage focuses more on its own pleasure in shooting the marbles than on following the rules of the game.

Around 5 years of age, the child enters the second stage of moral development, **moral realism,** in which rules are regarded as sacred and unchangeable. Children now use rules as guidelines for proper and acceptable behavior. This is the age when the often-heard refrain "It's not fair!" first appears. Rules are viewed as absolute extensions of higher authority, handed down by God or by parents. At this stage children also judge whether an action is good or bad in terms of its consequences, rather than the intentions of the actor. For example, a child at this

moral realism
The second stage in Piaget's development of moral reasoning during which children approximately 5 years old regard rules as sacred and unchangeable.

By studying the changes in the way children use rules in playing games, Piaget was able to distinguish different stages in children's development of moral reasoning.

stage would consider a child who accidentally breaks five teacups to be naughtier than the child who intentionally breaks one teacup. Children view punishment as a natural consequence of breaking rules and often suggest very harsh and severe punishments for bad acts.

By about 10 years of age, children demonstrate more mature moral reasoning in the third stage, known as **autonomous morality.** They shift from a blind acceptance of rules and authority to growing awareness that rules are made by people. Children realize that the purpose of rules is to help people meet their needs; if rules do not serve this purpose, they can be changed. Often children at this stage readily make up their own rules as they play games or modify existing ones. There is a shift in children's judgment of behavior. Actions are judged by the person's intentions and not by the consequences of the behavior. Now the child who purposely broke one teacup would be judged as naughtier than the child who accidentally broke five teacups. Punishment is now perceived as a way to teach the offender that his or her actions are inappropriate. Children at this age also believe that punishment should lead to some restitution to the victim of the inappropriate action. For example, a 10-year-old may suggest that the child who purposely broke the teacup pay for a new one and be made to wash the dishes for a week.

While researchers agree with the overall sequence of Piaget's theory of moral development, they question his view that young children ignore intention when making moral judgments (Yuill & Perner, 1988). Children as young as 3 have been found to be sensitive to other people's intentions and at age 4 distinguish between lying and telling the truth (Bussey, 1992). Children know it is wrong to tell lies.

autonomous morality

The third and more mature stage in Piaget's development of moral reasoning during which children have a growing awareness that rules are designed to help and meet people's needs.

FOCUS ON CULTURE

Teaching children right from wrong is an important task found in all cultures. However, the specific behaviors that are designated "right" and "wrong" vary considerably from culture to culture. For example, in some cultures it may be considered good manners to burp to show your appreciation of a meal, while in others, to do so would be rude. Understanding cross-cultural comparisons of moral development requires that researchers and students suspend their own culturally derived moral standards so as not to bias their perceptions of cultures that differ from their own.

Kohlberg's Theory of Moral Development   Inspired by Piaget's work, Kohlberg studied children of differing ages and developed a theory of moral reasoning in which he also postulated that children go through different stages of moral reasoning as their cognitive skills mature. Kohlberg (1963, 1964, 1976) originally based his theory on extensive analysis of interviews with boys ranging from 10 to 16 years of age who were presented with 10 hypothetical moral dilemmas. Each dilemma consisted of a story and a series of probing questions related to the issue presented. The following is an example of one of Kohlberg's dilemmas:

> In Europe a woman was near death from a special kind of cancer. There was one drug that the doctors thought might save her. It was a form of radium that a druggist in the same town had recently discovered. The drug was expensive to make, but the druggist was charging ten times what the drug cost him to make. He paid

$200 for the radium and charged $2,000 for a small dose of the drug. The sick woman's husband, Heinz, went to everyone he knew to borrow the money, but he could only get together $1,000 which is half of what it cost. He told the druggist that his wife was dying and asked him to sell it cheaper or let him pay later. But the druggist said, "No, I discovered the drug, and I am going to make money from it." So Heinz got desperate and broke into the man's store to steal the drug for his wife. (Kohlberg & Gilligan, 1971, pp. 1072–1073).

Was Heinz correct in stealing the drug? What would you do if you were Heinz and why?

Similar moral dilemmas have been developed for use with non-American subjects. For example, one such story developed for East Africans (Edwards, 1978) contained a story about a man named Daniel whose secondary school fees had been paid by his older brother Lester. Later, when Daniel is older and has a son of his own who is about to go off to school, his older brother has a serious accident. Daniel is poor, yet he wants to help his brother by paying the school fees for Lester's son. But to do so would mean that his own son could not go to school. What should he do?

What most interested Kohlberg was not the answer to such questions but the reasoning behind the answer. He proposed that moral reasoning develops in a three-level, six-stage, culturally universal sequence that is summarized in Table 7–5.

Children between the ages of 4 and 10 seem to function at the level of *pre-conventional moral reasoning* in which morality is based on anticipated rewards or punishments. A good act is one that is rewarded and a bad act is one that is punished. In Stage 1 of Level I, children focus on the physical consequences of their actions. Here a child may reason that Heinz should not steal the drug because he might be jailed, or that he should steal the drug because it is not really worth $2,000. In Stage 2 children reason that good acts serve one's own purpose. Thus a child may reason that Heinz should steal the drug because he needs it to save his wife's life, or that he should not steal it because the druggist is simply trying to earn a living.

During Level II, *conventional morality,* there is a shift in reasoning. At this level, children conform to and maintain the laws and convictions that have been developed by one's family and society. A child at Stage 3 might say that Heinz should not steal the drug because it would not be his fault if his wife died—he did what he could to help her—or that he should steal the drug because saving her life is part of being a good person. At Stage 4 the reasoning for or against stealing the drug would be based on either Heinz's duty to his wife or his duty to uphold the law, which prohibits theft.

During middle childhood, Level I (preconventional) morality generally predominates. However, Kohlberg (1963, 1964) did report that 40% of his 10-year-old subjects functioned at Level II (conventional) moral reasoning. (A more detailed discussion of Levels II and III will be presented in Chapter 9.)

Evaluating Kohlberg's Theory   While Kohlberg's ideas have generated a great deal of interest and many research projects on moral development, they have also been criticized. One criticism leveled by Gilligan (1982) is that Kohlberg's ideas are based on a male perspective on morality. (Recall that Kohlberg's views were

KOHLBERG'S LEVELS OF MORALITY

LEVEL I: PRECONVENTIONAL MORALITY

Stage 1: Obedience and Punishment Orientation

Obeys rules set by authority to avoid punishment; obedience is for its own sake. Does not consider the interests of others or recognize that they differ from the actor's; does not relate two points of view. Actions are considered physically rather than in terms of psychological interests of others.

Stage 2: Individualism, Instrumental Purpose, and Exchange

Follows rule only when it is in one's interests and meets ones needs; recognizes that others can do the same. Aware that each person has interests to pursue, and that these interests may conflict, so that judgments of right are relative.

LEVEL II: CONVENTIONAL LEVEL

Stage 3: Mutual Interpersonal Expectations, Relationships, and Interpersonal Conformity

Lives up to what is expected by significant others in the role of daughter, brother, friend, and so on. Being "good" means having good motives and keeping mutual relationships. Believes in the Golden Rule. Aware of shared feelings, agreements, and expectations that take priority over individual interests.

Stage 4: Social System and Conscience

Conforms blindly to rules or laws for the good of the institution or society, except in extreme cases where laws conflict with other fixed social duties. Takes the point of view of the system that defines roles and rules. Considers individual relations in terms of their place in the system.

LEVEL III: POST CONVENTIONAL OR PRINCIPLED MORALITY

Stage 5: Social Contract Orientation

Sees rules and laws as relative to the group that makes them and agrees to uphold them because of the social contract to make laws for the welfare of all people's rights. Considers moral and legal points of view; recognizes that they sometimes conflict and finds it difficult to integrate them.

Stage 6: Universal Ethical Principles Orientation

Follows self-chosen ethical principles, which are valued above laws or social agreements. When laws violate these principles, one acts in accordance with the universal principles of equality of human rights and respect for the dignity of human beings as individual persons.

TABLE 7–5

Source: From "Moral Stages and Moralization: The Cognitive Developmental Approach," by L. Kohlberg. In *Moral Development and Behavior,* ed. by T. Licknona, 1976, New York: Holt, Rinehart & Winston. Adapted with permission.

developed from boys' responses to moral dilemmas.) Kohlberg defined the highest standard of moral development in terms of a masculine focus on rules and justice. In contrast, women are more likely to be concerned with the social-interpersonal aspects of a situation when making moral judgments. Using Kohlberg's system of assessing the level of moral reasoning, girls would be judged to be less mature than boys in their moral development if they placed concern and caring for others above the value for laws. However, researchers who have examined Gilligan's claim have not found evidence that Kohlberg's measures underestimate the moral maturity of females (Walker, 1991). Furthermore, Kohlberg's approach incorporates concerns about both caring and justice in evaluating the maturity of moral judgments.

Kohlberg maintained that his three levels of moral development were universal—that is, they could be applied to people from all cultures. Nisan and Kohlberg (1982) studied the moral development of people in Turkey and found evidence for the sequence of stages proposed by Kohlberg. However, there were differences within the Turkish population: City dwellers were judged to be at a higher level of morality than people who lived in rural areas. People from technological societies and urban settings move through Kohlberg's stages more quickly and advance to higher levels than people from isolated villages or nontechnological societies (Snarey & Keljo, 1991). Other researchers have reported that the moral standards of other cultures are not always consistent with those of American and other Western cultures. For example, in one study on moral reasoning (Vasudev & Hummel, 1987), Indian subjects with the highest level of morality relied on collective solutions to moral dilemmas rather than their individual consciences to reach a solution.

RECAP

During middle childhood, concrete operational thinking emerges. It is characterized by the ability to decenter attention, reverse thoughts, conserve, and classify. Cross-cultural differences have been noted in children's ability to conserve. Improving cognitive skills allow children to appreciate and use humor and perceive the perspectives of other people. Piaget believed that moral reasoning develops with cognitive maturity and precedes moral behavior. Kohlberg proposed three levels and six stages of morality. Critics of his theory have questioned the universality of Kohlberg's stages and have suggested that females may be underrepresented, but these criticisms have not been substantiated.

INFORMATION PROCESSING

My grandmother used to say "Little pitchers have big ears" whenever children were present while the grown-ups were talking. It was her way of signaling the adults to be mindful of what they said because the children were listening and were likely to remember and, worse, repeat what they heard. As children mature, they become better able to pay attention to events and conversations around them; they also remember more of what they learn. Both of these growing skills help them become more efficient in problem solving. Together, attention, memory, and problem solving skills allow children to process information more efficiently, and this, in turn, influences their school performance and general knowledge of the world around them.

It is difficult to separate the influence of children's ability to think rationally as a concrete operational thinker from memory, attention, and problem solving. For example, Brown and her colleagues (Brown, Bransford, Ferrara, & Campione, 1983) report that children use their newly developed classification skills to aid their memory—by grouping objects together, children can remember more. For example, as Sienna learned how to classify the coconut shells using several criteria such as color and texture, she was also able to remember what type of shells she wanted to look for on the beach to add to her collection. Without the categories, it would be harder for her to remember which particular type of shell she had.

ATTENTION

Children are not only able to remember information better as they get older, they also become more attentive to specific sources of information. While younger children are easily distracted by irrelevant information, older children are able to filter out extraneous details and focus on the necessary information. They develop strategies that allow them to scan material to select the desired piece of information (Miller & Bigi, 1977).

Children also become more selective in the way they direct their attention—they can concentrate on a task at hand. More complex cognitive tasks can be attempted because children are better able at directing their attention to appropriate elements of a task. For example, multiplying 3 by 4 is a simpler cognitive task than multiplying 32 by 14 because the solution requires fewer steps. To successfully complete the more complex task, the child must selectively focus on the processes of multiplication, carrying, and addition. This ability to selectively focus attention increases with age (Kail & Bisanz, 1982) and is expressed in numerous areas in elementary school.

MEMORY

Children who attend school daily are presented with tasks that not only demand their attention, but also require them to commit information to memory. With practice, by age 6 or 7, children's capacity for memory improves significantly. This increase results primarily because they begin to use strategies that permit greater recall.

The ability to recall information is the product of two activities: **encoding,** or processing information into a set of cues to aid recall, and **retrieval,** the ability to recall information from long-term memory. When new information is acquired it is stored in memory so that it can be retrieved later. Forgetting occurs when this information cannot be retrieved—a result of a storage or a retrieval problem, or both. In one study, older children forgot less than younger children because they were better able to retrieve information (Brainerd, Kingma, & Howe, 1985). School-age children remember things better because they recite the items they want to remember, a process that cognitive psychologists call **verbal rehearsal.** In

encoding
A memory process in which information is stored using cues that later can be used to retrieve information for recall.

retrieval
A memory process referring to the ability to access information from long-term memory.

verbal rehearsal
Reciting items to be remembered.

FOCUS ON CULTURE

In nonindustrialized countries, some children do not attend school regularly. As a result they have less deliberate practice in verbal rehearsal and other memory strategies. Yet it would be inaccurate to conclude that unschooled children have poor memory skills. When information is important and relevant to their daily lives, such as the names of different weaving patterns, children who do not attend school have been found to have good memory skills (Rogoff & Waddell, 1982).

one study only 10% of children ages 6 and younger spontaneously used verbal rehearsal to recall items in a picture. However, 60% of the 7-year-olds and over 85% of the 10-year-olds used verbal rehearsal (Flavell, Beach, & Chinsky, 1966).

mnemonic device

A strategy used to recall information from short- or long-term memory.

chunking

A coding strategy for storing and retrieving information.

Memory Strategies   The use of **mnemonic devices,** strategies to aid recall, increases with age during middle childhood. Older children generally acquire and use more strategies and are more adept at selecting a strategy to match the memory task (Miller, Haynes, DeMarie-Dreblow, & Woody-Ramsey, 1986). For example, if children are asked to remember the names of the people in their class, they might choose a different strategy if they were in a large class and had lots of names to remember (for example, they might attach a unique cue to each name and rehearse the list). If they only had a few names to remember they might make up a little rhyme or song that included all the names. Not until about age 10 do children become adept at using mnemonic strategies (Kail, 1979). Verbal rehearsal is one such strategy for remembering that is frequently used by school-age children. Between the ages of 6 and 9, children refine their use of **chunking,** a coding strategy for storing and retrieving information. For example, it may be difficult to recall a long string of numbers such as 0 3 7 2 8 9 5 1 0. However, when these numbers are grouped, as in 037-28-9510, they are easier to store and recall.

These Greek schoolchildren are exposed to a variety of lessons and activities that encourage the development of memory skills.

clustering

Grouping items to be remembered into relevant classes.

Another strategy involves **clustering,** or grouping items to be remembered into relevant classes. In an experiment on memorization strategies (Neimark, Slotnik, & Ulrich, 1971), children from first to sixth grades were shown sets of pictures related to four categories: animals, furniture, clothing, and transportation. Without telling them that all the pictures belonged to these four categories, the experimenters asked the children to arrange the pictures in any way that would help them remember the pictured objects. Children from the first to the third grades usually made no effort to classify the pictures. However, the older children made increasingly greater efforts to categorize the pictures. Furthermore, the more proficient they were in organizing the pictures into classes, the better they were able to recall the pictures at a later time.

Making a sentence out of the first letters of an otherwise meaningless sequence is another common coding strategy that aids memory. Ian, for example, was unable to recall the names of the lines on his music staff until his teacher taught him the sentence "Every Good Boy Does Fine."

COGNITIVE STYLE

cognitive style

A person's particular pattern of thought and the behavior used to respond to cognitive tasks.

My husband and I respond to problems very differently. I am likely to jump right in with possible solutions, correcting my approach according to what happens; my husband is likely to ponder the problem for quite a while before attempting a solution. Despite our different styles of thinking, between the two of us we usually solve the problem. **Cognitive style** refers both to a person's particular pattern of thought and to the behavior used to respond to cognitive tasks (Kogan, 1983).

A cognitive style reflects an individual's personality and preference, not his or her ability or intelligence. For example, when Ian looks at a group of buildings he thinks about how each building may be used (a functional understanding), whereas his cousin Adam notices the age and architectural styles of the buildings (a structural understanding). Both boys are equally logical and intelligent, but they differ in their style or manner of understanding the buildings. Each boy reflects a different style of learning. An example of a cognitive style is field dependence versus independence.

field dependent style

A person's difficulty in separating a relevant feature from the context or field in which it is embedded.

field independent style

A person's ability to ignore the irrelevant perceptual information in order to consider an object or even an experience separately from its field.

Field Dependence versus Independence
Some children are more influenced than others by perceptual information that, though irrelevant to a particular problem, is nonetheless present. People who are **field dependent** have difficulty separating a relevant feature from the context or field in which it is embedded. Those who are **field independent,** on the other hand, can ignore irrelevant perceptual information and consider an object or even an experience separately from its field. One way in which this cognitive style is identified is by using the Embedded Figures Test, in which the subject is asked to locate a geometrical figure embedded in a larger one (see Figure 7–1). Compared to field-independent children, field-dependent children are less able to ignore the irrelevant background lines and shapes and thus have more difficulty with this task.

Research suggests that people become more field independent as they move through middle childhood and adolescence (Witken, Goodenough, & Karp, 1967). In addition, field-independent children generally are more successful in academic and problem-solving areas (Witken & Goodenough, 1981), including skills such

FIGURE 7–1

An item from the Embedded Figures Test used to measure field independence and dependence.

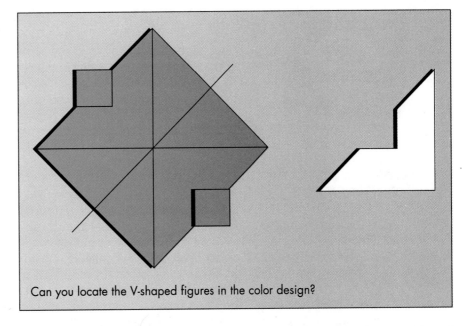

Can you locate the V-shaped figures in the color design?

as conservation, placing objects in a series, spatial perspective taking, and formal operations (Brodzinsky, 1985). Other research suggests that field-dependent people may be more skillful in social domains because they are adept at depending on other individuals for cues about how to act in situations in which there are no clear standards (Witken & Goodenough, 1977).

IQ TESTS

intelligence quotient (IQ)
A measure of a person's intelligence or mental capabilities.

In the United States, children are evaluated on the basis of their mental capabilities as early as the first grade. The most frequent assessment made of schoolchildren is that of intelligence. Educators use measures of the child's basic mental capabilities to guide class placement and curricula.

The first practical test to measure the mental capabilities of schoolchildren was published in 1905 by Alfred Binet. Binet had been commissioned by the Paris school system to develop a test to identify those children who were unable to benefit from normal classroom instruction. The test he developed consisted of a variety of items keyed to particular skills appropriate to each age level from 3 to 15 years of age. Binet assumed that those children who could pass the items appropriate for their age would also benefit from the schooling. Those who could not were given special instruction separate from the regular school curriculum.

Binet's test was brought to the United States and adapted by Lewis Terman at Stanford University; it has since been known as the Stanford-Binet intelligence test. Items of the Stanford-Binet include naming common objects, identifying parts that are missing from familiar figures, sorting, remembering numbers in a series, defining words, and copying figures. A series of items must be answered correctly for the child to receive credit for each age level. By assessing the highest age level for which the child passed most of the items, the child's **mental age (MA)** can be determined. For example, a child who passes most of the 10-year-old items

mental age
The highest age level for which a person passes most of the items on an IQ test.

Education Perspective

DO SCHOOLS CONTRIBUTE TO CHILDREN'S COGNITIVE DEVELOPMENT?

One of the developmental tasks of middle childhood is the acquisition of specific practical skills that prepare children to take their place in the world of adults. In many cultures the abilities to read, to write, to communicate with others, and to manipulate numbers are essential skills for success. In other cultures, more applied skills such as weaving, woodworking, farming, or tailoring may be vital to the economic survival of the family.

Depending on the culture, children receive their education in either formal or informal settings (Greenfield & Lave, 1982). In an informal education system children acquire skills in a number of ways, including apprenticeships, deliberate instructions from relatives or village elders, observation and demonstrations, and trial and error. However, in many cul-

tures, formal education systems offer children the opportunity to learn skills. Formal education is conducted outside the home, in schools in which trained teachers apply a common curricula.

Many assume that formal schooling enhances cognitive development. But does it? Stevenson (1982) attempted to find out by comparing the memory and cognitive performance of two groups of children in Peru—those who attended school and those who did not. In Peru, school attendance is compulsory, but only about 53% of 6-year-old children are in

school. Thus, Stevenson was able to study school attenders and nonattenders in three different types of settings: an isolated mountain village, a rain forest community, and a shantytown built on the outskirts of Lima. The study revealed that schooling did in fact make a difference. Those children who attended school scored much higher on memory and cognitive tasks.

Cross-cultural studies comparing achievement in Japan, Taiwan, and the United States (Stevenson & Lee, 1990; Stevenson, Chen, & Lee, 1993) shed some light on which aspects of formal education contribute to

deviation IQ
An IQ score derived by comparing the difference between a child's score and the average score of children of the same age.

would have a mental age of 10. Mental age is then divided by the child's chronological age to determine the IQ score, one that is used as a measure of intelligence or mental capabilities.

A different and more common way to measure IQ is to compute the **deviation IQ.** A deviation score is calculated by comparing the child's raw score on test items to the scores of children the same chronological age. By determining how much greater achievement. Japanese and Chinese children were studied because they have surpassed American children on measures of achievement, especially in mathematics. Significant cultural differences were found in the school and home environments of a sample of first- and fifth-grade children in Sendai, Japan; Taipei, Taiwan; and Minneapolis, Minnesota. Much greater emphasis was placed on academic activities among the Chinese and Japanese children than among the American children. Both at school and at home, more time, attention, and importance were placed on children achieving high academic standards in the Chinese and Japanese cultures. In Japanese and Chinese schools more specific time was spent in academic activities and less in social activities.

American parents seemed less concerned with their children's academic achievement and more interested in their cognitive growth than were Japanese and Chinese parents. Chinese and Japanese parents assisted the schools in promoting achievement by setting higher standards for their children, providing them with evaluations of their performance, and encouraging them to work hard. The Asian parents were more realistic about what their children could accomplish academically, socially, and cognitively than were the American parents who often overestimated what their children could accomplish. American parents were more likely to stress innate ability rather than hard work as the means for academic achievement.

Many cultures have informal schooling that resembles an apprenticeship in which children learn how to use tools and acquire practical skills.

the child's score differs from the average score of his or her peers, a deviation IQ score can be calculated.

An IQ score of 100 is considered to be average or the norm; most people would have a measured IQ score within the range of 90 to 119. An IQ score of 125 would be considered to be superior. IQ scores above 150 (very superior) are very rare; only about 0.23% of the population have scores this high. People with an IQ

Intelligence is often measured using standardized tests such as the Wechsler Intelligence Scale for Children—Revised Edition (WISC—R).

between 80 and 60 would be considered borderline mentally defective; IQ scores below 59 would be considered mentally defective and are rare in the population (about 0.63%).

David Wechsler developed a series of IQ tests that are similar to the Stanford-Binet. Each test is designed for use with a particular age group. The Wechsler Adult Intelligence Scale—Revised (WAIS—R) is used to assess people age 15 or older; the Wechsler Intelligence Scale for Children—Revised (WISC—R) is designed for children ages 6 to 16, and the Wechsler Preschool Primary Scale of Intelligence (WPPSI) is designed for children between ages of 4 to 6½. One difference between the Wechsler series and the Stanford-Binet is that the Wechsler IQ tests are divided not by age, but by skills needed to perform the various tasks on the test—divided into verbal and performance skills. Within each of these areas various subtests are used to measure specific abilities.

The Stanford-Binet and the Wechsler IQ tests are examples of *standardized tests*. They are administered individually according to a set standard of instructions. The score that a child receives is translated into an IQ score by comparing the child's performance with the standardized group performance.

Interpreting IQ Scores

Typically, children who score high on IQ also do well in school. This finding should not be too surprising since the tests were originally developed to predict school performance. However, IQ tests have been used to predict overall mental abilities instead of just school performance. As a result, they have been subject to much criticism and debate.

Some argue that the tests are culturally biased in favor of white, middle-class American children for whom most of the tests were originally developed. Some of the standardized tests questions assume that children have had specific experiences that children from a low socioeconomic setting or a different culture may not have had. Culture is believed to influence cognition by determining the information processing styles commonly used and the kinds of activities or practices in which a person would typically engage (Miller-Jones, 1989). For example, one question asks "What is the advantage of keeping money in banks?" This question would be difficult for children who have no money or opportunity to use banks. It has been recommended that measures of ability should include multiple tasks that are within the cultural domain of the test taker (Miller-Jones, 1989).

Other critics of IQ tests cite the heavy emphasis placed on what the child has already learned and not on the child's ability to learn new ideas. In fact, IQ tests measure achievement as well as ability. Some psychologists have suggested that the test be relabeled as a test of school ability or academic aptitude, instead of intelligence (Reschly, 1981). The new labels might avoid the implication that the tests are an index of overall innate ability.

Another criticism of IQ tests is that they place too much emphasis on verbal and logical cognitive skills and do not measure such talents as creativity or artistic or musical aptitude (Ellison, 1984; Gardner, 1983). Furthermore, children who are not proficient in English and those with language disorders are likely to be mislabeled as mentally retarded on the basis of their IQ score since performance on the test is heavily dependent on language skills.

Measures of intelligence vary not only from person to person, but also for the same person when measures are taken at different times in their development. Children experience spurts in their intellectual development as they do in their physical development. Typically, there is a spurt in intellectual growth at age 6 and again around age 10 or 11. However, by about age 10, IQ scores stabilize and one can make fairly accurate predictions about intellectual ability in adolescence and adulthood using the IQ score. For example, in one study, IQ scores taken at age 10 and IQ scores measured at age 18 were very similar (Honzik, MacFarlane, & Allen, 1948).

Although IQ scores have been overused and misinterpreted by those who have equated the IQ with general intelligence, the tests do serve a useful purpose when used correctly—to help predict school achievement. Using the IQ score as one guide, educators can identify children who can benefit from a specialized program of instruction tailored to meet their needs and abilities. IQ scores can be used to identify the slow learner, who may require more individualized programs, or the gifted child, who may be overlooked in the classroom.

RECAP

During the school years children gradually increase their abilities to attend to information, store it in memory, and retrieve it. By using mnemonic devices such as verbal rehearsal, chunking, or clustering, children are able to recall greater and more complex amounts of information. As children learn, they develop individual cognitive styles, including varying degrees of field dependence or independence. IQ tests are used to determine student ability and as a guide for class placement and curricula. The interpretation of IQ tests as a measure of intelligence has been criticized because of the tests' built-in biases.

THE LEARNING ENVIRONMENT

Acquiring new information and skills is a central part of children's activities during middle childhood. In all cultures, there are identified systems for educating children. Whether the learning environment is located in a community-based school, a village compound, or the home of a master artisan, much of children's time and attention is focused on learning and perfecting skills that will eventually help them to be productive members of their community. Schools in the United States and many Western cultures are formal institutions that are structured to provide a set curriculum and a somewhat standard code of conduct. But, despite the seeming uniformity of schools, children's learning experiences vary. Some children do well, while others fall behind. Some schools are effective in promoting learning, while others are not. The importance of the learning environment goes beyond the acquisition of knowledge. As a result of their school experiences children form beliefs about themselves as learners—beliefs that endure throughout adulthood.

THE SCHOOL EXPERIENCE

When the first day of school came around, both of my children could not wait to go. They looked forward to meeting their teachers and friends and getting their room assignments. They had their schoolbags, notebooks, and pencil cases ready several days before the opening of school. But not all children approach school with the same enthusiasm. For one thing, some schools, particularly in inner-city settings, are frightening places to some children. Unfortunately, in the United States the notion of the school as a safe haven for children is open to question. In some inner-city schools, children come to the classroom with weapons; gangs harass and attack nonmembers. Drug dealers hang around school yards to sell their wares. In an attempt to confront these hazards, schools have installed metal detectors and screens, established drug-free zones, and posted guards. While these efforts may prevent problems from occurring, they also call attention to the dangers within the school. In addition, many inner-city schools are older buildings that are often in need of physical repair; lead-based paint chips, vandalism, and poorly lit hallways contribute to the impression of decline. Children who attend unsafe schools may be distracted from their lessons by the challenges of avoiding the hazards in their school. In sharp contrast are schools in affluent suburban neighborhoods, which are frequently safer, brighter, and more spacious and better equipped.

Schools differ in the way they structure the learning environment. Over the years there have been two major shifts in prevailing ideas about how best to organize schools to promote learning. During my elementary school days, we were taught by rote and put in hours of practice on the multiplication tables. Teachers expected obedience and conformity and used strong disciplinary measures to obtain it. All children were taught the same lessons; those who did not learn as quickly were required to practice more. The classrooms were orderly, quiet, and filled with children working at their desks. My children, however, were educated in schools that placed greater emphasis on individualized learning in classrooms that were open and often noisy and colorful. The lessons were tailored to meet the needs of individual children. Children were given a choice about what they wanted to learn and the way they wanted to learn it. These different learning environments represent two contrasting approaches to education: the *traditional approach,* which focuses more on the achievement of academic skills, and the *open classroom,* which emphasizes the needs of the individual learner and is not limited to academic subjects.

The approach taken by schools at any given time is very much influenced by cultural and historical events. Back in the 1950s, when I was in grade school, most schools were organized to teach the three *R's* of reading, writing, and arithmetic. Later, schools shifted their emphasis to teaching children social and emotional skills. Today, because of national drops in SAT (Scholastic Aptitude Test) scores, schools are putting more emphasis on teaching the basics.

FUNCTIONS OF SCHOOL

Schools perform a variety of functions. First, they provide a setting in which children can learn the basic skills necessary for success in their culture. Typically, these skills include reading, communication skills, writing, computing, and arithmetic. The particular skills and subjects taught in school are dictated by the culture. For example, skill in foreign languages is important in cultures that are commercially active with people from different language cultures. In the United States, little emphasis is placed on foreign language skills in the elementary schools.

Schools are a major socializing agent for children. Instructors are expected to teach children how to follow orders, how to get along with other children and adults, and how to handle disputes. Parents and politicians argue about the extent of the teacher's responsibility. For example, children learn about how their bodies work, but not about sexuality or reproduction. In Great Britain, the only subject that is consistently required of students across school districts is religion, while in the United States the Constitution requires the separation of church and state, meaning that religious instruction cannot take place in public schools.

Schools are also the place where children learn about their culture. For example, children in the United States learn about the War of Independence and the Civil War and discuss the meaning of democracy and the Constitution. They also study and celebrate such holidays as Thanksgiving and Martin Luther King's Day. Other ethnic and religious events may also be discussed, but probably not to the degree to which they are studied in their native cultures.

FOSTERING LEARNING IN SCHOOL

What are the ingredients for effective schools? Certainly, a safe and inviting setting is important for preparing students to learn. But once children are in school and are presented with their lessons, what factors contribute to their success? Educational researchers have spent many hours attempting to identify the conditions that encourage children to become good learners. Obviously, teachers are an important element in the learning process. Effective teachers are typically those who are able to inspire students to want to learn, who set high enough standards for them to improve their skills, and who are lively enough in the classroom to hold students' interests. Good teachers like their jobs and love to learn themselves. They believe in their students' abilities to learn and convey that in their interactions with them. Of course, the size of the classroom will influence the type of interaction that teachers will be able to have with their students. Generally, smaller classes (less than 15 to 20 pupils per teacher) foster greater academic achievement than larger classes (Finn & Achilles, 1990).

Parents are another important ingredient in children's education. In the United States, many school systems in the United States are asking parents to join them in a partnership to help their children to do well in school (Epstein, 1990; National Commission on Excellence in Education, 1983). Parents display their involvement in their children's schooling in three ways (Grolnick & Slowiaczek, 1994). One is by their behavior; by going to school to meet their child's teachers and participating in classroom events and open houses. By being involved at school, parents demonstrate to their children the importance of education and gain information to help them guide their children.

Secondly, parents convey their personal and positive interest in how their children are doing in school through their comments and emotional reactions. Even though my daughter Sarah is a junior in college, she still likes it when I hang some of her "good" school work on the refrigerator! However, not all parental reactions are helpful. In one study (Ginsburg & Bronstein, 1993), researchers found that the more parents were involved in overseeing and helping with their children's homework—reminding them to do it, insisting that they complete it before they could do other activities—the poorer their children's grades and the more dependent they were on other people to tell them what to do. Furthermore, the more children were offered rewards for good grades, the lower their grades were. Apparently, parental overinvolvement can encourage dependence on extrinsic rewards for success and reduce children's ability to motivate themselves. Finally, parents reinforce the value of learning in the home by providing children with books, games, and other educational materials. Children influence their own learning. It probably would not surprise you to find out that how well a student behaves in the classroom will have an effect on the grades he or she receives from the teacher. In one study (Alexander, Entwisle, & Dauber, 1993) researchers found that classroom behavior in the first grade affected later academic performance in the second and fourth grades. "Teacher's pets" are more likely to receive positive evaluations from their teachers, which in turn reinforce their desire to do well in school. Children who want to do well in school are also more likely to select friends with a similar motivation (Kindermann, 1993). Furthermore, students who are involved in school activities are much more engaged in their own learning and earn higher grades than students who are less involved (Skinner, Wellborn, & Connell, 1990).

LEARNING DISABILITIES

In most cultures, by age 6 children start school and learn the basic reading, writing, and arithmetic skills. While most children readily acquire these fundamental skills, some experience considerable difficulty in the learning process. Compared to their peers, they may be two or more grade levels behind in reading or arithmetic skills. Years ago, such children would probably have been mislabeled as lazy, low achievers, or mentally deficient. Today, however, most American teachers are aware of the possibility that these children may have a learning disability.

The term **learning disability** refers to an inability to learn, and is used to include a variety of problems related to the basic processes necessary for school

learning disability
A problem in learning involving one or more of the basic processes that are necessary for understanding and using language and numbers.

Children with learning disabilities have normal mental aptitudes but for unknown reasons are unable to express their proficiency in their actual school performance.

achievement and comprehension. The term is difficult to define precisely because the specific disorders can vary from person to person and the symptoms may not be obvious early in development. These problems usually are not identified until children start school, where they are expected to perform specific learning tasks such as reading, drawing, taking tests, and writing. Learning-disabled children have normal mental abilities but for unknown reasons are unable to express their ability in their actual performance.

CHARACTERISTICS OF LEARNING-DISABLED CHILDREN

In the United States, estimates of the incidence of learning disabilities among children vary greatly, from 1% to over 30% (Hallahan & Kauffman, 1982). Twice as many boys as girls are affected by some form of learning disability (Freiberg, 1991). Some children have multiple difficulties that are obvious as soon as they enter school, while for other children the symptoms may be more subtle. The difficulties in learning may not emerge until later in childhood, adolescence, or even adulthood, when learning tasks become more complex and demanding. Many children never outgrow these difficulties; approximately 5 to 10 million American adults struggle with learning disabilities (Schulman, 1986).

While there is no universally agreed upon definition of the specific characteristics of learning-disabled children, commonly reported behavioral characteristics do exist (Meier, 1971). The most obvious attribute is that these children are unable to perform specific cognitive skills at grade level (see Table 7–6).

One common type of learning disability is **dyslexia,** inability to read as a result of difficulties in combining information from different sensory systems. For example, the child may not be able to distinguish the letter "b" from the letter "d" or may have difficulty associating the sound of a letter with its appearance. Other children with dyslexia may not be able to organize the words they see into a sentence or cannot distinguish between phrases like "in front of" and "in back of." **Dysgraphia** refers to difficulty in translating ideas or sounds into written letters and words. Some children, for example, display mirror writing—that is, writing

dyslexia

The inability to read as a result of difficulties in combining information from different sensory avenues.

dysgraphia

The inability to translate ideas or sounds into written words.

TYPES OF LEARNING DISABILITIES	
TYPE	**DESCRIPTION**
Aphasia	Inability to speak or comprehend what is said
Dyslexia	Inability to read or spell
Dysgraphia	Difficulty in writing
Dyscalcula	Inability to calculate numbers
Dyskinesia	Motor difficulties, poor coordination, and awkwardness
Attention deficit hyper-activity disorder (ADHD)	Unusual energy and restlessness, short attention span, and inability to complete work

TABLE 7–6

dyscalcula
The incapacity to mentally manipulate numbers or calculate.

from right to left and backward instead of left to right. Inability to learn basic arithmetic skills because of the incapacity to mentally manipulate numbers is called **dyscalcula.**

Some children with learning disabilities have very short attention spans and are very easily distracted by events going on around them. Sometimes these children are themselves distracting to others in a classroom because they constantly move about in an exaggerated way and are easily upset. A significant number of learning-disabled children have deficient gross and fine motor coordination, or *dyskinesia*. They are clumsy and have difficulty performing such motor actions as hopping on one foot, skipping, or walking a balance beam.

EFFECTS ON CHILDREN

While learning disabilities are usually not considered to be a result of emotional or behavioral disturbances, they do have an effect on children's personalities. Children with undiagnosed learning disabilities often develop behavior problems as a result of frustration at school. Children with learning disabilities also experience a loss of self-esteem as a result of their "failures" in school. Learning-disabled children tend to perceive themselves as less competent and less able to control their academic achievement (Grolnick & Ryan, 1990). They feel that their academic success or lack of it is under the control of other people rather than themselves. Other researchers (Hall & Haws, 1989) have found that children with learning disabilities had higher scores on a children's depression scale.

The negative effects of not being able to learn or complete school tasks as a result of a disability can be even more pronounced when children compare themselves to their peers who are not learning disabled (Renick & Harter, 1989). When learning-disabled children compare themselves with peers who are also learning-disabled, they have higher perceptions of themselves and their academic competence. This finding underscores the need to better train educators to deal with the needs of all children, disabled or not. Many people are unfamiliar with the specific abilities and limitations associated with learning disabilities and consequently underestimate the capabilities of learning disabled children.

CAUSES

Since we do not know what causes learning disabilities, perhaps they can be better understood by defining what does *not* cause them. The difficulties in academic performance found among learning-disabled children are not the result of mental deficiency or retardation. In fact, learning-disabled children typically score normal or above on IQ tests. Nor are these deficits the result of physical disabilities or uncorrected sensory handicaps such as poor vision or hearing loss.

One explanation of learning disabilities is that these difficulties are a result of a developmental lag. Many of the specific difficulties observed in school-aged, learning-disabled children are normally observed in less developmentally mature preschool-age children. For example, most preschoolers reverse or rotate letters of the alphabet, such as "b" for "d" and "q" for "p." While mirror writing, poor motor coordination, short attention span, and distractibility are all frequently observed in younger children, many of these characteristics are reduced or disappear between the ages of 5 and 7. However, it is not until the age of 12 that most hyperactivity and attentional problems decrease in learning-disabled

attention deficit hyperactivity disorder (ADHD)
Unusual energy and restlessness, short attention span, and inability to complete work.

Health Perspective

TREATING CHILDREN WITH ATTENTION DEFICIT DISORDERS

Teachers may be the first to call attention to a child who does not adjust well to the classroom routine. In the latest revision of diagnostic classification (American Psychiatric Association, *Diagnostic and Statistical Manual of Mental Disorders,* 1994) *hyperactive* was changed to **attention deficit hyperactivity disorder (ADHD).** The new term more precisely describes the symptoms of probably the most commonly diagnosed disorder in childhood (Minde, 1983).

The primary feature of attention deficit disorders is the child's inability to maintain attention. In school these children have short attention spans, are easily distracted, and seem inattentive. They do poorly on tests that require focused attention (Landau, Lorch, & Milich, 1992). They may daydream a lot and consequently may have difficulty in the classroom and at home, although it is not unusual for ADHD children to display attentional difficulties in one setting and not in another.

A second characteristic of ADHD children is their very low tolerance for frustration. They give up easily on tasks, may respond physically and aggressively when upset, and generally have difficulty delaying gratification. In short, they act very immaturely compared to their peers.

A third characteristic relates to the former label of hyperactive. ADHD children display an excessive level of aimless activity. They fidget, run and jump around, and appear restless. The problem with ADHD behaviors is heightened in school settings where children are expected to pay attention and not be disruptive. Typically, their school performance suffers and they have trouble getting along with other children and sometimes with their teachers (Henker & Whalen, 1989). Furthermore, hyperactive children often become poorly adjusted adults (Cantwell, 1972).

There are several hypotheses about the cause of ADHD. One possibility is that the disorder is the result of genetic defects. Parents of ADHD children tend to have been described as overactive in their early years and to have more psychiatric problems than parents of normal children (Morrison & Stewart, 1973). Boys are much more likely to have ADHD than girls (Hynd, Horn, Voeller, & Marshall, 1991). While this gender difference may be explained by socialization, particularly in the classroom, some researchers hypothesize that it is more likely a result of biological or genetic factors.

Attention deficit disorder has been treated with drugs, which reduce some of the symptoms. Stimulants such as Dexedrine and Ritalin have been prescribed to help children increase their attention spans and calm themselves down. The use of such drugs with ADHD children is controversial. The stimulants must be taken in frequent and often high doses, and they often have immediate negative side effects such as reduced appetite and insomnia. For some children, a long-term side effect of the stimulant is a slowdown in growth (Puig-Antich, Greenhill, Sassin, & Sachar, 1978). Although the drugs may work in the short term, there is no firm evidence that using these drugs has long-term educational or psychological benefits for ADHD children.

A second type of treatment involves cognitive behavior modification using rewards and punishment. Hyperactive children who are trained how to think ahead and to control their behavior have been shown to decrease their disruptiveness while under treatment, but these changes in behavior do not seem to generalize to nontreatment settings. The most effective treatment approach for ADHD children seems to be a combination of cognitive behavior modification and medication.

No single treatment approach has proven to be successful in curing attention deficit disorders, and controversy continues regarding the cause of ADHD. However, there is agreement among professionals that children with this disorder are best helped when they are diagnosed at an early age.

There is considerable variation in the incidence of dyslexia from one country to another. The United States has a very high rate; Japan has a very low rate. Italy has a lower rate than the United States (Lindgren, DeRenzi, & Richman, 1985). What explanations can you offer for these differences?

children. Yet not all of the problems associated with learning disabilities go away with maturity. Some learning disabilities continue into adulthood and throughout the lifespan; what changes is the person's ability to cope with the limitations.

Some researchers believe that these developmental and learning deficiencies are the result of some neurological dysfunction. In the past, the term **minimal brain damage** was used to explain neurological developmental delay resulting in learning deficiencies and other behavioral disorders. Brain damage can occur as a result of birth trauma or accidents, or it may be the result of a genetic brain dysfunction. The view that learning disabilities are produced by slight abnormalities in brain development is controversial. Many psychologists believe that the relation between brain functioning (an area still not fully understood) and learning disabilities is an indirect and complex one (Naylor, 1980).

minimal brain damage
A neurological developmental delay resulting in learning deficiencies and other behavioral disorders.

Children with attention deficit hyperactivity disorder (ADHD) are often disruptive in a classroom and cannot learn as well themselves because they are easily distracted by their surroundings.

TREATMENT

The best approach to helping children who are likely to experience extended difficulty in learning is to diagnose the disability early enough in their schooling to prevent the buildup of frustration and loss of self-esteem resulting from poor performance. Once the disability is recognized, usually by alert teachers, parents, or pediatricians, learning-disabled children benefit from individualized instruction in a setting designed to reduce distraction and increase attentiveness. Individual education plans are developed for each child that take into account the academic skills the child lacks and the resources that are available to minimize failure and enhance learning. Learning-disabled children need to learn early that they can succeed at school. By tailoring the lessons and instruction to the child's particular abilities, teachers and parents can help offset the difficulties presented by learning disabilities.

BRIEF REVIEW

Physical development during middle childhood is more uniform as children grow taller and leaner. Fine and gross motor coordination improves as children practice physical activities. Physical fitness and skills contribute to the child's self-concept and help establish lifelong habits.

According to Piaget, children attain the level of concrete operational thinking at about 6 to 7 years of age. They are able to reverse their thinking and decenter. Conservation and classification skills develop throughout the period from ages 6 to 12.

Children's appreciation of humor is closely linked with their level of cognitive development. Being able to understand and tell a joke adds to children's sense of competence.

During the concrete operational period, children lose their egocentric perspective and are able to consider other viewpoints besides their own. Social cognition refers to the child's growing awareness of other people and understanding of their motives.

Children shift in their understanding of morality at about age 6. Piaget described three stages of moral reasoning: premoral judgment, moral realism, and autonomous reasoning. Kohlberg's three levels and six stages of morality refine Piaget's early work. Children in middle childhood reason for the most part on Level I, preconventional morality. Kohlberg's theory has been criticized for its bias toward males and its lack of universality. Adults help children acquire moral behavior by reinforcing their behavior.

Children become more capable of processing information about the world. As children grow older, their attention span increases while they are less easily distracted. Their memory skills increase throughout the period from 6 to 12 years through the use of more efficient strategies.

Children develop their own style of processing information and solving problems. One cognitive style that has been studied is field dependence versus independence.

The IQ test was originally developed to predict school performance and is used in many schools to guide educators in their programs for children. Two popular standardized tests are the Stanford-Binet and the Wechsler IQ series. IQ tests have been criticized for being too narrowly constructed and biased. IQ scores stabilize at about age 10.

Schools vary in the type of learning environment they provide children. The function of schools include teaching children culturally valued cognitive and social skills. Two approaches to education have dominated the American system: the traditional emphasis on achievement and the open classroom emphasizing social-emotional skills. Teachers, parents, and children themselves all contribute to successful learning in school.

Some children have difficulty learning school subjects because they have some form of learning disability. While the causes of learning disabilities are not fully understood, psychologists and teachers recognize the importance of early diagnosis and treatment.

KEY TERMS

attention deficit hyperactivity disorder (ADHD) (286)
autonomous morality (270)

chunking (275)
class extension (264)
class intension (264)

clustering (276)
cognitive style (276)
concrete operations (260)

decentration (261)
deviation IQ (278)
dyscalcula (286)
dysgraphia (285)
dyslexia (285)
encoding (274)
field dependent style (276)
field independent style (276)
formal operations (260)

horizontal decalage (264)
intelligence quotient (IQ) (277)
learning disability (284)
mental age (277)
minimal brain damage (288)
mnemonic device (275)
moral behavior (268)
moral realism (269)

moral reasoning (268)
obesity (258)
physical fitness (257)
premoral judgment (268)
retrieval (274)
reversibility (261)
social cognition (268)
verbal rehearsal (274)

REVIEW QUESTIONS

If you can answer these questions, you have a good understanding of the material in this chapter. If a question seems difficult, go back to the text and review the topic.

1. Describe the motor development accomplishments of school-age children.

2. Why is middle childhood an important time in the development of physical fitness? What are the consequences of obesity for children?

3. Describe the cognitive characteristics of the concrete operational thinker. What is meant by horizontal decalage?

4. Describe at least three different tasks that are used to test the development of conservation in children.

5. What cognitive changes influence the appreciation and use of humor in middle childhood?

6. What is social cognition? Give an example of it.

7. Distinguish between moral reasoning and moral behavior. Describe Piaget's three stages of development of moral reasoning.

8. How does Kohlberg's theory of moral reasoning differ from Piaget's?

9. Describe Kohlberg's three levels of morality; give an example of each. Offer two criticisms of Kohlberg's theory.

10. Describe three strategies children use to aid their recall of information.

11. Distinguish between field independent and field dependent styles of thinking.

12. Why is it important to be cautious about using IQ tests to predict overall mental abilities? What are some other criticisms of the use of IQ tests?

13. Describe three ways in which parents can demonstrate involvement in their children's schooling.

14. What are learning disabilities? Describe how this type of disability affects self-esteem in children.

15. How are learning disabilities treated? What is ADHD and why is it a problem in school?

OBSERVATIONAL ACTIVITY

CLASSIFICATION SKILLS AND COLLECTIONS
Collecting things is a familiar part of childhood. Children collect all sorts of items, from stamps, rocks, stickers, and dolls to baseball cards, model airplanes, and bottle caps. As children develop a greater understanding of classes and relations between classes, they apply this knowledge to organize their collections. Because children still think in fairly concrete terms, it is sometimes easier for them to demonstrate their classification skills than it is to discuss them.

For this activity, you will need to find a child between the ages of 7 and 12 who has at least one collection of things. You may have a younger sibling, relative, or neighbor who would be willing to show you his or her favorite collection or collections. You will need to look at the child's collection and make some observations.

1. Ask the child to explain how the objects in the collection are arranged. What dimensions are used to sort the different items?

2. Notice the way the child has grouped the objects. Ask the child to explain how he or she knows where to place a new addition to the collection.

3. Are there subgroupings in the collection? Ask the child if there are categories that could be combined within the collection (for example, baseball cards from the different teams in the American League).

4. Ask the child to explain what he or she likes about collecting things. In what ways do they enjoy their collection? What does the child do with his or her collection?

After you have fully absorbed the details of the child's collecting, review your notes and describe the child's collection as an example of classification skills. What can you say about the benefit of collection for school-age children? What did you learn for yourself in doing this activity? Take a look at your own collections and ask yourself the same questions you asked the child in this activity.

CHAPTER 8

Middle Childhood: Personality and Social Development

It was a rainy Saturday afternoon and 12-year-old Loreen was baby-sitting for her younger siblings and cousins. Loreen lived with her sister and two younger brothers in an apartment building in a big city; her aunt and three cousins lived in the same building. The television set was broken and the children were getting bored. Finally, Loreen pulled out the Monopoly game and set it up on the kitchen table. Right away, Leroy, the oldest and biggest cousin, appointed himself banker. Immediately, James, age 7, protested: "That's not fair! You were the banker the last time!" As they argued about who should be the banker, Loreen distributed the play money. Her 10-year-old sister Kristal meanwhile picked her favorite playing piece, the Scotty dog, and then set about organizing her piles of play money.

The bickering finally stopped as Leroy and James resolved their argument—Leroy would be the banker since he was better at making change, and James would be in charge of passing out the deeds to the property. Fortunately, the order of the players was determined by a roll of the dice, and it was not long before they were all involved in moving their pieces along the board, acquiring property, and amassing their fortunes. Loreen congratulated herself for getting the kids to behave, and occupied herself by reading a magazine. In a few hours her aunt would be back from work and then she could meet her friends.

With her youngest sister, Elena, tied to her back with a shawl, 8-year-old Juanita joined several of her other sisters outside their adobe house in Juxtlahuaca, Mexico. They were watching two of their male cousins wrestle. At first the boys were pretend fighting; each boy was trying very hard to appear strong, but at the same time neither wanted to harm the other. The audience of girls added to the challenge of winning the match.

While the boys rolled over and over on the ground, Juanita gently rocked back and forth to soothe her baby sister. Her siblings were cheering the boys on and laughing at the spectacle they were creating. One boy pulled the other to the ground and in doing so, tore his shirt. This provoked the other boy to anger, and the pretend fight soon escalated from rough-housing to combat. Despite all of the commotion, no parent or adult interfered. The dominant boy would prevail and earn the respect of his peers for his strength.

PERSONALITY

personality
The consistent and unique pattern of social and emotional behavior and abilities that define an individual.

Now that my two children are adults, they frequently talk about their childhood memories. Among other memories, Adam remembers the time when I caught him and his friend Josh smoking cigars behind the garage; Sarah remembers the sleepover birthday party she went to when all of the girls ended up fighting with each other. The years from 6 to 12 are the times people remember the best when they consider their lessons from childhood. Unlike memories of the early childhood years, most people can recall many of the specific events and people from their school days. These memories help form their self-concept and shape their **personality**—that consistent and unique pattern of social and emotional behavior and abilities that define an individual. The successes and failures in the classroom, playground, village, and backyard become part of each person's self-concept. Especially significant during the school years is the impact of friends, relatives, elders, and teachers, because children are more aware of other people and their views of them as individuals.

Middle childhood is also a time when children rationally consider themselves as well as their world. Concrete operational thinkers are capable of simultaneously perceiving themselves as other people see them and as they would like to be. They are able to combine information about themselves from a variety of sources and areas. For example, cousin Leroy's view of himself is enhanced by his skill at counting out money, the admiration he receives from his cousins, and his physical size.

FOCUS ON CULTURE

The types of social interactions children and adults have is limited by their physical settings and their activities within these settings. In many cultures, age and gender may determine whether restrictions or expectations will influence particular activities. For example, in the Muslim culture, women and girls are not allowed to enter a mosque to pray. Many countries segregate their schools by gender and social class or caste. In many cultures girls are expected to stay near the home and care for younger children, while boys are expected to spend their nonschool time outside of the home working with older children and adults in the family or community business (Whiting & Edwards, 1988). These different types of experiences affect children's views of self within the culture.

THE LATENCY STAGE

According to Freud, the period from 6 to 12 years of age is the latency stage. *Latency* refers to the psychosexual stage in which children's sexual desires are latent or submerged. Because children are not distracted by unconscious desires to satisfy sexual urges, they are able to dedicate their energies to academic and intellectual achievements. Children avoid relationships with members of the opposite sex and instead seek out the companionship from peers of the same sex. It is during the latency stage that children develop their superegos as they become more adept at making cognitive distinctions between right and wrong. Through their interactions with family members, peers, and other adults, particularly in school, children gradually acquire values that help them develop their conscience.

THE STAGE OF INDUSTRY VERSUS INFERIORITY

The period from 6 to 12 years of age also corresponds to Erikson's (1963) fourth stage of psychosocial development, *industry versus inferiority.* During this period, children develop a view of themselves as workers, as people who can make things that have significance in the culture at large, and in the classroom, home, or play yard in particular. Children's multiple views of self become part of their adult personality.

During middle childhood, children in all cultures receive instruction about how to get along within their communities. In American culture, most instruction is accomplished through formal education in school. In other cultures, instruction occurs in less formal settings. This is the age when the young are taught how to hunt, cook, make clothing, and care for animals. In fact, in many rural cultures, children perform important work for the family and community in which they live. For example, it was Juanita's job to make the tortillas that were a part of the family's daily meals. In more industrialized cultures, children acquire work skills in school subjects: reading, writing, arithmetic, and computing skills. But social skills are also important; while Loreen was helping her aunt by baby-sitting her cousins, she was also learning how to take care of children, a skill that will help her with her own family in the future.

Regardless of the type of work the specific culture demands, all children acquire a sense of their own ability to be useful and industrious workers. Children develop a sense of industry as a result of their productivity. To the extent that they are able to apply their mastery of the tools of their culture to real problems, they develop a sense of their creative ability. For example, 7-year-old James took great pride in being able to read. Having this skill puts him on the same level as older children and adults. He is now able to do "real" work, not pretend work. He can use his reading skills to help his mother at the grocery store or to play Monopoly with his peers.

Success and tangible accomplishments in school or in sports provide children with evidence of their ability to initiate and complete a task. When children enter the first grade, they often bring an eagerness and enthusiasm to demonstrate their newly developed skills. Because they are focused on accomplishments, they often

During the period from ages 6 to 12, children in all cultures receive instruction in the ways of the world. In some cultures this might be instruction on preparing foods; in other cultures, it might mean learning how to use a computer.

admire adults because of their talents. When my daughter Sarah was 7, for example, she was in awe of my cooking skills. She would tell everyone, "My mother makes the best cookies in the world!" When she was able to make cookies on her own under my instruction and guidance, she was able to value her own accomplishments. "Taste the cookies I made! They're better than Mom's!"

Unfortunately, not all children find an area in which to demonstrate their competence. Instead, some children experience repeated failure or are made to feel like failures. Some parents always find something wrong with what their children have done. Consequently, these children form a view of themselves as inadequate, incompetent, and inferior. Believing that they cannot succeed, these children are easily discouraged from trying out new skills or from persevering on a task long enough to achieve success. They often give up on a project before it is begun.

Negative resolution of this stage of psychosocial development may be the result of several factors. Children may have accumulated failures because they have selected projects or tasks that are too difficult for their present levels of mastery. Children may be attempting to meet the unrealistic expectations of parents or older siblings who are pressuring them to achieve before they are ready. Another negative influence occurs when children's accomplishments are unrealistically compared to others and thereby diminished. Often school-age children will use rigid standards to evaluate their own accomplishments. For example, when I praised artwork that Sarah brought home from school, she objected by saying, "Mine was not as nice as Winnie's; hers was much neater!"

FOCUS ON CULTURE

Being a productive and contributing member of a group is an adult characteristic that has its roots in middle childhood. In many nonindustrialized countries, children are an economic resource for parents. Children help produce, transport, and sell the goods and products that contribute to the family's survival. At the same time, children gain mastery in the trades they will most likely enter when they reach maturity. School-aged children in highly industrialized countries, however, often must wait until adolescence or early adulthood before they gain practical experience in adult work.

THE DEVELOPMENT OF SELF

Do you remember when you first began to think about yourself and wonder what others thought of you? It probably was during your elementary school days. Between the ages of 6 to 12 children's views of themselves expand considerably. With the decline of egocentricity in the concrete operational period, children begin to comprehend other people's perspectives and distinguish between their own desires, needs, and points of view and those of others. **Self-concept** refers to people's sense of their own identity, including an awareness of their physical characteristics and psychological traits. Throughout middle childhood, self-awareness changes as children develop the cognitive skills that allow them to make more detailed comparisons and distinctions between themselves and others. Older children not only are more aware of other people's views of them, but they are better able to integrate these views with their own self-awareness to form a more complex and meaningful concept of self.

self-concept
A person's sense of his or her identity, including physical and psychological traits; the way a person views oneself.

During the school years, children develop more complex ways of defining themselves. This boy defines himself through his interest and skill at baseball.

Changes in Self Awareness The developmental changes in self-concept were the focus of research by Broughton (1978), who asked children such questions as "What is the self?" and "What is the mind?" From the children's answers, Broughton distinguished two levels of self-awareness in school-age children. In early childhood, the self is regarded in physical terms. For example, Juanita might distinguish herself as different from her cousin Gabriela because she has bushy eyebrows and a flat nose, while Gabriela has a rounded nose and thinner eyebrows. The self-definitions of younger children may include their possessions and toys as well as physical characteristics of their bodies. Gender, age, size, and appearance are critical features that young children use in defining the self (Damon, 1983). Physical activities are also included in children's views of themselves.

By about age 8, a shift occurs in the way children view themselves. According to Broughton (1978), at this age children begin to distinguish between mind and body—between what they think and feel and what they do or how they look. Older school-age children describe the self in psychological rather than physical terms.

Using a different procedure, Selman (1980) found a similar developmental shift in children's self-concept. He presented children with the following dilemma:

> Eight-year-old Tom is trying to decide what to buy his friend Mike for a birthday party. By chance, he meets Mike on the street and learns that Mike is extremely upset because his dog Pepper has been lost for 2 weeks. In fact, Mike is so upset that he tells Tom, "I miss Pepper so much that I never want to look at another dog again!" Tom goes off, only to pass a store with a sale on puppies. Only two are left and these will soon be gone. (1980, p. 94).

The children are asked to decide whether or not Tom should buy the dog for Mike. Using children's responses, Selman has identified three levels of self-awareness in children (see Table 8–1). In the first level, *physicalistic* conception of self, children view "self" only in physical terms, including their actions. When Mike says he doesn't want to see a puppy again, young children interpret this statement to mean just that. They do not make any distinction between feelings and actions.

The second level of self-awareness emerges around age 6, when children begin to distinguish between subjective inner states and more material outer states. Selman called this level *awareness of distinction* between actions and intentions. Children recognize the difference between a person's psychological and physical experience but believe that the two types of experiences are consistent with each other. So they interpret Mike's psychological experience of missing his dog to be consistent with his physical or behavioral reaction of saying he doesn't want another puppy. When Mike says he never wants to look at another dog, he means it. Children at this level do not believe that people can distort their outward expression of their inner feelings and psychological experience. They do not yet reflect on their own inner thoughts and feelings.

It is not until the third level, at age 8, that children recognize that a person's inner psychological experience may not be consistent with physical or outer appearance. At this level, which Selman calls the *emergence of an introspective self* and the second-person perspective, children realize that Mike may really want another puppy even though outwardly he has indicated that he does not.

Children now learn to manipulate their inner states and external appearance. For example, in playing Monopoly, Leroy may very much want to buy Park Place but does not express this desire in his behavior because he does not want cousin James to recognize his plan and thwart it by buying it before he does. Leroy's strategy is based on his recognition of the distinction between inner and outer aspects of the self and his awareness that others use his external reactions to judge what he is thinking.

During middle childhood children become more aware of personal characteristics in others and use them as standards to evaluate themselves and others

SELMAN'S STAGES OF SELF-AWARENESS IN CHILDREN		
STAGE	**AGE IN YEARS**	**CHARACTERISTICS**
Physicalistic conception of self	Less than 6	Views self in physical terms, including actions; does not distinguish between actions and feelings
Awareness of distinction between actions and intentions	6	Distinguishes between feelings and actions, but believes the two are consistent with each other; does not expect people to distort their actions to hide their feelings
Emergence of an introspective self	8	Recognizes the differences between feelings and thoughts and actions; learns to manipulate inner states and outward behavior

TABLE 8–1

(Rholes & Ruble, 1984). Ruble (1983) found that children's use of social comparisons of competence to define themselves increases dramatically after the age of 7. Furthermore, children develop a more differentiated view of themselves as they grow older (McCandless & Evans, 1973). Instead of simply describing themselves as "good" or "bad" as younger children do, children in the later part of middle childhood describe themselves in more specific ways: "I'm good at team sports but not so good at individual events," or "Most of the time I get along well with my friends except when I have to choose between spending time studying or playing." Children also become more self-critical as they get older (Harter, 1983). Nine- and 10-year-old children are particularly sensitive to correction and embarrassment in part because they themselves are so self-critical.

self-esteem

An affective evaluation of oneself expressed as positive or negative.

Self-Esteem   Do you like yourself? If you do, you probably have high self-esteem. According to Damon (1983), **self-esteem** is an affective evaluation of one's self, generally assessed in terms of positive or negative traits. While the self-concept—the cognitive aspect of self—changes with the child's ability to understand events, the child's evaluation of self seems to be more stable throughout middle childhood.

James (1890) was one of the first psychologists to study self-concept and the evaluation of self. He believed that a person's self-esteem was a result of three factors: (1) the extent to which one's successes or achievements meet one's aspirations; (2) the degree to which one's achievements or successes are also valued by communal standards of success or status; and (3) the extensions of the self—the material possessions and reputation a person has accumulated. If we achieve our aims, society views them positively, and we value our acquisitions, we will have high self-esteem.

Since James's early formulation, other researchers have studied self-esteem, particularly in children. The research of Coopersmith (1967) is notable. Coopersmith studied 85 fifth- and sixth-grade boys and their mothers to determine the antecedents of self-esteem. He interviewed the mothers and children separately, and asked each child to fill out his Self-Esteem Inventory (SEI).

Children with high self-esteem are more likely to be popular, outgoing, and friendly with their peers.

Children were asked to read a variety of statements and check whether each of these is "like me" or "unlike me." The statements classified the degree to which they felt sorry about themselves, were proud of their school achievements, felt they were popular with their peers, got along with their parents, and so on. Coopersmith found that boys' self-esteem did not change very much over the 3-year period studied. Boys who had a positive view of themselves at 10 also viewed themselves positively at age 13.

Coopersmith found that boys with high self-esteem were more independent and creative than those with low self-esteem. They did better in school and were more likely to be assertive, socially outgoing, and popular. They would also express their views on a topic even when they anticipated criticism for their beliefs. Furthermore, they were less conforming yet had fewer difficulties in forming friendships when compared to other children. Coopersmith noted that boys with high self-esteem seemed to lack a self-consciousness that would impede them from presenting themselves in a confident manner. Children with low self-esteem did not display the same degree of self-confidence.

Although Coopersmith studied self-esteem in boys, his findings have been generalized to girls as well. Other researchers (Harter, 1983, 1990; Piers, 1977; Rosenberg, 1979) using different scales of self-esteem derived from samples composed of both genders have generally supported Coopersmith's results.

A review of the research on self-esteem (Wylie, 1979) suggests that self-esteem generally becomes more positive during adolescence. Furthermore, self-esteem is relatively consistent over time; children with a high self-esteem in early adolescence maintained it through early adulthood (Block & Robins, 1993). However, unlike adults, children develop different views of themselves depending on their experiences in different settings. Adults may form different opinions about themselves as a result of different experiences, but they are able to integrate them into a global evaluation of themselves that describes their self-esteem. As children begin to form an evaluation of themselves, they often form separate and distinct versions of their self-esteem.

body esteem
A person's evaluation of his or her body.

One specific type of self-esteem is **body esteem,** which refers to a person's evaluation of his or her body. In normal-weight children, overall self-esteem does not systematically change with age nor is it related to body esteem. However, for overweight children between the ages of 11 and 17 the relationship between self-esteem and body esteem is closely linked (Mendelson & White, 1985). Those children who had low self-esteem also had a low body esteem. For younger overweight children (8- to 10-year olds) there was no relationship between body esteem and

FOCUS ON CULTURE

Children who grow up as members of minority groups often have to balance their views of self against the racial and ethnic attitudes prevailing in the broader culture. Bicultural children who grow up in families that value and teach their ethnic heritage are likely to develop higher levels of self-esteem than children who must confront racial and ethnic biases without family support (Allen & Majidi-Ahi, 1989). African American children, for example, are likely to have higher levels of self-esteem when they live in cohesive ethnic communities (Powell, 1985).

FOCUS ON CULTURE

In some areas of the United States, children have an opportunity to interact with children from different ethnic backgrounds and cultures in the classroom. Within ethnically diverse school settings, children can form friendships with cross-ethnic peers and thus expose themselves to new experiences (Howes & Wu, 1990). An ethnically diverse classroom forces children to learn more about other cultures and customs, and, by comparison, to learn about their own cultural heritage.

self-esteem. Mendelson and White also found that overweight boys suffered low self-esteem between the ages of 11 to 13, while overweight girls' self-esteem suffered more in late adolescence.

Parental Influence on Self-Esteem

When my children were young I wanted to provide them with experiences that would help them feel good about themselves as they grew up. My interest in being a supportive parent grew out of my knowledge of the research literature that suggests that parents have a strong influence on their children's self-esteem (Baumrind, 1971, 1991; Coopersmith, 1967). In his study, for example, Coopersmith examined the characteristic behaviors of the boys' parents. He found that certain child-rearing practices were related to high self-esteem in the children. Parents of such children were more accepting and affectionate; they took an interest in their children's activities and friends and were generally more attentive to them. They were also strict, set clear limits on behavior, and enforced rules in a firm and decisive manner. However, they did not use coercive kinds of discipline; they were more likely to deny privileges than to use physical punishment or withdrawal of affection to control their children. These parents were also more likely to include a rationale along with punishment.

Coopersmith believed that parents who set and enforced clear limits on acceptable behavior were also the parents who accepted their children's views and allowed them to exercise more self-control as opposed to parental control of behavior. They allowed their children greater individual expression. They believed that children should have a say in making family plans and were more likely to allow their children to set their own bedtimes. Children whose parents present no limits or ambiguously defined ones are unlikely to know what is expected of them and, therefore, tend not to evaluate their own behavior. According to Coopersmith (1967), "parents who have definite values, who have a clear idea of what they regard as appropriate behavior, and who are able and willing to present and enforce their beliefs are more likely to rear children who value themselves highly" (p. 236).

One final finding from Coopersmith's study is that the parents of children with high self-esteem children were themselves active, poised, and relatively self-assured. They had high self-esteem and confidence in their ability to cope with the responsibilities and duties of child rearing. Interestingly, the mother's work history was found to influence self-esteem. The higher the child's self-esteem, the more likely it was that the mother was regularly employed and satisfied with her job.

RECAP

During Freud's latency stage, children develop their academic skills and their conscience. According to Erikson, during middle childhood the crisis of industry versus inferiority is resolved. Children change the way they view themselves as they mature; they move from a physicalistic view of self to one that involves psychological traits and experiences. During this time children expand their view of self and begin to evaluate themselves; they also evaluate themselves differently depending on the setting of their experiences. Self-esteem is influenced by the way children are treated by their parents, peers, and family.

SOCIALIZATION

When my daughter Sarah went to school for the first time, she was a little reluctant to leave me. Even though I worked while she was young, we still had spent a lot of time together. However, it didn't take long before Sarah couldn't wait to go to school. She had made lots of friends and looked forward to playing with them during recess. During her elementary school years, it became obvious that her parents were not the only influential force in her life. More and more she relied on her brother Adam to give her advice and show her how to behave when she was uncertain.

During the school years there is a notable shift in children's social behavior. They spend less time under the direct scrutiny and instruction of their parents and

Competition for grades may encourage students to look at other children's work. Younger children glance at their neighbors for the answers; older children look to see how their work compares with that of their peers.

more time playing with siblings and peers or learning in the classroom from their teachers. The impact of parents on children's behavior is augmented by what children learn as a result of play and school interactions. Like parent-child relationships, child-child relationships are not static or unidirectional; the child not only is affected by others but, in turn, elicits certain reactions from siblings and peers. For example, Leroy liked to bully his brother James, who would respond by crying; James's behavior caused his mother to yell at Leroy. If you have siblings, you already know that sisters and brothers profoundly influence one another. Siblings are powerful socializing agents because they share our lives for the duration of childhood, and their influence extends well into adulthood.

THE IMPACT OF SIBLINGS

Juanita spent many hours with her sisters—especially Elena, because she was responsible for minding her. Children between the ages of 2 and 10 spend countless hours of play and other activities with their siblings. In the United States, more than 80% of children have one or more brothers or sisters. The impact of siblings on each other's lives is further enhanced by the trend in industrialized countries toward smaller families. With fewer children in a family, siblings have more intense relationships with each other (Bank & Kahn, 1982). Siblings serve as powerful behavioral models and teachers for each other (Azmitia & Hesser, 1993). They are a source of support and comfort in times of distress and help teach social roles (Lamb, 1982b).

Birth Order   Beulah harshly reprimanded her sister Kit for using too much butter on her bread. Kit, being 3 years Beulah's junior, reluctantly gave in to her older sister's authority and used less butter. This scenario may sound familiar to those

During middle childhood children spend less time with their parents and more time with their peers.

of you who have experienced the pecking order among siblings. You might be interested to know that Beulah is 90 years old and Kit is 87! Even though siblings establish their status with each other in early and middle childhood, their birth order can affect their relationship throughout their lifespan.

birth order

A person's rank in a family relative to the number of siblings based on the order of birth.

The impact of **birth order** on behavior and development has been studied by many researchers. Research suggests that firstborn children are more likely to be high achievers. They are more likely to go to college, score higher on IQ tests, and generally do better in school (Sutton-Smith, 1982). They are also judged to be more active than later-born children (Eaton, Chipperfield, & Singbeil, 1989). Other studies suggest that firstborn children are more conservative, more dominant, more dependent on others' approval, more affiliative, and more responsible than later-born children.

The effects of birth order are influenced by the siblings' genders and by the spacing between siblings (Minnett, Vandell, & Santrock, 1983; Sutton-Smith & Rosenberg, 1970). For example, second-born siblings often model their behavior after the firstborn, but the amount of imitation is greater if the older sibling is of the same sex. Furthermore, while the tendency to imitate an older sibling is very common for females, it is less often the case for males. Some males seem to counteract the influence of their older sisters by asserting themselves through gender-role behaviors. They may use physical aggression to reverse the dominant role the older sister has as a result of age (Sutton-Smith & Rosenberg, 1970).

Generally, older and firstborn siblings exercise more power over younger siblings, while later-born siblings acquire more social skills in negotiating with and accommodating others (Bryant, 1982). Older siblings assume the role of teacher and manager more often than younger siblings; younger siblings, like Kit, generally comply with their older sibling's role of teacher and guide (Brody, Stoneman, MacKinnon, & MacKinnon, 1985). Furthermore, female school-age siblings are more likely than male siblings to assume the role of teacher.

Children without siblings have earned an undeserved reputation for being more self-centered, less cooperative, and less likely to get along with people than children who have siblings. However, research studies do not always support this view. In one study, only children were found to be more likely to be cooperative rather than competitive in games (Falbo, 1982, 1979). Children who grow up without brothers and sisters score higher in self-esteem, have higher motivation to achieve, and, consequently, do better in school (Falbo, 1992). A country's culture and customs may influence the behavior of only children. For example, in mainland China, there is a strictly enforced one-child family policy. In comparing 180 matched pairs of only and sibling children, Jiao, Ji, and Jing (1986) found that children without siblings were more egocentric whereas children with siblings were more persistent and cooperative and were held in higher prestige by their peers. The researchers concluded that only children, being the sole targets of parental attention and family resources, did not have to learn to cooperate with others in a communal setting as did children with siblings. But, a later study involving over 4,000 Chinese children failed to find any differences in personality between only children and children with siblings (Falbo & Poston, 1993). Like Western firstborn children, only children scored higher on tests of academic achievement.

Sibling Interactions When our daughter Sarah was born, our son Adam immediately assumed the role of "older brother." He was very proud of his new baby sister, especially when we let him push her in her stroller. As Adam and Sarah grew older, their relationship changed somewhat. Adam continued to relate to Sarah as the authoritative older brother, but Sarah soon learned how to garner her own power by teasing and baiting Adam. She knew when to scream and when to smile, and the best Adam could do was to control his temper. Later, when they both approached young adulthood, their relationship mellowed and they became friends.

Siblings interact with each other in ways that are different from parent-child interactions (Buhrmester & Furman, 1990). For example, children generally behave in a more negative manner toward each other than parents do toward children (Baskett & Johnson, 1982). Even though some older siblings assume the role of baby-sitter for their younger siblings, they do not make good substitute parents (Bank & Kahn, 1982). For one thing, older siblings, even some adolescents, do not possess the cognitive maturity or experience to function effectively in the role as parent. They cannot impart values as parents do, nor do they demonstrate the degree of emotional poise characteristic of adult caregivers. Second, younger siblings tend to resist the older sibling's efforts to provide care (Baskett & Johnson, 1982), and will often behave more disruptively when under the care of siblings than when cared for by parents or other adults. Also, older siblings do not have access to the same resources as adults when caring for younger children. Their power base is considerably different from the parents', and younger siblings are likely to recognize this fact. For example, when Loreen attempted to control her sister's spitting, she was stopped by her sister's angry retort, "You can't make me!"

Younger siblings often have great admiration for their older siblings, a sentiment that is not usually reciprocated. Rather, older siblings view their younger siblings as an annoyance. Furthermore, older siblings do not report the same degree of intimacy toward their younger siblings that younger siblings express toward them (Burhmester & Furman, 1990). Yet the wider the age difference between siblings, the more likely it is they will develop a nurturing and affectionate relationship. The closer in age siblings are, the more likely it is that their relationship will be antagonistic and quarrelsome.

Sibling rivalry or jealousy is a common occurrence in childhood. Children often see themselves in competition with each other for their parents' attention, affection, or praise. Adler (1928) maintained that the "dethroning" of the firstborn child by a second child is bound to produce jealousy and hostile aggression. If parents respond to the aggressive behavior by punishing the transgressions, children often devise less obvious ways of getting back at their rivals through such actions as tattling or teasing.

Parents often find themselves caught in the middle of sibling conflict. By admonishing one sibling for inappropriate behavior, they may be inadvertently providing the other sibling with ammunition for a later taunt ("Ha, Ha, you got caught!"). One study (Dunn & Kendrick, 1982) found that following the birth of the second baby, mothers spent less time with and were less sensitive to the needs and interests of their firstborns. The researchers also found that firstborns of mothers who talked to the older sibling about the care and needs of the new baby as a person and valued the older child's participation in caregiving developed a more positive approach to the new sibling. Thus one way to reduce sibling rivalry among children is for parents to provide individual attention to each sibling based on the child's needs.

Sometimes parents actually foster the sibling rivalry by drawing comparisons among them. For example, telling one child that his school work is not as good as

sibling rivalry
Children's perceived competition for parents' attention, affection, or praise.

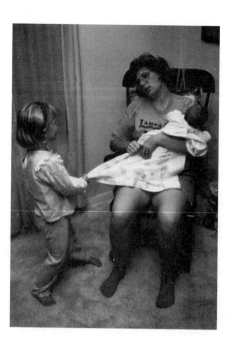

Sibling rivalry is exacerbated by who parents ignore the needs of one child in favor of another.

his sister's may intensify the brother's rivalrous feelings. Recognizing the child's achievements independently from his sister's provides the child with the recognition he desires without contributing to sibling rivalry.

Sibling interaction is marked not only by a negative tone but by positive feelings as well (Dunn, 1983). As early as 3 years of age, siblings have been known to have warm, positive, and helpful reactions toward each other. For one thing, older siblings often function as teachers for younger siblings. This is especially true in nonindustrialized or rural cultures where older siblings care for younger siblings on a daily basis. Sometimes, siblings are in a better position than parents to teach their younger siblings because they are on a similar level of understanding and can communicate with them more effectively (Cicirelli, 1977).

Sibling interactions are different from peer interactions. With siblings, children are able to practice different social roles that they cannot practice with their peers. For example, in two different studies (Stoneman, Brody, & MacKinnan, 1984; Brody, Stoneman, & MacKinnan, 1982) in which siblings and peers were observed playing, it was found that older siblings assumed the dominant role of manager-teacher with their siblings, the equalitarian role of playmate in their peer interactions, and a combination of dominant and equalitarian roles when

FOCUS ON CULTURE

Generally, when people use the term *sibling* they are referring to people who are related as brother or sister by blood lines or marriage. However, in many Native American Indian cultures, the term *brother* or *sister* is used to refer to people from the same tribe or to those living within the immediate community. Children who grow up in communal or extended family settings are likely to have "siblings" who are technically not related but who function in the same social capacity as genetic brothers and sisters.

interacting with peers and siblings together. By switching from one social role to another in play with peers and siblings, children acquire more experience and sophistication in seeing themselves in various social roles.

PEER INTERACTIONS

Characteristics   Who were your playmates during your elementary school years? Most likely you played with children who were the same sex as you and were around your own age. During middle childhood, children throughout the world interact primarily with others of their own sex and race (Edwards & Whiting, 1988; Maccoby, 1988; Sagar, Schofield, & Snyder, 1983). With the exception of sibling interactions, children are more likely to play with other children of the same age. In part, this is due to the greater familiarity and availability of classmates, but it may also reflect similarity in interests and cognitive maturity.

Likewise, peer interactions are qualitatively different from adult-child interactions. Children seek out other children for companionship, affection, and for amusement, whereas adult interactions are more often based on the child's need for protection, care, or instruction (Damon, 1983). Unlike parent-child relationships, children usually choose their own friends and freely end the relationship when they are dissatisfied with the interactions. Children are more likely to practice and refine their social skills with each other than with adults because of their more equal status.

Functions of the Peer Group   Peers serve a variety of functions during middle childhood. Williams and Stith (1980) have identified five functions of the peer group (Table 8–2). For one thing, peers provide *companionship*—someone to share company, time, and conversation. Through the subculture of peers, children

FUNCTIONS OF PEER GROUPS

FUNCTION	DESCRIPTION
Provide companionship	Peers are playmates, sharing time, conversation, and activity.
Provide a testing ground for new behavior	Children try out antisocial or prohibited behaviors with peers; peers provide opportunities to practice cooperation and negotiation.
Convey knowledge	Peers provide new information about games, the world, dress and manners, and school lessons.
Teach rules and logical consequences	Peers establish their own rules and punish those who disobey them.
Reinforce gender role behaviors	Peers accept those who conform to social norms and provide an audience for children's social roles.

TABLE 8–2

Source: From *Middle Childhood Behavior and Development* (2nd ed), by J. Williams and M. Stith, 1980, New York: Macmillan. Adapted with permission.

learn jokes, riddles, and games and enhance their collections of baseball cards and comic books. In addition, peers pass along the numerous games and superstitions that are a part of childhood. Juanita and her friends spend hours practicing the string game of Cat's Cradle, a game that has been known around the world for generations.

Second, peers provide a *testing ground for new behavior*—particularly behaviors that adults are likely to prohibit. Cursing, spitting, and performing acts of bravado are more readily practiced with peers, especially when these acts are likely to win admiration. Older children, particularly between the ages of 10 and 13, are more likely to engage in antisocial activities as a result of peer influence (Bixenstine, DeCorte, & Bixenstine, 1976). By looking to their friends for approval, children form an alliance that provides a buffer to the adult world. The peer group offers encouragement and the opportunity for children to be independent from their parents' values and standards. It also provides opportunities to acquire positive social skills such as cooperation and negotiation.

Third, peers help *communicate knowledge,* not only knowledge of children's games but more worldly knowledge as well. Children more readily accept information (and misinformation) from their peers. For example, from a friend at day camp Leroy learned how to carve a whistle from a piece of wood, and Juanita learned from her friend Carlos how to use a calculator. Many school systems are recognizing the benefits of peer instruction for both the teacher and the learner. Not only do peers deliberately impart knowledge to each other, but they also provide potent models of behavior. Because children are more likely to imitate models they perceive as similar to themselves, they learn more readily from their peers. The effects of modeling are easily seen in later childhood, when children imitate each other's manner of dress and gestures.

The peer group *teaches rules and logical consequences,* from which children learn specific codes of conduct. Often peers apply harsh consequences for

Peers provide companionship for one another; they play games together, develop new rules, and share good times.

violating these codes of acceptable behavior, however. Peer-generated rules cover a wide range of behaviors and are usually couched in negative terms: don't tattle, don't be a teacher's pet, don't cheat on a friend. Children often form informal clubs structured by a set of special rules. For example, members must live within walking distance of each other and swear loyalty to each other. If you follow these "rules" you become an accepted member of the group; if you move out of the neighborhood or are found to be disloyal, you are out the club.

Finally, peers also help *reinforce gender-role behaviors.* During the elementary school years, children are acutely aware of the differences between boys and girls as a result of peer pressure. A girl who acts like a boy or plays with boys is likely to not gain acceptance into the "girl's club." Children also learn about sexuality through peer discussions, particularly during later childhood. Through peer relations, children gain experience meeting new friends and telling them about themselves. Friendships in particular provide a context for the growth of a child's social self, a context within which the child can learn which presentation of self is socially acceptable and which is not (Fine, 1981). For example, a boastful child may learn from friend that bragging annoys others; hence the child may refrain from such behavior in new social groups. By developing the social skills necessary for getting along with others, children acquire a more varied and positive definition of themselves. Ten-year-old Loreen describes herself as a nice person because she is helpful to her friends in school. This view of herself with respect to her friends will probably generalize to other situations later in life.

Sex Differences in Peer Interaction

Children's birthday parties are a good setting in which to get a snapshot of peer interactions in middle childhood. If you are fortunate enough to watch one in action, you might notice that most, if not all, of the children at the party are of the same sex. Girls play with girls, and boys with boys, and usually the two do not interact unless they are grouped together by adults. At no time in development are sex groupings more prominent than in middle childhood. Children are more likely to segregate by sex when there are many peers from whom to select their playmates. If little or no choice exists, children will play with peers of the opposite sex (Edwards & Whiting, 1988). Same sex groupings are also more likely to occur in settings that are not structured or supervised by adults (Lockheed & Klein, 1985).

Boys and girls differ in the kinds of activities they prefer in play. Boys are more likely to engage in rough-and-tumble activities involving physical contact (Humphreys & Smith, 1987; Maccoby, 1988). They play in larger groups that demand more space, such as streets, playgrounds, or public areas. Girls are more likely to play in smaller and more intimate groups, usually inside. They are more concerned with cooperating with their peers and promoting friendships. They are less confrontational or directive in their styles of interaction with their same sex peers than are boys. Given a choice, girls will avoid interacting with boys, in part because boys are more likely to assert themselves using power techniques of pushing, grabbing, or threatening (Maccoby, 1990).

popularity
The degree to which a child is liked and accepted by his or her peers.

Popularity

One aspect of children's peer relationships that has been a prevalent area of research is **popularity,** the degree to which a child is liked and accepted by his or her peers. In any group of children there are usually some who are popular and accepted by the majority of their peers, and there are a fair number who have either few friends or none at all. Some children are openly rejected by their peers, while others are simply neglected. Furthermore, it appears that low-status or rejected children maintain their unpopularity over the years of middle childhood and into adolescence (Hymel, Rubin, Rowden, & LeMare, 1990; Kupersmidt & Coie, 1990; Parker & Asher, 1987). The children who had a low status within their peer groups during the third and fifth grades were found to have a similar low status 5 years later (Coie & Dodge, 1983).

What factors account for the differences in social status among schoolchildren? One frequently used technique for studying social relations among peers is **sociometry.** Patterns of attraction and rejection among children in a group are determined on the basis of the children's answers to such questions as "Who in the class is your best friend?" "Which of your classmates do you like the least?" "Who would you like to go on a picnic with?" and "Who are the ones that aren't liked by others?" The children's answers can be charted graphically by drawing a colored arrow to indicate a child's preference for a particular child and drawing a different colored arrow to indicate a child's dislike or rejection of a child (see Figure 8–1). On the basis of the resulting charts, called **sociograms,** researchers can identify the **stars,** or popular children (those who receive positive choices from other children), the **isolates,** or neglected children (those who are neither positively nor negatively chosen), and the **rejects** (those who are actively disliked) (Hartup, 1982). Another peer status category that is sometimes identified is **controversial children** (those who are highly liked by some of their peers and highly disliked by others) (Dodge, 1983). Table 8–3 summarizes the different categories of peer status.

A number of characteristics and traits have been associated with popular and unpopular children. Popular children are physically more attractive (Dodge, 1983; Kleck, Richardson, & Ronald, 1974). Not surprisingly, they also appear to be friendlier, more outgoing, more cooperative, and nicer than unpopular children (Putallaz & Sheppard, 1990). Popular children also achieve more academically and have higher IQs than unpopular children.

Rejected or unpopular children have few friends and are likely to act more aggressively and exhibit more behavior problems than popular children (French &

sociometry

A quantitative method of studying social relations among peers.

sociogram

A diagram representing social acceptance and rejection among a group of people.

stars

Those children who receive many positive choices from other children in a sociometry test.

isolates

Neglected children who are neither positively nor negatively chosen.

rejects

Those children who are actively disliked.

controversial children

Children who are highly liked by some of their peers and highly disliked by others.

FIGURE 8–1

A sociogram. Popular children, such as Adam, have many arrows pointing to their names; unpopular children, such as Keith, have none.

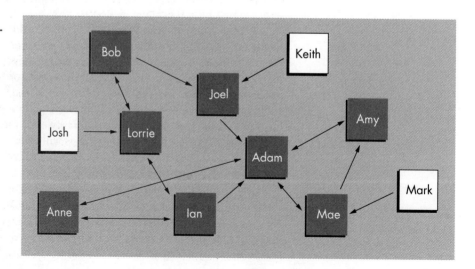

PEER POPULARITY	
PEER STATUS	**DESCRIPTION**
High status: popular "stars"	Liked by peers, attractive, friendly, praised by teachers, and cooperative
Low status: unpopular, aggressive "rejects"	Actively disliked by peers; engage in aggressive and socially disruptive behavior; hyperactive and inattentive
Low status: unpopular "isolates"	Withdrawn, anxious, submissive, and ignored by peers; neither positively nor negatively chosen by peers
Controversial status	Highly liked by some peers, actively disliked by others

TABLE 8–3

Waas, 1985; Kupersmidt & Coie, 1990). They are less self-confident, more disruptive in class, and less liked by teachers (Wentzel & Asher, 1995). In a study conducted by Ladd (1983), popular, average, and rejected third- and fourth-graders were observed during recess periods. The unpopular, rejected children spent less time in prosocial behavior and more time in antagonistic and unoccupied behaviors than the other children. They spent more of their time playing with either younger children or other unpopular children.

Unpopular children are less likely to join groups. When they do attempt to be included in social groups, they pick small groups over larger ones (Putallaz & Wasserman, 1989). Unpopular children are also more likely to have an uncommon and unattractive first name (McDavid & Harari, 1966). Negative peer status during middle childhood is associated with later problems in adjustment (Hartup, 1983; Hymel, Rubin, Rowden, & LeMare, 1990; Kupersmidt & Coie, 1990). For example, unpopular children are at risk for later dropping out of high school (Parker & Asher, 1987).

Recently researchers have begun to make distinctions among peer rejected or unpopular children; they question the assumption that all unpopular children are rejected for the same reasons (French, 1990; Hymel, Bowker, & Woody, 1993). While many children, especially boys, are rejected by their peers because of their aggressive behavior, others achieve low status because they are anxious, withdrawn, and submissive. Unpopular girls frequently have poor academic records in addition to being withdrawn and anxious (French, 1990).

In sociometry, children are asked to make judgments about peers. However, these judgments are usually made of peers they already know well—that is, their friends and those children who have attained some notoriety in the class, usually for negative behavior. Furthermore, these choices are made on the basis of reputation and about what they believe to be true about their peers rather than on the actual observed behaviors of the children. Another drawback to this technique is that teachers can influence children's preferences for their peers (White & Kistner, 1992). Children who receive negative attention and disapproval from the teacher are less likely to be preferred by their peers. Conversely, children who receive praise from teachers are more likely to be have a higher status. (The Research Perspective discusses alternative techniques for assessing popularity.)

Research Perspective

STUDYING CHILDREN'S FRIENDSHIPS

Suppose you were interested in finding out more about what children look for in a friend. How would you go about doing it? You might find a group of children and ask them to describe the qualities they seek when selecting their friends. However, this would probably produce a list of ideal qualities, rather than actual characteristics. The task of studying children's preferences among their peers is more complicated than it appears. Over the years a number of different approaches have been used to study children's peer preferences and friendships.

Sociometry has been used by a number of researchers. Chil-dren are asked to indicate which three or four of their peers they consider to be their best friends or to name the children they like most within a particular group (often the class). They are also asked to name the peers they like least. The number of nominations children receive is used as the measure of their acceptance and popularity. Chil-dren who receive no nomina-tions or who are often named in the category of "least liked" are identified as poorly accepted or rejected children. The problem with this approach is that chil-dren often fail to name peers whom they like or accept be-cause they are not their friends or even "best" friends. Thus some children may be well-liked by their peers, but are not nom-inated because they are not cat-egorized as "friends."

A different approach is to give children a list of all of their classmates and ask them to in-dicate how much they like to play with each peer, using a 5-point rating scale. Average ratings for each child are then computed to reflect their popu-larity. Then children are asked to name a limited number of their peers as their friends. This procedure allows researchers to distinguish between children who are unpopular and those who do not have friends. One study using this technique (Parker & Asher, 1993) found that children with low average ratings had best friends and were satisfied with those rela-tionships. Without breaking down the assessment into popu-larity and friendship measures, this distinction would not have been made.

Once children's social status has been determined, it is use-ful to observe them in action, usually in the classroom or playground. Video segments of peer interactions provides re-searchers with a detailed sketch of the behavioral differences among children who are ac-cepted or rejected by their

One question remains difficult to answer: Are unpopular children aggressive or withdrawn because they are disliked by their peers, or did their behavior cause them to be disliked? It is likely that popularity and the style of social interaction are bidirectional, each influencing the other (Asher, 1983; Dodge, 1983; Rubin, 1983). In order to answer the question of what causes children to have high or low status with their peers, researchers have observed the development of peer sta-tus in groups of unfamiliar children (Coie & Kupersmidt, 1983; Dodge, 1983; Putallaz, 1983; Rabiner, Keane, & MacKinnon-Lewis, 1993). Popular and unpopu-lar children appear to differ in their mastery of social competencies. For example, rejected children are frequently pessimistic about their ability to be accepted by new peers. Expecting failure, they often engage in behaviors that reduce their pop-ularity or acceptance. However, social competencies can be changed. In one study, rejected children who were encouraged to expect success in interacting with new peers. While this technique has been helpful in identifying many of the characteristics associated with rejected and popular children, it does not help researchers differentiate between behaviors that contribute to or result from rejection or acceptance. To correct this problem, researchers have turned to studying peer rejection using experimentally created peer groups of children who were previously unacquainted (Coie & Cillessen, 1993). Typically, the created peer groups are asked to work on a structured project or problem to solve that requires their interaction, and observations are made about how they respond to the task and to each other. An equal number of high- and low-status children are assigned to the created groups so that a comparison can be made of the behavioral differences between accepted and rejected children. Using this technique, researchers have determined that low peer status is related to such behaviors as aggressiveness, social intrusiveness, disruption, and fearfulness.

One of the reasons for the interest in studying friendship patterns in children is to gain insight on what contributes to and sustains peer rejection in the hopes of reversing its immediate and long-term negative consequences. Researchers are using longitudinal designs to follow specific children and to identify the extent to which behavioral patterns that earn children a low status continue into adulthood.

Rejected and isolated children spend less time with their peers, unlike popular children who are friendlier and more outgoing.

peers were more liked than rejected children with more pessimistic views of their ability to be liked by a new social group (Rabiner & Coie, 1989).

Social Competencies and Peers One reason some children are unpopular is because they lack social skills. Popular children, on the other hand, seem to acquire their status as a result of **social competence.** Asher (1983) has described three dimensions of socially competent performance.

The first dimension is *relevance*—children who gain entry into ongoing interactions seem to be able to read the social situation and adapt their behavior to the flow of interaction. They are poised and comfortable with their peers and seem to know what to say at the right time. A second dimension of competence is *responsiveness*—children who are effective with peers respond more positively to other children's initiations of contact. Generally, popular children are approached

social competence

The ability of popular children to display relevance, responsiveness, and understanding of the process of relationships in social interaction.

more frequently by other children and approach others less often. A third dimension is *understanding of the process of relationships*—high-status children recognize that relationships are built over time, not in the moment. As a result, they are likely to form a friendship slowly and in a less direct fashion. Whereas unpopular children are more likely to immediately initiate play with a new peer, or even to ask, "Will you be my friend?" popular children are more likely to start a relationship by suggesting an after-school bike ride and to let the friendship build over time.

Development of Children's Friendships   Children's understanding of friendship changes with age. It is not until the end of childhood that children can fully appreciate the meaning of friendship. In an interview study in which 130 children (ages 6 to 14) were asked questions like "What is a friend?" and "How do you make friends?" Youniss and Volpe (1978) found that 6- and 7-year-olds defined friends as playmates with whom they shared toys and physical activities. Nine- and 10-year-olds, however, spoke of friends as persons who respond to each other's needs—those who can be relied on for comfort and support.

Based on numerous open-ended interviews with people aging from 3 to 45, Selman (1981) presented a developmental theory that identifies five stages in children's ability to make and sustain friendships (see Table 8–4). The first stage (ages 3–7) is labeled *Stage 0* because children do not really form friendships. Rather, a close friend is someone who lives nearby and with whom the child happens to be playing with at the time. In this stage, described as *momentary playmateship,* friends are valued for their toys, physical attributes, and proximity. In *Stage 1* (ages 4–9), a close friend is someone who does what one wants. This stage is

SELMAN'S STAGES IN THE DEVELOPMENT OF CHILDREN'S FRIENDSHIPS

STAGE	AGE	CHARACTERISTICS
0	3–7	No real friendships are formed; rather, children have momentary playmates.
1	4–9	Close friends are those who do what child wants, providing one-way assistantship.
2	6–12	The reciprocal nature of friendships is acknowledged. However, the friendship is a fair-weather one that dissolves with disagreement or dispute.
3	9–15	Mutual intimacy and understanding are present in the friendship, which is exclusive and possessive.
4	12+	The interdependent and autonomous quality of friendship is acknowledged; friendships grow and change with the individuals.

TABLE 8–4

Source: From "The Child as a Friendship Philosopher: A Case Study in the Growth of Interpersonal Understanding," by R. L. Selman, 1981, in S. R. Asher and J. M. Gottman (Eds.), *The Development of Children's Friendships,* Cambridge: Cambridge University Press. Adapted with permission.

Popular children build their friendships with peers by being responsive and positive to others. Over time, the contact they have with their peers builds into friendships that develop as they acquire new social competencies.

Childhood friendships often are formed among playmates who share physical activities.

labeled *one-way assistance* because a friend is seen as important because he or she performs specific activities that the child wants accomplished. If the friend does not assist, then the child is likely to reply, "You are not my friend!" *Stage 2* (ages 6–12) is labeled *fair-weather cooperation* because children become aware of the two-way reciprocal nature of friendships. When friends disagree or argue, the friendship dissolves. *Stage 3* (ages 9–15) is labeled *intimate and mutually shared relationships.* Friendships are seen as a basic means to develop mutual intimacy and support. Friends share personal problems and secrets and do not dissolve their relationship because of disagreement or conflict of ideas. Friendship at this stage is exclusive and possessive; hence cliques develop. Finally, in *Stage 4,* the highest stage of development (age 12 to adulthood), friendships are characterized by an autonomous, interdependent quality. Friendships can grow and change as each person accepts the other's need to establish relations with others for personal growth. Friends still rely on each other for emotional support, but they are not possessive or clinging in their relationships.

FOCUS ON CULTURE

Children who are physically, mentally, or emotionally handicapped not only must cope with their specific disabilities but may also have difficulty establishing and maintaining friendships with their peers. In the United States many handicapped children are taught in the same classroom with nonhandicapped children. What are the possible merits and drawbacks to this policy with respect to children's peer interactions and friendships?

THE IMPACT OF MEDIA

This is probably difficult to believe, but one year my family and I decided not to have a television set in our home. Adam and Sarah were 16 and 12 respectively and had grown up with their favorite television shows. However, we went to live in a different country for a year, where all of us had broken our TV-watching habits. Upon our return to the United States, we wanted to see how long we could go without watching television. During our year of media abstinence, we talked to each other, learned new card games, read books and newspapers, and listened to music. There were no squabbles about who was going to watch what. However, when the Olympics came around, we succumbed and bought a television set.

Today, more than 98% of American families have at least one television set; some have two or more. Children spend a significant amount of their time watching TV programs or videos. One estimate is that children under 2 spend an average of 2½ hours per day, every day, watching television. For 8- to 10-year-olds, the amount of viewing time increases to an average of 4 hours per day (Liebert, Sprafkin, & Davidson, 1982). Based on these national averages, it is estimated that by high school graduation, the average child will have spent 15,000 hours watching TV. According to the *Annual Nielsen Report on Television* (Nielsen, 1990), children between the ages of 6 and 11 spend an average of 25 hours per week watching television. Boys watch more television than girls, and the programs they watch are more violent and action-packed (Huesmann & Eron, 1986; Huston, Wright, Rice, Kerkman, & St. Peters, 1990; Singer & Singer,

1981). Children between the ages of 2 and 6 spend an average of 28 hours, 20 minutes per week watching television.

These figures for television viewing are startling. It appears that children are spending as much time in front of the TV as they are in direct classroom instruction. The choices of programming has expanded considerably over the past years, and the ready availability of home videos has made the range of programming practically limitless. In addition to television, children spend their time playing a growing variety of computer games, many of which are viewed on the television monitor. Handheld computer toys provide portable entertainment for many children (and some adults). Clearly, media and especially television are important socializing agents in American culture. Let's take a closer look at television's impact on children (also see Table 8–5).

Questionnaire and diary studies indicate that systematic viewing of television begins at 2 years, reaches a high level during the preschool and early school years, declines during adolescence and adulthood, and then rises to a relatively high level among elderly people (Anderson, Lorch, Field, Collins, & Nathan, 1986). Anderson and his colleagues videotaped families in their TV viewing rooms and found that children spent about one third of their time with the television on while they were engaged in other activities such as playing with toys, reading, or interacting with parents. The TV in this case is background noise, much like elevator music. When the content becomes fast-paced, loud, and lively, children's attention is redirected to the television.

Effects of TV on Cognitive and Affective Development   Television programs are carefully produced to capture and hold the viewer's attention. The format of commercial TV programs, particularly children's shows, contains rapid-fire, action-packed sequences that are highlighted by audio and visual special effects.

TELEVISION'S IMPACT ON CHILDREN	
Viewing behavior	Begins as early as age 2 and occupies a significant portion of children's daily activity
Appeal	Captures and sustains children's attention with rapid-fire, colorful, and action-packed programs
Educational benefits	Exposes children to worlds far beyond their immediate environment, conveys information and new skills, and facilitates language development, especially if adults watch along with their children
Emotional impact	Can help children deal with fears by exposing them to models who cope with fears
Violence and aggression	Exposure to televised violence is associated with increased physical and verbal aggression
Stereotypes	Promotes racial, ethnic, and gender stereotypes
TV behavior	Promotes passivity and snacking; interferes with discussions, physical activity, and schoolwork

TABLE 8–5

Taken in large doses, this format may impair imagination and creativity because children cannot process the disconnected elements (Singer & Singer, 1983). Children's attention is especially captured by the television format of cartoons (Huston et al., 1990; Wright & Huston, 1983). Children spend endless hours, particularly on Saturday morning, watching the humorous (and often violent and aggressive) adventures of animated cartoon characters. The faster the pace of the program, the more receptive children are to it. It has been suggested that the format of children's programs can be arousing to them and can lead to aggressive behavior, even when the content of the program is nonviolent (Huston et al., 1981). The slow-paced, laid-back style of *Mr. Rogers* is not as well-received by children. However, once children are exposed to the *Mr. Rogers* show, studies indicate that they do acquire more prosocial behavior (Comstock & Paik, 1991; Singer & Singer, 1983).

Research on the effects of TV viewing on development suggests that it influences both learning and behavior; this can be beneficial. A study of cognitive development of children who watch *Sesame Street* (Ball & Bogatz, 1972) concluded that 3- to 5-year-olds from a variety of backgrounds acquired simple and complex cognitive skills as a result of watching *Sesame Street*. Those who watched the most gained the most, and 3-year-olds gained more than 5-year-olds.

Television has a rich and, as yet, untapped potential for educating and enhancing children's development (Singer & Singer, 1983). It is an excellent vehicle for presenting new ideas and information about cultures beyond the child's (or adult's) immediate experience. Children can, for example, learn about life in the Himalayas by watching a TV special. However, the benefits to children from many "good" television programs may depend on the presence of an adult (Singer, Singer, Desmond, Hirsch, & Nicol, 1988; Singer & Singer, 1981). Adults who watch the shows with children provide guidance and help children understand them. Young children can also learn about the use of their language by listening

Studies have reported that American children spend as much time in front of the television as they do in direct classroom instruction.

to television; often children imitate many of the jingles and sayings they hear on television in their play (Rice, 1983).

Some of the more recent children's programs on American television have attempted to help children deal more effectively with their fears. For example, by watching a television character overcome a fear of animals, children are able to deal more effectively with their own fears. However, what is learned from television depends on the child's level of cognitive development. First- and second-graders, for example, are not yet able to follow a complex plot line from one scene to the next, so they may miss the moral lesson contained in many TV programs (Rubinstein, 1983). Furthermore, before age 9, children believe much of what they see on TV to be true or real. On their own, without adult interpretation, they do not distinguish fantasy from reality very well (Eron, 1980, 1982). Thus, they may acquire misinformation about the world when they watch cartoons or very unrealistic programs. Heavy television viewing may also interfere with other activities that contribute to children's learning. Such activities as reading, playing games, constructing things, or discussing their ideas with others are considerably reduced when children spend many hours a day watching television.

Violence and Aggression   Perhaps the most studied issue regarding the media is the effect of televised violence and aggression on children's behavior. The results of research studies support the view that violence portrayed on television leads to aggressive behavior by children. By observing highly attractive models engaging in a variety of aggressive and physically violent behaviors, children are encouraged to act in a similar fashion (Bandura, Ross, & Ross, 1963). The extent to which children imitate aggressive acts on TV also is influenced by the age of the child. The time when children are most likely to learn aggressive behaviors from watching televised aggression is between 8 and 9 years of age (Eron, Huesmann, Brice, Fischer, & Mermelstein, 1983). Also, if children are already predisposed to aggressive behaviors, they are more likely to imitate aggression seen on TV. When

Video games that use combat activities in which the player receives a higher score for killing opponents are a concern because violence and aggression are reinforced.

parents watch aggressive or violent shows with their children and discuss the events afterward, this seems to reduce the negative effects and enhance the positive effects of TV.

Fortunately, many television stations provide announcements for parents concerning the impact on children of the program they are about to see. Similarly, parental warnings are being placed on home and some music videos with graphic reference to violent behaviors. Many of the popular computer video games contain vivid scenes in which the main characters engage in dramatic and violent aggressive behavior. As a result of the public concern about the relationship between media violence and aggression, manufacturers of video games have created a rating system to inform parents about the content of their games. But, the ratings are only useful when parents supervise their children's exposure to this media.

Social Beliefs and Behaviors   Another potent way in which media affect social behavior is through the presentation of gender-role models and other ethnic stereotypes. Girls who consistently see women portrayed as helpless victims or homemakers are likely to accept this view as part of their gender role. Concern over racial, ethnic, and gender-role stereotypes on television has resulted in attention being given to the way people are represented on television. However, commercials still seem to flagrantly reinforce limiting social stereotypes—for example, by portraying men as helpless in the kitchen or women as ignorant about mechanical things.

FOCUS ON CULTURE

The predominance of television in the lives of children and adults is a characteristic of American society. The majority of children in other parts of the world grow up without television in their homes or communities. Furthermore, in cultures that have television, there is less variety in programming compared to what is available in the United States. The number of television sets per home is also smaller, thus reducing the amount of time children have sole access to the TV set.

ADJUSTMENT PROBLEMS

During the elementary school years all children experience some difficulty in the process of growing up. While most children learn to deal with the stresses and challenges confronting them in school or with their peers, some experience problems in making these adjustments. Other children have difficulty because of physical or psychological handicaps that interfere with normal adjustment.

Research has shown that referrals to mental health facilities increase significantly during the school years and that most of the problems reported are school-related (Achenbach, 1978). About 33% of children between the ages of 6 and 12 have some form of emotional problem, and boys are 4 times as likely as girls to have difficulty. However, most of the problems children experience while growing up are resolved without professional help; only about 10% of school-age children are seen by professionals.

There are several reasons for the increase in referred emotional problems during middle childhood. For one thing, some problems have their origins in early childhood and are not considered problematic until children enter school. For example, aggressive behaviors are a commonly reported problem that becomes more apparent when the child goes to school. During early childhood children are normally more aggressive, and the problem behavior may not have been identified or may have been dismissed with the hope that the child would grow out of it. By the school years, problem behaviors that may have only affected the child's parents and a few neighborhood children may be affecting the entire classroom. Thus, as children enter school it is more likely that their problems will come to the attention of professionals, if for no other reason than because they are now observed by more people and can be more readily compared to their peers.

Another reason for an increase in adjustment problems during middle childhood is that there are more adjustments to make. As children mature and demonstrate their abilities to understand and cooperate with others, parents and teachers place greater social, cognitive, and emotional demands on them. The second-grader may find that it is no longer acceptable for her to throw a tantrum when things do not go her way. Now she may be expected to control her emotions and cooperate with others.

In addition, because children are able to consider future events and the influence that other people have on them, they are likely to react more strongly than younger children in anticipation of an event. For example, a recent study (Silverman, Greca, & Wasserstein, 1995) found that children between the ages of 7 and 12 worried most about personal harm (e.g., being robbed, stabbed, or shot), school (e.g., school performance or being called on in class), and health (e.g., parents' health, operations, or getting AIDS). By about age 9 children worry about the threat of a nuclear war (Escalona, 1982; Schwebel, 1982). In one study (Chivian, Mack, & Waletzsky, 1983) 98% of Soviet children and 58% of American children said they were "worried" or "very worried" about a nuclear attack. They worried about how they would be able to live without families, friends, and teachers to love and take care of them.

Another source of stress for school-age children concerns changes in the family structure. Many mothers decide to go to work when their children enter school. An increasing number of children live in families disrupted as a result of separation and divorce. Single-parent families and families combined through marriage are further examples of changes in the family structure that may result in a stressful period for children. While some of these changes may actually be beneficial in the long run (such as when both parents are happily employed), children often react to the transitional and temporary upheaval with disturbing behavior and emotional problems. The loss of family members or friends through death is another stressful change (see Chapter 17).

Parent-child relationships typically become problematic during the latter part of middle childhood. By age 9 or 10 children become critical of grown-ups, especially their parents and teachers. "No more pencils, no more books; no more teacher's dirty looks!" is a refrain heard more frequently among fourth- and fifth-graders than among first- and second-graders. As children begin doing more things on their own and turning to their peers instead of adults for approval, tension often develops between parents and their children. Parents may interpret the child's indifference toward them as a threat to their authority and react in a negative and controlling manner. Children may also react negatively to parents by talking back with angry sarcasm as a way of defining themselves as separate individuals.

Education Perspective

THE HURRIED CHILD

Teachers who motivate their students to learn are generally considered to be good and effective. But is there a danger in overemphasizing achievement or pushing children to accomplish things at an earlier age? Are the pressures of competition too big a burden for children?

Some American psychologists and educators think so. David Elkind (1981), a child psychologist, has written about the pressures on children to grow up. He argues that today, unlike many other cultures, we are pressuring our children to mature as never before. "Hurried children" and "children without childhood" are common euphemisms for this phenomenon.

Elkind observes this process operating in numerous ways. Chief among them is the pressure for early intellectual attainment. Beginning sometimes in infancy, but more often in the preschool years, American parents and educational specialists attempt to accelerate children's acquisition of academic skills. The general feeling among parents and teachers is that we must begin very early in children's lives if we wish to maximize their intellectual potential.

In addition to the pressures for early academic achievement, Elkind observes pressure on children to grow up quickly in their dress and behavior. According to Elkind, Americans encourage children to look, dress, and even act like adults well before they are capable of handling it emotionally. For example, we often see young and early school-age children in miniature versions of adult dress. Well known American designers have even begun producing high-priced fashions for infants and toddlers. The problem for children occurs when they associate looking older with needing to act or feel like an adult. Thus, they are encouraged to not be a child. The message is that it is better to be an adult.

The media have contributed to the pressure on children to grow up. Promotion of teenage sexuality is an everyday occurrence in television, film, music, literature, and advertising. Even children's play and sports activities are not exempt from this "pressure cooker" atmosphere—consider the proliferation of specialized camps for such sports as baseball, basketball, football, skating, wrestling, gymnastics, and the like. In these environments, the carefree camp atmosphere of bygone days has been replaced by daily rigorous routines to foster highly specialized competitive athletic skills. This emphasis on competition can also be seen in organized sports such as Pee Wee hockey, Little League baseball, and high school athletic programs.

What effect does this pressure to grow up have on children? One common reaction is intense anxiety. Pressured by parents, teachers, and even peers to perform and achieve beyond their years and often their abilities, many children respond to the stress by becoming highly anxious—most often because they believe they cannot live up to the expectations of others. Sometimes children

Peer status can be another source of frustration for schoolchildren. Children frequently react to stress by behaving aggressively, and unpopular children are often excluded or rejected because of their aggressive behavior. Thus, stress or difficulty in one area of a child's life, such as poor grades, may lead to further problems if the child reacts aggressively and thus invites peer rejection.

Children living in families in which one or both parents suffer from psychiatric disorders are more vulnerable to emotional disorders and are more likely to feel a sense of helplessness in response to a lack of control in their lives.

Undue pressure to grow up may also produce a premature structuring of the child's life. In this case, the child spends so much time involved in highly specialized activities (e.g., sports, music, etc.) that he or she does not have the opportunity to develop other aspects of the self. The case of Bobby Fischer is a good example. Overspecialized as a chess grandmaster while still an adolescent, Fischer was a socially inept recluse in his late twenties.

Elkind argues that many of the negative consequences of hurrying children to grow up do not emerge until adolescence. Elkind cites teenage experimentation with sex, drugs, and alcohol, and the testing of adult authority both in and outside of the home, as examples of reactions to the pressures to grow up too soon.

What can parents or teachers do to alleviate some of the pressure on "hurried" children? The answer is to slow down the pace by establishing reasonable standards of achievement and by encouraging more cooperative interactions in and outside of the classroom. Teachers can help relieve the pressure by showing children that they do not have to perform or be "stars" to be accepted. Many times children's advanced achievements blind teachers and parents to the fact that these children do not respond emotionally in the same way as adults.

Elkind argues that we must give our children the time they need to grow up—we must not deny them their childhood. The pressures on children today are great enough without the additional ones associated with hurrying them toward adulthood. "Feelings and emotions have their own timing and rhythm and cannot be hurried," he writes. "Growing up emotionally is complicated and difficult enough under any circumstances but may be especially so when children's behavior and appearance speak adult while their feelings cry 'child'" (p. 11).

Elkind believes that some children are encouraged to look, dress, and act like adults well before they are emotionally ready.

have a diagnosed psychiatric problem themselves (Rutter, 1979b; Weissman et al., 1984). However, when children have access to a caring adult and a supportive social network such as their schools, the stressful effects of having to cope with a disturbed parent are greatly reduced. In fact, research on young children of manic-depressive parents suggests that these children may acquire such social competencies as empathy and helpfulness as a result of having to cope with their parents (Zahn-Waxler, Cummings, McKnew, & Radke-Yarrow, 1984).

RESILIENT CHILDREN

Of equal interest to developmental researchers are children from stressful family and social environments who rise above their misfortunes and develop normally. Children of emotionally disturbed parents who do not display emotional problems, abused children who develop close personal relationships, and orphaned children who bear no emotional scars are but a few examples of children who seem to be **resilient** or invulnerable to the effects of stressful experiences.

resilient children
Children who are invulnerable to the effects of stressful experience.

The personality and social factors that distinguish resilient children from vulnerable children are yet to be fully understood (Garmezy & Rutter, 1983); however, two factors do seem to be important. The availability of social support from a caring adult friend or relative frequently helps to offset the negative effects of stress. The second factor is the child's ability to understand and cope with the situation. As a group, resilient children are friendly, independent, and have high levels of self-esteem; they also get along well with other children and do well in school. Thus, a combination of social support and personal strength seem to provide children with some protection from the negative effects of difficult conditions.

ADJUSTMENT REACTIONS OF CHILDREN

Aggression   One of the more common behavior problems in middle childhood is physical and verbal aggression. Boys are more likely than girls to respond to frustration by bullying their peers, having tantrums, or engaging in destructive actions. Boys who are experiencing stress and who have coercive relationships with their mothers are likely to be socially less competent and more aggressive than their less stressed peers (MacKinnon et al., 1994). Often the child who is not doing well academically or who experiences frequent failures displaces his or her frustration by acting aggressively. Hyperactive children and children with learning disabilities also often act aggressively toward their peers.

Children who behave aggressively tend to attribute hostile intentions to others, particularly when the situation is ambiguous (Dodge & Frame, 1982; Dodge & Somberg, 1987). Moreover, children who are rejected by their peers are more likely than socially accepted children to offer an aggressive solution when presented with a problem (Dorsch & Keane, 1994). In many cases children's aggression stems from inept and immature attempts to make contact with others and to gain attention. Social-learning theorists believe that learning to channel aggressive actions in socially appropriate ways is a major aspect of socialization during the school years. As we have pointed out in this and earlier chapters, aggression—like many other behaviors—is maintained by the consequences it elicits. The aggressive boy, for example, not only learns that hitting or bullying someone results in his getting his way, but he also learns that adults will pay attention to him—even if the attention is negative. Children also learn to be aggressive by watching others engage in aggressive actions. Again, many television programs provide children with numerous examples of modeled aggression. Parents who physically punish their children are also teaching them to be aggressive with others.

Aggression is a social event that involves at least one other person. Some researchers (DeRosier, Cillessen, Coie, & Dodge, 1994) have examined the extent to which the social setting can elicit aggressive responses from children. Settings in which there is a lot of physical activity, competition, and aversive behavior (such as verbal abuse, grabbing, shoving) seem to encourage more aggressive behavior. As we saw in the vignette at the beginning of the chapter, rough and tumble play can often escalate into overt aggression when one child misinterprets the intentions of another (Smith & Boulton, 1990). Children's groups that are friendly and cohesive are less likely to provoke misunderstandings that escalate into aggression.

The best treatment approach for discouraging aggressive behaviors in children is to change the consequences of those actions. Withdrawing reinforcing attention from a child who is acting aggressively reduces the frequency of aggressive behavior. A procedure also used with younger children, the **time out,** is often effective: The disruptive child is removed from the setting and placed in a socially isolated and nonstimulating environment for a specified period. When the time is up, the child is allowed to return to the original social setting. So long as his or her behavior is appropriate—that is, nonaggressive—the child is allowed to remain with the others.

In addition to reducing negative aggressive behaviors, intervention approaches should also teach the child more acceptable ways of dealing with frustrations. Exposing children to people who demonstrate greater maturity and control of their emotions while frustrated can also help children learn the necessary alternatives to aggression.

time out

A strategy for changing behavior by removing a person from the setting in which the behavior to be changed is reinforced.

FOCUS ON CULTURE

In Balinese culture, children—especially infants—are believed to be almost godlike (Reader, 1988). Children are worshiped for their innocence and indulged by their parents throughout childhood so as not to mar their state of near perfection. For example, Balinese parents will carry their children until they can walk, rather than have them crawl on the ground as animals do. Special rites are performed when the first tooth is lost and when permanent teeth erupt to guarantee their safe passage from one stage of childhood to another.

---

childhood stress

Children's reactions to a variety of stressful situational and developmental changes in their lives.

Fear and Anxiety　**Childhood stress** is a term that is used to describe children's reactions to a variety of situational and developmental changes in their lives (Miller, 1982). Two commonly experienced stress reactions are fear and anxiety. Fear is a natural reaction to real or imagined danger. When children do not understand or cannot control events in their lives, they are likely to perceive them as dangerous. The specific events or things that are frightening to children change, however, as they develop a better understanding of their world.

In a 5-year study of children ranging in age from 5½ to 14½, Maurer (1965) found that fear of animals, particularly snakes, was almost universal. As children got older, their fears diminished. For example, fear of the dark usually disappears by age 7, while fear of nonexistent monsters and ghosts disappears by age 10. Older children are more likely to fear realistic events. Fear of natural hazards increases with age. As we mentioned earlier, a common fear among school children today is a fear of nuclear war and annihilation (Yudkin, 1984).

Children also report fears of social situations involving possible embarrassment, such as forgetting their lines in the school play.

It is generally understood that fears are learned. Sometimes as a result of a previous trauma or accident, a child may be conditioned to fear similar situations or events. Other times children acquire fears through observational learning—for example, by watching someone else express fear of particular objects or events. When Juanita noticed her sister's fearful reaction to spiders, she soon acquired a similar fear. When children express fears, they often elicit a more nurturant and attentive response from adults. In doing so they may learn that being afraid has advantages.

Anxiety, like fear, is a response to a felt danger, which may or may not be real. However, anxiety is usually not directed toward a specific object or situation. Often children are unaware of what specifically is worrying them. They may experience physical reactions such as an uneasy feeling in their stomach, headache, fatigue, or difficulty in breathing, or they may simply experience a deep apprehension. Children facing hospitalization for surgery or medical tests often experience anxiety that interferes with their recuperation. In one study (Melamed & Siegel, 1981), children who were scheduled for surgery were shown a film about a 7-year-old boy as he prepared for a hernia operation. The boy in the film, while anxious, demonstrated his ability to cope with his initial fears. Watching this film helped to reduce the children's preoperative anxiety.

Childhood Depression

Ordinarily, you might not think of children as being depressed, partly because it conflicts with your belief that childhood is a happy time. However, psychologists recognize that some children are not at all happy; in fact, they suffer from **childhood depression**—they are very sad and experience a diminished sense of their own self-worth.

childhood depression
Children who experience extreme sadness and a diminished sense of their own self-worth.

Children do not express depression in the same ways as adults. The way they express a sense of despair corresponds to their age. Younger children, for example, may stop growing, have a poor appetite, and be listless, while school-age children may manifest their depression through hostile and aggressive behavior toward their parents. Often discontented and dissatisfied with their lives, such children derive no pleasure from their activities. Sometimes their depression is masked by vague physical symptoms such as headaches, stomachaches, and dizziness. Some children are so depressed that they are suicidal.

FOCUS ON CULTURE

Children who grow up in war zones confront dangers on a daily basis. Children's immediate reaction to living with the chronic fear of invasion, starvation, or assassination is a form of post-traumatic stress disorder in which they respond by being hyperaggressive or withdrawing (Garbarino, Kostelny, & Dubrow, 1991). Children who live in inner-city environments that are riddled with gang fights and drive-by shootings—in effect, also war zones—must cope with the stress of walking the streets or going to school. The long-term consequences of growing up in chronically dangerous environments (assuming that they survive) are that children's worldview changes to expect conflict and violence.

Childhood depression seems to be a reaction to a loss of an object, person, or state of well-being. Loss of a parent not only has a devastating effect on young children (Bowlby, 1973; Bradley, 1979), but may predispose thm to depression in adulthood (Seligman, 1975).

Another factor contributing to childhood depression is a hostile, overly critical, or unstable family environment. When parents are constantly fighting with each other, when the child is consistently belittled, or when there is considerable disruption in the family, as with separation or divorce, some children respond with depression. The most effective therapy for a depressed child in such situations involves restoring order and reducing the adverse qualities of the home environment (Bakwin & Bakwin, 1972).

BRIEF REVIEW

The child's personality is influenced by many experiences during middle childhood. The evaluations of significant others become part of the child's view of self.

According to Erikson, children during the school years must resolve the crisis of industry versus inferiority. In doing so they form an attitude about their ability to work and be productive.

Self-concept is composed of several aspects: The child's physical appearance (including gender and activities), the child's psychological experience (including feelings), and the child's social sense of self.

Children's self-esteem is influenced by their successes and accomplishments and by the degree of firm, affectionate direction they receive from their parents. Self-esteem is related to body esteem.

Siblings play an important role in each other's development as models of behavior, as sources of comfort, and as competitors for parental attention. Sibling interactions provide a way for children to learn how to get along with others.

The order in which children are born can affect their achievement and social interactions. Despite the fact that only children do not have to learn to cooperate or share resources with siblings, their social and personality development is normal.

Peer interactions are different from parent-child interactions and are more frequent during the school years. Peer groups serve several functions, including providing social approval, companionship, and a source of knowledge.

Popularity is influenced by the degree of acceptance by others. Factors in acceptance are friendliness, prosocial behavior, attractiveness, and social competence. Rejected and unpopular children are often aggressive and lack social skills.

Children's understanding of friendship changes during childhood. Selman's theory of friendship includes five stages in which children develop abilities to make and sustain friendships.

The media, and especially television, is a significant and pervasive socializing agent that influences children's aggression, social attitudes and behavior, and general knowledge.

Children's reactions to stress depend upon the degree of family and social support, their ability to understand events, and on their own personal strengths.

Some children have difficulty in making the many adjustments to school and family circumstances. Some common problems include aggressive behaviors, anxiety and fears, and childhood depression.

KEY TERMS

birth order (304)

body esteem (300)

childhood depression (326)

childhood stress (325)

controversial children (310)

isolates (310)

personality (294)

popularity (309)

rejects (310)

resilient children (324)

self-concept (296)

self-esteem (299)

sibling rivalry (305)

social competence (313)

sociogram (310)

sociometry (310)

stars (310)

time out (325)

REVIEW QUESTIONS

If you can answer these questions, you have a good understanding of the material in this chapter. If a question seems difficult, go back to the text and review the topic.

1. According to Erikson, what is the significance of school success on children's personality during middle childhood? What is the impact of failure on children's personality development?

2. Distinguish between self-awareness, self-concept, and self-esteem.

3. Describe Selman's three levels of self-awareness.

4. Describe the differences between children with high and low self-esteem. In what ways do school experiences contribute to self-esteem?

5. What influence do parents have on children's self-esteem?

6. In what ways do firstborns differ from latter-born siblings? What is sibling rivalry and how is it maintained in the family?

7. Describe the ways in which peer interaction in middle childhood differs from adult-child interactions. Distinguish between the ways boys and girls interact with their peers.

8. What are the five functions of peer groups? Give an example of each function.

9. How do researchers assess peer status among children? What behaviors distinguish popular children from rejected children?

10. Describe three dimensions of social competence in children.

11. Describe and give an example of each of Selman's five stages in the development of friendships.

12. How does television viewing affect children's cognitive development? Their emotional and social development?

13. What reasons explain the increase in reported adjustment problems during middle childhood?

14. What are the characteristics of a depressed child?

OBSERVATIONAL ACTIVITY

SCHOOLYARD PEER INTERACTIONS

One of the ways researchers learn about friendship patterns in children is through naturalistic observation. While observing children's social interactions in a classroom or in the laboratory may provide some useful information about how peers relate to one another, children's behavior in these settings is usually structured or constrained by the presence of adults or formal activities.

In the playground, however, more spontaneous social interactions are possible. Schoolchildren often make friends and establish their status among their peers through their interactions in the school yard. The focus of this activity is to gain a better understanding of how children interact with their peers and form social groups.

You will need to locate a school yard so that you can observe children playing either before school or during recess or lunch breaks. Your local YMCA/YWCA may also have playgrounds where groups of school-age children play. You will need to observe the same group of children for a period of 3 to 5 days. Watch the children playing for at least 20 minutes

each visit. On each visit make note of the following behaviors among the children:

1. Type of play: Solitary play in which children play alone; associative play in which two or three children use the same toys or equipment but are independent of each other; or cooperative play in which children share toys or organize their activities with each other.

2. Aggression: Verbal aggression such as shouting, name calling, sneering, and taunting, and physical aggression such as hitting, shoving, tripping, or spitting.

3. Prosocial behaviors: Helping, listening, cooperating, and affectionate displays such as touching, hugging, and winking.

4. Social approaches: The way in which children gain entry into an existing group of children. Does the child wait his or her turn to speak? How many entry attempts does each child make? What does the child say in

attempting to gain entry into the group? What is the reaction of the children in the group?

On the basis of your observations draw some conclusions about the kinds of behaviors used by children to gain peer acceptance. Did you notice which children were the most and least popular in the playground? What behaviors distinguish these children from each other? Share your observations about children's social interactions with your classmates. Compare your observations. What did you learn about yourself by doing this activity?

The Transition Years

dolescence is easy to recognize but hard to define. Typically this period includes the years from ages 12 to 18. However, age is not always a useful marker, since individuals vary considerably in their pace of development. Adolescence represents the junction of the routes from childhood and to adulthood. Some of the most challenging terrain in the journey through life can be found in the adolescent years. Dramatic physical changes seem to occur abruptly; with new cognitive skills come expanded vistas and the ability to consider the road ahead. The course to maturity is further defined by the acquisition of values and moral reasoning skills that will guide adolescents into adulthood.

Amidst competing and conflicting pressures from parents, peers, and the community, teenagers face the challenge of defining themselves and who they want to become. They expand the social networks they began in childhood and learn to balance their view of self with their desire for acceptance by their peers. Many view adolescence as a dress rehearsal for adulthood, because it is during this time that life decisions are considered and new behaviors are tested. As you read the next two chapters, keep in mind that attitudes and commitments made in adolescence help shape the character of young adulthood. As teenagers take steps to define themselves and become independent, they are also charting their route through early adulthood.

CHAPTER 9

Adolescence: Physical, Cognitive, and Moral Development

David's 14th year certainly presented a lot of changes. He seemed to grow overnight; just last week he measured his height and found he was taller than his mother. He was looking forward to the time when he would surpass his father's height. As his voice grew deeper and lower, people on the telephone often mistook David for his father.

His body was changing in other ways. The light peach fuzz under his arms and in his groin area was becoming coarser and thicker. Furthermore, his interests were beginning to turn from comic books to girls as he fantasized about his first sexual encounter.

David's mother was both surprised and delighted that he had changed his attitude and behavior about personal appearance and hygiene. During his 13th year he had abandoned showers. Now it was difficult to get him out of the bathroom. He spent what seemed like hours in the shower or gazing in the mirror at his changing body. He regularly worked out with the weight set he bought with his birthday money; he wanted to be strong and have big muscles by the time summer came around.

Sixteen-year-old Krista had spent her entire life in Estonia, but it was only in the last few years that she began to think and talk about the political climate of her country. When she was younger she could not understand why adult relatives would spend so much time talking about political issues. But now she thought more about her own future and what kind of life she wanted to live.

Krista was able to consider the different implications of living within a democratic political system. During her earlier years, Estonia was under a communist government that restricted free speech and innovation. Her country's rejection of communism and acceptance of a free market economy occurred at the same time that Krista emerged into adolescence and sought to become independent of her parents' influence. She wanted to be free to form her own opinions and make her own decisions.

Krista joined a group of teenagers who debated political issues and helped organize political rallies. Despite her seemingly radical stance, however, Krista was not certain about which political model was best. She only knew what she didn't like about the one she had lived in; with much fervor and thought, she would argue and debate the merits of other political systems. Her parents were both impressed and distressed by Krista's ability to reason about the future of Estonia. Yet, despite their differences of opinion on some issues, they knew that Krista had already accepted many of their values about life.

PHYSICAL AND SEXUAL DEVELOPMENT

When I was 12 I could not wait to be 13 because that would mean that I was a "teenager." Physically, however, I already looked like a teenager. I was as tall as I am now, and had reached sexual maturity. I was clearly an adolescent. Most people in the United States equate adolescence with the teenage years. But some people confuse the terms *adolescence* and *pubescence*. Adolescence can be roughly defined as the period from the onset of puberty or sexual maturity to adulthood, a period during which many physical, psychological, and social changes occur. Pubescence, however, is the shorter period of adolescence during which an individual achieves sexual maturity (Chumlea, 1982). Pubescence lasts from 2 to 4 years and is accompanied by both physical and psychological changes; adolescents' bodies become capable of functioning sexually, and their attitudes and behavior become more adultlike.

The outward signs of puberty—the development of sex organs and a mature body type—are not the first physical changes in adolescence, however. Many months before those outward signs become visible, the body is changing in unseen ways, particularly in its hormonal makeup, which prepares the way for sexual maturity and the ability to procreate.

PHYSICAL GROWTH

There is a wall in our kitchen on which we have recorded the changes in the height of our children. When Adam was almost 13, his height was recorded on the wall many times—but height was just one of the many physical changes we witnessed as Adam emerged into adolescence. Human beings grow most rapidly at two times during their lives: before the age of 6 months and again during adolescence. The second period of accelerated growth, often called the **adolescent growth spurt,** usually lasts 2 to 3 years (Barnes, 1975; Tanner, 1990).

adolescent growth spurt
The period of acceleration of growth that occurs in early adolescence.

The most obvious physical alterations in the adolescent are changes in height and weight, body proportions, and the development of secondary sexual characteristics, which include body hair, breast development, and changes in voice (see Table 9–1). All of these changes are closely controlled and integrated by the central nervous system and the endocrine (hormonal) system (Chumlea, 1982).

In girls, the adolescent growth spurt in height usually begins between the ages of 9 and 11 and reaches a peak at an average of $12\frac{1}{2}$ years. The spurt in weight gain follows the height gains. Growth slows down and usually ceases completely between the ages of 15 and 18. The growth spurt in boys generally begins about 2 years later than it does in girls and lasts for a longer time. The male growth spurt in height begins between the ages of 11 and 12, reaches a peak at about age 14, and slowly declines until the age of 20 or 21 (Malina, 1991).

Different parts of the teenager's body grow at differing rates, so that at times adolescents look a bit awkward. Growth during adolescence violates the proximodistal (from the center of the body outward) trend characteristic of other developmental growth periods. Big feet and long legs are the early signs of a changing body. First the hands and feet grow, then the arms and legs, and only later do the shoulders and chest grow to fit the rest of the developing body. The stereotype of the gangling and clumsy teenager may be fueled by an awkward-appearing body.

Other changes in body proportion also occur. The trunk widens in the hips and shoulders, and the waistline drops. Boys tend to broaden mostly in the

CHARACTERISTIC PHYSICAL CHANGES DURING ADOLESCENCE

FEMALE CHANGES	AGE
Increases in height	Peak by age 12
Increases in body fat	Peak by age 17
Emergence of breast buds	10
Growth of breasts	8–13; peak by age 16
Increase in muscle strength	12.5
Pubic hair appears	10–15
Pubic hair development complete	14–18
Onset of menstruation (menarche)	12.5
First ovulation	13.5

MALE CHANGES	AGE
Increases in height	Peak by age 13
Increases in muscle strength	Peak by age 14.5
Pubic hair appears	12
Pubic hair development complete	18
Testes and scrotum grow larger	11
Penis growth begins	10.5–14.5
Penis growth completed	12.5–16.5
Facial hair appears	16
Voice lowers	15
First ejaculation of semen	13

TABLE 9–1

Source: Ages are approximate averages and do not reflect the variability in physical development characteristic of normal adolescents.

shoulders, girls in the hips. One part of the adolescent's body that does not undergo much change is the brain. By about age 10 the brain has reached its adult size. However, the shape of the head and face change so that adolescents look more like adults. The forehead becomes wider and higher and the size of the head relative to the body is smaller than it was in childhood.

One of the earliest changes in both sexes is the addition of a layer of subcutaneous (under the skin) fat in the hips and legs. This fat soon diminishes in boys, but not in girls. By 17 years of age girls have 2 to 2½ times as much body fat as boys. In contrast, **lean body mass** (total body weight less total body fat), or LBM,

lean body mass (LBM)
Total body weight less body fat.

The adolescent growth spurt results in an uneven rate of growth for different parts of the body.

is significantly greater in boys than in girls. In girls LBM peaks around age 15, whereas in boys LBM continues to increase into late adolescence or early adulthood (Forbes, 1972). (See Figure 9–1.)

Growth in lean body mass in adolescence is due to an increase in muscle mass. In turn, greater muscle mass causes increases in strength and motor performance. In girls, strength increases gradually throughout adolescence, eventually leveling off between 16 and 18 years. In boys, the strength increase follows the growth path of girls until about age 13, when there is a dramatic rise in strength (Malina, 1979, 1991). The effect of this rise is that, from the adolescent period on, most males are significantly stronger than most females.

Heredity, health, and nutrition influence the timing of the adolescent growth spurt in several ways. Genetic patterns exert a strong influence on growth. However, the genetic program can be altered by health and nutrition. The rapid growth in muscle and bone tissue during adolescence requires additional calories and nutrients such as proteins and calcium. Children who are healthy and adequately nourished mature earlier and grow bigger than children who are malnourished or afflicted by disease (Eveleth & Tanner, 1976). Nutrition also affects the secretion of hormones by the endocrine glands. A growth hormone released by the pituitary gland is primarily responsible for the rapid growth at the beginning of adolescence. The thyroid gland aids in this development by releasing larger amounts of the hormones that permit the conversion of food into tissues and energy. The gonads—the ovaries in the female and the testes in the male—are stimulated by hormones secreted by the adrenal glands and the pituitary. The gonads generate sexual development, but they also play an important role in stimulating the physical development that occurs before the visible signs of puberty appear.

FIGURE 9-1

Changes in 50th percentiles of Lean Body Mass (LBM) in boys and girls.

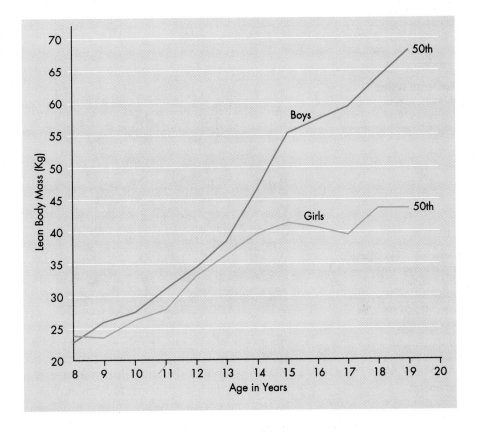

PUBERTY

puberty
The stage of development when the individual reaches sexual maturity and becomes capable of reproduction.

secondary sex characteristics
Physical features other than genitals that distinguish women and men.

Perhaps the first sign you had that you were entering **puberty** was the eruption of pubic hairs. Most women remember quite vividly the time they started their first period—another sign of pubertal growth. The production of semen and the growth of the penis and testes in boys, and the onset of menstruation in girls, are often taken as signs of the onset of puberty. However, these obvious changes in sex organs are accompanied by other changes in the body. **Secondary sex characteristics** include nongenital physical features such as body hair, breast development for girls, increased activity of the sweat glands, and changes in voice and skin texture. All of these changes in sexual characteristics are influenced by hormonal changes that occur as a result of the growth spurt.

FOCUS ON CULTURE

Poverty is a significant and persistent contributor to malnutrition and consequently has an impact on growth (Lozoff, 1989) that has no geographical boundaries. Growing up in poverty has a similar impact on growth for adolescents living in affluent countries and in poor ones. Impoverished adolescents may be deprived of the additional calories needed to sustain the adolescent growth spurt. They also may have had a history of malnutrition throughout childhood, which can have the cumulative effect of slowing or arresting development in adolescence.

hormones
Chemical substances that are released into the bloodstream from endocrine glands.

endocrine system
A complex arrangement of glands throughout the body that secrete different types of hormones.

Adolescent boys experience a rapid increase in muscle and bone tissue that requires additional calories and nutrients for adequate growth.

androgens
Hormones that are produced by the adrenal glands and by the male sex glands, the testes.

estrogens
Hormones produced in the adrenal glands and in the female sex glands that influence the development and maintenance of sex characteristics.

prepubescent stage
A stage of pubertal development in which secondary sex characteristics begin to develop but reproductive organs do not produce ova or sperm.

pubescent stage
In pubertal development, the stage when secondary sex characteristics continue to develop and the reproductive organs become capable of ova and sperm production.

postpubescent stage
A stage in pubertal development in which the secondary sex characteristics are well developed and the sex organs are capable of adult functioning.

Hormonal Influences   The physical changes that occur in puberty are stimulated by **hormones,** chemical substances that are released into the bloodstream by the endocrine glands. The **endocrine system** is a complex arrangement of glands throughout the body that secrete different types of hormones. The pituitary gland, located in the brain, serves as a master gland and regulates the production and secretion of many hormones. The pituitary gland, in turn, is regulated by a higher portion of the brain known as the hypothalamus.

Many hormones affect pubertal change, but two general classes of hormones are of particular importance: **androgens** and **estrogens.** While the levels of these hormones is different for males and females, androgen and estrogen are present in both sexes. Androgens are hormones that are produced by the adrenal glands and by the male sex glands, the testes. Androgen production increases dramatically in adolescence. Androgens are responsible for the adolescent growth spurt in females and the production of underarm and pubic hair. Androgen levels are higher in males than females and influence the development of sex characteristics in boys. Estrogens are also produced by the adrenal glands and in the female sex gland, the ovaries, and influence the development and maintenance of sex characteristics.

About 1 to 2 years before the outward signs appear, androgens and estrogens begin circulating throughout the body and set the stage for the emergence of the striking physical and mental changes of adolescence. The ways in which hormones trigger puberty's onset and the specific changes associated with it is not precisely known.

Pubescence can be divided into three stages. In the **prepubescent stage,** the secondary sex characteristics begin to develop, but the reproductive organs do not yet produce ova and sperm. In the **pubescent stage,** the secondary sex characteristics continue to develop and the reproductive organs become capable of producing ova and sperm. In the **postpubescent stage,** the secondary sex characteristics are well developed and the sex organs are capable of adult functioning.

The age of onset of puberty differs depending on sex. The great majority of American girls usually have their first menstrual period—an event known as

menarche
The first occurrence of menstruation.

menarche—between the ages of 10 and 17; the mean age is 12.7 years (Tanner, 1991b), although poor nutrition can delay the onset of menarche. For example, girls living in underdeveloped countries begin their first period at an older age than girls living in industrialized countries (Tanner, 1991b). The age of menarche is also influenced by genetic factors (Graber, Brooks-Gunn, & Warren, 1995); if a girl's mother reached menarche at an early age, then chances are she will too.

Puberty seems to occur with greater variability for boys than for girls. Boys produce their first ejaculation of seminal fluid at about age 13 (Jorgensen & Keiding, 1991). Throughout the world, girls generally mature sexually and physically about 2 years earlier than boys.

primary sex characteristics
Refers to organs necessary for reproduction.

Primary Sex Characteristics   **Primary sex characteristics** refer to the organs necessary for reproduction. The male testes are present at birth, but are only about 10% of their mature size. They grow rapidly during the first year or two of puberty, then grow more slowly, not reaching their mature size until the age of 20 or 21. Shortly after the testes begin to develop, the penis starts to lengthen, and the seminal ducts and prostate gland enlarge. Although the penis is capable of erection by means of contact from birth, only during adolescence does it begin to erect spontaneously or in response to sexually provocative sights, sounds, or thoughts.

The female's uterus, fallopian tubes, and vagina grow rapidly throughout puberty. The ovaries also grow; although they begin to function about midway through puberty, they do not reach their full adult size until the age of 20 or 21. The ovaries produce ova and secrete the hormones needed for pregnancy, menstruation, and development of the secondary sex characteristics. Following menarche, menstruation may initially occur at irregular intervals; for 6 months to 1 year or more, ovulation may not always occur.

SECONDARY SEX CHARACTERISTICS

The secondary sex characteristics are not directly related to reproduction. The first sign that David's body was changing was the sparse patches of lightly colored, straight pubic hair he noticed while showering. About a year or two later, his pubic hair took on the characteristically dark, curly appearance that is typical of adult secondary sexual characteristics. Axillary (underarm) and facial hair begin to appear when the pubic hair has almost fully grown in. Like pubic hair, this hair is at first lightly colored, fine, and sparse. Few boys find that they need to shave before they are 16 or 17. Hair also appears on the arms, legs, and shoulders, and, later, the chest. Body hair continues to develop for some time, often into adulthood, with the amount and density determined by heredity.

Perhaps the most noticeable change in boys, however, is the deepening of the voice. David sounded like his father well before he became similar to him in size. This is because typically by the time a boy is 13, his voice has begun to take on a huskier tone, a change that is caused by enlargement of the larynx and lengthening of the vocal cords. Voice change generally is complete by age 17 or 18.

Girls' secondary sex characteristics generally develop in the same sequence as boys, with the exception of breast development. The first indication of approaching sexual maturity in a girl is "budding" of the breast (Chumlea, 1982). Occurring at an average age of 10 or 11, the bud stage involves a slight elevation of the nipple and increasing fullness of the surrounding areola. Before menarche there is an increase in the amount of fat underlying the nipple and the areola, and the

One of the early signs of secondary sexual development in girls is the emergence of breast buds at about age 10 or 11.

For boys, the emergence of facial hair is a clear sign of secondary sexual development.

Before menarche, girls' breasts are in the budding stage. After menarche, the breasts become larger and rounded.

breast rises in a conical shape. After menarche the breasts become larger and rounded with the development of the mammary glands. In addition to breast development, there are also noticeable changes in the size and shape of the hips, which grow wider and become rounded. This development is caused by enlargement of the pelvic bone and increases in subcutaneous fat. Coinciding with these changes is the emergence of pubic hair, which has the same texture and appearance as boys'.

In both sexes, the skin becomes coarser and thicker during puberty, and the pores enlarge. The sebaceous, or fatty, glands in the skin become active at this time and produce an oily secretion, as persons suffering from acne know all too well. The sweat glands in the armpits also begin to function, even before the axillary hair appears, and this results in increases in the amount and odor of perspiration. Many teenagers are embarrassed by the large underarm sweat rings that occur when they least want to appear "uncool." Perhaps this is why David began taking long showers after a preadolescent period of avoiding them. Another telltale sign (or odor) of adolescence is sweaty, smelly feet and shoes, especially sneakers. Fortunately, the activity of the sweat glands decreases later in adolescence.

FOCUS ON CULTURE

In some cultures, the passage from childhood to physical maturity in adolescence is noted by rites and customs that serve different purposes. In some cultures, the symbolic rites, such as confirmation and bar mitzvah, are performed to mark an individual's passage to a new social status in life. After the rite, the individual is accepted as an adult member of the community. In other cultures, the rite of passage ceremony is more physical, such as facial scarring or male circumcision, and is meant to test adolescents' courage and readiness to separate from their families and accept their adult status. Whether physical or symbolic, most rites of passage involve a period of instruction and preparation for the tasks and responsibilities of adulthood.

VARYING RATES OF DEVELOPMENT

If you have ever attended a seventh- or eighth-grade assembly you would immediately notice the vast differences in size and shape of the students. Not only do the girls appear to tower over the boys, but within each of the sexes there is considerable variability in physical growth. Within any group of adolescents one can observe significant variations in physical maturity, as well as concomitant variations in emotional, social, and cognitive development.

Early and Late Maturation   Among the many adjustments that adolescents must make, certainly one of the most important is integrating a "new" body into an emerging picture of the self. This is a time of increased preoccupation with physical appearance (Collins & Plahn, 1988; Dorn, Crockett, & Peterson, 1988), and when many people report considerable dissatisfaction with the way they look (Rosenbaum, 1979; Simmons & Rosenberg, 1975). Who we are is very much related to how we look physically. For adolescents, who seem to be growing and changing physically almost overnight, self-image is greatly affected. Furthermore, the age and rate at which an adolescent grows can have an impact on his or her self-evaluation.

Research has shown that boys who mature early have distinct advantages over those who mature late (Alsaker, 1992; Jones, 1957, 1958; Mussen & Jones, 1957). They tend to excel at sports, achieve greater popularity, and become leaders in student government and extracurricular activities (Brooks-Gunn & Peterson, 1983; Simmons & Blyth, 1987). Early-maturing boys also tend to be more poised, relaxed, and good-natured, and they are more interested in girls. In adult life they are likely to be more successful vocationally.

In contrast, late-maturing boys not only are smaller and less well developed than almost everyone in their age group, but also they are not very interested in dating, and when they do become interested in girls, they often lack social graces or are rebuffed by the prettiest and most popular girls. These boys also are more likely to be characterized as impulsive, restless, and lacking in self-confidence. In adulthood, however, many of these disadvantages disappear or are compensated

There is considerable variation among boys in their rate of physical growth. Some boys seem to grow taller overnight, while their peers may take another year to catch up to them in height.

for by other traits. As adults, late-maturing individuals tend to be insightful, independent, curious, and less bound by rules and routines. They are also less conventionally successful (Brooks-Gunn & Reiter, 1990; Jones, 1965; Peskin, 1973).

Early-maturing boys are more likely to be treated as adults because they look more like adults than do late-maturing boys. Pressured by adult expectations to act like adults, early-maturing boys run the risk of prematurely adopting a personal and career identity (Livson & Peskin, 1980) before they have had a chance to fully explore their possible choices. Thus, early-maturing boys tend to be more conventional in their career choices and less adventurous in their view of self. Late-maturing boys have more time to explore and experiment with their options before becoming fixed in their identity. They are free to choose career paths that are unique to them and are not restricted to those defined by the previous generation.

In one longitudinal study (Blyth, Bulcroft, & Simmons, 1981) early maturation in girls (as defined by onset of menstruation) was found to be a mixed blessing, whereas early maturation in boys (as measured by rate of growth in height) was found to have positive effects. Blyth's 5-year study tracked American girls and boys from the 6th to the 10th grade. Early-maturing girls did not perform as well academically, had more reported school behavior problems, and were more dissatisfied with their bodies during the 9th and 10th grades. However, early-maturing girls were also found to be more independent and sexually active than their late-maturing peers; they dated earlier and had their first experience with sexual intercourse earlier (Phinney, Jensen, Olsen, & Cundick, 1990).

In part, the psychological significance of puberty is a product of the times and culture in which adolescents mature. Current opinion and values will affect the status of adolescents who are earlier or later in their physical maturation. In the United States during the 1960s, when the first longitudinal data on maturation rates were collected (e.g., Jones, 1965, 1957; Mussen & Jones, 1957), not nearly as much importance was placed on teenagers' looking like adults as is the case today. At that time the **age of majority,** the age at which people are considered to be legally responsible for themselves, was 21 and most of the men and all of the women had reached physical maturity. Today, however, the age of legal majority has been lowered to 18, pressuring many men to look like adults at an earlier age than did their counterparts who were born a generation earlier.

age of majority
The age at which people are considered to be legally responsible for themselves.

The Impact of Menarche

No area of adolescent female development has been marked by as much psychological and sociocultural significance as menarche—the first menstruation. In about half of the world's cultures this event is celebrated with elaborate rituals and ceremonies (Paige & Paige, 1981). But what is the meaning of menarche for the young female? And what factors influence her adjustment to this maturational event?

Psychological theories vary in their characterization of the impact of menarche (Grief & Ulman, 1982). The meaning of menarche must be understood in the context of the culture in which it occurs. In some cultures, menstruation is celebrated as the passage to fertility. In others, such as in the United States, the event often goes unmarked and ignored socially. Some have suggested that the first menstruation is inevitably traumatic; others have described the event as a positive experience in a girl's development. Research by Ruble and Brooks-Gunn (1982) has yielded results that tend to support a more moderate position. That is, when asked about their first menstrual experience, adolescent girls described both

In some cultures, initiation rites mark the young person's passage into adulthood. This young woman is preparing for the ceremony that will acknowledge her physical maturity.

negative (e.g., upset) and positive (e.g., excited) reactions. The researchers also noted that young adolescents who received greater preparation and had more knowledge about menarche prior to experiencing it were likely to have more positive reactions to their first menstrual period and to be less self-conscious than girls who were poorly prepared.

Girls' physical and emotional reactions to menstruation are also affected by their attitudes about having periods. Girls who believe that menstruation is a painful experience are more likely to have painful menstrual cramps (Gunn & Peterson, 1984). Furthermore, girls' adjustment to menstruation is influenced by whether they see themselves as fitting in with their social peers. Girls who perceived themselves to be early or late in beginning to menstruate had less positive feelings about puberty than girls who perceived themselves as "on time" (Dubas, Graber, & Peterson, 1991). Whether a girl is "on time" in beginning to menstruate is based more on cognitive and social than biological considerations. First, girls must be able to assess their own status with regard to menarche. This may be a more difficult task than it seems, since menstruation may be very irregular at first. Then she must compare her menarche with what she believes to be the norm. If some of her friends have not yet begun to menstruate, a girl who is a late maturer will not feel out of step. However, the early maturing girl may feel awkward about starting her period when none of her friends have. Thus, ballet dancers who were on time in development with respect to their general peer group but were ahead of their dancing peers had a more difficult adjustment to puberty (Brooks-Gunn & Warren, 1985).

secular growth trends
Variation in physical growth patterns that characterize populations over a period of time.

Secular Growth Trends   Biologists use the term **secular growth trends** to describe changes in the general directions of human physical growth throughout the world (Roche, 1979). To measure secular growth trends, biologists record the height, weight, and body changes in defined groups—usually national ones—over long periods, usually several decades.

Due in most part to improved nutrition and health care, children in different parts of the world seem to be reaching puberty earlier than their parents did, and growing taller and heavier as well (Tanner, 1991a). For example, records show that in the United States, a young man will, on the average, be 1 inch (2.5 cm) taller and 10 pounds (4.5 kg) heavier than his father. A young woman will probably be almost an inch taller than her mother and 2 pounds (0.9 kg) heavier, and will reach menarche 10 months earlier than her mother did. Today's adolescents are also reaching full adult height earlier than their ancestors. At the turn of the century girls reached full height at the age of 18, whereas the modern girl stops growing at age 17. A century ago, boys did not reach full height until age 23 or 24, but now an adolescent boy stops growing around the age of 20.

There is a genetic limit to growth; in developed countries the growth trend has reached a plateau. Among the middle and upper classes in the United States, children no longer outpace their parents in physical maturity. Among European populations, the age of menarche has decreased over the past century from a range of 15 to 17 years to between 12 and 14 years (Tanner, 1991b). In less developed countries, however, menarche still occurs relatively late. For example, Eveleth and Tanner (1976) reported that in New Guinea first menstruation occurs between 15.5 and 18.4 years of age.

Although no one is certain what causes secular growth trends, they are generally believed to be both environmental and genetic in origin. There is, for example, some apparent relationship between crop production, urbanization, family size, and mortality. This relationship does not clearly indicate cause, however. Important factors in secular growth trends are improved health and better care during childhood. Genetic factors, altered by such events as a change in immigration and marriage patterns, may also be important, as may changes in socioeconomic status, eating patterns, and environmental stress (Malina, 1979).

RECAP

Physical growth occurs at a rapid rate during adolescence and is characterized by changes in height, weight, strength, and body proportion. The onset of the adolescent growth spurt is influenced by heredity, nutrition, and health. Pubescence, the development of sexual maturity, is triggered by hormonal changes and occurs in three stages. Girls and boys differ in the age of onset and type of primary and secondary sex characteristics that emerge during puberty. Early and late maturation during adolescence has differing personality and social consequences for males and females. The significance of menarche for girls varies according to the cultural context. Physical growth differs over time and across cultures.

SEXUAL ATTITUDES AND BEHAVIOR

Not only are adolescents' bodies becoming more like those of adults, but their interest in sexual behavior increases sharply over the period from ages 12 to 18. For many teenagers in early adolescence, sexual explorations are tentative and generally self-centered. The 12- or 13-year-old, for example, usually is more concerned with meeting his or her own needs for sexual stimulation than satisfying another

mutuality

A concern for meeting the needs of both oneself and one's partner.

person. Later in adolescence, on the other hand, sexual relationships are more often based on **mutuality**—a concern for meeting the needs of both oneself and one's partner.

HETEROSEXUAL BEHAVIOR

One national survey (see Figure 9–2) found that more than 65 percent of white males and 60 percent of white females reported having sexual intercourse by the time they were 18. Sixty-five percent of African American males reported having intercourse by the age of 16, and 60 percent of African American females reported having sexual intercourse by age 17 (Michael, Gagnon, Laumann, & Kolata, 1994).

It is important to remember that compared to previous generations, teenagers today are more willing to talk about their sexual behavior. However, Dreyer (1982) notes that the growing acceptance of sexual expression among adolescents is not unconditional. Although the vast majority of adolescents approve of premarital sexual intercourse, they do so only within a relationship that is loving and affectionate. Promiscuous behavior and sexual exploitation are considered unacceptable by most adolescents.

Although research evidence has documented substantial increases in acceptance of adolescent sexual behavior, actual participation by young people in such behavior is considerably more modest. In fact, Siegel (1982) has suggested that changes in adolescent sexual behavior are better characterized as evolutionary

FIGURE 9–2

Age and sexual intercourse. *Source:* From *Sex in America,* by Robert T. Michael, John H. Gagnon, Edward O. Laumann, and Gina Kolata, 1994, Boston: Little, Brown, & Company.

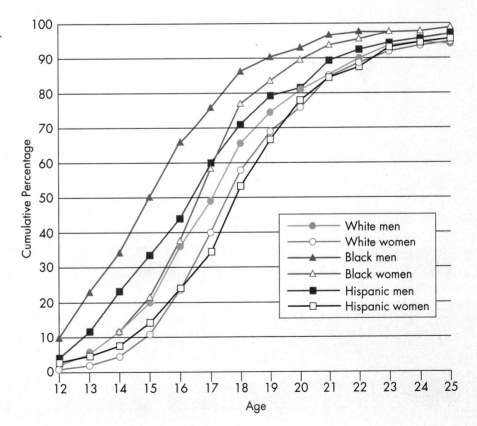

Sexuality emerges in full bloom during adolescence. It is a time for exploring sexual feelings and developing sexual relationships.

(implying a steady, gradual change) rather than revolutionary (implying a sudden and dramatic change).

In one study (Zabin, Hirsch, Smith, & Hardy, 1984) involving 3,500 American junior high and high school students, 83 percent of the sexually active students thought that the best age for first sexual intercourse was older than the age at which they had experienced it themselves. Eighty-eight percent of the teenage mothers thought that the best age for first birth was older than the age at which they had had their first baby. In other words, the adolescents' attitudes toward sexual behavior, or their values, were not in keeping with their actual behavior.

The greatest changes in adolescent sexual behavior over the past few generations have occurred for girls. Dreyer (1982) reports that from 1925 to 1979 the percentage of high school girls who had experienced premarital sexual intercourse more than quadrupled, from 10 percent in 1925 to 44 percent in 1979. Boys also showed an increase in premarital coitus over this time span, from 25 percent in 1925 to 56 percent in 1979. The less dramatic rise in sexual intercourse for boys clearly reflects the fact that, until recently, boys have enjoyed substantially more freedom in the expression of their sexuality—hence, their rates of sexual behavior have always been higher than those for girls.

FOCUS ON CULTURE

In the United States, most adolescents learn about sexual behavior and techniques from their equally uninformed peers. But on the island of Mangaia in the South Pacific, teenagers receive direct and explicit instruction from adults (Marshall, 1987). Boys and girls are encouraged to have sexual experiences with several partners before marriage. Girls are encouraged and taught how to have orgasms at a young age. Among the Kikuyu people in Kenya, with the approval of their parents, young boys and girls practice a type of preintercourse lovemaking. The couple lie down together in an embrace and fondle and rub each other everywhere but in the genital area (Worthman & Whiting, 1987).

HOMOSEXUALITY

The first reliable data on homosexual behavior came from the research of Kinsey and his colleagues (Kinsey, Pomeroy, & Martin, 1948, 1953). Their studies showed that a surprisingly large number of people had had some homosexual experience during their lives—about 37 percent of males and 19 percent of females. For most of the males and about half of the females these experiences had begun during adolescence. It was also found, however, that most of these people were not exclusively homosexual. Many of them had had both homosexual and heterosexual contacts during the same general time period, and felt comfortable in both. Also, many who engaged in homosexual activity in adolescence or early adulthood gave it up later on. Most of them were never identified as homosexuals by their heterosexual friends or coworkers.

In a more contemporary study, 15 percent of boys and 10 percent girls reported having had a homosexual experience (Dreyer, 1982). Studies of adolescent homosexuality indicate that such sexual experiences are usually more frequent before age 15, and more likely for boys than for girls (Hass, 1979; Sorensen, 1973). Most young people are quite tolerant of homosexuality. In a questionnaire study, nearly 70 percent of the 16- to 19-year-olds accepted sexual relations between two women, and only slightly less accepted such relations between two men (Hass, 1979).

Adolescence is the time when many teenagers make decisions about their sexual behavior—that is, whether they will meet their sexual needs with a person of the same sex or the opposite sex (Herdt, 1989; Herdt & Boxer, 1993; Savin-Williams, 1990). Because of the pervasive bias against homosexuality in many cultures, many youths may be reluctant to acknowledge their sexual feelings for same-sex partners. Those who do openly acknowledge their lesbian or gay preferences are more likely to experience discrimination and sometimes verbal and physical violence both at school and at home (Pilkington & D'Augelli, in press; Remafedi, 1987). The impact of this victimization on the mental health of gay and lesbian youth can be reduced when family members provide emotional and social support for their children who acknowledge that their sexual orientation is homosexual. Gay and lesbian adolescents who have a high sense of self-worth are more immune to the negative consequences of prejudice and violence (Hershberger & D'Augelli, 1995).

TEENAGE PREGNANCY

Each year in the United States almost 1 girl in 10 between ages the ages 15 and 19 gets pregnant; 4 out of 5 of these pregnancies are unintended (Ambuel, 1995). The rate is almost twice as high among African American teenage girls as among Caucasians. These U.S. rates are the highest among the industrialized nations of the world. In France the rate is 43 per 1,000, in Sweden 35 per 1,000 (Mall, 1985). The increase in sexual activity does not account for these differences, since sexual activity has increased among teenagers in other countries.

Almost half of sexually active teenagers fail to use contraception or use it occasionally, thus putting them at risk for an unwanted pregnancy (Santelli & Beilenson, 1992). Once a teenager gets pregnant for the first time, the odds are that she will be pregnant again within 3 years. In 1989, there were 233,000 unintended pregnancies, 161,000 births, and 162,000 abortions among teenagers between the ages of 15 and 17 (Ambuel, 1995).

Teenage pregnancy creates risks for both mother and child. The babies of teenage mothers have twice the normal chance of being born prematurely or with low birthweights, neurological defects, or birth injuries. These babies run 2 to 3 times the normal risk of dying in infancy. The younger the mother, the greater the risk. Teenage mothers themselves are 60 percent more likely than women in their twenties to suffer complications or death during pregnancy or delivery. Hemorrhage, miscarriage, toxemia, and anemia are the most frequent complications. However, these risks are more likely to be due to low socioeconomic levels than to biological inadequacies (Roosa, 1984). When the labor and delivery experiences of 2,700 low- and middle-income teenage and older mothers were compared, teenage mothers were not found to be at risk. Instead, low-income mothers, especially the older mothers, were at a greater risk for labor complications.

Babies require long-term care. Whereas the majority of unmarried teenagers, particularly Caucasian teenagers, once gave up their babies for adoption, only a small percentage do so today (Dreyer, 1982). The care of the child is frequently shared by the grandparents with whom the teenage mother lives. Most of these mothers do not marry the father of their child (Children's Defense Fund, 1991).

Approximately one third of all teenage mothers are married at the time their baby is born. But the likelihood of these marriages breaking up within 6 years is 3 times greater than it is for older couples. Due to their relative lack of education and their own immaturity, teenage couples often cannot meet the responsibilities of raising a child. They often have difficulty completing their high school studies, and without a diploma their chances for job security are limited. Furthermore, teenage parents must deal with all the difficulties of working parents while they are in school. Someone must care for their child and the

Teenage pregnancy creates risks for both mother and child. This teenager is seeking counseling about her impending labor and delivery and to help her make decisions about the care of her unborn child.

parents (or single mother) must share work or school demands with the demands of a new baby.

Adolescent fathers as a group have not been studied as systematically as teenage mothers, primarily because it is more difficult for researchers to identify them. The studies that have been done reveal that adolescent fathers are quite concerned about their newborn children; many young fathers are interested in caring for their children (Elster & Hendricks, 1986). They want to play a meaningful role in the lives of the teenage mother and child, while at the same time ensuring the financial stability of their young families by completing their schooling. The stresses adolescent fathers experience are similar to those of the adolescent mother. They must deal with the transition to parenthood while also adjusting to a relationship as a couple, often while still living in their parents' home. All new couples must make these adjustments, but adolescents must do so before they have matured socially and psychologically.

Contraceptive Use   Before the advent of effective female contraceptives, fear of pregnancy was a powerful deterrent to premarital sex. The invention and general availability of the Pill and other contraceptive devices led to a marked increase in sexual activity among teenagers as well as in society as a whole. Nonetheless, almost half of all sexually active teenagers do not use any sort of contraceptive technique at the time of their first intercourse, and only 20 percent report using some means of birth control with any consistency (Dreyer, 1982; Santelli & Beilenson, 1992). Having unprotected sex puts the individual at risk for unwanted pregnancies and sexually transmitted diseases. In one study (Arnett, 1990) of junior and senior high school students in Atlanta, Georgia, those who reported that they engaged in sexual intercourse without using

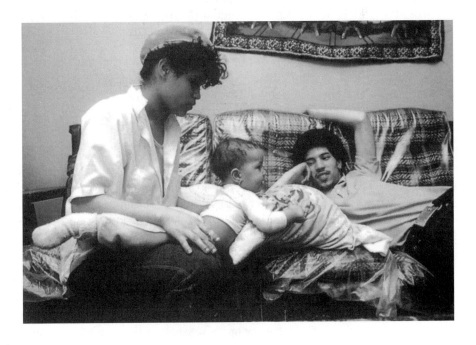

Teenage fathers are frequently concerned about and involved with their children.

Education Perspective

THE IMPORTANCE OF SEX EDUCATION

Sexually transmitted diseases (STD) include a variety of highly contagious viruses and bacteria that are passed from one person to the next through sexual contact. Gonorrhea, syphilis, and AIDS are examples of STDs. With the increase in teenage pregnancies and the dangers associated with sexually transmitted diseases, the need to educate young people about safe sexual behavior is becoming more apparent to educators, parents, and health officials (Brooks-Gunn, Boyer, & Hein, 1988; Centers for Disease Control, 1990; Flora & Thoresen, 1988). Yet the issue of what and when to teach children and adolescents about sex has sparked controversy in many communities and households. Many states now have mandatory sex education classes; however, the content of these classes varies from discussion of sexual anatomy to child care and family planning. Many do not explicitly discuss sexual behavior and contraception. Although sex education classes do not seem to influence adolescents' choices about having sex, there is evidence that sexually active teenage girls who have taken sex education courses are less likely to become pregnant (Zelnik & Kim, 1982). The habits and attitudes that teenagers establish concerning their sexual behavior could have drastic and long-term effects, particularly when it comes to sexually transmitted diseases.

Sexually active adolescents, either heterosexual or homosexual, can reduce their risk of contracting a sexually transmitted disease by taking certain precautions. The Public Health Service recommends the following steps:

1. Recognize that abstinence or a stable sexual relationship with one person (monogamy) is the best protection against sexual transmission of the AIDS virus.

2. Do not have unprotected sex with multiple partners or with people who have had multiple partners.

3. Do not have unprotected sex with anyone who has the AIDS virus. Protected sex involves using a latex condom from the start to the finish of sexual intercourse.

4. Avoid sexual activities that could cause cuts or tears in the skin.

5. Do not have sex with prostitutes or drug abusers.

6. Do not use intravenous drugs or share syringes.

Not only is it important to teach teenagers how to protect themselves against sexually transmitted diseases, there is a need to teach people to act responsibly toward others. If you have been exposed to someone

---

sexually transmitted disease (STD)

Diseases spread through sexual intercourse.

contraception also scored high on a scale that measured the degree to which they sought out exciting or arousing experiences. Adolescents' failure to use contraception adds risk and excitement to their lives.

There are other reasons that adolescents do not use contraception (see Table 9–2). One survey of African American teenage girls (Scott-Jones & Turner, 1988) found that despite having had formal discussions and instruction from their parents about reproduction and contraception, their reproductive knowledge and use of contraceptives was poor. The most prominent reason for failing to use contraceptives is the inability of the adolescent girl or boy to accept the fact that she or he is sexually active. It is all too easy to rationalize that the first sexual with AIDS or some other STD, anyone with whom you have sexual intercourse is equally exposed and needs to be informed of that risk before you engage in sexual behavior.

Education programs aimed at informing adolescents about AIDS and other sexually transmitted diseases can help prevent their transmission. Programs that provide specific information about the diseases and that encourage teenagers to talk about how they can protect themselves and their partners need to be tailored to different populations and age groups (Flora & Thoresen, 1988).

However, being informed about sexually transmitted diseases is useful only if behavior is modified accordingly. A study (Roscoe & Kruger, 1990) of 300 adolescents revealed that despite their knowledgeability about AIDS and its transmission, only about one third of the teenagers had altered their sexual behavior as a result.

According to Scales (1981), sex education programs should "provide young people with the skills, knowledge, and attitudes that will enable them to make intelligent choices and decisions" (p. 220). However, many teenagers do not discuss their sexuality with teachers in their sex education classes because they are afraid that teachers will tell their parents or other teachers. Other teenagers are reluctant to ask questions about sex in class because they are concerned about what their peers will think of them. If sex education programs are to have a positive impact on sexual behavior, they must address these concerns.

Sex education classes help to inform teenagers about the dangers of sexually transmitted diseases and ways to prevent them.

encounter as an accident that is unlikely to be repeated. Because the early stages of adolescent sexual behavior are characterized by infrequent coitus, this belief is easily maintained, resulting in ineffective contraceptive use. Other teenagers erroneously believe that they will not become pregnant unless they want to, are in love with their partner, or have sexual intercourse very often. The use of contraception increases when teenagers have strong reasons not to get pregnant; teenagers with high educational aspirations are more likely to use contraception effectively (Miller & Moore, 1990).

Teenagers who consider or use contraceptive methods must deal with several issues. Many girls rely on their partners for contraceptive protection, especially for

REASONS ADOLESCENTS FAIL TO USE CONTRACEPTIVE METHODS

Desire to tempt fate and run the risk of pregnancy

Limited or no knowledge of reproduction

Unwillingness to accept one's active sexuality

Erroneous beliefs that pregnancy will occur only if one is in love, wants to get pregnant, or has intercourse often

Unquestioned reliance on one's partner for contraceptive protection

Fear of parents finding out about one's contraceptive use

Belief that contraception will take the romance out of sexual intercourse

TABLE 9–2

the first experience of intercourse (Elster & Hendricks, 1986). At first boys take the lead in providing contraceptive protection, but as they become more sexually experienced, they abdicate this responsibility (Pleck, Sonenstein, & Swain, 1988). In a survey of African American inner-city junior and senior high school males (Jemmott & Jemmott, 1990), 97 percent of the boys said that they had had sexual intercourse once. Seventy-eight percent reported not using any contraception during their first sexual experience and 54 percent reported not using contraception during their most recent sexual experience.

Some adolescents misunderstand how fertility relates to the menstrual cycle. Some who understand the situation correctly, and would like to obtain a prescription for the Pill or be fitted with a diaphragm or an IUD (intrauterine device), are afraid of what their parents might do if they found out. Adolescents who perceive that their parents are supportive of contraceptive use are more likely to use contraception effectively (Baker, Thalberg, & Morrison, 1988; Green, Johnson, & Kaplan, 1992; Jorgensen & Sonstegard, 1984).

Finally, some adolescents have an idealistic view of sexual behavior and think it is unromantic to prepare for intercourse in advance. There are also those who imagine that pregnancies happen only to other people. In large part these beliefs are related to characteristics of adolescent cognitive development that we will discuss shortly.

RECAP

Once puberty has occurred, adolescents display increasing interest in sexual behavior. It is during this time that teenagers develop their sexual orientation. The frequency of unmarried teenage pregnancies has risen over the years, in part due to the increase in sexual activity and the reluctance of teenagers to use effective methods of contraceptives. Teenage pregnancies carry risks for both mother and child. Sex education is one way to prevent the spread of sexually transmitted diseases by affecting changes in sexual behavior.

COGNITIVE DEVELOPMENT

formal operational thought
Piagetian ability to address problems on an abstract level, form hypotheses, and reason from propositions that are contrary to fact.

Adolescence is a time of change, both physical and cognitive. The physical changes associated with adolescence are easy to spot. The psychological changes require a closer examination. In particular, patterns of thought change during adolescence (see Table 9–3). Adolescents' exposure to the world is broader than it was during childhood; they have learned more skills as a result of formal and informal education, and their social networks have extended well beyond their homes and immediate neighborhoods. But, the difference between the way children and adolescents think is qualitative as well as quantitative. Adolescents are capable of thinking abstractly and hypothetically; they think in terms of the future, not just the present. "What if I were to make the soccer team? What if governments required people to protect the environment? What if I were able to live independently of my parents?" Adolescents like Krista and David question, debate, and argue their ideas with parents, peers, elders, and themselves.

One of the major achievements of early adolescence is the attainment of what Piaget calls **formal operational thought** (Inhelder & Piaget, 1958). Concrete operational children are largely concerned with the here and now, with what is apparent to their senses, and with problems that can be solved by trial and error. During adolescence most people become better able to deal with problems on an abstract level, to form hypotheses, and to reason from propositions that are contrary to fact.

FORMAL OPERATIONS (11–15 YEARS)

According to Piaget, it is not until the period of formal operations—the fourth and last stage of cognitive development, which is reached between the ages of 11 and

CHARACTERISTICS OF THE ADOLESCENT THINKER
FORMAL OPERATIONAL THOUGHT
Able to think logically about abstract ideas
Can formulate and systematically test hypotheses
Conceives of time well into the future; is able to plan
Able to use symbols and metaphors
Explores ideas and conceives of ideal situations and people
EGOCENTRISM
Thinks others are focused on their perspectives
Self-absorbed and concerned about being evaluated
Creates an imaginary audience
Displays willingness to reveal aspects of the abiding or enduring self
Displays reluctance to reveal aspects of the transient or temporary self
Creates a personal fable in which he or she plays the leading role

TABLE 9–3

15—that a person can think flexibly enough to consider abstract universals such as freedom and justice and to grasp their intrinsic qualities. Children develop the ability to generalize before the age of 11, but they are not yet ready to understand abstract characteristics such as congruence and mass. By the age of 15 or so, most individuals can appreciate these abstract concepts. By this time they can also begin to think and operate on the level of theory, rather than being constrained by the observable facts or the apparent reality of a situation (Braine & Rumain, 1983; Moshman & Neimark, 1982; Neimark, 1982).

For example, most elementary-school-age children, given the statements "Cows are larger than cats" and "Cats are larger than mice," would have little trouble concluding that "Cows are larger than mice." However, these same children would most likely reject the argument that "Mice are larger than cats, and cats are larger than cows; therefore, mice are larger than cows." The difficulty they would have in accepting the logic of the latter statement is that it runs counter to their everyday, observable experience—that is, they have never seen mice larger than cows. Young children simply cannot separate the form and content of a problem. By contrast, the adolescent, having achieved the level of formal operations, is able to make this separation, and consequently can analyze the logical implications of purely hypothetical situations or statements.

Problem-Solving Skills   My twin sister Mary teaches algebra and calculus to high school students and loves it. She gets most excited when her students finally grasp the elements of how to solve algebraic formulas or see how the information they are learning in calculus could be applied to real life problems. She tells me that some of her students never seem to understand the abstract equations, while others seem to catch on right away. What my sister is talking about are the variations in her students' abilities to think abstractly and solve hypothetical problems.

Formal operational abilities are manifested in numerous areas of a person's life, particularly in the realm of scientific problem solving. In one of Piaget's experiments, for example, subjects were shown an object hanging from a string that

By age 15, most teenagers can understand abstract concepts. Understanding algebraic formulas may take longer, depending on individual abilities.

acted as a pendulum when released from a height. This pendulum could be modified by changing several factors: the length of the string, the weight of the object, the height at which the pendulum was released, and the force with which it was pushed. Subjects were asked to find out which of these factors determines how rapidly the pendulum swings. (The experimenter knew, of course, that the length of the string was the key factor and that testing any one variable would necessitate controlling all the others if accurate results were to be obtained.)

Children in the earlier stage of concrete-operational thought began their experiments by physically manipulating the various factors that could influence the rate of swinging. They were more analytic and systematic in their approach than younger, preoperational children, and they made careful and objective observations of what happened. But their inferences could at best be only partially correct because they had not planned for any sort of control, nor were they capable of extrapolating beyond directly observable results. In one case, a child compared a pendulum made with a long string and a heavy weight with one that had a short string and a light weight. The child concluded that both weight and length were important. A truly scientific approach would have entailed using the same length of string, the same height, and the same force for both pendulums while varying only the weight.

When working at peak capacity, formal operational adolescents would use just this sort of scientific approach. They do not simply plunge into the experiment, nor is their thinking bound by immediately observable results. Adolescents first consider all of the possibilities, or hypotheses, about what makes the pendulum swing faster. They are able to imagine that one or some combination of factors is involved, and they can deduce what might occur if different possibilities are tested. Thus, before even starting an experiment, they are capable of devising a detailed plan or design for systematically testing each alternative.

This change in the ability to thoroughly consider a problem without actually performing all of its intervening steps can also be seen in the adolescent's day-to-day life. David, for example, was interested in building a wooden case to hold his air rifle. In thinking about his problem, he realized that there were many possible ways to build the case. After careful consideration, he decided on a specific design and drew up a set of plans for building the case. He thought about how it might look from different perspectives (e.g., top view, side view), and what materials would be needed (including their cost). Then he presented his proposal to his father to obtain money to complete his project. Unlike a younger child, David was able to consider a number of possible solutions to the problem of building his rifle case. Through mental deliberations he was able to decide on the best possible solution.

Adolescents also develop a more mature notion of time. They can view time and the distant future concretely and are able to set realistic long-term goals. I recall when my daughter Sarah and her friend Liz were seniors in high school and were talking about how they would travel across country during the summer between their freshman and sophomore year in college. They were not yet in college, but they could think about what they would like to do after the end of their first year. With the ability to conceive of time far into the future comes a new, sometimes poignant awareness that life is an ongoing process of growth, aging, and death. It is not surprising, then, that teenagers often think about how they would like to die and often enjoy reading science fiction novels.

Piaget also found that the individual's ability to deal with symbols develops significantly during the stage of formal operations, particularly in the use and interpretation of metaphor (Cometa & Eson, 1978), interpretation of art (Seefeldt, 1979) and poetry (Hardy-Brown, 1979). For the first time, the individual can use symbols to represent other symbols, as in algebra.

The adolescent's increased freedom in forming hypotheses often creates problems in making decisions, however. Seeing not one but many alternatives can often lead to doubt and confusion about one's own judgment. It often causes external conflict, too, especially with parents and other authority figures (Weiner, 1977). You can probably remember when you first began to challenge your parents' decisions about such things as curfews or the use of the family automobile. Adolescents often demand to know the reasoning behind decisions and also want to present the virtues of their opinions and those of their peers. They are not likely to accept a decision without questions and some debate, and are also likely to challenge religious, political, and social values. Remember Krista's interest in debating the merits of differing political ideologies with her parents. We will take a closer look at the relationship between adolescents and their parents in Chapter 10.

Adolescent Idealism

At one time, my son Adam wanted to be a rock guitarist. He spoke confidently about his ability to make it as a rock star. He was 13 and was taking lessons on his Stratocaster electric guitar. He grew his hair long and wore worn jeans and a stereo headset. He promised me front row tickets at his concerts once he went on tour.

Adam's interest in music and his dream of becoming a rock star reflected his growing abilities to think abstractly about his future. During the formal operational period, adolescents are able to think about and construct ideal families, societies, and religions. The ability to generate and consider hypotheses expands the future for adolescents. For many, adolescence is the time when they draw their initial blueprint for life.

As a formal operational thinker, the adolescent is freed from the bonds of personal experience and present time to explore ideas, ideals, roles, beliefs, theories, commitments, and theoretical possibilities. In one study, researchers (Stiles, Gibbons, & Schnellmann, 1987) asked a group of American ninth-graders to identify qualities of the ideal man and the ideal woman. The "ideal man" was described by girls as the "chivalrous football player" (kind, honest, fun-loving, smiling, and bringing flowers); boys described the "ideal man" as "the frowning football player" (fun-loving, frowning, and engaged in sports). The "ideal woman" was described by boys as the "smiling sunbather" (good-looking, sexy, smiling, and engaged in leisure activities); this contrasted with the girls' view of the "ideal woman" as the "smiling hard worker" (kind and honest, intelligent, smiling, and having adult responsibilities). With experience, adolescents refine their ideals; however, until they change, these ideals guide them in their gender and social development.

Like Krista, many adolescents recognize that there are alternatives to the way things are presently done, and they want to find ways to end human suffering, poverty, social inequity, and false belief. Utopian solutions to the world's problems—New Age solutions, planned communities, Eastern religions, and new forms of consciousness—find many adherents among adolescents. Adolescent thinkers are very philosophical in their approach to the world. There is increasing

Interest in ideologies and religions increases during adolescence and young adulthood, when standards of right and wrong are considered and adopted.

emphasis on the distinctions between the physical and the mental, between reality and appearance, and between subjectivity and objectivity.

Limitations of Piaget's Theory   It should be noted that several researchers regard the work of Piaget and Inhelder only as "a good first approximation" for studying the cognitive development beyond the stage of concrete operations. Studies of older adolescents and adults in Western cultures show that formal operations may not be attained by all individuals (Commons, Miller, & Kuhn, 1982; Keating, 1991; Leadbeater, 1991); only between 40 to 60 percent of first year college students reason at the level of formal operational thought. Also, some people apparently attain it only in certain areas of expertise. Even Piaget (1972) notes that

FOCUS ON CULTURE

Preparation for adulthood begins in childhood with exposure to adults modeling roles and behaviors that define maturity within the culture. In many industrialized countries today, family networks are smaller and disconnected from the communities in which they live. As a consequence, it is more difficult for children to observe and acquire adult skills; even when they reach puberty they may not have had an opportunity to practice adult roles. However, in nonindustrialized and agrarian cultures, children's transition to adulthood is smoother and occurs earlier because they are embedded in social networks that include young and old adults; thus, teenagers not only observe adult roles, but assume them.

Do you think that 18-year-olds are mature enough to decide on who will run the government?

different individuals may attain formal operations at different ages, and the manner and age at which it is displayed may depend on aptitude and experience.

Piaget used scientific problems, such as the pendulum experiment, to test abstract thought and reasoning. He recognized that solving different problems demands different levels of thought. Cultures that are not heavily dependent on science, however, may still provide opportunities for formal operational thought to develop. For example, island cultures that depend upon navigation for survival demand that people learn how to judge their location at sea by using the stars and referencing themselves against standard points on the horizon, a task that relies heavily on formal operational skills. There is a need for more comprehensive studies and more objective experiments to ascertain the components of formal operational thought and to determine how variables such as class, culture, gender, IQ, education, and training affect the course of formal operational development.

ADOLESCENT EGOCENTRISM

adolescent egocentrism

The tendency of adolescents to believe that other people are as preoccupied with their behavior, ideas, and appearance as they are.

One of the most difficult aspects of being a parent of adolescent children is their self-absorption. Both of my children went through a period during their adolescence when they seemed to believe that the world was or should be organized around their needs and wants. They seemed to take little or no interest in the needs of other people, namely me. This type of attitude is fairly characteristic of adolescents and, if you think about it for a moment, understandable. New things capture our attention. The same can be said about adolescents who appear to be quite absorbed in themselves. Given the changes that are taking place in their bodies and in the way they think, it is no wonder teenagers seem overly concerned with their thoughts and appearance. This preoccupation with self is an example of adolescent egocentrism.

Adolescents, seeking to find out who they are, become very self-absorbed. While they take into account the thoughts of others, they assume that these thoughts are all directed toward themselves. Specifically, **adolescent egocentrism** refers to individuals' beliefs that other people are as preoccupied with their behavior and appearance, thoughts, and ideas as they themselves. Thus, adolescents are constantly evaluating and measuring themselves in terms of other people's reactions. For example, if a teenager has a small pimple, it may seem huge to the adolescent who is absorbed in his or her appearance; at the same time the pimple is overlooked by others. Teenagers anticipate that others will immediately be as aware of and as critical of those things they themselves fault—typically, things involving the way they look or act. Similarly, they expect others to be just as cognizant of and concerned with those things they find attractive or appealing—even a slight gesture or personal mannerism. Thus, when parents express a negative reaction—to rock music or a style of clothing, for example—the adolescent is often surprised or confused. From their perspective, *everyone* should want to wear high-top sneakers!

imaginary audience

A term used to describe adolescents' belief that they are the focus of others' attention.

Adolescents, then, feel as if they are in a personal "fish bowl" and are continually creating what Elkind (1978) calls an **imaginary audience,** before whom they perform. In reality, adolescents are probably not the focus of attention, though their overly developed self-consciousness leads them to imagine that they are. When young people meet, each one is playing to the audience and is at the same time an audience for the others. This testing of images takes the place of

Adolescents, searching to discover who they are, often become self-absorbed and pre-occupied with their physical appearance.

abiding self
An individual's willingness to reveal to others characteristics of the self that are assumed to be relatively stable or unchanging.

transient self
An individual's willingness to reveal to others characteristics of the self that are temporary or vary over time.

substantial interpersonal communication. Clothing, gestures, hairstyles, even the music one listens to—all become part of the image.

Elkind (1978) has identified two components of the imaginary audience. One component centers on the individual's willingness to reveal to others characteristics of the self that are assumed to be relatively stable or unchanging (e.g., personality, intelligence, etc.); Elkind refers to this component as the **abiding self.** The second component of the imaginary audience is the person's willingness to reveal to others characteristics of the self that are assumed to be temporary or to vary over time (e.g., inappropriate dress or behavior, a bad haircut, etc.); this component is referred to as the **transient self.**

Elkind and Bowen (1979) predicted that adolescents would be more reluctant to reveal aspects of the abiding self than to reveal aspects of the transient self. They also predicted that young adolescents would be less willing than younger children and older adolescents to reveal either aspect of themselves. To test these hypotheses, the researchers administered a questionnaire to 697 students in the 4th, 6th, 8th, and 12th grades that measured willingness to reveal specific aspects of the self.

The results of the study confirmed their hypothesis. Generally, subjects scored higher (or exposed themselves less) on items measuring the abiding self than on those measuring the transient self. Furthermore, self-consciousness about aspects of the abiding self, but not the transient self, was associated with lower self-esteem. In addition, subjects in the 8th grade were more concerned with what others thought of them than were subjects in the 4th, 6th, or 12th grades. Finally, girls showed greater overall self-consciousness about revealing themselves to others than did boys. These results, backed by similar results from a study by Gray and Hudson (1984), confirm the validity of the concept of imaginary audience and the heightened sensitivity of young adolescents to the perceived reactions of others.

In addition to the imaginary audience, many adolescents begin developing what Elkind (1967) calls the personal fable, an ongoing, private, imaginary story,

personal fable
The development by adolescents of an imaginary, ongoing, private story in which they themselves play the leading role.

often full of exaggerations, in which they themselves play the leading role. As part of the **personal fable,** adolescents come to believe that their thoughts and feelings are unique—that they are the only ones ever to experience such euphoria or anguish. This belief in one's own specialness is often tied in with a sense of immortality.

According to Elkind, the imaginary audience provides a way of testing reality and one's self-concept. In time adolescents begin to perceive that there is a difference between their concerns and those of others. This usually happens when the stage of formal operations has been established (about the age of 15 or 16). At this time adolescents can begin to develop true relationships, in which they find that others share many of the same pains and pleasures. The extreme self-interestedness associated with the personal fable is thus slowly, though probably never completely, overcome. Elkind suggests that establishing a sense of intimacy with another person serves as a replacement for the personal fable.

RECAP

For many people, adolescence is the time in which formal operational thinking emerges, allowing teenagers to think abstractly, formulate and test hypotheses, and reason about hypothetical and ideal situations. Criticisms of Piaget's theory center around the limitations of the methodology and tests used to assess formal operational thought in other cultures. Adolescents are also egocentric in their view, believing that others are as interested in their perspectives as they are. They construct an imaginary audience to which they reveal aspects of self, and they create their own personal fable about their lives.

MORAL REASONING

The same mental skills that adolescents apply in creating hypotheses about their world also influence the way they reason about right and wrong and good and bad. The ability to think abstractly and to consider alternatives allows adolescents to think about moral issues from broader perspectives. Part of achieving independence includes questioning and considering the beliefs and values they had previously accepted as true and right. In the process of challenging parental beliefs, adolescents begin to shape their own moral standards and, according to Kohlberg, ascend to higher levels of morality (see Table 9–4).

While most elementary-school-age children reason at Kohlberg's preconventional level of morality—in which moral judgments are based on whether the anticipated outcomes of a behavior will be rewarded or punished—during early adolescence there is a shift to Level II, **conventional morality.** Moral reasoning at the conventional level draws upon people's ability to think beyond the immediate personal consequences of actions to consider the impact of those actions on other people and social systems.

conventional morality
Kohlberg's second level of moral reasoning; morality is viewed as the desire to preserve harmonious interpersonal relationships and to obey existing formal rules, laws, and standards in a society.

Like the preconventional level, conventional morality comprises two stages. The first stage—Stage 3—involves a focus on mutual caring and affection. At this stage, people are concerned with living up to other people's expectations of them

KOHLBERG'S LEVELS OF MORALITY

LEVEL I: PRECONVENTIONAL MORALITY

Stage 1: Obedience and Punishment Orientation

Obeys rules set by authority to avoid punishment; obedience is for its own sake. Does not consider the interests of others or recognize that they differ from the actor's; does not relate two points of view. Actions are considered physically rather than in terms of psychological interests of others.

Stage 2: Individualism, Instrumental Purpose, and Exchange

Follows rules only when they are in one's interests and satisfy individual needs; recognizes that others can do the same. Aware that each person has interests to pursue, and that these interests may be in conflict, so that "right" is relative.

LEVEL II: CONVENTIONAL LEVEL

Stage 3: Mutual Interpersonal Expectations, Relationships, and Interpersonal Conformity

Lives up to what is expected by significant others in the role of daughter, brother, friend, and so on. Being "good" means having good motives and respecting mutual relationships; believes in the Golden Rule. Aware of shared feelings, agreements, and expectations that take priority over individual interests.

Stage 4: Social System and Conscience

Conforms blindly to rules or laws for the good of the institution or society, except in extreme cases where laws conflict with other fixed social duties. Takes the point of view of the system that defines roles and rules. Considers individual relations in terms of their place in the system.

LEVEL III: POSTCONVENTIONAL OR PRINCIPLED MORALITY

Stage 5: Social Contract Orientation

Sees rules and laws as relative to the group that makes them and agrees to uphold them because of the social contract to make laws for the welfare of all. Considers moral and legal points of view; recognizes that they are sometimes in conflict and finds it difficult to integrate them.

Stage 6: Universal Ethical Principles Orientation

Follows self-chosen ethical principles, which are valued above laws or social agreements. When laws violate these principles, acts in accordance with the universal principles of equality of human rights and respect for the dignity of individual persons.

TABLE 9–4

Source: From Kohlberg, L. (1984). *The Psychology of Moral Development*. New York: Harper & Row.

as sons or daughters, friends, or siblings; they want to be considered "a good person" by others. The golden rule, "do unto others as you would have them do unto you" guides their thinking and actions. Doing right means maintaining mutual trust and loyalty; betraying trusts and disrespecting relationships is considered wrong.

The second stage within this level—Stage 4—involves a focus on "law and order." Right and wrong are evaluated in terms of conformity to societal rules and regulations. If a behavior violates the law, it is wrong; if it adheres to the law, it is right. Furthermore, at this level it is the "letter" of the law rather than the "spirit" that is most important. Thus, if a law were enacted that inadvertently benefited certain groups of individuals to the detriment of others, the person still would consider adherence to the law essential—or morally correct—even if some people suffer as a result. For example, if a person caught in the act of a crime is not informed at the time of the arrest of his or her right to an attorney and to remain silent, then by law, any conviction would have to be invalidated. The spirit of this law is to protect the innocent, but the application of the law sometimes benefits the guilty.

Although the majority of adolescents (and adults) typically reason at the conventional level of morality, the ability to reason abstractly and to conceptualize alternatives—both of which broaden remarkably during middle to late adolescence—increases the possible range of moral judgments. For example, the national debate about abortion laws has generated much discussion on the rights of the unborn and of women's right to choose what happens to them. People may take a stand on one side of the issue and still be able to make fine distinctions about when an abortion may be right or wrong. At this time there is increased awareness of potential conflicts among socially acceptable standards and between the rights of the individual and societal laws. Such conflicts are not readily handled by Stage 4 (law and order) reasoning. If adolescents (or adults) recognize the inadequacy of Stage 4 reasoning, they will reach for the next level of moral development, **postconventional morality.**

postconventional morality

Kohlberg's third level of moral reasoning; morality is based on appeals to social agreements and democratic principles and to basic principles of ethics and human rights.

At Level III, postconventional morality, the individual defines moral values and principles apart from the authority of the groups or persons holding these principles, and apart from his or her own identity with these groups. At this level people control their decisions internally; that is, they base their decisions on their own evaluation and standards of what is right, rather than by conforming to social pressures and expectations. Thus, adolescents and adults may choose to disregard rules or laws that to them are not appropriate or valid. For example, an individual at this stage may personally disagree with a law requiring them to register their firearms and choose to ignore it if they disagree with the intent of the law.

The postconventional level is subdivided into two distinct stages: the social-contract orientation and the universal principle orientation. In the social-contract orientation (Stage 5) an action is considered to be moral when it conforms with a set of rules that have been agreed to by the whole society. The person at this stage believes that if a law or rule is unfair or unjust, it must be changed in a democratic and constitutional manner and in accordance with social rules, not by breaking a law.

A person with the universal-ethical-principle orientation (Stage 6) determines what is right or wrong using a set of self-chosen ethical principles. These principles are abstract; they include justice, equality of human rights, and respect for the dignity of individual persons. People at this level rely on their conscience to reason morally, and regularly review the standards upon which they base their decisions.

The level at which a person reasons about moral issues may vary from one situation to another. For example, people who usually reason at the postconventional level may regress to the conventional level when their beliefs about individual rights are challenged by or are in conflict with rules established by authority figures. Many people who were morally opposed to the war in Vietnam nevertheless did not refuse the draft—an action that would have put them in conflict with the government and the law. Such backsliding is not uncommon during a period when people are forming their values and beliefs. Cultural beliefs also may influence the quality of moral judgments. People who live in cultures that value the community needs over the individual—such as India—rely on collective rather than individual decisions of their conscience to solve moral dilemmas (Vasudev & Hummel, 1987).

Although people may function at different levels of moral reasoning, their moral development is typically upward and occurs gradually in a sequence of stages (Snarey, Reimer, & Kohlberg, 1985). However, not all people reach the highest stage of postconventional morality. As adolescents (and adults) move from conventional to postconventional levels of moral judgment, there is an overall tendency to display increased moral behavior. In essence, then, adolescents tend to "practice what they preach" (or believe).

FOCUS ON CULTURE

Some studies (Edwards, 1982; Kohlberg & Kramer, 1969; Tietjen & Walker, 1985) indicate that people living in small communities within nontechnological societies rarely go beyond Stage 3 in Kohlberg's system. People in these cultures have face-to-face interactions with other members of their community and often are isolated from other tribes or societies. When moral judgments are made, their frame of reference is limited to within their village; there is no larger social system to consider. Kohlberg's system for assessing moral reasoning was developed within a socially more complex, industrialized culture where people must get along with people they do not know and live by rules that are made without reference to their particular needs. So the measures of moral reasoning may not apply very well to nontechnological societies.

Parental Influence on Moral Development   Every society has established ways of ensuring that the values of the culture are maintained across generations. Values and moral principles help guide people in their judgments and actions throughout their lives. A key part of the socialization process that began in early childhood includes helping young people acquire a set of beliefs and values that guide their actions. It is during adolescence that teenagers deliberately consider and examine the ideals and principles that will ultimately be part of their philosophy of life. As you will learn when we take a closer look at the way adolescents and their parents get along, many parents worry about whether or not their teenage children will make the "right" decisions on their own. Parents are concerned that adolescents will be persuaded by their peers to drink, experiment with drugs, or engage in other prohibited behaviors. With increasing maturity come more opportunities for adolescents to apply their values and moral reasoning in real life situations.

When Kohlberg (1969) introduced his theory, he downplayed the role of the family in the development of moral reasoning and focused more on the role of peers and schools. Today, many psychologists believe that Kohlberg underestimated the role parents play in their children's moral development. Parents serve as powerful models of moral reasoning and behavior for their children.

Research Perspective

CROSS-CULTURAL MORAL JUDGMENTS

Do people universally apply their own moral standards to other cultures, or do they judge them according to the moral standards of those particular cultures? Wainryb (1993) designed and conducted a study to answer this question. Moral judgments involve a set of prescriptions or *moral beliefs* about what ought to happen, which are based on a set of *informational beliefs* concerning a situation. For example, a person's judgment about the morality of abortion is based on that person's informational beliefs about what constitutes human life. Thus, in order to effectively study the way that people make judgments about events in other cultures, Wainryb maintained that re-

searchers must control for the informational beliefs underlying those judgments. She hypothesized that when the subjects in her study were asked to make moral judgments about other cultures, they would change (i.e., contextualize, relativize) their personal moral judgments according to the *informational beliefs* of the different cultures. But, when they were presented with a culture that held *moral beliefs* that were different from their own, Wainryb hypothesized that subjects would apply their own standards to judge the morality of the event described.

To test her hypotheses, Wainryb asked a sample of 72 children enrolled in the 6th, 10th, and college levels of school to make moral judgments about a series of different situations. She began by assessing the way her subjects made moral judgments within their own cultures. In Situation 1, subjects were asked to judge an event in which there were no competing considerations (re-

ferred to as *moral baseline*):

> Mr Clark came back from work feeling tired and frustrated. Mr Clark spanked his 8-year-old son John, although John had done nothing wrong. Was that alright or not alright? Why?

Subjects were also presented with a task within their own culture in which additional consideration had to be given to the informational beliefs presented. In Situation 2, subjects were given an *informational baseline* example:

> An 8-year-old boy, Tom, misbehaved when visiting his grandparents. His father told him not to do that again. Tom did it again, and his father spanked him for repeatedly misbehaving. Was that alright or not alright? Why?

The tasks that involved judgments for cultures *different* from the subjects' paralleled the baseline situations. Situation 3 assesses the evaluation of an event similar to the moral baseline:

Experimental studies have shown that children benefit by their exposure to the more complex moral arguments their parents can provide (Rest, Turiel, & Kohlberg, 1969; Walker, 1982).

The way in which parents discipline their children has been found to influence the level of moral reasoning; children whose parents taught them to take another person's perspective in order to appreciate the full consequences of their actions were more likely to function at an advanced level of moral reasoning (Buck, Walsh, & Rothman, 1981). By encouraging their children to consider other perspectives, parents provide an opportunity to practice cognitive skills that allow children to reconsider their own moral judgments. The more give-and-take discussions parents have with their children about decision

There is a country where people have a tradition that children have to make their parents happy and believe that it is alright for a father to spank his child to make himself happy. In that country, a child did nothing wrong but his father spanked him just to make himself happy. Was that alright or not alright? Why?

One of two sets of tasks were used to assess subjects' application of their own standards to events in different cultures using different informational assumptions. This was to guarantee that the assumptions would be different from their own. If subjects believed that physical punishment was not an efficient way of teaching children, they were asked to respond to Situation 4:

> There is a country where people believe that children who misbehave are possessed by an evil spirit and that the only way to get rid of the spirit and make the child be good is by spanking the child. A father in that country spanked his son

repeatedly for misbehaving. Was that alright or not alright? Why?

If subjects believed that physical punishment was an efficient way of teaching children, they were then asked to respond to Situation 5:

> There is a country where people believe that the angels guarding the child are scared off when the child is spanked and, therefore, the only way to make the child be good is to say a prayer. A father in that country spanked his son for repeatedly misbehaving. Was that alright or not alright? Why?

In total there were three sets of questions that were presented; the baseline questions were asked first, followed by the culturally manipulated set of questions. The subjects were questioned individually and their responses were tape-recorded for later analysis.

Wainryb found support for her hypotheses. Her subjects generalized their own moral standards to different cultures even when those cultures held moral beliefs that differed from their own. That is, when presented with Situation 3, they responded that the father had done wrong (spanking the child to make himself happy). However, when subjects were provided with information about the *context* in which these moral beliefs occurred, they were more likely to change the standards they applied in making moral judgment to match the cultural context. Thus, children who approved of physical punishment nevertheless responded that the father had done wrong in Situation 5 (scaring the guardian angels), while those who did not approve of physical punishment felt that the father's action in Situation 4 (spanking to rid the evil spirit) was justified. There were no differences in reasoning among the three age groups of subjects.

making, the more likely that children will reason at higher levels of moral development (Walker & Taylor, 1991).

Speicher (1994) studied family patterns of moral judgments by using data collected from parents who participated in the Oakland Growth Study, a longitudinal study begun in the late 1930s (Jones, 1939a, 1939b). The offspring of participants in the longitudinal study were compared with their parents on levels of moral reasoning obtained by using the Kohlberg Moral Judgment Interview procedure. Speicher found consistent patterns across different generations in a family. During adolescence, parents' moral judgment was related to their offspring's moral reasoning; the mother's level of moral reasoning was a stronger predictor of the daughter's moral reasoning. If the mother reasoned at the level of social contract, then it was likely that her children reasoned at this level as well. During early adulthood the father's level of moral reasoning was a better predictor than the mother's level for both male and female offspring.

The Role of Schools in Moral Development

While adolescents often take on the attitudes and values of their parents, many people believe that schools should participate in the moral education of children and teenagers. In fact, in its early history in America, moral education was the main objective of schools. Today, high schools provide an appropriate setting for students to explore and discover their values and moral standards. Studies have shown that moral development—the ability to reason and make moral judgments—is enhanced by formal education (Colby, Kohlberg, Gibbs, & Lieberman, 1983; Rest & Thoma, 1985). In part, this is because students who go on to college or further education are generally reinforced for thinking about issues, including moral issues.

The process of moral development can be stimulated in the high school and even junior high classroom. In most schools students are exposed to and governed by a body of rules and regulations that guide the behavior of all people within the school. These rules function as moral principles; students learn what is right and wrong within the school context.

However, the school community can be used more effectively to help teenagers develop their values. In some schools teachers not only encourage their students to obey and respect school rules, but they also encourage them to participate in establishing or changing the rules to fit the needs of the school as a group. The teacher acts as a facilitator in active discussions on controversial issues or moral dilemmas. Take, for example, the issue of whether teachers should be allowed to smoke in school. The facilitator-teacher would make sure that students expressed their views on the question while helping them to identify the values underlying their views. Through open discussion of the issues, students also benefit from hearing several different points of view. This process of stimulating discussion and identifying one's personal values is called **values clarification.**

values clarification
The process of stimulating discussing and identifying one's personal values.

Kohlberg (1976) has advocated the use of give-and-take peer discussions of moral dilemmas as one way of increasing moral reasoning skills. The teacher's role is critical to the process. Teachers represent authority, and by their involvement in the discussion group they communicate to students the importance of having values and of applying them in a responsible way in the school community. The goal of moral education is not to teach specific virtues or values, but to teach teenagers a process by which they can identify their values and increase their level of moral reasoning. By exposing them to a realistic set of dilemmas within the school community, teachers can assist students in their moral development.

FOCUS ON CULTURE

People who leave their homelands in search of better economic and political climates often bring with them the values they acquired within their native cultures. But the children of immigrants often adopt the values of their new culture—which may conflict with their parent's beliefs. For example, in one study (Nguyen & Williams, 1989), the longer Vietnamese teenagers had lived in the United States, the greater the likelihood that their values about family life would differ from their parents'. What kinds of problems might immigration create for parents who want to raise their children to be morally responsible?

THE SCHOOL ENVIRONMENT

In many communities throughout the United States there is an ongoing debate among school board members and parents about how to deal with the difficulties children in early adolescence encounter as they make the transition from elementary to middle, junior, or high school. The most obvious difficulty is the wide variability in size and physical maturity among students. Some school boards argue that children in early adolescence should be segregated from older adolescents; they have established two systems: grades K–8 and 9–12 (high school). Others argue for a more gradual shift by creating a middle or intermediate school before high school (e.g., grades K–4, 5–8, 9–12).

Often students' school performance declines as a result of the transition to a new school (Simmons & Blyth, 1987). In part, the difficulty of this transition depends on the size and location (urban or suburban) of the school (Simmons & Blyth, 1987; Simmons, Carlton-Ford, & Blyth, 1987). As concern about violence in schools increases, it is not surprising that the transition to high school is more difficult in urban settings (Seidman, Allen, Aber, Mitchell, & Feinman, 1994).

The shift to high school represents a major and often difficult change in the adolescent's learning and social environment. As children progress through school, they form opinions about themselves as learners; they develop attitudes about school and their ability and desire to achieve in this environment (Eccles & Midgley, 1989). Part of the difficulty in making the transition to high school may be due to the mismatch between the needs of adolescents and the characteristics of the schools they enter. In contrast to elementary schools, junior high schools place greater emphasis on teacher control and discipline and provide fewer opportunities for decision making, choice, and self-management. Junior high school students are extremely regimented; their teachers spend more of their time maintaining order and less time teaching than do elementary school teachers. For example, while elementary school students may be allowed to get out of their seats

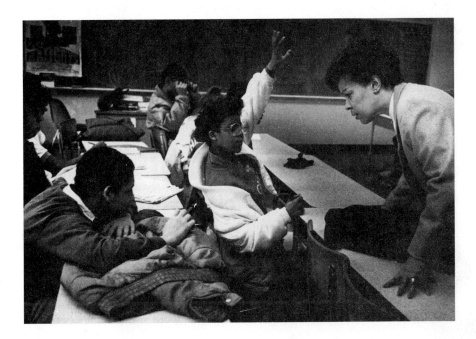

Students in junior high school may perceive their teachers to be less friendly and supportive compared with their elementary school teachers.

to participate in different activities, junior high school students are usually restricted to their seats for an entire class period. Thus, the same time that adolescents are expressing a desire to be more autonomous and practice emerging decision-making skills, they are thrust into a learning environment that restricts their opportunities for making informed choices (Eccles et al., 1993).

A second feature associated with junior high schools is that, compared to elementary schools, they are less personal and friendly places. Teachers are less supportive and less trusting of their students in the junior high school environment. Furthermore, there is less emphasis on individualized teaching and more emphasis on whole-class instruction. Frequently students are evaluated against the performance of the entire class, regardless of their abilities to compete. Not surprisingly, these classroom practices increase adolescents' concern about their status with their peers.

In response, teachers in the middle school feel less effective compared to elementary school teachers. For example, seventh grade teachers in a junior high school felt less confident about their ability to teach students mathematics than sixth grade elementary school teachers, even when the seventh grade teachers were more qualified as math specialists than the sixth grade teachers (Midgley, Feldlaufer, & Eccles, 1989). The effect of this lack of confidence is that students end up with lower expectations for success in mathematics, poorer grades, and greater perceptions that mathematics is difficult. Students of instructors who are confident of their teaching abilities do not experience these declines.

As you may well recall, junior high school is considered to be more challenging than elementary school. However, this appears to be unfounded. During the

---

HOW THE JUNIOR HIGH SCHOOL DIFFERS FROM THE ELEMENTARY SCHOOL ENVIRONMENT

Places more emphasis on teacher control and discipline

Provides fewer opportunities for student decision making and self-management

Provides less personal and positive teacher-student relationships

Employs more whole-class instruction

Engages in more public evaluation of student's work

Teachers tend to feel less effective and confident

Classwork is less cognitively challenging

Uses a higher standard in judging performance

Students' performance is judged by peer comparison rather than by measuring individual progress

TABLE 9–5

Source: From "Development during Adolescence: The Impact of Stage-Environment Fit on Young Adolescents' Experiences in Schools and in Families," by J. S. Eccles, C. Midgley, A. Wigfield, C. M. Buchanan, D. Reuman, C. Flanagan, and D. MacIver, 1993, *American Psychologist, 48,* pp. 92–94. Adapted with permission.

first year of junior high school, the work students are given requires lower cognitive skills than their elementary school work (Eccles et al., 1993). Much of the classwork in junior high schools involves copying material from the board or textbook to worksheets. Despite the lowered levels of demand, however, teachers in junior high school apply more stringent standards when evaluating student performance and assigning grades than elementary school teachers. Thus, while students' grades decline when they enter junior high school, their performance on standardized achievement tests does not depreciate (Kavrell & Petersen, 1984). Table 9–5 summarizes how the junior high school differs from the elementary school environment.

Another reason that schools are important during adolescence is that they provide a meeting place for teenagers to maintain their peer relationships. In the next chapter you will learn more about the social context of adolescence.

BRIEF REVIEW

Even before the sex organs change in appearance, hormonal changes are preparing the body for adulthood. Soon a dramatic change takes place in height, weight, and body proportions; this is known as the adolescent growth spurt. There are always variations in physical, emotional, and intellectual development within any adolescent age group.

Puberty is the period during which an individual reaches sexual maturity—which is not necessarily synchronous with other areas of development. In the prepubescent stage, secondary sex characteristics begin to develop. The reproductive organs begin producing ova or sperm. In the postpubescent stage, the sex organs become fully capable of adult functioning. Spontaneous erection in the male in response to sights, sounds, and thoughts first occurs during adolescence. The appearance of breasts and menstruation in girls, voice change in boys, and body hair in both sexes heralds sexual maturity.

Adolescents reach puberty at an earlier age than teenagers born several generations ago. The secular growth trends are believed to be influenced by biological and environmental factors.

The physical changes that the adolescent experiences have important consequences for psychological development, particularly for self-concept. Early-maturing boys generally excel at sports, in social activities, and in areas of leadership in comparison to late-maturing boys. The impact of timing of maturation is less clear-cut for girls.

Girls' reactions to the onset of menstruation, or menarche, are influenced by their expectations and by the amount of information they have. The degree to which a girl thinks she is developmentally on time in physical maturation depends on her social context.

More and younger teenagers are sexually active than ever before. The greatest change in adolescent sexual behavior has occurred for girls. Adolescents may also experiment with homosexual behavior. Boys under the age of 15 are more likely to have homosexual experiences.

Although a sizable percentage of teenagers engage in sexual intercourse, many remain ignorant of proper contraceptive use. Two consequences of unprotected sexual behavior are a rising birthrate and an increasing incidence of sexually transmitted diseases among teenagers.

Most schools have sex education programs for high school students. However, the content in these courses varies considerably and often does not include enough information on how to prevent pregnancy or the spread of sexually transmitted diseases. Ideally, sex education programs would involve parents.

The ability to deal with abstractions and to reason deductively develops during what Piaget calls the stage of formal operations, which emerges between the ages of 11 and 15. Individuals' abilities to consider many alternatives leads them to question their own ideas and to challenge authority figures and traditional beliefs. It also causes them to become self-absorbed and demonstrate self-importance—forms of egocentrism that Elkind describes as the imaginary audience and the personal fable.

Changes in cognitive development facilitate changes in moral reasoning. According to Kohlberg, the early period of adolescence is characterized by conventional morality—reasoning based on winning approval and maintaining the status quo. During middle to late adolescence, however, the range of moral judgments broadens for many people as they enter the period of postconventional morality. Here moral reasoning is based on self-accepted principles of ethics and justice.

Parents influence their children's level of moral reasoning by providing them with examples of higher levels of moral reasoning and opportunities to consider different perspectives when making moral judgments. Likewise, schools can provide real-life opportunities for informed decision making.

The transition from elementary to middle or junior high school is difficult for many adolescents because the school environment has not been structured to accommodate the cognitive and social skills that emerge during early adolescence.

KEY TERMS

abiding self (359)
adolescent egocentrism (358)
adolescent growth spurt (334)
age of majority (342)
androgens (338)
conventional morality (360)
endocrine system (338)
estrogens (338)
formal operational thought (353)

hormones (338)
imaginary audience (358)
lean body mass (LBM) (335)
menarche (339)
mutuality (345)
personal fable (360)
postconventional morality (362)
postpubescent stage (338)
prepubescent stage (338)

pubescent stage (338)
puberty (337)
primary sex characteristics (339)
secondary sex characteristics (337)
secular growth trends (343)
sexually transmitted diseases
  (STD) (350)
transient self (359)
values clarification (366)

REVIEW QUESTIONS

If you can answer these questions, you have a good understanding of the material in this chapter. If a question seems difficult, go back to the text and review the topic.

1. Distinguish between adolescence and puberty.

2. Describe the changes that occur for males during the adolescent growth spurt. Describe the changes that occur for females.

3. What are the characteristic changes that occur within the three stages of puberty?

4. Give an example of a secular growth trend. What factors help explain secular growth trends?

5. What are the advantages and disadvantages of being an early-maturing male? What are the advantages and disadvantages of being an early-maturing female?

6. Discuss the impact of menarche for young women.

7. In what ways has adolescent sexual activity changed over the years? What factors help explain the changes?

8. List precautions that can be taken to reduce the chances of contracting a sexually transmitted disease.

9. What are the risks associated with pregnancy for teenage mothers? For teenage fathers? For the child?

10. What reasons do teenagers offer for their failure to use contraceptive devices to prevent unwanted pregnancies?

11. What are the distinguishing characteristics of formal operational thought?

12. How does adolescent egocentrism differ from egocentrism during the preschool period? What is an imaginary audience? Give an example of the two components of the imaginary audience.

13. Distinguish between conventional and postconventional morality. Describe the stages within each of these levels.

14. In what ways do parents and the school influence moral reasoning during adolescence?

15. Describe the ways in which the school environment does not meet the developmental needs of adolescents. What changes need to be made?

OBSERVATIONAL ACTIVITY

ADOLESCENT PROBLEM SOLVING

During adolescence, people are better able to deal with problems on an abstract level, to form hypotheses, and to reason from propositions. One demonstration of these emerging problem-solving skills can be seen using Piaget's pendulum experiment described in this chapter.

You will need to find three teenagers between the ages of 14 and 16 who are willing to participate in a problem-solving experiment. For materials, you will need a piece of string about 4 feet long and several small objects of different weight to attach to the end of the string. To construct the pendulum, attach one of the weighted objects to the string and affix the string to the ceiling or the top of a table or bookcase. Be sure to leave enough room to swing the pendulum. Proceed as follows:

1. With your subject watching, release the pendulum by pulling the string back a certain distance and pushing the weighted object. Point out to the subject that the pendulum can be modified by changing several factors: the length of the string, the weight of the object, the height at which the object is released, and the force with which it is pushed.

2. Ask the teenager to find out which of these factors determines how rapidly the pendulum will swing. The purpose of this experiment is not to determine if the person can figure out the correct answer (the length of the string), but rather to determine the process by which the person solves the problem.

3. Take note of the teenager's strategy for solving the problem. Does the person systematically test one factor at a time and hold the others constant? Does the person consider the problem before manipulating the pendulum or does he or she just plunge in? Ask the teenager if he or she has any hypotheses or guesses about what influences the speed of the pendulum. Does the person have a plan for testing out these ideas?

After testing each teenager separately, compile your observations of their approaches to the problem. Compare your observations with those reported in this chapter. What conclusions can you draw about adolescent problem-solving ability? What did you learn from doing this activity?

CHAPTER 10

Adolescence: Personality and Social Development

At 18, Louis was preparing to graduate from the Santa Fe Indian School, where he had spent the past 4 years. He planned to study teaching at the University of New Mexico so that he could teach in the Pueblo reservation school.

Although he was a Cochiti Pueblo Indian, it was only recently that he had begun to learn more about and appreciate his Native American heritage. He had spent his early years living on the reservation, listening with fascination to the ancestral stories told to him by his elders. He had learned about Pueblo gods and spirits that still were believed to live in the mountains that surrounded the reservation. But during his elementary school years he had gone to the public schools, where his education about his culture had come to a halt.

During high school Louis immersed himself in his ethnic heritage. He learned more about the struggles of his people as they were gradually forced off their ancestral lands. He learned about their talents. He learned how to make clay figures in the tradition of his ancestors and how to talk with his elders in their native tongue. He had identified an important part of himself—and was eager to learn more.

Seventeen-year-old Erika was apprehensive as she entered the camp director's office. Ever since she was a camper, she had admired the counselors and wanted to become one herself. She had been gaining useful work experience by baby-sitting, and she had even organized a play group for neighborhood children. Now all she had to do was to convince the director that she was a good choice for the position. Erika's mother and stepfather were supportive and encouraging. They were pleased that she had taken the initiative in seeking a job. It was a clear sign of her growing independence and maturity.

The camp director looked at Erika and said, "Well, tell me why you should be the one to fill this position." Erika, feeling self-conscious but assertive, replied, "Well, I've always enjoyed being with children, and my friends and family agree that I am good with them. I like to dance, listen to music, and swim, and I think I would make a great camp counselor. . . ."

In adolescence one searches more urgently than ever before for the answers to basic questions. This sense of urgency reflects, in part, the rapid and varied transformations—in body, thought, and emotions—that the adolescent encounters during this stage of life (see Table 10–1). It also reflects the search for solutions to pressing problems regarding the self. Erika and Louis, like other adolescents, will find that there is no final solution, or closure, to the search for personal identity. The answers they achieve during adolescence are just one part of a dynamic and mobile construction that will change and grow as they do. This does not mean, however, that personal identity is unattainable. It simply means that one's perception of self is likely to be more fluid than fixed, and that during periods of rapid change, such as adolescence, there is likely to be greater crisis over who one "really" is.

Your teenage years may still be quite fresh in your mind. You may have younger teenage siblings; or you may be returning to school after raising your own family, which now includes teenagers. You therefore can think of adolescents you have known and realize that they are not all the same; adolescents vary considerably in behavior and in their reactions. For some teenagers, this is a difficult period of conflict and adjustment; for others, it is a relatively smooth transition.

ADOLESCENT TURMOIL: FACT OR FICTION?

The journey from ages 12 to 18 encompasses many changes: changes in physical shape, the emergence of sexuality, broader and more abstract ways of thinking, and more intense relationships with peers. But is this journey necessarily a rugged one? If you ask people to describe the adolescent years, no doubt they will use such terms as "upsetting," "full of turmoil," "intense," "troubling," or "difficult." Ever since G. Stanley Hall's classic work on adolescence (1904) we have come to expect considerable personal upheaval during this period of life. The conception of adolescence as a time of storm and stress is a foundation of many of our theories of development, particularly psychoanalytic theories. Anna Freud (1958), for example, portrays the adolescent as experiencing revived and intensified sexual and aggressive drives, feelings, and fantasies. The intensification of inner drives, she says, results in considerable emotional upset as the adolescent strives to control the impulses and desires that are pressing for expression. Similar pictures of normal adolescent crises are described by Blos (1979) and Erikson (1968).

Other theorists and researchers (Buchanan, Eccles, Becker, 1992; Larson, 1991) believe that psychological turmoil is not typical of most adolescents and that the course of development during this period is more often a continuation of earlier ways of adaptation rather than a dramatic emergence of new adaptive modes (Douvan & Adelson, 1966; Offer, 1969; Offer, Ostrov, & Howard, 1981). Adolescents

DEVELOPMENTAL TASKS OF ADOLESCENCE
Establish a personal identity
Achieve a mature gender identity
Achieve emotional independence from parents and other adults
Form mutual relationships
Explore, select, and prepare for an occupation
Develop a personal ideology and ethical standards
Assume membership in the larger community
Accept changes in one's body and sexuality
TABLE 10–1

Source: From R. Havighurst (1974). *Developmental Tasks and Education.* New York: McKay. Adapted with permission.

do not differ from adults in the overall rate of severe psychological problems, which is typically between 15 and 20% of the population (Powers, Hauser, & Kilner, 1989).

DO ADOLESCENTS SEE THEMSELVES AS INVULNERABLE?

One commonly accepted stereotype of adolescents is that, compared to children and adults, they are bigger risk-takers. This perception is based on statistics that show that teenagers engage in more risky behaviors and experience the negative consequences of their actions more than do adults (Office of Technology Assessment, 1991). For example, one out of seven teenagers has a sexually transmitted disease (Sunenblick, 1988); this is twice the rate for adults in their 20s (Hein, 1989). Teenagers' tendency to engage in high-risk behaviors is generally explained by the assumption that, compared to adults, adolescents see themselves as invulnerable. They underestimate and ignore the possible negative consequences of their actions and focus only on the possible benefits. The theoretical basis for this hypothesis comes from Elkind's (1967) concept of a personal fable in which adolescents see themselves as heros in their own lives. However, very little empirical support has been offered for the claim of adolescent invulnerability. In one study (Quadrel, Fischhoff, & Davis, 1993) groups of low-risk teenagers, adults, and high-risk adolescents in treatment homes were asked to assess the chances of bad events happening to them and to others. Subjects were asked to rate the probability that in the next five years they would be in an automobile accident, become an alcoholic, have an unwanted pregnancy, get mugged or injured in an explosion, or become ill as a result of exposure to an environmental toxin. All three groups saw themselves as facing less risks than other people. However, teenagers were no more likely to see themselves as invulnerable than adults. In fact, parents were viewed as less vulnerable by both parents and teenagers, partly because, as adults, they were seen as having more control over their lives.

Similar results were reported in a different study (Beyth-Marom, Austin, Fischhoff, Palmgren, Jacobs-Quadrel, 1993) in which parents and their adolescent children were asked to list the possible consequences of engaging or not engaging in risky behaviors such as drinking and driving, having sex, and smoking marijuana. Parents and their teenage children generated similar lists of outcomes; both indicated that there would be more bad than good consequences of engaging in risky behaviors.

What other reasons might explain teenagers' relatively high rate of unsafe behaviors? Perhaps it is that their need for adventure and excitement outweighs their need for caution. Sensation seeking, a desire for novel and intense experiences, is highest during adolescence (Zuckerman, Eysenck, & Eysenck, 1978). Driving a car at high speeds, having unprotected sex, and using illicit drugs are high risk behaviors that also fulfill a need for sensation (Arnett, 1992). The type of risky behaviors may be influenced by the cultural context. For example, in Denmark, where the legal age for driving a car is 18 and many people rely on bicycles for transportation, sensation-seeking Danish adolescents were found to have a high rate of operating bicycles at high speeds while intoxicated (Arnett & Balle-Jensen, 1993).

Personal Perspective

CHALLENGING VIEWS: A GENDER DIFFERENCE?

Being able to speak freely and openly about one's ideas is generally recognized as a healthy quality that emerges in adolescence. High school students who challenge the thinking of their teachers, ask questions in class, and openly argue or disagree with their teachers are likely to gain the respect of their teachers and enhance their own self-esteem. The high school experience thus provides many opportunities for teenage boys and girls to prove themselves and to enhance their self-confidence.

However, results from an extensive survey conducted by the American Association of University Women (AAUW) revealed some startling differences in self-esteem between male and female adolescents. The survey sampled over 3,000 adolescents from the 4th to the 10th grades and found that girls experienced a significantly larger drop in self-esteem as they moved from early to mid-adolescence than did boys. About 60% of the 8- and 9-year-old girls surveyed were confident and assertive and felt positive about themselves; this compared to 67% of boys the same age. By the time they reached their sophomore year in high school, however, a gender gap in self-esteem emerged. Only 29% of the girls felt positive about themselves, compared to 46% of the boys (Frieberg, 1991). Other researchers have found similar gender differences: From early to late adolescence, the self-esteem of males tends to increase while it decreases in females (Block & Robins, 1993).

One of the consequences of reduced self-esteem is that adolescents are less assertive and more inhibited about their ideas, feelings, and interests. Adolescence is viewed by many as a dress rehearsal for adult life. It certainly is a time for making career and personal choices that can have a lifelong impact. The reported steep decline in female self-esteem comes at a time when there are more opportunities for women

SOURCES OF STRESS DURING ADOLESCENCE

While research has discredited the notion that all adolescents endure a period of storm and stress, this does not mean that adolescence is a stress-free stage of development. What factors contribute to the rocky road along which some teenagers must travel? As you learned in Chapter 9, making the transition from elementary to junior high school can be very stressful. Some teenagers must cope with a number of changes such as entering puberty, divorce of parents, and a new school and friends simultaneously; multiple negative events increase the risk that teenagers will experience emotional distress (Larson & Ham, 1993). Furthermore, parental and societal expectations about school performance increase with age and can be a further source of stress. However, parental pressure to achieve success in school does not always produce stress. A study (Crystal et al., 1994) compared Japanese, Chinese, and American high school students on a variety of measures of adjustment. The researchers found that Asian students reported higher levels of parental expectations and lower levels of parental satisfaction with their academic achievement than American students. However, Japanese and Chinese students reported less stress and academic anxiety than American students. American students who were identified by the researchers as high achieving indicated more frequent feelings of stress than low achievers.

and more female role models to support and encourage adolescent girls to seek those opportunities. Hence, there is much cause for concern about the relative decline in self-esteem and confidence of adolescent girls—particularly because the workforce of tomorrow depends upon both males and females contributing their talents.

Why is there a drop in self-esteem in teenage girls? Gilligan (1982) cites a "crisis of connection" for teenage girls, who must learn to deal with shifting cultural expectations as they enter adolescence. Gilligan argues that parents and teachers do not interfere with or suppress preadolescent girls when they show their feelings, say what they think, or disagree. However, as girls emerge into adolescence a different standard of behavior seems to apply. Teenage girls are expected to be "perfect"—to be considerate of other people's needs, to focus on developing harmonious relationships with peers and elders, and to be quiet and calm. Girls who do not live up to these ideals suffer a loss of attention, popularity, and love (Moses, 1990). According to Gilligan, an adolescent girl must learn how to resolve the conflict between listening to her own "voice" and adjusting to the expectations others have of her.

For some teenage girls this conflict is reduced if their parents are supportive of their being assertive, autonomous, outgoing, and nonconforming. Based on longitudinal data, researchers Vaughn, Block, and Block (1988) found that parents who were in agreement on how to raise their children were more likely to have daughters who were outspoken and assertive during adolescence. Their daughters were also more likely to have high self-esteem. The researchers suggest that family harmony may be one key to the development of competence and autonomy for adolescent girls.

The AAUW report called on teachers to help raise self-esteem in teenage girls by focusing on their interests and talents, challenging them to speak out in class, and encouraging them to explore more demanding academic pursuits such as math and science.

The social context contributes significantly to the amount of stress adolescents experience in their lives (Jessor, 1993). Adolescents are embedded simultaneously in three social contexts: the family, the school, and the neighborhood, all of which are embedded within a larger sociocultural environment that is shaped by political and economic factors. For example, a teenager living in a poor single-parent household in an inner-city neighborhood is likely to be exposed to different kinds of stress—in the form of crime, violence in the schools, and family disruption—than a teenager living in a two-parent family in a safer neighborhood. Even within intact families, severe economic distress can result in increased parental conflict and family stress. In a study of adolescents and their parents in a rural, impoverished Midwest area, the researchers (Conger, Ge, Elder, Lorenz, & Simons, 1994) found that economic pressures were directly related to parent-adolescent conflicts that were characterized by hostile attempts to manipulate and control by verbal threats and criticisms.

ADOLESCENT SELF-ESTEEM

If you get lost or confused during a journey, does this affect your self-confidence? Similarly, to what extent do the stresses and challenges of adolescence affect self-esteem? During adolescence, self-esteem is at its lowest between the ages of 12 and

FOCUS ON CULTURE

The extent to which adolescence is stressful depends on cultural expectations and practices. In her classic study of growing up in Samoa, Margaret Mead (1928) could find no evidence to support the view that adolescence is inherently stressful. The only characteristics that distinguished Samoan adolescent girls from their younger siblings were bodily changes. Mead believed that Samoan society was responsible for this relatively smooth passage to adolescence; she attributed it to Samoan sexual attitudes, which are more relaxed than those of Western societies, and to the absence of an abrupt transition from childhood to adolescence. Later study of the Samoans, however, found evidence that adolescence was not as smooth as Mead suggested (Freeman, 1983).

13 (Harter, 1990). This corresponds to the period when physical changes are more dramatic and conflict with parents is most intense. Physical appearance is a significant contributor to teenagers' sense of self-esteem (Damon, 1991); hence they worry about how they look. Early adolescence is also when many teenagers switch from elementary to a middle school, a difficult transition for many students (Eccles et al., 1993). Self-esteem improves throughout adolescence (Mullis, Mullis, & Normandin; 1992) as teenagers become more comfortable with themselves and their peer group.

While self-esteem may fluctuate, self-concept appears to remain fairly stable. Dusek and Flaherty (1981) conducted a 3-year longitudinal study of the stability of self-concept in samples of adolescents ages 12 to 18 using a self-report questionnaire. These investigators found very little evidence that adolescents' self-concept undergoes dramatic change. On the contrary, the changes observed were gradual in nature. Similar results were found in a longitudinal study of adolescents' self-concept and self-esteem. Adolescents maintained a stable and slightly positive sense of themselves throughout this 6-year study (Savin-Williams & Demo, 1984).

The overall findings suggest that while some adolescents experience emotional turmoil during their journey toward adulthood, emotional upheaval is certainly not a universal phenomenon. For some individuals the passage through adolescence is accompanied by feelings of self-doubt, resentment of parents, avoidance of responsibility, and social anxiety. For others, however, the reaction to the physical and social role changes associated with adolescence is much less dramatic. As in every period of development, individual differences in coping strategies and adjustment is the rule.

RECAP

While earlier theorists believed that adolescence was a period of storm and stress, many contemporary researchers disagree. Adolescents do not see themselves as less vulnerable than adults, but they do engage in more risk-taking behaviors. The stresses that adolescents experience are the result of simultaneous demands by the social, family, and school contexts. Adolescents' self-esteem is influenced by their ability to cope with the changes and expectations they encounter.

ADOLESCENT IDENTITY

Experienced travelers will tell you that no matter what their destination, they usually learn something about themselves in their travels. As people travel, they meet new people with different experiences, expectations, and views of life—which prompts travelers to question their own perspectives and goals. Adolescence is similarly filled with new opportunities to learn about oneself. In their own unique ways, Erika and Louis are involved in the process of self-discovery. Erika's realization of her talents and interests, and Louis's involvement with his Pueblo heritage are examples of their attempts to identify and define themselves.

According to Erikson (1968), adolescence is the stage of development during which the crisis of identity is most acute. The major task of the individual at this time is the formation of a secure **ego identity**—one's perceptions and feelings about oneself. Ego identity has three major components:

ego identity
According to Erikson, psychosocial achievement during adolescence that results in a stable and unified sense of self.

1. A sense of unity among one's self-perceptions; the views one has of oneself are not disjointed;

2. A sense of continuity of self-definition over time; one's sense of self does not change readily but evolves into a richer self-understanding; and

3. A sense of the mutuality between one's self-perceptions and those held by others; one's self-view is influenced by the reactions of others and vice versa.

self-diffusion
A feeling that one lacks definition, commitment, and a sense of integration or togetherness.

Failure to achieve such an identity results in **self-diffusion**—a feeling that one lacks definition, commitment, and a sense of integration or togetherness. Ego identity is reflected in the way teenagers speak about themselves and one another. They often use terms relating to how "together" they are and whether they have "found" themselves or not.

During the early stages of adolescence there is an increase in self-awareness (Harter, 1983; 1990). The self becomes an object of study and interest. This change in orientation toward the self is largely due to the physical changes associated with puberty, as well as to the pressures society places on adolescents to make role choices. For example, high schools in the United States encourage students to begin planning for the future by choosing college-oriented versus noncollege-oriented courses. In doing so, students may for the first time be forced to consider their individual skills, goals, preferences, and potential place in society. In many other countries, the decision about whether a child will go on to higher education and college is made as early as age 12 on the basis of examinations or teacher recommendations. In some countries, decisions about vocation are made for children by their parents.

Heightened self-awareness also is related to the emerging cognitive skills associated with formal operational thinking (Elkind, 1978). The capacity for abstract, hypothetical thought allows the adolescent to speculate endlessly about the many possibilities the self may assume. This ability contrasts dramatically with the almost unquestioning self-acceptance that characterizes elementary school children. Consider the musings of 14-year-old Adam: "Now that I am playing the guitar I could be a rock star. . . . I know I'd start off first with my own group and we would make our own video so that people would want to buy our records. . . . But if I didn't make it as a rock star, I could also see myself as a guitar teacher."

For most people, the transition from childhood to adolescence is marked by trading dependency on their parents for dependency on their peers (Steinberg &

For Colin, age 13, skateboarding provides a way for him to define himself and to earn the esteem of his peers. In addition to collecting bruises, he has won prizes with his skateboarding maneuvers.

Silverberg, 1986). Conformity to the peer group may be very intense. Adolescents may identify so completely with the heroes of the peer group that they seem initially to lose their own emerging identities. By trying out various characteristics on peers and observing their reactions, adolescents hope to get a better understanding of their own identity. My nephew Colin is a good example; as he entered early adolescence he started to specialize in skateboarding. He read about the talents and stories of infamous skateboarders and imitated their dress (baggy trousers and shirts, shaggy hair, half-shaven). His life revolved around his skateboarding activities.

Establishing one's identity is a process that can take up to 10 years to complete (Waterman, 1985). The adolescent latches on to one view of self, tries it on for size, wears it around the neighborhood of peers, and then discards it for another. Each identification becomes part of the total view of self, and all identifications must be woven together into a coherent, consistent, and unique view of self (Conger, 1978).

ETHNIC AND RACIAL IDENTITY

Even before Louis entered high school he was aware of his status as a Pueblo Indian. He felt the sting of ethnic prejudice as some of his Pueblo peers dropped out of school rather than face the cultural and socioeconomic gap that existed between them and their Anglo teachers and peers. Louis was very proud of his ethnic heritage; it became a part of his quest to forge an identity for himself. In forming his identity he must blend his experience of self with his Native American heritage and

ethnic or racial identity

A sense of belonging to an ethnic or racial group that becomes part of one's thoughts, feelings, and behaviors.

history. **Ethnic or racial identity** refers to a sense of belonging to an ethnic or racial group that becomes part of one's thoughts, feelings, and behaviors. The awakening of ethnic or racial identification may occur at any point in adulthood. Very often, however, it occurs in adolescence.

Forging a racial or ethnic identity is a complex and difficult process for members of minority groups (Spencer & Markstrom-Adams, 1990). Minority adolescents must develop a view of self both within the dominant culture and within their own racial or ethnic group. This may be difficult when racial and ethnic discrimination has created a climate of distrust and resentment and numerous negative stereotypes. Often, adolescents must choose between identifying with people outside of their own group or identifying with that group and accepting the negative characteristics attributed to it (Spencer & Markstrom-Adams, 1990). Adult role models who have achieved a healthy racial or ethnic identity may not be available. This is especially true for teenagers who are removed from their cultural heritage through immigration or migration.

Parents are a critical link in racial and ethnic socialization (Thornton, Chatters, Taylor, & Allen, 1990). They give their children the guidance necessary to help them affirm their race or ethnicity. Racial and ethnic identity involves learning about one's heritage and traditions; it also involves learning about the restrictions placed on the individual and the skills necessary to cope with stereotypes and discrimination. On the basis of data from a national survey of African Americans, Thornton and his colleagues (1990) found that older African American parents were more likely than younger African American parents to value racial identity as important to their children's development. Furthermore, mothers were more likely than fathers to educate their children about race. Mothers living in

Interest in one's ethnic identity frequently occurs in adolescence and early adulthood.

neighborhoods with an equal mix of African Americans and whites were more likely to teach their children about race than were mothers in neighborhoods with few white residents.

Schools are another potent source of information about one's ethnic or racial heritage. Unfortunately, many schools do not offer students the opportunity to learn more about cultures other than the dominant one. Teachers need to be trained and sensitized to the importance of teaching about those cultures. Within the schools there must be greater recognition of the importance of ethnic and racial pride for development of self-esteem and identity.

SEARCHING FOR ORIGINS: ADOPTED ADOLESCENTS

ego continuity
The sense that one's current self-perceptions are firmly connected to the self-perceptions of the past.

One problem of identity for the adolescent is establishing a sense of **ego continuity**—a sense that one's current self-perceptions are firmly connected to the self-definitions of the past and to the anticipated self-perceptions of the future (Erikson, 1968). For most adolescents, the development of ego continuity is difficult enough, given the rapid changes associated with this period; for adopted adolescents, however, the problem is compounded by lack of knowledge about their origins.

At the time of adoption, most adoptive parents are given very little information about the child's birth parents or family history; in turn, the birth parents are told little about the adoptive parents. This procedure, which is followed by most adoption agencies, is considered to be in the best interests of all involved parties. However, this assumption is being challenged by a number of activist groups—in particular, the Adoptees Liberty Movement Association (ALMA), the Orphan Voyage, and Concerned United Birthmothers (CUB). These groups, and others, have argued that the sealing of records at the time of adoption not only violates the basic rights of individuals to know about themselves (and their offspring in the case of CUB members), but could set the stage for serious psychological difficulties related to the adoption experience.

Researchers have begun more systematic attempts to survey and assess the difficulties and needs of adopted youths and their adoptive parents. The *Service and Mental Health Needs of Adopted Adolescents* national study asked a sample of youths and their adoptive parents a series of open-ended questions about adoptive families (Sharma, 1992). Six major themes emerged:

1. Adolescents felt an overwhelming sense of gratitude for their adoption.

2. Adopted teenagers expressed a sense of feeling different or of not belonging.

3. Teenagers were concerned about their lack of information about their birth parents.

4. Teenagers expressed curiosity about the lives of their birth parents.

5. Adoptive parents wanted help with parenting skills, especially with such questions as "How much of my child's behavior is due to the adoption and how much is typical adolescent behavior?"

6. Both adopted teenagers and their adoptive parents were concerned about the public attitudes about adoption and how they would be perceived by others.

FOCUS ON CULTURE

In many Native American Indian tribes it is not unusual for grandparents to assume custodial care of their grandchildren when family trauma such as death, divorce, unemployment, disability, or illness separates parents from their children (Weibel-Orlando, 1990). This adoptive relationship can also be assumed at birth when the parents are dead or otherwise absent, with the expectation that the grandchildren will then care for their custodial grandparents when they become elderly. Often, children grow up knowing only their grandparents as caregivers; in the process they learn more about their cultural heritage. Many custodial grandparents welcome the opportunity to teach their grandchildren the traditional way of life in their tribes.

Researchers have pointed out that adopted children are at greater risk for psychological and academic problems than nonadopted children (Bohman, 1970; Brodzinsky, Schechter, Braff, & Singer, 1984). Problems related to identity development may be particularly troublesome in adolescence and young adulthood (Lifton, 1979; Sorosky, Baran, & Pannor, 1978). Sants (1964) has coined the term **genealogical bewilderment** to describe the feelings of incompleteness that are often experienced by adolescent adoptees trying to connect with their past. For nonadopted adolescents these connections are clear—there is a known family history. For most adoptees, however, there is a large void when it comes to one's ancestry.

Thoughts and fantasies about birth parents and the circumstances surrounding the original relinquishment are a normal part of development for the adopted child and adolescent. Nevertheless, adoptees often keep their thoughts and feelings to themselves because they do not want to hurt their adoptive parents, and in some cases out of fear that expressing these thoughts and fantasies will make them real.

Our discussion of identity is not over; in Chapter 11 we will learn more about the development of a mature identity.

genealogical bewilderment
Found among some adopted adolescents, the feelings of incompleteness and disconnectedness from one's genealogical or biological past.

RECAP

According to Erikson, adolescence is the period during which the crisis of ego identity is resolved. Failure to form a sense of self results in self-diffusion. Self-awareness increases during adolescence and teenagers often identify with peer groups and folk heroes as a way of defining themselves. For some adolescents, forging an ethnic or racial identity is central to their overall sense of self. Adopted adolescents need to learn more about their biological parents in order to establish a sense of ego continuity.

ADOLESCENTS AND THEIR PARENTS

During my early years as a parent, I worried about my children's journey through their teenage years because of the stories I had heard about how difficult it would be. Media images of teenagers as moody, rebellious, and self-centered added to my apprehension. However, as I look back on my experiences as a mother of two teenagers, I can say it was not that bad; in fact, I enjoyed some parts of their

Contrary to a popular misconception, adolescence is not necessarily a time of turmoil and stress. For many, it is a time of fun, exploration, and new identities.

journey. It was a time of unpredictable change and conflict, but we also shared interesting discussions about rules and expectations and devised creative compromises. As a parent I found it helpful to remember that my adolescent children's journey would lead them to adulthood, when they would no longer require their parents as guides. I tried to redefine my role to show them how to guide themselves.

One of the major themes of adolescence is separation; teenagers seek to define themselves as separate and different from their parents. In fact, many teenagers (and some adults) do not like to think that they are similar to their parents in any way. Yet the identity a person establishes is influenced in many ways by their parents.

Not all parents welcome their teenagers' seemingly abrupt attempts to separate from them. Many parents fear that their adolescent children will reject all of their beliefs and values in favor of radical and self-interested ones.

During the 1960s and early 1970s, when dissent and dispute over political issues were common, the term "generation gap" was coined to refer to adolescents' generalized disenchantment with their parents' way of life (Conger, 1981; Conger & Peterson, 1984; Yankelovitch, 1974). However, most adolescents got along with their parents and generally agreed with their views. Today there is even stronger evidence that adolescents and their parents are not natural enemies (Hamid & Wylie, 1980; Offer, Ostrov, & Howard, 1981; Peterson, 1987; Steinberg, 1987; Yankelovitch, 1981). When researchers examine the changes that occur in the same parent-child relationship over time (using a longitudinal design) rather than comparing groups of children of different ages (using a cross-sectional design), they generally find a pattern of continuity in parent-child relationships even though parents and teenagers may differ on specific issues (Galambos, 1992; Nally, Eisenberg, & Harris, 1991).

While adolescents may differ with their parents on issues such as hairstyles, clothing, music, and curfews, they are more likely to adopt their parents' views on broader social, moral, and political issues and values. During the teenage years, when adolescents direct more of their time and attention toward their peers, parents continue to have a strong influence on them (Youniss & Smollar, 1985). A study of 180 adolescents (Hunter, 1985) found that the frequency of discussions with parents remained unchanged between the ages of 12 and 20. However, Hunter also found that the relationship between parents and adolescents was not a mutual one. Parents tended to seek to explain their views to their teenagers rather than trying to understand the adolescents' views. The adolescents' friends, on the other hand, were willing both to explain their own views and to try to understand those of others.

Often tied to the assumption of differences and conflicts between generations is the notion that ideas and ideals are passed only from the older generation to the new generation. However, a review of the research literature (Bengston & Troll, 1978; Hagestad, 1984) suggests that the values and attitudes of youth may actually exert some influence on parental behavior and viewpoints. In some cases, the children may serve as a connection to the "larger world" and the prevailing social and cultural mood of the times. This may be particularly important for immigrants' adolescent children, who may be more attuned to their new culture. Thus, not only do adolescents learn from their parents, but parents learn from their offspring. This finding is consistent with the bidirectional models of parent-child interaction that are popular with developmental psychologists today (Bell & Harper, 1980; Belsky, 1981).

PARENT-ADOLESCENT CONFLICT

Even though the generation gap has been greatly exaggerated, conflict between teenagers and their parents does exist and contributes to the rough terrain associated with adolescence. Despite their love for one another, most teenagers and their parents may find themselves in an antagonistic relationship (Steinberg, 1987). The results of one study suggest that the sources of rebellion include the lack of sufficient freedom for adolescents to make their own decisions in areas such as clothing, hairstyle, and choice of friends; their desire to provoke greater parental interest and concern ("to get my parents to pay attention to me"); and their feelings of being criticized excessively. Interestingly, most of the teenagers questioned did not want absolute freedom in decision making; rather, they preferred their parents to be interested and actively involved in their lives (Clemens & Rust, 1979).

As children move from preadolescence to adolescence, they challenge the scope and domain of parental authority and control over their lives. Most of the challenges concern mundane, everyday details of family life such as chores and getting along with family members. Smetana (1988) asked adolescents and parents to read a list of fictional family scenarios in which parents exerted their authority over their teenage children (e.g., choices of friends, clothes, and leisure activities). Teenagers were more likely to judge the parent's actions in the hypothetical situations as transgressions on the teenager's right to make personal choices while parents tended to judge the same issues as examples of parents' exerting their rightful authority. A similar difference was found when adolescents and parents were asked to justify their own positions on disputes over daily tasks, such as doing chores and homework and getting along with others in the family, rather than hypothetical disputes (Smetana, 1989). Adolescents were more likely to interpret the disputes as personal issues outside the realm of parental control or regulation. Parents, on the other hand, viewed the disputes as involving social convention—their disciplinary jurisdiction. Refusal to dress according to social convention, for example, would be seen by the teenager as a personal prerogative and by the parent as a violation of social convention.

The degree of conflict between adolescents and parents can vary. Adolescents who have accepted many of the values of a traditional family (such as obedience and cooperation) show greater acceptance of parental control than adolescents who reject these values. Authoritative parents who show willingness to distribute family power as the child matures appear to have more effective interactions with their children than parents who are overly permissive or authoritarian (Baumrind, 1978). Authoritative parenting has also been found to facilitate academic achievement in adolescents (Steinberg, Elmen, & Mounts; 1989). Difficulties in school, social relationships, and other areas appear to occur more frequently in adolescent families in which there is "parental hostility, rejection, or neglect" (Conger, 1977). In one study (Feldman & Wentzel, 1990), adolescent boys whose parents' style of parenting was child-centered were better liked by their peers than boys whose parents used a harsh disciplinarian style. In a different study, sixth and seventh graders who perceived their parents as exerting a lot of control over them and who were not allowed to participate in family decision making were more likely to turn to their peers for support and advice (Fuligni & Eccles, 1993). It appears that parents who give their teenagers more of a say in family decision making, but who do not surrender their authority, have fewer conflicts with their adolescents (Smetana, 1995).

Some adolescents may challenge their parents' authority. In turn, some parents may react arbitrarily or coercively to the changing needs of their child. For example, when 15-year-old Laura wanted to attend a party in the next town, her parents objected, saying she was too young. Laura went to the party anyway, telling her parents that she was spending the night at a friend's house. When her parents learned of her disobedience and deception, they grounded her for 2 months: she was not allowed to talk on the telephone or visit with her friends. Her parents also refused to discuss the problem with her, preferring instead to allow her to "feel the effects of her deception." By cutting off communication with their daughter, Laura's parents are missing the chance to teach her the importance of being honest and of working out a mutually agreeable solution to the problem of how she can express her need to be independent and trustworthy.

Pressures from the outside world may worsen the parent-child conflict. For example, Flanagan (1990) found more conflicts between parents and adolescents in families experiencing economic hardships caused by unemployment than in families in which parents were employed.

The developing sexuality of the adolescent may also add to problems in relationships with parents. Difficulties inevitably arise because the child matures sexually while still living within the family structure. In some cultures, the onset of physical maturity signals the time for adolescents to leave home and establish themselves apart from their parents. However, in industrialized societies it is more difficult for adolescents to achieve this type of economic independence. Steinberg

(1987) believes that one factor contributing to parent-adolescent conflict is that teenagers are physically ready to leave home before they can be economically independent from their parents. So they bicker and squabble with their parents about petty issues such as keeping a room clean, putting out the garbage, and choosing hair and dress styles.

There is some evidence that teenagers' squabbling is related to pubertal changes (Graber, Brooks-Gunn, & Warren, 1995; Steinberg, 1988). Early-maturing adolescents quarrel with their parents at an earlier age than do their late-maturing peers (Steinberg, 1987). During early adolescence (between ages 11 to 13) parents report the most difficulty and strain with their teenagers. This is especially true for parents who are less involved in their careers; parents who are highly invested in their work are less bothered by their first-born adolescent's emergence into puberty and heterosexual dating (Silverberg & Steinberg, 1990).

Establishing Independence and Autonomy

In many ways, the voyage through life evolves around the individual's quest to become independent and autonomous. Becoming independent is a gradual process, begun in early childhood with the first "No!" and continued throughout childhood with the development of self-care skills. Likewise, during adolescence a teenager does not wake up one morning and declare himself or herself autonomous or independent. Rather, independence is achieved in steps. Often adolescents may not be aware of their movement toward separateness from their parents or their reliance on others for answers and direction until they have already accepted responsibility for their own actions. Likewise, some teenagers or young adults may consider themselves independent but discover that when they move away from home they may still need to rely on their parents for emotional support when faced with new decisions or uncertainties (such as buying a new car or changing jobs).

One of the difficulties American college students face is realizing how much they have relied on their parents for advice, for help in making decisions, or for basic support services such as laundry or housekeeping. Parents of college students also undergo changes as they accept their adolescents' maturity and independence. Parents who derive their importance solely from their role as caregivers may experience more difficulty in surrendering control of their adolescents. For example, mothers who are employed full-time are more accepting and supportive of their teenagers' growing independence (Hoffman, 1979, 1989).

autonomy
The many different characteristics and behaviors concerning the ability to feel, think, and act for oneself independent of one's parents.

The term **autonomy** refers to many different characteristics and behaviors concerning the ability to feel, think, and act for oneself independently of one's parents. It is not a single or simple characteristic, nor is it always expressed in the same way by the same person (Steinberg & Silverberg, 1987). In one study (Moore & Hotch, 1981), college freshmen were asked how they knew when they had left home and could consider themselves to be independent from their parents. The students' responses fell into eight categories (listed in Table 10–2). While some students accept the physical separation from their parents and personal control over their decisions, they may have some difficulty accepting an emotional separation from their parents.

HOW DO YOU KNOW YOU HAVE LEFT HOME?

CATEGORY	EXAMPLES
Personal control	Less parental control; makes own decisions; must do things for self; feels mature
Economic independence	Financial independence; has a job
Residence	Has all of his or her belongings; lives in a different place; moved to an apartment
Physical separation	Physical distance from home and family
School affiliation	Dorm is the center of life; considers school to be home
Dissociation	Won't go back home each summer; has broken the ties
Emotional separation	Has feeling of being a visitor (no sense of belonging) at home; doesn't feel close to family
Graduation	Has graduated from high school or college

TABLE 10–2

Source: From "Late Adolescents' Conceptualizations of Home-Leaving" by D. Moore and D. F. Hotch, 1981, *Journal of Youth and Adolescence, 10.* Adapted with permission.

RECAP

Despite the fact that adolescents are seeking to separate themselves from their parents, the quality of parent-child relationships during adolescence is an extension of relationships developed during childhood. Conflict between parents and adolescents does occur, often centering on issues of personal autonomy. Parenting styles, hormonal changes, and external pressures can influence the degree of this conflict. The road to independence broadens during adolescence as teenagers assume more personal responsibility.

ADOLESCENT PEER RELATIONS

When my children became teenagers, their use of the telephone became the focal point of family conflict. My husband and I deliberately chose to have only one telephone line in the house as a way of encouraging us all to learn how to share resources. However, we underestimated the number and length of phone calls our children would receive. I never realized how many friends they had until I had to fight my way to the phone! Conversations with their peers was a central part of their after-school lives and helped establish their circle of friends and acquaintances.

THE SOCIETY OF ADOLESCENTS

Parents and the mass media have much to say about the "youth culture" and the "adolescent subculture." But does such a subculture actually exist? Is it a by-product of cultural values and customs? Or have adults merely created a convenient stereotype as a means of explaining adolescent behavior? A classic study of midwestern American high school students by Coleman (1961) suggests that the adolescent subculture is indeed a reality, and that it has fostered substantial differences between itself and the adult culture. These differences, according to Coleman, alienate high school students from their parents and the academic goals of their school, and orient them toward their peers.

More recent observers of the adolescent social scene, however, have been critical of the picture portrayed in Coleman's report (McClelland, 1982). Although acknowledging the reality of an adolescent "society," contemporary sociologists and psychologists suggest that this subculture is neither unified nor separate from the adult culture. According to McClelland, high schools serve as "the meeting place of a wide variety of subcultural strains, some of which oppose parents and the school, others of which do not, and all of which reflect one element or another of the complex adult culture" (p. 412). Thus, while adolescents organize themselves into social systems around such distinctive cultural features as clothing, hairstyles, music, and recreational activities, the separation attempt from the world of adults is highly variable from one group of adolescents to another. Furthermore, the separation is not necessarily a revolt against institutions or norms—it is more often the way adolescents articulate their own needs and create a context in which to work out mutual problems.

Adolescents generally prefer the company of their friends to that of their families. As children move from pre-adolescence to adolescence they spend considerably less time with their families and more time either by themselves or in the

Although teenagers differ from their parents on some issues such as dress and hairstyles, they are more likely to adopt their parents' views on broader social, moral, and political issues and values.

company of friends (Larson & Richards, 1991). According to one study (Csikszentmihalyi & Larson, 1984) adolescents spend more time talking to peers than in any other single activity, and they describe themselves as most happy when engaged in these interactions. The world of the adolescent is not limited to friends, however. On the contrary, their social milieu is a large one—they mix socially not only with their many acquaintances but also with relative strangers (see Figure 10–1). Thus, adolescent society in our culture serves as a bridge to the mobile adult society, where they will be confronted with a wide variety of colleagues and occupations. Peer interactions in extracurricular activities also mirror the procedures by which organizations operate in the adult world. The adolescent learns how to deal with the power hierarchies within student government and other group activities.

Authority in many adolescent organizations, however, tends to be lateral rather than vertical. That is, adolescents tend to spread authority among group members and are reluctant to assume positions of authority over their peers. They see their interrelationships more as a fellowship than as a vertical power arrangement with one person having authority over another.

Adolescent society differs from adult society in other ways, too, but these differences are mainly superficial. For example, adolescent society thrives on fads, distinctive modes of dress, and slang. Feeling that they are not fully accepted as individuals in adult society, they create a group identity that gives them a sense of belonging to the larger world. Despite this show of distinctiveness, however, researchers (Newman, 1982) have observed that normal adolescents do not differ much in moral and ethical attitudes from their parents. In most cases they conform to parental standards of achievement and vocational preferences.

Peer Group Composition   Teachers and those who have an opportunity to observe young adolescents can readily describe the changes in the structure of the

Adolescents spend much of their time talking among friends and classmates.

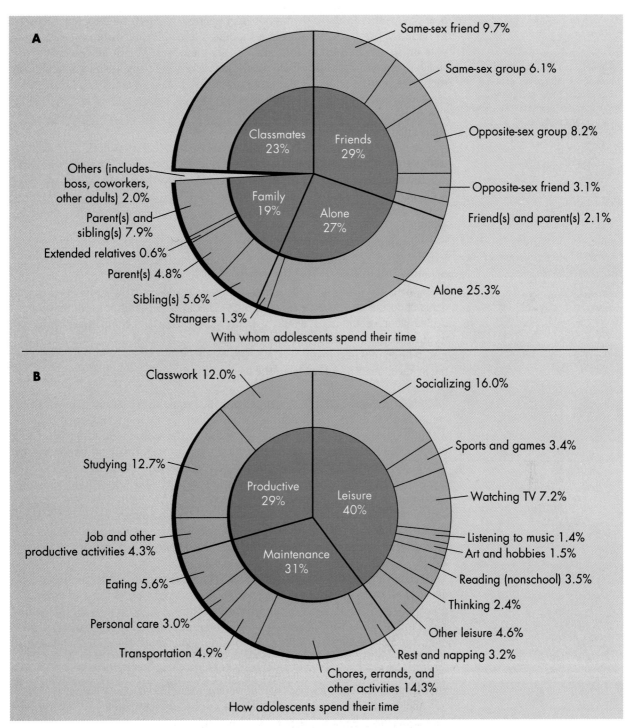

A

Classmates 23%

Friends 29%

Same-sex friend 9.7%

Same-sex group 6.1%

Opposite-sex group 8.2%

Opposite-sex friend 3.1%

Friend(s) and parent(s) 2.1%

Others (includes boss, coworkers, other adults) 2.0%

Family 19%

Alone 27%

Parent(s) and sibling(s) 7.9%

Extended relatives 0.6%

Parent(s) 4.8%

Sibling(s) 5.6%

Strangers 1.3%

Alone 25.3%

With whom adolescents spend their time

B

Classwork 12.0%

Socializing 16.0%

Studying 12.7%

Productive 29%

Leisure 40%

Sports and games 3.4%

Watching TV 7.2%

Job and other productive activities 4.3%

Maintenance 31%

Listening to music 1.4%

Art and hobbies 1.5%

Reading (nonschool) 3.5%

Eating 5.6%

Thinking 2.4%

Personal care 3.0%

Other leisure 4.6%

Transportation 4.9%

Rest and napping 3.2%

Chores, errands, and other activities 14.3%

How adolescents spend their time

FIGURE 10–1

How and with whom adolescents spend their time.

clique

A small informal group of people with similar social class, education, age, and interests who spend a lot of time together.

crowd

A large, informal group formed by two or three cliques.

mutual role taking

The ability to keep both one's own view and that of another in mind simultaneously; usually emerges in adolescence.

peer groups they form. In the prepubescent period, children band together loosely in same-sex groups without even a thought about their opposite-sex peers. In a year or so, as interest in the opposite sex increases, young adolescents form smaller, same-sex groups, or **cliques.** They congregate together in school, call each other on the phone, and engage in mutually planned activities. Later, these same-sex cliques start to interact with other opposite-sex cliques (Dunphy, 1963). Over time, individual members of these cliques may start to date or form friendships outside of the cliques.

The clique provides a setting for intimate personal relationships that formerly were found primarily in the family. Clique members are bound together by geographic closeness, age, education, heterosexual interest, degree of social and personal maturity, and similar social backgrounds as well as by mutual interests and similar academic orientation. Clique membership rarely cuts across socioeconomic class lines.

Surrounding the clique is the larger and less rigidly defined **crowd.** The crowd is held together by its orientation to the future, the social background of its members, and their personality types. The loosely organized college-bound, career-oriented group of high school students would constitute one crowd; students choosing a vocational track in high school and oriented toward blue collar, skilled-labor occupations would generally constitute a second crowd; athletes would constitute another. In later adolescence, the crowd disappears and is replaced by cliques of romantic couples (see Figure 10–2). In some high schools ethnic or racial identities may form the basis of a different set of cliques.

Adolescent Friendships   Peer groups provide people with a group with which to compare themselves. More personal and supportive relationships emerge from within the peer group in the form of friendships. Typically, adolescents have one or two close friends with whom they share their most intimate and intense feelings and concerns. Often these concerns center around other members of the clique. In friendships people are usually more open and honest and less self-conscious; individuals hesitate less about revealing their doubts, anxieties, and resentments. There is less role-playing to gain social acceptance and more mutual support. Adolescent friendships often substitute for parental support as teenagers seek greater independence from their families (Levitt, Guacci-Franco, & Levitt, 1993).

Friendships are usually based on similar social backgrounds, interests, and personality characteristics (Hartup, 1983). For example, outgoing and energetic people are likely to base their friendship on a common interest in team sports and dance music. Friendships between widely different personality types are less common. Intimate friendships first arise in early adolescence (Berndt, 1982). Compared to younger children, adolescents are more willing to share their personal thoughts and feelings with friends (Berndt, 1981b). They also have more actual knowledge about close friends than do younger children (Diaz & Berndt, 1982).

Adolescent intimacy is related, in part, to the emerging ability of the individual to engage in **mutual role taking.** According to Selman (1981), only when adolescents are capable of keeping both their own view and that of another in mind simultaneously, will they be able to achieve a level of intimacy within a social relationship. Other researchers (Douvan & Adelson, 1966) have explained the emergence of intimate friendships during adolescence in terms of the psychosexual

FIGURE 10–2

Stages of adolescent peer group development.

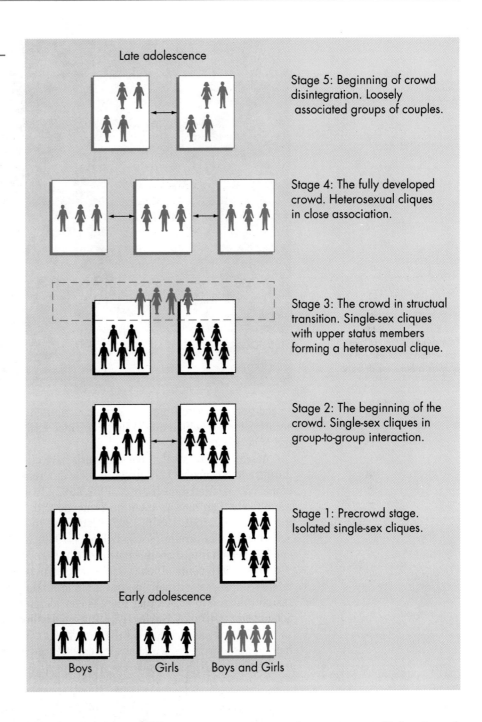

Late adolescence

Stage 5: Beginning of crowd disintegration. Loosely associated groups of couples.

Stage 4: The fully developed crowd. Heterosexual cliques in close association.

Stage 3: The crowd in structural transition. Single-sex cliques with upper status members forming a heterosexual clique.

Stage 2: The beginning of the crowd. Single-sex cliques in group-to-group interaction.

Stage 1: Precrowd stage. Isolated single-sex cliques.

Early adolescence

Boys   Girls   Boys and Girls

changes that accompany puberty. Such relationships serve as vehicles through which adolescents can express their feelings about the changes—particularly sexual ones—they are experiencing. Thus, adolescent friendships help young people cope with the impulses and drives that are demanding expression during this period. According to Berndt (1982), adolescent intimacy also can enhance self-esteem by showing the individual that others respect his or her ideas and feelings.

Friendships during adolescence can enhance self esteem and provide a basis for defining oneself.

In addition, intimate friendships can contribute to one's social skills and sense of security, both of which are likely to enhance intimate relationships in later periods of development.

Research suggests that boys and girls have different conceptions of friendship during adolescence and are likely to show different patterns in their development of intimate relationships (Berndt, 1982, 1992). In describing a best friend, girls are more likely than boys to mention someone with whom they can share intimate information (Berndt, 1981b, 1992). Compared to boys, girls seem to prefer interaction in smaller groups (Savin-Williams, 1980), and they are less likely to accept another person into their intimate circle of friends.

Contrary to popular belief, adolescents generally are not fickle in their social relationships—they usually do not jump around from one friend to another. Research evidence indicates that there is considerable stability in friendship during adolescence (Berndt & Hoyle, 1985; Tuma & Hallinan, 1979)—and certainly more so than during early childhood (Berndt, 1981a). These close, stable relationships help to ease the stresses and strains experienced by adolescents in their passage from childhood to adulthood.

FOCUS ON CULTURE

Researchers (DuBois & Hirsch, 1990) studying interracial friendship patterns among African American and white students attending an integrated high school found that 80% of the students reported having a close friend who was of a different race than them. However, only 28% of them saw that friend outside of school. The home setting also affected interracial friendships; it was more common for African American students who lived in integrated (as opposed to segregated) neighborhoods to have a friend of different race.

Intimate friendships first arise in early adolescence and are fostered by a willingness to share personal thoughts and feelings with each other.

Popularity   Membership in the clique and the crowd, as well as other adolescent subgroups, is determined by popularity. Popularity, in turn, may be enhanced by membership in the "right" clique. Lack of popularity or peer-group approval can be excruciatingly painful for an adolescent. Knowing who you are involves knowing what others think of you. Although parental interest and involvement is important in the development of self-esteem, the perceptions and reactions of peer-group members also strongly affect how adolescents perceive themselves.

One researcher (Ringness, 1967) found that possession of a pleasing personality was the most crucial factor in achieving popularity. Another study, however, found that physical attractiveness is the most important factor, at least for adolescents who are perceived by others as highly attractive or unattractive (Cavior & Dokecki, 1973). In other words, highly attractive individuals are popular, in large part, because of their attractiveness. Similarly, unattractive individuals are unpopular because of their lack of attractiveness. The same study suggests that for adolescents of average attractiveness a reciprocal effect may occur: Attractiveness generates popularity, and popularity then enhances the perception of attractiveness. Standards for physical attractiveness appear to be based on cultural definitions that are acquired at an early age (Cavior & Lombardi, 1973; Cross & Cross, 1971).

Athletic prowess, scholarship, knowledge of popular culture, (e.g., music, dress), and other attributes may supplement personality qualities and attractiveness in achieving popularity, but in themselves they are not sufficient to produce peer acceptance. Many studies have tried to identify the personality and behavioral characteristics associated with social acceptance and popularity. Among the characteristics identified were being helpful, friendly, the "life of the party," and conforming to peer norms; being flexible, tolerant, and sympathetic; being sensitive to the feelings of others; acting naturally and confident without being conceited; and possessing initiative and drive (Hartup, 1983).

Some personality types seem more likely than others to be rejected. Adolescents who are ill at ease and lack self-confidence may try to disguise their discomfort by aggressive or conceited behavior. Being timid, nervous, or withdrawn alienates other people, as does making excessive demands for attention.

FOCUS ON CULTURE

Establishing friendships and being accepted into peer groups is more complicated for adolescents with physical disabilities such as blindness, deafness, or paralysis. Those who have been labeled as disabled since birth or early childhood may not have had the benefit of positive disabled adult role models. Often they must confront other people's stereotypes about disabled people. Their nondisabled peers may feel uncomfortable around them. Deaf and blind children are often unable to respond and communicate effectively with their peers, and this creates more discomfort.

Youngsters who were popular in childhood generally continue to be popular in adolescence, in part because they began adolescence with a relatively stable self-concept.

Conformity   A strong interest in being accepted by one's peers and establishing friendships may seem to encourage greater conformity during adolescence. Strictly speaking, **conformity** is simply following the norms of one's family, society, or peer group. This is not always as easy as it sounds, however, because these various sets of norms sometimes conflict with one another. For example, adolescents may be torn between meeting their parents' expectation that they spend time with family and the peer expectation that they demonstrate their independence from parents and spend time away from the home. Ultimately, the individual must choose among them and adopt only the ones that are personally suitable. Children learn most of the norms of their society by the age of 11 or 12. In adolescence, they begin to evaluate these norms in relation to themselves and their evolving value systems.

conformity
Behaving according to family, society, or peer group norms.

Stereotypes about adolescents suggest that they are a highly conforming group of individuals. Pressure from peers is said to unduly influence the adolescent's choice of dress, mannerisms, values, judgments, and so forth. While it is certainly true that peers play a major role in the choices an adolescent makes, it is also true that others, particularly parents, exert considerable influence.

Are adolescents more likely than younger children to conform to peers? Apparently not, for research generally suggests either a peak in conformity in middle childhood followed by a decline in adolescence, or a continuous decline in conformity beginning in early childhood (Hartup, 1983). Thus, there is a tendency for individuals to think and act for themselves that increases with age (O'Brien & Bierman, 1988).

At any age, however, the degree of conformity varies with the situation (Hartup, 1983). Under conditions of stress, for example, people are much more likely to conform to group norms than when they are not stressed. Conformity is also more prevalent in complex tasks than in simple tasks, as well as in tasks in which an achievement orientation is fostered, such as school exams. In addition, the presence of a nonconformist in the group is likely to induce nonconformity in other group members, particularly if that person is admired and respected by the others. Finally, people with high self-esteem are much less likely to conform to peer pressure than those with low self-esteem.

Perhaps adolescents develop solidarity with their peers as a means of coping with the adult world looming on the horizon. Constantly reminded of the dire consequences of dropping out of school, getting poor grades, hanging out with the wrong crowd, and so forth, adolescents may feel that the safest thing to do is to follow the group. On the other hand, strong conformity to peer norms may reflect the sudden absence of parental control or support that the child relied on in earlier years (Baumrind, 1978). Rather than seeing a coercive adult world, some adolescents may perceive an uncaring one that allows them to flounder through feelings of insecurity and stress.

RECAP

Peer relationships become more important during adolescence, but are not significantly different from the adult culture. Large informal crowds and more informal cliques are formed. Adolescent friendships are based on intimate relationships and supplement the support teenagers receive from their families. Popularity among adolescents is often based on personality and physical characteristics. Adolescent conformity to peer pressure is not as great as the media portrayals suggest. The degree of conformity varies with the situation and the individual.

VOCATIONAL CHOICES

"What do you want to be when you grow up?" is a question frequently asked of adolescents. It is also one of the more difficult ones to answer. Even before they have completed high school, many teenagers feel the pressure from parents, teachers, and even their peers to define some future occupation for themselves. In the not-too-distant past, vocational "choice" was dependent on social class and birth. An artisan's son had few alternatives but to assume his father's trade; a peasant's son could only aspire to vocations that were appropriate to his social class; and women had no socially approved options beyond the roles of household manager, wife, and mother. In nearly all cases personal needs and desires were subordinated to the demands of a rigidly structured economy and society.

Today both men and women have a wider margin of freedom in the choice of careers. Yet various factors may make the job choice difficult and may impose limitations on one's actual range of choices. Those without sufficient education or training—high school dropouts, for example—will probably be limited to

FOCUS ON CULTURE

In cultures around the world, women have fewer vocational opportunities compared to men. In many Arab countries, boys constitute the majority of students in the high schools; in higher education men outnumber women three to one (Seager & Olson, 1986). Adolescent and adult women living in rural nontechnological countries spend most of their time taking care of the home and family. In Asia and Africa almost all women who are employed work in farm or field work.

low paying unskilled jobs, no matter what career they desire. Adolescents from economically or socially disadvantaged homes may not even be aware of the full range of career possibilities, for they lack or have limited interactions with role models outside their primary relationships.

Women and ethnic minorities are still affected by discrimination in the job market, although the situation has improved somewhat in the past decade or so. Women also continue to be influenced by negative self-perceptions. Despite progress toward changing gender-role stereotypes, some women still may have difficulty seeing themselves as engineers, dentists, or astronauts. These influences can affect their choice of occupation.

CHOOSING A CAREER

Parents and family members provide the first models of what workers do and how one feels about work. The socioeconomic level of the family still largely determines the vocational aspirations and attitudes of the child because it shapes the child's ideas about the kinds of work available and notions about what is a "good job." It is usual for children of professionals to assume careers, for example, and for parents who are unemployed or underemployed to pass these difficulties on to their children both by example and because of the economic realities of their lives. For example, a teenager from a poor family may quit school to take a job that will help support the family.

In high school, guidance counselors and teachers play pivotal roles in adolescents' career choices. When teenagers enter high school they are typically channelled into either a college preparatory or a vocational curriculum by teachers and guidance counselors. Even before they have begun to think about career choices, their curricula may make it difficult for teenagers to consider careers that require a college education. Since most colleges require specific high school courses such as algebra, a lab science, and foreign language as a condition for admission, teenagers who have avoided these courses are less likely to be accepted by a college. However, some high schools recognize the problem with "tracking" adolescents too early; they offer career planning courses to help guide juniors and seniors in the choice of a career. By bringing representatives from different careers into the classroom to talk about their career paths, teachers provide students with valuable role models and help stimulate their thinking about vocational choices.

ADOLESCENT EMPLOYMENT

When my son Adam was 16 he got a summer job working at the local supermarket; it gave him extra money and helped him structure his time over the summer months. However, when school began in September, he continued to work part-time. I was concerned that the time he spent on his job would interfere with his school work. My concerns were short-lived: by the time wrestling practice began in December, Adam quit his part-time job.

Many parents and adults support the idea of adolescent employment; they argue that working helps teenagers develop such traits as initiative,

Some researchers believe that having a job during adolescence helps to develop such traits as initiative, autonomy, and self-reliance.

autonomy, and self-reliance. Employed youths are said to be more responsible, not only on the job but also in their family and peer relations. Employment is also thought to facilitate social competence and understanding among teenagers.

Do empirical studies support this positive picture of the effects of working on adolescents? Only in part, say Greenberger and Steinberg, who, in collaboration with several other colleagues, have been investigating the impact of employment on teenagers (Greenberger, Steinberg, & Ruggiero, 1982; Greenberger, Steinberg, & Vaux, 1981; Steinberg, Fegley, & Dornbusch, 1993; Steinberg, Greenberger, Garduque, Ruggiero, & Vaux, 1982). These researchers report that working is associated with greater personal responsibility—such as punctuality, dependability, self-reliance, and positive work orientation—but not greater social responsibility. For example, cooperation, tolerance, and commitment among adolescents are unaffected by working.

Adolescent employment has a number of negative consequences for young people. In particular, working during the school year decreases the teenager's involvement with and commitment to activities and relationships in nonwork settings. Adolescents who work are more often absent from school, spend less time on homework and in extracurricular activities, and report that they enjoy school less. Teenagers who work more than 20 hours a week experience a drop in grade point average (Steinberg, Fegley, & Dornbusch, 1993). In addition, teenagers who work show less emotional closeness with peers and, in the case of employed girls, less emotional closeness with family members as well. This "distancing" from the family parallels the gains in autonomy that are especially striking for employed girls. Working also has been shown to lead to more materialistic attitudes among employed boys and among teenagers in general; compared to teenagers who work less than 20 hours a week, teenagers who work excessive hours are more likely to skip breakfast, exercise less, smoke cigarettes and marijuana, and consume alcohol and cocaine (Bachman & Schulenberg, 1993).

Gottfredson (1985), using data collected from a large and ethnically diverse sample, found slightly different results. Work experiences available to students did not affect commitment to education or attachment to school or parents. Moreover, teenage employment did not increase delinquency or have a detrimental effect on students' involvement with extracurricular activities. When work experience is carefully coordinated with the school curriculum, such as when students are expected to report on their work to their teachers, it can lead to a decrease in school dropouts and an increase in learning and school attendance.

Overall, the impact of employment on adolescents is determined by the type of job, the age of the teenager, the amount of support from the school and family, and the teenager's sex and socioeconomic status. The emerging consensus among researchers who are studying the impact of adolescent employment on development is that negative consequences of employment are related to *how much* a teenager works and not to whether the teenager works or not. Students who work more than 20 hours a week are more likely to experience declines in school performance and social relationships. Working shorter hours while in school may help teenagers acquire important work skills and earn extra money to make the experience worthwhile (see Table 10–3).

BENEFITS AND DISADVANTAGES OF ADOLESCENT EMPLOYMENT

BENEFITS	DISADVANTAGES
Encourages initiative and self-reliance	Decreases involvement with relationships
Helps establish independence and autonomy	Increases absences from school
Generates extra spending money	Encourages materialism
Encourages greater personal responsibility	Does not encourage greater social responsibility
Provides exposure to certain career paths	Distracts from school work and enjoyment of school
When coordinated with school curriculum, can lead to decrease in dropouts and increase in learning and school attendance	Reduces leisure time and encourages substance abuse

TABLE 10–3

RECAP

Choosing a career is a process that develops over time but has its roots in adolescence. Vocational choices are influenced by parents, schools, and socioeconomic and political factors. Adolescent employment was once considered to be beneficial to students but now is being questioned. School performance, social relationships, and adjustment may be adversely affected when teenagers work too many hours.

PROBLEM BEHAVIOR

One of the reasons I did not look forward to my children's adolescence was that I associated this period of development with problem behavior. Images of teenage rebellion, juvenile delinquency, runaway children, and drug abuse clouded my expectations of adolescence. Teenagers have greater opportunity than younger children to break family and societal rules because they have more autonomy and travel over a wider range (usually in automobiles). While most teenagers traverse adolescence without significant difficulties, some respond in maladaptive ways. However, with the exception of dropping out of school, most of the antisocial behavior and mental health problems exhibited by adolescents are not the exclusive domain of that age group. Certainly adolescents have no monopoly on drug abuse and alcoholism, and such problems as depression, schizophrenia, and obesity cut across all age levels. Psychologists and other social scientists disagree about whether these problems have specific characteristics when they originate in adolescence, but most agree that the physical and psychological upheavals that young people experience during this period make teenagers more susceptible to some of these disorders than they might be at other times of life (Ge, Lorenz, Conger, Elder, & Simons, 1994; Kovacs, 1989; Larson & Ham, 1993). In this section, we will look briefly at several problem behaviors and disorders that may appear during adolescence.

DEPRESSION

In a survey of Canadian high school students (Ehrenberg, Cox, & Koopman, 1990), 31.4% of those sampled were found to be mildly to clinically depressed. The researchers reported that their findings were similar to the rates of depression found in samples of adolescents in the United States and the United Kingdom. Melancholy and feelings of dejection are relatively common emotions during adolescence. In fact, there is a marked rise in the prevalence of depression-like symptoms during this period (Kovacs, 1989; Rutter & Garmesy, 1983).

Adolescent depression is characterized by a constellation of behaviors, most of which are also found in depressed adults (Carlson & Cantwell, 1982; Robbins, Alessi, Cook, Poznanski, & Yanchyshyn, 1982). Included among these behaviors are boredom and restlessness; irritability; disturbances in eating and sleeping; ruminations or obsessions; and hypochondria (imaginary ill health). In addition, depressed teenagers may have a poor self-image, which frequently leads to antisocial behavior that produces further depression and guilt and reinforces their belief that they are bad, ugly, or inferior. In one study (Daniels & Moos, 1990), depressed youths reported more acute stressors and less social support available to them than did healthy teenagers. Adolescent depression also has been linked to an increased likelihood of suicide threats and attempts.

Many of the symptoms of depression, such as moodiness, restlessness, boredom and impetuousness, are frequently observed in normal nondepressed adolescents. However, the depressed adolescent can be distinguished by three characteristics: (1) depressed teenagers act in such a way as to call attention to their problems—they "cry for help"; (2) their behavior is markedly different from their previous behavior; and (3) usually there has been a specific loss in their lives (Weiner, 1982).

Although depressive symptoms are slightly more prevalent among males during childhood (Rutter, 1986), they are more prevalent among females during adolescence (Nolen-Hoeksema, 1987). After age 13, girls experience a greater number of depressive episodes than boys (Brooks-Gunn, 1991; Nolen-Hoeksema, Girgus, & Seligman, 1991). One reason for this difference may be that, compared to boys, girls experience stressful life events more frequently during this period and respond more strongly to them with depressive symptoms. Data from a 4-year longitudinal study (Ge et al., 1994) that compared life events and depressive symptoms in boys and girls during early adolescence revealed that after age 13, girls reacted more strongly to stressful life events. Girls also were exposed to a greater number of stressful and uncontrollable life events. Examples of such events include the death of a pet, friend, sibling, or parent; serious financial difficulties in the family; marital difficulties between the parents; a parent's loss of a job; changing schools; and a sibling having a problem with the law. The researchers also found that adolescent girls who did not have warm and supportive mothers were more likely to respond to such life events with depressive symptoms.

adolescent depression
A devalued self-image in adolescence accompanied by behaviors such as boredom, restlessness, irritability, and eating and sleeping disturbances.

Research by Seligman and Peterson (1983) suggests that depressive feelings are quite stable in childhood and early adolescence, at least over a period of up to 6 months. Adolescents with diagnosed depression usually recover from the episode for which they were referred for help, but they frequently have related difficulties in their academic performance and social relationships (Kovacs, 1989). About two thirds of the teenagers with a history of depression will suffer additional bouts of depression while still in their teens (Kovacs & Gatsonis, 1989). We do not know, however, whether depressed children and adolescents will grow up to be depressed adults.

Psychotherapy seems to be the chief tool for treating depression in teenagers. Antidepressant drugs, which are often administered to depressed adults with good results, seem to be less effective with adolescents. The depressed teenager is usually eager to obtain help and frequently responds well to therapy. The problem lies in identifying the need for treatment. Often teachers and parents may mistake the depressed adolescent's behaviors as simply "growing pains."

FOCUS ON CULTURE

Living in poverty is stressful for families, especially those with children, and this stress has an impact on reported depressive symptoms in adolescents. One study (Lempers & Clark-Lempers, 1990) found that depressive symptoms, delinquency, and drug use increased for teenagers when their families experienced economic stress; during these stressful times less parental support was available to teenagers, especially girls. For many families economic stress and turmoil is a long-lasting event, especially if they live in political or social conditions that prevent their escape from poverty.

ADOLESCENT SUICIDE

Suicide in the United States is the second leading cause of death among teenagers (Brody, 1992); automobile accidents is the first. Experts consider the statistics on suicide to be underestimates of the actual number of adolescent suicides. Because of the embarrassment felt by family members, many adolescent suicides are listed as accidental deaths. Suicide attempts are also underreported. Although girls more often attempt suicide, boys are more often successful in completing the act (see Figure 10–3).

Many reasons have been offered to explain these statistics. Some claim that adolescence is typically a time of special anxiety and frustration that can trigger impulsive acts including suicide. While certain researchers (Powers, Hauser, & Kilner, 1989) suggest that emotional crisis and stress are not the norm in adolescence, strong competition for good grades, good jobs, and the "good life" may be exerting unreasonable pressure on young people in the United States.

Faced with strong family and cultural expectations to excel in sports, school, and the job market, some adolescents may feel cut off and detached from "normal" teenage life; driven by their desire to excel, they do not have time for leisure and stress-reducing activities (Husain & Vandiver, 1984). Suicide rates are highest in technological cultures such as Japan and the United States and lower in rural, less technological countries that stress religious values. In part, this may be due to a sense of alienation created in highly

FIGURE 10-3

Suicide rates for 15- to 19-year-olds by race and gender group. Source: From "Adolescent Suicide Prevention: Current Research and Social Policy Implications" by A. Garland and E. Zigler, 1993, *American Psychologist, 48,* pp. 170.

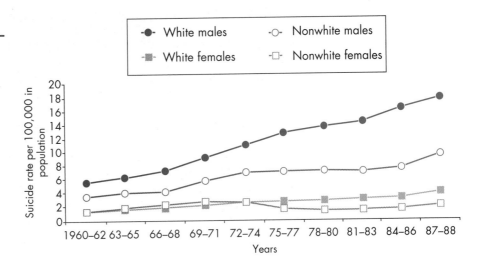

competitive and mobile technological cultures where materialism is valued over personal relationships. Overwhelmed by the competitiveness of their culture and by their sense of powerlessness, some adolescents may see suicide as the only way out of their dilemma.

Also implicated in suicide is the quality of family life. Divorce or the death of a parent, for example, makes adolescents feel insecure or abandoned. Even within intact families, adolescents who attempt suicide are described by family members as depressed and displaying behavior problems (King, Raskin, Gdowski, Butkus, & Opipari, 1990). Compared to other teenagers, teenagers who attempt suicide are also less likely to be living with their mothers and to have fewer and less supportive relationships with other people.

Excessive parental pressure to succeed can contribute to a distorted self-image and loss of esteem, even if the child "fails" in minor ways. Some studies, such as those of suicidal adolescents from multiple foster-home placements, indicate that continuity of care may be even more important than the quality of family life (Glaser, 1978).

Danger Signs of Adolescent Suicide Statistics on suicide are based on reports of people who succeed in killing themselves. At the point at which a suicide is detected, there is no longer any chance of prevention. The only means of prevention is to identify individuals who are likely to attempt suicide. Some people display signals before they attempt suicide. However, most high school students are poorly informed and sometimes misinformed about the warning signs of suicide in their peers (Norton, Durlak, & Richards, 1989).

Early warning signs of suicide among adolescents are presented in Table 10-4. If a teenager displays any of these behaviors, what can be done to intervene? Talking directly with the person about suicide is the first step. If a person is considering killing him- or herself, the question "Are you planning to kill or hurt yourself?" will bring the issue out into the open. An attentive listener who is supportive and nonjudgmental can help the adolescent consider alternatives to suicide. In situations in which a suicidal adolescent is under extreme emotional pressure, it is important that someone stay with him or her until the

DANGER SIGNS FOR ADOLESCENT SUICIDE

1. A preoccupation with death in music, drawing, or writing

2. Talking of suicide, or using threats such as "I wish I were dead" or "Life is not worth living"

3. Giving away prized possessions and attempting to put one's life in order

4. Experiencing recent losses such as the death of a family member or friend, parental divorce, or the end of a love relationship

5. Withdrawing from family and friends

6. Disturbance in eating, sleeping, and personal hygiene habits

7. Having a series of accidents or physical complaints

8. New or increased instances of alcohol and/or drug abuse

9. Truancy and poor school performance

10. Sudden changes in mood and behavior

11. A history of suicide attempts

TABLE 10–4

Suicide is the second most common cause of death among teenagers. Danger signs of impending suicide include long-standing depression, changes in sleep patterns, social withdrawal, and drug use.

immediate crisis is resolved. After the crisis has subsided, weekly or biweekly sessions with a therapist or physician may be needed.

EATING DISTURBANCES

A second problem area for teenagers that has serious psychological and fatal implications involves eating disorders. Being overweight or underweight may appear to be a strictly physical problem, but in adolescence these conditions may result from emotional disturbance or cause emotional problems. One study of adolescents categorized as "overweight," "underweight," or "average" in physique found evidence of a correlation between physical appearance and self-esteem (Hendry & Gillies, 1978). Self-concept and self-perception are partly shaped by **body concept,** which, in turn, is influenced by the reactions and expectations of others regarding different body builds.

body concept
One's perceptions and feelings about the physical aspects of oneself.

Physical appearance is an important contributor to self-worth throughout childhood and early adolescence (Harter, 1987). Early in life, children become aware of the body images that are valued in their culture and begin to judge their own physiques according to these standards. Both overweight and underweight children's self-concepts thus are vulnerable to injury or distortion. In adolescence the problem may be especially acute, since this is a time when the individual's identity is coming into focus. Adolescents are particularly self-conscious about their changing bodies.

The physiological factors that may lead to abnormal body weight include: (1) poor dietary habits and too little exercise; (2) a genetic predisposition (Holland, Hall, Murray, Russell, & Crisp, 1984); (3) an excessive number of fat cells acquired in early childhood, and (4) a hormonal imbalance. Obesity may result from any of these conditions, but it is frequently seen in people who have emotional problems as well (Stults, 1977).

The list of psychological factors that might be involved in obesity is almost endless, but one writer on the subject feels that there is a more basic underlying reason for eating disturbances. Bruch (1961, 1973) believes that the fundamental problem of seriously over- or underweight people is the inability to recognize one's own bodily needs—essentially, inability to differentiate hunger from satiety—and that this incapacity stems from a child's earliest eating experiences.

> If . . . a mother's reaction [to her child's hunger] is continuously inappropriate, be it neglectful, oversolicitous, inhibiting, or indiscriminately permissive, the outcome for the child will be a perplexing confusion. When [the child] is older he [or she] will not be able to discriminate between being hungry and being sated, or suffering from some other discomfort (Bruch, 1961).

anorexia nervosa
A psychological disorder, chiefly affecting adolescent girls, that is characterized by voluntary restriction of food intake and results in chronic undernutrition and, occasionally, death.

Included in Bruch's studies of eating disorders is a condition that primarily (but not exclusively) affects adolescent girls: **anorexia nervosa.** One of the few psychiatric disorders that can result in death, anorexia is characterized by voluntary restriction of food intake, resulting in chronic undernutrition and weight loss. Whereas most underweight adolescents may desire an average body and may feel self-conscious about their appearance, anorexics pursue thinness with a vengeance.

Health Perspective

THE BINGE-PURGE SYNDROME

In 1980 the American Psychiatric Association designated bulimia as a psychiatric disorder. The disorder is characterized by episodic, uncontrollable binge eating. A person diagnosed as bulimic hoards and eats very large quantities of food in short periods of time. Usually the food consumed is high in calories and can be easily ingested (e.g., ice cream, candy, cake, and cookies). One study estimated that bulimic individuals average 3,415 calories in a typical binge episode; a few bulimics reported bingeing on 5,000 calories ten times a day, for a daily total of 50,000 calories (Mitchell, Pyle, & Eckert, 1981). Sometimes the binge eating is followed by self-induced vomiting or by the use of laxatives or diuretics to purge the body of the binge food. Patients who resort to vomiting or laxative abuse run the risk of dehydration and other serious medical conditions, including death (Leon, 1991; Lucas, 1991; Russell, 1979).

Ninety percent of bulimics are female (Katzman, Wolchik, & Braver, 1984; Pope, Hudson, Yurgelun-Todd, & Hudson, 1984; Striegel-Moore, Silberstein & Rodin, 1986). One study of American high school students (Dasey, Nelson, & Aikman, 1990) reported that 6% of those surveyed were bulimic. Bulimic women are more likely to be college educated. Boarding schools and colleges, especially those in which dating is heavily emphasized, have a higher prevalence of bulimia than other settings (Squire, 1983; Rodin, Striegel-Moore, & Silberstein, 1986). Most bulimics are not extremely overweight; many are of normal weight or about 10 to 30 pounds overweight. Bulimics are aware of their abnormal eating behavior and are usually ashamed and depressed about their binge episodes.

The rise in reported cases of bulimia has been attributed to several factors, including cultural emphasis on thinness, physical fitness, and physical attractiveness (Striegel-Moore et al., 1986). A prolonged history of repeated dieting attempts may increase the risk of bulimia (Polivy & Herman, 1985). Denying oneself particular foods may encourage later binge eating of the forbidden food. Bulimia may also be influenced by genetic and hormonal factors. Early-maturing girls are at risk for chronic eating disorders (Graber, Brooks-Gunn, Paikoff, & Warren, 1994). Women who are heavier than their peers are also more likely to develop bulimia (Boskind-White & White, 1983; Fairburn & Cooper, 1983; Johnson, Stuckey, Lewis, & Schwartz, 1982; Timmerman, Wells, & Chen, 1990). Further, many bulimics have a genetic history of depression and other mood disorders within their family, suggesting that personality and genetic makeup may be contributing factors (Johnson & Maddi, 1986).

The treatment of bulimia depends upon whether the patient is underweight or normal-to-overweight. Underweight bulimics must be carefully monitored, usually in a hospital, to prevent dehydration. Normal or overweight bulimics are treated with psychotherapy combined with a nutritionally sound weight maintenance diet. Some bulimics respond well to antidepressant medication. The ultimate goal of treatment is to eliminate the binge and purge behaviors and to establish normal, healthy eating habits.

The cause of anorexia is not fully understood. It is generally viewed as a complex disorder influenced by the interaction of physiological changes, psychological stresses, and cultural expectations. Hormonal and physiological changes associated with puberty seem to be contributing factors. Anorexia is more commonly diagnosed in preadolescent and adolescent girls; early-maturing girls are at greater risk for eating problems in part because they are likely to be heavier than late-maturing girls (Brooks-Gunn, 1988; Graber, Brooks-Gunn, Paikoff, & Warren, 1994). Bruch (1977) associates anorexia with an almost delusionary body concept and an overdemanding family situation. The families are usually financially and socially successful, and the parents project an image of marital happiness. Yet this image often masks serious dissatisfaction between the couple, which the child feels she is expected to resolve or change.

Cultural factors have been suggested as a cause of eating disorders. Female gender roles are influenced by the ideal female portrayed in the media. Anorexia and **bulimia,** a disorder in which binge eating is followed by induced vomiting, are often a severe reaction to cultural pressures on females to be thin in order to considered attractive. In American culture, being overweight is a condition that invites negative sanctions and stigma, particularly for females. The ideal American female beauty is usually depicted as slender and relatively fat-free, a condition that is unrealistic to expect during adolescence, when female body weight and fat increase with sexual and physical maturity.

The typical anorexic may start out in prepuberty being slightly overweight. More commonly, she simply fears becoming "fat" and begins to reduce her food intake drastically and to exercise frantically. Anorexics deny all feelings of hunger, yet they are preoccupied with food. They may eat ravenously from time to time, only to remove the food by means of enemas, self-induced vomiting, or diuretics. Eventually the anorexic's psychological and physiological functions become distorted. They have great difficulty sleeping and may become hypersensitive to sound, light, temperature, and pain. Hyperactivity often masks a feeling of exhaustion, although anorexics deny such fatigue. They also deny that their emaciated appearance is abnormal. In fact, they usually continue to perceive themselves as overweight. These symptoms are often accompanied by increasing social isolation and a fierce preoccupation with school studies.

Although once considered a rare phenomenon, anorexia has become much more common in the past 20 years. According to Bruch, early diagnosis of anorexia and an integrated treatment program are very important. In chronic anorexia, hospitalization and the use of intravenous feeding may also be necessary.

CONDUCT DISORDERS

In recent years, the American public has been shocked by an apparent increase in the number of violent crimes conducted by teenagers and children. Psychologists refer to violent behaviors such as murder and fighting among gangs as **conduct disorders.** Conduct disorders are defined as those persistent behaviors that violate the basic rights of others and/or the norms of society. Typically, they involve much more serious crimes than those associated with **juvenile delinquency,** a term used to describe children and adolescents who engage in illegal acts. While most teenagers will admit to breaking some laws, these offenses often include minor offenses such as petty theft, shoplifting, vandalism, or possession of marijuana. In contrast, teenagers with conduct disorders are guilty of such violent crimes as homicide, rape, robbery, and assault. According to one source (U.S. Department of Justice, 1992) about 12% of violent crimes and 22% of theft and burglary are committed by adolescents. In the United States, 14% of murders,

bulimia
An eating disorder characterized by episodic, uncontrollable binges in eating, sometimes followed by self-induced vomiting.

conduct disorder
A form of psychopathology in which the individual persistently violates the basic rights of others and/or the norms of society.

juvenile delinquency
A term used to describe children and adolescents who engage in illegal acts.

15% of rapes, and 43% of automobile thefts were committed by people under the age of 18 (U.S. Bureau of the Census, 1992).

Who are these young people that so readily violate the norms of our society? What kinds of factors are associated with conduct disorders? And what is the relationship between adolescent conduct disorders and adult criminality? Conduct disorders occur more frequently among boys than girls (Robins, 1991). Adolescents who engage in misconduct did so during childhood, but their behaviors may not have been as antisocial (Dryfoos, 1990). For example, in childhood they may have failed in school, had poor peer relationships, and initiated sexual ctivity at an early age; in adolescence their misconduct might involve vandalism, drug use, and fights. During both periods of development, the individual appears to lack the ability to regulate or restrain his or her behavior (Feldman & Weinberger, 1994).

Some researchers (Dodge, 1990; Grych & Fincham, 1990; Kadzin, 1992; Patterson, DeBaryshe, & Ramsey, 1989) trace the origins of antisocial behavior to family stress, marital problems, inconsistent and poor parental discipline, and insensitivity to children's needs. A study by Patterson and Stouthamer-Loeber (1984) found that parents of delinquent boys were not very interested in or aware of their son's whereabouts and behavior, suggesting that parental indifference may be a factor contributing to their behavior. Some parents directly model antisocial behavior for their children, reinforcing deviant behavior as it occurs. In the process they are also failing to model self-restraint, an important characteristic often lacking in people with an antisocial personality.

Others researchers suggest that while the family plays some role in conduct disorders and delinquency, the causal link is far from clear or direct. It is not simply a case of malfunctioning families producing delinquent adolescents. Many of the crimes are drug related; either the offenders commit violent crimes to pay for drugs, or they lose their inhibitions while under the influence of drugs and alcohol

There is increasing concern about the number of teenagers involved in violence.

(McMurran, 1991). Violent acts, such as fighting or using a weapon, and serious violations of the law, such as burglary, may be influenced by poverty and external pressures, including high unemployment or a high crime rate (Johnstone, 1978). Exposure to graphic violence in the media has also been identified as a factor in increased violence (Synder, 1991).

What about the long-term stability of conduct disorders? Will today's young delinquents grow up to become tomorrow's hardened criminals? While most anti-social teenagers do not become antisocial adults, the origins of criminal adults' lifestyles can usually, but not always, be traced to antisocial attitudes and behavior in childhood and adolescence (Robins, 1978; Windle, 1991).

FOCUS ON CULTURE

Although boys commit nearly four times as many delinquent acts as girls (Robins, 1991), the rate of female delinquency in the United States has been increasing steadily, especially for crimes involving aggressive behavior such as theft, vandalism, and drug use. What changes in our culture during the past decade or so may account for the increase in arrests of females for delinquent acts?

SUBSTANCE ABUSE

Adolescence is viewed by many as a time of experimentation, exploration, and discovery. It is also the time when teenagers try one or several of the many licit (e.g., nicotine and alcohol) and illicit (e.g., marijuana, cocaine, and crack) drugs (Newcomb & Bentler, 1989). In the United States and other countries these drugs are readily available and often condoned or even glamorized in advertising. Probably no area in the teenager's life is of more concern to parents, and to a growing number of teenagers themselves, than the use and abuse of drugs. Widespread concern stems from findings indicating that long-term use of these drugs is associated with health problems (in some cases leading to death), academic failure, delinquency, psychological maladjustment, and rejection of societal values and standards (Sutker, 1982).

The most frequently used drugs among adolescents are alcohol, nicotine (in cigarettes), and marijuana (Johnston, Bachman, & O'Malley, 1994; Sutker, 1982). Most teenagers first experience alcohol, drugs, or tobacco in the middle school grades (Jackson & Hornbeck, 1989). In an annual study of over 15,000 high school students by Johnston, Bachman, and O'Malley (1994) it was found that almost all seniors reported some drinking, and more than 40% have tried marijuana or some other illegal drug. Experimentation with other drugs such as amphetamines, cocaine, and barbiturates, while not uncommon, was certainly less frequent than use of alcohol, cigarettes, or marijuana.

A distinction should be drawn between occasional use and experimentation with substances and abuse of those substances (Newcomb & Bentler, 1989). Substance abuse occurs when use results in negative reactions and adverse consequences to oneself or others, such as automobile accidents, peer rejection, or withdrawal. Use of drugs in inappropriate settings (such as using alcohol while driving or marijuana in school or at work) may also be defined as abuse. People vary in their tolerance for and ability to respond appropriately while using drugs; therefore abuse cannot be defined simply in terms of quantity or frequency of use.

Most professionals agree that the best way to deal with substance abuse is through education and drug prevention programs. Adolescents initially take drugs for a variety of reasons. The desire for peer acceptance is strong, particularly when teenagers have not acquired the social skills to say no to friends who offer them drugs. Teenagers are more likely to use drugs if they have low self-esteem, are exposed to an adult or relative who uses drugs, or whose families are in low socioeconomic circumstances or have high levels of emotional stress or disturbances (Newcomb & Bentler, 1989).

Alcohol   Alcohol is the most frequently used (and abused) drug among teenagers in the United States. Opinions are divided on the dangers or advantages of letting teenagers and children become acquainted with alcohol. Those in favor point out that few alcohol problems are found among Italians, Spaniards, Chinese, Lebanese, or orthodox Jews, who are traditionally exposed to wine or beer early in life as part of family meals and celebrations. For them, drinking is no proof of adulthood, and it is not regarded as either a virtue or a vice, or as the focus of any occasion. While abstinence is socially acceptable, excessive drinking or drunkenness is not.

For teenagers in this country, alcohol acquires numerous connotations beyond being a pleasant accompaniment to meals and conversation. It often becomes a symbol of independence, adulthood, virility, or defiance; and if these have to be demonstrated to oneself or others, they provide incentives for an immoderate use of alcohol. This may lead first to drunkenness and ultimately to alcoholism.

In the United States, 92% of high school seniors reported having had some experience with alcohol and 66% reported using it within the past month. Five percent said they were daily drinkers and 37.5% reported at least one heavy

A serious consequence of teenage alcohol use is drunk driving. Many students have formed volunteer groups such as Students Against Drunk Driving (SADD) to help reduce the number of teenage auto accidents.

drinking binge (five or more drinks in a row) (Newcomb & Bentler, 1989). Consistent use and abuse of alcohol creates numerous problems for the young drinker, not the least of which is an addiction to alcohol. When adolescents become dependent on alcohol, they develop academic problems and tend to abuse other drugs as well (Burkett, 1980; Chase, Jessor, & Donovan, 1980).

A major concern related to alcohol use is driving under the influence. The number of people killed by drunk drivers has caused many states to raise both the legal drinking age and the age at which one can obtain a driver's license. Adolescents are being encouraged to decline a ride from someone who has been drinking. Many high school students have formed volunteer groups to provide a safe ride home from a party to any teenager who does not want to accept a ride from a person who has been drinking.

For teenagers who seek help with their drinking problems, group therapy and individual counseling are available. Programs that involve the teenager's family are more likely to prove successful. Alcoholics Anonymous (AA) helps people of all ages, including an increasing percentage of teenagers. Many high schools include classes on drug and alcohol awareness in their curricula.

Nicotine   Not too long ago, the Marlboro Man was an American symbol of virility and strength. However, after actively campaigning about the dangers that cigarette smoking and nicotine impose on people's health and lives, one of the men who was a model for this advertisement died from lung cancer. Yet, despite the demonstrated medical evidence linking nicotine with cancer and lung and heart diseases, about one in every five high school seniors are daily smokers (Newcomb & Bentler, 1989). Many of these adolescents began smoking prior to the 10th grade, and some begin as young as 9 years of age.

Adolescents are more likely to become smokers if one or both of their parents are smokers. If their friends also smoke, they are likely to smoke with them, even though they are aware of the health hazards. With continued use, nicotine is addictive. Thus, the teenager who starts smoking to be a part of a group may find it very difficult to stop when peer acceptance is no longer an issue.

Adolescents are more likely to begin smoking if one or both of their parents are smokers and if their friends also smoke.

Nicotine is likely to be the first drug that young people try and the one with the most lasting effects on their health. Numerous education programs exist to help smokers quit the habit and to prevent teenagers from starting to smoke. Additional efforts focus on reducing the settings in which smoking is permitted. For example, many high schools have banned smoking throughout their campuses. Posters and television commercials with testimonials from popular athletes and pop stars remind teens and preteens to "be smart and cool" and not smoke.

Marijuana   Almost 40% of the young adults in the United States have experimented with marijuana at one time in their lives (Johnston, O'Malley, & Bachman, 1994). Marijuana use creates a feeling of relaxation and heightened sensitivity to sensations. While the intoxication lasts, it impairs certain functions, especially the processing of new information and its transfer from short-term to long-term memory. It also diminishes the ability to make judgments and respond to new situations. People who drive under the influence of marijuana are a menace to themselves as well as others because they take too long to respond to unexpected events; the greater the demands of the situation, the less they are able to cope. Additional dangers are that the impairment may last for several hours after the "high" has passed, and that simultaneous consumption of alcohol multiplies the impairment, rather than merely adding to it. Because marijuana is smoked, prolonged use increases the risk of lung cancer.

Another drawback of marijuana is its effect on learning. It has been amply proven that materials and concepts studied in an undrugged state are significantly better understood (Clark, Hughes, & Nakashima, 1970; Klonoff, Low, & Marcus, 1973) and remembered than those studied while "high" (Tinklenberg & Darley, 1975). There is also some concern that the development of social and intellectual pursuits may be impeded by frequent use of marijuana, since it gives teenagers the option of artificial relaxation as an alternative to learning how to deal with difficulties and frustrations.

Despite concerns that marijuana use is the first step along the path to hard drug use, the majority of those who try marijuana do not become abusers of other drugs. A 14-year longitudinal study (Shedler & Block, 1990) distinguished between adolescents who were frequent users of marijuana and those who either abstained or experimented with the drug. Adolescents who were frequent users of marijuana (once a week or more) had a history of maladjustment and personality problems that preceded their drug use. Adolescents who had experimented with marijuana (used it once or a few times) were the best adjusted psychologically. Abstainers who had never tried marijuana or any other drug were more anxious and lacking in social skills when compared to the other adolescents in the study. The researchers concluded that marijuana abuse is a symptom, not a cause, of personal and social maladjustment.

THE OVERALL TERRAIN OF ADOLESCENCE

After reading about the variety of behavior problems associated with adolescence, you may mistakenly conclude that they represent the norm rather than the exception. The majority of adolescents do not end up in trouble, nor are they likely to engage in misconduct. On the contrary, if you attend a high school graduation or watch a school athletic competition or concert you will get a more representative view of the overall terrain of adolescence. Just as any reputable tour guide might point out areas of a city or region that may be dangerous to uninformed travelers, I have pointed to the possible dangers of adolescence so that you will be prepared to respond to or help adolescents avoid these problems.

BRIEF REVIEW

While earlier theorists believed that adolescence was by nature a time of "storm and stress," research studies have not supported this view. There are notable stresses that adolescents are exposed to during this transitional period, but not all teenagers respond maladaptively. Research does not support the belief that adolescents have stronger perceptions of invulnerability than adults. Adolescent self-esteem is influenced by their abilities to cope with the physical and psychological changes and expectations placed on them.

According to Erikson, during adolescence the individual must establish an integrated identity or remain troubled by self-diffusion. An important aspect of identity for adolescents is awareness of ethnic or racial origins.

Although many adolescents experience emotional upheaval over identity and parent and peer relations, others pass through this period with considerably less stress and strain. Adopted adolescents may have more difficulty establishing their identity if they are uncertain about their birth history.

Even though adolescents and their parents experience conflicts, the majority of teenagers get along with their parents. The conflicts that do occur concern choice in hair and dress styles, independence, and sexuality. Parents who are overly controlling are more likely to have conflicts with their adolescents.

In order to establish their own identity, people must become independent of their family. They must find other ways to meet their material and emotional needs, make their own decisions about how to behave, and must form their own values.

The peer group is an important agent of socialization during adolescence, one that often conflicts with the standards and values of the family. Intimate friendships begin to emerge in adolescence and become a vehicle through which the individual copes with the stresses associated with this period.

Popularity is related to many factors in adolescence, but particularly to physical attractiveness and personality. The pursuit of popularity often leads adolescents to conform to group pressures. Some degree of conformity with peers is normal, and indeed unavoidable, because some guidance is necessary during the period in which personal values are formed.

Because most young people have such a wide variety of vocational choices, a career decision is often difficult, although guidance counseling and publications on various vocations can be a great help. Gender stereotyping imposes vocational limitations on women and deprives them of much of the encouragement that is received by men.

Adolescents who work gain useful social and work skills. However, youth employment may have negative consequences for some adolescents, depending on the type of job and support they receive from school and family.

Adolescents are prone to many of the same social and psychological problems as adults, including suicide, depression, eating disorders, conduct disorders, and substance abuse. The three most frequently abused drugs among teenagers are alcohol, nicotine, and marijuana.

KEY TERMS

adolescent depression (401)
anorexia nervosa (405)
autonomy (387)
body concept (405)
bulimia (407)
clique (392)

conduct disorder (407)
conformity (396)
crowd (392)
ego continuity (382)
ego identity (379)
ethnic or racial identity (381)

genealogical bewilderment (383)
mutual role taking (392)
juvenile delinquency (407)
self-diffusion (379)

REVIEW QUESTIONS

If you can answer these questions, you have a good understanding of the material in this chapter. If a question seems difficult, go back to the text and review the topic.

1. Describe the three major components of ego identity. What happens if a person does not form an identity?

2. What role do parents play in helping adolescents establish their ethnic and/or racial identities?

3. Discuss the impact of being adopted on the development of ego continuity.

4. Is adolescence a time of turmoil? Support your answer.

5. What factors contribute to parent-adolescent conflict? Is conflict inevitable during this period?

6. What is meant by autonomy during adolescence?

7. Discuss the difference between a clique and a crowd. Describe the stages of adolescent peer group development.

8. What makes an adolescent popular with peers? Do adolescents conform to peer influence? Explain.

9. Describe the developmental process involved in making a career choice.

10. What are the benefits to the adolescent of being employed while in school? What are some possible disadvantages?

11. Describe the symptoms associated with adolescent depression.

12. Describe the danger signs of adolescent suicide. What can be done to prevent teen suicide?

13. What factors influence the development of eating disorders?

14. What factors contribute to the development of conduct disorders?

15. What factors account for the use and abuse of substances such as alcohol, nicotine, and marijuana during adolescence?

OBSERVATIONAL ACTIVITY

ADOLESCENT FRIENDSHIPS

Peer relations and friendships are an important part of an adolescent's life. Teenagers prefer to spend more of their time away from family and in the company of their peers. Intimate friendships begin to emerge in early adolescence and become part of a teenager's identity. Girls and boys have different conceptions of friendship and are likely to behave differently with their friends.

The purpose of this activity is for you to gain a better understanding of adolescent friendships. You will need to locate four male and four female teenagers and interview them about their ideas of friendship. It would be best to interview the teenagers individually. Use the following questions to structure your interviews.

1. How would you define a friend? What characteristics do you look for in a friend?

2. Think about three of your own friends and describe the characteristics you like in them.

3. What do you like to do with your friends? What activities do you engage in with your friends?

4. Why is it important to have friends? What role or functions do friends play in your life?

5. Are you more likely to interact with your friends individually or in groups? How many friends are you usually with at one time?

6. How does having a friend or friends influence the way you see yourself?

After completing your interviews, compare the responses of the girls and boys. Notice the differences in their conceptions of friendship. How are they similar? Summarize the teenagers' views on friendship and compare them with those reported in the text. How do the teenagers' views compare with your own views? What did you gain from doing this activity?

The Decision Years

It is usually not until early adulthood that people begin to make and act on decisions about who they are and the type of life they want to live. Adulthood marks the beginning of a different kind of journey than the one experienced in childhood and adolescence. While the rate of development is comparatively slower, the terrain of adulthood is punctuated by diverse experiences and demands that have been created by the life choices people have made. Each decade of adulthood represents a milestone in life's journey; adults celebrate their passage by assessing their successes and shortcomings. To better understand the changes and challenges of adulthood, developmentalists subdivide this portion of the lifespan into three phases, each approximately 20 years in length: early, middle, and late adulthood.

In the following chapters, topics change to reflect a shift in emphasis toward the importance of social, family, and occupational development in adulthood. In earlier phases of the lifespan it made sense to group topics by presenting information about physical and cognitive changes in one chapter and social and personality development in another. However, at this point in our journey, it is useful to employ a different organization. Personality is influenced by physical and cognitive changes. Chapter 11 will explore the physical, cognitive, and personality influences on development. At the same time that adults become accustomed to the changes in body and mind, they are also making deliberate and mutually influential choices about how they spend their time—and with whom they spend it. People establish relationships with others who serve as their traveling companions in life. Changes in the social, family, and work aspects of their lives require a focused presentation. Thus, Chapter 12 concentrates on family and occupational development.

CHAPTER 11

Youth and Early Adulthood: Physical, Cognitive, and Personality Development

By the time Aura was 18 years old she was married to Carlos. Both of them had grown up in Guatemala City; their families had known each other for years. Carlos was a student at the university, and Aura followed in her mother's footsteps by raising three children and creating a home for her family. For many years, Aura derived much satisfaction as a mother and wife. But as she approached 30 she began to question her future goals. The political climate in Guatemala had changed for the worse. Soldiers with guns were becoming too common a sight in the city. People were uncertain about their future under the increasingly militant government. Out of fear and frustration, some of her friends had immigrated to the United States and other countries. When her husband raised the possibility of leaving, Aura was willing. By the time she was 34, she was ready to redefine her view of herself and the life she wanted to live.

By most people's standards Peter was an eligible bachelor. He was 32, popular, physically fit, good-looking, and single. But Peter was not interested in marriage. Just the previous spring, he and Jeannie had broken off their steady relationship when they realized that each had different life goals. Jeannie wanted to get married and talked of the challenge of maintaining her career and becoming a mother. Peter, however, didn't think he was established enough in his career to make a commitment to a wife and children. How could he take on that responsibility, he wondered, when he was still focused on what he wanted to do with his life? The fact that Peter also occasionally questioned whether he really was an adult yet only reinforced the idea that he was not ready for a serious commitment to someone else. By settling into a career path and developing his career identity, Peter hoped to become more secure about himself—to feel more responsible and adultlike. Intuitively, he knew this decision not to pursue a long-term love relationship also meant that he was considering whether he wanted to live his life as a bachelor rather than as a married man.

CHANGE DURING ADULTHOOD

The detailed study of adulthood is a relatively new addition to the field of developmental psychology. Until recently, most researchers focused on the earlier stages of life, particularly childhood. Those who studied early adult development tended to view all of adulthood, from age 18 to the end of life, as one large period. Despite the fact that there is an obvious difference in experiences and capabilities among 20-, 40-, 60-, and 80-year-old people, very little distinction was made among these age periods.

Today, however, as a result of an increase in research in adult development, the adult portion of the lifespan is typically subdivided into three periods: early adulthood (from 18 to 40 years), middle adulthood (from 40 to 65 years), and late adulthood (from 65 years onward). As was true for earlier portions of the lifespan, changes occur in these periods in a variety of areas: physical, cognitive, social, and personality. In addition, new areas of growth assume significance during adulthood: career and vocational changes, family relations, and the significance of life and death.

The challenge for me in preserving the chronological journey of a "guidebook" that captures important events and characteristics is made more difficult by the multidimensional quality of the changes in adulthood. For example, changes in personality can influence adults' view of themselves, the quality of their relationships, and their ability to solve life's problems. Change can mean decline or improvement or both, depending on the specific aspect we are considering. For example, as you will see, some cognitive skills increase while others decline across adulthood. Moreover, there are significant differences in our knowledge about various aspects of adult development. Much more is known about information processing in late adulthood than in middle adulthood; more studies are focused on sexual intimacy during early adulthood than in late adulthood. My solution to the problem of providing an accurate and representative discussion of adulthood development is to highlight certain aspects of change as they occur in one specific period, and to remind you that such changes also occur during the other stages. As we enter each new area of adult development, I will provide a quick overview of the changes that occur across the entire span of adulthood.

INFLUENCES ON ADULT DEVELOPMENT

For many years now, I have thought of myself as an adult. When I remember my childhood and even my adolescent years, it is difficult to reconcile the two images I have of myself. There seems to be a gap; my childhood seems separate and different from my current life.

This perception is a common one for adults. There appears to be little continuity between adults' experiences today and their experiences as children. This gap is due partly to the selective way in which we recall our personal histories. But it is also a product of the changing influences that affect development across the lifespan. In adulthood, historic events such as changing economies or war, and specific events in an individual's life such as a traumatic accident or unexpected winnings, are likely to have a greater influence on development compared to events that normally occur as a result of maturation.

For example, depending on when you were born, you would have experienced differing economic and social times, which would have influenced your life

Nonnormative events such as the bombing of the Oklahoma City federal building can have a greater influence on people's lives than age-normative events.

FOCUS ON CULTURE

During the Persian Gulf War in 1991, American women soldiers were sent to Saudi Arabia. Dressed in army fatigues and boots, these young women presented a sharp cultural contrast to typical Arab women, who wore long veils to cover their faces and bodies and severely restricted their contact with men other than their husbands and male relatives. The political event of war called attention to the lifestyles of women in different cultures. Western newswomen who lived in the Middle East were able to interview Arab women about their perspectives on war and their roles as women. While many American women viewed the Arab women's role as restrictive, the Arab women did not. Many had grown up with the expectation that they should be protected from the attention of men other than their husbands.

War and other history normative events can have a profound influence on the lives of adults.

choices. People who were born in the United States in 1912 experienced an economic depression when they were in their 20s, wars in their 30s and 50s, and peace and prosperity in their 40s. A complete study of changes in their development across the lifespan must include these critical events. People who were born in 1936 experienced very different social-historical events when they entered adulthood. We would expect to find differences between the 1912 and 1936 cohorts as a result of the times and events they experienced.

WHAT IS AN ADULT?

How do you know that you are an adult? By your age? In the United States, a person is considered to be a legal adult at age 18. However, parents of some 18-year-olds may not agree with this classification. In U.S. society, adulthood is defined in terms of social roles and behavior rather than age or physical maturation. Thus, being an adult means no longer being a child, teenager, or student; it means being a worker, spouse, or parent.

In the United States, leaving one's family home is considered part of the transition to adulthood. People leave home because they marry, relocate through their work, or seek to establish their independence from parents (Goldscheider & Goldscheider, 1994). People vary considerably in the timing of these events—in other words, they attain adult status at different times. Some 20-year-olds, for example, are students; others, like Aura, are already parents. Some are worrying about exams and forming relationships, while others are budgeting their incomes and raising their children. Some men and women enter the job market immediately after graduating from high school; others, such as developmental psychologists, do not undertake full-time employment until the age of 27 or 28.

PERCEIVED AGE

perceived age
How old a person feels.

Perceived age, or how old a person feels, is another influence on adult development. Clearly, our perceptions of ourselves reflect many different aspects of our

In many cultures, marriage is an event that signifies the emergence of the couple into adulthood.

lives—chronological age, physical maturity, assumed roles, psychological adjustment, and so on. Some people, like Aura, may feel and act like adults at age 17 or 18. Others, such as Peter, may still be struggling with conflicts between their unfulfilled needs and desires from childhood and their emerging adult personalities in their mid- to late 20s. As people grow older, their subjective experience of age may change. Younger adults are more likely to feel older while older adults are likely to report feeling younger than their chronological age (Barnes-Farrell & Piotrowski, 1989; Montepare & Lachman, 1989).

Peter's confusion about his adult status was a by-product of his unwillingness to make a commitment. In many cultures, early adulthood is the time when people usually form serious personal commitments, marry, start families, and assume a job or make meaningful use of their time. During this period people define their relationship to society through love, work, and play. Adults in American culture are often defined as people who are in charge of their own lives; they earn their own keep. They make the decisions, both important and petty, about their own lives independent of other people's dictates, and they accept the responsibility for and the consequences of these decisions. How long this takes to accomplish varies—for many people the break between adolescence and adulthood is not a moment in time but a long and gradual process.

It is important to keep in mind that the meaning and timing of adulthood is culturally defined. In many nontechnological cultures, middle to late adolescence is the time when people marry, have children, and become productive contributors to their communities. In some cultures, marriages are arranged at birth and the choice of an occupation is dictated by family needs rather than individual interests. In U.S. culture, independence is an important defining characteristic of adulthood. In other cultures, obedience to the family supersedes individual interests (Simic, 1990).

YOUTH: AN OPTIONAL PERIOD

You may have no trouble perceiving Aura as an "adult." At age 18, she was a married woman with a child and a job, and had already undertaken some of the tasks and responsibilities of adulthood. What about Peter? Is he the so-called "eternal

FOCUS ON CULTURE

How old you feel also depends on how long you expect to live. If you live in an industrialized country, where life expectancy is in the 70s, you may still consider yourself to be young at age 35 or 40. In many nontechnological countries— Ethiopia, Afghanistan, or Nepal, for example— life expectancy is below 45 years (Seager & Olson, 1986); if you lived in one of these countries you might perceive yourself as old at age 35.

adolescent," who is in a state of indecision well into his 20s or 30s? How do we classify the 25-year-old student who is dependent on the support of his parents and the evaluation of his professors? What about the 30-year-old community activist who has chosen to explore and challenge the political system? Clearly, as we have noted, individuals assume adult roles on very different schedules.

The concept of **youth** has been introduced to deal with the post-adolescent period of life that sometimes precedes adulthood (Keniston, 1970). This concept is unique to Western technological societies. It refers to an optional period of development that stretches from the point at which the person is legally an adult (generally at 18) to the point at which he or she actually undertakes adult work and family roles. For example, one may legally be an adult—old enough to vote, drive, drink, and join the armed forces—yet not feel "grown up" until some 5 to 10 years later when one is able to support oneself and a family.

From a historical standpoint, youth, like adolescence, is a rather new period of life. Unlike adolescence, however, which can be defined both biologically and socially, the period of youth is exclusively a social phenomenon that has emerged in response to several cultural factors (Kimmel, 1980). For example, the rate of technological change and increasing societal complexity require extended preparation by young adults before they can become effective workers or professionals. Never before has postgraduate study been so acceptable, or seemed so necessary. And never before has it seemed so difficult for the nonspecialist to find entry into the workforce. The result for many young people is a period of *moratorium,* corresponding to the apprentice, college and graduate school years, though often including travel, self-study, job hopping, "dropping out," and other forms of exploratory behavior.

The period of youth is also related to the wider range of available options in lifestyles and social roles. At no other time in American history have people had such a diversity of choices regarding how they live their lives. However, socioeconomic levels affect the extent to which a young person is able to make these choices. For many, youth may be a luxury they cannot afford. Their sense of well-being may be derived more from settling into adulthood than from exploring their personal boundaries or discovering their capabilities.

Youths may reject such conventional ideas as "settling down" or following the routes to adulthood taken by the previous generations. For example, a woman may realize that she has no wish to follow in her mother's footsteps as "someone's wife"; instead she may choose to remain single and pursue a career in marketing. A man may decide, after self-analysis, that the 9-to-5 work routine he has been taught to respect is not for him—that the life of a carpenter in Vermont makes more sense. Often adults become suddenly aware that they do not want to follow the paths set by their parents.

youth
An "optional" period of development in which an individual is legally an adult but has not yet assumed adult work and roles.

Youth is a period of time when people can explore their life choices; sometimes this might mean taking a long trip or just "dropping out" for a while.

There is also, for most young adults, a new need to forge intimate relationships outside the family, and perhaps outside traditional forms—such as by joining a religious community or sect. Many feel a need to make commitments to moral, political, or religious ideologies on the basis of their own experiences rather than their parents' choices. For example, a youth may join a different church or political party than the one to which the rest of the family belongs.

Because the concept of youth is a relatively new and optional period within the lifespan, it has not been fully integrated into our understanding of early adulthood. Furthermore, the period of youth is not found in all societies. This is particularly the case in cultures that distinguish between childhood and adulthood with rites of passage and clearly defined adult roles and responsibilities. It is enough to say that during the uncharted period between adolescence and middle adulthood, certain psychosocial developments occur. As these developments are described, we refer to a period of "early adulthood" with the understanding that for some people, it is appropriate to identify a more tentative, exploratory period of "youth."

RECAP

The age and tasks that define adulthood vary by culture and time. Despite a slowing down in the rate of physical change, people continue to grow throughout the adult years in many dimensions. Perceived age influences a person's behavior and development. Youth is the developmental period between adolescence and adulthood that is influenced by culture, opportunity, and history. Tasks of youth concentrate on establishing oneself as a responsible and independent person who can establish intimate relationships.

IDENTITY

At age 18, Aura knew what was important to her—she was a mother and wife. But several years later she was questioning who she really was and what she wanted to make of her life. Youth and young adults often find themselves searching for meaning in their lives. During adolescence they tackled the basic issue of identity and some may have achieved a self-definition, even if only temporary. As young adults, they are often preoccupied with the expansion of self into society. By establishing new friendships, joining volunteer groups and social clubs, and finding new ways of defining themselves through their interests and activities, they seek to broaden their definition of who they are.

In youth and early adulthood, individuals begin to stabilize their identity. Especially if they are attending college, young people are likely to find themselves changing the identity they forged in adolescence (Waterman, Geary, & Waterman,

College students have many opportunities to question their identities and role in society. The self image that emerges during the college years can last a lifetime.

1974). As a result of challenges during the freshman year, the student may re-examine many values and self-images. A new form of identity crisis will probably occur. Whereas the adolescent asks, "Who am I?" the young adult tends to ask, "Where am I going—and with whom?" Youth or early adulthood is the period in which a person tackles the question of how to find a place in society. The person begins to establish a personal lifestyle, and to make commitments, more often than not in the belief that decisions are irreversible (Sheehy, 1976)—which, of course, they are not.

IDENTITY STATUSES IN EARLY ADULTHOOD

You will recall from Chapter 10 that Erikson (1968) identified the adolescent years as the time when people focus on establishing their identities. However, Marcia (1966, 1980) has suggested that the resolution of the identity crisis in youth and young adulthood is more complex than the description offered by Erikson. Marcia has identified two factors as critical to the resolution of identity in this period: (1) the existence of a personal crisis in such areas as occupation, religion, or politics, and (2) the person's degree of commitment to issues in these areas. Marcia defines a crisis as a time when a person is confronted with several meaningful alternatives in life and must choose one. Combining these two factors, crisis and commitment, Marcia identified four possible resolution patterns of the identity crisis that he termed **identity status** (see Table 11–1).

Identity achievers are individuals who have made personal decisions or commitments in response to experienced crises in some areas of their lives (e.g., occupational, religious, or political). Their choices may or may not agree with their parents' desires and viewpoints. Rather, their commitment is based on a true decision-making process regardless of parental wishes. A young woman who decides to pursue a career as an environmental biologist as a result of her long involvement with a wildlife organization would be an example of an identity achiever. Compared with the other identity statuses, identity achievers tend to be more flexible and display high levels of moral reasoning (Marcia, 1991).

In contrast, individuals characterized by **identity foreclosure** make lifestyle and value decisions without experiencing a crisis or making a personal commitment. These individuals give in to parental desires and points of view out of emotional or financial pressure, fear of disapproval, or feelings of inadequacy and incompetence. Consider the young man who enters the family business because it is "expected of him." Marcia believes that although such individuals may appear to have strong ideological and career commitments, they actually lack a strong ego

identity status

According to Marcia, the specific resolution patterns the person adopts to resolve identity issues of crisis and commitment.

identity achievers

According to Marcia, individuals who have confronted various crises in life and who have made firm commitments to values, ideals, life patterns, and so on.

identity foreclosure

According to Marcia, an identity status characterized by avoidance of personal crisis; these individuals identify instead with the values and ideals of parents and other significant figures.

MARCIA'S ADULT IDENTITY STATUS		
	CRISIS	**NO CRISIS**
Commitment	Identity achievers	Foreclosure
No commitment	Moratorium	Identity diffuse

TABLE 11–1

This young man has made a conscious and deliberate decision to enter the field of digital electronics and is learning the skills he needs to reach his goal. He can be described as an identity achiever.

moratorium

According to Marcia, an identity status characterized by heightened personal crisis but no firm commitment with regard to specific values, ideals, life pattern, and so on.

identity diffuse

According to Marcia, a type of individual who has avoided personal crisis in areas of identity and who shows no firm commitment to specific values, ideals, and so on.

identity because they have avoided personal confrontation and crisis in these areas. They tend to be more inflexible and rigid than people in other identity statuses (Marcia, 1991).

Unlike identity achievers and foreclosers, individuals who are categorized as being in **moratorium** or as identity diffuse show no evidence of commitment. On the contrary, they are indecisive about life decisions and values. Individuals in moratorium are, however, at the height of crisis about these issues. They are struggling to achieve a degree of consistency about who they are and where they are going. Peter, the young man in our opening example, may be described as being in moratorium, since he is still struggling with the question of who he is and where he is going with his life. Individuals in the moratorium status are often more anxious and have ambivalent feelings toward their parents (Marcia, 1991).

Identity diffuse individuals appear less concerned or preoccupied with these issues; not only are they uncommitted to specific lifestyles or values, but they also show no evidence of personal crisis regarding these matters. For example, the young man who takes the first job that he sees because it is convenient rather than exploring possible career paths or other jobs may be categorized as identity diffuse. Individuals who remain at this status are likely to have other problems in adjustment; some may be angry and hostile, others are alienated and rebellious (Archer & Waterman, 1990; Frank, Pirsch, & Wright, 1990; Marcia, 1991).

DEVELOPMENTAL ASPECTS OF ADULT IDENTITY

One problem with categorizing people into any classification system—including Marcia's ego-identity statuses—is that it tends to foster a rigid, unchanging view of people. Of course, this is not the nature of human beings, nor is it the way in which Marcia intended the construct of ego identity to be interpreted.

Waterman (1982) has presented a model that describes the pattern of ego-identity development. His model suggests that individuals begin in a confused state of diffusion. Over time, they can either remain in a diffuse state or move forward in one of two directions. One possibility is to latch on to an identity suggested by parents or other significant figures without really considering other courses of action—in other words, a foreclosure pattern. Aura, at age 18, for example, never really questioned her family's expectation that she would marry and raise children as her occupation, without considering other career choices. A second possibility is to begin to consider a number of alternative life paths and to enter a state of moratorium while exploring further goals.

People who adopt a foreclosure pattern can either maintain this identity status as they move into adulthood, or change in one of two ways. Should their earlier commitments suddenly become challenged by life events, and consequently lead them to consider alternative values and lifestyles, these individuals would then move into a state of moratorium. Thus, provoked by political and economic changes in their country, Aura and Carlos began to consider other options regarding where and how they and their children could live. On the other hand, should the challenge to previous commitments not lead to an active consideration of alternative life paths, the individual would regress to a diffuse state of identity. In this state, people remain indecisive about what they want to do with their lives.

Having reached the level of moratorium—where one is clearly in crisis over life commitments—two patterns of identity adjustment are possible. The more beneficial pattern involves the transition from a state of moratorium to a state of identity achievement, in which specific identity commitments are based on personal evaluation of many available options. Aura, for example, may decide after much consideration to leave Guatemala for the United States. The second, less desirable, transition from the moratorium level involves a regression to a state of diffusion resulting from an inability to form a meaningful commitment.

Finally, Waterman (1982) suggests that having reached the state of identity achievement, the individual can still take any of several paths. As long as the person's commitments remain satisfying and firm, it is likely that a pattern of identity achievement will be maintained. However, should the person's values and lifestyle be challenged by life events, it is likely that he or she will regress to either a state of moratorium, where alternative courses of action are reconsidered, or, in rarer cases, to a state of diffusion, where no life alternatives seem worthwhile. For instance, a woman who has achieved an identity as a mother may revert to a level of moratorium when her children go off to school or leave home; many aerospace engineers found themselves questioning the value of their career choice when politics and a declining economy curtailed space programs.

One study has highlighted the way in which environmental conditions can foster the development of identity in young adults. Adams and Fitch (1983) examined the influence of the psychological climate on the identity development of college students within eight different university academic departments: business administration, engineering, elementary education, art, psychology, family and child development, forestry, and outdoor recreation. Students rated the degree to which the department's atmosphere (including its organization, curricula, and philosophy) emphasized such issues or characteristics as practicality, community or group welfare, awareness of societal concerns, propriety or conventional standards, and scholarship. Measures of ego identity and ego functioning were also collected.

The researchers found, among other things, that the general atmosphere of the university department can play an important role in fostering ego identity. Departments emphasizing awareness of societal issues were significantly more likely to facilitate development of ego identity than were departments characterized by other qualities. In commenting on this result, Adams and Fitch note that a focus on societal issues tends to broaden one's perspective and foster exploration of one's thoughts and ideas. In other words, it creates conflict and thus challenges the individual's conceptions of self—exactly the type of situation Marcia suggests is the basis of identity development. Instructors who encourage students to debate the impact and value of efforts to protect environmental resources, for example, may also provoke their students to examine their own views on the issue. Examining one's beliefs is an important component of identity development.

It is clear that as people enter adulthood they show considerable variation in identity development: Some remain diffuse; others move into a foreclosure or moratorium pattern; still others move forward to achieve a firm and personally created sense of self. In turn, these individual differences in identity are reflected in differences in personality and adjustment. Adult identity must be thought of as a lifelong process—an ever-changing aspect of the human being that responds to and reflects the unique experience of the individual's life.

> ### RECAP
>
> The process of establishing an identity begins in adolescence but is not complete until adulthood. Marcia has described four identity statuses: achievement, foreclosure, moratorium, and diffusion. During early adulthood, the pattern of identity development may vary, depending on whether environmental conditions encourage the individual to explore and carefully commit to an identity.

PHYSICAL DEVELOPMENT

By the time people reach early adulthood—their 20s and early 30s—they are physiologically at the peak of their life. Not all physical systems (e.g. muscular, skeletal, hormonal) peak at the same time; each system has its own unique pattern and rate of development. Early adulthood is characterized by both maturation and decline. Yet, when we consider the body as a whole, it is clear that this period is one of optimal biological functioning.

During early adulthood most people reach their full height, women at approximately age 17 or 18 and men somewhat later, usually age 21 (Roche, 1979; Roche & Davila, 1972). Maximum weight, in contrast, generally is not achieved until middle adulthood (Kent, 1976). Peak physical strength usually follows the attainment of mature stature but is not achieved until the mid- to late 20s. The capacity for vigorous activity requiring not only strength but speed, coordination, and endurance also is greatest during this period. Most Olympic and professional athletes, for example, fall in this age group. One study found that all of those competing in short-distance running, jumping, or hurdling—sports that demand high agility and speed—were between 18 and 30 (Tanner, 1964). The age at which athletes reach their peak in skill varies according to the sport (Fries & Crapo, 1981).

Most, but not all, athletes reach their prime in a sport during early adulthood. Can you think of some sports in which middle-aged adults normally perform better?

Gymnasts reach their peak in adolescence, while golfers do better in later adulthood. Thereafter, physical strength declines gradually—by approximately 10% between the ages of 30 and 60 (Troll, 1975).

A number of sensory and neural functions also attain optimal levels during young adulthood. Visual acuity and hearing are sharpest around age 20, the former remaining relatively constant into the middle adult years and the latter showing a very gradual decline over the same period. In addition, full brain weight and mature brain-wave patterns are achieved during early adulthood.

Young adults are the healthiest individuals in our society. In fact, they are much more likely to die from violent causes—accidents, suicide, or homicide—than from diseases. Still, some of the health problems of later life are discernible in this age group. These early manifestations of disease processes, which researchers have labeled "silent disease," include rheumatic fever, atherosclerosis, emphysema, lung cancer, cirrhosis of the liver, kidney disease, and arthritis. People under stress are more likely to engage in poor health practices such as drinking, smoking, or eating poorly (Cohen & Williamson, 1988; Conway, Vickers, Ward, & Rahe, 1981). These poor health practices may lead to greater susceptibility to diseases and disorders (see Cohen & Williamson, 1991, for review). Disorders included in this category are hypertension, drug and alcohol abuse, mental depression, ulcers, and obesity.

Perhaps because people are at their fittest during this period, they are less likely to practice preventive health habits such as proper nutrition, rest, and regular physical examinations. It is usually not until middle adulthood that people start to think about themselves in terms of health issues (Hooker & Kaus, 1994). Yet it is during early adulthood that people can more easily change health habits that can affect their lives later on. Stopping smoking, establishing a personal exercise program, and regulating weight are habits that can contribute significantly to good health in middle and late adulthood.

Young adults are particularly vulnerable to the spread of the AIDS virus, especially if they are sexually active with more than one partner. The AIDS epidemic has widespread implications for young adults as they select dating and marriage partners. Without knowledge of a partner's sexual history, a person may become exposed to the AIDS virus and unknowingly pass it on to others. Although most early cases of AIDS in the United States were reported by men who had anal sex with other men, there is growing concern that the virus is spreading to heterosexuals. The number of new AIDS cases resulting from heterosexual contact is increasing about 1½ times faster than the number of new cases in all other high-risk groups (Health Information Network, 1987). Precautions against contracting AIDS include using a condom and restricting sexual activity to one partner. Intravenous drug users are warned against using syringes that are not sterile.

Optimal biological functioning has important implications for the personal, social, and occupational adjustment of young adults. Indeed, in occupations that rely on physical and sensory abilities, early adulthood is considered the prime of life. A construction worker or foot soldier, for example, may be said to be in his or her occupational prime at 20 or 25, and past it at 40. For some individuals there is no drop in measurable performance with advancing age, however. Musicians such as Arthur Rubinstein and Pablo Casals and artists such as Pablo Picasso and Georgia O'Keeffe were still at the height of their powers in their mid-80s with little diminution even as they approached their 90s.

Personal Perspective

PREMENSTRUAL SYNDROME

Every month approximately 30 to 40% of the adult female population reports physical and psychological symptoms just prior to the onset of their menses (Rose & Abplanalp, 1983). Physical symptoms include breast tenderness and swelling, abdominal bloating, retention of water, backaches, and headaches. Psychological symptoms include depression, irritability, anxiety, and hostility. In addition, changes in energy level, eating and sleeping habits, and interpersonal activity are also commonly reported. Taken together, these symptoms have come to be known as **premenstrual syndrome (PMS).**

Recognition of an association between behavior and mood changes, tension, and the onset of menstruation is not new. As

long ago as 1931, Frank described the abrupt physical and psychological changes occurring just prior to menstruation as a clinical disorder. However, because of the prevailing societal attitudes regarding menstruation, both among physicians and the general public, little attention was given to the problem at that time.

Today, attitudes have changed. Abplanalp (1983) notes that detailed descriptions and discussions of premenstrual distress and other "female problems" have been widely reported in newspapers and magazines across the country. Premenstrual syndrome has become an important health issue for women, who increasingly are going public with their problems and demanding treatment.

What causes PMS? Most researchers have focused on the relationship between hormone fluctuation and physical and psychological symptoms. Carroll and Steiner (1978), for example, proposed that PMS resulted either from high prolactin and low estrogen levels

(producing premenstrual depression) or from high prolactin and low progesterone levels (producing premenstrual anxiety and irritability). In contrast, Dalton (1964, 1977) is a forceful proponent of the theory that women who suffer from PMS have a deficiency of progesterone relative to estrogen during the premenstrual days. Unfortunately, as Rose and Abplanalp (1983) point out, there is no firm, consistent evidence linking a specific hormonal abnormality to premenstrual distress. Nevertheless, the search goes on.

A number of studies have questioned the concept of a negative premenstrual syndrome caused entirely by physical factors. Ruble at Princeton University conducted a study of premenstrual symptoms in which the subjects in the experiment were duped into thinking that they were either premenstrual or intermenstrual—halfway in their cycle from the onset of menstruation—when, in fact, they were all about 6 days from the time of their monthly

premenstrual syndrome (PMS)
Physical and psychological symptoms that include breast tenderness, abdominal swelling, water retention, irritability, anxiety, and depression.

For women, reproductive capacity is also at its peak during young adulthood. Biologically speaking, the best age for a woman to become pregnant for the first time is in her 20s. This is because the organs and physiological systems involved in reproduction are better developed and coordinated during young adulthood than either earlier or later in life. Additionally, adolescent pregnancies are more difficult when proper prenatal care is not obtained. During young adulthood, women are more likely to produce fertilizable eggs; their hormone cycle related to reproduction is more regular; and their uterine and pelvic environment is more conducive to sustaining a pregnancy and facilitating a safe delivery. Though many women comfortably bear children during their teenage years or into their early period (1977). Ruble hypothesized that the women who thought they were premenstrual would be more likely to experience premenstrual symptoms than those who thought they were not premenstrual.

In the first phase of the experiment, the women were hooked up to a large oscilloscope (a machine that translates bodily electrical activity into a visible wave form on a screen) that, they were told, would be able to determine their places in their menstrual cycle. On a random basis they were then told they were premenstrual or intermenstrual; the control group was told nothing. They were then administered a menstrual distress questionnaire. The "premenstrual" group scored significantly higher than the "intermenstrual" group in three of the four predicted symptoms: water retention, pain, and change in eating habits. An unanticipated finding was that the "premenstrual" group scored higher on sexual arousal.

Commenting on these findings, Ruble (1977) said that "the results did not suggest that women never experience pain or water retention, nor that such symptoms never accompany the premenstrual phase." Rather, the findings seemed to indicate that women, because of cultural attitudes, associate such symptoms with the premenstrual phase so that they tend to look for such symptoms when they are premenstrual as well as to think they are premenstrual if they experience these symptoms.

There may also be a conditioned bias in women's recollection of their moods during the premenstrual portion of their cycle. In one study (McFarlane, Martin, & Williams, 1988), three groups of subjects (men, women whose menstrual cycles were altered by oral contraceptives, and women with normal menstrual cycles) were asked to record their moods on a daily basis for 70 days. Later, the women were asked to recall their average mood during each day of the week and phase of their menstrual cycle. Using daily mood records as a measure of emotional stability, normally cycled women reported more pleasant moods during their menstrual cycle than did the other subjects. However, when recollected reports of moods were used, women recalled more unpleasant moods during the premenstrual phase of their cycle than they had actually recorded at the time.

Most women develop coping routines if they experience monthly pain or negative feelings, such as keeping busy or making time for a little extra sleep to combat fatigue. Usually these strategies are successful. Regular exercise and increasing exercise during the premenstrual period seems to help relieve some of the symptoms. Cutting down on caffeine, carbohydrates, and salt also has lessened some PMS symptoms. Only a very small percentage of women—perhaps as little as 5% (Rose & Abplanalp, 1983)—appear to develop symptoms so severe that they require professional help. More research is needed to identify the causes and treatment of premenstrual syndrome.

FOCUS ON CULTURE

Cultures vary in the degree to which their members are physically healthy. Bond (1991) examined the relationship between cultural values and the overall physical health of the population. Countries with social norms supporting tolerance of and harmony with others, trustworthiness, and noncompetitiveness reported higher levels of cancer, circulatory diseases, and ulcers. In contrast, countries that valued the establishment of small in-groups such as family over more egalitarian acceptance of others were found to be healthier. Countries that valued material gain over self-restraint and self-sacrifice reported higher levels of coronary heart disease.

and mid-40s, their fertility is not as high; delivery is sometimes more difficult; and there is a greater incidence of defects in their infants than in infants born to mothers in their 20s.

Except in rare cases of disease, disfigurement, or abnormal growth, physical development is usually taken for granted by young adults. It is in middle adulthood that observable signs of aging begin to generate concern, and physical skills begin to be measured against past performance. In other words, the optimal physical characteristics of early adulthood tend to be noticed only in retrospect, during the middle and elderly years of life.

RECAP

Most people are at their peak of physiological functioning and health during early adulthood. But this is also the time adults acquire habits that may enhance or interfere with later health and fitness. Vulnerability to AIDS is high in this age period. Biologically, the best time to bear children is during early adulthood, when fertility is high and the hormonal environment is stable.

COGNITIVE DEVELOPMENT: HOW ADULTS THINK

Peter made a point of taking care of his body; he worked out at the gym regularly. But of equal importance to him was his intellectual development. He wanted to learn new skills that he could apply in his career; he wanted to challenge his own abilities. Like physical skills, certain intellectual abilities appear to peak during the early adult years. Research indicates that tasks requiring quick response time, short-term memory, and the ability to perceive complex relations are performed most efficiently during the late teens and early 20s (Craik & Rabinowitz, 1984; Gillund & Perlmutter, 1988). Certain creative skills, particularly those involving the development of unique or original ideas or products, also reach their highest level during young adulthood (Lehman, 1953; Simonton, 1988). Most other abilities, however, continue to develop beyond this age period. Intellectual skills related to verbal ability and social knowledge, for example, show increases well into the 50s and possibly later (Horn & Donaldson, 1980). These are skills that improve with education and experience across the lifespan.

LIFESPAN CHANGES IN COGNITION

The first 18 to 20 years of life are spent in preparation for the journey through adulthood. Children establish deliberate strategies for organizing information, solving problems, and learning. They acquire a language, expand their capacity for memory, and learn to think rationally and logically. During adolescence, the ability to think abstractly emerges. During adulthood, cognitive development continues, though not at the dramatic rate that was observed during childhood and adolescence. All along their journey adults continue to acquire new information and develop more efficient ways of organizing it; they refine and establish their own style of thinking; they become more knowledgeable and wiser. Changes in thinking, information processing, and knowledge occur in all stages of adulthood but are more noticeable in some portions of adulthood than in others. In this chapter I will highlight some of the changes that emerge in the way adults think. In Chapter 13 you will learn more about the changes that occur in information processing; Chapter 15 will focus on the different types of knowledge acquired during adulthood. Even though I have chosen to highlight selected aspects of cognition at different stages of adulthood, keep in mind that all three components—thinking, processing, and a base of knowledge—contribute to a person's ability to know and adapt to the world.

COLLEGE AND THINKING SKILLS

Some people enter college directly from high school with the expectation that they will learn new skills and be intellectually stimulated. More and more "older" students are returning to college to acquire new skills and to experience the pleasure (and challenge) of learning. Does a college education provoke changes in adult cognitive growth? This was the focus of a classic study conducted by Perry (1970, 1981). Based on intensive interviews of Harvard University and Radcliffe College students over their college careers, Perry was able to identify some patterns of cognitive change.

Perry's subjects were students who entered college from high school. He found that when these students begin attending college, they see the world in dualistic, polar terms. They assume that every question has a "right" answer that is known by some authority, often the teacher or the text. Over time, through discussion, debate, and instruction, college students move from this simplistic view of truth to one in which several competing points of view can be seen as valid. Students discover that there is a diversity of opinion; truth is no longer viewed as absolute and singular, but rather as multiple and infinite. Over the course of their college career, students come to view knowledge as relative to one's values and culture. Students emerge from college with a willingness to commit themselves to life values that become part of their identities.

It would be interesting to repeat Perry's study of cognitive changes in college using a nontraditional, older group of students. Would their patterns of thinking change in the same way that those of the younger group of students did? Probably not, since many older students may already be thinking more globally when they enter or return to college. Unlike 18-year-old freshmen, many nontraditional students have already incorporated their life values into their sense of self and are using college as a vehicle for reaching their goals.

PIAGET'S THEORY

You will recall that in earlier segments of the lifespan, we used Piaget's theory to provide a way of describing some of the changes that occurred in cognition. Originally, Piaget's scheme of cognitive development ended in adolescence with the period of formal operations (characterized by hypothetical reasoning and abstract thought). Piaget stated that this stage was reached between ages 12 and 15, which is true for many people. However, in later writings Piaget (1972) suggested that the period of formal operations may not develop or become consolidated until late adolescence or young adulthood (ages 15 to 20) and that it may be expressed more narrowly than was first supposed. For example, a young adult may demonstrate hypothetical reasoning in one particular field of specialization, but not in other fields. Thus, a financial analyst may show highly developed reasoning as she isolates the causes of poorly performing subsidiaries, yet may be unable to apply the same logical skills in figuring out an equitable vacation schedule for the workers in her office.

Empirical research has documented that not everyone can use formal thought to generalize from one field to another. DeLisi and Staudt (1980) found that college students could express formal operational principles much more easily within their own major than in other areas. For example, physics students were quite successful on a task dealing with the isolation of variables determining the frequency of oscillation of a pendulum. In contrast, they had considerable difficulty applying formal operations in tasks involving political socialization and literary styles. Political science majors, on the other hand, were most successful on the political socialization task and relatively unsuccessful on the other two tasks, while English majors were successful in applying formal operations only on the literary styles task.

What are some of the factors that determine the variability in development and expression of formal operational thought? Undoubtedly, cultural factors such as technology play a crucial role. Societies with advanced computer technologies are more in need of individuals who are capable of high-level abstract thought. Consequently, such societies are likely to provide avenues for the development and eventual expression of this type of cognition. One such avenue is higher education. Research indicates a positive relationship between number of years of schooling and understanding of formal operational principles (Papalia, 1972). Another factor related to formal thought is intelligence. As one might expect, people who are more intelligent are more likely to develop and use formal operations.

Cultures with more advanced technologies are more likely to encourage the development of formal operational thought. However, even nontechnological cultures provide avenues for abstract thought and problem solving. Knowledge of navigation by the skies and sun enables this Tahitian to kayak about the islands with ease.

It has been widely argued that not all adults, perhaps no more than half, think at the level of formal operations (Arlin, 1975). Adults who are said not to function at this level tend to fall into certain groups, such as the aged (Papalia, 1972), especially in non-Western societies (Dasen, 1972), and in some studies, women (Elkind, 1961, 1962; Leskow & Smock, 1970). Other researchers, however, have suggested that certain response tendencies, and the characteristics of the tests themselves, do not allow everyone to display their competence equally (Brodzinsky, 1985; Neimark, 1981; Overton & Newman, 1982). For example, if a person is uninterested in the task, or is highly anxious about being evaluated, or if the skills needed to perform the task are "rusty" from disuse, performance is likely to be poorer than if the person is motivated, shows only moderate evaluation apprehension, and is well-practiced in the skills necessary to perform the task.

cognitive style
A person's habitual approach to problem solving.

In addition, both Brodzinsky and Neimark have argued that **cognitive style,** a person's habitual approach to problem solving, affects performance on Piagetian-type tasks, including those measuring formal operations. For example, people who are reflective—that is, those who are cautious, systematic, and use planning in their approach to solving problems—do well on such tasks. So, too, do field-independent people, who are better able to distinguish relevant from irrelevant information in problem-solving contexts. However, people who are impulsive in responding to problem situations, and those who are field dependent—that is, those who have difficulty recognizing and isolating relevant information—do relatively poorly on these tasks.

BEYOND FORMAL OPERATIONS

Formal operational thinkers engage in logical, systematic, hypothetical deductions to figure out the best solution to a problem. But some researchers (Basseches, 1984; Labouvie-Vief, 1980; Riegel, 1984) criticize Piaget's description of adult thinkers as leaving little room to explain or describe other adult ways of thinking. For example, adults often can accept inconsistencies and generate unlikely solutions to problems because of their experience with practical problems—such as resolving conflicts in interpersonal relationships—that are not always logically solved. Another limitation of Piaget's theory is that it doesn't account for changes in thinking as a result of the specific environment or situation. In Piaget's theory, changes in thought are seen as changes in the person's cognitive structures. However, a lifespan approach sees cognitive growth as occurring in many different areas and caused by multiple factors—a process that occurs in an ever-changing environment (Labouvie-Vief & Chandler, 1978). Viewed from a lifespan-contextual perspective, there is no fixed end point to cognitive growth. If the environment or context is sufficiently stimulating, change is possible throughout life (Rebok, 1987). To adequately describe cognitive development in adulthood, a stage beyond formal operational thought is needed.

problem finding
According to Arlin, the ability of the person to generate new and relevant questions about the world; linked to postformal levels of reasoning.

Problem Finding   Arlin (1975, 1977, 1984), has identified a fifth stage of cognitive development, termed **problem finding,** in which the individual is able to generate new and relevant questions about the world. In problem finding, a person poses new problems rather than just attending to old ones. A problem finder might also discover new ways of looking at old problems in order to make new solutions possible. For example, instead of looking at trash as something that has to be removed, a problem finder might focus on how trash could be put to good use or consider how to prevent trash from accumulating. Arlin believes that problem finding might be the process that links Piagetian cognitive structures to creativity. Arlin's data suggest that formal operations is a necessary, but not sufficient, condition for problem finding. However, others have questioned the validity of this fifth stage on both empirical and logical grounds (Commons & Richards, 1978; Fakouri, 1976).

Dialectical Thought

dialectical process
According to Riegel, a characteristic of mature thought in which the individual recognizes, accepts, and even seeks out intellectual conflict or challenge.

A second suggestion for an additional form of adult thought comes from the work of Riegel (1973b, 1975). According to Riegel, adult thought is characterized by a **dialectical process**—that is, a recognition and acceptance of, even a desire for, conflict or contradiction. Riegel criticizes the notion that formal operational thought—the highest stage in Piaget's theory—is the most mature form of thinking. He is especially critical of the view that mature thought seeks equilibrium—a tensionless state where "everything fits together." According to Riegel, mature thought seeks not balance or lack of tension, but intellectual crisis. The mature mind needs constant stimulation. It welcomes the apparent contradiction that accompanies two or more opposing viewpoints, for this fosters the growth of intellect. Dialectical thinkers seek to discover what is missing from existing ways of ordering and making sense of the world; they wish to create new orderings that include ideas and observations that did not fit in earlier versions (Basseches, 1984).

Riegel notes that dialectical thinking can occur in any one of Piaget's stages, although the content of the dialectical process is much less complex at lower stages. The young child, for example, at first attributes absolute qualities to characteristics such as *big, small, heavy,* and *light.* A person is either big or small, heavy or light. Later on, however, children become aware of a conflict with respect to these qualities. An older sister is big when compared to oneself, but at the same time she is small when compared to Mom. How can a person be both big and small? The young child resolves this apparent contradiction by recognizing that certain characteristics have a relative quality—that is, they can be understood only in a particular context, or in relation to something else. This resolution not only solves the immediate problem for the child—understanding how someone can be both big and small at the same time—but also provides the child with the cognitive ingredients necessary to view the world in a broader, more sophisticated sense.

According to Riegel, youths and young adults, like young children, engage the world through a dialectical process, although at a much higher level. The contradictions that are confronted are more often on the level of abstract ideas. Mature adults struggle with conflict in their lives in such areas as morality, ethics, politics, religion, and the meaning of life. Yet they do not necessarily need to resolve the contradictions they confront. According to Riegel (1973b), in maturity "the individual accepts these contradictions as a basic property of thought and creativity." Dialectical thought in adults increases with age (Kramer, 1986).

A Contextual Model of Adult Cognition

Adults spend a fair amount of their time and effort in solving practical problems; by assuming such roles as worker, parent, and supervisor, adults assume the responsibility of making real-life decisions and choices. Without the benefit of deliberate instruction, adults solve life's problems by combining what they have learned with what they know about the circumstances and settings in which the problems occur. Schaie (1994) points out that adults differ from children and adolescents in the goals to which they prefer to apply their cognitive skills. While children and adolescents spend their time learning what they need to learn in order to succeed in school, adults prefer to direct their intellectual skills to solving practical problems, ones that are relevant to their life goals. Thus, the context in which problems arise becomes more important to the adult thinker. Consider the following story used in a study by G. Cohen (1979):

> Downstairs, there are three rooms: the kitchen, the dining room, and the sitting room. The sitting room is in the front of the house, and the kitchen and dining room face onto the vegetable garden at the back of the house. The noise of the traffic is very disturbing in the front rooms. Mother is in the kitchen cooking and Grandfather is reading the paper in the sitting room. The children are at school and won't be home till tea time. (p. 416)

Who was being disturbed by the noise? If you said "Grandfather" you would be responding the way the college students in Cohen's study did. However, when Labouvie-Vief (1985) asked older adults the same question, many of them interpreted the story differently depending on the context they were using. For example, some thought that Grandfather was deaf and therefore was not disturbed by the traffic noise; otherwise he would have left the sitting room. The level of cognitive maturity present in the older adults' reasoning is more complex. Labouvie-Vief (1982) believes that adult thought that includes a consideration of the context and the practical real-life implications of an event is more sophisticated than formal operational thought. Being an adult involves making logical choices and decisions on the basis of the responsibilities and commitments made to oneself and to one's family. What may appear to be a logical choice for one person may not be logical for another person in a different context. Perhaps you have faced the dilemma of responding to a multiple-choice item in which the "correct" answer would depend on the specific situation you imagine. In this case, context has become an important part of your thinking.

Characteristics of Mature Adult Thought   Although there is no consensus among developmental theorists on the existence and nature of a qualitatively distinct postformal stage of cognitive development, an increasing number of research studies have documented changes in adult thinking that are not easily explained using Piaget's theory (Commons, Richards, & Armon, 1982; Kramer, 1986). In reviewing the literature on adult thought, Kramer (1983) has identified three characteristics.

First, adult thinking is *relativistic*. Unlike adolescents, who tend to think of the world in absolutist ways, adults are more likely to accept the existence of mutually incompatible systems of knowledge. This results, in part, from the adult's expanding social world, which includes many differing, and potentially incompatible, viewpoints and roles.

A second feature of adult thought is the realization that *contradiction* is an inherent aspect of reality. No longer is there a need for necessarily resolving cognitive conflicts or contradictions. On the contrary, as Riegel (1973b) notes, the mature thinker not only accepts contradiction in reality, but actually is drawn to

WOMEN'S WAYS OF KNOWING

Much of what we know about adult cognitive development has been learned from studies of college students, most of whom have been men. Today there is growing support among psychologists and social scientists for more research on how men and women differ in their understanding of and response to their world. Data collected on men are no longer considered sufficient to use as a guide to understanding female development.

Belenky, Clinchy, Goldberger, and Tarule (1986) conducted intensive interviews of 135 women from rural and urban American communities with the aim of establishing a model of female development based on women's experiences in adulthood. They were interested in learning about how women saw themselves and how this self-concept affected the way they viewed reality. Belenky and her colleagues used an interview/case study approach to gather data on the women, who represented a diverse population—from college students in private and public institutions to women enrolled in parent education classes offered through family agencies.

The researchers asked the women a variety of questions developed from those used by Perry (1970) in his interviews with college students. The questions were aimed at learning about the women's backgrounds and their views of themselves, their gender, their relationships with others, and their educational experiences. They also sought to determine the women's views of morality and their ways of knowing about the world. Regarding their ways of knowing, Belenky and her colleagues asked the women questions such as: "In learning about something you really want to know, can you rely on experts? How do you know someone is an expert? What do you do when experts disagree? How do you know what is right/true?"

The women's responses were tape recorded and intensively analyzed. Based on their responses, the women were grouped into one of five categories that reflected their ways of knowing. Women grouped in the "silence" category experienced themselves as mindless, voiceless, and controlled by external authority figures. Women grouped in the "received knowledge" category conceived of themselves as capable of receiving and reproducing knowledge from all-knowing external authorities, but not capable of creating knowledge on their own. Women in the "subjective knowledge" category saw knowledge and truth as a personal, intuitive, and private experience. They listened to their "inner voice" and distrusted logic, analysis, or abstractions. Women in the "procedural knowledge" category were invested in the learning experience and applied objective procedures to obtain and communicate truth and knowledge. Women in this category actually spoke in a different voice, using a more deliberate, systematic, and measured approached to knowledge. Finally, women grouped in the "constructed knowledge" category viewed all knowledge as contextual, saw themselves as creators of knowledge, and valued their subjective and objective strategies for knowing.

The work of Belenky and her colleagues calls attention to the need to learn more about the ways women differ from men in their cognitive development. Knowledge of gender differences will enable educators to refine their approaches to their students in order to cultivate growth.

it. Kramer (1986) presented young, middle-aged, and older adults with a series of formal operational tasks and two lifelike dilemmas to solve. She found that older adults (60- to 75-year-olds) were more accepting of contradictions and the relativistic assumptions in the problems than were the young (17- to 25-year-olds) or middle-aged (40- to 55-year-olds).

The final characteristic of adult thought, according to Kramer, is the tendency to *integrate,* or synthesize, contradictory knowledge into an overriding and more inclusive whole—what Commons, Richards, and Kuhn (1982) have called *metasystems.* Kramer (1986) maintains that the ability to make sense out of contradictions requires that people function at the level of formal operational thought, but that this type of thought alone is not sufficient. Thus, whereas the adolescent is restricted to the development of a single abstract system of thought organized around formal operational principles, the mature adult thinker begins to view knowledge as the integration and coordination of multiple, potentially incompatible systems of beliefs. For the mature thinker, therefore, the existence of vastly different conceptions of religion, which are often contradictory in their description and explanation of spiritual and earthly matters, is no longer so perplexing as it once was. Instead of looking for the single, correct answer to questions, whether in religion or other areas, the adult thinker recognizes that knowledge is always a synthesis or integration of different points of view. Each experience, looked at from a different angle or from a different perspective, yields new information and new insights. Thus, knowledge is ever changing.

MORAL DEVELOPMENT

I became a parent during my late 20s; by the time I was 30 I was raising two children. Raising my children made me keenly aware of the importance of clarifying

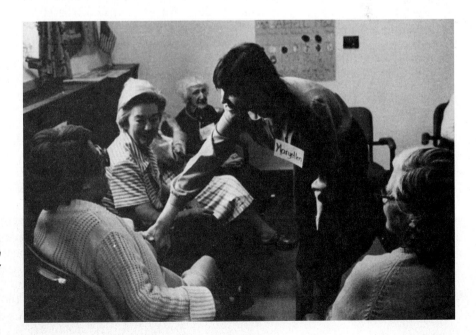

By volunteering in an adult health center, this young woman is likely to be more concerned about the welfare of others. Experiences such as these can affect a person's moral development.

my moral values. I thought about what I wanted to teach my children about right and wrong; in other words, I was concerned about their moral development.

Moral development, or the development of a personal value system, is closely related to cognitive development. It appears that a certain logical ability is necessary in order to reason at a given moral level. For example, Kohlberg (1984, 1973) has argued that one must reach the formal operational level of cognition before engaging in conventional or postconventional moral reasoning.

However, the higher levels of moral development seem to require more than just the achievement of a particular level of cognitive reasoning. They require certain kinds of personal experiences as well. For example, leaving home and entering a college environment typically exposes one to conflicting values, emotional choices, and new perceptions of self. Many college students react with skeptical relativism, arguing that what is right is merely relative and depends on the person, his or her needs and circumstances, and so on. This position reflects the student's new awareness of diversity in values and people. As students consolidate their identity, however, they achieve a higher level of moral judgment. They may proceed to the social contract orientation of Kohlberg's Stage 5 and, in rare cases, to the universal ethical principles orientation of Kohlberg's Stage 6.

The discussion of the two stages of the postconventional level in Chapter 9 notes that only about 28% of all moral judgments made by 16-year-olds were postconventional. Subsequent research suggests that the college experience is critical to these stages of moral development. For example, in one study none of the subjects who went directly to the adult occupations, bypassing the stage we called "youth," showed evidence of Kohlberg's highest moral stage (Kohlberg & Kramer, 1969).

Other studies, however, suggest that the critical factor is adult life experiences rather than educational attainment. Such experiences enable people who have not been to college to "catch up" to their more educated peers (Papalia & Bielby, 1974). A study by Lonkey, Kaus, and Roodin (1984) found that adults who reasoned at the Stage 6 postconventional level of morality were better able than adults who reasoned at the conventional level to deal constructively with significant losses in their lives, such as the death of a family member or the end of a relationship. Thus life experiences can provide a training ground for moral development and can also be better understood and accepted as a result of a higher level of moral reasoning. Kohlberg believes that the experience of sustained responsibility for the welfare of others is critical to higher levels of moral reasoning.

Criticisms of Kohlberg's Theory   Kohlberg's theory has come under attack (Murphy & Gilligan, 1980). Most researchers accept the first two levels, but according to Murphy and Gilligan, too many people show retrogression to an earlier stage rather than movement to a higher one. This lack of fit between the predictions of Kohlberg's theory and actual research results prompted Murphy and Gilligan to call for a revision of the adult aspects of the theory.

Kohlberg (1984) and others believe that achievement of formal operations is a sufficient cognitive foundation for the development of postconventional morality. Murphy and Gilligan (1980), however, argue that a more advanced, postformal level of reasoning underlies postconventional moral thought. The shift from adolescence to young adulthood, according to these authors, is accompanied by a shift in the way in which formal thought is applied to moral issues.

As noted earlier, adolescents use formal logic in an absolutist way when dealing with moral and ethical issues. Adults, because of their greater experience with moral conflict and choice, are more inclined to appreciate the "gray" areas of life—that is, to recognize and accept multiple perspectives in considering moral situations. Thus, according to Murphy and Gilligan, the absolutism of adolescent logic gives way to a more relativistic approach to moral dilemmas during young adulthood. For example, when asked whether his moral beliefs had changed since he entered college, one person in Murphy and Gilligan's study answered that as a result of trying to practice his beliefs he had become

> more considerate, taking into account other people's feelings and other people's lives and how you as a person affect their lives. And seeing whether your effect is a good effect or a bad effect. And before, I didn't really care about that too much. My first responsibility was mainly to myself, and the other just went along. (Murphy & Gilligan, 1980, p. 99)

Another criticism of Kohlberg's research, discussed in Chapter 7, is the description of women in research studies as functioning at a lower level of moral reasoning according to Kohlberg's scoring system. Gilligan again (1982) contests Kohlberg's theory, this time regarding gender bias in assessing moral reasoning. She argues that Kohlberg's theory is focused on concepts of justice and not on concepts of caring. According to Gilligan, men and women use different perspectives in defining morality. Women more often than men resolve moral dilemmas by seeking a solution that deals with the social relationships of the people involved. Men, on the other hand, are more likely to seek a "just" solution. For example, in the Heinz drug-stealing dilemma (introduced in Chapter 7), high-scoring women are more likely to emphasize Heinz's responsibility for his wife's care (Stage 4 reasoning) whereas high-scoring men are likely to emphasize the value of human life over money (Stage 6 reasoning). The problem is not so much with Kohlberg's theory as with the dilemmas that are presented to assess moral reasoning. When women are presented with a dilemma that pits justice against caring, they more often focus on caring. When other dilemmas are used that are centered on justice alone, they reason on the basis of justice.

Although controversy continues to surround the nature and origin of Kohlberg's advanced moral stages, it is generally agreed that while postconventional morality may begin to develop during late adolescence, it is not until adulthood—when people have finally attained the freedom to make their own life choices and have begun to assume responsibility for others—that this higher form

FOCUS ON CULTURE

Kohlberg's claim that moral reasoning develops through the same stages in all cultures has been the subject of debate and research (Boyes & Walker, 1988; Snarey, 1985). While acknowledging that the cognitive criteria Kohlberg used to define each stage of moral reasoning hold true across cultures, critics express concern that the measures used do not accurately capture significant moral concepts in every culture. In particular, they believe that there is a bias in Kohlberg's theory in favor of the moral concepts prevailing in urban middle-class populations in complex societies (Snarey, 1985).

of moral thought is established. According to Kohlberg (1973), while people may become aware of moral principles during adolescence, it is not until adulthood that a commitment to their ethical use develops. It is then that people make serious commitments—to themselves, to others, to ideas, and to ideologies. It should be noted that in response to his critics and based on his longitudinal research, Kohlberg (1984) later questioned the existence of Stage 6, in which universal ethical principles guide an individual's behavior and moral reasoning. Kohlberg's ideas for his theory were derived from interviews conducted with men whom he later identified as an "elite" sample, trained in moral leadership. When he sought to find empirical support for the existence of Stage 6 among other samples, he was unable to identify people at this level of moral reasoning. Despite this failure, however, Kohlberg continued to propose Stage 6 as the ideal goal of moral development.

RECAP

Cognitive development continues in adulthood with the emergence of more complex ways of thinking and processing information and a broader range of knowledge. Thinking skills become more complex and relativistic over the course of a college education. Not all adults achieve the level of formal operational thought, but some function at a higher level— engaging in relativistic thinking, seeking out contradiction, and being able to integrate complex and divergent pieces of information. Adult life experiences contribute to a higher level of moral thought. Gilligan and others have criticized Kohlberg's theory because it does not describe all types of moral development, especially for women.

PERSONALITY AND ADJUSTMENT

For the most part, personality researchers have focused more of their attention on studying specific personality traits and behaviors than on studying how personality changes over the adult portion of the lifespan. Most of the subjects used in personality research are young adult college students who receive course credit for participating in studies. There has been relatively little longitudinal research on personality over the adult years. However, adults continue to change and mature throughout the lifespan. The nature of these changes varies, depending on the individual's experiences, life events, and personality. For example, people who are more extraverted (that is, assertive, positive, and outgoing) are more likely to be satisfied with their lives regardless of life events or age (Costa & McCrae, 1984).

Recently, however, more researchers have assumed a lifespan perspective and are beginning to study personality in adulthood. Several questions about adult personality development have emerged: Are there predictable changes in adult development over the lifespan? Is there a set order for these life changes? How important are life events in the development of adult personality? In this section we will review some of the findings of research on these questions.

Era of late adulthood: 60–?

Era of middle
adulthood: 40–65

Late adult transition:
Age 60–65

Culminating life structure
for middle adulthood: 55–60

Age 50 transition: 50–55

Entry life structure for
middle adulthood: 45–50

Era of early
adulthood: 17–45

Mid-life transition:
Age 40–45

Culminating life structure
for early adulthood: 33–40

Age 30 transition: 28–33

Entry life structure for
early adulthood: 22–28

Era of preadulthood: 0–22

Early adult transition:
Age 17–22

FIGURE 11–1
- - - - - - - - - - - - - - - - -

Developmental periods in the
eras of early and middle
adulthood.

life structure
*A combination of interrelated so-
cial and occupational roles that
are adapted to the individual's
personality and skill at selected
points in adult life.*

DEVELOPMENTAL TASKS OF EARLY ADULTHOOD

On the basis of clinical observations and questionnaire data from a study of 524 men and women, Gould (1978) proposed seven developmental stages in adult life; they are described in Table 11–2.

Another view of adult developmental tasks is presented by Levinson (1978, 1980, 1986). In his book, *Seasons of a Man's Life* (1978), Levinson reported on his study of 40 men and the changes they experienced during their adult lives. Levinson suggests that at selected points in life each adult creates a life structure made up of a combination of interrelated social and occupational roles that are adapted to the individual's personality and skills. A **life structure** reflects a person's priorities and the pattern of choices he or she makes. It answers the question, "What is my life like now?"

Because life circumstances change, our life structure is not always stable. Aura, for example, changed her view of her life in response to political uncertainty in her country. In different periods in people's lives their life structures are in states of transition (see Figure 11–1). Levinson believes that it is during these transitional periods that people alter their life priorities, change attitudes and beliefs, and construct new values to carry them into new phases of their lives.

According to Levinson, early adulthood embraces a series of developmental periods leading to the mid-life transition. Levinson (1986) refers to the first three periods of early adulthood (approximately between the ages of 17 to 33) as the *novice phase* because they provide an opportunity to build a life structure that, though it may not be suitable throughout life, will guide people out of adolescence. During the novice stage, the men in Levinson's study dealt with four types of tasks: forming a dream of what their lives would be like, establishing mentor relationships, selecting an occupation, and establishing love relationships. Typically,

		GOULD'S DEVELOPMENTAL STAGES OF ADULT LIFE
STAGE	**AGE RANGE**	**DEVELOPMENTAL TASKS**
1	16–18	Desire to escape from parental control
2	18–22	Leave family; establish peer group relationships
3	22–28	Develop independence; commit self to career and family
4	28–34	Transitional questioning of life goals; reevaluation of marriage and career commitments
5	34–43	Urgent awareness of time running out; realignment of life goals
6	43–53	Settling down; acceptance of one's life
7	53–60	Acceptance of past; greater tolerance; general mellowing

TABLE 11–2

Source: From *Transformations: Growth and Change in Adult Life,* by R. Gould, 1978, New York: Simon & Schuster.

Mentors provide powerful examples of how to live one's life. This young man is following his father's example in work and play.

men's dreams centered on their careers; their success in their careers was directly related to the quality of the mentor relationships they established.

Following Levinson's scheme, the *early adult transition* marks the bridge between pre-adulthood and adulthood. The *entry life structure* for early adulthood indicates the time when people establish their initial way of living (e.g., get married or remain single, begin a career, choose a place to live). The confusion that Peter expressed about his career and commitment to marriage might suggest that he was at this point in adulthood. During the *age 30 transition* people get a chance to reappraise their earlier life plan and modify it (e.g., switch jobs, get married, have children, buy a house). The last early adulthood period according to Levinson is the *culminating life structure for early adulthood.* It is at this point that adults seek to realize the goals and dreams they established in their early 20s.

The *mid-life transition* represents the great divide between early adulthood and middle age. At this point a person may be in search of a better life structure than the one used in earlier years. Levinson does not describe what is a "normal" or "appropriate" life structure; in fact he doesn't believe that one period is more advanced than another. Instead, Levinson's periods represent the developmental tasks on which everyone must work in successive periods of their lives. Another distinguishing feature of Levinson's theory of adult development is his recognition of the continuous nature of development within a stage model. Levinson provides flexibility in his model with the addition of chronologically overlapping transitional periods. People do not alter their life structures overnight; instead they change gradually.

Women's Development in Adulthood   Levinson developed his theory of adult psychosocial development from a study of men. Later, other researchers used Levinson's biographical interviewing methods to study women's psychosocial development during adulthood (Roberts & Newton, 1987). While women's lives were described by changes that were similar to those identified for men, researchers reported some notable differences.

The Dream.   During Levinson's novice stage, the shape of women's dreams was formed by what they did *not* want to do as much as by what they *did* want to do with their lives. Unlike men, only a small percentage of women reported dreams that focused on an occupation. Rather, women dreamed of marriage first and then a career. While men saw themselves as independent achievers in occupational roles, women's dreams contained images of themselves in relation to other people such as husbands, children, or colleagues. Many of the women split their dreams between achievement and relationships.

The Mentor.   According to Levinson, mentors play an important role in men's lives; a mentor functions as teacher, role model, guide, and motivator. Women experience less mentoring than men, perhaps because of the scarcity of women available in the workplace to fill the mentor role. Furthermore, the quality of mentoring that occurs for women depends on the type of dream they form. If their dreams are centered on relationships, their mentors are likely to be a husband or boyfriend; if their dreams focus on individual achievement, their mentors are frequently professional associates.

The Occupation.   Men begin the process of establishing their occupations in early adulthood and spend several years developing their credentials, skills, and values to promote their occupational choices. Typically, they have achieved some status on the job by the time they reach the age 30 transition. Women take much longer to establish their careers; this process can extend well into mid-life. For women in the study who chose to marry and raise children in their 20s, the process of identifying an occupation and pursuing it did not begin until their early 30s. Even women who identified their careers early in their adult lives experienced a slowdown in occupational development when they took time out to have children. Furthermore, career success had less to do with women's personal happiness and satisfaction than the quality of their love relationships. Once they had fulfilled their relationship dreams, they could focus on their achievement dreams.

LIFE EVENTS AND ADJUSTMENT

Another way to look at adult development is to examine how adults confront and deal with important life events. Hultsch and Plemons (1979) argue that particular

Life events such as the birth of a child require some adaptation and can be stressful to some individuals. Graduation from college is an important life event for many people in their early adulthood.

life event

A personal experience that requires a significant change in the ongoing life pattern (such as divorce, a family member's death, and serious illness).

life events and transitions underlie many of the behavioral changes and adjustment patterns commonly found among adults.

At the most general level, a **life event** is any experience that is deemed noteworthy or significant by the individual and by the culture. More specifically, however, Holmes and Masuda describe it is an event "whose advent is either indicative of or requires a significant change in the ongoing life pattern of the individual" (1974, p. 46). An example is Aura and Carlos's decision to immigrate to the United States. Some life events are experienced by virtually all adults in our society—for example, entrance into the world of work, or a family member's death or illness. Other events are experienced only by certain people—for example, induction into military service or war, immigration, resettlement, the death of one's child, imprisonment, or chronic unemployment.

Within this perspective, all life events are viewed as potentially stressful, and hence, require some adaptation on the part of the individual. Certainly this makes sense when one is talking about such experiences as death of a spouse, divorce, loss of a job, and so on. However, life event theory suggests that even experiences that are generally regarded as positive—marriage, birth of a child, promotion, and the like—can create stress and thus require some psychosocial adaptation. Nevertheless, the more personally catastrophic the event, the greater the stress felt by the individual and the greater the need for adjustment.

In young adulthood, the individual is confronted with a number of important life events and developmental transitions. The more common ones—some of which will be discussed in this chapter as well as in Chapter 12—include the development of intimate relationships, leaving the family, marriage, pregnancy, the birth of a child, divorce, entrance into the job market, change in financial status, change in social activities, and so on. Lowenthal, Thurnher, and Chiriboga (1975) found that although young adults generally report exposure to more life events than middle-aged and older adults, they also report more positive stresses than the other two groups, whereas the older adults report more negative ones. These and other researchers (Dyal & Chan, 1985) also found that the greatest stresses in the lives of youth and young adults concerned education, dating and marriage, and changes in residence.

Lowenthal and his colleagues point out, however, that the mere occurrence of an event is not the critical factor in determining its impact on the person. The person's perception of the event appears to be more important. For example, two individuals can have the same stressful job yet experience it quite differently; one may view the demands of the job as manageable, while another person may worry about his or her ability to live up to others' expectations. These investigators found that individuals who are exposed to high stress and who perceive their lives as highly stressful are likely to feel "overwhelmed." In contrast, adults who are exposed to the same high levels of stress but who perceive their lives as unstressful are likely to feel "challenged." These findings suggest that the stress of life events does not reside within the event per se, or within the individual, but rather represents a mixture of the two.

Timing and Sequencing of Life Events

Progress in the journey through adulthood is often measured by success in adopting roles that define adults—worker, spouse, parent, and so on. People do not always adopt these roles at the same ages, however. Whereas some individuals leave the family at age 18, others may still live at home at age 28. Some never leave home.

Generally speaking, most people and cultures have a sense of whether they are "early," "on time," or "late" with regard to the adoption of specific adult roles (Keith, 1990). Research suggests that being "off time" with respect to role adoption usually is upsetting for adults (Bourque & Back, 1977; Lowenthal, Thurnher, & Chiriboga, 1975). For example, failing to achieve a promotion at a time when one's peers are moving up the career ladder is likely to be experienced as stressful and personally disruptive.

The order in which people choose to do things also varies during this period. In the past, fairly rigid customs prevailed. Young women were expected to marry and bear children soon after finishing high school—if their education even reached that far. Young men were expected to finish their education and military service, and then get a job. Only after these steps were taken were they expected to marry and have children. Over the past few decades, however, the timing and order (or sequencing) of life events in the United States have become less clear-cut for both sexes. Do these deviations from the customary order of life events in the young adult period make a difference in people's lives?

One researcher (Hogan, 1978) examined the order of three live events— completing schooling, taking a first job, and marrying—among 33,500 men born between 1921 and 1950. Most men, it was found, followed the expected order of these life events, although socioeconomic and ethnic differences were found. White males were less likely to follow the expected pattern because they completed their education much later than other groups of men. African American men were

FOCUS ON CULTURE

The life events that mark adulthood and their timing is culture-specific. Some events, such as the birth of children, are linked to health and physical maturity, which can be adversely affected by the economic resources within the country. In some Asian and Indian cultures, people may be married as children, years before they are capable of reproduction. Other events are tied to the needs of the culture. For example, people who live in agrarian cultures enter the workforce at a much younger age than people living in industrialized societies.

more likely to marry, and Hispanic men were more likely to work before finishing their education. Men who deviated from the usual order of life events experienced a higher rate of marital separation and divorce. Marital disruption was 17% higher among those who married before finishing high school.

The effects of early and delayed childbirth have been the most frequently studied aspects of deviation from the expected order of life events among women. Researchers have found that 10% of women questioned became pregnant before finishing high school, and 40% of the live births to these women occurred before marriage (Green & Polleigen, 1977). One consequence of this disruption in life events was that 80% of those who gave birth to a child did not finish high school.

Other research has found that if a woman marries after becoming pregnant and before completing high school, she is likely to have a greater number of children and to have them closer together. Her marriage is also 2 to 3 times more likely to end in divorce. At the other extreme, women who postpone their first pregnancy until after their education is completed and after they have been married a year or two are more likely to work before the birth of their first child and to expect and get more help from their husbands (Presser, 1978; Scanzoni, 1975).

Intimacy between two people is expressed in different ways depending on cultural expectations.

RECAP

Personality development in adulthood is influenced by the accomplishment of age-specific tasks and life events. Gould and Levinson have proposed stages to describe the timing of these tasks across adulthood. Men and women differ in the complexity and focus of the life events that define their life structures. The timing and order of life events varies among individuals and cultures.

INTIMACY

intimacy
According to Erikson, a critical psychosocial achievement for young adults; a relationship quality characterized by warmth, mutuality of feeling, and deep commitment.

From the beginning of life, **intimacy,** both physical and emotional, is critical to development. Infants and their parents, the middle-school girl and her best girlfriend, the young boy and the grandfather with whom he lives are all examples of intimate relationships that occur in the course of development. In early adulthood, however, a new kind of intimacy becomes possible. This is the intimacy that is freely chosen by two equal persons who have worked through the adolescent crises, know who they are, and are willing to share themselves with each other.

Erikson theorized that the ability to become intimate with another person—the central psychosocial task for the young adult in this theoretical model—awaits the resolution of the identity crisis during adolescence. In other words, it is only after one has achieved a sense of identity that it becomes safe to risk fusing this identity with that of another person.

Researchers who measure ego identity and intimacy in adults have largely supported Erikson's hypothesis, at least for males. For females, the relationship between identity and intimacy may be more complex, particularly since many women define themselves in terms of their relationships (Roberts & Newton, 1987). As Marcia (1980) notes, identity in females is closely tied to interpersonal areas—that is, to areas promoting intimacy. Thus, whereas males may be likely to develop a sense of identity in areas of achievement and then transfer this identity to interpersonal areas, for some females the development of identity and intimacy may develop in a more concurrent fashion (Gilligan, 1982); other researchers have found that some women, like men, achieve intimacy after identity, while others achieve intimacy before identity (Dyk & Adams, 1990; Schiedel & Marcia, 1985; Whitbourne & Tesch, 1985).

INTIMACY AND ATTACHMENT

During my childhood I formed a close bond with my twin sister Mary. We shared friends, school experiences, family upsets, and our developmental changes. It was quite a change in my life when we went our separate ways after graduating from the same college. I sought a replacement for my attachment relationship with my twin and found it with my husband.

According to some developmental psychologists, the foundation of adult intimacy can be traced to the early attachment bonds between infants and other human beings, particularly their parents (Shaver & Hazan, 1987; Troll & Smith, 1976). For some individuals, these early socio-emotional relationships produce a sense of security and trust, and the desire to be close to others. The quality of attachments formed in early infancy becomes the working model for what to expect and how to relate to others in an intimate relationship. People who form secure attachments in childhood are more likely to trust themselves and their partners in intimate relationships in adulthood (Kobak & Hazan, 1991). Individuals who established insecure attachments with their caregivers are likely to be less comfortable in adult intimate relationships. Their emotional insecurities interfere with their ability to form or maintain mature adult relationships based on respect and mutuality. Instead they seek out relationships based on dependencies that are not mutual.

Attachment is a lifelong process that influences the frequency and quality of all interpersonal relationships including sexual relationships (Bowlby, 1969). Some researchers have even suggested that when we become attached to groups, ideas, or objects, the critical factor in all of these examples is a strong emotional involvement (Kalish & Knudtson, 1976).

While attachment is a pervasive and enduring process throughout life, the nature and object of our attachments change with age. From your journey through the earlier portions of the lifespan you saw examples of attachment among family members and peers and the emergence of tentative heterosexual attachments in adolescence. In young adulthood new forms of attachment develop. These attachments, some strong and others weak, are the bonds of adult life—the bonds by which people find meaning in their lives.

Sexual Intimacy

Before the resolution of the identity crisis, attempts at sexual intimacy are usually of the searching, self-serving kind in which people are primarily interested in meeting their immediate sexual or security needs. Sexual relationships are not likely to develop into deep personal commitments, especially since the individuals do not have a clear idea of themselves, let alone their sexual partners.

By contrast, the intimacy of early adulthood is characterized by mutuality; ideally, one cares for the other person as much as one cares for oneself. Mutuality entails willingness to make sacrifices and compromises. It involves mature sexual functioning in genital love, which, as defined by Erikson, involves choosing a partner with whom one is willing to work, play, and establish a family. In sexually intimate relationships individuals experience a desire to make lifelong commitments. For example, couples may decide to have children as a natural extension of their mutual care and affection.

Naturally, researchers have been interested in determining when young people achieve mature sexual intimacy and what variables affect the outcome. It seems that the potential for mature sexuality occurs for most people in young adulthood rather than during adolescence. Yet, although most people begin to establish sexual relationships in early adulthood, not everyone experiences sexual intimacy. Sexual union can be the all-encompassing development described by Erikson, or, reduced to its most common denominator, it may become a mere physical event (Masters & Johnson, 1975). It appears that the outcome of the identity crisis and the resulting strength of the ego influence the quality of sexual intimacy.

In one study, for example, college students who scored high on ego identity were found to score high on intimacy as well. These students were able to share worries and express anger as well as affection toward their partners (Orlofsky,

Marcia, & Lesser, 1973). On the other hand, students who scored low on identity measures were shown to have developed alternatives to intimacy—*stereotyped* relationships, or relationships characterized as *pseudo-intimate*.

In **stereotyped relationships,** the partner is treated more or less as a sexual object, and the person seeks not intimacy, but sex for its own sake. In **pseudo-intimate relationships** the commitment is usually more permanent. The couple look and behave like partners, but the relationship is largely based on convenience. For example, a woman may couple with a man because he provides status; a man may couple with a woman because she bolsters his ego. On the emotional level, however, the couple hardly communicates. A typical statement of the pseudo-intimate partner is, "My partner meets my needs and doesn't make demands on me, so why should I complain?"

The opposite of intimacy in Erikson's model is **isolation.** Some young people isolate themselves from close personal or sexual relationships with others. In some cases this is an indication of emotional disturbance. For example, a man may have been so psychologically damaged by a parent's having abandoned him that he is unable to engage in satisfactory interpersonal relationships. In another case, a woman may be in a state of identity moratorium. The problems involved in breaking free from her parents or choosing a career may leave her little energy or desire to get involved with another person in either a sexual or a nonsexual relationship.

While people may desire sexual intimacy, not everyone is comfortable with the idea of engaging in sexual intercourse as a means of establishing intimacy. Some are cautious about catching AIDS or other sexually transmitted diseases and choose to wait until they have established a relationship before becoming sexually intimate.

NONSEXUAL INTIMACY

Heterosexual love relationships are not the only kind of intimacy that is first achieved in early adulthood. New relationships with peers and elders become possible in response to what White (1975) calls the "freeing of relationships" from childhood expectations. Adults are no longer perceived in terms of parental stereotypes but are appreciated as people in their own right. "For the first time," says a returning college student, "I was able to talk to my mother and my older brother as if they were real people—or friends." In large part this is because in young adulthood people begin to have experiences that they can truly share with their parents—getting married, obtaining a job, buying a house, creating a family, and so on. These are experiences that are common to all adults and consequently serve to bring the generations closer.

Early adulthood is the period of the lifespan when people tend to have the most friends and acquaintances (Antonucci, 1985). Young adults are more likely to have the time to devote to making and maintaining friendships. Later, the number of friends one has decreases, in part because of conflicting demands from work and family obligations. As people grow older, their number of friends diminishes further as a result of relocation, declining health, or death.

Adult friendships display some gender differences. Male friendships are more likely to be based on shared activities and interests; women's friendships are more likely to be based on a mutual sharing of intimate information and feelings. Men are more likely to participate in activities such as sports with their friends. Women

stereotyped relationship
A relationship in which the partner is treated more or less as a sexual object and the person seeks not intimacy but sex for its own sake.

pseudo-intimate relationship
A permanent commitment in which a couple looks and behaves like partners, but the relationship is based largely on convenience.

isolation
According to Erikson, a feeling that one is disconnected from others, empty, and abandoned; this quality often develops in the absence of true, intimate relationships.

are more likely to spend their time talking with their friends and sharing confidences (Huyck, 1982).

Mentor relationships or psychological apprenticeships to older people may be formed during this period (Keniston, 1970). At work or in college and graduate school, mentors—teachers, advisers, or "parental figures" who may be 8 to 15 years older than the young person—become important as they guide, instruct, and encourage people in their lives (Levinson, Darrow, Klein, Levinson, & McKee, 1977; Roberts & Newton, 1987). Finally, the quality of friendship changes. Whereas adolescents tend to choose friends who remind them of themselves or of what they want to become, young adults choose people for their own sakes; that is, they have more respect for individual differences.

BRIEF REVIEW

Because of the complexity of life experiences and challenges, adulthood can be divided into three stages: early, middle, and late adulthood. The meaning of adulthood is defined by culture and history. Youth is the term used to cover the period between age 18 and that time when individuals adopt adult commitments, identities, and lifestyles.

A major task for young adults is the stabilization of ego identity. Marcia proposes four separate identity statuses in youth and young adulthood: achievement, foreclosure, moratorium, and diffusion. Identity is an ever-changing quality that is sensitive to a person's many life experiences.

In early adulthood, people attain their biological and physiological peaks in terms of speed, coordination, strength, endurance, and health. For women, early adulthood is the best biological time to bear children. The ability to perform cognitive tasks that require quick response time, short-term memory, and perception in complex relations is also at its sharpest.

Piaget's period of formal operations (the period characterized by hypothetical reasoning and abstract thought) may not develop until late adolescence and is expressed more narrowly than was first supposed. The existence of a cognitive stage beyond formal operations called the postformal stage has been suggested. Three characteristics of thought have frequently been identified with postformal thinking: Thinking is relativistic; contradiction is seen as an inherent aspect of reality; and contradictory knowledge is integrated into higher-order, more inclusive systems of knowledge. Adults consider the context and practical real-life implications of an event. Based on their experiences, adults may interpret situations differently.

Moral development requires both cognitive development and personal experience to foster its growth. In youth and young adulthood, challenges to one's values and ideology, as well as resolution of identity issues, are likely to influence moral reasoning and behavior.

Moral development advances to higher levels in adulthood as a result of life experiences. Criticisms of Kohlberg's theory have been directed at its assessment of women's moral development and at the way postconventional morality ignores the use of multiple perspectives in resolving moral dilemmas.

Personality development in adulthood is affected by the accomplishment of specific developmental tasks. Developmental tasks or stages have been presented by Erikson, Gould, and Levinson. Men and women differ in the way they deal with adult tasks.

Patterns of adjustment in young adulthood are influenced by the type of events people encounter during this time. Life event theory suggests that both positive (e.g., marriage) and negative (e.g., divorce) life events are potentially stressful and require readjustment by the person. The timing and order of experiencing life events varies considerably from one person to another, which, in turn, makes a difference in the subsequent life of the individual.

During adulthood, intimacy based on mutuality is established. In Erikson's model, the opposite of intimacy is isolation. People may isolate themselves from close friendships and contacts, either because of some emotional disturbance or because they are in a moratorium state. Intimacy in nonsexual as well as sexual relationships can be fully realized at this time of life.

KEY TERMS

cognitive style (437)

dialectical process (438)

identity achievers (427)

identity diffuse (428)

identity foreclosure (427)

identity status (427)

intimacy (451)

isolation (453)

life event (448)

life structure (445)
moratorium (428)
perceived age (422)

premenstrual syndrome
  (PMS) (432)
problem finding (437)

pseudo-intimate relationship (453)
stereotyped relationship (453)
youth (424)

REVIEW QUESTIONS

If you can answer these questions, you have a good understanding of the material in this chapter. If a question seems difficult, go back to the text and review the topic.

1. List and give examples of the three types of influences on development across the lifespan.

2. What factors affect a person's perceived age?

3. In what ways is the period of youth distinguished from the period of early adulthood? How do the developmental tasks for these two periods differ?

4. Describe the four patterns of identity statuses offered by Marcia. Give an example of each. In what sequences do people achieve their identity? Give an example of each sequence.

5. Describe the status of physical capabilities during early adulthood. What impact do these capabilities have on later development?

6. What factors account for the variability among adults in the development of formal operational thought?

7. Describe three different types of cognitive skills that are believed to develop after formal operational thought. Identify three characteristics of mature adult thought.

8. Describe Kohlberg's postconventional level of morality. What criticisms have been raised against Kohlberg's theory of moral development?

9. Describe Levinson's developmental stages of adult life. Contrast the experiences of men and women in these stages.

10. Give examples of significant life events in your culture. What is the impact of the timing and sequencing of life events on adult personality development?

11. How are intimacy and attachment related? Distinguish between intimacy and isolation.

12. What are the differences between sexual and nonsexual intimacy? Describe gender differences in nonsexual intimacy.

OBSERVATIONAL ACTIVITY

THE MEANING OF ADULTHOOD

People have different conceptions of adulthood. For some people, being an adult means being self-supporting. For others, perceived age or how they feel influences their definition of adulthood. Accomplishing certain life events such as getting a job or getting married signals adulthood for some people.

To gain a more detailed understanding of the ways people define adulthood, interview 10 young adults between the ages of 20 and 30. Be sure to select a varied sample of people—male and female, college students and those who do not attend college, married and single people. Interview your respondents individually and ask them the following questions:

1. What does it mean to be an adult? What do you consider to be important characteristics of adults?

2. Are there certain roles or behaviors that are generally expected of adults?

3. Consider the following life events: getting a job, getting married, moving out of your parents' home, starting a

family, completing your education, and buying your own house. What do you think is the best age for a person to accomplish these different events? In what order should one complete them?

4. Are there times when you feel like an adult and other times when you don't? Explain.

Before you interview the people you have selected, answer the questions yourself. When you have completed all of the interviews, compile your findings and summarize them. Are there differences between men and women in their definitions and expectations of adulthood? Do college students differ from non-college students in their responses? Are there differences in responses between the married and single people? What other differences can you identify? How do your own answers compare with your respondents' answers? What did you gain from this activity?

Early Adulthood: Family and Occupational Development

It had been 5 years since Cathy and her first husband, Tim, had ended their 4-year marriage. They began their relationship as high school sweethearts, but they seemed to drift apart as they grew older and developed different interests. Their divorce was not complicated by children or property. Still, the process of ending their relationship was a stressful time for Cathy. Her parents and brother and sister were a source of support as she established a new life for herself as a single woman. She went back to school and completed her training to become a nurse.

After her divorce Cathy dated, and eventually she met and fell in love with Mark. Even though her parents held different values, they did not interfere or object when Mark and Cathy began living together. When Cathy was 32, she and Mark decided that they wanted to have a child before it was too late. So they decided to get married.

Yael and Ari had known each other since their childhood days in the kibbutz outside of Tel Aviv, Israel. Yael left the kibbutz for 6 years to study education at the University of Haifa, but later returned to work in the community school. Ari never left the kibbutz; instead he apprenticed himself to the collective's manager and gradually developed the skills he needed to serve as a manager himself. Although they differed in educational experience, Yael and Ari viewed each other as equals. They took pride in their abilities to contribute to the economic success and survival of the kibbutz that had been their family.

With Yael's return, she and Ari rekindled their friendship with a new sparkle—that of courtship. Members of the community teased them about being inseparable. So it came as no surprise when they asked permission to share a room within the kibbutz. This request effectively signaled their intention to marry. When the request was granted, they knew that their "marriage" had been sanctioned by the community.

Ari and Yael's decision to marry and their joint commitment to their work roles in the kibbutz are typical of early adulthood, when many people begin to make commitments to personal relationships and their work. By contributing to the care of others, young adults like Cathy and Mark also broaden their view of themselves and add a new dimension to their journey of life.

FAMILY LIFE

I grew up in a large family that continues to be relatively close even though we are spread out over several states. Despite the fact that I am well into middle adulthood, my mother still considers me "one of the kids." My husband and I have created our own family with our children, Adam and Sarah. I am also considered a member of my husband's extensive family (he has eight sisters). Some members of my family have died; others have left through divorce. But, the sense of family remains an important part of my life.

Across cultures, the family serves as an important influence of development. The size, composition, and function of families varies, but the roles adults play within their family unit contributes to their sense of competence and personal significance.

FOCUS ON CULTURE

Although many people in our culture accept and expect that a new family begins when adult children leave home, marry, and have children, these expectations are not the same in all cultures or subcultures. What constitutes a family is influenced by history and cultural beliefs. For example, to Asians who engage in ancestor worship, the family includes not only living but deceased relatives; family members have an obligation to honor the memory of their ancestors in their daily lives. To many Native Americans, family membership is defined by membership in the tribe rather than by direct parentage. In Yugoslavia, it is common for at least one of the adult children to remain with the nuclear family, bringing his or her spouse into the family through marriage.

The family is one of the most popular and enduring of all social groupings. Although the specific nature and function of families may vary from culture to culture, from generation to generation, and from family to family, the significance and importance of belonging to a family increases throughout the lifespan. As people become adults, they become more aware of the role that families play in their lives and attempt to strengthen their ties to their relatives (Carstensen, 1992).

In our culture, children and, to a lesser extent, adolescents are frequently the objects or recipients of care, direction, and instruction from parents and older family members; in early adulthood, however, we become the agents of socialization and the caregivers to our own and other people's children. As people leave their original families and establish their own nuclear families, they perpetuate a process that began hundreds of years ago—the family life cycle. For most people the knowledge that they are participating in this cycle of life is reassuring and inspiring. One of the warmest wishes to a newly married couple is that they live to see their children's children marry and continue the family tradition they hope to perpetuate by marrying.

THE NATURE OF THE FAMILY

At this point you are probably aware that what constitutes a family in one culture may be different in another. "What is a family?" and "What role does the family play in the lives of parents and children?" are complex questions. To begin with, families can be defined either structurally or functionally. *Structural* definitions focus on the pattern of organization that characterizes this societal unit. Specifying each of the family members and their relation to one another would constitute a structural approach to understanding families. By contrast, a *functional* definition of the family focuses more on family activities and the role the family plays in the lives of its members (Garrett, 1982).

The structural definition of a family is defined by the culture. On the Israeli kibbutz, and in other cultures, a family does not require a legal marriage. Yael and Ari were viewed as married by virtue of sharing a room. In other cultures, the presence of children, within or outside of marriage, is sufficient to define a family. The United States Census Bureau defines a family as two or more people who are related by marriage, blood, or adoption who are living together. Although most families in the United States are formed initially by a man and woman marrying and subsequently having children, the stability of this family unit is becoming increasingly shaky.

Norton and Moorman (1987) report that American young people are marrying at later ages than they did in the previous generation. Furthermore, they project that about 56% of all women will end their first marriage in divorce. Separation and divorce rates peaked in the 1980s, resulting in a large number of single parent households. Furthermore, since the majority of people who divorce also remarry, there has been a rise in blended or stepfamily arrangements. In addition, 10 to 15% of couples generally find that they have a fertility problem (Rathus, 1983), leading them either to remain childless or to adopt children. There are also those adults who choose not to have children, as well as those who never marry, and those who choose to live together—with a person of the opposite or the same sex—without the societal sanction of marriage. The point is that the "traditional American family," while not actually a myth, represents fewer and fewer family arrangements in today's world. And, when one considers the radical changes that are taking place in role adoption, both within and outside of the home (for example, greater sharing of family roles by husbands and wives, and the entrance of women into the workforce), the notion of "traditional" family life would seem to be losing even more of its meaning.

FOCUS ON CULTURE

The economic health and stability of a country has an impact on the structure of families. Extended families are much more common in agricultural societies, because the productivity of family farms is increased when adult offspring continue to live with the family and farm the land. In nonindustrialized countries without social security programs for the elderly, extended families ensure that older family members will be cared for by younger members. In contrast, nuclear families are the norm in industrialized countries, where adults often may be required to relocate for employment.

FUNCTIONS OF THE FAMILY

Regardless of the structure of the family and the specific roles played by its members, the family, as a social unit, serves a number of important functions that bind family members together and, at the same time, link them to the greater community (Garrett, 1982). First, families are the context for legitimate procreation; they are the legal unit responsible for the care of children born in that unit. A second function of families is to socialize its members, to train both the adults and children to get along with other people. Usually, children are the primary targets of socialization, although couples with or without children have a socializing effect on each other. Parents nurture, care for, and teach children the skills and behaviors necessary for effective coping in the world outside the home. By contrast, adults experience more indirect socialization as they interact with each other and with their offspring. It is well known that the behavior and attitudes of parents are shaped by the responses they produce in their children (Belsky, 1984a; Bell & Harper, 1977); for example, when our daughter Sarah was a teenager and a vegetarian, my husband and I reduced meat from our diets. This example is considered to be an indirect socialization effect since children usually do not intentionally try to alter their parents' behavior in the same way that parents intend to shape their children's behavior.

Families also are an important source of support and encouragement, especially during times of stress or turmoil. Cathy, for example, was helped during her divorce from Tim by her family's support of her choice to end the marriage. Support can take the form of emotional caring, financial assistance, or direct help such as baby-sitting. The only way some families can survive economically is by living together and pooling their financial resources. In times of loss, as you will learn when you reach Chapter 17, family support helps individuals in their bereavement. Family members can also serve as a referral source or consultants for specific problems of daily life. For example, adult children frequently help their aging parents navigate the bureaucracy of social or medical services and provide guidance on financial matters.

Finally, families also function to foster a companionship between marital partners. In so doing, the family unit facilitates intimacy among its members and provides a basis for physical and emotional support. Family members share leisure activities, celebrate holidays together, and listen to one another's problems. They are not only relatives, but also good friends.

CHANGES IN FAMILY LIFE

Just as people change as they mature, families undergo changes across the lifespan. An individual's lifespan begins at birth and ends at death. However, the lifespan of families is a bit more difficult to delineate. In many Western cultures, the family life cycle begins with marriage and ends when the surviving spouse dies. At this point, another second- or third-generation family may have been established along with a new family cycle. But in cultures that define families as intergenerational, it is more difficult to specify when the family life cycle has ended. Furthermore, an increasing number of families today are "blended" through remarriage or extended through the addition of grandparents or other relatives or nonrelatives. Children who divide their time between their divorced parents may be members of two distinct family units.

One way to examine families is to view them from a developmental or life cycle perspective. Basic to this perspective is the assumption that family life can be characterized as a series of stages, each with unique developmental tasks and conflicts to be confronted and resolved (Nock, 1982). The traditional **family life cycle** begins with marriage; it ends with the process of bereavement of the surviving spouse. Between these points are a series of stages describing different family structural patterns, role expectations, and life events that challenge family members and demand new patterns of coping from all of them.

Carter and McGoldrick (1980) developed a model to describe a family life cycle (see Table 12–1). Their model differs from the traditional family life cycle by conceptualizing the family as the emotional unit that holds people together. A new family life cycle begins when the unattached young adult comes to terms with his or her family of origin and formulates personal life goals, including the decision whether to have a family of his or her own. Carter and McGoldrick's family life cycle model recognizes the emotional and developmental changes that families endure over a lifetime.

family life cycle

Beginning with marriage and ending with the death of the surviving spouse, the changes in growth and development that mark the life of the family.

CARTER AND MCGOLDRICK'S FAMILY LIFE CYCLE MODEL

STAGE	EMOTIONAL ELEMENT	FAMILY CHANGES
Between families: The unattached young adult	Accepting parent-offspring separation	Separating self from family of origin; developing intimate peer relationships; establishing oneself in work
Joining of families: Newly married couple	Committing to a family	Forming a marital relationship; changing relationships with extended family and friends to include one's spouse
Family with young children	Accepting new members into the family	Adjusting to marriage to make room for children; assuming the parenting role; changing relationships to include parenting and grandparenting roles
Family with adolescents	Increasing family boundaries to include children's dependents	Changing parental roles to allow children to separate; refocusing marital and career goals; shifting concerns to older generation
Launching children and moving on	Accepting many exits from and entries into the family	Changing marital relationship to accommodate the empty nest; developing adult-to-adult relationships with children; accepting in-laws and grandchildren; dealing with the disability or death of one's parents
The family in later life	Accepting the shifting generational roles	Maintaining marital relationship in the face of physiological decline; supporting the older generation; dealing with loss of spouse

TABLE 12-1

Source: From "The Family Life Cycle and Family Therapy: An Overview," by E. Carter and M. McGoldrick, 1980, in *The Family Life Cycle: A Framework for Family Therapy,* New York: Gardenier Press. Adapted with permission.

Most families are formed with the addition of children to a partnership, regardless of a legal marriage. During the family's early stages, activity centers on child-rearing tasks. However, across the family life cycle the amount of time people spend in families with children is relatively small; in enduring marriages, almost half of a family life cycle occurs after the children are gone. Thus, family adjustments during the young-adult period, such as the use of leisure time, are not necessarily appropriate for later periods.

Family life cycle models have been criticized because of their limited scope and their inability to capture the dynamic quality of family life. While the models are useful for describing changes in traditional families through the life cycle, some fail to take into account the considerable proportion of people who divorce or become widowed, who remarry, or who have second families. Many of these people will spend some years as single parents or may bring up children not their own. Carter and McGoldrick's model (1980), however, has been extended to include additional phases for families that experience divorce and remarriage.

Another limitation is that the models fail to acknowledge the overlap and interaction of family life cycles across generations. For example, a family composed of a young couple with preschool children could be classified in the new-parent

FOCUS ON CULTURE

A "traditional" American family is composed of a mother, a father, and their offspring and is usually maintained in one household. Despite the increase in "nontraditional" families over the past 25 years, researchers have tended to focus on traditional families. What factors might bias researchers to study one type of family rather than another? How might this bias impact social policy or people's attitudes toward "nontraditional" families?

intergenerational relations

The relations between members of a family from different generations.

stage. At the same time, however, the couple remain part of a different family as children of their own middle-aged or aging parents, and thus could be categorized in a later stage of development. Thus, the impact of life cycle events on people must be viewed within the broader perspective of **intergenerational relations**— that is, the relations between members of a family from different generations. In other words, to understand the development and adjustment of the adult at any particular life cycle phase, one must understand the "fit" between the expectations and experiences a person has derived from the family of origin and those derived from the family he or she has created. There is more to say about intergenerational relations in Chapter 14.

Family life cycle models are also insensitive to the cultural context of family. Ideally, a different family life cycle model should be constructed according to the traditions and expectations of each culture studied. Unfortunately, all too frequently a Western family life cycle model is used to judge family development in non-Western cultures. For example, in many pre-industrial countries it is rare for children to spend their entire childhood with their natural parents; high rates of adult mortality often result in the creation of stepfamilies (Hewlett, 1991). Even within Western cultures, family life cycle models are limited; they do not reflect the different timing and structure of family variations that may apply to ethnic subcultures. For example, within African American families it is common for families living within one household to include three generations, all of whom affect the life of the family. Furthermore, because family life cycle models represent average family changes, they do not capture the circumstances or events that shape individual families.

RECAP

Family life is important in early adulthood development. What constitutes a family is culturally defined and usually involves marriage or a blood relationship. Families provide a context for legitimate procreation, for socialization, and companionship. Families are a source of support during times of crisis or transition. Carter & McGoldrick describe stages in the development across the family life cycle. While these stages help describe different phases of family life, they do not consider changes in the family or intergenerational relationships. Family life-cycle models are also insensitive to cultural and individual differences in families.

Health Perspective

FAMILY THERAPY: HELPING FAMILIES COPE

Families consist of individuals of different ages and with differing needs who are bound together by birth and/or residence. Numerous and complex social and emotional interactions among family members create the potential for conflict or harmony, depending on each member's expectations and behaviors. People usually have difficulty thinking about their families objectively; most people's knowledge of family structure is limited to their own experience and they have no basis of comparison. Furthermore, many people find it awkward to talk with family members about their expectations regarding how they should interact with one another. But, communication among family members is important in order for families to function in a productive and healthy fashion.

This is especially true in the United States today, where there is a growing concern about changing family structures and roles within the family. Not only are families smaller, but many experience divorce, single parenthood, and remarriage. For example, in the United States the number of single-parent families has increased from 3.8 million in 1970 to 10.5 million in 1992 and the number of stepfamilies has increased dramatically (Martin, 1994a). These challenges to family life have led to an increase in the popularity of family therapy as a way to heal some of the problems created within families and to help family members learn how to deal more effectively and supportively with one another.

Family therapy was developed in the late 1950s by Virginia Satir (1967). It operates on the assumption that when one member of the family has problems that result in psychological symptoms, all family members share the problem and discomfort in some way. Satir called her type of therapy *conjoint family therapy* because she viewed the family as an integral system in which each member contributes to the functioning of the family. Sometimes a family member's contribution results in a psychological disturbance or symptoms for which the person may seek or be asked to seek help. That family member then becomes the *identified patient (IP)*. Rather than focus on the identified patient as the only one with a problem, family therapists treat the whole family as a unit.

The family therapist usually sees all family members in a group to discuss their views of the problems within the family in general and their reactions to

MARRIAGE

My husband of 30 years has been my traveling companion along my journey through adulthood. We married during our senior year of college and have been fortunate enough to change together over the years of our married life. Marriage is a legal, and for some a religious, union of a man and a woman. About 80% of adults in the United States make a commitment to each other in marriage some time during their adult years (Norton & Moorman, 1987).

In agreeing to marry, couples assume legal and social responsibilities to care for one another as long as they are married. Over the past 10 years, the age at which people marry has increased and the marriage rate has declined. In 1991, the median age for first time marriage was 26.3 for men and 24.1 for women (U.S. Bureau of the Census, 1992). Furthermore, women with higher levels of education (college and postgraduate) are marrying even later in order to first establish their careers (Houseknecht, Vaughan, & Statham, 1987; Spanier, Roos, & Shockey, 1985).

the identified patient in particular. The therapist observes the patterns of communication or lack of communication among the family members. Special attention is placed on the function that the identified patient's disturbances play in the family members' interactions. Family roles are identified and destructive behaviors are noted. The family therapist then helps family members adjust their relationships to one another to help the family serve its function of promoting growth for all of its members.

For example, the therapist might observe that one member of the family dominates the discussion and does not listen when other family members speak. The therapist may intervene and suggest a change in behavior that will allow all members to be heard. This change in turn may provoke other reactions. The previously silenced family members may express their hidden resentment about not having been recognized within the family.

Frequently, family therapists find that the identified patient is actually the scapegoat for the family. So long as the identified person is seen as the sole source of difficulty, the other family members do not have to change. Satir observed that family members often interfered with or attempted to sabotage the identified patient's therapy—as if they did not want that person to get well. Rather than trying to change that person and return him or her to a dysfunctional family, the family therapist assists the family as a whole to change for the better. For example, a child who is unusually aggressive at school may be referred to family therapy for help; the therapist may notice that the parents fight with each other about how the child should be disciplined. The hostile relationship between the parents is a major part of the child's problem and interferes with the child's progress in therapy.

While it frequently takes a family crisis before the family members recognize the need for help, the benefits of family therapy continue long after the initial crisis has been resolved. The goals of family therapy may shift to include a discussion of the beneficial aspects of the family and an appreciation of the individual members. Communication patterns can be improved and new strategies for solving family problems can be developed.

Finally, family therapy has also been used to help couples decide whether they are well-suited for an enduring marriage (Edwards, 1995). Even couples who may seem incompatible due to differences in personality or backgrounds can learn how to get along better within their marriage by learning how to deal with conflict and different expectations.

Although the age at which people marry for the first time has risen since the last generation, many young adults may experience pressures from family, friends, and even themselves to get married "on time." Each society has a typical timetable for major adult life experiences, including marriage. What really matters is the individual's perception of whether he or she is marrying "late." Most people who marry also have children; since childbearing age is limited by biological factors, many women over the age of 30, like Cathy, may experience greater pressures to get married because they believe time is running out. Nevertheless, marriage today, or at least the traditional early marriage, appears to be but one of several possible lifestyle choices. Although most young adults still choose to get married, an increasing number of men and women are making the choice to remain single, or to postpone marriage until their late 20s or 30s.

FOCUS ON CULTURE

While the first-marriage age is rising in many Western cultures, the same cannot be said in other cultures. In Bangladesh, for example, 70% of females between the ages of 15 and 19 are married; 100% of uneducated 15- to 19-year-old girls in Guyana are married (Seager & Olson, 1986). Generally, women marry youngest in countries where there are limited opportunities for economic independence. In countries that limit the number of children per family, such as the People's Republic of China, adults may be encouraged to delay marriage until they are older as a way of keeping family size low.

MATE SELECTION

As high school sweethearts, Cathy and her first husband, Tim, were sure they had found their mates for life. They really didn't look around at other possible marriage partners. In contrast, Yael and Ari had spent some time dating other people before they decided to marry. One of the most obvious problems to be faced in regard to marriage is the choice of a partner. The field seems large enough; there are millions of unattached people in the world. Realistically, however, the range of selection for each person is limited. All the while one is seeing, meeting, and going out with potential partners, a selective screening process is taking place. In the end, people seem to choose their mates from a narrow group of individuals who are much like themselves.

physical attractiveness
A factor found to be the most influential in the mate selection process.

Three factors influence the mate-selection process: physical attractiveness, propinquity, and homogamy. **Physical attractiveness** has been found to be the best predictor of mutual liking between new acquaintances. In a study at the University of Minnesota, male and female freshmen were matched randomly at a dance. The freshmen were rated for physical attractiveness. Results showed that the higher the attractiveness rating of each person in the matched couple, the more they liked each other and the more they wanted to see each other again. The correlation between attractiveness and liking was even higher when the rating was done by the subjects themselves (Walster, Aronson, Abrahams, & Rottmann, 1966). Research studies have also found that men tend to value physical attractiveness more than women when selecting possible mates (Kenrick, Groth, Trost, & Sadalla, 1993; Kenrick, Sadalla, Groth, & Trost, 1990). People are attracted to others who are physically similar to them, especially in the face (Hinsz, 1989).

In establishing a relationship, personality traits and other characteristics gain more prominence—and may even weaken the effects of physical attraction (Kenrick, Neuberg, Zierk, & Krones, 1994; Mathes, 1975). A study of the continuing effects of physical attractiveness in marriage revealed that husbands, but not wives, were less attracted to spouses who became less physically attractive with age (Margolin & White, 1987). In a survey in which men and women were asked to rate various physical, social, and personality characteristics in terms of their importance in selecting a romantic partner, males placed greater importance on physical characteristics while females emphasized characteristics such as warmth, honesty, and faithfulness (Nevid, 1984).

People usually select as marriage partners people who are familiar to them in social and personality characteristics.

In the Hena, a premarriage ceremony, this Jewish couple announce their intention to marry. In New Guinea it is the custom for a man to offer a gift of a pig to the family of the woman he wishes to marry. This ritual announces the couple's intention to marry to the families and community.

propinquity
Nearness; one of the factors that is influential in the mate selection process.

homogamy
The general practice of choosing a mate who is similar to oneself in social or personality characteristics.

Propinquity means nearness. Ari and Yael worked together on the kibbutz and got to know each other better as a result of their daily opportunities to talk about what mattered to them. People are more likely to choose a mate from among those who live or work nearby, if only because they are more likely to meet such people and have a greater opportunity to get to know them.

Homogamy refers to the general practice of choosing a mate who is similar to oneself in social or personality characteristics. Marriage choices in the United States, for example, tend to be homogamous. Thus, people will tend to choose a partner from the same race and ethnic group, religion, and social class; partners also tend to share the same age, level of education, and values. Some factors are stronger than others, however. Judging by the relatively fewer interracial marriages, race would seem to be the single most powerful factor in homogamous mate selection. Religion is also important; people tend to marry within their religious community, although interreligious marriages are becoming more common. In countries where religious differences have created a history of political disputes, such as Northern Ireland and Pakistan, resistance to interreligious marriages is particularly high (Donnan, 1990). Social class also exerts a strong influence. However, when people marry outside of their own class, men tend to marry women of lower social class, while women tend to marry men of higher social class.

In American culture parents may influence the selection of a marriage partner, but they do not make the initial or ultimate choice. However, the practice of arranged marriage is still found in many nonindustrialized cultures and within some ethnic groups in the United States. Usually these marriages are based on family economic and social status rather than romantic love, and many are arranged long before the prospective bride and groom reach puberty. Furthermore, the practice of *polygyny,* or the marriage of two or more wives per husband, is found in many nonindustrialized countries. According to Muslim religious laws, for example, men are permitted to have up to four wives. In contrast, *polyandry,* in which a woman has more than one husband, is rare.

Courtship

My husband and I are both psychologists and I attribute that fact to our courtship. We met during our undergraduate years; we had different academic majors, but we shared an interest in psychology. To have more time to get to know each other, we took lots of psychology courses. By the time we entered graduate school in psychology we were married. While our courtship may seem unique, it was typical for our time. In your grandparents' time, mate selection in the United States would usually begin with casual dating, then lead to "going steady," becoming engaged, and finally getting married. Today, however, it is obvious that not all couples who date progress to the other phases of courtship, nor do they follow the same sequence. Becoming a "serious" couple is a process that depends on many factors.

Murstein (1970, 1976, 1982), has developed a three-stage theory of marital choice, known as **stimulus-value-role theory.** The first stage is the **stimulus (S) stage,** during which the person responds to certain stimulus values or characteristics in the other person. These characteristics include the person's physical attractiveness, reputation, adopted roles, and other information. Generally, the stimulus stage involves brief contacts with the other person and is a time for forming initial impressions.

If each person evaluates the other in approximately equal ways, they may progress to the **value comparison (V) stage** of courtship. In this phase the couple engages in conversations aimed at gathering information about each other. While my husband and I were taking classes together and getting to know each other, we were in the values comparison stage. Most of the information gathered during this stage focuses on the couple's interests, attitudes, beliefs, needs, values, and their past. Murstein notes, however, that the couple is unlikely to have developed sufficient intimacy by this stage to share their innermost feelings and thoughts. What is accomplished at this stage is mutual acceptance. Generally, some consensus develops as to what constitutes the important values of the relationship. For example, my husband and I both agreed on the importance of family, helping other people, and hard work; we both loved the seashore and folk music and supported the same political candidates.

If a couple has survived the stimulus and value comparison stages, they may (but do not necessarily) move on to the **role (R) stage.** It is at this point that the couple begins to plan for marriage or for a long-term commitment such as living together. In so doing, they evaluate the compatibility of their individual roles, as well as the "fit" between these roles and their perceptions of the way they want their relationship to develop. This also is a time when the partners share their intimate feelings and behaviors and begin talking about what they want in a spouse and co-parent, or whether they want children at all.

stimulus-value-role theory
Murstein's theory of courtship: The process begins with people responding to the overt characteristics of others; it progresses to value comparison; and eventually leads to an evaluation of role compatibility as the couple seriously considers marriage.

stimulus (S) stage
The stage in the stimulus-value-role theory in which a person responds to certain stimulus values or characteristics of another.

value comparison (V) stage
The second stage in the stimulus-value-role theory in which the couple engages in conversation aimed at gathering information about each other.

role (R) stage
The third stage of the stimulus-value-role theory in which the couple usually begins to plan for marriage or for a long-term commitment such as living together.

FIGURE 12-1

Stages of courtship.

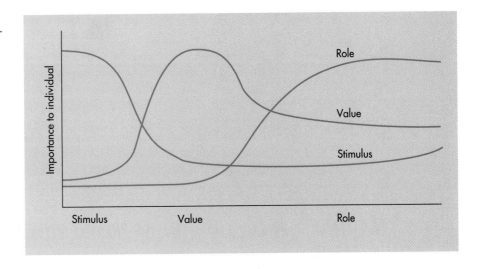

Murstein notes that the stimulus, value comparison, and role stages are not actually separate (see Figure 12–1). In other words, individuals within a couple relationship continue to respond to certain characteristics of their partner beyond the initial stage of courtship. However, those characteristics play a more important role during the early part of this process. Similarly, there is a constant comparison of values, interests, needs, and so on throughout the development of a relationship, although such comparisons are more important during the middle phase of the courtship. Other researchers (Windle & Lerner, 1984) believe that the comparison process takes place very early in a relationship and does not last for months or years as suggested by Murstein.

One of the more important insights gained from Murstein's stimulus-value-role theory of marital choice is that individuals do not necessarily have to be similar to have a successful relationship. Murstein (1982) points out that what is more important is that there be equity in the rewarding power of the partners. In other words, regardless of his or her characteristics, each individual in a relationship must have the ability to meet the needs of the other person. In some relationships, this may result when couples share similar interests and characteristics. In other relationships, it may result when each person complements the interests and characteristics of the other, as when one person likes to cook and another likes to clean up.

FOCUS ON CULTURE

In the United States, young adults get to know each other away from the watchful eyes of their parents or relatives. In Spain, Italy, and Latin America, however, it is not unusual for couples to be accompanied by chaperones to supervise their courtship. Courtship rituals may also be influenced by religious customs that may prohibit sexual relations between unmarried individuals.

RECAP

Most couples who marry do so in early adulthood. Mate selection is influenced by physical attractiveness, propinquity, and homogamy. Cultural factors can also influence mate selection. According to Murstein, couples first respond to each other during courtship based on perceived characteristics (stimulus stage), then gather more detailed information about each other's values and beliefs (values comparison stage), and finally evaluate the compatibility of their desired roles (role stage). Equity between the partners is an important factor in successful relationships.

MARITAL ADJUSTMENT

Establishing a Healthy Marital Relationship

Successful marriages do not just happen; they evolve as a result of a thoughtful courtship and deliberate attention to one another after the marriage. Marriage offers the individual the benefit of a committed and supportive partner. The partnerships that endure are usually ones in which each person gives more than they expect to get out of the relationship. While no marriage is without its conflicts or difficulties, successful marriages are characterized by many more positive interactions than negative ones. A mutual and common regard for one another adds to the pleasure of being married and may help to sustain the couple during stressful times in their lives. Often, successfully married couples are good friends as well.

Over the 20-year period that constitutes early adulthood, married couples experience a number of changes in their lives that can affect the nature and quality of their relationship. Career development and the addition of children to the family may compete with the time couples have to give each other. If their marriage is to survive these challenges, couples must periodically examine their needs together and make appropriate changes.

Resolving Marital Conflict

Even in the best of marriages, conflicts occur. An important component of any relationship is the ability to resolve disputes. Agreement may not be possible, but couples must be able to discuss their differences and at the very least agree to disagree. This involves effective communication *before* their disagreements have escalated into ugly, heated arguments. The ultimate failure in conflict resolution occurs when one or both partners refuses to talk about the issue. Sometimes marital disputes are resolved without the benefit of professional counseling; other times the problems are allowed to accumulate, thus making it difficult for couples to separate the problems themselves from their emotional reactions to the disputes. At this point, counseling can be helpful.

Sexual Adjustment

Another source of difficulty for some married couples is the nature of sexual adjustment and commitment. For some couples, the issue of sexual compatibility is raised before marriage. In the United States, premarital sex is common: 79% of men and 63% of women of college-age students sampled in one study indicated that they had engaged in premarital sexual intercourse (Robinson, Ziss, Ganza, & Katz, 1991). This represents a substantial increase in the incidence of premarital sex for women over the past few decades (Bell & Coughey, 1980; Robinson et al., 1991). The increase in premarital sexual experience for men has not been nearly as dramatic, primarily because it was higher than women's to begin with. Yet, despite the fact that many couples enter marriage with sexual experience, many must face sexual adjustments within a marriage or committed relationship.

Sex, like other social behavior, is learned. However, people who engage in sex are usually weighed down by all kinds of psychological and emotional baggage. They have ideas about how they should feel and how they should behave. Some people believe that if they are in love, satisfying sexual relations will follow naturally. These types of strongly held notions must often be discarded when adjusting to a sexual relationship. Couples have to discover in practice what causes sexual arousal for them and what sexual acts they are comfortable with, and then be able to communicate and coordinate their preferences with those of their partners. The issue of what constitutes permissible sexual technique may arise as partners gain experience with one another. New contraceptive planning may be necessary as the couple considers long-range plans for or against having children.

Even if the couple has lived together before marriage and has resolved some of these issues, new issues may arise. As Garrett (1982) observes, the trap of a dull and routine sex life needs to be avoided. Seduction must play a continuing role in the couple's sex life if this aspect of their marriage is to remain satisfactory. Unfortunately, for some couples the sexual excitement they experienced before marriage diminishes in the face of the routine they develop as husband and wife (Garrett, 1982). Marital fidelity is another new issue that must be addressed. Are the partners expected to be faithful to one another in the traditional sense, or are casual sexual encounters or even extramarital affairs to be tolerated, in theory or in practice?

Despite the change in attitude toward premarital sexual activity in recent years, there is little change in regard to extramarital sex. More than 90% of the American couples interviewed in a recent survey (Michael, Gagnon, Laumann, & Kolata, 1994) indicated that they considered extramarital sex to be wrong, although a small proportion of those surveyed indicated that sexual activity should not be regulated or judged at all. There is some feeling that extramarital sex may be "OK" if both partners agree to it or if it is part of the initial marriage contract or understanding. What most find unacceptable is lying and deception; if a partner lies about his or her extramarital involvement, this compromises the intimacy between them. Nevertheless, from 50 to 75% of all married men eventually commit adultery; so do from 25 to 43% of married women by the time they are 54 years of age (Thompson, 1983). In only one of five marriages is the spouse aware of it (Hunt, 1974). Men are most likely to engage in an extramarital affair during the first 5 years of a marriage, while women are most likely to have an affair after being married 15 to 20 years (Broderick, 1982).

Sexual activity is much more frequent among newly married couples. The longer couples are married, the less they engage in sexual intercourse. Results from a recent survey (Michael et al., 1994) suggest that about 40% of married

Sharing domestic chores is particularly important when both husband and wife have careers.

people have sex with their partner 2 or more times a week. The average monthly frequency of sexual intercourse for newlyweds is 15, while for couples married for 15 years, the average monthly frequency of sexual intercourse is 6 times.

MARITAL AND WORK ROLES

Perhaps the most difficult transition my husband and I made during our early years of marriage was figuring out our roles: We discussed, debated, and sometimes argued about who would be responsible for the financial tasks, meal preparation, decision making, and so on. Eventually, we were able to agree about how best to define our relationship with each other.

Especially significant for young couples living in industrialized countries in the 1990s are issues involving gender and work roles. It has become increasingly more common for both marriage partners to work outside the home, which has also produced a change in marital work roles (Gilbert, 1994). Overall, men's participation in family work has increased, more so in the area of parenting than in household work. According to Gilbert (1994), in more than one third of two-career families husbands and wives share equally in the household work and child care.

When marital satisfaction is measured, employed wives appear to be more satisfied and to perform more effectively than wives who do not work outside the home. Husbands of employed wives reported greater agreement with their wives over important issues (such as friends and sexual relations) and were more likely to solve disagreements in an egalitarian manner. Booth (1977) found that husbands whose wives were employed showed no more signs of stress and marital discord than did husbands whose wives were full-time homemakers. If anything, Booth concluded, husbands of employed women were happier and experienced less stress. They more often reported their wives as "loving" and "less critical." According to Booth, when stress does appear, it is likely to be the result of a transition period—for example, wives entering the workforce and employed women who became homemakers showed more signs of stress.

FOCUS ON CULTURE

In their book *American Couples,* Blumstein and Schwartz (1983) suggest that for relationships to be satisfying and long-lasting at least one member must be *relationship centered* rather than *work centered.* This expectation is consistent with the gender stereotypes of women as relationship oriented and men as task oriented. It also collides with reality, as the majority of American women enter the workforce while continuing family and domestic activities. How might relationships be affected when both partners are involved in careers?

Ideally, when both husband and wife work, they must balance the demands of their jobs with regular household chores such as cleaning, cooking, and laundry. Women feel more justified in asking husbands to help with housework and child care when they themselves are employed. Typically, a husband is more likely to involve himself fully in family work if his wife makes a major financial contribution to the household. However, other research that compared the work activity of husbands and wives around the house has found that husbands spend a much *shorter* time actually engaged in household tasks than do wives (1½ hours a day for men compared to 5 hours for women), and that wives generally are responsible for, and perform, most of the household and child-care tasks, as well as meal preparation (Maret & Finlay, 1984; Pleck & Rustad, 1980; Walker, 1970). Husbands, in turn, spend their time on traditionally masculine-oriented tasks such as washing the car and making repairs, which occur less frequently than the tasks for which wives are responsible.

When a married couple has children, they must balance their work roles with their marital and parental roles. A crucial factor in the success with which dual-earner families share their work is the gender-role attitude of the spouses, particularly the wives. In one study, Barnett and Baruch (1987) reported that the wife's attitude toward the male role was a major predictor of the husband's participation in child care and housework. When the wife's attitude was open to new and reversed gender roles, her husband did more; when it was traditional and fixed, he did less.

RECAP

Successful marriages result when people make a commitment to one another to communicate and cooperate. Conflict resolution involves willingness to resolve disagreements. Married couples must adjust to one another sexually; extramarital sex is viewed as an impediment to marital satisfaction. Work roles within marriages must be determined by each couple. People in dual-career marriages must find a way to balance their career and family roles. Women who work outside the home typically experience more satisfaction in their marriage.

DIVORCE

When Cathy and Tim married, they pledged to love, honor, and cherish each other until they died, not realizing at the time that they might not be able to live up to that pledge. The stresses and strains commonly found in marriages frequently lead to separation and divorce. However, cultural and religious beliefs may prevent or limit the use of divorce as a solution to difficult marriages. For example, for years divorce had been prohibited by law in Northern Ireland and the Republic of Ireland and in other Roman Catholic cultures, although couples may live separate lives while married.

The United States has the world's highest divorce rate. More than 60% of all U.S. couples who marry today can be expected to divorce (Bumpass, 1990). Over the past 20 years, the biggest increases in divorce rates in the United States have occurred among couples in their early adult years (after 9 or more years of marriage) and among those in middle adulthood (after 20 or more years of marriage) (Glenn, 1991); the greatest increases in the overall divorce rate have occurred since 1965. The typical divorced person is between 35 and 39 years of age (Norton & Moorman, 1987). The divorce rate is higher among the poor, the working class, the poorly educated, and those who marry outside of their social class or religion (Garrett, 1982). In the United States, divorce is more common in the west than in the east.

Nobody knows for certain what accounts for this number of divorces. Glenn (1991) suggests that the reason for the decline in marital success in the United States is that people have come to believe that marriages won't last; he maintains that fewer people today believe that marriage will last until the death of a spouse. Because they expect marriages to end, people are less likely to invest in their marital relationships; in this way they contribute to a social emotional context in which divorce is more likely to occur. Other reasons cited for divorce include unmet emotional needs and growing apart as a couple, lifestyle differences, boredom with the marriage, and conflicting or demeaning relationships (Gigy & Kelly, 1992).

One of the best predictors of divorce is age at first marriage. Teenage marriages, for example, are nearly twice as likely to fail as marriages that occur when the couple are in their 20s (Norton & Moorman, 1987). The tendency for early marriages to end in divorce and for marriages generally to break down in the early years suggests that an underlying developmental issue may involved. One or both of the marital partners may not have succeeded in becoming emotionally free from parents or in making a commitment to his or her own values or occupation. Not having done so makes it difficult to establish a mutually satisfactory relationship.

Women who marry after a premarital birth or give birth within 7 months after marriage are more likely to end their marriages in divorce. Further, first marriages of women over 30 are the most stable, although those who do divorce tend to do so sooner than women who marry at a younger age (Norton & Moorman, 1987). Also, several studies have suggested that the marriages of people whose parents divorced are more likely to end in divorce than those whose parents had stable marriages (Glenn & Kramer, 1987; Glenn & Shelton, 1983; Kobrin & Waite, 1984; Mueller & Cooper, 1986).

Research suggests that divorce is highly stressful, and second only to the death of a spouse in terms of the need for a major reorganization of one's life (Holmes & Rahe, 1967). It is not just the divorce itself that is stressful, however. Chiriboga and Cutler (1980) found that women reported equally high levels of

Divorce is stressful for adults because, in addition to the breakup of a relationship, it often results in moving out of one home and reestablishing a new one.

stress during the period before the decision to divorce and the period of separation itself. By contrast, men reported the least stress in the predecision period, somewhat greater stress during separation, and an even higher degree of vulnerability in the period after the divorce. Other research suggests that postseparation adjustment is related to the individual's preparedness for divorce. The person who initiates the divorce proceedings, takes a more active role in the decision-making process, and generally is better prepared for the divorce shows a higher level of adjustment in the postseparation phase (Helgeson, 1994; Wallerstein & Blakeslee, 1989; Wallerstein & Kelly, 1980).

Emotional reactions to separation and divorce are highly variable, and to a great extent are dependent on the nature of the process that preceded it (Kelly, 1982). The happy wife who comes home to find a note taped to the refrigerator will react with shock; the wife who has been locked in self-destructive conflict with her husband for years may well react with relief. There is much evidence, though, that both will suffer a great deal of pain and will need time to "mourn" the relationship. Some people are never able to adjust to divorce. They react to the breakup of their marriages with profound depression and anguish; some even contemplate suicide. However, not all couples that divorce end up as enemies. Some remain friends and maintain contact with each other through their mutual interest in their children (Ahrons & Rogers, 1987).

Most divorced people eventually remarry. About one quarter do so within a year; within 3 years, one half are remarried; within 9 years, three quarters have married again (Norton & Moorman, 1987). Men tend to remarry sooner than women. Although divorce rates are higher for second marriages, the majority of those who marry again remain married. Many see divorce as a growth experience that has allowed them to find not only a new and more suitable partner but greater awareness of themselves.

RECAP

Not all marriages endure; divorce rates have increased in the United States over the past 20 years. Reasons for divorce vary, but the expectation that marriages will not last increases the chances of separation and divorce. Teenage marriages and marriages after a premarital birth are more likely to end in divorce. Divorce is stressful for all involved. Emotional reactions to divorce vary, depending on the situation before the divorce. Most divorced people eventually remarry.

NONMARITAL LIFESTYLES

A great deal has been written in recent years about alternatives to marriage such as cohabitation, remaining single, living in a commune, living an open homosexual life, having and raising children without a spouse, and adopting a child as a single parent. Each of these nonmarital lifestyles—which are chosen by relatively few individuals—provides life satisfactions, problems, and developmental possibilities that are only beginning to be studied by psychologists and other social scientists. Perhaps the most common of these alternatives is cohabitation before or instead of marriage.

COHABITATION

cohabitation

Situation where an unmarried couple lives together and maintains a sexual relationship.

When Ari and Yael asked permission to share a room within their kibbutz, they did so with the intention of making a commitment to each other—a commitment that had the force of marriage. Unlike Ari and Yael, not all couples who decide to live together actually do so as a prelude to marriage. An increasingly common lifestyle in many Western cultures is **cohabitation,** in which an unmarried couple live together and maintain a sexual relationship (Michael et al., 1994). Living together may result from a dating relationship. In some cases, the couple does not make a deliberate decision to live together; they gradually drift into the relationship. Other relationships constitute a "trial" marriage during which each partner works at emotional commitment, but with the security (and insecurity) of knowing that one or the other can pack up and leave. Some couples live together for unromantic reasons. They may share living quarters for financial or other reasons and subsequently develop a sexual relationship. And in still other cases a couple may live together because the partners cannot legally marry—for example, because they are of the same sex or because one or both partners are married to another person.

No one knows for certain how many unmarried adults live together. Estimates, however, place the figure at about 4% of the American population; about 10% of single adults in their 20s and 30s have cohabited (Bumpass & Sweet, 1988). The rate of cohabitation is higher in other countries, such as Sweden, where 15% of unmarried couples live together.

Reiss (1980) has suggested that cohabiting couples fall into two broad categories. For one group of cohabitants, living together is simply another form of courtship, not an alternative to marriage. The primary feature of these couples is their attitude toward having children while living together—generally, they are against it. Macklin (1978) notes that in this type of relationship, should pregnancy occur, the couple would be likely either to have an abortion or to get married. Thus in the eyes of these individuals, parenthood is reserved for marital relationships. The second, and by far the smaller, group of cohabitants believes it is acceptable to bear children within their relationship. Thus, these individuals tend to view cohabitation as an alternative to marriage rather than as part of the courtship process. *Nonlegal marital cohabitation*—as Reiss (1980) calls this pattern—involves a desire for a lifelong commitment to one's partner along with a desire to develop the same type of family environment, including children, that is found in marital relationships.

For many young adults, cohabitation forms the basis for the decision to marry. However, many such relationships do not end up in marriage and last an average of 18 months. Some research suggests that cohabitation may interfere with a healthy marriage; marital instability and divorce rates are higher among couples who have lived together prior to marriage than for those who did not (Bumpass & Sweet, 1988; Thompson & Colella, 1992).

SINGLEHOOD

Peter came close to entering a committed relationship, but ultimately he realized that he was not ready for marriage. In avoiding marriage, Peter also embraced the possibility of remaining single. Although 25 may be the age by which many American young people plan to be married, about 56% of all men and 39% of all women in the United States find themselves single on their 25th birthday. At 30, the percentages are approximately 25 and 16, respectively (World Almanac and Book of Facts, 1995). A significant number of people in our society are single through much of their early adulthood.

Garrett (1982) has argued that two different decision-making processes can lead a person to singlehood. One involves the "push" toward singlehood as a way of avoiding marriage. The alternative is the "pull" of singlehood in response to its perceived benefits. In other words, some people remain single because of their fear of being "trapped" in marriage and becoming bored with their partner; or because they equate marriage with limited sexuality, inhibited self-growth, social isolation, and limited mobility within a career. In each case, singlehood is a response to the perceived negative qualities of marriage. By contrast, other people choose to remain single because of the perceived advantages singlehood affords: freedom for individual change, greater mobility, self-sufficiency, a greater variety of experiences, sexual freedom, and increased career opportunities. In one study (Goldscheider & Waite, 1987), women who left home in early adulthood to live on their own were less likely to get married than women who continued to live at home.

Single people tend to live in, or be drawn to, urban centers, where opportunities for employment and social interaction are high. They tend to associate with other singles and to be concerned with establishing relationships that meet their needs for intimacy, companionship, and emotional support (Stein, 1980). Indeed, it may be that the well-adjusted single person enjoys richer friendships characterized by greater age and ethnic diversity than do married couples in the same age range.

Single people tend to live in urban centers, where there are more opportunities for employment and social activities.

Homosexual Lifestyles

Over the past 20 years, increasing numbers of men and women have openly declared their homosexuality. Many of these individuals are married and have children; others are single and living alone or with a lover. Despite the greater openness, the number of homosexuals in the U.S. population is difficult to determine. Estimates range from 3 to 10% of the total population (Patterson, 1995). Of course, the definition of homosexuality affects this estimate. More conservative estimates usually reflect the number of people who are mainly or exclusively homosexual; more liberal estimates include not only these individuals but also those who have sporadic homosexual encounters and/or are bisexual.

As homosexuals "come out of the closet," many of the myths regarding their lifestyle are being challenged. One in particular involves the notion that all homosexuals are promiscuous and unable to form lasting intimate relationships. Bell and Weinberg (1978), however, found considerable variability in the lifestyles of gay men and lesbians. Specifically, five different life patterns were identified, accounting for over 70% of their sample.

Some homosexuals (28% of lesbian women and 10% of gay men) form **close couple** relationships that resemble marriage. These relationships are characterized by a high level of intimacy and fewer social and psychological problems than other types of homosexual relationships. They are similar to those of heterosexual couples. Kurdek (1994) found that among a sample of gay, lesbian, and heterosexual married and unmarried couples, length of the relationship was a better predictor of satisfaction than sexual preference. But unlike heterosexual couples, lesbian and gay couples share household tasks more equally. Approximately equal percentages of gay men (18%) and lesbian women (17%) live as **open couples:** These couples live together, but are less committed to the relationship than close couples. They also are likely to have affairs outside the relationship. Homosexuals in open relationships, although not as well adjusted as those in close relationships, are nevertheless comparable in adjustment to heterosexuals. Other homosexuals live a "single" life arranged around homosexual activities. These **functionals,** as Bell and Weinberg refer to them, account for 15% of gay men and 10% of lesbians. In general, these individuals tend to be social and political, and are well adjusted—second only to homosexuals in close-couple relationships.

A fourth group of gays, which includes 12% of the men and 5% of the women, are called **dysfunctionals.** Generally, these individuals live alone and are troubled by their homosexuality and the stigma associated with it. As a result, the incidence of sexual, social, and psychological problems is higher for this group than for other homosexual groups.

The final group of homosexuals identified by Bell and Weinberg are the **asexuals** (16% of gay men and 11% of lesbians). These individuals tend to be older, to be sexually inactive or less interested in sex, and to have difficulty forming intimate relationships. Research has also found consistent gender differences in the lifestyles of homosexuals. Overall, lesbians tend to have fewer sexual partners than do gay men (Patterson, 1994). They also are more concerned with romantic love and affection in their relationships.

close couple

A type of homosexual relationship that resembles marriage and includes a high level of intimacy.

open couple

A type of homosexual relationship in which the couple lives together, but are less committed to the relationship than close couples.

functionals

Homosexual individuals who live a "single" life, arranged around homosexual activities.

dysfunctionals

Homosexual individuals who live alone and are troubled by their homosexuality.

asexuals

Homosexual individuals who tend to be older, sexually inactive (or less interested in sex), and have difficulty in forming intimate relationships.

Gay rights organizations have taken on the challenge of educating homosexuals and heterosexuals about AIDS.

Since the mid-1980s, when the deadly AIDS virus first emerged among sexually active gay men and intravenous drug users, there has been considerable concern among gays and heterosexuals about the impact this disease may have on people's tolerance and acceptance of gay people in general. It is now recognized that susceptibility to the AIDS virus is not at all limited to gay people or intravenous drug users. Despite this fact, many people continue to associate AIDS with homosexuality. Out of their fear of AIDS, some people may shun normal contact with gay people—even though the virus is not spread by touching or by sharing food or drink. Nonetheless, gay people, especially gay men, who are sexually active need to take precautions to avoid the spread of the disease. Many health centers offer confidential AIDS testing and telephone hot lines have been established in many cities to provide information and advise people how to protect themselves against AIDS.

RECAP

Increasingly, young adult couples are living together. Some do so as a preliminary to marriage, others for convenience. While most adults marry, some choose to remain single. Single people associate with each other and establish relationships that meet their needs for intimacy and companionship. Some adults choose a lesbian or gay lifestyle. Life patterns among homosexual people are similar to heterosexual lifestyles. Some form close relationships, while others opt for a single lifestyle. A smaller number of gays remain alone or uninvolved in any sexual relationship.

PARENTING

In the course of their lives, most human beings become parents either through choice or chance. Some adults are unable to have children because they are infertile. To meet their desire to have children they turn to adopting children or acting as foster parents. In preindustrial countries where adult mortality is high due to accidents and deaths during childbirth, it is not uncommon for infertile adults to assume stepparent or foster parent roles as a way of satisfying their parental needs while also supporting orphaned children or an economically overburdened family. For example, in Oceania the proportion of households in which foster parenting occurs ranges from 12% in Tonga to 83% in a community of Tuvalu (formerly the Ellice Islands) (Hewlett, 1991). Similarly, among Native Americans in the Arctic, about 25% of all children live in some kind of foster care arrangement.

Fertility Motivation

Even before my husband and I were married, we discussed our interest in having children. Fortunately, we agreed that we wanted children. What we did not discuss was *why* we wanted children. At the time, it seemed to me that having children was what I was "supposed" to do. This was before reliable birth control measures were readily available; so our choices about whether to have children and how many were constrained. Today, couples have more choices and means to act on their choices. Researchers who study **fertility motivation** have examined the factors that influence people's motives and decisions regarding whether to have children. They have found that the value of children to parents differs across cultures and individuals, and so do the reasons for having children.

What motivates couples to make the transition to parenthood? The answer depends in part on economic factors. In many societies, people want children because of their economic benefit to the family. Generally, people living in rural areas in preindustrialized societies are more likely to value children because they can participate in family work or take care of them in their old age. In an

fertility motivation
People's reasons or motives for wanting children.

One way many people meet the mid-adulthood need of generativity is to become a parent and care for children.

extensive study comparing the value of children to parents in different cultures (Arnold et al., 1975), Filipino respondents living in the Philippines and Hawaii scored highest for valuing children for their economic benefit; Taiwanese and Thai parents scored next highest. Expectations of economic benefits from children were lowest in Japan.

In the United States and other industrialized societies, children are not seen as an economic family resource; instead, the expenses associated with having and raising a child may be a reason not to have children. Many couples desire to have children to reduce perceived social pressure to have children—particularly pressure from their own parents, the prospective grandparents. Once couples have had one child, they are more likely to cite as a reason for having another child their delight in children for their own sake. Others want children for the emotional comfort they believe their children may provide them in old age or because they desire heirs to whom they can bequeath their resources, ideas, and values. Children may also be seen as a way to "make it all worthwhile"—to do some good. Those who decide to have children in their 30s tend to mention feelings about their own mortality and the need for someone who will outlive them.

In one study (Gormly, Gormly, & Weiss, 1987), college students who indicated they wanted to have children at some point in their lives were asked to describe their reasons why. Their responses were coded into nine categories that are presented in Table 12–2. Most of the students' reasons reflected an interest in establishing an identity or social network, needs that may not yet have been fulfilled during their late teens and early 20s. For young adults who delay childbearing until their late 20s or early 30s, the reasons for wanting children may reflect different needs, such as a need to nurture or care for others.

MOTIVATIONS FOR PARENTHOOD AMONG COLLEGE STUDENTS

RANK	PERCENTAGE	MOTIVE
1	48.29%	To expand myself, have someone to follow me
2	47.91	To achieve adult status or social identity
3	45.25	To provide a family for myself
4	32.70	For the fun and stimulation children bring
5	23.19	To be able to influence or control someone
6	19.39	Because it is the morally correct thing to do
7	8.37	To compete or compare myself with others
8	6.84	For the sense of accomplishment or creativity
9	4.56	For the economic benefit

TABLE 12–2

Source: From "Motivations for Parenthood among Young Adult College Students," by A. Gormly, J. Gormly, and H. Weiss, 1987, Sex Roles, 16, 31–39.

Not all motives for having children are good ones. Social workers placing children with a couple for adoption tend to be critical of such motives as having a child to improve the marriage or prevent the marriage from deteriorating. Some people want a child as an escape from boredom or from an unsatisfactory job. Some see a child as a form of social status. Finally, some women, either single or unhappily married, want a child because in the absence of adult intimacy they need someone with whom to form a genuine attachment.

People's motives for wanting children can influence their parenting goals. Hoffman (1987) compared the child-rearing patterns of over 3,000 parents from eight countries with the value they placed on having children. She found that parents who wanted children for their economic benefit were more likely to stress obedience in raising their children. People who valued children for the love and companionship they would provide stressed congeniality. Other parents, who wanted children to strengthen their marriage, emphasized independence in their child-rearing goals.

FOCUS ON CULTURE

Population control is a worldwide issue. In the United States the birth rate is near the zero population growth rate of two children, representing one per parent. However, in many other countries where birthrates are either too high or too low, governments have established population control policies and laws. For example, in China severe sanctions are applied to couples who have more than one child. In contrast, other societies promote larger families either by forbidding contraception for religious reasons, as is the case in Roman Catholic or Muslim cultures, or by offering economic bonuses and privileges to couples who have more children, as in Quebec, Canada.

ADJUSTMENT TO PARENTHOOD

The day I became a mother for the first time was a very exciting time in my adult life. The day after I became a mother, I realized the change becoming parents would have on the lives of my husband and myself. There may be no good way of knowing in advance how parenthood will impact personal and social adjustments. The transition to parenthood has been described as a crisis point in the life of the couple, requiring adjustments for which they are often not prepared (Rossi, 1968). In one study of over 2,500 adults, the birth of the first child was rated as the sixth most stressful life event out of 102 possible events (Dohrenwend, Krasnoff, Askenasy, & Dohrenwend, 1978). Young girls living in preindustrialized societies often learn child-care skills by caring for younger siblings; some even attend the birth of their siblings. But in most industrialized societies very little is done to practically prepare people for parenthood, either before or after the child arrives. Furthermore, the transition to parenthood is an abrupt one. One day the couple are by themselves, and the next day they have "another mouth to feed"—a human being for whom they are responsible. The transition is even more abrupt when an unplanned pregnancy occurs. Childbirth and parent education programs help reduce the stress of the transition for some people, but the majority of parents do not have access to or interest in these programs.

Parenthood disrupts the two-person routine of the married couple and frequently interrupts the career of the wife while placing time constraints on the husband. The arrival of an infant restricts the parents' activities outside of the home, as well as their privacy within. Communication of feelings and ideas between the parents is sharply curtailed, perhaps because of the increased demands on parents' time. Indeed, one researcher found that young parents talk to each other about half as much as newly married couples—and their talk tends to focus on the child (Schulz, 1972).

Evidence suggests that marital satisfaction decreases with the arrival of the first child (Belsky, Spanier, & Rovine, 1983; Emery & Tuer, 1993; Miller & Sollie, 1980). The quality of marital relationships continues to decline as additional children are added to the family, particularly for women (Belsky, Spanier, & Rovine, 1983). In the later stages of family life, particularly after the departure of the children from the home, marital quality increases once again (Alpert & Richardson, 1980; Schram, 1979). However, the drop in marital satisfaction with the arrival of children does not occur for all couples. Hoffman and Mavis (1978) reported that if children are planned and desired, they can strengthen the marital relationship.

A healthy marriage can affect the quality of parenting that parents give to their children. One study (Cox, Owen, Lewis, & Henderson, 1989) found that couples in a close and intimate marital relationship displayed greater sensitivity and warmth and held more positive attitudes toward their babies than did couples in a less intimate or close marital relationship. Research by Umberson (1987) suggests that married couples with children may be healthier than adults who are not married or have no children—perhaps because they needed to be healthy to live up to their parental responsibilities.

Some adults choose to begin their families by adopting children. Adoptive parents often experience a more abrupt transition to parenthood than couples who become parents through pregnancy, because they may have had less predictable routes to parenthood (Levy-Shiff, Goldshmidt, Har-Even; 1991). During the early probationary months of parenting, their legal status as guardians may not yet be secure. Moreover, some adoptive parents may have to deal with biases against adoption as a route to parenthood. These difficulties compound those all adults must make in their transition to parenthood. Despite the problems associated with adoption, however, adoptive parents have been found to have more positive expectations and more satisfying experiences in their transition to parenthood than biological parents (Levy-Shiff et al., 1991).

The birth of a child to a couple who have been childless for many years or for couples who remarry at a later age may require additional adjustments. Women and men may feel a bit "out of step" with peers who started their families at a younger age. In the case of reconstituted families, the birth of a baby may create feelings of rivalry or even a sense of betrayal in children from a previous marriage.

The new status of parenthood necessarily leads to new relationships between the couple and society. New mothers seek out other new mothers for companionship and advice. Many new parents show increased pleasure in the company of their own parents as well, going to them for emotional and material support as well as for baby-sitting services. Parenthood also brings renewed contact with institutions that may have been ignored during single life and early marriage. As the child progresses through early childhood, parents begin evaluating the parks and libraries and especially the schools of their neighborhoods. For some, this leads to community activism, perhaps on behalf of better playground maintenance or in opposition to indecent advertising and violence on television. For others, dissatisfaction with the neighborhood can lead to major changes in lifestyle. A move from city to suburb, for example, will have a considerable effect on a family's consumption and commuting patterns.

RECAP

The decision to bear or adopt children is one way to meet the need to provide for the next generation. Reasons for wanting children are culturally influenced and range from wanting someone to love, enjoy, and influence to increasing the family's economic stability. Parenthood requires major adjustments by the couple and can be disruptive and stressful. Marital satisfaction declines during the early parenting years. Parenthood also enriches the life of the couple.

OCCUPATIONAL DEVELOPMENT

Two of the most important decisions adults make originate in early adulthood: the decision to marry and/or raise a family and the selection of one's career. The choices people make about their careers as young adults can alter the path they take through life. A large part of the person's identity is connected to their work, which occupies about 40 years of the typical person's life. "What do you do for a living?" is a commonly asked question. An occupation provides people with much more than a means of supporting themselves and their family. It gives them a way of defining themselves within their community and earning social status. The work environment offers adults a social network of acquaintances whom they might not ordinarily meet. Many adults gain enormous personal satisfaction from their work; they are able to learn new skills and demonstrate their competence and mastery. Work helps people structure their time and provides economic stability.

SUPER'S THEORY OF OCCUPATIONAL DEVELOPMENT

Perhaps you are at the beginning of your career; you may be in the process of switching to a new one. Finding and launching a meaningful career takes time; in fact, it may take years to achieve one's career goals. **Occupational development** refers to the changes people experience that culminate in their choice of a career. The concept of occupational development is more applicable to industrialized countries than nonindustrialized ones. Adults living in nontechnological or rural agricultural countries have fewer, if any, choices about what they will do to make a living. Often, occupational choice gives way to economic necessity. For example, within rural nontechnological cultures, young men reach physical maturity already knowing that they will make their living as farmers or animal herders, and young women can expect their work role to include child care and maintenance of the family home.

occupational development
The changes people experience that culminate in their assumption of a chosen career.

But for many people living in industrialized societies, the choice of a career is not a one-shot decision made in early adulthood. The life cycle imposes many different tasks at different periods of life; consequently, people develop and change in respect to their vocations. Donald Super (1957, 1963) has suggested that people go through five stages of occupational development (see Table 12–3). During adolescence (14–18 years) there is a crystallization of one's ideas about work. At this time the person is likely to be exposed to many different occupational areas through the media, schooling, family, friends and relatives, and firsthand experience in part-time jobs. While this is going on, the adolescent is comparing possible career paths with his or her skills, interests, personality characteristics, and so on.

The second stage (18–21 years) involves the specification of a particular occupational preference and the beginning of job training. Frequently, this involves specialized education such as that found in vocational training centers or in career-oriented college programs. For some people, like Ari, an apprenticeship to an older person may provide the specialized training needed to assume an occupation.

After specifying a particular career path, the next step in the occupational development process (21–24 years) is the implementation of training and entry into the first job. This step marks a major change in self-perception for some people; by adopting the worker role, many young people begin to see themselves as adults for the first time. When Ari got the job of collective manager on the kibbutz, he reached this level of occupational development.

Following the implementation phase, workers enter into the stage of job stabilization (24–35 years). This is the time when people become established in their fields and begin to develop job reputations—such as "good worker," "reliable," "a potential leader," "overly cautious," or "lacks motivation."

The fifth stage in Super's model (35 years and older) is the period of consolidation and advancement within a field or on the job. This stage represents the greatest span of time within the person's career; it is also the time when most individuals are at their peak earning power.

SUPER'S THEORY OF OCCUPATIONAL DEVELOPMENT

AGE*	STAGE	DESCRIPTION
14–18	Crystallization	Consideration of career paths
18–21	Specification	Selection of a particular career preference, beginning of job training
21–24	Implementation	Entry into the job market
24–35	Stabilization	Establishment of reputation as a worker
35+	Consolidation and advancement	Promotion and/or recognition for work

TABLE 12–3

*Ages are approximate and do not apply to later career changes.

During the phase of job stabilization people become established in their jobs and take pride and pleasure from their work.

Super's theory provides a way of thinking about the steps involved in career development. But for many women the sequence of steps may not fit easily into Super's stages. For one thing, women frequently pursue two careers, one as mother and one in the workforce. Today, large numbers of women are selecting career paths that include both working outside the home and planning for a family (Archer, 1985a, 1985b). Women's occupational development thus is more complex than men's because of their combined career and family roles.

Many women interrupt their careers to have or care for children. However, an uninterrupted career is an important ingredient in occupational success. A 7-year longitudinal study of women who were between the ages of 30 and 44 at the start of the study found that women who worked continuously had the highest salaries (Van Velsor & O'Rand, 1984). Furthermore, those who worked before having children and then returned to the same type of job after their children entered school earned higher salaries than those who switched jobs or entered the job market after they had had children. Women who work continuously are also more likely to be promoted than women who have breaks in their work patterns (Betz, 1984). Continuous commitment to occupational choice may be difficult, if not impossible, for some women who also have family commitments.

MOVING FROM COLLEGE TO CAREER

College provides many people with the skills and credentials to advance their career goals. But a college education is no job guarantee. For some young adults, going to college is way of exploring their career interests. Some people enter college with a specific career in mind, only to change their minds after learning more about the requirements or scope of the career. Other students know only that they will need a college degree to advance in any career, and they delay their choice of major as long as they can. But as graduation nears, the reality of having to find a job (and repay college loans) stimulates students to think carefully about what they want and don't want to do for a living.

To be successful, students' career goals must match the current job market. Some occupations are in greater demand than others, and students who have acquired necessary technological skills will have an advantage over those who lack them. Once in the job market, people discover the value of being able to confidently present themselves to prospective employers. Many of these skills can be acquired in college, but all too frequently, students don't realize the importance of these skills until after they graduate. Careful planning in college can help students in their job search after graduation. For example, internships give students an opportunity to acquire relevant job skills and refine their career interests while earning college credit.

RECAP

Occupational development involves selection of, preparation for, and entry into a career. Super proposed five stages of occupational development: crystallization, specification, implementation, stabilization, and consolidation and advancement. Women's career development may not follow the same progression owing to conflicts with family responsibilities. While a college degree is an important credential, it is no guarantee of a job. College can help students clarify their career goals and acquire relevant job skills.

CAREER CHOICE, SELF-CONCEPT, AND GENDER-ROLE IDENTITY

After Cathy's divorce from Tim, she struggled with the question of who she really was and how she wanted to live her life. Part of her answer included a career as a nurse. When an individual takes a first serious full-time job, in many cases it represents an implementation of his or her self-concept. For example, a person whose self-concept includes the qualities of empathy, genuineness, and understanding may well become a mental-health professional assuming that these personality characteristics are suited to such a career. The same person would be less likely to choose a career as a computer programmer, since interpersonal skills are less useful in such a job. Research using trait description checklists has shown that there is a high correlation between people's self-concepts and the occupations to which they aspire (Holland, 1973).

Self-concept influences more than one's initial occupational choice. Havighurst (1982) notes that following entry into the first job there may be some floundering as the young person finds that his or her initial career choice is not as satisfying as expected. Perhaps the job requirements were inappropriately evaluated; perhaps the person's self-evaluation was inadequate. Whatever the reason, the "fit" between the job requirements and the individual's self-concept is poor, leading the person to seek employment in another field. Levinson, Darrow, Klein, Levinson, and McKee (1977) have emphasized that reevaluation of the match between one's career and self-concept can take place at any point in the life cycle.

As people experience significant life events—marriage, parenthood, separation or divorce, death of a loved one—their self-concept is likely to change. Such a change can initiate a crisis regarding career commitment as one begins to question the fit between one's new sense of self and one's occupational goals.

Gender role is an important aspect of career-choice identity. People in their 20s today find that entrance into many occupations is determined less by gender than it used to be. Women who had assumed that they would enter a stereotypically feminine "caring" profession, such as teaching, nursing, or social work, are being encouraged to reconsider their options. For some young women this has meant taking the risk of expressing abilities and lifestyles their parents believed to be "masculine." Women have become mine workers, engineers, corporate managers, firefighters, and ministers—not always without some social and interpersonal stresses. A mother, for example, may caution her "manager" daughter that success may stand in the way of personal fulfillment in marriage. Or male coworkers may harass a female steelworker on the job, making it difficult for her to work comfortably.

When your grandparents (or great-grandparents) were young adults, they probably approached their work roles with a different view than that of many couples today. In the past, it was expected that men would be employed until they retired and women would be involved in maintaining the home and caring for the family. Today, however, men and women are both in the workforce, and many share in child care and household responsibilities. Moreover, it is much more difficult for one employed spouse to change jobs without a significant impact on the other employed spouse and other family members. Today, couples with children are less likely to place job or career interests above family concerns. A survey of managers in large corporations found that even in this high-achieving group there was growing reluctance among younger managers to uproot their families for the sake of a promotion. There was also more openness to the possibility of second careers, suggesting that identity was less rigidly tied to the job or the company than in earlier generations (Williams, 1977). A related phenomenon is the tendency of men and women to prefer jobs that offer maternity or paternity leave enabling them to care for newborn children.

Many more women are selecting career paths. Unfortunately, there are not as many role models for women as there are for men.

OCCUPATIONAL STRESS

When several workers in a section of a large corporation started calling in sick, the manager wondered what was happening in that department. An investigation revealed that the workers were expected to work quickly and precisely; the workload was heavy and workers were penalized for not keeping up with their coworkers. Furthermore, the work space was hot and very noisy. Several workers complained of headaches and general fatigue; others were noticeably irritable and a few reported themselves to be depressed. Clearly, the workers in this section were experiencing the effects of stress.

occupational stress
Adverse mental or physical health reactions that result from work-related conditions such as workload, pace, schedule, physical and social settings, and health hazards.

Occupational stress refers to adverse mental or physical health reactions that result from work-related conditions such as workload, pace, schedule, physical and social settings, and health hazards. Stress in the workplace and its impact on the individual worker has become a prominent issue, particularly in countries that depend upon a healthy and productive workforce for their economic and political stability (Keita & Jones, 1990). For individuals, the amount of stress they experience on the job can affect not only their decision to stay on the job, but their mental and physical health as well.

Stress in the workplace can be the result of excessive noise, a demanding work schedule, or unpleasant coworkers.

Personal Perspective

SEXUAL HARASSMENT ON THE JOB

In 1991, law professor and attorney Anita Hill accused Supreme Court nominee Clarence Thomas of engaging in sexually harassing activities. The issue of sexual harassment was immediately thrust into national attention when the Senate held hearings to determine whether these charges should interfere with his confirmation. Surveys suggest that approximately one of every two women will be harassed at some point during their academic or working lives (Fitzgerald, 1993). **Sexual harassment** is a violation of the federal Education Act (Title IX), the Employment Act (Title VII), and the Civil Rights Act of 1964,

and of many state laws as well. Under the law, there are two forms of sexual harassment: *quid pro quo,* in which sexual favors are made a condition of continued employment or advancement, and *hostile environment,* in which unwelcome sexual advances, requests for sexual favors, or other verbal or physical conduct of a sexual nature is perceived as hostile and impedes a person's work performance. Hostile sexual behaviors are defined from the point of view of the beholder; from a legal perspective, this is interpreted to mean behaviors that a "reasonable" person would expect not to occur in a given situation. For example, while a man may think that calling a female employee "sweetheart" or "honey" and giving her a pat on her backside may be complementary, most "reasonable" people would consider these behaviors to be demeaning and abusive. When a boss or supervisor displays such

behavior, the employee may not feel free to confront or complain about it out of fear of being fired or passed over for promotion. Other examples of sexual harassment include subtle pressure for sexual activity, sexual remarks about an individual's body or sexual activities, or overt threats or offers concerning a person's job that are tied to sexual activity.

Although illegal, sexual harassment continues to be a problem for many women and some men. Sexual harassment can occur between a male harasser and a female victim, a female harasser and a male victim, or people of the same sex. By far the largest number of complaints involving sexual harassment are filed against male harassers by female employees. One study (Gutek, Cohen, & Konrad, 1990) reported that more than 53% of the women employed by Los Angeles County reported that

sexual harassment
Situations in which sexual favors are made a condition for employment or advancement, or in which sexual advances or behaviors create a hostile environment that impedes a person's performance.

What factors contribute to occupational stress? Most jobs have been designed from the point of view of the employer rather than the worker. Some attention has been given to changing the work setting or job demands with the aim of increasing production and job efficiency. However, the long-term impact of specific jobs on workers' health or satisfaction has been neglected (Levi, 1990). In many settings, the worker must fit the job; no effort is made to fit the job to the worker.

Jobs that offer workers little control over their work are more likely to produce stress (Sauter, Murphy, & Hurrell, 1990). Workers who have little or no say in decision making or who cannot control their work flow, such as those on an assembly line, are at greater risk for job dissatisfaction, emotional distress, and other negative reactions (Spector, 1986).

Lack of job security and an uncertain career future are also associated with increased stress. People who work in jobs that make heavy demands on their time and energy and who are unclear about what is expected of them are vulnerable to they had been sexually harassed on the job at some point. The study also reported that 10% of women and less than 1% of men have quit their jobs as a result of sexual harassment.

The impact of sexual harassment can be traumatic. In addition to the disruption of her career, a woman who suffers on-the-job harassment often experiences discomfort and guilt. Harassment also erodes self-confidence and self-esteem.

Unfortunately, many instances of sexual harassment occur as a result of miscommunication and misunderstandings between men and women. Over the years, the standard of acceptable public conduct has changed dramatically from the time when female secretaries were portrayed in the media as sitting on their bosses' laps and responding to their every need. Today, men and women need to communicate more openly about the effects of their behaviors (intended or un-intended) on each other. So, for example, when a man tells jokes of a sexual nature in the workplace that make a woman feel uncomfortable, the woman should communicate her disapproval directly to the man by saying "I don't think that kind of joke is appropriate for the office." If the behavior persists, harsher steps need to be taken, such as notifying the offending person in writing about the effects of the behavior or filing formal charges with a grievance officer or supervisor.

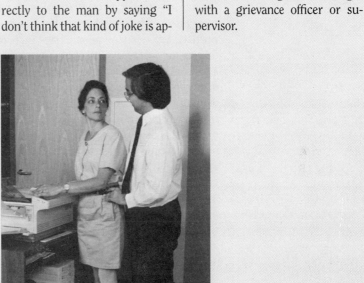

Unwanted sexual advances can create a hostile environment, making it difficult for a person to perform their work.

stress (LaCroix & Haynes, 1987). Examples of stressful jobs include situations where a supervisor fails to provide specific instructions or where a worker reports to two supervisors with conflicting expectations. Clearly defined expectations and goals and constructive feedback on job performance can help reduce this stress.

Workers who can strike a healthy balance between work, play, and family life are best able to counter the impact of occupational stress (Custer, 1994). The presence of a supportive social network on the job is another factor that seems to reduce occupational stress. When people have access to supportive coworkers and supervisors to help them accomplish their jobs or to deal with the stresses inherent in the job, they report less stress (Sauter et al., 1990).

The nature of the job can also contribute to the stress of working. Jobs that involve working with hazardous materials or are inherently dangerous, such as bomb squads, are obviously stressful and have an effect on long-term health. But other less obviously stressful jobs also present health hazards. For example, jobs involving repetitive movement such as constant typing on a computer keyboard can produce repetitive strain injuries in which the hands become numb and the wrists ache; in some cases surgery is required to restore normal functioning. Excessive exposure to video display terminals has also been identified as an occupational hazard.

WOMEN AND ETHNIC MINORITIES IN THE WORKPLACE

Numerous studies have found that the workplace is a major source of stress in men's lives, while the home offers a benign, stressless setting (Baruch, Beiner, & Barnett, 1987). Many people have incorrectly assumed that a similar relationship occurs for women. With the increase in the number of women entering careers and working outside of the home, it was predicted that a rise in job stress–related disorders would be found for women. However, a longitudinal study of American women found evidence to the contrary. The researchers found that participation in the workforce had beneficial effects on health for unmarried women and for married African American women, and no effect on health for white married women (Waldron & Jacobs, 1989). When women have a positive attitude about employment, when they want to work and accept their work role, they actually have better health (Repetti, Matthews, & Waldron, 1989). This is due in part to an increase in family income and greater access to health care as a result of being employed. The stresses associated with work are further reduced for married women when their husbands share the burdens of maintaining the home. For many women, working also provides a richer social network from which to derive support in times of need.

Job discrimination and prejudice can be sources of occupational stress for women and ethnic minorities (Keita & Jones, 1989). Overt or subtle racism and sexism can create an unpleasant work atmosphere. Much more research is needed to assess systematically the interaction of occupational stress with race, gender, and class. In addition, some women may face additional stress on the job due to sexual harassment.

FOCUS ON CULTURE

In just one generation, gender roles in many Western cultures have changed to include a wider range of career options for women and men. However, institutions such as professional schools, corporations, and certain industries do not change as quickly as individuals. What kinds of problems might a person have to confront when entering a career that has traditionally been associated with a specific gender (e.g., a male nurse or a female manager)?

TWO-PROVIDER FAMILIES

I began my career as a mother at the same time as my career as a psychology professor. My husband and I shared child-care responsibilities and worked out a schedule that would give each of us time to prepare for our classes and grade papers. When the children had school vacations or when one of them got sick, we would decide which of us could more easily stay home with them. It was a challenging part of our lives, sometimes frustrating, but ultimately rewarding.

One of the more important social trends of the past few decades is the increase in the number of women in the workforce and, consequently, the growing number of two-provider, or dual-earner, families. In the United States, more than half of the married women with children are employed, including 61% of women with children under age 6 ("U.S. Children and Their Families," 1991).

While many women would prefer to stay home and care for their children, they often must assume the additional responsibilities of work in order to support their family. In the case of single mothers, there frequently is no choice but to work. Moen (1982) notes that the majority of dual-earner couples see their situation as an economic necessity rather than an option. In addition, a declining birthrate has freed more women from the responsibility of child care at an earlier stage of their adult lives. Changes in societal attitudes concerning female and male roles have also helped women make the transition into the work world. Once there, these more flexible attitudes have opened up a greater range of career opportunities for women.

Much has been written about the relationship between work and the family, and the special costs and benefits found in two-provider households (Moen, 1982). The trend today is for more and more young women to look to both career and family relationships as sources of personal satisfaction (Regan & Roland, 1985). But there are costs associated with this choice. One of the more difficult problems faced by dual-earner couples is how to manage their time. There is only so much time in the day, and if both spouses work, less time can be allocated to other activities—child care, social activities, hobbies, and just being together as a couple. Managing work and family life also requires a great deal of energy. As Moen (1982) observes, the stresses and strains of work can be great, particularly for individuals who are moving up the career ladder. The physical and emotional drain that results can interfere with satisfactory adjustment areas of life outside of work.

role overload

A condition in which a person takes on, or is expected to take on, the responsibilities associated with many roles; this produces increased stress in the individual.

The meshing of work and nonwork roles also produces **role overload** for many people, particularly women. Although husbands of employed wives are more likely to contribute in household tasks and help with child care than husbands of non-employed wives (Patterson, 1994), women still do more of the household chores (Maret & Finlay, 1984). The additional strain on women produced by role overload can contribute to the development of marital dissatisfaction among dual-career couples. This is particularly true if the husband is not supportive of the woman's entry into the workforce.

It should be noted, however, that two-provider families are not necessarily doomed to greater conflict than single-earner families. In a study (Benin & Nienstedt, 1985) examining the causes of happiness and unhappiness among homemakers, working wives, and their husbands, it was found that in dual-earner families, marital satisfaction and job satisfaction were equally important in determining a person's happiness. For both single- and dual-earner families, marital happiness was the most important determinant of overall happiness. Job satisfaction (or lack of it) was the most important determinant of unhappiness. Employed wives' level of happiness (but not their husband's) varied, depending on their life cycle stage. When their children are young, women are likely to experience more strain as they balance family and work demands. Benin and Nienstedt's findings are similar to those earlier of Hoffman and Nye (1974), who found that when employed wives in middle-class families enjoy their work, the dual-earner couple actually experiences greater marital satisfaction than single-earner couples.

For many women the decision to work when their children are young is a difficult one to make. Research suggests that one of the factors influencing the decision is the woman's perception of the effects of separation from the infant. Hock (1978) found that women who planned to return to work were less anxious about the separation and more trusting of others to care for their infants than were nonworking women. In contrast, women who had not planned to return to work following childbirth, but who subsequently changed their minds, were more anxious about separating from their infants than nonworking mothers (Hock, Christman, & Hock, 1980). Even fathers, who have been socialized to define themselves through their jobs, experience anxiety about leaving their children for work. One team of researchers (Deater-Deckard, Scarr, McCartney, & Eisenberg, 1994) studied the separation anxiety and concerns of 589 dual-career couples and found that fathers and mothers of the children between the ages of 1 and 5 reported similar levels of separation anxiety.

FOCUS ON CULTURE

Cultural values and gender expectations can profoundly influence the ease with which women with children enter the workforce. In many cultures, including our own, there is a stereotypical expectation that the responsibility for child care rests with the mother even if she is also working outside the home. In Sweden, by contrast, responsibility for child care is assumed to be jointly shared by the mother and father. Thus, paternity as well as maternity is offered to workers (Trost, 1983). Swedish day-care nurseries are readily available to single and married parents, and parents may work a 6-hour rather than an 8-hour day in order to spend more time with their young children.

The motivation for working following childbirth plays a major role in the subsequent adjustment of the mother and, in turn, the rest of the family. When work is viewed as an avenue of self-expression and development, women are much more likely to be successful in integrating occupational and family roles than when women work primarily for financial reasons. When adequate substitute child-care and other support systems are available to the woman who wants to work, there is better integration of work and parental roles. Some women who work to help support their families cannot afford, or do not have available, the kind of support they need to meet day-to-day household responsibilities—child care, cleaning, shopping, cooking, and so on. For these women, the period of early adulthood is often marked by task overload and accompanying feelings of frustration and despair, especially if they did not choose to work or have children.

Although families in which both spouses work face many difficulties, there are some important benefits that must not be overlooked. One of these is the financial security provided by two incomes instead of one. With more money coming in, dual-earner families are better able to meet their material needs as well as obtain some of the "extras" that make life more enjoyable—vacations, a second car, a new stereo system, additional toys for the children, and so on. Working also broadens the person's social network. In fact, one of the major complaints of nonemployed women is their sense of social isolation (Ferree, 1976). Finally, work serves as a basis for consolidation of identity and evaluation of the self. It has long been known that identity in men is tied closely to their occupational positions. In recent years, however, we have come to recognize that this is also true for women—although possibly not to the same extent. Research indicates that employed women, if they enjoy their jobs, report more positive self-esteem, higher levels of competence, and greater life satisfaction than nonemployed women.

BRIEF REVIEW

Family life has many different periods during which new developmental tasks or issues arise. Early adulthood is the time during which many people form their own nuclear family by having or adopting children. Adults continue to be members of and influenced by their birth families throughout their lives.

Social scientists define families both structurally—in terms of who the family members are and how they are related to one another—and functionally. Families provide a context for legitimate procreation, socialization, support, and companionship.

The life cycle of a traditional nuclear family begins at marriage and ends with the death of the remaining spouse. Families undergo change throughout the lifespan as a result of marital separation, divorce, the departure or return of adult children, death, and/or remarriage. Stage models that represent these changes in the family life cycle are limited because they do not account for intergenerational relationships and nontraditional family structures.

The age at which people marry and the way they marry are influenced by social norms. Some of the factors affecting the courtship process are physical attractiveness, propinquity, similarity in background and values, achievement of rapport, mutual self-disclosure, role-taking ability, and the fitting together of roles and needs.

The newly married couple must learn to deal with conflict in a mature way and to make adjustments in areas dealing with money, sex, relatives, and the possibility of children. Adjusting to their new roles as husband and wife usually requires some personal change. Most young people today prefer a marital relationship of shared responsibilities. When both partners work, there seems to be more satisfaction in the marriage.

Among American couples who marry today, nearly one in three can be expected to divorce. Most divorces occur within the first 7 years of marriage. After a divorce, people seem to need to rework their lives and identities. Whereas most divorced people make adjustments to their new status and eventually remarry, many find it difficult.

Most Americans marry at least once, yet cohabitation is an increasingly common arrangement. Other people remain single throughout much or all of their young adulthood. Women who remain single exhibit better mental health and fewer neurotic tendencies than married women or single men. Today, a growing number of men and women are openly declaring and living homosexual lifestyles.

The reasons for having (or not having) children vary from one couple to another. The arrival of the infant restricts parental activities and privacy, imposes a financial burden on the family, and often disrupts the career of the wife. Marital satisfaction decreases with the birth of the first child, although it often increases again in later stages of family life. However, if the children are wanted and planned for, they can strengthen the marriage.

People first enter the work world during young adulthood and begin the process of moving up the occupational ladder. Super described the changes in occupational development as a series of stages, each with its unique tasks or issues. The transition from college to a career is not necessarily smooth or automatic. Initial job choice is influenced by one's self-concept and gender-role identity.

Occupational stress can affect the mental and physical health of workers. Sources of occupational stress include the demands and pace of the job, the degree of control a worker has over work conditions, job security, and the degree of supportive social networks on the job.

Some women experience an increase in health as a result of working. Married women whose husbands share in domestic duties experience less stress from work. Women benefit from work because they have greater access to health-care facilities, increased family incomes, and richer social networks to rely upon for support. Sexual harassment and discrimination due to race or gender contribute to stress on the job.

Families with two providers are finding that there are many costs as well as benefits to this lifestyle. Personal motivation for working and job satisfaction are two important factors in the adjustment of these families.

KEY TERMS

asexuals (478)
close couple (478)
cohabitation (476)
dysfunctionals (478)
family life cycle (461)
fertility motivation (480)
functionals (478)

homogamy (467)
intergenerational relations (463)
occupational development (484)
occupational stress (489)
open couple (478)
physical attractiveness (466)
propinquity (466)

role overload (493)
role (R) stage (468)
sexual harassment (490)
stimulus (S) stage (468)
stimulus-value-role theory (468)
value comparison (V) stage (468)

REVIEW QUESTIONS

If you can answer these questions, you have a good understanding of the material in this chapter. If a question seems difficult, go back to the text and review the topic.

1. Describe the concept of the family life cycle. What factors or events influence the changes a family experiences?

2. Explain the difference between a structural and functional definition of family. Give an example of each.

3. What are the three functions common to families?

4. Describe the three factors that influence mate selection. Describe and give an example of each of the three stages in Murstein's stimulus-value-role theory of marital choice.

5. What factors influence success in balancing work and marital roles? Do they differ for men and women?

6. What effect does divorce have on adults? What factors reduce the stressfulness of a divorce for adults?

7. Describe the two general categories of cohabitation. How do they differ?

8. What are the advantages and disadvantages reported for adults who remain single?

9. Describe the five lifestyle patterns found for homosexual men.

10. What motivates people to want to become parents? What are the adjustments adults must make in their transition to parenthood?

11. Describe the sources of occupational stress. Do men and women differ in their experience of stress on the job?

12. Describe and give an example of each of Super's five stages of occupational development.

13. Explain the relationship between gender-role identity, self-concept, and career choice.

14. Explain the rise in two-provider families. What factors contribute to role overload?

OBSERVATIONAL ACTIVITY

THE VALUE OF CHILDREN TO YOUNG ADULTS

In the past three decades, with the rise of the women's movement and the increase in dual-career families, the decision of whether or not to have children has become a prominent issue. More and more young adults are consciously weighing both the costs and benefits of raising children before committing themselves to a decision concerning parenthood or even marriage.

Interview five married couples and five men and five women who are not married about the value of having children. Ask your respondents the following questions:

1. What do you think are the benefits of having children?

2. What are the drawbacks?

3. Should people be married before having children?

4. If you do want to have children, when in your life would you like to have them? What factors would influence your decision to have a child?

5. What influence would your career plans have on your interest or decision to have or not have children?

6. What changes in your life would you expect following the birth of a child?

After completing your interviews, compare the responses you received with those of your classmates. What are the major benefits and costs of parenthood for today's young adults? How many people plan to remain childless? What factors appear to be important in this decision? How do you interpret the data on the costs and benefits of parenthood in light of the changes that have taken place in society over the past few decades?

The Reassessment Years

At this point in the journey through life, you will meet experienced travelers. Between ages 40 and 60, people emerge with a variety of experiences and lessons they have accumulated in their travels. For many people, middle adulthood is the best part of the journey. Their children may be grown or close to independence; many middle-aged adults have earned their place within their communities. Some people look upon their middle-adulthood years as a time to reconsider the choices they made in earlier stages of life. Greater confidence and wisdom gained from a wealth of life experiences may stimulate people to break tradition and venture down new paths by changing their lifestyles or careers. At the same time, the physical signs of aging may begin to show. The impact of these changes varies from person to person and from one culture to another. Health concerns become more prominent as habits acquired in the earlier part of the lifespan show their effects. This is also the time when many people experience the death of their parents and the decline in health of some of their peers. With the end of life's journey in sight, many people come to terms with the reality that their journey is finite and one-directional.

The middle-adulthood period is a period of challenge and change. The next two chapters consider the impact of the physical, cognitive, and personality changes during middle adulthood and the changes that occur in family and career.

CHAPTER 13

Middle Adulthood: Physical, Cognitive, and Personality Development

As she looked into the mirror, 45-year-old Karen noticed how gray her hair was becoming. Other signs of aging were also visible: The wrinkles around her eyes and mouth, the age spots on her hands, and the thickening of her waistline were all signs that she had reached middle age. Even though Karen did not particularly like the idea, she acknowledged that she was now a middle-aged woman. Not too long ago, she mused, this label had applied to her own mother. Still, with two children ready to enter college and her own parents now official Senior Citizens, Karen recognized that she could not deny the obvious—she had made the transition from the "young generation" to middle adulthood.

Actually, Karen was not distressed about entering the middle years of life. For one thing, she felt young, and despite the physical changes she had begun to notice, she still felt attractive. Certainly, she and her husband continued to have frequent and satisfying sexual relations. If anything concerned Karen about getting older, it was the uncertainty about how she would spend the rest of her life. Karen needed to commit herself to something meaningful, to be creative and to push herself into new areas.

Even though Seamus was the same age as Karen, he felt much older. In fact, he had felt middle-aged when he was in his 30s. Perhaps it was because of the different life he led. Seamus had spent his entire life in County Cork in Ireland. For generations his family supported themselves and their community by harvesting peat and raising dairy cows. Seamus and his wife Maura had been married more than 25 years and had fulfilled their religious obligations to have children. All but the last two of their six children were married. Their child-rearing days had been over for some time.

Seamus and his wife very seldom had sex now. Because he and his wife were devout Catholics, they were not comfortable with the idea of having sex just for the pleasure of it. Instead, their energies were channeled into helping their village of Sneem develop a program to teach the Gaelic language and culture to young children and teenagers. Seamus wanted to be able to pass on what he had learned about his ethnic heritage. It was important to him, and now he had the time to devote to it.

When considered from a lifespan perspective, development during the middle-adulthood years is a challenge to describe and explain. The changes in physical characteristics, cognition, and one's outlook on self and life are affected by the life experiences of 40 or more years. These cumulative experiences must be examined within their cultural context.

Events occurring as far back as early childhood can have an impact on the quality and meaning of life in middle adulthood. For example, the quality of care a person received during childhood may influence the stability of the person's marriage and family in middle adulthood (Franz, McClelland, & Weinberger, 1991). Significant social, cultural, and historical changes such as war, famine, or natural disasters can alter the individual's life experiences. Middle-aged women living in Western societies today, for example, have far more career opportunities available to them than their mothers did during their middle-adult years. The impact of such broad cultural changes will depend on the individual's life course.

Genetic and biological influences also contribute to the changes that occur during middle adulthood. The timing of the transition from young adulthood to middle adulthood varies from one person to another. Some people, like Seamus, perceive themselves to be middle-aged in their 30s; others, like those in a study by Busse and his colleagues (Busse, Jeffers, & Christ, 1970), continued to view themselves as young or middle-aged well into their 60s. Regardless of such differences in perceptions, though, this period of life poses new tasks and challenges.

PHYSICAL DEVELOPMENT

PHYSICAL CHANGES

As Karen noticed while looking in the mirror, the obvious signs of physical aging are most evident on the exterior of the body. In middle age, the skin loses some of its elasticity, laugh lines become facial wrinkles, and the waistline becomes flabbier due to declines in muscle tone and flexibility. Hair begins to thin and often turns gray or white, especially in the armpits and pubic area. The percentage of body weight that is fat also increases significantly in middle adulthood, in both men and women, although the problem of obesity is more often found in women (Weg, 1977).

Muscular strength and coordination declines slowly, but steadily, from young adulthood onward (Spirduso & MacRae, 1990). Troll (1982) notes that between the ages of 30 and 80, maximum muscular strength in men declines 42%. This does not mean, however, that middle-aged or even older people are incapable of activities that require muscular effort. People like Seamus who are accustomed to physical work will continue to be productive even into their late 50s and early 60s, particularly if they have engaged in regular physical activity in earlier stages of their lives.

With increasing age, there is a noticeable reduction in breathing efficiency; the person is more easily winded when running or climbing. The heart muscle, which declines in strength over the period, must work harder to achieve less. This is especially true of people who are overweight or have **atherosclerosis,** a degenerative condition involving thickening and hardening of portions of artery walls. Both conditions are more common in the late 50s.

Marked changes also occur in the sensory systems. Visual acuity peaks in early adulthood and remains relatively stable until the fourth decade, after which there

atherosclerosis
A degenerative condition involving thickening and hardening of portions of artery walls.

presbycusis

A progressive loss of hearing, especially for tones of high frequency, caused by degenerative changes in the auditory system; the most common auditory problem associated with aging.

is a slow but steady decline (Timiras, 1972). In almost all cases, however, problems of visual acuity can be corrected with glasses. The size of the pupil becomes smaller around age 50, resulting in less light entering the eyes. This means that the person may need brighter lighting to see adequately. At this time, problems with depth perception, recovery from glare, and adaptation to darkness also are observable (Troll, 1982). The most common auditory problem associated with increasing age is **presbycusis,** a progressive loss of hearing, especially for tones of high frequency, that is caused by a deterioration in the auditory system. This condition affects men more often than women (Corso, 1977), perhaps from greater exposure to loud noises through work. Living or working in urban environments that have loud noises from automobile traffic, sirens, trains, jet airplanes, or construction contributes to gradual hearing loss. Under ordinary circumstances, however, hearing loss has little impact on the day-to-day life of the middle-aged or older adult. Some loss of taste, smell, and sensitivity to touch also occurs in the late 40s and 50s but is not generally noticed by the individual until later in life.

During middle age, the nervous system undergoes changes which, under ordinary circumstances, have a minimal effect on behavior, perception, and intelligence during middle age. Brain weight decreases after age 20, gradually at first and more rapidly in later life. However, studies using electroencephalograms (EEGs), which record the electrical activity of the brain, show little difference between healthy young and old people in many instances (Bromley, 1974). Simple reflex time remains about the same from 20 to 80 years of age (Hugin, Norris, & Shock, 1960). However, reactions to complex stimuli such as finding a hidden figure in a puzzle or recognizing a specific combination of tones require more complex transmissions of neural impulses and thus become slower with age. There also seems to be a generalized slowing down of bodily functions and processes (Timiras, 1972).

Although the middle years bring a gradual decline in physical functioning from the peak reached in the 20s, the human organism does not experience a sudden reversal from growth to decline. Even in early life, both processes are taking place. For example, heart (cardiovascular) diseases of middle age are the result of cumulative rather than sudden conditions. For the average person, cardiac output (as measured in a state of rest) begins to decline not in middle age but around 19 or 20, at the rate of about 1% a year (DeVries, 1975); perhaps at age 50 a problem may be noticed when the person tires quickly or easily loses his or her breath. Similarly, some medical authorities claim that the first lesions of atherosclerosis are laid down in the first years of life (Timiras, 1972). Midlife, then, is not a sharp turning point; it simply marks the point at which the balance begins to shift, gradually and inevitably, from growth to decline.

FOCUS ON CULTURE

The impact of the physical changes associated with aging depends on the value a culture places on age. In China, where elderly adults are held in high esteem, growing old is viewed more positively than in a culture that values youth. How does the culture in which you were raised value growing old? How is this value communicated?

Sexual Development

Menopause and the Climacteric   During middle adulthood, men and women undergo a number of changes in their reproductive and sexual organs, a process generally referred to as the **climacteric.** These changes are linked to a decrease in the production of gonadal or sex hormones—specifically, estrogens and testosterone that are produced, respectively, by the ovaries and testes. Although the pituitary gland continues to send strong messages to the gonads, and although the adrenal glands, thyroid, and pancreas continue to function as before, the gonads become less productive in the middle-adult years.

For women, the mid-40s mark the beginning of a decline in estrogen and progesterone levels. The decrease in estrogen levels eventually leads to **menopause,** the cessation of the menses, when women stop menstruating and can no longer bear children. The cessation of menstruation takes place over a period of from 2 to 5 years. The decline in estrogen levels results in thinning of the vaginal walls, reduction in the vaginal lubrication response during sexual arousal, cessation of ovulation and menstruation, and shrinking of the ovaries and uterus.

The way in which these changes are experienced somewhat parallels adolescent development. Girls experience a clear beginning of "womanhood" in the first menstruation (menarche), but for the first year or so the menstrual cycle may be anovulatory, which means that the young girl may be infertile or only irregularly fertile. During the climacteric, women again experience relatively clear signs of change in the form of menopause. Twelve consecutive months without menstruating is experienced, on the average, at age 50 (Weideger, 1976), although there is wide individual variation. Again like the adolescent girl, the older woman is irregularly fertile; she may be anovulatory in one cycle, and fertile in the next. Thus, it is possible for a woman to become pregnant during menopause. Menopausal changes are not experienced primarily in terms of sexual activity; that is, a woman can enjoy sexual intercourse regardless of her fertility status. In fact, Hyde (1979) reports that for many women menopause is sexually liberating because the fear of pregnancy is eliminated.

A number of unpleasant symptoms have been correlated with menopause. Some women experience hot flashes, facial flushing, and profuse sweating, symptoms that are related to changes in the capacity of blood vessels to constrict or dilate to maintain body temperature. Other complaints associated with menopause include dizziness, headaches, irritability, depression, insomnia, and weight gain. Some of these symptoms are due to changes in dream-rich REM sleep, when women are awakened by hot flashes and sweating; the loss of sleep contributes to irritability and depression. Approximately 30% of all menopausal women seek medical attention for one of these symptoms (Weideger, 1976). But changes in the way people view menopause and new treatment approaches have altered the impact of menopause on many women's lives.

Myths of Menopause   There was a time when most people expected that menopausal women would be crippled with symptoms of depression and volatile emotional reactions. While some women do experience shifts in their emotional and psychological states before and during menopause, today there is better understanding of the complex changes women experience during this period. In addition to changes in hormone production and menstruation, middle-aged women

---

climacteric

Changes in the reproductive and sexual organs that usually accompany middle age.

menopause

The cessation of ovulation and menstruation signaling the loss of fertility in women that usually occurs between ages 45 and 55.

also experience changes in their roles within the family as their children grow to independence. As you will learn in Chapter 14, many women also assume the job of caring for their aging parents during the same period. Thus, shifts in emotional states could well be related to these and other social changes.

Many women go through menopause with very few problems. Studies that look at a woman's actual menopausal status rather than using age as a measure of menopause find that menopause is unrelated to such symptoms and traits as depression, anxiety, self-esteem, and satisfaction with life (Neugarten, 1979). In fact, some women object strongly to the medical-model approach to menopause, which stereotypes this biological state as a disease. Goodman (1980) reminds us that menopause refers to the cessation of menstruation, which sometimes, but certainly not always, is accompanied by unpleasant physical symptoms. She found that the same symptoms are often present in premenopausal women. The only difference Goodman found between menopausal and premenopausal women, after adjusting for age differences between the groups, was that the former more often had surgery related to female disorders. No difference was found for the incidence of sweating, headaches, nervous tension, and other "common menopausal symptoms." Only a small percentage of women have symptoms so severe that they are prohibited from performing their daily routine (Neugarten, Wood, Kraines, & Loomis, 1963). Yet the stereotype remains in our society, often contributing unnecessarily to problems in midlife adjustment.

In a number of non-Western cultures, menopause and the succeeding period of life for women are viewed differently; in some African cultures they are seen as positive life events (Lock, 1991). In Nigeria, for example, postmenopausal women are allowed to enter male groupings as persons of power (Hotvedt, 1983). In many societies, postmenopausal women are afforded greater freedom to speak their minds and travel because they are no longer seen as "contaminated" by menstruation (Posner, 1979). Clearly, the attitudes of a culture regarding menopause have a profound effect on women's experience of this biological event.

Hormonal Replacement Therapy

osteoporosis
A condition that results in the thinning of the bones in old age.

One long-term effect of a decreased level of estrogen is **osteoporosis,** a condition in which bones become thinner and hence more fragile and breakable. Although the effects of osteoporosis are more visible in late adulthood, the condition begins much earlier. Likewise, the disease is more readily prevented by steps taken in early and middle adulthood. Adding calcium to the diet and starting an exercise program such as walking, running, bicycling, or dancing are two measures that are recommended for preventing osteoporosis. Women who begin menopause at an early age because their ovaries have been surgically removed are at a higher risk for the disorder. In high-risk cases, doctors recommend the administration of a combination of the hormones estrogen and progesterone to reduce the risks of thinning bones.

Today, many physicians recommend the use of hormone replacement therapy (HRT) to reduce other menopausal symptoms such as hot flashes, thinning of the vaginal walls, and problems with bladder control. More important, however, hormone replacement is recommended for the long-term protection against heart attacks. The use of estrogen slows atherosclerosis, the process by which arteries are narrowed by the accumulation of fatty plaques. Estrogen prevents plaque from growing by regulating the body's production of "good cholesterol," or HDL, and reducing the levels of LDL, the "bad cholesterol." Some studies have found that women who took estrogen after menopause were only half as likely to die of a heart attack as women who did not take hormones (Barrett-Conner & Bush, 1991).

Earlier medical studies showed a strong correlation between prolonged use of estrogens as part of an estrogen replacement therapy program and the incidence of cancer of the breast and endometrium (the lining of the uterus) (Antunes et al., 1979; Hoover, Gray, & Cole, 1976; Nathanson & Lorenz, 1982). But when estrogen is combined with progesterone, the risks of developing cancer are significantly reduced. Women who are already at risk for cancer because of their family history or previous diagnoses of breast cancer are advised against HRT. The use of estrogen replacement in menopausal women is a controversial treatment because the long-term implications are not fully known. The decision must be made by weighing the advantages against the medical risks.

Male Climacteric Despite the fact that both men and women experience a change in their reproductive systems with age, popular terms describing this event have been developed only for women. Women's climacteric is referred to as menopause, but there is no comparable term for men. Yet there are clear changes in male reproductive and sexual organs during the middle-adult years.

male climacteric
Changes in the reproductive and sexual organs that usually accompany middle age; unlike females, it often goes unnoticed in males.

The **male climacteric** occurs at about the age of 50, when men experience a gradual decline in testosterone levels. This decline results in a slight decrease in the number of healthy, active sperm and in the size of the testicles; a reduction in the force of ejaculation and the volume of fluid ejaculated also is experienced, along with an enlargement of the prostate gland (Weg, 1975). Middle-aged males also find that they require more time and stimulation to achieve an erection, and experience a longer period between erections, than they did in adolescence and young adulthood. On the other hand, middle-aged men can usually maintain erections for longer periods. Unlike the case for women, the climacteric has little effect on male fertility status; most men remain fertile throughout life. In fact, one consequence of remarriage is that men become fathers during middle adulthood because they tend to marry younger women who are still in their childbearing years.

Although some men report a sudden increase in insomnia, irritability, headaches, and other "menopausal" symptoms in middle age, the majority seem unaware of the physical changes that are taking place. The climacteric, if experienced at all, usually is felt as a falling off of desire (less frequent and spontaneous erections) or decline in the ability to have an erection (usually caused by impotence anxiety). Seldom does a man consult a doctor about the climacteric. Unlike women, men do not usually have an ongoing relationship with a physician who is especially concerned with reproductive functions.

Midlife Male and Female Sexuality In the past, it was more or less assumed that middle-aged people did not approach sex with anything like the vigorous interest of the young. Whether due to fatigue, impotence (or the fear of it), or declining physical attractiveness, the middle-aged person was thought to experience a diminution of desire. Today, however, it is understood that this stereotype is an oversimplification of the facts. With good health, good spirits, and an available and interested partner, sexual activity can be a vital part of the life of the middle-aged and older adult.

To some extent, sexual expression in midlife (as in adolescence and early adulthood) is influenced by changing cultural expectations. Middle-aged people today are more willing to respond honestly to researchers' questions about sex, and have more relaxed attitudes toward sexual matters than their counterparts in the 1960s and 1970s. They also express their sexuality in more varied ways than did the middle-aged people Kinsey interviewed in his groundbreaking research over 40 years ago. The average frequency of marital intercourse for couples in all age groups has increased from the time of Kinsey's report (Kinsey, Pomeroy, & Martin, 1948, 1953) to Hunt's sampling (1974). The increase is proportionately greatest for people over age 55. Moreover, the 35-to-44 age group in the 1974 sampling was more active than the 26-to-35 age group a generation ago (Hunt & Hunt, 1975).

Nevertheless, there are differences between the sexuality of youth and middle age. Sometime between the ages of 46 and 55 (see Table 13–1), the majority of men and women become aware of a decline in sexual interest and activity (Michael,

CHANGES OVER TIME IN FREQUENCY PER WEEK OF MARITAL COITUS: MALE AND FEMALE ESTIMATES COMBINED

Kinsey (1948, 1953) Study

AGE	MEDIAN FREQUENCY PER WEEK
16–25	2.54
26–35	1.95
36–45	1.40
46–55	.85
56–60	.50

Hunt (1974) Study

AGE	MEDIAN FREQUENCY PER WEEK
18–24	3.25
25–34	2.55
35–44	2.00
45–54	1.00
55+	1.00

TABLE 13–1

Source: From *Sexual Behavior in the 1970s,* by M. Hunt, 1974, Chicago: Playboy Press; and *Sexual Behavior in the Human Male,* by A. C. Kinsey, W. B. Pomeroy, and C. C. Martin, 1948, Philadelphia: Saunders; and *Sexual Behavior in the Human Female,* by A. C. Kinsey, W. B. Pomeroy, and C. C. Martin, 1953, Philadelphia: Saunders.

Health Perspective

MIDLIFE PREGNANCY

Although most women start and complete their families during their early adulthood years, more women in industrialized societies are delaying both marriage and childbearing until they have settled into a career. The result of these trends is that more women are choosing to have a child during their middle-adulthood years. In contrast, most midlife pregnancies in the past were the result of unplanned conceptions.

At one time, pregnancy after the age of 35 was considered to be a high-risk situation for both mother and child. However, with careful prenatal care and a nutritious diet, there is no longer a greater risk to pregnant women over the age of 35 than to younger women. There are some risks for the infant, however. There is a greater likelihood of stillbirth or a neonatal death; the fetus tends to be smaller during pregnancy, increasing the risk of miscarriage, stillbirth, or premature birth; and there is a greater chance of neonatal morbidity—that is, that the infant will have central nervous system problems or respiratory problems related to the birth itself. As mentioned in Chapter 2, the incidence of Down syndrome is related to the mother's age. The chances—about one in 1,000 at age 30—escalate to less than one in 100 by about age 45.

Despite these somewhat alarming statistics, the infant mortality rates for older mothers are low. In the United States, the mortality rate for infants of mothers over the age of 35 is still only 47 per 1,000 births—more than twice the national infant mortality rate but still an unlikely event. Furthermore, infant mortality rates for high-risk pregnancies differ depending on the mother's number of previous pregnancies. The highest risk is to a mother over the age of 35 who has had more than one child (referred to as *multiparous*). If she is poor, in poor health, and perhaps malnourished during her pregnancy, such a woman has a poor chance of having a healthy baby in midlife. An older, middle-class woman in excellent health who is having her first child (referred to as *primigravida*) usually seeks out the best available care during her pregnancy and should have no problems. It is important to note that general health and socioeconomic

Gagnon, Laumann, & Kolata, 1994; Pfeiffer, Verwoerdt, & Davis, 1972). Although middle-aged men and women experience complete and satisfying sexual relationships, sexual response is usually slower, characterized by more leisurely and imaginative foreplay. While the older male may require prolonged physical stimulation before he achieves erection (Kaplan, 1977), such activity may actually enhance intimacy between the partners.

There are a number of reasons that middle age brings new sexual satisfaction to some couples. For women, there is reduced fear of pregnancy and, after ages 50 to 55, little fear at all. Birth control can be safely ignored, although the use of condoms to protect against sexually transmitted diseases may be necessary for couples who have more than one sexual partner. With the launching of the children from the home, privacy increases, promoting sexual expression and other forms of communication that enhance intimacy and sexual response. Men and women may differ in their peak years for sexual activity and enjoyment (Lips, 1988). In the United States, for example, men are more likely to enjoy their sexuality during their late adolescent and early adulthood period. Women, on the other hand, seem to peak in enjoyment of their sexuality in the middle adulthood period.

status are better predictors of the outcome of a pregnancy than age.

Another statistic that climbs for mothers over age 35 is the rate of deliveries by caesarean section. One explanation is the greater readiness of obstetricians to perform caesareans on older mothers. Obstetricians generally believe that a caesarean will prevent many of the complications that might arise during the delivery of a child by an older woman. Rather than judge each case on its own merits, some obstetricians prefer to play it safe and remove the infant surgically.

Bearing children in midlife changes the social makeup of the family. In situations involving second marriages, the birth of a baby can help establish a sense of family in the relationship. The advantage of a midlife pregnancy is the psychological

maturity a woman and her husband can bring to the experience. An older woman knows herself better, has a greater depth of experience, and can handle problems that arise

more wisely and with greater strength. She should not be threatened by the idea that at 35 or 40 she is "too old" to bear and rear children of her own.

Today, more women are delaying having children until they have established themselves in their career. With good medical care this woman will probably have a healthy baby even though she is over 35.

Cultures vary in their support of pleasurable and guiltless sexuality among people of all ages. Seamus, for example, was raised with the expectation that intercourse and other sexual activity should be done in secret and for the purpose of reproduction, not for the pure pleasure of it. In the South Pacific island of Yap and among the Mangaians in Polynesia, sexuality is freely encouraged among unmarried people so long as they do not produce children. Once people marry, they are expected to engage in sexual intercourse to produce offspring (Reader, 1988). This practice of openly encouraging sexuality is a common one in many cultures (Lips, 1988).

FOCUS ON CULTURE

One important facet of a culture is its religious beliefs. In what ways might the religion of the culture affect people's views regarding sexuality?

What other aspects of a culture might influence the culture's support of sexuality?

This recently married middle-aged couple enjoys the joy of loving each other.

HEALTH AND AGING

My twin sister and I share many traits; we even are aging at a strikingly similar pace. We were the same age when our hair turned gray, when we needed reading glasses, and when we began to develop facial wrinkles. We experienced these changes at the same time because we share the same genetic makeup and the rate and type of physical change are partly determined by heredity. Thus there are families whose members seem to be particularly long-lived. Insurance companies and other actuarial accounts show that a person whose same-gender parent suffered a condition such as cardiovascular disease or breast cancer is at risk of developing the same condition by virtue of heredity. Even family photographs reveal similarities in facial wrinkles from one generation to the next. In short, how people age and to which diseases they are vulnerable are partly influenced by their genetic history.

Aging is not merely a biological process, however. Environmental factors are also involved. For example, one study has shown that a series of life changes—death of a spouse, divorce, change of job or residence—may be so stressful as to result in rapid aging or increased vulnerability to a variety of disease processes (Rahe, Mahan, & Arthur, 1970). Moreover, statistics show that married people, especially men, tend to live longer than their unmarried counterparts; that middle-class whites live longer than poor whites or members of minority groups; and that certain Russian peasants who live in cohesive social structures live longer and have more vigorous lives than certain urban American populations (Benet, 1976).

Combined with other developmental changes, gender is an important variable in predicting health in middle age. For example, up until age 50, women as a group show fewer signs of the effects of atherosclerosis on coronary and cerebral functioning. However, after menopause, the rate of heart disorders increases for women to a level similar to that for men. Older men are more likely to experience acute, life-threatening illnesses, while older women are more likely to suffer from

arthritis
A painful disease in which the joints swell and become disabled.

chronic illnesses (Grambs, 1989). **Arthritis,** a painful disease in which the joints swell and become disabled, occurs much more frequently in women than in men. The first signs of arthritis occur in middle adulthood and continue throughout the person's life. The disease affects about 50% of people over the age of 65, most of whom are women (Moskowitz & Haug, 1986).

Ethnicity and Health   Health is an important factor in an adult's general sense of well-being (Tran, Wright, & Chatters, 1991) and overall cognitive functioning (Field, Schaie, & Leino, 1988). A person's health in middle adulthood is the result of a variety of influences that occur at different times throughout the lifespan. Inadequate prenatal and perinatal care and nutrition increases the risk to the developing nervous system, and this can have an effect on overall health throughout a person's life. As you learned in Chapter 11, young adulthood is the time when people develop attitudes and habits that can promote or reduce health in later years. Access to medical care and health insurance is also important, particularly to people in middle and late adulthood.

ethnic group
Social group defined by either race, religion, or national origin.

A person's ethnic origins may also be a significant factor affecting health (see Table 13–2). **Ethnic groups** are social groups defined by either race (such as African American, Native American, or Asian American), religion (such as Jewish, Muslim, or Hindu), or national origin (such as Mexican American, Irish American, or Polish American). Although there are numerous ethnic groups in the United States, only recently have researchers begun to examine the relationship between ethnicity and overall health.

While heart disease and cancer are the two leading causes of death among American adults, African American adults—especially males—have a much higher rate of death from these diseases (Fingerhut & Makuc, 1992; Markides & Mindel, 1987). During middle adulthood African American males are much more

Although the size, composition, and function of families varies from one culture to the next, the roles that people play within their families are an important influence on self-esteem and sense of meaning.

HEALTH CHARACTERISTICS BY AGE, RACE, AND ETHNICITY IN THE UNITED STATES, 1976–1977

AGE, RACE OR ETHNICITY	PERCENTAGE SELF-REPORTED HEALTH AS FAIR OR POOR	PERCENTAGE WITH HEALTH INSURANCE COVERAGE	MEAN DISABILITY DAYS IN BED
All Ages			
Total	12.3%	88.6%	7.0
Black	19.1	83.5	8.9
Hispanic	12.8	75.7	7.8
White	11.0	90.8	6.6
Under 17 years			
Total	4.2	87.9	5.2
Black	7.5	83.3	4.4
Hispanic	6.0	76.4	6.8
White	3.0	90.8	5.1
17–44 years			
Total	8.4	85.8	5.5
Black	16.1	81.2	8.3
Hispanic	12.1	72.4	6.9
White	6.6	88.1	4.9
45–64 years			
Total	22.1	90.2	8.6
Black	38.4	83.8	14.5
Hispanic	28.3	77.3	10.4
White	19.3	92.0	7.6
65 years and over			
Total	30.6	97.9	14.8
Black	44.1	95.5	19.4
Hispanic	36.5	95.7	19.2
White	28.3	98.4	14.0

TABLE 13–2

Source: From *Aging and Ethnicity* (p. 74), by K. Markides and C. Mindel, 1987, Newbury Park, CA: Sage Publications. Adapted with permission.

vulnerable to hypertensive disease (high blood pressure). African Americans are disadvantaged when it comes to access to health care, days of disability, and self-reported health status, particularly in middle adulthood (see Table 13–2).

It is more difficult to collect ethnicity-related health data among Hispanic Americans because the criteria used to define this population are less precise. For example, researchers may select the health records and death certificates of people with Spanish surnames as one way to define the ethnic population. However, there are Hispanic Americans who do not have Spanish surnames and non-Hispanics who do. Nonetheless, some studies have found that Hispanic Americans have a lower rate of death from heart disease and cancer when compared with whites, but a higher rate of death from infectious and parasitic diseases and from diabetes mellitus (Markides & Mindel, 1987).

The term *Native American* actually refers to many ethnic groups or tribes, each of which has its own social customs and geographic location. Because of the large number of different tribes, less is known about the health of Native Americans in general. However, researchers studying the Navajo Indians found these Native Americans had a lower life expectancy when compared to the total American population. Carr and Lee (1978) reported that in 1973 Navajo men had an average life expectancy of 58.8 years compared to the 71.8 years for Navajo women. For Navajo men, the leading cause of death was death by accident (most frequently in a motor vehicle), followed by heart disease, respiratory diseases, and cirrhosis of the liver. The researchers explained the high incidence of death by accident in terms of the conditions of life on the reservation. Navajo men must spend more time driving on dangerous reservation roads, sometimes while under the influence of alcohol. Diabetes affects a proportionately larger number of Native American Indians and is a major cause of death for members of a number of tribes (Markides & Mindel, 1987). Rates of death and disability from diabetes are increased by poor access to medical treatment early on in the course of the disease.

Not all ethnic groups in the United States are disadvantaged with regard to health. For example, Asian Americans have relatively better health in adulthood than the U.S. population in general. However, members of ethnic groups who are also poor, have limited access to medical care because they do not speak the language of the health-care providers, or live too far from an adequate health-care facility are likely to have poorer health throughout their lifespan.

Nutrition   The way people conduct their lives plays a major role in the extent to which they can offset the physical changes that accompany aging. Belloc and Breslow (1972) reported that seven personal habits are related to the health status and longevity of middle-aged and older adults. Habits that reduce health and longevity include smoking cigarettes, drinking immoderately, sleeping less than 7 hours a night (and to a lesser degree, more than 9), failing to eat breakfast, weighing too much (and to a lesser degree, too little), failing to exercise on a regular basis, and snacking between meals.

The mortality rate of men engaging in four or more of these habits was 4 times higher than those who had none of them; among women, the death rate was doubled. Moderate alcohol consumption (one or two drinks per sitting) was positively associated with good health; teetotalers had slightly higher death rates. Complete lack of exercise doubled the death rate for both men and women, but there was no difference between moderately active and very active people. Even a

The risk of cancer and other diseases is reduced by eating a nutritious diet, especially one that includes fibers found in whole grains and cereals.

little exercise kept people healthier than no exercise at all. For this reason, many corporations are including as part of their job benefits access to exercise programs and facilities at the work site.

More important than all the other health habits first mentioned, however, may be a proper diet. Not only is it best to eat only at meal times, but the calories eaten should be chosen carefully. According to the U.S. Surgeon General's report on diet and disease, the typical American diet is too high in fats, sugar, cholesterol, and salt, and too low in fiber. Scientists have estimated that as many as half of human cancers are diet related. A high intake of fats is associated with cancers of the breast and colon and may promote the growth of other cancers as well. The risk of colon cancer is reduced by eating fiber, which is found in whole grains (bran) and cereals, and fresh fruit and vegetables.

MIDDLE-ADULTHOOD STRESS

As I got older, it seems I got busier; I also took on more responsibilities within my family and in my career. On some days, my hectic pace and conflicting demands added to the level of stress I felt. But, fortunately, as I got older I also learned how to organize my life so that I was not pressured as much. I also learned some ways of reducing stress, such as exercising regularly, using humor, and getting enough sleep at night.

stress
A person's aversive physiological and psychological reactions to demanding, disturbing, or threatening situations.

Stress refers to a person's aversive physiological and psychological reactions to demanding, disturbing, or threatening situations. Stress is a common experience in middle adulthood and has received increased attention. Theorell and Rahe (1974), for example, have noted a positive relationship between the incidence of heart attacks and the number and type of such major changes in the person's life as death of a spouse, divorce, loss of a job, or retirement. Throughout life, people must adjust to numerous stressful events and transitions, many of which occur during middle adulthood. Not all of these events are necessarily negative ones. For example, in a scale of stressful life events developed by Holmes and Rahe (1967), marriage and the birth of a child are ranked among the top stressors (see Table 13–3). Both of these events, while generally cause for celebration, require people to make changes in the ways they lead their lives and define themselves. These events often result in additional related changes, such as a change in family income and place of residence.

Holmes and Rahe's Social Readjustment Scale is widely used in the United States to assess the level of stress in people's lives. People are asked to check off the events that have occurred during the past 6 or 12 months. A total stress index is then derived by summing all the stress values associated with the checked life events; the more events in people's lives, and the more changes they had to make, the greater their levels of stress. According to Holmes and Rahe, the higher the score, the more the person is at risk for a major health problem. A score over 300 is likely to be associated with a major life crisis and a significant decline in health (Holmes & Masuda, 1974).

Not included in Holmes and Rahe's listing of stressful events are the daily and chronic *hassles* that seem to erode the quality of life and contribute to a person's level of stress (Lazarus & DeLongis, 1983; Lazarus & Folkman, 1984). Getting stuck in traffic jams, misplacing one's keys, arguing with sales clerks or adolescent children—although relatively trivial compared to the death of a spouse or close friend, when experienced on a daily basis, these hassles can combine to affect one's emotional well-being. The 10 most frequently reported hassles among American

Job stresses can contribute to a shorter lifespan, particularly if people do not develop leisure activities and healthy lifestyles to counteract stress.

THE SOCIAL RE-ADJUSTMENT RATING SCALE

RANK VALUE	LIFE EVENT	STRESS
1	Death of a spouse	100
2	Divorce	73
3	Marital separation	65
4	Jail term	36
5	Death of a close family member	36
6	Personal injury or illness	53
7	Marriage	50
8	Fired at work	47
9	Marital reconciliation	45
10	Retirement	45
11	Change in health of family member	44
12	Pregnancy	40
13	Sex difficulties	39
14	Gain of new family member	39
15	Business readjustment	39
16	Change in financial status	38
17	Death of a close friend	37
18	Change to different line of work	36
19	Change in number of arguments with spouse	35
20	Mortgage over $10,000	31
21	Foreclosure of mortgage or loan	30
22	Change in responsibilities at work	29
23	Son or daughter leaving home	59
24	Trouble with in-laws	29
25	Outstanding personal achievement	28
26	Wife beginning or stopping work	26
27	Beginning or ending school	26
28	Change in living conditions	25

Cont'd

THE SOCIAL RE-ADJUSTMENT RATING SCALE—cont'd		
RANK VALUE	**LIFE EVENT**	**STRESS**
29	Revision of personal habits	24
30	Trouble with boss	23
31	Change in work hours or conditions	20
32	Change in residence	20
33	Change in schools	20
34	Change in reaction	19
35	Change in church activities	19
36	Change in social activities	18
37	Mortgage or loan less than $10,000	17
38	Change in sleeping habits	16
39	Change in number of family get-togethers	15
40	Change in eating habits	15
41	Vacation	13
42	Christmas	12
43	Minor violations of the law	11

TABLE 13–3

Source: From "The Social Readjustment Rating Scale" by T. H. Holmes and R. H. Rahe, 1967, *Journal of Psychosomatic Research, 11,* 213–218.

middle-aged adults are listed in Table 13–4. Depending on one's residence and socioeconomic status, some events may be more or less troublesome. For example, a person who lives in a noisy and crowded apartment complex may be bothered more by the physical environment than someone who lives in a more spacious or tranquil setting. Other common sources of stress during middle adulthood include role conflicts for employed parents or dual-earner families; changes in the size and composition of the household through divorce, remarriage, or the exit of adult children; and the physical and mental decline of one's parents. Events such as parents' aging, children leaving home, and divorce and remarriage are more likely to occur during the early part of middle adulthood; they may even occur simultaneously.

A life event may be a source of stress for one person and not for another. There is wide variation in the meaning attached to life events by different individuals—and in how they react to those events. For example, the birth of child may be stressful to someone who is worried about being able to care for an infant; another person who has been trying for a long time to get pregnant may be elated by the

TEN MOST FREQUENT HASSLES AMONG MIDDLE-AGED ADULTS

1. Concern about weight

2. Health of a family member

3. Rising price of common goods

4. Home maintenance

5. Too many things to do

6. Misplacing or losing things

7. Yard work or outside home maintenance

8. Property, investments, or taxes

9. Crime

10. Physical appearance

TABLE 13–4

Source: From "Little Hassles Can Be Hazardous to Your Health," by R. Lazarus, 1981, *Psychology Today* (July), p. 61.

childbirth. Thus, it is not so much that specific life events are stressful; what is significant is how a person's stress level is influenced by the way in which he or she copes with the combined stresses of living.

Type-A Behavior: A Factor in Heart Disease

Whereas the leading causes of death for American young adults are accidents and suicide, during middle adulthood death results primarily from cardiovascular diseases and cancer. Cardiovascular diseases have been associated with heredity, diet (particularly foods high in cholesterol and fat), smoking, overweight, and lack of exercise. However, 50% of all heart-disease cases cannot be linked to any known causal factor. Scientists have identified a pattern called Type-A behavior as one possible missing link as a major contributor to coronary heart disease (Cooper, Detre, & Weiss, 1981).

According to Matthews (1982), the **Type-A behavior** pattern, which was first identified by Friedman and Rosenman (1974; Rosenman & Friedman, 1983) in their work with middle-aged cardiac patients, is not a personality trait, but a continuum of behaviors associated with varying degrees of risk for heart disease. At

Type-A behavior
A behavioral and emotional pattern associated with coronary heart disease; includes explosive and accelerated speech, impatience with delay, excessive competitiveness and achievement striving, restlessness, undue irritability, and a chronic sense of time urgency.

FOCUS ON CULTURE

Much of the information we have about health issues is the result of research conducted on men. Despite the fact that sex differences exist in the onset, frequency, and death rates of certain diseases, there continues to be limited research on women's health (Rodin & Ickovics, 1990). Why do you suppose that women's health has not been studied with the same degree of interest as that of men?

one end of the continuum are the Type-A related behaviors, which include explosive, accelerated speech, impatience with delay, excessive competitiveness and striving for achievement, restlessness, and excessive irritability. The Type-A pattern also is characterized by a chronic sense of urgency—the person feels that there is just too much to do and not enough time to do it. In response to the time pressure and the need for achievement, Type-A people find themselves in a constant struggle to control and master their environment. In addition, this pattern is associated with a heightened pace of living—Type-A individuals move, walk, and even eat rapidly and often attempt to accomplish two tasks simultaneously. Compulsive in their quest to accumulate tangible evidence of their success, Type-A people measure their self-worth by how fast they achieve high-status goals. They also possess an aggressive drive that may become free-floating hostility. A simple conversation or sporting event, for example, can become a hostile, angry struggle. At the other end of the continuum are **Type-B related behaviors,** which are directly opposite to the Type-A behaviors—a relaxed, unhurried approach to the world, low aggressiveness, low-to-moderate need for achievement, and so on.

Type-B related behavior

In contrast to Type-A behavior, a relaxed, unhurried approach to the world, characterized by low aggressiveness and low-to-moderate achievement striving.

The link between Type-A behavior and heart disease is based on four findings: (1) the presence of Type-A behavior patterns in individuals already afflicted with coronary heart disease; (2) the extreme vulnerability of people displaying Type-A behaviors to later be diagnosed with heart disease: Type-A behavior is associated with at least twice as many cases of heart disease as Type-B behavior (Jenkins, Rosenman, & Zyzanski, 1974); (3) the presence of certain coronary biochemical abnormalities in Type-A persons; and most important, (4) successful experiments in which Type-A behavior was induced, following which coronary biochemical changes were found. Other research suggests that Type-A people are so busy and preoccupied that they may ignore important physical symptoms. This may actually contribute to the risk of heart disease by preventing them from seeking medical attention or altering their behavior to reduce tension (Matthews & Brunson, 1979; Weidner & Matthews, 1978). Although the stereotype of the Type-A person is the hard-driven, compulsive male executive, research evidence suggests that women who exhibit this behavior pattern are also at greater risk for heart disease (Eisdorfer & Wilkie, 1977).

Other studies have focused on the risks to Type-A and Type-B people of having a second heart attack. Researchers have found that Type-A people recover more quickly and are less likely to die from their first heart attack than Type-B people (Case, Heller, Case, & Moss, 1985). Ragland and Brand (1988) examined the health records of men involved in a longitudinal study of coronary disease. The men were selected because they had already had one heart attack. The researchers looked at the differences between Type-A and Type-B people in incidence of and response to a second heart attack. They found that Type-A people had a better chance of surviving a second heart attack than did people who displayed Type-B behavior. The researchers suggested that the Type-A people might have changed their behaviors as a result of their first heart attack.

Other research (Steinberg, 1988) suggests that the Type-A behavior pattern is likely to have had its origins in early childhood, when the characteristic behaviors are likely to be interpreted as temperament. Such dimensions of temperament as low activity, negative mood, low sensory threshold, and high adaptability are associated with adult the Type-A behavior pattern for males. For Type-A females, early temperamental characteristics include high activity, high motivation for achievement, and impatience and negative mood. That early temperamental characteristics are associated with the adult Type-A behavior pattern does not mean that all children who display these characteristics will grow up to be Type-A adults. Throughout the course of development from childhood to middle adulthood, socialization and life experience can interact with temperament to affect behavior patterns.

RECAP

Changes in appearance and physiological functioning begin to show during middle adulthood. Middle-aged men and women experience the climacteric, a decline in the production of sex hormones. Menopausal symptoms vary and are influenced by cultural expectations. Sexuality, while not as frequent, is an important part of most people's lives. Health during this period is related to hereditary factors as well as to the health habits acquired during earlier stages of adulthood. People from different ethnic groups report varying degrees of health. Diet and nutrition are environmental factors that are related to longevity and health. Stress is a big contributor to poor health. People who are described as displaying a Type-A personality are more vulnerable to heart disease.

COGNITIVE DEVELOPMENT

Some researchers have found that the creative abilities of middle-aged adults increased with their levels of self-esteem.

One thing I like about being middle-aged is that after many years of practice in learning new skills (such as the use of computers), and comprehending new ideas. I have discovered how I can best approach new information. The older I got, the more information I acquired, and along with this expansion of my knowledge has come the need to develop new techniques to organize it so I could remember it when I needed it. By the time I reached 50, I was actually somewhat surprised to see myself as a fairly efficient learner; I had fallen under the common misconception that with advancing age came declining intellectual skills.

My misconception about cognitive functioning in midlife is a by-product of the earlier assumption that intelligence, like muscular strength or height, is fully developed by late adolescence or the early 20s. This assumption recognizes the physical basis of intelligence—that is, the brain and related neurological foundations. More recent work has suggested that although some aspects of intelligence may develop only until young adulthood, intellectual development continues into later adulthood. Some cognitive skills, such as wisdom and being able to cope with problems in daily life, may not even appear until mid- or late adulthood (Baltes, 1987). Furthermore, depending upon how intelligence and cognitive ability are defined and measured, different conclusions can be drawn about whether there is an overall decline in cognitive development with age (Salthouse, 1982). Many of the earlier theories of intellectual and cognitive development grew out of either an interest in test development (psychometric movement) or an interest in the formation of cognitive capabilities in childhood and young adulthood (e.g., Piagetian theory).

Today, lifespan-development researchers are taking a new look at cognitive and intellectual development. A lifespan perspective views intellectual development as a multifaceted process that can proceed in different directions at different ages (Baltes, 1987). Knowledge and understanding are also influenced by culture. An example of cultural influence on cognitive development was presented in Chapter 11 when we discussed women's ways of knowing. Women who are educated in cultures based predominantly on a male perspective are likely to be channeled by their teachers and parents into ignoring or devaluing their unique ways of knowing about the world. In contrast, when cultures view male and female cognitive approaches as equally valid, their educational programs are more likely to be designed to encourage women to explore, develop, and apply their cognitive skills.

INFORMATION PROCESSING

In Chapter 11, I spoke of the difficulties in presenting a comprehensive picture of cognitive development during the adult years due to the number of gradual changes that occur over this period of 50 or more years. In that chapter I described some of the changes that occur in the way adults organize their thoughts. In this chapter I direct your attention to the way people process the vast amounts of information they are exposed to during their adult years. All along their journey through this period, adults are challenged by new terms, names, addresses, numerical sequences, concepts, and procedures that they must remember and retrieve to be able to function. For example, I must be able to recall a variety of passwords and numbers that will allow me to access my computer files, bank account, and telephone credit card. On the job, I need to remember the names of students I currently teach and those I taught last semester. The lists of information that must be processed grow longer every day.

Information Processing Models   Researchers typically use one of two models to help organize their thinking about the way people process information. Both of those models draw comparisons to the way information is processed by a computer. *Structural models* describe the various structures that are used to take in, store, and retrieve information. They draw comparisons to computer hardware, especially regarding different types of memory. Three types of memory storage structures are used to describe human information processing. First, information is taken in through **sensory memory,** a short-lived receptacle for visual, sensory, or auditory stimuli. This information is converted to **working memory** (also known as primary or short-term memory) for a period of time ranging from several seconds to several minutes. In working memory, information may also be manipulated or rehearsed to permit better immediate recall (Baddeley, 1986, 1992). Working memory can be compared to the random access memory (RAM) of a computer. Later, information is transferred to **secondary** (or long-term) **memory,** where it can be retained from several minutes to several weeks, months, or years. Birthdates, events, facts, theories, and stories are examples of information that is stored in secondary memory for an extended period—similar to data stored on a computer's hard drive.

While the structural model of memory has been useful in stimulating much research, it does not fully account for how information is *processed*. It describes memory as if it were an object or structure rather than focusing on the active process of remembering (Craik, 1994). The second model for understanding memory focuses on the different ways in which information is processed.

sensory memory
Short-lived receptacle for visual, sensory, or auditory stimuli.

working memory
Storage of information for a period of a few seconds up to several minutes; also referred to as short-term or primary memory.

secondary memory
Storage of information for extended periods of time, from several minutes to several years; also known as long-term memory.

Remembering is viewed as a pattern of mental activity that results when information is perceived and ultimately stored for later retrieval. Using the computer analogy, processing resembles the different types of software programs that manipulate and transform external data. The distinction between structural and processing models of memory is important to our discussion of the changes that occur in people's ability to process information as they get older. Since the time when Galton demonstrated that reaction time declines with age (Koga & Morant, 1923), numerous studies have demonstrated that memory too declines with age (Light, 1991; Salthouse, 1992). One of the reasons for this decline is that as people age, they lose some of their capacity to rapidly execute cognitive operations that help them store information for retrieval (Salthouse, 1991). Some of the processing that goes on while information is still in working memory is essential for reasoning and learning tasks (Campbell & Charness, 1990; Light, 1991; Salthouse, 1990). Thus, changes in a person's ability to quickly absorb and respond to information can have an impact on what new skills they learn and how they learn them. It is important to note that there is a lot of variability in adult cognitive skills. While many studies report declines in cognitive skills with age, others report no changes, and others identify skills in which older adults do better than younger adults (Craik, 1994; West, Crook, & Barron, 1994). The question, then, is not whether older adults can remember and learn, but how they process information in the context of learning and under what conditions information processing is improved or impaired.

Sensory Perception and Attention

Before information can be processed, it must be noticed. Research has shown that older adults have greater difficulty processing perceptual information than younger and middle-aged adults. For one thing, visual information is processed more slowly, and processing speed is influenced by the nature of the material to be processed (Clancy & Hoyer, 1994; Hoyer & Plude, 1980). Older adults have more difficulty than young adults in detecting patterns that are embedded within a complex background (Comalli, 1970). For example, if a familiar geometric pattern such as a triangle is hidden within a complex design, the older adult will take longer to identify it than will a younger person. At the same time, if the material to be scanned relates to a person's area of expertise, no age differences emerge. Clancy and Hoyer (1994) asked young and middle-aged medical laboratory technicians to pick out specific bacterial shapes from among an array of specimens, a task they were quite experienced in doing. There were no age-related differences in their performance of the task. When they were asked to perform a similar task that did not involve this area of expertise, younger adults did better that older adults.

Researchers have suggested that age-related perceptual-processing deficits may be linked to problems in attention (Stankov, 1988). Two components of attention are worth mentioning: divided attention and selective attention. **Divided attention** refers to the ability of the individual to process more than one source of information simultaneously—for example, being able to attend to multiple conversations at a social gathering. **Selective attention,** by contrast, refers to the person's ability to attend to relevant information while ignoring irrelevant information—for example, focusing on a conversation with one particular individual while ignoring all the other conversations and background noises that are going on in the immediate environment.

divided attention

A person's ability to process more than one source of information simultaneously.

selective attention

A person's ability to attend to relevant information while ignoring irrelevant information.

Research has shown that older adults are at a particular disadvantage in comparison to younger adults in situations where they must divide their attention between two or more information sources (Craik, 1977). Selective attention deficits among older adults also have been found, but only when it is difficult to differentiate between relevant and irrelevant information—that is, when the two forms of information are highly similar (Farkas & Hoyer, 1980). Thus, an elderly person may have trouble listening to a television news report while other people in the room are talking. Another reason that older people do not do as well as younger people on selective attention tasks is that they take longer to process the information (Madden, 1985).

Memory   Once information has been selected, it must somehow be stored, so that under appropriate conditions it can be retrieved and acted upon. Whether we are talking about a laboratory experiment involving nonsense words or a more realistic and meaningful problem such as trying to remember which grandchild's birthday falls on January 15, it is obvious that memory is involved. Most research suggests that working memory capacity—the number of words, letters, numbers, or bits of information a person can remember in correct order—does not usually decline with age (Craik, 1977; Hartley, Harker, & Walsh, 1980). What changes is the nature of the conditions under which working memory is evoked. Both older and younger adults are capable of remembering the same number of items, but only under ideal or undemanding conditions. To the extent that the person is required to reorganize the stimulus material (e.g., repeating the list backward), or divide attention between the "to-be-remembered list" and some other component of the task (Dobbs & Rule, 1989; Hultsch & Dixon, 1990), the older adult is likely to show decrements in working memory. Furthermore, the more cognitively complex the task the more difficulty older adults experience when compared with younger adults (Salthouse, 1992). When older adults are asked to recognize information they have learned, or when the material to be remembered is relevant to their experiences, they show no declines. For example, in one study (Morrow, Leirer, Altieri, & Fitzsimmons, 1994) older and younger pilots and nonpilots were asked to read typical air traffic commands and then to repeat these commands, a routine activity for pilots but not for nonpilots. The researchers found no age-related differences on this task; in tasks that were not related to airline expertise, the younger subjects did better than older subjects.

With respect to secondary memory, the research shows that older people have significantly more problems in remembering material that is no longer actively attended to or focused upon. This deficit has been linked to three distinct components of memory: perceiving and absorbing, storing, and retrieving information. In each of these areas, older adults perform less well than younger adults (Craik, 1994; Hartley, Harker, & Walsh, 1980). However, when different tests are used to measure recall, older adults do as well as younger adults (Adams, 1991; Fisk, Hertzog, Lee, Rogers, & Anderson-Garlach, 1994). When adults were asked to recall the set of visual images they had seen on a computer from a task they performed 16 months earlier, younger adults did better; but when they are asked to demonstrate the procedures that they learned on the original task (pressing a series of computer keys in response to target labels that were flashed on the screen), younger and older adults did not differ. Thus, it is important to use a variety of measures to assess capabilities when studying age differences in memory.

LEARNING IN MIDDLE ADULTHOOD

pacing
In information processing, the amount of time the person is allowed to examine the stimulus and/or to make a response.

It is clear that adults continue to learn as they age. However, it is also clear that learning is highly influenced by a number of factors. One of the most important factors is **pacing**—the amount of time the person has available to examine the stimulus and/or make a response. It has often been thought that fast-paced conditions place older adults at a significant disadvantage because of their slower reaction time; increasing time for inspection and response would decrease the performance difference between younger and older adults, and possibly eliminate it altogether. Research does indicate that learning in the elderly is adversely affected by fast-paced conditions. However, when learning occurs at a slow pace and when elderly adults are allowed to pace themselves, their performance improves. On the other hand, increased performance under self-paced conditions still does not equal the level of performance of younger adults (Arenberg & Robertson-Tchabo, 1977; Perlmutter & List, 1982).

Other factors besides pacing may also contribute to the performance decrement of older adults in learning tasks. According to Eisdorfer and his associates, the reason older people perform less well than younger people is that they are physiologically overaroused—that is, overly anxious and nervous—a condition that is known to interfere with the learning process. When elderly subjects have been administered drugs to lower autonomic nervous system arousal and thereby reduce their levels of anxiety, their performance has improved substantially—although still not to the level of younger subjects (Eisdorfer, 1968; Eisdorfer, Nowlin, & Wilkie, 1970).

The meaningfulness of the material to be learned also influences the performance of older individuals. Again, experience seems to affect how easily new tasks are learned. In one study (Czaja & Sharit, 1993) women ranging in age from 25 to 70 were given a series of computer interactive tasks of varying degrees of complexity and pacing (data entry, modifying a file, and an inventory management task). Both age and experience affected the women's performance. While older women took longer to perform the tasks, those who had had experience with computers made fewer errors and reported less fatigue. Hulicka (1967) found that many older subjects resent having to learn material they cannot understand or that they find uninteresting. In her experiment, the vast majority of older adults refused to participate because the material was viewed as "nonsense." When one considers that many learning experiments employ nonsense syllables and other patently uninteresting and meaningless stimuli, one may question whether performance decrements with age on these tasks represent decreased ability or simply lack of interest and motivation.

FACTORS THAT INFLUENCE CHANGES IN COGNITIVE SKILLS

Many of the studies that report age-related changes in cognitive skills rely on cross-sectional designs to compare the performance of people representative of different age groups. Longitudinal research, however, studies people over time and provides more insight into the factors that may influence such changes.

Education Perspective

MIDDLE-AGED STUDENTS

In 1978, 13% of all adults between the ages of 35 and 54 were enrolled in some kind of formal education. Both men and women are returning to school; however, women make up the majority of returning students. Today, the figures are much higher. Many of these returning students are single mothers who are seeking to improve their career opportunities and financial earnings. For others, middle adulthood corresponds with the time when their children are well on their way to independence and they are seeking new intellectual and personal challenges. It is also a time when individuals may be able to consider a career shift, particularly if they are in a dual-career family. For many who select education as their major focus of study, it is an opportunity to meet their need for generativity by using their knowledge and skills to educate children.

For middle-aged adults who enter college after years of being out of the classroom, the initial prospect of being a student may be stressful. Most of their classmates and some of the faculty may be younger than they are. The role of student is one more role that they must balance with those of spouse, parent, worker, and member of a community. They may experience feelings of uncertainty about their ability to do well "at their age." They may also be aware of some of the changes in their ability to process information quickly. Would this put the older student at a disadvantage in a classroom full of 18- to 20-year-olds?

Apparently not. Research studies show that the typical older student, after an initial period of adjustment, does better in college than the typical 18-year-old. One reason for their superior performance may be that older students usually have clearer personal goals and greater motivation. Furthermore, older students have accumulated a vast array of general information and problem-solving skills that can readily be applied to their studies.

Adult students are usually conscientious about their education. They attend all their classes, read and prepare their assignments, and seek ways to apply their classroom knowledge in the real world. They are more likely to bring their vivid experiences into their classes or to challenge lecture material when it seems to contradict their understanding. Adult students actively involve themselves in their education. Regardless of whether adult students are enrolled in college to complete a degree, acquire professional training, or stimulate their intellectual curiosity, they illustrate the potency of lifelong learning.

New teachers who are middle-aged are likely to have an advantage in the classroom because they do not look like novices and because their life experiences can often be put to good use in the classroom.

FACTORS THAT REDUCE THE RISK OF COGNITIVE DECLINE IN OLD AGE

FACTOR	EXAMPLES
Living in favorable conditions	High socioeconomic status and education, careers that are rewarding and complex, above average salaries, and intact families
Substantial involvement with complex and stimulating activities	Extensive reading, travel, attending cultural events, pursuit of continuing education, clubs, and professional organizations
Absence of cardiovascular and other chronic diseases	Good health that does not interfere with an active lifestyle
A self-reported flexible personality in midlife	Seeing oneself as adaptable to different circumstances and people
Marriage to a spouse with high cognitive status	An intellectually stimulating spouse will increase cognitive responding
Maintenance of high levels of perceptual processing speed into old age	People who practice their perceptual and motor skills will maintain their abilities to respond
Rating one's self as satisfied with life in middle adulthood	Being satisfied with one's life accomplishments

TABLE 13–5

Source: From "The Course of Adult Intellectual Development," by K. W. Schaie, 1994, in *American Psychologist, 49,* p. 310.

While adults as a whole decline in their cognitive functioning with age, there are some individual exceptions. Using data gathered from the Seattle Longitudinal Study begun in 1956, Schaie (1994) offers a list of factors that account for these individual differences in cognitive functioning. The seven factors that are displayed in Table 13–5 suggest that people who are active, flexible, educated, and satisfied with their lives seem to be less subject to cognitive declines as they age. This suggests that middle adulthood is a good time for people to take stock of their lives and make the necessary changes to increase their abilities to adapt in later stages of their journeys through life.

RECAP

To fully appreciate the complexity of cognitive development in adulthood a lifespan perspective must be used. Information processing involves the active manipulation and storage of stimuli. Changes in the way adults process information increase with age; while capacity for information remains fairly constant, processing becomes slower and more difficult—especially for demanding, complex, and nonrelevant tasks. While memory skills seem to decline with age, experience and expertise reduce age-related cognitive deficits. Decrements in learning and performance are related to pacing, physiological changes, the meaningfulness of the learning, and the motivation of the learner.

PERSONALITY DEVELOPMENT

In middle adulthood I changed the focus of my career, developed greater self-confidence, became more tolerant of disagreements, and learned how to negotiate more successfully with other people. I consider these changes to be helpful modifications in the way I approach myself and others; in other words, changes in my personality broadened my view of myself.

To some people, changes in personality in midlife seems improbable. They believe that middle-aged people are "set in their ways" or, to put it more positively, have achieved a welcome stability of personality. Some middle-aged people agree with this view. In one study (Gould, 1972), subjects in their early 40s showed a striking agreement with the statement, "My personality is pretty well set." The same group tended to agree with statements such as "It is too late to make any major changes in my career," or "Life doesn't change much from year to year."

On the other hand, observation suggests that middle age can be a period of extraordinary growth and change. The old saying, "Life begins at 40," supports this position, as do many popular and scholarly descriptions of the **midlife crisis,** a term used to describe the reactions (usually stressful) of middle-aged adults when they become aware of the limited time they have left in their lives. Midlife crises need not necessarily be stressful; they may represent a transition that results in a more satisfying life. For example, when Karen realized she was getting older, she took the opportunity to think creatively about what she really wanted to do with her life, something she hadn't asked herself seriously since her late adolescence and youth. Indeed, many writers compare the onset of middle adulthood with adolescence, using the term **middlescence** to refer to this often troubled period. Middlescence is seen as an opportunity to carry forth and resolve the identity crisis of adolescence. It is a second chance to "do your own thing, sing your own song, to be deeply and truly yourself," in one middle-aged writer's popular statement (LeShan, 1973).

PERSONALITY STABILITY AND CHANGE

Let us examine the issue of personality change in adult development more closely, focusing on the effect of aging on personality. Do individuals show systematic changes in such aspects of personality as character structure, values, and beliefs as they move from young adulthood to midlife, and finally to old age? Or is personality stable across the adult lifespan?

Measuring Personality Change

At first glance, it would appear that these questions would be easy to answer—simply by measuring some trait or cluster of traits at one age, say 20, and then again at a later age, say 40. If personality were stable, one would expect people to remain the same over the 20-year period—that is, the hostile-aggressive 20-year-old should also be hostile-aggressive at 40; the warm, nurturant young adult should develop into a warm, nurturant middle-ager. If personality changes with increasing age, however, different results would be expected.

Unfortunately, the answer to the question of personality stability versus change is not so easily discerned. Personality represents a complex interaction of traits and behaviors and is difficult to measure over time. Many theorists differentiate between genotypic and phenotypic continuity with respect to personality (Livson, 1973; Neugarten, 1977). **Genotypic continuity** refers to the stability of

midlife crisis
Term used to describe the usually stressful reactions of middle-aged adults alerted by the limited duration of their lifespans.

middlescence
The onset of middle adulthood.

genotypic continuity
The degree of continuity or similarity of a person's underlying personality structure over time.

an underlying personality structure or pattern of traits—a structure that may be expressed, however, in different behaviors at different times. Thus, a hostile-aggressive person may be physically assertive and verbally caustic during young adulthood—directly confronting people, arguing constantly, and even occasionally getting into fights. During middle age, however, the same person may express hostility in more indirect, passive-aggressive ways—for example, by repeatedly "forgetting" to invite a colleague to join the group at lunchtime, or by "misplacing" an important report that the boss needs for a conference presentation. In this example, it is assumed that the basic structure or trait pattern of personality—that is, hostility—is stable over time; only the types of behavior that represent that hostility have changed.

phenotypic continuity

The degree of continuity or similarity in a person's overt behavior or characteristics over time.

Phenotypic continuity, in contrast, refers to the degree of similarity in overt behavior at two different times. In the hostility example, phenotypic continuity would be low since the overt behaviors representing hostility have changed dramatically from early to middle adulthood. Thus, it should be clear that the lack of similarity in overt behavior from one time to another is not necessarily evidence of instability or change. Likewise, similarity in behavior does not necessarily imply continuity or stability. Two identical behaviors can be based on different underlying motives. For example, workers who offer help to colleagues may do so because of a genuine desire to assist others, or because they need to inflate their own self-images by drawing attention to their coworkers' incompetence and inferiority in specific areas—a passive-aggressive "put down" of others.

relative stability

The ordered distribution of personality scores of a sample of subjects across a period of time. In personality research, refers to whether people maintain the same score, or level of functioning, from one evaluation to another.

Another important distinction should be made between the relative and absolute stability of personality dimensions. **Relative stability** refers to the ordered distribution of personality scores of a sample of subjects across a period of time. A personality trait or behavior would be relatively stable if the ordered ranking among individuals on a personality test remained reasonably constant from one measurement period to another. Thus, subjects who scored higher on a personality trait than other subjects would still score higher at some future time regardless of whether the overall group of subjects increased, decreased, or remained the same with respect to the trait.

absolute stability

Describes a situation where a person maintains the same score or level of functioning from one evaluation of personality traits to another.

Absolute stability, in contrast, refers to whether people maintain the same score, or level of functioning, from one evaluation to another. For example, since people increase their levels of self-awareness from childhood to middle age, the absolute stability of this component of personality is low. Note that any behavior or trait that changes with development has low absolute stability.

It is also difficult to distinguish between differences in personality that are due to *development* and those that are due to *cohort,* or generational, effects. Most people's personalities would change as a result of development as they progressed through the lifespan. Generational effects would be observed only for a particular cohort of people who lived through a specific historical period—for example, people who were young during World War II, or those who were members of the "now" generation in the 1960s. Woodruff and Birren (1972) examined personality changes in adolescents who were tested in 1944 and then retested 25 years later when they were in middle age. To examine cohort differences, the personality scores of the subjects also were compared to a set of scores of adolescents and youth tested in 1969. The researchers found that personality changes from adolescence to middle adulthood were small in comparison to the differences due to cohort experiences. The major difference between the adolescents tested in 1944 and those tested in 1969 were that the 1944 adolescents scored higher in self- and social adjustment than the 1969 adolescents.

Personality Stability   Aside from these theoretical and methodological problems, much of the research evidence supports the assumption of personality stability in adulthood. This is particularly true of studies that have utilized longitudinal designs (Costa & McCrae, 1977, 1980b, 1984; Costa, McCrae, & Arenburg, 1980; Haan & Day, 1974; Leon, Gillum, Gillum, & Gouze, 1979; Schaie & Parham, 1976; Woodruff & Birren, 1972). Some of the most stable characteristics include values (aesthetic, religious, economic, social, and political) and vocational interests.

Some researchers, such as Costa and McCrae (1980b, 1984; McCrae & Costa, 1994), argue that personality remains remarkably stable in adulthood. Costa and McCrae conducted a longitudinal study using data on men between the ages of 20 and 90 and tested their subjects every 6 years. On the basis of the data the researchers categorized personality traits into three major dimensions: *neuroticism,* including such characteristics as anxiety, depression, hostility, and impulsiveness; *extraversion,* including such traits as attachment, outgoing personality, assertiveness, and excitement seeking; and *openness* to ideas, fantasies, feelings, and values. When measured over time on these clusters of traits, the men were found to be remarkably consistent in their personalities. Men who were highly extraverted in young adulthood described themselves as extraverted in later adulthood.

Another longitudinal study of adult personality development was reported by Haan (1981). The investigator was among a group of researchers (Eichorn, Clausen, Haan, Honzik, & Mussen, 1981) who examined data on physical, mental health, and personality for several groups of men and women; the data were collected at intervals from early adolescence (and in some cases, from childhood) through middle age. Haan's contribution to this massive research effort was an investigation of the relative stability and developmental changes in six common personality dimensions. The first dimension studied, cognitive investment, indicated ease and skill in dealing with intellectual matters, deliberate reflectiveness, and interest in personal achievement. The second dimension, emotional under-over control, was a bipolar dimension. One extreme represented a pressured, dramatic, and aggressive approach to interpersonal exchanges; the other extreme, an emotionally bland, constricted, and submissive approach. The third dimension, open-closed self, represented degree of openness to one's own thoughts, feelings, and experiences, as well as ease of self-expression. The fourth dimension, nurturant-hostile, was defined, on the one hand, by warmth, consideration, and responsiveness to other people and, on the other hand, by hostility, suspiciousness, and wariness of others. The fifth dimension, *heterosexuality under-over control,* referred to variations in expression of sexuality. At one extreme are individuals who are impulsive and self-indulgent in their sexual relations and who tend to eroticize most situations; at the other extreme are individuals who are overcontrolled, aloof, fearful, intellectualized, and asexual in character. The last dimension studied was termed *self-confidence* and dealt with the degree of poise, assertiveness, productivity, self-satisfaction, and confidence displayed in interpersonal relations. Developmental change was observed, however, for emotional under-over control. Finally, a rather complex developmental pattern was noted for under-over controlled heterosexuality. Following a peak in undercontrolled sexuality in adolescence, people became more controlled in young adulthood, only to show a resurgence in self- and sexual expression at midlife, perhaps coinciding with reduced concern about pregnancy.

In summarizing her findings, Haan emphasized that from adolescence to middle adulthood, people change slowly while maintaining a reasonable degree of continuity with their past. In other words, personality development is characterized by a low degree of absolute stability (since people often increase or decrease in their level of functioning with age) and a moderate degree of relative stability. Thus, Haan's findings supported other researchers' conclusion that adult personality, despite periods of change, remains generally stable over time. Adult personality development is not, generally speaking, characterized by large and pervasive changes in beliefs, attitudes, and values. In particular, the midlife crisis, if it is experienced at all, involves more of a reshaping and reorganization of existing personality characteristics than a complete transformation of the person into a "new human being."

FOCUS ON CULTURE

Most of what we know about personality development is derived from longitudinal research using people in industrialized societies. Most of the subjects studied have been literate, white males. Very little is known about adult personality development in nonindustrialized countries. How is our understanding of stability in personality development limited by the type of data collected in these longitudinal studies?

DEVELOPMENTAL TASKS OF MIDDLE ADULTHOOD

Although the evidence suggests that basic personality structure does not change much during adulthood, certainly the developmental tasks confronting adults do. Moreover, some theorists have speculated that the way in which people cope with life crises may well undergo some transformation as they are confronted with the new tasks of middle adulthood.

generativity versus stagnation
According to Erikson, the primary psychosocial crisis of middle age. Generativity refers to a concern for establishing and guiding the next generation; in the absence of generativity, a feeling of personal impoverishment, boredom, or stagnation occurs.

Erikson's Theory   In Erikson's psychosocial scheme, the central crisis for middle-aged adults is the resolution of **generativity versus stagnation.** Generativity involves the concern for establishing and guiding the next generation. For some individuals, generativity is expressed in the context of the family, through loving and nurturing relationships with spouse and children. For others, it is found in job productivity or in mentorship to younger workers—guiding and helping them in their career development. In some cultures, generativity may be achieved through ritualistic passing down of traditions, rites, and customs to the next generation. Generativity is a person's link with the future—the means by which one can transcend one's own mortality.

The opposite of generativity in Erikson's theory is stagnation, a feeling of personal impoverishment, boredom, and excessive concern or preoccupation with the self. Erikson points out that the experience of generativity is more difficult for adults who have not become parents. However, it is not essential that adults foster the development of their own biological offspring. In a longitudinal study of infertile men (Snarey, Son, Kuehne, Hauser, & Vaillant, 1987), it was found that infertile men who became fathers, either by adoption or birth, were more likely to be generative in middle adulthood than were infertile men who remained childless. The infertile men who had become adoptive fathers experienced a higher level of generativity than did fertile men. Perhaps because of their intense interest and persistence in overcoming their reproductive disabilities, infertile men put more effort into taking care of others.

Peck's Theory   The work of Peck (1968) echoes some of the themes of Erikson's theory. Peck outlines four major challenges or tasks for middle-aged adults who are attempting to cope with the changes taking place both within and outside themselves:

1. People must come to value wisdom over physical strength and attractiveness; they must acknowledge and accept their inevitable physical decline and rely more on experience, knowledge, and mental processes for life satisfaction.

2. They must redefine relationships; other people, including spouses, should increasingly be viewed as individuals and companions.

During middle adulthood people involve themselves in activities that reflect their civic and social responsibility.

Relationships, on the whole, become broader, more social, and less sexualized at this time.

cathected flexibility
The capacity to shift one's emotional investment to new people or activities.

3. Middle-aged adults must also be able to demonstrate what Peck calls **cathected flexibility**—that is, the ability to shift one's emotional investment to new people or activities. This capacity becomes especially important in middle age because of the increased exposure to "breaks" in relationships during this time—parents die, children grow up and leave home, certain activities (such as vigorous athletics) may have to be put aside. To adjust to these changes, middle-aged people must be able to "let go" of relationships—with parents, children, a job—and reinvest themselves in something new.

4. Peck suggests that successful adjustment to middle age also requires remaining mentally flexible and open to new experiences or ways of doing things. If people continue to rely on well-worn ideas or answers, they may become slaves to the past. Instead of controlling their lives, their lives may control them.

Havighurst's Theory   Another perspective on midlife challenges is offered by Havighurst (1974). He notes that developmental tasks arise from changes within the person, from societal pressures, and especially from pressures derived from the person's own values, standards, and aspirations. Middle age is a unique time of life. At no other point in the lifespan does the person have as much influence upon society. And yet it is also the time when society makes its greatest demands on the person (see Table 13–6). Middle-aged adults must cope with important tasks at home—for example, assisting teenage children to become responsible, happy adults while maintaining a harmonious relationship with a spouse. They face pressures at work and must reach and maintain a satisfactory level of occupational performance. And at the same time, they are asked by society to accept and fulfill their social, tribal, or civic obligations and responsibilities.

HAVIGHURST'S DEVELOPMENTAL TASKS OF MIDDLE AGE

1. Achieve adult civic and social responsibility

2. Establish and maintain an economic standard of living

3. Develop adult leisure-time activities

4. Assist teenage children to become responsible and happy adults

5. Relate to one's spouse as a person

6. Accept and adjust to the physiological changes of middle age

7. Adjust to one's aging parents

TABLE 13–6

Source: From *Developmental Tasks and Education,* 3rd ed., by R. J. Havighurst, 1974, New York: McKay.

Many adults define themselves as the "sandwich generation," as they respond to the needs of their own children and those of their aging parents. The middle-aged person, according to Havighurst, must also find new outlets for their leisure time that reflect changes in body, interests, values, financial status, and family structure.

Levinson's Theory   Daniel Levinson's (1986) theory of life-course development was introduced in Chapter 11; his work on occupational development was discussed in Chapter 12. In his theory, Levinson addresses the major transitions from one period of the lifespan to the next. During middle adulthood, which roughly corresponds to the years from 40 to 65, adults become "senior members" of their community and assume the responsibility for their work and for the development of the next generation of adults. From Levinson's perspective, the middle-adult years are the time for consolidation of interests, goals, and commitments. The transition to middle adulthood actually begins in the early to mid-40s (see Figure 11–1 in Chapter 11). This period represents a bridge between the early and middle years of adulthood—or, as Levinson notes, between the past and the future. It is a time when people take stock of themselves. Questions reminiscent of the adolescent period, such as "Who am I?" "Where am I going?" and so on, become important again. The individual begins to evaluate personal achievements in light of previous goals, and to reorganize those goals in light of both current and anticipated achievements.

According to Levinson, successful resolution of this midlife transition necessitates working through discrepancies between what is and what might be. For individuals who are able to acknowledge and accept the realities of their life structure, a new level of stability emerges as they enter middle adulthood, usually between the ages of 45 and 50. Levinson notes that during this period qualities such

In middle adulthood people have more time to develop new talents and interests. Adult school evening programs offer people many opportunities to develop new leisure activities.

as wisdom, judiciousness, compassion, and breadth of perspective often emerge. He also notes that men who reported good relationships with mentors in their early years are likely to become effective mentors themselves at this time, guiding and nurturing the development of younger, less experienced coworkers. A note of caution about generalizing from Levinson's conclusions: since he derived his theory primarily from the experiences of men, it may not apply as well to women as a whole.

Overview of Adult Development Theories   Each of the preceding theorists derived their ideas about adult personality development from observations and interviews with selected adults. Unlike other theories that have more precisely defined terms and whose ideas are more readily tested in controlled experimental settings, these theories have not been tested by research studies. Their usefulness is measured instead by the ideas they have generated about the changes adults experience throughout their lives.

Although each of these theorists portrays the tasks of middle age in somewhat different ways, a common thread runs through their writings. Each sees middle adulthood as a time of continued challenge for the individual—challenge that may require considerable adjustment in areas such as self, family relations, social interactions, career development, and leisure activity. Yet successful adjustment to the tasks of midlife, as to all periods of development, is dependent upon many factors and takes many forms. Middle-aged adults are not a homogeneous group. Each person is a unique individual with unique experiences, and each will adjust to the challenges of midlife in his or her own way. Some people approach this part of their lifespan with enthusiasm and vigor, while others view it as the beginning of the end. I know people my age who seem to have lost their interest in doing new things; they are worried about their health and seem to be waiting for that fatal heart attack or diagnosis of an incurable disease. They are no fun to be around. In contrast, I have middle-aged friends who are taking dancing lessons for the first time and planning trips to new places. They don't feel old or worry about getting older; life is just too short.

BRIEF REVIEW

Middle age is accompanied by a gradual physical decline from the peak reached in the 20s. The individual does not experience a simple reverse from growth to deterioration; both processes have been taking place since early in life. The meaning of these changes depends upon the values of the culture in which people live.

As people enter the middle years of life, concerns regarding physical health become more common. Cardiovascular diseases and cancer are the two leading causes of death during this time. Ethnicity can have an effect on overall health during middle age. In the United States, ethnic groups vary in terms of access to medical care, adequate living conditions, and attitudes toward health.

Stressful life events such as the death of a spouse, divorce, or change of jobs can contribute to health problems. Daily hassles and multiple stresses occur often and can erode a person's sense of well-being. Individuals react to stress in different ways; the most adaptive approach is to actively evaluate one's priorities and make appropriate changes.

Research indicates that emotional and personality factors—particularly Type-A behavior—are major contributors to the health problems of middle-aged adults. Type-A behavior patterns may have their origins in childhood and are linked to heart disease in adulthood.

One effect of aging is the climacteric, the changes in the reproductive and sexual organs that result from a decrease in the production of gonadal hormones. For women, the decline in estrogen and progesterone levels brings a clear signal of biological change: menopause. Menstruation gradually ceases over a period of a year or two. For men, the results of a decline in testosterone levels are less obvious.

Changes in the way adults process information increase with age; while capacity for information remains fairly constant, processing becomes slower and more difficult—especially for demanding, complex, and nonrelevant tasks. Experience and expertise reduces age-related cognitive deficits. Learning continues to be important during middle adulthood, but the pace of learning may slow down. A number of factors have been associated with individual differences in the rate of cognitive decline in old age.

It is difficult to determine whether adult personality is basically stable, or whether people undergo major personality changes across the lifespan. Some theorists have suggested that although the basic personality structure or trait pattern of the individual remains essentially the same across the adult years, the behaviors representative of the underlying structure may well change. Most research, particularly those studies using longitudinal designs, supports the assumption of personality stability in adulthood. Some of the most stable characteristics include values and vocational interests.

There are a variety of different views concerning mid-life personality development. Most theorists do agree, however, that middle adulthood is a time of challenge for the individual—challenge that may require considerable adjustment in such areas as the self, family relations, social interactions, career development, and leisure activity.

Erikson sees the midlife crisis as one of generativity, a concern for the next generation, versus stagnation, a sense of boredom and preoccupation with the self. Other views of middle-adulthood development have been proposed by Peck, Havighurst, and Levinson.

KEY TERMS

absolute stability (528)
arthritis (511)
atherosclerosis (502)
cathected flexibility (532)
climacteric (504)
cognitive investment (522)
divided attention (522)
ethnic group (511)
generativity versus stagnation (530)

genotypic continuity (527)
male climacteric (506)
menopause (504)
midlife crisis (527)
middlescence (527)
osteoporosis (505)
pacing (524)
phenotypic continuity (528)
presbycusis (503)

relative stability (528)
selective attention (522)
secondary memory (521)
sensory memory (521)
stress (514)
Type-A behavior (518)
Type-B related behavior (519)
working memory (521)

REVIEW QUESTIONS

If you can answer these questions, you have a good understanding of the material in this chapter. If a question seems difficult, go back to the text and review the topic.

1. Describe the physical signs of aging that occur during middle adulthood.

2. How do heredity and the environment affect health and aging? In what ways do men and women differ in health during middle adulthood?

3. In what ways do ethnic groups vary with regard to health in the United States? What factors can explain ethnic variation in health?

4. What role does nutrition play in health during middle adulthood?

5. Distinguish among highly stressful life events, mildly stressful life events, and chronic everyday hassles with regard to their impact on health. Cite two examples for each life event category.

6. What are the distinguishing characteristics of Type-A behavior? What is the relationship between Type-A behavior and heart disease?

7. Describe the symptoms associated with female and male climacterics. What cultural factors affect the experience of menopause for women?

8. In what ways does sexual activity change during middle adulthood? How do cultural attitudes affect middle-aged sexuality?

9. Describe the different types of memory involved in information processing. What is the difference between structural and process models of memory?

10. Compare the differences between older and younger adults in their ability to remember information.

11. What factors help explain individual differences in degree of decline of cognitive skills as people age?

12. Distinguish between genotypic and phenotypic continuity in personality development. Give an example of each.

13. Distinguish between relative and absolute stability of personality traits. How are developmental differences in personality different from cohort or generational differences?

14. What three characteristics were used in Costa and McCrae's longitudinal study of personality? How stable were these traits?

15. What were the six traits studied in Haan's longitudinal study and how stable were they over time?

16. What are the developmental tasks of middle adulthood described by Havighurst? How does his view of this period differ from Erikson, Levinson, and Peck?

OBSERVATIONAL ACTIVITY

HOW OLD IS OLD?

How old will you be when you start to "get old"? Perceptions of age, especially relative age such as young, middle-aged, and elderly, are based on many social, cultural, and personal experiences. Some of these experiences are objective in nature, such as the satisfaction with life goals one has achieved, or the perception of time left to pursue those goals. Because people differ in their experiences, perceptions of the aging process vary considerably among people.

Develop a short questionnaire with the purpose of ascertaining the perceptions people have about age.

1. Ask, for example, at what age does a person stop being young? When is a person middle-aged? When is a person old?

2. Keep track of such data as age, gender, and ethnic grouping. Direct your questions to about 40 people.

3. Tabulate your results.

4. What differences in perception of aging did you find for different age groups, males versus females, or among ethnic groupings?

5. Do single adults view aging differently than married adults?

6. What factors seem to be most influential in a person's perception of aging?

Summarize your data and draw some conclusions. Finally, answer this question: Is it really true (based on your findings) that you are as young or as old as you feel, or as you perceive yourself to be?

CHAPTER 14

Middle Adulthood: Family and Occupational Development

Josie was known by many in her neighborhood as "Nanny." At age 61 she had 4 grown children and 10 grandchildren, 3 of whom she was now helping to raise. Her involvement with her grandchildren was out of necessity as well as out of caring. Her youngest daughter was a single parent of three children and needed help in raising her family. Josie had been living alone since her husband Walter died 4 years ago, and she wanted to make sure her grandchildren had a proper religious upbringing. So Josie invited her daughter and grandchildren to live with her.

But it was in her role as the director of the children's choir in her church that Josie best came to be known as "Nanny." Every Saturday and Sunday Josie would lead her grandchildren and the other children as they sang hymns, offering words of encouragement and hope. She was an inspiration to many people in the African American community because of her steadfast dedication to helping children through music. It was always a special moment for her whenever any of the former choir members returned to thank her for her direction and encouragement. Many of the children she leads today are the children of former choir members.

At age 55, John, too, was at a good point in his life, but for different reasons. He enjoyed his work as a high school English teacher, especially since he had recently begun concentrating on helping his students improve their writing skills. For years he had taught American literature, but he really wanted to teach creative writing.

It was a bit ironic that he should be so enthusiastic about effective writing, since as a student he did not do particularly well in writing courses. However, his father had insisted that he acquire good writing skills, often insisting: "You cannot call yourself educated if you cannot put your thoughts on paper." John silently chuckled whenever he heard himself repeating the same message to his 10th-grade students.

His second wife Helen was his good companion and friend. Often when John was frustrated with some student's lack of progress, Helen would encourage him to find a way to help the student. He valued her input and involvement in this new facet of his teaching career. They both looked forward to sharing even more of their lives together as they got older.

John's interest in and dedication to his work and Josie's involvement with her family and community represent different ways of addressing the psychosocial tasks of middle adulthood. As we saw in Chapter 13, middle age brings with it a new sense of challenge—in Erikson's (1968) scheme, a challenge of *generativity versus stagnation.* Nowhere is this challenge better expressed than in the context of family, community, and work life.

In middle age there is a broadening of interests and a turning outward toward others. Having found their own place in society, mature adults like John and Josie reorient their energies toward the future—to the next generation. The issue of generativity involves the need to teach and otherwise become responsible for the development of that generation. Within the family, middle-aged parents provide encouragement and support as their offspring prepare to leave home and make their own ways. The middle-aged worker expresses generativity not only in managing people and policies, but in training and guiding one or several younger employees in **mentor relationships.** Thus, the fruits of middle age, according to Erikson, are found primarily in relationships based upon generativity.

Midlife identity may also be linked to adults' desire to make an impact—to leave their mark. As they watch the next generation emerge, middle-aged adults cannot escape the realization that their remaining years are limited. As they experience the death or decline of relatives from older generations, adults seek meaning in their lives. Are they part of a continuous cycle of families that produce new families? What contributions will they leave behind for those who follow?

Not all adults are successful in achieving generativity, however. For some, family life is a constant source of frustration and irritation. Previous or ongoing emotional problems may prevent them from engaging in supportive, friendly relationships with spouse, children, or friends. At work, too, some people are

mentor relationship

When an older, more experienced worker guides the training and development of a younger worker.

Generativity involves an interest in passing on to others the lessons of life learned from experience. This Kenyan storyteller shares an adventure with family and villagers.

unable to interact effectively with others. A woman may become disillusioned because she believes her work or ideas are unappreciated by her superiors. A man may feel defeated because he has failed to achieve some career goal established earlier in life. For such people, the midlife journey may be a rough one. If they are unable to reach out to others, their lives may take on the hollow feeling of stagnation.

FAMILY LIFE

At the start of my travels through middle adulthood, our children were both teenagers, my parents were both alive and fairly active, and I was not even thinking about getting older. Ten years later, both of our children are adults, my father has died and my mother requires daily care, and my husband and I are enjoying a new life without any children in the house. My story is not an unusual one. The nature of family life changes dramatically during middle age.

In many industrialized countries, it is common for adults to have married in their 20s, with their children born soon thereafter. Thus, by the time they are in their early 40s, their oldest children may have completed their formal education and be ready to try life on their own. For some families, the exit of young adult children from the household creates a very different day-to-day family atmosphere. Without the parade of teenagers and young adults using the phone, watching TV, or listening to music, the house is likely to be quieter. In a few more years, the youngest child may be launched into society as an independent adult, leaving the middle-aged couple by themselves. In other families, adult children may continue living in their parents' home or return home after a few years on their own at college or in a nonmarital relationship. As was the case for Josie, some adult children return home with their own children. Nonetheless, most couples will spend fully one half of the family life cycle living together without children in their household.

Many middle-aged couples are in the launching stage of the family life cycle. Their family is no longer expanding, but instead gets smaller as adolescent and young adult children mature. The point when family composition and functions change depends on several factors: the age at which the couple married and began childbearing, the number and spacing of children, whether they experience divorce and remarriage, the presence of stepchildren, and even the decision to remain childless.

Stereotypes portray the middle-aged couple as guiding their first child into the adult world. However, this image does not fit couples who delayed having their first child until their mid-30s, or remarried couples who have a child after their children from previous marriages are already teenagers or adults. People who marry and have children at a young age may have seen their adult children leave the family nest, only to experience their return in times of financial need or marital breakdown. Single-parent families and those in which extended family members (e.g., grandparents, aunts, uncles, and cousins) live in the household may experience a different sequencing and timing of events in the family life cycle.

The impact of these changes can only be understood within the culture in which they occur. American culture places a high value on independence and self-determination. However, in other cultures, expectations about how families change across the lifespan may differ dramatically. Simic (1990) illustrated this difference in a comparative study of intergenerational ties in American and Yugoslavian families. According to Simic, children raised in American families are taught to value self-determination and an individual's right to privacy. Children are given their "own space" in the form of their own bedroom and in terms of time alone. Furthermore, children are encouraged to develop social relationships outside of the family, particularly during adolescence. Thus, when children reach adulthood, it is expected that they will establish themselves separately from their families.

By contrast, Yugoslavian children are taught to value family and kinship ties. According to Simic, most Yugoslavian families expect that children will maintain a reciprocal relationship with their parents and relatives throughout their lives. Families anticipate the availability of their children to care for their economic, medical, and emotional needs. Privacy is not encouraged and children are encouraged to identify more with their families than with peers outside the family. As children develop into adulthood there are no sharp breaks with their families. Rather, the family grows to accommodate new generations of family members. It is expected that unmarried adult children will remain in the family home; married children often live on the family property or very close by. As a result of these cultural expectations and practices, Yugoslavians regard their obligations to their parents as a lifelong moral imperative and parents receive their children's care without a sense of dependency or guilt.

FOCUS ON CULTURE

People who immigrate to a new country face the challenge of living in a different culture. They must adjust to new languages, foods, and ways of doing business. They must balance their own cultural values and expectations with those of the new culture. For immigrant parents the challenge is even greater. For example, if they immigrated from a rural village that valued cooperation and community to an inner-city environment in which they are viewed as outsiders, they must struggle to communicate their value of cooperation while teaching their children how to survive in a totally different environment. Often, immigrant parents cling to the values and customs from their homeland while their children acquire conflicting values from their new peers.

INTERGENERATIONAL RELATIONS

As Hagestad (1982) has observed, the phrase "parents and children" is likely to evoke a picture of young to middle-aged adults interacting with children between the ages of 1 and 16. Less often do we think of young and middle-aged adults as the children of aging parents.

While families have become smaller, life expectancy has increased. There is a sizable percentage of multigenerational families that include parents, children, grandparents, and in some cases, great-grandparents. Parents maintain simultaneous relationships with their adult offspring and their own parents. Family life-course theorists speak of the various levels of parent-child relationships as **generational stations** (Hagestad, 1982).

generational stations
The various tiers of parent-child relationships that exist within a family.

Until recently, social scientists showed little interest in intergenerational relations. In part, this neglect stemmed from a narrow view of primary familial relationships. Rather than conceiving of parent-child relations as a lifelong process, most researchers focused almost exclusively on the early period of the family life cycle—the period when the couple rears young children, up to the

Families have become multigenerational as a result of increased life expectancies.

point when those children leave the family home and establish their own household. Furthermore, the cultural value of independence encouraged the belief that once young adults were out on their own, they no longer depended upon their parents for contact or help. We now know, however, that adult children and their parents maintain a reasonably high level of contact throughout their adult lives and that the relationship is usually beneficial to both (Parish, Hao, & Hogan, 1991; Walker & Pratt, 1991).

In studying intergenerational relations, two questions are frequently asked: "What is the degree to which one generation influences the development of the other?" and "Are the intergenerational influences observed primarily *unidirectional* (i.e., parents guiding and shaping the behavior and adjustment of their children) or *reciprocal* (i.e., parents and children mutually affecting each other's development)?"

Bengston and Troll (1978), in discussing the relationship between young adults and their parents, emphasize that family socialization in adulthood is a complex, interrelated process characterized by continuous feedback and a system of mutual influences. Moreover, they also note that intergenerational transmission of values, standards, and patterns of behavior are affected not only by the specific characteristics of the individuals involved, but by factors outside of the family—for example, the specific historical period in which the people live and their ethnic and cultural backgrounds. People who grew up during the Great Depression, a time when material goods and money were hard to come by, learned the value of being resourceful. As a result, they are more likely to continue to value hard work and resourcefulness in later adult life and to pass these views on to their own offspring either by example or by socialization (Elder, Downey, & Cross; 1980). Josie's commitment to her grandchildren and to the children in her church choir was influenced by the belief in her African American community that everyone shares in the responsibility to look after the welfare of people within their neighborhood.

The bidirectional nature of intergenerational influences is supported by the research of Hagestad (1984). Hagestad studied relationships across three generations of adults in 150 families—aged parents, middle-aged parents/children, and young-adult children. In areas as varied as diet and health practices, political attitudes, and childrearing views, Hagestad found evidence of socialization influences both up and down the generational lines. Not only did parents influence their children's views, but children had an impact on their parents' views.

Hagestad found that advice up the generational chain from middle-aged children to older parents mostly concerned health or practical matters such as household management and use of time. Older parents gave their middle-aged children advice on health, work, and money matters. The youngest generation tried to influence their middle-aged parents regarding health matters, social attitudes, and how to keep up with the changing times. Children (of all ages) were more likely to get their parents to change than parents were to get their children to change.

In reviewing the literature on intergenerational transmission, Troll and Bengston (1982) report that most researchers have focused on attitudes, values, and orientations in five areas: politics, religion, sex, work, and lifestyles. For example, similarity in political-party preference has been found to be consistently high across generations. Thus, American parents who identify themselves as Democrats usually have adult children who also identify themselves with the Democratic party. General political orientation and values—liberalism, egalitarianism, dedication to causes, and so forth—also show cross-generational continuity. Research on religious affiliation and religious values also has found a consistently high similarity between parents and their adult children. This similarity may be influenced by the sanctions found in many religions that require adults to raise

Middle adulthood is significant in the study of intergenerational relations. Middle-aged adults are influenced from both the top down (their parents) and the bottom up (their children).

FOCUS ON CULTURE

In industrialized cultures such as the United States and Europe, it is not unusual for people to move from one city, state, or country to another to maintain their jobs or advance their careers. By contrast, in rural or agricultural societies in which generations of people have worked the same soil, there is less opportunity for mobility and greater interdependence among people. How might the economy of a country affect adults' expectations about family life? How might a rapid change in a country's economic standard affect family life?

their children within that faith. In Western societies less intergenerational similarity has been reported for gender roles, lifestyle, and work orientation.

In studying intergenerational relations, the middle-adult period takes on special significance (see Table 14–1). Middle-aged adults, sometimes referred to as the *sandwich generation,* provide the link between the younger and older generations. Being in the middle of the family line also means that one is likely to be influenced both from the top down (elderly parent to middle-aged child) and the bottom up (adolescent or young-adult child to middle-aged parent). Consequently, during middle age the individual may find it necessary to integrate seemingly discrepant family roles into his or her sense of self. This psychosocial task poses considerable challenge for some middle-aged persons.

Families with Adolescents   There is an ironic twist in life's journey; just as adolescents are growing into physical maturity, many of their parents are experiencing changes in their own lives. Most teenagers are on the verge of adult life at the

CHARACTERISTICS OF INTERGENERATIONAL RELATIONS DURING MIDDLE ADULTHOOD

ADOLESCENT CHILDREN	ADULT CHILDREN	GRANDCHILDREN	AGING PARENTS
Assisting children make the move toward independence	Accepting children as adults	Defining the type of grandparent they want to be	Changing the direction of support to their own parents
Dealing with their own aging at a time when children come to maturity	Assessing their effectiveness as parents	Coming to terms with the image of grandparent	Providing physical, emotional, and financial support
Serving as career role models	Expanding their family to include in-laws	Providing guidance and encouragement to their children in their parenting roles	Creating a responsible relationship that is sensitive to parents' need for independence
Providing support to teenage parents	Staying in touch with children who may live far away	In some cases, serving as surrogate parents	Deciding on alternative care should it be necessary
	Dealing with the empty nest and the return of adult children to the family home		

TABLE 14–1

same time that their parents are in the middle of adulthood. In Chapter 10 the nature of the adolescent-parent relationship was discussed primarily from the perspective of the developing teenager; here we discuss it from the parent's perspective. As adolescents seek to establish their independence and autonomy within the family, their parents more often than not are also facing the personal challenge of defining themselves within a much broader context. Middle-aged parents who can see the end of their active role as parents may be asking themselves the same question as their adolescent children: "Who am I, and what do I want to do with my life?"

In addition to resolving whatever conflicts exist between themselves and their growing children, middle-aged parents of adolescents must also come to terms with their own inner conflicts (Steinberg & Silverberg, 1987). One such conflict, discussed in Chapter 13, is that adults may not want to accept the decline in their physical capabilities—which is made more apparent when they compare themselves to their physically mature (and strong and youthful) adolescents. Teenagers are not only younger-looking and stronger, they also have more energy than middle-aged adults. Recognizing that their adolescent children are functioning at a different physiological and developmental level helps parents "let go" of their children.

In American culture, the emergence of adolescents as independent and autonomous is like the final exam or report card for parenting. Some American parents may set an overall long-term goal of assisting their children to become independent and self-sufficient (Ryff, Lee, Essex, & Schmutte, 1994). Adolescence and youth offer the first developmental opportunities to measure such goals. With "success as parents" in their sights, many parents focus their energies on supporting and assisting their adolescents in their search to establish identities, identify career choices, and prepare themselves for the adult world. Parental assistance in career exploration can be critical for adolescents seeking to identify their adult career paths (Grotevant & Cooper, 1988).

Parents serve not only as role models for career orientations, but also as a source of encouragement, information, and financial support. In one survey (Hedin, Erickson, Simon, & Walker, 1985) American adolescents named their parents as the most important influence on their thinking about careers, more so than their high-school guidance counselors. Mothers are more influential than fathers in career exploration. Children whose mothers had established careers are much more likely to enter less traditional careers and to have high career aspirations (Hoffman, 1979, 1989; Rollins & White, 1982; Shapiro & Crowley, 1982). Although fathers serve as a source of information and expectations about careers, daughters are less likely to enter into candid discussions with their fathers about their career concerns or hopes (Youniss & Smollar, 1985).

As adolescents assume adult roles such as workers or parents, their parents may have greater influence on them. Stevens (1984) looked at the role middle-aged African American grandmothers played in the lives of their teenage daughters who became mothers. He found that the presence of the grandchild provided a context in which the grandmothers could teach their daughters about infant development. The grandmothers not only modeled appropriate parenting behavior, they also served as childrearing consultants for the teenage mothers. In families without grandchildren, socialization of parenting skills is less likely to occur.

The impact of intergenerational influence is not limited to grandmothers. In one study (Oyersman, Radin, & Benn, 1993) grandfathers who lived in the same household with a teenage daughter and her young child were found to have a

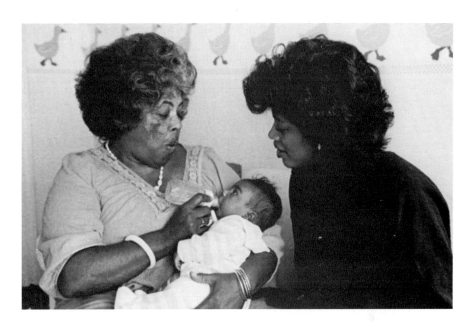

This grandmother is modeling appropriate parenting behaviors for her teenage granddaughter, the mother of the young infant.

direct influence on the cognitive and developmental adjustment of their grand-children. Nurturing grandfathers enhanced the baby's compliance with the mother's requests and reduced the number of negative outbursts the child displayed.

Thus, while the parents of adolescents may experience some conflicts, it is not necessarily a time of continual stress and strain. If middle-aged parents see their role as influencing rather than intruding in their adolescents' lives, this period can be one in which both parent and child accomplish some important developmental tasks.

Families with Adult Children   In cultures that value independence there comes a point in the family life cycle when parents and children begin to "let go" of one another. Parents begin to accept the fact that their children are independent, self-reliant individuals who are recognized by the outside community as legal adults. As children are launched into adulthood, parents begin to match their long-held hopes and dreams for their children with the realities of their adult children's lives. Many parents measure their own self-worth and well-being against the accomplishments and adjustments of their adult children. In one study (Ryff et al., 1994), parents' sense of self-acceptance, purpose in life, and mastery were all linked to how well-adjusted they thought their adult children were.

This stage of parenting, which almost always occurs in middle adulthood, is a poorly researched phase of family life (Hagestad, 1982). It is often referred to as the *postparental* period, as if the exit of children from the family home and into the world relieves adults of all parental responsibilities, obligations, and needs. In reality, people do not cease to be parents simply because their children no longer live with them—just as adults, regardless of age, are still their parents' children even though they may be married, have children of their own, and lead relatively autonomous lives.

The relationship between middle-aged parents and their adult children is different from parent-child relationships of earlier periods of the family life cycle

(Hess & Waring, 1978; Thompson & Walker, 1984). Since both parents and children are adults, they are in some ways social equals, at least insofar as privileges and responsibilities are afforded them by their adult status. Independent living, increasing financial autonomy, establishment of one's own family, and recognition by peers and coworkers all bolster the status of the young-adult child and, in turn, help to realign the power imbalance that characterized the earlier parent-child relationship.

Another difference between parent-child relationships and those of earlier periods of life is that primary emotional investments and obligations are redirected toward new individuals. For young adults, concerns for spouse and children take precedence over concerns for parents. Likewise, middle-aged parents begin to focus more attention on each other and less on their independent, and relatively self-reliant, adult children. For many American middle-aged adults, their level of satisfaction and contentment in life is not dependent on having regular contact with their adult children, even when they enjoy the company of their children and grandchildren (Cicirelli, 1982; Lee & Ellithorpe, 1982; Lee & Ihinger-Tallman, 1980).

The introduction of in-laws may also complicate parent-child relations at this time. Middle-aged parents often find that they must share their children's time, energy, and emotional investments with the parents of their daughter- or son-in-law. For some, this realization accompanies a sense of resentment and jealousy.

Finally, parent-child relationships are more voluntary than they once were. Independent living means that a greater effort must be made for parents and adult children to maintain their relationship. Some adult children may live in a different town, state, or country than their parents, making contact more difficult. Increasingly, parent-child interaction is part of leisure-time activity rather than daily routine.

Despite these changes, research suggests that parent-child relationships remain important for people during this stage of the family life cycle (Walker & Pratt, 1991). Troll, Miller, and Atchley (1979) point out that generally the ties between adult children and their parents are close. Young adult children, such as Josie's daughter, frequently rely on their parents for financial help, child care, and emotional support. In turn, middle-aged parents derive emotional satisfaction from their relationship with their adult children, as well as companionship and a sense of generativity. They have produced independent, responsible, and loving offspring who will carry on after they are gone. Middle-aged parents also share vicariously in the accomplishments of their adult children—at work, at home, and at play. They take pride in their daughter's graduation from medical school and their son's promotion within the company; they share the joy of their children's marriages and the birth of grandchildren. For some middle-aged adults, the success of their children becomes an avenue for fulfilling some of their own unmet needs and goals. For example, a mother who plays a musical instrument may derive great satisfaction from her daughter's career as a musician. Parents are even more satisfied with themselves when their adult children exceed their own level of attainment and accomplishment (Ryff et al., 1994).

Yet the *empty nest* of family life—as this period has been called—is not without its problems. Some parents experience considerable stress when their children finally leave home for good. The **empty-nest syndrome** may be a factor in depression in middle-aged women, especially if the woman has not established alternative ways of deriving meaning and satisfaction from her life once her active parenting role has ended. One study (Bart, 1970) found that women who had

empty-nest syndrome
An emotional pattern, including depression and loss of self-worth, that some middle-aged adults experience after their children leave home.

Families across the Lifespan

A family is a group of people who share a special relationship that influences their lives. Family members are often related to each other by birth or marriage and share common values. Typically, but not exclusively, that relationship involves the rearing of children and the care of elderly members. Some families are small; others are large and include members from several generations. Although membership in a family lasts a lifetime, changes can and do occur. Just as people change as they mature, so too do families change as their members enter different stages of the lifespan. Death, divorce, or remarriage can alter the size and well-being of individual families. The role of family members is also determined by cultural expectations and influenced by social and economic changes.

devoted themselves to their role as mother experienced the loss of a meaningful role in their family when their children grew up and no longer needed their care. Mothers are not the only ones who may be upset by the departure of the children from the home. Lewis and his colleagues (Lewis, Frenau, & Roberts, 1979) found that 22% of their sample of fathers reported considerable unhappiness over the departure of the last child from home. Older fathers who had few children, who were more involved in nurturing relationships, and whose marriages showed evidence of problems were the most affected by the absence of children.

More recent studies have shown that the empty-nest syndrome is not as common as it was in the early 1970s. Many middle-aged parents are happy to see their children leave the nest. Women who have juggled parental and work roles may find it much easier to deal with the transition to having fewer roles to fulfill (Bee, 1987). Furthermore, in the majority of marital satisfaction studies, couples report the most satisfaction during the empty-nest period. Many parents greet the departure of their children with a sense of relief and psychological well-being (Harkins, 1978; Ryff et al., 1994).

Some adult children return home after having lived away from the family. Researchers Aquilino and Supple (1991) examined the satisfaction of American

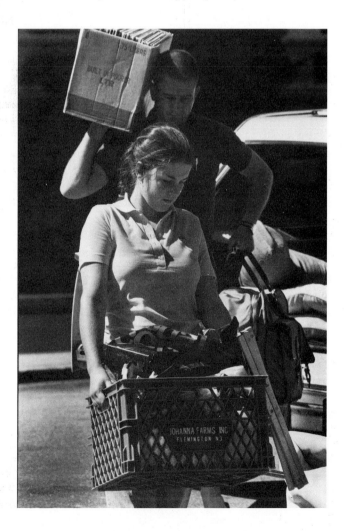

In most Western societies there comes a time when adult-aged children leave home to establish their independence. Middle-aged parents are often ready to "let go" of their children and begin their post-parental roles. For some parents, however, the process of letting go is more difficult.

Personal Perspective

MAKING THE RETURN TO THE NEST EASIER

When parents launch their children from the nest, most do so with the expectation that their children will be gone for good. While leaving home has become a transition that marks emergence into adulthood, returning home is becoming more and more common. Furthermore, the age at which young adults leave their family home to start on their own has risen since 1980 (Goldscheider & Goldscheider, 1994). Adult children extend their stay at home by attending college and graduate school for more years than was typical of previous genera-

tions. Many also marry at later ages. Adult children may also return to the family home because of unwed pregnancy, divorce, inability to find employment, or the high costs of housing. In most cases they return because they are unable to support themselves on their own.

While many parents are not eager to have their adult children return, they tend to welcome them back in an effort to support them on a temporary basis. The return may be a time of conflict and ambivalence for both the parents and the returning children. For the parents, the return may be taken as a sign that their children are not doing well and consequently that they have not fulfilled their obligations as effective parents. Parents may have become accustomed to their restructured lives without children or young adults in the home. They may re-

sent the loss of privacy and spontaneity. The problems associated with the return of adult children are even more pronounced when the returning offspring is accompanied by grandchildren (Aquilino & Supple, 1991).

Adult children may also feel constrained by living in their parents' home and view it as a threat to their newly acquired sense of independence and autonomy. The family home abounds with memories of their younger years, making it harder for them to feel like adults while they are living under their parents' roof. Parents and their adult children represent differing generations with different interests and needs. Even without the challenges associated with living with one's parents, this generational gap could be a source of conflict.

The question most middle-aged adults ask when their

middle-aged parents when their adult children lived at home with them. They found that parental satisfaction with having adult children (ages 19 to 34) at home depended on the degree of parent-child conflict. When the adult children were also financially dependent upon their parents there was greater conflict and less satisfaction with the living arrangements. Overall, however, the majority of parents in Aquilino and Supple's study were highly satisfied with having their adult children live with them.

FOCUS ON CULTURE

When adults divorce and remarry, there often is conflict and confusion among family members about how to stay in contact with ex-relations. For example, when a stepparent does not want to include the ex-spouse's parents in family gatherings, the grandparents' role is restricted.

What are the common assumptions or stereotypes in American culture concerning marriage, family relationships, and divorce that might contribute to the strained relationships among families in which divorce and remarriage have occurred?

children return home is "How will we survive?" There are a number of ways in which potential conflicts can be reduced or eliminated. If the move back to the family home is considered to be a temporary one by both parents and children, the tensions are automatically reduced, especially if a specific time frame is agreed upon in advance. The longer the stay, the greater the need for both parents and children to talk about their expectations regarding the arrangement.

The nature of the parent-child relationship must change from earlier stages of life when the parents assumed responsibility for the feeding, clothing, and medical needs of their children. Now both parents and children need to be aware of and respect each other's personal boundaries. The reentry works best when there is a mutual re-spect for one another's right to privacy. Conflicts occur when children "borrow" things without asking or when parents open their children's mail or enter their bedrooms without knocking. There needs to be an equitable agreement about the sharing of domestic responsibilities. Usually the parents are in a better financial situation than the returning children; in lieu of a financial contribution to the running of the household, the returning adult may perform domestic duties such as laundry, food preparation, or yard work. Whatever the arrangement, both parents and children must see it as a fair exchange. There should be a discussion about how they will share resources and space in the house. When disputes arise, family members must be willing to talk with one another until a solution is found that preserves each person's sense of autonomy and personal space without compromising the relationship.

Conflicts are considerably reduced when returning offspring are not financially dependent upon their parents. Unemployed adult children who live with their parents not only have little or no money, they also are home more than adult children who are out working. Parents often become impatient and dissatisfied with the housing arrangements when they see their adult children at home instead of pursuing employment.

If parents and children work to establish an adult relationship, the return to the nest does not have to be unpleasant. Rather, a mutually beneficial situation emerges in which parents get to enjoy their children as adults and children experience the satisfaction of being treated as adults.

Keep in mind that adults' reactions to their children's departure from the family home is dependent upon the cultural values attached to independence and kinship. The cultural expectations that prevail in the United States and other industrialized nations cannot be used to understand or evaluate family patterns in cultures that do not share these expectations.

Relationships with Aged Parents As middle-aged adults are freed from the responsibilities and obligations of raising children, some of their time, energy, and concern will be transferred to their own parents, who are now in the later years of life. Today, in the United States and other industrialized countries, large numbers of middle-aged people have older parents who live into their 80s and 90s. Just two generations ago, middle-aged adults usually were the oldest surviving members of the extended family—that is, their own parents were no longer alive.

Furthermore, the nature of involvement with aging parents is different today than it was even a few decades ago. Today's middle-aged adults are the first cohort of offspring who are relatively free from the responsibilities and obligations of providing at least minimum income maintenance and health care to their aging parents. Federally subsidized income (Social Security) and health care (Medicare and Medicaid), better retirement plans, planned retirement communities, and so on have softened (but certainly not eliminated) the impact of retirement and aging on the older person. In turn, this has reduced the burden on middle-aged children for caring for aging, and possibly ailing, parents. Many elderly people today not only enjoy relatively good health but are also financially better off than they were in the past (Aldous, 1987).

This is not to say that middle-aged adults are entirely free of responsibilities toward the older generation. Indeed, many middle-aged adults provide emotional and physical support, and often assume financial responsibility for many aspects of their parents' lives (Walker & Pratt, 1991). In fact, there is sometimes a reversal of the roles of parents and children as middle-aged people become providers and nurturers for their aging parents. This is usually true, though, only when the parents are well into their later years. Most research indicates that older parents do not want to be dependent upon their middle-aged children; on the contrary, they show a strong preference for remaining independent as long as possible (Yankelovich, Skelly, & White Inc., 1977). Regardless of this attitude, however, research indicates that contact between adult children and their aged parents is important and beneficial for older people's psychological well-being (Alpert & Richardson, 1980; Aldous, 1987).

There are difficult decisions to be made by the children of aged parents. How long can you let old people live alone who are not in good mental or physical condition? Can you put your own mother or father in a nursing home, no matter how well-managed? There is a delicate line between taking over and destroying older people's sense of their own independence and protecting them from physical harm. These issues will be discussed further from the perspective of elderly people in Chapter 16.

Grandparenthood   A good friend of mine is an aerobics instructor who conducts several classes a day, runs her own business, and still has time to enjoy her three grandchildren. Most people are surprised to learn that she is a grandmother because she doesn't look old enough. She married at age 18, had her first child by the time she was 19, and was just turning 40 when her daughter married. By the time she was 45 she was a grandmother. Although the media represent grandparents as gray-haired, wrinkled, and bespectacled old people whose favorite pastimes are sitting in a rocking chair or baking cookies or cakes for the family, today this image is not appropriate (Troll, 1980). With the changes in fertility and mortality patterns, and shifts in population characteristics over the past century, one is more likely to become a grandparent early in middle age than later. Troll (1983) notes that in American culture, the typical age at which people become grandparents is around 49 to 51 years for women and 51 to 53 years for men. Furthermore, teenage pregnancies often produce grandparents who are in their early to mid-30s. Thus, first-time grandparents are likely to be healthy, working at full-time jobs, and living independent and active lives. In fact, a few middle-aged people find it difficult at first to accept the grandparent role—they may feel that it casts a shadow of age on the youthful self-image they are maintaining.

Research suggests that grandparents play an important role in family systems. They provide the younger generations with emotional support and with advice concerning basic values, lifestyle, occupation, education, and parenting (Troll,

1980). Grandparents, especially maternal grandmothers, have been shown to be extremely important for promoting well-being in single-parent families, particularly those in which the mother is a teenager (Oyserman et al., 1993; Stevens, 1984; Tinsley & Parke, 1983; Walker & Pratt, 1991). Often grandmothers provide child care while the single parent is working. Similarly, Hetherington, Cox, and Cox (1982) found that the adjustment of mother-headed households following divorce was greatly affected by the contributions of grandparents.

Just as individuals differ in their personalities and styles of parenting, so, too, do their grandparenting styles vary. In what has become a classic study, Neugarten and Weinstein (1964) identified five styles of interactions with grandchildren among white, middle-class grandparents in their 50s and 60s (see Table 14–2).

Neugarten and Weinstein also noted that many grandparents experience a sense of biological renewal—a feeling of carrying on the family line—as well as a sense of emotional self-fulfillment in their new family role. The older mother may relive her pregnancy, delivery, and early mothering through the early parenting experiences of her daughter or daughter-in-law. The new grandfather, in turn, may realize that he has the time and interest for his grandchildren that he never had for his own children. Many people find grandparenting easier and preferable to parenting. It is not uncommon, in fact, to hear grandparents say that they are better grandparents than they were parents.

The role and impact that grandparents have within their families is influenced by cultural values, customs, and expectations. For example, several studies (Cherlin & Furstenberg, 1986; Pearson, Hunter, Ensminger, & Kellam, 1990; Tolson & Wilson, 1990) have reported on the role of the grandmother in African American families. Pearson and her colleagues reported that in about 10% of the

GRANDPARENTING STYLES	
STYLE	**CHARACTERISTICS**
Formal	Shows interest in the grandchild and occasionally provides special gifts or services, such as baby-sitting, but does not interfere in the raising of the child; leaves the parenting to the parents.
Fun-seeker	An informal, leisurely orientation toward grandparenting; assumes the role of playmate and expects mutually gratifying experiences with the grandchild.
Surrogate parent	Grandparent (almost always the grandmother) assumes the child-care responsibilities while the parents are working.
Reservoir of family wisdom	Grandparent (usually the grandfather) adopts an authoritarian role in the family; all family members, including parents, are subordinate to him; he dispenses resources, knowledge, and advice to others.
Distant figure	Has little consistent relationship with the grandchild; visits on holidays or special occasions; adopts a benevolent but emotionally distant role.

TABLE 14–2

Some grandparents assume the role of playmate with their grandchildren. This type of grandparent is referred to as the fun-seeker.

families they examined, the grandmother lived in the home and played a significant role in parenting. However, African American families are not all the same; they represent different family structures (e.g., one- versus two-parent, extended or nuclear), social classes, cultural and historical roots, and family climates (Tolson & Wilson, 1990). Thus, caution must be used in generalizing across all families.

Native American Grandparent

The term *Native American* is used to refer to members of over 500 Indian tribes found in the United States, Canada, and Mexico. Each one of these tribes has a distinct culture and history. Using interviews and naturalistic observations, anthropologist Weibel-Orlando (1990) examined the grandparenting styles of 28 Native American grandparents. Her sample consisted of men and women representing the Sioux, Creek, Seminole, Choctaw, and Chicksaw tribes. Among the data she collected was information about the quality and intensity of the grandparents' relationships with their grandchildren, their perceptions of the role of grandparent, how accessible they were to their grandchildren, and the degree to which the grandparents were a part of the family. An analysis of the data collected revealed five different styles of grandparenting.

The least frequent style, **distanced grandparent,** describes grandparents who live far away from their grandchildren and visit them infrequently. The distanced grandparents live a very different lifestyle than their grandchildren and share very little of their culture with them. According to Weibel-Orlando, this style of grandparenting is rare within Native American communities and is a result of the migration of Native Americans to urban centers.

The **ceremonial grandparent** also lives away from grandchildren, but has regular, planned visits with his or her grandchildren. The visits of grandparents are important family and social occasions. Ethnic ceremonies and celebrations signify the importance of the grandparent's position in the family and community. The ceremonial grandparent has time-limited contact with grandchildren, during which the grandchildren display their respect and love through ceremonial actions.

distanced grandparent
A grandparent who lives far away from and who infrequently visits the grandchild.

ceremonial grandparent
A grandparent who lives far away from the grandchild yet maintains regular and planned visits.

fictive grandparent
A grandparent who takes in foster children or adopts children when there are no biological grand-children.

custodial grandparent
A grandparent who takes on complete responsibility of raising grandchildren because some family trauma has left them without a suitable guardian.

cultural conservator grandparent
A grandparent who actively solicits their children to allow their grandchildren to live with them for extended periods of time.

Should there be no biological grandchildren, Native Americans become **fictive grandparents** by taking in foster children or adopting children. This occurred only with women in Weibel-Orlando's study. Some fictive grandmothers have biological grandchildren but are not able to have the kind of contact and influence with them that they would like. Taking other children as their grandchildren helps them meet their need to pass on their culture or have grandchildren around them for comfort or care.

In the fourth style, **custodial grandparents** take on the complete responsibility for raising their grandchildren because the children lack a suitable guardian. Sometimes the grandparents serve as the primary caregivers willingly, sometimes out of a moral obligation to the welfare of the children involved.

In contrast to custodial grandparents, **cultural conservator grandparents** actively solicit their children to allow their grandchildren to live with them for extended periods. They want to expose their grandchildren to the tribal way of life. This style is currently the most popular style of grandparenting among Native Americans, in part because many Native Americans recognize that much of their culture has been diluted because of the migration to urban centers.

RECAP

Midlife represents a time of change within the family as children mature and leave the home, although the nature of these family changes depends upon the culture. Middle-aged adults participate in bidirectional, multi-generational relationships with their parents, their adolescent or adult children, and grandchildren. Adults assume different roles and challenges with their adolescent and adult children, and with their aging parents. While some parents enjoy the benefits of the empty nest, others experience considerable distress. The degree to which adults participate in caring for their aging parents depends on the culture and the historical context. Different styles of grandparenting emerge in middle adulthood.

MIDLIFE MARITAL ADJUSTMENT

Midlife is the juncture of life's journey at which many people take stock of their lives and their relationships. Their children either have left the home or soon will do so. With the advent of the empty-nest stage of the family life cycle, the husband and wife enter a new phase of married life. The absence of children from the home allows couples to refocus their attention on each other and their marriage. This is a time when couples rediscover one another—and sometimes recognize the gulf that lies between them. At this time couples also reexamine the way in which they communicate and the activities and goals they share.

Probably the most frequently studied aspect of midlife marriage is marital adjustment. One early and important study suggested that most couples become progressively disenchanted over the course of a marriage (Pineo, 1961). More recent studies, however, show an upturn in marital satisfaction in the later stages of married life. As Figure 14–1 indicates, both husbands and wives consider the stage when children are in school to represent a low point in their marriage, whereas the later stages are viewed positively (Berry & Williams, 1987; Huyck, 1982;

Schram, 1979). Although the period after children have left home is often stressful, the dissatisfaction seems to concern the children and/or parenting, rather than the marriage or spouse.

What accounts for the rise in marital satisfaction during this period of life? To begin with, research suggests that the role strain experienced during the earlier years of marriage is lessened (Spanier & Lewis, 1980). Women, in particular, are freed from the burden and pressures of coordinating work and parenting roles. For many middle-aged adults renewed interest in sex, discussed in Chapter 13, also is likely to enhance intimacy between marital partners.

Another factor that may explain the greater marital satisfaction of middle-aged and elderly adults is that couples who are least satisfied with their marriage have already separated or divorced by this time. Hence, the "marital survivors" represent a select group of individuals who are more satisfied and better adjusted. If this interpretation is true or even partly true, the research findings regarding lifespan marital satisfaction are a result of a statistical trend rather than a reflection of true developmental changes in marital relationships.

Finally, couples who have invested considerable time and energy in one another—as is true for middle-aged and elderly adults—are the most likely to place a high value on their relationship. They are more inclined to see things in a similar, or at least in a compatible, way. After many years of knowing each other, couples may be pretty good at anticipating each other's answers to a questionnaire on marital satisfaction.

FIGURE 14–1

Marital satisfaction.
Source: B.C. Rollins and H. Feldman, Marital satisfaction over the family life cycle. *Journal of Marriage and the Family, 32* (1970), p. 26. Copyright 1970 by the National Council on Family Relations, 1910 West County Road B, Suite 147, St. Paul, Minnesota 55113. Reprinted by permission.

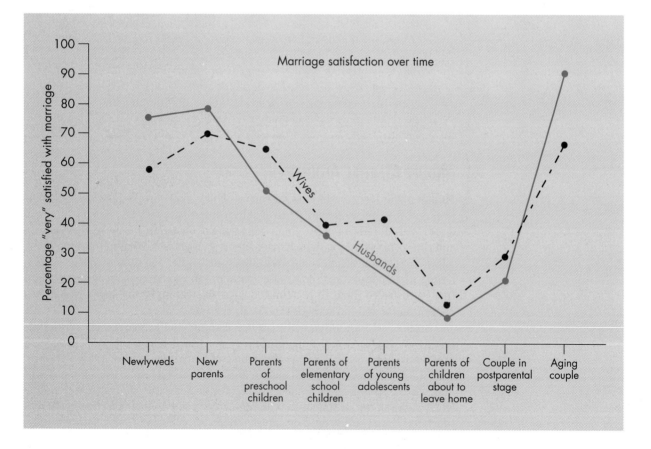

Marital Styles   My husband John is also my best friend, my colleague, and my biggest supporter. And I am the president of his fan club. Although we may not be typical of couples who have been married more than 30 years, the style we have developed in our relationship works well for us. We consider our marriage to be a happy one. What constitutes a happy marriage? Is there some optimal form of marriage toward which all of us should be striving? It is obvious that people differ in their personalities, interests, needs, fantasies, and life goals. In turn, marital adjustment is, in part, determined by the kind of characteristics the husband and wife bring to the marriage relationship. Does marital happiness, however, necessarily imply that the husband and wife share the same personality, interests, and needs? Some researchers believe so (Clore & Byrne, 1977) while others have argued that marital adjustment is determined by **complementarity** in the relationship—that is, the two individuals possess different and yet compatible traits. Most research suggests that complementarity theory is inadequate for explaining mate selection and adjustment in the early stages of marriage. Other researchers have speculated that the longer the couple remain together, the more likely the marriage relationship will be characterized by complementarity of roles. Furthermore, as we noted in Chapter 12, Murstein (1982) has suggested that the most satisfying interpersonal relationships do not necessarily occur between the most similar individuals, but between partners who are equally capable of meeting the other's needs. Research also suggests that marital satisfaction is highest in egalitarian couples, where power is distributed relatively equally between the partners, and lowest in couples headed by dominant wives (Gray-Little & Burk, 1983).

complementarity
A measure of marital adjustment in which the two individuals possess different and yet compatible traits.

Types of Marriages   Just as there are individual differences among people, there are differences among the types of marriages that people establish. As people mature and change with time, they also change the way they interact with each other

Some researchers suggest that the sharing of similar interests contributes to stable marriages.

in relationships. Family changes such as the birth of a child or the departure of a young-adult child can also affect the way married people relate to each other. Thus, marriages can develop in many ways depending on the life events and personalities involved.

Cuber and Harroff (1965) studied over 400 marriages that had lasted at least 10 years. None of the husbands and wives had seriously considered separation or divorce, so these marriages would be considered to be "good" ones. There was considerable variation in the types of relationships established in the marriages. Nonetheless, Cuber and Harroff identified five basic types of marriages, which are described in Table 14–3.

marital companionship

An aspect of marital life characterized by caring, emotional attachment, trust, commitment, and a sharing of interests.

Companionship and Marriage   If asked to name a key factor for determining a couple's marital satisfaction, many people would respond: sexual compatibility. Although this aspect of marriage certainly is important for the couple's happiness, research suggests that **marital companionship** is an even more important factor (Garrett, 1982).

Companionship implies more than simply spending a great deal of time with one's spouse. It involves caring, emotional attachment, trust, commitment, and a sharing of interests. In terms of the marital styles described by Cuber and Harroff (1965), one is more likely to find companionship in vital and total marriages. One reason companionship relations are linked to marital satisfaction is that they provide marital partners with a haven for venting the pressures, tensions, and frustrations that build up in daily life. Garrett (1982) observes that in the security of such a relationship, spouses can "blow off steam" without fear of criticism,

TYPES OF MARRIAGES	
NAME	**CHARACTERISTICS**
Conflict-habituated	Considerable conflict and tension expressed in arguing and bickering, which has become a habitual but acceptable pattern.
Devitalized	While the couple assert they love each other, the marriage lacks its original zest and vitality. There is now little passion or intimacy. Despite an appearance of disenchantment, the couple still view their marriage as a good one.
Passive-congenial	Couple are content and comfortable, and there is little effort at improving or changing the marriage. Conflict is avoided; partners have little to do with each other.
Vital	The marriage is vibrant and exciting. The couple are highly involved with each other, particularly in areas related to family life—such as finances, child care, and recreational and social activities.
Total	Like the vital marriage, there is a high degree of involvement between husband and wife, only to a greater and more complete extent.

TABLE 14–3

reprisal, or rejection. Couples who mutually provide each other with a willing and interested listener and offer encouragement and occasional advice also brings a balance to the marital relationship and promotes a sense of mutuality within the couple.

What factors contribute to marriages that endure over time? Only recently have researchers focused on what works in relationships as well as what doesn't. In one study (Levenson, Carstensen, & Gottman; 1993), researchers recruited 35 middle-aged couples who were satisfied in their marriage and 47 middle aged couples who were dissatisfied; they also studied a similar sample of older satisfied and dissatisfied couples. They found that couples who were older and also had been married for a longer time had fewer conflicts and were more satisfied than the middle-aged couples. This was because many of the middle-aged couples were still raising children, which increased the potential for disagreement and conflict in the marriage. They also found that older couples derived more enjoyment than middle-aged couples in talking about their families, vacations, activities, and dreams. Satisfied couples of both age groups were healthier than dissatisfied couples and disagreed with each other less.

DISRUPTIONS IN MARRIAGE

Family Violence   Law-enforcement officials in the United States estimate that every year from 2 to 3 million women are physically assaulted by male partners (Straus & Gelles, 1990). Research from prevalence studies suggests that between 21 and 34% of women will be slapped, kicked, beaten, choked, or threatened or attacked with a weapon by an intimate adult partner (Browne, 1993). This physical violence cuts across socioeconomic and racial lines (Tavris & Offir, 1977).

domestic violence
A situation in which one commits acts of aggression against a spouse or other family member.

Domestic violence involves physical abuse against family members, most commonly husbands against their wives. It is frequently seen as a misuse of power by men over women (Walker, 1989). Men who mistakenly believe that they are entitled to control the women in their lives often resort to physical violence as a means of exerting their power. Some cultures still maintain the belief that men have the right to control and beat their wives. In many societies men play the dominant role in determining and administering the laws that sanction spouse abuse.

Unchecked violence between intimate partners tends to grow worse with time. Even when outside help is secured, the violence usually continues after a cooling-off period. Furthermore, women who have been the victims of violence are likely to experience repeated victimizations in the future (Koss, 1990). Battered women are less skilled at protecting themselves and have lower self-esteem. Women are likely to be socially conditioned to see the victim role as a female characteristic and the aggressor role as a male characteristic (Pagelow, 1979).

What kind of women are victims of their husbands' beatings? Any woman may find herself in such a situation and have difficulty extricating herself from it. Despite the danger to herself and to her children, she may stay with her husband because of her lack of financial resources, dependence, or terror. She may also stay for the sake of the children or because she has nowhere else to go.

In many communities, shelters for battered wives provide women with an alternative to staying in the home and enduring domestic violence. Self-help groups help women validate their perceptions, regain their self-confidence, and build new skills to protect themselves and their children from future violence. Victims find

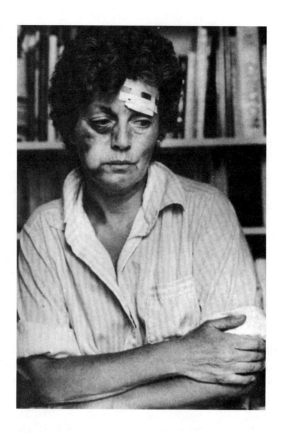

Battered wives need help in breaking away from a destructive relationship. Often wives stay with physically abusive spouses because they lack financial resources to leave.

psychological and legal counseling in these shelters as well as help in establishing a new life for themselves and their children. Greater emphasis is now being given to training law enforcement personnel on ways to identify domestic violence at early stages (Koss, 1990; Walker, 1989).

Midlife Divorce   More than half of all marriages in the United States end in divorce; approximately 15% of these divorces occur after 15 years of marriage, and therefore involve middle-aged partners (Norton & Moorman, 1987). Divorce by couples married for more than 20 or 25 years was formerly uncommon; today nearly everyone knows at least one couple who has divorced after many years of marriage.

Divorce in midlife occurs for many reasons. For some couples it is a response to the stresses of midlife career crises or extramarital affairs. For many others,

FOCUS ON CULTURE

Battered women are often mothers as well as wives. Financially dependent on their husbands, they often stay in a destructive marriage for the sake of their children. But their children are also victims as they witness domestic violence. For children who watch their mothers being beaten by their fathers, what effect might that experience have on gender role development?

however, it reflects differences in the individual growth and development of the marital partners. Troll (1982) has presented a model of couple adjustment that is based on the fit between the individual growth patterns of each partner. According to this model, the marriage has the best chance of remaining intact if both individuals either remain stable in personality, or grow (or even deteriorate) in similar and compatible ways over time.

Marital discord, in contrast, is likely to result from any pattern reflecting a deteriorating fit between the couple. This can occur (1) when one spouse remains stable and the other grows (or deteriorates) in personality; (2) when both spouses' personalities change in the same direction but at different rates; or (3) when the partners' personalities change in the opposite direction. Take, for example, the case of a couple in which the wife has established a new career after her children have left home. The husband, meanwhile, has spent the past 20 to 30 years on the job and is now more interested in traveling or spending leisure time with his wife. In this case, the spouses are changing in different and possibly incompatible directions.

Historical trends and expectations may also be linked to the rising divorce rate during midlife. Many of today's middle-aged divorced people claim to have married at the socially prescribed time of their lives without giving much thought to whether they wanted to marry or not. They did what was expected of them. Now social attitudes have changed and these couples have an opportunity to rethink their decisions and make corrections. One study (Norton & Moorman, 1987) found that women who marry after age 30 are less likely to divorce than women who marry in their early 20s. By delaying marriage until personal and career goals are established, women may be less likely to have second thoughts about their marriages in midlife.

For many middle-aged couples, divorce is seen as a growth experience. Their divorces lack many of the problems experienced by younger divorcing couples, such as young children, economic sacrifice, and disapproval of parents. On the other hand, the couple may have built up a more extensive household and made investments and purchases together. There are joint checking and savings accounts, and the house and car may be jointly owned. The couple has also developed a larger network of mutual friends, and these relationships may be strained by the separation.

Divorce at midlife, as in earlier points in development, is painful. It is typically followed by loneliness, self-doubt, mood swings, and many practical adjustments in living (Kelly, 1982). For example, the divorced woman may be starting to date at the time that she begins to experience doubts about her attractiveness. She also is expected to consider sexual relations after a number of years of intimacy (or the painful lack of it) with one partner. Fear of sexual inadequacy may also inhibit the divorced middle-aged male from pursuing new relationships.

If midlife divorce is almost always followed by uncertainty and stress, it is also usually followed by remarriage, on average, within 3 years after being divorced. Middle-aged men are more likely to remarry than women (Reiss, 1980), very often to a younger never-married woman. Of those adults who remarry, about half will divorce a second time (Glick, 1984; Norton & Moorman, 1987). However, for couples who remarry at midlife, married life is more successful (Hunt & Hunt, 1975; Norton & Moorman, 1987). Although the risk of divorce among remarried couples is higher than for first marriages, the majority of remarried people report that they are happier than they were in their first marriages. This generalization may hold especially well for midlife marriages that are not plagued by custody and stepparent arrangements.

Widowhood   People's journey through life is enhanced by spouses and partners who offer companionship and direction. What happens when a partner dies? Widowhood is usually associated with old age, but, according to Troll (1982), in the United States there are more than 90,000 widows under age 45, and half of all widows are younger than 60. The gap between the number of widowed men and women is growing. DiGiulio (1989) reports that 50 years ago widowed women outnumbered widowed men by a 3-to-1 ratio; today that ratio has grown to 5 to 1. Worldwide, women are outliving men by an ever widening margin (Seager & Olson, 1986), with the result that widowhood is beginning to be seen as an inevitable and almost universal phase of life—and one frequently associated with middle age.

Many of the problems of widowhood are related to the problems of later adulthood. (Indeed, a woman may define herself as "old" after she loses her husband.) Among the problems unique to the middle-aged widow, however, is the fact that she may be the first, or one of the first, in her social or work group to lose her husband. Her friends are still married, and she may consequently come to think of herself as the fifth wheel at any social occasion. Friends may be insensitive, alternately exhorting her to socialize and then forgetting to invite her. She also tends to be less willing than older women to resign herself to life without masculine companionship and sexuality, yet she may be unable to meet single men (especially widowed men) who can understand her experience. Consequently, for many women widowhood can be an extremely lonely period of life (Troll, 1982).

For some women, remarriage may be a useful coping response to the difficulties of widowhood. Gentry and Shulman (1988) found that women who had

Midlife divorces often are followed by remarriage, usually within 3 years after the divorce.

remarried following the death of their husband reported fewer current concerns than widows. Remarriage was much more likely for women who had been widowed for 2 years and were in their 50s. Remarriage may not be a realistic response for older women or for women who live within a culture that prohibits widows from remarrying. Widowhood in late adulthood will be discussed further in Chapter 16.

FOCUS ON CULTURE

Compared to middle-aged men, middle-aged women have a higher incidence of depression, more so than at any other period of the lifespan. Separation, divorce, and death of one's spouse are a few life events that may contribute to depression. Why should women be more susceptible to depression at this age than men?

SINGLEHOOD

Approximately 5% of all middle-aged adults in the United States are single people who have never been married. Relatively little research has been done on this group, and almost none on the positive aspects of its adjustment. Ordinary observation, however, produces many examples of single people who, in the absence of immediate family obligations, have achieved an especially intense career commitment. Others choose to remain single to preserve their privacy and maintain a flexible lifestyle that may include a network of close friends.

Single middle-aged people must contend with specific problems. They must confront the stereotypes associated with being a "spinster" or "bachelor." Many people assume that if a person is not married there is something wrong with him or her; they fail to view singlehood as an active choice but rather see it as a decision by default. If single people are not already part of an extended family network, they must plan for a late adulthood that does not include support from, or involvement with, children. They are also less protected against illness or misfortune. For example, if they become mentally disturbed they are more likely to be hospitalized than are married people, who may be cared for by their families.

The single, middle-aged person, however, is not usually a loner. Most single people develop close relationships with friends—single as well as married. Singles, particularly women, also often maintain close contact with family members.

The motives for remaining single typically are somewhat different for males and females. Never-married women are better educated, come from higher socioeconomic groups, and are more achievement-oriented than single men. Moreover, it appears that the majority of middle-aged single women have refused marriage proposals (Havens, 1973). In contrast, Spreitzer and Riley (1974) report that successful, achievement-oriented men are the least likely to remain single. In traditional and even many nontraditional marriages, women take primary responsibility for household and child care. Under these circumstances, it is hardly surprising that achievement-oriented women differ from achievement-oriented men in marital status.

<hr>

RECAP

Changes in middle adulthood marriage parallel those that occur in the family life cycle. Several different types of marriages emerge, depending on the personalities of the partners and the stresses they experience. Long-lasting marriages are characterized by mutual interests and respect, companionship, and satisfaction with life. Domestic violence involves an abusive partner physically attacking a spouse or other family member. Battered wives require the help and support of their communities to break the cycle of abuse. Midlife divorce occurs because couples have grown apart and have lost their reasons for staying together. Divorce at midlife, although painful, can encourage growth, while widowhood in middle adulthood is frequently a very lonely experience. Some adults actively choose to remain single and establish networks of friends as an alternative to a marital relationship.

<hr>

OCCUPATIONAL DEVELOPMENT

During my early 20s and 30s I directed most of my time toward my dual career as a college professor/researcher and parent. As my responsibilities as a parent lessened during my 40s I developed my career as an author and therapist. Now, in my 50s, I have a career as a college administrator. I fully expect to continue my occupational development over the next 10 years of my work life. Work adds meaning and resources to life's journey; meaningful work contributes to a person's sense of generativity.

The beginning of the chapter introduced John and described his enthusiasm for teaching writing. John provides another example of how people in middle adulthood find new opportunities to develop through work. Middle-aged people produce goods, ideas, plans, and policies at a higher rate than they did earlier. They may also achieve generativity by teaching what they know to others, usually younger people. The worker, like the parent, wants to contribute something to the community to be inherited by younger generations. On the other hand, when people have no opportunity, or take no opportunity, to impart their skill, experience, or care to others, they may suffer from a sense of stagnation. They will feel alienated both from what they produce and from what they leave behind. In short, one of the key components of identity and self-esteem, especially for men, is occupational status (Tamir, 1982).

OCCUPATIONAL ADVANCEMENT

In midlife, people are concerned with reaching and maintaining a satisfactory level in their career (Havighurst, 1982; Super, 1963). Advancement at this stage may mean moving from in-depth involvement in a specialty to a managerial or supervisory function. For example, the assembly-line worker becomes a supervisor; the clerical worker becomes the office manager; the research chemist becomes director of a unit. Or it may mean that workers have the confidence and experience to strike out on their own, starting their own businesses or functioning as freelance consultants. Havighurst (1982) suggests that one important career task at this time is achieving a flexible work role that is perceived as interesting, productive, and financially satisfactory.

Similar observations have been offered by Levinson and his coworkers, who have also noted that the middle-adult period is a time for self-evaluation regarding career development (Levinson, Darrow, Klein, Levinson, & McKee, 1977). Past goals are now revived in light of current achievements. Individuals who have achieved, or believe they will achieve, previously established career goals are likely to feel satisfied with themselves and to display a positive self-image. Conversely, the recognition that one is unlikely to achieve a desired occupational level—for example, corporate vice president, department chairperson, division manager, factory supervisor, and so on—typically leads to a reevaluation of life goals and often to a reevaluation of the self. Individuals who have difficulty readjusting their career goals and aspirations to the realities of their particular life situations may feel frustrated, stagnant, and personally impoverished. They are also more likely to change jobs or opt for early retirement.

During middle adulthood, most men and women attain the highest status and income of their careers. Yet men and women show striking differences in advancement with increasing age, with women lagging behind, especially in income. For the older woman, discrimination at the workplace becomes particularly evident as she fails to be promoted or given salary and responsibility increases commensurate with her male counterparts. Between the ages of 35 and 65, men's average yearly earnings are nearly double those of women. Furthermore, this gender difference in income is not completely accounted for by differences in occupation. Within all major occupational groups, women's earnings are far below those of men.

Middle-aged women find greater satisfaction in their lives as a result of their careers than do men.

Part of the reason for the discrepancy in salary levels between men and women is that women more often drop out of the workforce to establish their families and, in so doing, delay their career advancement. Studies of successful women (Betz, 1984; Van Velsor & O'Rand, 1984) suggest that women who work continuously are more likely to achieve a higher occupational status than women who switch or temporarily leave their jobs. However, even women with the same amount of work experience are paid less than men.

Personality and Occupational Advancement   In addition to discrimination and role conflict, what differentiates the individuals who advance within their respective careers from those who do not? Having a college degree makes a big difference; college-educated people advance earlier and go further in their careers. In one 20-year longitudinal study of AT&T executives, Bray and Howard (1983) found that men who rose higher in the corporation were more committed to the job, were more interested in success, showed higher achievement motives, and were more forceful and dominant than their less successful colleagues. There was no difference between these groups in life satisfaction. Regardless of their position on the corporate ladder, the executives were basically satisfied with their lives. Although Bray and Howard studied men, similar results have been found with women who work in companies similar to AT&T, prompting the conclusion that it is individual differences in personality rather than sex differences that explains who rises up the managerial ladder and who does not (Ritchie & Moses, 1983).

In a different study, Clausen (1981) found that occupational success for men during middle age was associated with a host of personality factors, not only during midlife but during the adolescent years as well. Personality variables in adolescence that predicted midlife career success included intellectual capacities and interests and qualities such as ambition, productivity, dependability, low self-indulgence, and objectivity. Midlife personality variables associated with career success included intellectual capacities and interests, dependability, objectivity, tolerance for uncertainty, low hostility and self-defeating attitudes, ambition, incisiveness, and flexibility in roles. Thus, it would appear that occupational achievement is to a great extent tied to motivational and personality variables—and presumably to competence. Yet, we must remember that the harsh realities of the world—sexism, racial and ethnic discrimination, and even favoritism—are factors in determining who gets a promotion or a raise.

JOB SATISFACTION

During midlife both men and women become acutely aware of the decreasing time remaining to accomplish their goals. For individuals who are within reach of their goals, this stage of occupational development is experienced as exciting, challenging, and rewarding. For others, however, the large gulf between their aspirations and their achievements may trigger a midlife crisis (Levinson et al., 1977).

In middle age, most people are seeking some assurance of job stability. They are less likely than younger workers to voluntarily leave their jobs (Byrne, 1975). This may reflect the fact that older people generally take fewer risks than younger ones. But it also represents satisfaction with the work itself. The highest percentage of satisfied workers are over 40 (Rhodes, 1983). These workers are significantly more satisfied than young adults, not only with their jobs but with the monetary

FOCUS ON CULTURE

According to Erikson's theory of psychosocial development, people's attitudes toward work and their views of themselves as workers are formed not in adulthood but in childhood, when they learn to value their productivity and ability to contribute to the community. In rural or agrarian cultures children are important contributors to family income and survival. By contrast, children in industrialized societies do not enter the world of work until late adolescence or young adulthood. How might these two different paths affect the development of positive work attitudes in adulthood?

job satisfaction
A measure of an individual's happiness with his or her occupation.

rewards and challenges they provide (Quinn, Staines, & McCullough, 1974; Tamir, 1982). In fact, the basis of **job satisfaction** differs between younger and older workers—at least for white-collar employees. For the younger group, dissatisfaction with the job is likely to be tied to salary; for the older group, it is more likely to be related to lack of challenge and insufficient resources to get the job done. In contrast, for blue-collar workers, income level is an important factor in job satisfaction for both younger and older workers.

Middle-aged career women find satisfaction in their lives as a result of their jobs. Coleman and Antonucci (1983) found that working women scored significantly higher on most measures of well-being than nonemployed women. They also had higher self-esteem, less psychological anxiety, better physical health, and greater marital satisfaction than women who were homemakers. In addition, working women expressed greater happiness and life satisfaction. On the other hand, there were no differences between working and nonworking women in depression, degree of satisfaction with their role as parents, and interest in life.

These findings are in general agreement with those other studies that have focused on the impact of work on women (Kessler & McRae, 1982; Northcott, 1981). They also are compatible with the results of research on the impact of work on men (Tamir, 1982). For example, one study (Barnett, Marshall, & Singer, 1992) compared the impact of changes in the quality of the job-role on women's level of psychological distress. The researchers found that as status and quality of a job declined, women who did not have partners or children experienced much higher levels of distress when compared with mothers or women with partners. When women take on multiple roles (e.g. worker, spouse, and parent), they have access to more resources and opportunities for rewards. Instead of deriving their sense of well-being from one source—that is, from their work—women with partners or children rely on multiple sources and thus are less affected by a decline in the rewards they obtain from work.

Coleman and Antonucci (1983) note that work may not have the same meaning for men and women. As a group, women's psychological adjustment, unlike men's, is less affected by salary and occupational prestige. Furthermore, the positive benefits of employment are reduced for working mothers whose spouses do not share household and child-care responsibilities for young children (Kessler & McRae, 1982).

RETRAINING AND SECOND CAREERS

In rapidly changing technological societies, many middle-aged workers find that the skills learned earlier in their careers do not serve them as well as they once did. Technological advances have radically changed the world of work for both white-collar and blue-collar workers. The manual typewriter, for example, is gone; it has been replaced by the computer; the telephone has been enhanced by voice and electronic mail. Comparable changes are taking place in virtually every area of occupational life. In the face of such changes, workers, particularly those who are middle-aged, are becoming increasingly aware of the need for retraining. Businesses and corporations are spending millions of dollars each year to upgrade their employee's skills. Community colleges across the country have developed courses in response to the demand for job-related education.

In some cases, however, simply upgrading one's skills is not enough. Among the serious problems encountered by middle-aged workers are job obsolescence, unemployment, and age discrimination in hiring and promotion. Not infrequently, the middle-aged worker becomes obsolete as businesses incorporate innovative and cost-efficient technological changes into their operations. In automotive plants, for example, computerized robots now do assembly-line work that used to be done by many workers. Other middle-aged adults have lost their jobs as a result of "downsizing" and "reengineering" designed to reduce the costs of doing business.

With the pressures of providing for others reduced by a shrinking family, some middle-aged adults use this phase of their life to retrain for a second career—perhaps pursuing a lifelong dream.

WOMEN'S WORK AND FAMILY ROLES IN MIDLIFE

Midlife represents a period of change, particularly for women. It is a time when women reassess their decisions regarding the balance they may have struck earlier in their lives between their parental and marital responsibilities and their career interests. However, only recently have psychologists and sociologists taken a systematic look at the factors that affect women's work life during middle adulthood.

It is commonly assumed that women's employment decisions are influenced by their family obligations. But in what ways do parental and marital roles affect work decisions during midlife? How do transitions in these roles, such as an empty nest, divorce, or death of a spouse, affect women's employment? To answer these questions, Moen (1991) examined the life course of a sample of middle-aged American women for a period of 10 years beginning in 1970.

Moen hypothesized that women's participation in the workforce during the 1970s would be influenced by their prior life experiences and expectations. The youngest women in Moen's study (aged 35 to 44) entered their adulthood in the late 1950s, when women were expected to stay home and maintain the family. Similar expectations existed for women (aged 45 to 54) who entered adulthood during the late 1940s and early 1950s. The third age group in Moen's study were women (over age 54) who reached adulthood during the Great Depression, during which anyone who could get a job, male or female, took it for the sake of family survival.

The stage of the family life cycle was a second major variable that Moen examined. Some of the women in the study no longer had children at home; others still did. Moen also noted the marital status of the women over the 10-year study. In addition, she collected information on the women's health and educational backgrounds, factors that have traditionally been associated with continuous participation in the labor force.

Moen found that the women's marital status, transitions in their marital status, and the presence of children in the home had an impact on their participation in the workforce. Unmarried women were more likely to remain fully employed over the 10-year period. Women who remained married were less likely to be continuously employed than women whose marriages dissolved during the period studied. The presence of children in the home was a greater impediment to the younger women (aged 35 to 44) than to women in the other age groups. However, across all age groups, the emptying of the family nest appeared to have little effect on women's employment. The two factors that were most associated with women's reduced involvement in work were poor health and marriage. Increased education promoted women's labor force participation throughout the period.

What do these findings suggest about middle-aged women today? Do they suggest a pattern for women who will reach midlife in the next 10 to 20 years? The answer is not clear. Today, women who are employed outside the home are likely to continue to work once their children leave the household. Many will be better prepared psychologically and economically to continue working when they reach midlife. But the decision to work will depend on the quality of the available job opportunities, the timing of marital and parental transitions, and the woman's health.

Middle-aged workers who lose their jobs may find it difficult to obtain other positions. Sweetland (1978) has reviewed some of the factors working against the rehiring of middle-aged and older workers. They include (1) unfavorable employer attitudes, (2) the need to pay higher salaries to older workers, (3) the reluctance of older workers to relocate, and (4) the fact that older workers tend to have less education and technological skills than younger workers. Regardless of the reasons, prolonged unemployment in midlife may cause serious loss of identity, status, and health, as well as loss of income.

In response to the pressures of job obsolescence or job dissatisfaction, a small but growing percentage of middle-aged people are making career changes. Free from the responsibility of supporting children, some people take an early exit from their life's work and begin a new one. The change may also be provoked by a fear that time is running out for "doing something important or meaningful." Sometimes the change is made to pursue a dream that was put aside in order to obtain a secure livelihood.

These midlife feelings seem to be largely responsible for the phenomenon of second careers. More and more people in their 30s and 40s are attempting to find more satisfaction in their work lives. Of course, not everyone is equally receptive to retraining and career change. Research indicates that the people who are most interested in such change are those who are concerned with the social-psychological aspect of jobs and are strongly motivated to achieve, but see little chance of advancement in their current job and consequently are less satisfied with what they are doing (Sheppard & Belitsky, 1966). In other words, they want to get ahead and/or do a good job, but they do not see much chance of accomplishing their goals in their current positions.

INTEGRATING WORK AND LEISURE

Even before people look ahead to retirement, the question of "What will I do with my time?" becomes particularly relevant (Gould, 1978). During middle age, people often have more time for leisure activities, especially after their children leave the family home. Integrating work, family, and leisure becomes an important goal for the middle-aged adult. John is able to combine his career, family, and leisure interests by traveling in the summer with his wife, Helen, and collecting material to use in his creative writing classes. Yet in our society leisure is not given a high priority. Many people are skeptical of those who seem to have too much time for hobbies, sports, or community work. According to Gordon, Gaitz, and Scott (1977), however, leisure activities often help to bridge role conflicts at different stages of the life cycle. Thus, people may use leisure activities to achieve goals or to satisfy needs not met in other aspects of their life—particularly on the job. The owner of a neighborhood gas station, for example, might find an outlet for his tendency to dramatize by joining a local theater group; a middle-aged social worker might spend her winter weekends on the ski patrol and her summer weekends marking new trails for the forest service.

People seek leisure activities for several reasons (Gordon, Gaitz, & Scott, 1977). Relaxation is the least intense form of leisure and may include napping, taking a sauna, and daydreaming. Leisure can also be a form of *diversion* from daily chores or activities; watching television, playing board or card games, or talking with friends on the telephone are examples. As in work, some leisure

FOCUS ON CULTURE

Leisure involves time that is not devoted to work or family responsibilities. In most industrialized societies the amount of time people spend in work is frequently limited by contractual arrangements, as is the number of years re- quired before retirement must occur. How would the concept of leisure fit into societies or- ganized around hunting-gathering or agricul- tural activities? When would workers in these societies retire?

activities take on a more intense quality when people use them to improve themselves. *Developmental pleasures* include leisure activities that require prac- tice and skill, such as weight training or playing a musical instrument. In *creative pleasures,* people might devote a fair amount of their free time to creative en- deavors. Sometimes these creative activities spill over into work, as when a worker is asked to organize the office holiday party because his hobby is gourmet cook- ing. Finally, people may seek out *sensual pleasures* in their leisure activities. Such pleasures can include massage, rhythmic dancing, contact sports, aerobic exercise, or even high-risk and exciting activities such as motorcycle racing or bungee-jumping.

The nature of leisure activity changes as one enters midlife. Between the ages of 30 and 44, leisure time is most often spent with the family. When adult children leave the home, however, more time is spent in personal, expressive activities, in which the family is not included (Gordon, Gaitz, & Scott, 1977). Watching televi- sion, gardening, visiting friends, walking, reading, and camping are examples of popular activities in midlife.

Finally, the question of leisure time also becomes important as plans are made for retirement. Individuals who are deeply involved in leisure pursuits may be ea- ger to retire; those who "live for their work" may find retirement traumatic. Once again, leisure activities may help the person to deal with role changes—in this case, with the change from worker to nonworker.

BRIEF REVIEW

The changes to family life in middle adulthood depend upon the family structure, marital status, and cultural expectations concerning independence from the family.

Intergenerational relations become increasingly signifi- cant during middle adulthood. Being in the middle of the fam- ily line means that the middle-aged adult is influenced both by top-down (elderly parent to middle-aged child) and bottom-up (adolescent or young-adult child to middle-aged parent) fam- ily processes. Research indicates greater intergenerational transmission of political and religious values and orientations than gender roles, lifestyles, and work orientations.

The composition of the family changes dramatically dur- ing middle adulthood. After years of sharing their lives with their children, middle-aged partners find themselves alone to- gether. Before the children leave, the parents must deal with

the conflicts encountered in raising adolescents. They must support adolescents in their search for identity, help them with their career exploration, and prepare them to take their places in the adult world. Guiding their children is a part of the resolution of Erikson's crisis of generativity versus stag- nation.

For most parents, the empty-nest phase of the family life cycle signifies freedom and is experienced as a relief. For some mothers or fathers, however, the absence of their children is difficult to bear—part of their self-definition and reason for living is gone. Some adult children return to their family home after having been out on their own, a situation that can create conflict and stress.

Relations between middle-aged parents and their adult children are closer than is generally assumed. Each relies on the other for support and psychological well-being. In middle age, a parent-child role reversal sometimes occurs, with the middle-aged child caring for and supporting aging, dependent parents. Most older people, however, neither want nor need to be dependent upon their adult children.

Becoming a grandparent for the first time today is more of a middle-aged than old-aged event. Grandparents play an important role in the family system, offering emotional support, child care, and advice on basic values, lifestyle, occupation, and parenting. Research indicates that grandparents play a particularly beneficial role in the adjustment of single-parent families, especially those involving teenage mothers. Just as there are styles of parenting, so too are there styles of grandparenting that people begin to adopt during this period. These styles are influenced by geographical, psychological, and cultural factors.

Most research suggests that marital satisfaction is high during middle adulthood, particularly in the post-parenting phase of the family life cycle. When problems do arise, they are often related to differential growth of partners, finances, sexual boredom, and work pressures.

Successful marriages assume many forms, from couples who are totally involved and committed to one another, to couples whose bickering and fighting form the basis for marital continuity. Although some investigators suggest that the longer a couple remains together, the more likely it is that their relationship will be characterized by complementarity of roles, most research indicates that marital adjustment is linked to a couple's complementarity regarding interests, attitudes, and personality. One factor that is particularly important for successful marital adjustment is the development of a companion relationship with one's spouse, which involves mutual caring, trust, commitment, and open communication.

In the United States violence against women has increased, particularly physical battering by their husbands. Socialization practices that foster a dominant, assertive role in men and a submissive, passive role in women also foster family violence.

Midlife divorce is becoming a more common phenomenon, particularly as cultural attitudes toward marriage and divorce become more flexible. Divorce during middle age, as at any other time, is painful and is usually followed by lone-liness, self-doubt, mood swings, and many practical adjustments in living. Most people who divorce in midlife do remarry.

Many women lose their husbands before the age of 60—thus, widowhood is often a middle-aged event. Middle-aged widows must deal with such problems as meeting new male companions, starting new sexual relationships, maintaining old friendships, and adjusting to reduced finances.

For many adults, generativity is achieved not only through family relations, but also on the job by the development of ideas, products, plans, and by acting as mentors to others. In middle age, most people are concerned with reaching a satisfactory level in their jobs and advancing in their careers. They also are concerned with evaluating their level of achievement in light of past, current, and future goals and aspirations. Because of gender discrimination on the job, women lag far behind men in occupational status and income.

Research suggests that personality and motivational factors play an important role in a person's occupational success. The traits most frequently associated with career success are intellectual competence, high achievement orientation, forcefulness, dominance, commitment, ambition, dependability, low hostility and self-defeating attitudes, and objectivity.

Middle-aged people generally are the most satisfied workers; moreover, among white-collar workers, satisfaction less often is tied to income than is true for younger or blue-collar workers.

Technological advances have radically changed the work world, both for white-collar and blue-collar workers, and have resulted in the need for retraining for many middle-aged adults. Should the middle-aged worker lose his or her job, that person is often faced with serious problems in getting rehired by another company. Many prejudices exist in the business world that discourage the hiring of middle-aged and older workers.

For adults in industrialized societies, midlife is the time to pursue leisure activities. Leisure activities often help people to adapt to role changes and to find satisfaction and interest that may be absent in other areas of their lives—especially on the job. Leisure activities are usually pursued for relaxation, diversion, personal development, creativity, and for sensual pleasure.

KEY TERMS

ceremonial grandparent (554)

complementarity (557)

cultural conservator
   grandparent (555)

custodial grandparent (555)

distanced grandparent (554)

domestic violence (559)

empty-nest syndrome (548)

fictive grandparent (555)

generational stations (542)

job satisfaction (567)

marital companionship (558)

mentor relationship (540)

REVIEW QUESTIONS

If you can answer these questions, you have a good understanding of the material in this chapter. If a question seems difficult, go back to the text and review the topic.

1. Describe the ways in which the family changes for adults during middle adulthood. In what ways are these changes influenced by cultural values? Give an example.

2. What are the questions researchers frequently ask about intergenerational relations? In what ways do adults influence their adult children? In what ways do adult children influence their parents?

3. What conflicts must middle-aged parents of adolescents resolve?

4. Describe the ways in which the relationship between middle-aged parents and their adult children differs from the parent-child relationship in earlier periods of the lifespan.

5. What is the empty-nest syndrome? Do all adults experience it? Explain with examples.

6. Name and give an example of each of the five styles of grandparenting identified by Neugarten and Weinstein. Describe the five styles of grandparenting found among Native Americans.

7. Why does marital satisfaction increase during middle adulthood? Name and describe the five types of marriages identified by Cuber and Harroff.

8. What is domestic violence? What factors help explain why women are more likely to be physically abused by their spouses?

9. Discuss Troll's concept of *fit* as it relates to midlife divorce.

10. What are the problems a widow must resolve during middle adulthood? Identify the special concerns of middle-aged adults who remain single.

11. Discuss the significance of generativity to occupational advancement. What personality factors are related to occupational advancement?

12. In what ways do women differ from men in job satisfaction?

13. Why do some middle-aged people seek second careers?

14. Discuss the motives for pursuing leisure activities in middle adulthood.

OBSERVATIONAL ACTIVITY

VOCATIONAL DEVELOPMENT

Vocational development takes many forms. Some people choose a job or career early in adulthood and stick with it through their entire working lives. Others try a variety of jobs before settling into the particular one they believe is right for them. Still other people find that after many years of commitment to a job, they have become dissatisfied or bored, leading to consider a midlife vocational change.

Interview 5 to 10 middle-aged working men and women about the nature of their vocational development. Ask each of them the following questions:

1. Describe your job history, starting with your first full-time job.

2. How satisfied have you been with your job development?

3. Have you thought seriously about switching jobs recently?

4. What factors might influence your decision to change your job during this time of your life?

On the basis of the data collected, speculate on the societal, situational, and personality factors that influence the course of one's working life. Are there differences in vocational development for men and women? For blue-collar versus white-collar workers? What factors may contribute to these differences?

The Golden Years

Change is a constant companion in life's travels. As people make their way through life they acquire friends, accumulate knowledge, learn new skills, and discover new aspects of themselves. The journey through late adulthood is accompanied by changes in the shape and functioning of the body that may influence the ways people think about themselves and their lives. While many of these physical changes represent a loss or decline of some sort, late adulthood is characterized by growth in practical knowledge and wisdom.

As people approach the end of their journey, they contemplate their lives: The effects of earlier physical and psychological changes and life events and accomplishments give meaning to the lives of some, while for others they produce a sense of despair. People show considerable variability in the way they adjust and adapt to the process of growing older.

In Chapter 15 you will examine the ways in which the body changes and the different types of knowledge and abilities that emerge in late adulthood. You will also discover some of the ways in which people in late adulthood adapt to these changes. Issues of identity and personality adjustment will also be discussed. In Chapter 16 the focus turns to changes in family life and social relations. Since late adulthood is the time when most people retire, you will also learn more about how people shift their perspective in response to these changes in their work roles.

CHAPTER 15

Late Adulthood: Physical, Cognitive, and Personality Development

Despite the fact that she had been disabled by arthritis since her late 40s, 65-year-old Minnie did not feel old. To her, the word *elderly* had always seemed to apply to others. The residents of the nearby nursing home, who often visited the park across the street, and her parents, who had passed away just a few years ago—they were the elderly.

By contrast, Minnie saw herself as healthy and, despite her crippled joints, still actively involved in events within her community. Her mind was clear and quick, and she was eager to learn new things. Furthermore, she and her husband were still active socially as well as sexually.

Minnie knew she was growing older, but she was determined to make the most of the time she had left. She decided to enroll her husband and herself in an adult education course on horticulture. They both wanted to have a hobby to share in their retirement years together, and since they had enjoyed raising children, Minnie thought they might enjoy raising plants as well.

Minnie was a youngster compared to Mu Qi. At 91, Mu Qi was the oldest person in the city of Taijen, China. He began his life as a farmer's son and was married by prearrangement to Yin-wei when he was barely 16. They later moved to the city, where he worked as a gardener and repairer for the university. He was strong and tall then.

Now he was neither. His back was curved and he had lost most of the strength in his large muscles. Yet he still worked. When he retired 12 years ago, the university honored his years of service by giving him a part-time job collecting books in the library. Mu Qi found his life very satisfying. Without any formal education, he taught himself English and now he was teaching it to his grandchildren. He was venerated by his family and community. He had produced sons, so he had fulfilled his obligations to continue his ancestry. He could face the end of his long life without fear.

THE IMPACT OF GROWING OLDER

When my grandmother turned 75, she needed to complete a physical exam before she could renew her driver's license. And since she prided herself on being able to get around in her big, old car, she went for a check-up. Her doctor told her she was in pretty good shape, and aside from a slightly enlarged heart that was typical for her age, she was healthy. However, what my grandmother focused on was that her doctor had told her she was old; from that moment on she considered herself to be an old woman who needed to be very careful about her health.

As people get older, they are inevitably surrounded by reminders of their advancing age and mortality. For some individuals, such as my grandmother and Minnie, these reminders are at odds with their *perceived age*—that is, the general age with which one identifies. It can come as a shock to people to realize that society has defined them as old simply because of the number of years they have lived. For other adults, however, self-perceptions of aging come relatively early in their lives. The graying of hair and wrinkling of skin experienced in middle age, for example, are sufficient for some individuals to redefine themselves as old—or, at least, as "getting on in years."

Not everyone is as fortunate as Mu Qi, who was growing older in a culture that esteems old age. Some people experience the unpleasant effects of discrimination and prejudice because of their age. **Ageism** refers to any situation in which people are judged negatively not because of their behavior or personality but because of their age. Negative stereotypes of the elderly persist in American culture and in many Western societies. Mandatory retirement underscores the image of older employees as less efficient than younger ones. Older people are inaccurately described as feeble or rigid. The elderly are sometimes perceived as children who require instruction and supervision (Arluke & Levin, 1984). Although some older adults may be physically or mentally disabled and require more care, most of the elderly do not fit the stereotype of helpless, mindless, or passionless people.

The esteem or status attached to being old varies from culture to culture. In the United States today, people wish to live long and healthy lives, but they do not want to be elderly. Compared to men or married women, single, divorced, or widowed women are particularly vulnerable to ageism (Kimmel, 1988). One study (Kite, Deaux, & Miele, 1991) found that among college students, age stereotypes were more pronounced and negative than gender stereotypes. To be old, female, and poor in the United States puts an individual at risk for inadequate diagnoses and poor treatment of mental health problems (Rodeheaver & Datan, 1988). Despite an increase in research and knowledge about individual differences and diversity among the elderly, ageist bias persists in psychological research, textbooks, and public policies (Kimmel, 1988; Schaie, 1988; Whitbourne & Hulicka, 1990).

In Japan and China the elderly have a much higher social status. People can expect to be revered and well cared for in their old age. Most elderly Japanese and Chinese people, like Mu Qi, live with their children and grandchildren and have a place of honor in the household. This is especially true for men, since they are seen as the link to the family's ancestors. The Japanese reverence for the elderly is even institutionalized in a national holiday, Respect for Elders Day.

Many non-Western cultures do not use chronological age to define the onset of old age. Instead, certain behaviors or events—such as the birth of a grandchild, the onset of menopause, or the inability to continue work—mark the passage to old age. In the !Kung culture in Africa, entering old age is perceived as a positive mark of maturity and spiritual growth (Sokolovsky, 1990). To signify their respect

ageism
Any situation in which people are prejudicial on the basis of age.

Although she is old, this Japanese woman leads a satisfying and productive life as a seamstress.

for this maturity, the community gives the elderly control over their most precious resource in their dry terrain: water.

The effects of ageism are subtle but can have a significant impact. To view older adults negatively is to increase our own fears about growing older and reduce the services we provide them. For elderly people who incorporate the negative stereotypes about themselves, the effects of ageism can be lowered self-esteem, greater unhappiness, and depression. Like other forms of prejudice such as racism and sexism, ageism is reduced by education and increased contact with vital and healthy elderly adults. As an increasing proportion of the U.S. population is over 65, it is even more important to eliminate negative stereotypes attached to being old. In fact, people over 65 are the fastest growing segment of the American population, making them a strong political and economic force.

FOCUS ON CULTURE

In the United States and many other Western societies, old age is defined in terms of chronological age, usually 65. In other cultures, old age is defined according to some functional change in the individual's life, such as the birth of grandchildren or menopause. In what ways might defining people in terms of chronological age increase ageism?

People older than 65 comprise the fastest growing segment of the American population, thus making them a political and economic power.

AN AGING POPULATION

In the past two decades, numerous sectors of our society have focused increased attention on the behavior and adjustment of the older adult. To the physician, the psychologist, the urban planner, the economist, the politician, and even to themselves, older people have become a "hot topic." For example, advanced medical technology has not only increased the average life expectancy, it has raised serious medical, legal, and ethical questions regarding the definition of death in terminal patients—many of whom are older adults. In addition, the age at which people ought to retire and the meaning of retirement have become important economic issues.

Due in part to advances in medical technology and to the postwar baby boom, the number of people over the age of 65 increased eightfold between 1900 and 1995. The aging of the population will continue into the next century. By the year 2030, one in five Americans will be over 65 (Heckler, 1985). Furthermore, due to overall increases in income and improved medical care, the elderly will not only live longer, they will be healthier and financially better off.

Many colleges are recognizing the importance of providing educational programs for older students. Many offer tuition waivers for people over age 65. It is not unusual to see a retired person working at a fast-food restaurant or collecting tickets at the local cinema. Health-and-fitness facilities now offer special aerobic exercise programs for "senior citizens." Thus, the shifting age of the population has focused more attention on the needs and characteristics of older adults.

PHYSICAL DEVELOPMENT

For me, the earliest sign of aging occurred during my 20s, when I noticed a growing number of grey hairs. In my 40s, age spots began to appear on my hands; now, in my 50s, I am detecting more and more facial and neck wrinkles. I know my body is aging. As people age, they experience numerous structural and functional changes in the body—changes that, while they may begin earlier, have their most significant impact during late adulthood.

Theories of Aging

Despite the physical signs of aging, some people live to their 90s, while others die much younger. Over the centuries, people have sought the answer to the question of aging: What factors accelerate aging to the point of death? Although there is an increased vulnerability to cancer and such cardiovascular diseases as heart failure, arteriosclerosis (clogging of the arteries), and hypertension, it is not clear exactly what part age plays in these processes. Practically everyone who has studied the aging person has remarked upon the difficulty of separating the effects of aging per se from the effects of disease or the gradual degenerative changes that develop with the passage of time. For example, is arteriosclerosis a disease or a degenerative process that only becomes evident in older people? Is heart failure the result of a disease process or the effect of age alone (Fries & Crapo, 1981; Timiras, 1972)?

As you might expect, a number of theories have attempted to explain the complex processes involved in aging (Shock, 1977). These theories generally fall into one of two general categories: (1) genetically controlled aging and (2) cellular errors not under genetic control.

Genetically Controlled Aging   My mother-in-law's mother lived to be 96 years of age; my mother-in-law is now 84 and walks to the grocery market regularly. Her longevity seems to be part of her genetic heritage. Many researchers believe that aging is controlled by our genetic blueprint, the DNA pattern that was established at the moment of conception. The average lifespan is a characteristic that varies by species; some have longer lifespans than others (e.g., humans live longer than dogs and cats). Moreover, just as individuals differ in their genetic makeup, so too

Longevity has a strong genetic component; these sisters are all in their 80s.

Hayflick limit
The predefined number of times a cell can replicate itself.

do they differ in the way their bodies age. Each person has a unique genetic clock that limits the amount of energy he or she has to pursue an active life and controls the sequences of physiological growth and decline; prompted by the DNA code, our bodies undergo hormonal changes that stimulate either the growth or decline of body systems. Aging is viewed as a normal and natural sequence that ultimately results in death. Hayflick (1970, 1977, 1980) has shown that after 50 or so divisions, human cells normally die. The inability of cells to replace themselves indefinitely means that over time the basic building block of life contained in our cells (i.e., DNA) will be used up, thus resulting in physiological decline and, ultimately, death (Rockstein & Sussman, 1979). The **Hayflick limit,** which refers to the number of times a cell can replicate itself before it ceases to be able to reproduce itself, has repeatedly been confirmed in humans and many other species. The genetically controlled aging theory helps explain the fact that longevity runs in families, provided people do not die from accident or debilitating disease.

cellular error
Theory that explains aging and eventual death as resulting from the accumulated effects of errors that occur in the sequence of the transfer of information at the cellular level.

Non-Genetic Cellular Errors Supporters of the theory of **cellular error** maintain that aging and eventual death are the result of the accumulated effects of errors that occur in the sequence of the transfer of information at the cellular level. Information originally stored in the genetic code must be transformed into biochemical processes. With increased age, errors occur; either the wrong biochemical message is sent or none is sent at all. As biochemical errors increase over time, cellular functioning deteriorates. The basic genetic code, carried in molecules of DNA, may also be damaged or altered over the years by radiation or other chemicals or drugs. Furthermore, there is some evidence to suggest that the cellular mechanisms that normally repair damaged DNA may deteriorate with age, resulting in an accumulation of genetic errors (Mclearn & Foch, 1985). Species or organisms that have a more efficient cell repair capacity are likely to live longer (Sacher, 1978).

wear-and-tear theory
A theory that compares the human organism to a machine and human cells to machine parts to explain the process of aging.

The **wear-and-tear theory** also focuses on nongenetic cellular error. This theory compares the human organism to a machine and human cells to machine parts, arguing that human cells wear out with prolonged use just like machine parts. A variation of the wear-and-tear theory is the **stress theory** of aging, which suggests that stressful life events reduce the energy capacities of the organism. The accumulation over time of the minor impairments caused by stress leads to a deterioration of the body's ability to adapt (Shock, 1977).

stress theory
Theory that stressful life events decrease the energy of an individual and lead to the deterioration and aging of the body.

Another error can occur when the body is unable to deliver adequate levels of oxygen or nutrients to the cells, thus creating a state of **deprivation** that results in aging at the cellular level. This kind of deprivation may be related to certain disease states, such as arteriosclerosis. The cells begin to deteriorate under these deprived conditions and eventually die.

deprivation theory
A theory that aging is due to the inadequate delivery of essential nutrients and oxygen to cells.

Aging has also been linked to another type of cellular error that occurs as a result of the accumulation of **free radicals.** In the process of metabolism, the body breaks down and recombines molecules within the cell; some of the electrons within these molecules do not attach themselves to any specific atoms. These free radicals within the cell are highly unstable and may combine with other cellular molecules with damaging results, especially when DNA molecules are combined. They can limit the body's ability to repair itself and may even damage the immune system. An excess of free radicals is believed to be a factor in diseases such as cancer, diabetes, and arthritis.

free radicals
Unstable molecular by-products of metabolism that contribute to the aging process.

PHYSICAL CHANGES IN LATE ADULTHOOD

During late adulthood numerous physical changes become obvious; other changes in organs and body functions may not be as apparent but their impact is felt. Most, but not all, of the physical changes that occur are described in terms of decline. These changes represent a normal part of growing older (Huyck & Hoyer, 1982).

senescence
The normal degenerative processes accompanying aging; also known as primary aging.

secondary aging
The acceleration of senescence, or primary aging, by environmental factors such as disease, trauma, or stress.

postural stoop
A slump of posture found in old age, with the head projected forward and lower limbs and hips flexed.

osteoporosis
A condition that results in the thinning of the bones in old age.

Postural stoop is caused by years of poor posture, shrinking muscles and tendons, and thinning of bones.

Primary Aging **Senescence** (or primary aging) refers to the period of the lifespan when the body weakens and declines rather than grows (Rockstein & Sussman, 1979), marking the deterioration of physical, social, and cognitive processes. Unlike disease, senescence occurs in all people across all cultures—although, of course, the timing and patterning of the decline varies from one person to another. The gradual loss of neural tissue and the slowing down of central nervous system activity with increasing age are two examples of senescence. Another example is the weakening of the body's immune system. Thus, as people age, they are more likely to catch diseases and have more difficulty recuperating from their illnesses.

Senescence is a gradual process. The resulting changes in structure and functioning are slow to emerge, unlike the sudden changes associated with accidents, stress, or disease. Senescence also takes place at many levels within the same individual. Thus, researchers have identified anatomical, biochemical, physiological, and behavioral changes that occur with advancing age. Finally, although senescence is distinct from disease, it is important to note that disease, and other extrinsic factors such as trauma and stress, can accelerate senescence and ultimately lead to death. Sometimes the death of a lifelong spouse or friend, or a move to a smaller apartment, may be so stressful that older people begin to deteriorate physically. The acceleration of senescence due to external environmental factors is referred to as **secondary aging.** Other factors that contribute to secondary aging include poor dietary habits, drug and alcohol abuse, and exposure to fatal diseases such as AIDS.

Physical Appearance The most obvious changes occurring in old age are demonstrated in physical appearance. The wrinkles and gray hair that began to appear during middle age become more pronounced. Decreases in fat and muscle tissue result in inelastic skin that tends to hang in folds. The craggy, lined, and weathered features of the aged person's face are a popular subject for photographers. Loss of hair—including scalp, axillary, and body hair—also accompanies aging in both sexes. There is also an increase in *age spots,* or irregular skin pigmentation, and teeth may be lost due to weakening gums (Rossman, 1980).

One of the most pronounced changes in physical appearance during old age is **postural stoop.** This characteristic slump, with head projected forward and lower limbs and hips flexed, is probably caused by years of poor posture and diet made worse by shrinkage of muscles and tendons, increased calcification of ligaments, compression of spinal discs, and thinning of bone. Older people also show a decrease in height that is related to spinal disc compression and probably to postural stoop as well.

Osteoporosis, a condition that results in the thinning of the bones, affects some postmenopausal women (and a few men) and may result in a "dowager's hump" or hunchback as well as decreased height. Because their bones are thinner, older women afflicted with osteoporosis are more likely to experience cracked or broken bones during a fall. Fortunately, the disease can be prevented by increased consumption of calcium and exercise programs beginning early in young adulthood and continuing into late adulthood.

Sensory-System Changes   Nearly all the sensory systems show reduced efficiency in old age. In many cases, the loss is simply a continuation of the problems that arose in middle age, now occurring at a faster rate. For some people, however, the progress of middle-aged sensory problems is halted while new complaints arise. In the area of vision, for example, changes in the lens that produced far-sightedness in middle age now stabilize. On the other hand, new changes affecting the retina and nervous system result in decreased visual acuity and color vision (Fozard, Wolf, Bell, MacFarland, & Podolsky, 1977). Many older people also have considerable difficulty seeing in the dark and require greater illumination to see things clearly. However, older people are also more sensitive to glare. Driving in bright sunlight or in the evening against bright headlights can be hazardous for some people.

Visual disorders are more commonly diagnosed in late adulthood, even though the disorders have their origin in middle adulthood. The most common visual disability of old age is **cataracts,** which are produced by the formation of an opaque covering of the lens. **Glaucoma** occurs when the pressure within the eye builds up and gradually damages the optic nerve. This disorder begins in middle adulthood, but the symptoms are not obvious until permanent damage has been done to the retina, usually in old age. The best prevention of glaucoma is detection in middle adulthood, before damage occurs. Nearly 60% of the elderly suffer from cataracts and 1 to 3% suffer from glaucoma (Crandall, 1980).

cataracts
Visual disability commonly diagnosed in late adulthood that is produced by the formation of an opaque covering of the lens.

glaucoma
Visual disorder commonly diagnosed in late adulthood that occurs when pressure within the eye builds up and gradually damages the optic nerve.

Because their bones are thinner, older people are more likely to break their bones during a fall.

presbycusis

A progressive loss of hearing, especially for tones of high frequency, caused by degenerative changes in the auditory system; the most common auditory problem associated with aging.

Another common sensory disorder associated with aging is loss of hearing. Both the degree and the variability of self-reported hearing problems increase with age, especially after age 50 (Arlinger, 1991; Slawinski, Hartel, & Kline, 1993). Older people report difficulty in listening to speech when there is background noise such as a television or other conversations. According to Corso (1977), 17% of people aged 65 or older show signs of advanced **presbycusis**—hearing loss due to degenerative changes in the auditory system. This loss is primarily restricted to high-frequency sounds, including many speech sounds. Many speakers try to compensate for the older person's auditory handicap by talking loudly, but this only serves to obscure the intelligible sounds. To promote effective communication with the hard-of-hearing, one should actually lower one's voice, since this reduces pitch—the vocal quality that poses the most trouble for the aged. The potential importance of hearing loss for the elderly is documented by research showing that aged people with reduced hearing are significantly more likely to perform poorly on tests of intellectual functioning than are people with normal hearing (Granick, Kleban, & Weiss, 1976; Lindenberger & Baltes, 1994) and to experience less satisfactory personal relationships (Humes & Roberts, 1990).

There is some evidence that the senses of taste and smell also decline with age. The number of taste buds on the tongue decreases sharply from young adulthood to old age (Bee, 1987), making it more difficult for elderly people to discriminate between tastes. In one study, for example, Grzegorczyk, Jones, and Mistretta (1979) found that among a sample of adults between the ages of 23 and 92, the ability to detect the taste of salt declined significantly with increasing age. The sense of smell is closely related to taste. A study of over 2,000 people between the ages of 5 and 99 found that the sense of smell was best between the ages of 30 and 60, less acute between the ages of 60 and 80, and sharply lower thereafter (Doty, Shaman, & Dann, 1984). Engen (1977) has cautioned, however, that loss for taste and smell may be due primarily to some pathological condition, or to chronic habits such as smoking. In any event, the older person who has trouble tasting and smelling things is likely to be less interested in food, and this can lead to nutritional problems—a serious issue for many individuals in later life.

If many of these sensory changes suggest a pessimistic picture of late adulthood, it should be pointed out that except in advanced states—which usually occur only in very old age—these physical changes typically do not prevent a person from living a normal life. In technological societies, better medical facilities, amplified telephones, hearing aids, and eyeglasses have helped the elderly live quite comfortably despite the reduced efficiency of their bodies.

FOCUS ON CULTURE

It is primarily under conditions of stress that the age-related losses appear to make a significant difference in the adjustment of older people (DeVries, 1975). Technological societies are better equipped to offer people alternatives to these losses. On the other hand, technological societies are likely to be place more stresses on older individuals.

Organ Functioning   Not only do older people worry about how aging has affected the way they look and their ability to see, hear, and taste things, but many also worry about how their heart, lungs, and brain are working. Certainly with the slowing down of the body's ability to heal itself comes a greater possibility for problems within the body's organs. Minnie's father, for example, was often heard to say, "My ticker just isn't what it used to be" and "These bones can't take it anymore."

Aging is accompanied by marked reductions in the efficiency and ease with which the body's organs function. The cardiovascular system (heart and blood vessels), in particular, manifests significant changes. The heart, like other muscles in the body, requires a longer time to contract, thereby increasing blood circulation time. Fatty concentrations (cholesterol) in the heart and arteries also reduce blood flow throughout the body; degeneration of the blood vessels leads to increased blood pressure (Kohn, 1977). Yet these changes, while most evident in later life, do not originate during this period. Losses in cardiac output (the amount of blood the heart can pump through the body) are evident from early adulthood on.

Other organ systems also show reduced efficiency in late adulthood. Vital lung capacity decreases with age. Older people frequently report shortness of breath, particularly after mild exercise such as climbing stairs or raking the yard (Klocke, 1977). Changes in the gastrointestinal system, such as deterioration of the mucous lining in the intestinal tract, and reduction of gastric juices, contribute to the frequent intestinal and digestive complaints of the elderly. Normal immune functions also decline with age, and may be related to an increased incidence of cancer or other diseases in the elderly (LaRue & Jarvik, 1982; Makinsdan, 1977; Teller, 1972).

As mentioned earlier, bone tissue deteriorates in older people. Chemical changes in the bone result in a thinning and weakening of bony material, particularly in the long bones found in the arms and legs. These changes increase the older person's susceptibility to fracture and prolong the healing process when breaks occur.

It is estimated that there are about 10 billion neurons, or nerve cells, in the brain at the point of maximum growth. As we age, a vast number of these cells die—anywhere from 20,000 to 100,000 cells per day after the age of 30 (Huyck & Hoyer, 1982). Undoubtedly, this neural loss accounts, in part, for the decrease in brain size that is observed with increasing age. Rockstein and Sussman (1979) report that by the time a person reaches 90 years of age, there may be as much as a 20% reduction from maximum brain weight.

Other brain changes occur on a microscopic level. Some of the more important changes concern the gradual accumulation of residue or waste products in the brain—specifically, *lipofuscan* and *argyrophilic plaque*. Researchers (Rockstein & Sussman, 1979) have speculated that the buildup of these waste products may be linked to the development of *dementia*, a syndrome that will be discussed in detail later in the chapter.

Central Nervous System and Behavior   The effects of aging on the central nervous system have been well studied. On the average, older people are found to be slower to respond to stimuli than young people. This reflects a basic change in the speed with which the central nervous system processes information (Birren, 1974; Birren, Woods, & Williams, 1980; Marsh & Thompson, 1977). Whereas

As the nervous system ages, re-action time slows down. Should these cyclists need to stop suddenly, it might take them a little longer to react than it did when they were younger.

young people appear to be quick or slow depending upon the demands of the situation, older people characteristically require more time to process information. When rapid decisions or movements are called for—avoiding an oncoming bicycle, for example—the older person may be unable to make the appropriate response. Older people are prone to falls and other accidents that might be avoided by quick movements and readjustments.

The slowing down of the central nervous system appears to be significant in several areas. For instance, it may account for some of the difficulties older people experience in memory retrieval and learning. It may also explain some age-related differences in intelligence-testing situations in which speed is a factor. The slowing down of responses may even affect personality and adjustment, undercutting the self-confidence with which older people manage themselves in a fast-paced urban environment—or in a fast-paced clinical interview. This slowing down may contribute to rigidity in behavior or to the reduced risk taking that seems to be characteristic of older people.

Although the slowing down of the nervous system normally affects many kinds of behavior, this fact is not related to the stereotype of the slow-paced, shuffling elder. The older person may take a split second too long to grab hold of the banister (and therefore fall) but will not necessarily take longer than a younger person to walk up the stairs and along the hallway. It is primarily when old people have to change the direction of their movement in response to new information that impairment occurs (Welford, 1959). When older people are accustomed to rapid and finely coordinated movement (if such movements do not represent new kinds of decisions), their responses may be so quick as to astonish the unpracticed young. Arthur Rubinstein, Vladimir Horowitz, Claudio Arrau, and Rudolf Serkin are examples of well-known pianists who continued to interpret

George Burns had entertained people well into his late 90s. He demonstrated that a slowing of the nervous system does not mean that older people lose their ability to perform.

difficult compositions—even at prestissimo tempos—into their late 70s, 80s, and even 90s. With regular practice, the older person loses little, and what is lost in response time is often compensated for by experience.

RECAP

The impact of growing older is influenced by cultural attitudes and ageism. Because more people are living longer, the elderly have become a significant political force. Theories of aging center on two types of explanations: those based on genetically programmed changes and those based on nongenetic cellular errors. Evidence of senescence can be found in visual, auditory, smell, and taste sensitivity. Physical signs of aging include postural stoop, wrinkles, and loss of hair. Organ functioning shows reduced efficiency, and bone tissue deteriorates. The general slowing of response behavior in late adulthood is due to declines in central nervous system functioning.

HEALTH FACTORS IN LATE ADULTHOOD

Among the most serious problems confronting the older person is increased susceptibility to disease. This is particularly true of chronic or long-term conditions, from which most people over 65 suffer. Yet relatively few of these individuals are seriously restricted in their mobility. When all things are taken into consideration, most older people are in reasonably good health. Only 4 to 5% of the elderly in the United States are in chronic-care facilities, hospitals, mental institutions, or nursing homes. The remaining 95 to 96% of the aged live in the community and are able to "get around" despite their chronic conditions (Harris, 1978). In many cultures, the elderly continue to live and, like Mu Qi, work independently well into late adulthood. This should not be surprising, since people who make it to late adulthood represent the sturdiest of the population; they have a lifelong history of surviving stresses, diseases, and traumas.

The prospect of illness is nevertheless a real threat to the aging adult. Older individuals are less likely to bounce back from an illness; once admitted to the hospital, they are likely to stay longer than a younger person. They are also more likely to die from the illness (Harris, 1978). Even acute or temporary conditions, which elderly people contract less frequently, generally are more serious for older people. Influenza, for example, can progress to pneumonia, and possibly death, in an aging adult.

The most common chronic conditions restricting activity in individuals aged 65 and older are heart disease, arthritis, hypertension, visual impairments, and orthopedic problems (Harris, 1978). Although all of these conditions take a significant toll on the aged, some people find that the secondary effects—that is, effects that go beyond the purely physical ones—are even more difficult to live with. The dependence on others that often accompanies these chronic conditions can be extremely frustrating, particularly for people who are used to "doing for themselves."

FOCUS ON CULTURE

An individual's willingness to accept the care and help of younger people is a by-product of his or her personality and cultural expectations regarding the aged. In the United States, there is a strong value on self-determination and independence, which creates a dilemma for the frail elderly. By contrast, in Japan and China, older people know that others will take care of them as a sign of respect. The importance placed on different stages of the lifespan varies across cultures and can have a profound effect on a person's self-concept and esteem.

Exercise and Health In 1991, John Kelley ran his 60th Boston Marathon. He was 83 years old. One minute after the race his pulse was a healthy 64 beats per minute, well below the normal pulse of a person at rest. Although running a 26-mile race is not prescribed for all people in their 70s and 80s, walking, jogging, running, and swimming are recommended not only for people in late adulthood, but for all men and women who live sedentary lives. Regular exercise improves mental abilities (Clarkson-Smith & Hartley, 1988, 1990; Hawkins, Kramer, & Capaldi, 1992; Powell, 1974) and helps to combat the degeneration of the cardio-vascular (heart and blood vessels) and pulmonary (lung and breathing) systems. Even after years of neglecting their bodies, people can make remarkable comebacks. One man who did not start jogging until he was 67 holds 14 world track-and-field records for his age category (Crandall, 1980).

To a large degree it has been found (Wessell & Van Huss, 1969) that losses in physiological functioning in older people may be related as much to inactivity—a sedentary lifestyle—as to age itself. Wessell and Van Huss coined the term **hypokinetic disease** (*hypo* = under, *kinetic* = motion) to describe loss of function due to inactivity. DeVries, an exercise physiologist, points out that there are three

hypokinetic disease
A condition in which physical functioning declines due to inactivity.

People in late adulthood who continue to be physically active are likely to benefit from being fit.

causes of physiological losses in older people: the processes of aging itself, undetected incipient diseases, and hypokinetic disease. Of the three, hypokinetic disease is reversible. DeVries (1970) set up a vigorous exercise training regimen in a retirement community. One hundred and twelve volunteers, men between the ages of 52 and 87 (mean age 69), exercised at calisthenics, jogging, and stretching or swimming for 1 hour three times a week. As a result, they were able to increase their capacity to transport oxygen throughout their body by 30 to 35%. Significant improvement was also found in both systolic and diastolic blood pressure. A group of men with heart trouble who were placed on a modified program of milder exercise showed similar gains. In a subsequent study (Adams & DeVries, 1973), older women aged 52 to 79 participated in a vigorous exercise program for 3 months and also showed significant improvement in physiological functioning.

It is recommended that elderly people who want to engage in more than vigorous walking in a regular exercise regimen should consult a physician or a physical education expert, particularly if they have lived a sedentary life. Furthermore, since it is the large muscles—such as those in the legs, arms, and back—that influence heart and lung capacity as well as the other factors mentioned above, it is recommended that a personal exercise program consist of natural activities such as walking, jogging, running (or a combinations of these), or swimming. For example, a 30- to 60-minute daily walk can bring about marked improvement in physical condition for elderly men and women.

The best way to assure physical fitness in late adulthood is to begin a program of exercise in early or middle adulthood and stick to it on a regular basis. The later a person begins an exercise program, the less effect it will have on increasing maximum skill or physical function (Denney, 1982). While exercise will not cure all that ails elderly people, a physically active life can enhance the prospects that one will reach one's full biogenetic potential for longevity (Bortz, 1982).

MENTAL HEALTH AND AGING

Two categories of mental disorders have a significant impact on the aging adult: **functional disorders** and **organic brain syndromes.** The common feature of these two conditions is that they produce substantial cognitive and personality changes. Functional disorders are those for which there is no apparent physiological or biological basis. Organic brain syndromes, in contrast, are the result of biological changes.

Depression   The most common functional disorders in the elderly are depression, paranoid reactions, hypochondriasis, and chronic anxiety (Butler & Lewis, 1982; Heidrich & Ryff, 1993; Pfeiffer, 1977). Of these, **depressive reactions** are the most frequent. Depressive symptoms include extreme sadness, social withdrawal, inhibition, lowered self-esteem, pessimism, indecision, and, occasionally, a slowing down of mental processes as well as physical movement. The incidence of depression rises sharply among adults over the age of 70 (Kessler, Foster, Webster, & House, 1992). Sometimes depressive symptoms are overlooked because they are mistakenly seen as a natural consequence of aging. This is unfortunate because, if properly diagnosed, the depressed individual can be helped by counseling. The suicide rate for the elderly, which is linked to depression, is higher than for any other age group—especially for white males. Moreover, when an older adult attempts suicide, there is roughly one chance in two that he or she will succeed, whereas

functional disorders
Mental disorders for which there is no apparent physiological or biological basis.

organic brain syndromes
Mental disorders caused by organic or biological factors.

depressive reaction
One of the most frequent functional disorders in the elderly, characterized by extreme sadness, social withdrawal, inhibition, lowered self-esteem, pessimism, indecision, and occasionally, a slowing down of mental processes as well as physical movement.

Loss of a loved one or friend is a common factor in depression among the elderly.

the ratio is one in seven for young adults (Pfeiffer, 1977). It is important to keep in mind that most of the research on depression among the elderly has been conducted using people living in Western societies. Depression among the elderly may not be as common for people living in cultures in which the elderly have greater dignity and control over their lives.

Loss is a common factor leading to depression in the elderly. For some people, loss of physical vigor and stamina, especially when it is due to a chronic, immobilizing illness, can trigger a depressive reaction. Loss of sensory function (sight, hearing, taste, or smell) can contribute to paranoid feelings and social isolation, two conditions that increase depression (Charatan, 1981). Depression can be a reaction to the death of friends and relatives, to the loss of a peer group or status after retirement, or to having to relocate to a smaller, more affordable residence.

Depression can be treated by individual or group psychotherapy, sometimes in combination with antidepressant drugs. Aerobic exercise programs and increased social activity also help reduce depression and anxiety in old people (Emery, Hauck, & Blumenthal, 1992).

Although many forms of psychopathology increase with advancing age (Butler & Lewis, 1982), it would be a mistake to assume that most older adults suffer from emotional problems. Romaniuk, McAuley, and Arling (1983), for example, found that only 18% of elderly adults living in a retirement community reported definite or extensive symptoms of functional psychological disorders. In addition, only 10% reported feeling lonely often, and only 6% rated their life satisfaction as poor. Separate ratings by interviewers generally confirmed the overall positive adjustment reported by the elderly themselves. Ninety-seven percent of these older adults were rated as being pleasant and cooperative, 94% as showing good common sense in making judgments, 89% as having the ability to cope with everyday problems, 89% as being mentally alert, and 76% as showing enjoyment of life.

The investigators also noted that mental health among the elderly was significantly related to perceived physical health, education, income, and marital status. Individuals who viewed themselves as physically healthy also rated themselves, and were rated by others, as emotionally healthy. Moreover, older adults with greater education and higher incomes also showed less evidence of psychological problems. Finally, married elderly adults fared much better psychologically than their widowed or nonmarried counterparts. Elderly women who saw themselves in meaningful roles such as mentors or volunteers and interacted with a reference group of family and friends also reported higher levels of well-being and fewer symptoms of emotional distress (Heidrich & Ryff, 1993).

FOCUS ON CULTURE   Information on mental health among the elderly is primarily collected in public hospitals and clinics. In the United States, access to psychiatric care is influenced by socioeconomic status and geographical location (Snowden & Cheung, 1990). Furthermore, most psychiatrists are white males—very few represent ethnic minority groups. How might national statistics on psychiatric disorders among the elderly be influenced by the way data is collected? What other sources of information need to be examined to get a clearer picture of mental health issues among the elderly?

dementia

A type of organic brain syndrome characterized by a variety of behaviors including decreased mental functioning, changes in mood and social skills, and a deterioration in personal habits.

Dementias   **Dementia** is the most common organic brain syndrome occurring in the elderly. This condition refers to a broad constellation of behavioral and psychological symptoms associated with diffuse or general brain loss of unknown origin. Over the course of the disease, brain weight can be reduced by as much as 15 to 30%. Typical symptoms include errors in intellectual and social judgment, mood changes, memory impairment, disorientation with respect to time and space, general confusion, loosening of inhibitions, and deterioration of personal habits. The behavior of 80-year-old Elmer is an example. His adult children became concerned when they noticed that he was not dressing as neatly as he had in the past. His usually well-kept hair always seemed in need of a shampoo. Just last week, Elmer lost his Social Security check and forgot to turn off the stove when he went to bed. When his son asked him about these problems, he seemed confused as to which day it was and when the problems had occurred. It was clear to those who knew and loved Elmer that he was declining mentally.

Alzheimer's disease

A form of dementia characterized by the slow deterioration of the brain.

The most common form of dementia is **Alzheimer's disease** (AD), named after the German physician who first described the condition in 1907. In Alzheimer's disease, a progressive and irreversible deterioration of the brain tissue, primarily in the cerebral cortex, results in increasing deterioration in mental functioning and social behavior. Until recently, the term *Alzheimer's disease* was reserved for people under the age of 60 who showed signs of dementia, while the term *senile* was applied to people over the age of 60 with the same symptoms. Today, however, the latter term is no longer used. Not only is it imprecise and blurred by negative stereotypes of the elderly, but it also appears that the onset of Alzheimer's disease may begin in middle adulthood but not be clearly diagnosed until the person is older (Emr & Schneider, 1985).

The risks of developing Alzheimer's disease increase dramatically with age. The prevalence of the disease among people age 65 or older is 6%; for people age 75 and over the incidence is 10%, and for people age 85 and older the incidence is 20%. People with Alzheimer's may live for 15 years or more with this disease, which has been classed as one of the leading causes of death for elderly Americans

(Heckler, 1985). With the numbers of elderly people projected to increase significantly in the next century, Alzheimer's disease has been targeted as a major health issue (Rickards, Zuckerman, & West, 1985).

Several symptoms of Alzheimer's disease appear in a stage-like sequence. In the early stages, some of the symptoms such as forgetfulness and confusion may be overlooked or accepted as normal signs of aging—another negative consequence of ageism. Patients may show memory or cognitive deficits. Like Elmer, they may be confused and even forget the names of close family members. As the condition progresses, people may experience personality changes, insomnia, loss of appetite, and depression. They may be unable to control their bodily functions, which adds to the difficulty of caring for them. Frequently, patients with Alzheimer's disease will show signs of depression as a result of their deteriorating condition and the stresses that result.

At present, there is no accurate test to diagnose the disorder until a brain autopsy is performed. Work is in progress on several behavioral tests that can be used to detect early signs and symptoms of Alzheimer's (Hostetler, 1987). These tests assess memory, people's ability to use and understand language, and their ability to control voluntary movements.

The cause of Alzheimer's disease is not yet known, although there are several possibilities under investigation (Khachaturian, 1985). Heredity, toxic-waste accumulations, autoimmune responses, trauma, and slow-growing viruses have been suggested as possible causes. There is a link between Alzheimer's disease and Down syndrome: Families with Alzheimer's disease have three times the likelihood of having a Down syndrome child (Ball, 1987).

multi-infarct dementia (MID)
A form of dementia characterized by sporadic decline in cognitive functions caused by a series of strokes or ministrokes.

The second most common form of dementia is called **multi-infarct dementia** (MID). It was formerly referred to as *cerebral arteriosclerosis* because it was thought that the dementia symptoms were caused by hardening of the arteries that carry blood to the brain. With reduced blood flow, specific damage and deterioration in brain tissue would result, producing cognitive and emotional deterioration. However, it is now believed that the symptoms, which include increased irritability, fatigue, headaches, and memory losses, are caused by strokes or mini-strokes brought on by arteriosclerosis. The onset of this disease, which is usually sudden, often affects more men than women, and may occur as early as the mid-50s. Because a person erratically suffers multiple strokes over the years, there is a corresponding pattern of decline and recovery of cognitive skill. Ultimately, the brain can no longer compensate for the stroke damage and death results (Reisberg, 1981).

RECAP

Chronic diseases contribute to a decline in health in late adulthood. Exercise contributes to physical and mental health. Lack of activity can result in loss of function, a condition referred to as hypokinetic disease. Two categories of mental disorders include functional disorders, which have no known physiological basis, and organic brain syndromes, which are the result of changes in the brain. Depression is the most common functional disorder; dementias are the most common organic brain disorders. Alzheimer's disease and multi-infarct dementia are the most common forms of dementia.

Health Perspective

CARING FOR PATIENTS WITH ALZHEIMER'S DISEASE

It is a fear that many people have—that their minds will stop working before their bodies do. When Alzheimer's disease begins, the victim looks well. Yet, someone who is physically active and capable of hauling groceries may not be able to do a simple task such as making a telephone call or preparing a cup of tea. The person can talk and recall past events, but may be unable to remember what was said 10 minutes earlier. The early symptoms of the disease are mistaken for forgetfulness and may produce frustration and irritation among family members who are affected by the victim's lapses of memory. Later, as the disease becomes progressively worse, disturbing changes in personality emerge.

From the point of view of the health-care provider, not only the Alzheimer's victim but members of the family need attention. In the earlier stages, which may linger for many years, the primary care providers are the families. Often the emotional needs of family members are ignored as they attempt to meet the increasing physical and psychological needs of the victim. When patients are severely impaired, the burden placed on the family is frequently overwhelming. Alzheimer victims eventually become incapable of taking adequate care of their bodies—they must be washed, bathed, and cared for in the same way as young children. Victims often become so confused that they wander off, sometimes in the middle of the night. Thus, they must be watched carefully. All the while, the spouse or adult children are dealing with the difficulties of relating to a loved one who is changing before their eyes.

The stress of caring for dementia victims often has negative psychological, social, and health consequences for the caregivers. People vary in their abilities to provide sustained care without themselves suffering a decline in health and well-being. People with optimistic outlooks who have low anxiety levels are less likely to be stressed or experience declines in their physical health (Hooker, Monahan, Shifren, & Hutchinson, 1992).

At some point, the victim and family members require outside assistance and support. In less technological societies, members of the extended family and the community help out. One source of help for people living in industrialized countries is a **respite worker.** As the name implies, respite

COGNITIVE DEVELOPMENT

respite worker
A person who gives primary care providers a temporary break or rest from the continuing care of a chronically ill family member.

On the one hand, people often think of older adults as being slower to respond both physically and mentally; on the other, they recognize that wisdom often comes with age and experience. This paradox is most pronounced in cultures that focus more attention on the young than on the old and that value intellectual abilities. American culture is particularly preoccupied with intelligence; by far the most frequently studied component of intellectual functioning in the aged is their performance on standard IQ tests.

Cognitive development during adulthood involves changes in the way people think and process information, and in the depth and breadth of their accumulated knowledge and skills. In earlier chapters on development during adulthood we looked at the differences in ways of thinking (Chapter 11) and in speed and efficiency in processing information (Chapter 13). Now, we turn our attention to the qualitative differences that emerge during adulthood in accumulated knowledge care is any service that gives the primary care providers a temporary break or rest from the continuing care of a chronically ill family member. Adult day-care programs are another alternative to full-time care in the home. Staffed by specially trained workers with medical backup, these programs help reduce the need for hospitalization and reduce the stress on family members (Burdz, Eaton, & Bond, 1988).

The significance of Alzheimer's disease and its impact on the family may vary from one culture to another. The behavior of some Alzheimer's patients may be misinterpreted as evidence of "craziness within the family" and a source of embarrassment, which prevents the caregivers from getting help. For example, relatives of Hispanic Alzheimer's victims are often reluctant to publicly discuss their problems in caring for the patients. In Florida, ethnic self-help groups that function as surrogate families have emerged to help Latino families cope more effectively with caring for family members afflicted with Alzheimer's disease (Henderson, 1990).

Another source of support is available through the Alzheimer's Disease and Related Disorders Association (ADRD). Founded by relatives who have had to cope with the disease, this national group has local chapters that provide afflicted families with a forum in which to discuss their concerns and frustrations and from which they can derive help and information.

Alzheimer's disease creates two victims: the person with the disease and the family members who care for the sufferer. Alzheimer's patients require constant attention and personal hygiene care.

and wisdom. One question that is of particular interest is whether people get "smarter" or more intelligent with age. At what age do these changes occur and in what ways are they manifested?

CHANGES IN INTELLIGENCE WITH AGE

The intelligence quotient (IQ) has long been used to measure intelligence in school-age children. Standardized intelligence tests measuring IQ have also been given to large adult populations such as military recruits. When different age groups are tested in a cross-sectional design, age-related differences in patterns of abilities emerge. In an early large-scale administration of a standardized intelligence test, Jones and Conrad (1933) discovered that individuals about 20 years of age scored higher than middle-aged and older adults; at the time this was interpreted to mean that intelligence began a long decline at age 20. In later cross-sectional studies of adult intelligence, however, the average peak of performance seemed to occur between 25 and 35 (Schaie, 1979, 1983, 1994; Schaie & Willis, 1993).

However, there is a problem with the cross-sectional design; we cannot assume that the differences between age groups are solely the result of aging. Younger subjects may score higher than middle-aged subjects not because they are more intelligent, but because of such variables as profound cultural changes, more formal education, better nutrition, and greater access to information through computers and television. Just as important is the fact that most younger people are used to being tested, particularly with standardized tests. The higher scores, then, may represent *generation* or *cohort* effects as opposed to (or in addition to) effects of physiological aging.

The possibility of large cohort effects for intelligence is impressively illustrated in a study by Flynn (1984). This investigator showed that every Stanford-Binet and Wechsler intelligence test standardization sample from 1932 to 1978 established higher norms than its predecessor. As Flynn notes, the obvious interpretation of this pattern is that representative samples of Americans did better and better on IQ tests over a period of 46 years, the total gain amounting to a rise in mean IQ of 13.8 points, a relatively large increase. What is unclear is whether the finding means that people today are more intelligent than people tested 40 to 50 years ago, or whether people today are simply better test takers.

In order to minimize generation effects and gain a clearer picture of changes in intelligence over time, some researchers have conducted longitudinal studies. In these studies, the same individuals are tested and retested at different points in their lifespan. The results show little or no decline in intelligence in middle age. In fact four major studies showed that middle-aged adults performed better than they had as young adults (Bayley & Oden, 1955; Eichorn, Hunt, & Honzik, 1981; Nisbet, 1957; Schaie, 1979, 1983). Measurements of intellectual abilities in late adulthood reveal much greater variability; some abilities decline, some remain constant, and some improve with age (Schaie, 1989).

The longitudinal studies have their own biases, however. For one thing, highly motivated and healthier individuals are more likely to remain in the study (which may continue for 20, 30, or even 40 years). The results, then, may reflect intelligence as it operates in more vital and thoughtful individuals. A second point is that longitudinal studies may be affected by changes in environment. For example, if testing were to become much more frequent during a given decade, all respondents tested after that time might do better—on the basis of their experience in the testing situation—than they had done 20 years earlier. Similarly, being given the same or similar tests repeatedly over time sensitizes people to the test-taking situation—that is, they learn how to take tests, and consequently, may do better on later tests. In each case, an increase in test scores would reflect more than aging.

A study by Schaie and Hertzog (1983) supports the belief that little, if any, significant decline in intellectual functioning takes place during middle adulthood. Using a sequential design (which combines the advantages of cross sectional and longitudinal design) that allowed them to separate age effects from cohort effects, these investigators noted that marked decreases in most areas of intellectual performance do not occur until after 60 years of age. When declines were observed prior to 60, they did not appear to be, in the authors' words, "of sufficient magnitude to be practically important." Perhaps the best conclusion regarding intelligence is that decreases in performance, if they exist at all, are certainly not universal (Schaie, 1994). A note of caution, however. Most of the longitudinal tests on intelligence have been conducted on people in Western industrialized societies. The impact of culture on intellectual functioning over the lifespan is largely unexplored at this time.

DIFFERENT TYPES OF ABILITIES

In order to test intelligence, researchers must define what it is they are testing. Over the years, the concept of intelligence has included a large number of factors such as verbal and reasoning abilities, long- and short-term memory, general information, knowledge, and quickness of response. Most researchers recognize the need to distinguish between abilities that appear to be the result of deliberate instructions and absorption of one's culture, such as knowledge about history or a large vocabulary, and those abilities that are acquired as a result of learning how to learn, such as being able to solve problems. Several models of intelligence have been developed to reflect these different types of cognitive abilities.

One such model divides intelligence into two patterns, referred to as fluid and crystallized intelligence (Cattell, 1963; Horn, 1972; Horn & Cattell, 1966). **Crystallized intelligence** is culturally derived—that is, it is a result of accumulated knowledge and of problem-solving techniques learned initially in school and more generally through direct instruction, socialization, and experience; crystallized abilities involve a knowledge of one's language and of the skills and technology of one's culture. Examples of crystallized intelligence include such abilities as vocabulary, general information, social judgment, reasoning ability related to formal logic, and mechanical knowledge such as use of tools and understanding of mechanical principles.

Fluid intelligence refers to strategies for processing information and involves abilities such as seeing relationships among stimulus patterns (like putting puzzles together), drawing inferences about such relationships, and comprehending their implications. As Horn (1982) notes, this component of intelligence represents the fundamental features of reasoning, abstraction, and problem solving that are not dependent on direct training and socialization within a culture. Research suggests that fluid intelligence is directly linked to the condition of the nervous system (Anstey, Stankow, & Lord, 1993). This finding explains why fluid intelligence is more affected than crystallized intelligence by hereditary factors and by injury to the central nervous system.

What is the relevance of fluid and crystallized intelligence to aging? As Figure 15–1 demonstrates, fluid intelligence peaks between the ages of 20 and 30 and declines thereafter. Crystallized intelligence, on the other hand, increases as one gets older (Horn, 1982; Horn & Donaldson, 1980). Thus, with age, people decline in their ability to process information, but improve in their ability to produce knowledge.

Baltes and his colleagues (Baltes, Smith, & Staudinger, 1992) have proposed a dual-process model of intelligence that builds on the earlier distinction between fluid and crystallized intelligence. Baltes's model distinguishes between the mechanics and pragmatics of intelligence. The **mechanics of intelligence** is similar to

crystallized intelligence
Abilities that depend on the individual's acquisition of information and skills important to his or her culture.

fluid intelligence
Abilities that enable a person to perceive relationships, draw inferences, conceptualize abstract information, and comprehend implications.

mechanics of intelligence
Part of the dual-process model of intelligence that pertains to the biologically and genetically controlled basic means of processing information.

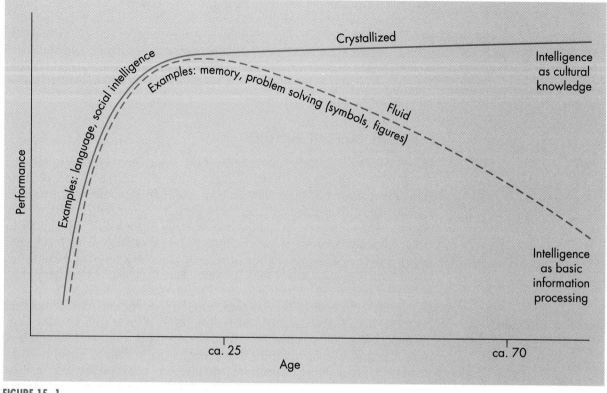

FIGURE 15-1

Changes in fluid and crystallized intelligence over the adult years.

pragmatics of intelligence
Part of the dual-process model of intelligence that describes culturally dependent, practical knowledge and applications that accumulate with age.

fluid abilities and refers to the means of processing information that are influenced by the neurological status and genetic makeup of the adult. With aging, there is a decline in cognitive mechanics. Examples of the mechanics of intelligence include visual and motor memory, categorization skills, and sensory discrimination.

In contrast, cognitive pragmatics improve with age. **Pragmatics of intelligence** refers to knowledge about facts and procedures; the knowledge is rich in content, embedded in culture, and derived from a variety of experiences. Expertise, wisdom, common sense, and specialized skills are all examples of pragmatic intelligence. Pragmatic intelligence is similar to crystallized intelligence, but covers a much wider range of skills and abilities; these abilities are typically passed on from one generation to the next within cultures through direct instruction and indirect socialization in the form of family stories and role models.

FOCUS ON CULTURE

The image of the "wise old person" who contributes to the community is a dominant theme in several non-Western cultures and in many Native American tribes. People within these cultures value the experiences and ideas that their elderly members pass on to them. In what ways might cultural values enhance the cognitive well-being of elderly people?

Aging brings about a decline in cognitive mechanics as a result of genetically programmed changes. These declines are more pronounced in middle and late adulthood, when sexual and physical maturity also declines. On the other hand, cognitive pragmatics are not dependent on genetics but rather on the experience cultivated within the culture. To the extent that cultures provide opportunities for people to access and practice new skills and knowledge, such as by going to college, there are gains in cognitive pragmatics well into late adulthood.

INTERPRETING AGE-RELATED COGNITIVE DECLINE

If intellectual performance does decrease during late adulthood—even if only in select areas—it appears that the decrease is not experienced equally by all people. One interesting theory is that "age is kinder to the more able"—that is, people with high ability show less decline in old age than do people with low ability. Since higher abilities tend to be related to higher education levels (and higher income levels), it has also been suggested that well-educated individuals experience less, if any, decline. One 20-year follow-up of 80-year-old subjects supports both these hypotheses—at least for a sample that included a wide range of intellectual abilities (Blum & Jarvik, 1975).

intellectual plasticity
The range of intellectual performance a person displays under different environmental conditions.

The researchers suggest that keeping oneself mentally active throughout life, including the older years, provides protection against intellectual decline: "Use it or lose it." This view is supported by the work of Schultz, Kaye, and Hoyer (1980) and Denney (1982), who found that individuals who continued to use their cognitive abilities on a regular basis into their older years were much less likely to show a decline in intelligence. The work of Baltes and Willis (1980) is also relevant to this issue. They have been concerned with the older adult's degree of **intellectual plasticity,** which they define as the range of intellectual performance a person displays under different environmental conditions. Using extensive training procedures to enrich the intellectual functioning of their subjects, Baltes and Willis have shown that older people have a relatively high level of intellectual plasticity—that is, their performance of unexercised abilities can be improved considerably through intervention and training. Thus, loss as a result of disuse can be regained by deliberate training.

These results have obvious practical implications for the education and re-training of the elderly. Recall that Mu Qi taught himself to read and speak English in late adulthood. It is not unusual to discover elderly students enrolled in adult-education courses that are offered in many communities, or in painting or poetry classes presented in retirement complexes. There is a growing trend for elderly people to continue their education. At least 1 out of every 20 adults over the age of 60 is enrolled in an educational class of some sort. In the United States, specialized programs for the elderly have emerged. One such program is the Elder-hostel, a network of colleges and universities that provide short-term inexpensive courses for retired people, who live in dormitories while attending college classes. If a person is provided with opportunity and encouragement, the ability to learn continues throughout the lifespan.

Other researchers believe that health-related factors and neurological intactness are associated with performance decrements in the elderly. In what has become a classic study, Birren and his colleagues (Birren, Butler, Greenhouse, Sokoloff, & Yarrow, 1963) examined physiological, intellectual, and personality

At least one of every twenty adults older than 60 is enrolled in an educational class of some sort. This woman received her degree at age 104!

functioning in young and elderly men. The latter were grouped into two categories: those who were in optimal health in every regard, and those who were without obvious clinical symptoms but were found to have mild forms of disease through extensive examinations. In the majority of areas measured, members of the less healthy, older group were functioning not only below younger subjects, but also below optimally healthy, older subjects. In the area of intelligence, the less healthy group obtained poorer scores than the healthy older group on 21 of 23 tests. Of particular interest, however, was the fact that on tests of verbal intelligence both older groups outperformed the younger group, whereas on tests measuring psychomotor speed (e.g., reaction time) the reverse was found. This pattern supports the hypothesis that verbal conceptual ability does not ordinarily decline with age and, in fact, may continue to increase, whereas skills dependent upon speed of central nervous system transmission do show age-related decline.

The study by Birren and his associates is important because it points to the adverse impact of disease, even a mild degree of disease, on the adaptive functioning of older people. When the elderly are free of disease, there is relatively little difference between the old and the young, with the major exception of a slowing down of central nervous system activity.

Another factor that has been linked to cognitive deficits in the elderly is their level of social interaction. Individuals who are isolated socially, as many older people are, have less opportunity to practice their intellectual skills than individuals who are more active. Limited contact and conversation with other people prevent the elderly from receiving information and feedback from others, which is

Elderly people who live in institutional settings typically perform less well on tests of cognitive skills.

competence

What an individual knows or is capable of doing under ideal conditions.

performance

A person's actual level of functioning in a situation or particular task.

important for correcting misperceptions, reducing egocentrism, and in general, stimulating cognitive growth.

The impact of social interaction on cognitive functioning in the elderly is well documented in the work of Dolen and Bearison (1982). These researchers found that the level of social interaction among a group of American subjects aged 65 to 89 years was a more sensitive predictor of social-cognitive reasoning than the subjects' ages. They suggested that their findings provided evidence to support programs designed to facilitate mental functioning in the elderly through enhanced social activity. Minnie and Mu Qi remain vital and alert in part because of the many family and social activities in which they are involved.

One other interpretation of the relatively low test scores achieved by the elderly rests on the distinction between **competence** and **performance** (Flavell & Wohlwill, 1969). Technically, competence is defined as what the individual knows or could do, whereas performance represents what the individual actually does in executing the task at hand. Utilizing this distinction, some psychologists suggest that the decreased performance of the elderly does not necessarily indicate decreased competence. For example, older people may perform poorly because they are not motivated. They may be put off by experimental procedures and awkward questionnaires. They may be unable to relate to younger researchers, or even to hear or understand the instructions. In some areas, their competence may be high, but their skills may be rusty. Older subjects may be in a position similar to that of the person who remembers having mastered Latin or the violin: They are still capable of functioning at a high level, but probably cannot do so at the present moment.

With each advancing year, the greater is the possibility that skills will fall into disuse. The decline in cognitive functions in the elderly may thus represent an increasingly wider gap between competence and performance, rather than a degeneration in ability. If this is so, then the performance of older people might be

Research Perspective

MEASURING WISDOM

While most people accept the notion that wisdom comes with age, very little effort has been made to define and measure it. Wisdom is considered to be related to but much more encompassing than intelligence or expertise. A person can be intelligent according to standardized IQ tests but not necessarily be considered wise. Similarly, an expert can accumulate a lot of information and skills about a narrowly defined body of knowledge without being deemed wise. Recently, researchers (Baltes & Staudinger, 1993; Birren & Fisher, 1990; Sternberg, 1990) have directed their attention to identifying what characteristics define a wise person, what behaviors and processes indicate wisdom, and how they can be measured.

Baltes and his colleagues (Baltes, Smith, & Staudinger, 1992; Baltes & Staudinger, 1993) suggest that there are commonly accepted characteristics associated with wisdom. First of all, wisdom is the result of experience and thus increases with age. Secondly, wisdom rep-

resents expert knowledge that can be applied to everyday living. Wisdom also involves a sense of wanting to seek out solutions that will contribute to the common good. Wise people are able to put their personal needs and desires aside and consider a problem from the perspective of the larger group or community. Thus, wisdom is considered to be both a value and a virtue.

Baltes went beyond these general assumptions to propose five criteria that define wisdom (see Figure 15–2). Wise people are knowledgeable about the essence of the human condition; they are sensitive to the impact of culture and socialization and to the uncertainties in life. They recognize that different developmental pathways through life exist, each of which are equally valid. They appreciate the changes that people go through in their journeys through life and have developed strategies for dealing with these changes. Wise people are self-aware; they recognize and accept their strengths and weaknesses and do not expect that they will always have the "right" answers. They see themselves and others as fallible, but capable of changing as a result of their mistakes.

Thus defining wisdom, the researchers developed a series of

dilemmas to measure wisdom-related knowledge and skills in different age populations. The dilemmas dealt with life problems such as the following: Imagine that a good friend of yours calls you up and tells you that she can't go on anymore and has decided to commit suicide. What would you be thinking about? How would you deal with this situation?

Other dilemmas dealt with such problems as a 15-year old who wanted to get married, a 60-year old woman's conflict between family and career needs, and a 28-year old man who must decide whether to take a job that will require his family to relocate. The researchers scored their subjects responses to these dilemmas using the criteria illustrated in Table 15–1 on page 604. Only about 5% of the subjects' responses were rated as "wise," providing support for the commonly held belief that wisdom is a rare characteristic. Much to the researchers surprise, younger and older adults did not differ in their overall performance (Staudinger, Smith, & Baltes, 1992). But older adults did score higher than young adults on dilemmas that were specific to their own age group; furthermore, older adults were fairly well represented among the group of people who scored highly on wisdom.

FIGURE 15–2

A model of wisdom as expert knowledge and behaviors.

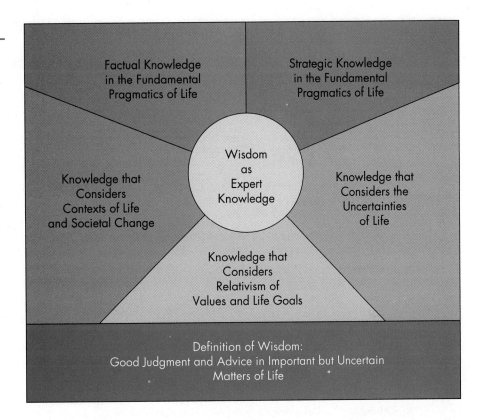

Factual Knowledge in the Fundamental Pragmatics of Life

Strategic Knowledge in the Fundamental Pragmatics of Life

Wisdom as Expert Knowledge

Knowledge that Considers Contexts of Life and Societal Change

Knowledge that Considers the Uncertainties of Life

Knowledge that Considers Relativism of Values and Life Goals

Definition of Wisdom:
Good Judgment and Advice in Important but Uncertain Matters of Life

improved relatively easily. For example, more appropriate rewards might be introduced to counter poor motivation; short-term retraining might be expected to result in higher functioning for skills that have fallen into disuse.

CREATIVITY

While most researchers interested in intellectual functioning across the lifespan have focused on the skills and knowledge represented in standardized intelligence tests or Piagetian-type measures, others have sought to examine the more creative aspects of human functioning (Sternberg & Lubart, 1992). One researcher (Lehman, 1953) studied the quality of the creative work of recognized artists and scientists and found that his subjects made fewer high-quality creative contributions as they became older. Creative breakthroughs were more often the work of young adults; there was a falling off in the quality of creative productions in middle age. Another researcher (Dennis, 1966) studied productivity—that is, the number of contributions, regardless of quality—made by men who had lived to 80 years of age. He found that artists, such as musicians and poets, reach their peak productivity earlier than scientists and scholars. However, scientists and scholars whose creative work involved extensive collection and evaluation of data, such as historians and geologists, were especially productive in middle and late adulthood.

What factors might be related to the decline in creativity of artists from young adulthood through old age, and to the later productivity of scientists and scholars? Bromley (1967) measured creativity in three groups of adults with mean group

WISDOM-RELATED CRITERIA FOR EVALUATING RESPONSES TO DILEMMA OF 15-YEAR-OLD GIRL WHO WANTS TO GET MARRIED IMMEDIATELY: WHAT SHOULD SHE DO AND CONSIDER?

CRITERION	EXAMPLES
Factual knowledge	Who, when, where; examples of possible different situations; multiple options (forms of love and marriage)
Procedural knowledge	Strategies of information search, decision making, and advice giving; timing of advice; monitoring of emotional reactions; cost-benefit analysis scenarios; means-ends scenarios
Lifespan contextualism	Age-graded contexts (e.g., issues of adolescence); culturally graded contexts; idiosyncratic contexts across time and life domains (e.g., terminal illness); interrelations, tensions, priorities of life domains
Relativism	Religious and personal preferences; current versus future values; historical period; cultural relativism
Uncertainty	No perfect solution; optimization of gain versus loss; future not fully predictable; backup solutions

Abbreviated Examples of Responses

Low wisdom score	A 15-year old girl wants to get married? No, no way. Marrying at age 15 would be utterly wrong. One has to tell the girl that marriage is not possible. It would be irresponsible to support such an idea. No, this is just a crazy idea.
High wisdom score	Well, on the surface, this seems like an easy problem. On average, marriage for 15-year-old girls is not a good thing. I guess many girls think about it when they fall in love for the first time. And, then, there are situations where the average case does not fit. Perhaps in this instance, special life circumstances are involved, such as that the girl has a terminal illness. Or this girl may not be from this country. Perhaps she lives in another culture and historical period. Before I offer a final evaluation I would need more information.

TABLE 15–1

Source: From "The Search for a Psychology of Wisdom," by P. Baltes and U. Staudinger, 1993, *Current Directions in Psychological Science, 2,* pp. 75–80.

divergent thinking

A measure of creativity that includes originality, the ability to think of many different ideas appropriate to a situation, and the ability to change and transform ideas from one state to another.

preference for complexity

A measure of creativity regarding the degree to which people seek out intricate and complicated problems and find pleasure in solving them; it has been found to decline with increasing age.

ages of 27, 47, and 67 years. Creativity was measured by asking the subjects to produce unique or novel arrangements and sortings of different colored and shaped blocks. Bromley found that the number of unique responses declined with increased age. People in the 67-year-old mean age group produced only 50 to 60% of the number of responses produced by those in the 27-year-old mean age group. Since all of the subjects were of superior intelligence (their IQ scores ranged from 121 to 123), the researcher excluded the possibility that declines in creativity were due to declines in intelligence. Rather, the age differences were interpreted as a reflection of the combined decline in three cognitive skills: persistence, flexibility of thought, and abstraction.

Alpaugh and Birren (1977) identified two variables that are related to a decline in the creative contributions of older people: divergent thinking and a preference for complexity. **Divergent thinking** includes originality, the ability to think of many different ideas appropriate to a situation, and the ability to change and transform ideas from one state to another. **Preference for complexity** means that people seek out intricate and complicated problems and find pleasure in solving them. Working with a cross-sectional sample of American subjects from 20 to 83 years of age, carefully controlled for education, Alpaugh and Birren found systematic declines in preference for complexity and divergent thinking with increasing age, whereas their measures for intelligence remained constant. They concluded, therefore, that in addition to declines in such factors as energy and vigor, declines in creative production across the lifespan—as related to cognitive processes—can be explained in terms of a decrease in divergent thinking and preference for complexity rather than any decline in intelligence per se.

Other researchers, however, have not confirmed a linear decline in divergent thinking from young adulthood through the elderly years. Jaquish and Ripple (1981) observed that middle-aged adults performed better than younger and older adults on a variety of divergent thinking tasks. Furthermore, these researchers reported that the creative abilities of their middle-aged and elderly subjects were positively correlated with self-esteem. That is, people who had high self-esteem were more likely to be creative. Minnie, described at the beginning of the chapter, is a good example. She felt good enough about herself to consider a creative solution to how she would spend her time during late adulthood.

There are some problems in studying creativity across the lifespan. Measures of creativity in early adulthood may not be equivalent to measures used for an older and more experienced adult population (Romaniuk & Romaniuk, 1981). For example, on a task that asks subjects to think of unusual uses for common objects such as a hammer, knife, or plastic cup, people from different ages or cohort levels may have different levels of experience with the objects. Furthermore, the meaningfulness of the task may vary considerably from one age group to another. What may be a fun and challenging task to a child or teenager may be perceived as trivial and boring to an adult. This may explain Bromley's (1967) finding that creativity declined with age when he asked his subjects to make designs with colored blocks. Thus, while it appears that creativity declines in old age, it is also clear that different measures are needed to fully assess the range of creative skills available to people in late adulthood.

RECAP

The question of whether intelligence (as measured by IQ) declines with age has been studied for many years. Cross-sectional research suggests that there is a drop in IQ with age, while longitudinal and sequential design research suggests that there is little significant decline. Two types of cognitive abilities have been proposed: those dealing with the mechanics of understanding and interpreting information (fluid intelligence) and those dealing with acquisition of culturally dependent and practical skills and knowledge (crystallized intelligence or cognitive pragmatics). Fluid abilities decline with age while crystallized abilities improve. Age differences in intelligence are related to changes in the neurological and biological status of the individual, to people's motivation to perform, and opportunities to learn new skills. Creativity peaks at different times during adulthood, depending on the skills involved, and appears to decline in late adulthood.

PERSONALITY DEVELOPMENT

Old age brings new challenges and new tasks to be faced and mastered. Most older individuals are just as successful or unsuccessful in confronting and handling the developmental tasks of late adulthood as younger individuals are in dealing with the tasks of their respective periods of life. Furthermore, the styles of adjusting are, if anything, more variable during the later years than earlier in life. This is not to deny, however, the seriousness of the problems confronting the aged. Declining health, loss of functions, widowhood, financial problems, loss of social status, social isolation, susceptibility to crime, and impending death are but some of the real problems older Americans face today. Yet face them they do. In fact, the success most older people have in meeting the challenges of old age speaks to a resilience not usually associated with this period in the minds of most individuals. Late adulthood is a time of continued psychological growth—even in the face of physiological decline. In many ways, old age is the time when people reflect on and appreciate their journey throughout life. As they near the end of their travels, they can remember and evaluate their experiences and accomplishments. To what extent did they learn the things they wanted to? What lies ahead in the remainder of life's journey?

DEVELOPMENTAL TASKS IN LATE ADULTHOOD

With an awareness that their travels will end, elderly adults face a new set of developmental tasks. Several people have theorized about what these tasks encompass.

Erikson's Theory

During old age, according to Erikson, people experience the crisis of **ego integrity versus despair** (Erikson, 1963). Integrity is experienced as emotional acceptance of one's life with all of its limitations and with a full awareness of the shortness and finality of life (Erikson, 1976). Despair occurs when people believe that time is now too short—that there is no further chance of finding an alternate path to an acceptable life. As in earlier stages, there is an inner struggle. Even the person who enters old age with a high degree of integrity experiences occasional despair at the thought of death—and disgust at the futility and pettiness of human life. As in the earlier psychosocial stages of Erikson's theory, it is the ratio that is important. The person who achieves a favorable ratio of integrity over despair in the last years attains wisdom: "the detached and yet active concern with life itself, in the face of death itself" (Erikson, 1976).

Stimulated by their own experiences of old age, Erik Erikson and his wife, Joan, elaborated on the challenges in the last stage of personality development (Goleman, 1988). They viewed old age as the time when people integrate into their current lives the lessons they have learned from earlier stages of their lifespan. These well-digested lessons of life become part of wisdom in old age (see Table 15–2). If people have been able to achieve positive resolutions in earlier stages, a sense of integrity and completeness emerges that offsets the despair that physical decline may produce.

Associated with the task of developing ego integrity is a process called the **life review.** As people reach the end of their lives, some organize their memories and reinterpret the actions and decisions that have shaped the course of their lives. Ideally, the life review is a positive experience resulting in integration of the personality. For some, the life review leads to less ego involvement with one's own

ego integrity versus despair
According to Erikson, the primary psychosocial task of late adulthood; ego integrity represents an emotional integration and acceptance of one's life; despair expresses itself as a feeling that one's life has lacked real meaning.

life review
In old age, the process of organizing memories and reinterpreting actions and decisions that have shaped a person's life.

ERIKSON'S STAGES OF DEVELOPMENT

STAGE	CONFLICT AND RESOLUTION	CULMINATION IN OLD AGE
Old Age	Integrity versus despair; wisdom	Existential identity; a sense of integrity strong enough to withstand physical disintegration
Adulthood	Generativity versus stagnation	*Caritas* (charity), caring for others, and agape (love), empathy and concern
Early Adulthood	Intimacy versus isolation; love	Sense of the complexity of relationships; value of tenderness and loving freely
Adolescence	Identity versus confusion; fidelity	Sense of the complexity of life; merger of sensory, logical, and aesthetic perception
School Age	Industry versus inferiority; competence	Humility; acceptance of the course of one's life and unfulfilled hopes
Play Age	Initiative versus guilt; purpose	Humor; empathy; resilience
Early Childhood	Autonomy versus shame; will	Acceptance of the cycle of life, from integration to disintegration
Infancy	Basic trust versus mistrust; hope	Appreciation of interdependence and relatedness

TABLE 15–2

Source: From D. Goleman, "Erikson, in His Own Old Age, Expands His View of Life," 1988, *The New York Times,* pp. C1, C14. Adapted with permission.

situation and to more concern with the world in general, a quality associated with wisdom (Baltes & Staudinger, 1993). For others, life review produces nostalgia and perhaps a touch of regret. In still others, it engenders anxiety, guilt, depression, and despair: Instead of reflecting on a full life, the person feels cheated and enraged (Butler, 1971). Often, elderly people share their thoughts about their lives with relatives and friends as they go through the life review process. Some non-Western societies, like the !Kung and Balinese people, institutionalize this process of life review as a privilege of the elderly. Elders are expected to pass on the wisdom they have gained to younger members of the community.

Peck's Theory   According to Peck (1968), continued psychological growth in the aging years centers on the outcome of three major developmental tasks. In late adulthood, most people must come to grips with *occupational retirement*. They must be able to find personal satisfaction and self-worth beyond the work activities that have been important for self-definition in earlier periods. Peck summarizes this issue in the question that he believes each person must ask him- or herself during late adulthood: "Am I a worthwhile person only insofar as I can do a full-time job; or can I be worthwhile in other, different ways—as a performer of several other roles, and also because of the kind of person I am?" (Peck, 1968). To the extent that older people can redefine themselves meaningfully in areas other than work, they are more likely to face the future with greater interest, vitality, and a sense of integrity. Having a hobby or interests beyond their work often helps people in making this transition.

As this woman spends time with her grandchild, she reflects on her own life as mother and, later, grandmother. A life review helps people develop a sense of integrity.

A second theme of old age concerns inevitable *physical decline.* People who define happiness and well-being primarily along physical dimensions are often seriously disturbed by the bodily changes they experience in old age—even more than by the changes in middle age. They become so preoccupied with their physical decline that they may experience a profound sense of despair and disgust with themselves and with life itself. Older people, according to Peck, must shift their values away from the physical domain (if they have not already done so) and into the domain of interpersonal relations and mental activities. It is through these areas of human functioning, Peck says, that the elderly are most likely to experience feelings of satisfaction and fulfillment.

The final theme emphasized by Peck is directly linked to *human mortality.* Each person in old age must face the realization of impending death; he or she must try to accept not only the inevitability of fate, but also find meaning in it. This may well be the most significant and challenging task confronting the aging adult. Like Erikson, Peck believes that the answer is to be found in the feelings of satisfaction with their families and accomplishments. For some, the answers are derived within their cultural and religious values. Balinese people, for example, believe that they will be reborn into their families several generations removed. Thus the ending of their physical lives is not feared since it is viewed as a transition to another form of their spiritual life.

Overview of Theories   It is obvious that there are many common threads in the portrayals of old age by Erikson and Peck, as well as by other theorists

(Havighurst, 1974; Neugarten, 1973). Each views the central developmental tasks of this period in terms of the challenges of declining health, reduced generativity, acknowledgment and acceptance of one's mortality, and, above all, the integration of feelings about the self and life in general. Not so obvious, however, is the assumption made by these researchers that success in meeting these challenges depends, to a great extent, on the success experienced with earlier developmental tasks.

ETHNICITY, SOCIAL IMAGE, AND SELF-CONCEPT

As noted at the beginning of this chapter, the image of old age in modern Western societies has not been a positive one. Take a quick glance at birthday greeting cards and you will notice how many funny (but not so funny) references there are to the negative qualities associated with growing older. These negative images not only affect older people, they influence the way younger people view older adults. Several attitudinal studies have shown that young people perceive the old as lonely, resistant to change, and failing in physical and mental powers (Brewer, Dull, & Lui, 1981; Hummert, 1990; Schmidt & Boland, 1986). The attitudes of American high school and college youth toward the elderly and their social role are mostly negative. The older the adult, the more unpleasant he or she appears to the younger subject (Hickey & Kalish, 1968).

Most of the research on old age among Hispanic people has involved Mexican Americans. Mexican Americans perceive the onset of old age as occurring earlier in the lifespan than do non-Hispanic people (Becerra & Shaw, 1984). In part, this may be because they equate the beginning of old age with poor health, which occurs earlier in the lifespan for Mexican Americans, many of whom have poor access to health care and adequate nutrition. For some, the onset of old age is marked by the ending of their work roles; if their jobs are physically demanding, they most likely will end their work at an earlier age than most people. Despite a cultural expectation that their families will care for them in old age, Mexican Americans do not differ from Anglos in viewing old age as undesirable (Markides & Mindel, 1987).

In traditional Japanese families, men at the age of 60 are ceremoniously honored with the rank of elder. They have earned the freedom to enjoy the leisure of their old age. Wives who have achieved the age of 60 are awarded a new power and authority in their position as the mother-in-law (Kiefer, 1990). The prestige and power that the Japanese elderly experience affects their expectations of aging. Perhaps the honor and gratitude offered to elderly family members can explain the relatively low rates of mental illness among elderly Japanese Americans (Kikimura & Kitano, 1981).

As for the elderly themselves, probably one of the most difficult things about aging is learning to define oneself as old. One 10-year longitudinal study found that nearly half of the subjects 65 years and older identified themselves as middle-aged (Turner, 1979). Unfortunately, the elderly cannot help but agree with some of the negative cultural stereotypes of old age. After all, they themselves have held these stereotypes most of their lives. A man who is biased against women, or a white man who dislikes African Americans, is never himself in the position of transforming into the object of his own prejudice. However, a young person *does* eventually become an old person. Activist groups that represent the elderly say that they must combat stereotypes held by the elderly about themselves as well as stereotypes held by younger generations. Still, the fact that some studies have found a decrease in self-concept and self-esteem in old age must be interpreted with caution.

Kaplan and Pokorny (1970) argue that it is not aging per se that influences self-concept, but rather events that the elderly experience during this phase of life—for example, declining health, lower income, and living alone. In support of this position, Flanagan (1981) found that the two most important factors influencing quality-of-life ratings among elderly Americans were lack of money and health problems. Older adults who are in poor health and lack adequate financial resources are more likely to experience problems in adjustment and to have negative views of themselves and of aging.

Regardless of long-held prejudices, older people must at some point face up to thinking of themselves as "old" and adjust their self-concepts accordingly. Many factors enter into the definition. One is awareness of social norms. According to the classic study by Neugarten and her associates, an "old" man is between 65 and 75 years of age; an "old" woman, between 60 and 75 (Neugarten, Moore, & Lowe, 1965). These age-norm differences are reinforced and perpetuated by social policy. For example, in the United States, under most circumstances people become eligible for Social Security at age 65. In some cities, they may receive special senior citizen passes to the movies or on intercity transportation upon reaching their 60th or 55th birthdays. All these "rites of passage" may be expected to contribute to a person's awareness of advancing age.

Double Jeopardy: The Aged Minority Group Member

Elderly Americans are members of a disadvantaged group. Ageist attitudes have contributed to the perception that older people have less money, less power, less ability, more health problems, and a limited future. Even when these stereotypical views do not apply specifically to the individual, they do affect the social services and resources available to them as elderly people. Thus, an older person is seen as being "in jeopardy." This jeopardy has its roots in false beliefs about the elderly. Thus, many physicians fail to diagnose problems of the elderly because they see them as unable to change or benefit from treatment because they are old. Older people are frequently denied access to more appropriate health care because they cannot afford to pay for the services (Rodeheaver & Datan, 1988).

Being a member of a minority group is another form of jeopardy. Racial and ethnic prejudice and discrimination have a long history in the United States. African Americans, Hispanic Americans, Native Americans, and Asian Americans have had to bear the burden of unfavorable stereotypes, job and housing discrimination, and racial and ethnic inequality throughout their lives. In addition, sexist attitudes have restricted opportunities and limited resources for women. Women constitute the majority of the elderly in the United States because they outlive men. They also are likely to be poor, widowed, and expected to carry the burden of caregiving responsibilities within their families (Rodeheaver & Datan, 1988).

The concept of *double jeopardy* refers to the risks associated with having double, or in the case of minority women, triple membership in a subculture that has received unequal treatment. The term was originally used to refer to the situation of African Americans who entered old age with the disadvantages associated with prejudice and discrimination—namely poverty, poor health, and limited resources to solve these problems. Double jeopardy is now applied to women and ethnic minorities who have not enjoyed the privileges and opportunities afforded to white males. Other subgroups, such as the physically and mentally disabled elderly, could also be viewed as being in a double jeopardy situation.

The health of African American aged people is poorer than that of elderly whites. African Americans have higher rates of hypertension, dental problems, and diabetes than do whites. Elderly African Americans, and especially African American women, have less money than whites, which further restricts their access to medical and mental health care. However, the extended kinship network of African American families provides greater support and care for their elderly than that provided by white families.

Research concerning aged Mexican Americans suggests that although they suffer from poverty, poor nutrition, and limited education, they appear not to suffer as much as African Americans from poorer health in old age (Markides & Mindel, 1987). Finally, most Native American elderly live on reservations and are out of reach of many of the services that other communities make available to the aged. As a group, Native Americans are the poorest in the United States. Their life expectancy is shorter and they also suffer from poor health and nutrition.

What is remarkable about individuals in double jeopardy situations is not that they suffer from prejudice and discrimination, but how well they cope under these disadvantaged social and economic conditions. More research is needed to identify the strengths and characteristics that make these people psychological survivors in old age.

PERSONALITY, SOCIAL INTERACTION, AND ADJUSTMENT

With respect to personality adjustment, it is clear that age is a poor index of differences between people (Neugarten, 1977). Work and family roles, financial resources, and physical health appear to be more important to adult adjustment than the exact number of birthdays that the individual has survived. In an attempt to understand the way in which older people handle the many changes they experience (in themselves, at work, with their families, and so on) psychologists (Moos & Lemke, 1985) have investigated older people's perceptions of, and interactions with, their particular environments—environments that have become increasingly risky, dangerous, and complex in modern technological societies.

Studies of elderly subjects suggest that people gradually reduce or simplify their interactions with others as they age. Older adults, for example, assume fewer roles such as homemaker, worker, or volunteer (Neugarten, 1973, 1977; Palmore, 1981); they engage less often in family and community activities. The drop-off in social interaction, however, is not a sharp one, but rather a gradual decline in each successive age group following the mid-50s (Havighurst, Neugarten, & Tobin, 1968). This is not, of course, a function of personality alone. Older people may have fewer opportunities to interact with others. Keep in mind that in cultures in which the elderly have higher status and in which community members are more interdependent, there may be no decline in social involvement with age—in fact, their interactions may even increase.

Furthermore, the fact that older people show a decline in social interaction should not be construed to mean that friends and social relationships, in general, are unimportant to them. Friends often help the older adult adjust to, and

Maintaining an active life enhances the chances of successful aging in late life. These active senior citizens belong to a cross-country ski club and enjoy regular outings.

interiority
A tendency of an older person to become increasingly preoccupied with his or her inner life.

disengagement theory
An explanation of the changes in elderly people that lead to reflection, self-exploration, and a reduction in social and psychological investments; gradual disengagement of the person from society is said to lead to a sense of well-being and satisfaction; the opposite of activity theory.

compensate for, the many losses experienced during aging. Thus, friendship and social interaction can be an important factor in the adjustment of the elderly (Tesch, 1983).

Preoccupation with one's inner life seems to become more intense in old age, leading some theorists to describe increased **interiority** as a developmental change of this period (Neugarten, 1973). Older people tend to move toward more self-centered positions. They are concerned more with their own individual problems and less with the problems of the outside world (Leon, Gillum, Gillum, & Gouze, 1979). Some researchers have proposed a **disengagement theory** to account for this change. Disengagement theory predicts a decrease in role activity and gradual physical and psychological detachment from others with increasing age. The process seems to be a reciprocal one between the elderly person and society. As individuals gradually disengage themselves from society, society offers them fewer roles. If the two processes occur at about the same time, then a good adjustment to aging is likely. However, if a person is cut off from society prematurely by forced retirement and loss of social contacts, there are likely to be problems in adjustment. Gradual disengagement of the person from society is said to lead to a sense of psychological well-being and satisfaction (Cumming & Henry, 1961).

Disengagement theory has been criticized on several points. The predictions that high activity would be associated with low morale and that disengagement is inevitable have not been supported by research studies (Maddox, 1968; Palmore, 1981; Reichard, Livson, & Peterson, 1962). The tendency for older adults to withdraw from social interaction is not universal. It is influenced not only by age but by the health or well-being of their spouse, their financial status, their work environment, and the culture. People who maintain social contacts are more likely to do so because the social environment is supportive. Other researchers have found that disengagement occurs about two years before people die (Lieberman & Coplan, 1970).

activity theory

The belief of some researchers that maintaining an earlier level of activity results in successful aging; the opposite of disengagement theory.

Some researchers have proposed an **activity theory** that suggests the opposite of disengagement theory: Maintaining earlier levels of activity results in successful aging. With declining mobility and incomes, older people may have to replace more strenuous or expensive activities with equally enjoyable events. The key element in activity theory is involvement and engagement. Research findings suggest that much depends on the individual's style of aging. Some people can easily relinquish tasks and responsibilities, while others cannot. Some other people are depressed by any reduction in social opportunities. Still others who have long had low levels of interaction accompanied by high satisfaction show relatively little change as they grow older. Personality type and long-standing lifestyles seem to predict the way in which individuals adapt to society as they age.

BRIEF REVIEW

In old age, people undergo numerous physical, cognitive, and socioemotional changes. The variation among the elderly in the extent and patterning of change is considerable.

Ageism occurs when people are negatively judged on the basis of age alone. The negative consequences of ageism can affect the overall experience of growing older. Cultures vary in the esteem they associate with aging.

The aging process cannot be satisfactorily explained by a single theory. Aging can be a result of (1) an accumulation of errors that occur in the transformation at the cellular level; (2) the wear and tear on the body over the years; (3) an inadequate delivery of essential nutrients to the cells, which then deteriorate and die (deprivation theory); (4) a breakdown in the immune system; (5) an accumulation of stresses over the years; or (6) an accumulation of metabolic wastes. It is unclear whether the explanatory factors are causes or symptoms of aging. Research has shown a definite link between heredity and longevity.

Senescence refers to primary aging—the normal age-related changes that occur in response to biological decline. Changes in physical appearance include wrinkles, graying of hair, hair loss, age spots, loss of teeth, and postural stoop. The major systems of the body—cardiovascular, pulmonary, digestive, and neural—continue to decline in efficiency. There is an acceleration in sensory decline, particularly in hearing. Secondary aging refers to decline that results from external factors such as stress, abuse, or disease.

A slowing down of the central nervous system accounts for many of the problems manifested by the elderly in movement and mental functioning. A regular and moderate level of physical activity and exercise can help slow down the aging process while helping older people to feel better.

Older people are more susceptible to disease and less likely to recover quickly. In old age, people are more likely to suffer from such mental disorders as depression, chronic anxiety, and hypochondriasis. Older white males have the highest suicide rate of any group of individuals. Loss is a common factor in depression in old age.

Dementia is a common condition in old age characterized by declines in physical, cognitive, and personality behaviors as a result of brain deterioration or damage. Alzheimer's disease, the most common dementia, is a chronic and progressive disorder that can last for 10 to 15 years or more before the victim dies. Multi-infarct dementia refers to brain damage as a result of a series of strokes or mini-strokes brought on by reduced blood flow to the brain.

Some theorists propose two components of intelligence. Peaking in early adulthood, fluid abilities are closely related to neurophysiological intactness. Crystallized abilities, which are the result of acculturation, remain unchanged or even increase during middle age. Cognitive mechanics decline with age, while cognitive pragmatics increase with age and experience. Declines are not experienced equally by all people. Better-educated and brighter individuals tend to experience little if any decline in intelligence.

Many factors affect the ability of older people to perform well on intelligence tests, including the pacing of the problems, an over-arousal of the autonomic nervous system, and a lack of motivation. Some researchers do not believe that intelligence declines in older people who are healthy and socially active. Other researchers believe that the cognitive changes that do take place are adaptive for the development and expression of wisdom.

Some expressions of creativity decline with age. Divergent thinking and preference for complexity also decline with age and may contribute to the decline in creativity. Different kinds of creativity may emerge at different ages. According to Erikson, the crisis of old age is that of ego integrity versus despair. Most old people continue to grow psychologically as they face the challenges of old age. Old people must adjust to retirement, physical aging, and the inevitability of their own deaths. Compounding these problems is the negative image of age held by most members of society, including the aged themselves.

There are two opposing theories concerning the best means of adapting to old age. The disengagement theory suggests that old people can adjust to aging best by reducing their involvement with other people and situations and becoming more interested in themselves. Other researchers, however, do not agree. They feel that activity and involvement keep a person healthy and youthful. The way they have lived their lives seems to predict the adaptation to aging of individual old people.

KEY TERMS

activity theory (613)
ageism (578)
Alzheimer's disease (592)
cataracts (584)
cellular error (582)
competence (601)
crystallized intelligence (597)
dementia (592)
depressive reaction (590)
deprivation theory (582)
disengagement theory (612)
divergent thinking (604)

ego integrity versus despair (606)
fluid intelligence (597)
free radicals (582)
functional disorders (590)
glaucoma (584)
Hayflick limit (582)
hypokinetic disease (589)
intellectual plasticity (599)
interiority (612)
life review (606)
mechanics of intelligence (597)
multi-infarct dementia (MID) (593)

organic brain syndromes (590)
osteoporosis (583)
performance (601)
postural stoop (583)
pragmatics of intelligence (598)
preference for complexity (604)
presbycusis (585)
respite worker (594)
secondary aging (583)
senescence (583)
stress theory (582)
wear-and-tear theory (582)

REVIEW QUESTIONS

If you can answer these questions, you have a good understanding of the material in this chapter. If a question seems difficult, go back to the text and review the topic.

1. What is ageism? How does it affect the quality of life for elderly people? Cite examples of cultural variations in ageism.

2. Describe and give examples of the two types of theories offered to explain aging.

3. Distinguish between primary and secondary aging. Give examples of each. At what stage in the lifespan does primary aging begin?

4. Describe the changes in the functioning of the sensory system that occur in late adulthood. In what ways can these declines be accommodated?

5. What are the signs of an aging nervous system? Cite some examples.

6. Discuss the impact of a sedentary life on health during late adulthood. What recommendations are offered to elderly people who need to increase physical activity?

7. Distinguish between functional disorders and organic brain syndromes. Cite an example of each, and describe the symptoms and treatment for each disorder.

8. What are the symptoms of Alzheimer's disease? What is known about its cause and cure?

9. What are the limitations in using cross-sectional research to study the decline in IQ among the elderly? Discuss the impact of intellectual activity on cognitive development in late adulthood.

10. Describe the difference between crystallized and fluid intelligence. How do cognitive mechanics differ from cognitive pragmatics?

11. How can the age-related declines in cognitive skills be explained? Offer at least four interpretations. Why is it important to distinguish between performance and competence in testing the elderly?

12. Describe the positive lessons that can be learned from earlier stages of life that contribute to a sense of integrity and wisdom during old age.

13. What developmental tasks are associated with late adulthood? How does the treatment of elderly within a culture affect the individual's sense of self in old age?

14. Compare disengagement theory with activity theory of adjustment to late adulthood.

OBSERVATIONAL ACTIVITY

MEDIA STEREOTYPING OF THE AGED

The image of old age in our society is anything but positive. Among other things, older people are said to be lonely, fearful, sexless, rigid, self-centered, and "out of date." Research, however, suggests that most of these stereotypes do not accurately represent the majority of older adults. Why then do the stereotypes persist? Some people believe that the media play a major role in fostering the continuation of such stereotyping.

Observe a random selection of television shows during prime time over a 2-week period. Focus on the roles and behaviors of older adults in these shows, as well as other people's behavior toward the elderly.

1. To what extent are the elderly portrayed as figures of authority? As wise people?

2. Are most older adults on television active and vigorous or are they portrayed as passive and unenergetic?

3. What role does sexuality play in the lives of older television characters?

4. Are the stereotypes attributed to the aged different for men and women? Different for individuals according to racial group or social class?

5. What are the attitudes of most younger adults toward the elderly in the majority of television shows? Do they perceive the elderly as competent and adaptable or as "senile" and unchangeable?

From your observations, draw some conclusions concerning the role of television in perpetuating negative stereotypes about the elderly. Are any subgroups of older adults more likely to be stereotyped than others?

CHAPTER 16

Late Adulthood: Family Life, Social Relations, and Retirement

At 81 years of age Hajiya Asabe was in the *tsohuwa* (old woman) stage of her life. She was a Hausa Muslim living in Kaduna, Nigeria. In addition to being the oldest, she was the most powerful and respected woman within her compound. Hajiya Asabe served as the link between the younger women in her compound and the outside world, from which the women were secluded according to social and religious custom.

The younger women were dependent upon her for news about women and families in other compounds and for the goods she brought them from the market. Whenever a dispute arose, Hajiya was the one to whom people turned for help. She set the standards for how men and women were to behave within the compound. Hajiya assisted in birth and death rites, naming ceremonies, and arranging marriages.

As an old woman she could enter the mosque to pray alongside the men. But most important, Hajiya enjoyed her freedom in old age. She was free from caring for children, husband, and mother-in-law. She was free to earn her own money as a midwife. She used her wealth to finance a pilgrimage to Mecca, a lifelong quest that earned her additional status among her people.

In contrast, Bill's life had not been a smooth one. His first marriage lasted only a few years. His second marriage lasted longer—15 years—and produced three children, but eventually it too dissolved. As with his first marriage, Bill was unable to fully comprehend the basis for his wife's decision to end the marriage.

Although Bill was defensive about his two divorces, he did acknowledge that he placed his desire for success ahead of his family. Ever since his late teens, he wanted more than anything to be successful in his career. In fact, he more than wanted it; he seemed to "need" it. Over the years, he buried himself in his career and eventually started his own accounting firm. After many years, Bill had achieved his goal of success, at least financially.

Now, at age 69, Bill worries about his forthcoming retirement. He regrets that he has no one with whom to share his success. He never remarried after his second divorce, and his relationship with his children is distant. In essence, he is alone. The thought of death frightens him. For Bill, the aging years have been years of loss and loneliness.

Bill and Hajiya Asabe represent two very different approaches to old age. Their individual adjustments have been influenced by choices they made in earlier stages of life and by the customs and expectations of their cultures. For most people who continue their life journey into late adulthood, the quality of their lives is heavily affected by the context of their family life and social relations. Certainly the changes in physical and cognitive capabilities that accompany aging influence the type of lifestyle people adopt during the last period of the lifespan. But their successful adjustment will more often center on how they spend their time after retirement.

FAMILY LIFE

My father died at the age of 75, leaving my mother as the head of our large family. In the years that followed, my mother has taken on an even more central role in the family. She is the one who gathers and disseminates information about the activities, accomplishments, and sometimes difficulties of my siblings and myself, our children, and close family friends. Her involvement in our family life not only helps keep us all connected but also provides her with an important incentive that keeps her life meaningful.

Because they have watched their own parents travel into old age, married couples who enter late adulthood together know that they can anticipate some fairly major changes in the composition and function of their families when they reach late adulthood. Retirement and the death of a spouse are two such changes that will have a profound impact on the quality of family life. For people who never married, or for those who have divorced and remarried, the last stage in the family life cycle may differ. Some people choose not to retire, or begin a second career after retirement. Some, who married and had children in their 40s, may still have teenage children living with them as they approach retirement.

In Western cultures, improved medical care, better nutrition, and a greater number and quality of social services have helped to ease the burdens of aging for older adults, thereby facilitating longer lifespans. In the past, it was rare for an individual to live into the late 70s, 80s, or 90s. Now it is relatively common. While earlier generations of married couples never even dreamed of living past the age of 60, today many couples are reaching late adulthood together and experiencing the joys and problems of older married life (Weishaus & Field, 1988). Family life in late adulthood is also influenced by the dramatic changes in the nature and function of families brought about by the trend toward smaller families and increased rates of divorce and remarriage. The ease with which older people cope with and/or benefit from these changes depends on their personal circumstances and the values of the culture in which they live.

MARRIAGE IN LATE ADULTHOOD

Imagine being married to the same person for 40, 50, or even 60 years. Perhaps you've seen newspaper photos of smiling elderly couples celebrating their "golden" wedding anniversaries. The quality of married life in old age is generally good. Like the smiling golden-anniversary couple, most couples who enter late adulthood together feel especially fortunate. In one important study, the majority of older American couples described this time as the happiest period

This special couple has enjoyed more than 50 years of sharing their lives in marriage. Their golden anniversary party provides a way for family members to celebrate this event.

of their marriage (Anderson, Russell, & Schumm, 1983; Stinnett, Carter, & Montgomery, 1972; Weishaus & Field, 1988).

What factors determine love and marital satisfaction in old age? Are the factors the same as those found for younger couples? Researchers asked a sample of young, middle-aged, and older American adults to rate a variety of statements in terms of how well the statements described their current love relationship (Reedy, Birren, & Schaie, 1981). The results of the study indicated that older couples rated emotional security and loyalty as more characteristic of their love relationship, and sexual intimacy and communication as less characteristic, than do younger couples (see Figure 16–1). The authors suggested that "over time, satisfying love relationships are less likely to be based on intense companionship and communication and more likely to be based on the history of the relationship, traditions, commitment, and loyalty" (p. 61).

Beyond these age differences, the study also found remarkable similarity among age groups in what couples find satisfying within their love relationship. All age groups rated emotional security as most important, followed by respect, communication, help and play behaviors, sexual intimacy, and loyalty. Reedy, Birren, and Schaie (1981) concluded that "there is considerably more to love than sex and that at any age, emotional security—feelings of concern, caring, trust, comfort, and being able to depend on one another—is the most important dimension in the bond of love" (p. 62).

The adjustment of the older couple represents, of course, many years of being with and learning about themselves and each other. After years of being together, each partner has learned to ignore small irritations and accept what cannot be changed. In addition, as people get older, they often are less emotionally involved with situations and events, and this may contribute to a more easygoing relationship in their marriage. So too does the tendency to "block out" conflict and other

FIGURE 16–1

The importance of specific characteristics for a good relationship across adulthood.

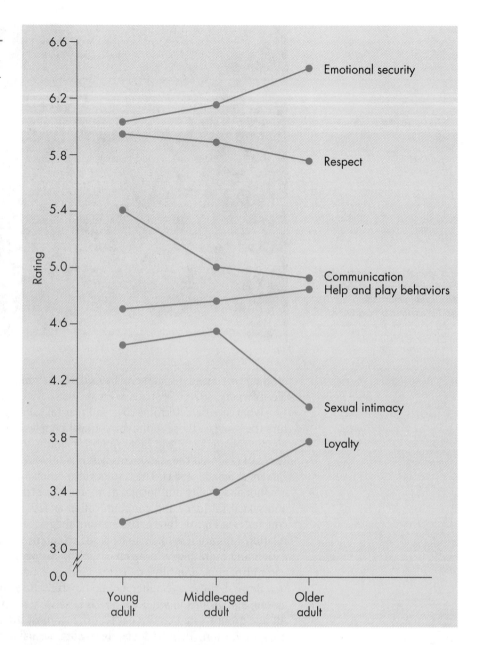

stressful situations. While the elderly frequently are confronted with stressful life events, they generally are successful in coping with them—usually by "distancing" themselves psychologically from such events (Chiriboga & Cutler, 1980). In so doing, the elderly experience less disruption in their lives, including their marriage.

The two factors that give the older marriage its unique character are the gradual shift in focus away from the children along with the retirement of the husband and wife from occupational life. Depending on cultural expectations, these events may give the couple greater freedom from outside responsibilities and obligations. They may only be expected to support and sustain each other. Death has usually relieved them of responsibilities toward their own parents; and for many their

Older marriages are often very satisfying because couples have more time to spend with each other and learn to enjoy new activities together.

children usually ask only that their parents remain self-sufficient, something which many elderly people would prefer in any case. Consequently, husbands and wives often find that they have more time for each other during this period than at any other time in their marriage—a factor that can enhance marital happiness.

Although older couples have more time to spend with each other, the amount of love actually expressed in a marriage declines over time (Swensen, Eskew, & Kohlhepp, 1981). However, for couples who have had a history of sharing their time and interests, who do not have a highly gender-typed division of labor within the family, and who have learned to cope with interpersonal conflicts by discussion and negotiation, the later years of marriage prove to be loving and positive ones (Ade-Ridder & Brubaker, 1983; Atchley, 1980; Atchley & Miller, 1983; Swensen, Eskew, & Kohlhepp, 1981).

However, like Bill, not all married people enjoy a satisfactory relationship in later life. The degree of marital satisfaction depends upon the quality of the couple's transition to retirement (Higginbottom, Barling, & Kelloway, 1993). When people are unhappy about their postretirement lives, they also are more likely to be dissatisfied with their marriage. This is especially true for couples who have not shared domestic duties throughout their marriage or who have not spent much time with each other before retirement. A wife who has been primarily responsible for the running of the household may consider her retired husband to be an inconvenience at first. New daily routines and household responsibilities must be established now that both spouses are at home. For women who have maintained a career and are now retired along with their husbands, there is an additional adjustment to be made: how to spend their time and how to divide the domestic chores with their spouse. Early in retirement, both husband and wife may find new tensions in their relationship as they tackle meal preparation and housecleaning with the same interest that characterized their work roles. Husbands may be unwilling to assume household activities that had been performed by their wives. Even though husbands spend more of their time on housework after retirement than at any other period of their lifespan, wives continue to do more housework than do their husbands (Rexroat & Shehan, 1987).

Illness also tends to strain the marital relationship, reduce sexual interaction, and perhaps introduce a new dependency relationship as the spouse takes on the role of nurse or caregiver. Poverty is another source of marital discontent, especially when encountered for the first time in the later years. In the United States, retirement brings with it a substantial reduction in income. Consequently, the older couple must make drastic adjustments in their standard of living—adjustments that may strain the marriage if they have not previously developed adequate processes for making decisions. For example, a couple that has had difficulty talking with each other about how they will spend their money may find the postretirement budget a source of conflict. The financial strain of old age is not felt in societies that assume the responsibility for providing shelter, food, and care for the elderly.

One factor that may help to explain the success of some late marriages is an interesting gender-role reversal that characterizes some older couples. It frequently has been noted that parenthood and occupational life sharpen gender-role distinctions in many couples. As couples enter into later life, however, the demands of parenthood and work lessen, often leading to a marked reduction of gender-role differences. Some men begin to recognize and express their more affiliative, nurturant, and emotional needs, while women become more assertive (Gutmann, 1977; McGee & Wells, 1982; Neugarten, 1968). These changes are likely to reduce tension between the couple, allowing for greater ease of communication and increased sharing of feelings—both of which are likely to facilitate marital satisfaction.

Finally, marriage is not only quite satisfying during this age period, it is psychologically and biologically beneficial. Research indicates that older individuals who are married are less likely to experience loneliness and depression than are the unmarried elderly (Tibbitts, 1977). They also show less evidence of mental illness (Gove, 1973), and they are likely to live longer (Civia, 1967). Marital adjustment increases an individual's physical, psychological, and social well-being and can help to counteract the negative influence that family strains and other stressful life events bring to later life (Lavee, McCubbin, & Olson, 1987).

FOCUS ON CULTURE

Cultures vary in the function and importance placed on marriage. In some societies, marriage is primarily the vehicle through which children are produced. Once the childbearing years are over, older adults may no longer need to stay married. Unsatisfactory marital relationships are dissolved or ignored. People are then free to establish nonmarital relationships to meet their social and emotional needs without the stigma of a "failed marriage."

SEXUALITY IN LATE ADULTHOOD

Contrary to the stereotyped view of the elderly as sexless people, there is sex after 60, 70, and even 80. In his 90s, actor George Burns took pride in talking about his interest in women. At one time in many Western societies, any older man who acknowledged or displayed a sexual attraction to women would be described as a "dirty old man" or "perverted." The strongly held belief that older adults do not (or should not) enjoy sexual relations is contradicted by more current and representative research (Kay & Neelley, 1982) that supports the view that many people can and do enjoy their sexuality well into old age.

Throughout the lifespan, sexuality is expressed in different ways and is affected by various cultural and life events. For example, the birth of a child usually reduces the frequency of sexual intercourse. Likewise, the illness of a spouse may limit the types of sexual activity engaged in by the couple. When sexuality is viewed more broadly to include pleasurable intimate physical contact between couples, the stereotype of the sexless elderly person becomes even more absurd (Laws, 1980). Even though the frequency of sexual intercourse declines with age, older adults are interested in sexual pleasures and indulge in them with warmth and dignity (Comfort, 1980).

Why, then, the persistent stereotype of sexless older adults? One reason is that until recently little research focused on older people, especially people over the age of 75. Sex among the elderly has been somewhat of a taboo topic in the United States (Laws, 1980). Gerontologists have been reluctant to survey older people about their sexual behavior because they themselves found it difficult to imagine that people at their parents' age or older would be interested in sexual relations. With little research to build on, the topic of sexuality was ignored until fairly

Most people who are healthy and have an available and willing partner continue to show an interest in sexual relations during later adulthood.

recently. The research of Masters and Johnson (1966, 1981) included a study of the sexual behaviors of men and women over age 60. They found that people who maintained active sexual relations during early stages of their lives were more likely to continue to be sexually active in later life. In a large questionnaire study by a consumer's magazine, 81% of married women and 50% of unmarried women over age 70 reported at least some sexual activity during the past month. For men over the age of 50, the figures were 81% for married men and 75% for unmarried men. Since the respondents in this study were all subscribers and readers of the magazine, they were, as a group, better educated and represented the middle class. Nonetheless, other studies have reported similar results (Butler & Lewis, 1976; Palmore, 1981) to support the existence of sexuality after age 60.

The experience of sexuality in old age is influenced by physiological functioning and by cultural expectations about sexual activity. Some cultures actually encourage sexuality among elderly people. In some African societies, the elderly are the sexual teachers or advisors of the young. For example, among the !Kung, elderly women are allowed considerably more sexual freedom than younger women. Among the Abkhasians of the Soviet Union, a region that has a disproportionate number of long-lived people, it is believed that a man is capable of sexual activity until he is 100 years old (Benet, 1974). For centuries, Hindu Indian and Chinese sages believed that sexuality offered a means of achieving eternal youth.

The nature of sexual activity in old age changes as a result of biological and physiological changes that take place with aging. The reduction in hormone levels (testosterone for men and estrogen for women) that began in middle adulthood continues to alter the structure and functioning of reproductive organs in old age. For women, the walls of the vagina become thinner, shorter, and less expansive. Vaginal lubrication also decreases, thereby leading to occasional pain during intercourse. Orgasm is generally shorter and less intense as well (Weg, 1978). For men, more direct stimulation is necessary to achieve erection; and the time required to reach full erection is longer, sometimes as long as 30 to 40 minutes (Runciman, 1975). Older men also experience longer times between erections, and less intense orgasms. However, they are better able to control ejaculation; that is, they are able to maintain erections longer. In many cases, this increases the man's ability to satisfy his partner while enhancing his own pleasurable sensations (Masters & Johnson, 1966).

Sexuality in old age may be complicated by medical problems, however. Cardiovascular problems, diabetes, hypothyroidism, arthritis, alcoholism, drug dependence, and obesity, to name a few health-related factors, frequently contribute to decreased sexual desire and, at times, even to **impotence,** the inability to produce an erection. Some prescription drugs used in the treatment of hypertension can cause impotence. Certain surgical procedures also are linked to sexual problems in the elderly. Radical surgery for cancer of the colon or the rectum frequently leads to impotence in older men—sometimes because of surgical damage to the nerves that cause an erection, but more often because of the negative impact of surgery on sexual self-image. Similarly, older women sometimes lose interest in sexual activity following a hysterectomy or mastectomy, not because of some medical complication, but because of the myths surrounding the surgery (Jacobson, 1974). They falsely believe that removal of the uterus or a breast causes loss of sexual desire or automatic sexual unattractiveness.

Although the myth that the elderly are not interested in sex has been discredited, older people continue to be adversely affected by it. For example, friends

impotence

A man's inability to produce an erection.

and relatives may react with consternation if an older widow or widower conducts an obviously sexual affair. As a result, many older couples court in an atmosphere of secrecy, referring to "companionship" as their main reason for dating.

FOCUS ON CULTURE

One of the vicious cycles perpetuated by ageism is reduced sexuality among the elderly. Believing sexuality to be inappropriate for their age, many elderly hide or inhibit their sexual feelings, thus contributing to the erroneous belief that they are sexless. How can this self-fulfilling prophecy be stopped? What values or beliefs within our culture maintain the view of elderly as asexual?

RELATIONS WITH FAMILY MEMBERS

Relations with Adult Children   When my widowed mother was in her mid-70s her health started to fail and it became difficult for her to take care of the family home. But rather than having her move out, my younger, unmarried brother moved in. This solved two problems: my mother's need for security and my brother's need for housing. My older brother took care of my mother's bills and banking. The rest of the family either visited or called my mother regularly to see if she needed any special help. Thus, my mother was able to maintain a somewhat independent lifestyle, while at the same time staying connected to her family. Her situation is not unusual. The majority of elderly people in the United States prefer to live independently, while actively maintaining close connections within their family network (Cicirelli, 1982; Neugarten & Neugarten, 1993; Thompson & Heller, 1990; Troll, Miller, & Atchley, 1979). With changes in family size and increased longevity, more older people are living within an extended family network that can span several generations. About one-half of all persons aged 65 years and over with surviving children belong to families spanning four generations (Shanas, 1979). Most of these family members live within easy driving distance, thus making it easier for an elderly person to live alone but not without assistance from family members (Shanas, 1980).

Whereas at the turn of the century over 60% of the population over the age of 65 lived with their children, today's figures suggest that the figure is below 15% (Smith, 1981; Shanas, 1980). Partly, these shifts are due to increased longevity. Today, most people over the age of 65 live with their spouses. Further, there has been an improvement in the standard of living for older couples. Elderly couples are not as financially strapped as their predecessors because, as a group, they are better educated and often have the benefit of two salaries or pensions (Aldous, 1987).

Older people rely primarily upon their children in times of illness, and they receive an almost instantaneous response (Shanas & Sussman, 1981; Sussman, 1960, 1965). Most adults are eager to help their aging parents by assisting them in shopping and visits to the doctor, or by acting as their spokesperson when dealing with insurance companies or the IRS. Older parents usually are not emotionally or financially dependent upon their children. The relationship is one in which they give as well as receive. Among the types of aid that older parents give their children are emotional support, money, services such as baby-sitting or legal advice, and household services such as shopping, cleaning, and house repairing. A study of near-elderly couples (people who were close to retirement or recently retired) found that older parents provided their adult children with child-care and house-and-yard-care services, financial assistance in the form of loans or gifts, and transportation (Aldous, 1987). The study also found that near-elderly parents were more likely to maintain contact with and provide support and services to adult children who had the greatest need for their attention—namely their divorced or single adult children. Although some elderly people may not be physically or financially able to do so, the number of older parents who help their children tends to exceed those who receive help from their children (Riley, Riley, & Johnson, 1968). Troll, Miller, and Atchley (1979) suggest that this pattern is likely to continue until the parents' health or financial condition deteriorates.

As independent and self-sufficient as older people wish to be, there does come a time in their lives when they need to accept help from their children and others. There is also a point at which the help received far outweighs the help given. At such times, a role reversal takes place, with adult children becoming caregivers to their own aging—and usually ailing—parents. Approximately 8% of the elderly in the United States are housebound, with much of the caregiving being provided by their adult children (Huyck & Hoyer, 1982). Daughters, in particular, are likely to take on this responsibility, both for their own parents and their in-laws (Troll & Turner, 1980).

Hajiya, introduced at the beginning of this chapter, enjoyed the freedom and status of being an elderly woman within her family compound. In her Nigerian Muslim community it was expected that should she need help, she could count on her children and community to provide it. In many other countries, and especially in nonindustrialized societies, it is more common to find the elderly living with their adult children. In Yugoslavia, for example, children are expected to cater to their aging parents and grandparents. Similarly, in Japan, elderly people often live with their children, although this pattern is changing with an improvement in the Japanese economy and increased urbanization (Martin, 1988).

Ethical Dilemmas in Caring for Elderly Parents

While most adults are prepared to accept the responsibility for caring for children while they are unable to care for themselves, few are prepared to fill a similar role for their aging parents. Yet, most of the elderly who require care depend upon family members, usually their adult children, for assistance. Adults must deal with a variety of ethical dilemmas when their parents or close relatives become dependent upon them (Martin, 1994a). They must first determine the extent of the obligation they feel: What constitutes care, and how much financial burden are they expected to bear? With few clear guidelines, this decision can be a difficult one, especially when the family's resources are limited. Secondly, while most adults agree that family members should share the care of elderly parents, they do not always agree about what to do about family members who do not pull their weight or even refuse to help. How to balance the care of one's aging parents with other family and work obligations is another dilemma that must be resolved. Once adults enter into a caregiving relationship with their parents, they usually continue until their parents die or must be institutionalized. For some people this can be a fairly long period. In order to be able to provide meaningful and continued care, adults must learn to set reasonable limits on how much time and money they can afford to spend.

FOCUS ON CULTURE

The behaviors that constitute elder abuse must be understood within a cultural context. For example, among the Kililui of Papua New Guinea, the frail elderly participate in a death-hastening ritual that signifies that they are close to dying and socially dead; they may isolate themselves from others and refuse food or drink. In other cultures, aged members are ignored, abandoned or neglected, and sometimes killed when they become unable to work or function. None of these behaviors are considered abusive.

Perhaps the most difficult dilemma for adults is how to know when it is time to step in and make decisions for their parents. This decision is made easier when elderly parents and their children discuss the possible options for their care *before* they become incapable of making their own decisions. For example, emergency medical decisions are easier to make if parents have provided their children with some guidance about the extent of extraordinary efforts that should or should not be taken to prolong their lives. In order for people to resolve the dilemmas surrounding the care of their aging relatives they must be committed to making choices that support and maintain the independence and autonomy of their elderly relatives. The care of elderly parents or relatives should be shared fairly and in an open and nonmanipulative manner.

RECAP

Family life in late adulthood has been extended as a result of greater longevity. Marriages that last into late adulthood are more satisfying because of the emotional security, respect, and loyalty they offer. With a shift in focus away from children and the retirement of one or both partners, late adulthood marriages offer increased freedom. Sexuality continues in late adulthood, with some changes in intensity due to hormonal changes. Older adults may be hampered in their sexual expression by ageist stereotypes and illness. Most older adults prefer to live independently from their children but remain in contact with them. At some point in late adulthood, elderly parents may have to depend on their children for help. This creates a series of ethical dilemmas that adults must resolve in order to provide their aging parents or relatives with appropriate care.

Relations with Grandchildren   By the time most people reach late adulthood, their grandchildren are no longer young children; they are adolescents, or older. Since life expectancy has increased, and people now reach advanced age in better health and with greater vitality than ever before, grandparents are likely to have considerable influence upon younger family members (Hagestad, 1982). Grandmothers, in particular, are likely to have an influential relationship with their grandchildren, if for no other reason than that they live longer than grandfathers. In African American and Native American families many grandmothers assume the responsibility for raising their grandchildren.

Health Perspective

ELDER ABUSE

Although abuse of children and wives has received a lot of public attention in the United States, abuse of the elderly has only recently become a matter of public concern (Quinn & Tomita, 1986). The greater life expectancy brought on by improved medical technology presents many families today with the responsibility for caring for elderly parents and relatives in a culture that has not prepared them to fully accept this role. Sometimes family members are frustrated by the often unwanted financial and emotional burdens of caring for elderly relatives who cannot take care of themselves or who have not planned for their extended retirement years. This frustration is occasionally expressed in elder abuse. As in child and spouse abuse, the elderly victim is often dependent upon the perpetrator for his or her basic needs and often lives in the same household.

Elder abuse is defined not in terms of acts of violence or neglect, nor does it address the perpetrator's relationship to the abused (as is the case with battered wives); rather, it refers to the age of the victim. Thus, a woman who had been abused by her husband during her middle-adulthood years could continue to be a victim of elder abuse in her old age (Steinmetz, 1990). Although abuse occurs across all age groups, studies have found the typical elderly victim to be female, over the age of 75, and frail (Steinmetz, 1990).

Elder abuse includes a variety of inappropriate behaviors, which are described in Table 16–1. Although abuse of the elderly has been reported in both public and private institutions, more often than not the elderly are abused by members of their own families. Furthermore, elder abuse is far less likely than child abuse to be reported to the authorities. Since children in the United States must be educated, suspicions of child abuse are likely to be reported by teachers and other adults who come into contact with the child. The elderly, however, are often housebound and away from the public view. Ageist attitudes may also contribute to psychological and financial abuse and the violation of basic rights of the elderly. Sometimes adult children view their aging parents as incapable of making their own decisions, and take over all decision making for them without consulting them or securing their consent (Cicirelli, 1990).

Careful study is needed to identify the specific signs of elder abuse. More importantly, adults need to be educated about the aging process with the aim of reducing and preventing abuse. Families caring for elderly family members may need short-term respite help or external support services to help them cope with the stresses of caring for a dependent elderly relative.

elder abuse
Various behaviors inflicted on elderly people.

One study (Thomas, 1986) assessed the degree of satisfaction with grandparenting among a sample of American grandmothers and grandfathers. Overall, grandmothers reported greater satisfaction with their roles than did grandfathers. The grandmothers who reported relatively high levels of responsibility for the care of their grandchildren also reported higher levels of satisfaction with their roles. This is not to deny the influence of grandfathers, who are often seen as reservoirs of family wisdom and cultural heritage, and are especially likely to have an impact on their grandsons (Hagestad, 1978).

Grandparents vary widely in their degree of involvement with their grandchildren—some are intensely involved, whereas others appear totally uninterested. Furthermore, grandparents' involvement is specific to each grandchild;

FORMS OF ELDER ABUSE

1. *Physical abuse,* including bruises, broken bones, blood clots, dehydration, malnutrition, cuts, burns, and death

2. *Financial abuse,* including loss of bank accounts, pension checks, homes, and other valuables

3. *Violation of basic rights,* including the right to practice one's religion, open one's mail, or talk on the telephone

4. *Psychological abuse,* including threats of abandonment or institutionalization, verbal harassment, and denigration

5. *Self-abuse and neglect,* including unwillingness to seek appropriate medical or psychiatric help

TABLE 16–1

Source: From "Elder Abuse and Neglect," by M. Quinn, 1987, in G. L. Maddox (Ed.), *The Encyclopedia of Aging,* New York: Springer.

they may be very involved with some grandchildren and less involved with others, depending on the amount of contact they have with them. Chapter 14 noted that grandparents often play a significant role in the well-being and adjustment of the family unit, particularly in situations following life stresses such as divorce and unplanned and/or unwanted pregnancy (Troll, 1983). Of interest, however, is the common finding that the well-being and morale of grandparents is unrelated to the amount of contact they have with their grandchildren. Life satisfaction among the elderly has more to do with friendship patterns—and presumably marital patterns—than it does with grandparenting patterns (Troll, Miller, & Atchley, 1979).

Grandparents and adolescent and adult grandchildren often acknowledge the ways in which they try to influence one another. Moreover, they admit that their attempts are often successful—but only in certain areas (Troll, 1980). Interestingly, both groups realize that there are some areas in which influence should be avoided—sexuality and religion, for example. Hagestad (1978) uses the term *demilitarized zone* in reference to these sensitive areas. She suggests that family members, including those from different generations, go to great lengths to avoid interpersonal conflict. By not attempting to influence one another within these sensitive areas, which obviously will vary from one family to another, grandparents and their grandchildren avoid disrupting the stability of familial relationships.

Divorce disrupts family bonds, sometimes resulting in a change in grandparents' relationships with their grandchildren. Bill, introduced in the opening story, had little to do with his children following his divorce and as a result had no contact with his grandchildren. One 40-month longitudinal study of grandmothers following the divorce of their children (Johnson, 1988) found that most grandmothers provided considerable assistance to both their children and their grandchildren. A decline in contact was noted, however, for paternal grandparents.

Since many divorced people often remarry, divorce can also result in a much larger network of relatives. Geographic proximity and the quality of the relationship between the grandparents and the custodial parent following a divorce greatly influence the amount of contact they have with their grandchildren. Grandparents who live close by to children who are custodial parents are likely to have greater contact with their grandchildren (Matthews & Sprey, 1984).

LIFE ON ONE'S OWN

Singlehood   About 5% of adults in the United States over the age of 65 have never married (U.S. Bureau of the Census, 1988). Men are more likely than women to remain single into late adulthood. Older people who have never married are in the special situation of having neither children nor grandchildren. Their adjustment to old age has been of interest not only to developmental researchers but to every happy single person who has heard the threatening question "But who will you turn to when you are old and sick?"

But elderly single people do not find old age especially lonely. Single older people appear to feel less lonely than those who are unhappily married or widowed. Whether that is because they prefer their solitude or simply because they have learned to make use of other emotional resources probably depends upon the individual. Single older people do tend to maintain closer relationships with siblings than do those who marry and have families (Shanas et al., 1968). Bonds between sisters are usually strongest. Many single people have friends with whom they spend a great deal of time (Cargan & Melko, 1982) and to whom the can turn when they want companionship. One study (Essex & Nam, 1987) found that loneliness in never-married women is not affected by their relationships with family and friends, but rather by the quality of their health; when their health is poor, never-married older women are more likely to report feeling lonely.

Single people rely on friends and siblings for companionship and support.

Widowhood In industrialized countries, widowhood represents the greatest emotional and social loss suffered by individuals in the normal course of the life-span. People who live in nontechnological societies are even more likely to experience other major family losses, such as the death of a parent in childhood, or the death of a young child. More than 50% of the women in the United States over the age of 65 and nearly 70% of women over the age of 75 are widowed (Neugarten & Neugarten, 1993). The corresponding percentages for men are much lower. The gender difference in widowhood reflects the higher mortality rate of men, and the fact that older men are much more likely to remarry following the death of their spouse than are older women.

Widowhood represents first a traumatic experience to be endured, followed by a new social status. The death of the spouse is an emotional emergency; only later is the bereaved person in a position to adjust, so far as is possible, to a new status and lifestyle that is influenced by cultural values and expectations.

Still, many widows outlive their husbands for what amounts to one or more generations. After adjusting to the actual death of her spouse, the widow must then establish a new relationship with society. Some cultures have expectations for how widows should conduct their lives. For example, in India a widow is expected to dress in white and mourn for a period of at least a year. In the United States, however, there are no set social roles for widows or widowers. According to Lopata (1973, 1979), who has studied widowhood in depth, the woman has several options. One option is to return to the medium or high levels of activity she enjoyed before being widowed. This may be difficult if her activities depended on the presence of a spouse, as is often the case for educated middle-class women. It can also be difficult for financial reasons. Many widows live at or below the poverty level. A second possibility is that the woman can choose to enter a new role and develop new friends (including widows like herself). Or, she can retreat into isolation. Lopata suggests that the first two solutions, or some combination of them, are ideal from the widow's standpoint.

A more immediate and practical problem for the widow is where she will live (most often expressed in the question "What will you do now?"). The widow can live alone, adopt some form of communal living, live with one of her married children, or remarry (Lopata, 1971). About one-half of Lopata's sample of 301 Chicago women lived alone, primarily because they wanted to be free and independent. Those who lived with relatives or let rooms were more often than not the heads of the household. Only 10% lived with married children, usually the least preferred alternative.

From 1969 to 1974, a demonstration project called the *Widow-to-Widow Program* was conducted through Harvard University (Silverman, 1985). The purpose of the program was to reduce the risks of mental and physical decline for widows who were in the process of transition following the death of a spouse. The program was designed as an outreach program in which widows who had already made a successful adjustment in their transition from spouse to widow to single person made contact with a recently widowed person. One-to-one contact would typically be made about 3 to 6 weeks after the death of the spouse, the time when most relatives and friends would have stopped visiting the widow in the belief that she no longer needed support.

The goals of the program centered on helping the widow make changes in her life by providing practical information about bereavement; financial, legal, and housing matters; and community and social services available to her. The new widow also received emotional support from and discussed coping strategies with the widow aide, who could readily share some of her own experiences. Usually the widow aide would be a neighbor or someone from the widow's immediate community. Today, numerous programs for widows in the United States and Canada are based on the Widow-to-Widow Program (Osterweis, Solomon, & Green, 1984).

One controversial question that has generated considerable research is whether widowhood affects men and women differently. Women are less likely than men to remarry following the death of their spouse. Widows are also undoubtedly less well-off financially than widowers. On the other hand, the literature on psychological and physical adjustment following loss of a spouse suggests that men generally suffer more than women. In reviewing the research in this area, Stroebe and Stroebe (1983) conclude that while women may display more physical and emotional problems following the death of a spouse, men who lose their wives are worse off. These researchers suggest that the gender difference is most easily explained in terms of greater difficulty in coping with new roles and less social support for older men than older women. The widower must find comfort for his loss while at the same time learning to care for a household and himself. According to a study conducted by DiGiuolo (1989), more women than men report a feeling of relief following the death of a spouse. Widowhood provided these women, particularly those who were middle-aged, with a sense of having a new lease on life. For older widows the relief they experienced came from no longer having to care for a chronically ill spouse.

INSTITUTIONALIZATION

The possibility that Hajiya might end her life in a nursing home or institution is very remote; for Bill, it is not. In many cultures, the idea of placing an elderly relative in an institution is unthinkable. But in the United States and other industrialized countries, it is a solution to the problem of providing care for people who cannot adequately take care of themselves. Some older people who are unable to live in family or home environments are placed (or place themselves) in institutions variously referred to as nursing homes, geriatric hospitals, hospitals for the chronically ill, and old-age homes.

The issue of institutionalized care of older persons receives a great deal of media attention in the United States, with the result that many people believe that institutionalization is widespread. As we have seen, the majority of older people live independently, usually less than an hour's drive from one of their children. Only about 5% of people in the United States live in nursing homes (Johnson, 1987). If we include other forms of institutions, however, such as psychiatric or extended-care medical facilities, perhaps as many as 20% of the elderly are institutionalized at some point (Johnson, 1987).

The typical nursing-home resident is approximately 80 years old, white, and female (Butler & Lewis, 1982). Between 85 and 90% of those who enter nursing homes eventually die there. The average length of stay in a nursing home is 1.6 years, with one-third of the residents dying within the first 12 months. Most nursing-home residents suffer from chronic physical illnesses, often

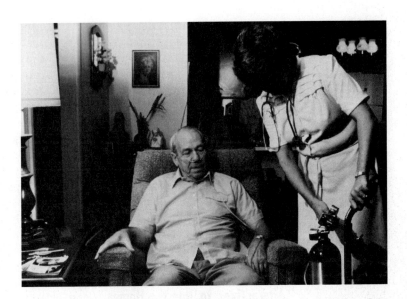

This nursing home health-care worker is instructing an elderly client about the use of his medical equipment.

some form of cardiovascular disease. Psychiatric disorders are also common, either as primary conditions or as secondary conditions to physical illness. Unfortunately, little psychiatric care is provided for most nursing home residents (Butler & Lewis, 1982).

The reasons for entering nursing homes and other long-care facilities are varied. Some older people enter voluntarily. A debilitating condition may make it impossible for some people to maintain themselves at home. Because of the strong value placed on independence in our culture, aging adults may be unwilling to become dependent on their children, seeking instead the impersonal comfort of institutionalized care. Some older people assert their independence by deciding to enter an institution (and even selecting the institution) before they become unable to care for themselves. Married couples occasionally close their home and admit themselves to a facility together—if they can afford it.

In many other cases, institutionalization seems not to be a decision but an involuntary action on everyone's part. The middle-aged offspring say they have no choice. They may be unable, financially or physically, to care for the chronically ill parent in their homes. Even if resources exist, they may feel unable to accommodate the parent without destroying their own family relationships (including, perhaps, the relationship with their ailing parent). Whatever the justification, the son or daughter often feels guilty.

The assumption underlying these feelings is that all institutions for the elderly are unpleasant and dehumanizing places. They are often described as places where one goes to die, and yet the institutions are so varied that it is difficult to make generalizations. They range from small convalescent homes run by religious orders to large proprietary nursing homes run by operators with "tender loving greed" (Mendelson, 1974). Some nursing homes provide basic nursing care while others offer an additional range of physical and recreational activities.

Because most older people do not reside in nursing homes or other institutions, it is often asked whether those individuals who do become institutionalized differ physically, socially, or psychologically from those who do not. In one of the most comprehensive studies on this question, Tobin and Lieberman (1976) found that, surprisingly, there was little difference between the two groups. Nursing-home residents were neither more dependent in personality nor more lacking in a confidant or close friend than were same-age residents of the community. Furthermore, both groups seemed to be characterized by the same kind of physical, social, and economic losses. The researchers found that institutionalization was most likely to occur when the person's physical condition showed evidence of increased deterioration, and there was a lack of adequate care facilities (or inability or unwillingness to provide it) within the family or the community.

Some older people adapt well to institutionalization and communal life. If admission is voluntary, if the older person has had a part in planning it, or if, in fact, it offers solutions to loneliness or other life problems, adjustment may be relatively smooth (Schulz & Brenner, 1977). To the extent that family and staff members support and encourage independent behaviors (such as self-care), life in institutional settings does not have to result in total passivity and decline (Baltes & Wahl, 1992).

Alternatives to Nursing Homes   Most elderly Americans do not want to live in a nursing home and would prefer to live independently. Likewise, most families dread the thought that they might have to place their parents in an institution. Fortunately, several alternatives to institutionalized nursing-home care exist. Many cities now offer some type of residential setting for the elderly (Moos & Lemke, 1985). For instance, some apartment complexes are rented only to the elderly and provide specialized leisure and social programs and medical services to their residents. Typically, residents in these specialized settings report that they like being able to socialize and participate in the planned activities (Lawton, 1981). The costs of living in housing specially designed for the elderly are usually lower since many receive state and federal funds. Residents are offered independence and security, ingredients that contribute to higher morale and a more active lifestyle.

Some elderly people live in specially built additions to the homes of their adult children. Commonly referred to as "mother-in-law apartments" or "granny flats," these arrangements allow older people privacy and independence without being cut off from their families. Some elderly people are able to continue living in their own homes with the help of daily visits from nurses who provide home care and social-welfare workers who help with bathing, dressing, and meal preparation. Many communities offer "meals on wheels" programs that deliver well-balanced, low-cost meals to people who are unable to cook for themselves. Sometimes a worker is hired to live with an aging person to provide care and security.

With smaller families and fewer offspring to provide assistance and increasing numbers of people living past retirement, the need for more flexible housing and living arrangements for the elderly is likely to become an even more important issue. The population of never-married people or child-free married couples will increase in the future, thereby increasing the number of older adults who cannot rely on adult children to provide for their care (Lawton, 1981). In such situations family members such as siblings or nieces and nephews may consider several alternatives besides placing the aging person in an institution.

Research Perspective

LOCUS OF CONTROL IN NURSING-HOME CARE

Health-care professionals who work in nursing homes are well aware of the negative effects of institutionalization on the elderly. Rapid decline in health is often observed upon admission; mortality is high among first-year residents. As we have seen, the aged person is especially vulnerable in periods of stress. Lieberman (1961) suggests that it is entering the institution (rather than living in one) that dramatically upsets the individual's equilibrium.

Entering a nursing home often means surrendering personal control over many aspects of life. Even when the elderly person is in fairly good health, perceived loss of control can lead to poorer health, low morale, and depression (Abramson, Seligman, & Teasdale, 1978; Fawcett, Stonner, & Zeppelin, 1980; Langer, 1985; Wolk & Kurtz, 1975). For example, patients in nursing homes often do not select their own rooms; rooms are assigned to them. Meals are usually served at preselected times, and visitors are allowed only during defined hours. Although the rules and operation of nursing homes are designed to meet the needs of elderly patients, many of whom require medical attention, the loss of independence and sense of control over one's life often cause further deterioration.

The importance of perceived control for the elderly is highlighted by the research of Langer and Rodin (1976). These researchers were interested in the influence of personal decision making and responsibility on the well-being of nursing-home residents. They designed an experiment in which one group of residents (the "responsibility" group) was encouraged by the staff to make decisions for themselves and given the responsibility of caring for plants. The other group of residents (the "no responsibility" group) was assured that the staff were there to make their decisions and take responsibility for them; they were not given plants to care for. The residents who were encouraged to take control of their own lives by making decisions and assuming responsibility showed significant improvement in mental alertness. They also were rated as more active and happier. Of the group that was not encouraged to assume personal responsibility for themselves, 71% showed evidence of debilitation. Furthermore, in an 18-month follow-up of this research, Rodin and Langer (1977) found that the "responsibility" group continued to be psychologically and physically healthier than the "no responsibility" group. The "responsibility" group even had a lower mortality rate. This research suggests that increased choice and responsibility and a sense of personal control can have a profound impact on the elderly and may even slow down some of the negative effects of aging and institutionalization.

Rather than refer to the people who enter nursing homes as *patients,* many health-care workers use the term *client.* Some nursing homes encourage their clients' independence and individuality by allowing them to decorate their rooms with their own furniture and plants. Some allow the residents to have a private phone in their rooms and to have unlimited visitors.

The layout and design of the nursing care facility can also contribute to a greater sense of independence and self-control. Since many elderly people have difficulty seeing, large signs and other visual aids strategically placed around the halls and buildings can make it easier for clients to move about unassisted. Flexible and frequent scheduling of activities, especially stimulating and active ones, further adds to the quality of life by giving people more choices in how to spend their time each day.

RECAP

During late adulthood grandparents vary in their degree of involvement with grandchildren, from minimal contact to assuming parental responsibilities. Divorce and remarriage complicates this relationship. Elderly single people do not necessarily find late adulthood lonely but rather rely on close friends and relatives for contact and support. More women than men lose their spouses during late adulthood and must cope with the problems of singlehood and bereavement simultaneously. While most elderly people are cared for in their homes, some are institutionalized, either voluntarily on involuntarily. Numerous care arrangements in the home provide alternatives to institutionalization.

SOCIAL RELATIONS

social convoy
A group of people who spend time together over the lifespan.

"Grow old along with me! / The best is yet to be. . . ." Robert Browning's familiar lines remind us that people age within a social context. Life's journey is enhanced by the friends and acquaintances who share our experiences, offer advice and support, and provide us with a frame of reference. Whether it is a circle of friends in a retirement home or a close-knit family, the aging process is made easier when people are connected to a social group. Antonucci (1985) used the term **social convoy** to refer to the people who travel together with us through life. People in the social convoy could include long-time friends, neighbors, teachers, or coworkers.

SOCIAL INTEGRATION VERSUS SOCIAL ISOLATION

When my parents retired, they joined a group of friends on a variety of cruises. Every year they would take a 2-week trip with these friends and spend the rest of the year planning the trip and talking about it afterwards. Even when they were no longer physically up to the rigors of travel they maintained contact with their travel friends. Their cruise adventures enriched my parents' social experience and kept them engaged in life.

social integration versus isolation
The degree of interpersonal activity and organizational participation in which a person engages, and the degree of social-emotional support the person receives from others in these activities.

　　Social integration versus isolation generally refers to the degree to which people seek out and are involved in social groups and organizations. It also refers to the extent of the person's social network and the degree of social support derived from that network (Kahana, 1982). Does the aged person belong to a social club or religious group, participate in programs for the elderly in the community, or keep abreast of what is happening in the local and national news? To what extent does the elderly person make use of the help that is available? Older people worry about losing their mobility by not being able to drive or travel; they can stay connected with friends through telephone calls and letters. In the age of information technology, some senior citizens are using the Internet to maintain contact with old friends and meet new ones.

　　It is important to distinguish between *voluntary* and *involuntary* social disengagement. People who choose to withdraw or, conversely, choose to remain active are much more likely to feel satisfied with their life situations than are people who are forced by personal or external circumstances to adopt particular lifestyles

Older people can maintain their involvement with the community by volunteering their time to help others. These seniors enjoy helping out at the local soup kitchen.

against their wills (Lowenthal & Boler, 1975). In essence, voluntary decision making allows individuals to feel more in control of their lives.

Another important factor contributing to people's social adjustment to aging is what social involvement means to the individual (Liang, Dvorkin, Kahana, & Mazian, 1980). For some individuals, social involvement is extremely important. In fact, it is through these activities that some individuals develop and maintain their sense of identity during the adult years. For example, even though Bill was planning on retiring from his work, he was not going to give up his involvement with professional business organizations. He needed to maintain his identification with the business world because it had been such an important part of his life. For other individuals, however, continued social involvement is much less significant—at least insofar as it affects identity and self-esteem. Thus, to understand the importance of social relations for successful adaptation in late adulthood, one must understand the personal meaning that social interaction and social roles have for the elderly, both at the present stage of life and earlier times.

Research also indicates that frequency of social participation per se is a poor predictor of life satisfaction and morale among older adults (Lemon, Bengston, & Peterson, 1972). More important than the number of social contacts a person has or the number of organizations he or she belongs to is the quality of the individual's social relations. The importance of close companions or confidants has often been linked to successful adjustment in the elderly (George, 1987). The most important companions for the elderly, besides one's spouse, are siblings and friends.

SIBLINGS

Between 75 and 80% of people in late adulthood have living brothers and sisters. Even very old people are likely to have a surviving sibling; however, smaller

These elderly twins are fortunate to share a lifetime together. Siblings provide companionship and are an important source of comfort during late adulthood.

families may eventually change the likelihood of having a sibling in late adulthood. In a sample of Midwestern older adults, those over 80 years of age still had, on the average, one living sibling (Cicirelli, 1979, 1982). Contact with brothers and sisters is relatively frequent among the aged, although it obviously depends on the distance between residences.

Relationships with siblings play an important role in the life of the aging adult, particularly for individuals who have lost a spouse, are divorced, or never married. Siblings often provide the support and help that normally would come from a spouse. They act as confidants; share family occasions, holidays, and recreational activities; aid in decision making, homemaking, and home repairs; boost morale; lend money in times of financial need; and provide nursing care and emotional support in times of illness. It is understandable, therefore, that the majority of older people feel "close" or "extremely close" to at least one of their siblings (Cicirelli, 1979, 1980, 1982; Depner & Ingersoll-Dayton, 1988; Scott, 1983).

Research suggests that the influence of siblings on older adults differs, 1979). Generally, female siblings exert a greater influence on both men and women. They are more effective in preserving family relationships and providing emotional support. Furthermore, the presence of sisters tends to reduce the threat of aging for the older man; that is, older men seem happier and less affected by economic and social insecurities when they have living sisters. For aged women, the presence of sisters results in greater concern about social skills, social relationships outside of the family, and community activity. In other words, sisters tend to create a more challenging environment for the older woman.

FRIENDS

Although much has been written about the meaning and role of friendship in childhood and adolescence, there is very little information about the importance of friends for adults, especially older adults (Tesch, 1983). Nevertheless, common

FOCUS ON CULTURE

In a longitudinal study that looked at the social motives that affect people's lives, Veroff, Reuman, and Feld (1984) found that as American women grew older their desire for affiliation declined. This decline was not found for older men, however. Their subjects were aged 21 or older when they were first studied in 1957; they were studied again in 1976. If you consider that men and women are socialized to the culture of their gender, what explanations can you offer for the differences between men and women in their interest in being with people?

sense would suggest that for most people friends are important. Unlike relatives, friends are selected on the basis of shared interests and compatibility. McCormick (1982) notes that friends serve a number of functions. Friends provide approval, affection, and emotional support during difficult times. Friends also encourage self-disclosure, as well as mutual trust, respect, and obligation. In addition, friends offer aid, advice, and services; and they may provide new information and experiences.

In old age, friendships help to compensate for many of the personal and social losses experienced by the individual (Hess, 1972). In times of grief and sorrow the elderly often seek to share their experiences with others, particularly those who also have gone, or are going, through similar situations. This may explain why older people, more than middle-aged adults, tend to choose friends who are close to their own age (Lopata, 1977; Norris & Rubin, 1984; Stueve & Fischer, 1978). The importance of friendships to the elderly is highlighted by research showing that life satisfaction is more closely linked to interaction with friends than to interaction with relatives (Philblad & Adams, 1972; Wood & Robertson, 1978). Furthermore, the willingness to think about the welfare of others and to provide support enhances the quality of friendships among older adults (Jones & Vaughan, 1990).

Friendship patterns in old age differ for men and women. Older men generally report more friends than older women, although they tend to spend less time with their friends and reveal less about themselves to their friends than women do (Dickens & Perlman, 1981; Powers & Bultena, 1976; Reisman, 1981). Older men also report more cross-sex friendships than do women (Booth & Hess, 1974). As Troll (1982) has noted, this may imply that it is easier to be friends with women than with men. That is, women may be more receptive to self-disclosure and sharing of confidences than men—characteristics that promote close, intimate friendships. Or it may simply mean that with fewer men surviving into old age, women have less opportunity than men to develop cross-gender friendships.

RECAP

Social relationships continue to be an important part of late adulthood. People vary in their degree of involvement with friends and group activities, ranging from socially integrated to isolated. Contact and involvement with siblings is common among the elderly, especially after the death of a spouse. Friends provide approval, emotional support, and assistance; they help compensate for some of the personal losses that occur in late adulthood. Friendship patterns differ for elderly men and women.

RETIREMENT

retirement
The end of one's work or occupational life.

In most industrialized countries, people typically enter the workforce in young adulthood and spend the next 40 to 50 years working. Late adulthood is the time when people end their occupational lives with **retirement.** When the time comes for them to stop working, some people find the change disruptive. The equivalent of retirement in nontechnological societies is when people no longer contribute to the work of the community. Generally, a person in the United States is considered retired if he or she is employed less than full-time year round and if at least part of his or her income is derived from a pension earned through prior years of employment. Thus, being retired is not the same as being unemployed. Many older people, after retiring from their primary job, take on part-time work—sometimes for financial reasons, but often because they feel more satisfied "doing something." Why do people retire? What significance and impact does the retirement role have for the older person? In this section we address these and other questions.

FOCUS ON CULTURE

Retirement is a term that does not apply equally well in all cultures or societies. For example, when Hajiya turned 60 she entered old age, but she did not stop being productive; to the contrary, she increased her contribution to the community. However, retirement is more common in modern technological societies that have an interest in older people leaving the workforce. By urging workers to retire, new positions, usually at lower salaries, are opened up for younger workers.

THE DECISION TO RETIRE

Retirement age in the United States is often described as an "artifact" of Social Security and other pension systems. As many psychologists, physicians, and social planners note, chronological age is a poor indicator of a person's ability or desire to work. Adopting a particular age, such as 70, as the normal retirement age allows employers to dispense with higher-paid older workers and enables younger workers to enter and advance in occupational hierarchies. Most supervisors, when questioned, say that they would prefer a variable retirement age, to account for individual differences in employee ability and health.

How long people remain in their jobs depends on a complex set of issues and factors such as the degree of satisfaction derived from work, financial constraints, health, and social expectations (Cavanaugh & Park, 1993). Reasons for retiring vary from one individual to another. Contrary to what most people think, retirement is less often forced on people than it is a voluntary decision. Between 40 to 50% of people who retire do so by choice (Palmore, Burchett, Fillenbaum, George, & Wallman, 1985). People from lower socioeconomic groups, however, are less likely to retire voluntarily than are people from middle- and high-income groups, primarily because the former are less financially secure.

Those who choose to retire usually do so because they have adequate financial resources, good pension plans, a desire to spend more time with family, or dislike of their jobs (Swan, Dame, & Carmeli, 1991). Age norms also influence a person's decision to retire. Some individuals may realize that they have reached the age when people expect them to retire. The desire to be part of the "retirement crowd," to join the activities of friends and relatives who have already retired, may be an additional inducement to finally stop working.

Involuntary retirement, on the other hand, usually results from the mandatory retirement policy of the company and is often associated with a poor adjustment following retirement. In one study (Swan et al., 1991) people who were forced to retire perceived their health to be poorer, reported a greater number of illnesses, and experienced more fatigue and depression when compared to people who retired voluntarily. For some people, poor health is the reason for voluntary retirement. As people age, chronic physical problems such as cardiovascular disease, arthritis, and pulmonary disease begin to take their toll, and prevent, or at least inhibit, older workers from effectively doing their job. In fact, the primary reason given for *early retirement*—that is, retirement prior to mandatory retirement age—is declining health. It is often difficult for older people to adjust to the combination of poor health and forced retirement.

Not all workers retire, or retire completely. Like Bill, self-employed people—artists, professional scholars, private practitioners in medicine and psychology, independent artisans and contractors, among others—are not affected by mandatory retirement. Furthermore, as we have noted, some adults retire from one job only to take up a second—usually part-time—job. A study by Flanagan (1981) indicated that as many as 16% of men and 12% of women in their late 60s to early 70s work either full-time or part-time. When asked to name the most important characteristics of a job for them, these older adults reported the following: The job should be something at which they are competent or do well; the job should be meaningful, challenging, and interesting; coworkers and the work environment should be pleasant; and supervisors should be friendly and interested in their welfare.

Early Retirement Even though federal legislation has raised the mandatory retirement age in the United States from 65 to 70 and some employers have eliminated any age requirement, many people are electing to retire early—that is, before they have to and even before they reach their 60s. Actual retirement age in major industries averages about 58 (Stagner, 1982). The major factors influencing an early retirement decision are financial status and health. People in poor health or with an ailing spouse are more likely to retire early if they have private pension and retirement benefits to supplement their Social Security benefits (which alone are not adequate to support a family in retirement). Many people retire early so that they can direct their time and energy to developing a postretirement second career. For example, a study of college professors who had taken early retirement found that more than half of them had planned specific projects such as writing a book or doing research (Kell & Patton, 1978).

Other workers leave their jobs early because they do not like their work. These are people who cannot wait to leave jobs that for them may be boring and require hard physical work under difficult or hazardous conditions. Some workers are offered inducements to retire earlier, such as a year's salary in the form of a bonus. Usually, employers who offer such inducements are hoping to make room for younger workers to advance or wish to make substantial changes in the organization. With the added financial incentive, older workers who are already close to retiring may decide to leave early. In some cases, early retirement is not an option but the result of being laid off or fired. As mentioned earlier, people who are forced to leave work usually have a more difficult time making the adjustment from work to retirement.

Some jobs are arduous and dangerous, making early retirement an attractive option.

THE PROCESS OF RETIREMENT

Although retirement is often marked by celebrations and good-bye parties, it is actually a process that takes place gradually over time. Bill, for example, has been preparing for his retirement for several years. For some time he had been setting money aside for the day when he would no longer be working.

Atchley (1977) has suggested that the retirement process consists of seven phases, which are listed in Table 16–2. He notes, however, that not everyone necessarily goes through all seven phases; nor must they complete the phases in the same order. Variability in age of retirement and reasons for retiring means that the process of retirement will be somewhat different from one person to another. Still, Atchley's model is useful for understanding the developmental tasks confronting the older person who is undergoing the transition from worker to nonworker.

PHASES OF RETIREMENT

Preretirement

Remote: Little thought or preparation for retirement

Near-Retirement: Active planning for retirement

Postretirement

Honeymoon: Initial enthusiasm for retirement activities

Disenchantment: Disappointment over retirement plans

Reorientation: Reevaluation of goals and strategies

Stability: Long-term goals are made and implemented

Terminal: Retirement loses its significance

TABLE 16–2

Source: From *The Social Forces in Later Life,* 3rd ed., by R. C. Atchley, 1977, Belmont, CA: Wadsworth.

remote phase

A phase in the retirement process before retirement where adults work intensely and enjoy the fruits of their labor: job status, financial security, and competence. Little is done to prepare for retirement.

near-retirement phase

A phase in the retirement process when people begin thinking and planning for the time they will end their work.

honeymoon phase

A phase in the process of retirement characterized by initial enthusiasm, excitement, and feelings of euphoria immediately following retirement.

The first, or **remote phase,** occurs long before retirement, usually in the early part of middle adulthood. For most adults, this is a time of intense activity at work, and a time for enjoying the fruits of one's labor—job status, financial security, feelings of competence, and so forth. Thoughts about retirement, if they exist at all, are vague; little is done to prepare for retirement at this time. However, this is the best time for people to begin to plan for their retirement years by saving and investing money to finance their activities after they (or their spouses) stop working.

As people move closer to the retirement event, they enter the **near-retirement phase.** This usually is a time for more active planning for retirement. Some workers—only a minority of those eligible—attend preretirement programs, in which they are counseled about retirement and learn how to plan for this phase of life. According to Atchley, this is a time of mutual disengagement at work. Duties and obligations are gradually given up and shifted to younger workers. This period ends with the actual retirement. Bill would be described as being in this phase.

The transition from worker to nonworker is often accompanied by initial enthusiasm, by feelings of excitement and even euphoria. This is the **honeymoon phase**—the first of the postretirement phases. During this time, people often begin to implement the many activities they had long planned for—for example, a trip across the country, visiting relatives or children, beginning the many house repairs that were put off in the past, developing a garden, reading and writing, or just plain relaxing. Not all people who retire, however, experience the excitement and enthusiasm of this early retirement period. Older adults who have been forced to retire, either because of company policy or owing to poor health, and those whose financial situation prevents them from engaging in the activities they had planned, usually feel a sense of dissatisfaction, frustration, and even anger.

disenchantment phase

A phase in the retirement process when a retiree's plans are beyond their means and they feel "let down" and often depressed.

reorientation phase

The phase in which retired people come to grips with the reality of their retirement and reevaluate their goals and ways of achieving them.

stability phase

A phase in the retirement process for determining and then implementing long-term choices or goals.

terminal phase

The final phase in the retirement process when retirement loses much of its significance or meaning for the person.

Even those who initially go through a honeymoon phase will usually find that some of their plans are beyond their means, or that the plans are not as satisfying as they had expected. When this happens, a transition to the **disenchantment phase** occurs. The retiree feels "let down" and often depressed.

For most adults, disenchantment does not last forever. Atchley suggested that as people move through the postretirement years they enter a **reorientation phase** during which they come to grips with the reality of retirement and its meaning for them. This is a time for reorienting oneself to the future and for reevaluating one's goals and the means of achieving them.

The next phase of retirement is termed the **stability phase.** Although Atchley indicates that it typically follows a period of disenchantment and then reorientation, he notes that some older people enter this phase immediately after the honeymoon period. This phase is a time for determining and then implementing long-term choices or goals.

The final phase of retirement is the **terminal phase.** This is a time when retirement loses much of its significance or meaning. Other factors, such as serious illness or impending death, assume more importance. In this case, the older adult puts aside the role of retiree and becomes preoccupied with the role of sick, disabled, or dying person. For other adults, however, the terminal phase takes on a much different perspective. Dissatisfaction with retirement goals and activities—including those associated with extended leisure—sometimes leads the older individual to seek out employment once again, usually a part-time job and often one that is totally unrelated to his or her earlier careers. Thus, the individual has come full circle, from worker to nonworker to worker once again. For example, about 2 years after my father retired, he grew bored and restless. He took a part-time job as a counter clerk in the local butcher's shop and still had time to travel with my mother.

Even though the Queen Mother of England was no longer a reigning monarch, she maintained an active life in retirement by visiting English cathedrals.

ATTITUDES TOWARD RETIREMENT

A number of factors influence people's attitudes toward retirement. First is the amount of choice they can exercise in the matter, which varies with the occupation. People who are self-employed, such as novelists, carpenters, or physicians, have the option of working well beyond normal retirement age. A schoolteacher can choose to retire after 20 or 25 years. Members of trade unions may be able to take advantage of a "flexible retirement" clause that allows them to work past normal retirement or provides an early retirement option. Other workers have no choice but to accept their retirement "gold watch" at the specified moment.

Interacting with these factors, of course, is job satisfaction. Unskilled workers (who show less job satisfaction) are likely to opt for early retirement if they are given this option. People who are bored with their work or unhappy with the control exercised over them by supervisors or coworkers also may look favorably on retirement (Troll, 1982). Other workers, particularly those in white-collar and professional jobs, are more likely to choose retirement at 65 or later. Who, then, is discontented? Those for whom adjustment is most difficult are competent at and enjoy their work but are forced to retire before they wish to do so.

Adjustment is also difficult for those who do not have adequate savings or retirement income. Many retired people find that their "nest eggs" and fixed retirement incomes amount to much less than they had foreseen. For the person who has always been poor, postretirement poverty is just "one more economic insult." For the majority of retirees, it represents deprivation and discontinuity with the working years. Reduced resources represent a difficult adjustment for retirees, perhaps a scrapping of plans for travel and other recreation. For retired people generally, a high level of morale may be possible only if their economic status compares favorably with that of working adults (Bromley, 1974).

FOCUS ON CULTURE

Retirement assumes an entirely different meaning if it is perceived as a change from one way of arranging one's time and activities to another. Women who have remained out of the workplace and have focused their energies on family activities naturally reorient their activities as their families change. A similar, more gradual shift in activities occurs for older adults living in nontechnological and agricultural societies.

Leisure Activities in Retirement Perhaps most important to retired people in terms of their attitude and adjustment to retirement is the issue of what they are going to do with their time. Their options include leisure, hobbies, or recreation, part-time employment, voluntary service, socializing, or doing nothing (which might mean anything from watching television to contemplating the meaning of life). Though doing nothing might be a reasonable choice after a lifetime of labor—there are societies that recognize an older person's privilege to sit and think—this is not considered to be an admirable choice in American culture.

Many people begin a leisure activity or hobby in middle adulthood, sometimes in anticipation of retirement. **Leisure** refers to nonwork or nonobligatory time

leisure
Nonwork or nonobligatory time during which people engage in activities that they enjoy.

during which people engage in activities that they enjoy. An activity such as cooking a meal may be work for one person and a leisure activity for another. It all depends on whether the person feels obliged to do the activity. Thus, retired people may take pleasure in volunteering their time to counsel teenage mothers or teach English to immigrants because they have made the choice to do so freely and not because they needed to work for money or because their services were required in some way.

Rather than continuing a work-related role, some older people develop new roles in voluntary services. There is ample opportunity. Among the many governmental agencies known to value the work of older people are the Veterans Administration Volunteers Service, Foster Grandparents, the Small Business Administration, VISTA, and the Peace Corps. Opportunities for general community service differs, of course, with each community. Some cities have agencies that place older people in other city agencies, matching their skills and interests to an agency's needs. Even small towns and rural areas have self-help programs that depend upon the volunteer efforts of retired residents.

Most people who volunteer their time do so within a 10-year period before and just after retirement (McPherson, 1983). Furthermore, they are likely to have higher levels of education and better health than nonvolunteers. Many people are limited in the leisure activities they can pursue because of lack of transportation, limited funds, or declining health (Burrus-Bammel & Bammel, 1985). People who live in an age-segregated residential community have more opportunities to engage in more leisure activities because they do not have to travel and often have neighbors with similar interests.

Leisure activities in late adulthood help people maintain their interest in life. Walking is a leisure activity that also contributes to a healthy life.

The leisure activities that are most frequently reported by American adults over the age of 65 are socializing with friends and relatives, watching television, gardening, reading, and thinking—all of which (except gardening) are sedentary activities (McPherson, 1983). Most of the activities are home-based and can be done alone. The sedentary quality of leisure activities may represent a continuation of a nonactive lifestyle from earlier stages of adulthood or it may be the result of limited mobility due to disability or disease.

Whatever activities are chosen, most studies have found that people who are involved in leisure activities are more satisfied with their lives and adjust better to retired life. Leisure activities often bring people into contact with one another and create more variety in their lives. While it may be that people who have made a more satisfactory adjustment to old age are also more likely to spend time with other people and engage in leisure activities, keeping active in the postretirement years is nonetheless an important factor in successful aging.

THE PSYCHOLOGICAL IMPACT OF RETIREMENT

Because I want to learn more about the journey that lay ahead of me in late adulthood, I am interested in what happens to my older colleagues who have retired. With the exception of a friend who retired because of serious health problems, every one of my retired friends appears to be in better health and to be happier than they were when they were working full time. I am inspired by their example and look forward to the time when I will retire.

Even though retirement represents a major and potentially stressful change in a person's life, it does not seem to be associated with a decline in well-being. With the exception of people who retire because they are ill, health does not deteriorate after retirement. In fact, many people's health improves in the immediate postretirement years (Troll, 1982). Moreover, except for those who have retired involuntarily, retirement does not seem to be associated with low morale in most cases (Streib & Schneider, 1971). Nor does it lead to psychological impairment or mental illness (Lowenthal & Haven, 1968). Finally, following retirement, family members in different generations usually interact more and become closer (Friedmann & Orbach, 1974).

BRIEF REVIEW

Many of the adjustments to aging lie within the contexts of family, social relations, and work—such as the death of a spouse, retirement, and accommodating a reduced income. Most research seems to indicate that the quality of married life in old age is good. The two factors that characterize older married couples are the focus away from the children and retirement from work, leaving the husband and wife with more time for each other.

Poverty and illness place a strain on older married life. However, people benefit in old age from being married. They live longer, and experience less mental illness and loneliness where there is a spouse to buffer them from the stresses of old age.

Sexual activity is still important to old people. They enjoy sex but are often frustrated by the lack of an available and willing partner. Older adults focus less on sexual performance and more on sexual pleasure.

Most older people are neither abandoned nor isolated. They live independently of their children, and often nearby. Old people rely on their children in times of illness, but give—as well as receive—advice, emotional support, and services.

Relationships with grandchildren vary considerably from one older adult to another and from one culture to another. Research suggests that older adults and their adolescent and young-adult grandchildren mutually influence one another, but only in certain areas.

Adults who care for their elderly parents or relatives must resolve dilemmas focused on their degree and type of caregiving obligation. They must work out ways to share the care among other family members and set reasonable limits for the time and energy they can expend on caring for elderly parents or relatives. Open discussions about personal decisions that must be made are also important.

Widowhood represents the single greatest loss suffered by the aging individual. Most of those widowed are women over 75 years of age. Most prefer to maintain their independence despite the problem of loneliness. Other problems faced by widows are decreased income and decrease in social status.

Few older Americans live in nursing homes. People generally enter into some form of extended-care facility when their physical condition is increasingly deteriorating and there is no other care available. Mortality rates following institutionalization are high.

Alternatives to institutionalization for elderly include retirement or age-segregated residential communities, in-home care, and living in apartments attached or close to the home of adult children. Most elderly Americans value their independence but want to live in a secure setting.

Aging takes place in a social and cultural context. The impact of declining social roles and social relations on the elderly is determined by whether the withdrawal is voluntary.

Besides marital relations, and relations with children and grandchildren, the older adult is influenced by interactions with friends and siblings—both of which offer emotional support in times of crisis.

People retire for various reasons. Those who choose to retire usually do so because of adequate financial resources, good pension plans, a desire to spend more time with family, or dislike of the job. Involuntary retirement is associated with mandatory retirement policies and poor health.

Retirement is a process involving a number of phases. As individuals go through the phases, they develop, implement, reevaluate, and enact their plans for the retirement years. Some adults find retirement exciting and satisfying; others are disenchanted and depressed.

Attitudes toward retirement depend on the person's control over retirement, financial situation, job satisfaction, personality, degree of preretirement planning, and satisfaction with the activities he or she is engaging in during retirement. Leisure activities in old age are mostly confined to in-home sedentary activities. Some people volunteer their time to community groups. People who are actively involved in leisure pursuits are usually more satisfied with their postretirement life. Contrary to popular belief, retirement, though often stressful, is unrelated to declining health and psychological problems.

KEY TERMS

disenchantment phase (644)
elder abuse (628)
honeymoon phase (643)
impotence (624)
leisure (645)

near-retirement phase (643)
remote phase (643)
reorientation phase (644)
retirement (640)
social convoy (636)

social integration versus
*   isolation (636)*
stability phase (644)
terminal phase (644)

REVIEW QUESTIONS

If you can answer these questions, you have a good understanding of the material in this chapter. If a question seems difficult, go back to the text and review the topic.

1. What contributes to marital satisfaction in old age? Describe the two factors that change the quality of late-adulthood marital life. What factors strain or diminish marital satisfaction between older adults?

2. What physiological changes interfere with sexual activity in late adulthood? Why does the stereotype of sexless older adults persist?

3. How do cultural values influence the relationship older adults may have with their adult children? Describe the way that American older adults interact both with their adult children and with their grandchildren.

4. What adjustments must be made following the death of a spouse? Describe the Widow-to-Widow program. How do men and women differ in adjusting to the loss of a spouse?

5. List some reasons for entering nursing homes or other institutions. What are the disadvantages of institutionalization? What are the advantages?

6. What are the ethical dilemmas family members must face when caring for an elderly family member?

7. Describe alternatives within our culture to nursing homes. How do people in other cultures deal with caring for the elderly?

8. Describe the five types of elder abuse. What factors promote this abuse? How can it be prevented?

9. Discuss the meaning of social integration versus isolation; cite examples of each dimension. What factors influence the quality of social contact in late adulthood?

10. Describe the contributions of siblings in the quality of life in late adulthood. How do men and women differ in their sibling relationships in old age?

11. How do men and women differ in their friendship patterns in old age?

12. How is retirement an artifact of the culture and times? How do voluntary and involuntary retirement differ in terms of their impact for older adults?

13. Describe the seven phases of the retirement process; give an example of each.

14. What factors influence people's attitude toward retirement? What is the psychological impact of retirement to people in old age?

15. What activities are retired people in the United States most likely to pursue? What impact do these activities have on the quality of life in retirement?

OBSERVATIONAL ACTIVITY

ADJUSTMENTS TO RETIREMENT

Between the ages of 60 and 70, most people retire from the jobs they have held for many years. Retirement is a major life event for men and some women in their late-adult years. The ease and impact of leaving their jobs and adjusting to a new life at home vary from person to person. The degree of personal satisfaction during retirement also is influenced by many factors, including the extent of preretirement planning, financial resources, hobbies and meaningful activities available, and the degree of involvement with people.

In order to fully understand the impact of retirement on people, choose several retired individuals who are willing to be interviewed. Ask them the following questions:

1. How old are you and how long have you been retired? What kind of work did you do before retirement? Do you work part-time now?

2. At what point in your life did you make plans for your retirement? What sort of plans did you make? Were these preretirement plans helpful to you?

3. What do you like about your life now that you are retired? Are there things you do now that you couldn't do before retirement? Give examples.

4. What changes have you had to make in your life as a result of retirement? What has been the most difficult part of retirement for you?

5. If you are married, how has being at home affected your relationship with your spouse? Are you more involved in household tasks? Give examples.

After you have interviewed these people, summarize your findings and compare them to the findings of your classmates. What factors seem to be most important in the degree of satisfaction associated with retirement? How does retirement affect family relations? On the basis of your interview, what suggestions can you offer to help a person better prepare for retirement?

The End of the Journey

Death, like birth, is a one-time event. Although everyone dies at some point, people vary greatly in when and how they die. For some people, life's journey is a long and rich one; others end their travels abruptly through premature death. In many cultures and religions death is viewed as a natural part of the rhythm of living. When their bodies die, they believe, people continue their spiritual journey into the afterlife. In some religions, death is the means by which people are transformed from one form of life to another, perhaps as an animal or a different person. Other cultures use a chronological perspective to understand life; birth marks the beginning of a lifespan and death marks the end.

Death also affects the living. As older family members and friends die, we are reminded that our lifespan is limited. When someone dies prematurely in childhood or early adulthood, we are more acutely aware of the ways in which death is the result of our behavior, our biology, and our sociocultural environment. We want to know why certain people die so early in life, perhaps hoping to learn something that may help us forestall our own deaths. In this last chapter, some of the issues concerning death and the process of dying are examined from a lifespan perspective. The meaning of death and the effects of the loss of a loved one are also considered.

CHAPTER 17

The Final Journey of Life: Death, Dying, and Bereavement

At 40 years of age, Bob did not want to accept his doctor's diagnosis that he had a rare and fatal form of bone cancer. His first reaction was disbelief, followed by anger that such a fate should befall him in the prime of his life. There were still so many things he wanted to do. He mourned the fact that he had not married or had children of his own. An important part of his life had been his friends and his students. Now, all that had changed.

When Bob finally accepted the reality of his diagnosis, he decided to make the most of the time remaining to him by doing what he most enjoyed: teaching and traveling. He traveled to Nepal where he watched the funeral procession of a woman in a small village. The woman's family and friends were celebrating her passage to the next world with music and dance.

Returning to his beloved classroom, Bob was full of enthusiasm and new ideas and insights to pass on to his students. Over the next few months, his blood tests continued to indicate the progressive deteriorating effects of the cancer. A week after commencement ceremonies, Bob was hospitalized.

As each new treatment effort failed, he moved closer to accepting the reality of his imminent death. He took steps to ensure that he would die as he had lived, among friends and with grace and dignity. He asked one friend to be with him and to hold him as he died.

Over the last 3 months of his life, despite the pain and discomfort caused by his disease, Bob set his life in order so that he was ready to die. He contacted old friends with whom he had lost touch. So that there would be no bad will after he died, he buried old grudges, including settling an old quarrel with his brother. He wrote out explicit instructions for the settling of his estate. As he thought about his many friends and selected something special to leave each of them, he was filled with a deep sense of gratitude for the friendships he had made.

Perhaps as a result of what he had learned about death in Nepal, Bob left the following request in his will: "Throw a party for all the folks . . . a happy party—very happy. If I'm ready—as I am—then you can all celebrate that fact." By early October, he had set his life in order, said his good-byes, and made plans for his funeral. He was ready to die. A few days later, surrounded by a few close friends and in the arms of one of them, Bob died peacefully. He died as he had lived, with full involvement and dignity.

Until fairly recently, many people would have considered a discussion of death to be in poor taste or disrespectful. And with few exceptions, psychologists, sociologists, and physicians were equally quiet on the subject (Feifel, 1990). Little research had been done on dying people, and not much was known about the effects on the individual or the consequences to the friends and relatives left behind. Today more is known about this last period in the lifespan, although much more remains to be learned about its significance and consequences.

DEATH: THE FINAL STAGE OF LIFE

Most people do not like to think or talk about death, especially their own. Yet death is a major life event for all of us. While most people accept the reality that life is finite, they rely on cultural traditions to provide them with a way to define and deal with death. Just as cultures vary in the way they respond to aspects of living, so, too, do they differ in their approaches to understanding death.

THE CULTURAL MEANING OF DEATH

The meaning of death varies across cultures, depending on religious beliefs, customs, and traditions. For example, if you were raised in India or Bali or another non-Western culture, the title of this chapter would not make much sense to you: These cultures view death as a part of the natural rhythm of life that results in the rebirth of the person. Among the Indian Hindus, it is believed that as soon as one is born, dying begins; when people die, they continue to live in another form. Life begins before birth and continues after death (Almeida, 1991). In most Western cultures, death is viewed as the end of life. According to most Western religions, one may expect to enter the spiritual world of heaven or hell after death.

Among Polynesian peoples, on the other hand, death is viewed as a process of transition from the world of humans to the world of the supernatural ghosts or spirits of the dead (Counts & Counts, 1985). When a person is dying, it is believed that the ghosts from the supernatural world have entered his or her body. The Polynesian word *mate* means that the dying person has left this world and is on the way to the next.

The !Kung people of East Africa do not keep track of their chronological age, but rather identify people by the life transitions they have experienced. Infants, children, adolescents, and adults are distinguished from *na*, the old people. Those who are very old and near death are called "old/dead," or *da ki*, although death is not viewed as an exclusive characteristic of the old since infant mortality is high as well (Rosenberg, 1990).

Navajo Indians have especially strong fears of death and the ghosts that inhabit the dead. They bury their dead quickly to avoid being harmed by the evil spirits. Terminally ill people are often kept away from the family shelters to protect the family from ghosts (Markides & Mindel, 1987).

WHAT IS DEATH?

The distinction between life and death sometimes is not easily drawn. At one time the legal and medical definitions of death were based on the moment at which the heart stopped beating and breathing ceased. Today, as a result of advances in

FOCUS ON CULTURE

The meaning of life and death is affected by the degree of control people have in prolonging life and preventing death. Industrialized societies such as the United States provide greater access to medical technology than nonindustrialized, third-world countries such as Burma, Zaire, Bangladesh, or Somalia. What impact might additional choices in medical care and treatment have on an individual's approach to death?

electroencephalogram (EEG)
Medical apparatus used to measure the activities of a person's brain.

medical technologies, the issue of determining death is more complex. Pacemakers and cardiac resuscitation can restore and regulate heartbeat; respirators can maintain cardiovascular and respiratory functions. These processes may even be continued long after the brain has been irreversibly damaged and is no longer functional. Many physicians have advocated a new medical and legal definition of death based on the death of the brain. Even this does not present a completely clear-cut alternative, however, since the principal measure of brain activity, the **electroencephalogram (EEG),** is not in itself sufficiently accurate. People whose EEGs have remained flat for several hours have been known to recover. In conjunction with other factors, however—such as lack of spontaneous respiration and muscle movement and the passage of time—a flat EEG could become the guideline in determining death.

CAUSES OF DEATH ACROSS THE LIFESPAN

While most people associate death with old age, death can occur at any stage of life. Death can occur at the moment of birth—or even before birth in the case of stillbirths or miscarriages. Most infants who die do so within a few days of birth. Most die as a result of birth defects or because their bodies have not developed sufficiently to sustain life outside the uterus. One of the reasons average life expectancy in the United States has increased in recent years is that medical technology has improved dramatically. Many newborns who might have died at birth now survive longer. **Sudden infant death syndrome (SIDS)** is a tragic condition that results in the sudden death of seemingly healthy young infants. Death of an infant from SIDS is especially difficult for parents because they do not expect it in one so young.

sudden infant death syndrome (SIDS)
The sudden and unexpected death of seemingly healthy infants between the ages of 3 weeks to 1 year.

During childhood, death is more likely to be caused by accidents or illness. In the United States, the leading causes of accidental death for children include automobile accidents, poisoning, drowning, death by fire, and falls from heights. Major illnesses that cause childhood death are cancer, heart disease, and birth defects.

During adolescence, death is more likely to occur violently through homicide, suicide, or motor-vehicle accidents, which are often alcohol-related. While not the leading cause of death, the AIDS virus is more likely to affect younger people, especially those who are sexually active.

In early and middle adulthood, people living in industrialized countries most often die from motor-vehicle accidents, combat, homicide, and disease—primarily heart disease and cancer. In nontechnological societies, adults are more likely to die from infectious and parasitic diseases. By late adulthood, most people die of disease or, in some cases, suicide.

Death of an infant is especially difficult to accept, especially for parents, because it is not expected at such a young age.

premature death
When death occurs before a person has reached middle adulthood.

In industrialized countries, death that occurs before the person has reached middle adulthood it is considered to be **premature death.** Often, as in the case of accidents, suicides, and homicides, the death is sudden and unexpected. Part of the distress associated with premature death is a sense of lost time. People who die prematurely do not have as much time to live as those who reach old age. Although no one is really certain how long they will live, it is often difficult to accept a sudden death, particularly one that is perceived to be early.

DEVELOPMENTAL CONCEPTIONS OF DEATH

The impact of death varies with the person's age and ability to grasp its meaning. Chronological age influences a person's expectations of death as well as experience with death and bereavement. As children develop, they gradually acquire a mature understanding of the meaning of death. According to Speece and Brent (1984), a mature, adultlike understanding of the concept of death includes recognition of three aspects:

1. Death is irreversible and final,
2. Death represents the end of life, and
3. All living things die.

In the earlier stages of the life-span, death is more likely to occur as a result of an accident.

Infancy   Most of the research on children's understanding of death suggests that children under the age of 2 years do not comprehend death. Death represents the loss of a person in one's life. To the infant functioning at Piaget's sensorimotor level of cognitive development, an object or person that is gone is also forgotten. Until the development of object permanence is firmly established, the infant has no idea of permanent loss. The infant cannot conceive of the thing "not being" because it does not conceive of the "being" in the first place.

As infants achieve object permanence, they begin to react to the disappearance of objects and people. By the time they are about 10 months old, they have formed an attachment, usually to their parents or caregivers. They can now experience loss and separation, and consequently suffer separation anxiety. It is important to note that the child does not attain an understanding of time until at least age 6. A short separation will be experienced as a total loss, especially since the child wavers in his or her ability to understand that the caregiver is "somewhere else." Separation, then, remains a powerful analogy to death for the infant.

Very little is known about infants' actual experiences with bereavement. Of course, some infants do lose a parent or primary caretaker during the 1st year of life. From the infant's perspective, it makes little difference whether this loss is a permanent separation, a temporary separation (as in foster placement), or death. Loss or prolonged separation from the primary caretaker during infancy may affect the child's vitality and health. Studies of institutionalized children who have been deprived of warm, loving social contact report a higher mortality rate for such infants (Spitz, 1945).

Early Childhood   During the period from 2 to 6 years of age, children are able to form concepts; they are functioning at Piaget's level of preoperational thought. Preschool-age children discover that some things are called "alive" and begin to form concepts of life and death. At first, young children ascribe the quality of life to a great many things that are not alive, a process known as *animism*. This is particularly true for items with which children have little direct contact. The moon and clouds, for example, are "alive" because they are moving or changing. By the same logic, these objects can die. At this stage of development, life and death are temporary, reversible states.

Death continues to be viewed as a state similar to sleep. Death may also be equated with disappearance. Because of feeling so small relative to other objects in the environment, the child will occasionally express fears of being sucked away or absorbed by some larger process. Children at this stage are often afraid of disappearing down the bathtub drain, being sucked up in the vacuum cleaner, or disappearing up or down an escalator.

Although they do not understand the significance of death, young children may react with seriousness to dead objects and death-related phenomena. They are likely to be interested in burial and what happens to the body. Even when quite young, children may draw back from a dead animal with awe, saying "no more" or "all gone" (Kastenbaum, 1977). This action is like that of some higher birds and mammals, which react dramatically to the death or dying of a member of their own species (Lorenz, 1966) even though (we assume) they have no real understanding of death.

In a classic study, Nagy (1948) asked 378 Hungarian children between the ages of 3 and 10 years to tell her whatever came into their minds when she asked them the following questions: (1) What is death? (2) Why do people die? and (3) How do you recognize when someone is dead?

On the basis of the children's responses, she identified three developmental stages of death-related concepts for children between 3 and 10 years of age (see

STAGES OF DEVELOPMENT IN CHILDREN'S CONCEPTION OF DEATH

Stage 1: Children under 5 years of age did not see death as irreversible but rather as living on under changed circumstances. Eighty-six percent of the 3-year-olds, 50% of the 4-year-olds, and 33% of the 5-year-olds were at this level of conceptual development.

Stage 2: Children between the ages of 5 and 9 years personified death. Fourteen percent of the 3-year-olds, 50% of the 4-year-olds, and 67% of the 5-year-olds were found to be at this level of conceptual development.

Stage 3: Children beyond 9 years of age saw death as final and inevitable. No child 5 years of age or younger was classified at this conceptual level.

TABLE 17–1

Source: From "The Child's Theories Concerning Death," by M. Nagy, 1948, *Journal of Genetic Psychology, 73,* pp. 3–27.

Table 17–1). The young child sees death as reversible, a state in which dead people are simply living differently. For example, death was cited as a long sleep or a journey. Children believe that when people die they still possess the same life processes and consciousness as the living. Thus, toddlers may wonder whether a deceased relative thinks about them. Young children view death as a separation and ask where the dead person went. If a person goes away from the child, as when a relative moves, the child may consider the person to be dead. Furthermore, children at this age believe that dead people can come back to life or be reborn in another place.

Unfortunately, some children are forced to confront their own deaths in early childhood. It was once assumed that young children did not understand their predicament (and that this was probably a blessing). Research suggests, however, that the seriously ill child of 4 or 5 years may be aware of impending death. Anxiety takes the form of separation anxiety, loneliness, and fears of abandonment (Spinetta, 1974). The child will be greatly comforted by assurances that their mother will stay with them and "never leave." Though young children normally do not realize that death is irreversible, many terminally ill children do. One researcher found that the majority of children came to understand not only that they were dying, but that this was a final and irreversible process (Bluebond-Langner, 1977).

Middle Childhood By age 6 or so, the child has formed a more realistic concept about what it means to be alive and what it means to be dead. Somewhere between 6 and 9 years of age, the child perceives that it is not movement itself that defines life, but rather spontaneous, or internally generated movement (Safier, 1964). Thus, for example, a car is no longer seen as alive (or dead) simply because it moves; it is not alive because it does not move itself. A worm, however, is alive (or dead) because it moves (or doesn't move) of its own accord.

At this stage, death, too, is perceived more nearly in adult terms. Death is no longer seen as reversible. However, it is not yet seen as inevitable (Safier, 1964).

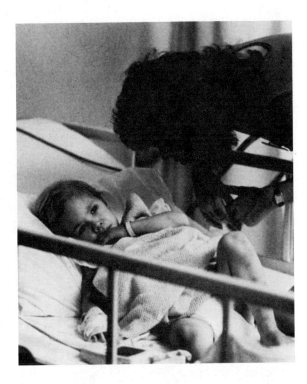

Even though this child is less than 5 years old, she may be aware of the seriousness of her illness. Some young children may even comprehend that they are going to die.

Death is still something that one can outwit. In particular, death is a person one can outwit—something akin to a bogeyman or a black angel (Nagy, 1948). Such personifications of death occur during Nagy's second stage. By making death humanlike, children are better able to understand it, because death is tangible, visible, and comparable to their experiences with people. Just as they have learned to manipulate and fool adults, children imagine that they can outwit or elude death. Children at this age believe that old or sick people are more likely to die because they cannot run or move fast enough to avoid the "death man." They think young children do not die because they are more active and because they are small enough to hide from death (Kastenbaum, 1967).

At about age 6, children begin to believe in their own personal mortality (Reilly, Hasazi, & Bond, 1983). Even though they recognize that they will die, most view their own deaths as a long way off. This awareness is related to the child's ability to use concrete operational thinking, particularly conservation. Children who have not achieved conservation typically do not believe in their own mortality; they are unable to accept the logical finality of death or their own mortality. Death-related experiences (e.g., the death of a parent, sibling, or close relation) also facilitate children's comprehension of their own mortality.

Children who experience a terminal illness in middle childhood appear to understand their predicament (Simeonsson, Buckley, & Monson, 1979). They are aware of hospital procedures and are able to acquire information on drugs and their side effects. Whereas the young child is concerned mostly with separation, the school-age child fears physical injury and mutilation (Natterson & Knudson, 1960). Older children, like adults, tend to fear the loss of normal bodily functions. Terminally ill children do not always verbalize their fears of death, one reason for

By the time children are 9 years old, they understand that death is final and irreversible.

the past belief that they did not understand their condition. However, it is now recognized that school-age children with a serious illness understand that they may die and need to be able to express their concerns and deal with their fears and anxiety (Furman, 1974).

At about 9 or 10 years of age, children enter the third stage described by Nagy, in which they achieve a firm, adult concept of death (although it may not operate at all times). Death and life are seen as internal processes that belong to people, animals, and plants. The child becomes concerned about the goodness and badness of people who died, about how they felt about dying, and so forth. These concerns are related to the child's growing capacity for self-knowledge. During this

FOCUS ON CULTURE

During middle childhood, children are better able to understand and accept religious beliefs concerning life and death. It is also the time when they can participate in death rituals within their culture. In many cultures, such as the Hindu or Jewish cultures, it is the custom for a dead person's children to perform a ritual such as lighting a funeral pyre or saying special prayers. Others, such as the Native American culture, believe children of all ages should be shielded from the harsh realities of death.

Attending the funeral of a loved one can help school-aged, concrete operational thinking children understand the meaning of death and loss.

period many children experience the death of a grandparent or distant relative, which makes death more real to them. Children who are concrete operational thinkers understand ideas and events better when they have a tangible, concrete way of conceptualizing them. While death can be viewed abstractly and philosophically by adults, it may not be by children. Discussing the death of relatives with children enables them to cope better with the loss of the relative and to gain a clearer understanding of death.

Adolescence and Youth   Adolescents operate at a higher level of abstract thinking than younger children, and most have attained a mature notion of time and of physical changes such as their own maturity and their parents' aging. Perhaps for the first time, they are facing the question of their personal future and setting long-range academic and vocational goals. These changes contribute to their new awareness of, and even interest in, death.

Adolescents understand death more or less the way adults do. However, their age makes their actual relationship to death different from that of older people. Adolescents and young adults are in an expansive period of life in which death is uncommon. Although mortality risk increases appreciably between the ages of 15 and 25, in the United States it remains relatively low (Kastenbaum, 1977). Not surprisingly, death for young people remains a distant event—something that happens to the elderly.

Adolescent egocentrism contributes to the fatalistic view of death shared by many teenagers. Adolescents often believe that they are immune from danger,

An adolescent's belief in his or her own immortality may be demonstrated by reckless behavior and risk taking.

that death won't happen to them. When young people think of death in relation to themselves or their peers, it tends to be closely bound up with ideas of fate or dramatic circumstances of violence that may support their personal fable. Death is not seen as a natural debilitating process: It is a cruel blow. (In fact, violent death, through accident or suicide, is the most common form of death in this period.)

Ordinarily, adolescents do not have a sense of longevity; length of life is not as important as its quality. Adolescents may be idealistic and willing to risk their lives for a cause. Risk-taking and reckless behavior among the young (particularly men) appears to be common in many cultures. Not all young persons are dominated by these attitudes toward life and death, but these attitudes are so often expressed by young people as to be characteristic of this age group.

Early Adulthood   Most young adults think very little about death on a personal level. Physical health is at a peak during early adulthood, and death may seem far off. It is only when people become aware of their own aging, usually in middle adulthood, that they start to think and worry about death. However, certain events and decisions that occur in early adulthood can cause people to think about the end of life. Marriage, for example, asks young adults to pledge themselves until "death do us part," to share the rest of their lifespan with one person. Young adults must also consider the possibility of having children. For some people—perhaps for all people at some level—this is experienced as a question of whether or not to extend themselves into the future, a future that includes their own death. Actually, becoming a parent affects one's relationship to death. During pregnancy, many prospective parents worry about the possibility that the baby or mother might die during childbirth. Upon birth, various rituals, such as naming the child after a deceased relative, remind the new parents of their place in the chain of generations. Indeed, thoughts of death and birth give rise to each other in many contexts, at many points in the lifespan (Kastenbaum, 1975). In countries with high infant mortality rates and poor prenatal care, pregnancy and birth can often mean an impending death of infant or mother or both.

Childlessness due to infertility or misfortune can be seen as a symbolic death. Spontaneous abortion (miscarriage), particularly in the later stages of pregnancy, may also be experienced as a death. Sometimes similar reactions follow induced

Naming a child after a recently deceased relative calls attention to the life-and-death cycle.

Education Perspective

DEATH EDUCATION

There is no easy way to eliminate the distress one experiences at the death of a friend or relative, or in anticipation of one's own death. However, information and awareness can help reduce the stress associated with death. People of all ages benefit from knowing more about how to cope with the grief that accompanies the loss of a close relative or friend.

Since Elisabeth Kubler-Ross, a leading expert on the psychology of dying, began her seminars on death and dying in the late 1960s, there has been a growing interest in educating people, young and old, about death and the dying process.

Death education, as this field of interest is called, does not morbidly dwell on death, but rather focuses on it as a natural consequence of life, a part of the life cycle found throughout nature. Being able to talk openly about death and to share their feelings helps people put their fears and anxieties about death into perspective. Death education can offer practical information about how to comfort and help dying and bereaved people as well as decrease the stress associated with a personal loss.

Throughout the United States—on college campuses, in medical schools, in elementary and secondary schools, and in adult-education programs—an estimated 20,000 death education courses have been initiated since the late 1960s (Durlak, 1978–1979). The specific content of the courses varies according to age and life experiences of the audience. For

elementary and middle-school children, the topics generally included are life cycles of plants and animals, death and separation, grief and its expression, and funeral and burial customs (Gibson, Roberts, & Buttery, 1982). Discussion of these topics may be stimulated by children's death-related experiences—for example, the death of a pet. Children's books that include the theme of death or loss may also be useful in stimulating discussion.

Similar topics are discussed in high school or college-level death education programs, but in more detail and with greater depth. The student is capable of considering the philosophical aspects of death, such as the right to die, suicide, human destiny, and accepting one's own death.

Death education occurs not only in schools but in the home as well. Death educators advocate that parents first examine

death education
Education programs that focus on the natural consequences of the life-death cycle and provide information on the process of dying and the importance of bereavement.

abortions—even women and men who are not opposed to abortion may suffer feelings of bereavement after ending a pregnancy.

Middle Adulthood   When I turned 50, I realized that I had a limited amount of time left in my life. While I did not dwell on the prospect of dying, I did consider what I wanted to achieve before I died. My response is typical of middle adulthood, during which people become sensitive to the aging process and their limited lifetime. Concern with death appears to peak during this period. In one study, the greatest fear of death was expressed by those in the 45-to-54 age group (Bengston, Cuellar, & Ragan, 1977).

Exactly *when* a person becomes more conscious of life's finitude probably depends on personal experience. The death or serious illness of a friend, co-worker, or parent can cause people to think more about their own mortality. In some cases the awareness grows slowly. In others it comes like a blow, inducing panic, crying spells, or temporary breakdown. In later middle age, fears of death their own feelings and ideas about death. With a clearer understanding of their own reactions, parents are in a better position to reassure their children when the subject of death arises. The best time to talk about death to children is when it is part of their immediate experience. By answering questions about death directly and honestly, the parent can help the child form a realistic concept of death. Saying that Grandma is sleeping when she is dead will only add to the child's misconceptions about what happens when someone dies. As with sex, children's interest and curiosity about death is a useful springboard for educating them on the topic. By not hiding the fact of death from children, and by openly discussing various aspects of death, parents and educators can help children learn how to cope with the reality of death in their lives.

As was the case for Bob, people who become terminally ill in middle age tend to experience their impending death as disruptive to their relationships and responsibilities. Whereas the young person may rage against the loss of experiences or ambitions, the middle-aged person is acutely concerned about the emotional survival of his or her family and important others. Unlike the elderly, the middle-aged person has had less time to make appropriate practical or emotional adjustments.

The death of a pet may be the first encounter that children have with death.

seem to be resolved—they tend to become more openly acknowledged and more fully integrated into the person's understanding of life.

Late Adulthood   The older person stands in a special relationship to death. Even when they are physically and mentally vigorous, older people realize that health is precarious and the amount of time left to them is relatively short. Death becomes a realistic concern, and a variety of activities may be undertaken in its preparation. These range from such practical matters as deciding upon the distribution of one's property to internal processes such as life review.

It is often assumed that the elderly, as a group, live in special fear of death. However, research suggests that this is not so. A classic study by Munnichs (1966) found that the most common orientations toward death in individuals aged 70 and older were acceptance and acquiescence. Another study suggests that elderly subjects were less preoccupied with death than middle-aged subjects (Bengston et al., 1977). There are several reasons why older adults are less fearful of death. Elderly people are reminded of death more frequently, as their peers and even younger people die. They are much more likely to have lost a spouse, sibling, or parents through death. They attend more funerals, visit more grave sites, and read obituaries more frequently. In addition, the elderly experience the decline in their own bodies, thus compelling them to think and talk more about their own death. By confronting the realities of death, they are better able to cope with their fears.

The Terminal Stage

terminal stage of life
The phase of life when a person becomes aware of his or her impending death.

Although the expected lifespan varies from one individual to another and is dependent on numerous life experiences and situations, older people generally have an idea about how long they will live. By accepting the reality of a life expectancy of 75 years or so, older people who live beyond that age generally consider themselves fortunate. As people approach their 70s, they do so with the realization that their lives are coming to a completion. The diagnosis of a terminal illness or the sudden loss of mental or physical capabilities may trigger awareness of the **terminal stage of life,** the time when a person becomes aware of his or her impending death.

Entering the terminal period also influences intellectual performance. Riegel and Riegel (1972) conducted a 10-year study of old people in Germany. The subjects included 190 males and 190 females ranging in age from 55 to 75. The investigators administered a battery of tests to the subjects, including an intelligence test, a word-association test, verbal achievement tests, and a number of attitude and interest tests. The findings showed that subjects whose performance on intelligence tests was below average were closer to death than their more successful peers. Riegel and Riegel analyzed the subjects' scores by going backward in age, starting with the time of death. They concluded that the decline in performance on intelligence tests was due to a sudden drop in ability that occurred within 5 years before the death of the subjects, a phenomenon termed **terminal drop.** Similar results have been found in other longitudinal studies (Palmore & Cleveland, 1976; Siegler, McCarty, & Logue, 1982; Suedfeld & Piedrahita, 1984).

terminal drop
A decline in intellectual performance that frequently occurs within 5 years before death.

For many older people, the terminal stage is characterized by loneliness. Spouses and peers die, one by one, leaving the survivor feeling bereft and depressed. Often an older person does not have time to recover from the passing of a loved one before another dies. This is particularly true for women, who tend to outlive men. When death takes one's spouse, the survivor is left to manage as well as possible and, often, to think about his or her own impending death.

FOCUS ON CULTURE

In China and other societies that engage in ancestor worship, a person who is very old and close to death is held in reverence because it is believed that he or she soon will become an ancestor. This treatment of the elderly contrasts with Western cultures that do not hold ancestors in special regard. Do you think that having a link with one's ancestors might help reduce the sense of loss and depression that is associated with dying?

> ### RECAP
>
> While the moment of death may vary according to legal and medical definitions, the meaning of death is rooted in the culture. Causes of death vary across the lifespan, with premature death defined as any death prior to middle adulthood. To understand the meaning of death people must accept that it is irreversible, represents the end of life, and occurs to all living things. With cognitive maturity children gradually develop an understanding of death, but it is not until middle childhood that children acquire a realistic conception of death. By middle adulthood, people begin to think about and deal with the prospect of their own death. Near the end of life, some people display a decline in intellectual functioning known as terminal drop.

THE DYING PROCESS

psychological process of dying
Begins when a person learns that he or she has a fatal physical condition and involves coming to terms with the reality of death.

physiological process of dying
The failure of the body to function.

Different cultures view death differently. In some, death is not a process but a moment of extinction. In others, it is likened to a journey to a long, restful wait before a final judgment day. Some cultures see death as the end of all experience; others perceive it to be the beginning of salvation.

A person's condition does not change from alive to dead in a single moment. In part because of technological advances, death is usually a slower process. The **psychological process of dying** begins when a person learns that he or she has a fatal physical condition, and includes the person's beliefs, behaviors, and emotions in response to the diagnosis. The **physiological process of dying,** the failure of the body to function, may have begun earlier. People who die suddenly as a result of accidents or heart attacks may never know that they are dying. Most people, however, are aware of their impending death (Kalish, 1981) and adjust their lives accordingly.

For some people, the diagnosis of a terminal disease signals the onset of dying. In the past, physicians and family members withheld the truth about a fatal condition from the dying person on the assumption that it was kinder to do so. Today, however, most physicians recognize that patients need to be told the truth about their condition so that they can make the necessary financial, psychological, and emotional adjustments (Schulz, 1978).

STAGES OF DYING

The best-known research on people's psychological reactions to dying was conducted by Kübler-Ross (1969), who interviewed and observed over 200 terminally ill patients. On the basis of her observations, she proposed a five-stage process of dying.

Stage 1: Denial and Isolation   The first reaction people usually have upon learning that they have a terminal condition is shock and numbness, followed by denial. They react to their serious illness (or loss) by saying, "No, it cannot be me." They may assert that the doctor is incompetent, the diagnosis mistaken. In extreme cases, the person may refuse treatment. Most patients who use *denial* extensively throughout their illness are people who have become accustomed to coping with difficult life situations in this way. Indeed, the habit of denial may contribute to the seriousness of the condition, as, for example, when a person refuses to seek medical attention at the onset of the illness. Ordinarily, patients rely on denial at the beginning of the illness and at other moments when they are unable to face reality. For most patients with a progressive disease, denial soon becomes difficult and other reactions begin to intrude.

Stage 2: Anger

The cry of the dying person at this stage is "Why me?" The patient feels *anger:* at fate, at God, at the powers that be, at every person who, unknowing, enters the patient's world. There is resentment of the healthy, particularly caregivers, for perceiving the patient as dying or as good as dead. This anger is likely to alienate others.

Stage 3: Bargaining

At this stage, terminally ill patients change their attitudes and attempt to *bargain* with fate. For example, Bob only wanted enough time to complete a trip to China and Near East before his disease got the best of him. Others may bargain with God for a certain amount of time in return for good behavior, stoicism, or cooperation in treatment. A man may promise to change his ways, perhaps to dedicate his life to the church. A woman may announce herself ready to settle for a less-threatening form of the same illness and attempt to bargain with the doctor over her diagnosis. If she submits gracefully to an unwanted medical procedure, might she be rewarded by not progressing to the next stage of the illness?

Stage 4: Depression

"When the terminally ill patient can no longer deny his illness, when he is forced to undergo more surgery or hospitalization, when he begins to have more symptoms or becomes weaker and thinner, he cannot smile it

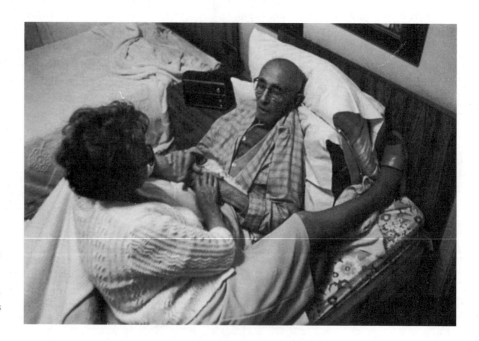

Dying people must come to terms with their impending death. The understanding support provided by loved ones can help the dying person express his or her feelings about the prognosis.

off anymore. His numbness or stoicism, his anger and rage will soon be replaced with a sense of great loss" (Kübler-Ross, 1969, p. 85). At this stage, people enter a deep *depression* over the losses they are incurring, such as the loss of their job, the depletion of their savings, or the loss of strength and alertness due to the disease. Dying people also are depressed about their impending death. During this stage they must be allowed to express their sorrow.

Stage 5: Acceptance   Finally, the dying person *accepts* death. The struggle is over and the person experiences "a final rest before the long journey." Bob's acceptance of death was reflected in the plans he made to celebrate his life and death. At this stage, patients are often tired and weak. They sleep often, and, in some cases, welcome the peacefulness they expect that death will bring them. People may limit the number of visitors they will see. Silence and constancy are appreciated, and they seem to detach themselves from the world around them in order to make death easier.

EVALUATING KÜBLER-ROSS'S THEORY

There is no doubt that Kübler-Ross has made an important contribution to people's awareness and understanding of the process of dying. Her theory and writings have provided a forum for dying people and their families to talk about death and understand their reactions. Those who care for the dying are sensitized to the emotional needs of their patients and better able to help friends and relatives through the difficult time as a result of being more knowledgeable about reactions to death.

However, the concept of stages of dying has been criticized on several points. One criticism is that the stages are not universal—not all terminal patients progress through the stages Kübler-Ross describes. For example, a woman may die during the denial stage because she refuses to consider any treatment alternative or because the course of her illness is too quick to grant her the time she needs to move beyond denial. Pattison (1977) found that anger and denial are prominent throughout the dying process, not just at the earlier stages. For some, depression is the dominant mood (Schulz, 1978). Others never accept their own death. Thus, people do not always experience the stages of dying in the order Kübler-Ross suggested, and some people never experience such a sequence at all.

Another criticism of the theory is that anger is often experienced repeatedly during the process of dying. Kübler-Ross herself acknowledged that patients do not limit their responses to any one stage; a depressed patient may have recurring bursts of anger. She notes, too, that all patients in all stages persist in feeling *hope*. Even the most accepting, most realistic patients leave open the possibility of recovery. For example, several days before his death Bob asked his doctors if there were any experimental drugs or procedures that might forestall the death he knew was at hand.

The nature of people's reactions to dying depends on many factors, such as the nature and suddenness of their deaths, the age at which dying occurs, their personalities, and cultural expectations surrounding death. The degree of loss associated with death often affects the intensity and duration of depression people experience. A person who is still relatively young at the time of death may experience a greater sense of loss than an older person who has lived a full life and has already lost a spouse. Those who have strong religious beliefs about life after death, rebirth, or heaven may find it easier to accept death than those who do not share such beliefs. Diseases that sometimes go into remission, such as cancer, may foster more denial than diseases that have no cure or remission, such as AIDS.

One final concern about Kübler-Ross's stages is that they may be overinterpreted by health-care professionals or relatives and applied to the dying person in a lockstep fashion. Expressions of anger by dying patients may reflect justified objections, particularly to aspects of their situations, and should not be dismissed as simply a reaction to the process of dying.

NEAR-DEATH EXPERIENCES

Do people experience life after death? What is it like? Throughout history, people have wondered about these questions. Religious beliefs attempt to provide answers—such as heaven, hell, purgatory, and nirvana. But, the true nature of life after death has eluded researchers because no one is able to report on the experience.

near-death experience (NDE)
The experience of people who come close to death but survive; a variety of common experiences have been reported.

clinical death
Death determined by the absence of a heart beat or brain activity.

Although it is impossible to study the experience of death itself, there have been attempts to understand the **near-death experience (NDE).** In a book titled *Life after Life,* Moody (1975) described the experiences of people who had come very close to death but had not actually died. Many of those he interviewed had been **clinically dead**—that is, they had no heartbeat or brain activity. Moody identified several common elements in people's accounts of their brushes with death. These included hearing the news that they were dead, hearing a buzzing noise, feeling peaceful and quiet, feeling oneself move out of one's body while traveling through a dark tunnel toward a bright light, seeing or feeling the presence of dead relatives or friends, experiencing one's life in review, and being aware that their time for dying had not come. Most of the people reported the experience as a positive one. Some did not want to return to living but wanted to stay with the light, which seemed to have powerful qualities.

Moody's interviews provided suggestive but unsystematic data on near-death experiences. Ring (1980, 1984) improved on Moody's work by establishing research procedures for studying NDEs. He developed a scale to measure the intensity of an NDE and compared the reports of subjects in his study. Ring (1989) reported that NDEs occur in about one in every three cases of people who have been clinically dead but were subsequently revived. Furthermore, he found that age, gender, socioeconomic status, and the type of death (e.g., automobile accident, surgery, illness) had no effect on whether a person had an NDE.

Near-death experiences have a powerful impact. Ring reported that many people have a renewed sense of purpose in their lives and are no longer afraid of death. Some individuals who had medical conditions seemed to improve, in part because of their more positive outlook on life (Sabom & Kreutziger, 1982). People who had NDEs as a result of suicide attempts were not likely to make another suicide attempt, but rather engaged in efforts to counsel others who were considering taking their own lives (Ring & Franklin, 1981–1982).

While there exists much controversy about how to explain NDEs, the reports seem to be consistent across a variety of studies. Critics of near-death experiences claim that the reports can be explained by known physiological processes (Siegel, 1980). For example, some NDE reports are similar to those of people under the influence of psychedelic drugs. Yet studies that compared the medical records of patients with NDEs could not support a physiological or biological explanation of their experiences (Sabom & Kreutziger, 1982). Thus, more study is needed to gain a clearer understanding of near-death experiences.

RECAP

Dying typically does not occur in a distinct moment, but rather is a process that has both psychological and physiological components. Kübler-Ross proposed five stages in the psychological process of dying: denial and isolation, anger, bargaining, depression, and acceptance. Critics question the universality and sequencing of the stages described by Kubler-Ross and worry that they may be overinterpreted by health-care professionals. Near-death experiences include a common pattern of reactions, such as travel through a dark tunnel to a light, seeing deceased relatives, experiencing one's life in review, out-of-body sensations, and feelings of peacefulness.

ISSUES IN THE CARE OF THE DYING

My father-in-law died at home in his own bed after an extended illness. His physician provided him with medication to alleviate his pain, and a visiting nurse checked in on him regularly. He was adamant about not wanting to die in a hospital. His whole life had revolved around his family and home, and it was this setting that gave him the most comfort in his dying days. Providing a comforting setting to dying people is an issue of concern to many people.

HOSPICE CARE

One significant outcome of Kübler-Ross's work with dying people is the awareness among physicians and health professionals of the dying person's need to be in contact with caring people who will listen as they share their concerns and prepare for death. Unfortunately, many individuals are often frightened or repelled by contact with dying people. Today, terminally ill patients in the United States and other technological countries are often isolated in sterile hospital wards and left to face the end alone, without the loving companionship of friends and family. Even adequate protection against pain is sometimes denied (Smyser, 1982).

Modern hospitals, geared to aggressive life-prolonging therapies, are simply not good places to die. An alternative to hospital treatment for the dying is a **hospice.** The modern hospice concept is based on the work of British physician Cicely Saunders. The idea was born out of her friendship with a Polish refugee who was dying of cancer in the noisy confusion of a busy London hospital. In 1967, Saunders founded St. Christopher's Hospice in southeast London for those afflicted with terminal cancer. St. Christopher's provides a pain-free, emotionally secure environment for dying patients. The atmosphere is warm and friendly, with plenty of sunlight and fresh flowers. Patients may bring in cherished possessions; one woman brought her antique collection. Visiting hours extend from 8 A.M. to

hospice
A homelike setting specializing in the care of the dying.

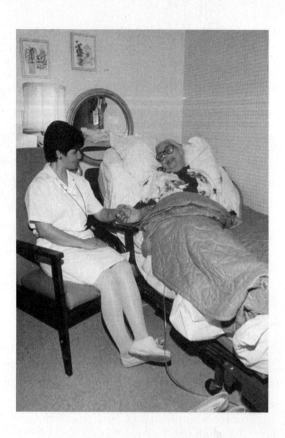

Hospice care provides dying people with the option of dying at home or in a homelike hospital setting.

Brompton mix

A mixture of painkillers given to dying patients to keep them relatively free of pain.

8 P.M., and family and friends help care for patients—holding their hands, giving them sponge baths, bringing special foods from home. Sophisticated use of analgesics keeps patients relatively pain-free. Saunders pioneered the use of the **Brompton mix,** containing such ingredients as heroin, cocaine, and gin, for the alleviation of cancer pain. If feasible, hospice patients may go home to die.

In the United States, the hospice movement has grown to more than 1,200 operational hospice programs (Osterweis, Solomon, & Green, 1984). Unfortunately, the availability of these programs is limited and waiting lists are long. Most medical insurance plans do not provide coverage for hospice care, thus limiting these programs to more affluent patients. Since most hospice programs depend on the help of a family member or friend to provide for the daily care of the dying person, not everyone may be able to participate.

Hospice care is just one way in which the needs of the dying person are met. The right to die with dignity or in the presence of loved ones can be accomplished in other ways. Like my father-in-law, some people are able to die at home with help and direction from trained medical and health practitioners. Not only is home care for the dying psychologically more acceptable to people because they are not isolated from their families, it is also considerably less costly than hospital or nursing home care.

EUTHANASIA

Every year in the Netherlands, between 2,000 to 6,000 people are helped to a "gentle death" by their physicians, who provide them with medication and instructions that allow them to end their own lives (Cooke, 1989). For years the Dutch have championed this right of dying people. While Dutch lawmakers do not condone the taking of life, they also recognize the doctor's duty to minister to the patient's right to die with dignity, and have established several criteria to help physicians determine whether "gentle deaths" are justifiable (see Table 17–2).

In the United States, Jack Kevorkian, a medical pathologist, has called attention to the question of **euthanasia.** Derived from the Greek words *eu* (good) and *thanatos* (death), the word *euthanasia* can be used to mean an easy and painless death, as well as the inducing of an easy and painless death for reasons assumed to be merciful. It is the second definition that has generated controversy. Dr. Kevorkian has assisted in the suicide deaths of several people who were not near death but in a state of continual and intractable pain. Dr. Kevorkian was brought to trial for his involvement in the deaths, and the publicity surrounding the legal proceedings stimulated a national debate about the rights of the dying person and the role of the physician in providing comfort. Because euthanasia is affected by so many factors—legal, moral, cultural, and historical—it is necessary to clarify the different meanings of the term. Many people differentiate between euthanasia by *omission* and euthanasia by *commission*—that is, ceasing the use of "extraordinary measures" in keeping a patient alive, versus actively ending someone's life. For instance, the Catholic Church, which is against euthanasia in general, makes an exception in cases where extraordinary measures are used to prolong life. As early as 1957, Pope Pius XII told a group of anesthesiologists that neither they nor their patients were morally obligated to use devices such as respirators to maintain life when there is no hope of recovery (Russell, 1977).

People who wish to ensure that no extraordinary medical attempts will be made to prolong their lives can draft living wills. **Living wills** are legal documents that describe people's wishes for the disposition of their own lives, should they later lose the ability to communicate or make decisions about medical treatments that merely prolong life when there is no reasonable expectation of recovery. The difficulty lies in deciding when there is "no reasonable expectation of recovery"; this decision usually is made by the attending physician. Most, but not all, states recognize the legality of a living will; some states recognize the wishes of the family as well as the patients in making decisions about life-sustaining efforts.

euthanasia
The act of inducing an easy and painless death for merciful reasons.

living will
A legal document by means of which people can express their wishes for the disposition of their own lives should they lose mental competence while dying.

CRITERIA FOR A "GENTLE DEATH"

There must be explicit and repeated requests from the patient.

The physical and mental pain must be severe and without hope of relief.

The patient's decision must be freely made and enduring.

Other options must be exhausted or refused by the patient.

The doctor must consult another physician.

The doctor must record all events leading up to the final hour of death.

TABLE 17–2

Source: From "The Gentle Death," by P. Cooke, 1989, in *Hippocrates, 3*, pp. 50–60.

FOCUS ON CULTURE

Cultures vary in their response to people who are near death. For example, on the Polynesian island of Niue, frail and dying elderly individuals are considered to be "nearly dead" and are subject to "death-hastening" behaviors such as abandonment and neglect (Barker, 1990). Among the Chukchi, a reindeer-herding society living in Siberia, old people may request to be killed when they become ill and can no longer function. Typically, the oldest son, daughter, or son-in-law stabs the old person in the heart with a knife (Glascock, 1990). In industrialized societies such direct death-hastening activities are rejected; instead frail or poor functioning old people are sometimes institutionalized and overmedicated, often without the knowledge or consent of the dying person.

Opponents feel that once voluntary euthanasia gains widespread approval, it could open the door to involuntary euthanasia. Furthermore, someone has to decide whether people who request euthanasia are competent to choose their fate, or are only temporarily depressed or affected by medication. Who would make this decision? Also, since our knowledge of medicine is far from perfect, it is difficult to decide when a given situation is hopeless. Many patients whose cases were deemed "hopeless" by physicians have recovered—in many cases, enough to lead normal lives. Lastly, some opponents hold that all life is a gift from God and only God can make the decision to end a life. The question remains: If individuals without hope for recovery wish their suffering and pain to end, do they have that right? Or is all life precious no matter what the financial or emotional costs?

While controversy surrounds the right to choose when one will die, there is little controversy about decisions to donate parts of one's body for organ replacement or scientific research. For some people, arranging for the donation of their vital organs after death is one way to ease their sense of loss at the approach of death. Elderly persons donate their corneas, younger people their hearts, kidneys, or lungs.

RECAP

Hospice care involves giving the dying person an opportunity to talk about his or her feelings and concerns in a supportive environment, as well as providing the means to alleviate pain. Family members assist in caring for their dying relatives. There is controversy over the value of euthanasia and assisted suicide as an alternative to painful dying. In the Netherlands, a gentle death is allowed, provided that physicians follow a set of criteria to determine its appropriateness. In the United States there is concern about the potential impact on the value of life if euthanasia were legalized. Living wills enable people to define the extent to which extraordinary efforts should be made to prolong their lives.

BEREAVEMENT

For several weeks after my father died, I was in a daze. I was constantly tired, cried easily, and had trouble concentrating on my work. I was mourning my loss. Fortunately, I was able to share my feelings and memories of my father with my

bereavement
The state or condition of loss, usually experienced through the death of a loved one.

grief
A person's emotional response to bereavement or the loss of a significant person.

mourning
The culturally prescribed, overt expression of grief and bereavement.

siblings and close friends. A year after my father's death, I was able to put his life and death into perspective and regain my own enthusiasm for life.

When someone close to us dies, we experience a state or condition of loss known as **bereavement.** The most significant bereavement occurs through death. However, bereavement may result from other losses, such as the loss of a love relationship through divorce or desertion; the loss of a child to adoption, abortion, or miscarriage; or the loss of a home through natural disaster, fire, financial upset, or relocation.

Grief is the emotional response to bereavement or the loss of a significant person. While it is true that grieving involves painful emotions and psychological suffering, bereaved people who do not grieve generally do not recover from their loss. One study found that during the process of bereavement, the survivors of all ages are at increased risk of dying prematurely or suffering physical and mental illness (Osterweis et al., 1984; Thompson, Gallagher-Thompson, Futterman, Gilewski, & Peterson, 1991). This is especially true for people who have experienced a high level of stress, lack of social support, and poor health prior to their loss (Murrell, Meeks, & Walker, 1991; Norris & Murrell, 1990).

CULTURAL DIFFERENCES IN BEREAVEMENT

Mourning refers to the culturally prescribed, overt expression of grief. While it is generally believed that the core experience of grief is much the same throughout the world, the way in which these feelings are approached and *expressed* is specific to the particular culture or subculture (Averill, 1968; Kastenbaum, 1977). Funeral practices and rituals, the length of bereavement, and the mourner's manner of dress and behavior are largely determined by the bereaved person's ethnic, cultural, or religious heritage. In China, for example, a funeral is a community event, with the degree of elaborateness reflecting the family's social status (Lee, 1991). A photo of the deceased person is displayed so that people can express their remorse about the loss. The purpose of the funeral is to give the deceased a good send-off to the next life. Hence, paper money, paper houses, food, and other material goods are burned along with the body. The noisier and more ornate the send-off, the greater the respect for the deceased. During the wake and funeral, relatives of the deceased are expected to wail and cry uninhibitedly, but after the funeral they are expected to control their emotions (Lee, 1991). The traditional period of mourning within Chinese families is 49 days, during which family members wear black cloth armbands. Daily prayers are recited in front of pictures of deceased relatives as part of ancestor worship.

Different customs govern the expression of grief in India. When a person dies, a close relative usually bathes and dresses the body in preparation for its reincarnation in the next life. The body is placed on a funeral pyre, which is lit by the oldest son. After cremation, the ashes are strewn in the River Ganges. Mourners are not expected to talk about their emotional reactions to the death and frequently participate in some form of self-sacrifice ranging from denial of food to offerings of money or prayers. At one time it was expected that a widow would commit suicide by throwing herself on the burning pyre with her husband's body; this practice is now forbidden by law. Women over the age of 25 are expected to remain in mourning for at least a year; some mourn throughout their lives (Almeida, 1991).

In the United States, mourning rituals are strongly influenced by people's ethnic and religious identification. For example, Jewish families must bury

Funeral and bereavement practices vary from culture to culture. Although the emotional experience of grief is the same, the way in which feelings are expressed depends upon the culture.

their dead within 24 hours of the death or as soon as possible. After the burial, family members begin a mourning period called *shiva*, which continues for 7 days during which special prayers are said and visitors pay their respects. Formal mourning may continue for a period ranging from 30 days to a year (Rosen, 1991).

Irish families consider death to be a very significant transition and go to great lengths to ensure a good celebration. It is not unusual for family members to drink, joke, and tell stories about the deceased person at the wake, a service in which the person's body is viewed by friends and relatives. However, once the funeral is over, family life goes back to normal and mourning is done in private (McGoldrick, 1991).

The nature of a person's emotional reactions to bereavement is also governed by cultural tradition and religion. In the United States it is commonly believed that the best thing to do after the loss of a loved one is to find a way to reduce one's attention to their loss, to find ways of "letting go of" one's attachment to the deceased (Stroebe, Gergen, Gergen, & Stroebe, 1992). In contrast, Japanese Shinto and Buddhist traditions dictate that emotional contact with the deceased should be maintained, since deceased relatives are believed to join ranks with other ancestors who continue to influence the lives of the living. Embedded within Japanese mourning rituals are numerous attempts to remain in contact with the deceased. Perhaps as a result of not having to sever emotional ties with loved ones, Japanese widows seem to have an easier time dealing with grief than widows in Western societies (Yamamoto, Okonoji, Iwasaki, & Yoshimura, 1969).

Native Americans in the Hopi tribe make every effort to avoid thinking about deceased loved ones; a successful mourning period is a short one in which people return to normal as soon as possible. This is because the Hopi believe that after death, people become ghosts in the afterworld. Because the spirits of the deceased are thought to bring trouble, every effort is taken to avoid memories of them (Stroebe et al., 1992).

THE EXPERIENCE OF GRIEF

Although people's reactions to the death or loss of a significant person vary depending on their age and personal circumstances, studies of bereaved people suggest certain commonalities in their grief reactions. In 1944, Lindemann described the grief reactions of over 100 bereaved people who had lost family members in the tragic Coconut Grove restaurant fire in Boston; these are summarized in Table 17–3. In addition to emotional reactions, research indicates that bereavement can produce changes in the respiratory, nervous, and hormonal systems and even alter the heart and immune systems (Bodnar & Kiecolt-Glaser, 1994; Osterweis et al., 1984).

COMMON SYMPTOMS OF BEREAVEMENT
Absentmindedness, difficulty in concentration, loss of memory
A feeling of tightness in the throat
Choking, with shortness of breath
A need for sighing
An empty feeling in the abdomen
Lack of muscular power
Insomnia and loss of appetite
An intense, subjective distress described as pain or tension
TABLE 17–3

Source: From "The Symptomatology and Management of Acute Grief," by E. Lindemann, 1944, *American Journal of Psychiatry, 101,* 141–148.

anticipatory grief

Grieving in expectation of a person's death.

Lindemann also noted a phenomenon he labeled **anticipatory grief,** in which one grieves in expectation of a person's death. When a relative or friend is very old or is afflicted with a terminal illness, people may begin the process of experiencing their loss of that person before the actual death. In most cases, anticipatory grief helps people cope more effectively with death and results in a better emotional adjustment during the bereavement period. Rando (1983) studied the experiences and adaptations of 54 parents for a period of 3 years following the death of a child from cancer. She found that parents who had experienced anticipatory grief were better prepared for the child's death and experienced less stress following the death. By grieving in advance of the child's death, these parents were able to participate more in the care of the sick child; this action helped them resolve their emotional reactions of guilt about their inability to help their dying child.

STAGES OF GRIEF

Several researchers have pointed out that people's reactions to death change over time (Averill, 1968; Bowlby, 1980; Parkes, 1972). Grief is not a fixed state but a process involving a succession of emotional reactions, each one affecting the next. By investigating the course of bereavement in widows, Parkes has identified four stages of grief.

In the first stage, usually directly after learning of the death, the bereaved persons experience *numbness* and little feeling. He or she may be in a state of shock or disbelief, may experience confusion, and may be dazed throughout the funeral and burial services. This stage usually is short in duration and is followed by the second stage, which is characterized by *yearning and protest.* The bereaved may pine for the lost relative with crying and weeping, or they may be angry and irritable. Accompanying these reactions may be a sense of anxiety and fear of making it on one's own, a need to relive memories of the deceased, and general restlessness and tension.

After a period of time, which varies from one person to the next but usually occurs within the 1st year after the death, the bereaved person enters the third stage of grief, which is characterized by *disorganization and depression.* The person may become apathetic and have no interest in the future. People in this stage may experience diminished appetite and other physical symptoms, or may be overwrought with guilt. Studies have found that people who were depressed prior to a loss or who experienced a loss through suicide are at greater risk of experiencing clinical depression during bereavement (Gilewski, Faberow, Gallagher, & Thompson, 1991; Norris & Murrell, 1990). Among elderly people higher mortality rates are commonly reported during this period of bereavement (Rowland, 1979). During this stage, bereaved people need the sympathetic support of friends and relatives, or they may need to talk with a professional in order to resolve their emotional reactions to their loss and get on with their lives.

The most important barrier to *recovery*—the final stage of grief that involves a resolution of one's loss—is the ability to express such emotions as anger, anxiety, or guilt. The length of time people spend in the disorganization and depression stage of grief is dependent in part on whether they are able to express their feelings about the death to a concerned listener. Spinetta and his colleagues (Spinetta, Swarner, & Sheposh, 1981) reported that the parents who effectively coped with the death of a child from cancer had someone to whom they could turn for help during their child's illness. Recovery from the loss of a loved one usually begins within 2 years of the death and is highlighted by the bereaved person's decision to get on with his or her life and to renew social contacts or initiate new activities. The person is able to establish new relationships and goals instead of hanging on to painful memories of the deceased. Memories of the deceased loved one are more likely to be pleasant ones (Futterman, Gallagher, Thompson, Lovett, & Gilewski, 1990), and the person experiences a sense of commitment to his or her own life and a deeper appreciation of human relationships.

People suffering from terminal illnesses experience numerous losses before they die. They lose contact with loved ones and friends, their jobs, and their normal activities; they lose control over their lives when they enter hospitals or nursing homes. The grief associated with these and other losses compounds the loss they feel at the approach of death.

DEATH IN THE FAMILY

According to a study by Osterweis, Solomon, and Green (1984), over 8 million Americans experience the death of a close family member each year. With the loss of a spouse, parent, sibling, or child comes a period of stress and bereavement for all members of the family. When a family member dies, the survivors must cope with their emotional reactions to the loss of a companion or loved one, while also taking over the roles and duties left vacant by the deceased person. For the new widow, the death of her husband may mean assuming the job of maintaining the family car, going to work, or dealing with lawyers. For the widower, the daily tasks of meal preparation or laundry may prove unsettling, at least initially. Adult children may step in to fill the roles of the deceased person. For some people, losing a parent may also signal a transition to adulthood when they realize that they can no longer rely on their parents for guidance or advice.

Young children and adolescents have special needs during the bereavement period. They may be concerned about who will take care of them. Often, the surviving parents may not be able to deal effectively with the immediate emotional needs of their children because they are overwhelmed by their own loss. This is a time when other, less emotionally stressed family members can provide assistance. The impact of the death of a loved one on the family depends on two factors: the emotional and social resources of the family and the degree of preparation for the death.

During bereavement, people suffer distress and need the support, reassurance, and assistance of others. The most valuable form of support is encouraging bereaved individuals to express their feelings about their loss (see Table 17–4).

The family whose members communicate openly, share their feelings, and show regard for one another is a rich resource to draw upon during bereavement. During the few days immediately following a death, family members help each other by talking about the life and death of the loved one, sharing the responsibility for the funeral and burial arrangements, and sharing their networks of friends as sources of support. Later, in the weeks and months following the death, family members can help each other deal with the sense of loneliness and depression by maintaining contact with one another.

Some families, however, are less fortunate. Relatives may live in different parts of the country and hence are unable to provide much mutual support. In

WAYS OF HELPING A GRIEVING PERSON	
TYPE OF HELP	**SUGGESTIONS**
Reach out	Show your interest and share your caring feelings. Express your sorrow; avoid cliches or saying "I know how you feel."
Listen	Be willing to listen; allow the person to talk freely about past memories and current feelings without fear of disapproval or judgment.
Ask how you can help	Be specific in your offer to help at home or work and be sure to follow up with action.
Remember important dates	Birthdays, anniversaries, and holidays are difficult times; don't let the person be isolated during them.
Suggest joint activities	Offer to do things with the grieving person; walking and other types of physical activity are helpful.
Encourage involvement	Help the person find new activities and friends; encourage social activities; be persistent but do not press for involvement prematurely.
Pay attention to warning signs	Signs that the grieving person is in distress include weight loss, talk of suicide, and lack of personal hygiene.

TABLE 17-4

Source: From *A Guide to Grief,* by the Hospice Council of Metropolitan Washington, 1994, Washington, DC: The Hospice Council of Metropolitan Washington, pp. 9–10.

other families, relationships among family members may be distant or even hostile. Families whose members characteristically deny the expression of emotions, or do not talk openly or listen to one another, lack sufficient emotional resources to draw upon during bereavement. Often, family members are angry with one another without realizing why. Unable to communicate freely about their feelings at having lost a loved one, some people may experience their distress in the form of mental or physical symptoms such as depression or fatigue that may require professional treatment (Osterweis et al., 1984). As a result of diminished emotional resources, many families turn to trained professionals for help, support, and information. Physicians, psychologists, clinical nurse specialists, social workers, and members of the clergy can offer such help to families.

The extent to which family members are prepared for a loved one's death is a critical factor in coping with bereavement. For most people an untimely or unexpected death is the most difficult with which to cope. A child's death is always considered untimely and premature and thus is often traumatic. Tragic or calamitous deaths due to war, accident, suicide, or murder intensify the grief experience. Very often families experiencing unexpected deaths may require the help of extended family members, friends, or professionals during the bereavement period.

In the case of an expected death, family members are aware of the impending death of a loved one as a result of either old age or terminal illness. The family often anticipates the changes in their lives that will follow the loss of that person. Family roles are often reorganized to accommodate the care of the dying family member, and the survivors are better prepared to deal with the changes in household routines following the death. Even with an expected death, however, family members still require loving support from each other to ease the distress caused by their loss and to reestablish meaningful lives.

BEREAVEMENT IN CHILDREN AND ADOLESCENTS

The effect of bereavement on young children has been studied mostly in retrospect—that is, through adult case studies. Numerous researchers have found that the loss of a parent during early childhood is associated with a greater-than-average tendency to suffer depression or commit suicide in adulthood (Bowlby, 1980). Early loss may even be associated with physical conditions such as cardiac disease (Lynch, 1977). Even before the age of 2, grief appears to be experienced and in some sense remembered. Physicians, psychiatrists, and psychologists occasionally encounter depressed patients who in midlife appear not to have completed the grieving process of early childhood.

Osterweis, Solomon, and Green (1984) report that when a parent or close relative dies, children frequently ask themselves three questions: Did I cause this to happen? Will it happen to me? Who will take care of me now (or if something happens to my parents)? These questions may or may not be expressed directly, but in either case children need to have the answers provided by a caring and trusted relative or friend. As irrational as these concerns may seem to adults, to children they are a reflection of their need for safety and care.

Unlike adults, who may also experience ambivalent feelings, children lack the cognitive ability and life experiences that would enable them to reject the anger they feel as part of their bereavement on rational grounds. Adults can help children during bereavement by providing information and support as they mourn their loss. The death of a pet sometimes enables children to learn to accept their emotional reactions to death and loss. Rather than quickly replacing the animal, parents need to respect the child's need to understand and feel the significance of the pet's death.

Bereavement in adolescence and youth usually means the death of a parent or the untimely death of a peer. As pointed out earlier, young people grieve and understand death as adults do. Still, bereavement at this point in the lifespan has a special significance. The person who is at the brink of establishing an adult identity may feel cheated out of sharing an adult relationship with the parent who has died. Deprived of the opportunity to share his or her achievements such as graduation or awards, the adolescent cannot enjoy the parent's recognition that he or she has become an adult.

If the young person loses a parent before having established an identity, development may be affected more directly. For example, a daughter's attempt to differentiate herself from her mother may become a source of guilt when separation is imposed by death. Concern for the remaining parent may cause her to alter her relationship with her family of origin—taking more adult responsibilities or slipping unhappily into childlike dependency.

Young people who lose a close friend, sibling, spouse, or lover are under "a heavy burden that comes out of season" (Shneidman, 1977). Even for the 20-year-old widower, physically in optimum health, bereavement can amount to a life-threatening condition. Temporarily at least, the loss of a spouse or lover may be so traumatic as to make any idea of future intimacy painful and impossible.

Most people who die in adolescence or youth are victims of accidents or suicide (Fuchs, 1974). The few who suffer through serious diseases are necessarily

The sudden and unexpected death of John F. Kennedy was difficult for many Americans to accept. As his father's casket passes, young John F. Kennedy Jr. salutes in tribute.

Health Perspective

WHEN A CHILD DIES

Perhaps the most sorrowful and anguishing event in any culture is the death of a child. The loss is felt most strongly by those who have taken care of the dying child—namely, the parents and sometimes the hospital nurses and staff. For parents of terminally ill children, the periods before and after a child's death are both difficult. Not only must they provide for the normal needs of their child for safety, love, and comfort, but they must also prepare themselves and their child for medical treatments and the eventual death. The experiences of parents whose children have died

in hospitals have shown that the ways in which nurses and staff members respond to the parents and the dying child can affect the length and severity of the grieving process. Sensitive, honest, and direct care in dealing with the parents before a child dies can help them to resume normal life afterward (Compassionate Friends, 1986).

The traumas associated with the death of a child have been compiled by Compassionate Friends, a nationwide support group for bereaved parents. When their child is dying, parents still want to care for him or her. Hospital personnel can help by letting parents participate as much as possible in the daily care of their child. Because dying children often are receiving treatment or being monitored by machines, nurses may need to

explain the equipment and procedures to parents beforehand so that parents (and perhaps siblings) are not frightened by the medical aspects of the treatment. Parents usually need and want to be with the child and can be a great comfort to a frightened child.

Sometimes nurses may be reluctant to tell parents what they know about the child's condition. Rather than try to protect them from the unpleasant news, nurses should tell parents the truth, including acknowledging what they don't know. If parents ask for the information, they are usually ready to hear it. Sometimes, parents may not be ready to accept bad news, and may use denial to try to cope with it. In this case, nurses and physicians need to patiently reaffirm the unpleasant reality, remembering that ultimately the parents will come to accept the situation.

aware of the great unfairness and untimeliness of death. The result is rage at lost opportunities and a fundamental uncertainty about what to do with the time remaining. Unlike the mature adult, the young person has not had to confront the hints of mortality that come with aging. A dying young man, for example, may be overwhelmed with disbelief at the seriousness of his condition. His situation is made more difficult by the inability of others to communicate with him and to accept the illness.

THE END OF THE JOURNEY

This discussion of death and the ways we adjust to it completes our travel across the lifespan. Death puts an end to further development or change. After a semester or more of studying the ways in which people adjust to physical, emotional, cognitive, and social changes, it may seem odd to come to an abrupt halt. Perhaps it is for the same reason that death is upsetting to people who have invested a lifetime in living.

Parents need to know it is okay and healthy to express their feelings. Sometimes nurses are able to help by showing their own feelings of sadness at the anticipated loss of a child. Using the child's name, being available for reassurance and information, and making it possible for parents to be with their child at the moment of death can help ease the parents' grief.

Nurses can further help bereaved parents by making them aware of the normal grieving process and telling them what emotional reactions they can expect to feel. For example, the birth or death anniversaries of the child are likely to be stressful for parents and they need to allow themselves time to take care of their emotional needs. It is important for nurses to also recognize their own grieving process, especially if they had become attached to the dying child. By allowing time to express feelings of sadness and frustration and finding a safe outlet for these feelings, nurses become more sensitive to the needs of others in bereavement.

Parents and family members who want to turn to a support group for help in absorbing the loss of a child can contact Compassionate Friends at (708) 990-0010.

The death of a child affects the whole family, parents and siblings alike. Families that openly share their feelings help each other overcome their loss.

I hope that your intellectual travel through the lifespan with this text and in your course has helped you to appreciate your own life journey. With a better understanding of the changes that occur throughout life and the forces that shape those changes, you may be able to readjust your life course to help you make the most of living. If you are successful in living your life to the fullest and helping others to do the same, then your life will have meaning and your ultimate death will not seem so abrupt. Enjoy your life!

BRIEF REVIEW

The meaning of death varies across cultures and is tied to the meaning of life. For some people death is the transitional event leading to rebirth and a new life. For other people death is viewed as the end of life.

The determination of death—the final stage of the life cycle—has become more complex as a result of advances in medical technology. Death can occur at any point in the lifespan, although the nature of death varies with age. Accidents and birth defects are more common causes of death in early childhood; in adolescence and young adulthood death occurs more frequently by violent means. During middle adulthood, people more often die from disease and accidents.

The impact of death varies with a person's age and cognitive ability. By the age of 10 months, infants have formed an attachment and are capable of experiencing loss and separation. Separation and sleep are both identified with deathlike experiences during infancy.

Young children define all things that move as "alive." Death is seen as reversible and similar to sleep. By age 6, death is perceived to be permanent, but it is not yet seen as inevitable. Instead, death is personified and children believe they can outwit or escape it. At 9 or 10 years, the child has an adult concept of death. Life and death are seen as internal processes that belong to all living things. Terminally ill children appear to understand their predicament.

Although adolescents appear to have an adult understanding of death, they view it as distant or remote from their experience. In young adulthood, marriage and deciding on parenthood help to define a person's relationship with death.

Concern with death peaks during middle adulthood as people become aware of their own physical limitations and experience the deaths of their parents. In late adulthood, death becomes a realistic concern as the elderly accept death as a natural part of living.

As people approach the limits of life expectancy, they enter the terminal stage of life and begin to anticipate dying. Some people experience a terminal drop in cognitive and intellectual skills just before the onset of death. Others experience isolation and loneliness as peers and spouses die.

Death is viewed as a process. Most people are aware that they are dying and make social and psychological adjustments as a result. Dying people need to be informed of their physical condition so that they can deal with their own death. Kübler-Ross describes five stages of adjustment that dying people experience: denial, anger, bargaining, depression, and acceptance. Criticisms have been expressed concerning the universality of Kübler-Ross's stages.

About one in three people who come close to dying, or who were clinically dead but were revived, have reported a near-death experience (NDE). Common to NDEs are hearing the pronouncement of death, a buzzing noise, an out-of-body experience while traveling in a tunnel toward a bright light, a personal life review, meeting people from their past, feelings of peace and quiet, and the awareness of being told to come back to life. Overall, NDEs are reported to be pleasant and have the effect of improving people's outlooks on life and reducing their fears of death.

Hospice care has been developed to help people through the dying process with dignity and with the presence of a concerned person. Some people make out living wills to ensure that no extraordinary medical efforts are used to prolong their lives.

Bereavement is a condition of loss during which people grieve and mourn the death of a loved one. Different cultural traditions influence mourning practices, while the experience of grief is believed to be universal.

Grief is an emotional reaction to loss and can be experienced in advance of an actual loss or death. People go through stages in their grief experience: numbness, yearning and protest, disorganization and depression, and recovery.

Children who experience the loss of a parent or close relative may experience emotional reactions similar to those of adults, but they do not possess the cognitive ability or life experiences to help them understand their emotional reactions.

KEY TERMS

anticipatory grief (678)
bereavement (675)
Brompton mix (672)
clinical death (670)
death education (664)
electroencephalogram (EEG) (655)
euthanasia (673)

grief (675)
hospice (671)
living will (673)
mourning (675)
near-death experience (NDE) (670)
physiological process of
    dying (667)

premature death (656)
psychological process of
    dying (667)
sudden infant death syndrome
    (SIDS) (655)
terminal drop (666)
terminal stage of life (666)

REVIEW QUESTIONS

If you can answer these questions, you have a good understanding of the material in this chapter. If a question seems difficult, go back to the text and review the topic.

1. Give an example of how the meaning of death changes from one culture to another.

2. Describe the major causes for death during infancy, childhood, adolescence, early and middle adulthood, and late adulthood.

3. List the characteristics that define a mature understanding of death. At what age do children begin to understand death? What factors influence the conception of death in infancy?

4. Compare and contrast the child's understanding of death during early and middle childhood. What three questions did Nagy use to study children's conception of death? Describe her three stages of development.

5. How do adolescents differ from adults in their understanding of death? What events in early adulthood provoke thoughts about death?

6. How do middle-age and elderly adults differ in their responses to death?

7. What are the aims of death education programs?

8. What impact does the diagnosis of a terminal disease have on some people?

9. Describe Kubler-Ross's stages of dying; give an example of each one. What are the criticisms that have been raised about Kubler-Ross's theory?

10. What is euthanasia? Discuss the concerns about euthanasia in our culture. What are living wills?

11. Distinguish between bereavement, mourning, and grief. Provide three examples of cultural differences in bereavement.

12. What are the commonly reported symptoms of grief? What is anticipatory grief? Describe Parkes's four stages of grief.

13. Describe the impact of death on families. What factors seem to reduce the impact of loss in families following a death?

14. Describe the effects of bereavement on children and adolescents.

OBSERVATIONAL ACTIVITY

BEREAVEMENT IN FAMILIES

Different cultures and religions have different rituals associated with death and bereavement. Funeral customs and memorial services are ritualized and prescribed to help ease the suffering of losing a loved one. The purpose of this exercise is for you to become more familiar with the customs and traditions associated with dying. To complete this activity, you will need to talk with priests, ministers, rabbis, and other religious or spiritual representatives in your community. You may have representatives of religious groups available on your college campus who would be able to provide you with information about funeral services and customs in different cultural groups. Often, hospitals have personnel on site to offer bereaved families help in making funeral arrangements. When you have located a sample of different ethnic and religious representatives, structure your discussions with them around the following questions.

1. What happens when a member of your community (congregation, synagogue, etc.) dies?

2. What rituals or traditions exist concerning death?

3. How long do people mourn the death of a loved one?

4. Are there specific social gatherings that typically occur when a person dies?

5. Are there specific times or days when funerals can or cannot occur?

You will probably generate more questions as you discuss these issues. When you have completed your interviews, summarize the responses and draw comparisons among the different religious and ethnic groups. Compare the bereavement practices with those from your own family or culture. Share what you have learned with other classmates.

Aaronson, L. S., & MacNee, C. L. (1989). Tobacco, alcohol, and caffeine use during pregnancy. *Journal of Obstetrics, Gynecology, and Neonatal Nursing, 18,* 279–281.

Abplanalp, J. M. (1983). Premenstrual syndrome: A selective review. *Women and Health, 8,* 107–123.

Abramson, L., Seligman, M. E. P., & Teasdale, J. (1978). Learned helplessness in humans: Critique and reformulation. *Journal of Abnormal Psychology, 87,* 49–74.

Abravanel, E., & Gingold, H. (1985). Learning via observation during the second year of life. *Developmental Psychology, 21,* 614–623.

Abroms, K., & Bennett, J. (1981). Changing etiological perspectives in Down's syndrome: Implications for early intervention. *Journal of the Division for Early Childhood, 2,* 109–112.

Achenbach, T. (1978). Developmental aspects of psychopathology in children and adolescents. In M. Lamb (Ed.), *Social and personality development.* New York: Holt, Rinehart & Winston.

Acredolo, L., & Feldman, P. (1979). The effect of active versus passive exploration on memory for spatial location in children. *Child Development, 50,* 698–704.

Adams, B. N. (1975). *The family: A sociological interpretation.* Chicago: Rand McNally.

Adams, C. (1991). Qualitative age differences in memory for text: A life-span developmental perspective. *Psychology and Aging, 6,* 323–336.

Adams, G. M., & DeVries, H. A. (1973). Physiological effects of an exercise regimen upon women aged 52–79. *Journal of Gerontology, 28,* 50–55.

Adams, G. R., & Fitch, S. A. (1983). Psychological environments of university departments: Effects of college students' identity status and ego stage development. *Journal of Personality and Social Psychology, 44,* 1266–1275.

Adelson, J. (1975). The development of ideology in adolescence. In S. Dragastin & G. Elder (Eds.), *Adolescence in the life cycle.* New York: Wiley.

Adelson, J. (1972). The political socialization of the young adolescent. In J. Kagan & R. Coles (Eds.), *Twelve to sixteen: Early adolescence.* New York: Norton.

Adelson, J. (1982). Rites of passage: How children learn the principles of community. *American Educator, 18,* 60–67.

Adelson, J., & O'Neil, R. P. (1966). Growth of political ideas in adolescence: The sense of community. *Journal of Personality and Social Psychology, 4,* 295–306.

Ade-Ridder, L., & Brubaker, T. (1983). The quality of long-term marriages. In T. H. Brubaker (Ed.), *Family relationships in later life.* Beverly Hills, CA: Sage Publications.

Adler, A. (1928). Characteristics of first, second, and third children. *Children, 3 (14),* Issue 5.

Adler, N., Boyce, T., Chesney, M., Cohen, S., Folkman, S., Kahn, R., & Syme, S. L. (1994). Socioeconomic status and health. *American Psychologist, 49,* 15–24.

Ahrons, C., & Rogers, R. (1987). *Divorced families.* New York: Norton.

Ahrons, C., & Wallisch, L. (1986). The relationship between former spouses. In S. Duck & D. Perlman (Eds.), *Close relationships, development, dynamics, and deterioration.* Beverly Hills, CA: Sage.

Ainsworth, M. (1967). *Infancy in Uganda: Infant care and the growth of love.* Baltimore, MD: Johns Hopkins University Press.

Ainsworth, M., Bell, S., & Stayton, D. (1971). Individual differences in strange situation behavior of one-year-olds. In H. R. Schaffer (Ed.), *The origins of human social relations.* New York: Academic Press.

Ainsworth, M., Blehar, M., Waters, E., & Wall, S. (1978). *Patterns of attachment.* Hillsdale, NJ: Erlbaum.

Alsaker, F. D. (1992). Pubertal timing, overweight and psychological adjustment. *Journal of Early Adolescence, 12,* 396–419.

Aldous, J. (1987). New views on the family life of the elderly and the near elderly. *Journal of Marriage and the Family, 49,* 227–234.

Alessandri, S. M., Sullivan, M. W., Imaizumi, S., & Lewis, M. (1993). Learning and emotional responsivity in cocaine-exposed infants. *Developmental Psychology, 29,* 989–997.

Alexander, K. L., Entwisle, D. R., & Dauber, S. L. (1993). First-grade classroom behavior: Its short- and long-term consequences for school performance. *Child Development, 64,* 801–814.

Allen, L., & Majidi-Ahi, S. (1989). Black American children. In J. Gibbs & Larke Nahme Huang & Associates (Eds.), *Children of color: Psychological interventions with minority youth.* San Francisco: Jossey-Bass.

Alley, T. (1983a). Growth-produced changes in body shape and size as determinants of perceived age and adult caregiving. *Child Development, 54,* 241–248.

Alley, T. (1983b). Infantile head shape as an elicitor of adult protection. *Merrill-Palmer Quarterly, 29 (4),* 411–427.

Allport, G. W. (1961). *Pattern and growth in personality.* New York: Holt, Rinehart & Winston.

Allport, G. W. (1968). *The person in psychology.* Boston: Beacon.

Almeida, R. (1991). Hindu Indian families. In F. Walsh & M. McGoldrick (Eds.), *Living beyond loss: Death in the family.* New York: Norton.

Alpaugh, P. K., & Birren, J. E. (1977). Variables affecting creative contributions across the adult life span. *Human Development, 20,* 240–248.

Alpert, J. L., & Richardson, M. S. (1980). Parenting. In L. Poon (Ed.), *Aging in the 1980s: Psychological issues.* Washington, DC: American Psychological Association.

Alsaker, F. D. (1992). Pubertal timing, overweight, and psychological adjustment. *Journal of Early Adolescence, 12,* 396–419.

Amazing births. (1984, January 23). *Time Magazine,* 30.

Ambron, S., & Salkind, N. J. (1984). *Child development* (4th ed.). New York: Holt, Rinehart and Winston.

Ambuel, B. (1995, February). Adolescents, unintended pregnancy and abortion: The struggle for a compassionate social policy. *Current Directions in Psychological Science, 4,* 1–5.

American Academy of Pediatrics Committee of Adolescence. (1988). Suicide and suicide attempts in adolescents and young adults. *Pediatrics, 81,* 322–324.

American Psychiatric Association. (1987). *Diagnostic and statistical manual of mental disorders* (3rd. ed., rev.). Washington, DC: Author.

American Psychiatric Association. (1994). *Diagnostic and statistical manual of mental disorders* (4th ed.) Washington, DC: Author.

Anastasi, A. (1958). Heredity, environment, and the question "how?" *Psychological Review, 65,* 197–208.

Andersson, Bengt-Erik. (1992). Effects of day-care on cognitive and socioemotional competence of thirteen-year-old Swedish schoolchildren. *Child Development, 63,* 20–36.

Anderson, D., Lorch E., Field, D., Collins, P., & Nathan, J. (1986). Television viewing at home: Age trends in visual attention and time with TV. *Child Development, 57,* 1024–1033.

Anderson, S. A., Russell, C. S., & Schumm, W. R. (1983). Perceived marital quality and family life cycle categories: A further analysis. *Journal of Marriage and the Family, 45,* 127–139.

Angoff, W. (1988). The nature-nurture debate, aptitude and group differences. *American Psychologist, 43,* 713–720.

Annis, L. F. (1978). *The child before birth.* Ithaca, NY: Cornell University Press.

Anstey, K., Stankov, L., & Lord, Stephen. (1993). Primary aging, secondary aging, and intelligence. *Psychology and Aging, 8,* 562–570.

Antonarakis, S. E., & Down Syndrome Collaborative Group. (1991). Parental origin of the extra chromosome in trisomy 21 as indicated by analysis of DNA polymorphisms. *New England Journal of Medicine, 324,* 872–876.

Antonucci, T. (1985). Personal characteristics, social support, and social behavior. In R. Binstock & E. Shanas (Eds.), *Handbook of aging and the social sciences.* New York: Van Nostrand.

Antunes, C., Stolley, P., Rosenshein, N., Davies, J., Tonascia, J., Brown, C., Burnett, L., Rutledge, A., Pokempner, M., & Garcia, R. (1979). Endometrial cancer and estrogen use. *New England Journal of Medicine, 300,* 9–13.

APA Journals, 1970–1989. *American Psychologist, 47,* 629–636.

Aquilino, W., & Supple, K. (1991). Parent-child relations and parents' satisfaction with living arrangements when adult children live at home. *Journal of Marriage and the Family, 53,* 13–27.

Archer, S. (1985a). Career and/or family: The identity process for adolescent girls. *Youth and Society, 16,* 289–314.

Archer, S. (1985b). Identity and the choice of social roles. In A. S. Waterman (Ed.), *Identity in adolescence: Processes and content.* San Francisco: Jossey-Bass.

Archer, S., & Waterman, A. (1990). Varieties of identity diffusions and foreclosures: An exploration of subcategories of the identity statuses. *Journal of Adolescent Research, 5,* 96–111.

Arenberg, D., & Robertson-Tchabo, E. A. (1977). Learning and aging. In J. E. Birren & K. W. Schaie (Eds.), *Handbook of the psychology of aging.* New York: Van Nostrand Reinhold.

Arlin, P. A. (1975). Cognitive development in adulthood: A fifth stage? *Developmental Psychology, 11,* 602–606.

Arlin, P. A. (1977). Piagetian operations in problem finding. *Developmental Psychology, 13,* 297–298.

Arlin, P. A. (1984). Adolescent and adult thought: A structural interpretation. In M. L. Commons, F. A. Richards, & C. Armon (Eds.), *Beyond formal operations: Late adolescent and adult cognitive development.* New York: Praeger.

Arlinger, S. (1991). Audiometric profile in presbycusis. *Acta Otolaryngological* (Supp. 476), 850–890.

Arluke, A., & Levin, J. (1984, August/September). Another stereotype: Old age as a second childhood. *Aging,* 7–11.

Arnett, J. (1990). Contraceptive use, sensation seeking, and adolescent egocentrism. *Journal of Youth and Adolescence, 19,* 171–180.

Arnett, J. (1992). Socialization and adolescent reckless behavior: A reply to Jessor. *Developmental Review, 12*, 391–409.

Arnett, J., & Balle-Jensen, L. (1993). Cultural bases of risk behavior: Danish adolescents. *Child Development, 64*, 1842–1855.

Arnold, F., Bulatao, R., Buripakdi, C., Chung, B., Fawcett, J., Iritani, T., Lee, S., & Wu, T. (1975). *The value of children: A cross national study: Vol. 1. Introduction and comparative analysis.* Honolulu, HI: East-West Population Institute.

Arnoldi, M. J. (1987). The legacy of a name among the Bamana of Mali. In A. Cohn & L. Leach (Eds.), *Generations: A universal family album.* New York: Pantheon Books.

Arthur, J. K. (1969). *Retire to action: A guide to voluntary service.* Nashville, TN: Abingdon.

Asher, S. (1983). Social competence and peer status: Recent advances and future directions. *Child Development, 54*, 1427–1434.

Aslin, R., Pisoni, D., & Jusczyk, P. (1983). Auditory development and speech perception in infancy. In P. H. Mussen (Ed.), *Handbook of child psychology: Vol. 2. Infancy and developmental psychology* (4th ed.). New York: Wiley.

Atchley, R. C. (1975). Dimensions of widowhood in later life. *The Gerontologist, 15*, 176–178.

Atchley, R. C. (1977). *The social forces in later life* (2nd ed.). Belmont, CA: Wadsworth.

Atchley, R. C. (1980). *The social forces in later life* (3rd ed.). Belmont, CA: Wadsworth.

Atchley, R. C., & Miller, S. (1983). Types of elderly couples. In T. H. Brubaker (Ed.), *Family relations in later life.* Beverly Hills, CA: Sage Publications.

Athanasiou, R., Shaver, P., & Tavris, C. (1970, July). Sex: Psychology Today reports back to readers on what they told when they filled out the sex questionnaire. *Psychology Today, 4*, 39–52.

Averill, J. R. (1968). Grief: Its nature and significance. *Psychological Bulletin, 70*, 721–748.

Axline, V. (1964). *Dibs: In Search of Self.* New York: Houghton Mifflin.

Azmitia, M., & Hesser, J. (1993). Why siblings are important agents of cognitive development: A comparison of siblings and peers. *Child Development, 64*, 430–444.

Bachman, J. G., & Schulenberg, J. (1993). How part-time work intensity relates to drug use, problem behavior, time use, and satisfaction among high school seniors: Are these consequences or merely correlates? *Developmental Psychology, 29*, 220–235.

Baddeley, A. D. (1986). *Working memory.* Oxford, England: Clarendon Press.

Baddeley, A. D. (1992). Working memory. *Science, 255*, 556–559.

Bahr, S. (1973). Effects of power and division of labor in the family. In L. Hoffman & G. Nye (Eds.), *Working mothers.* San Francisco: Jossey-Bass.

Baillargeon, R., & DeVos, J. (1991). Object permanence in young infants: Further evidence. *Child Development, 62*, 1227–1246.

Baker, S., Thalberg, S., & Morrison, D. (1988). Parent's behavioral norms as predictors of adolescent sexual activity and contraceptive use. *Adolescence, 23*, 265–282.

Bakwin, H., & Bakwin, R. (1972). *Behavior disorders in children.* Philadelphia: Saunders.

Ball, M. (1987). Pathological similarities between Alzheimer's disease and Down's syndrome: Is there a genetic link? *Integrative Psychiatry, 5*, 159–163.

Ball, S., & Bogatz, G. A. (1972). Summative research on Sesame Street: Implications for the study of preschool children. In A.D. Pick (Ed.), *Minnesota Symposium on Child Psychology* (Vol. 6). Minneapolis: University of Minnesota Press.

Baltes, M. M., & Baltes, P. B. (1977). The eco-psychological relativity and plasticity of psychological aging: Convergent perspectives of cohort effects and operant psychology. *Zeitschrift f er experimentelle und angewandte Psychologie, 24*, 179–197.

Baltes, M. M., & Wahl, H.-W. (1992). The dependency-support script in institutions: Generalization to community settings. *Psychology and Aging, 7*, 409–418.

Baltes, P. (1987). Theoretical propositions of life span developmental psychology: On the dynamics between growth and decline. *Developmental Psychology, 23*, 611–626.

Baltes, P., Smith, J., & Staudinger, U. (1992). Wisdom and successful aging. *Nebraska Symposium on Motivation, 39*, 123–167.

Baltes, P., & Staudenger, U. (1993). The search for a psychology of wisdom. *Current Directions in Psychological Science, 2*, 75–80.

Baltes, P. B., Reese, H. W., & Lipsitt, L. (1980). Lifespan developmental psychology. In M. Rosenzweig & L. Portor (Eds.), *Annual Review of Psychology* (Vol. 31). Palo Alto, CA: Annual Reviews.

Baltes, P. B., Reese, H. W., & Nesselroade, J. R. (1977). *Life-span developmental psychology: Introduction to research methods.* Monterey, CA: Brooks/Cole.

Baltes, P. B., & Willis, S. L. (1980). Enhancement of intellectual functioning in old age: Penn State adult development and enrichment project (ADEPT). In F. I. M. Craik & S. Treub (Eds.), *Aging and cognitive processes.* New York: Plenum.

Bandura, A. (1977). *Social learning theory.* Englewood Cliffs, NJ: Prentice-Hall.

Bandura, A. (1978). The self system in reciprocal determinism. *American Psychologist, 33*, 344–358.

Bandura, A., Ross, S. A., & Ross, D. (1963). Imitation of film-mediated aggressive models. *Journal of Abnormal and Social Psychology, 66*, 3–11.

Bank, S., & Kahn, M. (1982). *The sibling bond.* New York: Basic Books.

Banks, M. S., & Salapatek, P. (1983). Infant visual perception. In P. H. Mussen (Series Ed.), & M. Haith & J. Campos (Vol. Eds.), *Handbook of child psychology: Vol. 2. Infancy and developmental psychology* (4th ed.). New York: Wiley, 1983.

Barker, J. (1990). Between humans and ghosts: The decrepit elderly in a Polynesian society. In J. Sokolovsky (Ed.), *The cultural context of aging.* New York: Bergin & Garvey Publishers.

Barnes, H. V. (1975). Physical growth and development during puberty. *Medical Clinics of North America, 59*, 1305–1317.

Barnes, K. (1971). Preschool play norms: A replication. *Developmental Psychology, 5*, 99–103.

Barnes-Farrell, J., & Piotrowski, M. (1989). Workers' perceptions of discrepancies between chronological age and personal age: you're only as old as you feel. *Psychology and Aging, 4*, 376–377.

Barnett, R., & Baruch, G. (1987). Determinants of father's participation in family work. *Journal of Marriage and the Family, 49*, 29–40.

Barnett, R. C., Marshall, N. L., & Singer, J. D. (1992). Job experiences over time, multiple roles, and women's mental health: A longitudinal study. *Journal of Personality and Social Psychology, 62*, 634–644.

Barr, H. M., Streissgruth, A. P., Darby, B. L., & Sampson, P. D. (1990). Prenatal exposure to alcohol, caffeine, tobacco, and aspirin: effects on fine and gross motor performance in 4-year-old children. *Developmental Psychology, 26*, 339–348.

Barrera, M. E., Kitching, K. J., Cunningham, C. C., Doucet, D., & Rosenbaum, P. L. (1990). A 3-year early home intervention follow-up study with low birthweight infants and their parents. *Topics in Early Childhood Special Education, 10*, 14–28.

Barrera, M. E., Rosenbaum, P. L., & Cunningham, C. E. (1986). Early home intervention with low-birth-weight infants and their parents. *Child Development, 57*, 20–33.

Barrett, N. S. (1979). Women in the job market: Occupations, earnings, and career opportunities. In R. E. Smith (Ed.), *The subtle revolution: Women at work.* Washington, DC: The Urban Institute.

Barrett-Conner, E., & Bush, T.L. (1991). Estrogen and coronary heart disease in women. *Journal of the American Medical Association, 265*, 1861–1867.

Barrington, K. (1991). The natural history of the appearance of apnea of prematurity. *Pediatric Research, 29*, 372–375.

Barron, E. (1963). *Creativity and psychological health: Origins of personal vitality and creative freedom.* New York: Van Nostrand.

Bart, P. (1970). Mother Portnoy's complaints. *Trans-action, 8*, 69–74.

Baruch, G., Biener, L., & Barnett, R. (1987). Women and gender in research on work and family stress. *American Psychologist, 42*, 120–136.

Baskett, L., & Johnson, S. (1982). The young child's interactions with parents versus siblings: A behavioral analysis. *Child Development, 53*, 643–650.

Basow, S. A., & Howe, K. G. (1980). Role-model influence: Effects of sex and sex-role attributes on college students. *Psychology of Women Quarterly, 4*, 558–572.

Basseches, M. (1980). Dialectical schemata: A framework for the empirical study of the development of dialectical thinking. *Human Development, 23*, 400–421.

Basseches, M. (1984). *Dialectical thinking and adult development.* Norwood, NJ: Ablex Publishers.

Bauer, P.J., & Mandler, J. M. (1992). Putting the horse before the cart: The use of temporal order in recall of events by one-year-old children. *Developmental Psychology, 28*, 441–452.

Baumrind, D. (1967). Child care practices anteceding three patterns of preschool behavior. *Genetic Psychology Monographs, 75*, 43–88.

Baumrind, D. (1971). Current patterns in parental authority. *Developmental Psychology Monographs, 1* (Pt. 2).

Baumrind, D. (1977). Some thoughts about childrearing. In S. Cohen and T. J. Cominsky (Eds.), *Child development: Contemporary perspectives.* Itasca, IL: Peacock.

Baumrind, D. (1978). Parental disciplinary patterns and social competence in children. *Youth and Society, 9,* 239–276.

Baumrind, D. (1980). New directions in socialization research. *American Psychologist, 35,* 639–652.

Baumrind, D. (1991). The influence of parenting style on adolescents' competence and substance use. *Journal of Early Adolescence, 11,* 56–95.

Bayley, N. (1969). *Manual for the Bayley Scales of Infant Development.* New York: Psychological Corporation.

Bayley, N. (1993). *Bayley scales of infant development: II.* New York: Psychological Corporation.

Bayley, N., & Oden, M. H. (1955). The maintenancy of intellectual ability in gifted adults. *Journal of Gerontology, 10,* 91–107.

Bearison, D. J. (1974). The construct of regression: A Piagetian approach. *Merrill-Palmer Quarterly, 20,* 21–30.

Becerra, R., & Shaw, D. (1984). *The Hispanic elderly: A reference guide.* New York: Lanham.

Becker, H., & Epstein, J. (1982). Parent involvement: A survey of teacher practices. *The Elementary School Journal, 83,* 85–102.

Beckwith, L., & Parmelee, A. (1986). EEG patterns of preterm infants, home environment, and later I.Q. *Child Development, 57,* 777–789.

Bee, H. (1987). *The journey of adulthood.* New York: Macmillan.

Belenky, M., Clinchy, B., Goldberger, N., & Tarule, J. (1986). *Womens' Ways of Knowing.* New York: Basic Books.

Bell, A., & Weinberg, M. (1978). *Homosexualities: A study of diversity among men and women.* New York: Simon & Schuster.

Bell, R., & Harper, L. (1977). *Child effects on adults.* Hillsdale, NJ: Erlbaum.

Bell, R. Q. (1968). A reinterpretation of the direction of effects in studies of socialization. *Psychological Review, 75,* 81–85.

Bell, R. Q., & Harper, L. V. (Eds.). (1980). *Child effects on adults.* Lincoln, NE: The University of Nebraska Press.

Bell, R. R., & Coughey, K. (1980). Premarital sexual experience among college females, 1958, 1968, 1978. *Family Relations, 29,* 353–357.

Bell, S. M., & Ainsworth, M. D. (1972). Infant crying and maternal responsiveness. *Child Development, 43,* 1171–1190.

Belloc, N. B., & Breslow, L. (1972). Relationship of physical health status and health practices. *Preventive Medicine, 1,* 409–421.

Belsky, J. (1980). Child maltreatment: An ecological integration. *American Psychologist, 35,* 320–335.

Belsky, J. (1981). Early human experience: A family perspective. *Developmental Psychology, 17,* 3–23.

Belsky, J. (1984a). The determinants of parenting. A process model. *Child Development, 55,* 83–96.

Belsky, J. (1984b). Two waves of day care research: Developmental effects and conditions of quality. In R. C. Ainslie (Ed.), *The child and the day care setting.* New York: Praeger.

Belsky, J., Lerner, R., & Spanier, G. (1984). *The child in the family.* Reading, MA: Addison-Wesley.

Belsky, J., & Rovine, M. (1987). Temperament and attachment security in the strange situation: An empirical rapprochement. *Child Development, 58,* 787–795.

Belsky, J., & Rovine, M. (1988). Nonmaternal care in the first year of life and the security of infant-parent attachment. *Child Development, 59,* 157–167.

Belsky, J., Spanier, G. B., & Rovine, M. (1983). Stability and change in marriage across the transition to parenthood. *Journal of Marriage and the Family, 45,* 553–566.

Belsky, J., & Steinberg, L. (1978). The effects of day care: A critical review. *Child Development, 49,* 929–949.

Belsky, J., & Steinberg, L. (1979, July/August). What does research teach us about day care: A follow-up report. *Children Today,* 21–26.

Benawra, R., Mangurten, H. H., & Duffell, D. R. (1980). Cyclopia and other anomalies following maternal ingestion of salicylates. *Journal of Pediatrics, 96,* 1069–1071.

Bender, A. E. (1971). Nutrition of the elderly. *Royal Society Health Journal, 91,* 115–121.

Benedek, T. (1959). Parenthood as a developmental phase. *American Psychoanalytic Association Journal, 7,* 389–417.

Benet, S. (1974). *Abkhasians: The long-living people of the Caucasus.* New York: Holt, Rinehart & Winston.

Benet, S. (1976). *How to live to be 100.* New York: Dial Press.

Bengston, V., Cuellar, J., & Ragan, P. (1977). Stratum contrasts and similarities in attitudes toward death. *Journal of Gerontology, 32,* 76–88.

Bengston, V. L., & Troll, L. (1978). Youth and their parents: Feedback and intergenerational influence on socialization. In R. Lerner & G. Spanier (Eds.), *Child influence on marital and family interaction: A life-span perspective.* New York: Academic Press.

Benin, M., & Nienstedt, B. (1985). Happiness in single-and-dual-earner families: The effects of marital happiness, job satisfaction, and life cycle. *Journal of Marriage and the Family, 47,* 975–984.

Benn, R. (1986). Factors promoting secure attachment relationships between employed mothers and their sons. *Child Development, 57,* 1224–1231.

Bennett, S., & Dickinson, W. (1980). Student-parent rapport and parent involvement in sex, birth control, and venereal disease education. *Journal of Sex Research, 16,* 97–113.

Benson, J., Cherny, S. S., Haith, M.M., & Fulker, D. (1993). Rapid assessment of infant predictors of adult IQ: Midtwin-Midparent analysis. *Developmental Psychology, 29,*434–447.

Berardo, F. M. (1968). Widowhood status in the United States: Perspectives on a neglected aspect of family life-cycle. *The Family Coordinator, 17,* 191–203.

Berenson, G., Frank, G., Hunter, S., Srinivasan, S., Voors, A., & Webber, L. (1982). Cardiovascular risk factors in children. Should they concern the pediatrician? American *Journal of Diseases of Children, 136,* 855–862.

Berko, J. (1958). The child's learning of English morphology. *Word, 14,* 150–177.

Bernard, J. (1972). *The future of marriage.* New York: World.

Berndt, T., & Hoyle, S. (1985). Stability and change in childhood and adolescent friendships. *Developmental Psychology, 21,* 1007–1015.

Berndt, T. J. (1981a). Age changes and changes over time in prosocial intentions and between friends. *Developmental Psychology, 17,* 408–416.

Berndt, T. J. (1981b). Relations between social cognition, non-social cognition, and social behavior: The case of friendship. In J. H. Flavell & L. D. Ross (Eds.), *Social cognitive development: Frontiers and possible futures.* Cambridge: Cambridge University Press.

Berndt, T. J. (1982). The features and effects of friendships in early adolescence. *Child Development, 53,* 1447–1460.

Berndt, T. J. (1992). Friendship and Friends' Influence in Adolescence. *Current Directions in Psychological Science, 1,* 156–159.

Bernstein, A., & Cowan, P. (1975). Children's concept of how people get babies. *Child Development, 46,* 77–91.

Berry, R., & Williams, F. (1987). Assessing the relationship between quality of life and marital and income satisfaction: A path analytic approach. *Journal of Marriage and the Family, 49,* 107–116.

Bertenthal, B., & Fischer, K. (1978). Development of self-recognition in the infant. *Developmental Psychology, 14,* 44–50.

Betz, E. (1984). A study of career patterns of women college graduates. *Journal of Vocational Behavior, 24,* 249–263.

Beyth-Marom, R., Austin, L., Fischhoff, B., Palmgren, C., & Jacobs-Quadrel, M. (1993). Perceived consequences of risky behaviors: Adults and adolescents. *Developmental Psychology, 3,* 549–563.

Bhatt, R., Rovee-Collier, C., & Weiner, S. (1994). Developmental changes in the interface between perception and memory retrieval. *Developmental Psychology, 30,* 151–162.

Bielby, D. D., & Papalia, D. E. (1975). Moral development and perceptual role-taking egocentrism: Their development and interrelationship across the life span. *International Journal of Aging and Human Development, 6,* 293–308.

Biller, A. (1970). Father absence and the personality development of the male child. *Developmental Psychology, 2,* 181–201.

Birnbaum, J. (1971). Life patterns, personality, style, and self-esteem in gifted family-oriented and career-oriented women. (Doctoral dissertation, University of Michigan, 1971). *Dissertation Abstracts International, 32,* 1834B.

Birns, B. (1973). Individual differences in human neonates' responses to stimulation. In J. Stone, H. Smith, & L. Murphy (Eds.), *The competent infant.* New York: Basic Books.

Birren, J., Woods, A., & Williams, M. (1980). Behavioral slowing with age: Causes, organization, and consequences. In L. W. Poon (Ed.), *Aging in the 1980s.* Washington, DC: American Psychological Association.

Birren, J. E. (1974). Transitions in gerontology—from lab to life: Psychophysiology and speed of response. *American Psychologist, 29,* 808–815.

Birren, J. E., Butler, R. N., Greenhouse, S. W., Sokoloff, L., & Yarrow, M. R. (Eds.). (1963). *Human aging: A biological and behavioral study* (HSM Publication No. 71–9051). Washington, DC: U.S. Government Printing Office.

Birren, J. E., & Fisher, L. (1990). The elements of wisdom: Overview and integration. In R. J. Sternbery (Ed.), *Wisdom: Its nature origin and development*. Cambridge: Cambridge University Press.

Bixenstine, V., DeCorte, M., & Bixenstine, B. (1976). Conformity to peer-sponsored misconduct at four age levels. *Developmental Psychology, 12,* 226–236.

Bjork, E., & Cummings, E. (1984). Infant search errors: Stage of concept development or stage of memory development. *Memory & Cognition, 12,* 1–19.

Blasi, A. (1980). Bridging moral cognition and moral action: A critical review of the literature. *Psychological Bulletin, 88,* 1–45.

Block, J. (1983). Differential premises arising from differential socialization of the sexes: Some conjectures. *Child Development, 54,* 1335–1354.

Block, J., & Robins, R. (1993). A longitudinal study of consistency and change in self-esteem from early adolescence to early adulthood. *Child Development, 64,* 909–923.

Bloom, L. (1970). *Language development: Form and function in emerging grammars.* Cambridge, MA: MIT Press.

Blos, P. (1979). *The adolescent passage.* New York: International Universities Press.

Bluebond-Langner, M. (1977). Meanings of death to children. In H. Feifel (Ed.), *New meanings of death.* New York: McGraw-Hill.

Blum, J. E., & Jarvik, L. F. (1975). Intellectual performance of octogenarians as a function of education and initial ability. *Human Development, 18,* 364–375.

Blum, M. (1983). *The day care dilemma.* Lexington, MA: Heath.

Blumstein, P., & Schwartz, P. (1983). *American couples.* New York: William Morrow.

Blyth, D., Bulcroft, R., & Simmons, R. (1981, August). *The impact of puberty on adolescents: A longitudinal study.* Paper presented at the annual meeting of the American Psychological Association, Los Angeles.

Bodnar, J. C., & Kiecolt-Glaser, J. K. (1994). Caregiver depression after bereavement: Chronic stress isn't over when it's over. *Psychology and Aging, 9,* 372–380.

Bohman, M. (1970). *Adopted children and their families: A follow-up study of adopted children, their background environment, and adjustment.* Stockholm: Proprius.

Bolton, P. (1983). Drugs of abuse. In D. F. Hawkins (Ed.), *Drugs and pregnancy: Human tera to genesis and related problems.* Edinburgh: Churchill Livingston.

Bond, L. (1988). Teaching developmental psychology. In P. Bronstein & K. Quina (Eds.), *Teaching a psychology of people: Resources for gender and sociocultural awareness.* Washington, D.C.: American Psychological Association.

Bond, M. (1991). Chinese values and health: A cultural level examination. *Psychology and Health, 5,* 137–152.

Booth, A. (1977). Wife's employment and husband stress: A replication and refutation. *Journal of Marriage and the Family, 39,* 645–650.

Booth, H., & Hess, E. (1974). Cross-sex friendship. *Journal of Marriage and the Family, 36,* 38–47.

Bornstein, M. H. (1985). Human infant color vision and color perception. *Infant Behavior and Development, 8,* 109–113.

Bornstein, M. H., & Sigman, M. D. (1986). Continuity in mental development from infancy. *Child Development, 57,* 251–274.

Bortz, W. (1982). Disuse and aging. *Journal of the American Medical Association, 248,* 1203–1208.

Boskind-White, M., & White, W. (1983). *Bulimarexia: The binge/purge cycle.* New York: Norton.

Botwinick, J. (1966). Cautiousness in advanced age. *Journal of Gerontology, 21,* 347–353.

Botwinick, J. (1977). Intellectual abilities. In J. E. Birren & K. W. Schaie (Eds.), *Handbook of the psychology of aging.* New York: Van Nostrand Reinhold.

Bouchard, T. (1984). Twins reared together and apart: What they tell us about human diversity. In S. W. Fox (Ed.), *Individuality and Determinism.* New York: Plenum Press.

Bouchard, T., Lykken, D., McGue, M., Segal, N., & Tellegen, A. (1990). Sources of human psychological differences: The Minnesota study of twins reared apart. *Science, 250,* 223–228.

Bourque, L. B., & Back, K. W. (1977). Life graphs and life events. *Journal of Gerontology, 32,* 669–674.

Bower, D., & Christopherson, V. (1977). University student cohabitation: A regional comparison of selected attitudes and behavior. *Journal of Marriage and the Family, 39,* 447–453.

Bower, T. G. R. (1977). *A primer of infant development.* San Francisco: W. H. Freeman.

Bower, T. G. R. (1982). *Development in infancy* (2nd ed.). San Francisco: Freeman.

Bowerman, M. (1981). Language development. In H. C. Triandis & A. Heron (Eds.), *Handbook of cross-cultural psychology,* (Vol. 4, pp. 93–185). Boston: Allyn & Bacon.

Bowlby, J. (1969). *Attachment and loss: Vol. 1. Attachment.* New York: Basic Books.

Bowlby, J. (1973). *Attachment and loss: Vol. 2. Separation.* New York: Basic Books.

Bowlby, J. (1980). *Attachment and loss: Vol. 3. Loss, sadness, and depression.* New York: Basic Books.

Boyes, M., & Walker, L. (1988). Implications of cultural diversity for the universality claims of Kohlberg's theory of moral reasoning. *Human Development, 31,* 44–59.

Brachfeld, S., Goldberg, S., & Sloman, J. (1980). Parent-infant interaction in free play at 8 and 12 months: Effects of prematurity and immaturity. *Infant Behavior and Development, 3,* 289–305.

Bradley, R. H., Whiteside, L., Mundfrom, D. J., Casey, P. H., Kelleher, K. J., & Pope, S. K. (1994). Early indications of resilience and their relation to experiences in the home environments of low birthweight, premature children living in poverty. *Child Development, 65,* 346–360.

Bradley, S. (1979). The relationship of early maternal separation to borderline personality in children and adolescents: A pilot study. *American Journal of Psychiatry, 136,* 424–426.

Braga, L., & Braga, J. (1975). *Learning and growing: A guide to child development.* Englewood Cliffs, NJ: Prentice-Hall.

Braine, M. D. S., Heimer, C. B., Wortis, H., & Freedman, A. M. (1966). Factors associated with impairment of the early development of

prematures. *Monographs of the Society for Research in Child Development, 31*(4, Serial No. 106).

Braine, M. S., & Rumain, B. (1983). Logical reasoning. In J. H. Flavell & E. M. Markman (Eds.), *Handbook of child psychology: Vol. 3. Cognitive development.* New York: Wiley.

Brainerd, C. (1978). *Piaget's theory of intelligence.* Englewood Cliffs, NJ: Prentice-Hall.

Brainerd, C., Kingma, J., & Howe, M. (1985). On the development of forgetting. *Child Development, 56,* 1103–1119.

Brandwein, R. A., Brown, C. A., & Fox, E. M. (1974). Women and children last: The social situation of divorced mothers and their families. *Journal of Marriage and the Family, 36,* 498–514.

Braungart, R. (1980). Youth movements. In J. Adelson (Ed.), *Handbook of adolescent psychology.* New York: Wiley.

Bray, D., & Howard, A. (1983). The AT&T longitudinal studies of managers. In K. W. Schaie (Ed.), *Longitudinal studies of adult psychological development.* New York: Guilford Press.

Brazelton, T. B. (1973). *Neonatal assessment scale.* Philadelphia: Lippincott.

Brazelton, T. B. (1981). *On becoming a family.* New York: Delacorte Press/Seymour Lawrence.

Brecher, E. (1984). *Love, sex, and aging.* Boston, MA: Little, Brown.

Bretherton, I. (1985). Attachment theory: Retrospect and prospect. In Bretherton, I., & Waters, E. (Eds.), Growing points of attachment theory and research. *Monographs of the Society for Research in Child Development, 50*(1–2, Serial No. 209).

Brewer, G. S. (Ed.). (1978). *The pregnancy after 30 workbook.* Emmaus, PA: Rodale Press.

Brewer, M., Dull, V., & Lui, L. (1981). Perceptions of the elderly: stereotypes as prototypes. *Journal of Personal and Social Psychology, 41,* 656–670.

Brim, O., & Kagan, J. (1980). *Constancy and change in human development.* Cambridge, MA: Harvard University Press.

Broderick, C. (1982). Adult sexual development. In B. B. Wolman (Ed.), *Handbook of Developmental Psychology.* Englewood Cliffs, NJ: Prentice-Hall.

Brody, G., Stoneman, Z., & MacKinnon, C. (1982). Role asymmetries among school-aged children, their younger siblings, and their friends. *Child Development, 53,* 1364–1370.

Brody, G., Stoneman, Z., MacKinnon, C., & MacKinnon, R. (1985). Role relationships and behavior between preschool-aged and school age sibling pairs. *Developmental Psychology, 21,* 124–129.

Brody, J. E. (1979, October 4). Cancer agency head advises diet changes. *New York Times.*

Brody, J. E. (1992, June 16). Suicide myths cloud efforts to save children. *New York Times,* pp. B5, B6.

Brody, L., Zelago, P. R., & Chaika, H. (1984). Habituation-dishabituation to speech in the neonate. *Developmental Psychology, 20,* 114–119.

Brodzinsky, D. M. (1985). On the relationship between cognitive styles and cognitive structures. In E. Neimark & R. DeLisi (Eds.), *Moderators of competence.* Hillsdale, NJ: Erlbaum.

Brodzinsky, D. M., Messer, S., & Tew, J. (1979). Sex differences in children's expression and control of fantasy and overt aggression. *Child Development, 50,* 372–379.

Brodzinsky, D. M., Schechter, D. E., Braff, A. M., & Singer, L. M. (1984). Psychological and academic adjustment in adopted children. *Journal of Consulting and Clinical Psychology, 52,* 582–590.

Bromley, D. (1967). Age and sex differences in the serial production of creative conceptual responses. *Journal of Gerontology, 22,* 32–42.

Bromley, D. B. (1974). *The psychology of human aging* (2nd ed.). Middlesex, England: Penguin.

Bronfenbrenner, U. (1960). Freudian theories of identification and their derivatives. *Child Development, 31,* 15–40.

Bronfenbrenner, U. (1977). Toward an experimental ecology of human development. *American Psychologist, 32,* 513–531.

Bronfenbrenner, U. (1979). *The ecology of human development.* Cambridge, MA: Harvard University Press.

Bronfenbrenner, U., and Garbarino, J. (1976). The socialization of moral judgment and behavior in cross-cultural perspective. In T. Lickona (Ed.), *Moral development and behavior.* New York: Holt, Rinehart & Winston.

Brooks-Gunn, J. (1988). Antecedents and consequences of variations in girls; maturational timing. *Journal of Adolescent Health Care, 9,* 1–9.

Brooks-Gunn, J. (1991). How stressful is the transition to adolescence for girls? In M. E. Colten & S. Gore (Eds.), *Adolescent stress: Causes and consequences* (pp. 131–149), New York: Aldine de Gruyter.

Brooks-Gunn, J., Boyer, C., & Hein, K. (1988). Preventing HIV infection and AIDS in children and adolescents. *American Psychologist, 43,* 958–964.

Brooks-Gunn, J., & Furstenberg, F. (1988). Adolescent sexual behavior, *American Psychologist, 44,* 249–257.

Brooks-Gunn, J., & Matthews, W. (1979). *He and she: How children develop their sex-role identity.* Englewood Cliffs, NJ: Prentice-Hall.

Brooks-Gunn, J., & Peterson, A. (Eds.). (1983). *Girls at puberty: Biological and psychosocial perspectives.* New York: Plenum Press.

Brooks-Gunn, J., & Reiter, E. O. (1990). The role of pubertal processes. In S. S. Feldman & G. R. Elliott (Eds.), *At the threshold: The developing adolescent.* Cambridge, MA: Harvard University Press.

Brooks-Gunn, J., & Warren, M. (1985). The effects of delayed menarche in different contexts: Dance and nondance students. *Journal of Youth and Adolescence, 14,* 285–300.

Brooks, J. B. (1991). *The process of parenting.* Mountain View, CA: Mayfield Publishing Company.

Broughton, J. (1978). Development of concepts of self, mind, reality, and knowledge. In W. Damon (Ed.), *Social cognition: New directions for child development.* San Francisco: Jossey-Bass.

Brown, A. L. (1975). The development of memory: Knowing, knowing about knowing, and knowing how to know. In H. W. Reese (Ed.), *Advances in child development and behavior* (Vol. 10). New York: Academic Press.

Brown, A. L. (1979). Theories of memory and the problem of development: Activity, growth, and knowledge. In L. S. Cermak & F. I. M. Craik

(Eds.), *Levels of processing in human memory.* Hillsdale, NJ: Erlbaum.

Brown, A. L., Bransford, J., Ferrara, R., & Campione, J. (1983). Learning, remembering and understanding. In J. H. Flavell & E. Markman (Ed.), *Handbook of child psychology: Vol. 3. Cognitive Development* (4th ed.). New York: Wiley.

Brown, P. (1983). Teenage pregnancy: A national challenge, what are the facts? *Vital Issues, 32* (6).

Brown, R. (1970). The first sentences of child and chimpanzee. In *Psycholinguistics: Selected papers.* Glencoe, IL: The Free Press.

Brown, R. (1973). Development of the first language in the human species. *American Psychologist, 28,* 97–106.

Browne, A. (1993). Violence against women by male partners: Prevalence, outcomes, and policy implications. *American Psychologist, 48,* 1077–1087.

Bruch, H. (1961). Transformation of oral impulses in eating disorders. *Psychiatric Quarterly, 35,* 458.

Bruch, H. (1973). *Eating disorders.* New York: Basic Books.

Bruch, H. (1977). Anorexia nervosa and its treatment. *Journal of Pediatric Psychology, 2,* 110–112.

Bruck, K. (1961). Temperature regulation in the newborn infant. *Biologia Neonatorum, 3,* 65–119.

Bruner, J. (1978). From communication to language: A psychological perspective. In I. Markova (Ed.), *The social context of language.* New York: Wiley.

Bruner, J. (1984). Interaction, communication and self. *Journal of the American Academy of Child Psychiatry, 23,* 1–7.

Bryant, B. (1982). Sibling relationships in middle childhood. In M. E. Lamb & B. Sutton Smith (Eds.), *Sibling relationships.* Hillsdale, NJ: Erlbaum.

Buchanan, C. M., Eccles, J. S., & Becker, J. B. (1992). Are adolescents the victims of raging hormones? Evidence for activational effects of hormones on moods and behavior at adolescence. *Psychological Bulletin, 111,* 62–107.

Buck, L. Z., Walsh, W. F., & Rothman, G. (1981). Relationship between parental moral judgement and socialization. *Youth and Society, 13,* 91–116.

Bugental, D., Blue, J., & Cruzcosa, M. (1989). Perceived control over caregiving outcomes: Implications for child abuse. *Developmental Psychology, 25,* 532–539.

Buhrmester, D., & Furman, W. (1990). Perceptions of sibling relationships during middle childhood and adolescence. *Child Development, 61,* 1387–1398.

Bullock, M., & Lutkenhaus, P. (1990). Who am I? Self-understanding in toddlers. *Merrill-Palmer Quarterly, 36,* 217–238.

Bullough, V. L. (1981). Age at menarche. *Science, 213,* 365–366.

Bultena, G., & Powers, E. (1978). Denial of aging: Age identification and reference group orientations. *Journal of Gerontology, 33,* 748–754.

Bumpass, L., & Sweet, J. (1988). *Preliminary evidence on cohabitation* (NSFH working paper No. 2). Madison: University of Wisconsin-Madison, Center for Demography and Ecology.

Bumpass, L., & Sweet, T. (1991). The impact of family background and early marital factors on

marital disruption. *Journal of Family Issues, 12,* 22–42.

Burdz, M., Eaton, W., & Bond, J. (1988). Effects of respite care on dementia and nondementia patients and their caregivers. *Psychology and Aging, 3,* 38–42.

Burgess, R. (1979). Child abuse: A social interactional analysis. In B. B. Lakey & A. E. Kazden (Eds.), *Advances in clinical child psychology.* New York: Plenum.

Burke, R. I., & Weir, T. (1976a). Personality differences between members of one-career and two-career families. *Journal of Marriage and the Family, 38,* 453–459.

Burke, R. I., & Weir, T. (1976b). Relationship of wives' employment status to husband, wife, and pair satisfaction and performance. *Journal of Marriage and the Family, 1976, 38,* 279–282.

Burkett, S. (1980). Religiosity, beliefs and normative standards and adolescent drinking. *Journal of Studies on Alcohol, 41,* 662–671.

Burlin, F. (1976). The relationship of parental education and maternal work and occupational status to occupational aspiration in adolescent females. *Journal of Vocational Education, 9,* 99–104.

Burrus-Bammel, L., & Bammel, G. (1985). Leisure and recreation. In J. Birren & K. W. Schaie (Eds.), *Handbook of the Psychology of Aging* (2nd ed.). New York: Van Nostrand Reinhold.

Bushnell, I. W. R., Sai, F., & Mullin, J. T. (1989). Neonatal recognition of the mother's face. *British Journal of Developmental Psychology, 7,* 3–15.

Bushnell, E., Shaw, L., & Strauss, D. (1985). Relationship between visual and tactical exploration by 6-month-olds. *Developmental Psychology, 21,* 591–600.

Buss, A., & Plomin, R. (1984). *Temperament: Early developing personality traits.* Hillsdale, NJ: Erlbaum.

Busse, E. W., Jeffers, F. C., & Christ, W. D. (1970). Factors in age awareness. In E. Palmore (Ed.), *Normal aging: Reports from the Duke longitudinal study, 1955–1969.* Durham, NC: Duke University Press.

Bussey, K. (1992). Lying and truthfulness: Children's definitions, standards, and evaluative reactions. *Child Development, 63,* 129–137.

Butler, R. (1989). Mastery versus ability appraisal: A developmental study of childrens' observations of peers' work. *Child Development, 60,* 1350–1361.

Butler, R. N. (1971, December). Old age: The life review. *Psychology Today, 5,* 49.

Butler, R. N., & Lewis, M. I. (1976). *Love and sex after sixty: A guide for men and women for their later years.* New York: Harper & Row.

Butler, R. N., & Lewis, M. I. (1982). *Aging and mental health* (3rd ed.). St. Louis: Mosby.

Butterfield-Picard, H., & Magno, J. (1982). Hospice, the adjective, not the noun: The future of a national priority. *American Psychologist, 37,* 1254–1259.

Byrne, J. D. (1975, February). Mobility rate of employed persons into new occupations. Bureau of Labor Statistics, Manpower and Employment, Special Labor Force Reports. *Monthly Labor Review,* 53–59.

Calhoun, B. C., & Watson, P. T. (1991). The cost of maternal cocaine use: I Perinatal cost. *Obstetrics and Gynecology, 78,* 731–734.

Calkins, S. D., & Fox, N. A. (1992). The relations among infant temperament, security of attachment, and behavioral inhibition at twenty-four months. *Child Development, 63,* 1456–1472.

Cambell, J. I. D., & Charness, N. (1990). Age-related declines in working memory skills: Evidence from a complex calculation task. *Developmental Psychology, 26,* 879–888.

Campos, J. J., Bertenthal, B. I., & Caplovitz, K. (1982). The interrelationship of affect and cognition in the visual cliff situation. In C. Izard, J. Kagan, & R. Zajonc (Eds.), *Emotion and cognition.* New York: Plenum.

Campos, R. (1993, Fall). Relieving infant pain with comforting techniques. *SCRD Newsletter, 3,* 10, 12.

Cantwell, D. (1972). Psychiatric illness in the families of hyperactive children. *Archives of General Psychiatry, 27,* 414–417.

Caplan, T., & Caplan, F. (1983). *The early childhood years: The 2 to 6 year old.* New York: Putnam.

Carey, R., & Posavac, E. (1978–1979). Attitudes of physicians on disclosing information to and maintaining life for terminal patients. *Omega, 9,* 67–77.

Carey, S. (1977). The child is a word learner. In M. Halle, J. Bresman, & G. A. Miller (Eds.), *Linguistic theory and psychological reality.* Cambridge, MA: MIT Press.

Cargan, L., & Melko, M. (1982). *Singles: Myths and realities.* Beverly Hills, CA: Sage Publications.

Carlson, G. A., & Cantwell, D. P. (1982). Diagnosis of childhood depression: A comparison of the Weinberg and DSM III criteria. *Journal of the American Academy of Child Psychiatry, 21,* 247–250.

Carnegie Commission on Policy Studies in Higher Education. (1980). *Giving youth a better chance.* San Francisco: Jossey-Bass.

Caron, A. J., Caron, R. F., Caldwell, R. C., & Weiss, S. J. (1973). Infant perception of the structural properties of the face. *Developmental Psychology, 9,* 385–399.

Carpenter, G. (1975). Mother's face and the newborn. In R. Lewin (Ed.), *Child alive.* London: Temple Smith.

Carpenter, R. B., & Emery, J. L. (1974). Identification and follow-up of infants at risk for sudden death in infancy. *Nature, 250,* 729.

Carr, B., & Lee, E. (1978). Navajo tribal mortality: A life table analysis of the leading causes of death. *Social Biology, 24,* 279–287.

Carroll, B. J., & Steiner, M. (1978). The psychobiology of premenstrual dysphoria: The role of prolactin. *Psychoneuroendocrinol, 3,* 171–180.

Carruth, B. R., Goldberg, D. L., & Skinner, J. D. (1991). Do parents and peers mediate the influence of television advertising on food-related purchases. *Journal of Adolescent Research, 6,* 253–271.

Carstensen, L. L. (1992). Social and emotional patterns in adulthood: Support for socioemotional selectivity theory. *Psychology and Aging, 7,* 331–338.

Carter, E., & McGoldrick, M. (1980). The family life cycle and family therapy: An overview. In E. Carter & M. McGoldrick (Eds.), *The family life cycle: A framework for family therapy.* New York: Gardenier Press.

Carter, H., & Glick, P. C. (1970). *Marriage and divorce: A social and economic study.* Cambridge, MA: Harvard University Press.

Case, R., Heller, S., Case, N., & Moss, A. (1985). Type A behavior and survival after acute myocardial infarction. *New England Journal of Medicine, 313,* 737–741.

Cassidy, J., & Berlin, L. J. (1994). The insecure/ambivalent pattern of attachment: Theory and research. *Child Development, 65,* 971–991.

Caster, W. O. (1971). *The nutritional problems of the aged.* Athens, GA: University of Georgia Press.

Cattell, R. B. (1963). Theory of fluid and crystalized intelligence: A critical experiment. *Journal of Educational Psychology, 36,* 1–22.

Caughy, M., DiPietro, J., & Strobino, D. (1994). Day-care participation as a protective factor in the cognitive development of low-income children. Special Issue: Children and poverty. *Child Development, 65* (2), 457–471.

Cavanaugh, J., & Borkowski, J. (1980). Searching for metamemory memory connections: A developmental study. *Developmental Psychology, 16,* 441–453.

Cavanaugh, J. C., & Park, D. C. (1993). The graying of America: An aging revolution in need of a natural research agenda. *APS Observer* (Special Report No. 2), 3–24.

Cavior, N., & Dokecki, P. R. (1973). Physical attractiveness, perceived attitude similarity, and academic achievement as contributors to interpersonal attraction among adolescents. *Developmental Psychology, 9,* 44–54.

Cavior, N., & Lombardi, D. A. (1973). Developmental aspects of physical attractiveness in children. *Developmental Psychology, 8,* 67–71.

Centers for Disease Control. (1979). *Basic statistics on the sexually transmitted disease problem in the United States: Sexually transmitted disease sheet* (34th ed., HEW Publication No. CDC 79–8195). Atlanta: Author, 1–37.

Centers for Disease Control. (1990). *HIV-AIDS Surveillance Report.* Atlanta, GA: Author.

Charatan, F. (1981). Assessing, identifying and treating depressive illness in the elderly: I. *Carrier Foundation Letter, 68,* 1–5.

Chase, J., Jessor, R., & Donovan, J. (1980). Psychosocial correlates of marijuana use and drinking in a national sample of adolescents. *American Journal of Public Health, 70,* 604–612.

Chasnoff, I., Burns, W., Schnoll, S., & Burns, K. (1985). Cocaine use in pregnancy. *The New England Journal of Medicine, 313,* 666–669.

Chasnoff, I., Hunt, C., Kletter, R., & Kaplan, D. (1986). Increased risk of SIDS and respiratory pattern abnormalities in cocaine-exposed infants. *Pediatric Research, 1986, 20,* 425A.

Cherlin, A., & Furstenberg, F. (1986). *The new American grandparent.* New York: Basic Books.

Children's Defense Fund. (1991). *The adolescent and young adult fact book.* Washington, DC: Children's Defense Fund.

Chipuer, H. M., Plomin, R., Pedersen, N. L., McClearn, G. E., & Nesselroade, J. R. (1993). Genetic influence on family environment: The role of personality. *Developmental Psychology, 29,* 110–118.

Chiriboga, D. A., & Cutler, L. (1980). Stress and adaptation: Lifespan perspectives. In L. Poon (Ed.), *Aging in the 1980s: Psychological issues.* Washington, DC: American Psychological Association.

Chivian, E., Mack, J., & Waletzsky, J. (1983). What Soviet children are saying about nuclear war: Project summary. Mimeograph. The Nuclear Psychology Program. Harvard Medical School.

Chomsky, N. (1968). *Language and mind.* New York: Harcourt.

Chumlea, W. C. (1982). Physical growth in adolescence. In B. Wolman (Ed.), *Handbook of developmental psychology.* Englewood Cliffs, NJ: Prentice-Hall.

Cicchetti D., & Beeghly, M. (1990). *Children with Down Syndrome: A developmental perspective.* Cambridge, England: Cambridge University Press.

Cicirelli, V. G. (1976). Categorization behavior in aging subjects. *Journal of Gerontology, 31,* 676–680.

Cicirelli, V. G. (1977a). Family structure and interaction: Sibling effects on socialization. In M. McMillan & M. Sergio (Eds.), *Child psychiatry: Treatment and research.* New York: Brunner/Mazel.

Cicirelli, V. G. (1977b). Relationship of siblings to the elderly person's feelings and concerns. *Journal of Gerontology, 31,* 309–317.

Cicirelli, V. G. (1979). *Social services for the elderly in relation to the kin network.* Report to the NRTA-AARA Andrus Foundation, Washington, DC.

Cicirelli, V. G. (1980). Sibling friendship in adulthood: A lifespan perspective. In L. Poon (Ed.), *Aging in the 1980s: Psychological issues.* Washington, DC: American Psychological Association.

Cicirelli, V. G. (1990). Relationship of personal-social variables to belief in paternalism in parent caregiving situations. *Psychology and Aging, 3,* 458–466.

Cicirelli, V. G. (1982). Sibling influence throughout the life span. In M. E. Lamb & B. Sutton-Smith (Eds.), *Sibling relationships.* Hillsdale, NJ: Erlbaum.

Civia, A. (1967). Longevity and environmental factors. *The Gerontologist, 7,* 196–205.

Clancy, S. M., & Hoyer, W. J. (1994). Age and skill in visual search. *Developmental Psychology, 30,* 545–552.

Clark, L. D., Hughes, R., & Nakashima, E. N. (1970). Behavioral effects of marijuana: Experimental studies. *Archives of General Psychiatry, 23,* 193–198.

Clarke, A. (1952). An examination of the operation of residential propinquity as a factor in mate selection. *American Sociological Review, 17,* 17–22.

Clarke-Stewart, K. A. (1973). Interactions between mothers and their young children: Characteristics and consequences. *Monographs of the Society for Research in Child Development, 38* (1, Serial No. 153).

Clarke-Stewart, K. A. (1982). *Day care.* Cambridge, MA: Harvard University Press.

Clarke-Stewart, K. A., & Gruber, C. (1984). Day care forms and features. In R. C. Ainslie (Ed.), *The child and the day care setting.* New York: Praeger.

Clarkson, M., & Berg, W. K. (1983). Cardiac orienting and vowel discrimination in newborns, crucial stimulus parameters. *Child Development, 54,* 162–171.

Clarkson-Smith, L., & Hartley, A. (1988). Relationships between physical exercise and cognitive abilities in older adults. *Psychology and Aging, 4,* 183–189.

Clarkson-Smith, L., & Hartley, A. (1990). Structural equation models of relationships between exercise and cognitive abilities. *Psychology and Aging, 5,* 437–446.

Clarren, S. K., & Smith, D. W. (1978). The fetal alcohol syndrome. *New England Journal of Medicine, 298,* 1063–1067.

Clausen, J. A. (1981). Men's occupational careers in the middle years. In D. Eichorn, J. Clausen, N. Haan, M. Honzik, & P. Mussen (Eds.), *Present and past in middle life.* New York: Academic Press.

Clayton, R., & Voss, H. (1977). Shacking up: Cohabitation in the 1970s. *Journal of Marriage and the Family, 39,* 273–283.

Clayton, V., & Birren, J. E. (1980). Age and wisdom across the lifespan: Theoretical perspectives. In P. B. Baltes & O. G. Brim, Jr. (Eds.), *Life-span development and behavior* (Vol. 1). New York: Academic Press.

Clayton, V., & Overton, W. F. (1976). Concrete and formal operational thought processes in young adulthood and old age. *International Journal of Aging and Human Development, 7,* 237–245.

Clemens, P. W., & Rust, J. O. (1979). Factors in adolescent rebellious feelings. *Adolescence, 14,* 159–173.

Clifford, E. (1971). Body ratification in adolescence. *Perceptual and Motor Skills, 33,* 119–125.

Cline, H. F. (1980). Criminal behavior over the life span. In O. Brim & J. Kagan (Eds.), *Constancy and change in human development.* Cambridge, MA: Harvard University Press.

Clingempeel, W. G., & Segal, S. (1986). Stepparent-stepchild relationships and the psychological adjustment of children in stepmother and stepfather families. *Child Development, 57,* 474–484.

Clore, G. L., & Byrne, D. (1977). The process of personality interaction. In R. B. Cattell & R. M. Dreger (Eds.), *Handbook of modern personality theory.* New York: Wiley.

Cogswell, B., Cohen, J., Mikow, V., Kanoy, K., & Margolin, R. (1982). *Adolescents' perspectives on the health care system.* Chapel Hill: University of North Carolina.

Cohen, E., Gelfand, D., Dodd, D., Jensen, J., & Turner, C. (1980). Self-control practices associated with weight loss maintenance in children and adolescents. *Behavior Therapy, 11,* 26–37.

Cohen, G. (1979). Language comprehension in old age. *Cognitive Psychology, 11,* 412–429.

Cohen, J., & Eiduson, B. T. (1975). Changing patterns of child rearing in alternative life styles: Implications for development. In A. Davids (Ed.), *Child personality and psychopathology: Current topics.* New York: Wiley.

Cohen, R. (1983). Reading disabled children are aware of their cognitive deficits. *Journal of Learning Disabilities, 16,* 286–289.

Cohen, S., & Williamson, G. (1988). Perceived stress in a probability sample of the United States. In S. Spacapan & S. Oskamp (Eds.), *The social psychology of health.* Newbury Park, CA: Sage.

Cohen, S., & Williamson, G. (1991). Stress and infectious disease in humans. *Psychological Bulletin, 109,* 5–24.

Cohn, J., & Campbell, S., Matias, R., & Hopkins, J. (1990). Face-to-face interactions of postpartum depressed and nondepressed mother-infant pairs at 2 months. *Developmental Psychology, 26,* 15–23.

Cohn, J., & Tronick, E. (1983). Three-month-old infants' reaction to stimulated material depression. *Child Development, 54,* 185–193.

Cohn, J., & Tronick, E. (1988). Mother-infant face-to-face interaction: Influence is bidirectional and unrelated to periodic cycles in either partner's behavior. *Developmental Psychology, 24,* 386–392.

Coie, J., & Dodge, K. (1983). Continuities and changes in children's social status: A five-year longitudinal study. *Merrill-Palmer Quarterly, 29,* 261–282.

Coie, J., & Kupersmidt, J. (1983). A behavioral analysis of emerging social status in boys' groups. *Child Development, 54,* 1400–1416.

Coie, J. D., & Cillessen, A. (1993). Peer rejection: Origins and effects on children's development. *Current Directions in Psycholgical Science, 2,* 89–92.

Colby, A., Kohlberg, L., Gibbs, J., & Lieberman, M. (1983). A longitudinal study of moral judgment. *Monographs of the Society for Research in Child Development, 48*(1–2, Serial No. 200).

Coleman, J. S. (with the assistance of Johnston, J. W. C., & Jonassohn, K.). (1961). *The adolescent society: The social life of the teenager and its impact on education.* New York: Free Press.

Coleman, L. M., & Antonucci, T. C. (1983). Impact of work on women at midlife. *Developmental Psychology, 19,* 290–294.

Coles, R. (1967). *The children of crisis: A study of crisis and fear.* Boston: Atlantic-Little Brown.

Coles, R. (1970). *Erik H. Erikson: The growth of his work.* Boston: Little, Brown.

Colletta, N. D. (1978). *Divorced mothers at two income levels: Stress, support, and child-rearing practices.* Unpublished thesis, Cornell University, Ithaca, NY.

Collins, J., & Plahn, M. (1988). Recognition, accuracy, stereotypic preference, aversion, and subjective judgment of body appearance in adolescents and young adults. *Journal of Youth and Adolescence. 17,* 317–334.

Colman, N., Helliarachy, N., & Herbert, V. (1981). Detection of a milk factor that facilitates folate uptake by intestinal cells. *Science, 211,* 1427–1429.

Comalli, P. E., Jr. (1970). Life-span changes in visual perception. In L. R. Goulet & P. B. Baltes (Eds.), *Life-span developmental psychology: Research and theory.* New York: Academic Press.

Cometa, N. S., & Eson, M. E. (1978). Logical operations and metaphor interpretation: A Piagetian model. *Developmental Psychology, 49,* 649–659.

Comfort, A. (1980). Sexuality in later life. In J. E. Birren & R. B. Sloane (Eds.), *Handbook of mental health and aging.* Englewood Cliffs, NJ: Prentice-Hall.

Comfort, A., & Comfort, J. (1979). *The facts of love: Living, loving and growing up.* New York: Ballantine Books.

Commons, M. L., Miller, P. M., & Kuhn, D. (1982). The relation between formal operational reasoning and academic course selection and performance among college freshmen and sophomores. *Journal of Applied Developmental Psychology, 3,* 1–10.

Commons, M. L., & Richards, F. A. (1978, April). *The structural analytic stage of development: A Piagetian postformal operational stage.* Paper presented at the meeting of the Western Psychological Association, San Francisco, CA.

Commons, M. L., Richards, F. A., & Armon, C. (1982). *Beyond formal operations: Late adolescent and adult cognitive development.* New York: Praeger.

Commons, M. L., Richards, F. A., & Kuhn, D. (1982). Metasystematic reasoning: A case for a level of systematic reasoning beyond Piaget's stage of formal operations. *Child Development, 53,* 1058–1069.

Compassionate Friends, Inc. (1986). *Suggestions for medical personnel.* Oak Brook, IL: The Compassionate Friends, Inc.

Comstock, G., & Paik, H. (1991). *Television and the American Child.* San Diego: Academic Press.

Condon, W. S., & Sander, L. W. (1974). Neonate movement is synchronized with adult speech. *Science, 183,* 99–101.

Conel, J. L. (1939–1959). *The postnatal development of the human cortex* (Vols. 1–3). Cambridge, MA: Harvard University Press.

Conger, J. (1981). Freedom and commitment: Families, youth and social change. *American Psychologist, 36,* 1475–1484.

Conger, J., & Peterson, A. (1984). Adolescence and youth. In J. Adelson (Ed.), *Handbook of adolescent psychology* (4th ed.). New York: Harper & Row.

Conger, J. J. (1977). Parent-child relationships, social change, and adolescent vulnerability. *Journal of Pediatric Psychology, 2,* 93–97.

Conger, J. J. (1978). Adolescence: A time for becoming. In M. Lamb (Ed.), *Social and personality development.* New York: Holt, Rinehart & Winston.

Conger, R. D., Ge, X., Elder, G. H., Jr., Lorenz, F. O., & Simons, R. L. (1994). Economic stress, coercive family process, and developmental problems of adolescents. *Child Development, 56,* 541–561.

Congressional Record, U.S. House of Representatives, Full Hearing on enacted H.R. 2647, April 10, 1978.

Conway, T., Vickers, R., Ward, H., & Rahe, R. (1981). Occupational stress and variation in cigarette, coffee, and alcohol consumption. *Journal of Health and Social Behavior, 22,* 155–165.

Cooke, P. (1989). The gentle death. *Hippocrates, 3,* 50–60.

Cooper, C. D., Detre, T., & Weiss, S. M. (1981). Coronary prone behavior and coronary heart disease. *Circulation, 63,* 1199–1215.

Cooper, R., & Aslin, R. (1990). Preference for infant-directed speech in the first month after birth. *Child Development, 61,* 1584–1595.

Coopersmith, S. (1967). *The antecedents of self-esteem.* San Francisco: Freeman.

Corah, N. L., Anthony, E. J., Painter, P., Stern, J. A., & Thurston, D. L. (1965). Effects of perinatal anoxia after seven years. *Psychological Monographs, 79*(3, Whole No. 596).

Cordes, C. (1983). Researchers make room for father. *APA Monitor, 14,* pp. 1, 9–10.

Coren, S., & Halpern, D. F. (1991). Lefthandedness a marker for decreased survival fitness. *Psychological Bulletin, 109,* 90–106.

Corso, J. F. (1977). Auditory perception and communication. In J. E. Birren & K. W. Schaie

(Eds.), *Handbook of the psychology of aging.* New York: Van Nostrand Reinhold.

Costa, P. T., & McCrae, R. R. (1977). Age differences in personality structure revisited: Studies in validity, stability, and change. *International Journal of Aging and Human Development, 8,* 261–275.

Costa, P. T., & McCrae, R. R. (1980a). Objective personality assessment. In M. Storandt, I. C. Siegler, & M. F. Elias (Eds.), *The clinical psychology of aging.* New York: Plenum Press.

Costa, P. T., & McCrae, R. R. (1980b). Still stable after all these years: Personality as a key to some issues in adulthood and old age. In P. Baltes & O. Brim (Eds.), *Lifespan development and behavior III.* New York: Academic Press.

Costa, P. T., & McCrae, R. R. (1984). Personality as a lifelong determinant of wellbeing. In C. Z. Malatesta & C. E. Izard (Eds.), *Emotion in adult development.* Beverly Hills, CA: Sage Publications.

Costa, P. T., McCrae, R. R., & Arenberg, D. (1980). Enduring dispositions in adult males. *Journal of Personality and Social Psychology, 38,* 793–800.

Cotton, P. (1990). Sudden infant death syndrome: Another hypothesis offered but doubts remain. *Journal of the American Medical Association, 263,* 2865, 2869.

Counts, D. A., & Counts, D. R. (1985). "I'm not dead yet!" Aging and death: Process and experience in Kaliai. In D. A. Counts and D. R. Counts (Eds.), *Aging and its transformation.* Boston: University Press of America.

Cousins, N. (1976). *Anatomy of an illness.* New York: Norton.

Cowan, P. (1978). *Piaget with feeling: Cognitive, social and emotional dimensions.* New York: Holt, Rinehart & Winston.

Cox, M., Owen, M. T., Henderson, V.K., & Margand, N.A. (1992). Prediction of infant-father and infant-mother attachment. *Developmental Psychology, 28,* 474–483.

Cox, M., Owen, M. T., Lewis, J., & Henderson, V. K., (1989). Marriage, adult adjustment, and early parenting. *Child Development, 60,* 1015–1024.

Coyne, A. C., Whitborne, S. K., & Glenwick, D. S. (1978). Adult age differences in reflection-impulsivity. *Journal of Gerontology, 33,* 402–407.

Craik, F., & Rabinovitz, J. (1984). Age differences in the acquisition and use of verbal information. In J. Long & A. Baddeley (Eds.), *Attention and performance* (Vol. X). Hillsdale, NJ: Erlbaum.

Craik, F. I. M. (1977). Age differences in human memory. In J. E. Birren & K. W. Schaie (Eds.), *Handbook of the psychology of aging.* New York: Van Nostrand Reinhold.

Craik, F. I. M. (1994). Memory changes in normal aging. *Current Directions in Psycholgical Science, 3,* 155–158.

Crandall, R. C. (1980). *Gerontology: A behavioral science approach.* Reading, MA: Addison-Wesley.

Cravioto, J., DeLicardie, E. R., & Birch, H. G. (1966). Nutrition growth and neurointegrative development: An experimental and ecological study. *Pediatrics, 38* (Pt. 2), 319–372.

Crawford, M., & Marecek, J. (1989). Psychology reconstructs the female. *Psychology of Women Quarterly, 13,* 147–165.

Crittenden, A. (1983, November 13). New insights into infancy. *New York Times,* pp. 84–96.

Crittenden, P. (1985). Social networks, quality of child rearing, and child development. *Child Development, 56,* 1299–1313.

Crnic, K., Greenberg, M., Ragozin, A., Robinson, N., & Basham, R. (1983). Effects of stress and social support on mothers and premature and full-term infants. *Child Development, 54,* 209–217.

Crockenberg, S. (1983). Early mother and infant antecedents of Bayley Scale Performance at 21 months. *Developmental Psychology, 19,* 727–730.

Crockenberg, S., & Litman, C. (1990). Autonomy as competence in two-year-olds: Maternal correlates of child defiance, compliance, and self-assertion. *Developmental Psychology, 26,* 961–971.

Crockenberg, S., & Litman, C. (1991). Effects of maternal employment on maternal and two-year-old child behavior. *Child Development, 62,* 930–953.

Crockenberg, S., & McCluskey, K. (1986). Change in maternal behavior during the baby's first year of life. *Child Development, 57,* 746–753.

Cronbach, L. J. (1970). *Essentials of psychological testing* (3rd ed.). New York: Harper & Row.

Cross, J. F., & Cross, J. (1971). Age, sex, race, and the perception of facial beauty. *Developmental Psychology, 5,* 431–439.

Crosson, C. W., & Robertson-Tchabo, C. A. (1983). Age and preference for complexity among manifestly creative women. *Human Development, 26,* 149–155.

Crystal, D. S., Chen, C., Fuligni, A. J., Stevenson, H. W., Hsu, C., Ko, H., Kitamura, S., & Kimura, S. (1994). Psychological maladjustment and academic achievement: A cross-cultural study of Japanese, Chinese, and American high school students. *Child Development, 65,* 738–753.

Csikszentmihalyi, M., & Larson, R. (1984). *Being adolescent: Conflict and growth in the teenage years.* New York: Basic Books.

Csikszentmihalyi, M., Larson, R., & Prescott, S. (1977). The ecology of adolescent activity and experience. *Journal of Youth and Adolescence, 6,* 281–294.

Cuber, J. F., & Harroff, P. B. (1965). *The significant Americans.* New York: Appleton-Century-Crofts.

Cumming, E., & Henry, W. (1961). *Growing old: A process of disengagement.* New York: Basic Books.

Cummings, E., & Bjork, E. (1983). Perseveration and search on a five choice invisible displacement task. *Journal of Genetic Psychology, 142,* 283–291.

Cummings, E. M., Iannotti, R., & Zahn-Waxler, C. (1985). Influence of conflict between adults on the emotions and aggression of young children. *Developmental Psychology, 21,* 495–507.

Curtiss, S. (1977). *Genie: A psycholinguistic study of a modern-day "wild child."* New York: Academic Press.

Custer, G. (1994, October). Balance can counteract stress of work. *APA Monitor,* p. 49.

Czaja, S. J., & Sharit, J. (1993). Age differences in the performance of computer-based work. *Psychology and Aging, 8,* 59–67.

Dalton, K. (1964). *The premenstrual syndrome.* London: Heinemann.

Dalton, K. (1977). *The premenstrual syndrome and progesterone therapy.* London: Heinemann.

Dalton, K. (1980). Cyclical criminal acts in premenstrual syndrome. *Lancet, 2,* 1070–1071.

Damon, W. (1977). *The social world of the child.* San Francisco: Jossey-Bass.

Damon, W. (1983). *Social and personality development.* New York: Norton.

Damon, W. (1991). Adolescent self-concept. In R. M. Lerner, A. C. Petersen, & J. Brooks-Gunn (Eds.), *Encyclopedia of adolescence.* New York: Garland.

Daniels, D., & Moos, R. (1990). Assessing life stressors and social resources among adolescents: Applications to depressed youth. *Journal of Adolescent Research, 5,* 268–289.

Dannemiller, J. (1989). A test of color constancy in 9 and 20 week old human infants following simulated illuminant changes. *Developmental Psychology, 25,* 171–184.

Dasen, P. (Ed.). (1977). *Piagetian psychology: Cross-cultural contributions.* New York: Gardiner Press.

Dasen, P., Ngini, L., & Lavallee, M. (1979). Cross-cultural training studies of concrete operations. In L. H. Eckenberger, J. L. Lonner, & Y. H. Poortings (Eds.), *Cross-cultural contributions to psychology.* Amsterdam: Swets & Zeilinger.

Dasen, P. R. (1972). Cross-cultural Piagetian research: A summary. *Journal of Cross-Cultural Psychology, 3,* 23–39.

Dasey, C., Nelson III, W., & Aikman, K. (1990). Prevalency rate and personality comparisons of bulemic and normal adolescents. *Child Psychiatry & Human Development, 20,* 243–251.

DeAngelis, T. (1990, September). Panel calls child abuse a "national emergency." *APA Monitor,* pp. 18–19.

Deater-Deckar, K., Scarr, S., McCartney, K., & Eisenberg, M. (1994). Paternal separation anxiety: Relationships with parenting stress, child-rearing attitudes, and maternal anxieties. *Psychological Science, 5,* 341–346.

Deaux, K. (1984). From individual differences to social categories: Analysis of a decade's research growth. *American Psychologist, 39,* 105–116.

Deaux, K., & Major, B. (1987). Putting gender into context: an interactive model of gender-related behavior. *Psychological Review, 94,* 396–389.

DeCasper, A. J., & Fifer, W. P. (1980). Of human bonding: Newborns prefer their mothers' voices. *Science, 208,* 1174–1176.

DeFries, J. C., & Plomin, R. (1978). Behavioral genetics. *Annual Review of Psychology, 29,* 473–515.

DeFries, J. C., Plomin, R., Vandenberg, S. G., & Kuse, A. R. (1981). Parent-offspring resemblance for cognitive abilities in the Colorado Adoption Project: Biological, adoptive and control parents and one-year-old children. *Intelligence, 5,* 245–277.

DeLisi, R., & Staudt, J. (1980). Individual differences in college students' performance on formal operations tasks. *Journal of Applied Developmental Psychology, 1,* 201–208.

Den-Ouden, L., Rijken, M., Brand, R., Verloove-Vanhorick, P., & Ruys, J. H. (1991). Is it correct to correct? Developmental milestones in 555 "normal" preterm infants compared with term infants. *Journal of Pediatrics, 118,* 399–404.

Denham, S. (1986). Social cognition, prosocial behavior, and emotion in preschoolers: Contextual validation. *Child Development, 57,* 194–201.

Denney, N. W. (1982). Aging and cognitive changes. In B. Wolman (Ed.), *Handbook of developmental psychology.* Englewood Cliffs, NJ: Prentice-Hall.

Denney, N. W., & Cornelius, S. W. (1975). Class inclusion and multiple classification in middle and old age. *Developmental Psychology, 11,* 521–522.

Denney, N. W., & List, J. A. (1979). Adult age differences in performance on the Matching Familiar Figures test. *Human Development, 22,* 137–144.

Dennis, W. (1940). The effect of cradling practices upon the onset of walking in Hopi children. *Journal of Genetic Psychology, 56,* 77–86.

Dennis, W. (1966). Creative productivity between the ages of 20 and 80 years. *Journal of Gerontology, 21,* 1–18.

Dennis, W. (1973). *Children of the creche.* New York: Meredith.

Depner, C., & Ingersoll-Dayton, B. (1988). Supportive relationships in later life. *Psychology and Aging, 3,* 348–357.

Depner, C., & Ingersoll-Dayton, B. (1990). Supportive relationships in later life. *Psychology and Aging, 5,* 451–457.

DeRosier, M. E., Cillessen, A. H. N., Coie, J. D., & Dodge, K. A. (1994). Group Social Context and Children's Aggressive Behavior. *Child Development, 65,* 1068–1079.

de Villiers, P., & de Villiers, J. (1979). *Early language.* Cambridge, MA: Harvard University Press.

DeVries, H. A. (1970). Physiological effects of an exercise training regimen upon men aged 52–88. *Journal of Gerontology, 25,* 325–336.

DeVries, H. A. (1975). Physiology of exercise and aging. In D. S. Woodruff & J. E. Birren (Eds.), *Aging: Scientific perspectives and social issues.* New York: Van Nostrand Reinhold.

DeVries, H. A., & Adams, G. M. (1972). Electromyographic comparison of single doses of exercise and meprobamate as to effects on muscular relaxation. *American Journal of Physical Medicine, 51,* 130–141.

Diaz, R. (1985). Bilingual cognitive development: Addressing three gaps in current research. *Child Development, 56,* 1376–1388.

Diaz, R. M., & Berndt, T. J. (1982). Children's knowledge of a best friend: Fact or fantasy? *Developmental Psychology, 18,* 787–794.

Dickens, W., & Perlman, D. (1981). Friendship over the life-cycle. In S. Duck & R. Gilmour (Eds.), *Personal relationships: Vol. 2. Developing personal relationships.* New York: Academic Press.

DiGiulio, R. (1989). *Beyond widowhood: From bereavement to emergence and hope.* New York: Free Press.

Dinnerstein, D. (1976). *The mermaid and the minotaur: Sexual arrangements and human malaise.* New York: Harper & Row.

DiPietro, J. (1981). Rough and tumble play: A function of gender. *Developmental Psychology, 17,* 50–58.

DiVitto, B., & Goldberg, S. (1979). The effects of newborn medical status on early parent-infant interactions. In T. M. Field, A. M. Sostek, S. Goldberg, & H. H. Shuman (Eds.), *Infants born at risk.* New York: Spectrum.

Dobbs, A., & Rule, B. (1989). Adult age differences in working memory. *Psychology and Aging, 4,* 500–503.

Dodge, K. (1983). Behavioral antecedents of peer social status. *Child Development, 54,* 1386–1399.

Dodge, K. A. (1986). A social information processing model of social competence in children. In M. Perlmutter (Ed.), *Minnesota Symposium on Child Psychology* (pp. 77–125). Hillsdale, NJ: Erlbaum.

Dodge, K. A. (1990). Nature versus nurture in childhood conduct disorder: It is time to ask a different question. *Developmental Psychology, 26,* 698–701.

Dodge, K. A., & Frame, C. L. (1982). Social cognitive biases and deficits in aggressive boys. *Child Development, 53,* 620–635.

Dodge, K. A., & Price, J. M. (1994). On the relation between social information processing and socially competent behavior in early school-aged children. *Child Development, 65,* 1385–1397.

Dodge, K. A., & Somberg, D. R. (1987). Hostile attributional biases among aggressive boys exacerbated under conditions of threat to the self. *Child Development, 58,* 213–224.

Dodge, K. A., & Tomlin, A. (1987). Cue utilization as a mechanism of attributional bias in aggressive children. *Social Cognition, 5,* 280–300.

Dohrenwend, B., Krasnoff, L., Askenasy, A., & Dohrenwend, B. (1978). Exemplification of a method for scaling life events. *Journal of Health and Social Behavior, 19,* 205–229.

Dolen, L. S., & Bearison, D. J. (1982). Social interaction and social cognition in aging: A contextual analysis. *Human Development, 25,* 430–442.

Donaldson, M. (1978). *Children's minds.* New York: Norton.

Donnan, H. (1990). Mixed marriages in comparative perspective: Gender and power in Northern Ireland and Pakistan. *Journal of Comparative Family Studies, 21,* 207–225.

Dorn, L., Crockett, L., & Peterson, A. (1988). The relations of pubertal status to intrapersonal changes in young adolescents. *Journal of Early Adolescence, 8,* 405–419.

Dorsch, A., & Keane, S. P. (1994). Contextual factors in children's social information processing. *Developmental Psychology, 30,* 611–616.

Doty, R., Shaman, P., & Dann, M. (1984). Development of the University of Pennsylvania Smell Identification Test: A standardized microencapsulated test of olfactory function. *Physiology and Behavior, 32,* 489–502.

Douvan, E., & Adelson, J. (1966). *The adolescent experience.* New York: Wiley.

Doyle, A.-B., Champagne, M., & Segalowitz, N. (1978). Some issues in the assessment of linguistic consequences of early bilingualism. In M. Paradis (Ed.), *Aspects of bilingualism.* Columbia, SC: Hornbeam Press.

Dreyer, P. H. (1982). Sexuality during adolescence. In B. Wolman (Ed.), *Handbook of developmental psychology.* Englewood Cliffs, NJ: Prentice-Hall.

Drillien, C. M., & Ellis, R. W. B. (1964). *The growth and development of the prematurely born infant.* Baltimore: Williams & Wilkins.

Dryfoos, J. G. (1990). *Adolescents at risk: Prevalence and prevention.* New York: Oxford University Press.

Dubas, J., Graber, J., & Peterson, A. (1991). A longitudinal investigation of adolescents' changing perceptions of pubertal timing. *Developmental Psychology, 27,* 580–586.

DuBois, D., & Hirsch, B. (1990). School and neighborhood friendship patterns of Blacks and Whites in early adolescence. *Child Development, 61,* 524–536.

Duncan, G., Brooks-Gunn, J., & Kato Klebanov, P. (1994). Economic deprivation and early childhood development. *Child Development, 65,* 296–318.

Dunn, J. (1983). Sibling relationships in early childhood. *Developmental Psychology, 54,* 787–811.

Dunn, J., & Kendrick, C. (1982). *Siblings: Love, envy, and understanding.* Cambridge, MA: Harvard University Press.

Dunn, J., Plomin, R., & Daniels, D. (1986). Consistency and change in mother's behavior toward young siblings. *Child Development, 57,* 348–356.

Dunphy, D. C. (1963). The social structure of urban adolescent peer groups. *Sociometry, 26,* 230–246.

Durlak, J. (1973). A relationship between attitudes toward life and death among elderly women. *Developmental Psychology, 8,* 146.

Durlak, J. (1978–1979). Comparison between experimental and didactic methods of death education. *Omega, 9,* 57–66.

Dusek, J. B., & Flaherty, J. F. (1981). The development of the self-concept during the adolescent years. *Monographs of the Society for Research in Child Development, 1981, 46* (3–4, Serial No. 191).

Dutton, D. B., & Levine, S. (1989). Overview, methods, logical critique, and reformation. In J. P. Bunker, D. S. Gomby, & B. H. Kehrer (Eds.), *Pathways to health* (pp. 29–69). Menlo Park, CA: The Henry J. Kaiser Family Foundation.

Duvall, E. (1977). *Marriage and family development* (5th ed.). Philadelphia: Lippincott.

Dyal, J., & Chan, C. (1985). Stress and distress: A study of Hong Kong Chinese and Euro-Canadian students. *Journal of Cross Cultural Psychology, 16,* 447–466.

Dyk, P. H., & Adams, G. R. (1990). Identity and intimacy: An initial investigation of three theoretical models using cross-lag panel correlations. *Journal of Youth and Adolescence, 19,* 91–110.

Eagly, A. (1983). Gender and social influence. *American Psychologist, 38,* 971–981.

Eaton, W., Chipperfield, J., & Singbeil, C. (1989). Birth order and activity level in children, *Developmental Psychology, 25,* 668–672.

Eaton, W. O., & Enns, L. R. (1986). Sex differences in human motor activity. *Psychological Bulletin, 100,* 19–28.

Eccles, J. (1982, March). *Sex differences in math achievement and course enrollment.* Paper presented at the annual meeting of the American Educational Research Association, New York.

Eccles, J., Adler, T., & Kaczala, C. (1982). Socialization of achievement attitudes and beliefs: Parental influences. *Child Development, 53,* 310–321.

Eccles, J. S., & Midgley, C. (1989). Stage-environment fit: Developmentally appropriate classrooms for young adolescents. In R. E. Ames & C. Ames (Eds.), *Research on motivation in education* (Vol. 3, pp. 139–186). New York: Academic Press.

Eccles, J. S., Midgley, C., Wigfield, A., Buchanan, C. M., Reuman, D., Flanagan, C., & MacIver, D. (1993, February). Development during adolescence: The impact of stage-environment fit on young adolescents' experiences in schools and in families. *American Psychologist, 48,* 90–101.

Eckenrode, J., Laird, M., & Doris, J. (1993). School performance and disciplinary problems among abused and neglected children. *Developmental Psychology, 29,* 53–62.

Eckerman, C. O., & Whatley, J. L. (1977). Toys and social interaction between infant peers. *Child Development, 48,* 1645–1656.

Edwards, C. (1978). Social experience and moral judgment in East African young adults. *Journal of Genetic Psychology, 133,* 19–29.

Edwards, C. (1982). Moral development in comparative cultural perspectives. In D. Wagner & H. Stevenson (Eds.), *Cultural perspectives on child development.* San Francisco: W. H. Freeman.

Edwards, C., & Whiting, B. (1988). *Children of different worlds.* Cambridge, MA: Harvard University Press.

Edwards, R. (1995, February). New tools help gauge marital success. *APA Monitor,* p. 6.

Egeland, B., & Farber, E. (1984). Infant-mother attachment: Factors related to its development and changes over time. *Child Development, 55,* 753–771.

Eggebeen, D. J., & Hogan, D. P. (1990). Giving between generations in American families. *Human Nature, 1,* 211–232.

Ehrenberg, M., Cox, D., & Koopman, R. (1990). The prevalence of depression in high school students. *Adolescence, 25,* 905–912.

Eichorn, D. H., Clausen, J. A., Haan, N., Honzik, M., & Mussen, P. H. (Eds.). (1981). *Present and past in middle age.* New York: Academic Press.

Eichorn, D. H., Hunt, J. V., & Honzik, M. P. (1981). Experience, personality, and IQ: Adolescence to middle age. In D. Eichorn, J. Clausen, N. Haan, M. Honzik, & P. Mussen (Eds.), *Present and past in middle age.* New York: Academic Press.

Eiduson, B. T. (1978). Emergent families in the 1970's: Values, practices and impact on children. In D. Reiss & H. Hoffman (Eds.), *The family: Dying or developing.* New York: Plenum Press.

Eiduson, B. T., Cohen, J., & Alexander, J. (1973). Alternatives in child rearing in the 1970's. *American Journal of Orthopsychiatry, 43,* 721–731.

Eiduson, B. T., Kornfein, M., Zimmerman, I. L., & Weisner, T. S. (1982). Comparative socialization practices in traditional and alternative families. In M. Lamb (Ed.), *Nontraditional families: Parenting and child development.* Hillsdale, NJ: Erlbaum.

Eimas, P. D., & Miller, J. L. (1992). Organization in the perception of speech by young infants. *Psychological Science, 3,* 34–344.

Eisdorfer, C. (1968). Arousal and performance: Experiments in verbal learning and a tentative theory. In G. Talland (Ed.), *Human aging and behavior.* New York: Academic Press.

Eisdorfer, C., Nowlin, J., & Wilkie, F. (1970). Improvement of learning in the aged by modification of autonomic nervous system activity. *Science, 170,* 1327–1329.

Eisdorfer, C., & Wilkie, F. (1977). Stress, disease, aging, and behavior. In J. E. Birren & K. W.

Schaie (Eds.), *Handbook of the psychology of aging.* New York: Van Nostrand Reinhold.

Eisenberg, N., Wolchik, S., Hernandez, R., & Pasternack, J. (1985). Parental socialization of young children's play: A short term longitudinal study. *Child Development, 56,* 1506–1573.

Elder, G., Downey, G., & Cross, C. (1980). Family ties and life chances: Hard times and hard choices in women's lives since the 1930s. In R. Turner and H. Reese (Eds.), *Life-span developmental psychology.* New York: Academic Press.

Elkind, D. (1961). Quantity conceptions in junior and senior high school students. *Child Development, 32,* 551–560.

Elkind, D. (1962). Quantity conceptions in college students. *Journal of Social Psychology, 57,* 459–465.

Elkind, D. (1967). Egocentrism in adolescence. *Child Development, 38,* 1025–1035.

Elkind, D. (1978). Understanding the young adolescent. *Adolescence, 13,* 127–134.

Elkind, D. (1981). *The hurried child: Growing up too fast too soon.* Reading, MA: Addison-Wesley.

Elkind, D., & Bowen, R. (1979). Imaginary audience behavior in children and adolescents. *Developmental Psychology, 15,* 38–44.

Ellison, J. (1984, June). The seven frames of mind. *Psychology Today,* 20–26.

Elster, A., & Hendricks, L. (1986). Stresses and coping strategies of adolescent fathers. In A. Elster & M. Lamb (Eds.), *Adolescent fatherhood.* Hillsdale, NJ: Erlbaum.

Elster, A., & Lamb, M. (Eds.). (1986). *Adolescent fatherhood.* Hillsdale, NJ: Lawrence Erlbaum.

Emery, C. F., Hauck, E. R., & Blumental, J. A. (1992). Exercise adherence or maintenance among older adults: 1-year follow-up study. *Psychology and Aging, 7,* 466–470.

Emery, R., & Tuer, Mr. (1993). Parenting and marital relationships. In T. Luster & L. Okagalei (Eds.), *Parenting: An ecological perspective.* Hillsdale, NY: Lawrence Erlbaum.

Emler, N. P. (1983). Morality and politics: The ideological dimension in the theory of moral development. In H. Weinreich-Haste & D. Locke (Eds.), *Morality in the making: Thought, action, and social context.* New York: Wiley.

Emler, N. P., Renwick, S., & Malone, M. (1983). The relationship between moral reasoning and political orientation. *Journal of Personality and Social Psychology, 45,* 1073–1080.

Emr, M., & Schneider, E. (1985). Alzheimer's Disease: Research highlights. *Geriatric Nursing, 16,* 135–138.

Engen, T. (1977). Taste and smell. In J. E. Birren & K. W. Schaie (Eds.), *Handbook of the psychology of aging.* New York: Van Nostrand Reinhold.

Epstein, H. T. (1980). EEG developmental stages. *Developmental Psychology, 13,* 629–631.

Epstein, J. (1986). Friendship selection: Developmental and environmental influences. In E. C. Mueller & C. R. Cooper (Eds.), *Process and outcome in peer relationships.* Orlando, FL: Academic Press.

Epstein, J. L. (1990). School and family connections: Theory, research, and implications for integrating sociologies of education and family. *Marriage and Family Review, 15,* 99–126.

Epstein, J. L. (1993). Longitudinal effect of family-school-person interactions on student outcomes. In A. Kerckhoff (Ed.), *Research in*

sociology of educational and socialization (Vol. 4). Greenwich, CT: JAI.

Epstein, M. H., Cullinan, D., Lessen, E., & Lloyd, J. (1980). Understanding children with learning disabilities. *Child Welfare, 59,* 2–14.

Erikson, E. H. (1959). *Identity and the life-cycle: Selected papers by Erik H. Erikson.* New York: International Universities Press.

Erikson, E. H. (1963). *Childhood and society* (2nd ed.). New York: Norton.

Erikson, E. H. (1968). *Identity: Youth and crisis.* New York: Norton.

Erikson, E. H. (1976, Spring). Reflections on Dr. Borg's life cycle. *Daedalus, 105,* 1–28.

Eron, L. D. (1980). Prescription for the reduction of aggression. *American Psychologist, 35,* 244–252.

Eron, L. D. (1982). Parent-child interaction, television violence and aggression of children, *American Psychologist, 37,* 197–211.

Eron, L., Huesmann, L. R., Brice, P., Fischer, P., & Mermelstein, R. (1983). Age trends in the development of aggression, sex typing, and related television habits. *Developmental Psychology, 19,* 71–77.

Ervin, S. (1964). Imitation and structural change in children's language. In E. H. Lenneberg (Ed.), *New directions in the study of language.* Cambridge, MA: MIT Press.

Escalona, S. (1982). Growing up with the threat of nuclear war: Some indirect effects on personality development. *American Journal of Orthopsychiatry, 52,* 600–607.

Essex, M., & Nam, S. (1987). Marital status and loneliness among older women: The differential importance of close family and friends. *Journal of Marriage and the Family, 49,* 93–106.

Etaugh, C. (1980). Effects of nonmaternal care on children. *American Psychologist, 35,* 309–319.

Euthanasia Educational Council. (1974). *A living will.* New York: Euthanasia Educational Council.

Eveleth, P., & Tanner, J. (1976). *Worldwide variation in human growth.* Cambridge, England: Cambridge University Press.

The facts of adolescent life. (1979, February). *Parents Magazine, 54,* 69.

Fagan, J. (1982). Infant memory. In T. J. Field, A. Huston, H. C. Quay, L. Troll, & G. E. Finley (Eds.), *Review of human development.* New York: Wiley.

Fagot, B., Leinbach, M., & Hagan, R. (1986). Gender labeling and the adoption of sex-typed behaviors. *Developmental Psychology, 22* (4), 440–443.

Fagot, B., Hagan, R., Leinbach, M., & Kronsberg, S. (1985). Differential reactions to assertive and communicative acts of toddler boys and girls. *Child Development, 56,* 1499–1505.

Fairburn, C., & Cooper, P. (1983). The epidemiology of bulimia nervosa. *International Journal of Eating Disorders, 2,* 61–67.

Fakouri, M. E. (1976). Cognitive development in adulthood: A fifth stage? A critique. *Developmental Psychology, 12,* 472.

Falbo, T. (1979). Only children, stereotypes, and research. In M. Lewis & L. A. Rosenblum (Eds.), *The child and its family.* New York: Plenum.

Falbo, T. (1982). PAQ types and power strategies in intimate relationships. *Psychology of Women Quarterly, 6,* 399–405.

Falbo, T. (1992). Social norms and the one-child family: Clinical and policy implications. In F. Boer & J. Dunn (Eds.), *Children's sibling relationships* (pp. 71–82), Hillsdale, NJ: Erlbaum.

Falbo, T., & Poston, D. L. (1993). The academic, personality, and physical outcomes of only children in China. *Child Development, 64,* 18–35.

Fantz, R. (1958). Pattern vision in young infants. *Psychological Record, 8,* 43–49.

Fantz, R. L. (1961). The origins of form perception. *Scientific American, 204,* 66–72.

Fantz, R. L. (1965). Visual perception from birth as shown by pattern selectivity. *Annals of the New York Academy of Science, 118,* 793–814.

Farkas, M. S., & Hoyer, W. J. (1980). Processing consequences of perceptual grouping in selective attention. *Journal of Gerontology, 35,* 207–216.

Fawcett, G., Stonner, D., & Zeppelin, H. (1980). Locus of control, perceived constraint, and morale among institutionalized aged. *Aging and Human Development, 11,* 13–24.

FBI Law Enforcement Bulletin. (1978, Vol. 47, No. 5, May). 4–5. Federal Bureau of Investigation, U.S. Department of Justice, Washington, D.C.: Office of Public Affairs.

Featherman, D. (1983). Life-span perspectives in social science research. In P. Baltes & O. Brim (Eds.), *Life-span development and behavior: Vol. 5.* New York: Academic Press.

Federal Bureau of Investigation. (1984). *Crime in the United States.* Washington, DC: Federal Bureau of Investigation.

Feifel, H. (1990). Psychology and death: Meaningful rediscovery. *American Psychologist, 45,* 537–543.

Fein, G. C., Jacobson, J., Jacobson, S., Schwartz, P., & Dowler, J. (1984). Prenatal exposure to polychlorinated biphenyls: Effects on birth size and gestational age. *Journal of Pediatrics, 105,* 315–320.

Feingold, A. (1988). Cognitive gender differences are disappearing. *American Psychologist, 43,* 95–103.

Feldman, S., & Wentzel, K. (1990). The relationship between parenting styles, son's self-restraint, and peer relations in early adolescence. *Journal of Early Adolescence, 10,* 439–454.

Feldman, S. S., & Weinberg, D. A. (1994). Self-restraint as a mediator of family influences on boys' delinquent behavior: A longitudinal study. *Child Development, 65,* 195–211.

Fernald, A. (1989). Intonation and communicative intent in mother's speech to infants: Is the melody the message? *Child Development, 60,* 1497–1510.

Fernald, A., Taeschner, T., Dunn, J., Papousek, M., deBoysson-Bardies, B., & Fukui, I. (1989). A cross-language study of prosodic modifications in mothers' and fathers' speech to preverbal infants. *Journal of Child Language, 16,* 447–501.

Ferree, M. M. (1976). Working-class jobs: Housework and paid work as sources of satisfaction. *Social Problems, 23,* 431–441.

Feshbach, N. (1974). The relationship of child rearing factors to children's aggression, empathy and related positive and negative behaviors. In J. deWit & W. W. Hartup (Eds.), *Determinants and origins of aggressive behavior.* The Hague: Mouton.

Field, D., Schaie, K. W., & Leino, E. V. (1988). Continuity in intellectual functioning: The role of

self reported health. *Psychology and Aging, 3,* 385–392.

Field, T. (1978). Interaction behaviors of primary versus secondary caretaker fathers. *Developmental Psychology, 14,* 183–184.

Field, T. M., Cohen, D., Garcia, R., & Greenberg, R. (1984). Mother–stranger face discrimination by the newborn. *Infant Behavior and Development, 7,* 19–25.

Field, T., Woodson, R., Greenberg, R., & Cohen, D. (1982). Discrimination and imitation of facial expressions by neonates. *Science, 218,* 179–181.

Field, T. M., & Schanberg, S. A. (1990). Massage alters growth and catecholamine production in preterm newborns. In Nina Gunzenhauser (Ed.), *Advances in touch: New implications in human development.* Skillman, NJ: Johnson and Johnson.

Fine, G. (1981). Friends, impression management, and preadolescent behavior. In S. Asher & J. Gottman (Eds.), *The development of children's friendships.* New York: Cambridge University Press.

Fingerhut, L., & Makuc, D. (1992). Mortality among minority populations in the United States. *American Journal of Public Health, 82,* 1168–1170.

Finkelhor, D. (1994, Summer/Fall). Current information on the scope and nurture of child sexual abuse. *The Future of Children, 4,* 31–53.

Finn, J. D., & Achilles, C. M. (1990). Answers and questions about class size: A statewide experiment. *American Educational Research Journal, 27,* 557–577.

Fischer, D. (1987). *Growing old in America.* New York: Oxford University Press.

Fischer, K. (1987). Relations between brain and cognitive development. *Child Development, 58,* 623–632.

Fishkin, J., Keniston, K., & MacKinnon, C. (1973). Moral reasoning and political ideology. *Journal of Personality and Social Psychology, 27,* 109–119.

Fisk, A. D., Hertzog, C., Lee, M. D., Rogers, W. A., & Anderson-Garlach, M. (1994). Long-term retention of skilled visual search: Do young adults retain more than old adults? *Psychology and Aging, 9,* 206–215.

Fitzgerald, L. (1993). Sexual harassment: Violence against women in the workplace. *American Psychologist, 48,* 1070–1076.

Flanagan, C. (1990). Change in family work status: Effects on parent-adolescent decision making. *Child Development, 61,* 163–177.

Flanagan, J. (1981, August). *Some characteristics of 70-year-old workers.* Paper presented at the Annual Meeting of the American Psychological Association, Los Angeles.

Flavell, J. H. (1977). *Cognitive development.* Englewood Cliffs, NJ: Prentice-Hall.

Flavell, J., Beach, R., & Chinsky, J. (1966). Spontaneous verbal rehearsal in a memory task as a function of age. *Child Development, 37,* 283–299.

Flavell, J., Green, F., & Flavell, E. (1986). Development of knowledge about the appearance-reality distinction. *Monographs of the Society for Research in Child Development, 51*(1, Serial No. 212).

Flavell, J. H., Miller, P. H., & Miller, S. A. (1993). *Cognitive development* (3rd ed.). Englewood Cliffs, NJ: Prentice-Hall.

Flavell, J. H., & Wellman, H. (1977). Metamemory. In R. Kail & J. Hagen (Eds.), *Perspectives on the development of memory and cognition.* Hillsdale, NJ: Erlbaum.

Flavell, J. H., & Wohlwill, J. F. (1969). Formal and functional aspects of cognitive development. In D. Elkind & J. H. Flavell (Eds.), *Studies in cognitive development: Essays in honor of Jean Piaget.* New York: Oxford University Press.

Fleming, J. B. (1979). *Stopping wife abuse.* Garden City, NY: Anchor Press.

Flora, J., & Thoresen, C. (1988). Reducing the risk of AIDS in adolescents. *American Psychologist, 43,* 965–970.

Flynn, J. R. (1984). The mean IQ of Americans: Massive gains 1932 to 1978. *Psychological Bulletin, 95,* 29–51.

Fogel, A., Toda, S., & Kawai, M. (1988). Mother-infant face-to-face interaction in Japan and the United States: A laboratory comparison using 3-month-old infants. *Developmental Psychology, 24,* 398–406.

Foley, M., Johnson, M., & Raye, C. (1983). Age-related changes in confusion between memories for thoughts and memories for speech. *Child Development, 54,* 51–60.

Forbes, G. B. (1972). Growth of the lean body mass in man. *Growth, 36,* 325–338.

Fowles, B., & Glanz, M. (1977). Competence and talent in verbal riddle comprehension. *Journal of Child Language, 4,* 433–452.

Fox, G. L. (1979, May–June). The family's influence on adolescent sexual behavior. *Children Today,* 21–25.

Fox, J. H. (1977). Effects of retirement and former work life on women's adaptation to old age. *Journal of Gerontology, 32,* 196–202.

Fozard, J. L., Wolf, E., Bell, B., MacFarland, R., & Podolsky, S. (1977). Visual perception and communication. In J. E. Birren & K. W. Schaie (Eds.), *Handbook of the psychology of aging.* New York: Van Nostrand Reinhold.

Fraiberg, S. (1977). *Every child's birthright: In defense of mothering.* New York: Basic Books.

Frank, R. T. (1931). The hormonal causes of premenstrual tension. *Archives of Neurological Psychiatry, 26,* 1053.

Frank, S. J., Pirsch, L. A., & Wright, V. C. (1990). Late adolescents' perceptions of their relationships with their parents: Relationships among deidealization, autonomy, relatedness, and insecurity and implications for adolescent adjustment and ego identity status. *Journal of Youth and Adolescence, 19,* 571–588.

Franz, C., McClelland, D., & Weinberger, J. (1991). Childhood antecedents of conventional social accomplishment in midlife adults: A 36-year prospective study. *Journal of Personality and Social Psychology, 60,* 586–595.

Frazier, T., Davis, G., Goldstein, H., & Goldberg, I. (1961). Cigarette smoking: A prospective study. *American Journal of Obstetrics and Gynecology, 81,* 988–996.

Freeman, D. (1983). *Margaret Mead and Samoa: The making and unmaking of an anthropological myth.* Cambridge, MA: Harvard University Press.

Freeman, N., & Janikoun, R. (1972). Intellectual realism in children's drawings of a familiar object with distinctive features. *Child Development, 43,* 1116–1121.

Freiberg, P. (1991, January). Work and well-being. *APA Monitor,* pp. 24–25.

Freiberg, P. (1991, February). Study: Disorders found in 20 percent of children. *APA Monitor,* p. 36.

Freidrich, L., & Stein, A. (1974). Aggressive and prosocial television programs and the natural behavior of preschool children. *Monographs of the Society for Research in Child Development, 38*(4, Serial No. 151).

French, D., & Waas, G. (1985). Behavior problems of peer-neglected and peer-rejected elementary-age children: Parent and teacher perspectives. *Child Development, 56,* 246–252.

French, D. C. (1990). Heterogeneity of peer-rejected girls. *Child Development, 61,* 2028–2031.

Freud, A. (1958). Adolescence. *The Psychoanalytic Study of the Child, 13,* 255–278.

Freud, S. (1924). *A general introduction to psychoanalysis.* London: Boni and Liveright.

Frieberg, P. (1991, April). Self-esteem gender gap widens in adolescence. *APA Monitor,* p. 29.

Fried, B. (1967). *The middle-age crisis.* New York: Harper & Row.

Friedenberg, E. Z. (1959). *Vanishing adolescence.* Boston: Beacon.

Friedman, S., Jacobs, B., & Werthmann, M. (1981). Sensory processing in pre- and full-term infants in the neonatal period. In S. Friedman & M. Sigman (Eds.), *Preterm birth and psychological development.* New York: Academic Press.

Friedmann, E. A., & Orbach, H. L. (1974). Adjustment to retirement. In S. Arieti (Ed.), *American handbook of psychiatry: Vol. 1.* New York: Basic Books.

Friedmann, M., & Rosenman, R. H. (1974). *Type A behavior and your heart.* New York: Knopf.

Fries, J., & Crapo, L. (1981). *Vitality and aging: Implications of the rectangular curve.* San Francisco: W. H. Freeman.

Frodi, A., Lamb, M., Leavitt, L., Donovan, W. L., Neff, C., & Sherry, D. (1978). Fathers' and mothers' responses to the faces and cries of normal and premature infants. *Developmental Psychology, 14,* 490–498.

Fry, D. (1988). Intercommunity differences in aggression among Zapotec children. *Child Development, 59,* 1008–1019.

Fuchs, V. R. (1974). *Who shall live? Health, economics and social choice.* New York: Basic Books.

Fuligni, A. J., & Eccles, J. S. (1993). Perceived parent-child relationships and early adolescents' orientation toward peers. *Developmental Psychology, 29,* 622–632.

Furman, E. (1974). *A child's parent dies.* New Haven: Yale University Press, 1974.

Furrow, D., Nelson, K., & Benedict, H. (1979). Mothers' speech to children and syntactic development: Some simple relationships. *Journal of Child Language, 6,* 423–442.

Furstenberg, F. (1979). Premarital pregnancy and marital instability. In G. Levinger & O. Moles (Eds.), *Divorce and separation: Context, causes and consequence.* New York: Basic Books.

Furstenberg, F., Nord, C., Peterson, J., & Zill, N. (1983). The life course of children of divorce: Marital disruption and parental contact. *American Sociological Review, 48,* 656–668.

Fuson, K., Secada, W., & Hall, J. (1983). Matching, counting and conservation of numerical equivalence. *Child Development, 54,* 91–97.

Futterman, A. Gallagher, D., Thompson, L., Lovett, S., & Gileweski, M. (1990). Retro-spective assessment of marital adjustment and depression during the first 2 years of spousal bereavement. *Psychology and Aging, 5,* 277–283.

Galambos, N. L. (1992, October). Parent-adolescent relations. *Current Directions in Psycholgical Science, 1,* 146–149.

Galambos, S. J., & Goldin-Meadow, S. (1990). The effects of learning two languages on level of metalinguistic awareness. *Cognition, 34,* 1–56.

Gallahue, D. L. (1976). *Motor development and movement experiences for young children.* New York: Wiley.

Gallup, G. (1977). Self-recognition in primates. A comparative approach to the bidirectional properties of consciousness. *American Psychologist, 32,* 329–338.

Galton, F. (1869). *Hereditary genius: An inquiry into its laws and consequences.* London: Macmillan.

Garbarino, J., Kostelny, K., & Dubrow, N. (1991, April). What children can tell us about living in danger. *American Psychologist, 46,* 376–383.

Garcia-Coll, C. (1990). Developmental outcome of minority infants: A process oriented look into our beginnings. *Child Development, 61,* 270–289.

Gardner, H. (1974). Metaphors and modalities: How children project polar adjectives onto diverse domains. *Child Development, 45,* 84–91.

Gardner, H. (1980). *Artful scribbles: The significance of children's drawings.* New York: Basic Books.

Gardner, H. (1983). *Frames of mind: The theory of multiple intelligence.* New York: Basic Books.

Gardner, L. (1972). Deprivation dwarfism. *Scientific American, 227,* 17–25.

Gardner, W., Millstein, S., & Wilcox, B. (Eds.). (1990). *Adolescents in the AIDS epidemic.* San Francisco: Jossey-Bass.

Garland, A. F., & Zigler, E. (1993, February). Adolescent Suicide Prevention: Current Research and Social Policy Implications. *American Psychologist, 48,* 169–182.

Garmezy, N., & Rutter, M. (Eds.). (1983). *Stress, coping and development in children.* New York: McGraw-Hill.

Garner, P., Jones, D. C., & Palmer, D. J. (1994). Social cognitive correlates of preschool children's sibling caregiving behavior. *Developmental Psychology, 30,* 905–911.

Garrett, W. R. (1982). *Seasons of marriage and family life.* New York: Holt, Rinehart & Winston.

Garvey, C. (1990). *Play* (Enlarged ed.). Cambridge, MA: Harvard University Press.

Ge, X., Lorenz, F. O., Conger, R. D., Elder, G. H., Jr., & Simons, R. L. (1994). Trajectories of stressful life events and depressive symptoms during adolescence. *Developmental Psychology, 30,* 467–484.

Gelles, R. J., & Straus, M. A. (1979). Violence in the American family. *Journal of Social Issues, 35,* 14–38.

Gelman, R. (1979). Preschool thought. *American Psychologist, 34,* 900–905.

Gelman, R., & Gallistel, C. (1978). *The child's understanding of number.* Cambridge, MA: Harvard University Press.

Gelman, R., & Shatz, M. (1978). Appropriate speech adjustments: The operation of conversational constraints on talk to two-year-olds. In M. Lewis & L. A. Rosenblum (Eds.), *Interaction, conversation, and the development of language* (pp. 27–61). New York: Wiley.

Gelman, R., Spelke, E. S., & Meck, E. (1983). What preschoolers know about animate and inanimate objects. In D. Rogers & J. A. Sloboda (Eds.), *The acquisition of symbolic skills.* New York: Plenum, 1983.

Gelman, S., Collman, P., & Maccoby, E. (1986). Inferring properties from categories versus inferring categories from properties: The case of gender. *Child Development, 57,* 396–404.

Gentry, M., & Shulman, A. (1988). Remarriage and coping response for widowhood. *Psychology and Aging. 3,* 191–196.

George, L. (1987). Stress, social support, and depression over the life-course. In K. Markides & C. Cooper (Eds.), *Aging, stress, social support, and health.* London: Wiley.

Gergen, K. (1980). The emerging crisis in life-span developmental theory. In P. Baltes and O. Brim (Eds.), *Life-span development and behavior: Vol. 3.* New York: Academic Press.

Gesell, A. (1925). *The mental growth of the preschool child.* New York: Macmillan.

Gesell, A. (1954). The ontogenesis of infant behavior. In L. Carmichael (Ed.), *Manual of child psychology* (2nd ed.). New York: Wiley.

Gesell, A., & Thompson, H. (1929). Learning and growth in identical infant twins: An experimental study by method of co-twin control. *Genetic Psychology Monographs, 6,* 1–124.

Gibson, B., Roberts, P., & Buttery, T. (1982). *Death education: A concern for the living.* Bloomington, IN: Phi Beta Kappa Educational Foundation.

Gibson, E. J., & Walk, R. D. (1960). The visual cliff. *Scientific American, 202,* 64–71.

Gigy, L., & Kelly, J. (1992). Reasons for divorce: Perspectives of divorcing men and women. *Journal of Divorce and Remarriage, 18,* 169–187.

Gil, D. (1970). *Violence against children: Physical child abuse in the United States.* Cambridge, MA: Harvard University Press.

Gilbert, L. A. (1994, August). Current perspectives on dual-career families. *Current Directions in Psycholgical Science, 3,* 101–105.

Gilder, G. (1974). *Naked nomads.* New York: Quadrangle.

Gilewski, M., Faberow, N., Gallagher, D., & Thompson, L. (1991). Interaction of depression and bereavement on mental health in the elderly. *Psychology and Aging, 6,* 67–75.

Gilligan, C. (1982). *In a different voice: Psychological theory and women's development.* Cambridge, MA: Harvard University Press.

Gillund, G., & Perlmutter, M. (1988). Episodic memory and knowledge interactions across adulthood. In L.L. Light & M. Burke (Eds.), *Language, memory, and aging.* New York: Cambridge University Press.

Ginsburg, G. S., & Bronstein, P. (1993). Family factors related to children's intrinsic/extrinsic motivational orientation and academic performance. *Child Development, 64,* 1461–1474.

Ginzberg, E., Ginzberg, S., Axelrod, W., & Herna, J. (1951). *Occupational choice.* New York: Columbia University Press.

Gjerde, P., Black, J., & Black, J. (1985). The longitudinal consistency of matching familiar figures test performance from early childhood to preadolescence. *Developmental Psychology, 21,* 262–271.

Glascock, A. (1990). By any other name it is still killing: A comparison of the treatment of the elderly in America and other societies. In J. Sokolowsky (Ed.), *The culture context of aging*. New York: Bergin.

Glaser, B., & Strauss, A. (1965). *Awareness of dying*. Chicago: Aldine.

Glaser, B., & Strauss, A. (1968). *Time for dying*. Chicago: Aldine.

Glaser, K. (1978). The treatment of depressed and suicidal adolescents. *American Journal of Psychotherapy, 32*, 252–269.

Glausiusz, J. (1994). HIV: the babies who escape. *New Scientist, 142*, 38–42.

Gleitman, L., Newport, E., & Gleitman, H. (1984). The current status of the motherese hypothesis. *Journal of Child Language, 11*, 43–79.

Glenn, N. (1991). The recent trend in marital success in the United States. *Journal of Marriage and the Family, 53*, 261–270.

Glenn, N., & Kramer, K. (1987). The marriages and divorces of the children of divorce. *Journal of Marriage and the Family, 49*, 811–825.

Glenn, N., & Shelton, B. (1983). Pre-adult background variables and divorce: A note of caution about over-reliance on explained variance. *Journal of Marriage and the Family, 45*, 405–510.

Glenn, N., & Shelton, B. (1985). Regional differences in divorce in the United States. *Journal of Marriage and the Family, 44*, 641–652.

Glick, P. C. (1979). Children of divorced parents in demographic perspective. *Journal of Social Issues, 35*, 170–182.

Glick, P. (1984). Marriage, divorce and living arrangements. *Journal of Family Issues, 5*, 7–26.

Glick, P., & Lin, S. (1986). Recent changes in divorces and remarriage. *Journal of Marriage and the Family, 48*, 737–747.

Gold, D., & Andres, D. (1978a). Developmental comparison between adolescent children with employed and nonemployed mothers. *Merrill-Palmer Quarterly, 24*, 243–254.

Gold, D., & Andres, D. (1978b). Developmental comparisons between 10-year-old children with employed and nonemployed mothers. *Child Development, 49*, 75–84.

Gold, D., & Andres, D. (1978c). Relations between maternal employment and development of nursery-school children. *Canadian Journal of Behavioral Science, 10*, 116–129.

Gold, D., Andres, D., & Glorieux, J. (1979). The development of Francophone nursery children with employed and nonemployed mothers. *Canadian Journal of Behavioral Sciences, 11*, 169–173.

Goldberg, S. (1977). Social competence in infancy: A model of parent-infant interaction. *Merrill-Palmer Quarterly, 23*, 163–177.

Goldberg, S. (1979). Premature birth: Consequences for the parent-infant relationship. *Science, 67*, 214–220.

Goldberg, S., Brachfield, S., & DiVitto, B. (1980). Feeding, fussing and play: Parent-infant interaction in the first year as a function of prematurity and perinatal medical problems. In T. Field, S. Goldberg, D. Stern, & A. Sostek (Eds.), *High-risk infants and children: Adult and peer interactions*. New York: Academic Press.

Goldberg, S., & DeVitto, B. (1983). *Born too soon*. San Francisco: Freeman.

Goldberg, S., Perrotta, M., Minde, K., & Corter, C. (1986). Maternal behavior and attachment in low-birth-weight twins and singletons. *Child Development, 57*, 34–46.

Golden, M., Rosenbluth, L., Grossi, M., Policare, M., Freeman, H., & Brownlee, E. (1978). *The New York City infant day care study*. New York: Medical and Health Association of New York City.

Goldman, R., & Goldman, J. (1982). How children perceive the origin of babies and the role of mothers and fathers in procreation: A cross-national study. *Child Development, 53*, 491–504.

Goldscheider, F., & Goldscheider, C. (1994, March). Leaving and returning home in 20th century America. *Population Bulletin, 48*.

Goldscheider, F., & Waite, L. (1987). Nest-leaving patterns and the transition to marriage for young men and women. *Journal of Marriage and the Family, 49*, 507–516.

Goldsmith, H. H., & Campos, J. J. (1982). Toward a theory of infant temperament. In R. Emde & R. Harmon (Eds.), *The development of attachment and affiliative systems*. New York: Plenum Press.

Goldstein, E. (1979). Effects of same-sex and cross-sex role models on the subsequent academic productivity of scholars. *American Psychologist, 34*, 407–410.

Goleman, D. (1988, June 14). Erikson, in his own old age, expands his view of life. *New York Times*, pp. C1, C14.

Goodall, M. (1980). Left-handedness as an educational handicap. In R. S. Laura (Ed.), *Problems of Handicap*. Melbourne: Macmillan.

Goodman, M. (1980). Toward a biology of menopause. *Signs: Journal of Women in Culture and Society, 5*, 739–753.

Goodnow, J. J. (1962). A test of milieu differences with some of Piaget's tasks. *Psychological Monographs, 76*(36, Whole No. 555).

Gordon, C., Gaitz, C. M., & Scott, J. (1977). Leisure and lives: Personal expressivity across the life span. In R. Binstock & E. Shanas (Eds.), *Handbook of aging and the social sciences*. New York: Van Nostrand Reinhold.

Gormly, A., Gormly, J., & Weiss, H. (1987). Motivations for parenthood among young adult college students. *Sex Roles, 16*, 31–39.

Gortmaker, S., Dietz, W. H., Sobol, A. M., & Wehler, C. A. (1987). Increasing pediatric obesity in the United States. *American Journal of the Diseases of Childhood, 141*, 535–540.

Gottesman, I. (1991). *Schizophrenia genesis*. New York: Freeman.

Gottesman, I., & Shields, J. (1982). *Schizophrenia: the epigenetic puzzle*. Cambridge, England: Cambridge University Press.

Gottfredson, D. (1985). Youth employment, crime, and schooling: A longitudinal study of a national sample. *Developmental Psychology, 21*, 419–432.

Gottfried, A., & Bathurst, L. (1983). Hand preference across time is related to intelligence in young girls, not boys, *Science, 221*, 1074–1076.

Gottfried, A. E., & Gottfried, A. W. (Eds.). *Maternal employment and children's development: Longitudinal research*. New York: Plenum, 121–154.

Gould, L. X. (1972, December). A fabulous child's story. *Ms.*, 74–76, 105–106.

Gould, R. (1978). *Transformations: Growth and change in adult life*. New York: Simon & Schuster.

Gould, R. L. (1972). The phases of adult life: A study of developmental psychology. *American Journal of Psychiatry, 129*, 33–43.

Gouze, K., & Nadelman, L. (1980). Constancy of gender identity for self and others in children between the ages of three and seven. *Child Development, 51*, 275–278.

Gove, W. R. (1973). Sex, marital status, and mortality. *American Journal of Sociology, 79*, 45–67.

Graber, J. A., Brooks-Gunn, J., Paikoff, R. L., & Warren, M. P. (1994). Prediction of eating problems: An 8-year study of adolescent girls. *Developmental Psychology, 30*, 823–834.

Graber, J. A., Brooks-Gunn, J., & Warren, M. (1995). The antecedents of menarcheal age: Heredity, family environment, and stressful life events. *Child Development, 66*, 346–359.

Graham, F. K., Ernhart, C. B., Thurston, D. L., & Craft, M. (1962). Development three years after perinatal anoxia and other potentially damaging newborn experiences. *Psychological Monographs, 76* (Whole No. 522), 3.

Graham, S. (1992). Most of the subjects were white and middle class. Trends in published research on African Americans in selected APA Journals, 1970–1989. *American Psychologist, 47*, 629–639.

Gralinski, J. H., & Kopp, C. B. (1993). Everyday Rules for Behavior: Mothers' Requests to Young Children. *Developmental Psychology, 29*, 573–584.

Grambs, J. (1989). *Women over forty: Visions and realities* (rev. ed.). New York: Sprenger Publishing Co.

Granick, S., Kleban, M. H., & Weiss, A. D. (1976). Relationship between hearing loss and cognition in normally hearing aged persons. *Journal of Gerontology, 31*, 434–440.

Gray, W., & Hudson, L. (1984). Formal operations and the imaginary audience. *Developmental Psychology, 20*, 619–627.

Gray-Little, B., & Burk, N. (1983). Power and satisfaction in marriage: A review and critique. *Psychological Bulletin, 93*, 513–538.

Greeley, J. (1977). *Euthanasia: The debate*. Cincinnati: Pamphlet Publications.

Green, B. L., & Kenrick, D. L. (1994). The attractiveness of gender-typed traits at different relationship levels: Androgynous characteristics may be desirable after all. *Personality and Social Psychology Bulletin, 3*, 244–253.

Green, C. P., & Polleigen, K. (1977, August). *Teenage pregnancy: A major problem for minors*. Washington, DC: Zero Population Growth.

Green, L., & Horton, D. (1982). Adolescent health: Issues and challenges. In T. J. Coates, A. C. Peterson, & C. Perry (Eds.), *Promoting adolescent health: A dialogue on research and practice*. New York: Academic Press.

Green, V., Johnson, S., & Kaplan, D. (1992). Predictors of adolescent female decision making regarding contraceptive usage. *Adolescence, 27*, 613–632.

Green, W., Campbell, M., & David, R. (1984). Psychosocial dwarfism: A critical review of the evidence. *Journal of the American Academy of Child Psychiatry, 23*, 39–48.

Greenberger, E., O'Neil, R., & Nagel, S. K. (1994). Linking workplace and homeplace: Relations between the nature of adults' work and their parenting behaviors. *Developmental Psychology, 30*, 990–1002.

Greenberger, E., Steinberg, L., & Ruggiero, M. (1982). A job is a job is a job . . . or is it? *Work and Occupations, 9,* 79–96.

Greenberger, E., Steinberg, L., & Vaux, A. (1981). Adolescents who work: Health and behavioral consequences of job stress. *Developmental Psychology. 17,* 691–703.

Greene, J., Fox, N., & Lewis, M. (1983). The relationship between neonatal characteristics and three-month mother-infant interaction in high-risk infants. *Child Development, 54,* 1286–1296.

Greenfield, P. (1966). On culture and conservation. In J. S. Bruner, R. R. Ower & P. Greenfield (Eds.), *Studies in cognitive growth.* New York: Wiley.

Greenfield, P., & Lave, J. (1982). Cognitive aspects of informal education. In D. Wagner & H. Stevenson (Eds.), *Cultural Perspectives on Child Development,* San Francisco: W. H. Freeman.

Greenspan, S. (1984). *First feelings.* New York: Viking Press.

Grief, E. B., & Ulman, K. J. (1982). The psychological impact of menarche on early adolescent females: A review of the literature. *Child Development, 53,* 1413–1430.

Grollman, E. (Ed.). (1967). *Explaining death to children.* Boston: Beacon Press.

Grolnick, W., & Ryan, R. (1990). Self-perceptions, motivation, and adjustment in children with learning disabilities: A multiple group comparison study. *Journal of Learning Disabilities, 23,* 177–184.

Grolnick, W. S., & Slowiaczek, M. L. (1994). Parents' involvement in children's schooling: A multidimensional conceptualization and motivational model. *Child Development, 65,* 237–252.

Grossman, J.T. (1986). Congenital syphilis. In John L. Sever & Robert L. Brent (Eds.), *Teratogen update: Environmentally induced birth deficits risks.* New York: LISS.

Grossman, K., Grossman, K., Spangler, S., Suess, G., & Unzner, L. (1985). Maternal sensitivity and newborn orientation responses related to quality of attachments in Northern Germany. In I. Bretherton & E. Waters (Eds.), *Growing points of attachment theory and research. Monographs of the Society for Research in Child Development, 50*(1–2, Serial No. 209).

Grotevant, H., & Cooper, C. (1988). The role of family experience in career exploration: A lifespan perspective. In P. Baltes, D. Featherman, & R. Lerner (Eds.), *Lifespan development and behavior: Vol. 8.* Hillsdale, NJ: Erlbaum.

Grych, J. H., & Fincham, F. D. (1990). Marital conflict and children's adjustment: A cognitive-contextual framework. *Psychological Bulletin, 108,* 267–290.

Grzegorczyk, P. B., Jones, S. W., & Mistretta, C. M. (1979). Age-related differences in salt-taste acuity. *Journal of Gerontology, 34,* 834–840.

Gubrium, J. F. (1975). Being single in old age. *International Journal of Aging and Human Development, 6,* 29–41.

Gunn, J., & Peterson, A. (Eds.). *Girls at puberty: Biological psychological, and social perspectives.* New York: Plenum.

Gunther, J. (1949). *Death be not proud.* New York: Harper & Row.

Gurin, G., Veroff, J., & Feld, S. (1960). *Americans view their mental health.* New York: Basic Books.

Gutek, B., Cohen, A., & Konrad, A. (1990). Predicting social-sexual behavior at work: A contact hypothesis. *Academy of Management Journal, 33,* 560–577.

Gutmann, D. (1977). The cross-cultural perspective: Notes toward a comprehensive psychology of aging. In J. E. Birren & K. W. Schaie (Eds.), *Handbook of the psychology of aging.* New York: Van Nostrand Reinhold.

Haan, N. (1981). Common dimensions of personality development: Early adolescence to middle life. In D. Eichorn, J. Clausen, N. Haan, M. Honzik, & P. Mussen (Eds.), *Present and past in middle life.* New York: Academic Press.

Haan, N., & Day, D. (1974). A longitudinal study of change and sameness in personality development: Adolescence to later adulthood. *International Journal of Aging and Human Development, 5,* 11–39.

Haan, N., Smith, M. B., & Block, J. H. (1967). Moral reasoning of young adults: Political-social behavior, family background, and personality correlates. *Journal of Personality and Social Psychology, 10,* 183–201.

Hagerman, R. J., & Silverman, A. C. (Eds.). (1991). *Fragile X Syndrome: Diagnosis, treatment, and research.* Baltimore: The John Hopkins University Press.

Hagestad, G. O. (1978, August). *Patterns of communication and influence between grandparents and grandchildren in a changing society.* Paper presented at the World Congress of Sociology, Upsala, Sweden.

Hagestad, G. O. (1982, October). *Issues in the study of intergenerational continuity.* Paper presented at the National Council on Family Relations Theory and Methods Workshop. Washington, DC.

Hagestad, G. O. (1984). The continuous bond: A dynamic, multigenerational perspective on parent-child relations between adults. In M. Perlmutter (Ed.), *Minnesota symposia on child psychology: Vol. 17.* Hillsdale, NJ: Erlbaum.

Haith, M. (1980). *Rules newborns look by.* Hillsdale, NJ: Erlbaum.

Hakuta, K. (1987). Degree of bilingualism and cognitive ability in mainland Puerto Rican children. *Child Development. 58,* 1372–1388.

Hall, C., & Haws, D. (1989). Depressive symptomatology in learning-disabled and non-learning-disabled students. *Psychology in the Schools, 26,* 359–364.

Hall, G. S. (1904). *Adolescence: Its psychology and its relations to physiology, anthropology, sociology, sex, crime, religion, and education* (2 volumes). New York: Appleton.

Hallahan, D., & Kauffman, J. (1982). *Exceptional children: Introduction to special education* (2nd ed.). Englewood Cliffs, NJ: Prentice-Hall.

Halle, M. (1994, April 16). Probe cuts danger of suffocation at birth. *New Scientist, 142,* 22.

Halling, H. (1979). Suspected link between exposure to hexachlorophene and malformed infants. *Annals of the New York Academy of Sciences, 320,* 426–435.

Halverson, H. M. (1931). An experimental study of prehension in infants by means of systematic cinema records. *Genetic Psychology Monographs, 10,* 107–286.

Hamid, P., & Wylie, A. (1980). What generation gap? *Adolescence, 15,* 385–391.

Hammill, D., & Bartel, N. (1975). *Teaching children with learning and behavior problems.* Boston: Allyn and Bacon.

Hammond, D., & Middleton, R. (1984). Penile prosthesis. *Medical Aspects of Human Sexuality, 18,* 204–208.

Hanna, E., & Meltzoff, A. N. (1993). Peer imitation by toddlers in laboratory, home, and day-care contexts: Implications for social learning and memory. *Developmental Psychology, 29,* 701–710.

Harding, P. (1971). The metabolism of brown and white adipose tissue in the fetus and newborn. *Clinical Obstetrics and Gynecology, 14,* 685–709.

Hardy-Brown, K. (1979). Formal operations and the issue of generality: The analysis of poetry by college students. *Human Development, 22,* 127–136.

Hardyck, C., & Petrenovick, L. (1977). Left-handedness. *Psychological Bulletin, 84,* 385–404.

Harkins, E. B. (1978). Effects of empty-nest transition on self-report of psychological and physical well-being. *Journal of Marriage and the Family, 40,* 549–558.

Harlow, H. F. (1962). The heterosexual affectional system in monkeys. *American Psychologist, 17,* 1–9.

Harlow, H. F., & Harlow, M. K. (1966). Learning to love. *American Scientist, 54,* 244–272.

Harris, C. S. (1978). *Fact book on aging: A profile on America's older population.* Washington, DC: The National Council on the Aging.

Harris, L., and Associates, Inc. (1975). *The myth and reality of aging in America.* Washington, DC: The National Council on the Aging.

Harris, P. L., & Kavanaugh, R. D. (1993). Young children's understanding of pretense. *Monographs of the Society for Research in Child Development, 58*(1, Serial No. 231).

Harris, S. L., & Ersner-Hershfield, R. (1978). Behavioral suppression of seriously disruptive behavior in psychotic and retarded patients: A review of punishment and its alternatives. *Psychological Bulletin, 85,* 1352–1375.

Harrison, A. O., Serafica, F., & McAdoo, H. (1984). Ethnic families of color. In R. D. Parke (Ed.), *The family: Review of child development research* (pp. 7, 329–371). Chicago: University of Chicago Press.

Harrison, A. O., Wilson, M., Pine, C., Chan, S., Buriel, R. (1990). Family ecologies of ethnic minority children. *Child Development, 61,* 347–362.

Harter, S. (1982). The perceived competence scale for children. *Child Development, 53,* 87–89.

Harter, S. (1987). Determinants and mediational role of global self-worth in children. In N. Eisenberg (Ed.), *Contemporary topics in development psychology.* New York: John Wiley.

Harter, S. (1983). Developmental perspectives on the self-system. In E. M. Hetherington (Ed.), *Handbook of child psychology: Vol. IV. Socialization, personality, and social development.* New York: Wiley.

Harter, S. (1990). Issues in the assessment of the self-concept of children and adolescents. In A. LaGreca (Ed.), *Through the eyes of a child* (pp. 292–325). Boston: Allyn and Bacon.

Hartley, J. T., Harker, J., & Walsh, D. A. (1980). Contemporary issues and new directions in adult development of learning and memory. In

L. Poon (Ed.), *Aging in the 1980s: Psychological issues.* Washington, DC: American Psychological Association.

Hartshorne, H., & May, M. S. (1928–1930). *Studies in the nature of character* (Vols. 1–3). New York: Macmillan.

Hartup, W. (1970). Peer interaction and social organization. In P. Mussen (Ed.), *Carmichaels' manual of child psychology: Vol. 2.* New York: Wiley.

Hartup, W. (1982). Peer relations. In C. Kopp & J. Krakow (Eds.), *The child: Development in a social context.* Reading, MA: Addison-Wesley.

Hartup, W. W. (1983). Peer relations. In E. M. Hetherington (Ed.), *Handbook of child psychology: Vol. 4. Socialization, personality, and social development.* New York: Wiley.

Hashima, P. Y., & Amato, P. R. (1994). Poverty, social support, and parental behavior. *Child Development, 65,* 394–403.

Haskins, R. (1985). Public school aggression among children with varying day-care experience. *Child Development, 56,* 689–703.

Hass, A. (1979). *Teenage sexuality.* New York: Macmillan.

Havens, E. M. (1973). Women, work, and wedlock: A note on female marital patterns in the United States. *American Journal of Sociology, 78,* 975–981.

Havighurst, R. J. (1964). Youth in exploration and man emergent. In H. Borrow (Ed.), *Man in a world of work.* Boston: Houghton Mifflin.

Havighurst, R. J. (1974). *Developmental tasks and education* (3rd ed.). New York: McKay.

Havighurst, R. J. (1982). The world of work. In B. Wolman (Ed.), *Handbook of developmental psychology.* Englewood Cliffs, NJ: Prentice-Hall.

Havighurst, R. J., Neugarten, B. L., & Tobin, S. S. (1968). Disengagement and patterns of aging. In B. L. Neugarten (Ed.), *Middle age and aging.* Chicago: University of Chicago Press.

Hawkins, H. L., Kramer, A. F., & Capaldi, D. (1992). Aging, exercise, and attention. *Psychology and Aging, 7,* 643–653.

Hawkins, J., Pea, R., Glick, J., & Scribner, S. (1984). "Merds that laugh don't like mushrooms": Evidence for deductive reasoning by preschoolers. *Developmental Psychology, 20,* 584–594.

Hawley, T. L., & Disney, E. R. (1992). Crack's children: The consequences of maternal cocaine abuse. *Social Policy Report of the Society for Research in Child Development, VI*(4), 1–23.

Hawton, K., & Osborn, M. (1984). Suicide and attempted suicide in children and adolescents. In B. Lahey & A. Kazdin (Eds.), *Advances in clinical child psychology: Vol. 7.* New York: Plenum Press.

Hayes, C., & Kammerman, S. (1983). *Children of working parents: Experiences and outcomes.* Washington, DC: National Academy Press.

Hayflick, L. (1970). Aging under glass. *Experimental Gerontology, 5,* 291–303.

Hayflick, L. (1977). The cellular basis for biological aging. In C. E. Finch & L. Hayflick (Eds.), *Handbook of the biology of aging.* New York: Van Nostrand Reinhold.

Hayflick, L. (1980). The cell biology of human aging. *Scientific American, 242,* 58–66.

Haynes, H., White, B. W., & Held, R. (1965). Visual accommodation in human infants. *Science, 148,* 528–530.

Hazan, C., & Shaver, P. (1990). Love and work: An attachment-theoretical perspective. *Journal of Personality and Social Psychology, 59,* 270–290.

Health Information Network. (1987). *The facts about AIDS: A special guide for NEA members.* Washington, DC: Author.

Heckler, M. (1985). The fight against Alzheimer's disease. *American Psychologist, 40,* 1240–1244.

Hedin, D. Erickson, J., Simon, P., & Walker, J. (1985). *Minnesota youth poll: Aspirations, future plans, and expectations of young people in Minnesota* (Report AD-MR-2512). St. Paul: University of Minnesota, Center for Youth Development and Research.

Heidrich, S. M., & Ryff, C. D. (1993). Physical and mental health in later life: The self-system as mediator. *Psychology and Aging, 8,* 327–338.

Hein, K. (1989). AIDA in adolescence. *Journal of Adolescent Health Care, 10,* 10S–35S.

Helgeson, V. S. (1994). Long-distance romantic relationships: Sex differences in adjustment and breakup. *Personality and Social Psychology Bulletin, 20,* 254–265.

Helson, R. (1967). Personality characteristics and developmental history of creative college women. *Genetic Psychology Monographs, 76,* 205–256.

Henderson, J. N. (1990). Alzheimer's disease in cultural context. In J. Sokolovsky (Ed.), *The cultural context of aging.* New York: Bergin & Garvey Publishers.

Hendricks, L. (1983). Suggestions for reaching unmarried Black adolescent fathers. *Child Welfare, 62,* 141–146.

Hendry, L. B., & Gillies, P. (1978). Body type, body esteem, school, and leisure: A study of overweight, average, and underweight adolescents. *Journal of Youth and Adolescence, 7,* 181–195.

Henig, R. (1981, March 22). The child savers. *New York Times.*

Henker, B., & Whalen, C. K. (1989). Hyperactivity and attention deficits. *American Psychologist, 44,* 216–223.

Hennessy, K. D., Rabideau, G. J., Cicchetti, D., & Cummings, E. M. (1994). Responses of physically abused and nonabused children to different forms of interadult anger. *Child Development, 65,* 815–828.

Henshaw, S., & O'Reilly, K. (1983). Characteristics of abortion patients in the United States, 1979 and 1980. *Family Planning Perspectives, 15,* 5–16.

Herdt, G. (Ed.), (1989). *Gay and lesbian youth.* New York: Harrington Park Press.

Herdt, G., & Boxer, A. (1993). *Children of Horizons: How gay and lesbian teens are leading a new way out of the closet.* Boston: Beacon Press.

Herman, J., & Roth, S. (1984). Children's incidental memory for spatial locations in a large-scale environment: Taking a tour down memory lane. *Merrill-Palmer Quarterly, 30,* 87–102.

Hernandez, A. (1981). *Cardiac orienting response and habituation/dishabituation in term and preterm infants due to pure tone auditory stimuli.* Paper presented at the meetings of the Society for Research in Child Development, Boston.

Hershberger, S. C. & D'Augelli, A. R. (1995). The impact of victimization on the mental health and suicidality of lesbian, gay, and bisexual youths. *Developmental Psychology, 31,* 65–74.

Hess, B. (1972). Friendship. In M. Riley, M. Johnson, & A. Foner (Eds.), *Aging and society: Vol. 3. A sociology of age stratification.* New York: Russell Sage Foundation.

Hess, B., & Markson, E. W. (1980). *Aging and old age.* New York: Macmillan.

Hess, B., & Waring, J. M. (1978). Parent and child in later life: Rethinking the relationship. In R. Lerner & G. Spanier (Eds.), *Child influences on marital and family interaction: A life-span perspective.* New York: Academic Press.

Hess, R., & Camara, K. (1979). Post-divorce family relationships as mediating factors in the consequences of divorce for children. In T. E. Levitin (Ed.), Children of divorce. *Journal of Social Issues, 35,* 79–96.

Hess, R. D. (1968). Political socialization in the schools. *Harvard Educational Review, 38,* 528–536.

Hetherington, E. M. (1979). Divorce: A child's perspective. *American Psychologist, 34,* 851–858.

Hetherington, E. M., Cox, M., & Cox, R. (1982). Effects of divorce on parents and children. In M. Lamb (Ed.), *Nontraditional families: Parenting and child development.* Hillside, NJ: Erlbaum.

Hetherington, M., Stanley-Hagan, M., & Anderson, E. (1989). Marital transitions *American Psychologist, 44,* 303–312.

Hewlett, B. (1991). Demography and childcare in preindustrial societies. *Journal of Anthropological Research, 47,* 1–33.

Hickey, T., & Kalish, R. A. (1968). Young people's perceptions of adults. *Journal of Gerontology, 23,* 215–219.

Higginbottom, S. F., Barling, J., & Kelloway, E. K. (1993). Linking Retirement Experiences and Marital Satisfaction: A Mediational Model. *Psychology and Aging, 8,* 508–516.

Hill, R. (1964). Methodological issues in family development research. *Family Process, 3,* 186–206.

Hinsz, V. (1989). Facial resemblance in engaged and married couples. *Journal of Social and Personal Relationships, 6,* 223–229.

Hirsch, J. (1975). All number and size as a determinant of subsequent obesity. In M. Winick (Ed.), *Childhood obesity.* New York: Wiley.

Hock, E. (1978). Working and nonworking mothers with infants: Perceptions of their careers, the infants' needs, and satisfaction with mothering. *Developmental Psychology, 14,* 37–43.

Hock, E., Christman, K., & Hock, M. (1980). Factors associated with decisions about return to work in mothers of infants. *Developmental Psychology, 16,* 535–536.

Hofferth, S., Brayfield, A., Deich, S., & Holcomb, P. (1991). *National Child Care Survey, 90: National Association for the Education of Young Children (NAEYC) Study.* Washington, DC: The Urban Institute Press.

Hoffman, L. (1987). The value of children to parents and child rearing patterns. *Social Behavior, 2,* 123–141.

Hoffman, L. W. (1974). Effects of maternal employment on the child—a review of the research. *Developmental Psychology, 10,* 204–228.

Hoffman, L. W. (1979). Maternal employment: 1979. *American Psychologist,* 859–865.

Hoffman, L. W. (1989). Effects of maternal employment in the two parent family. *American Psychologist, 44,* 283–292.

Hoffman, L. W., & Mavis, J. D. (1978). Influences of children on marital interaction and parental satisfactions and dissatisfactions. In R. Lerner

& G. Spanier (Eds.), *Child influences on marriage and family interaction: A lifespan perspective.* New York: Academic Press.

Hoffman, L. W., & Nye, F. I. (1974). *Working mothers.* San Francisco: Jossey-Bass.

Hoffman, M. (1981). Development of moral thought, feeling and behavior. In E. M. Hetherington & R. Parke (Eds.), *Contemporary readings in child psychology* (2nd ed.). New York: McGraw-Hill.

Hoffereth, S., & Hayes, C. (Eds.). (1987). *Risking the future: adolescent sexuality, pregnancy and child bearing: Vol. 2. Working papers and statistical appendixes.* Washington, DC: National Academy of Sciences.

Hogan, D. (1978). The variable order of events in the life course. *American Sociological Review, 43,* 573–586.

Holden, C. (1980). Identical twins reared apart. *Science, 207,* 1323–1328.

Holden, C. (1983). Avoiding conflicts: Mothers as tacticians in the supermarket. *Child Development, 54,* 233–240.

Holland, A., Hall, A., Murray, R., Russell, G., & Crisp, A. (1984). Anorexia nervosa. A study of 34 twin pairs and one set of triplets. *British Journal of Psychiatry, 45,* 414–419.

Holland, J. L. (1973). *Making vocational choices: A theory of careers.* Englewood Cliffs, NJ: Prentice-Hall.

Holmes, L. (1978). How fathers can cause the Down's syndrome. *Human Nature, 1,* 70–72.

Holmes, T. H., & Masuda, M. (1974). Life change and illness susceptibility. In B. S. Dohrenwend & B. P. Dohrenwend (Eds.), *Stressful life events: Their nature and effects.* New York: Wiley, 1974.

Holmes, T. H., & Rahe, R. H. (1967). The social readjustment rating scale. *Journal of Psychosomatic Research. 11,* 213–218.

Holzman, D. (1992). A tool for all seasons. *Mosiac, 23*(2), 2–11.

Honzik, M., Macfarlane, J., & Allen, L. (1948). The stability of mental test performance between 2 and 18 years. *Journal of Experimental Education. 4,* 309–324.

Hooker, K., & Kaus, C. R. (1994). Health-related possible selves in young and middle adulthood. *Psychology and Aging, 9,* 126–133.

Hooker, K., Monahan, D., Shifren, K., & Hutchinson, C. (1992). Mental and Physical Health of Spouse Caregivers: The Role of Personality. *Psychology and Aging, 7,* 367–375.

Hooper, F. H., & Sheehan, N. W. (1977). Logical concept attainment during the aging years: Issues in the neo-Piagetian research literature. In W. Overton & J. Gallagher (Eds.), *Knowledge and development* (Vol. 1). New York: Plenum Press.

Hoover, R., Gray, L., & Cole, P. (1976). Menopausal estrogens and breast cancer. *New England Journal of Medicine, 295,* 401–405.

Horn, J. L. (1970). Organization of data on lifespan development of human abilities. In L. R. Goulet & P. B. Baltes (Eds.), *Lifespan developmental psychology: Research and theory.* New York: Academic Press.

Horn, J. L. (1972). Intelligence: Why it grows, why it declines. In J. Hunt (Ed.), *Human intelligence.* New Brunswick, NJ: Transaction Books.

Horn, J. L. (1982). The aging of human abilities. In B. Wolman (Ed.), *Handbook of devel-*

opmental psychology. Englewood Cliffs, NJ: Prentice-Hall.

Horn, J. L., & Cattell, R. B. (1966). Refinement and test of the theory of fluid and crystallized intelligence. *Journal of Educational Psychology. 57,* 253–270.

Horn, J. L., & Donaldson, G. (1980). Cognitive development in adulthood. In O. G. Brim, Jr., & J. Kagan (Eds.), *Constancy and change in human development.* Cambridge, MA: Harvard University Press.

Hospice Council of Metropolitan Washington (1994). *A Guide to Grief.* Washington, DC: The Hospice Council of Metropolitan Washington.

Hostetler, A. (1987). Alzheimer's trials hinge on early diagnoses. *APA Monitor, 18,* pp. 14–15.

Hotvedt, M. (1983). The cross-cultural and historical context. In R. B. Weg (Ed.), *Sexuality in later years.* New York: Academic Press.

Houseknecht, S., Vaughan, S., & Statham, A. (1987). The impact of singlehood on the career patterns of professional women. *Journal of Marriage and the Family, 149,* 353–366.

Howe, M. L., & Rabinovitz, F. M. (1991). Gest or another panacea? Or just the illusion of inclusion. *Developmental Review, 11,* 305–316.

Howes, C. (1985). Sharing fantasy: Social pretend play in toddlers. *Child Development, 56,* 1253–1258.

Howes, C. (1990). Can age of entry into childcare and the quality of childcare predict adjustment in kindergarten? *Developmental Psychology, 26,* 292–303.

Howes, C., & Olenick, M. (1986). Family and child care influences on toddler's compliance. *Child Development, 57,* 202–216.

Howes, C., & Rubenstein, J. (1985). Determinants of toddler experiences in day care: Age of entry and quality of setting. *Child Care Quarterly, 14,* 140–151.

Howes, C., & Wu, F. (1990). Peer interactions and friendships in an ethnically diverse school setting. *Child Development, 61,* 537–541.

Hoyer, W. J., & Plude, D. J. (1980). Attentional and perceptual processes in the study of cognitive aging. In L. Poon (Ed.), *Aging in the 1980s: Psychological issues.* Washington, DC: American Psychological Association.

Hudson, T. (1983). Correspondence and numerical differences between disjoint sets. *Child Development, 54,* 84–90.

Huesmann, L., & Eron, L. (Eds.). (1986). *Television and the aggressive child: A cross-national comparison.* Hillsdale, NJ: Erlbaum.

Hugin, F., Norris, A., & Shock, N. W. (1960). Skin reflex and voluntary reaction time in young and old males. *Journal of Gerontology, 14,* 338–391.

Hulicka, I. M. (1967). Age differences in retention as a function of interference. *Journal of Gerontology, 22,* 274–280.

Hultsch, D., & Dixon, R. (1990). Learning and memory and aging. In J. E. Birren & K. W. Schaie, (Eds.), *Handbook of aging* (3rd edition). New York: Academic Press.

Hultsch, D. F., & Plemons, J. K. (1979). Life events and life span development. In P. B. Baltes & O. G. Brim, Jr. (Eds.), *Life-span development and behavior* (Vol. 2). New York: Academic Press.

Hume, E. (1984, January 11). Gays see election as chance for gain: May be main political force this year. *Wall Street Journal,* p. 60.

Humes, J. E., & Roberts, L. (1990). Speech-recognition difficulties of the hearing-impaired

elderly: The contributions of audibility. *Journal of Speech and Hearing Research, 33,* 726–735.

Hummert, M. (1990). Multiple stereotypes of elderly and young adults: A comparison of structure and evaluations. *Psychology and Aging, 5,* 182–193.

Humphreys, A., & Smith, P. (1987). Rough and tumble friendship and dominance in school children. Evidence for continuity and change with age in middle childhood. *Child Development, 58,* 201–212.

Hunt, B., & Hunt, M. (1975). *Prime time: A guide to the pleasures and opportunities of the new middle age.* New York: Stein & Day.

Hunt, J. V., & Rhodes, L. (1977). Mental development of preterm infants during the first year. *Child Development, 48,* 204–210.

Hunt, M. (1974). *Sexual behavior in the 1970s.* Chicago: Playboy Press.

Hunt, M., & Hunt, B. (1977). *The divorce experience.* New York: McGraw-Hill.

Hunter, F. T. (1985). Adolescents' perception of discussions with parents and friends. *Developmental Psychology, 121,* 433–440.

Husain, S., & Vandiver, T. (1984). *Suicide in children and adolescents.* New York: SP Medical and Scientific Books, 1984.

Huston, A., Wright, J., Wartella, E., Rice, M., Watkins, B., Campbell, T., & Pitts, C. (1981). Communicating more than content: Formal features of children's television programs. *Journal of Communication, 31,* 32–48.

Huston, A., Wright, J., Rice, M., Kerkman, D., & St. Peters, M. (1990). Development of television viewing patterns in early childhood: A longitudinal investigation. *Developmental Psychology, 26,* 409–420.

Huston, A. C., Donnerstein, E., Fairchild, H., Feshbach, N. D., Katz, P. A., Murray, J. P., Rubinstein, E. A., Wilcox, B. L., & Zukerman, D. (1992). *Big world, small screen.* Lincoln, NE: University of Nebraska Press.

Huston-Stein, A., & Higgins-Trenk, A. (1978). Development of females from childhood through adulthood: Career and feminine orientations. In P. B. Baltes (Ed.), *Lifespan development and behavior* (Vol. 1). New York: Academic Press.

Huyck, M. H. (1982). From gregariousness to intimacy: Marriage and friendship over the adult years. In T. Field, A. Huston, H. Quay, L. Troll, & G. Finley (Eds.), *Review of human development.* New York: Wiley, 1982.

Huyck, M. H., & Hoyer, W. J. (1982). *Adult development and aging.* Belmont, CA: Wadsworth.

Hyde, J. S. (1979). *Understanding human sexuality.* New York: McGraw-Hill.

Hymel, S., Bowker, A., & Woody, E. (1993). Aggressive versus withdrawn unpopular children: Variations in peer and self-perceptions in multiple domains. *Child Development, 64,* 879–896.

Hymel, S., Rubin, K., Rowden, L., & LeMare, L. (1990). Children's peer relationships: Longitudinal prediction of internalizing and externalizing problems from middle to late childhood. *Child Development, 61,* 2004–2021.

Hynd, G. W., Horn, K. L., Voeller, K. K., & Marshall, R. M. (1991). Neurobiological basis of attention-deficit hyperactivity disorder. (ADHD). *School Psychology Review, 20,* 174–186.

Iannotti, R. (1978). Effect of role-taking experiences on role taking, empathy, altruism, and aggression. *Developmental Psychology, 14,* 119–124.

Iannotti, R. (1985). Naturalistic and structured assessments of prosocial behavior in preschool children: The influence of empathy and perspective taking. *Developmental Psychology, 21,* 46–55.

Inhelder, B., & Piaget, J. (1958). *The growth of logical thinking from childhood to adolescence.* New York: Basic Books.

Inhelder, B., & Piaget, J. (1970). *The growth of logic in the child: Classification and seriation.* New York: Humanities Press.

Isabella, R. A. (1993). Origins of attachment: Maternal interactive behavior across the first year. *Child Development, 64,* 605–621.

Istomina, Z. (1975). The development of voluntary memory in preschool-age children. *Soviet Psychology, 13,* 5–64.

Izard, C. E. (1979). *The maximally discriminative facial movement coding system (MAX).* Newark: University of Delaware, Instructional Resources Center.

Izard, C. E. (1991). *The psychology of emotions.* New York: Plenum.

Jacklin, C. (1989). Female and male: Issues of gender. *American Psychologist, 44,* 127–133.

Jackson, A., & Hornbeck, D. (1989). Educating young adolescents: Why we must restructure middle grade schools. *American Psychologist, 44,* 831–836.

Jacobson, J., Jacobson, S., Fein, G., Schwartz, P., & Dowler, J. (1984). Prenatal exposure to an environmental toxin: A test of the multiple effects models. *Developmental Psychology, 20,* 523–532.

Jacobson, L. (1974). Illness and human sexuality. *Nursing Outlook, 22,* 50–53.

Jacobson, S., Fein, G., Jacobson, J., Schwartz, P., & Dowler, J. (1985). The effects of intrauterine PCB exposure on visual recognition memory. *Child Development, 56,* 853–860.

Jacobson, S. W., Jacobson, J. L., Sokol, R. J., Martier, S. S., & Ager, J. W. (1993). Prenatal Alcohol Exposure and Infant Information Processing Ability. *Child Development, 64,* 1706–1721.

James, W. (1890). *Principles of psychology* (Vols. 1–2). New York: Holt.

Jaques, E. (1964). Death and the midlife crisis. *International Journal of Psychoanalysis, 46,* 502–514.

Jacques, J. M., & Chason, K. J. (1979). Cohabitation: Its impact on marital success. *Family Coordinator, 28,* 35–45.

Jaquish, G. A., & Ripple, R. E. (1981). Cognitive creative abilities and self-esteem across the adult life-span. *Human Development, 24,* 110–119.

Jemmott, L., & Jemmott III., J. (1990). Sexual knowledge attitudes and risky sexual behavior among inner-city Black male adolescents. *Journal of Adolescent Research, 5,* 340–369.

Jenkins, C. D., Rosenman, R. H., & Zyzanski, S. J. (1974). Prediction of clinical coronary heart disease by a test for the coronary-prone behavior pattern. *New England Journal of Medicine, 290,* 1271–1275.

Jessor, R. (1993, February). Successful adolescent development among youth in high-risk settings. *American Psychologist, 48,* 117–126.

Jiao, S., Ji, G., & Jing, Q. (1986). Comparative study of behavioral qualities of only children and sibling children. *Child Development, 57,* 357–361.

Johnson, C. (1987). The institutional segregation of the elderly. In P. Silverman (Ed.), *The elderly as modern pioneers.* Bloomington, IN: Indiana University Press.

Johnson, C. (1988). Active and latent function of grandparenting during the divorce process. *The Gerontologist, 28,* 185–191.

Johnson, C., & Maddi, K. (1986). The etiology of bulimia. *Adolescent Psychiatry, 13,* 253–273.

Johnson, C., Stuckey, M., Lewis, L., & Schwartz, D. (1982). Bulimia: A descriptive survey of 316 cases. *International Journal of Eating Disorders, 2,* 3–16.

Johnson, E., & Meade, A. (1987). Developmental patterns of spatial ability: An early sex difference. *Child Development, 58,* 725–740.

Johnson, J., & McGillicuddy-Delisi, A. (1983). Family environment factors and children's knowledge of rules and conventions. *Child Development, 54,* 218–226.

Johnson, J. S., & Newport, E. L. (1989). Critical period effects in second language learning: The influence of maturational state on the acquisition of English as a second language. *Cognitive Psychology, 21,* 60–99.

Johnston, L., O'Malley, P., & Bachman, J. (1986). *Drug use among American high school students, college students, and other young adults: National trends through 1985.* Rockville, MD: National Institute on Drug Use.

Johnston, L. D., Bachman, J. G., & O'Malley, P. M. (1979). *1979 highlights: Drugs and the nation's high school students: Five year national trends.* Rockville, MD: National Institute on Drug Abuse.

Johnston, L. D., Bachman, J. G., & O'Malley, P. M. (1985). Student drug use, attitudes, and beliefs: National trends 1975–1982. In M. Bloom (Ed.), *Life span development* (2nd ed.). New York: Macmillan.

Johnston, L. D., Bachman, J. G., & O'Malley, P. M. (1994). Monitoring the future study: Preliminary report of the 1993 findings (University of Michigan News and Information Services Press Release, January 17, 1994). Ann Arbor, MI: University of Michigan.

Johnstone, J. W. C. (1978). Juvenile delinquency and the family: A contextual interpretation. *Youth and Society, 9,* 299–313.

Jones, D. C., & Vaughan, K. (1990). Close friendships among senior adults. *Psychology and Aging, 5,* 451–457.

Jones, H. E. (1939a). The adolescent growth study: I Principles and methods. *Journal of Consulting Psychology, 3,* 157–159.

Jones, H. E. (1939b). The adolescent growth study: II Procedures. *Journal of Consulting Psychology, 3,* 177–180.

Jones, H. E., & Conrad, H. S. (1933). The growth and decline of intelligence: A study of a homogeneous group between the ages of ten and sixty. *Genetic Psychology Monographs, 13,* 223–294.

Jones, K. L., & Smith, D. W. (1973). Recognition of the fetal alcohol syndrome in early infancy. *Lancet, 2,* 999–1001.

Jones, K. L., Smith, D. W., Streissguth, A. P., & Myrianthopoulos, N. C. (1974). Outcome in offspring of chronic alcoholic women. *Lancet, 1,* 1076–1078.

Jones, M. C. (1924). A laboratory study of fear: The case of Peter. *Pedagogical Seminar, 31,* 308–315.

Jones, M. C. (1957). The later careers of boys who were early- or late maturing. *Child Development, 28,* 115–128.

Jones, M. C. (1958). A study of socialization patterns at the high school level. *Journal of Genetic Psychology, 93,* 87–111.

Jones, M. C. (1965). Psychological correlates of somatic development. *Child Development, 36,* 899–911.

Jones, R. (1977). *The other generation: The new power of older people.* Englewood Cliffs, NJ: Prentice-Hall.

Jorgensen, M., & Keiding, N. (1991). Estimations of spermarche from longitudinal spermaturia data. *Biometrics, 47,* 177–193.

Jorgensen, S., & Sonstegard, J. (1984). Predicting adolescent sexual and contraceptive behavior: An application and test of the Fishbein model. *Journal of Marriage and the Family, 46,* 43–55.

Judd, D. (1989). *Give sorrow words: Working with a dying child.* London: Free Association Books.

Kadzin, A. E. (1992). Overt and covert anti-social behavior: Child and family characteristics among psychiatric in patient children. *Journal of Child and Family Studies, 1,* 3–20.

Kagan, J. (1965). Impulsive and reflective children: Significance of conceptual tempo. In J. D. Krumholz (Ed.), *Learning and the educational process.* Chicago: Rand McNally.

Kagan, J. (1971). *Personality development.* New York: Harcourt Brace Jovanovich.

Kagan, J. (1981). *The second year: The emergence of self-awareness.* Cambridge, MA: Harvard University Press.

Kagan, J. (1982). *Psychological research on the human infant: An evaluative summary.* New York: W. T. Grant Foundation.

Kagan, J. (1984). *The nature of the child.* New York: Basic Books.

Kagan, J. (1989). Temperamental contributions to social behavior. *American Psychologist, 44,* 668–674.

Kagan, J., Kearsley, R., & Zelazo, P. (1978). *Infancy: Its place in human development.* Cambridge, MA: Harvard University Press.

Kagan, J., & Kogan, N. (1970). Individual variation in cognitive processes. In P. Mussen (Ed.), *Carmichael's manual of child psychology* (Vol. 1). New York: Wiley.

Kagan, J., & Snidman, N. (1991, August). Temperamental Factors in Human Development. *American Psychologist, 46,* 856–862.

Kahana, B. (1982). Social behavior and aging. In B. Wolman (Ed.), *Handbook of developmental psychology.* Englewood Cliffs, NJ: Prentice-Hall.

Kahn, R., & Antonucci, T. (1980). Convoys over the life course: Attachment, roles and social support. In P. Baltes and O. Brim (Eds.), *Life-span development and behavior* (Vol. 3). New York: Academic Press.

Kail, R. (1979). *The development of memory in children.* San Francisco: Freeman.

Kail, R., & Bisanz, J. (1982). Information processing and cognitive development. In H. Reese (Ed.), *Advances in child development and behavior* (Vol. 17). New York: Academic Press.

Kail, R., & Hagen, J. (1982). Memory in childhood. In B. Wolman (Ed.), *Handbook of developmental psychology.* Englewood Cliffs, NJ: Prentice-Hall.

Kalichman, S. C. (1993). *Mandated reporting of suspected child abuse: Ethics, law and policy.* Hyattsville, MD: American Psychological Association.

Kalish, R. A. (1981). *Death, grief, and caring relationships.* Monterey, CA: Brooks/Cole.

Kalish, R. A., & Knudtson, F. W. (1976). Attachment versus disengagement: A lifespan conceptualization. *Human Development, 19,* 171–181.

Kallman, F. J., & Jarvik, L. (1959). Individual differences in constitution and genetic background. In J. Birren (Ed.), *Handbook of aging and the individual.* Chicago: University of Chicago Press.

Kantner, J., & Zelnick, M. (1972). Sexual experiences of young unmarried women in the U.S. *Family Planning Perspectives, 4,* 9–17.

Kaplan, H. S. (1977). Sex at menopause. In L. Rose (Ed.), *The menopause book.* New York: Hawthorn.

Kaplan, H. S., & Pokorny, A. P. (1970). Aging and self-attitude: A conditional relationship. *International Journal of Aging and Human Development, 1,* 241–250.

Karp, I. (1987). Tragedy in birth: An African view. In A. Cohn & L. Leach (Eds.), *Generations: A universal family album.* New York: Pantheon Books.

Kastenbaum, R. (1967). The child's understanding of death: How does it develop? In E. Grollman (Ed.), *Explaining death to children.* Boston: Beaco.

Kastenbaum, R. (1969). The foreshortened life perspective. *Geriatrics, 24,* 126–133.

Kastenbaum, R. (1975). Is death a life crisis? On the confrontation with death in theory and practice. In N. Datan & L. Ginsberg (Eds.), *Lifespan developmental psychology: Normative life crises.* New York: Academic Press.

Kastenbaum, R. (1977). Death and development through the lifespan. In H. Feifel (Ed.), *New meanings of death.* New York: McGraw-Hill.

Kastenbaum, R., & Candy, S. E. (1973). The 4% fallacy: A methodological and empirical critique of extended care facility population statistics. *International Journal of Aging and Human Development, 4,* 15–21.

Kastenbaum, R., & Durkee, N. (1964). Young people view old age. In R. Kastenbaum (Ed.), *New thoughts on old age.* New York: Springer.

Katzman, M., Wolchik, S., & Braver, S. (1984). The prevalence of frequent binge eating and bulimia in a nonclinical sample. *International Journal of Eating Disorders. 3,* 53–62.

Kavrell, S. M., & Petersen, A. C. (1984). Patterns of achievement in early adolescence. In M. L. Maehr (Ed.), *Advances in motivation and achievement* (pp. 1–35), Greenwich, CT: JAI Press.

Kay, B., & Neeley, J. N. (1982). Sexuality in the aging: A review of current literature. *Sexuality and Disability, 5,* 38–46.

Kaye, H., & Marcus, J. (1978). Imitation over a series of trials without feedback: Age six months. *Infant Behavior and Development, 1,* 141–155.

Keating, D. P. (1991). Adolescent cognition. In R. M. Lerner, A. C. Petersen, & J. Brooks-Gunn (Eds.), *Encyclopedia of adolescence.* New York: Garland.

Keita, G. P., & Jones, J. (1990). Reducing adverse reaction to stress in the workplace: Psychology's expanding role. *American Psychologist, 45,* 1137–1141.

Keith, J. (1990). Age in social and cultural context: Anthropological perspectives. In R. H. Binstock & L. K. George (Eds.), *Handbook of aging and the social sciences* (3rd ed.). San Diego, CA: Academic Press.

Kell, D., & Patton, C. (1978). Reactions to induced retirement. *The Gerontologist, 18,* 173–179.

Keller, A., Ford, L., & Meachem, J. (1978). Dimensions of self-concept in preschool children. *Developmental Psychology, 14,* 483–489.

Kelly, J. B. (1982). Divorce: The adult perspective. In B. Wolman (Ed.), *Handbook of developmental psychology.* Englewood Cliffs, NJ: Prentice-Hall.

Kenrick, D. T., Groth, G. R., Trost, M. R., & Sadalla, E. K. (1993). Integrating evolutionary and social exchange perspectives on relationships: Effects of gender, self-appraisal, and involvement level on mate selection. *Journal of Personality and Social Psychology, 64,* 951–969.

Kenrick, D. T., Neuberg, S., Zierk, K., & Krones, J. (1994). Evolution and social cognition: Contrast effects as a function of sex, dominance, and physical attractiveness. *Personality and Social Psychology Bulletin, 20,* 210–217.

Kenrick, D. T., Sadalla, E. K., Groth, G. R., & Trost, M. R. (1990). Evolution, traits, and the stages of human courtship: Qualifying the parental investment model. *Journal of Personality, 58,* 97–117.

Keniston, K. (1970, Autumn). Youth: A "new" stage of life. *The American Scholar,* 631–654.

Keniston, K. (1971). *Youth and dissent: The rise of a new generation.* New York: Harcourt Brace Jovanovich.

Kenkel, W. F. (1966). *The family in perspective.* New York: Appleton-Century-Crofts.

Kent, S. (1976, March). How do we age? *Geriatrics,* 128–134.

Kerig, P. K., Cowan, P. A., & Cowna, C. P. (1993). Marital quality and gender differences in parent-child interaction. *Developmental Psychology, 29,* 931–939.

Kessler, R., & McRae, J. (1982). The effects of wives' employment on the mental health of married men and women. *American Sociological Review, 47,* 216–226.

Kessler, R. C., Foster, C., Webster, P. S., & House, J. S. (1992). The relationship between age and depressive symptoms in two national surveys. *Psychology and Aging, 7,* 119–126.

Khachaturian, Z. (1985). Progress on research on Alzheimer's disease. *American Psychologist, 40,* 1251–1255.

Kiefer, C. (1990). The elderly in modern Japan: Elite, victims, or plural players? In J. Sokolovsky (Ed.), *The cultural context of aging.* New York: Bergin & Garvey.

Kikimura, A., & Kitano, H. (1981). The Japanese American family. In C. H. Mindel & R. W. Habenstein (Eds.), *Ethnic families in America* (2nd ed.). New York: Elsevier.

Kilbride, P. (1980). Sensorimotor behavior of Baganda and Samia infants. *Journal of Cross-Cultural Psychology, 11,* 131–152.

Kimmel, D. (1988). Ageism, psychology, and public policy. *American Psychologist, 43,* 175–178.

Kimmel, D. C. (1980). *Adulthood and aging* (2nd ed.). New York: Wiley.

Kindermann, T. A. (1993). Natural peer groups as contexts for individual development: The case of children's motivation in school. *Developmental Psychology, 29,* 970–977.

King, C., Raskin, A., Gdowski, C., Butkus, M., & Opipari, L. (1990). Psychosocial factors associated with urban adolescent female attempts. *Journal of the American Academy of Child and Adolescent Psychiatry, 29,* 289–294.

Kinney, D. K., & Matthysse, S. (1978). Genetic transmission of schizophrenia. *Annual Review of Medicine, 29,* 459–473.

Kinsey, A. C., Pomeroy, W. B., & Martin, C. C. (1948). *Sexual behavior in the human male.* Philadelphia: Saunders.

Kinsey, A. C., Pomeroy, W. B., & Martin, C. C. (1953). *Sexual behavior in the human female.* Philadelphia, Saunders.

Kite, M., Deaux, K., & Miele, M. (1991). Stereotypes of young and old: Does age outweigh gender? *Psychology and Aging, 6,* 19–27.

Klahr, D., & Wallace, J. G. (1976). *Cognitive development: An information-processing view.* Hillsdale, NJ: Erlbaum.

Klaus, M., & Kennell, J. (1982). *Parent-infant bonding* (2nd ed.). St. Louis: Mosby.

Kleck, R., Richardson, S., & Ronald, L. (1974). Physical appearance cues and interpersonal attraction in children. *Child Development, 46,* 187–192.

Kleiman, D. (1984, February 15). When abortion becomes a birth: A dilemma of medical ethics shaken by new advances. *New York Times,* B1, B4.

Klein, R. (1985). Caregiving arrangements by employed women with children under one year of age. *Developmental Psychology, 21,* 403–406.

Klimes-Dougan, B., & Kistner, J. (1990). Physically abused preschoolers' responses to peers' distress. *Developmental Psychology, 26,* 599–602.

Kline, M., Tschann, J., Johnston, J., & Wallerstein, J. (1989). Children's adjustment in joint or sole physical custody families. *Developmental Psychology, 25,* 430–438.

Klocke, R. A. (1977). Influence of aging on the lung. In C. E. Finch & L. Hayflick (Eds.), *Handbook of the biology of aging.* New York: Van Nostrand Reinhold.

Klonoff, H., Low, M., Marcus, A. (1973). Neuropsychological effects of marijuana. *Canadian Medical Association Journal, 108,* 150–156.

Kobasa, S. C. (1979). Stressful life events, personality, and health: An inquiry into hardiness. *Journal of Personality and Social Psychology, 37,* 1–11.

Kobak, R., & Hazan, C. (1991). Attachment in marriage: Effects of security and accuracy of working models. *Journal of Personality and Social Psychology, 60,* 861–869.

Kobrin, F., & Waite, L. (1984). Effects of childhood family structure on the transition to marriage. *Journal of Marriage and the Family, 46,* 807–816.

Koga, Y., & Morant, G. M. (1923). On the degree of association between reaction times in the case of different senses. *Biometrika, 15,* 346–372.

Kogan, N. (1973). Creativity and cognitive style: A lifespan perspective. In P. B. Baltes & K. W. Schaie (Eds.), *Life-span developmental psychology: Personality and socialization.* New York: Academic Press.

Kogan, N. (1974). Categorizing and conceptualizing styles in younger and older adults. *Human Development, 17,* 218–230.

Kogan, N. (1982). Cognitive styles in older adults. In T. Fields, A. Huston, H. Quay, L. Troll, & G.

Finley (Eds.), *Review of human development*. New York: Wiley.

Kogan, N. (1983). Stylistic variation in childhood and adolescence: Creativity, metaphor, and cognitive styles. In J. H. Flavell & E. M. Markman (Eds.), *Handbook of child psychology: Vol. 3. Cognitive development*. New York: Wiley.

Kohlberg, L. (1963). The development of children's orientations towards a moral order: I. Sequence in the development of moral thought. *Vita Humana, 6,* 11–33.

Kohlberg, L. (1964). Development of moral character and moral ideology. In M. L. Hoffman & L. W. Hoffman (Eds.), *Review of child development research*. New York: Russell Sage Foundation.

Kohlberg, L. (1966). A cognitive developmental analysis of children's sex-role concepts and attitudes. In E. Maccoby (Ed.), *The development of sex differences*. Stanford, CA: Stanford University Press.

Kohlberg, L. (1973). Continuities in child and adult moral development revisited. In P. Baltes & K. W. Schaie (Eds.), *Lifespan developmental psychology: Personality and socialization*. New York: Academic Press.

Kohlberg, L. (1976). Moral stages and moralization: The cognitive development approach. In J. Lickona (Ed.), *Moral development and behavior*. New York: Holt, Rinehart & Winston.

Kohlberg, L. (1984). *The psychology of moral development*. New York: Harper & Row.

Kohlberg, L., & Gilligan, C. (1971). The adolescent as a philosopher: The discovery of the self in a postconventional world. *Daedalus, 100,* 1051–1086.

Kohlberg, L., & Kramer, R. (1969). Continuities and discontinuities in the childhood and adult moral development. *Human Development, 12,* 93–120.

Kohn, R. R. (1977). Heart and cardiovascular system. In C. E. Finch & L. Hayflick (Eds.), *Handbook of the biology of aging*. New York: Van Nostrand Reinhold.

Kolata, G. (1983). Huntington's disease gene located. *Science, 222,* 913–915.

Kolata, G. B. (1986). Obese children. *Science, 232,* 20–21.

Kopp, C., & Kaler, S. Risk in infancy. *American Psychologist, 44,* 224–230.

Korner, A., Zeanah, C., Linden, J., Berkowitz, R., Kraemer, H., & Agras, W. S. (1985). The relation between neonatal and later activity and temperament. *Child Development, 56,* 36–42.

Koss, M. (1990). The women's mental health research agenda. Violence against women. *American Psychologist, 45,* 374–380.

Kovacs, M. (1989). Affective disorders in children and adolescents. *American Psychologist, 44,* 209–215.

Kovacs, M., & Gatsonis, C. (1989). Stability and change in childhood onset depressive disorders longitudinal course as a diagnostic validator. In L. N. Robins, J. L. Fleiss, & J. E. Barrett (Eds.), *The validity of psychiatric diagnosis*. New York: Raven.

Kramer, D. (1986). Relativistic and dialectical thought in three adult age groups. *Human Development, 29,* 280–290.

Kramer, D. A. (1983). Post-formal operation? A need for further conceptualization. *Human Development, 26,* 91–105.

Krupnick, M. (1984, May). Incest: Identification and reporting. *Carrier Foundation Letter, 98,* 1–4.

Kubler-Ross, E. (1969). *On death and dying*. New York: Macmillan.

Kubler-Ross, E., & Warshaw, M. (1978). *To live until we say goodbye*. Englewood Cliffs, NJ: Prentice-Hall.

Kuchuk, A., Vibbert, M., & Bornstein, M. (1986). The perception of smiling and its experiential correlates in three-month-old infants. *Child Development, 57,* 1054–1061.

Kuczaj, II, S. (1982). Language play and language acquisition. In H. Reese (Ed.), *Advances in child development and behavior* (Vol. 17). New York: Academic Press.

Kuhlen, R. G. (1964). Developmental changes in motivation during the adult years. In J. E. Birren (Ed.), *Relations of development and aging*. Springfield, IL: Charles C. Thomas.

Kuhn, D., Nash, S., & Brucken, L. (1978). Sex-role concepts of two- and three-year-olds. *Child Development, 49,* 445–451.

Kuhn, T. S. (1970). *The structure of scientific revolutions* (2nd ed.). Chicago: University of Chicago Press.

Kupersmidt, J., & Coie, J. (1990). Preadolescent peer status, aggression and school adjustment as predictors of externalizing problems in adolescence. *Child Development, 61,* 1350–1362.

Kurdek, L. (1994). Lesbian and gay couples. In A. R. D'Augelli & C. J. Patterson (Eds.), *Lesbian, gay, and bisexual identities across the lifespan: Psychological perspectives*. New York: Oxford University Press.

Labouvie, E. W. (1975). The dialectical nature of measurement activities in the behavioral sciences. *Human Development, 18,* 396–403.

Labouvie, E. W. (1982). Issues in life-span development. In B. Wolman (Ed.), *Handbook of developmental psychology*. Englewood Cliffs, NJ: Prentice-Hall.

Labouvie-Vief, G. (1980a). Adaptive dimensions in adult cognition. In N. Datan & N. Lohmann (Eds.), *Transitions in aging*. New York: Academic Press.

Labouvie-Vief, G. (1980b). Beyond formal operations: Uses and limits of pure logic in life-span development. *Human Development, 23,* 141–161.

Labouvie-Vief, G. (1982). Dynamic development and mature autonomy: A theoretical prologue. *Human Development, 25,* 161–191.

Labouvie-Vief, G. (1985). Intelligence and cognition. In J. E. Birren & K. W. Schaie (Eds.), *Handbook of the psychology of aging* (2nd ed.). New York: Van Nostrand Reinhold.

Labouvie-Vief, G., & Chandler, M. (1978). Cognitive development and life-span developmental theory: Idealistic versus contextual perspectives. In P. Baltes (Ed.), *Life-span development and behavior* (Vol. 1). New York: Academic Press.

Labouvie-Vief, G., & Schell, D. A. (1982). Learning and memory in later life. In B. Wolman (Ed.), *Handbook of developmental psychology*. Englewood Cliffs, NJ: Prentice-Hall.

Lachiewicz, A. M., Spiridigliozzi, G. A., Gullion, C. M., Ransford, S. N., & Rao, K. (1994). Aberrant behaviors of young boys with fragile X syndrome. *American Journal on Mental Retardation, 98,* 567–579.

LaCroix, A., & Haynes, S. (1987). Gender differences in the health effects of work place roles. In R. C. Barnett, L. Biener, & G. K. Baruck (Eds.), *Gender and stress*. New York: Free Press.

Ladd, G. (1983). Social networks of popular, average, and rejected children in school settings. *Merrill-Palmer Quarterly, 29,* 283–307.

Ladd, G., & Oden, S. (1979). The relationship between peer acceptance and children's ideas about helpfulness. *Child Development, 50,* 402–408.

Lamaze, F. (1981). *Painless childbirth*. New York: Simon & Schuster.

Lamb, M. E. (1976). Interaction between eight-month-old children and their fathers and mothers. In M. Lamb (Ed.), *The role of the father in child development*. New York: Wiley.

Lamb, M. E. (1982a). Parent behavior and child development in nontraditional families: An introduction. In M. E. Lamb (Ed.), *Nontraditional families: Parenting and child development*. Hillsdale, NJ: Erlbaum.

Lamb, M. E. (1982b). Sibling relationships across the lifespan. In M. E. Lamb & B. Sutton-Smith (Eds.), *Sibling relationships*. Hillsdale, NJ: Erlbaum.

Lamb, M. E. (1982c). What can research experts tell parents about effective socialization? In E. Zigler, M. Lamb, & I. Child (Eds.), *Socialization and personality development* (2nd ed.). New York: Oxford University Press.

Lamb, M. E., Frodi, A., Hwang, C. P., Frodi, M., & Steinberg, J. (1982). Effects of gender and caretaking role on parent-infant interaction. In R. Emde & R. Harmon (Eds.), *The development of attachment and affiliative systems*. New York: Plenum.

Lamb, M. E., & Oppenheim, D. (1989). Fatherhood and father-child relationships: Five years of research. In S.H. Cath, A. Gurwitt, & L. Gunsberg (Eds.), *Fathers and their families* (pp. 11–26). Hillsdale, NJ: Erlbaum.

Lampl, M., Veldhuis, J. D., & Johnson, M. L. (1992). Saltation and stasis: A model of human growth. *Science, 258,* 801–803.

Landau, S., Lorch, E. P., & Milich, R. (1992). Visual attention to and comprehension of television in attention-deficit hyperactivity disordered and normal boys. *Child Development, 63,* 928–937.

Lane, B. (1964). Attitudes of youth toward the aged. *Journal of Marriage and the Family, 26,* 229–231.

Lane, D., & Pearson, D. (1982). The development of selective attention. *Merrill-Palmer Quarterly, 28,* 317–337.

Langer, E. (1985). Planning the middle against both ends: The usefulness of older adult cognitive activity as a model for cognitive activity in childhood and old age. In S. Yussen (Ed.), *The growth of reflection in children*. New York: Academic Press.

Langer, E. J., & Rodin, J. (1976). The effects of choice and enhanced personal responsibility for the aged: A field experiment in an institutional setting. *Journal of Personality and Social Psychology, 34,* 191–198.

Largman, R. (1976). *The social-emotional effects of age of entry into full time group care*. Unpublished doctoral dissertation, University of California, Berkeley.

LaRue, A., & Jarvik, L. (1982). Old age and biobehavioral change. In B. Wolman (Ed.),

Handbook of developmental psychology. Englewood Cliffs, NJ: Prentice-Hall, 1982.

Larson, R. (1991). Adolescent moodiness. In R. M. Lerner, A. C. Petersen, & J. Brooks-Gunn (Eds.), *Encyclopedia of adolescence.* New York: Garland.

Larson, R., & Ham, M. (1993). Stress and "storm and stress" in early adolescence: The relationship of negative events with dysphoric affect. *Developmental Psychology, 29,* 130–140.

Larson, R., & Richards, M. (1991). Daily companionship in late childhood and early adolescence: Changing developmental contexts. *Child Development, 62,* 284–300.

Laska, S. B., & Micklin, M. (1979). The knowledge dimension of occupational socialization: Role models and their social influences. *Youth and Society, 10,* 360–378.

Lasky, R., Tyson, J., Rosenfeld, C., & Gant, N. (1984). Maternal infant interactions at one year adjusted age in infants at low and high-risk as newborns. *Early Human Development, 9,* 145–152.

Lavee, Y., McCubbin, H., & Olson, D. (1987). The effects of stressful life events and transitions on family functioning and well-being. *Journal of Marriage and the Family, 49,* 857–873.

Laws, J. L. (1980). Female sexuality through the lifespan. In P. Baltes & O. Brim (Eds.), *Lifespan development and behavior* (Vol. 3). New York: Academic Press.

Lawton, M. (1981). Community supports for the aged. *Journal of Social Issues, 37,* 102–115.

Lazar, I., & Darlington, R. (with Murray, H., Royce, J., & Snipper, A.). (1982). Lasting effects of early education: A report from the consortium for longitudinal studies. *Monographs of the Society for Research in Child Development, 47*(2–3, Serial No. 195).

Lazarus, R. S. (1981, July). Little hassles can be hazardous to health. *Psychology Today, 58–62.*

Lazarus, R. S., & DeLongis, A. (1983). Psychological stress and coping in aging. *American Psychologist, 38,* 245–254.

Lazarus, R. S., & Folkman, S. (1984). Stress, appraisal, and coping. New York: Springer.

Lazarus, R. S., & Launier, R. (1978). Stress-related transactions between person and environment. In L. A. Pervin & M. Lewis (Eds.), *Perspectives in interactional psychology.* New York: Plenum.

Leadbeater, B. (1991). Relativistic thinking in adolescence. In R. M. Lerner, A. C. Petersen, & J. Brooks-Gunn (Eds.), *Encyclopedia of adolescence.* New York: Garland.

LeBel, J., & Zuckerman, B. (1981). Feeding problems, obesity. In S. Gabel (Ed.), *Behavioral problems in childhood: A primary care approach.* New York: Grune & Stratton.

Lee, E. (1991). Mourning rituals in Chinese culture. In F. Walsh & M. McGoldrick (Eds.), *Living beyond loss: Death in the family.* New York: Norton.

Lee, G., & Ellithorpe, E. (1982). Intergenerational exchange and subjective well-being among the elderly. *Journal of Marriage and the Family, 44,* 217–224.

Lee, G., & Ihinger-Tallman, M. (1980). Sibling interaction and morale: The effects of family relations on older people. *Research on Aging, 2,* 367–391.

Lee, J. A., & Pollack, R. H. (1978). The effects of age on perceptual problem-solving strategies. *Experimental Aging Research, 4,* 37–54.

Lehman, H. C. (1953). *Age and achievement.* Princeton, NJ: Princeton University Press.

Lemon, B. W., Bengston, V. L., & Peterson, J. A. (1972). An exploration of the activity theory of aging: Activity types and life satisfaction among in-movers to a retirement community. *Journal of Gerontology, 27,* 511–523.

Lempers, J., & Clark-Lempers, D. (1990). Family economic stress, maternal and paternal support and adolescent distress. *Journal of Adolescence, 13,* 217–229.

Lempers, J. D., Flavell, E. R., & Flavell, J. H. (1977). The development in very young children of tacit knowledge concerning visual perception. *Genetic Psychology Monographs, 95,* 3–53.

Lenneberg, E. (1967). *Biological foundations of language.* New York: Wiley.

Leon, G. R. (1991). Bulimia nervosa in adolescence. In R. M. Lerner, A. C. Petersen, & J. Brooks-Gunn (Eds.), *Encyclopedia of adolescence.* New York: Garland.

Leon, G. R., Gillum, B., Gillum, R., & Gouze, M. (1979). Personality stability and change over a 30-year period—Middle age to old age. *Journal of Consulting and Clinical Psychology, 47,* 517–524.

Lerner, J. (1976). *Children with learning disabilities* (2nd ed.). Boston: Houghton Mifflin.

Lerner, J., & Galambos, N. (1985). Maternal role satisfaction, mother-child interaction, and child temperament: A process model. *Developmental Psychology, 21,* 1157–1164.

Lerner, J., & Lerner, R. (1983). Temperament and adaptation across life: Theoretical and empirical issues. In P. Baltes & O. Brim (Eds.), *Lifespan development and behavior* (Vol. 5). New York: Academic Press.

Lerner, J. V., & Galambos, N. L. (1988). The influence of maternal employment across life: The New York longitudinal study. In A. E. Gottfried & A. W. Gottfried (Eds.), *Maternal employment and children's development* (pp. 59–83). New York: Plenum.

Lerner, R. M., & Korn, S. J. (1972). Development of body build stereotypes in males. *Child Development, 45,* 908–920.

LeShan, E. (1973). *The wonderful crisis of middle age.* New York: David McKay.

Leskow, S., & Smock, C. D. (1970). Developmental changes in problem-solving strategies: Permutations. *Developmental Psychology, 2,* 412–422.

Lester, B., Corwin, M. J., Sepkoski, C., Seifer, R., Peucker, M., McLaughlin, S., & Golub, H. L. (1991). Neurobehavioral syndromes in cocaine-exposed newborn infants. *Child Development, 62,* 694–705.

Lester, B., & Dreher, M. (1989). Effects of marijuana use during pregnancy on newborn cry. *Child Development, 60,* 765–771.

Lester, B., Garcia-Coll, C., Valcarcel, M., Hoffman, J., & Brazelton, T. B. (1986). Effects of atypical patterns of fetal development on newborn (NBAS) behavior. *Child Development, 57,* 11–19.

Levenson, R. W., Carstensen, L. L., & Gottman, J. M. (1993). Long-term marriage: Age, gender, and satisfaction. *Psychology and Aging, 8,* 301–313.

Levine, L. (1983). "Mine": Self-definition in two-year-old boys. *Developmental Psychology, 19,* 544–549.

Levine, M. (1974). Scientific method and the adversary model: Some preliminary thoughts. *American Psychologist, 29,* 661–677.

Levinson, D. (1978). *The seasons of a man's life.* New York: Knopf.

Levinson, D. (1980). Conceptions in the adult life course. In N. Smelser & E. Erikson (Eds.), *Themes of work and love in adulthood.* Cambridge, MA: Harvard University Press.

Levinson, D. (1986). A conception of adult development. *American Psychologist, 41,* 3–13.

Levinson, D., Darrow, C., Klein, E., Levinson, M., & McKee, B. (1977). Periods in the adult development of men: Ages 18 to 45. In A. G. Sargent (Ed.), *Beyond the sex roles.* New York: West.

Levitt, M. J., Guacci-Franco, N., & Levitt, J. L. (1993). Convoys of social support in childhood and early adolescence: Structure and function. *Developmental Psychology, 29,* 811–818.

Levitt, M. J., Weber, R. A., & Guacci, N. (1993). Convoys of social support: An intergenerational analysis. *Psychology and Aging, 8,* 323–326.

Lewis, M., & Brooks-Gunn, J. (1979). *Social cognition and the acquisition of the self.* New York: Plenum.

Lewis, R. A. (1973). A longitudinal test of a developmental framework for premarital dyadic formation. *Journal of Marriage and the Family, 35,* 16–25.

Lewis, R. A., Frenau, P. J., & Roberts, C. L. (1979). Fathers and the postparental transition. *The Family Coordinator, 28,* 514–520.

Lewit, E. (1992). Child indicators: Teenage child bearing. *The Future Children, 2,* 186–191.

Levi, L. (1990). Occupational stress: Spice of life or kiss of death? *American Psychologist, 45,* 1142–1145.

Levy-Shiff, R., Goldschmidt, I., & Har-Even, D. (1991). Transition to parenthood in adoptive families. *Developmental Psychology, 27,* 131–140.

Li, C. Q., Windsor, R. A., Perkins, L., Goldenberg, R. L., & Lowe, J. B. (1993). The impact on infant birth weight and gestational age of continued validated smoking reduction during pregnancy. *Journal of the American Medical Association, 269,* 1519–1524.

Liang, J., Dvorkin, L., Kahana, E., & Mazian, F. (1980). Social integration and morale: A reexamination. *Journal of Gerontology, 35,* 746–757.

Liaw, F., & Brooks-Gunn, J. (1993). Patterns of low-birth-weight children's cognitive development. *Developmental Psychology, 29,* 1024–1035.

Lieberman, A., Weston, D., & Pawl, J. (1991). Preventive intervention and outcomes with anxiously attached dyads. *Child Development, 62,* 199–209.

Lieberman, M., & Coplan, A. (1970). Distance from death as a variable in the study of aging. *Developmental Psychology, 2,* 71–84.

Lieberman, M. A. (1961). The relation of mortality rates to entrance to a home for the aged. *Geriatrics, 16,* 515–519.

Lieberman, M. A. (1965). Psychological correlates of impending death: Some preliminary observations. *Journal of Gerontology, 20,* 181–190.

Liebert, R., Sprafkin, J., & Davidson, E. (1982). *The early window: Effects of television on children and youth* (2nd ed.). New York: Pergamon.

Lifton, B. J. (1979). *Lost and found*. New York: Dial Press.

Light, L. L. (1991). Memory and aging: Four hypotheses in search of data. *Annual Review of Psychology, 42*, 333–376.

Lin, C., & Fu, V. (1990). A comparison of child-rearing practices among Chinese, immigrant Chinese, and Caucasian American parents. *Child Development, 60*, 429–433.

Lindemann, E. (1944). The symptomatology and management of acute grief. *American Journal of Psychiatry, 101*, 141–148.

Lindenberger, U., & Baltes, P. B. (1994). Sensory functioning and intelligence in old age: A strong connection. *Psychology and Aging, 9*, 339–355.

Lindgren, S., DeRenzi, E., & Richman, L. (1985). Cross-national comparisons of developmental dyslexia in Italy and the United States. *Child Development, 56*, 1404–1417.

Lips, H. (1988). *Sex and gender: An introduction*. Mountain View, CA: Mayfield Publishing.

Lipsitz, J. S. (1979, October). Adolescent development: Myths and realities. *Children Today*, 2–7.

Lipsitt, L. (1975). The synchronicity of respiration, heart rate and sucking behavior in the newborn. *Mead Johnson Symposium on Perinatal and Developmental Medicine: No. 6. Biological and clinical aspects of brain development* (pp. 67–72). Evansville, IN: Mead Johnson & Company.

Lipsitt, L., & Kaye, H. (1964). Conditional sucking in the human newborn. *Psychonomic Science, 1*, 29–30.

Livson, N. (1973). Developmental dimensions of personality: A lifespan formulation. In P. Baltes & K. W. Schaie (Eds.), *Lifespan developmental psychology: Personality and socialization*. New York: Academic Press.

Livson, N., & Peskin, H. (1980). Perspectives on adolescence from longitudinal research. In J. Adelson (Ed.), *Handbook of Adolescent Psychology*. New York: Wiley.

Lock, M. (1991). Contested meanings of the menopause. *The Lancet, 327*, 1270–1272.

Lockheed, M., & Klein, S. (1985). Sex equity in classrooms organization and climate. In S. Klein (Ed.), *Handbook for achieving sex equity through education*. Baltimore, MD: Johns Hopkins University Press.

Loeber, R., & Dishion, T. (1983). Early predictors of male delinquency: A review. *Psychological Bulletin, 94*, 68–99.

Loeber, R., & Stouthamer-Loeber, M. (1986). Family factors as correlates and predictors of juvenile conduct problems and delinquency. In M. Tonry & N. Morris (Eds.), *Crime and justice: A review of research* (Vol. 7, pp. 29–149). Chicago: University of Chicago Press.

Loehlin, J. C., & Nichols, R. C. (1976). *Heredity, environment and personality*. Austin: University of Texas Press.

Loftus, E., & Loftus, G. (1983). *Mind at play: The psychology of video games*. New York: Basic Books.

Lonetto, R. (1980). *Children's conceptions of death*. New York: Springer.

Lonkey, E., Kaus, C., & Roodin, P. (1984). Life experience and mode of coping: Relation to moral judgment in adulthood. *Developmental Psychology, 20*, 1159–1167.

Lopata, H. Z. (1971). Widows as a minority group. *The Gerontologist, 11*, 67–77.

Lopata, H. Z. (1973). *Widowhood in an American city*. Cambridge, MA: Schenkman.

Lopata, H. Z. (1977). The meaning of friendship in widowhood. In L. Troll, J. Israel, & K. Israel (Eds.), *Looking ahead: A woman's guide to the problems and joys of growing older*. Englewood Cliffs, NJ: Prentice-Hall.

Lopata, H. Z. (1979). *Women as widows: Support systems*. New York: Elsevier.

Lorenz, K. (1966). *On aggression*. New York: Harcourt.

Lowenthal, M. F., & Boler, D. (1975). Voluntary versus involuntary social withdrawal. *Journal of Gerontology, 20*, 363–371.

Lowenthal, M. F., & Haven, C. (1968). Interaction and adaptation: Intimacy as a critical variable. *American Sociological Review, 33*, 20–30.

Lowenthal, M. F., Thurnher, M., & Chiriboga, D. (1975). *Four stages of life: A comparative study of women and men facing transitions*. San Francisco: Jossey-Bass.

Lowry, E. H. (Ed.). (1967). *Growth and development of children*. Chicago: Year Book Medical Publishers.

Lozoff, B. (1989). Nutrition and behavior. *American Psychologist, 44*, 231–236.

Lucas, A. R. (1991). Eating disorders. In M. Lewis (Ed.), *Child and adolescent psychiatry: A comprehensive textbook*. Baltimore: Williams & Wilkins.

Ludemann, P., & Nelson, C. (1988). Categorical representation of facial expressions by seven-month-old infants. *Developmental Psychology, 24*, 492–501.

Luke, B. (1977, December). Maternal alcoholism and the fetal alcohol syndrome. *American Journal of Nursing*, 1924–1926.

Lynch, J. (1977). *The broken heart: Medical consequences of loneliness*. New York: Basic Books.

Maccoby, E. (1980). *Social development: Psychological growth and the parent-child relationship*. New York: Harcourt, Brace, Jovanovich.

Maccoby, E. (1984). Socialization and developmental change. *Child Development, 55*, 317–328.

Maccoby, E. (1988). Gender as a social category. *Developmental Psychology, 24*, 755–765.

Maccoby, E. (1990). Gender and relationships: A developmental account. *American Psychologist, 45*, 513–520.

Maccoby, E., & Jacklin, C. (1974). *The psychology of sex differences*. Stanford, CA: Stanford University Press.

Maccoby, E., & Jacklin, C. (1980). Sex differences in aggression. A rejoinder and reprise. *Child Development, 51*, 964–980.

Maccoby, E., & Jacklin, C. (1987). Gender segregation in childhood. In E. H. Reese (Ed.), *Advances in child development and behavior* (Vol. 20). New York: Academic Press.

Maccoby, E., & Martin, J. (1983). Socialization in the context of the family: Parent-child interaction. In E. M. Hetherington (Ed.) & P. H. Mussen (Series Ed.), *Handbook of child psychology: Vol. 4. Socialization, personality and social development*. New York: Wiley.

MacFarlane, A. (1975). Olfaction in the development of social preferences in the human neonate. *CIBA Foundation Symposium: Vol. 33. Parent-infant interaction*. Amsterdam: Elsevier.

MacFarlane, A. (1978, February). What a baby knows. *Human Nature*.

MacKinnon-Lewis, C., Volling, B. L., Lamb, M. E., Dechman, K., Rsbiner, D., & Curtner, M. E. (1994). A cross-contextual analysis of boys' social competence: From family to school. *Developmental Psychology, 30*, 325–333.

Macklin, E. D. (1978). Nonmarital heterosexual cohabitation. *Marriage and Family Review. 1*, 1–12.

Madden, D. (1985). Adult age differences in memory driven selective attention. *Developmental Psychology, 21*, 655–665.

Maddox, G. (1968). Persistence of life style among the elderly. In B. Neugarten (Ed.), *Middle-age and aging*. Chicago: University of Chicago Press.

Maddox, G. L. (1968). Retirement as a social event in the United States. In B. L. Neugarten (Ed.), *Middle age and aging*. Chicago: University of Chicago Press.

Madison, L. S., Madison, J. K., & Adubato, S. A. (1986). Infant behavior and development in relation to fetal movement and habituation. *Child Development, 57*, 1475–1482.

Magenis, R. E., Overton, K. M., Chamberlin, J., Brady, T., & Lovrein, E. (1977). Parental origins of the extra chromosome in Down's syndrome. *Human Genetics, 37*, 7–16.

Mahler, M., Pine, F., & Bergman, A. (1975). *The psychological birth of the human infant*. New York: Basic Books.

Main, M., & George, C. (1985). Responses of abused and disadvantaged toddlers to distress in agemates: A study in the daycare setting. *Developmental Psychology, 21*, 407–413.

Main, M., & Solomon, J. (1990). Procedure for identifying infants as disorganized/disoriented during the Ainsworth Strange Situation. In M. T. Guenberg, D. Ciccbetti, & E. M. Cummings (Ed.), *Attachment in the preschool years: theory, research and intervention*. Chicago: University of Chicago Press.

Makin, J. W., Fried, P. A., & Watkinson, B. (1991). A comparison of active and passive smoking during pregnancy: Long-term effects. *Neurotoxicology and Teratology, 13*, 5–12.

Makinsdan, T. (1977). Immunity and aging. In C. E. Finch & L. Hayflick (Eds.), *Handbook of the biology of aging*. New York: Van Nostrand Reinhold.

Malatesta, C., Culver, C., Tesman, J., & Shepard, B. (1989). The development of emotion expression during the first two years of life. *Monographs of the Society for Research in Child Development, 54*(1–2, Serial No. 219).

Malatesta, C. Z., Grigoryev, P., Lamb, C., Albin, M., & Culver, C. (1986). Emotion socialization and expressive development in preterm and full-term infants. *Child Development, 57*, 316–330.

Malatesta, C. Z., & Haviland, J. M. (1982). Learning display rules: The socialization of emotion expression in infancy. *Child Development, 53*, 991–1003.

Malina, R. M. (1974). Adolescent changes in size, build, composition and performance. *Human Biology, 46*, 117–131.

Malina, R. M. (1978). Adolescent growth and maturation: Selected aspects of current research. *Yearbook of Physical Anthropology, 21*, 63–94.

Malina, R. M. (1979). Secular changes in size and maturity: Causes and effects. In A. F. Roche (Ed.), Secular trends in human growth, maturation and development. *Monographs of the Society for Research in Child Development, 44* (3–4), 59–102.

Malina, R. M. (1991). Adolescent growth spurt: II. In R. M. Lerner, A. C. Petersen, & J. Brooks-Gunn, *Encyclopedia of adolescence.* New York: Garland.

Mall, J. (1985, March 17). A study of U.S. teenage pregnancy rates. *Los Angeles Times,* Part 7, p. 27.

March of Dimes Birth Defects Foundation. (1983). *Birth Defects.* White Plains, NY: Author.

Marcia, J. E. (1966). Development and validation of ego-identity status. *Journal of Personality and Social Psychology, 3,* 551–558.

Marcia, J. E. (1976). Identity six years later: A follow-up study. *Journal of Youth and Adolescence, 5,* 145–160.

Marcia, J. E. (1980). Identity in adolescence. In J. Adelson (Ed.), *Handbook of adolescent psychology.* New York: Wiley.

Marcia, J. E. (1991). Identity and self-development. In R. M. Lerner, A. C. Petersen, & J. Brooks-Gunn (Eds.), *Encyclopedia of adolescence.* New York: Garland.

Marcus, D. E., & Overton, W. F. (1978). The development of cognitive gender and constancy and sex role preferences. *Child Development, 49,* 434–444.

Marcus, G. F., Pinker, S., Ullman, M., Hollander, M., Rosen, T. J., & Xu, F. (1992). Overregularization in language acquisition. *Monographs of the Society for Research in Child Development, 57*(4, Serial No. 228).

Maret, E., & Finlay, B. (1984). The distribution of household labor among women in dual earner families. *Journal of Marriage and the Family, 46,* 357–364.

Margolin, L., & White, L. (1987). The continuing role of physical attractiveness in marriage. *Journal of Marriage and the Family, 49,* 21–27.

Markides, K., & Mindel, C. (1987). *Aging & ethnicity.* Newbury Park, CA: Sage Publications.

Markman, E., & Hutchinson, J. (1984). Children's sensitivity to constraints on word meaning: Taxonomic versus thematic relations. *Cognitive Psychology, 16,* 1–27.

Marsh, G. R., & Thompson. L. W. (1977). Psychophysiology of aging. In J. E. Birren & K. W. Schaie (Eds.), *Handbook of the psychology of aging.* New York: Van Nostrand Reinhold.

Marshall, D. (1987). Sexual behavior on Mangara. In D.J. Marshall & R.C. Suggs (Eds.), *Human sexual behavior.* New York: Basic Books.

Martin, B. (1975). Parent-child relations. In F. D. Horowitz (Ed.), *Review of child development research* (Vol. 4). Chicago: University of Chicago Press.

Martin, C., & Halverson, C. (1981). A schematic processing model of sex typing and stereotyping in children. *Child Development, 52,* 1119–1134.

Martin, C., & Little, J. (1990). The relation of gender understanding to children's sex-typed preferences and gender stereotypes. *Child Development, 61,* 1427–1439.

Martin, C. L., Wood, C. H., & Little, J. K. (1990). The development of gender stereotype components. *Child Development, 61,* 1891–1904.

Martin, J. B. (1987). Molecular genetics: Applications to the clinical neurosciences. *Science, 298,* 765–772.

Martin, L. (1988). The aging of Asia. *Journal of Gerontology, 43,* 599–5113.

Martin, S. (1994a, October). Aging of a loved one alters family dynamics. *APA Monitor,* p. 24.

Martin, S. (1994b, October). Balance can counteract stress of work. *APA Monitor,* p. 49.

Maslow, A. (1954). *Motivation and personality.* New York: Harper & Row.

Masnick, G., & Bane, M. J. (1980). *The nation's families: 1960–1990.* Cambridge, MA: Joint Center for Urban Studies.

Masten, A. (1986). Humor and competence in school-aged children. *Child Development, 57,* 461–473.

Masters, W. H., & Johnson, V. E. (1966). *Human sexual response.* Boston: Little, Brown.

Masters, W. H., & Johnson, V. E. (1975). *The pleasure bond: A new look at sexuality and commitment.* Boston: Little, Brown.

Masters, W. H., & Johnson, V. E. (1981). Sex and the aging process. *Journal of the American Geriatric Society, 29,* 385–390.

Masterson, J. F. (1967). *The psychiatric dilemma of adolescence.* Boston: Little, Brown.

Matheny, A., Riese, M., & Wilson, R. (1985). Rudiments of infant temperament: Newborn to 9 months. *Developmental Psychology, 21,* 486–494.

Mathes, E. (1975). The effects of physical attractiveness and anxiety on heterosexual adjustment over a series of five encounters. *Journal of Marriage and the Family, 37,* 769–773.

Matthews, J. (1990). Drawing and individual development. In R. M. Thomas (Eds.), *The encyclopedia of human development and education: theory research and studies.* Oxford: Pergamon.

Matthews, K., & Angulo, J. (1980). Measurement of the Type A behavior patterns in children: Assessment of children's competitiveness, impatience-anger, and aggression. *Child Development, 51,* 466–475.

Matthews, K. A. (1982). Psychological perspectives on the Type A behavior pattern. *Psychological Bulletin, 91,* 293–323.

Matthews, K. A., & Brunson, B. I. (1979). Allocation of attention and the Type A coronary-prone behavior pattern. *Journal of Personality and Social Psychology, 37,* 2081–2090.

Matthews, S., & Sprey, J. (1984). The impact of divorce on grandparenthood: An exploratory study. *The Gerontologist, 24,* 42–47.

Maurer, A. (1961). The child's knowledge of nonexistence. *Journal of Existential Psychiatry, 2,* 193–212.

Maurer, A. (1965). What children fear. *Journal of Genetic Psychology, 106,* 265–277.

Maurer, D., & Salapatek, P. (1976). Developmental changes in the scanning of faces by young infants. *Child Development, 47,* 523–527.

Mayer, J. (1975). Obesity during childhood. In M. Winick (Ed.), *Childhood obesity.* New York: Wiley.

Mayle, P. (1973). *Where did I come from?* Secaucus, NJ: Lyle Stuart.

McCabe, A., & Lipscomb, T. (1988). Sex differences in children's verbal aggression. *Merrill-Palmer Quarterly, 34,* 389–401.

McCall, R. B., & Carrigir, H. S. (1993). A meta-analysis of infant habituation and recognition memory performances as predictors of later IQ. *Child Development, 64,* 57–79.

McCall, R. B., Eichorn, D. H., & Hogarty, P. S. (1977). Transitions in early mental development. *Monographs of the Society for Research in Child Development, 42* (No. 3, Serial No. 171).

McCandless, B., & Evans, E. (1973). Children and youth: Psychosocial development, Hillsdale, IL: Dryden.

McCartney, K. (1984). The effects of quality of day-care environment on children's language development. *Developmental Psychology, 20,* 244–250.

McClelland, K. A. (1982). Adolescent subculture in the schools. In T. Field, A. Huston, H. C. Quay, L. Troll, & G. E. Finley (Eds.), *Review of human development.* New York: Wiley-Interscience.

McCormick, K. (1982). *An exploration of the functions of friends and best friends.* Unpublished doctoral dissertation, Rutgers University, New Jersey.

McCrae, R. R., & Costa, P. T. (1994). The stability of personality: Observations and evaluations. *Current Directions in Psychological Science, 3,* 173–176.

McCurdy, K., & Daro, D. (1994, April). *Current trends in child abuse reporting and fatalities: The results of the 1993 annual fifty states survey* (Working Paper No. 808, prepared by the National Center on Child Abuse Prevention Research). Chicago: National Committee for Prevention of Child Abuse.

McDavid, J., & Harari, M. (1966). Stereotyping of names and popularity in grade school children. *Child Development, 37,* 453–459.

McFarlane, J., Martin, C., & Williams, T. (1988). Mood fluctuations: Women versus men and menstrual versus other cycles. *Psychology of Women Quarterly, 12,* 201–223.

McGee, J., & Wells, K. (1982). Gender typing and androgeny in later life. *Human Development, 25,* 116–139.

McGhee, P. (1979). *Humor: Its origin and development.* San Francisco: Freeman.

McGoldrick, M. (1991). Irish families. In F. Walsh & M. McGoldrick (Eds.), *Living beyond loss: Death in the family.* New York: Norton.

McKain, W. C. (1972). A new look at older marriages. *Family Coordinator, 21,* 61–69.

McKee, L. (1987). The dieta: Postpartum seclusion in the Andes of Ecuador. In A. Cohn & L. Leach (Eds.), *Generations: A universal family album.* New York: Pantheon Books.

McKinney, J., Hotch, D., & Truhon, S. (1977). The organization of behavioral values during late adolescence: Change and stability across two eras. *Developmental Psychology, 13,* 83–84.

McKinney, J., & Moore, D. (1982). Attitudes and values during adolescence. In B. B. Wolman (Ed.), *Handbook of human development.* Englewood Cliffs, NJ: Prentice-Hall.

Mclearn, G., & Foch, T. (1985). Behavioral genetics. In J. E. Birren & K. W. Schaie (Eds.), *Handbook of the psychology of aging* (2nd ed.). New York: Van Nostrand Reinhold.

McMurran, M. (1991). Young offenders and alcohol-related crimes: What interventions will address the issues? *Journal of Adolescence, 14,* 245–253.

McPherson, B. (1983). *Aging as a social process.* Toronto: Butterworths.

McPherson, B., & Guppy, N. (1979). Pre-retirement life-style and the degree of planning for retirement. *Journal of Gerontology, 34,* 254–263.

Mead, M. (1928). *The coming of age in Samoa.* New York: William Morrow.

Meier, J. (1971). Prevalence and characteristics of learning disabilities found in second grade children. *Journal of Learning Disabilities, 4,* 1–16.

Melamed, B., & Siegel, L. (1981). Reduction of anxiety in children facing hospitalization and surgery by use of filmed modeling. In E. M. Hetherington & R. Parke (Eds.), *Contemporary readings in child psychology* (2nd ed.). New York: McGraw-Hill.

Meltzoff, A. (1959). Imitation of televised models by infants. *Child Development, 59,* 1221–1229.

Meltzoff, A. (1985). Immediate and deferred imitation in fourteen- and twenty-four-month-old infants. *Child Development, 56,* 62–72.

Meltzoff, A. (1988a). Infant imitation after a 1-week delay: Longterm memory for novel acts and multiple stimuli. *Developmental Psychology, 24,* 470–476.

Meltzoff, A. (1988b). Infant imitation and memory: Nine-month-olds in immediate and deferred tests. *Child Development, 59,* 217–225.

Meltzoff, A., & Moore, K. M. (1977). Imitation of facial and manual gestures by human neonates. *Science, 198,* 75–78.

Meltzoff, A., & Moore, M. (1983). The origins of imitation in infancy: Paradigm, phenomena and theories. In L. P. Lipsitt & C. K. Rovee-Collier (Eds.), *Advances in infancy research* (Vol. 2). Norwood, NJ: Ablex.

Mendelson, B., & White, D. (1985). Development of self-body esteem in overweight youngsters. *Developmental Psychology, 21,* 90–96.

Mendelson, E., Robinson, S., Gardner, H., & Winner, E. (1984). Are preschoolers' renamings intentional category violations? *Developmental Psychology, 20,* 187–192.

Mendelson, M. A. (1974). *Tender loving greed: How the incredibly lucrative nursing home "industry" is exploiting old people and defrauding us all.* New York: Knopf.

Meredith, H. V. (1978). Research between 1960 and 1970 on the standing height of young children in different parts of the world. In H. W. Reese and L. P. Lipsitt (Eds.), *Advances in child development and behavior* (Vol. 12). New York: Academic Press.

Meredith, H. V. (1982). Research between 1950 and 1980 on urban rural differences in body size and growth rate of children and youths. In H. Reese (Ed.), *Advances in child development and behavior* (Vol. 17). New York: Academic Press.

Meredith, H. (1987). Variations in body stockiness among and within ethnic groups at ages from birth to adulthood. In H. Reese (Ed.), *Advances in child development and behavior* (Vol. 20). New York: Academic Press.

Merewood, A. (1991, April). Sperm under siege: More than we ever guessed, having a healthy baby may depend on dad. *Health,* 53–57, 76–77.

Mergler, N. L., & Goldstein, M. D. (1983). Why are there old people? Senescence as biological and cultural preparedness for the transmission of information. *Human Development, 26,* 72–90.

Merriman, W., & Bowman, L. (1989). The mutual exclusivity bias in children's word learning.

Monographs of the Society for Research in Child Development, 54(3–4, Serial No. 220).

Messer, S. B. (1976). Reflection-impulsivity: A review. *Psychological Bulletin, 83,* 1026–1052.

Messer, S., & Schacht, T. (1986). A cognitive-dynamic theory of reflection-impulsivity. In J. Masling (Ed.), *Empirical studies of psychoanalytic theories* (Vol. 2). Hillsdale, NJ: Erlbaum.

Meyerhoff, M., & White, B. (1986, September). Making the grade as parents. *Psychology Today,* 30–45.

Michael, R., Gagnon, J., Laumann, E., & Kolata, G. (1994). *Sex in America: A definitive survey.* Boston: Little Brown.

Midgley, C., Feldlaufer, H., Eccles, J. S. (1989). Change in teacher efficacy and student self and task-related beliefs during the transition to junior high school. *Journal of Educational Psychology, 81,* 247–258.

Miller, B., & Gerard, D. (1979). Family influences on the development of creativity in children: An integrative review. *The Family Coordinator, 28,* 295–312.

Miller, B. C., & Moore, K. A. (1990). Adolescent sexual behavior, pregnancy, and parenting: Research through the 1980's. *Journal of Marriage and the Family, 52,* 1025–1044.

Miller, B., & Sollie, D. (1980). Normal stresses during the transition to parenthood. *Family Relations, 29,* 459–465.

Miller, M. (1982). *Childstress.* New York: Doubleday.

Miller, N., & Maruyama, G. (1976). Ordinal position and peer popularity. *Journal of Personality and Social Psychology, 33,* 123–131.

Miller, P., Haynes, V., DeMarie-Dreblow, D., & Woody-Ramsey, J. (1986). Children's strategies for gathering information in three tasks. *Child Development, 57,* 1429–1439.

Miller, P. H. (1983). *Theories of developmental psychology.* San Francisco: Freeman.

Miller, P. H. (1993). *Theories of developmental psychology* (3rd ed.). San Francisco: W. H. Freeman.

Miller, P. H., & Bigi, L. (1977). Children's understanding of how stimulus dimensions affect performance. *Child Development, 48,* 1712–1715.

Miller-Jones, D. (1989). Culture and testing. *American Psychologist, 44,* 360–366.

Milne, A. A. (1926). *Winnie-the-Pooh.* New York: E. P. Dutton.

Minde, K. (1983). Disorders of attention. In P. Steinhauer & Q. Rae-Grant (Eds.), *Psychological problems of the child in the family* (2nd ed.). New York: Basic Books.

Minnett, A., Vandell, D. L., & Santrock, J. (1983). The effects of sibling status on sibling interaction: Influence of birth order, age spacing, sex of child and sex of sibling. *Child Development, 54,* 1064–1072.

Mischel, W. Sex typing and socialization. (1970). In P. Mussen (Ed.), *Carmichael's manual of child psychology* (3rd ed., vol. II). New York: Wiley.

Mitchell, J., Pyle, R., & Eckert, E. (1981). Frequency and duration of binge eating episodes in patients with bulimia. *American Journal of Psychiatry, 138,* 835–836.

Miyake, K., Chen, S., & Campos, J. (1985). Infant temperament, mother's mode of interaction, and attachments in Japan. An interim report. In J. Bretherton & E. Waters (Eds.), *Growing points of attachment theory and research.*

Monographs of the Society for Research in Child Development, 50(1–2, Serial No. 209).

Moen, P. (1982). The two-provider family: Problems and potentials. In M. Lamb (Ed.), *Nontraditional families: Parenting and child development.* Hillsdale, NJ: Erlbaum.

Moen, P. (1991). Transition in midlife: Women's work and family roles in the 1970's. *Journal of Marriage and the Family, 53,* 135–150.

Molfese, D., Molfese, V., & Carrell, P. (1982). Early language development. In B. Wolman & G. Stricker (Eds.), *Handbook of developmental psychology.* Englewood Cliffs, NJ: Prentice-Hall.

Money, J., & Ehrhardt, A. (1972). *Man and woman, boy and girl: The differentiation and dimorphism of gender identity from conception to maturity.* Baltimore: Johns Hopkins University.

Montagu, M. F. A. (1962). *Prenatal influences.* Springfield, IL: Charles C. Thomas.

Montepare, J., & Lachman, M. (1989). "You're only as old as you feel": Self-perceptions of age, fears of aging, and life satisfaction from adolescence to old age. *Psychology and Aging, 4,* 73–78.

Monthly vital statistics report: Advance report of final natality statistics. *National Center for Health Statistics, 33* (Suppl. 6).

Moody, R. (1975). *Life after life.* Atlanta: Mockingbird Books.

Moore, D., & Hotch, D. (1981). Late adolescents' conceptualizations of home-leaving. *Journal of Youth and Adolescence, 10,* 1–10.

Moore, K., & Waite, L. (1977). Early childbearing and educational attainment. *Family Planning Perspectives, 9,* 220–225.

Moos, R., & Lemke, S. (1985). Specialized living environments for older people. In J. Birren & K. Schaie (Eds.), *Handbook of the psychology of aging* (2nd ed.). New York: Van Nostrand Reinhold.

Morgan, L. A. (1976). A reexamination of widowhood and morale. *Journal of Gerontology, 31,* 687–695.

Morrison, F., Lord, C., & Keating, D. (1984). Applied developmental psychology. In F. Morrison, C. Lord & D. Keating (Eds.), *Applied developmental psychology.* New York: Academic Press.

Morrison, I. (1975). The elderly primigravida. *American Journal of Obstetrics and Gynecology, 15,* 465–470.

Morrison, J., & Stewart, M. (1973). The psychiatric status of the legal families of adopted hyperactive children. *Archives of General Psychiatry, 28,* 888–891.

Morrow, D., Leirer, V., Altieri, P., & Fitzsimmons, C. (1994). When expertise reduces age differences in performance. *Psychology and Aging, 9,* 134–148.

Moses, S. (1990, November). Teen girls can have a "crisis of connection." *APA Monitor,* p. 26.

Moshman, D., & Neimark, E. (1982). Four aspects of adolescent cognitive development. In T. Field, A. Huston, H. C. Quay, L. Troll, & G. E. Finley (Eds.), *Review of human development.* New York: Wiley-Interscience.

Moskowitz R., & Haug, M. (1986). *Arthritis and the elderly.* New York: Springer Publishing Co.

Moursand, J. (1976). *Learning and the learner.* Monterey, CA: Brooks/Cole.

Mueller, D., & Cooper, P. (1986). Children of single parent families: How they fare as young adults. *Family Relations, 35,* 169–176.

Mueller, E., & Lucas, T. (1975). A developmental analysis of peer interactions in playgroup setting. In M. Lewis & L. A. Rosenblum (Eds.), *Friendships and peer relations*. New York: Wiley.

Mullis, A. K., Mullis, R. L., & Normandin, D. (1992). Cross-sectional and longitudinal comparisons of adolescents self-esteem. *Adolescence, 27*, 51–61.

Munnichs, J. (1966). *Old age and finitude*. Basel, Switzerland: Karger.

Murphy, J. M., & Gilligan, C. (1980). Moral development in late adolescence and adulthood: A critique and reconstruction of Kohlberg's theory. *Human Development, 23*, 77–104.

Murphy, L. B. (1972). Infants' play and cognitive development. In M. W. Piers (Ed.), *Play and development: A symposium*. New York: Norton.

Murrell, S. A., Meeks, S., & Walker, J. (1991). Protective functions of health and self-esteem against depression in older adults facing illness or bereavement. *Psychology and Aging, 6*, 352–360.

Murstein, B. I. (1970). Stimulus-value-role: A theory of marital choice. *Journal of Marriage and the Family, 32*, 465–481.

Murstein, B. I. (1976). *Who will marry whom? Theories and research in marital choice*. New York: Springer.

Murstein, B. I. (1982). Marital choice. In B. Wolman (Ed.), *Handbook of developmental psychology*. Englewood Cliffs, NJ: Prentice-Hall.

Musick, J. (1994, Fall). Capturing the child-rearing context. *SRCD Newsletter, 1*, 6–7.

Mussen, P. H., & Eisenberg-Berg, N. (1977). *Roots of caring, sharing and helping*. San Francisco: Freeman.

Mussen, P. H., & Jones, M. C. (1957). Self-conceptions, motivations, and interpersonal attitudes of late- and early-maturing boys. *Child Development, 28*, 243–256.

Myers, N., & Perlmutter, M. (1978). Memory in the years from two to five. In P. A. Ornstein (Ed.), *Memory development in children*. Hillsdale, NJ: Erlbaum.

Nagy, M. (1948). The child's theories concerning death. *Journal of Genetic Psychology, 73*, 3–27.

Nally, S., Eisenberg, N., & Harris, J. D. (1991). Consistency and change in maternal child-rearing practices and values: A longitudinal study. *Child Development, 62*, 190–198.

Nash, S. C., & Feldman, S. S. (1981). Sex role and sex-related attributions: Constancy and change across the family life cycle. In M. Lamb & A. Brown (Eds.), *Advances in developmental psychology* (Vol. 1). Hillsdale, NJ: Erlbaum.

Nathanson, C., & Lorenz, G. (1982). Women and health: The social dimensions of biomedical data. In J. Giele (Ed.), *Women in the middle years*. New York: Wiley.

National Audience Demographics Report 1985. (1985). Northbrook, IL: A.C. Nielsen Company.

National Center for Health Statistics. (1980). *Lifetables: Vital statistics of the United States, 1978* (Vol. II). Washington, DC: U.S. Government Printing Office.

National Center for Health Statistics. (1982). Advance report of final natality statistics. *Monthly Vital Statistics Report, 33* (Suppl. 6).

National Commission on Excellence in Education. (1983). *A nation at risk*. Washington, DC: U.S. Government Printing Office.

National Commission on the Reform of Secondary Education. (1973). *The reform of secondary education*. New York: McGraw-Hill.

National Commission on Youth. (1980). *The transition of youth to adulthood: A bridge too long*. Boulder, CO: Westview Press.

National Institute of Health, Osteoporosis. (1984). *Consensus development conference statement, 5* (3). Bethesda, MD: U.S. Government Printing Office, 4652.

National Panel on High School and Adolescent Education. (1976). *The education of adolescents*. Washington, DC: U.S. Government Printing Office.

Natterson, J., & Knudson, A. (1960). Observations concerning fear of death in fatally ill children and their mothers. *Psychosomatic Medicine, 22*, 456–466.

Naylor, H. (1980). Reading disabilities and lateral asymmetry: An information processing analysis. *Psychological Bulletin, 87*, 531–545.

Neel, N. P., & Alvarez, J. O. (1991). Maternal risk factor for low birth weight and intrauterine growth retardation in a Guatemalan population. *Bulletin of the Pan American Health Organization, 25*, 152–165.

Neimark, E. D. (1975). Intellectual development during adolescence. In F. Horowitz (Ed.), *Review of child development research* (Vol. 4). Chicago: University of Chicago Press.

Neimark, E. D. (1981). Confounding with cognitive style factors: An artifact explanation for the apparent nonuniversal incidence of formal operations. In I. Sigel, D. Brodzinsky, & R. Golinkoff (Eds.), *New directions in Piagetian theory and practice*. Hillsdale, NJ: Erlbaum.

Neimark, E. D. (1982). Adolescent thought: Transition to formal operations. In B. Wolman (Ed.), *Handbook of developmental psychology*. Englewood Cliffs, NJ: Prentice-Hall.

Neimark, E. D., Slotnik, N., & Ulrich, T. (1971). Development of memorization strategies. *Developmental Psychology, 5*, 427–432.

Nelson, C., & Dolgin, K. (1985). The generalized discrimination of facial expressions by seven-month-old infants. *Child Development, 56*, 56–61.

Nelson, G. (1993). Risk, resistance, and self-esteem: A longitudinal study of elementary school-aged children from mother-custody and two-parent families. *Journal of Divorce and Remarriage, 19*, 99–119.

Nelson, K. (1993). Events, narratives, memory: What develops? In C. S. Nelston (Ed.), *Minnesota symposia on child psychology: Vol. 26. Memory and affect in development*. Hillsdale, NJ: Erlbaum.

Nelson, K. (1990). Remembering, forgetting, and childhood amnesia. In R. Fivush & J. A. Hudson (Eds.), *Knowing and remembering young children*. Cambridge: Cambridge University Press.

Nelson, M., & Nelson, G. K. (1982). Problems of equity in the reconstituted family: A social exchange analysis. *Family Relations, 31*, 223–231.

Neugarten, B., & Neugarten, D. (1993). Policy issues in an agency society. In M. Storandt & G. Vandenblos (Eds.), *The adult years: Continuity and change*. Washington, DC: American Psychological Association.

Neugarten, B. L. (1964). *Personality in middle and late life*. New York: Atherton Press.

Neugarten, B. L. (1967). The awareness of middle age. In R. Owen (Ed.), *Middle age*. London: British Broadcasting Corporation.

Neugarten, B. L. (1968). Adult personality: Toward a psychology of the life cycle. In B. L. Neugarten (Ed.), *Middle age and aging*. Chicago: University of Chicago Press.

Neugarten, B. L. (1973). Personality change in late life: A developmental perspective. In C. Eisdorfer & M. P. Lawton (Eds.), *Psychology of adult development and aging*. Washington, DC: American Psychological Association.

Neugarten, B. L. (1977). Personality and aging. In J. E. Birren & K. W. Schaie (Eds.), *Handbook of the psychology of aging*. New York: Van Nostrand Reinhold.

Neugarten, B. L. (1979). Time, age, and the life cycle. *American Journal of Psychiatry, 136*, 887–894.

Neugarten, B. L., Moore, J. W., & Lowe, J. C. (1965). Age norms, age constraints, and adult socialization. *American Journal of Sociology, 70*, 710–717.

Neugarten, B. L., & Weinstein, K. K. (1964). The changing American grandparent. *Journal of Marriage and the Family, 26*, 199–203.

Neugarten, B. L., Wood, V., Kraines, R., & Loomis, B. (1963). Women's attitude toward the menopause. *Vita Humana, 6*, 140–151.

Nevid, J. (1984). Sex differences in factors of romantic attraction. *Sex Roles, 11*, 401–411.

Newcomb, M., & Bentler, P. (1989). Substance use and abuse among children and teenagers. *American Psychologist, 44*, 242–248.

Newcomb, P. (1979). Cohabitation in America: An assessment of consequences. *Journal of Marriage and the Family, 41*, 597–603.

Newcombe, N., & Huttenlocker. (1992). Children's early ability to solve perspective-taking problems. *Developmental Psychology, 28*, 635–643.

Newman, P. R. (1982). The peer group. In B. Wolman (Ed.), *Handbook of developmental psychology*. Englewood Cliffs, NJ: Prentice-Hall.

Newport, E. L. (1991). Contrasting conceptions of the critical period for language. In S. Carey & R. Gelman (Eds.), *The epigenesis of mind: Essays on biology and cognition* (pp. 111–130). Hillsdale, NJ: Erlbaum.

Nguyen, N., & Williams, H. (1989). Transition from East to West: Vietnam adolescents and their parents. *American Academy of Child and Adolescent Psychiatry, 28*, 505–515.

Nielsen, A. C. (1990). *Annual Nielsen report on television: 1990*. New York: Nielsen Media Research.

Niemi, R. G., & Sobieszek, B. I. (1977). Political socialization. *Annual Review of Sociology, 3*, 209–233.

Nisan, M., & Kohlberg, L. (1982). Universality and variation in moral judgment: A longitudinal and cross-sectional study in Turkey. *Child Development, 53*, 865–876.

Nisbet, J. D. (1957). Intelligence and age: Retesting with twenty-four year interval. *British Journal of Educational Psychology, 27*, 190–198.

Niswander, K. R., & Gordon, M. (Eds.). (1972). *The collaborative perinatal study of The National*

Institute of Neurological Diseases and Stroke: Women and their pregnancies. Washington, DC: U.S. Government Printing Office.

Nock, S. L. (1982). The life-cycle approach to family analysis. In B. Wolman (Ed.), *Handbook of developmental psychology.* Englewood Cliffs, NJ: Prentice-Hall.

Nolen-Hocksema, S. (1987). Sex differences in unipolar depression: Evidence and theory. *Psychological Bulletin, 101,* 259–282.

Nolen-Hocksema, S., Girgus, J. S., & Seligman, H. E. P. (1991). Sex differences in depression and explanatory style in children. *Journal of Youth and Adolescence, 20,* 233–245.

Norbeck, J. S., & Tilden, V. P. (1983). Life stress, social support, and emotional disequilibrium, in complications of pregnancy: A prospective, multivariate study. *Journal of Health and Social Behavior, 24,* 30–46.

Norman, J., & Harris, M. (1981). *The private life of the American teenager.* New York: Rawson Wade.

Norris, F., & Murrell, S. (1990). Social support, life events, and stress as modifiers of adjustment to bereavement by older adults. *Psychology and Aging, 5,* 429–436.

Norris, J., & Rubin, K. (1984). Peer interaction and communication: A life-span perspective. In P. Baltes & O. Brim (Eds.), *Life-span development and behavior* (Vol. 16). Orlando, FL: Academic Press.

Northcott, H. C. (1981). Women, work, health, and happiness. *International Journal of Women's Studies, 4,* 268–276.

Norton, A., & Moorman, J. (1987). Current trends in marriage and divorce among American women. *Journal of Marriage and the Family, 49,* 3–14.

Norton, E., Durlak, J., & Richards, M. (1989). Peer knowledge of and reactions to adolescent suicide. *Journal of Youth and Adolescence, 18,* 427–437.

NYCA. (1978). *Facts on alcoholism.* New York: National Council on Alcoholism.

Nyiti, R. (1976). The development of conservation in the Meru children of Tanzania. *Child Development, 47,* 1122–1129.

Nyiti, R. (1982). The validity of "Cultural differences explanations" for cross-cultural variation in the rate of Piagetian cognitive development. In D. Wagner & H. Stevenson (Eds.), *Cultural perspectives on child development.* San Francisco: W.H. Freeman.

O'Brien, M., & Huston, A. (1985). Development of sex-typed play behavior in toddlers. *Developmental Psychology, 21,* 866–871.

O'Brien, S., & Bierman, K. (1988). Conceptions and perceived influence of peer groups: Interviews with preadolescents and adolescents. *Child Development, 59,* 1360–1365.

O'Brien Caughy, M., DiPietro, J. A., & Strobino, D. M. (1994). Day-care participation as a protective factor in the cognitive development of low-income children. *Child Development, 65,* 457–471.

Ochs, E. (1982). Talking to children in Western Samoa. *Language in Society, 11,* 77–104.

O'Connell, M., & Rogers, C. (1983). Child care arrangements for working mothers: June 1982. *Current Population Reports* (Series P-23, No. 129). Washington, DC: U.S. Government Printing Office.

Oden, S., & Asher, S. R. (1977). Coaching children in social skills for friendship making. *Child Development, 48,* 495–506.

Offer, D. (1969). *The psychological world of the teenager: A study of normal adolescence.* New York: Basic Books.

Offer, D., & Church, R. B. (1991). Generation gay. In R. M. Lerner, A. C. Petersen, & J. Brooks-Gunn (Eds.), *Encyclopedia of adolescence.* New York: Garlang.

Offer, D., Ostrov, E., & Howard, K. (1981). *The adolescent: A psychological self-portrait.* New York: Basic Books.

O'Hara, D., & Kahn, J. (1985). Communication and contraceptive practices in adolescent couples. *Adolescence, 20,* 33–43.

Okun, M. A., & DiVesta, F. J. (1976). Cautiousness in adulthood as a function of age and instructions. *Journal of Gerontology, 31,* 371–376.

Okun, M. A., & Elias, C. S. (1977). Cautiousness in adulthood as a function of age and payoff structure. *Journal of Gerontology, 32,* 311–316.

Oldershaw, L., Walters, G., & Hall, D. (1986). Control strategies and noncompliance in abusive mother-child dyads: An observational study. *Child Development, 57,* 722–732.

Olds, D. L., & Kitzman, H. (1993). Review of research on home visiting for pregnant women and parents of young children. *The Future of Children: Home Visiting, 3,* 51–92.

Olmstead, A. H. (1975, August 13). From the journal of a newly-retired man. *New York Times,* p. 33.

Olson, G. M., & Sherman, T. (1983). Attention, learning and memory in infants. In P. H. Mussen (Ed.), *Handbook of child psychology, Vol. II: Infancy and developmental psychobiology* (4th ed.). New York: Wiley.

Olson, H. C., Sampson, P. D., Barr, H., Streissguth, A. P., & Bookstein, F. L. (1992). Prenatal exposure to alcohol and school problems in late childhood: A Longitudinal prospective study. *Development and Psychopathology, 4,* 341–359.

Oren, D. L. (1981). Cognitive advantages of bilingual children related to labeling ability. *Journal of Educational Research, 74,* 164–169.

Orlofsky, J. L., Marcia, J. E., & Lesser, I. M. (1973). Ego identity status and the intimacy versus isolation crisis of young adulthood. *Journal of Personality and Social Psychology, 27,* 211–219.

Oskamp, S., & Mindick, B. (1981). Personality and attitudinal barriers to contraception. In D. Byrne & W. A. Fisher (Eds.), *Adolescents, sex, and contraception.* New York: McGraw-Hill.

Osterweis, M., Solomon, F., & Green, M. (1984). *Bereavement: Reactions, consequences, and care.* Washington, DC: National Academy of Sciences, Institutes on Medicine.

Overton, W. F., & Newman, J. L. (1982). Cognitive development: A competence-activation/utilization approach. In T. Field, A. Huston, H. C. Quay, L. Troll, & G. E. Finley (Eds.), *Review of human development.* New York: Wiley-Interscience.

Overton, W. F., & Reese, H. W. (1973). Models of development: Methodological implications. In J. R. Nesselroade & H. W. Reese (Eds.), *Life-span developmental psychology: Methodological issues.* New York: Academic Press.

Oyserman, D., Radin, N., & Benn, R. (1993). Dynamics in a three-generational family: Teens, grandparents, and babies. *Developmental Psychology, 29* (3), 564–572.

Pagelow, M. D. (1979). Research on woman battering. In J. B. Fleming (Ed.), *Stopping wife abuse.* Garden City, NY: Anchor Press.

Paige, K. E., & Paige, J. M. (1981). *Politics and reproductive rituals.* Berkeley, CA: University of California Press.

Palkovitz, R. (1985). Father's birth attendance, early contact and extended contact with their newborns: A critical review. *Child Development. 56*(2), 392–406.

Palmore, E. (1981). *Social patterns in normal aging: Findings from the Duke longitudinal study.* Durham, NC: Duke University Press.

Palmore, E., Burchett, B., Fillenbaum, G., George, L., & Wallman, L. (1985). *Retirement: Causes and consequences.* New York: Springer.

Palmore, E., & Cleveland, W. (1976). Aging, terminal decline and the terminal drop. *Journal of Gerontology, 31,* 76–81.

Palmore, E. B. (1984). *Handbook on the aged in the United States.* Westport, CT: Greenwood Press.

Panek, P. E., Barrett, G. V., Sterns, H. L., & Alexander, R. A. (1978). Age differences in perceptual style, selective attention, and perceptual-motor reaction time. *Experimental Aging Research, 4,* 377–387.

Papalia, D. E. (1972). The status of several conservation abilities across the life span. *Human Development, 15,* 229–243.

Papalia, D. E., & Bielby, D. (1974). Cognitive functioning in middle- and old-age adults: A review of research based on Piaget's theory. *Human Development, 17,* 424–443.

Papousek, H., & Bernstein, P. (1969). The functioning of conditioning stimulation in human neonates and infants. In A. Ambrose (Ed.), *Stimulation in early infancy.* New York: Academic Press.

Parents on the brink of child abuse get crisis aid. (1983, April 17). *New York Times,* 1983, pp. 1, 29.

Parish, W., Hao, L., & Hogan, D. (1991). Family support networks, welfare, and work among young mothers. *Journal of Marriage and the Family, 53,* 203–215.

Park, D., Puglisi, J., & Smith, A. (1986). Memory for pictures. *Psychology and Aging, 1,* 11–17.

Parke, R. (1979). Father-infant interaction and infant social responsiveness. In J. Osofsky (Ed.), *The handbook of infant development.* New York: Wiley.

Parke, R., & Lewis, N. (1980). The family in context: A multilevel interactional analysis of child abuse. In R. W. Henderson (Ed.), *Parent-child interaction: Theory, research and prospect.* New York: Academic Press.

Parke, R., & Sawin, D. (1980). The family in early infancy: Social interactional and attitudinal analysis. In F. A. Pedersen (Ed.), *The father-infant relationship: Observational studies in a family setting.* New York: Praeger.

Parke, R., & Slaby, R. (1983). Aggression: A multilevel analysis. In E. M. Hetherington (Ed.), *Handbook of child psychology: Socialization, personality and social development* (4th ed.). New York: Wiley.

Parke, R. D. (1977). Punishment in children: Effects, side effects, and alternative strategies. In Harry L. Horn, Jr., and Paul Robinson (Eds.),

Psychological processes in early education. New York: Academic Press.

Parke, R. D., & Tinsley, B. J. (1987). Family interaction in infancy. In J. D. Osofsky (Ed.), *Handbook of infant development* (2nd ed.). New York: Wiley.

Parker, J., & Asher, S. (1987). Peer relations and later personal adjustment: Are low accepted children "at risk"? *Psychological Bulletin, 102,* 357–389.

Parker, J., & Asher, S. (1993). Friendship and friendship quality in middle childhood: Links with peer group acceptance and feelings of loneliness and social dissatisfaction. *Developmental Psychology, 29,* 611–621.

Parkes, C. M. (1970). The first year of bereavement: A longitudinal study of the reaction of London widows to the death of their husbands. *Psychiatry, 33,* 444–467.

Parkes, C. M. (1972). *Bereavement.* London: Tavistock.

Parmelee, A. H., & Stern, E. S. (1972). Development of states in infants. In C. Clemente, D. Purpura, & F. Mayer (Eds.), *Sleep in the maturing nervous system.* New York: Academic Press.

Parpal, M., & Maccoby, E. (1985). Maternal responsiveness and subsequent child compliance. *Child Development, 56,* 1326–1334.

Parten, M. (1932). Social play among preschool children. *Journal of Abnormal and Social Psychology, 27,* 243–269.

Patterson, C. J. (1994, April). Lesbian and gay families. *Current Directions in Psycholgical Science, 3,* 62–64.

Patterson, C. J. (1995). Sexual orientation and human development: An overview. *American Psychologist, 31,* 3–11.

Patterson, G. (1980). Mothers: The unacknowledged victims. *Monographs of the Society for Research in Child Development, 45*(5, Serial No. 186).

Patterson, G., DeBaryshe, B., & Ramsey, E. (1989). A developmental perspective on antisocial behavior. *American Psychologist, 44,* 329–335.

Patterson, G., & Stouthamer-Loeber, M. (1984). The correlation of family management practices and delinquency. *Child Development, 55,* 1299–1307.

Pattison, E. (1977). Death through the life cycle. In E. Pattison (Ed.), *The experience of dying.* Englewood Cliffs, NJ: Prentice-Hall.

Peal, E., & Lambert, W. (1962). The relation of bilingualism to intelligence. *Psychological Monographs, 76* (Whole No. 546), 1–23.

Pearce, K., & Denney, N. (1984). A lifespan study of classification preference. *Journal of Gerontology, 39,* 458–464.

Pearson, J., Hunter, A., Ensminger, M., & Kellam, S. (1990). Black grandmothers in multigenerational households: Diversity in family structure and parenting involvement in the Woodlawn community. *Child Development, 61,* 434–442.

Peck, R. (1968). Psychological development in the second half of life. In B. L. Neugarten (Ed.), *Middle age and aging.* Chicago: University of Chicago Press.

Pelton, L. (1978). Child abuse and neglect: The myth of classlessness. *American Journal of Orthopsychiatry, 48,* 608–617.

Pemberton, E. F. (1990). Systematic errors in children's drawings. *Cognitive Development, 5,* 395–404.

Perlmutter, M., & List, J. (1982). Learning in later adulthood. In T. Field, A. Huston, H. Quay, L. Troll, & G. Finley (Eds.), *Review of human development.* New York: Wiley.

Perry, W. (1970). *Forms of intellectual and ethical development in the college years.* New York: Holt, Rinehart & Winston.

Perry, W. (1981). Cognitive and ethical growth: The making of meaning. In A. Chickering (Ed.), *The modern American college.* San Francisco: Jossey-Bass.

Peskin, H. (1973). Influence of the developmental schedule of puberty on learning and ego functioning. *Journal of Youth and Adolescence, 2,* 273–290.

Peterson, A. (1987). Those gangly years. *Psychology Today, 21,* 28–34.

Peterson, A. C. (1979). Female pubertal development. In M. Sugar (Ed.), *Female adolescent development.* New York: Brunner/Mazel.

Pfeiffer, E. (1977). Psychopathology and social pathology. In J. E. Birren & K. W. Schaie (Eds.), *Handbook of the psychology of aging.* New York: Van Nostrand Reinhold.

Pfeiffer, E., Verwoerdt, A., & Davis, G. C. (1972). Sexual behavior in middle life. *American Journal of Psychiatry, 128,* 82–87.

Phelps, K. E., & Woolley, J. D. (1994). The form and function of young children's magical beliefs. *Developmental Psychology, 30,* 385–394.

Philblad, C., & Adams, D. (1972). Widowhood, social participation, and life satisfaction. *International Journal of Aging and Human Development, 3,* 323–330.

Phillips, D. A., Voran, M., Kisker, E., Howes, C., & Whitebook, M. (1994). Child care for children in poverty: Opportunity or inequity? *Child Development, 65,* 472–492.

Phillips, J. (1981). *Piaget's theory: A primer.* San Francisco: Freeman.

Phinney, V., Jensen, L., Olsen, J., & Cundick. (1990). The relationship between early development and psychosexual behaviors in adolescent females. *Adolescence, 25,* 322–332.

Piaget, J. (1926). *The language of the child* (M. Warden, Trans.). New York: Harcourt.

Piaget, J. (1929). *The child's conception of the world.* New York: Harcourt & Brace.

Piaget, J. (1952a). *The child's conception of number.* New York: Humanities.

Piaget, J. (1952b). *The origins of intelligence in children.* New York: International Universities Press.

Piaget, J. (1959). *The language and thought of the child* (3rd ed.). London: Routledge, Kegan Paul.

Piaget, J. (1965). *The moral judgment of the child.* New York: Free Press.

Piaget, J. (1967). *The child's conception of the world.* Totowa, NJ: Littlefield, Adams.

Piaget, J. (1969). *Psychology of intelligence.* Totowa, NJ: Littlefield, Adams.

Piaget, J. (1970a). The definition of stages of development. In J. Tanner & B. Inhelder (Eds.), *Discussions on child development* (Vol. 4). New York: International Universities Press.

Piaget, J. (1970b). Piaget's theory. In P. Mussen (Ed.), *Carmichael's manual of child psychology* (Vol. 1). New York: Wiley.

Piaget, J. (1971). *The child's conception of time* (A. J. Pomerans, Trans.). New York: Ballantine Books. (Original work published 1927)

Piaget, J. (1972). Intellectual evolution from adolescence to adulthood. *Human Development, 15,* 1–12.

Piaget, J., & Inhelder, B. (1969). *Psychology of the child.* New York: Basic Books.

Picariello, M., Greenberg, D., & Pillemer, D. (1990). Children's sex-related stereotyping of colors. *Child Development, 61,* 1453–1460.

Pickens, J., & Field, T. (1993). Facial expressivity in infants of depressed mothers. *Developmental Psychology, 29,* 986–988.

Piers, E. (1977). Children's self-esteem, level of esteem certainty, and responsibility for success and failure. *Journal of Genetic Psychology, 130,* 295–304.

Piers, E., & Harris, D. (1969). *The Piers-Harris children's self-concept scale.* Nashville, TN: Counselor Recordings & Tests.

Pilkington, N. W., & D'Augelli, A. R. (In press). Victimization of lesbian, gay, and bisexual youth in community settings. *Journal of Community Psychology.*

Pineo, P. C. (1961). Disenchantment in the later years of marriage. *Marriage and Family Living, 23,* 3–11.

Pleck, J., & Rustad, M. (1980). *Husbands' and wives' time in family work and paid work in the 1975–76 study of time use.* Wellesley, MA: Wellesley College Research Center on Women.

Pleck, J., Sonesnstein, F., & Swain, S. (1988). Adolescent males' sexual behavior and contraceptive use: Implications for male responsibility. *Journal of Adolescent Research, 3,* 275–284.

Pleck, J. H. (1977). The work-family role system. *Social Problems, 24,* 417–427.

Pleck, J. H. (1979). Men's family work: Three perspectives and some new data. *The Family Coordinator, 28,* 481–487.

Plomin, R. (1989). Environment and genes: Determinants of behavior. *American Psychologist, 44,* 105–111.

Plomin, R., & DeFries, J. C. (1980). Genetics and intelligence: Recent data. *Intelligence, 4,* 15–24.

Plomin, R., & Neiderhiser, J. (1992). Genetics and experience. *Current Directions in Psycholgical Science, 1,* 160–163.

Pohlman, E. (1970). Childlessness, intentional and unintentional: Psychological and social aspects. *Journal of Nervous and Mental Disease, 151,* 2–12.

Polivy, J., & Herman, C. (1985). Dieting and binging: A causal analysis. *American Psychologist, 40,* 193–201.

Pollit, E., Gorman, K. S., Engle, P. L., Martorell, R., & Rivera, J. (1993). Early supplemental feeding and cognition: Effects over two decades. *Monograph of the Society for Research in Child Development, 58* (7, Serial No. 235).

Pope, H. G., Jr., Hudson, J., Yurgelun-Todd, D., & Hudson, M. (1984). Prevalence of anorexia nervosa and bulimia in three student populations. *International Journal of Eating Disorders, 3,* 45–51.

Population Institute. (1978). *The youth values project: An inquiry conducted by teenagers themselves, into the attitudes, values, and experiences of teenagers in New York City regarding sex, contraception, and their life goals.* Washington, DC: Author.

Porter, F. L., Porges, S. W., & Marshall, R. E. (1988). Newborn pain cries and vagal tones:

Parallel changes in response to circumcision. *Child Development, 59*, 495–505.

Posner, J. (1979). It's all in your head: Feminist and medical models of menopause (strange bedfellows). *Sex Roles, 5*, 179–190.

Powell, G. (1985). Self concepts among Afro-American students in racially isolated minority schools: Some regional differences. *Journal of the American Academy of Child Psychiatry, 24*, 142–149.

Powell, R. R. (1974). Psychological effects of exercise therapy upon institutionalized geriatric mental patients. *Journal of Gerontology, 29*, 157–161.

Power, T., & Parke, R. (1983). Patterns of mother and father play with their eight-month-old infant: A multiple analysis approach. *Infant Behavior and Development, 6*, 453–459.

Powers, E., Bultena, G. (1976). Sex differences in intimate friendships in college. *Journal of Marriage and the Family, 38*, 739–747.

Powers, S., Hauser, S., & Kilner, L. (1989). Adolescent mental health. *American Psychologist, 44*, 200–208.

President's Science Advisory Committee. (1974). *Youth: Transition to adulthood.* Chicago: University of Chicago Press.

Presser, H. (1978). Social factors affecting the timing of the first child. In W. Miller & F. Newman (Eds.), *The first child and family formation.* Chapel Hill: Carolina Population Center.

Pressey, S., Janey, T., & Kuhlen, R. (1939). *Life: A psychological survey.* New York: Harper.

Price-Williams, D. (1961). A study concerning concepts of conservation of quantities among primitive children. *Acta Psychologica, 18*, 293–305.

Price-Williams, D. (1981). Concrete and formal operation. In R. Munroe, R. Munroe, & B. Whiting (Eds.), *Handbook of cross-cultural human development.* New York: Garland STPM Press.

Puig-Antich, J., Greenhill, L., Sassin, J., & Sachar, E. (1978). Growth hormone prolactin and cortisol responses and growth patterns in hyperkinetic children treated with dextroamphetamine: Preliminary findings. *Journal of American Academy of Child Psychiatry, 17*, 457–475.

Putallaz, M. (1983). Predicting children's sociometric status from their behavior. *Child Development, 54*, 1417–1426.

Putallaz, M., & Sheppard, B. H. (1990). Social status and children's orientations to limited resources. *Child Development, 61*, 2022–2027.

Putallaz, M., & Wasserman, A. (1989). Children's naturalistic entry behavior and sociometric status: A developmental perspective. *Developmental Psychology, 25*, 297–305.

Quadrel, M. J., Fischhoff, B., & Davis, W. (1993, February). Adolescent (in)vulnerability. *American Psychologist, 48*, 102–116.

Quay, H. C. (1982). Adolescent aggression. In T. Field, A. Huston, H. C. Quay, L. Troll, & G. E. Finley (Eds.), *Review of human development.* New York: Wiley-Interscience.

Quindlen, A. (1977, November 28). Relationships: Independence vs. intimacy. *New York Times*, p. 36.

Quinn, M. (1987). Elder abuse and neglect. In G. L. Maddox (Ed.), *The encyclopedia of aging.* New York: Springer.

Quinn, M., & Tomita, S. (1986). *Elder abuse and neglect: Causes, diagnosis, and intervention strategies.* New York: Springer.

Quinn, R., Staines, G., & McCullough, M. (1974). *Job satisfaction: Is there a trend?* (U.S. Department of Labor, Manpower, and Research Monograph No. 30). Washington, DC: U.S. Government Printing Office.

Rabiner, D., & Coie, J. (1989). Effect of expectancy inductions on rejected children's acceptance by unfamiliar peers. *Developmental Psychology, 25*, 297–305.

Rabiner, D. L., Keane, S. P., & MacKinnon-Lewis, C. (1993). Children's beliefs about familiar and unfamiliar peers in relation to their sociometric status. *Developmental Psychology, 29*, 236–243.

Racine, A., Joyce, T, & Grossman, M. (1992). Effectiveness of health care services for pregnant women and infants. *The Future of Children, 2*, 40–57.

Rader, N., Bausano, M., & Richards, J. (1980). On the nature of the visual-cliff-avoidance response in human infants. *Child Development, 51*, 61–68.

Radke-Yarrow, M., Cummings, E. M., Kuczynski, L., & Chapman, M. (1985). Patterns of attachment in two- and three-year-olds in normal families and families with parental depression. *Child Development, 56*, 884–893.

Ragland, O., & Brand, R. (1988). Type A behavior and mortality from coronary heart disease. *New England Journal of Medicine, 318*, 65–69.

Rahe, H., Mahan, J., & Arthur, R. J. (1970). Prediction of near future health change from subjects preceding life change. *Journal of Psychosomatic Research, 14*, 401–406.

Ramey, C., & Mills, P. (1977). Social and intellectual consequences of day care for high-risk infants. In R. Webb (Ed.), *Social development in childhood: Day care programs and research.* Baltimore, MD: Johns Hopkins University Press.

Ramey, C., & Smith, B. (1977). Assessing the intellectual consequence of early intervention with high-risk infants. *American Journal of Mental Deficiency, 81*, 318–324.

Ramsay, D. S., Campos, J. J., & Fenson, L. (1979). Onset of bimanual handedness in infants. *Infant Behavior and Development, 2*, 69–76.

Rando, T. (1983). An investigation of grief and adaptation in parents whose children have died from cancer. *Journal of Pediatric Psychology, 8*, 3–20.

Rapoport, R., & Rapoport, R. (1976). *Dual-career families re-examined: New integrations of work and family.* New York: Hoper-Colophon.

Rathus, S. A. (1983). *Human sexuality.* New York: Holt, Rinehart & Winston.

Read, M. (1968). *Children of their fathers: Growing up among the Ngoni of Malawi.* New York: Holt, Rinehart & Winston.

Reader, J. (1988). *Man on Earth: A celebration of mankind,* New York: Harper & Row.

Reaves, J., & Roberts, A. (1983). The effects of the type of information on children's attraction to peers. *Child Development, 54*, 1024–1031.

Rebok, G. (1987). *Life-span cognitive development.* New York: Holt, Rinehart & Winston.

Reedy, M. N., Birren, J. E., & Schaie, K. W. (1981). Age and sex differences in satisfying love relationships across the adult life span. *Human Development, 24*, 52–66.

Reese, H. W., & Overton, W. F. (1970). Models of development and theories of development. In L. R. Goulet & P. B. Baltes (Eds.), *Lifespan developmental psychology: Theory and research.* New York: Academic Press.

Regan, M., & Roland, H. (1985). Rearranging family and career priorities: Professional women and men of the eighties. *Journal of Marriage and the Family, 47*, 985–992.

Reichard, S., Livson, F., & Peterson, P. (1962). Adjustment to retirement. In B. Neugarten (Ed.), *Middle age and aging.* Chicago: University of Chicago Press.

Reid, P. T. (1993). Poor women in psychological research. *Psychology of Women Quarterly, 17*, 133–150.

Reilly, T., Hasazi, J., & Bond, L. (1983). Children's conceptions of death and personal mortality. *Journal of Pediatric Psychology, 8*, 21–31.

Reinert, G. (1979). Prolegomena to a history of life-span developmental psychology. In P. B. Baltes & O. G. Brim (Eds.), *Life-span development and behavior* (Vol. 2). New York: Academic Press.

Reinisch, J. (1981). Prenatal exposure to synthetic progesterone increases potential for aggression in humans. *Science, 211*, 1171–1173.

Reis, H. T., Lin, Y., Bennett, E., & Nezlek, J. B. (1993). Change and consistency in social participation during early adulthood. *Developmental Psychology, 29*, 633–645.

Reisberg, B. (1981). *Brain failure: An introduction to current concepts of senility.* New York: Macmillan.

Reisman, J. (1981). Adult friendships. In S. Duck & R. Gilmour (Eds.), *Personal relationships: Vol. 2. Developing personal relationships.* New York: Academic Press.

Reiss, I. L. (1980). *Family systems in America* (3rd ed.). New York: Holt, Rinehart & Winston.

Reissland, N. (1988). Neonatal imitation in the first hour of life: Observations in rural Nepal. *Developmental Psychology, 24*, 464–469.

Remafedi, G. (1987). Male homosexuality: The adolescent's perspective. *Pediatrics, 79*, 326–330.

Renick, M.J., & Harter, S. (1989). Impact of social comparison on the developing self perceptions of learning disabled students. *Journal of Educational Psychology, 81*, 631–638.

Repetti, R. Matthews, K., & Waldron, I. (1989). *American Psychologist, 44*, 1394–1401.

Reschly, D. (1981). Psychological testing in educational classification and placement. *American Psychologist, 36*, 1094–1102.

Rest, J. (1983). Morality. In P. H. Mussen (Ed.), *Handbook of child psychology: Cognitive development* (4th ed., Vol. 3). New York: Wiley.

Rest, J., & Thoma, S. (1985). Relation of moral judgment development to formal education. *Developmental Psychology, 21*, 709–714.

Rest, J. R., Turiel, E., & Kohlberg, L. (1969). Relations between level of moral judgement and preference and comprehension of the moral judgement of others. *Journal of Personality, 37*, 225–252.

Rexroat, C., & Shehan, C. (1987). The family life cycle and spouses' time in housework. *Journal of Marriage and the Family, 49*, 737–750.

Rhodes, S. R. (1983). Age-related differences in work attitudes and behavior: A review and conceptual analysis. *Psychological Bulletin, 93*, 329–367.

Rholes, W., & Ruble, D. (1984). Children's understanding of dispositional characteristics of others. *Child Development, 55,* 550–560.

Ricciardelli, L. A. (1992). Bilingualism and cognitive development: Relation to threshold theory. *Journal of Psycholinguistic Research, 21,* 301–316.

Riccuiti, H. N. (1993). Nutrition and mental development. *Current Directions in Psycholgical Science, 2,* 43–46.

Rice, M. (1983). The role of television in language acquisition. *Developmental Review, 3,* 221–224.

Rice, M. (1989). Children's language acquisition. *American Psychologist, 44,* 149–156.

Richards, M. P. M., & Bernal, J. F. (1971). Social interactions in the first few days of life. In H. Schaffer (Ed.), *The origins of human social relations.* New York: Academic Press.

Richards, M. H., & Duckett, E. (1994). The relationship of maternal employment to early adolescent daily experience with and without parents. *Child Development, 65,* 225–236.

Richardson, D. W., & Short, R. V. (1978). Time of onset of sperm production in boys. *Journal of Biosocial Science, 5,* 15–25.

Rickards, L., Zuckerman, D., & West, P. (1985). Alzheimer's disease: Current congressional response. *American Psychologist, 40,* 1256–1261.

Ricks, M. (1985). The social transmission of parental behavior: Attachment across generations. In I. Bretherton & E. Waters (Eds.), *Growing points of attachment theory and research, Monographs of the Society for Research in Child Development, 50*(1–2, Serial No. 209).

Riegel, K. (1984). In M. L. Commons, F. A. Richards, & C. Armon (Eds.), *Beyond formal operations: Late adolescence and adult cognitive development.* New York: Praeger.

Riegel, K. F. (1973a). Developmental psychology and society: Some historical and ethical considerations. In J. R. Nesselroade & H. W. Reese (Eds.), *Life-span developmental psychology: Methodological issues.* New York: Academic Press.

Riegel, K. F. (1973b). Dialectic operations: The final period of cognitive development. *Human Development, 16,* 346–370.

Riegel, K. F. (1975). Adult life crises: A dialectical interpretation of development. In N. Datan & L. H. Ginsberg (Eds.), *Lifespan developmental psychology: Normative life crises.* New York: Academic Press.

Riegel, K. F., & Riegel, R. (1972). Development, drop and death. *Developmental Psychology, 6,* 306–319.

Riger, S. (1992). Epistemological debates, feminist voices: Science, social values, and the study of women. *American Psychologist, 47,* 730–740.

Riley, M. W., Riley, J. W., Jr., & Johnson, M. F. (1968). *Aging and society: Vol. 1. An inventory of research findings.* New York: Russell Sage.

Ring, K. (1980). *Life at death.* New York: Coward, McCann & Geoghegan.

Ring, K. (1984). *Heading toward omega.* New York: Coward, McCann & Co.

Ring, K. (1989). Near-death experiences. In R. Kastenbaum & B.K. Kastenbaum (Eds.), *Encyclopedia of Death.* Phoenix, AZ: Oryx Press.

Ring, K., & Franklin, S. Do suicide survivors report near death experiences? *Omega, 12,* 181–182, 191–208.

Ringness, T. A. (1967). Identification patterns, motivation, and school achievement of bright junior high school boys. *Journal of Educational Psychology, 58,* 93–102.

Ritchie, R., & Moses, J. (1983). Assessment center correlates of women's advancement into middle management: A seven-year longitudinal analysis. *Journal of Applied Psychology, 68,* 227–231.

Ritter, J., Casey, R., & Langlois, J. (1991). Adults' responses to infants varying in appearance of age and attractiveness. *Child Development, 62,* 68–82.

Robbins, D. R., Alessi, N. E., Cook, S. C., Poznanski, E. O., & Yanchyshyn, G. W. (1982). The use of the research diagnostic criteria (RDC) for depression in adolescent psychiatric inpatients. *Journal of the American Academy of Child Psychiatry, 21,* 251–255.

Roberts, L. (1991). Report card on the genome project. *Science, 253,* 376.

Roberts, P., & Newton, P. M. (1987). Levinsonian studies of women's adult development. *Psychology and Aging, 2,* 154–163.

Robertson, J. F. (1977). Grandparenthood: A study of role conceptions. *Journal of Marriage and the Family, 34,* 165–174.

Robins, L. N. (1978). Sturdy childhood predictors of adult antisocial behavior: Replications from longitudinal studies. *Psychological Medicine, 8,* 611–622.

Robins, L. N. (1991). Conduct disorders. *Journal of Child Psychology and Psychiatry, 32,* 193–212.

Robinson, I., Ziss, K., Ganza, B., & Katz, S. (1991). Twenty years of the sexual revolution, 1965–1985: An update. *Journal of Marriage and the Family, 53,* 216–220.

Robinson, J. L., Kagan, J., Reznick, J. S., & Corley, R. (1992). The heritability of inhibited and uninhibited behavior: A twin study. *Developmental Psychology, 28,* 1030–1037.

Roche, A. F. (1979). Secular trends in stature, weight, and maturation. In A. F. Roche (Ed.), *Secular trends in growth, maturation, and development of children. Monographs of the Society for Research in Child Development, 44* (No. 3–4, Serial No. 179), 3–27.

Roche, A. F. (1981). The adipocyte-number hypothesis. *Child Development, 52,* 31–43.

Roche, A. F., & Davila, G. H. (1972). Late adolescent growth in stature. *Pediatrics, 50,* 874–880.

Rockstein, M., & Sussman, M. (1979). *Biology of aging.* Belmont, CA: Wadsworth.

Rodeheaver, D., & Datan (W. (1988). The challenge of double jeopardy: toward a mental health agenda for aging women. *American Psychologist, 43,* 648–654.

Rodger, J., & Rowe, D. (1988). Influence of siblings on adolescent sexual behavior. *Developmental Psychology, 24,* 722–728.

Rodgers, W., & Thornton, A. (1985). Changing patterns of first marriage in the United States. *Demography, 22,* 265–279.

Rodin, J., & Ickovics, J. (1990). Women's health: Review and research agenda as we approach the 21st century. *American Psychologist, 45,* 1018–1034.

Rodin, J., & Langer, E. J. (1977). Long-term effects of a control-relevant intervention with the institutionalized aged. *Journal of Personality and Social Psychology, 35,* 897–902.

Rodin, J., Striegel-Moore, R., & Silberstein. L. (1986). *A prospective study of bulimia among college students on three U.S. campuses* (First unpublished progress report). New Haven, CT: Yale University.

Rogoff, B., & Morelli, G. (1989). Perspectives on children's development from cultural psychology. *American Psychologist, 44,* 343–348.

Rogoff, B., & Waddell, K. (1982). Memory for information organized in a scene by children from two cultures. *Child Development, 53,* 1224–1228.

Rollins, B. C., & Feldman, H. (1970). Marital satisfaction over the family life-cycle. *Journal of Marriage and the Family, 32,* 20–37.

Rollins, J., & White, P. (1982). The relationship between mothers' and daughters' sex role attitudes and self concepts in three types of family environment. *Sex Roles, 8,* 1141–1155.

Romaniuk, J., & Romaniuk, M. (1981). Creativity across the life span: A measurement perspective. *Human Development, 24,* 366–381.

Romaniuk, J., & Romaniuk, M. (1982). Participation motives of older adults in higher education: The Elderhostel experience. *Gerontologist, 22,* 364–368.

Romaniuk, M., McAuley, W. J., & Arling, G. (1983). An examination of the prevalence of mental disorders among the elderly in the community. *Journal of Abnormal Psychology, 92,* 458–467.

Roosa, M. (1984). Maternal age, social class, and the obstetric performance of teenagers. *Journal of Youth and Adolescence, 13,* 365–374.

Roscoe, B., & Kruger, T. (1990). AIDS: Late adolescents' knowledge and its influence on sexual behavior. *Adolescence, 25,* 39–48.

Rose, R. M., & Abplanalp, J. M. (1983, June). The premenstrual syndrome. *Hospital Practice,* 129–141.

Rosen, B. C., & Aneshensel, C. S. (1978). Sex differences in the educational-occupational expectation process. *Journal of Social Forces, 57,* 164–186.

Rosen, E. (1991). Jewish families. In F. Walsh & M. McGoldrick (Eds.), *Living beyond loss: Death in the family.* New York: Norton.

Rosenbaum, M. B. (1979). The changing body image of the adolescent girl. In M. Sugar (Ed.), *Female adolescent development.* New York: Brunner/Mazel.

Rosenberg, H. (1990). Complaint discourse, aging and caregiving among the !Kung San of Botswana. In J. Sokolovsky (Ed.), *The cultural context of aging.* New York: Bergin & Garvey.

Rosenberg, M. (1965). *Society and the adolescent self-image.* Princeton, NJ: Princeton University Press.

Rosenberg, M. (1979). *Conceiving the self.* New York: Basic Books.

Rosenman, R., & Friedman, M. (1983). Relationship of type A behavior pattern to coronary heart disease. In H. Selye (Ed.), *Selye's guide to stress research* (Vol. 2). New York: Scientific and Academic Editons.

Rossi, A. S. (1968). Transitions to parenthood. *Journal of Marriage and the Family, 30,* 26–39.

Rossman, I. (1980). Bodily changes with aging. In E. W. Busse & D. G. Blazer (Eds.), *Handbook of geriatric psychiatry.* New York: Van Nostrand Reinhold.

Rovee-Collier, C. (1993). The capacity for long-term memory. *Current Directions in Psychological Science, 2,* 130–135.

Rovee-Collier, C. K. (1984). The ontogeny of learning and memory in human infancy. In R. Kail & N. E. Spear (Eds.), *Comparative perspectives on the development of memory.* Hillsdale, NJ: Erlbaum.

Rowland, K. (1979). Environmental events predicting death for the elderly. In L. Bugen (Ed.), *Death and dying: Theory, research, and practice.* Boston: W. C. Brown.

Rubin, J., Provenzano, F., & Luria, Z. (1974). The eyes of the beholder: Parents' views on sex of newborns. *American Journal of Orthopsychiatry, 44,* 512–519.

Rubin, K. (1983). Recent perspectives on social competence and peer status: Some introductory remarks. *Child Development, 54,* 1383–1385.

Rubin, K., Watson, K., & Jambor, T. (1982). Free-play behaviors in preschool and kindergarten children. *Child Development, 49,* 534–536.

Rubinstein, E. (1983). Television and behavior: Research conclusions of the 1982 NIMH Report and their policy implications. *American Psychologist, 38,* 820–825.

Ruble, D. (1977). Premenstrual symptoms: A reinterpretation. *Science, 197,* 291–292.

Ruble, D. N. (1983). The development of social comparison processes and their role in achievement-related self-socialization. In E. T. Higgins, D. N. Ruble, & W. W. Hartup (Eds.), *Social cognition and social behavior: Developmental perspectives.* New York: Cambridge University Press.

Ruble, D. N., & Brooks-Gunn, J. (1982). The experience of menarche. *Child Development, 53,* 1557–1566.

Rugh, R., & Shettles, L. (1971). *From conception to birth: The drama of life's beginnings.* New York: Harper & Row.

Runciman, A. (1975). Problems older clients present in counseling about sexuality. In I. M. Burnside (Ed.), *Sexuality and aging.* Los Angeles: University of Southern California Press.

Ruopp, R., & Travers, J. (1982). Janus faces day care: Perspective on quality and cost. In E. Zigler and E. W. Gordon (Eds.), *Day care: Scientific and social policy issues.* Boston: Auburn House.

Ruopp, R., Travers, J., Glantz, F., & Coelen, C. (1979). *Children at the center.* Cambridge, MA: Abt Associates.

Rupley, W., Garcia, J., & Longnion, B. (1981). Sex role portrayal in reading materials: Implications for the 1980's. *The Reading Teacher, 34,* 786–791.

Russell, C. S. (1974). Transitions to parenthood: Problems and gratifications. *Journal of Marriage and the Family, 36,* 294–301.

Russell, G. (1979). Bulimia nervosa: An ominous variant of anorexia nervosa. *Psychological Medicine, 9,* 429–448.

Russell, O. (1977). *Freedom to die: Moral and legal aspects of euthanasia* (Rev. ed.). New York: Human Sciences.

Russo, N.F. (1990). Forging research priorities for women's mental health. *American Psychologist, 45,* 368–373.

Rutter, M. (1986). The developmental psychopathology of depression: Issues and perspectives. In M. Rutter, C. E. Izard, & P. B. Read (Eds.), *Depression in young people: Developmental and clinical perspectives* (pp. 3–32). New York: Guilford Press.

Rutter, M. (1979a). Proactive factors in children's responses to stress and disadvantage. In M. Kent & J. E. Rolf (Eds.), *Primary prevention of psychopathology: Vol. 3. Social competence in children.* Hanover, NH: University Press of New England.

Rutter, M., & Garmesy, N. (1983). Developmental psychopathology. In E. M. Hetherington (Ed.), *Handbook of child psychology: Vol. 4. Socialization, personality, and social development* (4th ed.). New York: Wiley.

Rutter, M., Tizard, J., & Whitmore, K. (Eds.). (1970). *Education, health, and behavior.* London: Longmans.

Rychlak, J. F. (1968). *A philosophy of science for personality theory.* Boston: Houghton Mifflin.

Ryff, C. D., Lee, Y. H., Essex, M. J., & Schmutte, P. S. (1994). My children and me: Midlife evaluations of grown children and of self. *Psychology and Aging, 9,* 195–205.

Sabom, M.B., & Kreutziger, S. (1982). Physicians evaluate the near death experience. In C. Lundahl (Ed.), *A collection of near death research readings.* Chicago: Nelson-Hall.

Sacher, G. A. (1978). Longevity, aging, and death: An evolutionary perspective. *Gerontologist, 18,* 112–119.

Safier, G. (1964). A study in relationships between life and death concepts in children. *Journal of Genetic Psychology, 105,* 283–294.

Sagar, H. A., Schofield, J., & Snyder, H. (1983). Race and gender barriers: Preadolescent peer behavior in academic classrooms. *Child Development, 54,* 1032–1040.

Salkind, N., & Nelson, C. (1980). A note on the development of reflection-impulsivity. *Developmental Psychology, 16,* 237–238.

Sallade, J. B. (1973). A comparison of psychological adjustment of obese vs. non-obese children. *Journal of Psychosomatic Research, 17,* 89–96.

Salthouse, T. (1982). *Adult cognition: An experimental psychology of human aging.* New York: Springer-Verlag.

Salthouse, T. A. (1990). Working memory as a processing resource in cognitive aging. *Developmental Review, 10,* 101–104.

Salthouse, T. A. (1991). Mediation of adult age differences in cognition by reductions in working memory and speed of processing. *Psychological Science, 2,* 179–183.

Salthouse, T. A. (1992). Why do adult age differences increase with task complexity? *Developmental Psychology, 28,* 905–918.

Sameroff, A. (1983). Developmental systems: Contexts and evaluation. In P. H. Mussen (Ed.), *Handbook of child psychology: Vol. 1. History, theory and methods.* New York: Wiley.

Sameroff, A. J., & Cavanagh, P. J. (1979). Learning in infancy: A developmental perspective. In J. D. Osofsky (Ed.), *Handbook of infant development.* New York: Wiley.

Santelli, J. S., & Beilenson, P. (1992). Risk factors for adolescent sexual behavior, fertility, and sexually transmitted diseases. *Journal of School Health, 62,* 271–279.

Santrock, J. (1972). The relation of type and onset of father absence to cognitive development. *Child Development, 43,* 455–469.

Santrock, J., & Tracy, R. (1978). Effects of children's family structure status on the developmental stereotypes by children. *Journal of Educational Psychology, 70,* 754–757.

Santrock, J., & Warshak, R. (1979). Father custody and social development in boys and girls. *Journal of Social Issues, 35,* 112–125.

Santrock, J., Warshak, R., Lindberg, V., & Meadows, L. (1982). Children's and parents' observed social behavior in stepfather families. *Child Development, 53,* 471–480.

Sants, H. J. (1964). Genealogical bewilderment in children with substitute parents. *British Journal of Medical Psychology, 37,* 133–141.

Satir, V. (1967). *Conjoint family therapy* (Rev. ed.). Palo Alto, CA: Science and Behavior Books, Inc.

Sauter, S., Murphy, L., & Hurrell, J. (1990). Prevention of work-related psychological disorders: A national strategy proposed by the National Institute for Occupational Safety and Health CN10S4. *American Psychologist, 45,* 1146–1158.

Savin-Williams, R. C. (1980). Social interactions of adolescent females in natural groups. In H. C. Foot, A. J. Chapman, & J. R. Smith (Eds.), *Friendship and social relations in children.* New York: Wiley.

Savin-Williams, R. C. (1990). *Gay and lesbian youth: Expressions of identity.* New York: Hemisphere.

Savin-Williams, R., & Demo, D. (1984). Developmental change and stability in adolescent self concept. *Developmental Psychology, 20,* 1100–1110.

Scales, P. (1981). Sex education and the prevention of teenage pregnancy: An overview of policies and programs in the United States. In T. Ooms (Ed.), *Teenage pregnancy in family context: Implications for policy.* Philadelphia: (pp. 213–254). Temple University Press.

Scanlon, J. (1979). *Young adulthood.* New York: Academy for Educational Development.

Scanzoni, J. (1975). *Sex role, life styles, and childbearing.* New York: Free Press, 1975.

Scanzoni, J. (1980). Contemporary marriage types: A research note. *Journal of Family Issues, 1,* 125–140.

Scarr, S. (1984). *Mother care/other care.* New York: Basic Books.

Schacter, D., & Moscovitch, M. (1984). Infants, amnesics, and dissociable memory systems. In M. Moscovitch (Ed.), *Infant memory.* New York: Plenum.

Schacter, D., Moscovitch, M., Tulving, E., McLachlan, D., & Freedman, M. (1986). Mnemonic precedence in amnesic patients: An analogue of the AB error in infants? *Child Development, 57,* 816–823.

Schaefer, R., & Bayley, N. (1963). Maternal behavior, child behavior and their intercorrelations from infancy through adolescence. *Monographs of the Society for Research in Child Development, 28*(3, Whole No. 87).

Schafer, W. (1987). *Stress management for wellness.* New York: Holt, Rinehart & Winston.

Schaffer, R. (1977). *Mothering.* Cambridge, MA: Harvard University Press.

Schaie, K. W. (1974). Transitions in gerontology—from lab to life: Intellectual functioning. *American Psychologist, 29,* 802–807.

Schaie, K. W. (1979). The primary mental abilities in adulthood: An exploration in the development of psychometric intelligence. In P. B. Baltes & O. G. Brim, Jr. (Eds.), *Lifespan development and behavior* (Vol. 3, pp. 67–115). New York: Academic Press.

Schaie, K. W. (1988). Ageism in psychological research. *American Psychologist, 43,* 179–183.

Schaie, K. W. (1989). Individual differences in the rate of cognitive change in adulthood. In Vern L. Bengston and K. Warner Schaie (Eds.), *The course of later life.* New York: Springer.

Schaie, K. W. (1994, April). The course of adult intellectual development. *American Psychologist, 49,* 304–313.

Schaie, K. W. (Ed.). (1983). *Longitudinal studies of adult psychological development.* New York: Guilford Press.

Schaie, K. W., & Hertzog, C. (1982). Longitudinal methods. In B. Wolman (Ed.), *Handbook of developmental psychology.* Englewood Cliffs, NJ: Prentice-Hall.

Schaie, K. W., & Hertzog, C. (1983). Fourteen-year cohort-sequential analyses of adult intellectual development. *Developmental Psychology, 19,* 531–543.

Schaie, K. W., & Parham, I. A. (1976). Stability of adult personality: Fact or fable? *Journal of Personality and Social Psychology, 34,* 146–158.

Schaie, K. W., & Willis, S. L. (1993). Age difference patterns of psychometric intelligence in adulthood: Generalizability within and across ability domains. *Psychology and Aging, 8,* 44–55.

Schiedel, D. G., & Marcia, J. E. (1985). Ego identity, intimacy, sex role orientation, and gender. *Developmental Psychology, 21,* 149–160.

Schmeck, H. (1983, October 18). Fetal defects discovered early by new method. *New York Times,* p. C1.

Schmidt, D., & Boland, S. (1986). Structure of perceptions of older adults: Evidence for multiple stereotypes. *Psychology and Aging, 1,* 255–260.

Schoen, R., & Nelson, V. E. (1974). Marriage, divorce, and mortality: A life table analysis. *Demography, 11,* 267–290.

Schram, R. W. (1979). Marital satisfaction over the family life-cycle: A critique and proposal. *Journal of Marriage and the Family, 41,* 7–40.

Schulman, S. (1986). Facing the invisible handicap. *Psychology Today, 20*(2), 58–64.

Schultz, N. R., Jr., Kaye, D. B., & Hoyer, W. J. (1980). Intelligence and spontaneous flexibility in adulthood and old age. *Intelligence, 4,* 219–231.

Schulz, D. A. (1972). *The changing family: Its function and future.* Englewood Cliffs, NJ: Prentice-Hall.

Schulz, R. (1978). *The psychology of death, dying and bereavement.* New York: Addison-Wesley.

Schulz, R., & Brenner, A. (1977). Relocation in the aged: A review and theoretical analysis. *Journal of Gerontology, 32,* 323–333.

Schutter, S., & Brinker, R. (1992). Conjuring a new category of disability from prenatal cocaine exposure: Are the infants unique biological or caretaking casualities? *Topics in Early Childhood Special Education, 11,* 84–11.

Schwebel, M. (1982). Effects of the nuclear war threat on children and teenagers: Implications for professionals. *American Journal of Orthopsychiatry, 52,* 608–617.

Scott, J. (1983). Siblings and other kin. In T. Brubaker (Ed.), *Family relationships in later life.* Beverly Hills, CA: Sage Publications.

Scott-Jones, D., & Turner, S. (1988). Sex education, contraceptive and reproductive knowledge, and contraceptive use among black

adolescent females. *Journal of Adolescent Research, 3,* 171–187.

Seager, J., & Olson, A. (1986). *Women in the world: An international atlas.* New York: Simon & Schuster.

Sears, R., Maccoby, E., & Levin, H. (1957). *Patterns of child rearing.* Evanston, IL: Row Peterson.

Sears, R., Rau, L., & Alpert, R. (1965). *Identification and child rearing.* Stanford, CA: Stanford University Press.

Seavey, C., Katz, P., & Zalk, S. (1975). Baby X: The effects of gender labels on adult responses to infants. *Sex Roles. 1,* 103–109.

Seefeldt, F. M. (1979). Formal operations and adolescent painting. *The Genetic Epistemologist, 8,* 5–6.

Segal, J., & Yahraes, H. (1979). *A child's journey: Forces that shape the lives of our young.* New York: McGraw-Hill.

Seidman, E., Allen, L., Aber, J. L., Mitchell, C., & Feinman, J. (1994). The impact of school transitions in early adolescence on the self-system and perceived social context of poor urban youth. *Child Development, 65,* 507–522.

Seligman, M. (1975). Helplessness: On depression, development, and death. San Francisco: Freeman.

Seligman, M. E. P., & Peterson, C. (1983). A learned helplessness perspective on childhood depression: Theory and research. In M. Rutter, C. E. Izard, & P. Read (Eds.), *Depression in childhood: Developmental perspectives.* New York: Guilford Press.

Selman, R. (1980). *The growth of interpersonal understanding.* New York: Academic Press.

Selman, R. L. (1981). The child as a friendship philosopher: A case study in the growth of interpersonal understanding. In S. R. Asher & J. M. Gottman (Eds.), *The development of children's friendships.* Cambridge: Cambridge University Press.

Serbin, K., & Sprafkin, C. (1986). The salience of gender and the process of sex typing in three-to-seven-year-old children. *Child Development, 57,* 1188–1199.

Serbin, L., & O'Leary, K. (1975, December). How nursery schools teach girls to shut up. *Psychology Today, 9,* 56–58.

Shanas, E. (1979). Social myth as hypothesis: The case of the family relations of old people. *The Gerontologist, 19,* 3–9.

Shanas, E. (1980). Older people and their families: New pioneers. *Journal of Marriage and the Family, 42,* 9–18.

Shanas, E., & Sussman, M. (1981). The family in later life: Social structure and social policy. In R. W. Fogel, E. Hatfield, S. B. Kiesler & E. Shanas (Eds.), *Aging: Stability and change in the family.* New York: Academic Press.

Shanas, E., Townsend, P., Weddenburn, D., Friis, H., Hilhoj, P., & Strehouwer, I. (1968). *Older people in three industrial societies.* New York: Atherton.

Shantz, C. V. (1983). Social cognition. In J. H. Flavell & E. Markman (Eds.), *Handbook of child psychology: Vol. 3. Cognitive development* (4th ed.). New York: Wiley.

Sharma, A. (1992, March). *A comparison of adoptive and nonadoptive adolescents on psychological at-risk indicators.* Paper presented at the meeting of the Society for Research on Adolescents, Washington, DC.

Shapiro, D., & Crowley, J. (1982). Aspirations and expectations of youth in the United States. P. 2: Employment activity. *Youth and Society, 14,* 33–58.

Shaver, P., & Hazan, C. (1987). Being lonely, falling in love: Perspectives from attachment theory. *Journal of Social Behavior and Personality: Loneliness: Theory, research and applications* [Special issue], 2, 105–124.

Shaw, D. S., & Bell, R. Q. (1993). Developmental theories of parental contributors to antisocial behavior. *Journal of Abnormal Child Psychology, 21,* 225–249.

Shaw, D. S., Keenan, K., & Vondra, J. I. (1994). Developmental precursors of externalizing behavior: Ages 1 to 3. *Developmental Psychology, 30,* 355–364.

Shedler, J., & Block, J. (1990). Adolescent drug use and psychological health, *American Psychologist, 45,* 612–630.

Sheehy, G. (1976). Passages: Predictable crises of adult life. New York: Dutton.

Sheffield, M. (1972). *Where do babies come from?* New York: Knopf.

Sheppard, H., & Belitsky, A. (1966). *The job hunt.* Baltimore: Johns Hopkins Press.

Sherif, C. W. (1979). Bias in psychology. In J. A. Sherman & E. T. Beck (Eds.), *A prism of sex: Essays in the sociology of knowledge* (pp. 93–133). Madison: University of Wisconsin Press.

Shirley, M. (1933). The first two years: A study of twenty-five babies. *Child Welfare Monograph, 11*(7).

Shneidman, E. (1977). The college student and death. In H. Feifel (Ed.), *New meanings of death.* New York: McGrawHill.

Shock, N. W. (1977). Biological theories of aging. In J. E. Birren & K. W. Schaie (Eds.), *Handbook of the psychology of aging.* New York: Van Nostrand Reinhold.

Shucard, J. L., & Shucard, D. W. (1990). Auditory evoked potentials and hand preference in 6-month-old infants: Possible gender-related differences in cerebral organization. *Developmental Psychology, 26,* 923–930.

Sidorowicz, L., & Lunney, G. S. (1980). Baby X revisited. *Sex Roles, 6,* 67–73.

Siegel, M. (1973). Congenital malformations following chicken pox, measles, mumps and hepatitis. *Journal of American Medical Association, 226,* 1521–1524.

Siegel, O. (1982). Personality development in adolescence. In B. Wolman (Ed.), *Handbook of adolescent psychology.* Englewood Cliffs, NJ: Prentice-Hall.

Siegil, R. K. (1980). The psychology of life after death. *American Psychologist, 35,* 911–931.

Siegler, I., McCarty, S., & Logue, P. (1982). Wechsler memory scale scores, selective attrition, and distance from death. *Journal of Gerontology, 37,* 176–181.

Siegler, R. (1983). Information processing approaches to development. In P. H. Mussen (Ed.), *Handbook of child psychology: Vol. 1. History, theory and methods.* New York: Wiley.

Sigel, I. E., & Brodzinsky, D. (1977). Individual differences: A perspective for understanding intellectual development. In H. L. Hom & P. A. Robinson (Eds.), *Psychological processes in early education.* New York: Academic Press.

Sigel, R. S. (1979). Students' comprehension of democracy and its application to conflict situations. *International Journal of Political Education, 2,* 47–65.

Sigel, R. S., & Hoskin, M. B. (1981). *The political involvement of adolescents.* New Brunswick, NJ: Rutgers University Press.

Sigman, M., Neumann, C., Jansen, A., and Bwibo, N. (1989). Cognitive abilities of Kenyan children in relation to nutrition, family characteristics, and education. *Child Development, 60,* 1463–1474.

Silverberg, S., & Steinberg, L. (1990). Psychological well-being of parents with early adolescent children. *Developmental Psychology, 26,* 658–666.

Silverman, P. (1985). Widowhood and preventive intervention. In M. Bloom (Ed.), *Life span development: Bases for preventive and interventive helping* (2nd ed.). New York: Macmillan.

Silverman, W. K., Greca, A. M., & Wasserstein, S. C. (1995). What do children worry about? Worries and their relation to anxiety. *Child Development, 66,* 671–686.

Silverstein, L. B. (1991, October). Transforming the debate about child care and maternal employment. *American Psychologist, 46,* 1025–1032.

Simeonsson, R., Buckley, L., & Monson, L. (1979). Conceptions of illness causality in hospitalized children. *Journal of Pediatric Psychology, 4,* 77–84.

Simic, A. (1990). Aging, world view, and intergenerational relations in America and Yugoslavia. In J. Sokolovsky (Ed.), *The cultural context of aging.* New York: Bergin & Garvey Publisher.

Simmons, R., & Blyth, D. (1987). *Moving into adolescence: The impact of pubertal change in school context.* New York: deGruyter.

Simmons, R. G., Carlton-Ford, S. L., & Blyth, D. A. (1987). Predicting how a child will cope with the transition to junior high school. In R. M. Lerner & T. T. Foch (Eds.), *Biological-psychosocial interactions in early adolescence: A lifespan perspective.* Hillsdale, NJ: Erlbaum.

Simmons, R. G., & Rosenberg, F. (1975). Sex, sex roles, and self-image. *Journal of Youth and Adolescence, 4,* 225–258.

Simonton, D. (1988). Age and outstanding achievement: What do we know after over a century of research? *Psychological Bulletin, 104,* 251–267.

Simpson, J., Campbell, B., & Berscheid, E. (1986). The association between romantic love and marriage: Kephart (1967) twice revisited. *Personality and Social Psychology Bulletin, 12,* 363–372.

Singer, J., & Singer, D. (1983). Psychologists look at television: Cognitive, developmental, personality and social policy implications. *American Psychologist, 38,* 826–834.

Singer, J., Singer, D., Desmond, R., Hirsch, B., & Nicol, A. (1988). Family mediation and children's cognition, aggression, and comprehension of television: A longitudinal study. Journal of Applied *Developmental Psychology, 9,* 329–347.

Singer, J. L., and Singer, D. G. (1981). *Television, imagination and aggression. A study of preschoolers.* Hillsdale, NJ: Erlbaum.

Singer, L., Brodzinsky, D., Ramsay, D., Stein, M., & Waters, E. (1985). Mother-infant attachment in adoptive families. *Child Development, 56,* 1543–1551.

Skinner, B. F. (1938). *The behavior of organisms: An experimental analysis.* New York: Appleton.

Skinner, B. F. (1957). *Verbal behavior.* New York: Appleton-Century-Crofts.

Skinner, B. F., & Vaughan, M. E. (1983). *Enjoy old age.* New York: Norton.

Skinner, E. A., Wellborn, J. G., & Connell, J. P. (1990). What it takes to do well in school and whether I've got it: The role of perceived control in children's engagement and school achievement. *Journal of Educational Psychology, 82,* 22–32.

Slawinski, E. B., Hartel, D. M., & Kline, D. W. (1993). Self-reported hearing problems in daily life throughout adulthood. *Psychology and Aging, 8,* 552–561.

Slobin, D. (1972, July). Children and language: They learn the same way all around the world. *Psychology Today,* p. 18.

Slobin, D. (1975). On the nature of talk to children. In E. H. Lenneberg & E. Lenneberg (Eds.), *Foundations of language development* (Vol. 1). New York: Academic Press.

Slobin, D. (Ed.). (1982). *The cross-cultural study of language acquisition.* Hillsdale, NJ: Erlbaum.

Slocum, W. L., & Nye, F. I. (1976). Provider and housekeeper roles. In F. I. Nye, H. Bahr, S. Bahr, J. Carlson, V. Gecas, S. McLaughlin, & W. Slocum (Eds.), *Role structure and analysis of the family.* Beverly Hills, CA: Sage Foundation.

Smetana, J. (1988). Adolescents' and parents' conceptions of parental authority. *Child Development, 59,* 321–335.

Smetana, J. (1989). Adolescents' and parents' reasoning about actual family conflict. *Child Development, 60,* 1052–1067.

Smetana, J. (1995). Parenting styles and conceptions of parental authority during adolescence. *Child Development, 66,* 299–316.

Smilansky, S. (1968). *The effects of sociodramatic play on disadvantaged children: Preschool children.* New York: Wiley.

Smiley, S. S., & Brown, A. L. (1979). Conceptual preference for thematic or taxonomic relations: A nonmonotonic age trend from preschool to old age. *Journal of Experimental Child Psychology, 28,* 249–257.

Smith, D. (1981). Historical change in the household structure of the elderly in economically developed societies. In R. Fogel, E. Hatfield, S. B. Kiesler, & E. Shanas (Eds.), *Aging: Stability and change in the family.* New York: Academic Press.

Smith, P. K., & Boulton, M. (1990). Rough-and-tumble play, aggression, and dominance: Perception and behavior in children's encounters. *Human Development, 33,* 271–282.

Smith, P. K., & Daglish, L. (1977). Sex differences in parent and infant behavior in the home. *Child Development, 48,* 1250–1254.

Smith, S. N. (1979). Recent cross-ethnic research on the adolescent. *Journal of Negro Education, 48,* 302–323.

Smuts, A. B., & Hagen, J. W. (1985). History and research in child development. *Monographs of the Society for Research in Child Development, 50*(4–5, Serial No. 211).

Smyser, A. (1982). Hospices: Their humanistic and economic value. *American Psychologist, 37,* 1260–1262.

Snarey, J. (1985). Cross-cultural universality of social-moral development: A critical review of Kohlbergian research. *Psychological Bulletin, 97,* 202–232.

Snarey, J., Reimer, J., & Kohlberg, L. (1985). Development of social moral reasoning among kibbutz adolescents: A longitudinal cross-cultural study. *Developmental Psychology, 21,* 3–17.

Snarey, J., Son, L. Kuehne, V., Hauser, S., & Vaillant, G. (1987). The role of parenting in men's psychosocial development: A longitudinal study of early adulthood infertility and midlife generativity. *Developmental Psychology, 23,* 596–603.

Snarey, J. R., & Keljo, K. (1991). In a gemeinschaft voice: The cross-cultural expansion of moral development theory. In W. M. Kurtines & J. L. Gewirtz (Eds.), *Handbook of moral behavior and development* (Vol. 1, pp. 395–424). Hillsdale, NJ: Erlbaum.

Snow, C. E. (1981). The uses of initiation. *Journal of Child Language, 8,* 205–212.

Snowden, L., & Cheung, F. (1990). Use of inpatient mental health services by members of ethnic minority groups. *American Psychologist, 45,* 347–355.

Snyder, R. D. (1971). Congenital mercury poisoning. *New England Journal of Medicine, 284,* 1014–1016.

Sokol, R. J., Miller, S. I., & Reed, G. (1980). Alcohol abuse during pregnancy: An epidemiologic study. *Alcoholism, 14,* 135–145.

Sokoloff, B. (1987). Alternative methods of reproduction: Effects on the child. *Clinical Pediatrics, 26,* 11–16.

Sokolovsky, J. (Ed.). (1990). *The cultural context of aging.* New York: Bergin & Garvey.

Sontag, L. W. (1966). Implications of fetal behavior and environment for adult personalities. *Annals of the New York Academy of Sciences, 134,* 782–786.

Sontag, L. W., & Wallace, R. F. (1935). The effect of cigarette smoking during pregnancy upon the fetal heart rate. *American Journal of Obstetrics and Gynecology, 29,* 77–83.

Sorensen, R. (1973). *Adolescent sexuality in contemporary America.* New York: William Collins.

Sorosky, A. D., Baran, A., & Pannor, R. (1978). *The adoption triangle: The effects of the sealed record on adoptees, birth parents, and adoptive parents.* Garden City, NY: Anchor Press.

Sorce, J., Emde, R., Campos, J., & Klinnert, M. (1985). Maternal emotional signaling: Its effect on the visual cliff behavior of one-year-olds. *Developmental Psychology, 21,* 195–200.

Sosa, R., Kennel, J., Klaus, M., Robertson, S., & Urrutia, J. (1980). The effect of a supportive companion on perinatal problems, length of labor, and mother-infant interaction. *New England Journal of Medicine, 303*(11), 597–600.

Spanier, G. B., & Lewis, R. A. (1980). Marital quality: A review of the seventies. *Journal of Marriage and the Family, 42,* 825–839.

Spanier, G. B., Lewis, R. A., & Cole, L. C. (1975). Marital adjustment over the family life cycle: The issue of curvilinearity. *Journal of Marriage and the Family, 37,* 262–275.

Spanier, G. B., Roos, P., & Shockey, J. (1985). Marital trajectories of American women: Variations in the life course. *Journal of Marriage and the Family, 47,* 993–1003.

Speece, M., & Brent, S. (1984). Children's understanding of death: A review of three components of a death concept. *Child Development, 55,* 1671–1686.

Spector, P. (1986). Perceived control by employees: A meter-analysis of studies concerning autonomy and participation in decision making. *Human Relations, 39,* 1005–1016.

Speicher, B. (1994). Family patterns of moral judgment during adolescence and early adulthood. *Developmental Psychology, 30,* 624–632.

Spellacy, W., Miller, S., & Winegar, A. (1986). Pregnancy after 40 years of age. *Obstetrics and Gynecology, 68,* 452–454.

Spencer, M., & Markstrom-Adams, C. (1990). Identity processes among racial and ethnic minority children in America. *Child Development, 61,* 290–310.

Spiker, D., Ferguson, J., & Brooks-Gunn, J. (1993). Enhancing maternal interactive behavior and child social competence in low birth weight, premature infants. *Child Development, 64,* 754–768.

Spinetta, J. (1974). The dying child's awareness of death: A review. *Psychological Bulletin, 81,* 256–260.

Spinetta, J., & Rigler, D. (1972). The child-abusing parent: A psychological review. *Psychological Bulletin, 72,* 296–304.

Spinetta, J., Swarner, J., & Sheposh, J. (1981). Effective parental coping following the death of a child from cancer. *Journal of Pediatric Psychology, 6,* 251–263.

Spirduso, W. W., & MacRae, P. G. (1990). Motor performance and aging. In J. E. Birren & K. W. Schaie (Eds.), *Psychology of aging* (3rd ed.). New York: Academic Press.

Spitz, R. (1945). Hospitalism: An inquiry into the genesis of psychiatric conditions in early childhood. *Psychoanalytic Study of the Child, 1,* 53–74.

Spreitzer, E., & Riley, L. E. (1974). Factors associated with singlehood. *Journal of Marriage and the Family, 36,* 533–542.

Squire, S. (1983). *The slender balance: Causes and cures for bulimia, anorexia, and the weight-loss/weight-gain seesaw.* New York: Putnam.

Sroufe, L. A. (1978, October). Attachment and the roots of competence. *Human Nature,* 50–57.

Sroufe, L. A. (1979). Socioemotional development. In J. Osofsky (Ed.), *Handbook of infant development.* New York: Wiley.

Sroufe, L. A. (1985). Attachment classification from the perspective of infant caregiver relationships and infant temperament. *Child Development, 56,* 1–14.

Stagner, R. (1982). Postscripts and prospects. In A. S. Glickman (Ed.), *The changing composition of the work force: Implications for research and its application.* New York: Plenum.

Stankov, K. (1988). Aging, attention and intelligence. *Psychology and Aging, 3,* 59–74.

Stattin, M., & Klackenberg-Larsson, I. (1991). The short- and long-term implications for parent-child relations of parents' prenatal preferences for their child's gender. *Developmental Psychology, 27,* 141–147.

Staudinger, U. M., Smith, J., & Baltes, P. B. (1992). Wisdom-related knowledge in a life review task: Age differences and the role of professional specialization. *Psychology and Aging, 7,* 271–281.

Stein, A., & Friedrich, L. (1975). Impact of television on children and youth. In E. M. Hetherington, J. Hagen, R. Kron, & A. H. Stein (Eds.), *Review of child development research* (Vol. 5). Chicago: University of Chicago Press.

Stein, P. J. (1980). Singlehood: An alternative to marriage. In J. Henslin (Ed.), *Marriage and the family in a changing society.* New York: Free Press.

Stein, S. (1974). *Making babies.* New York: Walker.

Steinberg, L. (1987). Bound to bicker. *Psychology Today, 21,* 36–39.

Steinberg, L. (1988a). Reciprocal relation between parent-child distance and pubertal maturation. *Developmental Psychology, 24,* 122–128.

Steinberg, L. (1988b). Stability of type A behavior from early childhood to young adulthood. In P. Baltes, D. Featherman, & R. Lerner (Eds.), *Life-span development and behavior* (Vol. 8). Hillsdale, NJ: Erlbaum.

Steinberg, L., Elmen, J., & Mounts, N. (1989). Authoritative parenting, psychosocial maturity, and academic success among adolescents. *Child Development, 60,* 1424–1436.

Steinberg, L, Fegley, S., & Dornbusch, S. M. (1993). Negative impact of part-time work on adolescent adjustment: Evidence from a longitudinal study. *Developmental Psychology, 29,* 171–180.

Steinberg, L., Greenberger, E., Garduque, L., Ruggiero, M., & Vaux, A. (1982). Effects of working on adolescent development. *Developmental Psychology, 18,* 385–395.

Steinberg, L., & Silverberg, S. (1986). The vicissitudes of autonomy in early adolescence. *Child Development, 57,* 841–851.

Steinberg, L., & Silverberg, S. (1987). Influences on marital satisfaction during the middle stages of the family life cycle. *Journal of Marriage and the Family, 49,* 751–760.

Steinmetz, S. (1990). Elder abuse: Myth and reality. In T. Brubaker (Ed.), *Family relationships in later life* (2nd ed.). Newbury Park, CA: Sage Publications.

Stenberg, C., Campos, J., & Emde, R. (1983). The facial expression of anger in seven-month-old infants. *Child Development, 54,* 178–184.

Stern, G., Caldwell, B., Hersher, L., Lipton, E., & Richmond, E. (1969). A factor-analytic study of the mother-infant dyad. *Child Development, 40,* 163–182.

Stern, M., & Hildebrandt, K. (1986). Prematurity stereotyping: Effects on mother-infant interaction. *Child Development, 57,* 308–315.

Stern, M., & Karraker, K. H. (1989). Sex stereotyping of infants: A review of gender labeling studies. *Sex Roles, 20,* 501–522.

Sternberg, R. J. (1990). *Wisdom: Its nature, origin and development.* Cambridge: Cambridge University Press.

Sternberg, R. J., & Lubart, T. (1992). Buy low and sell high: An investment approach to creativity. *Current Directions in Psychological Science, 1,* 1–5.

Sternglanz, S. H., & Serbin, L. (1974). Sex role stereotyping in children's television programs. *Developmental Psychology, 10,* 710–715.

Stevens, J. (1984). Black grandmothers' and black adolescent mothers' knowledge about parenting. *Developmental Psychology, 20,* 1017–1025.

Stevens-Long, J. (1979). *Adult life: Developmental processes.* Palo Alto, CA: Mayfield.

Stevenson, H. (1982). Influences of schooling on cognitive development. In D. Wagner & H. Stevenson (Eds.), *Cultural Perspectives on Child Development.* San Francisco: W.H. Freeman.

Stevenson, H., Chen, C., & Lee, S. Y. (1993). Mathematics achievement of Chinese, Japanese, and American children: Ten years later. *Science, 258,* 53–58.

Stevenson, H., & Lee, S. (1990). Context of achievement: A study of American, Chinese, and Japanese children. *Monographs of the Society for Research in Child Development, 55*(1–2, Serial No. 221).

Stewart, R. (1983). Sibling attachment relationships: Child-infant interactions in the strange situation. *Developmental Psychology, 19,* 192–199.

Stiles, D., Gibbons, J., & Schnellmann, J. (1987). The smiling sunbather and the chivalrous football player: Young adolescents' image of the ideal woman and man. *Journal of Early Adolescence, 7,* 411–427.

Stinnett, N., Carter, L. M., & Montgomery, J. E. (1972). Older persons' perceptions of their marriages. *Journal of Marriage and the Family, 34,* 665–670.

Stinnett, N., & Walters, J. (1977). *Relationships in marriage and family.* New York: Macmillan.

Stipek, D. (1983). A developmental analysis of pride and shame. *Human Development, 26,* 42–54.

Stipek, D., Gralinski, J H., & Kopp, C. (1990). Self-concept development in the toddler years. *Developmental Psychology, 26,* 972–977.

Stipek, D., Recchia, S., & McClintic, S. (1992). Self evaluation in young children. *Monographs of the Society for Research in Child Development, 57*(1, Serial No. 226).

Stoddard, S. (1978). *The hospice movement: A better way of caring for the dying.* Briarcliff Manor, NY: Stein and Day.

Stoddart, T., & Turiel, E. (1985). Children's concepts of cross gender activities. *Child Development, 56,* 1241–1252.

Stoneman, Z., Brody, G., & MacKinnon, C. (1984). Naturalistic observations of children's activities and roles while playing with their siblings and friends. *Child Development, 55,* 617.

Stott, D. H., & Latchford, S. A. (1976). Prenatal antecedents of child health, development, and behavior: An epidemiological report of incidence and association. *Journal of the American Academy of Child Psychology, 15,* 161–191.

Straus, M. A., & Gelles, R. J. (1990). *Physical violence in American families: Risk factors and adaption to violence in 8,145 families.* (pp. 3–16). New Brunswick, NJ: Transaction.

Strean, L. P., & Peer, A. (1956). Stress as an etiologic factor in the development of cleft palate. *Plastic and Reconstructive Surgery, 18,* 1–18.

Streib, G. F. (1977). Social stratification and aging. In R. H. Binstock & E. Shanas (Eds.), *Handbook of aging and the social sciences.* New York: Van Nostrand Reinhold.

Streib, G. F., & Schneider, C. (1971). *Retirement in American society.* Ithaca, NY: Cornell University Press.

Streissguth, A., Barr, H. Sampson, P., Darby, B., & Martin, D. (1989). IQ at age four in relation to maternal alcohol use and smoking during pregnancy. *Developmental Psychology, 25,* 3–11.

Streissguth, A., Martin, D., Barr, H., Sandman, B., Kirchner, G., & Darby, B. (1984). Intrauterine alcohol and nicotine exposure: Attention and reaction time in four-year-old children. *Developmental Psychology, 20,* 533–541.

Streissguth, A. P., Aase, J. M., Clarren, S. K., Randels, S. P., LaDue, R. A., & Smith, D. F.

(1991). Fetal alcohol syndrome in adolescents and adults. *Journal of the American Medical Association, 265,* 1961–1967.

Striegel-Moore, R., Silberstein, L., & Rodin, J. (1986). Toward an understanding of risk factors for bulimia. *American Psychologist, 41,* 246–263.

Stroebe, M. S., Gergen, M. M., Gergen, K. J., & Stroebe, W. (October, 1992). Broken Hearts or Broken Bonds. *American Psychologist, 47,* 1205–1212.

Stroebe, M. S., & Stroebe, W. (1983). Who suffers more? Sex differences in health risks of the widowed. *Psychological Bulletin, 93,* 279–301.

Strong, L. D. (1978). Alternative marital and family forms: Their relative attractiveness to college students and correlates of willingness to participate in nontraditional forms. *Journal of Marriage and the Family, 40,* 493–503.

Stueve, A., & Fischer, C. (1978, September). *Social networks and old women.* Paper presented at the Workshop on Older Women, Washington, DC.

Stults, H. (1977). Obesity in adolescents: Prognosis, etiology, and management. *Journal of Pediatric Psychology, 2,* 122–126.

Stunkard, A., Thorkild, M., Sorenson, I., Hanis, C., Teasdale, T., Chakraborty, R., Schull, W., & Schulsinger, F. (1986). An adoption study of human obesity. *The New England Journal of Medicine, 314,* 193–198.

Suedfeld, P., & Piedrahita, L. (1984). Intimations of mortality: Integrative simplification as a precursor of death. *Journal of Personality and Social Psychology, 47,* 848–852.

Sunenblick, M. B. (1988). The AIDS epidemic: Sexual behavior of adolescents. *Smith College Studies in Social Work, 59*(1), 21–37.

Super, C. (1981). Behavioral development in infancy. In R. H. Munroe, R. L. Munroe, & B. B. Whiting (Eds.), *Handbook of cross-cultural human development.* New York: Garland.

Super, C. M. (1982, Spring). Secular trends in child development and the institutionalization of professional disciplines. *SCRD Newsletter,* 10–11.

Super, D. E. (1957). *The psychology of careers.* New York: Harper & Row.

Super, D. E. (1963). *Career development: Self-concept theory.* New York: College Entrance Examination Board.

Super, G., & Harkness, S. (1972). The infant's niche in rural Kenya and metropolitan America. In L. Adler (Ed.), *Issues in cross-cultural research.* New York: Academic Press.

Sussman, M. B. (1960). Intergenerational family relationships and social role changes in middle age. *Journal of Gerontology, 15,* 71–75.

Sussman, M. B. (1965). Relationships of adult children with their parents in the United States. In E. Shanas & G. Streib (Eds.), *Social structure and the family: Generational relations.* Englewood Cliffs, NJ: Prentice-Hall.

Sutker, P. B. (1982). Adolescent drug and alcohol behaviors. In T. Field, A. Huston, H. C. Quay, L. Troll, & G. E. Finley (Eds.), *Review of human development.* New York: Wiley-Interscience.

Sutton-Smith, B. (1982). Birth order and sibling status effects. In M. E. Lamb & B. Sutton-Smith (Eds.), *Sibling relationships: Their nature and significance across the life span.* Hillsdale, NJ: Erlbaum.

Sutton-Smith, B., & Rosenberg, B. (1970). *The sibling.* New York: Holt, Rinehart & Winston.

Svejda, M. J., Campos, J. J., & Emde, R. N. (1980). Mother-infant "bonding": Failure to generalize. *Child Development, 51,* 775–779.

Swain, I. U., Zelazo, P. R., & Clifton, R. K. (1993). Newborn infants memory for speech sounds retained over 24 hours. *Developmental Psychology, 29,* 312–323.

Swan, G. E., Dame, A., & Carmelli, D. (1991). Involuntary retirement, type A behavior, and current functioning in elderly men: 27-year follow-up of the Western Collaborative Group study. *Psychology and Aging, 6,* 384–391.

Swanson, J., & Kinsbourne, M. (1980). Food dyes impair performance of hyperactive children on a laboratory learning test. *Science, 207,* 1485–1487.

Sweetland, J. (1978). *Mid-career perspectives: The middle-aged and older population.* Scarsdale, NY: Work in America Institute.

Swensen, C., Eskew, R., & Kohlhepp, K. (1981). Stage of family life cycle, ego development, and the marriage relationship. *Journal of Marriage and the Family, 43,* 841–853.

Synder, S. (1991). Movies and juvenile delinquency. *Adolescence, 26,* 83–88.

Talland, G. A. (1965). Three estimates of the word span and their estimates over the adult years. *Quarterly Journal of Experimental Psychology, 17,* 301–307.

Tamir, L. (1982). *Men in their forties: The transition to middle age.* New York: Springer.

Tanfer, K. (1987). Patterns of premarital cohabitation among never married women. *Journal of Marriage and the Family, 49,* 483–497.

Tangri, S. S. (1975). Determinants of occupational role innovations among college women. In M. T. S. Mednick, S. S. Tangri, & L. W. Hoffman (Eds.), *Women and achievement: Social and motivational analysis.* Washington, DC: Hemisphere.

Tanner, J. M. (1964). *The physique of the Olympic athlete.* London: Allen and Unwin.

Tanner, J. M. (1970). Physical growth. In P. H. Mussen (Ed.), *Carmichael's manual of child psychology.* New York: Wiley.

Tanner, J. M. (1978). *Fetus into man: Physical growth from conception to maturity.* Cambridge, MA: Harvard University Press.

Tanner, J. M. (1990). *Foetus into man* (2nd ed.). Cambridge, MA: Harvard University Press.

Tanner, J. M. (1991a). Growth spurt, adolescent. In R. M. Lerner, A. C. Petersen, & J. Brooks-Gunn (Eds.), *Encyclopedia of adolescence* (Vol. 1), New York: Garland.

Tanner, J. M. (1991b). Menarche, secular trend in age of. In R. M. Ledner, A. C. Petersen, & J. Brooks-Gunn (Eds.), *Encyclopedia of adolescence* (Vol. 2), New York: Garland.

Taussig, H. B. (1962). The thalidomide syndrome. *Scientific American, 107,* 29–35.

Tavris, C., & Offir, C. (1977). *The longest war: Sex differences in perspective.* New York: Harcourt Brace Jovanovich.

Tavris, C., & Wade, C. (1984). *The longest war: Sex differences in perspective.* New York: Harcourt Brace Jovanovich.

Taylor, M., & Gellman, S. (1988). Adjectives and nouns: Children's strategies for learning new words. *Child Development, 59,* 411–419.

Teller, M. N. (1972). Age changes and immune resistance to cancer. *Advances of Gerontological Research, 4,* 25–43.

Terman, L. M. (1925). *Genetic studies of genius: Mental and physical traits of a thousand gifted children* (Vol. 1). Stanford, CA: Stanford University Press.

Terman, L. M., & Merrill, M. (1973). *Stanford-Binet Intelligence Scale: Manual for the third revision of form L-M.* Boston: Houghton Mifflin.

Termine, N., & Izard, C. (1988). Infants' responses to their mothers' expression of joy and sadness. *Developmental Psychology, 24,* 223–229.

Tesch, S. A. (1983). Review of friendship development across the life span. *Human Development, 26,* 266–276.

Teti, D. M., & Gelfand, D. M. (1991). Behavioral competence among mothers of infants in the first year: The mediational role of maternal self-efficacy. *Child Development, 62,* 918–929.

Theorell, T., & Rahe, R. H. (1974). Psychosocial factors and myocardial infarction: An inpatient study in Sweden. *Journal of Psychosomatic Research, 15,* 25–31.

Thomas, A., & Chess, S. (1977). *Temperament and development.* New York: Brunner/Mazel.

Thomas, J. (1986). Gender differences in satisfaction with grandparenting. *Psychology and Aging, 1,* 215–219.

Thompson, A. P. (1983). Extramarital sex: A review of the research literature. *Journal of Sex Research, 19,* 1–22.

Thompson, E., & Colella, U. (1992). Cohabitation and marital stability. *Journal of Marriage and the Family, 54,* 259–267.

Thompson, L., & Walker, A. (1984). Mothers and daughters: Aid patterns and attachment. *Journal of Marriage and the Family, 46,* 313–322.

Thompson, L. W., Gallagher-Thompson, D., Futterman, A., Gilewski, M. J., & Peterson, J. (1991). The effects of late-life spousal bereavement over a 30-month interval. *Psychology and Aging, 6,* 434–441.

Thompson, M., & Heller, M. (1990). Facets of support related to well-being: Quantitive social isolation and perceived family support in a sample of elderly women. *Psychology and Aging, 5,* 535–544.

Thompson, R. A., Lamb, M. E., & Estes, D. (1982). Stability of infant-mother attachment and its relationship to changing life circumstances in an unselected middle class sample. *Child Development, 53,* 144–148.

Thoresen, C., Eagleston, J., Kirmil-Gray, K., & Bracke, P. (1985, August). *Type A children.* Paper presented at the annual meeting of the American Psychological Association, Los Angeles.

Thornton, M., Chatters, L., Taylor, R., & Allen, W. (1990). Sociodemographic and environmental correlates of racial socialization by Black parents. *Child Development, 61,* 401–409.

Thurnher, M., Spence, D., & Lowenthal, M. F. (1974). Value conflict and behavior conflict in intergenerational relations. *Journal of Marriage and the Family, 36,* 308–319.

Tibbitts, C. (1977). Older Americans in the family context. *Aging, 6,* 270–271.

Tierney K., & Corwin, D. (1983). Exploring intrafamilial child sexual abuse: A systems approach. In D. Finkelhor, R. J. Gelles, G. T. Hotaling, & M. A. Straus (Eds.), *The dark side* of families: Current family violence research. Beverly Hills, CA: Sage Publications.

Tietjen, A., & Walker, L. (1985). Moral reasoning and leadership among men in Papua New Guinean society. Child Development, 21, 982–992.

Timiras, P. S. (1972). Developmental physiology and aging. New York: Macmillan.

Timmerman, M., Wells, L., & Chen, S. (1990). Bulimia nervosa and associated alcohol abuse among secondary school students. Journal of the Academy of Child and Adolescent Psychiatry, 29, 118–122.

Tinklenberg, J. R., & Darley, C. F. (1975). Psychological and cognitive effects of cannabis. In P. H. Cornell & N. Dorn (Eds.), Cannabis and man. New York: Churchill Livingstone.

Tinsley, B. R., & Parke, R. D. (1983). Grandparents as support and socialization agents. In M. Lewis (Ed.), Beyond the dyad. New York: Plenum.

Tisdale, S. (1987). Harvest Moon: Portrait of a nursing home. New York: Henry Holt.

Tobias, S. (1982, January). Sexist equations. Psychology Today, 15, 14–18.

Tobin, J., Wu, D., & Davidson, D. (1989). Preschool in three cultures. New Haven: Yale University Press.

Tobin, S. S., & Lieberman, M. A. (1976). Last home for the aged. San Francisco: Jossey-Bass.

Tolson, T., & Wilson, M. (1990). The impact of two- and three-generational Black family structure on perceived family climate. Child Development, 61, 416–428.

Townes, B., & Wold, D. (1979). Childhood leukemia. In E. Pattison (Ed.), The experience of dying. Englewood Cliffs, NJ: Prentice-Hall.

Townsend, C. (1971). Old age, the last segregation: The report on nursing homes (Ralph Nader's Study Group Reports). New York: Grossman.

Tran, T., Wright, R., & Chatters, L. (1991). Health, stress, psychological resources, and subjective well-being among older Blacks. Psychology and Aging, 6, 100–108.

Treas, J., & Van Hilst, A. (1976). Marriage and remarriage rate among older Americans. The Gerontologist, 16, 132–136.

Treffert, D. A. (1978). Marijuana use in schizophrenia: A clear hazard. American Journal of Psychology, 135, 10.

Troll, L. E. (1971). The family of later life: A decade review. Journal of Marriage and the Family, 33, 263–290.

Troll, L. E. (1975). Early and middle adulthood. Monterey, CA: Brooks/Cole.

Troll, L. E. (1980). Grandparenting. In L. W. Poon (Ed.), Aging in the 1980s: Psychological issues. Washington, DC: American Psychological Association.

Troll, L. E. (1982). Continuations: Adult development and aging. Monterey, CA: Brooks/Cole.

Troll, L. E. (1983). Grandparents: The family watchdog. In T. Brubaker (Ed.), Family relationships in later life. Beverly Hills, CA: Sage.

Troll, L. E., & Bengston, V. (1982). Intergenerational relations throughout the life span. In B. Wolman (Ed.), Handbook of developmental psychology. Englewood Cliffs, NJ: Prentice-Hall.

Troll, L. E., Miller, S. J., & Atchley, R. C. (1979). Families in later life. Belmont, CA: Wadsworth.

Troll, L. E., & Smith, J. (1976). Attachment through the life span: Some questions about dyadic bonds among adults. Human Development, 19, 156–170.

Troll, L. E., & Turner, B. F. (1980). Sex differences in problems of aging. In E. Gomberg & V. Franks (Eds.), Gender and disordered behavior. New York: Brunner/Mazel.

Trost, J. (1983). Parental benefits: A study of men's behavior and views. Social Change in Sweden, 28, 1–8.

Tronick, E. (1989). Emotions and emotional communication in infants. American Psychologist, 44, 112–119.

Tuckman, J., & Lorge, I. (1953). Attitudes toward old people. Journal of Social Psychology, 37, 249–260.

Tuma, N. B., & Hallinan, M. T. (1979). The effects of sex, race, and achievement on schoolchildren's friendships. Social Forces, 57, 1265–1285.

Turner, B. K. (1979). The self-concepts of older women. Research on Aging, 1, 464–480.

Turiel, E. (1978). Social regulations and domains of social concept. New Directions for Child Development, 1, 45–74.

Turkington, C. (1984, April). Parents found to ignore sex stereotypes. APA Monitor, p. 12.

Umberson, D. (1987). Family status and health behaviors: Social control as a dimension of social integration. Journal of Health and Social Behavior, 28, 306–319.

Unger, R. K. (1979). Female and male: Psychological perspectives. New York: Harper & Row.

UNICEF. (1975). Games of the world: How to make them, how to play them, and how they came to be. Zurich: Swiss Committee for UNICEF.

U.S. Bureau of the Census. (1992). Marital status and living arrangements: March 1991 (Current Population Reports, Series P20–461). Washington, DC: U.S. Government Printing Office.

U.S. Bureau of the Census. (1992). Statistical abstract of the United States, 1992 (112 ed.). Washington, DC: U.S. Government Printing Office.

U.S. Bureau of Labor Statistics. (1986). Rise in mothers' labor force activity includes those with infants. Monthly Labor Review, 109, 43–45.

U.S. Bureau of the Census. (1988). 1988 Marital status and living arrangements (Current Population Reports, Series 28, No. 433, p. 3). Washington, DC: U.S. Government Printing Office.

U.S. Bureau of the Census. (1980). Statistical Abstracts of the United States, 1980 (101st Annual Ed.). Washington, DC: U.S. Government Printing Office.

U.S. Bureau of the Census. (1981). Statistical Abstracts of the United States, 1981. Washington, DC: U.S. Government Printing Office.

U.S. Bureau of the Census. (1982). Statistical Abstracts of the United States, 1982–83. Washington, DC: U.S. Government Printing Office.

U.S. Bureau of the Census. (1983). Statistical Abstracts of the United States, 1982 (Vol. 83, 103rd Annual Ed.). Washington, DC: U.S. Government Printing Office.

U.S. Bureau of the Census. (1984). Statistical Abstracts of the United States 1983. Washington, DC: U.S. Government Printing Office.

U.S. Bureau of the Census. (1985). Households, families, marital status and living arrange-

ments: March 1985, Advanced Report (Current Population Reports, Series P–20, No. 402). Washington, DC: U.S. Government Printing Office.

U.S. children and their families: Current conditions and recent trends, 1984. (1991, Winter). SRCD Newsletter.

U.S. Department of Agriculture, Family Economics Research Group, Agricultural Research Service. (1988, Jan.). Child care arrangements of working women. Hyattsville, MD: Author.

U.S. Department of Commerce, Bureau of the Census. (1977). The sex differential in earnings by age, 1975 (Current Population Reports, Series P–60, No. 105). Washington, DC: U.S. Government Printing Office.

U.S. Department of Commerce, Bureau of the Census. (1979). Marital status and living arrangements, March 1978 (Current Population Reports, Series P–20, No. 338). Washington, DC: U.S. Government Printing Office.

U.S. Department of Health, Education and Welfare. (1978). Monthly vital statistics report: final mortality statistics, 1976. Washington, DC: U.S. Government Printing Office.

U.S. Department of Health, Education and Welfare, Public Health Service. (1979, Dec.). Facts about Down's syndrome for women over 35 (NIH Publication No. 80–536).

U.S. Department of Health and Human Services, Food and Drug Administration. (1979). Caffeine and pregnancy [Consumer memo] (Publication No. 80). Rockville, MD: Author.

U.S. Department of Justice. (1992). Crime in the United States. Washington, DC. U.S. Government Printing Office.

U.S. Department of Labor, Bureau of Statistics. (1977). Students, graduates, and dropouts in the labor market, October, 1976 (Special Labor Force Report No. 200). Washington, DC: U.S. Government Printing Office.

U.S. Department of Labor, Bureau of Labor Statistics. (1979). Monthly labor statistics, November, 1979. Washington, DC: U.S. Government Printing Office.

U.S. Department of Labor, Bureau of Labor Statistics. (1980). Perspectives on working women: A databook (Bulletin 2080). Washington, DC: U.S. Government Printing Office.

U.S. Department of Labor, Bureau of Labor Statistics. (1987, September). Monthly Labor Review. Washington, DC: U.S. Government Printing Office.

U.S. News and World Report. (1978, July 10). Why a surge of suicide among the young?

U.S. Office of Technology Assessment (1991). Adolescent health: Vol. 3. Crosscutting issues in the delivery of health and related services (Publication No. OTA-H-467). Washington, DC: U.S. Congress.

U.S. Public Health Service. (1984). National children and youth fitness study. Washington, DC: Office for Disease Prevention and Health Promotion.

Vaillant, G. E. (1977). Adaptation to life. Boston: Little, Brown.

Valdes-Dapena, M. (1980). Sudden unexplained infant death 1970 through 1975 (DHEW Publication No. 80–5255). Washington, DC: U.S. Department of Health, Education and Welfare.

van Den Boom, D. C., & Hoeksma, J. B. (1994). The effect of infant irritability on mother-infant interaction: A growth-curve analysis. *Developmental Psychology, 30,* 581–590.

VanderLinde, E., Morrongiello, B., & Rovee-Collier, C. (1985). Determinants of retention in 8-week-old infants. *Developmental Psychology, 21,* 601–613.

Van Velsor, E., & O'Rand, A. (1984). Family life cycle, work career patterns and women's wages at midlife. *Journal of Marriage and the Family, 46,* 365–373.

Vasudev, J., & Hummel, R. C. (1987). Moral stage sequence and principled reasoning in an Indian sample. *Human Development, 30,* 105–118.

Vaughn, B., Block, J., & Block, J. (1988). Parental agreement on child rearing during early childhood and the psychological characteristics of adolescents. *Child Development, 59,* 1020–1033.

Vaughn, B., Gove, F., & Egeland, B. (1980). The relationship between out-of-home care and the quality of infant-mother attachment in an economically disadvantaged population. *Child Development, 57,* 1203–1214.

Vega-Lahr, N., & Field, T. (1986). Type A behavior in preschool children. *Child Development, 57,* 1333–1348.

Veroff, J., Reuman, D., & Feld, S. (1984). Motives in American men and women across the adult life span. *Developmental Psychology, 20,* 1142–1158.

Vincent, C. E. (1964, August 8). Socialization data in research on young marrieds. *Acta Sociologica.*

Vinovskis, M. (1988). The historian and the life course: Reflections on recent approaches to the study of American family life in the past. In P. Baltes, D. Featherman, & R. Lerner (Eds.), *Life-span development and behavior* (Vol. 8). Hillsdale, NJ: Erlbaum.

Vishner, E. B., & Vishner, J. S. (1978). Major areas of difficulty for stepparent couples. *International Journal of Family Counseling, 6,* 71–72.

Vogel, D., Lake, M., Evans, S., Karraker, K. (1991). Children's and adults' sex-stereotyped perceptions of infants. *Sex Roles, 24* (9–10), 605–616.

Vogel, D. A., Lake, H. A., Evans, S., & Karraker, H. (1991). Children's and adult's sex-stereotype perceptions of infants. *Sex Roles, 24,* 605–616.

Vore, D. (1973). Prenatal nutrition and postnatal intellectual development. *Merrill-Palmer Quarterly, 19,* 253–260.

Vurpillot, E. (1968). The development of scanning strategies and their relation to visual differentiation. *Journal of Experimental Child Psychology, 6,* 632–650.

Vygotsky, L. (1962). *Thought and language.* Cambridge, MA: MIT Press.

Vygotsky, L. (1978). *Mind in society: The development of higher psychological processes.* Cambridge, MA: Harvard University Press.

Wachs, T., & Gruen, G. (1982). *Early experience and human development.* New York: Plenum.

Wagner, C. A. (1980). Adolescent sexuality. In J. F. Adams (Ed.), *Understanding adolescence: Current development in adolescent psychology* (4th ed.). Boston: Allyn Bacon, 1980.

Wainryb, C. (1993). The application of moral judgments to other cultures: Relativism and universality. *Child Development, 64,* 924–933.

Walberg, H. J. (1984). Families as partners in educational productivity. *Phi Delta Kappan, 65,* 397–400.

Waldron, I., & Jacobs, J. (1989). Effects of labor force participation on womens' health: New evidence from a longitudinal study. *Journal of Occupational Medicine, 30,* 977–983.

Walker, A., & Pratt, C. (1991). Daughters' help to mothers: Intergenerational aid versus caregiving. *Journal of Marriage and Family, 53,* 3–12.

Walker, K. (1970). Time spent by husbands in household work. *Family Economics Review, 14,* 8–11.

Walker, L. (1989). Psychology and violence against women. *American Psychologist, 44,* 695–702.

Walker, L. J. (1991). Sex differences in moral reasoning. In W. M. Kurtines & J. L. Gewirtz (Eds.), *Handbook of moral behavior and development* (Vol. 2, pp. 333–364). Hillsdale, NJ: Erlbaum.

Walker, L. J. (1982). The sequentiality of Kohlberg's stages of moral development. *Child Development, 53,* 1330–1336.

Walker, L. J., & Taylor, J. H. (1991). Family interactions and the development of moral reasoning. *Child Development, 62,* 264–283.

Wallach, M. (1973). Ideology, evidence and creative research. *Contemporary Psychology, 18,* 162–164.

Wallerstein, J. S. (1991). The long-term effects of divorce: The psychological tasks of the child. *American Journal of Orthopsychiatry, 53,* 230–243.

Wallerstein, J. (1987). Children of divorce: Report of a ten-year follow up of early latency age children. *American Journal of Orthopsychiatry, 57,* 199–211.

Wallerstein, J., & Blakeslee, S. (1989). *Second chances: Men, women, and children a decade after the divorce.* New York: Ticknor & Fields.

Wallerstein, J., Corbin, S., & Lewis, J. (1988). Children of divorce: A ten-year study. In E. Hetherinton & J. Arasteh (Eds.), *Impact of divorce, single parenting and stepparenting on children.* Hillsdale, NJ: Erebaum, 1988.

Wallerstein, J. S., & Kelly, J. B. (1980). *Surviving the breakup: How children and parents cope with divorce.* New York: Basic Books.

Walster, E., Aronson, V., Abrahams, D., & Rottmann, L. (1966). Importance of physical attractiveness in dating behavior. *Journal of Personality and Social Psychology, 4,* 508–516.

Walters, G., & Grusec, J. (1977). *Punishment.* San Francisco: Freeman.

Walton, G. E., & Bower, T. G. R. (1993). Newborns from "Prototypes" in less than 1 minute. *Psychological Science, 4,* 203–205.

Walton, G. E., Bower, N. J. A., & Bower, T. G. R. (1992). Recognition of familiar faces by newborns. *Infant Behavior and Development, 15,* 265–269.

Wapner, J., & Conner, K. The role of defensiveness in cognitive impulsivity. *Child Development, 57,* 1370–1374.

Washington, J., Minde, K., & Goldberg, S. (1987). Temperament in preterm infants: Style and stability. *Annual Progress in Child Psychiatry and Child Development,* 40–62.

Wasserman, G., & Stern, D. (1978). An early manifestation of differential behavior toward children of the same and opposite sex. *Journal of Genetic Psychology, 133,* 129–137.

Waterman, A. S. (1982). Identity development from adolescence to adulthood: An extension of theory and a review of research. *Developmental Psychology, 18,* 341–358.

Waterman, A. S. (1985). Identity in the context of adolescent psychology. In Alan S. Waterman (Ed.), *Identity in adolescence: Processes and contents. New directions in child development* (Vol. 30). San Francisco: Jossey-Bass.

Waterman, A. S., Geary, P. S., & Waterman, C. K. (1974). A longitudinal study of changes in ego identity status from freshman to the senior year of college. *Developmental Psychology, 10,* 387–392.

Watson, E. H., & Lowrey, G. H. (1967). *Growth and development of children* (5th ed.). Chicago: Year Book Medical Publishers.

Watson, J. B., & Raynor, R. (1920). Conditioned emotional reactions. *Journal of Experimental Psychology, 3,* 14.

Watson, M., & Amgott-Kwan, T. (1983). Transitions in children's understanding of parental roles. *Developmental Psychology, 19,* 659–666.

Waugh, W. C., & Norman, D. A. (1965). Primary memory. *Psychological Review, 72,* 89–104.

Waxman, S., & Kosowski, T. (1990). Noun mark category relations: Toddlers' and preschoolers' word learning biases. *Child Development, 61,* 1461–1473.

Weber, R. A., Levitt, M. J., & Clark, M. C. (1986). Individual variation in attachment security and strange situation behavior: The role of maternal and infant temperament. *Child Development, 57,* 56–65.

Weg, R. B. (1975). Changing physiology of aging: Normal and pathological. In D. S. Woodruff & J. E. Birren (Eds.), *Aging: Scientific perspectives and social issues.* New York: Van Nostrand.

Weg, R. B. (1977). More than wrinkles. In L. Troll, J. Israel, & K. Israel (Eds.), *Looking ahead: A woman's guide to the problems and joys of growing older.* Englewood Cliffs, NJ: Prentice-Hall.

Weg, R. B. (1978). The physiology of sexuality in aging. In R. L. Solnick (Ed.), *Sexuality and aging.* Los Angeles, CA: University of Southern California Press.

Weibel-Orlando, J. (1990). Grandparenting styles: Native American Perspectives. In J. Sololowsky (Ed.), *The cultural context of aging.* New York: Bergin & Garvey Publishers.

Weideger, P. (1976). *Menstruation and menopause: The physiology and psychology: The myth and the reality.* New York: Knopf.

Weidner, G., & Mathews, K. A. (1978). Reported physical symptoms elicited by unpredictable events and the Type A coronary-prone behavior pattern. *Journal of Personality and Social Psychology, 36,* 1213–1220.

Weiner, A. S. (1977). Cognitive and social-emotional development in adolescence. *Journal of Pediatric Psychology, 2,* 87–92.

Weiner, I. (1982). *Child and adolescent psychopathology.* New York: Wiley.

Weinraub, M., Clemens, L. P., Sockloff, A., Ethridge, T., Gracely, E., & Myers, B. (1984). The development of sex role stereotypes in the third year: Relationships to gender labeling, gender identity, sex-typed toy preference, and family characteristics. *Child Development, 55,* 1493–1503.

Weinraub, M., & Wolf, B. (1983). Effects of stress and social supports on mother-child interactions in single- and two-parent families. *Child Development, 54,* 1297–1311.

Weishaus, S., & Field, D. (1988). A half century of marriage: Continuity or change? *Journal of Marriage and the Family, 50,* 763–774.

Weisler, A., & McCall, R. (1976). Exploration and play. *American Psychologist, 31,* 492–508.

Weiss, R. (1979). Growing up a little faster: The experience of growing up in a single-parent household. In T. E. Levitin (Ed.), *Children of divorce. Journal of Social Issues, 35,* 97–111.

Weissberg, J., & Paris, S. (1986). Young children's remembering in different contexts: A reinterpretation of Istomina's study. *Child Development, 57,* 1123–1129.

Weissman, M., Prusoff, B., Gammon, G. D., Merikangas, K., Leckman, J., & Kidd, K. (1984). Psychopathology in the children (ages 6–18) of depressed and normal parents. *Journal of the American Academy of Child Psychiatry, 23,* 78–84.

Welford, A. T. (1959). Psychomotor performance. In J. E. Birren (Ed.), *Handbook of aging and the individual.* Chicago: University of Chicago Press.

Wellberg, H. (1984, February). Families as partners in educational productivity. *Phi Delta Kappan, 65,* 397–400.

Wellman, H. M., Cross, D., Bartoch, K. (1987). Infant search and object permanence: A meta analysis of the A-not-B error. *Monographs of the Society for Research in Child Development, 51*(3, Serial No. 214).

Wellman, H., & Estes, D. (1986). Early understanding of mental entities: A reexamination of childhood realism. *Child Development, 57,* 910–923.

"Wellness epidemic" spreads. (1987, November 8). *Trenton Times,* p. A10.

Wentzel, K. R., & Asher, S. R. (1995). The academic lives of neglected, rejected, popular, and controversial children. *Child Development, 66,* 754–763.

Werner, H. (1957). The concept of development from a comparative and organismic point of view. In D. Harris (Ed.), *The concept of development: An issue in the study of human behavior.* Minneapolis: University of Minnesota Press.

Wessel, J. A., & Van Huss, W. D. (1969). The influence of physical activity and age on exercise adaptation of men 20–69 years. *Journal of Sports Medicine, 9,* 173–180.

West, D. J. (1982). *Delinquency: Its roots, careers and prospects.* London: Heinemann.

West, R. L., Crook, T. H., & Barron, K. L. (1992). Everyday memory performance across the life span: Effects of age and noncognitive individual differences. *Psychology and Aging, 7,* 72–82.

Whalen, C., & Henker, B. (1986). Type A behavior in normal and hyperactive children: Multi-source evidence of overlapping constructs. *Child Development, 57,* 688–699.

Wharf, B. (1956). *Language, thought and reality.* New York: Wiley.

Whitbourne, S., & Hulicka, I. (1990). Ageism in undergraduate psychology tests. *American Psychologist, 45,* 1127–1136.

White, B. (1971). *Human infants: Experience and psychological development.* Englewood Cliffs, NJ: Prentice-Hall.

White, B. (1988). *Educating the infant and toddler.* Lexington, MA: Lexington Books.

White, K. J., & Kistner, J. (1992). The influence of teacher feedback on young children's peer preferences and perceptions. *Developmental Psychology, 28,* 933–940.

White, R. (1975). *Lives in progress* (3rd ed.). New York: Holt, Rinehart & Winston, 1975.

Whitbourne, S., & Hulicks, I. (1988). Ageism in undergraduate psychology text. *American Psychologist, 45,* 1127–1136.

Whitebourne, S. K., & Tesch, S. A. (November, 1985). A comparison of identity and intimacy statuses in college students and alumni. *Developmental Psychology, 21,* 1039–1044.

Whitehurst, G. and Valdez-Menchaca, M. (1988). What is the role of reinforcement in early language acquisition? *Child Development, 59,* 430–440.

Whiting, B., & Edwards, C. (1988). *Children of different worlds.* Cambridge, MA: Harvard University Press.

Whorf, B. (1956). *Language, thought and reality.* New York: Wiley.

Wierson, M., & Forehand, R. (1994, October). Parental behavorial training for child non-compliance: Rationale, concepts, and effectiveness. *Current Directions in Psychological Science, 3,* 146.

Wilcox, A. J., & Skjoerven, R. (1992). Birth weight and perinatal mortality: The effect of gestational age. *American Journal of Public Health, 83,* 378–382.

Wilkes, R., & Coles, R. L. (1978, March 26). Doctor of crisis. *New York Times Magazine.*

Wilkinson, A. C. (1984). Children's partial knowledge of the cognitive skill of counting. *Cognitive Psychology, 6,* 28–64.

Willems, E. P., & Alexander, J. L. (1982). The naturalistic perspective in research. In B. Wolman (Ed.), *Handbook of developmental psychology.* Englewood Cliffs, NJ: Prentice-Hall.

Williams, D. (1977). *The search for leadership.* Unpublished manuscript prepared for The Conference Board, New York.

Williams, J., & Stith, M. (1980). *Middle childhood behavior and development* (2nd ed.). New York: Macmillan, 1980.

Wilson, A. L., & Neidich, G. (1991). Infant mortality rates and public policy. *Social Policy Report of the Society for Research in Child Development, 5,* 2.

Wilson, R., & Matheny, A. (1983). Assessment of temperament in infant twins. *Developmental Psychology, 19,* 172–183.

Winch, R. F. (1974). Complementary needs and related notions about voluntary mate selection. In R. F. Winch & G. B. Spanier (Eds.), *Selected studies in marriage and the family.* New York: Holt, Rinehart & Winston.

Windle, M. (1991). Externalizing disorders (conduct problems). In R. M. Lerner, A. C. Petersen, & J. Brooks-Gunn (Eds.), *Encyclopedia of adolescence.* New York: Garland.

Windle, M., & Lerner, R. (1984). The role of temperament in dating relationships among young adults. *Merrill-Palmer Quarterly, 30,* 163–175.

Winick, M. (Ed.). (1975). *Childhood obesity.* New York: Wiley.

Winick, M. (1976). *Malnutrition and brain development.* New York: Oxford University Press.

Wiseman, R. (1975). Crisis theory and the process of divorce. *Social Casework, 56,* 205–212.

Witken, H. A., & Goodenough, D. R. (1977). Field dependence and interpersonal behavior. *Psychological Bulletin, 84,* 661–689.

Witken, H. A., & Goodenough, D. R. (1981). *Cognitive styles: Essence and origins.* (Psychological Issues: Monograph 51). New York: International Universities Press.

Witken, H. A., Goodenough, D. R., & Karp, S. A. (1967). Stability of cognitive style from childhood to young adulthood. *Journal of Personality and Social Psychology, 7,* 291–300.

Witken, H. A., Mednick, S., Schulsinger, F., Bakkestrom, E., Christiansen, K., Goodenough, D., Hirschhorn, K., Lundsteen, C., Owen, D., Philip, J., Rubin, D., & Stocking, M. (1976). Criminality in XYY and XXY men. *Science, 193,* 547–555.

Wolff, P. H. (1959). Observations on newborn infants. *Psychosomatic Medicine, 21,* 110–118.

Wolk, S., & Kurtz, J. (1975). Positive adjustment and involvement during aging and expectancy for internal control. *Journal of Consulting and Clinical Psychology, 43,* 173–178.

Women on Words and Images. (1975). *Dick and Jane as victims.* Princeton, NJ.

Wood, V., & Robertson, J. F. (1978). Friendship and kinship interaction: Differential effect on the morale of the elderly. *Journal of Marriage and the Family, 40,* 367–375.

Woodruff, D. S., & Birren, J. E. (1972). Age changes and cohort differences in personality. *Developmental Psychology, 6,* 252–259.

World Almanac and Book of Facts. (1995). New York: Pharos Books.

Worthman, C., & Whiting, J. (1987). Social change in adolescent sexual behavior, mate selection, and premarital pregnancy rates in a Kikuyu community. *Ethos, 15,* 145–165.

Wright, J., & Huston, A. (1983). A matter of form: Potentials of television for young viewers. *American Psychologist, 38,* 835–843.

Wyden, B. (1971, December 17). Growth: 45 crucial months. *Life,* 93–95.

Wylie, R. C. (1979). *The self-concept* (Vol. 2, Rev. ed.). Lincoln: University of Nebraska Press.

Yamamoto, J., Okonoji, K., Iwasaki, T., & Yoshimura, S. (1969). Mourning in Japan. *American Journal of Psychiatry, 126,* 74–182.

Yaniv, I., & Shantz, M. (1988). Children's understanding of perceptibility. In J. W. Astintion, P. L. Harris, & D. R. Olson (Eds.), *Developmental theories of mind.* London: Cambridge University Press.

Yaniv, I., & Shantz, M. (1991). Heuristics of reasoning and analogy in children's visual perspective taking. *Child Development, 61,* 1491–1501.

Yankelovich, D. (1974). *The new morality: A profile of American youth in the 70s.* New York: McGraw-Hill.

Yankelovich, D. (1981). *New rules: Searching for self-fulfillment in a world turned upside down.* New York: Random House.

Yankelovich, Skelly, & White, Inc. (1977). *Raising children in a changing society.* Minneapolis: General Mills.

Yarris, L. (1992). Unraveling the genetic message. *LBL Research Report, 17*(1), 2–15.

Yarrow, L. (1979). Everything you want to know about teen-agers (but are afraid to ask). *Parents Magazine, 54,* 68.

Yarrow, L. J., Rubenstein, J., & Pedersen, F. (1975). *Infant and environment.* New York: Wiley.

Yarrow, M. R., Campbell, J., & Burton, R. (1968). *Child rearing: An inquiry into research and methods.* San Francisco: Jossey-Bass.

Yllo, K. (1978). Nonmarital cohabitation: Beyond the college campus. *Alternative Lifestyles, 1,* 37–54.

Yonas, A., Granrud, C., & Pettersen, L. (1985). Infants' sensitivity to relative size information for distance. *Developmental Psychology, 21,* 161–167.

Young, R. D., & Avdze, E. (1979). The effects of obedience-disobedience and obese-nonobese type on social acceptance by peers. *Journal of Genetic Psychology, 134,* 43–49.

Younger, A. J., & Daniels, T. M. (1992). Children's reasons for nominating their peers as withdrawn: Passive withdrawal versus active isolation. *Developmental Psychology, 28,* 955–960.

Youniss, J., & Smollar, J. (1985). *Adolescent relations with mothers, fathers, and friends.* Chicago: University of Chicago Press.

Youniss, J., & Volpe, J. (1978). A relationship analysis of children's friendship. In W. Damon (Ed.), *Social cognition: No. 1. New directions for child development.* San Francisco: Jossey-Bass.

Yudkin, M. (1984, April). When kids think the unthinkable. *Psychology Today, 18,* 18–25.

Yuill, N., & Perner, J. (1988). Intentionality and knowledge in children's judgements of actor's responsibility and recipient's emotional reaction. *Developmental Psychology, 24,* 358–365.

Zabin, L. S., Hirsch, M. B., Smith, E. A., & Hardy, J. B. (1984). Adolescent sexual attitudes and behavior: Are they consistent? *Family Planning Perspectives, 16,* 181.

Zacharias, P., Rand, W., & Wurtman, R. (1976). A prospective study of sexual development and growth in American girls: The statistic of menarche. *Obstetrical and Gynecological Survey, 31,* 323–337.

Zahn-Waxler, C., Cummings, E. M., McKnew, D., & Radke-Yarrow, M. (1984). Altruism, aggression and social interaction in young children with a manic-depressive parent. *Child Development, 55,* 112–122.

Zahn-Waxler, C., Iannotti, R., & Chapman, M. (1982). Peers and prosocial development. In K. H. Rubin and H. S. Ross (Eds.), *Peer relationships and social skills in childhood.* New York: Springer-Verlag.

Zaslow, M., Pederson, F., Suwalsky, J., & Rabinovich, M. (1989). Maternal employment and parent-infant interaction at one year. *Early Childhood Research Quarterly, 4,* 49–478.

Zelnik, M., & Kantner, J. (1980). Sexual activity, contraceptive use and pregnancy among metropolitan-area teenagers, 1971–1979. *Family Planning Perspectives, 12,* 230–237.

Zelnik, M., Kantner, J., & Ford, K. (1981). *Sex and pregnancy in adolescence.* Beverly Hills, CA: Sage Publications.

Zelnik, M., & Kim Y. (1982). Sex education and its association with teenage sexual activity, pregnancy, and contraceptive use. *Family Planning Perspectives. 14,* 117–126.

Zelniker, T., & Jeffrey, W. (1976). Reflective and impulsive children: Strategies of information processing underlying differences in problem solving. *Monographs of the Society for Research in Child Development 41*(5, Serial No. 168).

Zelniker, T., & Jeffrey, W. (1979). Attention and cognitive style in children. In G. Hale & M. Lewis (Eds.), *Attention and cognitive development.* New York: Plenum.

Zelson, C. (1973). Infant of the addicted mother. *New England Journal of Medicine, 288,* 1393–1395.

Zelson, C., Lee, S. J., & Casalino, M. (1973). Neonatal narcotic addiction: Comparative effects of maternal intake of heroin and methadone. *New England Journal of Medicine, 289,* 1216–1220.

Zeskend, P., & Marshall, T. (1988). The relation between variations in pitch and maternal perceptions of infant crying. *Child Development, 59,* 193–196.

Zigler, E. (1980). Controlling child abuse: Do we have the knowledge and/or will? In G. Gerbner, C. Ross, & E. Zigler (Eds.), *Child abuse: An agenda for action.* New York: Oxford University Press.

Zigler, E. (1982). Controlling child abuse in America: An effort doomed to failure. In E. Zigler, M. Lamb, & I. Child (Eds.), *Socialization and personality development.* New York: Oxford University Press.

Zigler, E., & Gorden, E. (Eds.). (1982). *Day care: Scientific and social policy issues.* Boston: Auburn House.

Zill, N., & Peterson, J. (1982, January). *Trends in the behavior and emotional well-being of U.S. children: Findings from a national survey.* Paper presented at the meeting of the American Association for the Advancement of Science, Washington, DC.

Zimmerman, B. J. (1981). Social learning theory and cognitive constructivism. In I. Sigel, D. Brodzinsky, & R. Golinkoff (Eds.), *New directions in Piagetian theory and practice.* Hillsdale, NJ: Erlbaum.

Zuckerman, M., Eyzenck, S. B., & Eyzenck, H. J. (1978). Sensation seeking in England and America: Cross cultural, age, and sex comparisons. *Journal of Consulting and Clinical Psychology, 46,* 39–149.

PHOTOGRAPHS

Chapter 1: p. 3, © Anna Zuckerman/PhotoEdit; p. 8, © Martha Cooper/Peter Arnold, Inc.; p. 11, © Joel Gordon; p. 17, © StockUp Archive; p. 18, © Charles Anderson/Monkmeyer Press Photo Service; p. 19, © Jeffrey W. Myers/Stock Boston; p. 22, © Miro Vintoniv/Stock Boston; p. 26, © Cary Wolinski/Stock Boston; p. 32, © Peter Menzel/Stock Boston; p. 33, © Dennis Budd Gray/Monkmeyer Press Photo Service

Part Opener 1: p. 40, © Susie Fitzhugh/Stock Boston

Chapter 2: p. 43, © M. Shostak/Anthro-Photo; p. 44, © James Stevenson/Science PhotoLibrary/Photo Researchers, Inc.; p. 46, © Charles Mayer/Photo Researchers, Inc.; p. 46, © Robert Lee II; p. 49, © J. Wishnetsky/Comstock; p. 53, © Dr. Ram Verma/Phototake; p. 62, © Petite Format/Nestle/Science Source/Photo Researchers, Inc.; p. 64, © Petite Format/Nestle/Science Source/Photo Researchers, Inc.; p. 64, © Petite Format/Nestle/Science Source/Photo Researchers, Inc.; p. 65, © Petite Format/Nestle/Science Source/Photo Researchers, Inc.; p. 65, © Petite Format/Nestle/Science Source/Photo Researchers, Inc.; p. 69, © Fetal Alcohol Research Fund/Meese Photo Research; p. 74, © Phototake; p. 79, © Pat Hansen; p. 79, © Pat Hansen; p. 79, © Pat Hansen

Chapter 3: p. 85, © Robert Brenner/PhotoEdit; p. 89, © Hermine Dreyfuss/Monkmeyer Press Photo Service; p. 91, © George Goodwin/Monkmeyer Press Photo Service; p. 93, © Ed Lettau/Photo Researchers, Inc.; p. 93, © Charles Gupton/Tony Stone Worldwide/Chicago, Ltd.; p. 93, © Monkmeyer Press Photo Service; p. 95, © Beryl Goldberg, Photographer; p. 97, © Peter Menzel/Stock Boston; p. 103, © Lew Merrim/Monkmeyer Press Photo Service; p. 106, © Lionel J-M Delevingne/Stock Boston; p. 109, © Courtesy of Nadja Reissland, Phd.; p. 110, © Sandra Lord/Harcourt Brace & Co.; p. 113, © Robert Brenner/PhotoEdit; p. 115, © George Zimbel/Monkmeyer Press Photo Service; p. 121, © C. Ursillo/H. Armstrong Roberts

Chapter 4: p. 125, © I. Devore/Anthro-Photo; p. 127, © Ira Kirschenbaum/Stock Boston; p. 128, © Ann McQueen/Stock Boston; p. 131, © Ken Karp/Omni-Photo Communications, Inc.; p. 135, © Barbara Peacock/FPG; p. 137, © Bachmann/Photo Researchers; p. 142, © Elizabeth Crews; p. 143, © Jim Cummins/FPG; p. 146, © Elizabeth Crews; p. 150, © Image courtesy of Anne V. Gormly; p. 151, © Pat Hansen; p. 154, © Betsy Cole/The Picture Cube

Part Opener 2: p. 158, © Frank Siteman/Stock Boston

Chapter 5: p. 161, © John Kelly/The Image Bank; p. 167, © Dr. & Mrs. Ivan Jirak/Monkmeyer Press Photo Service; p. 167, © Brent Jones/Tony Stone Worldwide/Chicago, Ltd.; p. 168, © Image courtesy of Anne V. Gormly; p. 170, © 1985 Steve Elmore/West Stock; p. 171, © Lew Merrim/Monkmeyer Press Photo Service; p. 174, © Elizabeth Crews; p. 179, © Elizabeth Crews; p. 187, © Robert Brenner/PhotoEdit; p. 197, © Elizabeth Crews

Chapter 6: p. 205, © Alan Oddie/PhotoEdit; p. 208, © Peter Vandermark/Stock Boston; p. 209, © Image courtesy of Anne V. Gormly; p. 211, © Alan Carey/The Image Works; p. 212, © Steve Vidler/SuperStock; p. 215, © Alexander Lowry; p. 218, © 1991 J. Hangarter/Lightwave; p. 219, © Andy Sacks/Tony Stone; p. 223, © Ann L. Reed/Taurus Photos; p. 226, © Tom Pix/Peter Arnold, Inc.; p. 230, © Gail Meese/Meese Photo Research; p. 233, © David Young-Wolff/PhotoEdit; p. 235, © Erika Stone/Peter Arnold, Inc.; p. 237, © Judy Gelles/Stock Boston; p. 242, © James R. Holland/Stock Boston; p. 244, © Rick Kopstein/Monkmeyer Press Photo Service; p. 246, © Elizabeth Crews

Part Opener 3: p. 252, © Elizabeth Crews/Stock Boston

Chapter 7: p. 255, © Image courtesy of Anne V. Gormly; p. 256, © Image courtesy of Anne V. Gormly; p. 257, © Pam Hasegawa; p. 259, © Maria Paraskevas; p. 265, © Bob Daemmrich/Stock Boston; p. 267, © Pat Hansen; p. 269, © Bruce Roberts/Photo Researchers, Inc.; p. 275, © M.T. D'Hoste/SuperStock, Inc.; p. 278, © Jacques Jangoux/Peter Arnold, Inc.; p. 279, © Charles Kennard/Stock Boston; p. 279, © Owen Franken/Stock Boston; p. 284, © Elizabeth Crews; p. 288, © Grant LeDuc/Monkmeyer Press Photo Service

Chapter 8: p. 293, © Kathleen Marie Menke/Crystal Images/Monkmeyer Press Photo Service; p. 295, © Victor Englebert/Photo Researchers, Inc.; p. 295, © Robert A. Isaacs/Photo Researchers, Inc.; p. 297, © Image courtesy of Anne V. Gormly; p. 299, © Elizabeth Short; p. 302, © Robert Kalman/The Image Works; p. 303, © Joseph Schuyler/Stock Boston; p. 306, © C. Walterson/Meese Photo Research; p. 308, © Karen Preuss/The Image Works; p. 313, © David Tejada/Tony Stone; p. 315, © George Hunter/H. Armstrong Roberts; p. 315, © David Wells/The Image Works; p. 318, © Jim Whitmer/Stock Boston; p. 319, © Gail Meese/Meese Photo Research; p. 323, © Kathy Sloane

Part Opener 4: p. 330, © Grant LeDuc/Stock Boston

Chapter 9: p. 333, © Mathew Naythons/Stock Boston; p. 336, © Joel Gordon; p. 338, © Image courtesy of Anne V. Gormly; p. 339, © Hella Hammid/Photo Researchers, Inc.; p. 340, © Spencer Grant/Monkmeyer Press Photo Service; p. 340, © Rhoda Sidney/Monkmeyer Press Photo Service; p. 341, © Rick Kopstein/Monkmeyer Press Photo Service; p. 343, © David Gillison/Peter Arnold, Inc.; p. 346, © Image courtesy of Anne V. Gormly; p. 348, © Richard Hutchings/PhotoEdit; p. 349, © Katherine McGlynn/The Image Works; p. 351, © Joel Gordon; p. 354, © George White Location Photography; p. 359, © Image courtesy of Anne V. Gormly; p. 367, © The Image Works; p. 357, © Alex Borodulin/Peter Arnold, Inc.; p. 358, © Miriam White/The Stock Market

Chapter 10: p. 373, © Jerry Sinkovec/Artwerks; p. 380, © Image courtesy of Anne V. Gormly; p. 381, © Image courtesy of Anne V. Gormly; p. 384, © Image courtesy of Anne V. Gormly; p. 389, © Comstock, Inc./Sven Martson; p. 390, © Elizabeth Short; p. 394, © Elizabeth Short; p. 395, © Penny Tweedie/Tony Stone; p. 398, © Elizabeth Crews/The Image Works; p. 404, © Frances M. Cox/Stock Boston; p. 408, © Michael Hayman/Stock Boston; p. 410, © Spencer Grant/Stock Boston; p. 411, © Gail Meese/Meese Photo Research

Part Opener 5: p. 416, © Jean-Claude Lejeune/Stock Boston

Chapter 11: p. 419, © Janeart LTD/The Image Bank; p. 423, © Joel Gordon 1985; p. 423, © Porterfield-Chickering/Photo Researchers, Inc.; p. 421, © Win McNamee/Reuters/Bettmann; p. 422, © Photo Researchers, Inc.; p. 425, © Peter Menzel/Stock Boston; p. 426, © Peter Correz/Tony Stone; p. 428, © Fredrik Bodin/Stock Boston; p. 430, © Bob Daemmrich/Stock Boston; p. 436, © Bear Productions/The Image Works; p. 441, © Milton Feinberg/The Picture Cube; p. 446, © Image courtesy of Anne V. Gormly; p. 448, © Image courtesy of Anne V. Gormly; p. 450, © David W. Hamilton/The Image Bank

Chapter 12: p. 457, © Joel Fishman/Photo Researchers, Inc.; p. 458, © Liane Enkelis Photography/Stock Boston; p. 458, © Hub Willson/H. Armstrong Roberts; p. 446, © Ellis Herwig/The Picture Cube; p. 467, © Israel Talby/Israel Talby A.S.A.P.; p. 467, © Frank Perkins/ProFiles West, Inc.; p. 472, © Mike Malyszko/FPG; p. 475, © Joel Gordon; p. 477, © Tony Arruza/Tony Stone; p. 479, © Tom McHugh/Photo Researchers, Inc.; p. 480, © Paul Conklin/Monkmeyer Press Photo Service; p. 486, © Ted Horowitz/The Stock Market; p. 488, © Fred Herholdt/Tony Stone; p. 489, © Robert Eckert/Stock Boston; p. 491, © Steven Lunetta/StockUp

Part Opener 6: p. 498, © Karen Kasmauski/National Geographic

Chapter 13: p. 501, © Cesar Lucas/The Image Bank; p. 509, © Michael Keller/FPG; p. 510, © Image courtesy of Anne V. Gormly; p. 511, © Rob Gage/FPG; p. 514, © David Young Wolff/Tony Stone; p. 515, © Arlene Collins/Monkmeyer Press Photo Service; p. 520, © Charles Kennard/Stock Boston; p. 525, © Elizabeth Crews/The Image Works, Inc.; p. 521, © Paul Conklin/Monkmeyer Press Photo Service; p. 523, © Michael Kagan/Monkmeyer Press Photo Service

Chapter 14: p. 539, © Bill Aron/PhotoEdit; p. 540, © Douglas Jones/Globe Photos, Inc.; p. 543, © Elizabeth Crews; p. 544, © William Beermann/Superstock, Inc.; p. 547, © Elizabeth Crews/

Stock Boston; p. 549, © Peter Southwick/Stock Boston; p. 554, © Image courtesy of Anne V. Gormly; p. 557, © Andrew Brillant/The Picture Cube; p. 560, © Mimi Forsyth/Monkmeyer Press Photo Service; p. 562, © Estate of Sybil Shelton/Peter Arnold, Inc.; p. 565, © R. Llewellyn/SuperStock, Inc.; p. 568, © Joel Gordon

Part Opener 7: p. 574, © Barbara Alper/Stock Boston

Chapter 15: p. 577, © Pat Watson; p. 579, © Elizabeth Crews; p. 580, © Ron Chapple/FPG; p. 581, © Thomas Del Braise/The Stock Market; p. 583, © George Gardner/The Image Works; p. 584, © J. Wang/SuperStock, Inc.; p. 587, © Bob Daemmrich/The Image Works; p. 587, © UPI/Bettmann; p. 589, © Lori Adamski Peek/Tony Stone; p. 591, © Mark Mittleman/Taurus Photos; p. 595, © PhotoEdit; p. 601, © Jack Spratt/The Image Works; p. 608, © SuperStock, Inc.; p. 612, © Comstock, Inc./David Lokey

Chapter 16: p. 617, © David M. Grossman/Photo Researchers, Inc.; p. 619, © Image courtesy of Anne V. Gormly; p. 621, © Joel Gordon; p. 623, © Frank Siteman/The Picture Cube; p. 630, © Ron Chapple/FPG; p. 633, © D&P Valenti/H. Armstrong Roberts; p. 637, © David M. Grossman/Photo Researchers, Inc.; p. 638, © Martha Stewart/The Picture Cube; p. 642, © Image courtesy of Anne V. Gormly; p. 644, © Image courtesy of Anne V. Gormly; p. 646, © Dale Wittner/West Stock

Part Opener 8: p. 650, © Frank Siteman/Stock Boston

Chapter 17: p. 653, © Tomas Friedmann/Photo Researchers, Inc.; p. 656, © Bobbi Carrey/The Picture Cube; p. 659, © Renee Lynn/Photo Researchers, Inc.; p. 660, © Gale Zucker/Stock Boston; p. 661, © Bill Aron/PhotoEdit; p. 662, © James Carroll/Stock Boston; p. 663, © George White Location Photography; p. 665, © Michael Weisbrot/Stock Boston; p. 668, © Randy Matusow/Monkmeyer Press Photo Service; p. 672, © Steve Skjold/PhotoEdit; p. 676, © Bernard Pierre Wolf/Photo Researchers, Inc.; p. 676, © Victor Englebert/Photo Researchers, Inc.; p. 681, © Bettmann Newsphotos; p. 683, © Jeff Mitchell/REUTERS/Bettmann

Learning throughout Life Insert: p. 1, © Jeff Greenberg/Unicorn; p. 1, © Skjold/PhotoEdit; p. 1, © George White Location Photography; p. 1, © John M. Roberts/The Stock Market; p. 2, © David Young-Wolff/PhotoEdit; p. 2, © Elizabeth Hathon/The Stock Market; p. 2, © Bob Krist/The Stock Market; p. 3, © Julie O'Neill/The Picture Cube; p. 3, © 1995 PhotoDisc, Inc.; p. 3, © Kathy Sloane; p. 3, © Terry Wild Studios; p. 4, © Richard Levine; p. 4, © Palmer/Brillaint/The Picture Cube; p. 4, © Comstock; p. 4, © George White Location Photography; p. 4, © 1995 PhotoDisc, Inc.

Families across the Lifespan Insert: p. 1, © Jeff Greenberg/Unicorn; p. 1, © Myrleen Ferguson/PhotoEdit; p. 1, © Chuck Savage/The Stock Market; p. 1, © Erick Berndt/Unicorn; p. 2, © Steven Lunetta/StockUp; p. 2, © Tony Freeman/PhotoEdit; p. 2, © Deborah Davis/PhotoEdit; p. 3, © Roy Morsch/The Stock Market; p. 3, © David Young Wolffe/PhotoEdit; p. 3, © Michael Newman/PhotoEdit; p. 3, © Chip and Rosa María de la Cueva Peterson; p. 4, © Robert Holmes/Corbis; p. 4, © Laura Zito; p. 4, © Myrleen Ferguson/PhotoEdit; p. 4, © 1995 PhotoDisc, Inc.; p. 4, © Jean Higgins/Unicorn

FIGURES AND TABLES

FIGURE 1.1:   Reproduced, with permission, from the *Annual Review of Psychology*, Vol. 31, © 1980 by Annual Reviews, Inc.

TABLE 1.3:   CHILD DEVELOPMENT, S. Amborn & N. Salkind, © 1984 by Holt, Rinehart, & Winston. Reprinted with permission by the authors.

TABLE 1.8:   "Statement of the Division of Developmental Psychology of the American Psychological Association," 1986, © SOCIETY FOR RESEARCH IN CHILD DEVELOPMENT, pp. 1–3. Reprinted with permission.

FIGURE 2.4:   Figures from PSYCHOLOGY: SCIENCE, BEHAVIOR, AND LIFE by Robert L. Crooks and Jean I. Stein, copyright © 1988 by Holt, Rinehart, & Winston. Reproduced by permission of the publisher.

FIGURE 2.8:   Figures from PSYCHOLOGY: SCIENCE, BEHAVIOR, AND LIFE by Robert L. Crooks and Jean I. Stein, copyright © 1988 by Holt, Rinehart, and Winston. Reproduced by permission of the publisher.

TABLE 3.1:   From P.H. Wolff, "Observations on Newborn Infants," *PSYCHOSOMATIC MEDICINE*, 21, 1959, pp. 110–118. Used with permission of Williams & Wilkins.

FIGURE 3.1:   Reprinted by permission of the publisher from THE POSTNATAL DEVELOPMENT OF THE HUMAN CORTEX, VOLUME 1 by J. L. Conel, Cambridge, Mass.: Harvard University Press, Copyright © 1939 by the President and Fellows of Harvard College; Copyright renewed in 1967 by Jesse LeRoy Conel.

TABLE 5.1:   From Ernest H. Watson and George H. Lowery, *GROWTH AND DEVELOPMENT OF CHILDREN,* 5/e; data from tables 10-A through 10-D (pp. 89–92). Copyright © 1967 by Year Book Medical Publishers, Inc.

TABLE 5.2:   From MOTOR DEVELOPMENT EXPERIENCES FOR YOUNG CHILDREN (pp. 65–66), by D. L. Gallahue, 1976, New York: John Wiley & Sons. Adapted with permission.

FIGURE 5.4:   Adapted from Vurpillot, "The Development of Scanning Strategies and their Relation to Visual Differentiation." JOURNAL OF EXPERIMENTAL CHILD PSYCHOLOGY, 6, pp. 632–650.

TABLE 5.5:   Adapted with permission from B.L. White, EDUCATING THE INFANT AND TODDLER (p. 24). Copyright © 1988 Jossey-Bass Inc., Publishers. First published by Lexington Books. All rights reserved.

TABLE 5.6:   Reprinted with permission from PSYCHOLOGY TODAY magazine, Copyright © 1972 (Sussex Publishers, Inc.).

TABLE 5.8:   From S.L. Hofferth, A. Brayfield, S. Deich, and P. Holcomb, NATIONAL HEALTH CARE SURVEY, 1990, p. 59. Reprinted with permission by Urban Institute Press.

TABLE 6.4:   From D. Finkelhor, "Current Information on the Scope and Nurture of Child Sexual Abuse," *The Future of Children,* 4, (Summer/Fall), 1994, pp. 31-53. Adapted with permission of the Center for the Future of Children of the David and Lucile Packard Foundation.

TABLE 7.5:   From "Moral Stages and Moralization: The Cognitive Development Approach," by L. Kohlberg. In *Moral Development and Behavior,* ed. by T. Lickona, 1976, New York: Holt, Rinehart & Winston. Adapted with permission.

TABLE 8.2:   MIDDLE CHILDHOOD BEHAVIOR AND DEVELOPMENT, 2/e, by Williams/Stith, © 1980. Adapted by permission of Prentice-Hall, Inc., Upper Saddle River, NJ.

TABLE 8.4:   From R.L. Selman, "The Child as a Friendship Philosopher: A Case Study in the Growth of Interpersonal Understanding," THE DEVELOPMENT OF CHILDREN'S FRIENDSHIPS, ed. S. R. Asher & J. M. Gottman, 1981.

FIGURE 9.1:   From G. B. Forbes. "Growth of the lean body mass in man." *Growth 36* (1082): 325-338.

FIGURE 9.2:   From SEX IN AMERICA by Michael, et al. Copyright © 1994 by CSG Enterprises, Inc., Edward O. Laumann, Robert T. Michael and Gina Kolata. By permission of Little, Brown and Company.

TABLE 9.4:   Table adapted from ESSAYS ON MORAL DEVELOPMENT: (Vol. 11) by Lawrence Kohlberg.

TABLE 9.5:   From J.S. Eccles, S. Midgley, A. Wigfield, C. M. Buchanan, D. Reuman, C. Flanagan, & D. MacIver, "Development During Adolescence: The Impact of Stage-Environment Fit on Young Adolescents' Experiences in Schools and in Families," *AMERICAN PSYCHOLOGIST,* 48, 1993, pp. 92–94. Copyright © 1993 by the American Psychological Association. Reprinted with permission.

TABLE 10.1:   From *Developmental Tasks and Education,* 3/e by Robert Havighurst. Copyright © 1972 by Longman Inc. Reprinted by permission of Addison-Wesley Educational Publishers, Inc..

FIGURE 10.1:   Based on Czikszentmihaly and Larson, *Being Adolescent: Conflict and Growth in the Teenage Years* (New York: Basic Books, 1984).

TABLE 10.2:   From D. Moore & D. F. Hotch, "Late Adolescents' Conceptualizations of Home-Leaving," *Journal of Youth and Adolescence,* 10, 1981. Reprinted by permission of Plenum Press.

FIGURE 10.3:   From A. Garland & E. Zigler, "Adolescent Suicide Prevention: Current Research and Social Policy Implications," *American Psychologist,* 41, 1993, p. 170. Copyright © 1993 by the American Psychological Association. Reprinted with permission.

FIGURE 11.1:   From THE SEASONS OF A MAN'S LIFE by Daniel J. Levinson. Copyright © 1978 by Daniel J. Levinson. Reprinted by permission of Alfred A. Knopf, Inc.

TABLE 11.2:   TRANSFORMATIONS: GROWTH AND CHANGE IN ADULT LIFE. Copyright © 1978 by Roger Gould, M.D. Reprinted by permission of Author.

TABLE 12.1:   From E. Carter & M. McGoldrick, "The Family Life Cycle and Family Therapy: An Overview," THE FAMILY LIFE CYCLE: A FRAMEWORK FOR FAMILY THERAPY, © 1980 by Allyn & Bacon. Reprinted/adapted with permission.

FIGURE 12.1: From Bernard I. Murstein, *Who Will Marry Whom? Theories and Research in Marital Choice,* p. 123, © 1976. Used with permission of author.

TABLE 12.2: From A. Gormly, J. Gormly, & H. Weiss, "Motivations for Parenthood Among Young College Students," *Sex Roles,* 16, 1987, pp. 31–39. Reprinted with permission by Plenum Publishing Corporation.

TABLE 13.1: Reproduced with permissions from Playboy Enterprises, Inc., SEXUAL BEHAVIOR IN THE 1970s by Morton Hunt. Copyright © 1974 by Morton Hunt.

TABLE 13.1: From A. C. Kinsey, W. B. Pomeroy, & C. C. Martin, SEXUAL BEHAVIOR IN THE HUMAN MALE, © 1948. Reprinted by permission of The Kinsey Institute for Research in Sex, Gender and Reproduction, Inc.

TABLE 13.1: From A. C. Kinsey, W. B. Pomeroy, & C. C. Martin, SEXUAL BEHAVIOR IN THE HUMAN FEMALE, © 1953. Reprinted by permission of The Kinsey Institute for Research in Sex, Gender and Reproduction, Inc.

TABLE 13.2: K. Markides & C. Mindel, AGING AND ETHNICITY, p. 74, copyright © 1987 by Sage Publications, Inc. Reprinted by Permission of Sage Publications, Inc.

TABLE 13.3: Reprinted with permission From T. H. Holmes & R. H. Rahe, *Journal of Psychosomatic Research,* 11, "The Social Readjustment Rating Scale," 1967, pp. 213–218, Elsevier Science.

TABLE 13.4: Reprinted with permission from PSYCHOLOGY TODAY magazine, Copyright © 1981 (Sussex Publishers, Inc.) "Little Hassles Can Be Hazardous to Your Health" by R. Lazarus.

TABLE 13.5: From K. W. Schaie, "The Course of Adult Intellectual Development," *American Psychologist,* 49, 1994, p. 310. Copyright © 1994 by the American Psychological Association. Reprinted with permission.

TABLE 13.6: From *Developmental Tasks and Education,* 3/e by Robert Havinghurst. Copyright © 1972 by Longman Inc. Reprinted by permission of Addison-Wesley Educational Publishers, Inc.

FIGURE 14.1: From B. C. Rollins & H. Feldman, "Marital Satisfaction Over the Family Life Cycle," *Journal of Marriage and the Family,* 32, 1970, p. 26. Copyrighted 1970 by the National Council on Family Relations, 3989 Central Ave., NE, Suite 550, Minneapolis, MN 55421. Reprinted by permission.

TABLE 15.1: From p. Baltes & U. Staudinger, "The Search for a Psychology of Wisdom," *Current Directions in Psychological Science,* Vol. 2, 1993, pp. 75–80.

TABLE 15.2: From D. Goleman, "Erikson, in His Own Old Age, Expands His Views of Life." Copyright © 1988 by the New York Times Co. Reprinted by permission.

TABLE 16.1: From Maddox, et al, THE ENCYCLOPEDIA OF AGING, © 1987, Springer Publishing Company, Inc., New York 10012. Used by permission

FIGURE 16.1: From M. N. Reedy, et al, *Human Development,* 24, 1981, "Age and Sex Differences in Satisfying Love Relationships Across the Adult Life Span," pp. 52–66. Reprinted with permission of S. Karger AG, Basel, Switzerland.

TABLE 16.2: Phases of Retirement for R.C. Atchley, The Sociology of Retirements. Rochester, VT.: Schenkman Books, 1979.

TABLE 17.1: From *Journal of Genetic Psychology,* 73, 1948, pp. 3–27. "The Child's Theories concerning Death," by M. Nagy. Reprinted with permission of the Helen Dwight Reid Educational Foundation. Published by Heldref Publications, 1319 First Street N.W., Washington D.C., 20036-1802. Copyright © 1948.

TABLE 17.2: Excerpted from an article by Patrick Cooke. Reprinted with permission from HIPPOCRATES, © 1989.

TABLE 17.3: From *American Journal of Psychiatry,* 101, pp. 141–148, 1944, "The Symptomatology and Management of Acute Grief," by E. Lindemann. Copyright © 1944, the American Psychiatric Association. Reprinted by permission.

TABLE 17.4: A GUIDE TO GRIEF, 1994, pp. 9–10. Reprinted with permission of the National Hospice Organization.